Patterns in Prehistory: Humankind's First Three Million Years

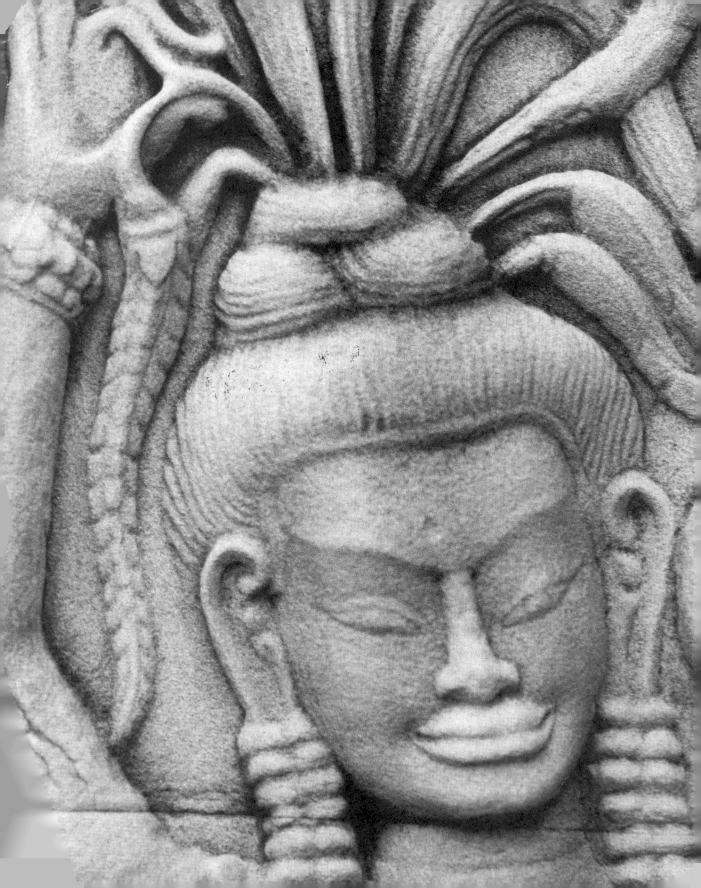

Patterns in Prehistory

Humankind's First Three Million Years

Fifth Edition

Robert I. Wenke
University of Washington

Deborah I. Olszewski
University of Pennsylvania

New York   Oxford
OXFORD UNIVERSITY PRESS
2007

Oxford University Press, Inc., publishes works that further Oxford University's
objective of excellence in research, scholarship, and education.

Oxford New York
Auckland Cape Town Dar es Salaam Hong Kong Karachi
Kuala Lumpur Madrid Melbourne Mexico City Nairobi
New Delhi Shanghai Taipei Toronto

With offices in
Argentina Austria Brazil Chile Czech Republic France Greece
Guatemala Hungary Italy Japan Poland Portugal Singapore
South Korea Switzerland Thailand Turkey Ukraine Vietnam

Published by Oxford University Press, Inc.
198 Madison Avenue, New York, New York 10016
http://www.oup.com

Library of Congress Cataloging-in-Publication Data

Wenke, Robert J.
  Patterns in prehistory: humankind's first three million years / Robert J. Wenke,
Deborah I. Olszewski. — 5th ed.
      p. cm.
  Includes bibliographical references and index.
  ISBN-13: 978-0-19-516928-7

    1. Prehistoric peoples. 2. Archaeology. I. Olszewski, Deborah. II. Title.

GN740.W46 2007
930.1—dc22

                                                            2005058961

Printing number: 9 8 7 6 5 4 3 2

Printed in the United States of America
on acid-free paper

FLIP

For David, Ilene, Lorence, Dennis, and Judy, with much gratitude
Robert J. Wenke

For Dr. Elizabeth Ann Morris, my first archaeology professor and the inspiration for my professional career
Deborah I. Olszewski

Contents

Preface

We find ourselves in a bewildering world. We
want to make sense of what we see around us
and to ask: What is the nature of the universe?
What is our place in it and where did it and we
come from? Why is it the way it is?

Stephen W. Hawking[1]

Our journey into the past several million years of human prehistory and early history—beginning about the time of the first appearance of stone tools and extending to the recent past—is an endeavor to see more clearly and to understand ourselves, modern human beings (*Homo sapiens sapiens*). Ours is a story of "fits and starts," of human ancestors and of societies that shed light on natural and cultural experiments, both those that succeeded and those that failed. The key, of course, is diversity, a characteristic of both modern humans and our ancestors before us.

APPROACHES TO PREHISTORY

The story of prehistory and early history is the story of all of us living today. Across the vast bounds of time and space, archaeology reveals glimpses into the variety of behaviors and adaptations of countless and nameless individuals and groups. When we reach the period of our earliest recorded history, we can put names to some of these individuals and groups, but others remain more obscure. It is thus the goal of archaeology to integrate evidence—stone tools, pottery sherds, animal bones, plant remains, and a myriad of other data—with theory to reconstruct the many behaviors that formed the archaeological record of hunter-gatherers, farmers, pastoralists, and members of early complex societies.

Theoretical approaches differ considerably within archaeology today, and this edition of *Patterns in Prehistory* offers examples of how these different approaches affect the interpretation of the data of the archaeological record. The overall strategy of this edition, however, is to present archaeological interpretation in the context of the scientific method. Interpretations of data using a particular theoretical approach, for example, can be contrasted with interpretations offered by a differing theoretical approach. In doing so, we can examine which of the explanations is currently better supported and how one or both of these explanations can be refined once a comparison is made. Scientific research, after all, is fundamentally a method of proposing explanations, testing them, and then revising the explanations so that the fit between data and theory becomes closer over time. That is the intention of this edition: to facilitate students' understanding of this approach to explanation and interpretation and the lively debates that result.

ORGANIZATION OF THE BOOK

The fifth edition of *Patterns in Prehistory* begins with background on the development and contributions of theories and archaeological methods. Next we introduce readers to the wide diversity of past societies through the use of several broad themes. These provide both numerous examples—some similar and some different—of the evidence and the interpretations that are used to arrive at a better understanding of our past and its relevance to us.

Themes

The themes that form the backbone of the organization of this edition are:

- Intellectual background: discusses the ideas and theories that have contributed to archaeological approaches to an understanding of the past
- Archaeological methods and techniques: describes the types of evidence collected by archaeologists, how these data are analyzed, and the technology used
- Culture: examines issues surrounding how culture develops and related models, the evidence for early culture, comparisons with nonhuman primates, and the archaeological record for early human ancestors
- Emergence of anatomically modern humans: presents information on human ancestors in the genus *Homo*, their migration into Eurasia, models for the origins of anatomically modern humans, and the colonization of the world outside of Africa, including the Americas, by modern humans
- Food-producing economies: discusses models for the origins of agriculture in the Old and New Worlds, with examples from Southwest Asia, Egypt, China, Mesoamerica, Andean South America, and North America
- Complex societies, civilizations, and states: examines models for the origins of complex societies, civilizations, and states, with examples from Southwest Asia, Egypt, the Indus Valley, China, Mesoamerica, Andean South America, temperate Europe, and North America

Arrangement of Chapters

Chapters from the previous edition of *Patterns in Prehistory* have undergone considerable reorganization. To help readers, we have introduced more, and more standardized, headings within chapters to serve as signposts through the text; we have repositioned data and discussions to create better flow of thought and readability; and we have introduced timelines in each chapter to provide a better comparative context.

Those chapters dealing with the intellectual heritage, archaeological methods and techniques, and the origins of culture (Chapters 1–3) of necessity have topical outlines that differ substantially from one chapter to the next. Chapter 1 examines the body of scientific thought and intellectual background that underlie theories used to explain the past. Chapter 2 deals with topics concerning how archaeologists gather information and analyze data. Chapter 3 presents theoretical background to understanding the appearance of culture, as well as examines the archaeological record of the earliest human ancestors.

The next two chapters (Chapters 4 and 5) continue the theme of the archaeological record of earlier prehistory. Chapter 4 examines models and data used to interpret early human ancestors, delves into the issues surrounding the origins of anatomically modern humans—us—and follows early humans as they colonize the Old World. Chapter 5 continues the colonization theme through discussion of the initial peopling of the New World and the adaptations of these early settlers.

An interlude is provided in the next two chapters (Chapters 6 and 7), as these stress theoretical background to two intriguing research problems. Chapter 6 examines the origins of agriculture and food-producing economies in the Old and New Worlds. Chapter 7, on the other hand, discusses the origins of complex societies in both the Old and New Worlds.

Chapters dealing with case studies of the development of complex societies (Chapters 8–15) examine, with slight deviation for the subject matter treated in Chapters 12 (later Old World complex societies) and 15 (early cultural complexity in North America):

- Timeline
- The ecological context
- The archaeological background for agriculture and early farming societies
- The archaeology of the major periods in the development of complex societies, civilizations, and states, as well as theoretical perspectives
- The role of art, religion, and writing systems in these societies
- The collapse, demise, disappearance, or transformation of early complex societies, civilizations, and states
- A summary and conclusions section

Finally, Chapter 16 provides an epilogue.

NEW TO THIS EDITION

In updating *Patterns in Prehistory*, we have drawn on Rob Wenke's revisions for the new edition, insightful comments from reviewers, and Deb Olszewski's expertise and research experience in the Middle East, American Southwest, and earlier periods of prehistory, as well as Deb's experience teaching with previous editions of *Patterns in Prehistory*. New materials for this fifth edition include:

- Expansion of graphic presentations, including 70 percent more photos and illustrations throughout the book, timelines added to all relevant chapters (Chapters 3–8 and 12), existing timelines updated (Chapters 9–11 and 13–15), and an overview timeline added to illustrate the temporal framework for the textbook.

- Facilitation of comprehension through reorganization of chapters to standardize presentation of information, streamlining of text, updating of chapter bibliographies and endnotes, and use of current spellings of names for places, cultures, objects, and people
- Updating of chapter information, including addition of material on technology such as Geographic Information System, global positioning system, and total stations (Chapter 2); discussion of biomechanical studies that model bipedalism in early human ancestors (Chapter 3); examination of site taphonomy in the context of recent revisions to interpretations of cultural activities at sites (Chapters 2, 3, and 4); the latest discoveries of fossils of human ancestors (Chapters 3 and 4); addition of the Pacific coast-hopping hypothesis and the Atlantic route idea for the initial peopling of the Americas (Chapter 5); consideration of the role of genetics in the interpretation of the origins of anatomically modern humans (Chapter 4), the colonization of the Americas (Chapter 5), and the spread of food-producing economies (Chapter 6); revision of information on local ecological contexts for the origins of agriculture (Chapters 6 and 10) and the origins of complex societies (Chapters 7 and 8); improved discussion of the Chinese Neolithic (Chapter 11); enhanced treatment of Iron Age Europe (Chapter 12); addition of recent ideas about the "collapse" of the Classic Maya (Chapter 13); corrected description of the European Conquest of Andean South America (Chapter 14); and expanded discussion of Chaco Canyon and interpretations of its significance in the American Southwest (Chapter 15).

FEATURES AND BENEFITS

The fifth edition of *Patterns in Prehistory* has retained the popular features and benefits that characterized its earlier editions, as well as added others that facilitate comprehension:

- Readability, accessibility, breadth, and humor; in-depth coverage of major complex societies, civilizations, and states with discussions that integrate theory and data for the reader; literary quotes that personalize the text; and discussion of major transitions in human prehistory, as well as colonization events, that examines the processes involved in the development of human culture, human behavior, and socioeconomic adaptations
- Chapter timelines that provide overviews to help the reader place events in context; examples of scholarly debates and varying interpretations that exemplify how theory and method are integrated to derive interpretations and how interpretations are revised over time; an augmented visual component that enhances reader comprehension of topics; and updated chapter bibliographies and endnotes that provide additional resources for students and instructors

NOTE ON DATES

Dates for archaeological sites, fossil human ancestors, origins of agriculture, and so forth are given in this edition in three forms. These are "years ago," corresponding to uncalibrated years before the present (b.p.), and "B.C.," corresponding to uncalibrated years before Christ. The difference between the two time scales is 1,950 years, which represents A.D. 1950, the benchmark date conventionally used in radiocarbon dating as the zero point for calculating radiocarbon ages (see Chapter 2). Thus, for example, a date of 10,000 B.C. can be roughly translated as 11,950 years ago. Dates given in this edition for "A.D." are often known calendric dates because they can be determined from cross-references to written documents from several of the early civilizations and states or have been calibrated.

As discussed in Chapter 2, conventional radiocarbon dates are known to fluctuate in accuracy for certain time periods. Researchers have been able to compensate for some of these fluctuations by using calibration (correction) curves. The original basis for calibration was founded on dendrochronology (tree rings; see Chapter 2), which can be used to calibrate dates in the period from 0 to 12,400 cal B.P.[2] Recent technical advances, especially use of data from marine records, currently allows the calibration of terrestrial radiocarbon dates in the period from 12,400 to 26,000 cal B.P.[3]

Several scholars working on archaeological materials from various parts of the world have published new calibrated sequences of dates for their regions (for example, see Chapter 5). These, however, do not always provide calibrated dates for individual sites, so that integrating the new calibrated sequences with the previously reported uncalibrated dates for some sites is not always straightforward. To promote clarity and minimal confusion about dates, this edition of *Patterns in Prehistory* continues to use the years ago and B.C. uncalibrated dates.

ACKNOWLEDGMENTS

This edition of *Patterns in Prehistory* would not exist without the dedication and hard work of Jan Beatty and Karen Shapiro at Oxford University Press. We thank them for their editing, support, insights, and the production of this edition. To have been brought to Jan's attention as the person to work on this edition, however, was through the efforts of Harold Dibble, to whom I owe an enormous debt of gratitude. The detailed comments provided by Professors Thomas Charlton (University of Iowa), Terence N. D'Altroy (Columbia University), Ronald Hicks (Ball State University), Kenneth G. Hirth (Pennsylvania State University), Laura J. Levi (University of Texas at San Antonio), Michael Malpass (Ithaca College), John Rick (Stanford University), Ralph M. Rowlett (University of Missouri – Columbia), Robert Santley (University of New Mexico), Andrew Sherratt (Sheffield University), Mark Tveskov (Southern Orgeon University), Rita Wright (New York University), and Paul Zimansky (Boston University) are also much appreciated, as they corrected various details both large and small, offered clarity of thought, and pointed the way to improved discussions.

Archaeologists often say that it is possible to know how another archaeologist will think about or interpret the past if they know his or her "kinship." They mean, of course, those professors with whom one studied, because like students everywhere, our perspectives partly reflect those of our teachers. Of the many professors I could mention, I will limit myself to two. As an undergraduate major in anthropology at Colorado State University, I was greatly influenced by Liz Morris. In the small and serendipitous world of archaeology, our association did not end there. We have remained friends over several decades, with one of my greatest surprises being when I found out that the Paleolithic stone artifact collections from the site of Warwasi, Iran—that I studied in the late 1980s—were from an excavation project in which Liz participated in 1960! During my graduate days at the University of Arizona, I was a student of Art Jelinek's, and thus explains my mainly Old World (and Paleolithic) focus. To Art, I owe insights into the nature of stone tool studies, exposure to Bordian systematics, and a penchant to see if explanations can be turned on their heads and reexamined.

Intellectual kinship involves not only those with whom we studied, but also lively interactions with friends and colleagues in the discipline over the years. In this regard, I would like to thank Patty Anderson, Mike and Margaret Barton, Ofer Bar-Yosef, Mark Baumler, Mary Bernard, Walt Birkby, Phil Chase, Anna Belfer-Cohen, J. Simon Bruder, Geof Clark, Nancy Coinman, Jason Cooper, Harold and Lee Dibble, John Dockall, Dave Doyel, Hans-Georg Gebel, Naama Goren-Inbar, Nigel Goring-Morris, Leslie Hartzell, Zeidan Kafafi, Kathy Kamp, Daphne Katrinides, Ian Kuijt, Cathy Lebo, Susan Lebo, Helen Leidemann, Heidi Lennstrom, Shannon McPherron, Andrew Moore, Dani Nadel, Maysoon al-Nahar, Mike Neeley, Gordon Nishida, Jane Peterson, Leslie Quintero, Gary Rollefson, Barb Roth, Utsav Schurmans, Alan Simmons, Peggy Trachte, John Whittaker, and Phil Wilke. This is, of course, only a partial list, and I also thank the rest of you who are not mentioned here by name. Finally, but not least, I extend thanks to countless students in my classes over the years for their refreshing perspectives and to the people of Jordan and Egypt, countries in which I have been fortunate enough to do the majority of my research.

My Old World research has been funded by the National Science Foundation, the Leakey Foundation, the National Geographic Society, the Wenner-Gren Foundation for Anthropology, the Fulbright Program, the University of Pennsylvania Museum of Archaeology and Anthropology, the American Philosophical Society, and the Joukowsky Family Foundation, and I am grateful to them for the research opportunities that resulted. In the New World, I have worked on a number of projects funded through Cultural Resource Management auspices, including some of the most memorable sites and regions of the American Southwest. Cultural Resource Management funding also provided me with opportunities to study the pre-Contact prehistory of Hawai'i.

Deborah I. Olszewski

NOTES

1. *A Brief History of Time: From the Big Bang to Black Holes*, 1988, p. 171. New York: Bantam Books.
2. http://calib.qub.ac.uk/calib/; The use of B.P. in caps is generally understood to refer to calibrated dates, while the use of b.p. in lowercase refers to uncalibrated dates.
3. http://calib.qub.ac.uk/calib/; it is becoming common to refer to calibrated dates using the designation of "cal B.P." or "cal B.C."

TODAY

A.D. 1500s	Spanish arrival in the Americas
A.D. 1476	Beginning of the Inka empire in South America
A.D. 1150	Beginning of the Aztec state in Mexico
A.D. 1000	Beginning of Hohokam, Ancestral Pueblo and Mogollon complex society in the North American Southwest
A.D. 800	Beginning of Mississippian complex society in the North American Southeast
A.D. 600	Initial date for colonization of Hawai'i
A.D. 600	Appearance of Wari and Tiwanaku states in South America
A.D. 300	Beginning of Classic Maya civilization in Mesoamerica
A.D. 1	Beginning of the Teotihuacán state in the Valley of Mexico and Moche civilization in South America
15 B.C.	Roman conquest of Europe
475 B.C.	Beginning of La Tène complex society in Europe
800 B.C.	Beginning of Halstatt complex society in Europe
1000 B.C.	Beginning of Mycenaean civilization in the Aegean
1300 B.C.	Appearance of Olmec complex society in Mesoamerica
1500 B.C.	Beginning of spread of Lapita Complex in the Pacific
1600 B.C.	Appearance of Shang civilization in China
2000 B.C.	Appearance of Minoan civilization in the Aegean
2000 B.C.	Origins of agriculture in Eastern North America
3100 B.C.	Beginning of Egyptian civilization
3200 B.C.	Beginning of Harappan civilization in the Indus Valley
3600 B.C.	Beginning of Mesopotamian civilization in the Middle East
5700 B.C.	Origins of agriculture in South America
6000 B.C.	Agriculture begins to spread into Europe from the Middle East

6500 B.C.	Origins of agriculture in Asia
7500 B.C.	Origins of agriculture in Africa
8000 B.C.	Origins of agriculture in Mesoamerica
8500 B.C.	Origins of agriculture in the Middle East
20–15,000 years ago	Beginning of colonization of the Americas by Paleoindians
32,000 years ago	Neandertals become extinct
40,000 years ago	Modern humans begin to colonize Europe; explosion of art and symbolism
60,000 years ago	Beginning of colonization of Australia by modern humans
100,000 years ago	Early modern humans begin to radiate out of Africa to the Middle East and Asia
160,000 years ago	Early modern humans (*Homo sapiens*) appear in Africa
230,000 years ago	Neandertals (*Homo neanderthalensis*) appear in Western Eurasia
1.7 million years ago	*Homo erectus* grade begins to migrate out of Africa to Eurasia
2.5 million years ago	Genus *Homo* appears in Africa
2.6 million years ago	First stone tools appear in Africa
3 million years ago	Beginning of radiation of Australopiths in Africa
5 million years ago	Australopith hominins appear in Africa

Prehistory, History, and Archaeology

History is philosophy teaching by examples.

Dionysius of Halicarnassus (c. 40 B.C.)

History is bunk.

Henry Ford

The archaeologist-adventurers of film and fiction never seem too concerned about what they are looking for or why they want it. "It" is usually something like a curse-protected pharaoh's tomb treasures or the biblical Ark of the Covenant—something intrinsically interesting and protected by enough snakes, traps, or villains to require a romantic hero for its discovery.

In this prosaic age it will come as no surprise to the reader that contemporary archaeology differs considerably from these fictional versions, as this book will make clear. Yet, in a sense, archaeology is in fact a uniquely interesting science. And certainly its origins are in rather romantic bygone eras. In the early 1800s, for example, the Italian adventurer Giovanni Belzoni looted dozens of ancient Egyptian tombs in Thebes (near modern Luxor) and sold their riches in Europe. Belzoni crept and crawled through miles of tunnels in the stinking, dusty air of these crypts, smashing hundreds of mummies as he went:

> [Al]though, fortunately I am destitute of the sense of smelling, I could taste that the mummies were rather unpleasant to swallow. After the exertion of entering into such a place, through a passage of . . . perhaps six hundred yards, nearly overcome, I sought a resting place. . . . [B]ut when my weight bore on the body of an Egyptian, it crushed like a band-box. . . . I sank altogether among the broken mummies, with a crash of bones, rags, and wooden cases. . . . [E]very step I took I crushed a mummy. . . . I could not pass without putting my face in contact with that of some decayed Egyptian; but as the passage inclined downwards, my own weight helped me on: however, I could not avoid being covered with bones, legs, arms, and heads rolling from above. . . . The purpose of my researches was to rob the Egyptians of their papyri.[1]

Even the more scholarly of the early archaeologists, if not so candidly larcenous as Belzoni, at least had a clear simple vision of what it was they were after and a rather romantic reason for their quest. In 1876, for example, the German Heinrich Schliemann, his imagination fired by his schoolboy readings of Homer (in the original Greek), ravaged the archaeological site of Hissarlik, in western Turkey, looking for the home of the heroes of the Trojan

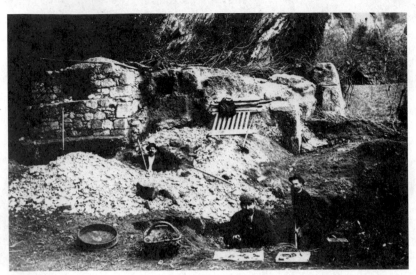

FIGURE 1.1 In the eighteenth and nineteenth centuries, archaeology was often more like organized looting of antiquities than scientific research. Here, workmen at a site near Les Eyzies, France, destroy a Paleolithic site while looking for nicely fashioned stone tools.

War, as chronicled in *The Iliad*. Schliemann's notebooks show that he made careful records of his finds and that he even had a primitive sense of analytical methods of archaeological excavation. He was ecstatic when he found gold masks affixed to decayed bodies in a cemetery at Hissarlik and concluded that these were the Trojan warriors. When he died, many years later, he was still happily unaware that what he had thought were the remains of Troy were probably of an altogether different era, and that he may have hacked right through the settlement occupied during the presumed period of the Trojan War.

The archaeology of today is significantly different from that of these nineteenth-century practitioners. If a professional archaeologist today were to excavate, for example, the parts of Troy that Schliemann left, she or he would make a detailed map so that everything found could be located to exact three-dimensional coordinates. And the actual excavations would require many more years than Schliemann spent, so that technical specialists could analyze pottery, animal and plant remains, architecture, and every other kind of find.

The most profound difference between the archaeology of Belzoni's and Schliemann's times and that of the present, however, is in research *objectives*: Almost all early archaeologists were looking for specific *things* (Figure 1.1). They seem to have had little sense of the importance of their finds except as curious and valuable relics of bygone ages. Most contemporary archaeologists, on the other hand, try to look beyond the objects they find to seek a more profound understanding of the past—and of ourselves in relation to the past.

WHAT ARE ARCHAEOLOGISTS LOOKING FOR? (THE MEANING OF THE PAST)

Archaeology is about Facts; if you want the Truth, go next-door to the Philosophy Department!

Professor Indiana Jones (dialogue from the film *Indiana Jones*)[2]

Most archaeologists spend years gathering small bits of stone, bone, and pottery that would not arrest the attention of a museum-goer for more than a few seconds; they then spend much of the rest of their lives in Hamlet-like reflection, asking themselves an endless and largely unanswered series of questions, such as: "What does all this stuff mean?" "What do these things tell me about what happened in the past and why it happened?" "What is the point of investigating the past?" "What can I hope to know about the people who made these things?" "Are there causal factors that we can identify that explain the course and nature of human history?" "Does the past have any relevance for our own lives?" "What does the past *mean*?"

This concern with the meaning of the past is one of the most difficult concepts for the non-archaeologist to understand about contemporary professional archaeology—and for many people it shatters an illusion that archaeology is just the pleasant pursuit of interesting relics in exotic locales. Most non-archaeologists, unsurprisingly, would be much more interested in, for example, viewing the gold masks that Schliemann found at Troy than in listening to professional archaeologists debate the inferred socioeconomic and political organization of the first millennium B.C. town at Tepe Hissarlik, where these masks were found. And yet it is just such debates, not the gold masks, that involve the kinds of questions central to contemporary archaeology.

Yet no one can comprehend what contemporary archaeology—or this book—is all about until one understands this relentless search for not just the artifacts of the past, but the patterns and meaning of our past. Most archaeologists are not just trying to answer specific questions, such as what our hominin ancestors first used stone tools for, or why the Neandertals disappeared, or how the ancient Egyptians built pyramids. In every archaeological excavation or research project many specific questions such as these are at issue, but the context of this research often involves the more abstract goals of trying to understand the factors that have determined the course of human history and the nature of our cultures, and thus not only to see patterns in the past but also to understand why those patterns appeared—and to explain in some sense the great variability in the world's long history of cultures.

It may seem odd that archaeologists even consider the possibility that something apparently so chaotic as human history may have some underlying pattern or meaning or explanation. How could a history that can be so radically affected by a single person like Adolph Hitler, or a blind yet potent natural process such as the end of the last Ice Age, ever be "explained" in general terms? But scholars throughout the ages have sought just such an explanation. The questions they have asked in this regard are many, difficult, and important for understanding ourselves and humanity: Is there some factor, for example, that explains why we seem to have evolved in the direction of ever greater brain size while our primate relatives, such as the chimpanzee, and all other animals seem to have retained relatively tiny brain-to-body size ratios? Why, after humans had lived for about two and a half million years as simple hunter-foragers, did some of our ancestors "suddenly" become farmers soon after about 10,000 years ago, and not just in the Old World but "independently" in the New World as well and at about the same time? Why were all ancient civilizations strictly organized in terms of social classes instead of according to the democratic ideals espoused by many philosophers over the millennia? Why does warfare seem to have been so common in history when there are such apparent advantages to cooperation and peace? Why did large cities appear in ancient civilizations in Mexico, China, Pakistan,

Mesopotamia, and elsewhere but not in aboriginal Australia, North America, England, or Hawaii? Does the archaeological record of the world indicate that human "races" differ in innate abilities and that cultures vary in their "accomplishments"? Do economic forces really "drive" history, as Karl Marx argued,[3] so that we can understand forms of religions and governments merely as by-products of these basic economic dynamics, or do great ideas and powerful individuals *decide* the course of history? Does "the past" really exist in some analyzable form and sense, or is what we call the past just our evanescent and unanalyzable imaginings about something irretrievably lost? Does the past tell us anything of interest about where we are going, about our future, and do we have any control over our future, or are we just "leaves on the stream" of time and circumstance?

Libraries around the world are filled with books that represent several millennia of attempts to answer these and related questions. Many complex theories of history have been propounded, but none has been shown to be a complete and powerful explanation of the human past. Reasonable people might suspect that, if these questions about the meaning and explanation of the past have not yielded powerful answers in all these millennia of study, then perhaps we are asking the wrong questions or perhaps the questions we are asking have no real answers. This book, in fact, is largely an attempt to chronicle part of the world's past and then review attempts to answer these many questions about the meaning of the past.

The very idea that we can aspire to understand and explain why history has turned out the way it has is one of the most hotly debated and complex issues in contemporary archaeology. British archaeologists Michael Shanks and Christopher Tilley, for example, argue that the human past can never be analyzed in terms of an empirical science that "explains" history, in the sense of answering in a scientific fashion the kinds of questions just posed about *why* history has turned out the way it has.[4] They argue first that the material remains of the past are just another "text," and thus, like any novel, the past can be understood differently by different people and also that every "reader" of every text, including the archaeologist who reads the archaeological record, is so bound by his or her own cultural biases and forms that there can be no such thing as an objective or definitive understanding of the past (Figure 1.2).

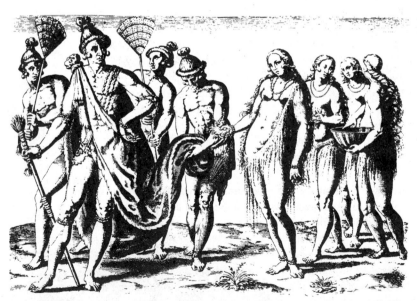

FIGURE 1.2 This sixteenth-century engraving of Florida Indians exemplifies ethnocentrism, or interpreting other cultures in one's own terms. The four women on the right are highly reminiscent of Italian Renaissance renderings of Venus and the Three Muses. Many European scholars of the last three centuries were ethnocentric in their analyses of ancient non-European cultures—most of which they assumed had incompletely evolved to the high level of European civilization.

Other scholars argue that the past can be analyzed scientifically and that with the future development of powerful theories, archaeology can be as much a science as geology, paleontology, or biology.[5]

Although we frequently shall return to these issues in this book, one thing seems clear—the primary problem in answering questions about the meaning of the past is not a lack of evidence. All over the world, museum shelves groan under the weight of ceramic pots, stone tools, and the broken skulls of our ancestors. Archaeologists have excavated everything from the first known human camps of two and a half million years ago to early twentieth-century Manhattan. And every year, archaeologists in the thousands spread out across the globe to excavate more remains of the past, and they then provide the results of their research to their colleagues and the world in the form of hundreds of thousands of books, articles, and lectures.

In the rest of this book, we will review thousands of these studies, but before wading into this sea of facts and figures, the reader should join archaeologists in musing on the point of all this sifting through the garbage of the past. These are complex issues, and to begin to analyze them it is necessary to consider the basic logical structure of archaeology as it traditionally has been practiced and some examples of archaeological analyses.

ARCHAEOLOGY AS THE RECONSTRUCTION OF EXTINCT CULTURES AND THEIR HISTORIES

The past is another country. They do things differently there.

L. P. Hartley[6]

Whether one views the past and the world's archaeological record as the product of a meaningless jumble of accidental events and concatenations of unrelated human decisions or as an explainable, even predictable developmental pattern, most scholars begin to try to understand the past by trying to reconstruct and describe it.

Reconstructions of the past are usually based on the principle known to the Romans as *ex ungue leonem*, literally, "from the claw, the lion," or the notion that from a part we can know the whole through the processes of analogy and inference. If one looks closely, for example, at the dinosaurs on display in various museums one can see that some of them comprise a very small amount of fossilized bone and a very much greater amount of plastic that has been inserted hopefully in place of the missing parts. And as scholars find new fossils, it is quite common, even today after centuries of research, for them to change the dinosaur reconstructions on exhibits to reflect new ideas about the arrangements of bones.

When we look at attempts to reconstruct entire cultures, not just bones, the principles are the same as in dinosaur reconstructions: We use the preserved parts to infer missing elements, based on our knowledge and speculations. In some situations the inferences one must make seem so obviously accurate and the evidence available seems so comprehensive that our interpretations seem particularly compelling. Archaeologists, for example, have carefully studied the remains found in the tomb of Egypt's Tutankhamun (Figures 1.3 and 1.4), and through a process of scientific analysis and inference we seemingly can know a lot

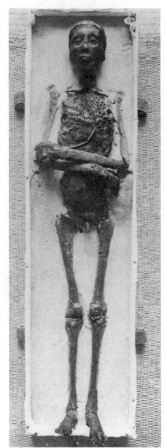

FIGURE 1.3 The contents of Tutankhamun's tomb provided a vivid picture of many aspects of ancient Egyptian life.

about this pharaoh and his culture. Studies of his teeth,[7] for example, indicate his genetic relationship to his relatives, some of whose mummified bodies have also been found; analyses of the food and wine with which his tomb was supplied appear to reflect both what he ate in this life and apparently hoped to eat in the next; analyses of the chariots, furniture, and jewelry reflect the arts and crafts of his age; and studies of the inscriptions on his tomb's walls and in contemporary documents offer descriptions of his religious beliefs and life-history.

What makes reconstructions such as that of Tutankhamun's life and times so vivid is not just the impressive preservation of objects; rather, it is that by analogy with our own lives we seem to understand so much about him. Most people of our own era, for example, still commit their dead to the earth with religious invocations offered in hope of some future resurrection. Even the thoughtful selection, in Tut's tomb, of dry and sweet wines from an impressive diversity of vineyards and vintages, all carefully labeled by estate, year, and chief vintner, seems so utterly human and part of the same fabric as our own lives.[8]

Reconstructions such as these, by means of analogy and inference based on our own lives and knowledge of history, offer satisfying accounts of the past in terms of our own experiences, and for many people they constitute all or most of what we can hope to learn about the past. We think we "know" Tutankhamun in a very real and personal sense. And for many people the "pleasures of ruins" they experience when they read about these reconstructions and interpretations require no great theoretical justification. Dull, indeed, would be the person insensitive to such pleasures. We do not know, and can never know, what really went on in Tutankhamun's mind, but by considering his tomb contents most of us think we can know a lot about his diet, the technology of his times, his place in the royal bureaucracy, and so on.

But are our analyses necessarily limited to these speculative reconstructions of Tutankhamun's life and times, or can we go further in attempting to understand Tutankhamun? We might, for example, consider him to have been just one example of the class-based state societies that existed all over the ancient world. Rich ancient tombs like Tutankhamun's have been found in China, Peru, Mexico, Iraq, and many other places. Thus Tutankhamun is part of a historical pattern in which all of the more complex "civilizations" of antiquity and today have been and continue to be organized on the basis of wealth and social classes. And thus, Tutankhamun brings us back to the most basic and important questions of historical analysis, such as: Why did these societies, Old and New World alike, all—largely independently—evolve social systems based on inherited privilege and wealth, in which the great mass of humanity labored mainly for the benefit of a small elite class?

By asking these grand questions about the past we need not sacrifice the pleasures and rewards of simply trying to reconstruct past times and cultures and their peoples' lives—people for whom we can feel a great deal of kinship and even sympathy. But even reconstructions of cultures that we know a great deal about raise important questions about archaeological inferences and about the "point" of such reconstructions. On about August 24, A.D. 79, for example, a group of people in an Italian coastal town concluded a funeral service for a friend by sitting down to a banquet. We can only wonder about what was said at the meal, but we know what food they ate, how they were dressed, and where they sat, because this town was Pompeii, and at some point in the banquet, poison gases from the eruption of the volcano of Vesuvius killed them all. They and their fellow citizens, and their neighbors in Herculaneum, were preserved in the midst of their daily activities (Figure 1.5). A half-cooked suckling pig, bread, and other foods were found in ovens; money was left near half-eaten meals in restaurants; wax tablets and papyri lay on library tables; bodies of townspeople were found curled over the children they were trying to protect; and in one case a woman's skeleton was found scattered over the floor of a room filled with volcanic ash, near the intact skeleton of a dog chained to a stake—suggesting that the dog slowly starved and eventually ate the body of its mistress.[9]

Written language aids greatly in "fleshing out" cultural reconstructions. Herculaneum's daily life was described in great detail in surviving documents;

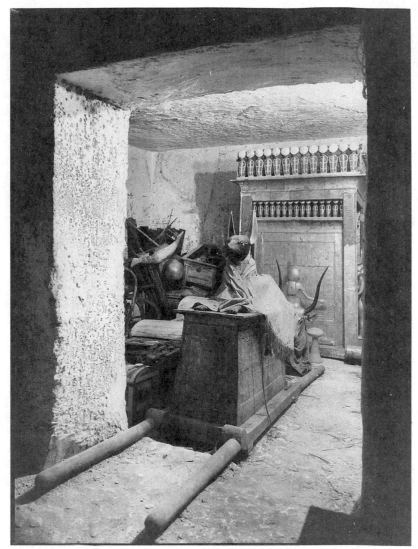

FIGURE 1.4   The entrance to the "Treasury" of Pharaoh Tutankhamun's tomb. The cloaked statue is a representation of Anubis, Lord of the West.

we even have graffiti on brothel walls describing the charms of particular prostitutes and other opinions common to such venues. In fact, Pompeii's and Herculaneum's destruction was recorded by people who took boats out to sea to watch it.

Whether an archaeologist is trying to reconstruct Pompeii or a two-million-year-old camp of early hominins in Africa, the intention is the same: Just as an ethnographer describes the daily life of the people he or she lives with and is studying, an archaeologist, substituting analogy and inference for direct observation, uses ancient objects to reconstruct as much as possible about the diet, technology, residences, burial practices, and beliefs—in short, the lifeways and cultures—of ancient peoples.

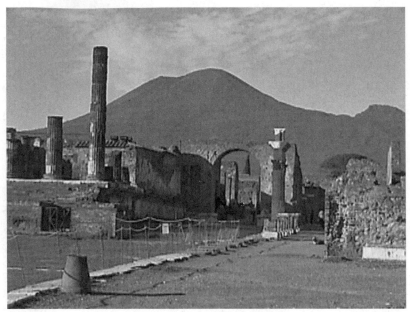

FIGURE 1.5 The eruption of Mount Vesuvius preserved Pompeii at a single moment in time. This is a rare occurrence that stands in contrast to how most archaeological sites are formed.

Compared to the riot of full life evident to the ethnographer, even analyses of towns like Pompeii may seem a pale and cold investigation into the dry stalks and stems of dead cultures. But the last several decades have seen major advances in the techniques of cultural reconstructionism (reviewed in chapter 2). An impressive array of electron microscopes, satellite imagery, chemical analyses, elaborate mathematical models, sophisticated computers, and other techniques are available to help the archaeologist make ever more persuasive inferences about the past.

But despite these many improvements, cultural reconstructions often include a large measure of speculation, particularly when dealing with extremely ancient societies, whose artifacts and lifeways may have no historical analogs and thus may require even more than the liberal amounts of imagination that inferences about more recent societies involve. And the possibilities for cultural reconstructions are essentially infinite: One can always excavate another site and fill in one more tiny bit of knowledge. Once the thrill of discovery has worn off, most archaeologists begin to wonder just how important it is to know, for example, whether this or that group ate more salmon than reindeer, or vice versa.

And of course there is really no way ever to confirm—to be certain—about one's reconstructions. The reconstruction of the dog at Herculaneum eating the body of his mistress may seem compelling, but one can imagine alternative interpretations; and reconstructions of less well-preserved and earlier sites are much less persuasive than those concocted about the living dead of Pompeii and Herculaneum. In short, one can make up extremely convincing stories about what happened at some ancient place, or what some ancient artifacts were used for, but we'll never be able to confirm such inferences conclusively—at least not in the way an astronomer's understanding of celestial mechanics is confirmed by the exact prediction of eclipses.

In this same context consider, for example, the remains of crocodiles we (Wenke) found while excavating in Egypt in 1981.[10] We discovered that one area that had been a few hundred meters from the shoreline of a lake in the late fifth millennium B.C. contained many crocodile bones but no crocodile skulls or teeth. Evidence indicated that this area was probably the site of a temporary camp, occupied in spring and fall, where people came to fish and hunt migratory birds. One evening, after a long day's field work, and inspired by one, perhaps two, "Stella" beers, we evolved the plausible notion that the ancient Egyptians were hunting these crocodiles for some unspeakable culinary purpose and, to aid in transporting the "edible" parts of their kills back to camp, they gutted the animals, cut off their heads and discarded them to rot on the shore, and then brought the rest of the carcass back to the site. Therefore, we conjectured, we had found no head bones in our excavations, just cut-up body bones.

Now, we could go back and "test" this hypothesis by excavating other sites to see if the same pattern is found elsewhere on the lake shore, or by checking the crocodile body bones carefully for cut marks, or in any number of other plausible ways. We could also generalize this specific idea and test some hypotheses about general cultural processes, such as the notion that hunters and gatherers tended to transport the shortest distance those animal parts with the least meat on them. Or we could generalize still further and test the notion that people tend to avoid work as much as possible.

A crucial problem with cultural reconstructions such as these is *equifinality*: One can imagine many different alternative explanations for our finding few crocodile head parts at this site, and very different factors and combinations of factors could produce extremely similar archaeological records; and in the end all that one could do is show that one hypothesis is more probable than the others. And such hypotheses would really only be particularly interesting in the context of some theory about ancient cultures—some set of generalized principles about the factors that determine the course of cultures in general, including our rag-tag bunch of ancient Egyptian crocodile hunters.

Thus, archaeological reconstructions of ancient cultures are probably as close to that staple of science fiction, "time travel," as humans are likely to achieve, and it is the powerful impulse to travel in time, at least cerebrally, that motivates many archaeologists. An archaeologist, given *one and only one* such time-travel opportunity, would probably have a difficult time choosing among so many interesting times and places. One could go, for example, to Africa's Olduvai Gorge about 1.7 million years ago to see how our early hominin ancestors made a living (a problem to which much of chapter 3 is devoted); or to France at about 50,000 years ago to document the relationship of Neandertals and our more direct human ancestors (see chapter 4); or to Egypt to determine once and for all how the pyramids were built (chapter 9); or to Pakistan's Indus Valley 4,000 years ago to learn what is contained in the thousands of Harappan written documents—one of the world's undeciphered scripts (chapter 10); or perhaps to London of the later nineteenth century, just to share a pitcher of beer with Charles Darwin or Karl Marx or another of the founding fathers of modern historical sciences.

But the important point here is that even if one could go back in time and study an extinct culture as its people lived it, one is still faced with the limits of cultural reconstruction and left with great questions of *why*—why was that culture of that form, and how did it evolve from previous human adaptations? └── *epistemology?*

Time, Causality, and Culture History

Very few things happen at the right time and the rest do not happen at all. The conscientious historian will correct these defects.

Attributed to Mark Twain, Herodotus, and others

Attempts to reconstruct the past may be "static" in the sense that in studying the long-dead citizens of Pompeii we may be interested only in how they lived on the day they were all killed.

But most attempts to analyze the past involve some sense of *sequence*, usually in the form of cultural changes over time. Reconstructing ancient cultures and putting them into chronological sequences are usually complementary parts of any archaeological research project.

The sense of time as infinitely stretching behind and ahead of us, as we ourselves flow along the stream of time, is very ancient. An accurate recognition of the awesome time-scale of the past, however, is relatively recent. Today nearly every educated person knows and accepts that our human ancestry extends back millions of years and that our civilizations have slowly evolved over thousands of years. But this sense of our place in time is really quite new. The recognition—or at least the widespread acceptance—of the idea that we, and our world, have been here for millions of years is only about a century old. Until the nineteenth century, most Western people accepted the biblical implication that the world was about 6,000 years old and that almost from the very beginning our ancestors had lived in towns, engaged in agriculture, and organized themselves in great states and empires. But nineteenth-century excavations deep below the ground levels of many European cities revealed the bones of animals long extinct, such as mammoths and cave bears—and amidst many of these bones were stone tools. By the early twentieth century the great antiquity of humankind was evident, and today almost all knowledgeable scientists accept that our earliest hominin, tool-using ancestors lived about two and a half million years ago.

This idea of reconstructing the histories of cultures works well when one is dealing with, say, the Roman Empire, where there are written records and the evidence of thousands of cities. But how do you write culture histories of prehistoric people who left no written records and of whom we have little more than the occasional skeleton and crude flint tools?

The main method of culture history is to make large collections of artifacts (the stone tools, pots, and everything else made or deposited by people) from each site (their houses, graves, or workplaces) and then make a lot of brave inferences about the cultural relationships among the people who made these pots, stone tools, or whatever.

Much culture history has been done on simple comparisons of artifacts. My associates and I (Wenke), for example, once walked the plains of southwestern Iran for five months, collecting bags of broken pottery from the thousands of ancient villages and towns to be found there. Most of these old settlements are now just mounds of decomposed mud bricks and garbage and are littered with thousands of scraps of broken pottery and stone. Through various dating methods (chapter 2), we knew the styles of pottery that were in use in different ancient periods in this part of the world. To the experienced analyst, for example, a fragment of a Sasanian (c. A.D. 225–640) clay pot is utterly different from a Late Uruk (c. 3200 B.C.) ceramic fragment (though both are impressively ugly). Each day we counted up the numbers of different types of pottery styles collected from each site. Sites that had very similar kinds of pottery were assumed to have been occupied at about the same time and to have interacted socially or economically; those with markedly different pottery styles were assumed to have been occupied at different times. On this basis, settlement maps for several successive periods of occupation in this area were inferred and a 3,000-year culture history reconstructed, complete with estimates of changes in population density, irrigation systems, possible wars, probable economic collapses—in other words, a rich, even emotionally moving, history of people known almost exclusively from 4,134 bags of pottery bits.

Such culture history "works" in the sense that through using these methods, we now know roughly what kinds of cultures inhabited most of the world during most of the past.

When we are dealing with the relatively slow change of styles in early stone tools, however, even with the help of modern chemical dating techniques we usually can form only rough categorizations of time into periods hundreds of thousands of years long.

It is unfortunate but probably inescapable that culture histories were often done in such a way that all the world's cultures were arranged like a giant ladder, leading to the pinnacle of Western societies. Because American and western European cultures of the nineteenth and early twentieth centuries were technologically the most "advanced," the archaeological record has often been viewed in terms of the way in which modern Western humans evolved from the first culture-bearing animals. Thus, cultural historical "explanations" of, for example, the appearance of agriculture and urban communities have tended to assume that these developments were the "natural" and inevitable products of prehistoric peoples who, like many Westerners, were constantly trying to improve their standard of living, and did so through technological development.

Such reconstructions of culture histories are prone to many problems. No histories, for example, are purely descriptive or entirely atheoretical. There cannot be an absolutely neutral and value-free history, particularly an archaeological "history," where interpretations frequently soar far beyond the evidence.

ARCHAEOLOGY AS A BODY OF THEORIES AND METHODS FOR EXPLAINING THE PAST

I shall certainly admit a system as empirical and scientific only if it is capable of being tested *by experience. These considerations suggest that not the verifiability but the* falsifiability *of a system is to be taken as a criterion of demarcation. . . .* It must be possible for an empirical scientific system to be refuted by experience.

Karl Popper[11]

Simply arranging archaeological sites in time and making inferences about the extinct societies that created them does not "explain" the past. But *can* we explain the past? What would we be trying to explain, and how? Take, for example, something as apparently simple as the origins of agriculture—a topic discussed in detail in chapter 6. After two and a half million years as hunter-foragers, about 10,000 years ago our ancestors began to domesticate plants and cultivate them. Farming did not appear in one place and then spread to the rest of the world; it developed in many different places at about the same time, in both the Old World and the New, and involved thousands of species, from yaks to cats, leeks to beets. Surely, one would think, with patient archaeological research one should be able to find the *causes* of agricultural origins—perhaps a combination of, for example, increasing human population densities, climate changes after the end of the last Ice Age, and improvements in technology. Evidence of such changes might be sought to show that they caused agriculture to occur—that they explain in effect why agriculture appeared in Southwest Asia about 10,000 years ago, and not 20,000 or 5,000 years ago, and why it was practiced first in Southwest Asia, and only much later in southwestern North America. And if we could explain agricultural origins in this fashion, it seems plausible that we might formulate similar explanations for the origins of writing, cities, warfare, state religions, and so on. And having constructed such explanations, one would think, we might be able to bring them together in a set of general propositions about people and history.

For centuries some scholars have worked on the premise that we can do more than just describe the past: We can understand it in terms of general principles—general principles to be formulated by some future Darwin of the historical sciences. After all, unlike ethnographers, who are limited to the study of societies as they exist today or existed in the recent past, archaeologists can study change over the long term, over the three million years of our history. It is this great time depth that is the primary resource and database of archaeology, for if it is ever possible to see the patterns in human history, and to define the determinants, it will likely require that we study the whole sweep of the human past in all its variety. When asked in the 1960s for his opinion about the overall historical impact of the French Revolution (almost 200 years earlier), Mao Zedong is reported to have said, "It's too early to tell." We expect major cultural dynamics to be long term. But we now have a vast and detailed knowledge about millions of years of the human past, and surely, one might assume, some major changes should be explainable.

In fact, however, as we will see in detail, there is nothing simple, nothing obvious about such attempts to explain the past. Archaeology is currently in the midst of a great identity crisis concerning such issues as whether or not we will ever be able to explain the past in these terms, and what "explanation" is. Physicist Steven Wolfram, for example, has recently argued that there are no simple cause-and-effect explanations of such phenomena as ancient civilizations.[12] Instead, he argues, complex systems that have a determinable time-span and an evolutionary trajectory can best be understood as algorithms. Many archaeologists have lost interest in older ideas of "explanation" and have focused instead on how we should *interpret* the past. These ideas will be considered at length throughout this book, but they are best understood in the context of their history.

A SHORT HISTORY OF ATTEMPTS TO UNDERSTAND THE PAST

It's about love, death, torture, infinity. It's a comedy.

Woody Allen

A hundred thousand lemmings can't be wrong.

Anonymous

The reader anxious to get to the blood, sex, and pyramids of prehistory may at this point recoil from a plunge into the philosophy of science and history, but it is simply impossible to understand what contemporary archaeologists are doing and why without a brief excursion into Western intellectual history. What contemporary archaeologists think about world history and how they go about interpreting it are inextricably linked to epistemological (i.e., studies of how we know and the nature and limits of our knowledge) traditions many centuries old. And beyond the relevance of these ideas to archaeology, the student will find that the ideas reviewed in this section permeate all of the humanities and social sciences in Western intellectual traditions.

The world's literature is littered with attempts to understand our place in the cosmos and make sense of our past. Ancient Near Eastern literature, especially as reflected in the comparatively late and derivative form of the Old Testament, envisioned a static, created world in which great changes came about through divine intercession, and where the ultimate explanation of events was in terms of God's will—which we see "as in a glass, darkly." For the devout Christian, Muslim, and many others as well, even if we could see the divine design of history more clearly, we would see that it is predestined, beyond the realm of human initiative. If one truly believes that the course of the world's events and history is an unintelligible expression of Divine Will, then history becomes simple post hoc description, not analysis—for analysis implies the search for knowable, testable causes.

As far as we know, the ancient Greeks were the first people to think profoundly (or perhaps they were simply the first to record their thoughts) about the problem of cause and effect in a supposedly divinely directed world. "We are all Greeks," it has been said, because so much of modern Western thought is ultimately traceable to ancient Greece. Some scholars feel that the Greeks were more deeply in debt to other cultures than we commonly suppose,[13] but in many ways it seems as if the Greeks simply thought about the world differently from their predecessors. Herodotus, for example, was the first, as far as we know, to travel widely and compile extensive descriptions of the people, cultures, and places of his world in a way that was *analytical.* In the fifth century B.C., for example, Herodotus visited Egypt and became intrigued by the question of why the Nile flooded each and every spring. He asked Egyptian scholars everywhere he went and found that the Nile rose and fell according to the will of the gods. Herodotus then preceded to analyze several reasonable alternative possibilities—all of them wrong—but all expressed mainly in terms of wind, rain, sun, and oceanic patterns, in other words, in terms of natural causes. In short, Herodotus analyzed, he did not just ascribe the Nile's flood to the inscrutable will of the gods. Similarly, in his late fourth-century B.C. history of the Peloponnesian War, Thucydides tried to explain how the struggle began. He described the personalities involved, the strategies of the warring powers, and the economic realities of the time. In short, by arranging the events and circumstances preceding the war in what he thought was a causal chain, he did what any modern historian would do in trying to explain the events of the past. Archaeologically based culture histories are founded precisely on this logic. Egyptians, Sumerians, and many others recorded aspects of their histories, but their surviving records do not treat the world or history in the same analytical fashion that the Greeks did. It is a mark of how culturally Greek most of us are that what Thucydides did seems so normal and natural to us as hardly to deserve comment. But in truth this sort of real-world explanation of the course of history seems to have been widely used first by the Greeks and became common in many other cultures only recently.[14]

Another central tenet of modern archaeology with Greek roots is evolution. Evolutionary theory was first clearly stated by Charles Darwin, and the ancient Greeks had only a vague sense of this idea. But already by the fifth century B.C. the Athenian scholar Empedocles had formulated a version of the principle of natural selection. And other Greek scholars developed rudimentary sciences of geomorphology and biology that contained

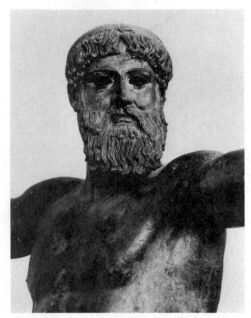

FIGURE 1.6   The ancient Greek view of the world was that it reflected the "perfection" of the gods in its symmetry and wholeness—attributes reflected in their art, as in this bronze figure from a Greek shipwreck of about 460 B.C.

glimpses of the fact that the world is very ancient and that plants and animals have changed over time.

These ideas of evolution and scientific analysis, however, were in some contrast to a concept much more central to the ancient Greek view of the world, the notion of the *Great Chain of Being*, or the *Scala Naturae,* which is founded on Greek ideas about the nature of God and "perfection." Greek philosophers found it inconceivable that the world they knew could have arisen by chance, because there seemed to be such a precise design in its every part. The intricate interdependence among plants and animals, the regularity of the seasons—the whole natural world—exhibited to them proof of the existence of a Supreme Intelligence; they therefore defined God as the perfect being who created and controls the world. The Greeks' conception of perfection, however, had a somewhat different connotation than it does for us, for they understood it to be in essence wholeness, or completeness (a concept vividly evident, for example, in classical Greek statues) (Figure 1.6).

Aristotle, in particular, formulated the idea of the world as a Great Chain of Being, perfect in its completeness (Figure 1.7). He concluded that the natural world was rationally ordered according to what he charmingly called "powers of soul," representing different levels within the perfectly whole universe. Thus, a horse is higher than a sunflower because a horse can think, after a fashion, and a man is higher than a horse because he can reason and apprehend God. Early European scholars were greatly influenced by the concept of the Great Chain of Being. They thought it impossible that there should be "missing links" in the chain or that any parts of the chain should cease to exist. God, being perfect, could not create an imperfect, that is, incomplete, universe; nor could His sustaining powers allow a whole level of this perfection to vanish. This notion was still at the very core of European culture when the English poet Alexander Pope (A.D. 1688–1744) wrote:

> Vast chain of being! which from God began
> Natures aethereal, human, angel, man,
> Beast, bird, fish, insect, what no eye can see,
> No glass can reach; from Infinite to thee,
> From thee to nothing.—On superior pow'rs
> Were we to press, inferior might on ours;
> Or in the full creation leave a void,
> Where, one step broken, the great scale's destroy'd—
> From Nature's chain whatever link you strike,
> Tenth, or ten thousandth, breaks the chain alike.

The idea of this Great Chain of Being pervades Western literature and science and continues well into our own time. It remains, for example, a major element in arguments by those who lead the repeated crusades to have the biblical story of Creation installed in American elementary education as a worthy alternative to evolution.

The concept of the Great Chain of Being, however, is impossible to reconcile with evolutionary theories and the discoveries of modern archaeology. And it is not simply a matter of the great antiquity of the human past, which has been revealed in the past century. For if God had created and sustained every bacterium, every sparrow, every Neandertal, how could it had happened that thousands of species had come into existence, flourished, only eventually to vanish? How could humans possibly have evolved from lower primate species and lived for millions of years as "subhuman" races now long since extinct?

It is easy to understand the attractiveness of the idea of the Great Chain. It placed humanity, the masterwork of the Creator, "but little lower than the angels." Furthermore, it "explained" why we are here and why the world seems so marvelously and intricately integrated and designed: God designed the world in every detail for His purposes and placed humankind in a position of stewardship over His creation. Yet in many ways, the last 200 years of Western philosophy have been a long struggle to come to terms with a gradual and profound loss of faith in the validity of the notion of the Great Chain of Being as evidence for the *Argument from Design,* as it came to be known in Western thought. This Argument from Design is the conviction that the intricacies and perfections of the world *prove* that humanity

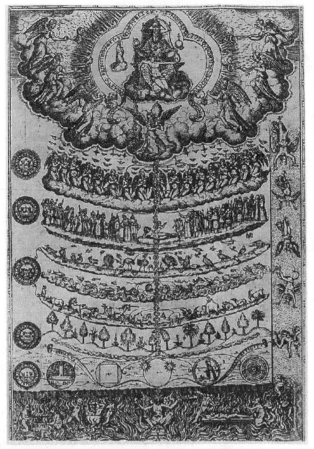

FIGURE 1.7   The Great Chain of Being placed humanity just lower than angels in a static view of the relationship between all living species.

and history are under divine control—that such a perfectly ordered and operating universe necessarily implies the existence of a creator and sustainer. This conclusion still has great power in the world, in both the Christian West and the Islamic East, for example, but it has been under assault for centuries.

The Enlightenment

Not until the "Enlightenment" of the seventeenth and eighteenth centuries were the intellectual foundations of modern archaeology securely established. Then, primarily in the eighteenth and nineteenth centuries, the *scientific method* was combined with *determinism, materialism,* and *evolutionism* to try to explain the world and history.

There can be no absolute definition of the scientific method, for rather than a method it is a state of mind along with a few assumptions. The key ideas are that most, if not all, things and events can be understood in terms of identifiable, measurable, physical forces, and that the best way to identify and measure these forces is to conceive ideas and then expose them to rejection through scientific experimentation or data analysis.

Although this sounds to most people like nothing more than common sense, history shows that it is a rather late and rare perception of the world. For most ancients and for many moderns, the world swarms with phenomena and forces that can never be understood by science; to them, in fact, precisely those aspects of human existence that cannot be scientifically understood or explained, such as why we are here and the nature and destination of the human soul, are the most important.

But, building on Greek ideas, seventeenth- and eighteenth-century scholars observed natural, social, and historical phenomena, devised hypotheses about their causes, and then tested these ideas by dropping balls from the tops of buildings (Galileo), flying kites in lightning storms (Franklin), and so on. What was scientifically essential in these analyses was that the ideas be exposed to falsification or contradiction by some sort of experimentation or alternative interpretation, that, above all, the explanation of something be considered not absolute, eternal truth, but just the best current hypothesis, subject to correction in the light of new research.

The materialist and determinist elements in this kind of science were the assumptions that the phenomena of this world—including historical and cultural phenomena—had some ultimate causation, that is, were in some way determined by knowable, measurable, material factors such as population growth, genetic mutation, infections, or gravity. If one accepted this view of the world, then one should look for explanations in the causal relationships and processes governing the attributes of phenomena, not in human decisions or divine agency. The evolutionary component was the notion that over time there had been and would continue to be an increase in complexity in the biological, historical, and political world—an ancient notion.

There is no necessary conflict between these ideas of Western science and religion. Few of the scholars of the Enlightenment were avowed atheists. Benjamin Franklin did important scientific research in the eighteenth century, but he was largely serious when he said that "wine is a continuing proof that God loves us very much and wants us to be happy." Thomas Jefferson, one of the most versatile intellects of the eighteenth and early nineteenth centuries, believed in God—as did many of his contemporaries—as a kind of a Great Clock-Maker, who set the universe in motion but does not often intrude upon its operation. Jefferson in fact "scientifically" edited the Bible to what he considered its essential and useful message, deleting everything he considered mythical and obscure, and produced *The Jefferson Bible,* a pamphlet of about forty-eight pages.

The Enlightenment scholars made brilliant advances in determining the physical mechanics of the universe and they avidly looked for the mechanics of human history, but most found no conflict between their science and their belief that God created these mechanics and set them into operation.

The Enlightenment was more than the crucible of modern science; it was in many ways the period in which the social perspective of the West first formed, particularly with regard to the notion of progress and conceptions of material culture. By the end of the eighteenth century, science had shown that the natural world was understandable in terms of the elegant (i.e., comprehensive yet reduced to the simplest possible terms) ideas of mathematics and physics. One result was that scholars everywhere began to apply the scientific method to the understanding of human history and the problem of cultural origins. For example, the Marquis de Condorcet (1743–1794), a French philosopher, proposed a series of universal laws he thought governed the history of human social organizations, and he went so far as to use his analysis to try to predict the future of the world.

Such direct applications of the physical science model to history might seem strange, but one must understand the eighteenth-century mind. "Common sense" tells us that history and culture are far too complex to explain in terms of simple mathematical laws, but common sense also tells us that we walk about on a flat earth, around which revolves the sun. The scholars of the Enlightenment had only recently been shown how treacherous common sense was and how the mysteries of the universe were being reduced to the commonplaces of science. Meanwhile, all around them great advances in the biological and historical sciences were being made.

In France, Georges Cuvier (1769–1832) undertook an extensive analysis of fossilized bones and concluded that hundreds of animal species had become extinct and that there seemed to be an evolutionary trajectory to the biological world. The French naturalist Jean Lamarck (1744–1829) published various arguments that the world was much older than the 6,000 years described in the Bible, and he arranged the biological world in a sequence, from human beings to the smallest invertebrates, in a way similar to later evolutionary schemes.

Scientific archaeology based on evolutionary and materialist assumptions was also emerging in the late eighteenth century, when P. F. Suhm published in 1776 a *History of Denmark, Norway, and Holstein,* based on the recognition that in many parts of Europe ancient people first made tools of stone, then of bronze, and finally of iron. This Three-Age System was first clearly stated and then developed by the Danish archaeologist Christian Thomsen in 1836 and by J. Worsae (1821–1885).[15] But its origins are much earlier. Lucretius (c. 98–55 B.C.), the great Roman scholar, wrote that "The earliest weapons were the hands, nails, and teeth; then came stones, and clubs. These were followed by iron and bronze, but bronze came first, the use of iron not being known until later." And as K. C. Chang has noted,[16] a near-contemporary of Lucretius, the Chinese scholar Yuan K'ang, stated essentially the same idea.[17]

Nineteenth-Century Evolutionism, Materialism, and Determinism

Excavations for the London Underground Railroad in the mid-1800s produced many curious finds, among them the bones of animals that sorely troubled the scientists of the time. Great elephant-like animals, standing 13 feet high at the shoulder, had left their skeletons amidst those of gigantic cave bears and many other animals that no longer lived in Britain—or anywhere else in the world. "Animals dead before the Noachian deluge," some concluded. But others sought scientific explanations. In England in the 1830s, William "Strata" Smith and Charles Lyell, among others, attempted to show that the earth was formed through the action of slow geological processes—processes still in effect. Lyell's contributions were particularly important because the dawning realization of the earth's great age had led some scientists and clergy to a belief in a series of "catastrophes," the last of which was Noah's Flood. Adherents of this position saw the fossil animal bones deep in the earth's strata as evidence that God had "destroyed" the world at various times with floods.

In 1848 John Stuart Mill published an evolutionary analysis of history that postulated a sequence of six stages: (1) hunting, (2) pastoralism, (3) Asiatic (by which he meant the great irrigation civilizations of China and the Middle East), (4) Greco-Roman, (5) feudal, and (6) capitalist. He complemented this classification with an extensive analysis of the economic factors determining these stages.

At about the same time Mill was writing, another Englishman, Herbert Spencer, applied the concepts of "natural selection" to human societies some years before Darwin applied them to the biological world, though his constructs were quite different from those eventually arising out of Darwinian thought.

Spencer was much influenced by Thomas Malthus, who in 1798 had noted that human societies—and indeed all biological species—tended to reproduce in numbers far faster than they increased the available food supply. For human groups, he postulated, this meant a life of struggle in which many were on the edge of starvation and more "primitive" societies lost out in the struggle for survival to the more "advanced" cultures. Spencer believed that eventually natural selection would produce a perfect society:

> Progress therefore, is not an accident, but a necessity. Instead of civilization being artifact, it is part of nature; all of a piece with the development of the embryo or the unfolding of a flower. The modifications mankind have undergone, and are still undergoing, result from a law underlying the whole organic creation; and provided the human race continues, and the constitution of things remains the same, those modifications must end in completeness. . . . So surely must the things we call evil and immorality disappear; so surely must man become perfect.[18]

Spencer's ideas permeated archaeological analyses of early civilizations and social forms, but they are now largely abandoned, for various reasons (see chapter 7). Some scholars consider Spencer to have been a racist whose notions of progress have misled a century of social science. But Spencer was a brilliant analyst, and he was operating on assumptions that seemed eminently reasonable in the nineteenth century: that history is subject to natural laws, that we can know these laws, and that—as Spencer's whole life experience showed him—applications of science to human affairs could only lead to progress. Thomas Huxley read a draft of Spencer's *Principles of Biology* (1864), and he and others convinced Spencer that "progress" was the wrong concept to apply to biological evolution, so Spencer used "persistence"; but in his ideas about human history he simply could not escape the notion that what history principally showed was "progress."[19]

CHARLES DARWIN

How very stupid not to have thought of that.

T. H. Huxley (referring to Darwin's ideas about evolution)[20]

On a warm Saturday afternoon in June 1860, about a thousand people gathered in Oxford, England, to witness a debate on Charles Darwin's (Figure 1.8) theory of biological evolution. For years Darwin had studied the animals and plants of South America, and he had formulated ideas about "descent with modification." But for various reasons he was reluctant to publish his views. Only when he knew that others were about to publish similar evolutionary analyses did he advance his opinion that for centuries the biological sciences had been in error concerning the origins and nature of biological species. Before Darwin, most scholars had assumed that all varieties of plants and animals were the direct product of God's creative might, and humankind itself was viewed as a special act of creation. In fact, as noted earlier, long before Darwin and continuing through his age and into our own, the Argument from Design, the idea that the intricacy, complexity, and interdependency of the universe point unmistakably to the existence of a Divine Creator, has been one of the major intellectual currents in Western civilization—and in other cultures as well.

But Darwin's research all but eliminated from educated Western thought the Argument from Design. On his travels through South America, Darwin had been particularly impressed by the great diversity of plant and animal life in the Galapagos Archipelago, near Ecuador. There he found islands geologically similar and within sight of one another, but nevertheless inhabited by significantly different species of plants and animals. Why should there be such diversity in such a small area?

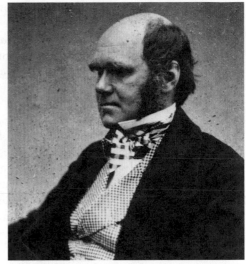

FIGURE 1.8 Charles Darwin (1809–1882) altered forever human conceptions of the dynamics of the physical world and the nature of history.

> It was evident (after some reflection) that such facts as these could only be explained on the supposition that species gradually become modified; and the subject haunted me. But it was equally evident that neither the action of the surrounding conditions, nor the will of the organism . . . could account for the innumerable cases in which organisms of every kind are beautifully adapted to their habits of life—for instance . . . a tree-frog to climb trees, or a seed for dispersal by hooks or plumes. I had always been much struck by such adaptations, and until these could be explained it seemed to me almost useless to endeavor to prove by indirect evidence that species had been modified.[21]

Darwin knew of course that for millennia farmers had used selective breeding to improve their animals in specific ways, such as increased milk production in cows. But these changes were the result of purposeful intervention in these animals' breeding patterns. How could such selection come about in the natural world?

Darwin was influenced by Malthus's idea of population and Adam Smith's concepts of economic competition, and he was much impressed with the importance of competition in all spheres of life: "Being well prepared to appreciate the struggle for existence which everywhere goes on from long-continued observation of the habits of animals and plants, it at once struck me that under these circumstances favorable variations would tend to be preserved and unfavorable ones to be destroyed."

With these observations and simple conclusions, Darwin provided the world with answers to a whole range of perplexing questions. Why was there such variety in the biological world? Because so many different environments were inhabited for so many millions of years, which allowed natural selection to shape biological populations to these varied environments. Why did animals and plants change over time? Because their environments had changed and some individuals were better equipped to survive and pass on their personal characteristics.

Darwin knew nothing about the genetic mechanisms we now recognize as the agencies through which biological diversity arises and on which natural selection operates, and he believed that characteristics acquired by an organism in its lifetime could be passed on to its offspring. We now know this to be a misconception. We also know that Darwin was deeply in debt intellectually to other scientists.[22] Moreover, great debates currently rage in theoretical biology about the mechanisms of evolution. Some scholars believe, for example, that existing biological systems, whether they be organisms, populations, or species, "constrain" the possible directions of evolutionary change in a way that cannot be accounted for in classical Darwinian ideas about natural selection.[23] But all this does not detract from his great contribution.

Darwin put in motion an intellectual revolution that has continued to the present and has battered the very foundations of Western ideas about the nature of God, humanity, and history. Through logic and evidence, Darwin and his contemporaries showed there had been millions of years in which the world had been dominated by reptiles, eons in which there were no people. Thus he forced people to wonder how God could be glorified by countless generations of snakes and lizards and dinosaurs breeding, fighting, and dying in primeval swamps, and why they should consider humanity a special act of creation if people, too, developed from earlier, simpler forms, from ancestors who were no more imaginative, intelligent, creative, or religious than any other animal.

As noted earlier, it is important to recognize that there is no *necessary* conflict of these ideas with Christianity or other religions; indeed, many founders of Western science remained true believers until their deaths. They simply assumed that God used the natural processes of the world to work out His Divine and Unknowable Plan. Thus the Austrian monk Gregor Mendel (A.D. 1822–1884) could serenely work out the genetic basis of biological evolution and still die untroubled in his faith. And Darwin thought that through evolutionary processes people would eventually become altruistic and profoundly civilized, and he himself said that he had "never been an atheist in the sense of denying the existence of God" (although he professed a rather muddled agnosticism).[24]

But the great mass of people were shocked and troubled by the implications of evolutionary theory. Evolutionary biology is now the only generally accepted theory of biology, and few scientists doubt its essential validity. But in that room at Oxford in 1860, Darwin and his advocate, Thomas Huxley, were reviled and ridiculed (Figure 1.9). This hostility characterized reaction to Darwinian ideas well into our own times, and it is not at all surprising that this should be so. In a sense, Darwin completed Galileo's revolution. Galileo showed that the earth was just one among an inconceivable number of celestial bodies, without apparent special claim to centrality; Darwin showed that today's human being is one of many related life-forms and is always a "transitional form," constantly changing, with no apparent claim to centrality in the universe.

As Stephen Jay Gould points out, however, evolutionary theory makes no pretense of explaining the ultimate nature or purpose of human existence—if it is humanly possible, at all, ever to answer such questions. Evolutionary theory simply supplies powerful explanations of change over time in human biology and society—leaving the problem of ultimate causation to some other forms of inquiry or to faith.

But to understand the vehemence and loathing in the initial reaction to evolutionary theory and its persistent controversial status, one must recognize that evolutionary theory goes beyond simply calling into question the argument that the design of the universe necessarily proves the existence of a divine creator and sustainer. The important point here is that the impact of evolutionary theory on how we view our universe and our past, present, and future has been profound and continues to reverberate through science and culture, and it calls into question some of the most cherished and ancient notions about human morality and worth.

It is important to note in this context, however, that evolutionary theory cannot *prove* that the Argument from Design is wrong. It simply provides an alternative explanation of how the biological and cultural history of earth might have happened. And as powerful as evolutionary, material-ist, and determinist theories have been in shaping our world, they will probably never eradicate nonscientific "knowl-edge." One of novelist G. García Márquez's characters says, "I don't believe in God but I'm afraid of Him," and we can find vestiges of the same thought throughout modern cultures.

One reason for this is that from some perspectives the evolution of life is so extraordinarily improbable. If the earth's orbit had been 5 percent closer to the sun, for example, the earth would have been far too hot for life to evolve; if the earth

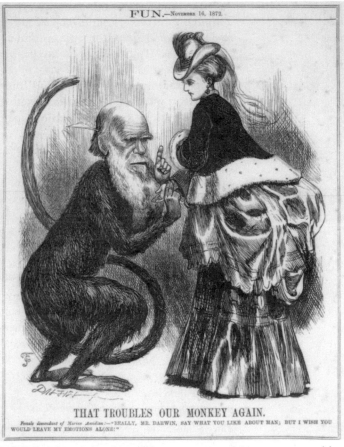

FUN.—November 16, 1872.

THAT TROUBLES OUR MONKEY AGAIN.

Female descendant of Marine Ascidian:—"REALLY, MR. DARWIN, SAY WHAT YOU LIKE ABOUT MAN; BUT I WISH YOU WOULD LEAVE MY EMOTIONS ALONE."

FIGURE 1.9 Many nineteenth-century cartoonists were amused by the idea of biological evolution.

were 1 percent farther out, all the water on the planet would be locked in glacial ice. It is easy to understand why many people through the ages have concluded that the earth was designed for humans. Some scientists accept that the complex chemicals constituting the self-replicating compounds necessary for biological life *could* have evolved by random processes, but consider the few-billion-year history of organic earth life to be too short for this to be a probable occurrence. Hence, some hypothesize that the earth passed through a space cloud of organic molecules, from which we are all descended.

But such subtle points were unknown to people of Darwin's age. Darwin and other evolutionists had posed cosmic questions and had provided compelling answers. Their arguments and research showed that not just biological species, but cities, ships, pyramids, farms, religions, parliaments—all things cultural—had evolved out of earlier, simpler forms; they implied that we have no special claim to centrality or exemption from the processes of the universe. And, perhaps most important, Darwin's ideas made it reasonable to ask whether or not there were principles with which to understand our cultural as well as our physical evolution.

It is important to recognize that Darwinian theory is more than just an abstraction about how the biological universe acquired its present form. In its application to cultures and history, Darwinian theory is profoundly political. When it was first widely accepted, in the late nineteenth century, some people justified rampant Western colonialism and exploitation in terms of the "survival of the fittest," implying that it was somehow natural and right that "higher" social systems control, coerce, and replace "primitive" ones.

Darwin was in some senses a "gradualist," who saw evolution operating at a constant rate, finely sifting through variations, perpetuating some, extirpating others. Biologists Niles Eldridge and Stephen Jay Gould countered the gradualist vision of evolutionary processes with a concept of "punctuated equilibrium," or periods of rapid change interspersed with long periods of much slower change. Here, too, the possible applications of these ideas are not just to biology. Evolutionists such as Eldridge and Gould, for example, have argued that gradualism has been used implicitly by some to justify a slow, gradual pace of social reform.

As we shall see, Darwinian principles are simply indispensable to understanding the subjects of chapters 3, 4, and 5 of this book. They are the only scientific basis we have for trying to understand how we evolved out of early nonhuman hominins and how we converted plants and animals into the power sources on which our societies have been based.

Much less clear, however, is the extent to which Darwin can help us understand the origins of civilizations and the basic dynamics of human history and society.

HISTORICAL MATERIALISM

[The purpose of critical materialism is] to help
men out of their self-made prison of
uncomprehending economic determinism.

Alfred Schmidt[25]

Schmidt's observation is, if true, perhaps the most powerful justification one could make of the contemporary importance of archaeology and historical analysis. Marxists and other determinists conclude that slavery, poverty, violence, and other ills of the world through history have been the result of economic determinants that have never been fully understood. They suggest that if these determinants can be analyzed and applied, then these ills will eventually disappear.

Archaeological analyses of the past have been greatly influenced by various notions about "determinism." Determinism, as applied to human history and culture, is the imprecise collective term for the idea that what happened in history was (partly, or largely, or entirely) the result of determining factors that are outside "free will" or the influences of divinities.

Although statues of Lenin and Marx have recently and literally been consigned to the "dustbin of history" in much of the world, along with the sociopolitical systems purportedly based on their philosophies, it does not necessarily follow that Marxist methods of historical analysis are entirely worthless. Even archaeologists who consider Marxism a bankrupt political ideology are in debt to Marxian thought in many of its elements of materialist determinism. Marxism, or at least materialist notions, are a "natural" for archaeology because archaeologists spend their lives amidst heaps of materials—the houses, stone tools, storage bins, pots, weapons, irrigation canals, and other items that constitute the technology of a central Marxian concept of the "means of production."

An early anthropological expression of evolutionary and materialist ideas that had considerable impact on studies of the past was the work of Lewis Henry Morgan (1818–1881), who divided history into a series of stages on the basis of initial uses of fire, bow and arrow, pottery, domesticated animals, writing, and so on. Karl Marx (1818–1883) (Figure 1.10) was influenced by Morgan and other earlier evolutionists, but the full impact of nineteenth-century evolutionism was achieved only when it was combined with Marx's ideas about material-ist determinism.

Certainly one of the most diverse—not to say solipsistic—associations of all time is that group of individuals who have tried to explain what Marx meant. People have killed each other in disputes over Marxian interpretations, and neo-Marxist variants on the basic Marxian ideology are so diverse as to defy summariza-tion. The student with a sense of humor and a good German dictionary is invited to read Marx's original description of the all-important "modes of production" and "relations of production," and then to follow the exegesis of these terms into the contemporary era. Scholars of every inclination, from Platonic idealism to existentialism, have claimed inspiration from Marxist theory.

But what has all this got to do with archaeology? Precisely this: Some of the most influential archaeologists of our century have used Marxian ideas in their analyses.[26] Often these forms of Marxism are quite different from what Karl Marx himself professed, but they are derived from nineteenth-century ideas about historical material ism and determinism.

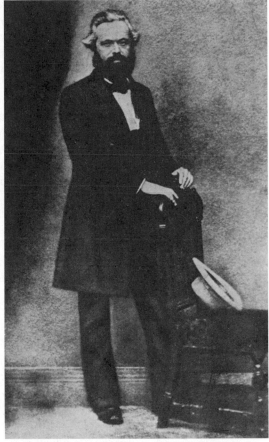

FIGURE 1.10 Karl Marx (1818–1883) profoundly influenced anthropology and archaeology by revealing the links between the economic basis of societies and their political institutions, social structures, and other cultural characteristics.

As we will see in chapter 7, Marx argued that much of human history could be understood on the basis of an analysis of how a society produces and distributes its wealth. He attempted to show that everything—wars, social classes, poverty, parliaments, religion, art—could be explained if one examined the technology, economy, and environment of a given society and the social relations people establish in relation to these economic and environmental factors. In recent years there have been numerous reworkings of Marxian theory, and the most recent archaeological expressions of these ideas stress the social relations that people enter into in producing and consuming goods. These, rather than just the blunt forces of climate, crops, and technology, are seen by Marxist archaeologists as the determinant factors of history. An important point of departure for some, more tradi-tional, Marxists is that historical analyses must be *comparative*. They "contend that a comprehensive view of all ancient societies, seen in relation to each other, will reveal general outlines of a regularity in the historical development of humanity"[27]; they assume that ancient human societies practiced an initial primitive communism, followed by the inevitable appropriation of surpluses in early agricultural communities, and the subsequent formation of "class society [by] strictly logical laws." They conclude that analysis of the forces that resulted "in the stratification of society into antagonistic classes" provides "the key for our understanding of the course of the subsequent history of ancient society," and that "all Marxist historians adhere to the concept that, in the final analysis, the relations of production are determined by the level of development of the means of production."

In contemporary Marxist archaeology[28] many of these assumptions and ideas are being debated. Contemporary Marxist archaeologists differ greatly in their perspectives, but many of them consider social conflict as major determinants of cultural change; they also are trying to create a "human-centered" view of the past, in which people are not just passive, reacting elements whose actions and beliefs are not simple products of external economic and environmental forces, but instead are themselves the agents of social dynamics and cultural changes.[29]

We will consider contemporary expressions of Marxist ideas in archaeology more fully in chapter 7. It is sufficient here to note that materialist determinism in various forms and philosophies has had a long and profound influence on archaeology. Moreover, Marxist ideas retain great potency in contemporary archaeology, especially among the post-processualists.

EARLY TWENTIETH-CENTURY ARCHAEOLOGY

To sum up: 1. The cosmos is a gigantic fly-
wheel making 10,000 revolutions a minute. 2.
Man is a sick fly taking a dizzy ride on it. 3.
Religion is the theory that the wheel was
designed and set spinning to give him the ride.

H. L. Mencken[30]

From the mid-nineteenth century to the beginnings of the twentieth, archaeology entered a remarkable era of Discovery and Decipherment[31]—this was the period in which Egyptian hieroglyphs and Mesopotamian cuneiform were first deciphered and major archaeological excavations were undertaken everywhere. In 1922 Lord Carnarvon and Howard Carter opened the tomb of Pharaoh Tutankhamun in Egypt and in the same year Sir John Marshall began excavating the great Harappan civilization in the Indus Valley; in 1926 Sir Leonard Woolley discovered the Royal Tombs of Ur in Mesopotamia; and all over the world at this time other marvelous archaeological discoveries were being made.

Archaeology made great progress in this era, but it was also a time in which archaeology was dominated by Europeans and Americans in an ethnocentric and imperialist way that even today gives the discipline a negative image in many parts of the world. The French and British in particular, but all Western nations to some extent, looted the antiquities of other lands, especially Greece, Turkey, Egypt, Iraq, and Iran. European governments collaborated with archaeologists to extract antiquities concessions from weak governments. When the British and French controlled Egypt, they always made one of their own citizens the director of the Egyptian antiquities service. Archaeologists, in turn, sometimes acted as spies for their governments.[32]

World War I with its horrible carnage, the Depression of the 1930s, and the other dismal events of this era disillusioned many intellectuals and caused them to doubt any notion of human social evolution—at least in the sense of a world growing more rational and moral, of *progress* in any sense. The first half of the twentieth century saw an age of existentialism and in many senses a rejection of rationalism. Darwinian notions of struggle and godlessness, the irrationality of world wars, all these destroyed for many people the last vestiges of the Argument from Design and resulted in a profound sense of cosmic isolation.

The philosophical currents of the early twentieth century produced in archaeology a largely nontheoretical discipline in which most scholars contented themselves with patient accumulation of artifacts and a minimum of interpretation. This period was the "Golden Age" of cultural reconstruction and culture history. In the United States the federal government invested considerable sums in archaeological investigations, in part as a way to employ people during the Depression. It was widely assumed that progress in explaining prehistoric cultural developments would be made only when much more archaeological evidence had been accumulated and the "facts be allowed to speak for themselves." Even by the 1930s, however, there was a growing frustration with the idea of an archaeology limited just to an endless series of inferences about how ancient people lived and how they were related culturally. And many scholars, such as the Marxist archaeologist V. Gordon Childe, continued to work on a science of history.[33]

One of the earliest and most influential attempts to move archaeology beyond simple data collection and description was Julian Steward's 1949 classic article, "Cultural Causality and Law: A Trial Formulation of Early Civilization."[34] Steward tried to relate worldwide similarities in the evolution of cities, writing, warfare, urbanism, and so on, to basic determinants of ecology, technology, and demography.

ARCHAEOLOGY 1960–1996

Every decoding is another encoding.[35]

The New Archaeology   After about 1960 there was a major revival of the idea of archaeology as a historical "science." In the 1960s some archaeologists tried to introduce into archaeology the logical methods they saw in physics and chemistry, on the premise that even if archaeology could not be entirely the same kind of science as these "natural sciences," they could at least use the same kinds of logic for analysis.[36]

Why would physics and these other sciences be so attractive as models for archaeologists, to the extent that archaeologists were accused of "physics envy"? Primarily because physics and the other natural sciences offer powerful *explanations*. Natural scientists use a limited number of principles, such as the principles of relativity, thermodynamics, and so on, and powerful mathematical formulations to explain much of the workings of the physical universe. We *know* what causes eclipses, thermonuclear explosions, malaria, and other natural processes to the extent that we can control these forces and make televisions, nuclear reactors, and genetically engineered plants and animals.

Attempts to understand the human past in terms of principles like those of physics have a long history in Western culture. Archaeologists have wanted to know what *caused* the first vaguely human animals to use stone tools, what factors drove these early hominins into the northern temperate latitudes, why people changed from hunting-gathering to agriculture, what forces impelled people to establish cities, develop written languages, wage international wars—in short, why history has turned out the way it has.

One of the most influential scholars in the attempt to make archaeology a powerful science has been Lewis Binford. While a student at the University of Michigan, Binford was impressed by anthropologist Leslie White's evolutionary, materialistic vision of anthropology.[37] In an influential and programmatic series of papers Binford argued that archaeologists should turn their attention from endless excavations and attempts to reconstruct ancient cultures and culture histories and concentrate instead on the study of general cultural processes. Binford particularly stressed the importance of problem orientation and testing hypotheses. He argued, for example, that the initial appearance of agricultural economies independently in different areas of the world was the result of climate changes, population growth, and various cultural adaptations of peoples in certain environments. He then related a wide range of archaeological data to his hypothesis in an effort to explain why agriculture appeared when and where it did.

Binford and many others sought to make archaeology an objective, empirical science in which hypotheses about all forms of cultural variability could be tested. This *New Archaeology* (also called *processual archaeology*) includes many diverse perspectives, methods, and ideas, but there are some common elements.[38] First, many archaeologists believe that *mathematics* can play a powerful role in archaeological analyses. Mathematical analyses of many different types have been applied to archaeological data, and some of these will be reviewed in later chapters. Second, almost all attempts to make archaeology a science have assumed that this would be an *evolutionary* science—at least in the sense that important differences between cultures represent development from simple to complex. The application of Darwinian ideas of evolution to human societies has in many ways just begun, and some archaeologists see great potential in this approach. Third, the New Archaeology also has stressed *cultural ecology,* in the sense that it looks for the causes of major cultural changes primarily in factors like climate changes, variability in the agricultural productivity of different environments, technological changes, and demographic factors. But most of the archaeologists of this era assumed that ancient cultures were complex integrated *systems*—that is, the patterns of cause and effect are complexly interrelated and are rarely unidirectional. Thus, if one were to consider why people in ancient Iraq first began cultivating plants, one would expect that the answer would involve many different factors, such as changes in population densities, climate fluctuations, evolving technologies, the genetic properties of certain plant genera, and so on. Human societies are assumed to have regulating mechanisms that promote the group's adaptation. Most human societies, for example, have developed means of birth control to regulate their population-to-resources balance; the intensity with which birth control is practiced can change as the resources change. To some extent then, the systems view of cultures is that they are self-regulating entities, open to influences from their environments. Explanations based on this model are often *functional* explanations: Just as a biologist might account for the evolution of the mammalian heart as a way to circulate blood, an archaeologist might account for the rise of state religions in all early civilizations by the functional benefits of a low-cost, ideological mechanism like religion to organize and control the mass of the population for military and economic purposes.

The goal of reformulating archaeology as a mathematical, evolutionary, ecological science for analyzing extinct complex cultural systems remains a strong theme in contemporary archaeology, but there has been a widespread loss of faith in the possibility of a "physics of history." Most archaeologists recognize that human history is in some ways fundamentally different from some of the material phenomena of the world, such as atoms. For one thing, human history is the product of *natural selection* in a way that does not seem true of the history of galaxies and subatomic particles (this point is discussed in later chapters). The human past by definition is a specific sequence in time and through a particular space—the planet earth—while the principles of physics and chemistry are applicable (at least theoretically) to all times and places. That the volume of a gas is determined by its pressure and temperature is assumed to be true now and forever, here and in the farthest reaches of the universe.

But biology, population genetics, ecology—these and other life sciences deal with a historical sequence of life-forms in a particular place, earth. Yet these are powerful mathematical explanatory disciplines, and some archaeologists continue the quest to formulate a science of archaeology that is similar to these disciplines. Unlike the natural sciences, however, there is no "theory" that unites and focuses the research of the many practitioners of archaeology in the same way that evolutionary theory and population genetics unite biologists and thermodynamics unites physicists. Some scholars, nonetheless, see the potential for a unifying theory for archaeology in Darwinian evolutionary theory, and we will consider this approach in more detail in chapter 7.

POST-PROCESSUAL ARCHAEOLOGY

Il n'y a pas hors-texte. [There is nothing outside of the text.]

Jacques Derrida.[39]

For the subjective idealism of scientistic archaeology we substitute a view of the discipline [of archaeology] as an hermeneutically informed dialectical science of past and present unremittingly embracing and attempting to understand the polyvalent qualities of the socially constructed world of the past and the world in which we live.

Michael Shanks and Christopher Tilley[40]

As these quotations illustrate, post-processual approaches to archaeology can be difficult to describe and understand. Indeed, it is one of the tenets of post-processualism that any attempt to summarize and capture the essence of the approach is doomed because there is no single approach, no unified perspective. The reader might wonder what all this theorizing has to do with the bones and stones of our ancient past: The point here is that many archaeologists say this theorizing has nothing to do with the study of our past, while, conversely, many post-processual archaeologists think it has everything to do with the study of the past.

The origins of post-processualism were described by Ian Hodder as an attempt to overcome perceived shortcomings in processual archaeology.[41] These include that processualists neglect the influence of culture, that they concentrate on norms rather than individuals, and that they rarely attempt to incorporte the ideas used by societies to structure how material culture fits into a society's world-view.

The post-processualists have found many different frameworks, but none that are "scientific" in the classical Western sense of that term. Most post-processualists believe that the search for an empirical science of artifacts is in essence a search for a unicorn, that archaeology can use a few scientific methods, such as radiocarbon dating, but that it will always be a humanistic enterprise and a fundamentally interpretive exercise, not an observational one.

The major flaw the post-processualists discern in the processualists is the assumption that archaeology can be a neutral, value-free, empirical science of artifacts. Young, for example, expresses this difference of opinion as, on the one hand, those who think that "history is what *happened* in the past," as opposed to the post-processualist notion that history "is what a living society *does* with the past."

Bruce Trigger,[42] drawing on the works of philosopher Larry Lauden, has identified and analyzed four main tenets of post-processualism in American and British archaeology. The first is the proposition that "no one perceives the world objectively: what we perceive, and even more what we interpret what we perceive, is influenced, either to some degree or entirely, by what we believe." A second related premise is what Trigger characterizes as the assumption that "sensory data or observational evidence is rarely capable of refuting strongly held beliefs." A third premise involves "holism"—the idea that "in order to understand any part of a system or issue we must first understand the whole." The fourth premise is the principle that "science is a social activity. This implies that science is only one source of knowledge among many, including common sense, religious beliefs, and perhaps even delusions."

As Trigger notes in his analysis, all of these premises are at least somewhat true, and few archaeologists would reject them totally. Contemporary disputes in archaeology revolve around the extent to which these premises are true and their implications for archaeological method and theory.

The abstract philosophical points that Trigger discusses are perhaps best illustrated by the work of British archaeologists Michael Shanks and Christopher Tilley.[43] Shanks and Tilley, drawing on the ideas of Derrida, Foucault,[44] and others, have argued that, just as one cannot assign a definitive single meaning to a text, one cannot make an empirically verifiable and definitive interpretation of the archaeological record. We create the past, they argue, and our interpretations of the past are limited by, and arise out of, our own cultural context.

This may seem an obvious point, that archaeologists' interpretations of the past are in part a function of their own sociocultural context. Archaeologists regularly report temples, social stratification, intensified storage, social class, warfare, states, and other "things" that do not, technically, exist. Our own culture determines to some extent what we make of the past. We can dig up people, sort through their feces, measure their bodies, sift their garbage for their food remains, translate their writings, measure their buildings, and do all kinds of scientific things to them, but in the end what we make of them will have a lot to do with our own lives and personalities.

Indeed, just as some ethnographers have concluded that human life and society have "only meanings rather than causes," some archaeologists think that the emphasis of archaeology should be on assessing the meaning of the past for ourselves, rather than on futile attempts to understand the causes of the patterns and trajectory of the human past.

These post-processual forms of archaeological theory have had somewhat less influence in the United States than in Britain and Scandinavia, but the issues they raise have become prominent in theoretical circles everywhere. Indeed, some elements of post-processual archaeology derive from the *post-modernist* perspective that can now be found in many academic disciplines, such as literary criticism, architecture, and sociology. Exactly what post-modernism is in anthropology and archaeology is difficult to define.[45] As archaeologist Ian Hodder wrote:

> It is thoroughly engrossing for an archaeologist, a student of cultural change, to be living through the apparent "birth" of a new cultural style. Yet it is surprising how difficult it is to define and understand what is happening. The more I try to tie down post-modernism, the less coherent it seems. . . . [T]he growth of the style seems bigger than any individual's attempt to characterize it. Ultimately it engulfs any attempt to fix it.[46]

Whatever else they have in common, post-processual archaeologists view archaeology as profoundly *political.* Archaeologist Mark Leone, for example, in his archaeological interpretations of the early history of Annapolis, Maryland, discusses how his archaeological work there has involved contemporary African Americans and how his interpretations of the archaeological data from that city do not necessarily match those of the African Americans. Of this experience he writes:

> American archaeologists have only just begun to accept the constructivist view of knowledge, which implies that data are not neutral. . . . We are not at all accustomed to negotiating truth values with nonarchaeologists who are affected by our work. However, such negotiating does not debase archaeology. . . . The eventual result will be a much richer archaeology. It will produce not a single interpretation of data, but many interpretations; not one uniformly useful literature, but many incommensurable literatures.[47]

The post-processual perspective raises many important issues and poses some significant problems. For example, if "science" cannot be applied to the archaeological record to evaluate competing claims to the truth, and if there can be many equally "true" readings of any text, then it would seem that one would have to accept that Native Americans who believe that the New World archaeological record shows that they originated in North America, not Asia, have a claim to the truth equal to that of the majority of archaeologists who believe that Native Americans first came to the New World between 10,000 and 20,000 years ago.

Are these equally valid ideas? Some post-modernists and post-processualists reject this absolute relativism, but if "positivist" ideas about scientific evaluation are inapplicable to archaeology, as some of these scholars believe, there can be no "correct" or most probably accurate reading of the past.

What archaeologists do may not be "science" in the classical sense of that term, but many archaeologists reject the idea that all readings of the past are equally valid in terms of their accuracy with regard to what actually happened in the past. All of the terms in the previous sentence are "loaded" in a sense. "Correct" does not necessarily have to be in relation to whether Native Americans originated in North America or not. Correctness, validity, and accuracy can be understood here to mean that they are both culturally constructed beliefs about the past.

In general, there seems little post-modernists and post-processualists agree on except, perhaps, their belief that archaeologists who think they are doing "science" are mistaken.

Agency and Landscape Archaeology   One expression of the frustration many contemporary archaeologists feel with traditional processualist archaeology is the immense growth of interest in such topics as "agency," and the use of this concept in such applications as Landscape Archaeology. These concepts are part of the post-processual movement in archaeology—although they need not entail a complete rejection of more traditional processual approaches.

The archaeological landscape in its simplest conception is the physical background and field on which ancient peoples lived and left their stones, bones, pots, houses, and so on. In contemporary archaeology, however, the notion of archaeological landscape goes beyond that sense, to emphasize the social and symbolic ways in which ancient peoples invested their worlds with meaning.[48] As Knapp and Ashmore note, "landscape is an entity that exists by virtue of its being perceived, experienced, and contextualized by people."[49] As an example, consider Egyptologist Janet Richard's analyses of landscapes in the Nile Valley. Richards notes that the ancient Egyptians used an area of the site of Abydos as a royal cemetery for many generations. She suggests that this location can be explained by the fact that it is in a dramatic setting, on the border between the two environments the Egyptians recognized as their world, the desert and the cultivated lands—Kemet and Deshret. She concludes that by intentionally positioning the cemetery in this area, they were reinforcing the ideology of the pharaoh as the unifier of Egypt. And in so doing they created a political arena that fostered the conservative ideology of ancient Egypt.

Many similar examples could be offered. Great tombs, temples, and other monuments often seem to have been placed, for example, with regard to their visibility. The implication is that these constructions were intended to remind the people living around them of the social interaction between people, the power of the state, and the ideologies of their societies. People of the early farming communities of the Neolithic in Europe, for example, built tombs, such as dolmens and passage graves. Although these were not necessarily highly visible in the landscape, they were intimately linked to daily activities in the settlements. Christopher Tilley proposes that these grave monuments were multilayered symbols "read" by the Neolithic people who constructed them.[50] The meaning of the tombs thus depends on the context in which they were perceived—tombs are markers for important landscape features such as the transition from a flat plain (low) to a mountain (high), or they can be seen as referents to ancestors and the past history of groups living in the area.

The notion of *agency* may seem obvious: It is the recognition that people are the agents of cultural construction and cultural change. The world's archaeological record was created by the perceptions and activities of billions of people. To many archaeologists we cannot interpret the past by considering people as just constants in equations driven by ecology, environment, and technology. These are simply constraining factors; we must also consider how people intentionally shaped their cultural worlds. In the American Southwest, for example, Feinman, Lightfoot, and Upham have suggested that people living in pithouse communities had two major choices in sociopolitical organization.[51] In some settlements, people adopted a corporate-oriented strategy that focused on rituals, ceremonies, and storage shared by the entire community, with few differences between households. People living in other pithouse settlements chose a network-oriented strategy that emphasized social differences between households through elaboration of architecture and accumulation of surpluses.

Sex and Gender in Archaeology   Another example of how contemporary archaeology has developed from its traditional forms involves the ideas of sex and gender. One of the most evident impacts of post-processualism in contemporary archaeology is the growing interest in gender and in what some have called *feminist archaeology*. Concepts and discussions of gender and sex long predate the current interest in these subjects, of course, and not all discussions of this topic are part of post-processualism. As we shall see in chapter 3, for example, a pivotal concept in most hypotheses about how the first hominins evolved involves the relationship of males and females in economic and other behavior; and in later prehistory scholars have studied everything from the "goddess" female figurines of Neolithic Europe to the status of women in ancient Egypt. But contemporary feminist archaeological studies from the post-processual perspective diverge from these traditional studies in several ways. Biological sex is a relatively simple and useful dichotomy (although there are, of course, ambiguities), and a trained archaeologist can determine the sex of a well-preserved skeleton with considerable reliability. The exaggerated sexual characteristics of Pleistocene female figurines leave no doubt as to the sexual and reproductive capabilities of the person or idea represented. But gender is a cultural construct and not so easily defined. The terms "lesbian," "homosexual," and "bisexual" roughly fit sexual practices, but perceptions of these genders differ radically in different societies. Even more abstract are the long-term historical dynamics that have shaped perceptions of gender and the processes of interactions of different genders and sexes.

Perhaps the most important element in post-processualist expressions of feminist archaeology involves the rejection of some forms of empiricism. Traditional archaeology long neglected many aspects of sex and gender because it appeared difficult to relate the bones and stones of the archaeological record to gender or sex. In excavating an Egyptian archaeological site, for example, one finds what looks like the remains of villages. There are mudbrick walls, floors of compacted sand filled with the bits and pieces of daily life, such as fragments of burnt bone and wheat, small bits of pottery, and so on, and there are also things that look like hearths, latrines, animal pens, and a thousand other remnants of a 5,000-year-old residence. Reasonable archaeological analyses can estimate when people lived here, what foods they ate, what tools they used, whom they traded products with, how big the community was, how they buried their dead, and many other aspects of the culture of which these people were a part. Inferring the gender of the people who used particular artifacts and the relationship of males and females in this extinct community could begin with generalizations made from the many ancient Egyptian paintings and texts, which indicate that men and women did very different kinds of work. Other resources that might help decipher gender-related tasks in this ancient society could potentially be found in ethnohistoric or ethnoarchaeological studies of life in Egyptian villages of the recent past. Such interpretations, however, might be regarded by a processual archaeologist as mere speculation that is on a lot less secure ground than estimates of diet based on recovered archaeological materials.[52]

Whatever the evidentiary basis of gender in the archaeological record, this topic carries with it some complex political and social implications. An enormous amount of evidence from archaeology, ethnography, and history shows that throughout the past women have been primary producers of much of the goods and services of all societies (Figure 1.11). Even in societies such as the Eskimo, where hunting is the primary source of food, women provide labor in the form of child care, food preparation, hide-processing, and many other

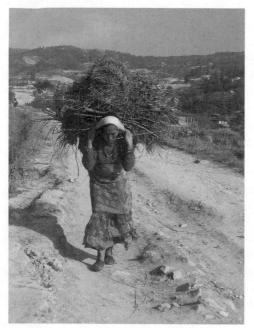

FIGURE 1.11   Both today and in the past, women have made substantial contributions to subsistence, goods, and services in society.

activities. In agricultural societies throughout history women have also provided much of the material wealth and available services in these societies, in the form of the toil of farming; the production of pottery, textile, and other craft goods; child care. and a thousand other activities.[53] Yet it also seems undeniable that throughout history these goods and services have often been appropriated by men outside the basic family unit, men who had the power to consume and redistribute this wealth. How does one explain this asymmetry, and is an attempt to explain it in terms of societal efficiency or biological factors necessarily an attempt to justify it? And if we write a world prehistory and history that concentrates on the people of power, the pharaohs, priests, and other male potentates, do we necessarily ignore and devalue the contribution of women?

These are important issues in contemporary archaeology, and whatever the ultimate long-term impact of post-processual ideas about archaeology as a political act and statement, considerations of gender have raised topics well worth contemplation.[54] Like all cultural elements, constructions of gender in societies, and their variations over time and place, cannot be treated in isolation. Gender roles can only be understood in relation to such other societal elements as social stratification, marriage and kinship systems, inheritance patterns, rituals, and so on.

SUMMARY AND CONCLUSIONS

So, where do we—and archaeology and world prehistory—go from here, in the midst of these contrasting ideas about the nature of inquiries into the past? What can we know about the past, and how should we go about knowing it?

As we have seen, answers have ranged from the notion that history is God's plan and ultimately unknowable to the idea that history can be the subject of scientific methods of analysis and ultimately can be explained in terms of general principles. Contemporary archaeologists include those who are working on complex computer models designed to extract historical processes, others who are trying to produce humanistic interpretations of ancient cultures, and others who believe they can't really scientifically "know" any thing about the past but are using it for contemporary political purposes.

In the face of these competing ideas about how the past should be analyzed, interpreted, and understood, many archaeologists have an eclectic position: They use ideas from many different sources and theoretical perspectives, on the assumption that a synthesis of this kind represents our best research strategy.

A good defense of an eclectic theoretical approach to archaeology is that offered by Bruce Trigger, in his recent calls for a "holistic" archaeology. Trigger notes:

I have argued that the future of archaeology lies not in replacing the ecological determinism of processual archaeology with the historical particularism that currently appears to be attracting many postprocessual archaeologists, but rather in effecting a synthesis of these seemingly opposed positions. The synthesis I have proposed involves trying to investigate as many of the factors that constrain human behavior as possible. These include not only the external factors championed by the processualists but also the cultural traditions without which human existence would be impossible.[55]

Ian Hodder[56] too has argued that there is no necessary conflict between processual and post-processual archaeology. He suggests that processual archaeology has made the essential contribution of demonstrating the constraints that ecology, demography, and technology have on societies; post-processualism, on the other hand, offers a way to include in archaeological interpretations such elements as ideas, gender roles, power relations, ritual, and so on.

The approach taken in this book is a "holistic" one in this same sense. It is a blend of many different perspectives and analyses. It must be remembered, however, that the various kinds of "knowledge" that are provided are not all fundamentally the same. A statistical comparison of stone tools from European sites of 20,000 years ago can produce a different kind of knowledge by different methods from that of an interpretation of the symbols these people painted on cave walls and engraved on stones and bones (although post-processualists might see these as fundamentally similar at some levels). Yet each can give us at least a sense that we understand the past better, in a way, and each can be an interesting and instructive exercise. An underlying assumption and premise of this book is that an archaeological inquiry into the past can be usefully and productively done in the form of "science," and that all interpretations of the past are not necessarily equally valid.[57]

Who Owns the Past?

Who controls the past controls the future; who
controls the present controls the past.

George Orwell[58]

In contemporary archaeology the vast majority of field work and publication is done by Western European and American archaeologists. Some of these scholars have begun to question their "right" to interpret the pasts of so many different cultures and peoples around the world.

If one takes the view that archaeology is a science, then one could at least argue that, like biology, chemistry, demography, and any other science, what matters is the quality of the science, not the ethnic or cultural identity of the person doing the analyses. Given the various intellectual trends in post-processual archaeology (as reviewed earlier), however, the reader will not be surprised to know that many archaeologists think that it is unethical to "appropriate" the pasts of others. Randall McGuire, for example, in reviewing the archaeology of North America, suggests:

> The time has come for archaeologists to reunite their object of study, the Indian past, with its descendants, and to ask about the needs of Indian people and address those needs. . . .
> [This will require] that all archaeologists initiate a process of dialogue with Indian peoples that will alter our perceptions of the past, how we deal with living Native Americans, . . .

and how we present our results to each other and the general public. . . . Most fundamentally, archaeologists need to recognize the contradictions between inclusion and exclusion and uniformity and diversity that are at the core of our national heritage. . . . Social evolutionists and material-culture analysts have failed to address these contradictions, the former by relegating Indian people to lower stages of evolution and the latter by refusing to acknowledge that artifacts from the past have power in the present because they present the image of a known past while their interpretation remains infinitely malleable.[59]

Such calls to political action and socially constructed interpretations will probably have limited impact on the many archaeologists who are trying to study topics such as the date, routes, and adaptations of the first human occupations of the New World; the possible role of people in the extinction of mammoths and other large animals the New World; the processes by which maize agriculture was established in North America; and the hundreds of other research topics that dominate professional North American archaeology today. It should be noted, however, that an increasing number of North American archaeologists are establishing working relationships with Native Americans and that these collaborations have led to interesting alternative hypotheses about the past, many of which can be scientifically evaluated.[60]

BIBLIOGRAPHY

Adams, A. B. 1969. *Eternal Quest.* New York: Putnam.

Alexander, R. D. 1987. *The Biology of Moral Systems.* Hawthorne, NY: Aldine de Gruyter.

Anschuetz, K. F., R. H. Wilshusen, and C. I. Scheick. 2001. "An Archaeology of Landscapes: Perspectives and Directions." *Journal of Archaeological Research* 9(2):157–211.

Ashmore, W., and A. B. Knapp. 1999. *Archaeologies of Landscape: Contemporary Perspectives.* Malden, MA: Blackwell.

Bamforth, D., and J. C. Spaulding. 1982. "Human Behavior, Explanation, Archaeology, History, and Science." *Journal of Anthropological Archaeology* 1(2):179–194.

Barzun, J. 2000. *From Dawn to Decadence: 500 Years of Western Cultural Life, 1500 to the Present.* New York: HarperCollins.

Bernal, M. 1987. *Black Athena: The Afroasiatic Roots of Classical Civilization, Vol 1: The Fabrication of Ancient Greece.* New Brunswick, NJ: Rutgers University Press.

Bevan, A. H. 2002/2004. "GIS, Archaeological Survey, and Landscape Archaeology on the Island of Kythera, Greece." *Journal of Field Archaeology* 29(1–2):123–138.

Betzig, L. L. 1986. *Despotism and Differential Reproduction: A Darwinian View of History.* Hawthorne, NY: Aldine de Gruyter.

Binford, L. R. 1968. "Archaeological Perspectives." In *New Perspectives in Archaeology,* ed. Sally R. Binford and L. R. Binford. Chicago: Aldine.

———. 1981. *Bones: Ancient Men and Modern Myths.* New York: Academic Press.

Bintliff, J. 1986. "Archaeology at the Interface: An Historical Perspective." In *Archaeology at the Interface,* ed. J. L. Bintliff and C. F. Gaffney. Oxford: BAR International Series 300.

———. 1993. "Why Indiana Jones Is Smarter Than the Post-Processualists." *Norwegian Archaeological Review* 26(2):91–100.

Brooks, D. R., and E. O. Wiley. 1988. *Evolution as Entropy: Toward a Unified Theory of Biology,* 2nd ed. Chicago: University of Chicago Press.

Brown, M., and J. Cave. 1989. *A Touch of Genius: The Life of T. E. Lawrence.* New York: Paragon House.

Brumfiel, E. M. 1994a. "Distinguished Lecture in Archaeology: Breaking and Entering the Ecosystem." *American Anthropologist* 94(3):551–567.

———. 1994b. "A Review of *Prehistory of the Americas* (by S. J. Fiedel, 1992, Cambridge: Cambridge University Press)." *Norwegian Archaeological Review* 27(2):132–134.

Butzer, K. W. 1982. *Archaeology as Human Ecology.* Cambridge: Cambridge University Press.

Ceram, C. W. 1967. *Gods, Graves, and Scholars.* New York: Knopf.

Chang, K. C. 1988. *The Archaeology of Ancient China.* New Haven, CT: Yale University Press.

Childe, V. G. 1936. *Man Makes Himself.* London: Watts.

Claassen, C. P., and R. A. Joyce, eds. 1997. *Women in Prehistory: North America and Mesoamerica.* Philadelphia: University of Pennsylvania Press.

Clifford, J., and G. Marcus, eds. 1986. *Writing Culture.* Berkeley: University of California Press.

Cohen, G. A. 1978. *Karl Marx's Theory of History. A Defense.* Princeton, NJ: Princeton University Press.

Coles, B., & J. Coles. 1986. *Sweet Track to Glastonbury: The Somerset Levels in Prehistory.* London and New York: Thames and Hudson.

Conkey, M. W., and J. M. Gero. 1991. "Tensions, Pluralities, and Engendering Archaeology: An Introduction to Women and Prehistory." In *Engendering Archaeology,* ed. J. M. Gero and M. W. Conkey. Oxford: Blackwell.

Daniel, G. 1967. *The Origins and Growth of Archaeology.* Baltimore: Penguin.

Daniel, G. E., and C. Chippendale, eds. 1989. *The Pastmasters.* London and New York: Thames and Hudson.

Derrida, J. 1976. *Of Grammatology.* Trans. G. C. Spivak. Baltimore: John Hopkins University Press.

———. 1978. *Writing and Difference.* Trans. A. Bass. London: Routledge & Kegan Paul.

Desmond, A. 1982. *Archetypes and Ancestors.* Chicago: University of Chicago Press.

Desmond, A., and J. Moore. 1991. *Darwin.* New York: Warner.

Diakonov, I., ed. 1969. *Ancient Mesopotamia.* Moscow: Nauka.

———., ed. 1991. *Early Antiquity.* Chicago: University of Chicago Press.

Dobres, M., and J. E. Robb. 2000. *Agency in Archaeology.* New York: Routledge.

Dongoske, K., M. Aldenderfer, and K. Doehner, eds. 2000. *Working Together: Native Americans and Archaeologists.* Washington, DC: The SAA Press.

Dunnell, R. C. 1980. "Evolution Theory and Archaeology." In *Advances in Archaeological Method and Theory,* Vol. 3, ed. M. B. Schiffer. New York: Academic Press.

———. 1982. "Science, Social Science, and Common Sense: The Agonizing Dilemma of Modern Archaeology." *Journal of Anthropological Research* 38:1–25.

———. 1986. "Methodological Issues in Americanist Artifact Classification." *Advances in Archaeological Method and Theory* 9:147–207.

Durham, W. H. 1990. "Advances in Evolutionary Culture Theory." *Annual Review of Anthropology* 19:187–242.

Earle, T. K., and R. W. Preucel. 1987. "Processual Archaeology and the Radical Critique." *Current Anthropology* 28(4):501–538.

Easterbrook, G. 1988. "Are We Alone?" *Atlantic,* August 1988, pp. 25–38.

Eiseley, L. 1946. *The Immense Journey.* New York: Time.

———. 1979. *Darwin and the Mysterious Mr. X.* New York: Harcourt Brace Jovanovich.

Faubion, J. D. 1993. "History in Anthropology." *Annual Review of Anthropology* 22:35–54.

Feder, K. L. 1990. *Frauds, Myths, and Mysteries: Science and Pseudo-Science in Archaeology.* Mountain View, CA: Mayfield.

Feinman, G. M., K. G. Lightfoot, and S. Upham. 2000. "Political Hierarchies and Organizational Strategies in the Puebloan Southwest." *American Antiquity* 65(3):449–470.

Feyerabend, P. 1993. *Against Method,* 3rd ed. New York: Verso.

Flannery, K. V. 1973. "Archaeology with a Capital 'S.'" In *Research and Theory in Current Archaeology,* ed. C. L. Redman. New York: Wiley.

Foley, D. 1990. *Learning from Capitalist Culture.* Philadelphia: University of Pennsylvania Press.

Foucault, M. 1979. *Discipline and Punish: The Birth of the Prison.* New York: Random House.

———. 1986. *The Foucault Reader.* Ed. P. Rabinow. Harmondsworth, England: Penguin.

Frayer, D. W., M. Wolpoff, A. G. Thorne, F. H. Smith, and G. G. Pope. 1993. "Theories of Modern Human Origins: The Paleontological Test." *American Anthropologist* 95:14–50.

Friedman, J. 1992. "The Past in the Future: History and the Politics of Identity." *American Anthropologist* 95(4):837–859.

Friedman, J., and M. J. Rowlands. 1977. *The Evolution of Social Systems.* Pittsburgh: University of Pittsburgh Press.

Gamble, C. 1994. *Timewalkers: The Prehistory of Global Colonization.* Cambridge, MA: Harvard University Press.

Gathercole, P., and D. Lowenthal, eds. 1994. *The Politics of the Past.* New York: Routledge.

Gellner, E. 1992. *Post-Modernism, Reason, and Religion.* New York: Routledge.

Gero, J. M., and M. W. Conkey. 1991. *Engendering Archaeology.* Oxford: Blackwell.

Gosden, C. 1994. *Social Being and Time.* Oxford: Blackwell.

Gould, R. A. 1995. *Recovering the Past.* Albuquerque: University of New Mexico Press.

———, ed. 1978. *Explorations in Ethno-Archaeology.* Albuquerque: University of New Mexico Press.

Gould, R. A., and P. J. Watson. 1982. "A Dialogue on the Meaning and Use of Analogy in Ethnoarchaeological Reasoning." *Journal of Anthropological Archaeology* 1:355–381.

Gould, S. J. 1977. *Ever Since Darwin.* New York: Norton.

———. 1988. "Kropotkin Was No Crackpot." *Natural History* 97(7):12–21.

———. 1989. *Wonderful Life.* New York: W. W. Norton.

Gould, S. J., and N. Eldredge. 1977. "Punctuated Equilibria: The Tempo and Mode of Evolution Reconsidered." *Paleobiology* 3:115–151.

Graber, R. B. 1994. *A Scientific Model of Social and Cultural Evolution*. Lanham, MD: University Press of America.

Graslund, B. 1987. *The Birth of Prehistoric Chronology*. Cambridge: Cambridge University Press.

Grayson, D. K. 1983. *The Establishment of Human Antiquity*. New York: Academic Press.

Haberman, J. 1970. "Toward a Theory of Communicative Competence." *Inquiry* 13(4):360–376.

———. 1979. *Communication and the Evolution of Society*. Boston: Beacon Press.

———. 1985. "The Theory of Communicative Action." In *Reason and the Rationalization of Society*, Vol. 1. Boston: Beacon Press.

Harris, J. E., and K. R. Weeks. 1973. *X-Raying the Pharaohs*. New York: Scribner's.

Harris, M. 1968. *The Rise of Anthropological Theory*. New York: Crowell.

———. 1979. *Cultural Materialism*. New York: Random House.

Harrold, F. B., and R. A. Eve. 1988. *Cult Archaeology and Creationism*. Iowa City: University of Iowa Press.

Hartley, L. P. 2002. *The Go-Between*. New York: New York Review Books.

Hawkes, C. 1954. "Archaeological Theory and Method: Some Suggestions from the Old World." *American Anthropologist* 55:55–68.

Hempel, C. B. 1966. *Philosophy of Natural Science*. Englewood Cliffs, NJ: Prentice-Hall.

Herrnstein, R. J., and C. Murray. 1996. *The Bell Curve, Intelligence and Class Structure in American Life*. New York: Simon and Schuster.

Hodder, I. 1985. "Postprocessual Archaeology." In *Advances in Archaeological Method and Theory*, vol. 8. ed. M. Schiffer. New York: Academic Press.

———. 1989. *The Meanings of Things*. London: Unwin Hyman.

———. 1991. "Postprocessual Archaeology and the Current Debate." In *Processual and Postprocessual Archaeologies, Multiple Ways of Knowing the Past*. ed. R. W. Preceul. Carbondale, IL: Center for Archaeological Investigations.

Hodder, I., M. Shanks, A. Alexandri, V. Buchli, J. Carman, J. Last, and G. Lucas. 1995. *Interpreting Archaeology: Finding Meaning in the Past*. London: Routledge.

Itzkoff, S. 1987. *Why Humans Vary in Intelligence*. Ashfield, MA: Paideia.

Jochim, M. A. 1998. *A Hunter-Gatherer Landscape: Southwest Germany in the Late Paleolithic and Mesolithic*. New York: Plenum.

Johnson, G. A. 1987. "Comment on T. K. Earle and R. W. Preucel. 1987. Processual Archaeology and the Radical Critique." *Current Anthropology* 28(4):517–518.

Jones, D. 1995. "Sexual Selection, Physical Attractiveness, and Facial Neoteny: Cross-cultural Evidence and Implications." *Current Anthropology* 36(5):723–748.

Kaplan, A. 1984. "Philosophy of Science in Anthropology." *Annual Review of Anthropology* 13:25–39.

Kirk, G. S., and J. E. Raven. 1966. *The Presocratic Philosophers*. Cambridge: Cambridge University Press.

Kitto, H. D. F. 1951. *The Greeks*. Edinburgh: Penguin.

Knapp, A. B., and W. Ashmore. 1999. "Archaeological Landscapes: Constructed, Conceptualized, Ideational." In *Archaeologies of Landscape: Contemporary Perspectives*, ed. W. Ashmore and A. B. Knapp. Malden, MA: Blackwell.

Kohl, P. L. 1981. "Materialist Approaches in Prehistory." *Annual Review of Anthropology* 10:89–118.

Krebs, J., and N. B. Davies. 1981. *Introduction to Behavioral Ecology*. Oxford: Blackwell.

Langer, W. L. (gen. ed.), P. MacKendrick, D. Geanakoplos, J. H. Hexter, and R. Pipes. 1968. *Western Civilization*. New York: Harper & Row.

Leach, E. R. 1984. "Glimpses of the Unmentionable in the History of British Social Anthropology." *Annual Review of Anthropology* 13:1–23.

Leone, M. 1995. "A Historical Archaeology of Capitalism." *American Anthropologist* 97(2):251–268.

Leone, M., P. B. Potter, Jr., and P. A. Schackel. 1987. "Toward a Critical Archaeology." *Current Anthropology* 28(3):283–302.

Ling, R. 1987. "A New Look at Pompeii." In *Origins*, ed. B. Cunliffe. London: BBC Books.

Lodge, D. 1984. *Small World*. London: Penguin.

Lovejoy, A. O. 1960. *The Great Chain of Being: A Study of the History of an Idea*. New York: Harper & Row

Marx, K. 1904. *The Critique of Political Economy*. Trans. I. N. Stone. Chicago: International Library Publication.

McGuire, R. H. 1992a. *A Marxist Archaeology*. San Diego: Academic Press.

———. 1992b. "Archeology and the First Americans." *American Anthropologist* 94(4):816–834.

Meek, R. L. 1953. *Marx and Engels on Malthus*. London: Lawrence and Wishart.

Meltzer, D. J., D. D. Fowler, & J. A. Sabloff, eds. 1986. *American Archaeology Past and Future*. Washington, DC: Smithsonian Institution Press.

Menken, H. L. 1977 (c. 1922). *Prejudices, Third Series, "Ad Imagininem dei creavit illium," Coda*. New York: Octagon Books.

Miller, D. 1987. *Material Culture and Mass Consumption*. Oxford: Basil Blackwell.

Morgan, L. H. 1877. *Ancient Society*. Reprint ed. 1964, ed. and with an introduction by L. A. White. Cambridge, MA: Harvard University Press.

Nelson, S. M. 1997. *Gender in Archaeology*. Walnut Creek, CA: Altamira Press.

Neiman, F. D. 1995. "Stylistic Variation in Evolutionary Perspective: Inferences from Decorative Diversity and Interassemblage Distance in Illinois Woodland Ceramic Assemblages." *American Antiquity* 60(1):7–36.

Nisbet, R. J. 1980. *History of the Idea of Progress*. New York: Basic Books.

Nordbladh, J., and T. Yates. 1990. "This Perfect Body, This Virgin Text: Between Sex and Gender in Archaeology." In *Archaeology After Structuralism*, ed. I. Bapty and T. Yates. London: Routledge.

O'Meara, J. T. 1989. "Anthropology as Empirical Science." *American Anthropologist* 91(2):354–369.

Orton, C. 1980. *Mathematics in Archaeology*. London: Collins.

Orwell, G. 1961. *Nineteen Eighty-Four: A Novel*. New York: New American Library.

Owen, L.R. in 2005. *Distorting the Past: Gender and the Division of Labor in the European Upper Paleolithic*. Tübingen: Kerns Verlag.

Paddayya, K. 1985. "Theoretical Archaeology—A Review." In *Recent Advances in Indian Archaeology*, ed. S. B. Deo and K. Paddayya. Poona, India: Deccan College of Post-Graduate and Research Institute.

Patterson, T. C., and C. W. Gailey, eds. 1987. *Power Relations and State Formation*. Washington, DC: American Anthropological Association.

Pauketat, T., and T. Emerson. 1991. "The Ideology of Authority and the Power of the Pot." *American Anthropologist* 93(4):919–941.

Pinsky, V., and A. Wylie, eds. 1995. *Critical Traditions in Contemporary Archaeology*. Albuquerque: University of New Mexico Press.

Popper, K. 1959. *The Logic of Scientific Discovery*. London: Hutchinson. (facsimile)

Pyne, K. A. 1996. *Art and the Higher Life: Painting and Evolutionary Thought in Late Nineteenth Century America*. Austin: University of Texas Press.

Read, D. 1996. Personal communication to Wenke.

Reeves, N. 1990. *The Complete Tutankhamun*. New York: Thames and Hudson.

Renfrew, C. 1978. "Trajectory, Discontinuity and Morphogenesis: The Implications of Catastrophe Theory for Archaeology." *American Antiquity* 43:202–222.

Richards, R. J. 1987. *Darwin and the Emergence of Evolutionary Theories of Mind and Behavior*. Chicago: University of Chicago Press.

Rindos, D. 1984. *The Origins of Agriculture*. New York: Academic Press.

Robertshaw, P., ed. 1990. *A History of African Archaeology*. Portsmouth, NH: Heinemann.

Rogers, J. D., ed. 1995. *Ethnohistory and Archaeology: Approaches to Postcontact Change in the Americas*. New York: Plenum Press.

Ross, E. B., ed. 1980. *Beyond the Myths of Culture: Essays on Cultural Materialism*. New York: Academic Press.

Rowlands, M., and K. Kristansen, eds. 1995. *Social Transformation in Archaeology*. New York: Routledge.

Sahlins, M. D., and E. R. Service, eds. 1960. *Evolution and Culture*. Ann Arbor: University of Michigan Press.

Salmon, M. H. 1982. *Philosophy and Archaeology*. New York: Academic Press.

Salmon, M. H., and W. C. Salmon. 1979. "Alternative Models of Scientific Explanation." *American Anthropologist* 81:61–74.

Salt, G. W., ed. 1984. *Ecology and Evolutionary Biology*. Chicago: University of Chicago Press.

Schiffer, M. B. 1981. "Some Issues in the Philosophy of Archaeology." *American Antiquity* 46:899–908.

———. 1987. *Formation Processes of the Archaeological Record*. Albuquerque: University of New Mexico.

Schmidt, A. 1971. *The Concept of Nature in Marx*. London: NLB.

Shanks, M., and C. Tilley. 1987. *Re-constructing Archaeology*. Cambridge: Cambridge University Press.

———. 1988. *Social Theory and Archaeology*. Albuquerque: University of New Mexico Press.

Skibo, J. M., W. H. Walker, and A. E. Nielsen, eds. 1995. *Expanding Archaeology*. Salt Lake City: University of Utah Press.

Spaulding, A. C. 1973. "Archeology in the Active Voice: The New Anthropology." In *Research and Theory in Current Archaeology*, ed. C. L. Redman. New York: Wiley.

Spencer, H. 1883. *Social Statics*. New York: Appleton.

Spriggs, M., ed. 1984. *Marxist Perspectives in Archaeology*. Cambridge: Cambridge University Press.

Spuhler, J. N. 1985. "Anthropology, Evolution, and 'Scientific Creationism.'" *Annual Review of Anthropology* 14:103–133.

Steward, J. 1949. "Cultural Causality and Law: A Trial Formulation of the Development of Early Civilizations." *American Anthropologist* 51:1–27.

Stone, P., and R. MacKenzie, eds. 1995. *The Excluded Past: Archaeology in Education*. New York: Routledge.

Tilley, C. 1996. *An Ethnography of the Neolithic: Early Prehistoric Societies in Southern Scandanavia*. New York: Cambridge University Press.

Toth, N., and K. D. Schick. 1986. "The First Million Years: The Archaeology of Protohuman Culture." *Advances in Archaeological Method and Theory* 9:1–96.

Trigger, B. G. 1984. "Archaeology at the Crossroads: What's New?" *Annual Review of Anthropology* 13:275–300.

———. 1985. "Marxism in Archaeology: Real or Spurious?" *Reviews in Anthropology* 12:114–123.

———. 1989. *History of Archaeological Thought.* Cambridge: Cambridge University Press.

———. 1991. "Distinguished Lecture in Archaeology: Constraint and Freedom." *American Anthropologist* 93(3):551–569.

———. 1991. "Post-Processual Developments in Anglo-American Archaeology." *Norwegian Archaeological Review* 24(2):65–76.

———. 1993. *Early Civilizations: Ancient Egypt in Context.* Cairo: American University in Cairo Press.

Turner, H. 1985. *Herbert Spencer: A Renewed Appreciation.* Beverly Hills: Sage.

UNESCO and S. J. de Laet, eds. 1994. *History of Humanity: Vol. 1, Prehistory and the Beginnings of Civilization.* New York: Routledge.

Vasicek, Z., and J. Malina, eds. 1990. *Archaeology Yesterday and Today.* Cambridge: Cambridge University Press.

Watson, P. J., S. A. LeBlanc, and C. L. Redman. 1971. *Explanation in Archeology.* New York: Columbia University Press.

———. 1984. *Archeological Explanation.* New York: Columbia University Press.

Wells, P. S. 1980. *Culture Contact and Culture Change.* Cambridge: Cambridge University Press.

Wenke, R. J. 1975–1976. "Imperial Investments and Agricultural Developments in Parthian and Sasanian Khuzestan: 150 B.C. to A.D. 640." *Mesopotamia* 10–11:31–217.

———. 1981. "Explaining the Evolution of Cultural Complexity: A Review." In *Advances in Archaeological Method and Theory,* Vol. 4, ed. M. B. Schiffer. New York: Academic Press.

———. 1987. "Western Iran in the Partho-Sasanian Period: The Imperial Transformation." In *The Archaeology of Western Iran,* ed. F. Hole. Washington, DC: Smithsonian Institution Press.

Wenke, R., J. Long, and P. Buck. 1988. "Epipaleolithic and Neolithic Subsistence and Settlement in the Fayyum Oasis of Egypt." *Journal of Field Archaeology* 15(1):29–51.

White, L. A. 1949. *The Science of Culture.* New York: Grove Press.

———. 1959. "The Concept of Culture." *American Anthropologist* 61:227–251.

Wolfram, S. 2002. *A New Kind of Science.* Champaign, IL: Wolfram Media.

Wylie, A. 1982. "An Analogy by Any Other Name Is Just as Analogical." *Journal of Anthropological Archaeology* 1:382–401.

———. 1989. "Matters of Face and Matters of Interest." In *Archaeological Approaches to Cultural Identity: One World Archaeology,* No. 10, ed. S. Shannen. London: Unwin-Hyman.

———. 1991. "Gender Theory and the Archaeological Record: Why Is There No Archaeology of Gender?" In *Engendering Archaeology,* ed. J. M. Gero and M. W. Conkey. Oxford: Blackwell.

Young, T. C., Jr. 1988. "Since Herodotus, Has History Been a Valid Concept?" *American Antiquity* 53(1):7–12.

Yoffee, N., and A. Sherratt, eds. 1993. *Archaeological Theory: Who Sets the Agenda?* Cambridge: Cambridge University Press.

NOTES

1. Quoted in Daniel, *The Origins and Growth of Archaeology,* p. 49.
2. From the film *Indiana Jones,* quoted in Bintliff, "Why Indiana Jones Is Smarter Than the Post-Processualists," p. 100.
3. See chapter 7 for a detailed discussion of this premise.
4. See, for example, Shanks and Tilley, *Social Theory and Archaeology.*
5. See, for example, Rindos, *The Origins of Agriculture*; Dunnell, "Evolution Theory and Archaeology."
6. Hartley, *The Go-Between.*
7. Harris and Weeks, *X-Raying the Pharaohs.*
8. Reeves, *The Complete Tutankhamun,* p. 203.
9. Ceram, *Gods, Graves, and Scholars,* pp. 8–9.
10. Wenke et al., "Epipaleolithic and Neolithic Subsistence and Settlement in the Fayyum Oasis of Egypt."
11. *The Logic of Scientific Discovery,* 1959.
12. *A New Kind of Science,* 2002.
13. Greek science and philosophy incorporated elements from other cultures. Metallurgy, geometry, mathematics, and many other arts and sciences all have long histories that predate classical Greek culture by millennia. Martin Bernal (*Black Athena*) and some other scholars have recently argued that Greek intellectual accomplishments were deeply and strongly rooted in Egyptian and Syro-Palestinian achievements, but few scholars agree with his conclusions. There simply is very little in ancient non-Greek cultures that seems to

presage the political brilliance of Pericles; the dramas of Aeschylus, Sophocles, and Aristophanes; the oratory of Demosthenes; the architecture of Mnesicles and Ictinus (designers of the Acropolis); the histories of Thucydides and Herodotus; and the philosophy of Socrates and Plato—among many other arts and sciences.

14. H. D. F. Kitto's *The Greeks* is a brilliant and literate summary of the ancient Greek contribution to Western thought.
15. Daniel, *The Origins and Growth of Archaeology*, p. 90.
16. Chang, *The Archaeology of Ancient China*, p. 5.
17. Reviewed in Graslund, *The Birth of Prehistoric Chronology*, p. 18.
18. Spencer, *Social Statics*, p. 80.
19. Desmond, *Archetypes and Ancestors*, pp. 100–101.
20. Attributed.
21. Darwin, quoted in Adams, *Eternal Quest*, p. 334.
22. Eiseley, *Darwin and the Mysterious Mr. X*.
23. *Evolution as Entropy*, by Brooks and Wiley.
24. Quoted in Desmond and Moore, *Darwin*, p. 636.
25. Schmidt, *The Concept of Nature in Marx*, p. 41.
26. E.g., V. G. Childe.
27. These and other quotes in this paragraph are from I. M. Diakonoff, *Early Antiquity*, pp. 1–27.
28. See, for example, R. McGuire, *A Marxist Archaeology*.
29. See B. Trigger's perceptive analysis, "Marxism in Archaeology: Real or Spurious?" Also see R. McGuire, *A Marxist Archaeology*; M. Spriggs, ed., *Marxist Perspectives in Archaeology*.
30. Menken, *Prejudices, Third Series*, "Ad Imagininem dei creavit illium," Coda.
31. Daniel, *The Origins and Growth of Archaeology*.
32. T. E. Lawrence (Lawrence of Arabia), for example, has been often been accused of spying for the British while working with Woolley in Mesopotamia (see Brown and Cave, *A Touch of Genius*).
33. G. Childe, *Man Makes Himself*.
34. *American Anthropologist* 51:1–27.
35. Variants of this postmodernist aphorism have been used by various scholars; see David Lodge's entertaining novel *Small World*, p. 328 and elsewhere.
36. See Watson, Redman, and LeBlanc, *Explanation in Archaeology*; also see Watson et al., *Archaeological Explanation*; Bamforth and Spaulding, "Human Behavior, Explanation, Archaeology, History, and Science"; Schiffer, "Some Issues in the Philosophy of Archaeology."
37. White, *The Science of Culture*.
38. Trigger, "Archaeology at the Crossroads: What's New?"; also see Bamforth and Spaulding, "Human Behavior, Explanation, Archaeology, History, and Science"; and Salmon, "Philosophy and Archaeology."
39. *Of Grammatology*.
40. Shanks and Tilley, *Re-Constructing Archaeology*, p. 243.
41. Hodder, "Postprocessual Archaeology."
42. See Trigger's "Post-Processual Developments in Anglo-American Archaeology," pp. 65–69.
43. See, for example, their *Social Theory and Archaeology*.
44. See, for example, Derrida, *Writing and Difference*, or Foucault, *The Foucault Reader*.
45. Ernst Gellner found it difficult to define post-modernism, but he leaves no doubt about his opinion of it, as seen in his *Post Modernism, Reason, and Religion*, pp. 22–23: "Post-modernism is a contemporary movement. It is strong and fashionable. Over and above this, it is not altogether clear what the devil it is. In fact, clarity is not conspicuous amongst its marked attributes. It not only generally fails to practise it, but also on occasion actually repudiates it. But anyway, there appear to be no 39 post-modernist Articles of Faith, no post-modernist manifesto, which one could consult so as to assure oneself that one has identified its ideas properly.... The movement and its ideas are ... a little too ethereal and volatile to be captured and seized with precision: perhaps the acute awareness of the movement that all meanings are to be deconstructed in a way which also brings in their opposites, and highlights the contradictions contained in them ... actually precludes a crisp and unambiguous formulation of the position."
46. Hodder, *The Meaning of Things*, p. 65.
47. Leone, "A Historical Archaeology of Capitalism," p. 213; see also Wylie, "Matters of Face and Matters of Interest."
48. Anschuetz et al., "An Archaeology of Landscapes: Perspectives and Directions."
49. Knapp and Ashmore, "Archaeological Landscapes: Constructed, Conceptualized, Ideational," p. 1.
50. Tilley, *An Ethnography of the Neolithic: Early Prehistoric Societies in Southern Scandanavia*, pp. 193–214. Tilley also notes that these Neolithic structures are "read" by modern observers, for example, as "sculptures" in the landscape.
51. Feinman et al., "Political Hierarchies and Organizational Strategies in the Puebloan Southwest," pp. 459–466.

52. As Dwight Read has observed, "Gender, as a cultural construct . . . is not observable; what is observable are its implications for how gender is embedded in the cultural system which leads, through the actions of individuals, to patterning in the observable world of material objects. The constant problem that archaeology faces is that the mapping from culture to patterning of material objects is never an isomorphism, is sometimes a homomorphism, and most often is a mapping which confounds multitudinous structuring processes. But this is a constant problem, not one peculiar to gender constructs."
53. Brumfiel, "A Review of *Prehistory of the Americas* (by S. J. Fiedel)."
54. For example, Gero and Conkey, *Engendering Archaeology*; Nelson, *Gender in Archaeology*.
55. Trigger, "Distinguished Lecture in Archaeology: Constraint and Freedom," pp. 562–563.
56. Hodder, "Postprocessual Archaeology and the Current Debate."
57. A similar position has been advocated by John Bintliff, who recently predicted the demise of most forms of post-processual archaeology, suggesting that "[t]he Theoretical Archaeology of the 1990s is undeniably going to be 'Cognitive Processualism,'" ("Why Indiana Jones Is Smarter Than the Post-Processualists," p. 100). The sense of cognitive Processualism as used by Renfrew and Bintliff is close to that of the holistic archaeology advocated by Bruce Trigger (see earlier) in that all useful methods of analysis are applied to the past, but in the context of an analytical science based on materialist perspectives.
58. *Nineteen Eighty-Four*.
59. McGuire, "Archaeology and the First Americans," p. 828.
60. Numerous examples of cooperative partnerships between archaeologists and Native peoples can be found in short contributions published in the "Working Together" section in *The SAA Archaeological Record* and its predecessor, *The SAA Bulletin*. See also Dongoske et al., eds., *Working Together: Native Americans and Archaeologists*.

2

Fundamentals of Archaeology

Though nothing can bring back the hour
Of splendour in the grass, of glory in the flower;
We will grieve not, rather find
Strength in what remains behind. . . .
William Wordsworth (1770–1850)

In *Intimations of Immortality*, Wordsworth recognized that humanity's hopes of immortality must lie elsewhere than in our physical selves or in our works; for these are transitory; and in the process of decay from the moment of conception. "Shades of the prison house begin to close upon the growing boy," he wrote, intimating that Death's grip is always there, always tightening.

Philosopher Bertrand Russell shared none of Wordsworth's hopes about our prospects of immortality, but he had the same sense of inevitable decay. When asked what he thought would happen to him after death, he cheerfully said, "When I die, I rot."

Perhaps the only people in the world who view the long record of the world's record of rot and decay with hope and optimism are archaeologists. In chapter 1 we reviewed some of the great theories of history and the past—the influential ideas about why history has turned out the way it has. Whatever one thinks of these theories, whatever one's view of the past, to assess these various ideas one must link them to the physical material remains of the past. In this chapter we shall consider the methods that have been developed to apply these great ideas to the material record of the past.

ARCHAEOLOGISTS AND THE PRACTICE OF ARCHAEOLOGY

Before considering in more detail how archaeology is done, let us consider who actually does it. When trapped in airplanes or up against the wall at a party, archaeologists who reveal their occupation often are told, "When I was growing up I wanted to be an archaeologist," or "It must be exciting to be an archaeologist!"

Few non-archaeologists realize, however, that most archaeologists have had to spend 10 years or more in college and graduate school in preparation for their profession, or that for every hour an archaeologist spends excavating, he or she spends hundreds of hours teaching university classes, raising money for research, analyzing artifacts, and writing research reports.

41

Most professional archaeologists in the United States have a Ph.D., a Doctor of Philosophy degree, the prize for an average of six years of post-graduate study. "Those who can, do, those who can't, teach" does not apply to archaeology: Many professionals hold teaching positions, although a growing proportion of archaeologists are employed by public agencies and private companies. The majority of North American archaeologists have been trained as anthropologists; a minority are language scholars, such as Egyptologists, Assyriologists, Classicists (e.g., specialists in ancient Greek and Roman cultures), art historians, and biblical scholars.

Anthropological archaeologists consider their discipline a social science, whereas language scholars such as Egyptologists often view their studies as part of the humanities. Language scholars tend to be particularly interested in relating archaeological remains to ancient written documents, such as the Bible, Greek and Roman texts, Egyptian hieroglyphic inscriptions, and so on. These different perspectives are not strictly separate, and anthropological concepts are beginning to be incorporated in the humanities, while some anthropologists also have mastered ancient languages. But, as in most academic disciplines, specialization is a necessary part of training. To be well trained in both anthropology and Egyptology, for example, requires at least 8–10 years of graduate study for those hardy few who attempt such extensive preparation.

The majority of North American archaeologists who are anthropologists are generally considered "social scientists," but both this term and "anthropology" are increasingly ambiguous. Anthropology literally means "the science (or study) of man," but that leaves rather a lot to be defined. Anthropology today continues to be divided among several specializations, each of which is at least marginally relevant to the study of world prehistory. *Biological anthropologists*[1] are concerned mainly with the evolution of, and variations in the physical attributes of, humans and primates. Some biological anthropologists search for the fossils of extinct forms of early humans, while others study the genetics of existing human groups; so me are *primatologists*, who analyze the behavior and other characteristics of nonhuman primates; others are specialists in the adaptation of human groups to different environments (especially in extreme environments, such as the high Andes Mountains). *Sociocultural anthropologists* focus on studies of living or recent human societies. They include an extremely diverse range of specialists, such as those who study the languages of nonliterate peoples, and others who do the traditional ethnological studies of human societies, analyzing the lifeways of selected groups, from the hunter-gatherers of the rain forests of the Amazon to the patrons of the bars of south Texas.[2] *Archaeologists* represent a third major specialization within anthropology. Most anthropological archaeologists have some graduate training in the other fields of anthropology, in addition to their concentrations in archaeological methods and theories. Most archaeologists also take advanced courses in statistics, geology, demography, and related disciplines.

The lines that used to separate anthropology, sociology, psychology, and other social sciences have blurred greatly in recent times. The concept of "culture"—the uniquely human intellectual and behavioral capacities (see chapter 3)—has been, and remains, for many anthropologists the connective tissue that incorporates them all in a single discipline, but for many anthropologists there is no strong theoretical structure that unites their discipline.

In Europe, Asia, and Africa, archaeology is often a separate university department— not connected with sociocultural anthropology or biological anthropology, as it is in the

United States. In those countries archaeology is often viewed as a form of history, or, in some cases, as a natural science like paleontology. But contemporary archaeology in the United Kingdom and in some other European countries has become increasingly viewed as social studies, and conversely, in North America, some centers of archaeology have separated and allied themselves more closely with the biological and geological sciences.

Archaeology as a discipline has long been dominated by North American and European scholars,[3] but India, Japan, China, Egypt, Argentina, and many other countries have long and productive traditions of archaeological research, and there is a growing internationalism to archaeology.

THE BASIC DATA OF THE PAST

People are messy animals. More than two million years ago, our ancestors began littering Africa with stone tools and smashed animal bones, and ever since we have been carpeting the world with layer upon layer of our own garbage. All this junk, collectively, from two-million-year-old stone tools to today's eternal aluminum beer cans, as well as the bones of our human ancestors and the remains of the plants and animals they ate, constitute the *archaeological record*.

Archaeologists see cosmic significance in the archaeological record. There is a "truth" of sorts embedded in the archaeological record, and archaeologists seek to clarify that truth. The major premise of archaeology is simple and unassailable: It is that much of what we will ever know about our origins, our nature, and even our destiny must be read in the patterns inherent in these layers of debris. Archaeologists assume that they can see in the contents, spatial arrangements, and depositional sequence of the world's garbage the reflections of the factors that have shaped our physical and cultural evolution.

This material archaeological record is the *only* evidence we have to understand more than 99 percent of our past—the period before written languages appeared. And even for the historical era, when we have written records of our past, the archaeological record is important: Whereas historical documents may be full of the usual human lies, propaganda, and misconceptions, the material remains are a physical record of what *did* happen, not what someone said happened or thought happened or wanted to have happened.

Artifacts, Features, and Sites

All academic disciplines have their own jargon, and archaeology is no exception. Archaeologists analyze the archaeological record primarily in terms of *artifacts*, which can be defined as things that owe any of their physical characteristics or their place in time and space to human activity. Thus, a beautifully shaped stone spear-point from a 20,000-year-old campsite in France is an artifact (Figure 2.1), but so is an undistinguished stone flake that some weary Native American pitched out of a Mississippi corn field a thousand years ago.

Nor do things cease to be artifacts because of their recent origins. For many years, archaeologist William Rathje[4] and numerous archaeology students at the University of Arizona studied the artifacts added each day to the Tucson municipal dump and littered along city roads, trying to discern how things are thrown away and what they say about the community that created the trash—and the implications such patterns of discard have for

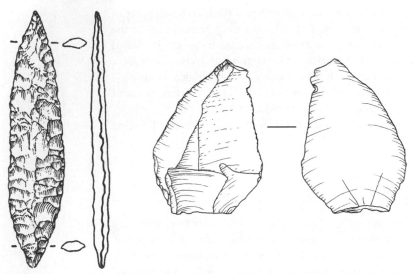

FIGURE 2.1   Stone artifacts include highly worked pieces such as the Solutrean point on the left, as well as undistinguished pieces such as the flake on the right.

understanding the patterns of discard in the past (they learned, among other things, that the average Tucson resident wastes astounding amounts of food; that in rural road litter, unsurprisingly, beer cans and contraceptives are often found together; and that food, newspapers, and other debris preserve extraordinarily well for years in municipal dumps).

These can include footprints left several million years ago when a few of our earliest bipedal ancestors strolled across a volcanic plain at Laetoli, in Tanzania (Figure 2.2)—or the astronauts' footprints on the moon.

Another common archaeological term is *feature*, which refers to a modification to a site that is not portable. They also can be the remains of a hearths, or a storage bin set into the corner of a complex of mudbrick walls (Figure 2.3). Features usually reflect inferred specific, sometimes repeated, activities, such as quarries and latrines.[5]

Perhaps the most common archaeological term is *site*, an imprecise term generally used to refer to relatively dense concentrations of artifacts and features. The ancient city of Babylon, in Iraq (Figure 2.4), which today comprises a huge mound of slowly dissolving baked brick buildings, millions of pottery fragments (known as "sherds" to archaeologists), and all the other debris of an ancient city is a site. But so too is any one of the many areas in Olduvai Gorge, Tanzania, where a few score stone tools and animal bones mark spots where 1.7 million years ago a few of our ancestors hungrily disassembled a killed or scavenged antelope.

Ancient village and town sites are often hard to miss because they are usually marked by remnants of walls and massive quantities of pottery and other debris. It is convenient to think of the archaeological record in this case as composed of many discrete sites representing different settlements, but, in truth, the whole world is littered with artifacts and features: What varies is simply the relative density of artifacts.

In recent years, archaeologists have also become interested in "nonsite" approaches.[6] This method records not only traditional, high-density sites, but also the intervening areas between sites where artifact density is low or nonexistent. By discovering what lies between sites, archaeologists can better understand the full range of behaviors across a landscape.

My colleagues and I (Olszewski), for example, use a nonsite landscape approach for our archaeological survey project (Abydos Survey for Paleolithic Sites, or ASPS) in the high desert of Middle Egypt. Stone artifacts of the Paleolithic period are extremely visible on the barren reaches of this landscape. We record the density of artifacts by taking a sample every 100 m that we walk. At each of these sample spots, we establish a circle of 2 m diameter and then collect every stone artifact that falls into that circle (Figure 2.5). Sometimes these sample circles are devoid of artifacts, in which case, we record a density of zero. The location of each sample circle is logged using a global positioning system (GPS) (see the section "Locating and Excavating Sites"). We then plot the density data for each circle and the circle's location using a mapping program, which allows us to examine patterning in the landscape. Our survey results from the 2002/2003 field season, for example, show that locations along the Wadi Umm al-Qaab[7] were preferentially used (higher density) compared to areas to the west, in the direction of the Wadi al-Jir (Figure 2.6). This may relate to the fact that the Wadi al-Jir is deeply entrenched and thus difficult to use as a pathway from the Nile Valley corridor into the high desert, while the Wadi Umm al-Qaab is a lot easier to walk. Looking at artifact density compared to features of landscape topography creates one layer than can be used in Geographic Information System (GIS) analyses (see the section on "Quantification and Computers in Archaeology").

The world's archaeological record is the raw material for the analysis of the past, but to find meaning in it we must bring to bear a wide range of analytical techniques and a body of theories, hypotheses, and ideas of many different kinds.

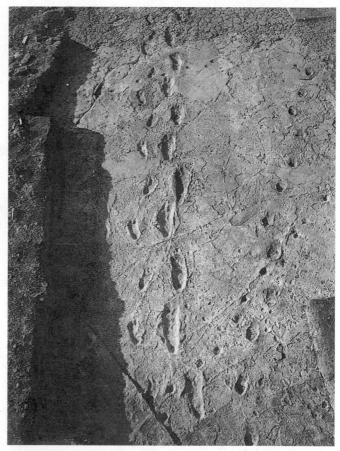

FIGURE 2.2   A trail of hominin footprints was found preserved in volcanic ash at Laetoli, Tanzania. These prints demonstrate that hominins were fully bipedal by 3.6 million years ago.

The Formation of the Archaeological Record

The "past" in a sense is simply the present archaeological record. This may sound like a Zen *koan* (a riddle without a solution whose purpose is to demonstrate the inadequacy of logical reasoning and provide enlightenment), but, in fact, the past *is* the present, in that we can only see the past in the present archaeological record.

The artifacts, features, and sites constituting the archaeological record vary widely in their contents and ages, but all must be understood to have been formed by a complex interplay not only of the activities of the people who created them but also of natural forces, such as erosion, volcanic deposits, and organic decay.[8] Studying archaeological sites from this perspective is called *taphonomy*.[9]

Any hopes we may have of explaining the past are necessarily linked to our ability to understand how the past—in the sense of the archaeological record—was created.[10]

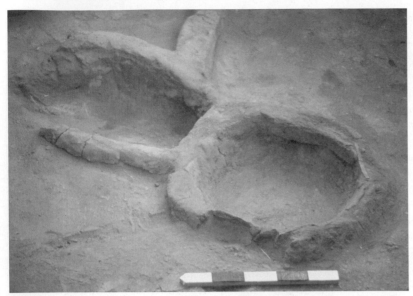

FIGURE 2.3   This feature is a set of clay-lined hearths from a pithouse (semi-subterranean dwelling) at an Ancestral Puebloan site in the American Southwest.

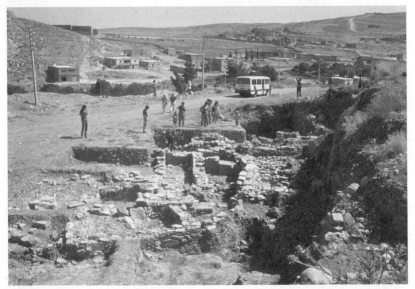

FIGURE 2.4   Architectural remains, such as these stone room walls at the Neolithic site of Basta in Jordan, are an example of an early farming village site.

Consider as an example the problem of understanding the origins of modern humans —that is, of us, *Homo sapiens sapiens*. Many "models" (i.e., sets of linked hypotheses about the causes of a particular development) of modern human origins have been formulated, but currently only one has the confidence of a majority of scholars: This model— described variously as the "African Origins," "Total Replacement," or "Eve" model[11] —is that modern humans evolved first and only in Africa, just a few hundred thousand years ago or less, and then migrated to the rest of the world, displacing all other hominin forms, and with little or no genetic interchange with them. An alternative model, commonly known as the "Multiregional Evolution" model,[12] and held by a minority of anthropologists, accepts that North Africa was a conduit for hominin migrations for millions of years but contends that modern humans arose out of gene flow among some or all of the many different human populations that had colonized Africa, Europe, and Asia many hundreds of thousands, perhaps millions, of years ago.

The evidence relevant to these "models" of human origins is discussed in chapter 4. The important point here is that to analyze this archaeological record we have to sort out a bewildering array of cultural and natural factors that produced the archaeological record of relevance here. Early *Homo sapiens* in Africa, for example, may have developed a simple advantage in toolmaking that made them slightly better than other forms of humans at making a living as hunter-foragers, with the long-term result that this slight advantage allowed them to supplant other groups. If so, then we should be able to see reflections of this supposed advantage in the stone tools, food remains, and other data of the archaeological record. We might look at the animal bones found in sites associated with early *Homo sapiens* in Africa, for example, and see if they show different, perhaps more efficient, hunting techniques, compared to those of Europe and Asia. The problem, however, is to sort out the natural and cultural factors that created these sites. At various South African sites, for example, human skeletal remains and tools have been found in caves along with animal bones. But

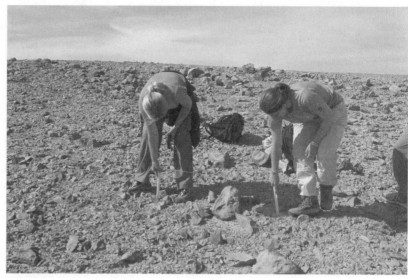

FIGURE 2.5 Systematic collection of surface artifacts is shown here as archaeologists establish a size-standardized circular collection unit during the Abydos Survey for Paleolithic Sites project.

we know that leopards and other "natural" predators regularly killed animals and brought them back to these cave dens. So how can we tell which animals were killed by people and which by other animals? One can use a low-power microscope to look at marks on some

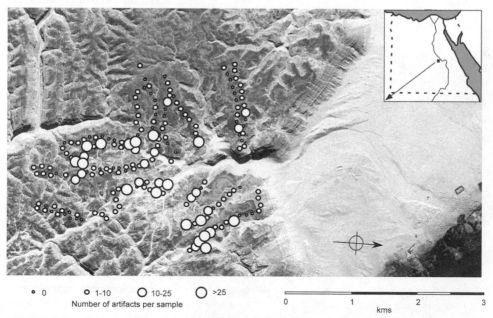

0   1-10   10-25   >25
Number of artifacts per sample

0   1   2   3
kms

FIGURE 2.6 This map shows the variable density of surface artifacts in the area surrounding the Wadi Umm al-Qaab, Egypt, recorded by the Abydos Survey for Paleolithic Sites project. Such information is a valuable clue to how the landscape was used by prehistoric groups.

bones and see evidence that they were butchered with stone tools, but what if a leopard killed this animal and humans simply scavenged it? While it is not always easy to differentiate marks left on bones by animal teeth from those made by humans with stone or bone tools, precise observations can reduce errors in identification to less than 5 percent.[13]

While we can use taphonomy to address broad questions about hominin behaviors, such as those described earlier, many archaeologists also employ this technique to study the nature of specific archaeological sites. One example is the research at the French site of Cagny l'Epinette.[14] Initial excavations and interpretations here identified a "living floor" of Lower Paleolithic age. This occupation surface was thought to be relatively pristine and was described as containing a thin, but dense, concentration of stone artifacts, as well as evidence for activity areas associated with the butchering of animals and other tasks. In effect, it is analogous to having a mini-version of a Pompeii-like situation, where behaviors are virtually frozen in time.

But is this living floor interpretation the correct explanation? Harold Dibble and his colleagues tested this in their new excavations at the site by carefully recording spatial information for artifacts and animal bones, as well as many details about the stone artifacts and sediments, such as the presence of fine gravel or larger cobbles in the dirt associated with the living floor artifacts and animal bones. Their results, which are supported by several lines of independent evidence, indicate that Cagny l'Epinette (Figure 2.7) is not a living floor, but the result of stream deposition. This can be seen, for example, in the edge damage on stone artifacts resulting from stream transport and the lack of very small stone artifacts, which because they are light in weight were carried farther away by stream action than the larger stone artifacts and animal bones. Other evidence includes the orientation of the artifacts,[15] which are mainly parallel or perpendicular to stream flow rather than randomly oriented as would be expected on a living floor; very little evidence in the form of cut marks on animal bones to indicate butchering; and the size match of the stone artifacts and natural materials such as cobbles. Because these cultural and natural materials are similar in size, and we know that hominins were not depositing the natural materials, this also suggests processes such as stream action. The recent research at Cagny l'Epinette has thus shown that it is not hominin behavior that is directly reflected at this site, but a combination of cultural and natural materials brought together through redeposition. Pompeii-like situations in archaeology are indeed quite rare.

There are many other ambiguities in the archaeo-

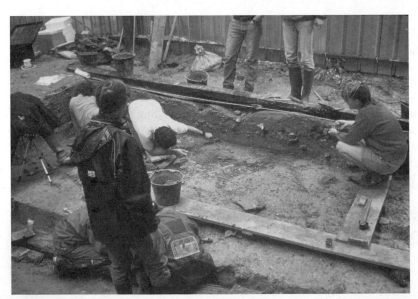

FIGURE 2.7   Excavations at the Lower Paleolithic site of Cagny l'Epinette, France.

logical record pertaining to modern human origins, and this complexity of disentangling cultural from natural factors is found in almost every archaeological project, whether the site is two million or 200 years old. And to the extent that there is brilliance and great creativity in the practice of archaeology, it is usually expressed in formulating some major problems in terms that can be "tested" effectively with archaeological data, whether from new excavations or from laboratory analyses.

The archaeological record is often viewed as "incomplete" because decay and other factors have changed it. But in a sense, the archaeological record is only incomplete if one looks at it as potentially a perfect reflection of the complete history of actions by the human societies that created it. It is what it is: the product of cultural and natural factors. The archaeological record can never be that perfect reflection; instead, it is itself a product of these forces, and in that sense it is not really "incomplete"—even though our knowledge of these forces must always be incomplete.[16]

Artifact Production and Preservation

> The innocent and the beautiful
> Have no enemy but time.
> *W. B. Yeats*[17]

The basic sequence of events that has produced the world's archaeological record is the same for stone tools as it is for today's best DataWhacker computer. In each case, people: (1) acquire the raw materials, (2) make some of these materials into artifacts by changing them (or simply altering their location) in some way, (3) use some of the artifacts, and (4) then discard them.

At each stage of this sequence, a variety of cultural and/or natural factors comes into play. In ancient Mesopotamia, for example, people lived primarily in houses made of mudbricks—made simply by mixing mud with straw and forming bricks by hand or in simple wood molds and leaving them to dry. Mesopotamia's intense sun, occasional rain, strong winds, and ground water seepage then began to degrade these bricks and the buildings created from them. Eventually the buildings were abandoned and a variety of cultural and natural factors continued to operate on them. Wooden roof beams, stone thresholds, and even some mudbricks, for example, were regularly carried away for a variety of reuses.

This process, of making and using—and reusing—things and then discarding them, is really no different today. For example, landfills around the world are currently filling up with the carcasses of typewriters and early generations of computers, many of which have been scavenged for spare parts. Although these machines may last longer than most of the remains of antiquity, all are subject to eventual obliteration through a combination of cultural and natural forces.

How quickly these materials are returned to their elemental chemical state is simply a matter of their composition and the conditions of preservation. The laws of thermodynamics assert that matter is never destroyed nor lost in the universe, but this is little consolation to the archaeologist looking, for example, at the smear of calcium that is all that is left of a corpse buried many millennia ago in the warm, wet soils of the Egyptian Delta. Even in drier, better-preserved contexts, a number of things can destroy archaeological remains. Floods wash them away, glacial ice sheets grind them to bits, rodents go out of their way to burrow through them, earthworms move them, and rivers and winds bury them under silt and sand.

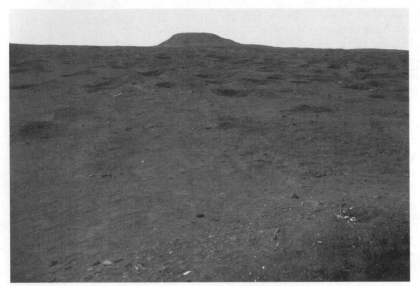

FIGURE 2.8 Looting of archaeological sites removes artifacts from their context and destroys sites. Seen here are the results of grave robbing at the site of el Brujor in Peru.

The greatest destruction, however, is caused by people. The gleaming limestone sheaths that originally enclosed each of the Egyptian pyramids were looted in medieval times and used as building materials. All over the ancient world, in fact, successive settlements were built on—and of—the remnants of earlier occupations. Still, our own generation is perhaps the worst despoiler of antiquities. In Rome, New York, and many other cities, for example, nearly every construction project disturbs the archaeological record of earlier times.

Industrialization at least has some possible benefits, but the same cannot be said for the other great destroyer of the past, looting. Illegal antiquities from around the world are openly on sale around the world. It is sad to relate, but even the mild fines and other penalties currently in force in some countries are only occasionally applied to people convicted of looting. And in many countries the primary looters are impoverished peasants who are simply trying to make a minimal living.

Looting destroys the only hope we have of analyzing cultural processes in the archaeological record because it obliterates the *context* of artifacts and features (Figure 2.8). Thus, for example, to study the origins of the first civilizations of Mexico, it is crucial to excavate sites in such a way that the goods people were buried with and the contents of their houses are meticulously recorded, so that the distribution of wealth in the community can be estimated. But once a looter has ripped through house floors to loot graves of their contents, the anthropological significance of the site is lost forever.

Context involves not only the relationship of specific artifacts and features to each other at a site but also their relationships to other types of data such as plant remains and animal bones. These spatial data provide valuable additional information about the organization of activities at sites.

Natural decay processes affect sites too, but if a site is not looted the effects of these natural processes can be discerned and taken into account in interpretations. Stone tools are almost indestructible, but organics—bones, hides, wood, plants, people, and so on—rot. The best preservation of organic remains occurs where there is not enough water, heat, pH balance, or oxygen for the chemistry of decay to occur. The best preservation is in dry caves, under thick layers of volcanic ash, or in peat bogs, permafrost, or deep, dark, cold water. Entire mammoths have been retrieved from frozen pits in Siberia, and well-preserved human corpses thousands of years old have been recovered from peat bogs (Figure 2.9), swamps, and in one case, a glacier in Europe.

No one knows how powerful the analytical equipment of the future will be, so archaeologists must consider the option of not digging some fraction of extremely important sites, in hopes that someday we will have equipment and techniques of vastly greater sophistication.

Archaeological Research Design

No matter what an archaeologist's academic orientation, anyone who metaphorically or actually dons the pith helmet chooses where to excavate or survey and then interpret what is found. Choosing the place to dig, for example, is usually not so speculative a procedure as imagined by non-archaeologists, who frequently ask, "How do you know where to look?" In modern archaeology, one rarely sets out on expeditions to remote places on the Micawberish assumption that something interesting will turn up—although many ancient remains are still found by accident or unsystematic exploration. But increasingly, archaeological remains are identified through a process of systematic survey. It does not take a trained archaeologist to find the pyramids of Egypt or Mexico, but most archaeological remains are less evident and accessible, such as those covered by drifting sand or alluvial soils, buried beneath contemporary settlements, or located in remote, untravelled areas.

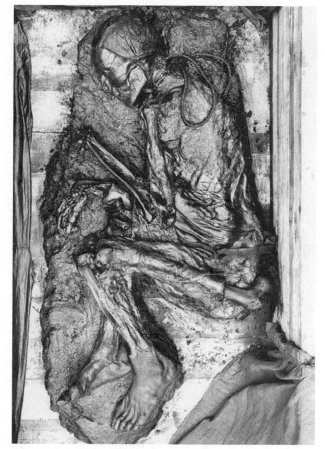

FIGURE 2.9   "Tollund man," a 2,000-year-old hanging victim from the peat bogs of Denmark, illustrates the "pickling" properties of weakly acidic environments.

Many archaeological surveys and excavations are done within the context of a specific intellectual question or problem. If one were interested in the origin of maize agriculture in ancient Mexico, for example, one would read the numerous articles on this subject, and then examine maps of where early varieties of maize have been found. One might then hypothesize some possible causes of the transition to maize agriculture. This process of hypothesis formation is one of the more creative aspects of the discipline. The goal for the archaeologist is to develop some novel ideas or ways of looking at a problem that lead him or her to look for certain kinds of data. One might, then, hypothesize that for various reasons maize was domesticated in lowland coastal areas and in the context of certain kinds of communities. One could then identify where relevant remains might be found and then design a program of surveys and/or excavations to study this problem in this area.

Only some archaeological research is in this *problem-oriented* format. Many contemporary archaeologists believe that such an approach unnecessarily limits archaeology to a dubious kind of empirical science. Instead they seek to understand the archaeological record in the terms they speculate the ancient peoples themselves viewed their world.

Archaeologists James Brady and Wendy Ashmore,[18] for example, focused on the conceptual world of the ancient Maya, of Mesoamerica. In their view the physical world of the Maya, especially the mountains, caves, and water sources, combine in the form of an animate and sacred landscape that continuously renews and re-creates the core beliefs and cosmic processes that the ancient Maya considered fundamental to their universe. They suggest that the ancient Maya built many structures in forms and placements that reinforced the king's power and the religious beliefs of the kingdom. Stone pyramids, for example, were considered forms of sacred hills, and artificial caves through which flood waters were channeled reinforced the notion of the king as an agent of the gods who governs life-giving irrigation waters.

The problem many archaeologists face in this regard is that, on the one hand, we have ample evidence that the physical worlds of the ancients *were* invested with symbolic significance that is far different from our own; but, on the other hand, we have face enormous difficulties in ever verifying our interpretations. In fact, many archaeologists believe that we can never verify, in an empirical sense, our attempts to reconstruct the symbolic significance of the Maya landscape or any other ancient place and time.

Often archaeological research is simply exploratory. One might select an area and do surveys to see if any important remains can be found there. Also, in recent years "problem-oriented" archaeological research has been complemented by rapid growth in "public" archaeology, or "CRM"—that is, cultural resource management. In many countries, governments stipulate that new construction must be preceded by an analysis of its impact on the historical and archaeological record, and then research is undertaken if significant remains are found. These efforts mitigate—offset—the destruction of portions of the archaeological record through the preservation of some sites from destruction or the careful excavation of those sites that will be destroyed. Hundreds, perhaps thousands, of archaeologists now are employed around the world as "public archaeologists" to do this kind of work.

"Public archaeology" is usually well funded by the relevant government, but other archaeological approaches are a different matter. Interesting ideas about the past are in no short supply in archaeology, but money to do the relevant research certainly is. In the United States, for example, an archaeologist can submit a written proposal for research funds to the U.S. National Science Foundation or the National Endowment for the Humanities, explaining precisely what kinds of archaeological evidence he or she hopes to find and why it is important. This proposal will be judged by a group of one's peers, and if it is successful (in recent years only about 15 percent of National Science Foundation archaeology proposals were funded), one then would receive the money and conduct the field research.[19] Most archaeologists who direct long-term research projects must spend months of each year trying to obtain funds to continue the project by writing proposals, administering grants received, requesting funds from corporations and private donors, and so on.

LOCATING AND EXCAVATING SITES

Actually locating sites might involve walking surveys, where 5 or 10 archaeologists, working from maps or aerial photographs, simply line up and walk over a selected area, recording sites as they are found. Aerial photographs and other photogrammetric techniques can often be used to reveal ancient agricultural fields, roads, and other features not visible from the ground. The CORONA satellite images (Figure 2.10), for example, which are a type of remote sensing, have recently been used to understand the history of settlement and ecology of Mesopotamia. Other remote sensing techniques include magentometry, and ground-penetrating radar that send signals that "bounce" off sub-surface anomalies such as structures, burials, or other features. Archaeologists can thus map these anomalies, often showing enough of the outline of the features so that their type can be identified, for example, a residential dwelling, without necessarily excavating.

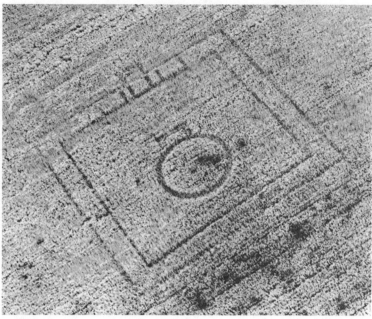

FIGURE 2.10   Aerial photographs often reveal archaeological remains that are not directly visible from ground level, as in the outline of this Roman temple on Hayling Island, Hampshire, England. Stone walls just below ground surface caused parching of grain just above them during the 1976 drought, revealing the outline of the temple wall.

Until recently, many archaeologists relied on placing marks (such as dots or Xs) on topographic maps or aerial photographs to record the location of the sites they found on surveys. This has dramatically changed, however, with the wide availability of GPS. GPS reads locational data by triangulating signals from orbiting satellites and thus records highly accurate spatial information, such as the universal transverse mercator (UTM) coordinates or, alternatively, longitude and latitude.[20] Moreover, GPS units are relatively inexpensive, portable and thus easy to use in the field, and capable of digitally storing information. At the end of each field day, these data are downloaded into computer software programs, a process that decreases the chance of error associated with handwriting data and later keyboarding that information into a computer application.

However they are located, archaeological sites can either be simply mapped and recorded, or they can be excavated—depending on the project's resources and objectives. The methods used to excavate archaeological sites depend on the kind of remains involved and the objectives of the archaeologist. Normally the first step is to make a careful map of the site so that objects and features found can be given precise three-dimensional coordinates, the *provenience* (Figure 2.11). Then the site is gridded into, say, 5-by-5 m blocks, and a sample of these blocks is selected for excavation. Actual digging is done with dental tools, paint brushes, trowels, shovels, bulldozers, or dynamite—depending, again, on the objectives and context.

Although many of the hand tools that archaeologists dig with at sites have remained the same for more than a hundred years, one of the most significant advances in recording information during excavation has come about due to the total station. A total station

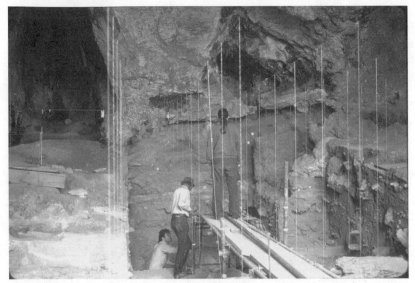

FIGURE 2.11   The Lower and Middle Paleolithic site of Abri Vaufrey, France, during excavations. Note the grid system demarcated using weighted strings suspended from above.

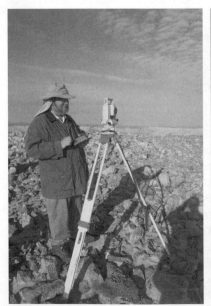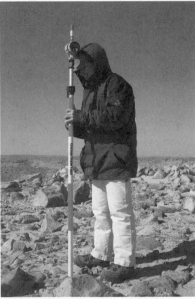

FIGURE 2.12   The use of total stations has revolutionized archaeological recording for both accuracy and speed. On the left, a crew member uses a small computer to coordinate information received from the total station. On the right, another crew member holds the prism pole at the point being recorded by the total station.

combines a theodolite (a survey instrument that measures horizontal and vertical angles) with an electronic distance meter (EDM) (Figure 2.12). The EDM shoots a laser beam to a reflective prism that is held at a specific point, for example, on a stone tool that has been uncovered. The prism bounces the laser beam back to the EDM, which uses the horizontal and vertical angle measurements from the theodolite and calculates the exact three-dimensional Cartesian coordinates (grid coordinates) of the point being measured.[21] Total stations can be linked to small computers, which automatically store the data, thus eliminating errors that occur when data have to be handwritten in field notebooks. Of course, these data can be downloaded into a mapping program each day. Being able to "see" the site (stone tools, animal bones, features, etc.) in plan and profile views as it is excavated on a daily basis is a great boon to decision-making in the field. Total stations can also be used to accurately map the surface of sites, for example, foundations of dwellings and other features, the natural topography of the site and its surrounding area, and the distribution of sites across the landscape.

Like every other profession, archaeology has its variants of Murphy's Laws: Veteran field workers know that the most important find will likely be made on the last day of the season, when there is no time or money to continue the excavations, and that particularly important finds are usually located in the most inaccessible places. Archaeology is also a lot of hard work, usually, and much of it takes place at uncongenial hours of the day and seasons of the year. Anyone who has dug a backyard trench for a sewer pipe on a hot August day has already experienced many of the thrills of field archaeology.

The simple mechanics of excavation are within the range of abilities of almost any healthy adult. The best field archaeologists tend to be those who have a good sense of spatial relationships and enormous patience. "God is in the details," said a great architect,[22] and the same is true of archaeology. One usually tries to excavate according to the *stratigraphy* (Figure 2.13) of the site, so that the different layers of debris are removed in the reverse sequence in which they were deposited—as opposed to simply digging the site by arbitrary levels and removing successive layers, each, say, 25 cm thick.

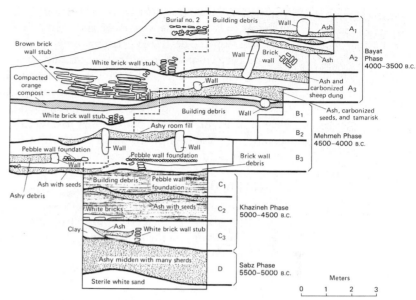

FIGURE 2.13 This profile drawing shows the depositional history of a community at Tepe Sabz, near Deh Luran, Iran, from about 5500 to 3500 B.C. Skill in field archaeology is largely the ability to discern and interpret such cultural layers in the confusing jumble of mudbrick, stones, ash, and other debris.

Thomas Jefferson may have conducted the first scientific stratigraphic archaeological excavation in history.[23] In 1784 he excavated a trench through a Native American burial mound near his home in Virginia and recognized that it had been built up over time by many burials and reburials. Jefferson was able to read a time sequence in the stratigraphy of the site, and he related the differences in preservation of the human bones to the relative time these people had been buried. Jefferson also applied his research to a specific problem: In Jefferson's time many people thought that the "mound-builders" were ancient Europeans, not Native Americans; Jefferson concluded that Native Americans may have been the builders of these mounds.

Modern stratigraphic excavation techniques are based on the same logic as Jefferson's. In Tabun Cave in Palestine, for example, Neandertals came each year for a few months and built fires, made tools, butchered animals, and generally lived out their presumably unremarkable lives. Rocks falling from the ceiling and animals bringing their prey back to the cave when people were not there added to the layers of debris. Thus the excavators,[24] who were interested in subtle changes in diet and tool manufacture over the whole history of the cave's occupation because they were looking for evidence regarding the relationship of the Neandertals to ourselves, had to tease apart layer after layer of debris, trying to separate layers that were the result of short time intervals. The excavators were, in effect, trying to see *change* in the way the Neandertals lived over thousands of years.

Aaron Copland described listening to one of Ralph Vaughn William's symphonies as like staring at a cow for 45 minutes, and although studying archaeological strata is even less eventful, it is one of the most important activities in archaeology. Stratigraphic analyses require that the analyst reconstruct the many different processes that produced the sequence of deposits, and this can require considerable skill, patience, and experience. In cave sediments, for example, one must try to discern faint traces of burrowing animals that may have tunneled in from the surface and whose burrows were subsequently filled with charcoal, ash, and artifacts that date to periods long after their stratigraphic position would suggest. Some of the most complex stratigraphy is found in the remains of early villages and towns in the Middle East, where mudbrick buildings were built and rebuilt and replaced in the same area over many centuries, so that the last, most recent community sat (or sits) atop 10 or more meters of compacted debris representing the remains of thousands of years of building and then abandoning houses, walls, streets, latrines, hearths, and the other facilities of ancient daily life.

Excavation techniques and stratigraphic analyses in such sites reward patience, work, and imagination. British archaeologist Sir Leonard Woolley, for example, while excavating Ur, in Mesopotamia, removed some debris and saw two holes in the ground where something had apparently rotted away. He poured them full of plaster and when the plaster had hardened, Woolley unearthed an almost complete cast of an ancient wooden musical instrument that had long since disintegrated (Figure 2.14). One of the pioneers in devising the techniques of excavating ancient cities was Sir Mortimer Wheeler, a British archaeologist whose excavations at sites in the Indus Valley (modern Pakistan) were done with great care to reveal a stratigraphic record that would allow him to understand how these cities grew and changed over time.[25]

Stratigraphic analyses are a fundamental part of field archaeology because they provide the primary data for looking at change over time in all aspects of cultures. The archaeologist knows that if he or she can detect disturbances and read the strata correctly, the lowest strata can be assumed to be earlier than the ones above it, and thus a form of "time" can be read in a stratigraphic sequence. Understanding the nature of these changes, however, requires analyses of the materials and artifacts found in these strata.

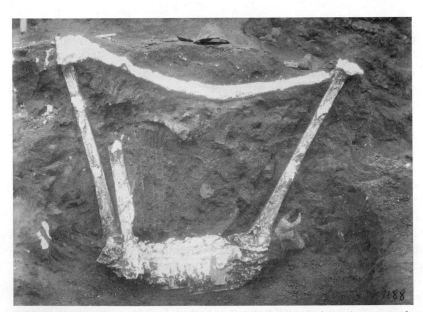

FIGURE 2.14   Sir Leonard Woolley's innovation of pouring plaster into a couple of unusual holes in the ground at the Mesopotamian site of Ur resulted in the recovery of a cast of a lyre.

ANALYSES OF THE PAST

A century ago, most archaeologists were "generalists" in that they were all broadly trained academically and could do most of the analyses their research required, including the excavations and laboratory analyses. The extreme specialization of modern culture, however, has had its impact on archaeology too, and today almost every professional has some kind of technical specialization or area of research in which she or he is particularly qualified. Every archaeological site is unique and nonrenewable, and many technical specialists are required to make the most of the evidence unearthed. Most excavation staffs today include geologists, botanists, palynologists (experts on plant pollen), architectural draftsmen, faunal experts (specialists in analyzing animal remains), artifact illustrators, and other specialists. Conserving finds once they are discovered has also become a highly technical specialty, requiring advanced training in chemistry and other sciences.[26] A few of these specializations are discussed here; others are considered in the context of specific archaeological problems in later chapters.

Reconstructing Ancient Environments and Cultural Ecologies

Archaeologists usually begin their analyses by trying to reconstruct the physical environments in which a particular segment of the archaeological record was formed. Climates and the world's geomorphology—the shape and constituents of land surfaces—have changed greatly over the several million years we and our ancestors have lived, and each archaeological analysis begins with an effort to reconstruct the physical world of the culture being analyzed.

Ancient climates can often be reconstructed from floral and faunal remains. The study of animal remains, or *faunal analysis*, is a complex discipline in which in most cases the archaeologist is trying to reconstruct human diet and local environments. Taphonomic[27] analyses usually are focused on the factors that decompose and in other ways change animal bones after the animal dies. Faunal analysts generally tally the numbers and kinds of animals represented by the remains they find, and then use statistical methods to estimate food values, the ages and sexes of the animals involved, and changes in diets and the physical characteristics of the animals being exploited.[28] One of the most prolonged and heated arguments in contemporary archaeology now involves analyses of marks (Figure 2.15) left by humans cutting up animals with stone tools: For reasons discussed in chapters 3 and 4, it is important in understanding the origins of our genus to study butchered animal bones to try to distinguish between cases in which people butchered animals they had killed themselves and those in which they butchered animals they scavenged from kills of other animals, such as lions and hyenas.[29]

Throughout the history of our genus, plants have been the main source of food for most humans, and so *floral analyses*—studies of the remains of plants—are an extremely important part of archaeology, particularly in studies of how domesticated plants and animals and agricultural economies evolved.[30] Carbon is chemically quite stable, so charred plants and seeds preserve well. Carbonized plant remains can be retrieved by *flotation*: Excavated sediments are mixed with water or some other fluid and the charred plant

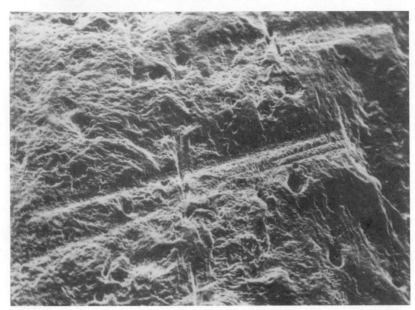

FIGURE 2.15 This animal bone from the FxJj; 50 site in Koobi Fora, Kenya, shows evidence of cut marks made by stone tools.

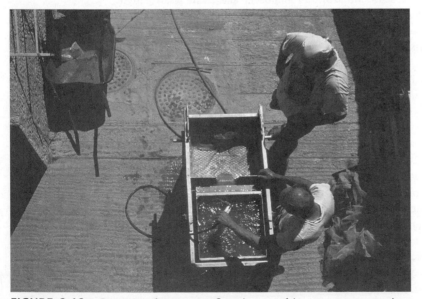

FIGURE 2.16 Crew members use a flotation machine to recover ancient carbonized plant remains.

fragments rise to the surface, where they can be skimmed off and identified (Figure 2.16).

The importance of such analyses lies in the fact that these plants indicate much about the climates and vegetation of the periods in which these animals lived. We shall see, for example, that there are debates about when and where various animals were domesticated (chapter 6).

Human bodies are treasure troves of information for archaeologists, particularly if they are mummified. For example, 11 naturally mummified bodies found in beach sand in northern Chile that date to about 1000 B.C. indicated when analyzed that, among other things, one of them is the earliest known coca leaf chewer, while other bodies showed the changes of the bones of the inner ear that are typical of people who spend a lot of time diving in cold water. In addition, they had the kinds of dental caries and missing teeth associated with the sticky starches of an agricultural diet —although about 40 percent of their diet came from marine resources.[31]

Studies of human *paleopathology*, in general, can tell us much about the demography and health of ancient peoples.[32]

A rapidly growing technical specialty within archaeology is *geoarchaeology*, the combination of archaeological and geological analyses.[33] Geology and archaeology form a "natural" marriage in many obvious ways, for both disciplines are concerned with the alterations of natural landscapes. Glaciers, changing rainfall patterns, and many other natural forces alter landscapes, and so, of course, do people. Geologists are broadly concerned with ancient physical environments, and archaeologists require knowledge of these environments to interpret their finds.

Geoarchaeological analyses involve many different kinds of questions and techniques. In the Egyptian Delta, for example, many of the earliest communities were built on large sand-gravel mounds created by the Nile as it deposited the sediments it carried. But many of these communities have been buried under many meters of sediments from all of the annual floods since that time, and by other factors as well. Moreover, the Nile tributaries in the Delta have changed course many times, leaving a maze of criss-crossed buried river channels. To find these buried sand-gravel mounds and the archaeological sites on them thus often requires complex geological analyses involving augering, satellite image analysis, and many other techniques.

Geoarchaeological analyses are sometimes required simply to determine if some alteration to the landscape or objects are of natural or human origin. Other geoarchaeologists deal with dating strata, reconstructing ancient temperature and rainfall patterns, and related problems.

Reconstructing the physical environment and cultural ecology of any particular site usually involves the coordinated efforts of many specialists. In some ancient sites, for example, such as the floors of caves, the archaeological record is principally one in which repeated seasonal occupations of an area have left strata containing small particles of bones, burned seeds and other plant remains, debris from making stone tools, and other remnants. Spilled food, human wastes, the manure of domestic animals—all these and many other factors associated with human life change the chemistry, texture, and contents of the surfaces on which people live. A geoarchaeologist might, for example, measure the chemical composition of a large sample of sediments taken from different areas of such a site and look for areas relatively high in nitrogen and the other by-products of organic decay. Other specialists would identify the plants and animals that lived or were consumed in the adjacent areas.

Artifact Analyses

Aside from ancient buildings, in sheer bulk the largest part of the archaeological record is made up of stone tools and pottery fragments (sherds). Stone tools are the earliest known artifacts, having been first used more than two million years ago, and they have remained in use to the present day. When a chunk of fine-grain stone is struck with sufficient force at the proper angle with another rock or with a wood or bone baton, a shock wave will pass through the stone and detach a flake of the desired size and shape. Classrooms all over the world are bloodied each year as instructors attempt to demonstrate this process, but with a little experience most become quite skilled. In analyzing ancient stone tools, many archaeologists have mastered the skills needed to make stone tools themselves. Few things are sharper than a fragment struck from fine-grain flint or from obsidian (volcanic glass). Obsidian is so fine-grained that flakes of it can have edges only about 20 molecules thick—hundreds of times thinner than steel tools. One archaeologist (the late Richard Daughtery, of Washington State University) convinced his doctor to use obsidian tools as well as standard surgical scalpels during his own heart surgery and claimed that the incisions made with obsidian healed faster.

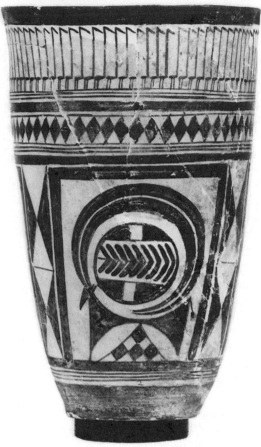

FIGURE 2.17 This "Susa A" style jar, from early fourth millennium B.C. Iran, exemplifies the hand-painted, highly decorated pottery styles that were widely distributed in Southwest Asia just before initial cultural complexity.

Through experimentation, some archaeologists are able to produce copies of almost every stone tool type used in antiquity. A common research strategy is to make flint tools, use them to cut up animals, saw wood, clean hides, bore holes, and so on, and then compare the resulting wear traces with the marks found on ancient artifacts. Sometimes electron-scanning microscopes are used to study minute variations in these use marks. Some rough correspondence can be found between the types of lithic uses and the characteristics of wear marks, but there are many ambiguities. Archaeologists have shown that the marks produced on stone tools by different uses can be subtle and often ambiguous.[34]

Ethnographic data from people who still use lithics, like Brian Hayden's study of stone use in the Mexican highlands and Polly Weissner's study of how the !Kung hunter-gatherers use styles of stone spear-points to identify their social groupings,[35] indicate that even crude-looking stone tools may reflect a great amount of social life and economic forces.[36]

Ceramics were in use much later than the first stone tools (appearing in quantity in many places about 10,000 years ago), but they were used in such massive quantities in antiquity that, for many archaeologists, life consists mainly of the slow sorting and analyzing of potsherds. Ceramic pots were first made by hand and dried in the sun or low-temperature kilns, but in many areas of the Old World, the invention of the potter's wheel and high-temperature kilns produced pottery that is nearly a form of glass and therefore all but indestructible (Figure 2.17).

Ceramics form such a large part of archaeologists' lives because ceramics express so much about the people who made them.[37] Pots are direct indicators of function, in that they show how diets and economies changed over time. David Braun, for example, has documented how pottery in the American Southeast changed in prehistoric times as a form of agriculture developed in which people boiled seeds of various native plants, and pottery was developed to withstand the heat and mechanical stresses of this kind of food preparation.[38]

Ceramics are almost always analyzed on the basis of their *style*. This idea of style is hard to define, but—as discussed later—changing styles are the basis on which archaeologists date much of the archaeological record. But for many archaeologists, ceramics styles are more than just convenient devices for dating—stylistic decoration of artifacts is the primary means by which one can enter the cognitive world of the ancients. Societies throughout history have invested their objects with styles that have profound and complex meanings and effects. As we will see in the case of the Maya (chapter 13) and every other early civilization, rulers used particular symbols and styles, such as in styles of dress, personal ornamentation, and inscriptions, as mechanisms through which they portrayed, communicated, and implemented their power. In all societies, styles fix social meaning and are powerful ways in which these groups define and construct their culture. Styles of objects, language, and personal behavior identify people in terms of gender, age group, ethnic group, socioeconomic class, and many other important ways.[39]

Although stone tools and ceramics make up much of the archaeological record, artifacts of wood, animal hides, metals, minerals, and almost everything else have been in use for thousands, and in some cases even millions, of years (Figure 2.18).[40]

ARRANGING ARTIFACTS

The novelist Luis Borges imagined an ancient Chinese classification of animals that included the following categories:

> (a) those that belong to the Emperor, (b) embalmed ones, (c) those that are trained, (d) suckling pigs, (e) mermaids, (f) fabulous ones, (g) stray dogs, (h) those that are included in this classification, (i) those that tremble as if they were mad, (j) innumerable ones, (k) those drawn with a very fine camel's hair brush, (l) others, (m) those that have just broken a flower vase, and (n) those that resemble flies from a distance.[41]

A zoologist working with this classification of animals might develop exquisite sensibilities, but he or she would have a difficult time using this system to study animal remains of archaeological interest. A fundamental procedure of science, or any form of analysis, is to construct classifications, or *typologies*, that facilitate certain kinds of research objectives. To understand how the world operates, we have to categorize it into groups of similar things and then discover the relationships among these groups. Modern chemistry or physics, for example, would be inconceivable were it not for classes such as electrons, atoms, and molecules, and the laws of thermodynamics. In the same way, evolutionary biology is possible only because of concepts of chromosomes, cells, and species, and the principles of population genetics. These notions about classification and analysis are quite straightforward and simple, but when we consider the kinds of data archaeologists work with, we find that archaeological classifications and analyses have differed somewhat from those of other disciplines.[42] The archaeologists' broken pottery, house foundations, and stone tools have not been organized in classifications in the same ways as the atom and the cell. A potassium atom is exactly the same thing to a Japanese chemist and an American chemist, but when a French archaeologist describes stone tools from southern France as "scrapers," those artifacts differ in many respects from North American "scrapers" as described by an American archaeologist. Archaeological classifications generally have been constructed with much more limited purposes than the units of the natural sciences. It is theory, whether biological, quantum, or Marxian, that tells the researcher how to break up the world for analysis, and in archaeology the only theories are relatively weak behavioral generalizations.

One of the most common classifications in archaeology has been in terms of *functional* types. Archaeologists, for example, frequently categorize the 1.75-million-year-old tools from Olduvai Gorge as "cleavers," "scrapers," and "choppers" (Figure 2.19). Such a classificatory system is based in part on ideas about how our earliest ancestors actually used these tools. Obviously, imagination plays a role in creating functional types, particularly when archaeologists are dealing with extremely old remains left by people very unlike known or

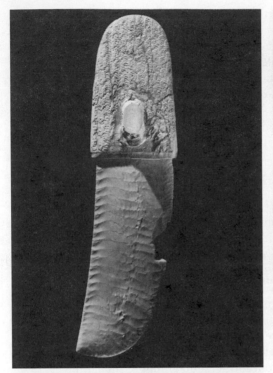

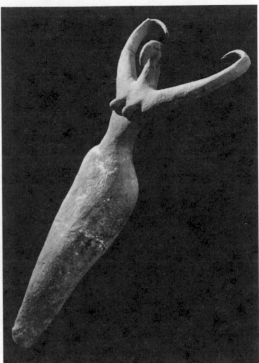

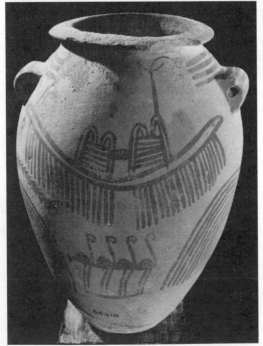

FIGURE 2.18 A great part of the world's archaeological record is composed of stone, wood, and clay artifacts. The flint knife depicted here dates from about 4000 B.C., from Egypt. Its ivory handle is carved with scores of delicate animal figures. The ceramic pot and figurine are also from Egypt, from about 3100 B.C.

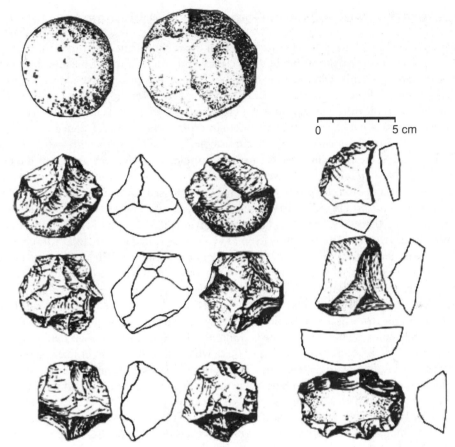

0   5 cm

FIGURE 2.19   Some examples of 1.75-million-year-old Oldowan stone tools.

existing cultures. The use of high-powered microscopes to study wear patterns on stone tools and other technical advances has given archaeologists more confidence in their ability to infer the functions of artifacts, but there will always be an element of speculation, inference, and error in these typologies.

Another widely used archaeological classificatory approach employs *chronological types*. Chronological (or "historical") types are artifacts whose combination of attributes is known to be limited to particular time periods. We have already noted that stylistic elements such as pottery decorations and house architecture have limited distribution in time, and by sorting artifacts into groups based on their similarity of stylistic elements we can often devise relative chronologies of archaeological remains.

While depending on chronological and functional types in most analyses, archaeologists continue to search for more powerful systems of arrangement. In contemporary archaeology, debates about the logic and mechanics of arranging and classifying artifacts into analytical units continue, with some stressing a statistical approach, others more formal methods, and yet others completely new ways of linking tool forms and tool types.[43]

Quantitative Methods and Computers in Archaeology

Once archaeologists have grouped the artifacts of the archaeological record into classes or types, they analyze the distribution of these classes and types through time and space. In a film scene, W. C. Fields, while dealing cards, was asked by a prospective player, "Is this a game of chance?" Fields—felonious eyes agleam—replied, "Not the way I play it!" Modern archaeology, on the other hand, is in many crucial ways a game of chance in the sense that we must use probability theory and statistics to interpret what we find. Chance in this sense enters directly into the formation of what archaeologists have to work with—the archaeological record. Some 1.7 million years ago, for example, an individual who from the neck down looked very much like ourselves made a light lunch of a cow-like animal (possibly killed and partially eaten by some other animal) and tossed some of its bones into some lakeside sediments, where the bones were preserved—cut marks intact—until Louis Leakey dug them out in the 1950s. Doubtless this same individual of 1.7 million years ago munched on other bones that were thrown away in areas where they rotted or were totally fragmented by hyenas, and have thus disappeared. And chance enters into not only the preservation of objects but also their discovery. Many major archaeological sites in European countries, for example, are within a short distance of major roads—a sign that there are probably many other sites that have not yet been discovered because no one has happened on them. Chance—or, more precisely, probability statistics—is also part of the analytical methods of modern archaeology. The costs in time and money of archaeology are such that even well-known sites, like the ancient Iranian city of Susa, where the biblical Esther lived 3,000 years after the city's founding, are so large that even a century of excavation has removed only a small fraction of the site. Even in Egypt, where centuries of excavations and reoccupation have destroyed many sites, hundreds of huge sites have been only partly excavated.

The only reasonable archaeological strategy in the face of such a massive archaeological record is to *sample*: to excavate some parts of some sites in the hope that these samples will accurately reflect the whole.

The essentials of statistical sampling are familiar to most people. Polling organizations regularly ask a few thousand people how they are going to vote in an election and use this information to make very reliable predictions about the voting behavior of the larger population (all the people who actually vote). Defining the target population—that is, what it is one is trying to estimate—is the key to valid statistical analyses. Introductory statistics professors are fond of citing the fact that the average adult human has one testicle and one breast. One of the reasons sampling works in elections is that pollsters *stratify* samples: They know from previous elections that people in the North vote differently from those in the South and that certain occupational groups are far more likely to vote than others. Thus, they break up, or stratify, their samples so that these and other subpopulations are proportionately represented. Then, by using procedures of statistical inference, they are often able to estimate election results quite precisely.

Archaeologists also use sampling theory and procedures. If they wish to know relatively straightforward information, such as the number and kinds of sites in a large region, they can divide the area up into subareas—perhaps stratifying it according to ecological zones—and then go out and record the number of sites in perhaps 10 percent of all the subareas. Excellent results are usually obtained from such procedures, if the objective is simply an estimate of site densities. One critical sampling problem derives from the great size and complexity of the archaeological record. Suppose, for example, that you have the idea that trade in items such as flint and obsidian was a key element in the rise of the first states of ancient Mexico. The only way to test your idea would be to determine if there had been a significant increase in the amount or kinds of these commodities at sites occupied just prior to or during the period when the first states appeared. To do this with statistical precision, you would have to excavate at least portions of a statistically valid sample of at least 30 or 40 sites—something just not feasible in today's archaeology. The result is that archaeologists are not purists when it comes to using statistics and probability models. Because so much of the residue of the past has decayed, and because of the high cost of gathering and analyzing archaeological data, archaeologists tend to misuse statistics and probability theory by making sweeping inferences on the basis of inadequate data. No Wall Street trader (or even drunk riverboat gambler) would bet on the odds that archaeologists do when testing their hypotheses; but archaeologists deal only in history and science, whereas gamblers and stockbrokers deal in money.

Archaeologists have opted for the only realistic compromise: They use statistical sampling techniques, knowing that they often don't meet the theoretical requirements of optimal statistical inference, but believing that useful—if not perfect—results can be obtained. Fortunately, most statistical sampling techniques are very "robust" in that one can strain their assumptions badly and still get quite reasonable results.

To a large extent, archaeological interest in sampling and many other aspects of modern archaeology are side effects of the invention and improvement of the modern computer. Applying even the simplest statistical description and inference to archaeology would be impossibly time-consuming without computers. Quantification in archaeology is not just a matter of sampling: It underlies most other methodological advances. The archaeological record is so complex that in most cases the archaeologist cannot see patterns in the welter of data without the aid of numerical summaries or quantitative presentation.

One example of new methodologies that help identify complex archaeological patterning is the Geographic Information System (GIS), which has been used by both processual and post-processual archaeologists. With this technique, spatial data, such as the location across the landscape of certain types of stone artifacts or the distribution of house sites and temples, are combined with nonspatial information, such as images or database records.[44] GIS is designed so that questions about the data can be asked and analyzed with statistics. In my (Olszewski) ASPS project in Egypt, for example, I might want to know where a certain type of stone artifact, such as a Levallois core, has been found. By setting up a query, I can generate a map showing the distribution of Levallois cores, along with descriptive database information about each of them. One advantage of GIS is that once I've generated this map, I can ask questions about it to generate other maps. For example, perhaps I want to know where the Nubian Levallois cores are in relationship to radial Levallois cores (Figure 2.20). If a pattern is present, then I can run additional queries and statistical analyses that will facilitate interpreting the pattern.

DATING THE PAST

Computers are useless. They can only give you answers.

Pablo Picasso (1881–1973)

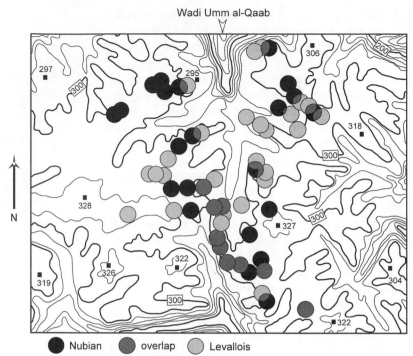

Wadi Umm al-Qaab

● Nubian   ● overlap   ○ Levallois

FIGURE 2.20 The distribution of Middle Paleolithic Levallois and Nubian cores in surface samples near the Wadi Umm al-Qaab, Egypt; collected by the Abydos Survey for Paleolithic Sites project.

The basics of excavating artifacts and features, classifying them, and counting them are relatively straightforward problems common to many sciences. But like other disciplines, archaeology involves many specialized forms of *measuring* artifacts and the rest of the archaeological record. This field is generically referred to as *archaeometry*.

Dating Methods in Archaeology

The primary importance of dating methods in archaeology is in analyzing cultural changes. To take an example, some have argued (chapter 6) that people first domesticated sheep and goats and began farming wheat and barley in the Middle East because human population densities had risen to the point that people could no longer survive on hunting and gathering alone. Other people suggest that rising population densities had little to do directly with the origins of agriculture in this area.

Our only hope of resolving such disputes—of testing hypotheses—about the mechanics of major cultural transformations is to look at the archaeological record. If we conduct archaeological surveys in the area of the Middle East where agriculture first appeared and determine what sites were occupied during what periods and how large they were, we can estimate population densities before, during, and after the period when agriculture first appeared—about 10,000 years ago. If we discover that there is no significant rise in population densities just before and during the period when we find the first domesticated plants and animals and agricultural implements, we might reject the idea that rising population densities were the important direct cause of this change. In short, our only hope of determining cause and effect in ancient cultures is to show correlations in time and space.

But how are we to date artifacts in order to show such correlations?

Archaeologists rely on two different kinds of dating methods. In some situations the objective is to obtain a *chronometric* date: that is, an age expressed in years, such as "that house was built 7,200 years ago." In many situations, chronometric dates may be difficult to obtain or simply unnecessary for the problem at issue, and for these situations archaeologists have devised several methods of *relative* dating, in which the objective is to arrange sites or artifacts in a sequence that reflects the order in which they were created—even though we may not know for certain the actual age of any of them.

CHRONOMETRIC DATING

Many archaeologists dream of a small pocket-sized device, stuffed with microchips and Star Trekian "dilithium oxide" crystals, which, when pointed at an artifact, will read out the object's exact date of manufacture. Fanciful as this may sound, modern physiochemical dating methods have been greatly improved in the last decade, and age estimates are becoming increasingly reliable.[45]

Perhaps the most precise and yet technologically simple form of chronometric dating is *dendrochronology*—the use of sequences of tree rings to infer time.[46] Most trees add a single "ring" each year to their circumference; thus, if we count the number of rings, the age of a tree can be precisely established. Normally the tree grows faster in wet years than in dry ones; therefore, over the centuries there is a unique series of changes in ring widths, and precise dates can be inferred by comparing cross sections of trees that overlapped in time (Figure 2.21). By comparing beams, posts, and other artifacts to cross sections taken from trees that live for long periods, it is often possible to determine the exact year in which the tree used to make the artifact was cut. But here's the rub: In dry climates tree trunks cut as lumber tend to be used and reused for very long times, so that the date that the tree actually was cut may be centuries earlier than the period it was used as a beam in some house. Also, since local climates vary, dendrochronological records must be built up for each region, and at present detailed records are available for the North American West, Europe, and the Near East.

The most widely used chronometric technique is ^{14}C (carbon-14 or radiocarbon dating), a method first outlined in the 1940s by Nobel laureate Willard Libby.[47] When solar radiation strikes the upper atmosphere, it converts a small amount of atmospheric nitrogen into the radioactive isotope ^{14}C. Wind and other factors spread this ^{14}C throughout the atmosphere, and because all living organisms exchange gases with the atmosphere, the ratio of ^{14}C in their cells is equal to that in the atmosphere. When the organism dies, the ^{14}C trapped in its cells begins to revert to nitrogen. This disintegration occurs because ^{14}C is unstable. Because we know that approximately half of any given quantity of ^{14}C will disintegrate in about 5,730 years, we can estimate the time an

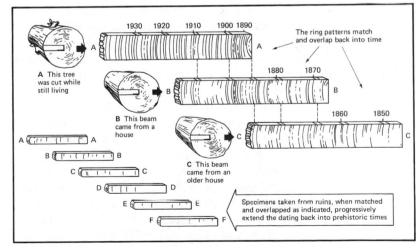

FIGURE 2.21 The most precise dates in archaeology are derived through dendrochronology. In many important areas of the world, however, a dendrochronological sequence has not been established, and in other areas, such as Mesopotamia, there are no native, long-lived species of trees.

organism has been dead by measuring the amount of ^{14}C against the stable isotopes ^{12}C and ^{13}C remaining in its cells. After about 50,000 years, too little persists to be measurable with standard laboratory methods, although with large samples and the most powerful equipment, reliable dates up to 100,000 years ago are theoretically possible.

Radiocarbon dating works best on wood and charcoal, but paper, leather, bone, skin, peat, and many other organic materials can also be dated by this method. Grains and grasses make excellent archaeological samples when charred by fire because they preserve well and are short-lived compared to trees.

The ratio of ^{14}C in the atmosphere has not been constant over the last 50,000 years, and thus ^{14}C dates have had to be "corrected" by measuring the ratio of ^{14}C in tree rings dated through dendrochronology. Fortunately, some trees, such as the bristlecone pine of northern California, live thousands of years; cores from their trunks can be dated through dendrochronology, and then each ring can be radiocarbon-dated to construct a "correction curve."[48] Logs found submerged in northern European bogs, where they have been preserved for thousands of years, have recently allowed the calculation of a radiocarbon correction curve extending back more than 7,000 years for that area. But samples dated by the ^{14}C method can still be contaminated with younger or older carbon sources, such as ground water or petroleum deposits.

Additionally, we also know that the amount of ^{14}C is not the same for all environments. The northern and southern hemispheres, for example, have different proportions of ^{14}C. These types of factors must be considered or accounted for by the laboratories that process samples for ^{14}C dating.

A major advance in radiocarbon dating was made in the 1970s when various researchers used particle accelerators (the AMS method, or accelerator mass spectrometry) to date samples. This method allows reliable dates to be obtained from samples the size of a match-head, whereas older methods require about a handful of carbon. Accelerator dating has other advantages: Samples can be more easily purified of contaminants, individual samples can be subdivided into very small amounts and tested for internal consistency, and older samples can be dated because problems involving background radiation have been obviated. Because accelerator dating can be done on such small samples, reliable dates can be obtained from the cooking soot on pots, dung, and other organic temper in pottery, slag, textiles, and many other materials.

In February 1989 an international team of 21 scientists reported the results of radiometric dating of the Shroud of Turin, a cloth that appears to bear the image of a man who has been whipped and crucified. For centuries, many people have believed that the Shroud was used to wrap the body of Jesus Christ. The scientists took three samples of cloth, each about 50 mg (about the size of a postage stamp), and sent them to three different laboratories, in England, Switzerland, and the United States. Using accelerator mass spectrometers, scientists at the three laboratories all concluded independently that the linen used for the Shroud was made about A.D. 1260–1390.

Interpretations of radiocarbon dates are rarely simple. The radiocarbon method was first applied by Libby to wood from the Pyramid of Djoser in Egypt, and over the years thousands of radiocarbon analyses of Egyptian materials have been made. In a recent attempt to refine the radiocarbon chronology of Egypt, I (Wenke) was part of a group of scholars[49] that retrieved hundreds of samples from the 22 major Egyptian pyramids and scores of temples and tombs. Because we were engaged in a decade-long project to try to define the basic mechanics of ancient Egyptian cultural change, one of the aims of this study was to determine when the Egyptian pyramids were built. Construction of the enormous pyramids and other monuments in the Nile Valley was obviously a critical part of this cultural change, since they must have required astounding investments of time and energy. But how do we know when they were built and what their relation in time was to fluctuations in the Nile floods, political developments in neighboring areas, and other important events?

Not a single ancient text from the age when the pyramids were built has ever been found that describes their construction, or even refers to them. Egyptologists have dated the pyramids primarily on the basis of names on inscriptions in temples and tombs in areas near the pyramids. Ancient king-lists have been found, and the length of reigns of specific kings are often given in inscriptions, so Egyptologists have been able to estimate the sequence of pharaohs and how long each ruled. Occasionally, a text would record a specific astronomical event in the reign of a specific king, such as the rising of the star Sirius at a particular time and place on the horizon. Such events can be precisely dated, so we know the dates of some rulers with great accuracy. Unfortunately, such astronomical observations have not been found for the period when the pyramids appear to have been built.

Most of the mortar used to bind the blocks of stone making up the pyramids appears to have been produced by burning gypsum to create a powder that was combined with water and other materials. Thus pieces of carbon from the fires can be found throughout this mortar. We thought that if these charcoal fragments could be dated, then we could estimate when the brush, trees, and so on, had been cut to get the fuel to burn the gypsum, and from this we could estimate the age of the pyramids. We also hoped that if we took a lot of samples in sequence, from the base to the top of each pyramid, we might arrive at some estimate of how long it took to construct them and the sequence in which they were constructed.

After having obtained the necessary research funds and permissions, we started at the first course of the Great Pyramid of Khufu and began extracting bits of carbon out of the mortar. Six months later we had just over a hundred samples from 17 of the largest pyramids. Some samples were about the size of a pea; others constituted roughly a handful of carbon. We sent the larger samples to the Radiocarbon Laboratory at Southern Methodist University for conventional radiocarbon dating, and we sent the smaller samples to a laboratory in Switzerland, to be dated with the recently developed AMS methods. The majority of our dates came out almost 400 years older than most Egyptologists would estimate as the ages for these various pyramids. We presented a paper on our results at a scientific conference and were informed by most Egyptologists and virtually everyone else that our radiocarbon dates had little or nothing to do with the ages of the pyramids. It was suggested that our dates came out too old because (1) the ancient Egyptians used old wood in the fires to produce the mortar, or (2) the carbon came from plants that naturally absorb relatively large amounts of radioactive carbon, or (3) the mortar itself had contaminated the carbon, or (4) the correlation curves we used were wrong. Because of "wiggles" in the correction curve, for example, for any particular sample one might be able to read three or more different dates from the graph, none of which is more likely than the other dates.

All these factors may, in fact, have played a role in producing our dates, and even though we tried to control for as many of them as we could, we still were in no position to conclude that the traditional Old Kingdom chronology is wrong. In 1994–1995 we returned to Egypt and collected hundreds of additional samples. This time, with botanical identifications of the materials analyzed and a more comprehensive sampling design, our initial results were confirmed in the sense that the radiocarbon chronology for the construction of the pyramids shows that most of the monuments we dated were built earlier than the historical chronology would suggest.[50]

In any case, as the preceding indicates, radiocarbon dating can be very useful, but interpretations of radiocarbon dates are usually difficult: Dates that agree with one's suppositions tend to find a ready audience, while dates that do not are often labeled "intrusive."

Another important form of archaeological dating is the potassium-argon method. Potassium-argon dating is based on the fact that a radioactive isotope of potassium (^{40}K), present in minute quantities in rocks and volcanic ash, decays into the gas argon (^{40}Ar) at a known rate (half of a given amount of ^{40}K will change into ^{40}Ar in about 1.3 billion years). Because ^{40}Ar is a gas, it escapes when rock is molten (as in lava), but when the rock cools, the ^{40}AR is trapped inside. By using sensitive instruments to measure the ratio of ^{40}K to ^{40}Ar, it is possible to estimate the time since the rock or ash cooled and solidified.

Because of the long half-life of ^{40}K (1.3 billion years), potassium-argon dating can be used to estimate dates of materials many millions of years old. The remains of our ancestors at Olduvai Gorge and other sites more than a million years old have been dated with the potassium-argon method.

Carbon-14 and potassium-argon dating remain the mainstays of chronometric dating, but archaeologists can now use many other techniques involving chemical changes, although most of these are subject to considerable error and many qualifications.[51]

Paleomagnetic dating is based on the fact that the north and south pole have "reversed" their magnetism many times. Today the north pole is positive and the south pole is negative, but these were reversed in some periods, such as for most of the period between about 700,000 and 1.6 million years ago. Magnetic rocks preserve a record of these changes in polarity. As a result, finds that are, for example, between two layers of magnetic rock can often be roughly dated.

Luminescence dating[52] has become increasingly important in archaeological research. The technique is based on the fact that commonly occurring crystalline minerals such as quartz and feldspars "soak up," in a sense the radioactivity of the naturally occurring radioactive elements in the sediments in which they are found. In this sense they *record* how long they have been exposed to these radioactive elements. When these minerals are heated to a high enough temperature (e.g., by firing pottery or using earthen ovens) or are "bleached" by sunlight the record of exposure to natural radiation is erased, setting their radiological "clocks" at zero. Once these materials cool, or in the case of sediments are removed from sunlight through burial, the minerals again begin to record their time in contact with their radioactive environment. Even sun-baked surfaces such as agricultural fields and natural soils will record the time of their own burial. In a dark laboratory the accumulated energy can be released as light and measured with a device called a photomultiplier. The earliest technique, thermoluminescence (TL, developed in the 1970s for pottery), uses heat to release the light. Optically stimulated luminescence (OSL), developed for application to sediments, uses one wavelength of light to release light of another wavelength. In both TL and OSL the researcher uses the luminescence record from the sample together with the rate of radioactivity decay in its environment to calculate the age of the sample. Recent technical advances have made possible OSL age determinations for single grains of sand. Age determinations from zero to one million years are possible with TL and OSL. Luminescence techniques can be used to date the last heating of an artifact or the burial of a surface. This has the great advantage of dating the actual construction of the artifact, or the burial of a site. The radiocarbon method, in contrast, dates the death of the organism—an event that may be very far removed from the creation of an artifact or its burial.

Electron spin resonance (ESR) dating is similar to luminescence dating in that the scientist measures the record of exposure to radiation. In ESR, samples of ancient teeth and some other materials are placed in a variable magnetic field and the energy interactions between the object and the magnetic field are measured. ESR is less destructive than other dating techniques, but like TL and OSL it can be applied to very tiny samples (less than 1 g).

Other methods of physical dating have been developed and applied to archaeological problems, and refinements of these methods continue. All of these techniques have inherent expected margins of error and all are still somewhat experimental. Thus, archaeologists tend, where possible, to use as many different techniques on as many samples as possible, in hopes that a clear pattern will be observed with all of the methods converging on approximately the same age estimates. In a recent analysis of Egypt in the period between about 170,000 and 70,000 years ago, scientists on a project directed by Fred Wendorf, Romuald Schild, and Angela Close applied an impressive array of different dating techniques, including uranium series dating of carbonates and tooth enamel; thermoluminescence dating of deposits, both with traditional techniques and the newer optical methods; electron spin resonance dating of tooth enamel and other materials; and amino-acid analyses of eggshells.[53]

RELATIVE DATING

To the novice, perhaps one of the most impressive things archaeologists can do is to be able to tell the approximate date, place of manufacture, and place of origin of a tiny sherd of pottery simply by looking at it.

This kind of relative dating involves the concept of "style." Artisans throughout history have invested their artifacts with characteristics that vary predictably over time and space, and the distribution of these stylistic elements tends to follow certain patterns, whether the objects involved are skirt lengths, musical forms, or stone tools. Styles originate in some small area, spread to adjacent ones, reach a peak in popularity, and then die out (Figure 2.22). To some extent, styles reflect rates of interaction and shared aesthetic preferences, and these are not always exact functions of time and distance. Dress styles in midtown Manhattan, for example, may be more similar to those on Rome's Via Veneto than to those in a small town in rural New Jersey, even though this pattern of stylistic similarity "reverses" their relative distances. And often a style dies out at its point of origin long before it reaches its ultimate dispersal.

Seriation, a type of relative dating, is often used where many surface collections of artifacts have been made. Several generations of archaeologists,[54] for example, have surveyed most of the area around Mexico City, identifying thousands of settlements dating from 12,000 years ago up to the Spanish Conquest. Most of these sites are small mounds whose surfaces were littered with pottery sherds and obsidian tools. The differences in style between a Late Aztec Black-on-Orange dish (c. A.D. 900) and Middle Formative plainware

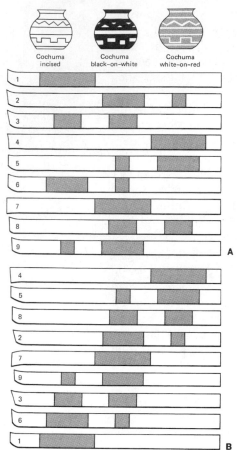

FIGURE 2.22 Relative seriation of nine archaeological sites on the basis of three pottery styles from the American Southwest. The percentage that each pottery style represents of the total pottery found at each site is represented by the width of the colored area on the strip of paper (A). Since most styles tend gradually to grow in popularity and then slowly die out, a seriation can be produced by arranging the paper strips in such a way that the three pottery styles have this "battleship shape" distribution through time. The inferred order of the nine sites is shown in B. Mathematical models and computer programs have been developed to sort scores of sites and pottery styles into these kinds of graphs. Such mathematical aids are often needed because the number of possible unique orderings of 9 sites is 9!, or 362,880.

jar (c. 550 B.C.) are so obvious that anyone can learn to date sites of these periods in a few days of study. On this basis, archaeologists have dated thousands of sites without excavating them, simply by grouping them into a relative seriation of four or five major periods. Carbon-14 dating can be used to provide a few absolute dates to anchor this sequence, and most chronologies based on changes in artifact styles are derived from excavations, in which the archaeologist can order the found pottery in time on the basis of stratigraphy. But pottery styles alone are all that is necessary to construct a seriation. Accurate relative seriations usually require massive quantities of data from artifacts of a highly decorated nature (like pottery) from a relatively small area, and they tend to be least precise when extended to largely undecorated objects such as early stone tools (Figure 2.23).

SUMMARY AND CONCLUSIONS

Having considered various elements of modern archaeological methods and theory, it is, perhaps, useful to consider an example of a specific archaeological project. As one such example, I (Wenke) offer the Fayyum Archaeological Project, which I codirected in Egypt in the 1980s. I offer this example not as a model of its kind, but simply as an illustration of the kind of archaeology that remains in some ways typical of contemporary archaeology.

The proximate cause of the Fayyum Archaeological Project, which was wholly conducted in Egypt, was in fact the Iranian Revolution. I had done archaeological research in Iran on several occasions in the early 1970s and was due to resume work there in 1979, on a day almost exactly between the shah's departure from Iran and the first seizure of the American Embassy by Islamic militants. I had received my first National Science Foundation grant and would probably have gone to Teheran despite the revolution, had the Iranians permitted—which they emphatically did not. Through a series of events too baroque to recount here, I had the good fortune to be able to work instead in Egypt.

I was hardly the first archaeologist forced to change geographical focus by political events. Political situations in many countries, from Peru to China, from Russia to Tanzania, have often rerouted archaeologists.

In 1980 I codirected excavations at el-Hibeh, a site on the Nile that was a major town during most of the first millennium B.C.[55] But I had long been interested in the origins of agricultural economies, and I was much impressed by some new ideas about agricultural origins in Egypt. Simply put, I was curious why wheat and barley farming appeared in Egypt so long—about 2,000 years—after it did in Southwest Asia. So while in Egypt I started searching for an area in which to investigate the origins of Egyptian agriculture.

Many of the most important sites in Egypt have been excavated for decades and are already being studied by other archaeologists; one cannot just decide to excavate this or that site. The late Professor Michael Hoffman suggested that I look

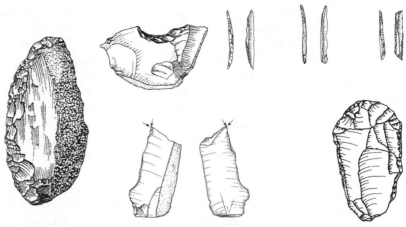

FIGURE 2.23 Many stone tool types are not good indicators of short time periods, and thus are not useful in seriation. On the left is a Middle Paleolithic sidescraper. The top row shows a Middle Paleolithic notch and Epipaleolithic microliths. The bottom row shows an Upper Paleolithic burin and an endscraper.

at unsurveyed parts of the Fayyum Oasis, in central Egypt. Years of work by other archaeologists had shown evidence of early agriculture at the site, but it was not being explored at that time.

Although my main interest was the origins of agriculture, I wanted to do a complete regional survey, to locate sites of all periods in this area. The remains of large towns of the last few centuries B.C., for example, can be found at many places in the research area. Archaeological projects in Egypt usually have on their staffs an Egyptologist—someone who reads ancient Egyptian writing—and I was fortunate enough to recruit a recent graduate from the Sorbonne (The University of Paris), Dr. Mary Ellen Lane, as codirector. With a representative of the Egyptian Antiquities Organization, we made several trips into the deserts of the southern Fayyum without finding much except a restaurant in the provincial capital, where I got deathly ill for only 90 piastres.

In the 1920s, the intrepid British archaeologist Gertrude Caton-Thompson had surveyed the southern edge of the Fayyum Lake, noting here and there scatters of Neolithic-style stone tools. One day, hiking through an area near where she had surveyed, we saw a large pile of bones. On inspection it proved to be the remains of a hippopotamus, and we were delighted to see that near it were stone projectile points ("arrowheads") of a Neolithic type. Within a few hours of surveying, it was evident that we had found a dense scatter of hearths, pottery, stone tools, and animal bones, and that the styles of artifacts suggested two periods of occupation: an "Epipaleolithic" period of occupation by hunter-foragers at about 7000 B.C., followed by an occupation by some of Egypt's earliest known farmers, at about 5500 B.C. Thus, we had the opportunity to study one of the most important cultural changes in Egypt, the transition from hunting-foraging to agriculture. Other archaeologists had worked in the Fayyum on this problem, but we had found a well-preserved part of the archaeological record there that we thought would give us new and important data to analyze this transition.

Back in Cairo, several weeks of library research convinced us that what we had was significant, and that we should try for our first field season in the summer of 1981—a year later. All we needed was $200,000, a staff of at least 20 trained archaeologists, and permission from the Egyptian government.

Famed felon Willie Sutton, when asked why he robbed banks, patiently explained, "That's where the money is." Archaeologists, too, must go where the money is, and in this era it is mainly in the hands of the government. After months of writing proposals, we received about $200,000 from the U.S. Agency for International Development and the U.S. National Science Foundation. We then recruited our staff of specialists in ancient plant remains, animal bones, and geology, and conscripted eight graduate students to assist with the demanding field work.

On June 4, 1981, we left Cairo in several jeeps and trucks to make the four-hour trip to the research area. We lived that summer and autumn in a large gray house that looked across a green palm grove and the blue of the Fayyum Lake to the white limestone cliffs on the northern edge of the Fayyum Oasis. Our villa—the country home of a wealthy Cairo family—was a lovely international-style building with every convenience except three: water, electricity, and a sewage system. But we bought a generator, the provincial governor graciously arranged for a water truck to visit us every three days, and we devised an entertaining method of periodically napalming our open cesspool.

"Tell me what you eat, and I will tell you what you are," said the French gastronome Brilliant-Savarin, but archaeological field projects usually do not usually offer much scope to express one's self in terms of the food one chooses to eat. Our budget and the remoteness of our field quarters meant that our diet was almost wholly composed of bread, canned tuna fish, a vile processed cheese by-product, rice, tomatoes, and several hundred chickens, who were executed on our kitchen steps and then converted into indescribable meals. "Fire-Cracked Veal" and "Dreaded Veal Cutlet" were occasional holiday treats. We bored each other constantly with food fantasies. The morbidity rates—physical and psychological—on archaeological projects are often high, especially when, as in our case, water for washing was scarce and the cook had nothing but contempt for the germ theory of disease. We totaled at least five different strains of parasitical and bacterial infections among our crew, and we lost many days to illness. There was also one emergency appendectomy (mine), performed in Cairo after a thought-provoking four-hour truck ride from the desert, greatly assisted by our geologist, Professor Fekri Hassan, now of the University of London, whose truck and driver got me to a Cairo hospital in record time. After the appendectomy it was determined that I had kidney stones, not appendicitis, but I was in no position to complain.

When we began our six months of field work, we geared most of our efforts to reconstructing as precisely as possible the ways of life of the people who had lived in the Fayyum in the Qarunian period (c. 6500 B.C.), just before the appearance of domesticated plants and animals in this region, and in the succeeding Neolithic Fayyum A period (c. 5000 B.C.), when the first agriculturalists appeared. We hoped to reconstruct the pattern of human settlement in the Fayyum between 7000 B.C. and A.D. 1500 and explain the changes in these settlement patterns over this long period.

We began by making a topographic map of the area in which we intended to work. We then devised a sampling program and collected every artifact in the sampling units defined, that is, in the hundreds of 5-by–5-m squares in our study area. The Fayyum is surrounded by the Sahara Desert, and the average temperature during most of this work was over 40°C

(104°F); by midday the stone tools were often so hot we would have to juggle them as we bagged them. Afternoons were spent back at the field camp, sorting, drawing, and photographing artifacts, drinking warm water, and drawing each other's attention to the heat. In some cases, "It's not the heat, it's the humidity" is not at all true. In September we began excavations, mainly of the hearths and pits that were the dominant feature of both the Qarunian and Fayyum A occupations. In most we found charred animal bones, some carbonized plant remains, and other debris.

To evaluate our "model" of how agriculture appeared in the Fayyum and why, we had to collect sufficient evidence to make statistical arguments about certain kinds of conditions and events in Fayyum prehistory. The details of these arguments are not relevant here, but it should be stressed that as in most archaeological projects, not all the information we had hoped would be there was actually found. But most of it was, and the preliminary analysis of this information was published in several journals and presented at various conferences.[56] We have since made occasional returns to the Fayyum to collect more information, in hopes that eventually we will produce a more complete analysis of this part of the world's archaeological record.

In Cairo, after the season was over, we delivered the artifacts to the Egyptian Museum and made preparations to leave. It is traditional, after the privations of the field, to treat oneself to some rest and relaxation, and some project members agonized between such choices as the Club Med's Red Sea beaches or the delights of Rome. Most of the crew just went home and enjoyed the luxury of sleeping past 4:00 A.M.

BIBLIOGRAPHY

Adams, W. Y., and E. W. Adams. 1991. *Archaeological Typology and Practical Reality: A Dialectical Approach to Artifact Classification and Sorting*. New York: Cambridge University Press.

Aitken, M. J. 1990. *Science-Based Dating in Archaeology*. London and New York: Longman.

Aldenderfer, M. S. 1998. "Quantitative Methods in Archaeology: A Review of Recent Trends and Developments." *Journal of Archaeological Research* 6(2):91–120.

Aldenderfer, M. S., and R. K. Blashfield. 1984. *Cluster Analysis*. Beverly Hills: Sage.

Ambrose, S. H., and M. J. DeNiro. 1986. "Reconstruction of African Human Diet Using Bone Collagen Carbon and Nitrogen Isotope Ratios." *Nature* 319:321–324.

Andel, T. H. van 1989. "Late Quaternary Sea Level and Archaeology." *Antiquity* 63(241):733–745.

Andersen, S. H. 1986. "Mesolithic Dugouts and Paddles from Tybrind Vig, Denmark." *Acta Archaeologica* 57:87–106.

Anderson, A., ed. 1989. *Prodigious Birds: Moas and Moa-hunting in New Zealand*. Cambridge: Cambridge University Press.

Anderson, D. G., and J. C. Gilliam. 2000. "Paleoindian Colonization of the Americas: Implications from an Examination of Physiography, Demography, and Artifact Distribution." *American Antiquity* 65(1):43–66.

Atkinson, T. C., K. R. Briffa, and G. R. Coope. 1987. "Seasonal Temperatures in Britain During the Past 22,000 Years, Reconstructed Using Beetle Remains." *Nature* 325:587–592.

Badekas, J., ed. 1975. *Photogrammetric Surveys of Monuments and Sites*. New York: Elsevier.

Bahn, P. G., and R. W. K. Paterson. 1986. "The Last Rights: More on Archaeology and the Dead." *Oxford Journal of Archaeology* 3:127–139.

Bailey, R. N., E. Cambridge, and H. D. Briggs. 1988. *Dowsing and Church Archaeology*. Wimborne, Dorset: Intercept.

Baillie, M. G. L. 1982. *Tree-Ring Dating*. Chicago: University of Chicago Press.

Baillie, M. G. L., and M. A. R. Munro. 1988. "Irish Tree Rings, Santorini and Volcanic Dust Veils." *Nature* 332:344–346.

Bard, E., B. Hamelin, R. G. Fairbanks, and A. Zindler. 1990. "Calibration of the [14]C Timescale over the Past 30,000 Years Using Mass Spectrometric U-Th Ages from Barbados Corals." *Nature* 345:405–410.

Barisano, E., E. Bartholome, and B. Marcolongo. 1986. *Télédétection et Archéologie*. Paris: CNRS.

Barker, P. 1986. *Understanding Archaeological Excavation*. London: Batsford.

Bass, G. F., ed. 1988. *Ships and Shipwrecks of the Americas: A History Based on Underwater Archaeology.* New York: Thames & Hudson.

Basset, C. A. 1987. "The Culture Thieves." *Science* 86, July/Aug: 22–29.

Battarbee, R. W. 1986. "Diatom Analysis." In *Handbook of Holocene Palaeocology and Palaeohydrology,* ed. B. E. Berglund, pp. 527–570. London: Wiley.

Baxter, M. J. 2003. *Statistics in Archaeology.* New York: Oxford University Press.

Beattie, O., & Geiger, J. 1987. *Frozen in Time.* London: Bloomsbury.

Beck, C., ed. 1995. *Dating in Exposed and Surface Contexts.* Albuquerque: University of New Mexico Press.

Behre, K-E., ed. 1986. *Anthropogenic Indicators in Pollen Diagrams.* Rotterdam and Boston: Balkema.

Behrensmeyer, A. K., and A. P. Hill, eds. 1980. *Fossils in the Making: Vertebrate Taphonomy and Paleoecology.* Chicago: University of Chicago Press.

Behrensmeyer, A. K., K. D. Gordon, and G. T. Yanagi. 1986. "Trampling as a Cause of Bone Surface Damage and Pseudo-Cutmarks." *Nature* 319:768–768.

Bimson, M., and J. C. Freestone, eds. 1987. *Early Vitreous Materials.* London: British Museum Occasional Paper 56.

Binford, L. R. 1964. "A Consideration of Archaeological Research Design." *American Antiquity* 29:425–441.

———. 1985. "Human Ancestors: Changing Views of Their Behavior." *Journal of Anthropological Archaeology* 4:292–327.

Binneman, J., and J. Deacon. 1986. "Experimental Determination of Use Wear on Stone Adzes from Boomplaas Cave, South Africa." *Journal of Archaeological Science* 13:219–219.

Blumenschine, R. J., J. A. Cavallo, and S. D. Capaldo. 1994. "Competition for Carcasses and Early Hominid Behavioral Ecology: A Case Study and Conceptual Framework." *Journal of Human Evolution* 27(1–3):197–213.

Blumenschine, R. J., C. W. Marean, and S. D. Capaldo. 1996. "Blind Tests of Inter-Analyst Correspondence and Accuracy in the Identification of Cut Marks, Percussion Marks, and Carnivore Tooth Marks on Bone Surfaces." *Journal of Archaeological Science* 23(4):493–507.

Boddington, A., A. N. Garland, & R. C. Janaway, eds. 1987. *Death, Decay and Reconstruction: Approaches to Archaeology and Forensic Science.* Manchester: Manchester University Press.

Bodner, C., and R. M. Rowlett. 1980. "Separation of Bone, Charcoal, and Seeds by Chemical Flotation." *American Antiquity* 45:110–114.

Bonani, G., H. Haas, Z. Hawass, M. Lehner, S. Nakhla, J. Nolan, R. Wenke, and W. Wölfli. 2001. "Radiocarbon Dates of Old and Middle Kingdom Monuments in Egypt." *Radiocarbon* 43(3):1297–1320.

Bower, J. 1986. "A Survey of Surveys: Aspects of Surface Archaeology in Sub-Saharan Africa." *The African Archaeological Review* 4:21–40.

Brady, J. E., and W. Ashmore 1999. "Mountains, Caves, Water: Ideational Landscapes of the Ancient Maya." In *Archaeologies of Landscape: Contemporary Perspectives,* ed. W. Ashmore and A. B. Knapp, pp. 124–148. Malden, MA: Blackwell.

Brain, C. K. 1981. *The Hunters or the Hunted? An Introduction to African Cave Taphonomy.* Chicago: University of Chicago Press.

Branting, S. 2002. "Modelling Terrain: The Global Positioning System (GPS) Survey at Kerkenes Dag, Turkey." *Antiquity* 76(293):639–640.

Brassell, S. C., et al. 1986. "Molecular Stratigraphy: A New Tool for Climatic Assessment." *Nature* 320:129–133.

Braun, D. P. 1983. "Pots as Tools." In *Archaeological Hammers and Theories,* eds. A. Keene and J. Moore. New York: Academic Press.

Brewer, D. J. 1987. "Seasonality in the Prehistoric Faiyum Based on the Incremental Growth Structures of the Nile Catfish (Pisces: *Clarias*)." *Journal of Archaeological Science* 14:459–472.

Brinkhuizen, D. C., and A. T. Clason, eds. 1986. *Fish and Archaeology: Studies in Osteometry, Taphonomy, Seasonality and Fishing.* Oxford: British Arch. Reports, Int. Series No. 294.

Bronitsky, G. 1986. "The Use of Materials Science Techniques in the Study of Pottery Construction and Use." In *Advances in Archaeological Method and Theory* 9, ed. M. B. Schiffer. New York: Academic Press.

Brothwell, D. 1986. *The Bog Man and the Archaeology of People.* London: British Museum Publications.

Buchanan, W. F. 1988. *Shellfish in Prehistoric Diet: Elands Bay, S.W. Cape Coast, South Africa.* Oxford: British Arch. Reports, Int. Series No. 455.

Bunn, H. T. 1981. "Archaeological Evidence for Meat-eating by Plio-Pleistocene Hominids from Koobi Fora and Olduvai Gorge." *Nature* 291:574–577.

Bunn, H. T., and E. M. Kroll. 1986. "Systematic Butchery by Plio-Pleistocene Hominids at Olduvai Gorge, Tanzania." *Current Anthropology* 27(5):431–452.

Carr, C., ed. 1989. *For Concordance in Archaeological Analysis.* Prospect Heights, IL: Waveland Press.

Carver, M. 1987. *Underneath English Towns: Interpreting Urban Archaeology.* London: Batsford.

Chappell, J., and N. J. Shackleton. 1986. "Oxygen Isotopes and Sea Level." *Nature* 324:137–140.

Clark, A. 1990. *Seeing Beneath the Soil: Prospecting Methods in Archaeology.* London: Batsford.

Coles, B., and J. Coles. 1989. *People of the Wetlands.* London and New York: Thames & Hudson.

Conkey, M., and C. Hastorf, eds. 1990. *The Uses of Style in Archaeology*. Cambridge: Cambridge University Press.

Cooke, W. D., and B. Lomas. 1987. "Ancient Textiles—Modern Technology." *Archaeology Today* 8(2):21–25.

Cotterel, B., and J. Kamminga. 1990. *Mechanics of Pre-Industrial Technology*. Cambridge: Cambridge University Press.

Courty, M-A., P. Goldberg, and R. MacPhail. 1990. *Soils and Micromorphology in Archaeology*. Cambridge: Cambridge University Press.

Crabtree, D. 1972. *An Introduction to Flintworking*. Pocatello: Occasional Papers of the Idaho State University Museum, No. 28.

Crabtree, P. J., and K. Ryan, eds. 1991. *Animal Use and Culture Change*. MASCA Research Papers in Science and Archaeology, supplements to Vol. 8. Museum of Applied Science, Center for Archaeology. Philadelphia: University of Pennsylvania Press.

Dahl-Jensen, D., and S. J. Johnsen. 1986. "Palaeotemperatures Still Exist in the Greenland Ice Sheet." *Nature* 320:250–252.

David, N., J. Sterner, and K. Gavua. 1988. "Why Pots Are Decorated." *Current Anthropology* 29(3):365–389.

Davis, S. J. M. 1987. *The Archaeology of Animals*. London: Batsford.

Deetz, J. 1967. *Invitation to Archaeology*. Garden City, NY: Natural History Press.

Dekin, A. A. 1987. "Sealed in Time: Ice Entombs an Eskimo Family for Five Centuries." *National Geographic* 171(6):824–836.

Dibble, H. L. 1987. "The Interpretation of Middle Paleolithic Scraper Morphology." *American Antiquity* 52:109–117.

Dibble, H. L., P. G. Chase, S. P. McPherron, and A. Truffreau. 1997. "Testing the Reality of a 'Living Floor' with Archaeological Data." *American Antiquity* 62(4):629–651.

Dormion, G., and J-P. Goidin. 1987. *Les Nouveaux Mystères de la Grande Pyramide*. Paris: Albin Michel.

Dorn, R. I., D. B. Bamforth, T. A. Cahill, J. C. Dohrenwend, B. D. Turrin, D. J. Donahue, A. J. T. Hill, A. Long, M. E. Macko, E. B. Weil, D. S. Whitley, and T. H. Zabel. 1986. "Carbon-Ratio and Accelerator Radiocarbon Dating of Rock Varnish on Mojave Artifacts and Landforms." *Science* 231:830–833.

Drennan, R. D. 1976. "A Refinement of Chronological Seriation Using Nonmetric Multidimensional Scaling." *American Antiquity* 41:290–320.

Dunnell, R. C. 1970. "Seriation Method and Its Evaluation." *American Antiquity* 35:305–319.

———. 1982. "Science, Social Science, and Common Sense: The Agonizing Dilemma of Modern Archaeology." *Journal of Anthropological Research* 38:1–25.

———. 1986. "Methodological Issues in Americanist Artifact Classification." *Advances in Archaeological Method and Theory* 9:149–207.

Dunnell, R. C., and W. Dancey. 1983. "The Siteless Survey: A Regional Scale Data Collection Strategy." *Advances in Archaeological Method and Theory* 6:267–287.

Enge, P. 2004. "Retooling the Global Positioning System." *Scientific American* (May):91–97.

Faegri, K., P. Ekaland, and K. Krzywinski, eds. 1989. *Textbook of Pollen Analysis*, 4th ed. London: Wiley.

Fowler, P. J. 1988/1989. "The Experimental Earthworks 1958–88." *Annual Report of the Council for British Archaeology* 39:83–98.

Fox, A. 2004. *Real Country: Music and Language in a Working-Class Culture*. Durham, NC: Duke University Press.

Gage, M. D., and V. S. Jones. 1999. "Principles of Ground-Penetrating Radar." *Journal of Alabama Archaeology* 45(1):49–61.

Gifford, D. P. 1981. "Taphonomy and Paleoecology: A Critical Review of Archaeology's Sister Discipline." In *Advances in Archaeological Method and Theory*, Vol. 4, ed. M. B. Schiffer. New York: Academic Press.

Gilbert, R. I., Jr., and J. H. Mielke, eds. 1985. *The Analysis of Prehistoric Diets*. New York: Academic Press.

Gould, R. A. 1995. *Recovering the Past*. Albuquerque: University of New Mexico Press.

Gould, R. A., and P. J. Watson. 1982. "A Dialogue on the Meaning and Use of Analogy in Ethnoarchaeological Reasoning." *Journal of Anthropological Archaeology* 1:355–381.

Gowlett, J. A. J. 1987. "The Archaeology of Radiocarbon Accelerator Dating." *Journal of World Prehistory* 1(2):127–170.

Grayson, D. 1984. *Quantitative Zooarchaeology: Topics in the Analysis of Archaeological Faunas*. Orlando: Academic Press.

Green, L. R., and F. A. Hart. 1987. "Colour and Chemical Composition in Ancient Glass: An Examination of Some Roman and Wealden Glass by Means of Ultaviolet-Visible-Infrared Spectrometry and Electron Microprobe Analysis." *Journal of Archaeological Science* 14:271–282.

Grün, R. 1989. *Die ESR-Alterbestimmungsmethode*. Heidelberg: Springer.

Guthrie, R. D. 1990. *Frozen Fauna of the Mammoth Steppe*. Chicago: University of Chicago Press.

Haas, H., J. Devine, R. J. Wenke, M. E. Lehner, W. Wolfli, and G. Bonani. 1987. "Radiocarbon Chronology and the Historical Calendar in Egypt." In *Chronologies in the Near East*, ed. O. Avrenche, J. Evin, and P. Hours. *British Archaeological Reports* 379:585–606.

Hall, A. 1986. "The Fossil Evidence for Plants in Mediaeval Towns." *Biologist* 33(5):262–267.

Harris, E. C. 1989. *Principles of Archaeological Stratigraphy*, 2nd ed. Orlando, FL: Academic Press.

Hastorf, C. A., and V. S. Popper, eds. 1989. *Current Palaeoethnobotany: Analytical Methods and Cultural Interpretations of Archaeological Plant Remains*. Chicago: University of Chicago Press.

Hayden, B., ed. 1987. *Lithic Studies Among the Contemporary Highland Maya*. Tucson: University of Arizona Press.

Heaton, T. H. E., et al. 1986. "Climatic Influence on the Isotopic Composition of Bone Nitrogen." *Nature* 322:822–823.

Hill, H. E., and J. Evans. 1987. "The Identification of Plants Used in Prehistory from Organic Residues." In *Archaeometry: Further Australasian Studies*, ed. W. R. Ambrose and J. M. J. Mummery. Canberra: Australian National University.

Hillman, G. C. 1986. "Plant Foods in Ancient Diet: The Archaeological Role of Paleofaeces in General and Lindow Man's Gut Contents in Particular." In *Lindow Man: The Body in the Bog*, ed. I. M. Stead et al. London: British Museum Publications.

Hillman, G. C., E. Madeyska, and J. Hather. 1988. "Wild Plant Foods and Diet at Late Palaeolithic Wadi Kubbaniya: Evidence from Charred Remains." In *The Prehistory of Wadi Kubbaniya, Vol. 2: Studies in Late Palaeolithic Subsistence*, ed. F. Wendorf et al. Dallas: Southern Methodist University Press.

Hillson, S. 1986. *Teeth*. Cambridge: Cambridge University Press.

Holden, C. 1987. "A Quest for Ancient Egyptian Air." *Science* 236:1419–1420.

Holliday, V. T., ed. 1991. *Soils in Archaeology: Landscape Evolution and Human Occupation*. Washington, DC: Smithsonian Institution Press.

Jelinek, A. 1982. "The Tabun Cave and Paleolithic Man in the Levant." *Science* 216:1369–1375.

Joukowsky, M. 1980. *A Complete Manual of Field Archaeology*. Englewood Cliffs, NJ: Prentice-Hall.

Jouzel, J., C. Lorius, J. R. Petit, C. Genthon, N. I. Barkov, V. M. Kotlyakov, and V. M. Petrov. 1987. "Vostok Ice Core: A Continuous Isotope Temperature Record over the Last Climate Cycle (160,000 Years)." *Nature* 329:403–408.

Kantner, J. 1997. "Ancient Roads, Modern Mapping: Evaluating Chaco Anasazi Roadways Using GIS Technology." *Expedition* 39(3):49–62.

Keeley, L. H. 1980. *Experimental Determination of Stone Tool Use: A Microwear Analysis*. Chicago and London: University of Chicago Press.

Kerisel, J. 1988. "Le Dossier Scientifique sur la Pyramide de Khéops." *Archéologia* 232 (Feb.):46–54.

Kimes, T., C. Haselgrove, and I. Hodder. 1982. "A Method for the Identification of the Location of Regional Cultural Boundaries." *Journal of Anthropological Archaeology* 1:113–131.

Klein, R. G. 1999. *The Human Career: Human Biological and Cultural Origins*. Chicago: University of Chicago Press.

Koike, H. 1986. "Prehistoric Hunting Pressure and Paleobiomass: An Environmental Reconstruction and Archaeozoological Analysis of a Jomon Shellmound Area." In *Prehistoric Hunter-Gatherers in Japan*, ed. T. Akazawa and C. M. Aikens. Tokyo: University Museum Bulletin 27, University of Tokyo.

Koike, H., and N. Ohtaishi. 1987. "Estimation of Prehistoric Hunting Rates Based on the Age Composition of Sika Deer (*Cervus nippon*)." *Journal of Archaeological Science* 14:251–269.

Körber-Grohne, V. 1988. "Microscopic Methods for Identification of Plant Fibres and Animal Hairs from the Prince's Tomb of Hochdorf, Southwest Germany." *Journal of Archaeological Science* 15:73–82.

Kukla, G. J. 1987. "Loess Stratigraphy in Central China." *Quaternary Science Reviews* 6:191–219.

Langford, M., G. Taylor, and J. R. Flenley. 1986. "The Application of Texture Analysis for Automated Pollen Identification." In *Proceedings of the Conference on Identification and Pattern Recognition*, Toulouse, June 1986, Vol. 2:729–739. Toulouse: Université Paul Sabatier.

Leakey, M. 1987. "Animal Prints and Trails." In *Laetoli, a Pliocene Site in Northern Tanzania*, ed. M. Leakey and J. M. Harris. Oxford: Clarendon Press.

LeBlanc, S. A. 1975. "Microseriation. A Method for Fine Chronological Differentiation." *American Antiquity* 40:22–38.

Lehner, M. 1983. "Some Observations on the Layout of the Khufu and Khafre Pyramids." *Journal of the American Research Center in Egypt* 20:7–29.

———. 1985. *The Pyramid Tomb of Hetep-heres and the Satellite Pyramid of Khufu*. Mainz am Rhein: Philipp von Zabern.

Lewenstein, S. 1987. *Stone Tool Use at Cerros. The Ethnoarchaeological and Use-Wear Evidence*. Austin: University of Texas Press.

Libby, W. F. 1955. *Radiocarbon Dating*. Chicago: University of Chicago Press.

Llobera, M. 2001. "Building Past Landscape Perception with GIS: Understanding Topographic Prominence." *Journal of Archaeological Science* 28(9):1005–1014.

Longacre, W. A., ed. 1991. *Ceramic Ethnoarchaeology*. Tucson: University of Arizona Press.

Loy, T. H. 1987. "Recent Advances in Blood Residue Analysis." In *Archaeometry: Further Australasian Studies*, ed. W. R. Ambrose and J. M. J. Mummery. Canberra: Australian National University.

Lyman, R. L. 1994. *Vertebrate Taphonomy*. New York: Cambridge University Press.

Mahaney, W. C., ed. 1984. *Quaternary Dating Methods*. Amsterdam: Elsevier.

Mannion, A. M. 1987. "Fossil Diatoms and Their Significance in Archaeological Research." *Oxford Journal of Archaeology* 6:131–147.

Marquardt, W. H. 1979. "Advances in Archaeological Seriation." In *Advances in Archaeological Method and Theory*, Vol. 1, ed. M. B. Schiffer. New York: Academic Press.

McBrearty, S., and A. S. Brooks. 2000. "The Revolution That Wasn't: A New Interpretation of the Origin of Modern Human Behavior." *Journal of Human Evolution* 39:453–563.

McPherron, S. P., and H. L. Dibble. 2002. *Using Computers in Archaeology: A Practical Guide*. New York: McGraw-Hill Mayfield.

———. 2003. "Using Computers in Adverse Field Conditions: Tales from the Egyptian Desert." *The SAA Archaeological Record* 3:28–32.

Mead, J. I., L. D. Agenbroad, O. K. Davis, and P. S. Martin. 1986. "Dung of *Mammuthus* in the Arid Southwest, North America." *Quarternary Research* 25:121–127.

Merkel, J., and I. Shimada. 1988. "Arsenical Copper Smelting at Batán Grande, Peru. *IAMS* (Institute for ArchaeoMetallurgical Studies) 12 (June): 4–7.

Minnis, P. E. 1987. "Identification of Wood from Archaeological Sites in the American Southwest." *Journal of Archaeological Science* 14:121–132.

Mithen, S., and M. Reed. 2002. "Stepping Out: A Computer Simulation of Hominid Dispersal from Africa." *Journal of Human Evolution* 43(4):433–462.

Montluçon, J. 1986. "L'électricité pour mettre à nu les objets archéologiques." *La Recherche* 17:252–255.

Moore, A. M. T., G. H. Hillman, and A. J. Legge. 2000. *Village on the Euphrates*. New York: Oxford University Press.

Nash, D. T., and M. D. Petraglia, eds. 1987. *Natural Formation Processes and the Archaeological Record*. Oxford: British Arch. Reports, Int. Series 352.

Noel, M., and A. Bocquet. 1987. *Les Hommes et le Bois: Histoire et Technologie du Bois de la Préhistoire à Nos Jours*. Paris: Hachette.

Noten, F. van, and J. Raymaekers. 1988. "Early Iron Smelting in Central Africa." *Scientific American* 258(6):84–91.

Odell, G. 2000. "Stone Tool Research at the End of the Millennium: Procurement and Technology." *Journal of Archaeological Research* 8(4):269–331.

———. 2001. "Stone Tool Research at the End of the Millennium: Classification, Function, and Behavior." *Journal of Archaeological Research* 9(1):45–100.

Ortner, D. J., and A. C. Aufderheide, eds. 1991. *Human Paleopathology: Current Syntheses and Future Options*. Washington, DC: Smithsonian Institution Press.

Orton, C. 2000. *Sampling in Archaeology*. New York: Cambridge University Press.

Parsons, J. R. 1971. *Prehistoric Settlement Patterns in the Texcoco Region, Mexico*. Ann Arbor: Memoir of the Museum of Anthropology, University of Michigan, No. 3.

Parton, J. 1874. *Life of Thomas Jefferson*. Boston: Houghton, Mifflin, and Co.

Pauketat, T., and T. Emerson. 1991. "The Ideology of Authority and the Power of the Pot." *American Anthropologist* 93(4):919–941.

Pearsall, D. M. 1989. *Paleoethnobotany*. New York: Academic Press.

Pearson, G. W. 1987. "How to Cope with Calibration." *Antiquity* 60:98–104.

Peters, C. P., and R. J. Blumenschine. 1995. "Landscape Perspectives on Possible Land Use Patterns for Early Pleistocene Hominids in the Olduvai Basin, Tanzania." *Journal of Human Evolution* 29:321–362.

Petrie, W. M. F. 1900. "Sequences in Prehistoric Remains." *Journal of the Anthropological Institute* 29:295–301.

Philip, G., D. Donoghue, A. Beck, and N. Galiatsatos. 2002. "CORONA Satellite Photography: An Archaeological Application from the Middle East." *Antiquity* 76(291):108–118.

Pickering, M. P. 1989. "Food for Thought: An Alternative to Cannibalism in the Neolithic." *Australian Archaeology* 28:35–39.

Pigeot, N. 1988. *Magdaléniens d'Etiolles: Economie de Débitage et Organisation Sociale*. Paris: Centre National de la Recherche Scientifique.

Piperno, D. R. 1987. *Phytolith Analysis*. Orlando, FL: Academic Press.

Potts, R. 1988. *Early Hominid Activities at Olduvai*. New York: Aldine de Gruyter.

Price, T. D., ed. 1989. *The Chemistry of Prehistoric Human Bone*. Cambridge: Cambridge University Press.

Pritchard, J. B., ed. 1987. *The Times Atlas of the Bible*. London: Times Books.

Rathje, W. 1981. "A Manifesto for Modern Material Culture Studies." In *Modern Material Culture: The Archaeology of Us*, ed. R. Gould. New York: Academic Press.

Read, D. 1989. "The Substance of Archaeological Analysis and the Mold of Statistical Method: Enlightenment Out of Discordance?" In *For Concordance in Archaeological Analysis*, ed. C. Carr. Prospect Heights, IL: Waveland.

Reeves, N. 1990. *The Complete Tutankhamun*. New York: Thames & Hudson.

Relethford, J. H. 2001. *Genetics and the Search for Modern Human Origins*. New York: Wiley-Liss.

Rice, P. M. 1987. *Pottery Analysis*. Chicago: University of Chicago Press.

Riley, D. N. 1987. *Air Photography and Archaeology*. London: Duckworth.

Rossignol, J., and L. Wandsnider, eds. 1992. *Space, Time, and Archaeological Landscapes*. New York: Plenum.

Rottländer, R. C. A. 1986. "Chemical Investigation of Potsherds of the Heuneberg, Upper Danube." In *Proceedings of the 24th International Archaeometry Symposium*, ed. J. S. Olin and M. J. Blackman, pp. 403–405. Washington, DC: Smithsonian Institution.

Rowley-Conwy, P. 1987. "The Interpretation of Ard Marks." *Antiquity* 61:263–266.

Russell, M. 1987. "Mortuary Practices at the Krapina Neadertal Site." *American Journal of Physical Anthropology* 72:381–397.

Sackett, J. R. 1982. "Approaches to Style in Lithic Archaeology." *Journal of Anthropological Archaeology* 1(1):59–112.

Sanders, W. T., J. R. Parsons, and R. S. Santley. 1979. *The Basin of Mexico: The Ecological Processes in the Evolution of a Civilization*. New York: Academic Press.

Scarre, C., ed. 1988. *Past Worlds: The Times Atlas of Archaeology*. London: Times Books.

Schick, K. 1992. "Geoarchaeological Analysis of an Acheulean Site at Kalambo Falls, Zambia." *Geoarchaeology: An International Journal* 7(1):1–26.

Schiffer, M. B. 1987. *Formation Processes of the Archaeological Record*. Albuquerque: University of New Mexico Press.

Schwarcz, H. P. 1994. "Chronology of Modern Humans in the Levant." In *Late Quaternary and Paleoclimates of the Eastern Mediterranean*, ed. O. Bar-Yosef and R. S. Kra, pp. 21–31. Tucson: Radiocarbon.

Sealy, J. C. 1986. *Stable Carbon Isotopes and Prehistoric Diets in the South-Western Cape Province, South Africa*. Oxford: British Arch. Reports, Int. Series No. 293.

Sease, C. 1988. *A Conservation Manual for the Field Archaeologist*. Archaeological Research Tools 4. Los Angeles: UCLA Institute of Archaeology.

Semenov, S. 1964. *Prehistoric Technology*. Trans. M. W. Thompson. London: Cory, Adams & Mackay.

Shackleton, N. J. 1987. "Oxygen Isotope, Ice Volume and Sea Level." *Quarternary Science Reviews* 6:183–190.

Shipman, P. 1983. "Early Hominid Lifestyle: Hunting and Gathering or Foraging and Scavenging?" In *Animals and Archaeology*, Vol. 1 of *Hunters and Their Prey*, ed. J. Glutton-Brock and C. Grigson. Oxford: British Archaeological Reports International Series, 163.

Sieveking, G., and M. H. Newcomer, eds. 1987. *The Human Uses of Flint and Chert*. Cambridge: Cambridge University Press.

Smith, A. B., and C. Poggenpoel. 1988. "The Technology of Bone Tool Fabrication in the Southwestern Cape of South Africa." *World Archaeology* 20(1):103–115.

"Special Radiocarbon Section: Six Articles." 1987. *Antiquity* 61:97–138.

Spence, C., ed. 1990. *Archaeological Site Manual*, 2nd ed. London: Museum of London.

Stead, I. M., J. B. Bourke, and D. Brothwell, eds. 1986. *Lindow Man: The Body in the Bog*. London: British Museum Publications.

Stein, J. K. 1983. "Earthworm Activity: A Source of Potential Disturbance of Archaeological Sediments." *American Antiquity* 48:227–289.

———. 1986. "Coring Archaeological Sites." *American Antiquity* 51:505–527.

Street, M. 1986. "Un Pompéi de L'âge Glaciaire." *La Recherche* 17:534–535.

Stuiver, M., and G. W. Pearson. 1986. "High-Precision Calibration of the Radiocarbon Time Scale, AD 1950–500 BC." *Radiocarbon 28 (2B), Calibration Issue: Proceedings of the Twelfth International Radiocarbon Conference, 1985*. Trondheim, Norway.

Taylor, R. E. 1987. *Radiocarbon Dating: An Archaeological Perspective*. Orlando, FL: Academic Press.

———. 1996. "Radiocarbon Dating: The Continuing Revolution." *Evolutionary Anthropology* 4:169–181.

Taylor, R. E., and M. J. Aitken, eds. 1997. *Chronometric Dating in Archaeology*. New York: Plenum.

Thomas, D. H. 1975. "Nonsite Sampling in Archaeology: Up the Creek Without a Paddle?" In *Sampling in Archaeology*, ed. J. W. Mueller, pp. 61–81. Tucson: University of Arizona Press.

———. 1986. *Refiguring Anthropology*. Prospect Heights, IL: Waveland Press.

Throckmorton, P., ed. 1987. *The Sea Remembers: Shipwrecks and Archaeology*. New York: Weidenfeld.

Toth, N. 1987. "The First Technology." *Scientific American* 256(4):104–113.

Traverse, A. 1988. *Paleopalynology*. Boston: Unwin Hyman.

Tsukuda, M., S. Sugita, and Y. Tsukuda. 1986. "Oldest Primitive Agriculture and Vegetational Environments in Japan." *Nature* 322:632–664.

Tylecote, R. F. 1987. *The Early History of Metallurgy in Europe*. London and New York: Longman.

Valladas, H., J-P. Chadelle, J-M. Geneste, J-L. Joron, L. Meignen, and P-J. Texier. 1987. "Datations par la Theremoluminescence de Gisement Moustériens du Sud de la France." *L'Anthropologie* 91:211–226.

Vandiver, P. B., O. Soffer, B. Klima, and J. Svoboda. 1989. "The Origins of Ceramic Technology at Dolni Vestonice, Czechoslovakia." *Science* 246:1002–1008.

Vaughn, P. 1985. *Use-Wear Analysis of Flaked Stone Tools*. Tucson: University of Arizona Press.

Verano, J. W., and D. H. Ubelaker, eds. 1992. *Disease and Demography in the Americas*. Washington, DC: Smithsonian Institution Press.

Villa, P., C. Bouville, J. Courtin, D. Helmer, E. Mahieu, P. Shipman, G. Belluomini, and M. Branca. 1986. "Cannibalism in the Neolithic." *Science* 233:431–437.

Walton, T. 2002. "GPS Use and Archaeological Site Recording." *Archaeology in New Zealand* 45(4): 293–296.

Waters, M. R. 1992. *Principles of Geoarchaeology: A North American Perspective.* Tucson: University of Arizona Press.

Weigelt, J. 1989. *Recent Vertebrate Carcasses and Their Palaeobiological Implications.* Chicago: University of Chicago Press.

Weisner, P. 1983. "Style and Social Information in Kalahari San Projectile Points." *American Antiquity* 48(2):253–277.

Welsh, F. 1988. *Building the Trireme.* London: Constable.

Wendorf, F., R. Schild, A. E. Close, and Associates. 1993. *The Middle Paleolithic of Bir Tarfawi and Bir Sahara East.* New York: Plenum Press.

Wenke, R. J. 1987. "Western Iran in the Partho-Sasanian Period: The Imperial Transformation." In *The Archaeology of Western Iran*, ed. F. Hole. Washington, DC: Smithsonian Institution Press.

Wenke, R. J., J. E. Long, and P. E. Buck. 1988. "Epipaleolithic and Neolithic Subsistence and Settlement in the Fayyum Oasis of Egypt." *Journal of Field Archaeology* 15(1):29–51.

Whallon, R., and J. A. Brown, eds. 1982. *Essays on Archaeological Typology.* Evanston: Center for American Archaeology Press.

Wheeler, A., and A. K. G. Jones. 1989. *Fishes.* Cambridge: Cambridge University Press.

Wheeler, M. 1954. *Archaeology from the Earth.* Baltimore: Penguin.

Wolpoff, M. H., J. Hawks, and R. Caspari. 2000. "Multiregional, Not Multiple Origins." *American Journal of Physical Anthropology* 112(1):129–136.

Wylie, A. 1982. "An Analogy by Any Other Name Is Just as Analogical." *Journal of Anthropological Archaeology* 1:382–401.

Yellen, J. 1991. "Small Mammals: !Kung San Utilization and the Production of Faunal Assemblages." *Journal of Anthropological Archaeology* 10:1–26.

NOTES

1. In recent years, the term *physical anthropology* has often been replaced by *biological anthropology*.
2. Urban anthropology is becoming an increasingly important area of study. See, for example, Fox, *Real Country: Music and Language in a Working-Class Culture.*
3. Including many scholars who teach at universities in Australia, New Zealand, and elsewhere.
4. Rathje, "A Manifesto for Modern Material Culture Studies."
5. The idea of "feature," although still common in archaeology, has been discarded by some archaeologists in favor of a terminology based on depositional stratigraphy; see, for example, Harris, *Principles of Archaeological Stratigraphy*, 2nd ed.
6. For example, Dunnell and Dancey, "The Siteless Survey: A Regional Scale Data Collection Strategy"; Thomas, "Nonsite Sampling in Archaeology: Up the Creek without a Paddle?"; Peters and Blumenschine, "Landscape Perspectives on Possible Land Use Patterns for Early Pleistocene Hominids in the Olduvai Basin, Tanzania."
7. *Wadi* is the local term for a canyon.
8. Schiffer, *Formation Processes of the Archaeological Record.*
9. The term *taphonomy* (see Reconstructing Ancient Environments and Cultural Ecologies) comes to archaeology from faunal analysis. Today this term is widely used in the context of reconstructing how archaeological sites are formed by both natural and cultural processes over time.
10. Schiffer, *Formation Processes of the Archaeological Record.*
11. See, for example, Relethford, *Genetics and the Search for Modern Human Origins*; McBrearty and Brooks, "The Revolution That Wasn't: A New Interpretation of the Origin of Modern Human Behavior."
12. Wolpoff et al., "Multiregional, Not Multiple Origins."
13. Blumenschine et al., "Blind Tests of Inter-Analyst Correspondence and Accuracry in the Identification of Cut Marks, Percussion Marks, and Carnivore Tooth Marks on Bone Surfaces."
14. Dibble et al., "Testing the Reality of a 'Living Floor' with Archaeological Data."
15. Orientation of artifacts is obtained by measuring the X, Y, and Z coordinates of the ends of elongated artifacts and bones, along with the strike (horizontal) and dip (vertical).
16. Dunnell, "Science, Social Science, and Common Sense: The Agonizing Dilemma of Modern Archaeology."
17. "In Memory of Eva Gore Booth and Con Markiewics," 1923.
18. Brady and Ashmore, "Mountains, Caves, Water; Ideational Landscapes of the Ancient Maya."
19. Currently the archaeology programs of the U.S. National Science Foundation and the U.S. National Endowment for the Humanities often face funding cuts through congressional action.
20. See Enge, "Retooling the Global Positioning System"; McPherron and Dibble, *Using Computers in Archaeology: A Practical Guide*, pp. 54–63. UTM stands for universal transverse Mercator, a grid system that

is placed over the entire world. It measures each grid in meters, so that a UTM reading gives you an Easting and a Northing, such as $E^{36R}75039$ $N^{34}24964$. This particular UTM corresponds to a location in west-central Jordan, just southeast of the Dead Sea.

21. See McPherron and Dibble, *Using Computers in Archaeology: A Practical Guide*, pp. 30–53.
22. This has been attributed to Mies van der Rohe and others.
23. Jefferson was once described as "a gentleman of 32 who could calculate an eclipse, survey an estate, tie an artery, plan an edifice, try a cause, dance a minuet, and play the violin." James Parton, *Life of Jefferson*.
24. Jelinek, "The Tabun Cave and Paleolithic Man in the Levant."
25. Wheeler, *Archaeology from the Earth*.
26. Sease, *A Conservation Manual for the Field Archaeologist*.
27. Lyman, *Vertebrate Taphonomy*.
28. Grayson, *Quantitative Zooarchaeology*.
29. Binford, "Human Ancestors: Changing Views of Their Behavior"; Bunn, "Archaeological Evidence for Meat-Eating by Plio-Pleistocene Hominids from Koobi Fora and Olduvai Gorge"; Shipman, "Early Hominid Lifestyle: Hunting and Gathering or Foraging and Scavenging?"
30. Moore et al., *Village on the Euphrates*; Piperno, *Phytolith Analysis*; Gilbert and Mielke, eds., *The Analysis of Prehistoric Diets*; Bodner and Rowlett, "Separation of Bone, Charcoal, and Seeds by Chemical Flotation."
31. Ortner and Aufderheide, eds., *Human Paleopathology: Current Syntheses and Future Options*.
32. Ibid.
33. See, for example, Holliday, ed., *Soils in Archaeology: Landscape Evolution and Human Occupation*.
34. Vaughn, *Use-Wear Analysis of Flaked Stone Tools*; Keeley, *Experimental Determination of Stone Tool Use: A Microwear Analysis*.
35. Hayden, *Lithic Studies Among the Contemporary Highland Maya*; Weissner, "Style and Social Information in Kalahari San Projectile Points."
36. See also, for example, Gould, *Recovering the Past*.
37. For an excellent review of the role of ceramics in archaeological analysis, see Rice, *Pottery Analysis*.
38. Braun, "Pots as Tools."
39. See, for example, papers by Hodder, Plog, Wiesner, and others in Conkey and Hasdorf, eds., *The Uses of Style in Archaeology*.
40. Information collected about artifacts is stored in databases. These can be relatively simple, such as records in software programs such as Access or Excel, or quite sophisticated, combining photographs of the artifacts, data on their location within a site, their measurements and other attributes, field notes describing them, and so on. One example of this type of database is at http://www.museum.upenn.edu/mis/index.html.
41. Jorge Luis Borges, *Other Inquisitions: 1937–1952*, quoted in Aldenderfer and Blashfield, *Cluster Analysis*, p. 7.
42. Adams and Adams, *Archaeological Typology and Practical Reality*.
43. See, for example, Whallon and Brown, *Essays on Archaeological Typology*; Read, "The Substance of Archaeological Analysis and the Mold of Statistical Method: Enlightenment Out of Discordance?" pp. 45–86; Dunnell, "Methodological Issues in Americanist Artifact Classification"; Adams and Adams, *Archaeological Typology and Practical Reality*; Dibble, "The Interpretation of Middle Paleolithic Scraper Morphology."
44. See McPherron and Dibble, *Using Computers in Archaeology: A Practical Guide*, pp. 188–215.
45. Beck, ed., *Dating in Exposed and Surface Contexts*.
46. Baillie, *Tree-Ring Dating*.
47. Libby, *Radiocarbon Dating*.
48. Taylor, *Radiocarbon Dating: An Archaeological Perspective*; Taylor, "Radiocarbon Dating: The Continuing Revolution." Until recently, radiocarbon dates were often published as a certain number of years before A.D. 1950, the benchmark year in which the method was first established. "BP" was often used for corrected radio-carbon dates, "bp" for uncorrected dates (the "bp" first referred to "before present" or even "before physics"; see Taylor, *Radiocarbon Dating: An Archaeological Perspective*, p. 5). These correction curves allow dates to be calibrated—adjusted to be more accurate—and they are often reported as cal BC or cal BP. Because not all dates can be calibrated, there is a wide range of how dates are reported in the archaeological literature.
49. Haas et al., "Radiocarbon Chronology and the Historical Calendar in Egypt."
50. Bonani et al., "Radiocarbon Dates of Old and Middle Kingdom Monuments in Egypt."
51. Mahaney, *Quaternary Dating Methods*; Taylor and Aitken, *Chronometric Dating in Archaeology*.
52. I (Wenke) am indebted to Dan Bush for the following discussion.
53. Wendorf, Schild, Close, et al., *The Middle Paleolithic of Bir Tarfawi and Bir Sahara East*.
54. Sanders et al., *The Basin of Mexico*.
55. I (Wenke) thank Maurice and Lois Schwartz, the National Science Foundation, and the U.S. Agency for International Development for their support of this research.
56. See, for example, Wenke et al., "Epipaleolithic and Neolithic Subsistence and Settlement in the Fayyum Oasis of Egypt."

The Origins of Culture

*What a book a Devil's Chaplain might write on
the clumsy, wasteful, blundering low & horridly
cruel works of nature!*

Charles Darwin

D arwin, somewhat ambivalently, concluded that a close study of nature and evolution argued powerfully for the nonexistence, or noninvolvement in human affairs, of a supreme deity. Darwin's analysis convinced him that the origins of the human species, like that of all other species, are to be found in blind and "cruel" competition at all levels—that is, in countless millennia of nature "red in tooth and claw" (a phrase coined by Alfred Lord Tennyson). Darwin was acutely aware of the impact of his ideas on revealed religions, and even today the reverberations of the conflict between evolutionary theory and some religious doctrines echo in some cultures, including the United States.[1]

In this chapter we consider our origins in the competitive world of Pleistocene Africa—how our genus, *Homo*, evolved out of more ancient primates in a complex mosaic of environments. In contemporary paleoanthropology one of the most interesting recent developments is the growing consensus that many of the hominins who lived before about 300,000 years ago were not the direct ancestors of us, *Homo sapiens*, genetically. Yet there are still many unresolved issues in these debates and analyses, and it is entirely possible that our current understanding of our pre–*Homo sapiens* past will be radically altered as new evidence is discovered.

THE PROBLEM OF CULTURAL ORIGINS

In the film *2001: A Space Odyssey* our chimpanzee-like African ancestors of some millions of years ago awake one morning to find themselves at the foot of a huge, black, perfectly smooth, monolith. Jabbering in fright and wonder, they contemplate its meaning. In a later scene, a descendant of these creatures, but still an ape-like primate, "discovers" tools—and murder—by using an animal leg bone to smash the skull of another ape. He throws the bone skyward in bloody triumph, where, spinning, it is transformed into a rotating twenty-first-century space station—carrying a man on his way to examine another—or perhaps the same—monolith, which has been found in an excavation on the moon.

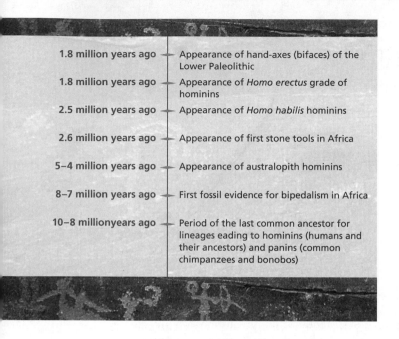

1.8 million years ago	Appearance of hand-axes (bifaces) of the Lower Paleolithic
1.8 million years ago	Appearance of *Homo erectus* grade of hominins
2.5 million years ago	Appearance of *Homo habilis* hominins
2.6 million years ago	Appearance of first stone tools in Africa
5–4 million years ago	Appearance of australopith hominins
8–7 million years ago	First fossil evidence for bipedalism in Africa
10–8 million years ago	Period of the last common ancestor for lineages eading to hominins (humans and their ancestors) and panins (common chimpanzees and bonobos)

Stanley Kubrick's powerful film of this classic Arthur Clarke story effectively uses the monolith as a symbol, perhaps of human evolution and enlightenment or of some cosmic intelligence. It leaves the viewer to muse on the nature of the possible driving force of human evolution: natural processes, God, extraterrestrial beings, or something else.

Anthropological analyses of the beginnings of tool-use and the nature and significance of our past and future have, perhaps, much less mythic power than *2001*, but the fundamental questions addressed are similar: What factors transformed us from just one kind of genera of African ape into space travelers, and what, if anything, does this transformation "mean"?

Long ago a Greek philosopher suggested we are the progeny of spores blown here millions of years ago through the illimitable reaches of space, and, perhaps, the answers to our questions of origins are, thus, truly, in the stars. Even today some scientists, impressed by the relatively short time between the formation of the earth and the complexity of contemporary human civilizations, consider it possible that life on earth derives ultimately from the accidental intersection of the earth's orbit with a cloud of complex chemicals brewed in some ancient stellar explosion.

Alternatively, people in every age have found great comfort in their sure and certain knowledge that we and the world are the result of Divine Creation and that there is Someone in Charge.

Whatever the value of such speculations, the major premise of anthropology is that one should begin any inquiry into our origins, history, and destiny with a consideration of real-world factors of climate, genetics, culture, and so on. The anthropological assumption is that with the careful sifting and analysis of the shattered fragments of our ancestors, their tools, and other material evidence, we can "know," in a scientific sense, at least something about our nature and our past. Indeed, in their search for human origins, anthropologists have concentrated on such embarrassingly ordinary subjects as chimpanzee sexual behavior and the cuisine of African hunter-gatherers.

THE NATURE OF CULTURE

Intelligence . . . is the faculty of making artificial objects, especially tools to make tools.
Henri Bergson[2]

If we take Bergson's definition literally, we might conclude that the earliest evidence for human "intelligence" dates to some time before 2.6 million years ago, in Ethiopia, where stone tools have been found under volcanic ash layers dated to that time.[3] But what are we trying to explain when we speak of the origins of culture? Anthropologists restrict the term "cultural" to human beings (although chimpanzees are sometimes called "proto-cultural"); thus the origins of culture are essentially the origins of those human qualities that make us a unique animal.[4] But it is more difficult than it might seem to reduce humanity to this or that constellation of attributes, to capture the essence of being human. In most religions, for example, a human fetus, whether six seconds or six months after conception, is human in the only way that really matters, being imbued with an immortal soul. But what observable, *measurable* qualities can we use to distinguish ourselves from other life-forms?

Most who address this question turn instinctively, as it were, to attributes of the human mind, and particularly to the unique qualities of human thought. Descartes's famous phrase *Cogito, ergo sum* ("I think, therefore I am") is a classic expression of this idea.

A traditional view is that humans are unique in their ability to manipulate symbols and that the evolution of this ability underlies all human achievements. Anyone who has seriously studied chimpanzees at play can feel a sense of kinship with these primates; the term *proto-cultural* seems hardly an exaggeration. But in analyzing the origins of culture, it is how we are *different* from other primates that is important, and in large part this difference resides in our mentality—our creativity, intuition, logic, aesthetics—all the powers of the human mind. Anthropologist Leslie White argued,[5] for example, that although chimpanzees are clever animals who can use tools and even can be taught to use plastic counters, computers, and sign languages to express emotions and desires, they are fundamentally different from us in two ways: First, they can never use symbols at an abstract level that would give them any understanding of concepts like "holy water" or the casting of a vote; second, even the smartest of nonhuman animals seem to pass relatively little new, learned knowledge from generation to generation in such a way that there is an observable long-term net increase.

For White these differences amounted to a qualitative difference between ourselves and all other animals, but one can also view them as quantitative. We simply do not know what a chimpanzee sees or what he or she "thinks," and White's distinction may be less sharp than it appears. Nonetheless, chimpanzees can smear canvasses with paint in an excellent imitation of "modern art," but they seem utterly untalented at more representational painting; and it seems highly unlikely that even chimpanzees can *respond* in great depth to aesthetics—can savor, for example, the vibrancy of a Van Gogh landscape or the sublime delicacy of a Ming porcelain jar. Their ability to pass new learned knowledge from generation to generation is a more complex problem. Japanese monkeys, for example, have been reported to have learned how to wash sand from handfuls of grain (Figure 3.1) and then instruct younger members of the group how to do this, but there is evidence that even such simple food-related behavior is partially genetically determined.[6] And even if it were not, such behavior is at a sufficiently low scale that it remains true that "the most characteristic part of being human is the ability to profit from the accumulated and transmitted experience of other human beings."[7]

Tooby and Devore have expressed this sense of the distinctiveness of human intelligence and behavior as a set of two kinds of primate characteristics, and have listed those

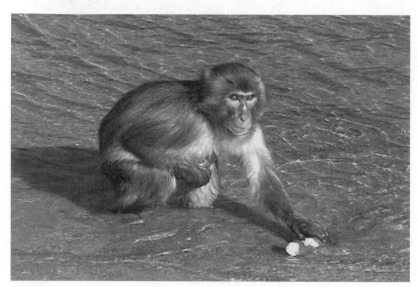

FIGURE 3.1   Japanese macaque washing sweet potatoes.

that are unique to humans and those that we share with other primates but to a much different degree.

Fifteen features on this list basically relate to a generalized sense of "intelligence" in combination with some emotional capacities, but the unfortunate reality is that, although we know that we modern humans are different from other primates, we must presume that our earlier ancestors were increasingly similar to other primates as one goes back in time, and we must also recognize that we will never know directly the symbolic capacities of our earliest ancestors: We must relate "intelligence" to material things that we can find and measure, and for the first several million years of the human clade, this means looking mainly at changes in the size and shape of hominin skulls and bodies, and, after about 2.6 million years ago, at stone tools and the remains of other objects on which our ancestors imposed their intellects. These indirect reflections of evolving symbolic abilities constitute "culture" for the anthropologist in an analytical sense.

One might question why a "moral" sense is not listed as a defining attribute of human mentality, as that characteristic has been the focus of theological definitions of humanity. In rural Southern colloquial American English, if one wants to disparage a person's knowledge of something, a common phrase is that "he knows about as much about it as a pig knows about Sunday." Even Mark Twain, no sentimentalist, said, "Man is the only animal that blushes—or needs to." But many scientists[8] have considered human moral systems to be learned, not innate, and to have evolved as extensions of the same symbolizing abilities that allow us to categorize "friend" and "foe."[9]

The paradox that we have only one tool with which to try to understand the origins of the human mind, namely, the human mind, is a bit of cosmic whimsy appreciated by philosophers of all ages. There is an embedded circularity to this form of the analysis that has led some to kick stones, wondering if they are really "there." Someone observed that "a fish would be the last creature to discover water,"[10] and we may be in similar circumstances—unable to see the reality in which we live because we can see no other reality. Readers interested in such topics and with much time to indulge their interest are referred to volumes 2–9 of Father Frederick Copleston's rewarding *History of Philosophy*.

What some researchers assume, however, is that our ancestors of about 8–10 million years ago were not much different from the chimpanzees one can see in any zoo today,[11] and, yet, today *we* are very different from all other apes. This knowledge of our deep antiquity and the nature of our physical and cultural evolution—and the search for an explanation for them—is relatively recent.

Early Studies of Human Origins

As discussed in chapter 1, the impact of the discovery of human antiquity was profound.[12] Many scholars lost their comforting faith in a recently created and human-centered world and were forced to peer instead into an abyss of millions of years, one that saw our slow emergence from rodents, reptiles, worms, and, ultimately, the same lifeless chemicals that appear to make up the rest of the universe.

By the end of the nineteenth century both Darwin's ideas (see chapter 1) about the biological evolution of the human species and the discovery of stone tools in association with the bones of extinct animals in extremely ancient geological strata had convinced many scholars of the great antiquity of humans. Nevertheless, as long as no bones were found that were recognized as those of a human ancestor intermediate between ourselves and other primates in physical form, it was still possible to cling to the idea that humans were an exception: that we were an extremely old species, older than had previously been suspected, but that we had not evolved as other species had.

Those who had studied Darwin and Lyell closely, however, knew it was just a matter of time before the first fossil "missing link" was found—or recognized in the bones that had already been found. The French scholar (and full-time customs inspector) Boucher de Perthes, grown old and tired of waiting, offered a 200-franc reward to the discoverer of the first "antediluvian" (meaning "before the flood") human in France. His enterprising workers were soon "finding" any number of such remains—all of which they had themselves put there, of course, in hopes of collecting the money.

Boucher de Perthes did not know that pre-modern hominins had already been discovered some years before but simply had not been recognized. A fragmentary Neandertal child's skull was found near Liège, Belgium, in 1829–1830, and in 1848 work at a quarry on Gibraltar revealed a skull whose receding chin, heavy brow ridges, and thick bones we now recognize as that of a Neandertal. Neither the Belgium or Gibraltar finds excited much interest at the time. In 1856, however, a skullcap and some limb bones were found in a cave in the Neander Valley near Dusseldorf, Germany (Figure 3.2). Although these remains were dismissed by the great German anatomist Rudolf Virchow as those of a deformed human, Johann Karl Fuhlrott, their discoverer, argued from the beginning that the remains were of an early form of human. But Virchow's opinion, and those of others who variously labeled it an ancient Celt, a victim of rickets, an idiot, or a Cossack, conspired to deny these bones their proper significance for many years. One French savant even suggested that the huge brow ridges of the Neandertal came about because

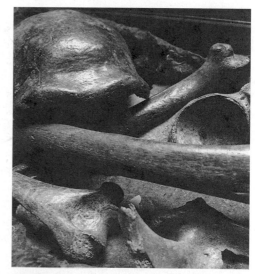

FIGURE 3.2 The remains of Neandertals were recovered from the Neander Valley, near Dusseldorf, Germany, in 1857. This evidence that ancient people were different from modern humankind was part of the assault by evolutionary ideas and evidence on traditional ideas about our place in the universe.

his deformed arm caused him such pain that he continually furrowed his brow, and the expression became ossified.

In 1886 two partial skeletons similar to the Neandertal specimen were recovered in a cave in Spy, Belgium, in direct association with stone tools and the bones of rhinoceroses, mammoths, and other animal species known to have been long extinct. Although Virchow also refused to accept these as ancient men, the tide of opinion had turned and scientists everywhere were soon looking eagerly for additional specimens of early hominins.

One of these was a young Dutch physician, Eugene Dubois, who spent years wandering the wilds of Sumatra without finding much of interest; only when he arranged a transfer to Java did he make his great discovery. In 1890 he unearthed a fragment of a lower jaw, and over the next few years he recovered a skullcap and a femur (thigh bone).[13]

For the next 30 years, controversy raged over Dubois's find, with some authorities again claiming it to be a deformed freak or a giant chimpanzee, while others recognized it as an early form of our genus and a direct ancestor of modern humans. Dubois's fossil had an approximate brain volume of 1,040 cm^3, about a third less than modern people but far more than any living primate. Scholars of the time recognized that if this animal were in fact a human ancestor, it was an ancestor considerably different from ourselves and from "Neandertal man" (whose cranial capacity was slightly larger than that of most modern humans).

In 1906 the German anatomist Gustav Schwalbe proposed three successive stages of hominin evolution: pithecanthropine (as represented by Dubois's fossils), Neandertal, and modern. It was apparent, however, that if this were the correct succession of hominin forms, there would have been many intermediate types not yet found.

The recognition of an earlier stage of hominin evolution did not come until the 1920s, when Raymond Dart discovered a nearly complete skull of a strange-looking child. It was encased in stone quarried from a mine at Taung, some 300 kilometers from Johannesburg, South Africa. The skull's shape, small volume, and primitive teeth convinced Dart he had found one of humankind's earliest, most primitive ancestors, which he labeled *Australopithecus africanus* ("Southern ape of Africa"). While Dart's conclusions were being challenged by some of the most influential scientists in Europe, another important find was made, this time in northeastern China, near Beijing, at a mining installation called Zhoukoudian (formerly rendered in English as "Choukoutien") (Figure 3.3). For centuries, fossilized bones from the area had been ground into powder and used, hopefully, as aphrodisiacs, and many specimens of great scientific significance have probably long since been consumed in the form of impotent aphrodisiacs and medical potions.[14]

A somewhat more scientific interest in these fossils was stimulated in 1921 when a single human-looking tooth from Zhoukoudian was given to the English anatomist Henry Black. He recognized it as belonging to an ancient form of hominin, and as a consequence, excavations at Zhoukoudian were begun. Altogether, the remains of about 40 individuals were found, including many skull fragments, and it was obvious that these individuals were similar in brain size, facial structure, and other characteristics to the hominin found by Dubois on Java. This supported Schwalbe's proposed pithecanthropine stage, and fossils of this type were accorded the name *Sinanthropus* or *Homo erectus* ("erect man").

Thus, by the 1930s at least some of the scientific community recognized four categories of early hominins: australopiths, *Homo erectus*, Neandertals, and modern humans. Since that time the arguments have focused not on *whether* humankind evolved from some sort

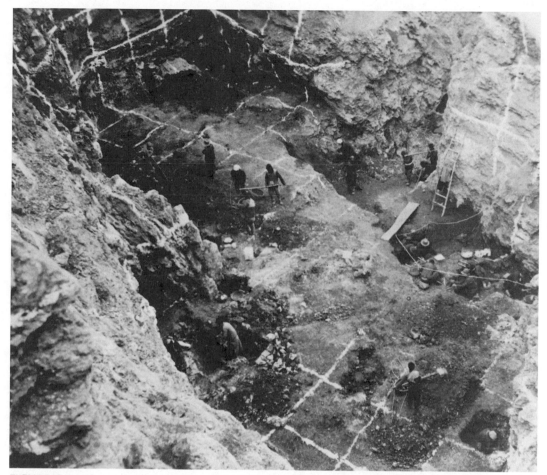

FIGURE 3.3 Excavations at Zhoukoudian, China. The rope enclosures on the right mark areas where hominin skulls were found.

of nonhuman ancestor, but on what these various ancestral forms are, how they are related genetically during their evolutionary histories, and what evolutionary mechanisms produced ourselves, *Homo sapiens sapiens*, from pre-human primates. It is somewhat ironic that many scholars today consider the Javanese *Homo erectus*, the Neandertals, and most of the australopiths to have been unrelated or only distantly related to our own ancestors (discussed in chapter 4), but the importance of these early finds is that they demonstrated that we had evolved from nonhuman primates.

We have many sources of evidence about our origins including the study of our primate relatives, the fossil bones of our ancestors, and the early stone tools and other physical traces our forebears left. But before we look at the collected evidence, we must consider the analytical principles we must use to interpret them—specifically, evolutionary theory. The basic premise underlying the study of human origins is that about six to eight million years ago our ancestors were animals something like chimpanzees, and that the forces of evolution changed us into what we are today. But what were these forces?

Evolutionary Theory

The origins of evolutionary theory in the writings of Darwin and others was reviewed in chapter 1, but a more detailed description of evolutionary principles and processes is required here in order to understand how they can be applied to the human past—and to the entire span of biological life on this planet.[15]

Evolutionary theory is a complex, often mathematically expressed discipline, and its major elements can only be briefly summarized here.[16]

As noted in chapter 1, Charles Darwin made the fundamental observations that still serve as the basic paradigm for evolutionary theory. He noted that many more animals and plants were bred than actually lived to reproduce themselves; further, he noted that there was much variation in the form and physical qualities of individuals in any species. He further inferred that there was some connection between these variations and the differing rates of success of individuals in living and reproducing. Finally, he concluded that "natural selection" was the process in which nature—in the form of different environments—selected some individuals to live and reproduce based on the relative "fitness" of individuals in these environments. Darwin then attempted to show how this general process had worked on innumerable generations to produce the awesome visible biological diversity of the world.

What Darwin did not know, however, was how variations in individuals arose and how they were passed on from generation to generation. The answers to these problems were supplied by geneticists, beginning primarily with Gregor Mendel (1822–1884). Mendel studied the inheritance of color and shape in peas, and in a series of convincing experiments showed that there were predictable patterns to the results of breeding plants of different characteristics.[17] Mendel and later scholars formulated what we now call the *particulate theory of inheritance*, which says that physical characteristics of individual organisms are passed from one generation to the next in the form of discrete particles (informally known as "genes") and that these particles retain their ability to express themselves even when they do not express themselves in every generation. The *law of segregation* stipulates that these particles are inherited in pairs, one of each from each of the parents.

The elixir of life, in the sense of evolutionary theory, is the substance known as DNA. Within the nucleus of every animal cell are chromosomes, thread-like structures composed of deoxyribonucleic acid, or DNA. DNA in turn is made of four *nucleotides*: guanine, cytosine, adenine, and thymine (Figure 3.4). These nucleotides combine in groups of three to form 20 amino acids, which are the building blocks for all protein formation. The arrangement, or sequence, of these bases determines the physical structure of all living things, from AIDS viruses to elephants (Figure 3.5). Except for the sperm or ova, every human cell, whether it be from the eyeball or toenail, contains the complete genetic code for that individual. If the DNA strand representing the entire code for a particular person were removed from a single cell and straightened, it would be about 6 feet long. The specific sequence of the DNA for any individual reader of this book would be unique and would fill about 125 books the size of the Manhattan telephone directory. DNA contains all the information required to direct the operation of a cell, in combination with another nucleic acid, RNA (ribonucleic acid). DNA has the ability to reproduce itself, and it also offers the potential for the main stuff of evolution, genetic change.

The two main sources of genetic variety are *meiosis* and *mutation*. Animal cells are constantly splitting (*mitosis*) and producing genetically identical copies of themselves, and thus growth and maintenance are accomplished. But in meiosis, egg and sperm cells are produced that carry only half the genetic code of the parent—in the case of humans, our 23 pairs of chromosomes total 46 total chromosomes in each body cell, but each egg and sperm cell carries only half the total, so each new person receives 23 chromosomes each from his or her father and mother. These genes are shuffled and then recombined in sexual reproduction, and thus the number of genetically

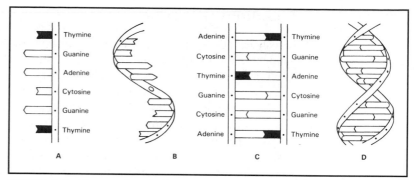

FIGURE 3.4 The genetic code determining the biological characteristics of species lies in the sequence of bases (thymine, guanine, adenine, cytosine) that links two strands of nucleotides to form the double helix that is DNA. (**A**) Bases in part of one strand of nucleotides. (**B**) Part of one strand twisted. (**C**) Complementary bases joined. (**D**) Two strands joined and twisted.

unique offspring possible for any human couple is determined by the equation $2^{23} \times 2^{23} = 2^{46}$, or about 70,000,000,000,000.[18] Each of us truly has won a lottery featuring odds against success that dwarf those of the financial kind.

Genetic variability is also produced by *mutations* in chromosomes—errors DNA makes in copying itself. The origins of mutations are not completely known, but some probably arise through the cosmic ray bombardment to which all living organisms are subjected. Early work on DNA involved exposing hapless populations of fruit-flies to radiation, producing monstrous combinations of eye colors, wing size, and other features. And there is reason to believe that industrial pollution, loss of ozone in the atmosphere, and other factors in the modern environment will lead to greater rates of mutation in all living things.

One illustration of the elements of evolutionary theory and its power to explain change in the natural world involves organisms too small to be seen with the naked eye—disease-causing bacteria. We all know of the importance of antibiotic medicines in fighting various diseases, such as *Staphylococcus* and *Streptococcus*. Strains of these bacteria can cause pneumonia or toxic shock, and the development of penicillin to combat them was considered a "miracle." During World War II, drug companies began mass-producing penicillin as part of the war

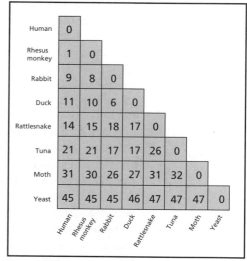

FIGURE 3.5 Amino acid sequences. Organisms (human, Rhesus monkey, rabbit, duck, rattlesnake, tuna, moth, yeast) differ in the sequence of amino acids in protein cytochrome *c*, an enzyme used in energy production. The higher the number shown, the greater the difference between any two.

effort, and by the time of the Korean War the use of this drug proved very effective.

Initially, bacterial infections were successfully killed off when patients were given penicillin. But like all organisms, bacteria also have variations in their genetic composition. Some of these variations are resistant to antibiotics such as penicillin. In evolutionary context, the use of antibiotics selects against those microbes that have no resistance to the antibiotic, but selects for those variants that have the genetic coding allowing the microbes to fight off the effects of the antibiotic. Somewhat quixotically, our societal practices actually help increase the reproductive success of antibiotic-resistant bacteria. This is what happens, for example, when people indiscriminately use antibiotics to treat viral infections—antibiotics aren't the solution to viruses, but taking antibiotics allows the survival and reproduction of drug-resistant bacteria in our bodies. When we do get a bacterial infection, those drug-resistant bacteria are that much more difficult to treat.

Medical research is thus constantly searching for new types of antibiotics—previous efforts have resulted in the development of tetracycline, erythromycin, and cipro, and many others—to replace those antibiotics that have become less effective. Other drug-resistant diseases most of us have heard about include tuberculosis and gonorrhea.

This example demonstrates all of the major elements of evolutionary theory. It explains biological changes in life-forms over time and space in terms of *natural selection*, at least in the simplistic sense of differential survival over time in organisms on the basis of their genetically determined characteristics. For natural selection to operate there must be *variability*, that is, differences between individuals in their physical form and the specific and unique genetic combinations each individual represents, so that over time there can be selection of characteristics, such as changes in drug resistance, brain size, instinctive migration, and so on.

It is important to recognize that evolution is not goal directed: These bacteria could not intentionally produce drug resistance to solve their problem; evolutionary processes simply and blindly sorted the genetic potential for different degrees of drug resistance on the basis of the advantage in reproduction and survival. The biological history of life on this planet is one of uncountable extinctions of species—which makes it clear that evolution does not "solve" all problems of adaptation.

But the reader should be aware that intense debates continue about the status of Darwinism and what is often called "neo-Darwinism." In general, biologists do not doubt the essential validity of Darwin's ideas, but they dispute heatedly the mechanisms involved. For example, a major book, *Evolution as Entropy*, by Brooks and Wiley, argues that natural selection is not the most important factor in directional change. Instead, they suggest that existing systems—whether these be organisms, populations, or species—present a configuration that constrains the possible "spaces" or directions in which evolution may take place. These are highly abstract and fundamentally mathematical arguments that are beyond the scope of this book.

APPLICATIONS OF EVOLUTIONARY THEORY TO THE PROBLEM OF HUMAN ORIGINS

Most genetic mutations seem to be "bad," in the sense that they reduce the chances of the individual carrying them to reproduce successfully. Other mutations are "good," in that they increase reproductive potential, or "fitness." But what is good or bad in evolution is measured entirely by reproductive success—and can be good or bad in different environments. For example, sickle-cell anemia—a genetic condition in which red blood cells are misshapen—is a common disease in Africa and the Mediterranean Basin. People who are born with a certain combination of the genes for this condition often die in childhood; but those with another genetic combination appear to have some protection against malaria.

Thus the gene for sickle-cell anemia has persisted because its presence in a population—although it results in the death of some people—helps others to live to reproductive age in zones of the world where malaria has long been a ferocious killer. "Natural selection," in this sense, is obviously no master or beneficent craftsman.

The spread and perpetuation of genetic mutations through biological populations are accomplished by various mechanisms. The variations in skin color in contemporary peoples, for example, seem to be the result of *migration* into different environments and subsequent adaptation. Dark skin offers a defense against skin cancers and other maladies that direct sunlight on human skin can produce, and so we see dark skin tones not just in Africa, but in the Indian subcontinent and far out into the Pacific Ocean island chains. But in humans the critical nutrient vitamin D is synthesized in the skin through the action of sunlight, and in relatively dark and cloudy climates a dark-skinned person with be at a disadvantage in times of scarcity of dietary sources of vitamin D—in winter months, for example. Early humans from Africa, whom we assume to have been dark-skinned, invaded environments where heavy pigmentation interfered with the synthesis of vitamin D, and eventually natural selection produced the blond, fair-skinned, blue-eyed human physical type typical of northern Europe: We must assume that small variations in skin pigmentation over thousands (replacement model) or millions (multiregional model) of years allowed those with lighter pigmentation to have a slightly greater reproductive "fitness" for living in more temperate environments

In this way, the world's "races" were formed, with natural selection acting on mutations in hundreds of genetically determined features. Geographical barriers have been a factor in channeling and constraining these migratory patterns: The Sahara, the Himalayas, and other natural barriers have restricted the matings between people in different areas to the point that modern "races" evolved. Most biological scientists reject the term "race" as imprecise and misleading. Patterns of evolutionary variability in people seem best understood in terms of *clines*, or gradients of variation through time and space that are not easily and discretely compartmentalized. Skin color, for example, varies greatly if one examines people on a cline from Sweden to South Africa, and these variations are only crudely described as "black" and "white." Also, some of the traits commonly used to identify "race," such as skin tone, eyelid shape, nose and lip shape, and so on, also show immense—and often independent—variation along gradients through time and space: That is, southern Indians, West Africans, some Pacific Islanders, and others share a relatively dark skin pigmentation but differ greatly in nose and lip shape, hair texture, and so on.[19]

Changes in physical form can also result from *sexual selection*: Once individuals choose mates nonrandomly with regard to some characteristics, evolutionary change can result. Gaudy colors and exaggerated features, such as represented by the male peacock, are probably the result of sexual selection, in which females choose mates partly on the basis of elaborateness of the display. Nor are these displays necessarily irrelevant to genetic "fitness," for they often correlate with superior health and genetic potential of some kinds. Some scientists believe that sexual selection was responsible for such features as the "exaggerated" size (by comparison to other primates) of human penises and female breasts.[20]

Modern population genetics is a complex mathematical discipline and is largely beyond the scope of this book. And many complex debates continue about the application of evolutionary theory to human evolution.[21] But for the study of cultural origins and the other physical changes we will consider here, including plant and animal domestication (chapter 6), the important points to remember are: (1) Genetic variability is constantly arising through various mechanisms; and (2) changing environments, sexual selection, and other factors "select" or act on this variability and differing reproductive success through time and space to produce evolutionary change.

Although modern cultures have erected some barriers to "natural selection" (few people in industrialized countries now die of appendicitis, for example), through our long evolutionary history we have been no less a product of evolutionary forces than any other life-form. Most modern human physical characteristics are the result of complex genetic interactions that involve a subtle, long-term balancing of the costs and benefits of genetic changes. Consider, for example, the average height of human beings. As professional basketball teams and the pygmies of central Africa demonstrate, humans can live perfectly normal lives as individuals 7 feet or 3 feet tall. So why, on the average, are people around the world between 5 and 6 feet tall? And why do they vary sharply in average height by sex and geographical location? Why are we not all about 4 feet tall or 7 feet tall? As it is with almost all human characteristics, the "environment"—nutrition, for example—is a factor in human height. The high-calorie diets of North America, for example, have produced generations of Asian Americans who are significantly taller, on average, than their parents. But height is also partially genetically controlled. And we must assume that we average between 5 and 6 feet and not between 7 and 8 feet or 3 and 4 feet because our average size made sense in complex evolutionary equations. With selective breeding and adequate nutrition, a group of people could probably have been bred to an average height of 7 feet or more, but the costs of maintaining that body mass obviously did not make evolutionary "sense." The pygmies of the African rain forests appear to have evolved in response to the very low food resources available in a tropical rain forest, where most of the energy is locked in forms of cellulose of no use to humans.

Consider another aspect of the human diet. There is overwhelming evidence that contemporary death rates from cancer and other diseases are directly related to the fact that most of us savage our evolutionary heritage with diets that simply do not meet the needs of the omnivorous hunter-gatherers that natural selection fashioned us to be. Every one of us is the direct descendant of tens of thousands of generations of people who were naturally selected to thrive on the omnivorous diets available to hunter-foragers as they radiated from Africa across the world. In many areas these diets would have been high in fiber and fruit, low on fat and salt—diets that involved eating many different species of animals and plants. Although our ancestors' diets varied greatly in different times and places, in most cases they would have been very different from the diets of most of us.[22]

Since our brief 9,000 years as farmers have had little effect on our basic physiology and metabolism, logic might tell us that we should eat as wide-ranging a diet as our hunting-foraging ancestors did. But, alas, evolutionary equations are complex. One might, for example, vastly increase one's vitamin C consumption on the grounds that ancient hunter-foragers had high concentrations of this vitamin in their diets, but the factors that improve an individual's chances of becoming a successful mother or father many times before age 40—an all-important accomplishment in evolutionary terms—may not be the same as those that produce fit and happy 70 and 80 year olds. Until about 10,000 years ago—or just yesterday in evolutionary terms—few people lived past 50. In terms of an individual's success in passing on his or her genes, what probably mattered most was to have children and successfully raise them on a diet of some meat, a lot of plant foods, and an exercise regime that modern medical science would consider dangerous.

In general, human physiology appears to have been selected over millions of years to operate on a diet of almost anything, particularly if there is some variety and moderation. Even Irish coffee, that perfect end to a field archaeologist's day, containing four basic food groups—fat, sugar, alcohol, and caffeine—can be tolerated as long as one scavenges widely among the other food groups the rest of the day. Yet Eskimos are reported to eat, during the long winter months, a diet consisting mainly of meat, augmented only with a few scraps of vegetation they find in the stomachs of seals and other animals they kill. And poor Hindu peasants have produced a population explosion on a meatless diet consisting mainly of vegetables, rice, oils, and sugar.

Whatever the diet of our ancestors, we must assume that we are walking, talking genetic packages that reflect what "worked" for hunters and gatherers, plus an unknown amount of "random" genetic change. So although every characteristic of every person cannot be accounted for in terms of its competitive value in passing on one's genes, a lot of what we are must be explained in exactly these terms. Thus, for example, our brain size averages about 1,450 cm³ because that size is a good balance between the advantages of greater intelligence and general cerebration and the high costs of large brains in terms of blood supply and the reduced mobility of the broadened female pelvis, which is needed for successful live birth of the cerebral monstrosities that we are.

There are very real problems with the "adaptationist" views of human evolution—the idea that most or all of what we are is the product of selected accumulated successful mutations. A lot of what we are, in fact, may be the result of random genetic variation, not the direct product of selection for a particular quality or trait. And it is almost impossible to find some trait or behavior that *cannot* be explained as the solution to some kind of imagined evolutionary problem or opportunity.[23] It is also often difficult to identify exactly what the *focus* of selection was for complex physiological or anatomical evolution. Hamilton, for example, suggests that many of the sex differences between men and women and between humans and other apes are the result of long-term selection for high levels of sex hormones—not to exaggerate our sexuality but to give us the stamina we needed as foragers who walked long and often to find food.[24]

With this simple introduction to evolution, it is easy to see why the Argument from Design—the theory that the universe *had* to have been created by a Divine Being because everything worked together in such harmony—was almost universally rejected by scientists from the late nineteenth century on, and why few professional research biologists and geneticists doubt that humans have evolved from single-cell animals and are genetically related to all other life-forms on this planet. Science has shown that (1) the chemistry of human genetics operates identically to that of other life-forms and (2) the differences between humans and other animals in the "spelling" of their DNA sequence is slight—depending on which aspects of DNA sequences are examined, there is only about a 1 percent difference between a person and a chimp, for example, and only 2 percent between a person and a mouse. In fact, the human DNA sequence contains bits of the same genetic code that produces or once produced mice, plants, ants, dinosaurs, and so forth—a situation that is exactly what one would expect, based on evolutionary theory.

Biological evolution can shape a world of great complexity and, in a sense, beauty. And although it is tempting to see "natural selection" as an active, quasi-intelligent force, shaping plants and animals for certain purposes and to meet certain requirements, this is a fundamentally flawed perspective. Natural selection does not "know" what will be required at some later date. Natural selection in this sense is simply differential rates of reproduction and survival.

If this is so, what is the key to long-term evolutionary success in a lineage? One important element seems to be the maintenance of genetic variability. A classic example of this is the problem caused by the introduction of rabbits into Australia. Without a natural predator, the rabbits multiplied to the point of becoming a major crop pest. Efforts to control them by introducing a rabbit disease killed millions of them, but because of genetic variability a few individuals were naturally immune. They survived and quickly reestablished a population that was more resistant to this disease.

As the AIDS epidemic demonstrates, Life with a capital L is a constant struggle between life-forms for survival. The AIDS virus's "strategy" involves rapidly changing forms and a late onset—afflicting many people long after they have already spread the virus to others. But some people will be naturally resistant to the virus, and even if the epidemic sweeps the world, these resistant individuals would be able to reestablish human populations. There is no reason to suspect that the AIDS virus will be the last one to sweep the world; in fact, it seems simply another of a long line of human afflictions, and there are likely much worse ones to come.

A discussion, such as this, of evolutionary theory as applied to us and our ancestors seems to lead inevitably to a consideration of eugenics—attempts to produce individuals with selected genetic characteristics, either through selective mating, abortion, or—now— direct manipulation of a person's genes.

People are understandably ambivalent about the idea of genetically selected traits. Based on what we know about genetically determined aspects of anatomy and physiology, for example, it seems manifestly evident that not even a lifetime of practice can make one another Mozart, that no amount of education will enable many of us to extend the insights of a Newton. Even something as seemingly effortless as the high-floating left-handed lay-up of the professional basketball player can never be acquired by most of us, even were we to spend a lifetime in practice.

But eugenics, of a sort, is already here. Every year human fetuses are aborted because genetic testing has shown that they would be born afflicted with Down's syndrome, cystic fibrosis, Huntington's disease, or some other malady. In China and India, untold numbers of fetuses are aborted because they are female. And there is every indication that these forms of "eugenics" will expand greatly. From a fetus's genetic structure, scientists can now, or soon will be able to, propose many other conditions an individual might have in later life, such as Alzheimer's disease, manic depression, breast cancer, some forms of bowel cancer, and obesity. Also, the recent mapping of the entire human genome probably will make it possible to predict occurrences of alcoholism, homosexuality, and many other conditions previously thought to be mainly consequences of choices people made.

Simply put, is such knowledge about genetics good or bad? Every reader of this book can expect to hear increasing debates on this point for the rest of his or her life, for the answer is complex and ultimately a matter of values. One might argue, for example, that our best "strategy" in long-term evolutionary equations is to maintain as much genetic diversity as possible—the antithesis of "eugenics" programs, in effect. For no one can predict what new genetic horrors will arise in AIDS-like viruses or some other disease, and it may well be that only a few individuals have natural genetic immunity to them. And it may be that some yet-to-be mutated natural resistance to skin cancer, to exposure to asbestos and organic pollutants, or to some newly mutated disease will be the key to our long-term survival as a species.

Evolution is in no sense "over" for us just because we currently are doing rather well.

THE ECOLOGICAL CONTEXT OF CULTURAL ORIGINS

In the bleak mid-winter
Frosty wind made moan,
Earth stood hard as iron,
Water like a stone;
Snow had fallen, snow on snow,
Snow on snow,
In the bleak mid-winter
Long ago.
Christina Rossetti (1830–1894)[25]

One of the central facts of human physical and cultural evolution is that many of the crucial developments of our species occurred in Africa between about 8 million and 10,000 years ago, a period in which world climates fluctuated greatly but were, on average, cooler than today. About 4.2 million years ago, some of our first bipedal (i.e., walking upright) ancestors appeared in Africa. By about 2.5 million years ago massive glaciers had spread over northern lands, such as Europe, and about 1.8 million years ago, when early forms of *Homo* were radiating from Africa, climates began fluctuating, with long periods of intense cold followed by periods that were nearly as warm as climates of today. This period of climatic fluctuation during the past 1.8 million years is known as the *Pleistocene* epoch, or the *Quaternary* period. The correspondence between this period of climatic change and our own development has led scholars for many years to suspect that somehow Pleistocene climatic changes directly shaped human evolution, perhaps by creating difficult and demanding environments that "selected" larger and more intelligent hominins. But the relationship between climatic changes and human changes seems to have been a very complex one.

For the modern individual, sheltered from climate by cities and central heating, the effects of winter are reduced to minor inconveniences, but for our Pleistocene ancestors, the brutal winters of hundreds of thousands of years ago made southern France, Italy, China, and other currently hospitable regions a challenge to hominin resourcefulness and tenacity. Advancing and retreating glaciers and the weather systems that drove them operated in slow but powerful pulses, alternately drawing hominin populations into some areas and evicting them from others, all the while mixing genes, eliciting adaptations, and shaping our cultural and physical evolution. In Africa, too, the great climatic changes of the Pleistocene occasionally changed large areas of formerly habitable land into vast deserts, and then later changed them back to forests and grassland.

Average worldwide temperatures have fluctuated more rapidly in the last 14 million years than ever before, and a world as warm as our own has been a rarity during the last 2.5 million years. There have been, however, occasional interglacials—periods often of

50,000 years or more when temperatures rose almost to present-day levels. Even during the main glacial periods, there were interstadials, short warming phases when the temperature rose but did not reach today's levels. Archaeologists use the term *Holocene* to refer to the last 10,000 years, which likely represents the latest interglacial period.

During the glacial periods themselves, ice sheets spread from the poles and from higher elevations to cover much of the higher latitudes. So much of the seas were locked in ice during the coldest periods that the sea level dropped by as much as 150 m, making dry land of coastal areas that today are many meters below the sea. Land bridges that facilitated the spread of peoples throughout the world formed between North America and Asia, Europe and Britain, and Southeast Asia and what are now offshore islands. Unfortunately, Pleistocene ice sheets have ground many critical archaeological sites to powder, and the rising seas of the post-glacial periods have covered thousands of others.

The great climatic shifts of the Pleistocene seem to have been caused by a combination of factors, including fluctuations in solar radiation, eccentricities in the earth's orbit, mountain-building activity, and changes in the earth's atmosphere.[26] But in the next several decades the world may see the invalidation of the cliché, "everyone talks about the weather, but nobody does anything about it." We seem to have been doing something to it since the Industrial Revolution. Various scientists have suggested that we are already seeing the results of the *Greenhouse Effect*—a dramatic warming of average world climates as a result of industrial pollution. Some meteorologists predict that by the mid-twenty-first century, and thus within the life span of some readers of this book, such coastal cities as New York will be partially flooded by rising sea levels.

Between about seven and two million years ago, early hominins lived in the tropics of Africa. We were all Africans, and we were all Africans much later—late, in any event, in our evolutionary story.[27] Even with evidence for hominin invasion of Europe and Asia before a million years ago (chapter 4), we must still look to the grasslands and forests of Africa for the environments of our origins.

The history of the hominins appears to represent adaptations to a wide variety of habitats and environments, including *savanna*, bushland, open woodland, and riverine forest, as well as a mosaic of these contexts.[28] Savannas are relatively flat, arid expanses with scattered trees and occasional water holes, and their mixed grasses, shrubs, and other plants usually support large herds of grazing animals such as zebras, buffaloes, and gazelles. Woodlands and forests represent somewhat more closed, but wetter environments compared to savannas.

The Evidence of Cultural Origins

We have four basic categories of evidence for analyzing human origins: (1) *paleontology*, the study of ancient forms of animal life, including the ancestors of humankind; (2) *archaeology*, the analysis of the archaeological record—the stones and bones and other evidence of past cultures used by our ancestors; (3) *primatology*, the study of our contemporary nonhuman relatives, the other primates, whose behavior patterns may give us clues to the behavior of our own ancestors and whose genetic composition can be compared through molecular biology with our own to address questions of our common descent; and (4) *ethnology*, particularly the study of contemporary or recent hunting-and-gathering peoples, whom we assume to be living in environments and patterns similar to those of our Paleolithic ancestors (although any contemporary human societies must be regarded as fundamentally different from those of our earliest ancestors).

Anthropologists use these four kinds of evidence to produce "models of cultural origins"—sets of related hypotheses about the factors that combined to change our ancestors from unremarkable primates to human beings.

PALEONTOLOGICAL EVIDENCE OF HUMAN ORIGINS

A brain weight of nine hundred grams is
adequate as an optimum for human behavior.
Anything more is employed in the commission
of misdeeds.

Earnest Hooten

One of the most difficult things for the people of the nineteenth century to accept was the idea that as a species we are the progeny of nonhuman primates. It is perhaps fortunate that they did not know then that an even earlier ancestor seems to have been a small, pink-nosed, libidinous, insect-eating animal whose modern form, the shrew, is on a pound-for-pound basis among the most ferociously effective predators known.

Taken as an overall sequence, is there any trend in the evolution of animal life on this planet that would help us understand the appearance of culture and our own physical type? One possible answer is suggested by the comparison of the ratio of brain size to body size in successive animal forms during the many millions of years before the first culture-bearing animals appeared. The anatomist Harry Jerison has devised an encephalization index by dividing the total brain volume of each animal by the two-thirds power of its body size. This simple index thus represents a scaled ratio of brain volume to overall size. Jerison's results give us an answer of sorts to our questions. The increase in average human brain size—from approximately 500 to approximately 1,450 cm^3 in only a few million years—has been extraordinarily rapid, but, overall, we seem to be a continuation of a process that began at least 600 million years ago, a process involving, in some animal forms, long-term natural selection for increased brain-to-body ratios and, presumably, mental capacity.

But we represent something more than just another species in this long-term evolutionary process, for we are truly monstrosities in terms of brain size. Jerison lists the "encephalization quotients" (which take account of the relationship and brain size across invertebrates) for a variety of primate individuals, including ourselves (Table 3.1), and it is clear that we are a radical departure from our nearest primate relatives.

Why should there be this long-term evolution of larger brain-body ratios? We assume that it must be because of the reproductive advantages conferred by this development. But

Table 3.1 Encephalization Quotients, or Brain-to-Body Ratios

Gorilla (male)	1.53	(172.4 kg body weight, 570 g brain weight)
Gorilla (female)	1.76	(90.7 kg body weight, 426 g brain weight)
Chimp (male)	2.48	(56.7 kg body weight, 440 g brain weight)
Chimp (female)	2.17	(44.0 kg body weight, 325 g brain weight)
Human (male)	7.79	(55.5 kg body weight, 1,361 g brain weight)
Human (female)	7.39	(51.5 kg body weight, 1,228 g brain weight)

with regard to human brain size, Jerison stresses that the important point to remember is that very advanced behavior can be governed by very small amounts of brain tissue. The behavioral adaptations of the lower vertebrates are as remarkable as those of mammals in many ways. Encephalization in mammals, in primates, and in the human species is not easy to explain as a correlate of the refinement of behavior. Information-processing of a kind that could be done only by very large amounts of neural tissue must have been evolving in the mammals. But the exact nature of that processing is difficult to demonstrate. Moreover, "rewiring" of brain tissue through evolutionary processes may result in behavioral changes without an increase in total size of brain.

In many fictional treatments of the future, people are portrayed with enormous heads and correspondingly impoverished physiques. Is this likely, given Jerison's data? Among the grimmer medical implements that was found in many delivery rooms in the last century was a device for crushing the head of the fetus if it was too large to deliver without killing the mother—a situation that, in the absence of medical intervention, may occur as frequently as a few times out of every 100 live births, according to some ethnographic accounts. Even experienced obstetricians[29] dreaded performing this procedure—now no longer necessary if the surgical skills to perform a Cesarean section are available. Mismatched fetal head size and maternal pelvic dimensions are expressions of the trend Jerison has identified, but human brain size, in fact, seems to have stabilized at about $1,450 \text{ cm}^3$ over the last 100,000 years. Yet 100,000 years is insignificant in the span of animal life on our planet, and encephalization ratios may well continue to increase—or decrease—during the next millions of years. The cliché "time will tell" still has some cogency in evolutionary studies. We too, no doubt, are in a sense "missing links" in the ancient evolutionary experiment that is the history of animal life on this planet.

One question we must address is: Why are people so much smarter than they apparently need to be just to survive and reproduce? As discussed in the next section, we have conclusive evidence that our ancestors, who had brains two-thirds of our size, successfully made stone tools and other implements, competed with a formidable array of other animals, and managed to colonize an area from Java to Spain. In the world of a half million years ago, or even 100,000 years ago, one needed a brain only a few hundred cm^3 bigger than that of a chimp to do very well indeed. Why then did we evolve the capacities for quantum mechanics, Arabic verb forms, Puccini arias, and the poetry of Ezra Pound?

Once again it must be stressed that when we ask such questions we must look almost exclusively at our lives as hunter-gatherers, that is, before 10,000 years ago. The agriculture and urbanization that appeared in the past 10,000 years is far too short a span to have produced significant differences in our genetically based mentalities, compared to our Pleistocene forebears.

Early Primates and the Australopiths

I don't know, but we call him "Bob"

Sam Ervin, former U.S. Senator (when asked what the
name of his horse was)[30]

To return to the paleontological evidence, bits and pieces of various animals have been placed into our family tree as far back as 20 million years ago (Figure 3.6), but there are huge gaps and many questions as to what particular primates are on our ancestral line.

Classifying extinct animals is even more contentious than classifying living ones, but in the traditional classification, we are members of the primate order and the anthropoid suborder, which includes humans, apes, and monkeys; the other primate suborder is the prosimians, which includes lemurs, tarsiers, and other similar animals. We are in the superfamily *Hominoidea* and the family *Hominidae*. The *Hominidae* are separated into three subfamilies, the *Ponginae* (including the orangutan), the *Gorillinae* (the gorilla), and the *Homininae* (common chimpanzees, bonobos, and humans and their ancestors).[31] The *Homininae* separated from the *Ponginae* and *Gorillinae* at some point in the distant past of the Miocene era (c. 25 to 10 million years ago), when primates included at least 16 genera of hominoids, some of which were forest-dwelling, quadrupedal animals who may have been on our genetic line. Within the *Homininae*, there are two tribes, the *Panini* (common chimpanzees and bonobos) and the *Hominini* (humans and their ancestors, including the australopiths). These two tribes separated from a common ancestor probably around 8 million years ago.

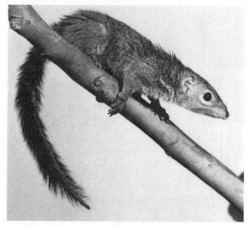

FIGURE 3.6 This species of Southeast Asia tree shrew resembles closely the small insectivorous ratlike animals believed to be ancestral to all primates, including ourselves.

This determination of when the human line split from that of other primates results from a combination of the fossil evidence with evidence from molecular biology.[32] These age estimates and sequences are based on estimates of rates of change in nuclear genetic materials and are known to vary widely in the animal kingdom (rates of change are much faster in rodents than in humans, for example). But several analytical techniques have produced similar estimates for the human/chimpanzee split. A crucial period in the evolution of culture appears to be between five million years ago, when the first australopiths appeared, and a million years ago, by which time all the world's hominins belonged to a single genus, *Homo*.

Paleoanthropologists recognize various genera and species of early hominins in the period between about 4.2 and 1 million years ago. These include a sometimes bewildering array of australopiths and early *Homo*. The relationship between these species—and which ones are on the line to modern humans—is not always clear-cut. The australopiths include *Ardipithecus ramidus*, *Australopithecus anamensis*, *Australopithecus bahrelghazali*, *Australopithecus afarensis*, *Australopithecus africanus*, *Australopithecus garhi*, *Paranthropus aethiopicus*, *Paranthropus robustus*, and *Paranthropus boisei*. Early *Homo* species during this range of time include *Homo rudolfensis*, *Homo habilis*, *Homo ergaster*, and *Homo erectus*.[33] These species seem to have differed in various anatomical details and the periods in which they existed, and they are probably most correctly displayed as a "bushy tree" in which lineage and descent is not yet precisely known (Figure 3.7).

The factors that identify Australopiths as probable members of the same tribe are: (1) They all were bipedal, walking upright on two legs all or most of the time—although they were perhaps not quite as well-suited anatomically for this means of locomotion as ourselves; (2) they all appear to have brains only slightly larger, if at all, than modern gorillas and chimps; (3) they all lived in Africa; and (4) they all had teeth that looked somewhat like ours and differed from those of gorillas and chimps in various details, such as flattened

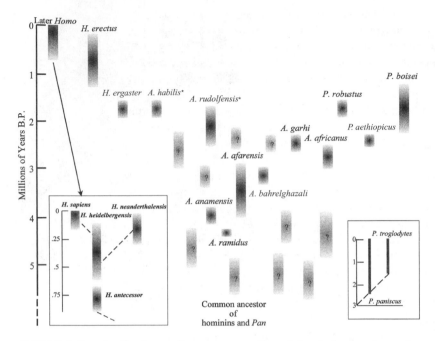

FIGURE 3.7 The "bushy tree" appearance of hominin phylogeny shows the existence of several contemporary hominin species and indicates the difficulty of assigning a particular species to the direct line leading to modern humans.

surface of molars—probably to facilitate grinding of foods. Scholars dispute whether or not any of the australopiths used stone tools. Their remains have been found with such tools but the association is ambiguous.

Early Australopiths Much of the story of cultural origins may have been "over" by 3.8 million years ago. Mary Leakey found human footprints of this age at Laetoli, Kenya, indicating that our ancestors were walking upright by that time, and new fossils such as *Australopithecus anamensis* suggest that bipedalism in the hominins may be at least 4.2 million years old. The tracks of two *Australopithecus afarensis* at Laetoli indicate that they may not have had quite the same smooth gait as modern humans do, as they seem to have a somewhat rolling walk in which the hips swiveled side to side more than they do when we walk. But they clearly show two bipedal creatures, both between about 1.4 and 1.5 m tall, who apparently walked across this surface at different times.

There is a sort of destiny in bipedalism: The hands are free to manipulate tools, the field of vision gives a slice of time and distance that rewards planning, and the arrangement of the limbs and cranium seems to require only additional brain tissue to "convert" a primate into something human.

But upright posture in the absence of tools—and there is no evidence for stone tool use until about a million years after the Laetoli footprints—means something else. It means that an animal with roughly our body shape (but about two-thirds our size) and with our approximate powers of vision, smell, locomotion, and so on, could compete in a world teeming with awesome predators. Without speed, claws, significant teeth, night vision, or protective coloration, these primates of 3.8 million years ago and earlier flourished. Walking across the same surface as the *Australopithecus afarensis* at Laetoli were tigers, rhinoceroses, elephants, and other animals that competed with the australopiths on these African plains, and one wonders how such an unprepossessing animal could survive in this environment. Perhaps they already possessed embryonic forms of the critical elements of cultural behavior: intelligence, protective human family relationships, and tool-use capabilities that were slightly better than that of the chimpanzees (who use sticks and unmodified stones).

If we had only the tracks at Laetoli as evidence of early australopiths, we would know little about this crucial stage in human evolution, but recent finds have produced the skeletal remains of a growing sample of these individuals—and possibly some of their ancestors. The earliest australopiths are a likely candidate as one of the founding species of the human line; they are represented by fossils that date to between 4.5 and 3 million years ago from several areas of north-central and east Africa.

In the Hadar region of Ethiopia we find the most substantial early remains, including "Lucy" (named after a Beatles song), a female 25- to 35-year-old hominin. About 3.18 million years ago, Lucy strode upright through the river valleys of Ethiopia, as part of a group of primates who were around 1.2 to 1.5 meters tall, but who varied greatly in size and morphological characteristics. No tools of any kind have been found associated with Lucy and her kin, and without tools, we cannot really know much about Lucy and her group—the "First Family," to use the name Donald Johanson, one of her discoverers, gave them. By counting the number of different bones, we know that there were at least 13 people in Lucy's group, 4 of them children. A few bits of geological evidence and the absence of other animal bones near the hominins raise the possibility that the First Family was trapped in a ravine by a flash flood, but we'll never really know.

But if "Lucy" and her group were bipedal, how far back in time does bipedalism go? Several recent finds have begun to illuminate this great transformation in the human past. Between 1990 and 1994, parts of 53 other early hominins were found in the Hadar region, including a particularly well-preserved skull that seems to confirm some of the interpretations of Lucy but raises other questions.[34] The age of the skull, about one million years before Lucy, was determined by its location between two layers of volcanic rock. Because the rock contains potassium, the rate at which potassium radioactively decays could be used to date each layer accurately (see chapter 2). The skull of this individual has an ape-like jutting jaw, small braincase, and thick protruding ridges above the eyes—a skull, in other words, that was much more ape-like than human-like.

Tim White has identified some of the earliest Ethiopian fossils as a new genus, *Ardipithecus ramidus*, on the premise that they are different from other early australopiths. This Middle Awash fossil suggests that this small-brained, upright-walking, pre-human species with an ape-like body existed until at least to Lucy's time without significant anatomical change. Whatever the evolutionary forces were that converted australopiths into us, at least as far as mentality is concerned, they appear either to have been slow processes or not in force at this time. Despite their human-like posture, the brain-to-body ratios of Lucy and her friends were such that it is highly probable they could have led full mental and spiritual lives in any municipal zoo: Lucy's brain was probably only slightly larger than a softball, and there is no evidence that she or her colleagues used tools or were cultural in significant ways. But the fact that these australopiths had brains insignificantly larger than apes is not conclusive evidence on this point. The human brain probably evolved both through getting bigger and by internal "rewiring," and we know little about how the latter might have come about.

Another recent discovery of fossils in Kenya supports the idea that by 4.2 million years ago, our ancestors already walked upright, on two legs. In August 1995, anthropologist Meave Leakey[35] reported the discovery in northwestern Kenya's Lake Turkana area of fossil hominin jaws, teeth, a piece of skull including the ear region, and a lower leg bone, all of which date to between 3.9 and 4.2 million years ago. The hominin species from which the fossils came has been named *Australopithecus anamensis*. Leakey said primitive features distinguishing the species from other known early human ancestors were in the crania and dentition and included almost parallel mandibular tooth rows set close together, large canines with long strong roots, wide flaring molar teeth, and a small elliptical external opening of the ear.

But she notes that in "contrast, the leg and arm bones have relatively modern morphology and the shape of the former indicates that at this early date, human ancestors were walking bipedally." Leakey said the newly found fossils had features consistent with their being a cross between "Lucy" and the earliest Hadar fossils that have been identified by Tim White as *Ardipithecus ramidus*.

Still another recent find provides cogent evidence about early human bipedalism. Few things are more pedestrian, literally or figuratively, than the human foot, but the archaeological record contains only one reasonably well-preserved set of four articulated hominin foot bones for the critical period when people were becoming (or already were) bipedal. These bones, from South Africa's Sterkfontein Cave, may date to 3.5 million years ago,[36] and they have set off another debate about the origins of human bipedalism (Figure 3.8). They appear to be those of an australopith, and they suggest that these hominins may have retained tree-climbing abilities far beyond what later humans had. One of the preserved bones is the beginning of the big toe, and it suggests that this individual had both ape-like and human-like locomotion abilities. There is no question that the basic anatomy is that of an upright-

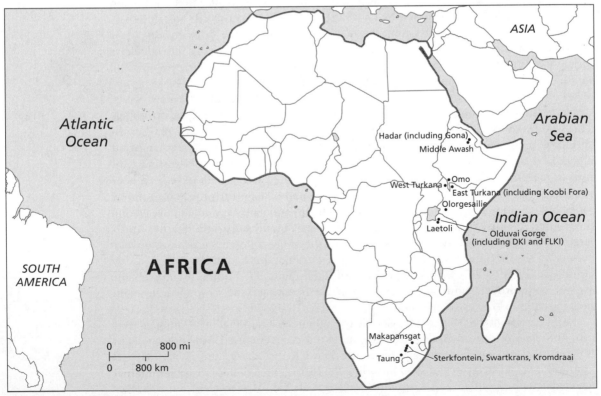

FIGURE 3.8 The distribution of some early hominin sites in Africa.

walking individual, but the big toe diverged sharply to the side, in the manner of apes, providing a highly flexible, opposable-toed foot that would allow the hominin to climb trees.

In summary of these recent finds, human bipedalism probably extends back to 4.2 million years ago and some unknown time earlier than that, but we still have only vague ideas about why this transformation occurred. In any case, the most important point about these australopiths is that they were *bipedal*, and whether or not bipedalism is the stimulus for all later evolution of "culture," our ancestors appeared soon after bipedalism, and there is reason to assume that this was not an accidental correlation.

The Appearance of *Homo*

*Monkeys are superior to men in this: when a
monkey looks into a mirror, he sees a monkey.*

Malcolm de Chazal

As in the case of most biological classifications, cutting the continuum of hominins into several groups and naming them differently, as in the case of *Australopithecus* and *Homo*, necessarily involves some degree of arbitrariness. Unless we have been badly misled by the data, what we call the first *Homo* arose out of the mix of australopith species and subspecies, and thus these different genera names are mainly collective descriptions of gradually accumulating anatomical differences.

That *Homo* did succeed the australopiths now seems clear. Major disputes remain about the relationship of the australopiths and early *Homo*, but the evidence generally supports the notion that, whatever the genetic relationship between the australopiths and early *Homo*, early *Homo* (1) appeared after about 2.5 million years ago—long after Lucy and her colleagues; (2) had a brain somewhat larger than the australopiths (i.e., c. 600 c³ or larger); (3) made stone tools—or at least some groups of them did; and (4) was the first hominin to leave Africa. Early *Homo* is usually assigned to *Homo habilis*, *Homo rudolfensis*, *Homo ergaster* or *Homo erectus*.

The earliest stone tools known are only between two and three million years old, and we might suspect that they are important markers of the transition to *Homo*. Primates of all kinds, including Lucy, no doubt, use sticks and unmodified stones for a variety of purposes, but making a stone tool requires that a recognition that sharp-edged pieces can be detached from an unworked lump of stone. Evidence suggests that the manufacture of stone tools was a rather late part of the whole transition to humanity, since bipedalism and even increasing brain size were well underway by the time the first stone tools apparently were made. Toth has suggested that "tool use in apes was not directly selected for in evolution but rather was a by-product of a general increase in problem-solving abilities through time."[37] But once humans could make stone tools, that ability became an important factor in the rate at which we evolved and spread throughout the world. The importance of tools to our ancestors can perhaps best be appreciated if one imagines oneself standing about 4 feet tall on the Serengeti Plain of two million years ago, trying to resolve into its component nutritious parts a small antelope one has just killed or scavenged from a temporarily napping lion. Already harried by vultures and other scavengers, one tries to rip into the body with one's teeth and nails. Even with Lucy's relatively stout dentition, it would have been difficult. The most nutritious parts—the liver, brain, and other internal organs—are protected by thick layers of skin, flesh, and bone that resist the puny tearing motions to which our ancestors would have been limited. But just a chip off one of the quartz pebbles abundantly scattered over this area would instantly have opened up life-saving rations for several individuals.

The first hominin to make and use stone tools was probably one of the australopith species (simple stone tools made by hitting one lava chunk with another have been found in Ethiopia under layers of volcanic ash that date to 2.5 million years ago[38]) or early *Homo*, but the species of the first tool-makers remains a matter of doubt and dispute. Some of these disputes could be resolved if we had many full skeletons of the earliest *Homo*, but we may never have adequate samples of this hominin. Most anthropologists have used the category *Homo habilis* to refer to the species from which *Homo ergaster* and thereby ourselves have descended, and the KNM-ER 1470 skull, dated to about 1.88 million years ago, is perhaps the best example of this category. *Homo habilis* is generally thought to have had a cranial capacity of about 600–650 cm³, halfway between some of the smaller australopiths and *Homo ergaster/Homo erectus*, but its taxonomic position will likely change on the basis of future finds.[39] A skull and some limb bones of *Homo habilis* recently discovered at Olduvai (a specimen known as OH 62) have been dated to about 1.8 million years ago, and raise some interesting questions about *Homo habilis* in general. First, this apparently female adult was only about 1 m tall (3 feet, 4 inches). Thus, she was up to a foot shorter than "Lucy," an australopith who lived about 1.3 million years before her, and whose height appears to have been somewhere between 3.5 and 4 feet. We might expect that human height had been increasing gradually but continuously, as we know that the general trend in hominins was certainly toward greater height. But OH 62 suggests this trend may not have been constant. Here, too, possible sample biases intrude. OH 62 may simply have been an exceptionally short person. But OH 62's skeletal anatomy looks very much like Lucy's, and in general she suggests that the australopiths and early *Homo* were only slightly different until after 1.8 million years ago.

In 1984 a group headed by Richard Leakey found a *Homo ergaster/Homo erectus* (known as KNM-WT 15000) near Lake Turkana,[40] Kenya, that seems well-dated to about 1.6 million years ago and is virtually complete. Such a modern and "brainy" hominin at this time is somewhat surprising, given the other known fossils (this find is discussed in more detail in chapter 4).

These many arguments about human lineage will doubtless continue for many more years, and all that really seems clear at this point is that from 3 to 1.5 million years ago, bipedal primates of about 1.25 to 1.75 m in height roamed the grasslands and forests, and that at least some of these animals made tools.

ARCHAEOLOGICAL EVIDENCE OF THE ORIGINS OF CULTURE

We can begin to look at the *archeological record* to determine how our ancestors actually lived and changed over time. As always, the problem here is one of poor evidence. Perhaps the only way in which we will understand the details of our origins would be if we found several Pompeii-like sites where volcanic eruptions had trapped early humans some two to three million years ago, toward evening, say, around a water hole on the East African savanna. Such a catastrophe might have killed thousands of animals, including some hominins. Without wishing any disaster to even these, our most distant hominin ancestors, such a volcanic event would be most scientifically useful if it happened just after these hominins had scavenged or hunted their food, butchered it with stone tools, and then dispersed into social groups to sleep off the meal. At present, however, our direct archaeological evidence about the initial period of the evolution of culture is extremely meager; we have only a few small sites, almost all of which are in southern and eastern Africa.

About five million years ago, a large lake covered about 130 km² of what today is the Serengeti Plain, in central East Africa. Countless generations of animals, including, no doubt, our hominin ancestors, lived near this lake, and today their fossilized bones are thickly distributed through the black clay of the ancient shoreline and lake bed. About a half million years before the appearance of culture-bearing animals in this part of the world, the lake and the adjacent areas were the scene of dramatic geological activity. Volcanoes near the lake had been erupting for millions of years, and in a particularly violent episode about a million and a half years ago, a volcano to the south of the lake covered it with a layer of ash and molten rock some 5 m thick. Similar eruptions occurred in succeeding millennia, and today we can measure the intensity of each volcanic episode by gauging the thickness of each superimposed ash level. Sometime during and after these volcanic eruptions, the climate of the area began a cycle of alternating dry and wet periods. These millions of years of volcanic activity and climatic change eventually covered the original lake and adjacent lands with a 100-m-thick deposit of sand, ash, and lake sediments, the surface of which is the present Serengeti Plain. Ancient floods cut down through this plain at several points, creating Olduvai Gorge and revealing in its cliffs and floor many concentrations of stone tools and animal bones. These sites represent by far our best archaeological record of human activities at the time of the emergence of the genus *Homo*.[41]

One such concentration, Site DK I, has been radiometrically dated to about 1.75 million years ago, making it one of the oldest in Olduvai Gorge. The site is composed of a layer several meters thick of bones, worked and unworked stone, and other debris. Because of the complex stratigraphy, it is difficult to separate this accumulation into different levels with any assurance that the divisions represent discrete hominin occupations.

The most prominent archaeological feature at DK I is a semicircle of stones (Figure 3.9) lying within a concentration of stone tools and animal bones. Measuring approximately 3 m in diameter and made of chunks of vesicular basalt, this feature was originally interpreted by some as a foundation for a windbreak or some other temporary structure, but the evidence is inconclusive. The tools found here are similar to the other materials from Beds I and II at Olduvai: hundreds of crudely flaked stones, some of them showing evidence of use, others simply by-products of the manufacturing process. Although it is tempting to see Site DK I as a "home-base" for hominins, the evidence suggests that natural processes played a major role in site formation.[42]

Another Olduvai site, FLK I, is particularly important because several hominin bone fragments were found in its various levels, including the remains of an early hominin that Louis Leakey named *Zinjanthropus*, which most now assign to *Parathropus boisei* and presumed by many anthropologists not to be a maker of stone tools. This "*Zinjanthropus* floor" covers an area of more than 1,036 m² and contains several thousand pieces of worked stone and about 3,500 identifiable mammal bones. Many stone artifacts and pieces of shattered bone are concentrated in a "working area" some 5 m in diameter, and a relatively clear arc-shaped area in the midst of all this debris suggests to some the remains of a temporary shelter. But just as with Site DK I, the FLK I site is likely the result of cultural and natural processes rather than a pristine living surface.

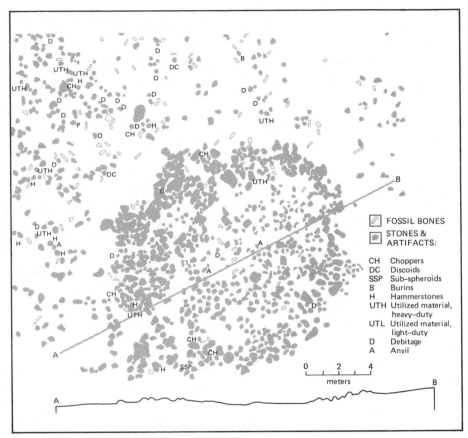

FIGURE 3.9   Site DK I. Plan of the stone circle and the remains on the occupation surface. Stones, including artifacts, are shown in gray. Fossil bones are shown in outline. A consideration of taphonomic processes makes the interpretation of this as a home base or a windbreak unlikely.

A few other sites in Africa have been shown to have stone tools that date to about 2 million years ago, including Koobi Fora, where crude stone tools appear to be at least 2.3 million years old.

These early stone tools from Olduvai, Koobi Fora, and a few other sites provide some indications about the nature of our ancestors. Studies of the Olduwan tools by Nicholas Toth indicate that already by 1.7 million years ago our ancestors at Olduvai had developed a preference for right-handedness.[43] Based on the marks left that indicate how they held the stone cores when they hit them to produce stone flakes, the Olduvai hominins seem to have the same proportions of right-handers—90 percent—as do modern populations. Toth also suggests that archaeologists may have been fundamentally wrong about the Olduvai tools in assuming that the big "core-tools" were the object of the tool-making: He studied wear patterns on the putative "hand-axes" from Olduvai and concluded that they rarely show any wear indicative of use—rather, it was the *flakes* that were the point of the tool-making, and the "hand-axes" and the core-tools were in many cases the by-products of tool manufacture.

The question of what these tools were used for is a central element in debates about the nature of our early evolution.

COMPARATIVE PRIMATOLOGY AND THE ORIGINS OF CULTURE

*Many researchers view human evolution as a
long corridor, where chimpanzees enter at one
end and modern hunter-gatherers exit at the
other.*

J. Tooby and I. Devore[44]

To use primate studies to investigate our origins, we must define clearly the ways in which we are different from them. Tooby and DeVore list six major areas in which we differ fundamentally from other contemporary primates: (1) bipedalism; (2) situation-appropriate, intensive male parental investment and an increase in female parental investment; (3) an unparalleled degree of hunting and meat consumption; (4) a change in life-history correlates: an extension of life span, an increase in the period of investment in offspring, a marked increase in the altriciality (i.e., the length of time the young remain in the direct care and physically with the parents) of human young; (5) an expansion of ecozones occupied, from tropical woodland and forest into savanna areas, but eventually including every other terrestrial ecozone; (6) concealed ovulation with continuous sexual receptivity.

Given that chimpanzees and ourselves share a common ancestor, perhaps as recently as six to eight million years ago, how did these differences arise?

While some scholars think studying contemporary primates will tell us little about our origins, others see in them prototypical behavior for everything that is human. McGrew,[45] for example, notes that culture in other species is studied by disciplines other than anthropology, such as psychology and zoology. These lend different views to how we define culture and how we recognize culture in nonhuman primates.

A major problem in applying primatological studies to the question of human origins, aside from the fact that poachers are killing off the last remaining wild groups of these animals, is that observing them is not a purely scientific procedure. Observers see aggression, dominance, and so on, partly as a projection of their own personalities, and thus models of cultural origins based on primate studies are inherently suspect.

To begin with the basic physical changes, to make a human out of a chimpanzee-like ancestor, the legs had to be lengthened greatly in relation to body size, the hip and knee joints had to be repositioned to allow bipedalism, and the spine had to develop an S-shaped curvature to cushion the brain against the shocks of bipedal locomotion. The face, jaw, and teeth had to be changed from the straight-row, prominent canines-and-incisors configuration of early primates to the curved human dental arch with reduced canines and incisors, and adapted to grinding rather than puncturing (Figure 3.10). In the long course of our evolution from apes, we lost most of our body hair, our sexual organs and behavior changed greatly, and our brains were greatly expanded and probably "rewired."

Consider first the simple matter of body size. A survey of numerous primate species indicates that a pronounced size difference between the sexes is relatively uncommon,[46] and thus "marked morphological and behavioral dimorphism is not a primitive characteristic of primates but has evolved in certain genera in relation to particular patterns of living."[47] One clue as to what patterns of living these might have been can be seen in the size

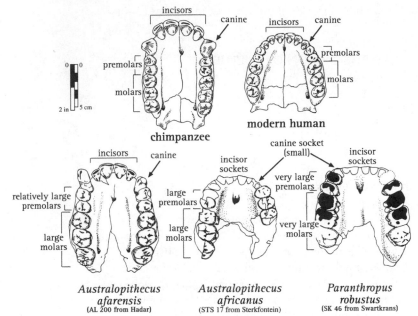

incisors — canine   incisors — canine

premolars

molars

0   0
2 in   5 cm

chimpanzee

premolars

molars

modern human

incisors — canine

relatively large premolars

large molars

incisor sockets

canine socket (small)

large premolars

large molars

very large premolars

very large molars

incisor sockets

Australopithecus afarensis
(AL 200 from Hadar)

Australopithecus africanus
(STS 17 from Sterkfontein)

Paranthropus robustus
(SK 46 from Swartkrans)

FIGURE 3.10   Teeth preserve best of all body parts. Note the difference between chimpanzees and hominins in the shape of the dental arcade. Other distinctive features include the presence or absence of a canine diastema and the size of the molars.

differences of the sexes in living nonhuman primates. Male and female gibbons, who spend most of their lives in trees, are almost identical in size; among chimpanzees, who spend some of their time on the ground, males are usually larger than females; and among gorillas, who are almost completely terrestrial, males average almost twice the size of females. Why should the physical size of the sexes show this association with terrain?

A probable factor in the evolution of both sexual dimorphisms and the overall increase in size of *Homo sapiens sapiens* of both sexes was the need for defense against predators. Our ancestors apparently evolved in environments where competition and pre-dation by large cats and other carnivores would have been significant, and thus it is not at all surprising that part of our evolution in these environments would have been in the direction of greater physical size. A human with a rifle, or even a crude spear, would have some reasonable defenses, but until tool-use reached this point there would no doubt have been strong direct selection for increasing physical size. Our earliest tool-using ancestors were only about 3 or 4 feet tall, weighing perhaps 60 or 70 pounds—not really a formidable competitor, given the other animals in its range. Today, on the African savannas, baboon populations are able to survive, despite occasional predation by leopards and lions, partly because they have retained impressive canine and incisor teeth and great physical strength. By 10 million years ago, however, our ancestors had probably lost these dental defenses. Another factor may have been females' preference for mating with larger individuals—who may have had greater ability to provide food and protection and to produce offspring with these same qualities.

But drawing conclusions about a primate's physical characteristics and, especially, social behavior on the basis of the characteristics of its physical environment is plagued with ambiguities and difficulties. In some animal species, sexual dimorphisms seem to be linked to differences in feeding strategies of males and females. While this may have been of some importance to our early primate ancestors, the kinds of food eaten by males and females probably overlapped considerably soon after tool-use began.[48] Nonetheless, early hominin males and females would probably have been under increasingly different selective pressures as soon as males began specializing in hunting and females in gathering—specializations that may have appeared only comparatively late and sporadically.

Another aspect of sexual dimorphism among humans is particularly intriguing when seen in comparison with nonhuman primates: namely, the secondary sexual characteristics that differentiate human males and females. Among human females, breasts are significantly larger than among males—in fact, the size, shape, and other differences distinguishing male and female breasts are much more pronounced than in any other mammal species, and only in humans do breasts first enlarge at puberty rather than at the first pregnancy.[49] Selection for increased breast size appears to have involved a complex set of factors, including the erotic role; Rose Frisch has even suggested that the disproportionate size of the human female breast may have evolved because of its role "as a cooling fin to get rid of body heat."[50] Breast size cannot be explained simply in terms of milk production, since size seems to have almost no relationship to effective functioning in human beings. Similarly, the human penis is far larger, relatively and absolutely, than that of any other primate, including the gorilla. In addition, human females have softer skin and higher voices than males and have lost more of their body hair—although compared to the other species of primates, males also have remarkably little body hair.

Many explanations have been offered for the origins of these characteristics. A primary difference, for example, between humans and other primates, and one that many people link directly to human origins, is that human females do not exhibit estrus; that is, women's receptivity to sexual intercourse does not seem to increase to any large extent with the rise in estrogen levels that precedes ovulation. How can we account for this? One suggestion is that

> in all probability the evolutionary development of hair reduction, increased skin sensitivity and tactile changes involving skin tension were [sic] all associated with increasing the tactile sensations of coital body contact, especially in the frontal presentation. Likewise the breasts of young women taken together with other features (limb contour, complexion, and the like) seem to represent the main visual sexual releasers for the male. While the latter features may have been due to straight-forward intersexual selection by ancient males the former features have probably been selected in both sexes for their effect in improving sexual rewards, in inducing sexual love, and in maintaining pair bonds. The same is also likely to be true for the presence of orgasm in women and the absence of the more typical mammalian estrus.[51]

Our loss of the body hair that our primate relatives retained is a more radical development than it might seem. Naked skins may increase sexual sensitivity, and hair loss even seems to have helped, paradoxically, in water conservation; but naked skins increase the risks of skin cancers and other diseases, and they also open the body to vermin in a way that no chimpanzee must live with.

Other basic differences between ourselves and other primates, and possible reasons for them, are evident if we compare baboons and chimpanzees. Baboons inhabit a diversity of environments, but our most reliable and complete information comes from savanna-adapted populations in central and east Africa. Within the baboon troop, the eldest males have almost unimpeded access to food and sex, and they protect their privileges with aggressive behavior. Younger males are allowed access to females only on the sufferance of more dominant males, although they are constantly testing this dominance by attempting to strike up meaningful relationships with concupiscent females. Often this will incite a dominant male to charge and make threatening gestures. Similarly, when desirable but limited food is available, such as fruit or a clutch of eggs, the dominant males and females take what they want first. A mother and child may share food, but there is no systematic food sharing between adult members of the group.

When baboon troops move across savanna or open environments, they typically position members according to age and sex. Adolescent males are on the periphery, dominant adult males are in the front-center, adult females are behind the adult males, and dependent young are stationed near the adult females. This is of course an excellent defensive formation, offering the best protection to the young and females, on whom the perpetuation of the group depends. There are many more adolescent males than necessary for reproduction, so although they would endure the most losses to predators, the stability of the group would not suffer much. Significantly, when the baboon troop moves into more forested areas, the positioning becomes much more fluid and dispersed, indicating, not too surprisingly, that terrain is an important determinant of behavior for baboons, and that savanna environments seem to put a premium on group cohesiveness and dominance hierarchies— although forest-dwelling chimpanzees, counterintuitively, perhaps, seem to exhibit *more* group hunting, tool-use, and forms of cooperation than savanna-dwelling chimpanzees.[52]

Some baboon groups seem to construct dominance hierarchies on the basis of length of residence in the troop, and in general baboons seem somewhat more variable and adaptable in dominance hierarchies and aggression than previously thought.

Thus, in trying to explain how culture-bearing individuals developed from our primate ancestors, we must look for factors or conditions that would work against these dominance hierarchies and promote the distinctive human family structure, with its food sharing, division of labor, and pair bonding.

The relevance of baboons to our own ancestry may be somewhat limited because we are much more closely related to chimpanzees. Chimpanzees also inhabit diverse environments, and generalizations about their behavior are as dangerous as in the case of baboons. The most studied chimpanzees are those of the Tanzanian forests, especially those of the Gombe Stream area.[53] In Gombe, many of these chimpanzee groups have been regularly fed by the people observing them, and since most groups are cut off by modern development from their complete range and interactions with more distant groups, we cannot expect these primates to be perfect reflections of chimpanzee behavior in the true natural state. But it is striking that the chimpanzees of this area behave very differently from the savanna-dwelling baboons. Access to food and sex is much less rigidly controlled, and the entire dominance hierarchy seems to be less in evidence. In one instance where a female was sexually receptive for a record 21 days, the males of the chimpanzee group, young and old alike, stood in line for her favors with only minor apparent bickering.[54] This is not always typical behavior, and the adolescents were effectively barred from mating with some females in many cases, but compared to baboons, chimpanzees are absolute libertines in sexual matters. Strictly speaking, chimpanzees do not have true estrus cycles, but they do have periods of greater and lesser sexual receptivity.

Similarly, there is also a diminution of territoriality. Chimpanzees run for kilometers along trails through the forests, often alone or with one or two others, and individuals frequently leave one small group to go live with another. So relaxed are chimpanzees, in fact, about sex and territoriality that they have aroused envious feelings in some human observers. "Chimpanzees, it seems, successfully achieve what *Homo sapiens* radicals only dream of: peaceful, non-competitive, non-coercive, non-possessive, egalitarian, jealousy-free, promiscuous, non-tyrannical communes."[55]

This may be a somewhat idealized picture. Chimpanzees have elaborate threat rituals and do menace each other according to a well-developed hierarchy. In addition, chimpanzees are the only animals besides ourselves who regularly use objects as weapons—usually wooden clubs or thrown rocks and debris.[56] They fight over food and females, and sometimes over rank, and they are the only other primates known to practice cannibalism, having been observed on several occasions eating young chimps alive.[57]

Tanner notes that wild chimpanzees place nuts on flat roots or stones and then break them open by hitting them with sticks or rocks, suggesting that "a fairly intelligent ancestral ape could have taken the step from such opportunistic tool use during foraging, to tool-making and more regular use of tools in plant gathering."[58] She also notes that female chimpanzees use tools more often than males in nut-cracking. Moreover, they generally use tools in more complex ways than males, and they teach their daughters to use tools and even supply them with tools.[59]

In reviewing hunting and meat-eating by chimpanzees, Boesch and Boesch-Achermann[60] note that the frequency of hunting in wild chimpanzees is quite variable, sometimes being dependent on group size and the number of adult males. There is also no clear evidence that meat-sharing for sexual favors is more common when females are in estrus. In addition, there seems to be a rudimentary sexual division of labor among chimpanzees, with male chimpanzees more adept at hunting and female chimpanzees spending more time nut-cracking or collecting termites and other invertebrates—a prelude, perhaps, to the sharp division of labor in human hunting and gathering groups.

ETHNOLOGY AND THE STUDY OF EARLY HOMININ ECONOMIES

With the evidence from Gona, Olorgesailie, Olduvai Gorge, and the few other sites of this time period (c. 2.6–1.0 million years ago), we must account for, among other developments: (1) the evolution of stone tool-use, (2) the approximate doubling of human brain size, (3) increased stature and changes in facial architecture and other physical features, and (4) the migrations of hominins throughout the warmer regions of the Old World.

Great controversies have erupted over the explanation of these changes, particularly about the *economic* basis of these transitions. What is at issue here is the very basis of almost all human evolution, since we must assume that we are mainly the physical products of the roughly two million years of natural selection on all the generations that connect us to the hominins of Africa. Arguments on these issues have centered on whether or not early *Homo* did no, some, or a lot of hunting, and how much like modern peoples they were in their social relationships.[61] It is not surprising, perhaps, that in trying to understand what those selective forces and environments were, anthropologists have depended heavily on ethnographic studies of people who until recently lived as hunter-foragers in the savannas of southern and eastern Africa, particularly the Kalahari Bushmen. Some feel, however, that the *behavior* of these modern-day hunter-gatherers may have almost nothing to tell us about our hominin ancestors. Edwin Wilmsen,[62] for example, suggests that almost everything we know about these people is contaminated by Western misperceptions. But the Kalahari hunter-gatherers and others at least illustrate some of the possibilities open to our ancestors in this kind of environment.

Studies of African savanna ecology suggest that *scavenging* could have been a significant part of early hominin repertoires. African savannas would seem to reward animals who are opportunists and generalists when it comes to food: An early hominin might well have adopted the principle of "eat it if it moves, or has reasonably recently moved." Schaller and Lowther spent a few days during the dry season on the Serengeti Plain and found a lot of edible meat in the form of a dead buffalo (which did not appear to have been killed by a predator), some lion kills, and a few incapacitated animals that could have been killed.[63] Blumenschine and his colleagues found that scavenging would have been possible and even rewarding, presuming that our ancestors went for the brains and marrow of lion kills and other casualties.[64] Small animals, such as juvenile Thompson's gazelles, persisted as carcasses for only about a day before some scavenger totally consumed them, but larger animals, such as adult buffalo, remained as significant food sources for about four days, after which even if they were not eaten by lions, hyenas, vultures, and so on, they were putrid to the point that their "market value" had plummeted.

Even without scavenging, our ancestors may have developed a way to subcontract some of the effort and risk of hunting to lions in a way that is right in line with our later history as one of the most selfish, exploitative, rapacious members of the animal family. O'Connell and his colleagues have shown that the Hadza, hunter-gatherers who live in northern Tanzania, sometimes scavenge simply by scaring lions away from kills by making a lot of noise.[65]

The Kalahari hunter-gatherers keep their population densities low and thinly distributed. The low level of productivity of their hot, arid environment, as manipulated by their simple technology (bows, arrows, digging sticks, and so forth), requires that they spend most of the year in groups of 25 people or less, often on the move from one camp to another. Most of their diet is made up of vegetable products, tortoises, and other small game, but occasionally giraffes and other large animals are killed, usually through cooperative hunting by several males. Although females provide the bulk of the group's food by gathering and processing plants and eggs, nestlings, turtles, and other small animals, men do all the hunting of large animals among most known remaining hunting-gathering societies, including the Bushmen and Australian Aborigines.

Kalahari Bushmen also illustrate the value of division of labor. We all know that it is better, in complicated tasks, to work as an integrated group doing different things than for everyone to do every task, whether the task involves getting a football downfield or building a supercomputer. The Kalahari split tasks into those that men do, those that women do, and those that everyone does, children included.

Hunter-gatherer economic life is also dominated by the principle of reciprocity: Food and other resources are exchanged among kinsmen, balancing out the periodic shortages that may afflict any member or nuclear family in the band.

Like most hunting and gathering societies, the Bushmen are at least somewhat territorial. They move often but always within a relatively restricted region, usually 25–30 kilometers in all directions from a central water hole or home base. Clearly, some degree of territoriality is an advantage if resources are not uniformly distributed; it is efficient to know where reliable sources of flint, vegetables, game animals, and water are within one's territory, and the group forced out of its territory is faced with unpredictable supplies and, perhaps, the hostility of the group on whose territory it is trespassing. Thus, any models or reconstructions we make regarding our early hominin ancestors should incorporate the assumption that they were probably at least loosely territorial.

Hunter-gatherer population densities are directly determined by resource availability and are maintained by methods of population control that seem harsh to us. The aboriginal population density of most of Australia (or at least these populations as they existed until recent decades), for example, can be predicted with a high degree of accuracy simply from the amount of average rainfall in the various areas. This balance between population and resources is maintained mainly by marriage rules and female infanticide. Birdsell reports that 15 to 30 percent of all babies are killed, usually by the grandmother, who places her hand over the infant's mouth and nose as it is born so that it never draws its first breath.[66] She acts out a group's unstated decision that keeps a mother from carrying more than one infant while she works.

Studies of !Kung infant breast-feeding may reveal the powerful controls on fertility rates that are available to a group simply through natural mechanisms. !Kung women breast-feed their babies as often as 60 times every 24 hours, including during the night when the mother is asleep, and there is some evidence that this frequency is necessary to produce and maintain the hormonal levels that suppress ovulation; a study of women in Scotland shows that they usually nurse their babies only six times in 24 hours and that this has less effect in suppressing ovulation.[67]

In her study of hunters and gatherers in New Guinea, Patricia Townsend observed that although women produce over 90 percent of one group's food, this society is strongly patriarchal.[68] Townsend found that the women in this group usually marry soon after puberty and have about six children. Malaria and other diseases kill off about 43 percent of the children early in life, but girls die from diseases at a much greater rate than boys, probably from malign neglect. If thought necessary, unwanted girls are killed by strangulation with a vine soon after birth.

Most hunter-gatherers keep their numbers at a level far below what could be supported in any average year, and it is the older people who remember the worst winters and the longest droughts that must be accommodated by the group's sizes. Someone said that when an old person dies it is like a library burning down, and this is true also among hunter-gatherers.

In summary, the Kalahari Bushmen and other contemporary hunter-gatherers may offer some general guidelines for interpreting the archaeological remains of our ancestors in these areas of Africa—even though we know that in mentality and many other ways they are profoundly different from early *Homo*.

MODELS OF CULTURAL ORIGINS

The distance is nothing; it is only the first step that is difficult.

Marquise de Deffand (remarking on the legend that St. Denis walked two leagues carrying his head in his hands)

Having compared nonhuman primates to ourselves, let us look at several attempts to formulate general explanations for the first stages of the evolution of culture. Many people have considered this problem, and it is a subject fraught with political implications, for it involves the basic nature of humanity and the forces that produce cultural change. No explanation for cultural origins is complete or conclusive, but many have points of interest.

A great difficulty in explaining the factors that produced humans out of a chimpanzee-like animal is that to do so one must try to reconstruct the patterns of natural selection that existed millions of years ago in ecosystems that no longer exist.

Some years ago, Owen Lovejoy argued that bipedalism as an evolutionary product is essentially a matter of sex and the economics of foraging.[69] As he notes, in some ways bipedalism seems an unlikely development; it is a slow method of movement, and an animal expends great amounts of energy just holding itself up. Also, because we evolved as a quadrupedal and semi-erect animal, bipedalism is in a sense an unnatural form of locomotion. Our spines evolved to serve as a cantilevered bridge-like structure, and even though this structure was successfully modified into a bipedal erect form, we are heirs to many problems, including slipped disks and other back problems, bunions, hernias, poor blood circulation in our legs and feet, and a shortened birth canal that means difficult births for many mothers. If bipedalism is so bad, why should it appear? Lovejoy argues that all apes are potentially semi-erect animals by virtue of natural selection for "handedness" —the constant use of the hand to forage for food. And if one's evolutionary niche does not reward great bursts of speed over the short run, bipedalism is quite effective for long periods of methodical hunting and gathering.

Lovejoy notes that through the later history of the primates, there has been an evolution in the reproductive strategy. The trend has been toward decreasing the number of offspring a female has but increasing the parental investment in each one, so that they have a better chance to survive and in turn reproduce. (Ecologists call this a *k-strategy*, as opposed to the *r-strategy* of an animal like the housefly, which has thousands of offspring, only a few of which survive.)

The heart of Lovejoy's argument is that bipedalism was selected over quadrupedalism in our ancestors because it was a way to increase reproductive success. It allowed our ancestors to have more offspring while maintaining a high level of parental investment in the form of food provision, protection, and training. This was accomplished by evolving an economic adaptation and social organization that allowed the mother to spend less of her energy getting her own food and more of her time taking care of offspring. Lovejoy argues that one way females could successfully raise several children born within a short time interval would be to induce the male to provide the female with food on a regular basis, to take part in other tasks of raising many children, and to do it all without competing with other males to the point that the group would break up into murderous, insanely jealous individuals. This meant that the dominance hierarchy and competition common in other primate groups had to be suppressed. One way in which this might occur is if individuals began to differ in perceived "attractiveness," so that qualities of physical appearance and personality played a role in sexual desirability and feelings of "love." The advantages of suppressed conflict in the human group might also be related to the fact that humans developed concealed ovulation and sexual receptivity.

Many people have criticized Lovejoy's model. As Kinzey notes, studies of chimpanzees show that it is the females, not the males, who most frequently share food with young chimps.[70] Another problem is that substantial differences in size between males and females in primates seem to be associated with competition between males in polygamous mating patterns, whereas Lovejoy proposes monogamous patterns for early hominins.

But if one argues, as various scholars have, that the negative aspects of bipedalism are compensated for by the increased intelligence and better tool-making abilities of our ancestors, how was it possible for bipedalism to appear before any significant increase in brain size and—presumably —intelligence took place? Recently, this question of the origins of bipedalism has emphasized several major avenues of research, including biomechanics, energetics, and ecological contexts.

Biomechanics[71] is the study of motion and the effects of forces on the body, for example, how bones are shaped in part by the actions of muscles on them. We know, for instance, that modern human babies are born with a femur (upper leg bone) that has a bicondylar[72] angle of zero degrees (Figure 3.11). As a growing child learns to walk, the femur begins to "knee-in" (develop the

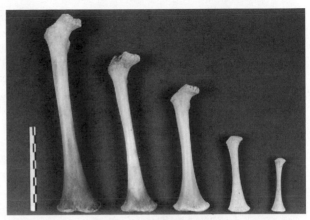

FIGURE 3.11 The epigenetic development of the bicondylar angle in the human femur is shown in this growth sequence from a seven-month fetus (right) to a seven-year-old child (left).

bicondylar angle) as a result of how the muscles and ligaments interact (create a mechanical load) on the condyles—by about eight years of age, a child achieves the adult bicondylar angle of 8 to 11 degrees.[73] This angle is important because it helps stabilize balance as a human walks. Close examination of the form of fossil hominin bones therefore offers clues as to whether or not they walked bipedally in the same way as modern humans.[74] While interpretations have varied, some researchers have suggested that the type of bipedalism that australopiths such as "Lucy" had was not exactly the same as ours today. Such studies are important in examining how bipedalism evolved in the hominins.

Some researchers have examined the energetics of bipedality to assess whether this was potentially significant in the origins of this type of walking. Leonard and Robertson,[75] for example, propose that energy savings are important to reproductive success in early hominins. Their model, which is based on a hypothetical reconstruction of "Lucy" (*Australopithecus afarensis*), suggests that walking bipedally results in an energy savings of 4 percent over short day ranges (distances traveled in the search for food) and 15 percent to 20 percent over large day ranges compared to nonhuman primates (monkeys and apes) that walk quadrupedally (using all four limbs). These energy savings could be used for growth and reproduction,[76] thus echoing some of Lovejoy's early ideas about the benefits of bipedalism.

Still other researchers have concentrated on the ecological contexts that may have facilitated the development of bipedalism. These studies often focus on the period of the last common ancestor (LCA) to hominins and chimpanzees, in the period around 8 to 10 million years ago. Common to all of these is the observation that environmental changes resulted in discontinuous habitats. That is, as open terrain in the form of wooded parklands and savanna grasslands developed due to worldwide climatic drying trends, the continuous forested areas in which the LCA lived were broken up by these more open contexts. Food resources would become more scattered as a result.

One explanation for the origins of bipedalism stresses that this context would lead to increased competition for food and aggression both between groups and within groups.[77]

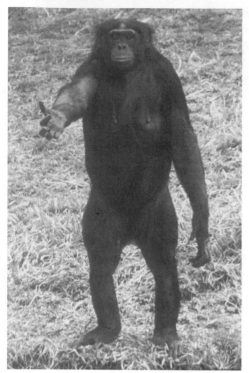

FIGURE 3.12   Bipedal behavior in a bonobo.

The development of bipedal displays, such as are seen in living chimpanzees (Figure 3.12), is a mechanism for peacefully resolving these conflicts, because actual attacks that lead to death or injury tend to occur rarely in these situations. Instead, the threat underlying the bipedal display is enough to prevent an actual attack. Males that have bipedal display behavior might thus be more successful in attracting mates, while females with this behavior might have more access to food resources as well as the ability to protect their young more effectively. Over time, the juveniles in the group add the "play" behavior of bipedal displays, and the wider spread use of this behavior leads to changes in anatomy that facilitate walking bipedally.

Other explanations for the origins of bipedalism in this context emphasize having the hands free to gather as well as carry food,[78] or the adoption of one type of LCA social organization, the large group.[79] Having a large group size, of course, is one way to outcompete smaller groups for resources simply by the force of sheer numbers and threat of aggression. The disadvantage of a large group is that it will eat up the resources in a given area at a much faster rate than a small group. This means that a large group will have to cover more distance on a daily basis in the search for food, and bipedalism is a strategy to accomplish this extended travel. The evolutionary line leading to chimpanzees, on the other hand, emphasized small group size and less daily distance to travel, thus leading to the retention of quadrupedal walking.

It is quite clear that bipedalism is very ancient, and that it originates long before stone tool-use. But, what of other behavioral patterns that might have lead to or accompanied the origins of culture? Food-sharing, for example, would tend to lengthen the period during which a female was sexually responsive, if sex served as an inducement to food-sharing. And this was an important evolutionary change in more ways than one. Human females are fertile for only a relatively unpredictable three days a month, so intercourse at least a few times a week would be necessary for successful fertility rates.

In an analysis of the link between sexual behavior and other aspects of culture, Donald Symons has addressed the problem of human origins on the basis of a sustained comparison of sexuality in men and women.[80] Symons summarizes the major differences between men and women in this regard as follows. (1) Intrasexual competition generally is much more intense among males than among females, and in preliterate societies competition over women probably is the single most important cause of violence. (2) Men incline to polygyny, whereas women are more malleable in this respect and, depending on the circumstances, may be equally satisfied in polygamous, monogamous, or polyandrous marriages. (3) Almost universally, men experience sexual jealousy of their mates. Women are more flexible in this respect, but in certain circumstances women's experience of sexual jealousy may be characteristically as intense as men's. (4) Men are much more likely to be sexually aroused by the sight of women and the female genitals than women are by the sight of men and the male genitals. (5) For men, physical characteristics, especially those associated with youth, are by far the most important determinants of women's sexual attractiveness. For females, physical characteristics are somewhat less important determinants of men's sexual attractiveness; political and economic prowess are more important, and youth is relatively unimportant. (6) Much more than women, men are predisposed to desire a variety of sex partners for the sake of variety (although one is reminded here of Cornelia Otis Skinner's remark that "Women's virtue is man's greatest invention"). (7) Among all cultures, copulation is considered to be essentially a service or favor that women render to men, and not vice versa, regardless of which sex derives or is thought to derive greater pleasure from sexual intercourse.[81]

In the absence of evidence for a genetic basis for these supposed traits, however, and given the fact that patriarchal societies have dominated human history, we cannot tell if any of these traits are biologically based or are, instead, cultural constructions. Opinions on this point vary. Admitting the great plasticity and potential for variability of human sexual behavior, Symons thinks that there is a strong biological, genetic, profoundly evolutionary basis to these apparent behavioral differences between males and females and these cultural aspects of sexuality. And this is what one would expect, given our evolutionary origins. For millions of years the evolutionary advantage has been with men who have had intercourse with as many young women as they could—provided that the resulting progeny could be raised to reproductive age. Lovejoy's model was based on initial monogamous pairings, but ethnographic evidence suggests that human mating patterns have been primarily polygamous for millions of years.

John Tooby and Irven DeVore have suggested that the various models of cultural origins and subsequent human evolution seem most plausible if we assume that our ancestors of several million years ago began to increase the time they spent hunting or scavenging other animals.[82]

They begin with *male parental investment*. As noted previously, it is highly unusual among primates for males to invest significant energy in providing their offspring with food, yet humans do. Tooby and DeVore note that, whereas it is not economically efficient to carry low-calorie vegetable foods long distances back to one's mate and offspring, meat is a concentrated form of high-calorie nutrition, and thus would be more advantageous to transport. Tooby and DeVore also point out that "male coalitions" may have developed because of the advantages of group hunting. Reciprocity, sharing, and exchange, too, may be linked to hunting. Tooby and DeVore argue that vegetable foods offer few evident rewards to the kinds of exchange, sharing, and reciprocity typical of all human groups. Vegetable foods come in many different forms and sizes, and animals tend to gather them on the basis of energy costs and immediate needs. But meat, "unlike vegetable foods, comes in discrete quantities: an entire animal is either captured or lost. . . . [V]ariability in hunting success, and the fact that meat comes in chunked quantities often in excess of what the capturers can readily consume, provides a ready explanation for food sharing, food exchange and risk sharing through deferred reciprocation among the larger social group."[83]

Regarding the pronounced sexual division of labor among humans, Tooby and DeVore suggest that extreme differentiation in the kinds of foods males and females gather is not feasible without food exchange between males and females. "If males changed from occasional to intensive hunting, one consequence would be the extreme sexual division of labor found among humans, with females exploiting the more [fixed, vegetable] food sources."[84] Similarly, they see stone tool-use as probably an adjunct to the requirements of animal butchering and hunting.

These forms of small-game hunting and scavenging would have rewarded group cooperation, reduced dominance hierarchies, improved communication systems, and encouraged the development of stone tools for processing meat and vegetable foods.

In general summary of these models, we have seen that bipedalism, human sexuality, social networks, terrain, hunting/scavenging, and various other factors may all be related in complex patterns of interaction, resulting in the kinds of animals represented by "Lucy" and the other Hadar fossils. These hominins need not have been major tool-users to have been "cultural" in fundamental ways.

Analyzing the Evidence

How can we go about integrating all this ethnographic, archaeological, primatological, and paleontological evidence and use it to understand our origins? To begin with, in an evolutionary analysis we must concentrate on those factors that might have allowed some individuals and not others to have survived to pass on their genes, so that over time our brain size increased and all the other dimensions of the human animal were formed. And once we start examining differential reproduction, we must look directly at how food was procured, shared, and consumed.

Initially, researchers vigorously debated whether early hominins hunted or scavenged animals based on observations of marks on animal bones and stone tools.[85] One might think that the simple conjunction of stone tools amidst piles of animal bones, some of which show obvious cut marks from being hacked at with stone tools, irresistibly would lead one to the conclusion that our ancestors butchered and ate these animals. But one archaeologist's stone-tool-cutting mark was another archaeologist's hyena-bite mark, and when it came to the statistics of the extent and significance of different kinds of bone alteration, entirely different interpretations arose.

Since then, numerous studies have examined not only the marks on animal bones, but also the availability of animal carcasses in the landscape.[86] These suggest that animal carcasses with plenty of remaining meat would have been especially available in the ecological niche along the woodlands margins (Figure 3.13). Unlike the open grasslands, where hyenas and other scavengers would make quick work of most existing carcasses including the bones, the woodland margins are not usually inhabited by these scavengers. Thus carcasses left behind by leopards that carry their prey up into the trees, or by other large cats, are more available in this setting. Additionally, the teeth of the large cats are not efficient at stripping off all the meat, so that early hominins observing the cats could approach the carcasses once the cats left them behind. Stone tools therefore provided "sharp teeth" for hominins to strip meat from bones and clearly offered an advantage in these circumstances. Of course, it is entirely possible that hominins also scavenged bones from these carcasses and cracked them open with hammerstones to obtain the greasy and nutritious marrow.

The stone tools of two million years ago include a diversity of forms, but most sharp-edged pieces are simple flakes. They certainly are adequate for butchering animals, whether hunted or scavenged. The absence of "spear-points" or anything resembling them strongly suggests that these early hominins had no means of killing large animals,

Ecological, zooarchaeological, and behavioral correlates of competition for larger mammal carcasses, as documented in the Serengeti ecosystem of northern Tanzania.

	Low competition	High competition
Ecosystemic variable (N. Tanzania)		
Habitat	Riparian woodlands	Non-riparian *or* non-wooded
Season and place (Serengeti only)	Dry in north, wet on plains	Wet in north? Dry on plains
Type of competing carnivore	Flesh-eater	Bone-cruncher
Carnivore:ungulate ratio	Low (Serengeti)	High (Ngorongoro)
Stratum	Arboreal	Terrestrial
Time of day	Mid-day	Dawn/dusk
Cause of death	Mass drowning	Predation by bone-crunching carnivore
Zooarchaeological traces		
Skeletal parts	Little differential destruction	Denser bones survive preferentially
Portions	High epiphysis:shaft fragment ratio	Low epiphysis:shaft fragment ratio
Species	Low carnivore:ungulate ratio; dominated by single species as in glut; more small species	High carnivore:ungulate ratio; high species diversity?; more large species
Age (mortality)	High neonate:adult ratio	Low neonate:adult ratio
Fragmentation	Low NISP:MNE or MNI	High NISP:MNE or MNI
Surface marks	Low incidence; single agent	High incidence; multiple agents
Behavioral strategy		
Timing of access	Planned search?; unrestricted access, including early in resource life	Opportunistic search?; access restricted to end of resource life
Processing/consumption	Energy limited?; complete consumption	Time limited?; consumption of highest net yield available
Transport	Process and consume where found	Transport easily removed parts to safe/concealed locale
Defense/pilfering	No strategies needed	Cooperative and/or artificial techniques
Predation risk from competitors	Lower	Higher

FIGURE 3.13 Opportunities for scavenging carcasses in the East African landscape are assessed using experimental and observational data.

although perhaps they could have used wooden spears—or, as noted earlier, they may not have hunted.

Why is it so important to know about the addition of meat to the diet? Here again we are dealing directly with the factors that shaped us physically and to some extent mentally. When anthropologists argue about the economy of early hominins they are arguing about one of the driving forces of human evolution.

COULD EARLY PLEISTOCENE HUMANS SPEAK?

Maybe. Academics are notorious for their maddening penchant for qualifying everything to the point of utter irresolution, but that's the nature of human analysis, and when we ask a question such as this, the correct answer has to be that it depends in part on how one defines "speech." Do chimpanzees, for example, speak? Clearly they communicate vast amounts of information to each other through noises they make, and they may well communicate far more than we think they do. If we take the reasonable position that human abilities to convey meaning through speech can all be placed on a continuum between the abilities of a chimpanzee and Winston Churchill, then we can ask when abilities equal to our own first evolved, and why.

Various scholars[87] believe that our contemporary fluency of speech appeared only after about 50,000 years ago and in only a limited number of hominin species (perhaps only one); others believe that even the tool-makers of Olduvai Gorge could communicate vocally with much greater fluency than chimpanzees. We'll probably never know much more about this issue than we do now. The areas of the human brain most associated with speech, Broca's and Wernicke's areas, both of which are located on the left side of the brain, were almost certainly not as developed in early hominins, given that their brains were much smaller than ours. But speech is not simply a matter of brain size. Unlike the anatomy of other animals, the human larynx (air passageway in the throat) and the pharynx (food passageway in the throat) converge low in the throat, so that we cannot breathe and swallow at the same time—something most of us occasionally prove by choking on food swallowed "the wrong way." The advantage to this odd configuration is that it provides a relatively large chamber over the vocal cords, permitting sound production of great variety. Some estimates of the extent to which early hominins were evolving this human sound apparatus have been made on the basis of computer models, but we simply do not have adequate samples of the relevant anatomy of early hominins to be sure of their resemblance to us in this regard.

Why would people have a better or worse chance of living and reproducing successfully based on their language abilities? Many possible reasons could be suggested. Just the knowledge conveyed from one person to another, or from one group to another about resource availability in distant areas, conflict resolution, technological methods, or any number of other matters could improve the chances of survival and reproduction. If the !Kung Bushmen are any guide in this matter, language would be an extremely important adaptive tool even in this low-tech era—and it would greatly mitigate the crushing boredom of this way of life as well.

SUMMARY AND CONCLUSIONS

We are but "pulvis et umbra," Horace said, "dust and shadow," and certainly this is true for the long line of fossils that connect us to our beginnings. Nor are the factors that have shaped our evolution entirely clear. Climate changes, scavenging, hunting, evolutionary change in the biology of our sexuality and mentality, bipedalism, tool-use—all these and many other factors seem to have been ingredients in the evolutionary experiment that is our past, but the evidence is far too slight to reduce us to some simple product of a few factors.

Even if we fight through all these issues of causation and taxonomy and eventually reach a consensus, we will be left with an equally important and profound question—the nature of the mode and tempo of human physical and cultural evolution. The question is this: Does evolution in such things as human cranial capacity (Figure 3.14), technological efficiency, administrative centralization, urbanization, and so forth, proceed gradually, with approximately the same rate of change, or are there long periods of stability punctuated by periods of rapid change? As Robert McC. Adams phrased it in the context of early states, does the simile of a "ramp" or of a series of "steps" best describe our evolutionary history?[88]

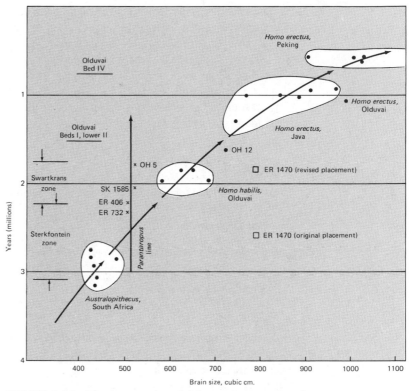

FIGURE 3.14   The increase in cranial capacity over time in our ancestors was enormous and rapid by evolutionary standards, but the rate of increase has slowed in the last 1,000,000 years, and we may have reached the limits allowed by the mechanics of human birth and locomotion.

This simple question involves some fairly murky political issues. Some fear that to consider human behavior as largely an adaptation and the result of natural selection means that human behavior is beyond social change, that aggression, racism, and so forth may be genetically inherent. Some people think the Marxian concept of dialectical development means that even in such matters as the physical changes from the australopiths to ourselves, we should look for a developmental pattern showing long periods of stability punctuated by periods in which physical characteristics changed relatively rapidly. Thus, Gould and Eldredge say that "no gradualism has been detected within any hominid taxon."[89] But J. E. Cronin and others who have analyzed the measurements on fossil hominins from four million years ago to ourselves found no evidence of "stasis" or "punctuation" and believe that the record of human evolution is best seen as an example of gradual change with some periods of varying rates of evolution.[90] To have any kind of conclusive test of these competing ideas, we need the remains of hundreds of early hominins, at least some of which fall in the time "gaps" for which we now have no information.

M. Henneberg has taken an interesting and novel approach to the lack of precise dates and the problem of the rate at which human cranial capacities increased. He plotted the estimated dates for a large group of human fossils from the past 3.5 million years against the date for each of these fossils that would be predicted based on the assumption that the increase in cranial capacity over time was gradual, at about the same rate—a rate estimated by a standard mathematical technique called regression.[91] The results suggest that the increase over time in human cranial capacities was in fact gradual and at about the same rate—if one assumes that some fossils are incorrectly dated.

As important as all these issues are, they are in a sense all just refinements on a basic advance in human intellectual history: Whatever the tempo of human evolution, we now know its modes, its mechanisms, and its results more clearly than a person of a century and a half ago would ever have thought possible.

BIBLIOGRAPHY

Adams, R. McC. 1966. *The Evolution of Urban Society*. Chicago: Aldine.

Alexander, R. D. 1975. "The Search for a General Theory of Behavior." *Behavioral Science* 20:77–100.

Anderson, P. 1983. "The Reproductive Role of the Human Breast." *Current Anthropology* 24(1):25–45.

Audette, R., and T. Gilchrist. 1999. *Neanderthin: Eat Like a Caveman to Achieve a Lean, Strong, Healthy Body*. New York: St. Martin's Paperbacks.

Bartlett, T. Q., R. W. Sussman, and J. M. Cheverud. 1993. "Infant Killing in Primates: A Review of Observed Cases with Specific Reference to the Sexual Selection Hypothesis." *American Anthropologist* 95(4):958–990.

Bergson, H. 1983. *Creative Evolution (L'Evolution Creatrice)*, authorized translation by A. Miller. Lanham, MD: University Press of America.

Bertram, B. C. R. 1979. "Serengeti Predators and Their Social Systems." In *Serengeti: Dynamics of an Ecosystem*, ed. A. R. E. Sinclair and M. Norton-Griffiths. Chicago: University of Chicago Press.

Binford, L. R. 1981. *Bones: Ancient Men and Modern Myth*. New York: Academic Press.

———. 1985. "Human Ancestors: Changing Views of Their Behavior." *Journal of Anthropological Archaeology* 4(4):292–327.

———. 1988. "Fact and Fiction About the Zinjanthropus Floor: Data, Arguments, and Interpretations." *Current Anthropology* 19(1):123–135.

Birdsell, J. B. 1972. *Human Evolution*. Chicago: Rand McNally.

———. 1979. "Ecological Influences on Australian Aboriginal Social Organization." In *Primate Ecology and Human Origins: Ecological Influences on Social Organization*, ed. I. S. Bernstein and E. O. Smith, pp. 117–151. New York: Garland STPM Press.

Blumenschine, R. J. 1987. "Characteristics of the Early Hominid Scavenging Niche." *Current Anthropology* 28(4):383–407.

———. 1995. "Percussion Marks, Tooth Marks, and Experimental Determinations of the Timing of Hominid and Carnivore Access to Long Bones at FLK *Zinjanthropus*, Olduvai Gorge, Tanzania." *Journal of Human Evolution* 29:21–51.

Blumenschine, R. J., J. A. Carvallo, and S. D. Capaldo. 1994. "Competition for Carcasses and Early Hominid Behavioral Ecology: A Case Study and Conceptual Framework." *Journal of Human Evolution* 27:197–213.

Blumenschine, R. J., C. W. Marean, and S. D. Capaldo. 1996. "Blind Tests of Inter-Analyst Correspondence and Accuracy in the Identification of Cut Marks, Percussion Marks, and Carnivore Tooth Marks on Bone Surfaces." *Journal of Archaeological Science* 23:493–507.

Boesch, C., and H. Boesch. 1981. "Sex Differences in the Use of Natural Hammers by Wild Chimpanzees: A Preliminary Report." *Journal of Human Evolution* 10:565–583.

———. 1984. "Possible Causes of Sex Differences in the Use of Natural Hammers by Wild Chimpanzees." *Journal of Human Evolution* 13:415–440.

Boesch, C., and H. Boesch-Achermann. 2000. *The Chimpanzees of the Taï Forest: Behavioural Ecology and Evolution*. New York: Oxford University Press.

Boesch-Achermann, J., and C. Boesch. 1994. "Hominization in the Rainforest: The Chimpanzee's Piece of the Puzzle." *Evolutionary Anthropology* 3(1):9–16.

Brace, C. L. 1967. *The Stages of Human Evolution: Human and Cultural Origins*. Englewood Cliffs, NJ: Prentice-Hall.

Brace, C. L., D. P. Tracer, L. Allen Yaroch, J. Robb, K. Brandt, and A. Russel Nelson. 1993. "Clines and Clusters Versus 'Race': A Test in Ancient Egypt and of a Death on the Nile." *Yearbook of Physical Anthropology* 36:1–31.

Brain, C. K. 1981. *The Hunters or the Hunted?* Chicago: University of Chicago Press.

Brooks, D. R., and E. O. Wiley. 1986. *Evolution as Entropy: Toward a Unified Theory of Biology*. Chicago: University of Chicago Press.

Brown, F., J. Harris, and A. Walker. 1985. "Early *Homo erectus* Skeleton from West Lake Turkana, Kenya." *Nature* 316:788–792.

Bunn, H. T. 1981. "Archaeological Evidence for Meat-Eating by Plio-Pleistocene Hominids from Koobi Fora and Olduvai Gorge." *Nature* 291:574–577.

Bunn, H. T., L. E. Bartram, and E. M. Kroll. 1988. "Variability in Bone Assemblage Formation from Hadza Hunting, Scavenging, and Carcass Processing." *Journal of Anthropological Archaeology* 7:412–457.

Bunn, H. T., and E. M. Kroll. 1988. "Reply to L. Binford 'Fact and Fiction About the Zinjanthropus Floor: Data, Arguments, and Interpretations.'" *Current Anthropology* 29(1):135–149.

Cashdan, E. 1983. "Territoriality Among Hunter Foragers: Ecological Models and an Application to Four Bushman Groups." *Current Anthropology* 24(1):47–66.

Clark, G. A. 1988. "Some Thoughts on the Black Skull: An Archaeologist's Assessment of WT-17000 (*A. boisei*) and Systematics in Human Paleontology." *American Anthropologist* 90(2):357–371.

Clarke, R. J., and P. V. Tobias. 1995. "Sterkfontein Member 2 Foot Bones of the Oldest South African Hominid." *Science* 269:521–524.

Clutton-Brock, T. H. 1989. "Female Transfer and Inbreeding Avoidance in Social Mammals." *Nature* 337:70–72.

Cohen, L. A. 1987. "Diet and Cancer." *Scientific American* 257(5):42–48.

Conroy, G. C. 1990. *Primate Evolution*. New York: W. W. Norton.

Cook-Deegan, R. M. 1994. *The Gene Wars: Science, Politics, and the Human Genome*. New York: W. W. Norton.

Cordain, L. 2002. *The PaleoDiet: Lose Weight and Get Healthy by Eating the Food You Were Designed to Eat*. Hoboken, NJ: John Wiley & Sons.

Cronin, J. E., N. T. Boaz, C. B. Stringer, and Y. Rak. 1981. "Tempo and Mode in Hominid Evolution." *Nature* 292:113–122.

Crook, J. H. 1972. "Sexual Selection, Dimorphism, and Social Organization in Primates." In *Sexual Selection and the Descent of Man 1871–1971*, ed. B. Campbell. Chicago: Aldine.

Davis, E. 2005. "Science and Religious Fundamentalism in the 1920s." *American Scientist* 93(3):253–260.

Devine, J. 1985. "The Versatility of Human Locomotion." *American Anthropologist* 87:550–570.

Dunbaar, R. I. 1988. *Primate Social Systems*. Ithaca, NY: Cornell University Press.

Eckhardt, R. B. 1988. "On Early Hominid Adaptation and Heat Stress." *Current Anthropology* 29(3):493.

Farraro, G., Trevathan, W., and J. Levy. 1994. *Anthropology. An Applied Perspective*. New York: West Publishing.

Ferris, T. 1988. *Coming of Age in the Milky Way*. New York: William Morrow.

Fialkowski, K. 1986. "A Mechanism for the Origin of the Human Brain: A Hypothesis." *Current Anthropology* 27(3):288–290.

Finkel, D. J. 1981. "An Analysis of Australopithecine Dentition." *American Journal of Physical Anthropology* 55:69–80.

Fisher, E. 1979. *Woman's Creation*. New York: McGraw-Hill.

Foley, R. 1987. "Hominid Species and Stone-Tool Assemblages: How Are They Related?" *Antiquity* 61:380–392.

Frisch, R. E. 1983. "Comment on P. Anderson, 'The Reproductive Role of the Human Breast.'" *Current Anthropology* 24(1):25–45.

Futuyma, D. J. 1992. "History and Evolutionary Processes." In *History and Evolution*, ed. M. H. Nitecki and D. V. Nitecki. Albany: State University of New York Press.

Goodall, J. 1986. *The Chimpanzees of Gombe*. Cambridge, MA: Belknap (Harvard University Press).

Gould, S. J. 1977. *Ever Since Darwin*. New York: Norton.

Gould, S. J., and N. Eldridge. 1977. "Punctuated Equilibria: The Tempo and Mode of Evolution Reconsidered." *Paleobiology* 3:115–151.

Grayson, D. K. 1983. *The Establishment of Human Antiquity*. New York: Academic Press.

Hamilton, M. E. 1984. "Revising Evolutionary Narratives: A Consideration of Alternative Assumptions About Sexual Selection and Competition for Mates." *American Anthropologist* 86(3):651–662.

Harcourt-Smith, W. E. H., and L. C. Aiello. 2004. "Fossils, Feet and the Evolution of Human Bipedal Locomotion." *Journal of Anatomy* 204(5):403–416.

Harding, R. S., and G. Teleki, eds. 1981. *Omnivorous Primates*. New York: Columbia University Press.

Harris, D. R., ed. 1980. *Human Ecology and Savanna Environments*. New York: Academic Press.

Harrison, T. 1978. "Present Status and Problems for Paleolithic Studies in Borneo and Adjacent Islands." In *Early Paleolithic in South and East Asia*, ed. F. Ikawa-Smith. The Hague: Mouton.

Henneberg, M. 1989. "Morphological and Geological Dating of Early Hominid Fossils Compared." *Current Anthropology* 30(4):527–528.

Hill, J. H. 1978. "Apes and Language." *Annual Review of Anthropology* 7:89–112.

Hughes, A. R., and P. V. Tobias. 1977. "A Fossil Skull Probably of the Genus Homo from Sterkfontein, Transvaal." *Nature* 65:310–312.

Ingold, T. 1988. *The Appropriation of Nature*. Iowa City: University of Iowa Press.

Isaac, G. 1977. *Olorgesailie; Archaeological Studies of a Middle Pleistocene Lake Basin in Kenya*. Chicago: University of Chicago Press.

Isbell, L. A., and T. P. Young. 1996. "The Evolution of Bipedalism in Hominids and Reduced Group Size in Chimpanzees: Alternative Responses to Decreasing Resource Availability." *Journal of Human Evolution* 30:389–397.

Itzkoff, S. 1987. *Why Humans Vary in Intelligence*. Ashfield, MA: Paideia.

Jablonski, N. G., and G. Chaplin. 1993. "Origin of Habitual Terrestrial Bipedalism in the Ancestor of the Hominidae." *Journal of Human Evolution* 24:259–280.

Jerison, H. J. 1983. "The Evolution of the Mammalian Brain as an Information-Processing System." In *Advances in the Study of Mammalian Behavior*, ed. J. F. Eisenberg and D. G. Kleinman, Special Publication No. 7. The American Society of Mammologists.

Johanson, D. C., and M. A. Edey. 1981. *Lucy: The Beginnings of Humankind*. New York: Simon and Schuster.

Jolley, C. J. 1970. "The Seed-Eaters: A New Model of Hominid Differentiation Based on a Baboon Analogy." *Man* 5:6–26.

Kauffman, S. 1993. *Origins of Order*. Oxford: Oxford University Press.

Kimbel, W. H., D. Johanson, and Y. Rak. 1994. "The First Skull and Other New Discoveries of *Australopithecus afarensis* at Hadar, Ethiopia." *Nature* 368:449–451.

Kinzey, W. G., ed. 1987. *The Evolution of Human Behavior: Primate Models*. Albany: State University of New York Press.

Kramer, P. A. 1999. "Modelling the Locomotor Energetics of Extinct Hominids." *Journal of Experimental Biology* 202:2807–2818.

Krebs, J., and N. B. Davies. 1981. *Introduction to Behavioral Ecology*. Oxford: Blackwell.

Kurland, J. A., and S. J. Beckerman. 1985. "Optimal Foraging and Hominid Evolution: Labor and Reciprocity." *American Anthropologist* 87(1):73–93.

Leakey, M. G., C. S. Feibel, I. McDougall, and A. C. Walker. 1995. "New Four-Million-Year-Old Hominid Species from Kanapoi and Allia Bay, Kenya." *Nature* 376:565–571.

Leakey, M. G., and R. E. Leakey, eds. 1978. *Koobi Fora Research Project: Vol. 1, The Fossil Hominids and an Introduction to Their Context, 1968–1974*. Oxford: Clarendon Press.

Leakey, R. E., and R. Lewin. 1977. *Origins*. New York: Dutton.

Lee, R. B. 1979. *The !Kung San*. Cambridge: Cambridge University Press.

Leonard, W. R., and M. L. Robertson. 1997. "Rethinking the Energetics of Bipedality." *Current Anthropology* 38(2):304–309.

———. 2001. "Locomotor Efficiency and the Origin of Bipedality: Reply to Steudel-Numbers." *American Journal of Physical Anthropology* 116:174–176.

Lewis, R. 1995. "The Rise of Antibiotic-Resistant Infections." FDA Consumer Magazine Web posting.

Lewontin, R. C. 1979. "Sociobiology as an Adaptationist Program." *Behavioral Science* 24:5–14.

Lieberman, L., and F. L. C. Jackson. 1995. "Race and Three Models of Human Origin." *American Anthropologist* 97(2):231–242.

Lieberman, P. E. 1991. *Uniquely Human: The Evolution of Speech, Thought, and Selfless Behavior*. Cambridge, MA: Harvard University Press.

———. 1998. *Eve Spoke: Human Language and Human Evolution*. New York: Norton.

Lieberman, P. E., E. S. Crelin, and D. H. Klatt. 1972. "Phonetic Ability and Related Anatomy of the Newborn and Adult Human, Neanderthal Man, and the Chimpanzee." *American Anthropologist* 74:287.

Lovejoy, O. 1980. "Hominid Origins: The Role of Bipedalism." *American Journal of Physical Anthropology* 52:50.

Maddison, W. P., and D. R. Maddison. 1992. *MacClade, Version 3, Analysis of Phylogeny and Character Evolution*. Sunderland, MA: Sinauer Associates.

Marean, C. W., L. M. Spencer, R. J. Blumenschine, and S. D. Capaldo. 1992. "Captive Hyaena Bone Choice and Destruction, the Schlepp Effect, and Olduvai Archaeofaunas." *Journal of Archaeological Science* 19:101–121.

Martin, K., and B. Voorhies. 1975. *The Female of the Species*. New York: Columbia University Press.

McBrearty, S., and A. S. Brooks. 2000. "The Revolution That Wasn't: A New Interpretation of the Origin of Modern Human Behavior." *Journal of Human Evolution* 39:453–563.

McGrew, W. 1992. *Chimpanzee Material Culture: Implications for Human Evolution*. Cambridge: Cambridge University Press.

———. 1998. "Culture in Nonhuman Primates?" *Annual Review of Anthropology* 27:301–328.

McHenry, H. M., and K. Coffing. 2000. "*Australopithecus* to *Homo*: Transformations in Body and Mind." *Annual Review of Anthropology* 29:125–146.

O'Connell, J. F., K. Hawkes, and N. B. Jones. 1988. "Hadza Scavenging: Implications for Plio/Pleistocene Hominid Subsistence." *Current Anthropology* 29(2):356–363.

Orchiston, D. W., and W. G. Siesser. 1982. "Chronostratigraphy of the Pleistocene Fossil Hominids of Java." *Modern Quaternary Research in Southeast Asia* 1:131–150.

Parker, S. T., R. W. Mitchell, and M. L. Boccia, eds. 1994. *Self-Awareness in Animals and Humans: Developmental Perspectives*. New York: Cambridge University Press.

Penny, D., L. R. Foulds, and M. D. Hendy. 1982. "Testing the Theory of Evolution by Comparing Phylogenic Trees Constructed from Five Different Protein Sequences." *Nature* 297:197–200.

Peters, C. P., and R. J. Blumenschine. 1995. "Landscape Perspectives on Possible Land Use Patterns for Early Pleistocene Hominids in the Olduvai Basin, Tanzania." *Journal of Human Evolution* 29:321–362.

Petraglia, M. D., and R. Potts. 1994. "Water Flow and the Formation of Early Pleistocene Artifact Sites in Olduvai Gorge, Tanzania." *Journal of Anthropological Archaeology* 13(3):228–254.

Pianka, E. 1974. *Evolutionary Ecology.* New York: Harper & Row.

Pilbeam, D., and S. J. Gould. 1974. "Size and Scaling in Human Evolution." *Science* 186:892–901.

Potts, R. 1987. "On Butchery by Olduvai Hominids." *Current Anthropology* 28(1):95–96.

———. 1988. *Early Hominid Activities at Olduvai.* Hawthorne, NY: Aldine de Gruyter.

Potts, R., A. K. Behrensmeyer, and P. Ditchfield. 1999. "Paleolandscape Variation and Early Pleistocene Hominid Activities: Members 1 and 7, Olorgesailie Formation, Kenya." *Journal of Human Evolution* 37(5):747–788.

Quiatt, D. D., and V. Reynolds. 1993. *Primate Behaviour: Information, Social Knowledge, and the Evolution of Culture.* New York: Cambridge University Press.

Quiatt, D. D., and J. Itani, eds. 1994. *Hominid Culture in Primate Perspective.* Niwot: University Press of Colorado.

Relethford, J. H. 2000. *The Human Species: An Introduction to Biological Anthropology,* 4th ed. Mountain View, CA: Mayfield.

Richmond, B. G., D. R. Begun, and D. S. Strait. 2001. "Origin of Bipedalism: The Knuckle-Walking Hypothesis Revisited." *Yearbook of Physical Anthropology* 44:70–105.

Rose, K. D. 1994. "The Earliest Primates." *Evolutionary Anthropology* 3(5):159–172.

Ruff, C. B., and J. A. Runestad. 1992. "Primate Limb Bone Structural Adaptations." *Annual Review of Anthropology* 21:407–433.

Ruvolo, M. 1997. "Genetic Diversity in Hominoid Primates." *Annual Review of Anthropology* 26:515–540.

Salt, G. W., ed. 1984. *Ecology and Evolutionary Biology.* Chicago: University of Chicago Press.

Schaller, G. B., and G. R. Lowther. 1969. "The Relevance of Carnivore Behavior to the Study of Early Hominids." *Southwestern Journal of Anthropology* 25:307–341.

Schrire, C., ed. 1984. *Past and Present in Hunter-Gatherer Studies.* New York: Academic Press.

Schwalbe, G. 1906. *Studien zur Vorgeschichte des Menschen.* Stuttgart: Scheizerbart.

Seaboook, J. 1994. "Building a Better Human." *The New Yorker,* March 18, pp. 109–114.

Semaw, S. 2000. "The World's Oldest Stone Artefacts from Gona, Ethiopia: Their Implications for Understanding Stone Technology and Patterns of Human Evolution Between 2.6–1.5 Million Years Ago." *Journal of Archaeological Science* 27(12):1197–1214.

Sevink, J., E. H. Hebeds, N. Priem, and R. H. Verschure. 1981. "A Note on the Approximately 730,000-Year-Old Mammal Fauna and Associated Human Activity Sites Near Isernia, Central Italy." *Journal of Archaeological Science* 8:105–104.

Shapiro, H. L. 1974. *Peking Man.* New York: Simon and Schuster.

Shefelbine, S. J., C. Tardieu, and D. R. Carter. 2002. "Development of the Femoral Bicondylar Angle in Hominid Bipedalism." *Bone* 30(5):765–770.

Shipman, P. 2003. "We Are All Africans." *American Scientist* 91(6):496–499.

Skelton, R. R., J. M. McHenry, and G. M. Drawhorn. 1986. "Phylogenetic Analysis of Early Hominids." *Current Anthropology* 27(1):21–43.

Small, M. F. 1988. "Female Primate Sexual Behavior and Conception." *Current Anthropology* 29(1):81–100.

———, ed. 1984. *Female Primates: Studies by Women Primatologists.* New York: A. R. Liss.

Smith, E. A. 1991. *Inujjuamiut Foraging Strategies: Evolutionary Ecology of an Arctic Hunting Economy.* Hawthorne, NY: Aldine de Gruyter.

Smith, K. C. 1992. "Neo-Rationalism Versus Neo-Darwinism: Integrating Development and Evolution." *Biology and Philosophy* 7:431–451.

Steudel-Numbers, K. L. 2003. "The Energetic Cost of Locomotion: Humans and Primates Compared to Generalized Endotherms." *Journal of Human Evolution* 44(2):255–262.

Strum, S. C., and W. Mitchell. 1987. "Baboon Models and Muddles." In *The Evolution of Human Behavior: Primate Models,* ed. W. G. Kinzey. Albany: State University of New York Press.

Speth, J., and D. Davis. 1976. "Seasonal Variability in Early Hominid Predation." *Science* 192:441–445.

Swaicki, R. M. 1978. "Unusual Response of DDT-Resistant Houseflies to Carbinol Analogues of DDT." *Nature* 275:443–444.

Symons, D. 1979. *The Evolution of Human Sexuality.* New York: Oxford University Press.

Tanner, N. M. 1987. "The Chimpanzee Model Revisited and the Gathering Hypothesis." In *The Evolution of Human Behavior,* ed. W. G. Kinzey. Albany: State University of New York Press.

Tattersall, I. 1992. "Species Concepts and Species Identification in Human Evolution." *Journal of Human Evolution* 22:341–350.

———. 1994. "How Does Evolution Work?" *Evolutionary Anthropology* 3(1):2–3.

Teleki, G. 1981. "The Omnivorous Diet and Eclectic Feeding Habits of Chimpanzees in Gombe National Park, Tanzania." In *Omnivorous Primates*, ed. R. S. Harding and G. Teleki. New York: Columbia University Press.

Testart, A. 1982. "The Significance of Food Storage Among Hunter-Gatherers: Residence Patterns, Population Densities, and Social Inequalities." *Current Anthropology* 23(5):523–537.

Thomas, D. H. 1986. *Refiguring Anthropology*. Prospect Heights, IL: Waveland Press.

Thorpe, S. K. S., R. H. Compton, M. M. Gunther, R. F. Ker, and R. M. Alexander. 1999. "Dimensions and Moment Arms of the Hind- and Forelimb Muscles of Common Chimpanzees (*Pan troglodytes*)." *American Journal of Physical Anthropology* 110:179–199.

Tooby, J., and I. DeVore. 1987. "The Reconstruction of Hominid Behavioral Evolution Through Strategic Modeling." In *The Evolution of Human Behavior: Primate Models*, ed. W. G. Kinzey. Albany: State University of New York Press.

Toth, N. 1985. "The Oldowan Reconsidered: A Close Look at Early Stone Artifacts." *Journal of Archaeological Science* 12:101–120.

Townsend, P. K. 1971. "New Guinea Sago Gatherers: A Study of Demography in Relation to Subsistence." *Ecology of Food and Nutrition* 1:19–24.

Van den Berghe, P. L. 1972. "Sex Differentiation and Infant Care: A Rejoindor to Sharlotte Neely Williams." *American Anthropologist* 74:770–772.

Van Lawick-Goodall, J. 1968. "The Behavior of Free-living Chimpanzees in the Gombe Stream Area." *Animal Behavior Monographs* 1:161–311.

———. "Some Aspects of Aggressive Behavior in a Group of Free-living Chimpanzees." *International Social Science Journal* 23:89–97.

———. 1973. "The Behavior of Chimpanzees in Their Natural Habitat." *American Journal of Psychiatry* 130:1–12.

Vertes, L. 1965. "Typology of the Buda Industry: A Pebble-Tool Industry from the Hungarian Lower Paleolithic." *Quaternaria* 7:185–195.

Von Koenigswald, G. H. R. 1975. "Early Man in Java: Catalogue and Problems." In *Australopithecus Paleoanthropology: Morphology and Paleoecology*, ed. R. H. Tuttle. The Hague: Mouton.

Watanabe, K. 1994. "Precultural Behavior of Japanese Macaques: Longitudinal Studies of the Koshima Troops." In *The Ethological Roots of Culture*, ed. R. A. Gardner, B. T. Gardner, B. Chiarelli, and F. X. Plooij, pp. 81–94. Dordrecht: Kluwer.

Wheatley, B. P. 1988. "Cultural Behavior and Extractive Foraging in *Macaca fasciculris*." *Current Anthropology* 29(3):516–519.

White, L. 1949. *The Science of Culture*. New York: Grove Press.

Williams, M., D. Dunkerley, P. De Deckker, P. Kershaw, and J. Chappell. 1998. *Quaternary Environments*, 2nd ed. New York: Oxford University Press.

Wilmsen, E. 1989. *Land Filled with Flies: A Political Economy of the Kalahari*. Chicago: University of Chicago Press.

Wolpoff, M. 1994. "How Does Evolution Work?" *Evolutionary Anthropology* 3(1):4–5.

Wolpoff, M., Xinzhi, Wu, and A. G. Thorne. 1984. "Modern *Homo sapiens* Origins: A General Theory of Hominid Evolution Involving the Fossil Evidence from East Asia." In *The Origins of Modern Humans: A World Survey of the Fossil Evidence*, ed. F. H. Smith and F. Spencer. New York: A. R. Liss.

Wood, B. 1987. "Who Is the 'Real' *Homo habilis*?" *Nature* 327:187–188.

Wood, B., and B. G. Richmond. 2000. "Human Evolution: Taxonomy and Paleobiology." *Journal of Anatomy* 196:19–60.

Woodburn, J. 1982. "Egalitarian Societies." *Man* (NS)17:431–451.

Yellen, J. E. 1976. "Settlement Patterns of the !Kung: An Archeological Perspective." In *Kalahari Hunter-Gatherers: Studies of the !Kung San and Their Neighbors*, ed. R. Lee and I. Devore. Cambridge, MA: Harvard University Press.

Zeleznik, S., A. W. Grele, J. Pollack, and I. Aloni. 1989. "On Systematic Butchery by Plio/Pleistocene Hominids." *Current Anthropology* 29(1):151–153.

NOTES

1. Recent news stories have discussed Federal and ACLU lawsuits against various school districts to maintain the separation of church and state, as well as state legislature attempts in at least nine states to introduce the teaching of "intelligent design" into school curricula as an alternative to the theory of evolution.
2. Bergson, *L'Evolution Creatrice*.
3. Semaw, "The World's Oldest Stone Artefacts form Gona, Ethiopia: Their Implications for Understanding Stone Technology and Patterns of Human Evolution Between 2.6–1.5 Million Years Ago."

4. Some researchers, for example, McGrew, "Culture in Nonhuman Primates?", argue that differences across primate species may be a matter of degree rather than kind. This would mean that in a broad sense, species such as chimpanzees and humans both have culture, although the specifics of the cultures will differ.

5. White, *The Science of Culture.*

6. Wheatley, "Cultural Behavior and Extractive Foraging in *Macaca fascicularis.*" The Japanese macaque "cultural tradition" of washing sweet potatoes, and later wheat, in salt water, appears to have persisted over several generations; see, for example, Watanabe, "Precultural Behavior of Japanese Macaques: Longitudinal Studies of the Koshima Troops."

7. Brace, *The Stages of Human Evolution*, p. 51.

8. See, for example, Alexander, "The Search for a General Theory of Behavior."

9. Alexander, "Evolution and Culture."

10. Variously attributed.

11. These types of assumptions, however, must be viewed with some caution because they imply that chimpanzees have not evolved appeciably over the past several million years.

12. Grayson, *The Establishment of Human Antiquity.*

13. Dubois's finds were eventually classified as *Homo erectus.*

14. Von Koenigswald, "Early Man in Java." See also Harrison, "Present Status and Problems for Paleolithic Studies in Borneo and Adjacent Islands," pp. 54–55.

15. Relethford, *The Human Species: An Introduction to Biological Anthropology*, is an up-to-date introduction to evolutionary theory as applied to people.

16. For the introductory student a good and well-illustrated introduction to evolutionary theory in anthropological applications is in Farraro et al., esp. pp. 59–71.

17. There's good reason to believe that Mendel falsified his data because his results are far too "perfect" mathematically and do not show the expected levels of "chance" variation, but this does not detract from his overall contribution. See Thomas, *Refiguring Anthropology*, pp. 288–291.

18. Birdsell, *Human Evolution.*

19. Brace et al., "Clines and Clusters Versus 'Race': A Test in Ancient Egypt and of a Death on the Nile."

20. Crook, "Sexual Selection, Dimorphism, and Social Organization in Primates."

21. See, for example, the exchange between Tattersall and Wolpoff, in *Evolutionary Anthropology*, 3(1), 1994.

22. Several examples of diet books based on presumed hunter-gatherer diets can be found, for example, Audette and Gilchrist's *Neanderthin: Eat Like a Caveman to Achieve a Lean, Strong, Healthy Body*, and Cordain's *The PaleoDiet: Lose Weight and Get Healthy by Eating the Food You Were Designed to Eat.*

23. Lewontin, "Sociobiology as an Adaptationist Program."

24. Hamilton, "Revising Evolutionary Narratives: A Consideration of Alternative Assumptions About Sexual Selection and Competition for Mates."

25. Rossetti was describing the day of Christ's birth here in *A Christmas Carol*, not the Pleistocene.

26. Williams et al., *Quaternary Environments.*

27. Shipman, "We Are All Africans."

28. Wood and Richmond, "Human Evolution: Taxonomy and Paleobiology."

29. I (Wenke) am indebted to Dr. Thomas Morgan for some anecdotes on this point.

30. Attributed.

31. This taxonomy is quite recent and recognizes the close genetic links between chimpanzees and humans. The older terminology used the word "hominid" to mean humans and their ancestors. With the taxonomic revisions, hominid now applies to gorillas, chimpanzees, humans and their ancestors. The correct term for humans and their ancestors is "hominin." See Wood and Richmond, "Human Evolution: Taxonomy and Paleobiology," pp. 20–21.

32. Conroy, *Primate Evolution.*

33. There is some disagreement among scholars regarding the exact placement of several of the hominins. For example, some researchers prefer to classify *Homo rudolfensis* and *Homo habilis* as *Australopithecus rudolfensis* and *Australopithecus habilis.* Other researchers place *Homo ergaster* with *Homo erectus.*

34. Kimbel et al., "The First Skull and Other New Discoveries of *Australopithecus afarensis* at Hadar, Ethiopia."

35. Leakey et al., "New Four-Million-Year-Old Hominid Species from Kanapoi and Allia Bay, Kenya."

36. Clarke and Tobias, "Sterkfontein Member 2 Foot Bones of the Oldest South African Hominid."

37. Toth, "The Oldowan Reconsidered: A Close Look at Early Stone Artifacts."

38. Semaw, "The World's Oldest Stone Artefacts from Gona, Ethiopia: Their Implications for Understanding Stone Technology and Patterns of Human Evolution Between 2.6–1.5 Million Years Ago."

39. See Clark, "Some Thoughts on the Black Skull"; also McBrearty and Brooks, "The Revolution That Wasn't: A New Interpretation of the Origin of Modern Human Behavior"; McHenry and Coffing, "*Australopithecus* to *Homo*: Transformations in Body and Mind"; Wood and Richmond, "Human Evolution: Taxonomy and Paleobiology."

40. Brown, Harris, and Walker, "Early *Homo erectus* Skeleton."

41. Potts, *Early Hominid Activities at Olduvai*. See also Peters and Blumenschine, "Landscape Perspectives on Possible Land Use Patterns for Early Pleistocene Hominids in the Olduvai Basin, Tanzania"; Potts et al., "Paleolandscape Variation and Early Plesistocene Hominid Activities: Members 1 and 7, Olorgesailie Formation, Kenya."

42. Petraglia and Potts, "Water Flow and the Formation of Early Pleistocene Artifact Sites in Olduvai Gorge, Tanzania."

43. Toth, "The Oldowan Reconsidered."

44. Tooby and DeVore, "The Reconstruction of Hominid Behavioral Evolution," pp. 215–217.

45. "Culture in Nonhuman Primates?"

46. Crook, "Sexual Selection, Dimorphism, and Social Organization in Primates," p. 235.

47. Ibid.

48. Pianka, *Evolutionary Ecology*.

49. Anderson, "The Reproductive Role of the Human Breast."

50. Frisch, "Comment on Anderson, P. 'The Reproductive Role of the Human Breast.'"

51. Crook, "Sexual Selection, Dimorphism, and Social Organization in Primates," p. 254.

52. Bosch-Achermann and Boesch, "Hominization in the Rainforest: The Chimpanzee's Piece of the Puzzle."

53. Goodall, *The Chimpanzees of Gombe*. Long-term studies of chimpanzees have also been undertaken in the Mahele Mountains National Park in Tanzania, in Bossou in Guinea, in the Kibale forest of Uganda, and in the Taï National Forest of Côte d'Ivoire; see Boesch and Boesch-Achermann, *The Chimpanzees of the Taï Forest*.

54. Van Lawick-Goodall, "Some Aspects of Aggressive Behavior in a Group of Free-living Chimpanzees."

55. Van den Berghe, "Sex Differentiation and Infant Care: A Rejoinder to Sharlotte Neely Williams," p. 772.

56. Van Lawick-Goodall, "Some Aspects of Aggressive Behavior in a Group of Free-living Chimpanzees."

57. Van Lawick-Goodall, "The Behavior of Free-living Chimpanzees in the Gombe Stream Area"; idem., "Some Aspects of Aggressive Behavior in a Group of Free-living Chimpanzees"; idem., "The Behavior of Chimpanzees in Their Natural Habitat."

58. Tanner, "The Chimpanzee Model Revisited and the Gathering Hypothesis," p. 20.

59. Ibid., citing Boesch and Boesch, "Sex Differences in the Use of Natural Hammers," and Boesch and Boesch, "Possible Causes of Sex Differences in the Use of Natural Hammers by Wild Chimpanzees."

60. *The Chimpanzees of the Taï Forest*, pp. 159–164, 204–205.

61. Binford, "Human Ancestors."

62. Wilmsen, *Land Filled with Flies: A Political Economy of the Kalahari*.

63. Schaller and Lowther, "The Relevance of Carnivore Behavior to the Study of Early Hominids."

64. Blumenschine, "Characteristics of the Early Hominid Scavenging Niche"; Blumenschine et al., "Competition for Carcasses and Early Hominid Behavioral Ecology: A Case Study and Conceptual Framework."

65. O'Connell et al., "Hadza Scavenging: Implications for Plio/Pleistocene Hominid Subsistence."

66. Birdsell, "Ecological Influences on Australian Aboriginal Social Organization."

67. Anderson, "The Reproductive Role of the Human Breast," p. 31.

68. Townsend, "New Guinea Sago Gatherers: A Study of Demography in Relation to Subsistence."

69. Lovejoy, "Hominid Origins: The Role of Bipedalism."

70. Kinzey, *The Evolution of Human Behavior: Primate Models*, p. x.

71. Biomechanics uses physics to examine the action of forces on the body. In addition to statistical analyses, many of these studies use computer modeling and computer-generated simulations.

72. The distal end of the femur (upper leg bone) articulates (meets) the proximal end of the tibia (large lower leg bone). At the distal end of the femur are lateral (toward the outside) and medial (toward the inside) condyles (rounded areas of bone that articulate with hollowed out areas on the proximal end of the tibia). In human bipedalism, the medial condyle grows at a faster rate than the lateral condyle, thus creating the bicondylar angle.

73. Shefelbine et al., "Development of the Femoral Bicondylar Angle in Hominid Bipedalism."

74. For example, see Kramer, "Modelling the Locomotor Energetics of Extinct Hominids"; Ruff and Runestad, "Primate Limb Bone Structural Adaptations"; Thorpe et al., "Dimensions and Moment Arms of the Hind- and Forelimb Muscles of Common Chimpanzees (*Pan Troglodytes*)"; Harcourt-Smith and Aiello, "Fossils, Feet and the Evolution of Human Bipedal Locomotion."

75. Leonard and Robertson, "Rethinking the Energetics of Bipedality," and "Locomotor Economy and the Origin of Bipedality: Reply to Steuden-Numbers."

76. Of course, not all researchers agree with Leonard and Robertson; see Steudel-Numbers, "The Energetic Cost of Locomotion: Humans and Primates Compared to Generalized Endotherms."

77. Jablonski and Chaplin, "Origin of Habitual Terrestrial Bipedalism in the Ancestor of the Hominidae."

78. Richmond et al., "Origin of Bipedalism: The Knuckle-Walking Hypothesis Revisited."

79. Isbell and Young, "The Evolution of Bipedalism in Hominids and Reduced Group Size in Chimpanzees: Alternative Responses to Decreasing Resource Availability."

80. Symons, *The Evolution of Human Sexuality*.
81. Ibid., pp. 27–28.
82. Tooby and DeVore, "The Reconstruction of Hominid Behavioral Evolution."
83. Ibid., pp. 223–224.
84. Ibid., p. 224.
85. Binford, "Fact and Fiction About the Zinjanthropus Floor: Data, Arguments, and Interpretations"; Bunn and Kroll, "Reply to L. Binford 'Fact and Fiction About the Zinjanthropus Floor: Data, Arguments, and Interpretations'"; Zeleznik et al., "On Systematic Butchery by Plio/Pleistocene Hominids."
86. Blumenschine, "Percussion Marks, Tooth Marks, and Experimental Determinations of the Timing of Hominid and Carnivore Access to Long Bones at FLK *Zinjanthropus*, Oduvai Gorge, Tanzania"; Blumenschine et al., "Competition for Carcasses and Early Hominid Behavioral Ecology: A Case Study and Conceptual Framework"; Blumenschine et al., "Blind Tests of Inter-Analyst Correspondence and Accuracy in the Identification of Cut Marks, Percussion Marks, and Carnivore Tooth Marks on Bone Surfaces"; Marean et al., "Captive Hyaena Bone Choice and Destruction, the Schlepp Effect, and Olduvai Archaeofaunas."
87. Reviewed in Lieberman, *Uniquely Human: The Evolution of Speech, Thought, and Selfless Behavior*.
88. Adams, *The Evolution of Urban Society*.
89. Gould and Eldredge, "Punctuated Equilibria: The Tempo and Mode of Evolution Reconsidered."
90. Cronin et al., "Tempo and Mode in Hominid Evolution."
91. Henneberg, "Morphological and Geological Dating of Early Hominid Fossils Compared."

4

The Origins of *Homo sapiens sapiens*

And how am I to face the odds
Of man's bedevilment and God's?
I, a stranger and afraid
In a world I never made.
                A. E. Houseman[1]

Viewed from space, earth's green and blue beauty is framed by the black infinity of the universe. This perspective has compelled many astronauts to reflect on our common humanity. A similar contemplation of community should arise when we look back archaeologically through the millions of years of our common human ancestry and meditate on the evidence in the fragmented bones and crude stone tools of our primate ancestors.

It is tempting to lapse into a sentimental vision of our ancestors pluckily fighting their way up a long dangerous road, and finally to "succeed"—to become "us." But human evolution was not like this. As in most evolutionary equations, the most intense competition was between individuals of the same species—we are all the progeny of people who "won," in the sense that their genes made it through the unforgiving sieves of time and circumstance, to reside in us. But chance, randomness, seems to have affected the biological universe in profoundly incalculable ways since the beginnings of our planet; we seem to be here by virtue in part of a chain of improbable accidental events.[2]

We can see traces of our origins in all the earth's ancient life-forms, from the earliest marine creatures through early mammals that lived tens of millions of years ago to our later primate ancestors—but only in the crucial interval of two to one million years ago did our genus, *Homo*, become the dominant primate in the world; and not until just a few hundred thousand years ago did humans appear whom we accord the honor of calling them, too, *Homo sapiens*. We reserve the ultimate accolade of "people like us," *Homo sapiens sapiens*, for only some of the humans who lived after about 150,000 years ago, and it was not until about 30,000 years ago that we alone came to constitute humanity.[3]

To follow the Socratic dictum to know ourselves, we must ask, what were the forces and circumstances that produced us, modern humanity, from the pre-human forms of our ancestors, and what does this knowledge tell us about ourselves and our future?

HUMAN EVOLUTION AND RADIATION: 1.8? MILLION TO CIRCA 300,000 YEARS AGO

When we left our African ancestors in chapter 3, at about 1.5 million years ago, some of them had cranial capacities approaching the low end of the normal modern range, they could make and use a variety of efficient stone tools, and some of them may have already been living far outside of Africa. Several localities outside of Africa are beginning to show quite convincingly that early hominins were able to leave the African continent and disperse into at least some areas of Eurasia; by shortly after a million years ago, our ancestors had colonized most of the southern edge of the Old World, from Africa to Indonesia. These were the habitats—rich in flora and fauna and with few seasonal differences in the availability of food—to which we, as tropical animals, were best adapted. But while our hominin ancestors were extending their range in the hot savannas of Africa and the warm margins of Europe and Asia, great fertile tracts of the world lay unknown and untouched by humans.

At some time between about one million and half a million years ago, however, humans were beginning to colonize more temperate northern environments. If there is any answer as to why they would begin to move out of the tropical environments they had

10,000 years ago	First documented appearance of bows and arrows
14,000 years ago	Appearance of fish weirs
20–12,000 years ago	Appearance of Mesolithic and Epipaleolithic industries
32,000 years ago	Neandertals become extinct
36,000 years ago	Appearance of the Chatelperronian Upper Paleolithic industry
40,000 years ago	Appearance of the Aurignacian Upper Paleolithic industry
50–45,000 years ago	Appearance of Upper Paleolithic industries
60–50,000 years ago	*Homo sapiens* begins to colonize Australia
100,000 years ago	Beginning of radiation of *Homo sapiens* from Africa to Eurasia
130,000 years ago	Neandertals well-established in Western Eurasia
160,000 years ago	Appearance of early forms of anatomically modern humans (*Homo sapiens*) in Africa
230,000 years ago	Appearance of early forms of Neandertals (*Homo neanderthalensis*) in Europe
300,000 years ago	Appearance of Middle Paleolithic industries
800,000 years ago	*Homo erectus* grade present in Spain
1.7–1.2 million years ago	*Homo erectus* grade present in Israel, Central Europe, and China
1.7 million years ago	Beginning of radiation of *Homo erectus* grade from Africa to Eurasia
1.8 million years ago	Appearance of handaxes (bifaces) of the Lower Paleolithic
1.8 million years ago	Appearance of *Homo erectus* grade of hominins

evolved in, it probably lies in the nature of the hunting-gathering band. Ethnographic studies suggest that human hunting-gathering bands with primitive technologies need large areas to support themselves, and also that one response to growing populations is for bands to split and for "daughter" groups to establish themselves in open territories on the original group's boundary.

Hundreds of thousands of years of this process of band division, coupled with slow evolution in the efficiencies of tools, would have populated the warmer ranges of the

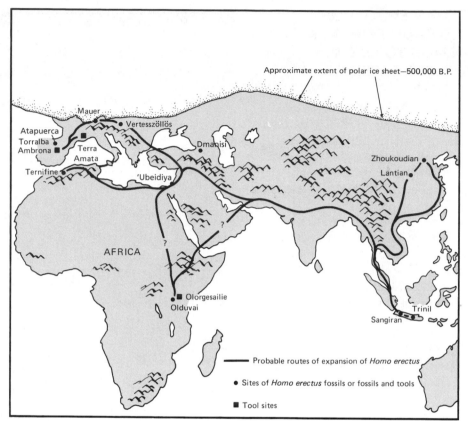

FIGURE 4.1   Distribution of *Homo erectus* sites. *Homo erectus* was the first hominin to invade temperate climates. Land bridges, now submerged, facilitated *Homo erectus* movements.

Old World and positioned human groups for colonization of more temperate latitudes (Figure 4.1).

Let us begin with the problem of which hominin actually did make the first forays into the Middle East and Asia, and then into the north. The most likely candidate would seem to be the hominin that, until recently, was commonly known as *Homo erectus*. Individuals generally classed as *Homo erectus* averaged just over five feet feet tall (about 1.5 meters), walked fully erect (though its body and legs differed in various proportions and shapes from ours), and had a cranial capacity that ranged between about 850 and 1,300 cm³.[4] Compared to us, these hominins had low foreheads, large brow ridges, thick cranial bones, and almost no chins (Figure 4.2).

Alas, physical anthropologists have had a great crisis of faith with regard to the species designation of "*Homo erectus*":

> Does *Homo erectus* exist as a true taxon or should it be sunk into *Homo sapiens*? Is it a palaeospecies that exists . . . as a segment of the line that emerged from *Homo habilis* and gave rise to *Homo sapiens*? Is *Homo erectus* an extinct form that had no part to play in the

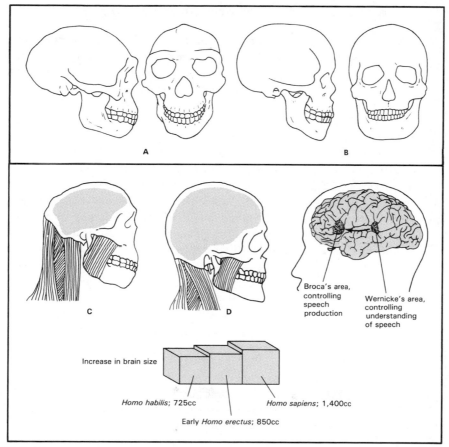

Broca's area, controlling speech production

Wernicke's area, controlling understanding of speech

Increase in brain size

Homo habilis; 725cc

Early *Homo erectus*; 850cc

Homo sapiens; 1,400cc

FIGURE 4.2   The *Homo erectus* skull (A) was long and low, with heavy brow ridges, no chin, and protruding jaws, compared to modern humans (B). In the transition from *Homo erectus* (C) to modern humans (D), the brain enlarged and the muscles controlling the head and neck were changed.

evolution of *Homo sapiens*? Is *Homo erectus* a good example of a "stasis event" . . . with little or no change in its form during its existence? Is there a clear cut example of *Homo erectus* in the European fossil record of man? Finally, are the Asian forms so far removed from the evolution of *Homo sapiens* in Africa to call into question the existence of *Homo erectus sensu stricto* in Africa at all?[5]

In view of these and other problems, some anthropologists have hypothesized that *Homo erectus* consisted of only the east Asian hominins who branched off from the main *Homo* line in Africa at about 1.5 million years ago, and that the African humans of this period should be called *Homo ergaster*.[6] Others classify almost all Asian, African, and European hominins of between about 1.5 and 0.5 million years ago as *Homo erectus*.

In what follows here, all of the humans who lived between about 1.5 and 0.5 million years ago are called *Homo erectus*, but this designation is likely to change as these taxonomies are refined.

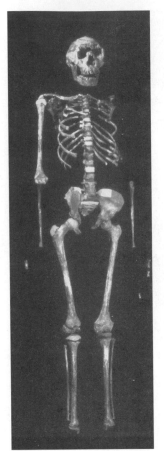

FIGURE 4.3 The Nariko-
tome boy (KNM-WT 15000)
from West Turkana, Kenya,
a *Homo ergaster* hominin
(*Homo erectus* grade).

Early Radiation and Migrations of *Homo*

By 1.5 million years ago, "culture" by any definition was present. Hominins with brainsizes on the low end of our own range had a stone tool repertoire indicating they could produce different forms for different purposes—often out of materials that had to be brought many kilometers to the place where the tools were made or used.

The 11-year-old boy who died on the western shore of Lake Turkana in northern Kenya about 1.6 million years ago, and whose skull and nearly intact skeleton (known as KNM-WT 15000) represent one of the best preserved and earliest *Homo erectus* individuals, seems to tell us much about our ancestors of this age (Figure 4.3). He was 1.6 meters (5 feet, 3 inches) tall—taller than many modern 11-year-olds. His cranial capacity, however, was 880 c^3, somewhat more than half our size, and his brow ridges were very thick. His skeleton appears very similar to ours, though, and this suggests that our ancestors developed a body much like ours long before their mentalities equaled ours.

No stone tools were found with this individual, but Acheulian-style (named after the French site at St. Acheul) stone tools associated with *Homo erectus* in Europe at a much later date (c. 600,000 years ago at the earliest) were apparently already present in many other East African sites more than a million years ago.[7] For example, at Koobi Fora, on Lake Turkana in Kenya, *Homo* remains and animal bones with what seem to be butchering marks have been found in substantial numbers, and there are small clusters of stone tools, some in concentrations about 5 to 10 m in diameter with from about 10 to 100 artifacts.[8]

The hand-axes and other stone tools associated with the early African *Homo erectus* are a major improvement on the tools associated with the australopiths of the previous million years, and this developing technology may have enabled hominins to radiate from warmer latitudes into colder, more demanding climates. The "Acheulian hand-axe" may not seem like a marvelous bit of technological advance, but it has several features that seem to reflect human intellectual evolution (Figure 4.4). First, it requires more processing—more actual steps of manufacture—than did the Oldowan chopper-style tools. Again, this might not seem like some major technological breakthrough, but in a rather abstract sense the Acheulian hand-axe requires that the maker "see" the possibilities of striking off numerous flakes—a sort of intuitive feel for the physics and geometry involved. Also, Acheulian hand-axes came in a variety of sizes and shapes. As we shall see, in some cases the best use of basalt, quartzite, flint, and other hard stones is to knock off a series of flakes, use them until the edges dull, and then strike off more flakes. In such a substantial tool it may have been functionally efficient and effective to get the proportions as close to the ideal size as possible. If one is simply going to smash open a cow femur for marrow, any rock not too heavy to lift or too small to transmit much force would be adequate, but one interpretation of Acheulian hand-axes suggests that they were beginning to converge on functionally optimal proportions and overall size.

What these functions were, however, remains unclear. Possibly these tools were used for a great variety of tasks, or they may have simply been cores to produce sharp-edged flakes; other archaeologists think they are specialized tools. Many are too heavy to have been hafted (attached to a spear or other piece of wood) easily, yet they are often found in association with animal bones. It is barely possible that this association with animal bones is accidental, but it seems more likely that one function of this tool was as a primary butchering tool.

Since Acheulian hand-axes are usually found with other types of stone tools (and were presumably used with a wide variety of wood and bone tools that did not preserve), and although they may not have been the "Swiss Army" knives of their generation, they were certainly an important tool. Their distribution is particularly impressive. They have been found (Figure 4.5) over most of western Europe, Africa, and India, and are also occasionally reported from China.

The economy of all humans of this time period remains more a matter of speculation than hard evidence and continues to be the source of sharply different interpretations. Some think *Homo erectus* was primarily a hunter and that the demands of the hunting way of life partially "drove" human evolution toward ourselves; others doubt *Homo erectus* did much more than scavenging and opportunistic hunting.

An interesting site in this dispute is Olorgesailie, near Nairobi, Kenya (Figure 4.6). Here many small concentrations of stone tools and bones are spread out along a peninsula in

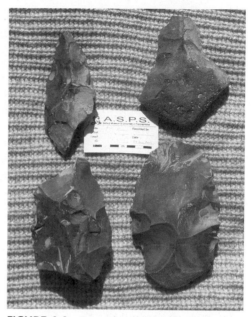

FIGURE 4.4 Examples of Acheulian hand-axes from the Abydos Survey for Paleolithic Sites project, Egypt.

an extinct lake. Most of the tools are cleavers and hand-axes, and some show considerable chipping and blunting wear. Mixed in with them are bones from several species of large mammals, including a hippopotamus and, curiously, 63 individuals of an extinct species of baboon (but no hominins). Potassium-argon dating of the Olorgesailie formation yields an age of about 480,000 years.[9]

Glyn Isaac suggested that ancient hominins encircled a troop of baboons here, perhaps at night, spooked them by making a lot of noise, and then systematically clubbed them to death as they tried to escape. Pat Shipman, too, has interpreted this site as the result of a hunting episode.[10] If Olorgesailie is a case of hominins hunting baboons, as some suggest, we may have been underestimating the linguistic and physical prowess of *Homo erectus*. It is instructive to try to imagine oneself about two-thirds our size, going out at night with stones and clubs to kill 63 baboons.

But Lewis Binford has questioned whether Olorgesailie—and most other early hominin sites—were places where hominins killed and butchered animals.[11] He suggests that the evidence from Olduvai and Olorgesailie may well be remains left by hominins who scavenged the kills of other animals, mainly for bone marrow, which they obtained by smashing bones with stone tools. He sees no evidence that early hominins shared food in complex patterns like humans or that they foraged from home bases.[12]

Again, the non-anthropologist might wonder why anthropologists take so seriously these debates about how people made a living in Africa half a million years ago, but from a certain perspective, we really *are* what we eat, and not only that, as modern humans we are very much a product of the natural selective forces that applied over the millions of years of our past and especially to such basic matters as to how we and our ancestors got our food.

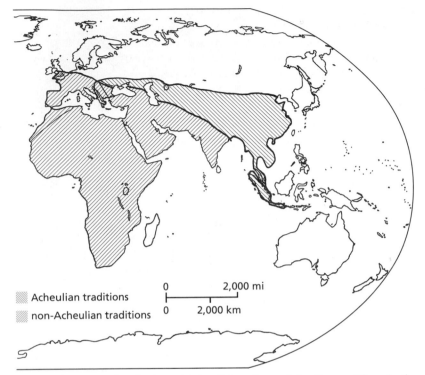

Acheulian traditions

non-Acheulian traditions

FIGURE 4.5   The distribution of Acheulian and non-Acheulian traditions in the Old World.

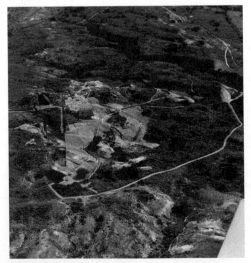

FIGURE 4.6   Aerial view of Olorgesailie, Kenya, an area with Early and Middle Stone Age sites.

The Invasion of Temperate Ecozones

One of the most interesting discoveries about these early *Homo*, however, is that some groups of them left Africa, apparently very soon after they first appeared there.

Finds from Israel, the Republic of Georgia, Pakistan, China, Java, and Spain indicate that hominins were distributed across the warmer regions of the world as early as 1.7 million years ago. The lowered seas of the Pleistocene would have facilitated this, opening rich coastal niches far out into the Southeast Asian archipelagos.

At various times in the past million years the climate of northern Europe and Asia was much warmer than it is at present. So warm were areas of Germany and France about 800,000 or 900,000 years ago that monkeys swarmed through dense forests there. But at other times the icy fingers of glaciers drew down out of the Alps and other mountain ranges, and great expanses of northern Europe were tundra.

One can imagine human groups probing northward during warmer periods—some of which lasted tens of thousands of years—and then their descendants being faced with equally long-term cooling trends. Probably no individual was conscious of the change, since it was so gradual, but kilometer by kilometer, year by year, they would have had to retreat or adapt. For our ancestors to invade the more northern climates, and to survive there during periods of expanding glaciers, would have required some form of clothing, seasonal hunting, and perhaps the use of fire.[13] If these early hominins had the use of fire, it could be used for keeping warm, cooking food, and evicting bears and other carnivores from caves and rock shelters—the safest and warmest places to live in northern latitudes.

Climate has had a strong impact on people physically and culturally until very recently, when modern technology began to moderate its direct effects. In the Pleistocene, moving into northern climates depended on people becoming whiter and stouter over many tens of millennia, through natural selection: Up to 80 percent of the energy value of food goes simply to maintain body temperatures, and it is an inescapable fact of physics that spheres lose heat more slowly than any another shape of equal volume. Even with the pervasive migrations of people during the last century, the relationship between body shape and mean temperature—as epitomized by the East African Watusi and the Arctic Inuit ("Eskimo")—is strong.[14]

The white skins of northern peoples have to do most directly with their dependency on vitamin D, which is present in some foods but can also be synthesized in humans by the action of sunlight on skin. But whiter shades of skin are also more susceptible to cancer, acne, and psoriasis than are darker tones, so for northern Europeans the selection for whiter skins—necessary to maintain vitamin D production in the long dark northern winters—was a mixed blessing.

The problems of living in northern climates go beyond simply keeping warm. In winter most of the plants suitable for human consumption die, and an animal like ourselves has only two ways to get food: store it—or hunt, fish, or scavenge other animals who *can* find suitable nutrition. On the African savannas and in other warm environments, women supply most of the food in hunting and gathering cultures, and even pregnant women, children, and the aged can gather much of their own food all year long. But such self-reliance would not have been possible in northern latitudes, where snow covered the ground for five to six months of the year. Clearly, strong social systems in which food-sharing and cooperative efforts were common would be important in adapting to these demanding temperate environments.[15]

The best evidence for hominins outside of Africa before one million years ago is found in four widely separated areas: the Republic of Georgia, China, Java, and Israel.

Ongoing work at the site of Dmanisi in the Republic of Georgia has yielded a treasure trove of early hominin remains.[16] The fossils (Figure 4.7) are very similar to the African *Homo ergaster* rather than Asian hominins. Numerous animal bones (which help provide a relative date for the site) and some stone tools similar to the Oldowan industry (chopper-chopping tradition) were also found, but Dmanisi is not a "living site"

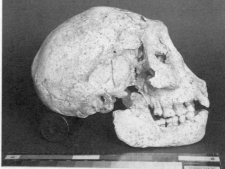
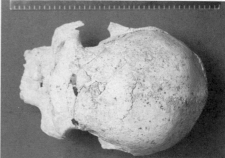
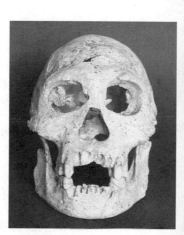

FIGURE 4.7   One of the *Homo ergaster* hominins from Dmanisi, Republic of Georgia, dating to about 1.7 million years ago.

—it represents materials that were redeposited from elsewhere in the landscape. Perhaps the most surprising discovery is the age of the site—the fossils are in deposits that are age bracketed between 1.77 and 1.85 million years ago. Dates for the underlying basalt layer (1.85 million years ago) were obtained using the potassium argon method and paleomagnetism (see chapter 2), which measures the magnetic fields of strata of rocks. The earth's magnetic field is known to have reversed polarity several times and the irregular timing of these events is well established. The overlying sediments at Dmanisi yielded paleomagnetic information that can be correlated to a change in the earth's magnetic poles from normal to reversed polarity at 1.77 million years ago.

The recent discovery of the northern Chinese site of Majuangou shows that hominins were present in this colder and drier area by 1.66 million years ago—thus making this site nearly as old as the evidence from Dmanisi.[17] No hominin fossils were found, but Majuangou was a lakeside site with stone tools such as cores and flakes (a chopper industry similar to the Oldowan), as well as animal bones including horse, hyena, rhinoceros, deer, gazelle, and ostrich. Some of the horse and deer bones were broken open with stone tools to extract the nutritious marrow.

The *Homo erectus* remains found in Java by Dubois are also comparably old. After redating the sediments where the finds were supposedly made, plus some sediments that had adhered to the fossils themselves, de Vos and colleagues are now confident that these remains date to about 1.7 million years ago.[18] But there will always be questions about these dates because the exact location these finds were made is not known with absolute certainty, and even sediments adhering to fossils might have come from older formations that had nothing to do with the fossils themselves. One of the most frustrating things about the record of *Homo erectus* in Java is that not a single fossil of this hominin has been found there in good association with stone tools.

'Ubeidiya (Figure 4.8), 3 km south of the Sea of Galilee in what is now Israel, comprised about 14 distinct archaeological assemblages, all probably dating to no later than 640,000 years ago, and perhaps much earlier, before 1.2 million years ago (and some dates on animal remains are as high as 2 million years).[19] The tools found here seem very similar to those from Middle and Upper Bed II at Olduvai Gorge, being mainly choppers, spheroids (rounded stones), hand-axes, and used flakes. Richard Klein notes that at different times in the Pleistocene, the eastern Mediterranean can be considered part of Africa—in the sense that the climate and animals there very closely resembled nearby areas of Africa.[20]

It is clear that early hominins were able to inhabit a great diversity of environments—they were a successful genus, expanding into new niches. The most conservative view and probably the most accurate one is that hominins evolved bipedalism, then tool-using and other cultural behavior in Africa, and then spread out along the warmer margins of the Old World in a long slow process of population growth

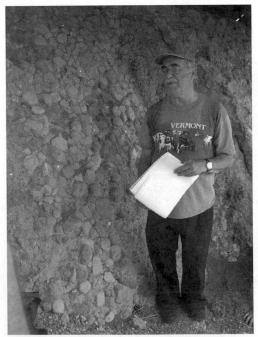

FIGURE 4.8 Ofer Bar-Yosef at the Lower Paleolithic site of 'Ubeidiya, Israel. Note the extremely tilted stratigraphic deposit.

and very gradual movements, as groups split and moved short distances away from one another, until hominins could be found from southern Africa to Java.

After one million years ago, there is widespread evidence of hominins in many areas outside of Africa, including, for the first time, in western Europe.

If *Homo* had reached northern China well before a million years ago, there seems to be no obvious environmental reason why they could not have invaded southern temperate Europe as well. Klein notes that some scholars believe that humans colonized most of temperate Europe only after

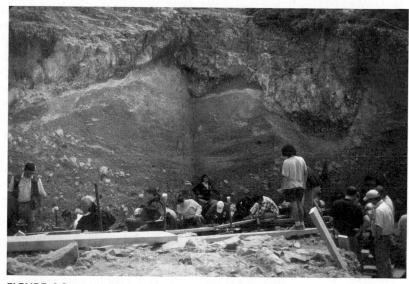

FIGURE 4.9   Excavations at the Lower Paleolithic Gran Dolina site at Atapuerca, Spain.

500,000 years ago, but recent human fossils found in Spain, at Cueva Victoria and Gran Dolina, "suggest that humans in fact arrived in Europe nearer to 1 million years ago."[21] At Gran Dolina (a cave site at a place called Atapuerca; Figure 4.9), for example, Eudald Carbonell and other Spanish scholars found what could be the oldest known European humans.[22] About 36 human bones, including cranial fragments, teeth, jaw, hand, and foot bones were recovered, representing at least four individuals, including an adolescent and a child. These fossils' ages were estimated using paleomagnetic dating. The Atapuerca fossils were found just below a magnetic reversal that is known to have happened 780,000 years ago.

If this date is accurate—and many scholars consider it to be—these fossils raise many questions. The bones do not seem to be very similar to *Homo erectus*. The Spanish researchers who found the fossils say they do not closely resemble any known form of human but could represent ancestors of the Neandertals (see later in this chapter). The Atapuerca fossils may represent one of many unsuccessful attempts to colonize Europe, as time after time people migrated into the area but did not persist, in the face of the severe winters and other challenges of Pleistocene Europe.

Another well-dated early European site is Isernia La Pineta, in central Italy, where volcanic deposits overlie deposits of stone tools associated with animal bones. Stone choppers, flakes, and scrapers were found here amidst bones from elephants, bison, and other animals, and the animals and volcanic deposits indicate a date of about 500,000 years ago and possibly much earlier.[23] A human thigh bone from Boxgrove in southern England has also been dated to about 500,000 years ago, and various other sites in Europe date to this age. For people to have colonized this far north, into England by 500,000 years ago, we might expect that they began to move out of the Mediterranean area by 600,000 years ago or earlier, and it is certainly possible, given the vagaries of preservation, that people were in northern Europe in substantial numbers by 700,000 years ago, or earlier. But based on the available evidence it seems likely people did not regularly and significantly inhabit northern temperate Europe until about 500,000 years ago.

If people were in Java 1.7 million years ago, however, we might expect dense concentrations along the routes out of Africa and along the southern coasts of Asia that date to this same period, but there is little evidence of this. A few stone tools found at Ban Mae Tha, Thailand, appear to date to 700,000 years ago, and the Lan-t'ien and Q'en-Xia-wo sites in central China contained fragments of *Homo erectus* that date to about 600,000 years ago, but there simply is little other credible evidence of human occupation of these more southern areas before about 900,000 years ago. It is possible that such factors as the sea level rise at the end of the Pleistocene drowned most of the pre-1-million-year-old sites along the southern approaches to Java, but it is also possible that the 1.7-million-year-old dates for the Indonesian *Homo erectus* hominins are wrong.

An important site for analyzing human colonization of temperate environments is Zhoukoudian (literally "Dragon Bone Hill"), a cave located 43 km southwest of Beijing. Using explosives, excavators managed to blast out and examine thousands of cubic meters of collapsed cave debris at the site between 1927 and 1937, and these excavations and later research revealed the remains of more than 40 hominins, as well as over 100,000 stone tools, countless animal bones, and many hearths and ash layers, all well stratified in a deposit that is an astonishing 50 m deep. Not all this was cultural debris—cave bears and other animals alternated with hominins in occupying the cave, and these other animals probably brought in many of the animals. But Zhoukoudian has more superimposed occupational layers than any other known *Homo erectus* site. Analysis of the fauna and hominins and various forms of dating (including fission track, uranium-thorium, paleomagnetism, and thermoluminescene) have produced conflicting age estimates. In a recent summary[24] of these dates, Wu Rukang and Jia Lampo conclude that the uppermost layers date to 230,000 years ago and the earliest levels to about 700,000 years ago.

The 14 skullcaps, 6 skull bones, 10 jaw fragments, 147 teeth, and assorted arm, leg, and hand bones found at Zhoukoudian all appear to have come from *Homo erectus*. Brain volumes average about 1,040 cm^3 and range between about 775 and 1,300 cm^3—somewhat larger than the *Homo erectus* from Java—and teeth sizes fall between ourselves and australopiths (actually, they are only slightly larger than contemporary native Australian populations). Based on the few leg-bone fragments recovered, it is estimated that the Zhoukoudian hominins averaged about 5 feet, 1 inch in height—which may seem short, but is only an inch or two less than the average height of most people of just a few hundred years ago.

Wu and Lampo note that every *Homo erectus* upper incisor found in China, including those from Zhoukoutian, Yuanmou, Yunxian, and Hexian, is "shovel-shaped"—that is, in cross section the tooth is curved like a shovel. They note that this feature is found in nearly as high frequencies in living Mongoloid populations, whereas it is at much lower frequencies elsewhere, and thus they conclude that the Chinese *Homo erectus* are the genetic ancestors of contemporary Chinese. This point is discussed at greater length later.

About 100,000 stone tools were retrieved from Zhoukoudian, most of them simple flakes and choppers made from quartz, but with some more specialized tools, as well, including flakes, drills, and augers. Over the course of the site's occupation, the simple chopper tools of the 700,000-year-old initial occupation were replaced by a variety of tools that included retouch and prepared core flaking.[25]

Zhoukoudian may have been a base camp from which hominins hunted and to which they brought back their kills to be cooked and eaten. The site includes hundreds of thousands of animal bones, mainly from deer, but also from elephants, rhinoceroses, beavers, bison, boars, and horses. The large quantities of charred hackberry seeds found at Zhoukoudian suggest that they were a dietary staple, and pollen analysis indicates that nuts from walnut, hazelnut, and pine would have been available. Such finds remind us that we see only a distorted picture of early hominin diets: They probably ate vastly greater quantities of plant foods than meat, but only when they used fire to cook plants do we find the traces of vegetable foods, and although pollen can show that some plants were available, many plant foods simply were not preserved in archaeologically recognizable forms.

Not a single skull from this site had an attached face, and the base of each skull was broken, perhaps to get at the brains. But numerous scholars have questioned the idea that these bone alterations indicate cannibalism.[26] Arens, for example, also rejects the notion that cannibalism was a common practice for very long in any culture, ancient or recent.[27] He may well be right, since ecologically, systematic cannibalism is a poor food-procurement strategy.[28] Compared to almost any other animals, people are hard to catch in relation to the amount of food they represent, and one risks depleting the stock extremely quickly if cannibalism is at all frequent.

Some of these questions about the Zhoukoudian humans could be answered if we still had their bones, but all the hominin remains disappeared while being transferred from Beijing to an American ship during the Japanese invasion of China prior to World War II. Although there are some mysterious indications that they have survived, to date no progress has been made in locating any of the fossils.[29] Fortunately, at the time of their discovery the great German anatomist Franz Weidenreich made excellent plaster casts of them all and described them in superlative detail.

Perhaps our best evidence of European adaptations hundreds of thousands of years ago comes from Torralba and Ambrona, located about 1.5 km apart in a deep valley 150 km northeast of Madrid (Figure 4.10). Given the many difficulties of discriminating between human scavenging and hunting, no single site can be taken as a convincing evidence of the general nature of early human life in Europe. But many regard Torralba and Ambrona as evidence that at least some groups in Middle Pleistocene Europe engaged in big-game hunting. Excavations at Torralba in the early 1960s by F. Clark Howell exposed about 300 m² of stratified archaeological deposits, from which were

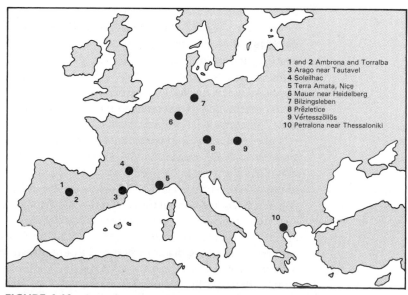

FIGURE 4.10   Some important *Homo erectus* sites in Europe.

collected hundreds of pollen samples, several thousand stone tools, and countless animal bones (but no human remains). The kinds of pollen found in these remains have convinced some scholars that Torralba dates to about 400,000 years ago, but some think it is only about 200,000 years old. Pollen analysis indicates the area was a cool, swampy valley when the site was inhabited.[30]

The remains of at least 30 elephants were found at Torralba, as well as about 25 deer, 25 horses, 10 wild oxen, and several rhinoceroses. The original interpretation of activities at this site suggested that most of the animals here were killed and butchered by hominins, based on the presence of disarticulated skeletons, the lack of elephant skulls and other meat-bearing bones which could have been carried elsewhere, and charcoal—possible evidence of setting fires to drive game—found mixed with bones and stone tools.

The process of driving animals into the swamps and killing and butchering them would have been quite a spectacle, with great clouds of smoke, shrieking, demented animals, and running, shouting hominins. But how could these ill-equipped people have killed these huge animals? Not a single obvious stone spear-point was found at the site, but Freeman suggests that the animals were either stoned to death with the many fragments of rock found amid the bone or dispatched with wooden spears.[31] It is a bit difficult to envisage any human, let alone *Homo erectus*, about to stone three or four large elephants to death, or to kill them with long-since-rotted wooden stabbing spears,[32] but if they did, it would have been a fantastic Hitchcockian scene played out in this Spanish valley hundreds of thousands of years ago.

As intriguing a picture as this ancient hunt may be, our better understanding of taphonomic processes in the formation of sites (see chapter 3) has led to a reinterpretation of Torralba. Some of the patterns in the disarticulated bones are almost certainly the result of the actions of slow-moving water, and at least some of the smashed and split animal bones are due to scavenging animals such as hyenas. The widely scattered charcoal is most likely due to a naturally occurring brush fire, not a fire set to drive game into the swamps.

That said, the stratigraphy at Torralba is complex, and the site may represent not one, but many different hunting episodes for some of the animals found there.[33] Those animal bones with no signs of butchering may be natural deaths or deaths due to nonhuman predation. The few animals with evidence of butchering may be what remains to us from those occasional hunting episodes, added to the "background noise" of natural deaths and other predators in the landscape.

Another important central European site is Vértesszöllös, a rock quarry west of Budapest, Hungary. A recent series of uranium dates put the site at about 185,000 years B.P.,[34] but it could be as old as 350,000. When the site was first occupied, it was on the banks of some hot springs, and several layers of human occupational debris have been found near these springs. Excavations in the 1960s uncovered about 3,000 stone tools, many smashed and burned animal bones, and the occipital bone from one hominin and a few teeth from another. The estimated cranial capacity of between 1,115 and 1,437 cm³ is large for a *Homo erectus*, and some consider this fossil to be an archaic form of *Homo sapiens*. No hearths have been found at the site, but burned bones here indicate the use of fire.

Nearly all the evidence reviewed to this point seems clear in indicating that some form of early *Homo* left Africa and colonized Europe and Asia between 1.7 and 0.5 million years ago; and most scholars see patterns of regional evolution, with some commonalties but also some differences appearing in human groups as they made their living in highly varied ways, exploiting small areas in a complex mosaic of adaptations that reached from England to southern Africa to Indonesia.

This consensus of scholarly opinion on our ancestors up to about 300,000 years ago evaporates, however, when the question of "what happened next?" is considered.

HOMO SAPIENS: MODELS OF ORIGINS

In their tool use, social systems, and economies, *Homo* of several hundred thousand years ago, as we know them from Zhoukoudian, Torralba-Ambrona, and the other sites described in the previous section, seem to have been similar to modern hunters and gatherers in many ways, yet there is something alien about these creatures. We look for artifacts expressing ritual or complex symbolism, but not a single figurine,[35] wall painting, rock carving, or even an elaborately made stone tool can be securely attributed to *Homo erectus*. Later, beginning at least 40,000 years ago, people made exquisitely crafted stone tools, some so delicately worked that even moderate use would ruin them—tools that must have been made in part simply for the pleasure of creating something beautiful. But the tools of *Homo erectus* are undeviatingly simple, efficient, utilitarian objects.

Perhaps even more revealing, there are no known *Homo erectus* burials or ritual dispositions of corpses. For at least the last 30,000 years, death has almost everywhere been an occasion for the outpouring of human emotion, and even the simplest hunters and gatherers during this span usually disposed of their dead by digging a hole and placing a few stone tools or bits of shell in with the body; but not a single *Homo erectus* anywhere in the world appears to have been even intentionally buried, let alone sent off to the next world with a few provisions and expressions of goodwill.

These various absences of stylistic behavior among *Homo erectus* can be interpreted in several different ways. *Homo erectus*, with his brain about two-thirds the size of our own, may simply have lacked the mental equipment to generalize and symbolize his experiences as we do. *Homo erectus*'s language skills, in particular, may have been quite limited.[36] On the other hand, *Homo erectus* may have had the potential for stylistic, religious, and social impulses but lived in circumstances that did not elicit such expressions. As Randall White has observed, the ethnographic record of material forms of representation like that of Pleistocene "art" suggests that these aesthetic expressions are about political authority and social distinctions,[37] and it may be that the social conditions in which such distinctions are important were just beginning to appear in the Middle and Late Pleistocene.

It is difficult to overstate the importance of the evolution of the capacity for aesthetic, ritual, and social feelings, for as we will see, it was precisely these mental characteristics that made possible the rise of great civilizations. Thus, we are particularly concerned in this chapter with the conditions under which these feelings first appeared (as reflected in the archaeological record) and with their concurrent important cultural developments. Richard Klein,[38] for example, suggests that the "explosion" of art about 30,000 years ago, in the form of figurines and highly stylized stone tools, as well as other evident cultural change, reflects the migrations of anatomically modern peoples throughout the world—the first people, he suggests, to have these mental powers.

The obvious question is: How were our ancestors changed by time and circumstance in these highly significant ways? To consider this question, we must turn to the contrasting hypotheses about modern human origins.

"I can't believe that!" said Alice. "Can't you?" the Queen said. . . . "Try again: draw a long breath, and shut your eyes." Alice laughed. "There's no use trying," she said: "one can't believe impossible things." "I daresay you haven't had much practice," said the Queen. "When I was your age, I always did it for half-an-hour a day. Why, sometimes I've believed as many as six impossible things before breakfast."

Lewis Carroll[39]

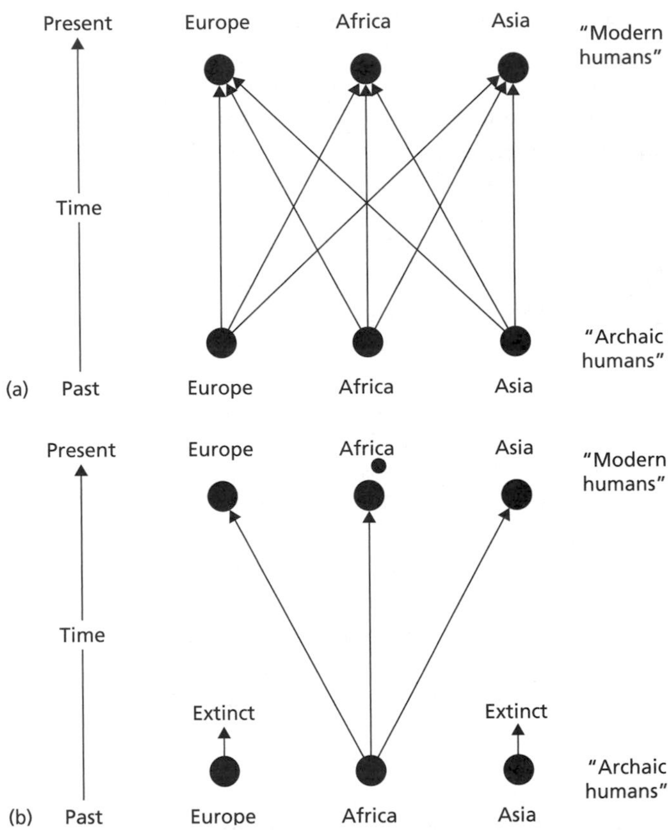

FIGURE 4.11 Two models for the origins of modern humans. a) Multiregional model. This model proposes that the ancestry of modern humans is from both African ancestors and archaic human populations outside Africa beginning about 150,000 years ago. b) Replacement or out-of-Africa model. This model proposes that the ancestry of modern humans is only from African ancestors about 150,000 years ago. All archaic humans outside of Africa became extinct and African modern humans replaced these archaic populations in areas outside of Africa.

The major contemporary "models" (that is, sets of linked assumptions, hypotheses, and interpretations of data) about how we changed from early African hominins into us, *Homo sapiens sapiens*, all require one to believe scenarios that, if not exactly impossible to believe, do require some dramatic leaps of faith.

Most models of modern human origins are variants of two basic contrasting hypotheses. One of these, which has become the majority view, is described variously as the *African Origins, Total Replacement, Noah's Ark,* or *Eve* model.[40] It stipulates that modern humans evolved first and only in Africa and only a few hundred thousand years ago or less, and then migrated to the rest of the world, replacing all other hominin forms, and with little or no genetic interchange with these other forms (Figure 4.11).

An alternative model, commonly known as the *Continuity, Multiregional Evolution,* or *Candelabra* model,[41] traces all modern populations back to what was ultimately an African source (but to a time when people lived only there), through a web whose genetic contributions to the present varied from region to region and from time to time (see Figure 4.11).[42] Thus, this model proposes that archaic humans in Africa and outside Africa contributed to the ancestry of modern humans. The basic idea of this hypothesis is that sometime between about one and two million years ago a generic *Homo* ancestor of ours spread out across the warmer latitudes of Africa, the

Middle East, Asia, and possibly the southernmost fringe of Europe. With the passage of the millennia these groups began to diverge somewhat as they adapted to local and different environments, but across the whole range of *Homo* they were evolving toward *Homo sapiens* as a result of "genic exchange" (i.e., gene flow through mating and migrations) that connected all human groups to some extent; and because they were under similar evolutionary selective forces, as generalized hunter-foragers, they all emerged in the last 30,000 years as one species, *Homo sapiens sapiens*—but with some of the physical differences that distinguish many modern Europeans, Africans, and Asians from each other.

These different views of the origins of modern humans have long histories. Louis Leakey, for example, argued[43] an African origins hypothesis in the 1960s against the then-predominate multiregional view, such as that advanced in the 1930s by Franz Weidenreich.[44] Weidenreich suggested that modern humans exhibit physical features that reflect continued gene flow throughout the world, but from at least four centers where the genetic continuity was sufficient to produce the differences observable in today's major "races."[45]

These competing models require some difficult assumptions. Since relatively few nonhuman species have evolved from one species into another over a wide range in a "convergent" fashion, for example, why would we expect humans to be different? One answer might be that if humans actually did evolve in the convergent worldwide pattern imagined by Weidenreich it was because they all shared a similar ecological niche—that is, "culture." If we ask how many migrants per generation would be required to sustain the gene flow to keep regional evolution convergent, estimates range as low as just one migrant per generation, but many scholars doubt that migrations and matings and convergent evolution were enough to produce *Homo sapiens sapiens* at about the same time and in about the same form in such widely separated areas as, for example, northern China and southern Africa.

This presumed pattern of convergent human evolution over a wide area and through great spans of time remains a problem for the Multiregional Evolution model, but, as we shall see, the African Origins model also requires some assumptions.

Whatever the ultimate accuracy of these models, different scholars using the same data have come to very different conclusions about which of these models best fits the data. Resolution of intellectual debates sometimes comes as much from a change in perspective (e.g., Darwin) as from additional data. Fundamental research continues on the nature of evolutionary processes, and this research, along with discoveries of new fossils and tools, will probably resolve these debates.

Molecular Biological Evidence of Modern Human Origins

The skulls and skeletons of our ancestors may seem the most direct evidence to assess hypotheses about human origins, but these bones are usually just mineral casts of formerly living individuals, and arguments about the meaning of subtle differences in size and shape of their features are endless and largely irresolvable. An alternative approach is to work backward—in effect, to look at today's people and see how their degree of biological relatedness fits various ideas about our origins.

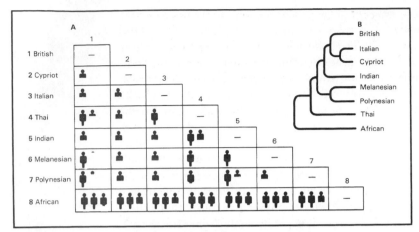

FIGURE 4.12 (A) Analyses of DNA have been used to suggest genetic distances among contemporary groups of people. In this figure the genetic distances between groups is based on a sample of 600 individuals from eight groups. Between any two groups, the fewer the symbols the shorter the genetic distance and the closer the presumed relationship. In (B) these data are arranged in a family tree. These data suggest all modern humans are genetic descendants of one small inbred group of prehistoric Africans.

Figure 4.12 presents one such form of analysis: It expresses the degree of biological similarity among contemporary peoples of the world. How did such different degrees of relatedness appear, and when, and what do these differences "mean"?

It is an inescapable fact of genetics that all the people alive in the world are genetically related and that at some point an individual existed whom we can all claim as an ancestor. The only points of debate are how long ago that ancestor lived, and where. Some scholars have argued on the basis of genetic evidence that all of us alive today have a common female ancestor who lived less than about 200,000 years ago. This African Eve model is based on the study of DNA taken from the mitochondria, which are features in human cells where energy to keep the cell functioning is produced. The term "mtDNA" stands for mitochondrial DNA; mtDNA is different from nuclear DNA in that it is all in the mitochondria of the mother's egg and therefore is not affected by the sperm's contribution to genetic inheritance as implanted during fertilization. Thus, mtDNA is inherited only through the mother. MtDNA is subject to random mutations at a higher rate than nuclear DNA, and these are expressed as minor mistakes in copying the genetic code that are then passed on to the next generation. Thus, we would not even expect two people from, for example, the same small isolated group of hunter-foragers in, for example, highland New Guinea to have identical mtDNA. And we would expect that differences in mitochondrial DNA would increase the longer any two people are separated in terms of a common ancestor, since the minor genetic mutations in mtDNA accumulate over time.

An analogy to accumulation of changes in mtDNA is the fate of last names in many Western cultures, where a child's last name usually comes only from the father. If a man does not have children or has only female children, his individual perpetuation of that last name is "lost" (although, of course, there are usually many others with that last name). Similarly, mtDNA is "lost" if a woman has no children or has only sons.[46]

In an early study to test the relatedness of contemporary human groups, Cann, Stoneking, and Wilson collected the placentas of 147 women in the United States, Asia, Europe, the Middle East, New Guinea, and Australia, and then separated the mtDNA from these samples and compared them. They concluded that everyone living today is descended from an African woman, a "mitochondrial Eve," who lived between 140,000 and 290,000 years ago—probably about 200,000 years ago. They identified Africa as the home of this woman because mtDNA is most variable in today's Africa, and thus these mtDNA differences appear to have been accumulating longest in Africa. If the estimate of about 200,000 years ago for a common maternal ancestor is correct, it is highly unlikely that the people who lived in Europe and Asia before about 200,000 years had anything to do with us, in terms of our biological ancestry. Since this study, other researchers have increased the sample of people studied and used various other methods of calculating genetic similarity (reviewed by Aiello[47]), and some have concluded that, indeed, the evidence shows that everyone in the world today is descended from a few Africans who lived a few hundred thousand years ago.

But many scholars have questioned these mtDNA and related studies. For these estimates to be accurate, at least three things must be true: (1) The generation time (i.e., the average number of years between mother and daughter's ages) must be accurately estimated; (2) the molecular "clock," in the sense of the rate at which genetic differences accumulate, must run equally as fast for us, the *Hominini*, as for other mammals; and (3) nucleotide substitutions must be constant over time. Each of these assumptions has been attacked by recent scholars, and, in any case, Don Melnick and Guy Hoelzer strongly caution about the use of the mtDNA clock, suggesting that various problems with it "render mtDNA unreliable for dating past evolutionary events."[48] Frayer and others[49] also strongly criticize assumptions about the mutation rate of mtDNA, and they argue that if the starting date of the "clock" is pushed back to 800,000 years ago for the origins of the mtDNA we now all share, then there would be a better fit between the molecular evidence and the fossil and archaeological records.

The details of these debates about the interpretation of graphs of genetic relatedness based on mtDNA are beyond the scope of this book—and beyond the grasp of those without specific kinds of mathematical expertise. Various mathematical techniques are required to measure similarity and to arrange these patterns of similarity in patterns that show descent and genetic relatedness, and disputes about the appropriateness of these techniques continue. Frayer and his colleagues[50] conclude, for example, that "There is no statistically reliable mtDNA evidence for an African, or any other single, geographically centered origin for Eve."

Although these debates have raged on in the literature for a couple of decades now, new genetic studies appear to be putting this argument to rest. Perhaps the best recent genetic support for the "Out of Africa" scenario has come from studies of mtDNA recovered from Neandertal (discussed later) fossils.[51] These appear to show that Neandertals differ from modern humans in more than 20 mtDNA mutations. Coupled with the mitochrondrial clock for mutation rates, this degree of difference suggests that Neandertals cannot be related to modern humans. If true, then Neandertals, and likely most other archaic *Homo* forms outside of Africa, did not contribute to the gene pool that constitutes us.

To evaluate these opposing models of human origins and interpretations of the genetic evidence, we can at least consider the ambiguous and fragmentary record of their bones and stone tools.

Fossil and Archaeological Evidence of Modern Human Origins: Testing the Total Replacement Model

Let us consider the Total Replacement model to be a "null hypothesis," in the sense that we can attempt to demonstrate that it is *not* true. Although some of the most vocal proponents of the Total Replacement model have recently questioned aspects of their model,[52] it at least has the virtue of clearly testable implications. If, for example, the Total Replacement model is accurate, we would expect to see various kinds of specific evidence.[53]

First, the earliest known *Homo sapiens sapiens* should be found in Africa, and there should be evidence that "modern" humans lived only in Africa prior to their appearance in the rest of the world.

A second testable implication of the Total Replacement model is that there should be no anatomical evidence of genetic mixing between the early modern Africans and the people they replaced. That is, except in Africa, there should be an absence of "intermediate" forms of humans—those whose physical forms appear as a blend of early *Homo* and *Homo sapiens sapiens*—in the period between about 400,000 and 30,000 years ago.

Third, everywhere outside of Africa the earliest modern humans should resemble these African ancestors and not the local people who had lived there first. Also, there should be evidence of a "rapid" change from early *Homo* to *Homo sapiens sapiens* in both the fossil and archaeological records as the replacement took place, and in a geographical pattern that reflects the routes they took out of Africa.

Fourth, in areas outside of Africa there should be no evidence of anatomical continuity spanning the time period before and after the replacement occurred: That is, we should not expect to see a pattern of continuous similarity in the physical types who lived, for example, in China at Zhoukoudian 300,000 years ago, 50,000 years ago, and today.

Fifth, we should look for some evidence as to why Africans were able to displace well-adapted hominins all over the Old World. We would expect some evidence in technology, skull size and shape, animal exploitation patterns, site densities and placement, or some other attribute of the archaeological record that would explain why this replacement was both rapid and complete. As Frayer and his colleagues note,[54] even the European conquest of the Americas, involving as it did far superior technology and the introduction of numerous lethal diseases, left many indigenous Native American hunter-foragers, from Alaska to Tierra del Fuego, and some have persisted even into the present day. So, what evidence is there that the early African *Homo sapiens sapiens* possessed some advantage that allowed them to drive into extinction all other humans?

It is important to note that all of these five categories of evidence are to some degree equivocal: What, for example, would an "intermediate" skull be, and what would "rapid" change look like in the archaeological record?[55] Different scholars have different ideas about what these kinds of terms mean. Also, given the vagaries of preservation and differences in the intensity of archaeological research (much more work has been done in western Europe, for example, than, say, Pakistan), we could be easily misled by sample biases. Moreover, whatever advantages the early African *Homo sapiens sapiens* had that allowed them to replace other hominin forms, if in fact that is what happened, these advantages may not be visible in the archaeological record, given our current knowledge of that record. If early Africans, for example, simply had a slightly greater fertility rate, perhaps because of some genetic mutation and minor cultural adaptation to this mutation, and no other advantages, it is possible that they could have supplanted all other hominins in a few hundred thousand years—although we would still have to explain why no interbreeding by adjacent groups took place, since such gene flow is the common pattern during the recent past. Finally, the basic logic of science stipulates that hypotheses cannot be "proven." One attempts to disprove them and in the end all that science can aspire to is pointing us toward the current "best" model—"best" being defined in terms of "fit" to the data and parsimony.

To "test" these five implications of the Total Replacement model requires that we examine a complex array of evidence, and the reader is forewarned that this review ends inconclusively: Reasonable scientists differ on interpretations of this evidence.

THE EVIDENCE FROM AFRICA

One implication of the Total Replacement model is that the earliest modern humans should appear in Africa. Does this appear to be true? Recent fossil discoveries by Tim White and his colleagues in Ethiopia suggest that this may be the case.[56] Several hominin crania recovered from Herto in the Middle Awash area—dated to between 160,000 to 154,000 years ago—have features that are intermediate between archaic *Homo* in Africa and anatomically modern humans. The combination of the age of these fossil hominins and their morphology may be strong evidence that they are the ancestors of modern humans.

Another example of early *Homo sapiens sapiens* is the fragmentary human remains from the Klasies River Mouth caves in South Africa (Figure 4.13), found in association with many stone tools, animal bones, and other evidence of repeated occupation.[57]

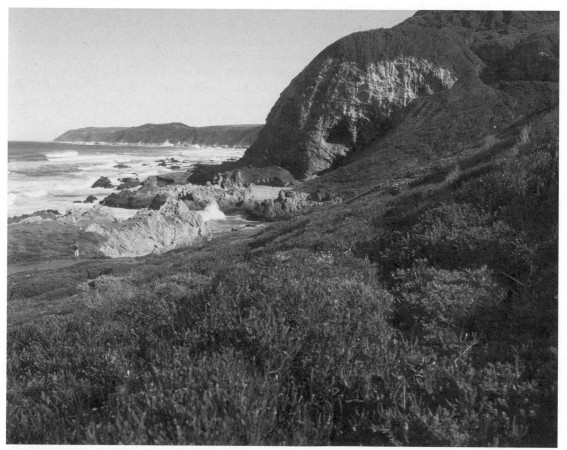

FIGURE 4.13   Overview of the Middle Stone Age site of Klasies River Mouth, South Africa.

Uranium series dates and correlations with dates from marine cores seem to place these remains between 125,000 and 95,000 years ago. Only some elements of the crucially important facial morphology are preserved on just four of the individuals represented by these bones. The scholars who have analyzed the Klasies human remains come to startlingly different conclusions. Some scholars see archaic features in many elements of these bones and little evidence for the "modern" features they would expect if these individuals were part of the population that, according to the Total Replacement model, preceded the appearance of modern *Homo sapiens sapiens* elsewhere in the world. The excavators of this site, R. Singer and J. Wymer, add that the many stone points found at the site indicate substantial hunting with hafted spears.[58]

Early hominin fossils of *Homo sapiens* have also been found at Bodo and Omo (Ethiopia); Laetoli (Tanzania); Kanjera (Kenya);[59] Kabwe, or Broken Hill (Zambia); Border Cave (South Africa); and several other sites, but in every case at least some scholars consider the dating unreliable or disagree on the degree of modernity evident in these highly fragmented finds.[60] Other scholars,[61] however, see a pronounced modern appearance in the African human fossils that span the period between about 200,000 and 100,000 years ago and conclude that the evolution of *Homo sapiens sapiens* was slow and continuous and had nearly run its course in Africa by 70,000 years ago.

But the Total Replacement model does not require that *Homo sapiens sapiens* appeared in East Africa as early as 100,000 years ago. Richard Klein has suggested that the *Homo sapiens sapiens* who actually replaced all other humans only appeared in Africa after 50,000 years ago, and perhaps only shortly before 30,000 years ago, when we see the spread across the Middle East and Europe of "art," in the sense of wall paintings, figurines, shell and bone ornaments, and beautifully crafted tools (see later), and when we also see standardized tool shapes and highly organized activity areas in the remains of archaeological sites:

> The fourth and most recent event occurred about 50,000 years ago and it was arguably the most important of all, for it produced the fully modern ability to invent and manipulate culture . . . a genetic mutation that promoted the fully modern brain. . . . [I]t allowed the kind of rapidly spoken phonemic language that is inseparable from culture as we know it today. . . . Fossil, archaeological, genetic, and linguistic evidence all point to Africa as the place where the 50,000-year-old behavioral breakthrough occurred. . . . Had the crucial mutation occurred first in Europe, the earliest evidence for modern behavior would be there, and students of human evolution today would be Neandertals marveling at the peculiar people who used to live in African and then abruptly disappeared.[62]

One interesting implication of Klein's hypothesis is that these *Homo sapiens sapiens* could also have replaced the supposedly modern-looking but much more ancient *Homo sapiens*, like those who lived at Herto, Klasies, Omo, and elsewhere in Africa 100,000 or more years ago (Figure 4.14). Klein suggests that the mutation that accounted for the ability of these *Homo sapiens sapiens* to replace all other forms after 50,000 years ago may have been just an increased ability to conceptualize and communicate—as perhaps is evident in "art" and the standardized tools they used and the way they organized their daily activities. Such changes may have had no reflections in the shape or size of human skulls and only very subtle reflections in the ways tools were made, used, and discarded.

Is there any artifactual evidence in African sites after 100,000 or between 50,000 and 30,000 years ago, as Klein suggests, for "art" and other improved conceptual skills? Tantalizing bits of evidence have been produced, but the evidence, as always, is ambiguous.

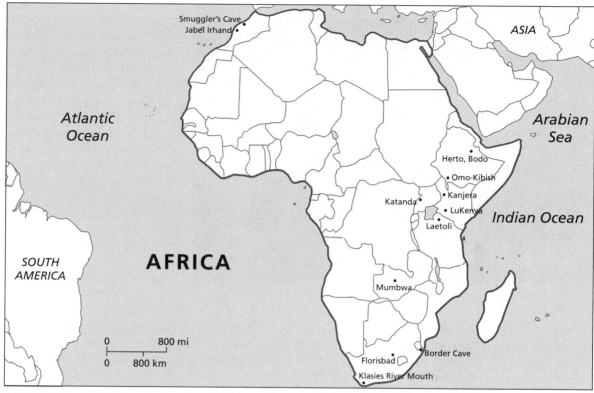

FIGURE 4.14   Early *Homo sapiens* sites in Africa. The dates of some sites are controversial. Most are thought to date beween 160,000 and 60,000 years ago.

Allison Brooks and her group report that they have found sophisticated bone tools, including barbed points that may have been used to spear catfish in rivers in Zaire as early as 90,000 years ago (Figure 4.15).[63] Fishing in this way seems to have been a very late development in Europe, so one might consider this as some evidence in support of the idea that *Homo sapiens sapiens* evolved in Africa, and only in Africa. Perforated ostrich eggshell ornaments, bones, stone points, and examples of the use of ochre (a mineral that is often red or yellow in color)—perhaps as a pigment—have been found, but it is difficult to argue definitively on the basis of this evidence that there is a clear reflection of greater cognitive powers than other humans outside of Africa at this time possessed.

   Thus, to some, the African evidence, in summary, is ambiguous. There are suggestions of a transition from archaic *Homo* to *Homo sapiens* at 160,000 years ago, but it is not certain that Africa is the *only* place this morphological change occurred, nor is there material evidence of some advantage that explains why Africans might have been able to drive into extinction all other hominins.

THE EVIDENCE FROM EAST ASIA AND AUSTRALIA

If the Total Replacement model is correct, at some point we should see a radical change in the human physical types who lived on this far periphery of early human adaptations. That

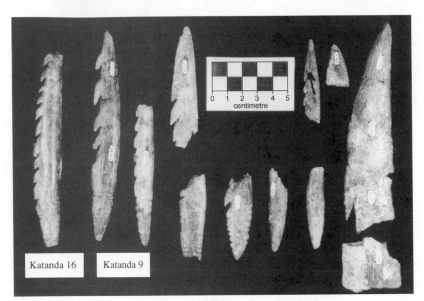

Katanda 16   Katanda 9

FIGURE 4.15   Bone harpoons from the site of Katanda, Zaire.

is, the people who almost certainly were in Indonesia and adjacent regions by about 900,000 years ago, for example, would have been abruptly replaced by *Homo sapiens sapiens* of the African type after about 100,000 years ago (and possibly much later). Moreover, there should be no evidence here of hybridization of Africans and Asians, nor any patterns of continuity in the physical evolution of indigenous Asian humans toward modern *Homo sapiens sapiens*. We might also expect some evidence of replacement in the tools and other aspects of the archaeological record.

Consider first the farthest periphery of the Late Pleistocene Old World—Australia. There is now persuasive evidence that people arrived there at least by 50,000 years ago, and possibly by 60,000 years ago.[64] If the "total replacement" occurred at about 200,000 years ago, then these early Australians might be expected to show little physical similarity to Chinese and other Asians of the hundreds of thousands of years before this time, such as those at Zhoukoudian and Java, because the Australians would have migrated to Australia as much as 140,000 years after the replacement of the world's population began. If, as Klein suggests, however, the replacement occurred after 50,000 years ago, then these Australians may be a mix of early and later peoples, some of whom were closely related to Africans of this period.

Some anthropologists think that the east Asian fossil and archaeological record constitutes persuasive evidence for the rejection of the Total Replacement model. Pope, Wolpoff, Thorne,[65] and others see strong similarity between the early Australians and the Javanese, for example, and all of them as very distinct from Africans of the same age (i.e., c. 400,000–50,000 years ago). They focus on physical traits such as the "shovel" shape of the cross- sections of human incisors, which occurs in high frequency in Asian populations and much lower frequencies in Africans.[66] Frayer and his colleagues conclude that there is a very distinctive combination of facial and cranial features in Java, for example, and that this "unique combination of regional features . . . was stable for at least 700,000 years, while other characteristics continued evolving. The more recent Java remains have expanded brains that reached the modern range."[67] These patterns of anatomical continuity would be expected on the basis of the Multiregional Evolution/Continuity hypothesis.

Advocates of the Multiregional Evolution/Continuity hypothesis also see strong evidence of continuity in the physical forms of humans in northeast Asia, as well as gradual regional evolution here of modern human brain capacities. Crania from Zhoukoudian, Dali, Jinniushan, and Yunxian and fragmentary finds from elsewhere form the basic evidence here.

Advocates of the Total Replacement model disagree with these interpretations.[68] Some have suggested that claims that early Asian humans show evolution toward "modern" *Homo sapiens sapiens* forms are based on a biased selection of only a few physical traits and inappropriate statistical manipulation of these data. They also stress the fragmentary and possibly biased record of fossils in Asia.

There is little evidence in the east Asian archaeological record of some obvious advantage in technology or other aspect of adaptation. From about 400,000 years ago onward, Asian stone tools show strong similarities, and some contrasts between Asian and African and European tools seem to go back far into prehistory. It is possible, of course, that invading Africans adopted the lithic technology of the groups they replaced, but this would seem unlikely.

In summary of the Asian evidence, scholars disagree entirely on the extent to which these data support the various hypotheses about human origins, and these debates turn on abstractions of statistical analyses of scarce and fragmentary human fossils. The stone tools of east Asia would seem to support the Multiregional Evolution/Continuity hypothesis in that east Asian forms seem to show similarity over hundreds of thousands of years as well as differences that distinguish them from those of other areas. But if replacement by Africans occurred in east Asia after 50,000 years ago, as Klein suggests, then the archaeological evidence becomes even more ambiguous. The few well dated and excavated sites of this period show some minor indications of greater use of "style" in the form of pierced shells and other artifacts. That these changes represent an African invasion, however, is far from clear.

THE EVIDENCE FROM WESTERN ASIA AND EUROPE

We know a great deal more about the prehistory of Europe and western Asia than of the rest of the world. One might optimistically think this fact would result in a much more uniform interpretation of this evidence, but in fact disagreements about the European and western Asian evidence are even more intense than those for Africa and east Asia.

About all scholars agree on is that (1) there were humans living in Europe and western Asia by 500,000 years ago but they were not *Homo sapiens sapiens*; (2) a distinctive form of human, the "Neandertals," who were different from us in important anatomical ways, lived in Europe and western Asia between about 130,000 and 30,000 years ago; and (3) by 30,000–27,000 years ago all the Neandertals and other distinctive physical forms of humans, except ourselves, *Homo sapiens sapiens*, had disappeared.[69]

To review this evidence requires discussion of a bewildering array of site names, fossil names, types of technologies, and so on. To focus all these data and to make them coherent, one can consider again the kinds of evidence stipulated earlier as to be expected on the basis of the Total Replacement model. That is, do we see various kinds of evidence in the European fossil and archaeological record that Africans invaded western Asia and Europe at some point after about 200,000 years ago and drove the indigenous people in these areas into extinction by virtue of some advantage in intelligence, technology, or other feature?

To set the stage for an examination of the evidence bearing on this question, we must go back to the beginning of human occupations in Europe and western Asia. As noted earlier, a few sites in the Middle East date, perhaps, to more than 500,000 years ago (e.g., 'Ubeidiya, in Israel), and some fragmentary finds of human bones and archaeological sites in Europe seem securely dated to before 500,000 years ago (see earlier). Other important hominin finds from the Middle East are discussed later in the context of the Neandertals.

To begin with the physical types of hominins that made these transitions, Chris Stringer (and his colleagues) and Erik Trinkaus have arranged most of the fossils between 500,000 and 30,000 into an order based on morphology.[70] Grade 1 hominins may be as old as 500,000 years, but dating these fossils has proved difficult in most cases. Some Grade 1 fossil specimens come from Europe. Trinkaus notes that some of these have been classified as *Homo erectus* and others seem to have Neandertal traits (see later), but as a group they seem to be consistent with a gradual change toward modern human forms (e.g., increased size of the cranial vault and decreasing mean dimensions of molars).

In Europe these Grade 1 hominins are followed by a group that seems to fall between the grades, in that they are quite archaic in some characteristics but also resemble slightly the Neandertals, who generally seem later in time than the Grade 1 group. A good example of these intermediate Grade 1–2 fossils is from Swanscombe, England, along the Thames River, not far from London. In 1935 workers in a cement plant uncovered a cranial bone from a gravel bank, and a year later another cranial fragment was found nearby that articulated perfectly with the first bone. Later, during excavations connected with preparations for the 1944 Allied invasion of France, another bone from the same skull was found just 25 m from the site of the first find. It is very possible, incidentally, that more hominin bones were included in the gravel used to make concrete for floating docks during the D-Day operation.

In the same gravel layers that produced these bones, excavators recovered the bones of extinct forms of elephants, deer, rhinoceroses, and pigs, which, together with subsequent chemical analysis and geological evidence, dated the Swanscombe fossils to between 400,000 and 250,000 years ago, when the abundance of horses, elephants, rhinoceroses, and other big-game species would have made England an ideal place for generalized hunting-and-gathering groups.[71] Nor is there any problem explaining how these hominins would have gotten there, since Britain and Ireland were physically joined to Europe by a land bridge at various times during the Pleistocene.

The Swanscombe cranial remains are probably those of a woman of 20–25 years of age, with a cranial capacity of about 1,325 cm^3—well within the range of modern humans.[72] Hand-axes roughly similar to those of the Acheulian assemblages of France and Africa are among the most frequent tools in the level where the skull was found, but lower levels contain only flakes and choppers. Similar flakes and choppers have been found elsewhere in England and are commonly referred to as the Clactonian assemblage.[73] A wooden object that looks like the shaped end of a spear was found at Clacton and is one of the earliest wooden artifacts recovered anywhere, dating to 400,000–200,000 years ago. Stone projectile points are not found at Swanscombe, Zhoukoudian, or any other site prior to about 150,000 years ago, and thus the wooden spear fragment—if that is what it was used for—may be a clue to how these Middle Pleistocene peoples managed to kill animals. If animals were trapped in bogs, they could have been killed by multiple stab wounds with wooden spears—although it could not have been pleasant work.

The Swanscombe hominin is usually considered part of a biological group that includes a fossil from Steinheim, Germany. This cranium, dated to about 250,000 years ago, probably belonged to a young woman whose brain size and facial features place her between *Homo erectus* and ourselves. Unfortunately, no artifacts were found with the Steinheim skull, so we cannot compare the site with the material from southern England. Nonetheless, the physical differences between this individual and *Homo erectus* at least raise the possibility that the transition from *Homo erectus* to *Homo sapiens* was well underway by 300,000 to 250,000 years ago and was taking place in more than one part of western Europe.

Excavations in a cave site in the French Pyrenees unearthed a skull (the Arago skull) and two mandibles (Figure 4.16) dated to about 200,000 years ago that seemed to fill the gap between *Homo erectus* and the European Neandertals.[74] The skull possesses some morphological characteristics of the east Asian *Homo erectus*, but lacks the incipient keel at the top of the skull usually found in these populations. The large size of the teeth and mandible and the structure of the chin seem to foreshadow the features of the "classic" (western European) Neandertal.

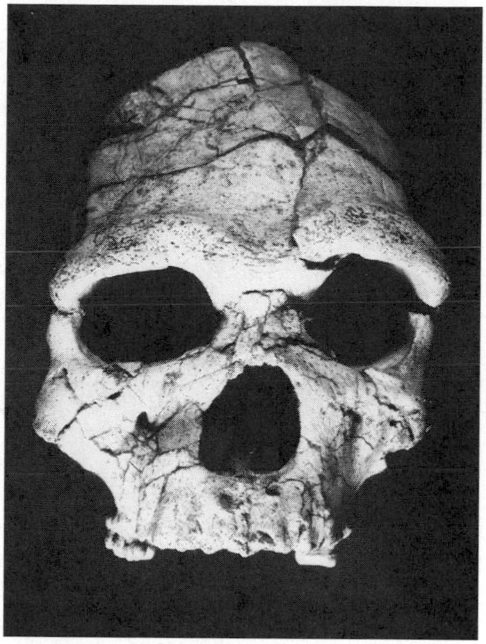

Late *Homo* remains have also been found at Bilzingsleben in eastern Germany, along with a somewhat atypical assemblage of very small tools with much larger implements, all quite different from the typical Acheulian assemblage. In fact, Svoboda has argued that the many small tools found at Arago, Vértesszöllös, and Bilzingsleben developed out of adapting to cold, open landscapes and thus could be expected to be different from the tools used in more forested environments.[75]

FIGURE 4.16   The Arago skull from France. This individual is now considered to be an early European Neandertal.

In general, tool technology, diet, site locations, and average group size in Europe about 200,000 years ago do not seem much different from those of several hundred thousand years earlier, but clearly, population densities were increasing, and as people moved into more diverse niches there was an increasing variety in the stone tools associated with them.

Until recently these various early European *Homo sapiens* were viewed as representatives of the changes that eventuated in us, *Homo sapiens sapiens*, but recent evidence raises many questions about this interpretation. A key element in interpreting these archaic *Homo* fossils is the Neandertals.

THE MIDDLE TO UPPER PALEOLITHIC PERIOD (C. 300,000–40,000 B.P.)

I held it truth, with him who sings
  To one clear harp in divers tones,
  That men may rise on stepping-stones
Of their dead selves to higher things.
       Alfred, Lord Tennyson, from
        In Memoriam[76]

There are multiple ways in which *Homo sapiens* diverged physically and behaviorally from pre-sapiens forms of *Homo* in the period between about 300,000–40,000 years ago.[77]

This is visible in many radical changes in human physical characteristics and material culture, including (1) an increase of average human brain size from about 1,100 to about 1,450 cm³ (although local variability was high, and the modern range of normal brain functioning is at least 1,000 to 2,000 cm³); (2) changes in physical form such that modern *Homo sapiens sapiens* have less robust skeletons, a more prominent chin, smaller or absent brow ridges, smaller teeth, a higher rounded skull, and other physical characteristics;[78] (3) increased human population numbers and densities—again with considerable local variation; (4) many technological innovations, including the atlatl (throwing stick), bone and wood tools of diverse types, and techniques for extracting a relatively great amount of cutting edge from a given amount of stone; (5) increased aesthetic expression in figurines, usually of bone or stone, beautiful wall paintings and rock carvings, burial techniques, and objects used for personal adornment; (6) a shift from generalized hunting patterns to concentrations in some areas on gregarious herd mammals like deer, reindeer, and horses; and (7) the appearance of artifact styles and trade in exotic items that bespeak the first manifestation of some sort of regional "ethnic" identity"[79] that exceeds by a wide margin the local band society—in short, changes that may reflect the "total restructuring" of social relationships during the period from the Middle to Upper Paleolithic.[80]

As noted earlier, the Total Replacement, African Origins, or Eve model contends that modern humans evolved first and only in Africa and only a few hundred thousand years ago or less, and then migrated to the rest of the world, displacing all other hominin forms, and with little or no genetic interchange with them. If this is true, then, as interesting as these many European and Asian fossils and sites of hundreds of thousands of years ago are, the people who left these remains had almost nothing to do with us in terms of our physical or cultural heritage.

This is a difficult premise for many anthropologists to accept because so much of what we think we know about human evolution has been based on sites such as Zhoukoudian in China, Toralba-Ambrona in Spain, and so on. If the African Origins model is correct, however, these sites were created by a form of human that has virtually nothing to do with us genetically, and probably little to do with us culturally.

Alternatively, the Multiregional Evolution, Continuity, or Candelabra models propose that sometime between about one and two million years ago a generic *Homo* ancestor of ours spread out across the warmer latitudes of Africa, the Middle East, Asia, and possibly the southernmost fringe of Europe; then, with the passage of the millennia, although these groups began to diverge somewhat as they adapted to local and different environments, across the whole range of *Homo* they were evolving toward *Homo sapiens* as a result of gene flow that connected all human groups to some extent and because they were all under similar evolutionary selective forces as generalized hunter-foragers, so that they all converged at about 30,000 years ago as one species, *Homo sapiens*—but with the physical differences that distinguish modern Europeans from, for example, modern Chinese.

For many archaeologists, one of the best test cases for resolving at least some aspects of the Total Replacement versus Multiregional Continuity ideas can be found in a relatively recent hominin group widely known to both archaeologists and the general public—the Neandertals. Our record of them is both abundant and long studied—Neandertals have provided one of the most numerous fossil bone assemblages for a hominin group, as well as more than 100 years of archaeological research on their sites.

The Neandertals

Nothing about the Neandertals seems simple. Evidence suggests they lived between about 130,000 and 30,000 years ago, but their precise period in history is difficult to define. Most of them seemed to have lived in Europe and western Asia, some as far east as central Asia and in much of the Middle East. The "Classic," or western, Neandertals were different from us and from their contemporaries in Africa, east Asia, and Australia in various physical characteristics, but scholars disagree on the extent and significance of these differences. Some think the Neandertals could speak with about as much fluency as we do, others think the Neandertals did not have the mentality or vocal apparatus for normal human speech. Scholars disagree perhaps most heatedly about what "happened" to the Neandertals: That is, are we descendants of the Neandertals, or did they lose out in competition with our ancestors?

Because they belonged to the first pre-modern human identified, the Neandertals received much of the initial hostility to the concept of human evolution. From the beginning, anthropologists, clergy, and others held that the Neandertals were an aberrant stage in human development, not directly related to our own—presumably superior— ancestors. Some scholars, however, suspected that the Neandertals were the connecting link between *Homo erectus* and at least some populations of *Homo sapiens sapiens*. In 1957 a conference on the Neandertal produced evidence that Neandertal brain size on the average was larger than that of some modern human groups and that there were no grounds for concluding that their brains were structurally inferior or that they did not walk fully erect. In fact, it was suggested that "if he could be reincarnated and placed in a New York subway—provided that he were bathed, shaved, and dressed in modern clothing—it is doubtful he would attract any more attention than some of its other denizens."[81]

Yet there are differences between ourselves and the Neandertals (Figure 4.17). The characteristics most frequently used to define them are (1) a receding or virtually absent chin; (2) large cheekbones and prominent brow ridges curving over the eye orbits and connecting across the bridge of the nose; (3) prognathism (protruding lower face); (4) a strong masticatory apparatus, including larger front teeth than are found in most modern human populations; (5) a short (average of perhaps 5 feet) but powerful stature, with thick and slightly curved long bones; and (6) a cranial capacity within the range of modern humans, though slightly larger on average for the classic "Western" type.

Erik Trinkaus has shown how the shapes and sizes of Neandertal teeth and heads vary in many obvious and also subtle ways from our own.[82] He interprets the projecting mid-face of the Neandertals as a feature selected by natural selection in part "to facilitate the use of the anterior teeth as a vise."[83] Neandertals would have had no problems with candied apples or corn on the cob, had they been available.

Based on their legs and lower bodies, Trinkaus suggested that the overall impression of Neandertal locomotor anatomy

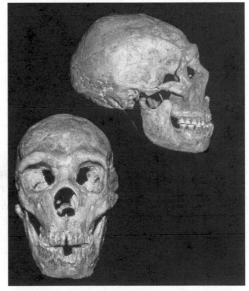

FIGURE 4.17 A Neandertal skull from Shanidar, Iraq.

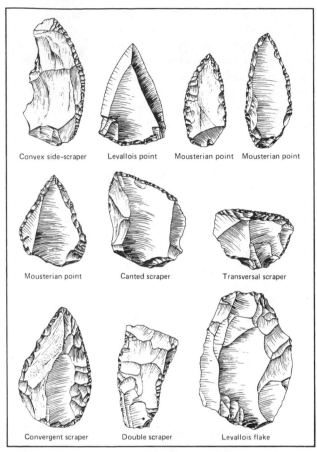

Convex side-scraper · Levallois point · Mousterian point · Mousterian point

Mousterian point · Canted scraper · Transversal scraper

Convergent scraper · Double scraper · Levallois flake

FIGURE 4.18 Some typical tool types of the Mousterian period. The Neandertals made effective stone tools for a variety of purposes.

is "one of great strength, as with the upper limb, but also one adapted for endurance for prolonged locomotion over irregular terrain." Trinkaus concludes that the anatomy of their legs "suggests that they spent a significant portion of their waking hours moving across the landscape . . . far more than did early modern humans."[84] The Neandertals would have been a bit short to be good offensive football linemen, but they would have made superstar wrestlers or baseball catchers, given their tremendous arm strength (though their ability to grip the ball might have been less than ours).

The Neandertals were adept stone tool-makers. Most of their tools belong to the Mousterian stone tool industry (named after the site of Le Moustier in southern France), which includes several distinctive stylistic and functional elements (Figure 4.18). The scores of Mousterian sites in the Dordogne region of southwestern France include cave sites, rock shelters, and "open-air" locations, and one of the largest and most complex Mousterian sites here is a cave in the Combe Grenal Valley, near the Dordogne River. Francois Bordes uncovered 64 superimposed occupational levels in this cave, spanning the period from about 85,000–45,000 years ago, with few long periods of abandonment. The lowest levels contained tools resembling the Acheulian tools found at Swanscombe, but all later levels had the classic Mousterian tools usually associated with Neandertals. More than 19,000 Mousterian implements were collected and analyzed from this cave, and the tools from different levels contrast sharply. Some levels contained many small flake-like pieces of stone, while others had concentrations of scores of "toothed" or "denticulated" tools. Moreover, analysis of the different levels revealed that certain types of tools tended to be spatially associated with a number of other types. That is, levels containing a relatively high number of points would usually contain relatively large numbers of scrapers and flakes—but few denticulates.

This diversity of tools may seem relatively unimportant, but it was the focus of a long debate that involved issues fundamental to the development of the discipline of archaeology and to contemporary views of human origins. The specific case of the Mousterian tools became part of a larger question: How are we to measure and interpret variability in ancient artifacts? For the Mousterian tools, François Bordes spent years in excavation and analysis to establish a typology that has been the framework for much of the work done on this period. Bordes classified all Mousterian tools into four categories, based on the relative frequencies of certain types.[85] Bordes considered various explanations of the diversity of Neandertal tools, such as that this variability reflected different time periods, climates, or seasons of the year. On the basis of the archaeological evidence, however, he rejected these possibilities and eventually concluded that the four different clusters of tools are the remains of four distinct cultural traditions, or "tribes," which developed certain kinds of tool manufacture and retained these distinctive expressions over the 100,000 years of the Mousterian period. Bordes's vision of the Mousterian was one in which different tribes of Neandertals wandered much of the Old World for generation after generation, through tens of thousands of years, each group maintaining its unique styles of tool manufacture and meeting the others infrequently and usually with hostility.

This vision was questioned by Lewis and Sally Binford, who assumed that Mousterian tool variability was largely a reflection of the different tasks Neandertals had to perform to meet successfully the demands of their environment.[86] They tried to test their interpretation by a statistical analysis of Mousterian tools from three widely separated sites: the Jabrud Rock Shelter near Damascus, Syria; Mughâret es-Shubbabiq Cave in Israel; and an "open-air" station near Houpeville, France. Each site contained several different levels, representing different occupations; the total number for all three sites was 16. Lithics from each site were classified in terms of Bordes's system and statistically analyzed for evidence that these groups of tools were used for different economic activities, rather than simply representing stylistic traditions. Factor analysis was the statistical method used to determine which of the tool types were usually found in proximity to one another in the various levels of the different sites. On this basis they defined several different "tool kits," whose presumed functions included tool preparation, wood-working, butchering, and various other tasks.

But the exact nature of Neandertal tool-making variability has remained a matter of dispute. A recent model proposed by Harold Dibble, for example, suggests that most of the variability in types of scrapers is the result of how often Neandertals resharpened these tools (Figure 4.19).[87] Imagine that you need a sharp-edged flake for some task. You strike an appropriate flake off a core and use it, but the edge dulls. To continued using the same piece, you resharpen (strike small flakes off) the dull edge. You now have a single-edge sidescraper (in the Bordian typology). You can continue to resharpen that same edge several times, or you can choose to use and then resharpen the opposite lateral side of the flake. Once you resharpen that second edge, you have a double sidescraper (in the Bordian typology). Dibble's model thus proposes that much of the variability we see in Mousterian scrapers is simply the result of how a stone artifact is resharpened, rather than linking those scraper shapes to activities or different groups of Neandertals.

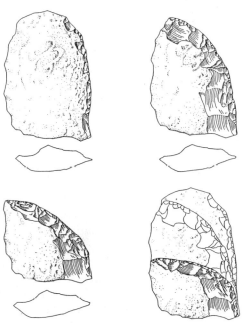

FIGURE 4.19 Dibble's scraper reduction model shows how a single sidescraper is transformed into a transverse sidescraper simply through the process of resharpening the tool.

NEANDERTAL CULTURE AND SOCIETY

As if the slurs cast on Neandertal intelligence and posture by early archaeologists were not enough, some anthropologists have questioned whether or not Neandertals were able to produce the range of sounds necessary for normal human speech. P. Lieberman and E. Crelin reconstructed the vocal apparatus of Neandertals using a computer simulation based on the measurement of a classic Neandertal, and using the vocal tracts of chimpanzees and human infants for comparison, they concluded that western European Neandertals would not have been able to make some vowels, such as *e*, and perhaps some labial and dental consonants, such as *b* and *d*.[88] Others doubt that the Neandertals could speak at all. Frayer and Wolpoff[89] challenge the old idea that the size and shape of the hyoid bone and other Neandertal anatomy are sufficiently different from that of modern humans to be used as evidence that the Neandertals had any less linguistic ability than we do. Lieberman[90] also has recently revised his earlier opinion about the speech of early hominins, contending that they likely did have language.

Archaeologists have long believed that, whatever their verbal fluency, the Neandertals were at least human enough to bury their dead. Excavations at La Chapelle-aux-Saints, in France, revealed a Neandertal corpse apparently laid out in a shallow trench, with a bison leg placed on his chest, and the trench filled in with bones, tools, and other debris—perhaps representing offerings of meat and implements. At La Ferrassie, France, a Neandertal "cemetery" was found, where a man, a woman, two children, and two infants seem to have been buried. A flat stone slab was on the man's chest, the woman was in a flexed position, and, toward the back of the cave, the skull and skeleton of one of the children were buried in separate holes, about 1 m apart. At Teshik-Tash, in Siberia, a Neandertal child was buried in a grave with goat skulls whose horns seemingly had been jabbed into the ground. At Shanidar Cave in Iraq, the soil near a Neandertal's body contained massive quantities of flower pollen. Ralph Solecki, the excavator, and Arlette Leroi-Gourhan, the palynologist, concluded that the skeleton had been buried with garlands of flowers.

But in these and other cases the evidence is at least somewhat equivocal. Even in the best of circumstances, archaeological excavation is a messy, ambiguous business of judging the significance of faint changes in the texture and color of sediments, and the Neandertal cave burials are notoriously difficult to excavate and interpret. Such caves have been homes not just to people but to hundreds of thousands of generations of cave bears, rodents, and other animals, and the natural processes of roof fall and sediment accumulation make for a confusing stratigraphic sequence. Thus, where one excavator may see a Neandertal carefully buried in a pit with a rock slab placed on his chest, another may observe evidence of a Neandertal who simply expired and was covered with rocks falling from the cave roof and by other debris. Thus some scholars see no evidence that any Neandertals were intentionally buried, while others believe that the Neandertals invested death with human-like emotion and ritual.[91] Richard Klein, for example, suggests that the Neandertals did in fact bury their dead, but probably only as a matter of hygiene and without any or much ceremony.[92] Lawrence Straus concludes[93] that Neandertal burial was a rare event, but he also makes the useful point that it is not at all clear than even *Homo sapiens sapiens* always buried their dead.

There is good evidence that Neandertals were not insensitive to the plight of the handicapped. Some Neandertals evidently suffered terribly from arthritis or had lost limbs and so could not have contributed much to the group's food supply. Yet, they must have been supported by the rest of their society. Despite these touching displays of societal concern, there is also some evidence that Neandertals killed, butchered, and perhaps ate one another. At Krapina in Yugoslavia, excavations revealed 20 Neandertals—men, women, and children—whose skulls and long bones had been smashed and split in suspicious ways. But Trinkaus and others question whether cannibalism was actually practiced.[94]

All Neandertals were apparently hunters and gatherers, but they must have varied considerably throughout their range in the kinds of resources they exploited. The archaeological record is no doubt biased because most Neandertal sites found and excavated are those made evident by masses of animal bones associated with stone tools; the remains of plant foods and wooden tools, of course, do not preserve nearly so well and are not as easily found.

Neandertal population densities appear to have been low, and it is likely that most Neandertals lived with the same group of 25 or 50 people their whole lives, from time to time meeting other bands for mate exchanges. They were skilled hunters, locked into seasonal migrations with the animals they hunted, but in most habitats they probably foraged widely for eggs, birds, plants, and other small resources. They competed quite successfully with other predators for game, but must have occasionally lost out to the zoological carnival of horrors whose ranges they shared. Giant cave bears, saber-toothed cats, and wolves occasionally "selected out" an unfortunate Neandertal: "Some days you eat the bear, some days the bear eats you" was probably no empty cliché to them.

Trinkaus[95] examined 40 nearly complete Neandertal skeletons as well as bones from 166 other Neandertals, from both Europe and the Middle East, and compared their estimated age at death to the age at death for a variety of other groups, including ethnographically observed groups like the Yanomamö hunter-gatherers of South America and the !Kung Bushmen of southern Africa, as well as archaeologically retrieved skeletons from North America, Japan, Mexico, and elsewhere. Noting all the biases and other problems in estimating time of death and other factors, Trinkaus concluded that the Neandertals experienced relatively high "young adult mortality"[96]—meaning that a higher percentage of Neandertals died during their young adult years than did in these other groups. Trinkaus suggests that these mortality patterns may be the result of various factors, including a relatively high level of adaptive stress. Almost all Neandertals would have been required to have a high degree of mobility, except infants in arms.

NEANDERTALS AND *HOMO SAPIENS SAPIENS*

William Golding, in his novel *The Inheritors*, imagined a world of the past in which peaceful, egalitarian, vegetarian Neandertals faced oblivion at the hands of villainous, meat-eating, beer-drinking *Homo sapiens sapiens*. This literary version of the Total Replacement model is studded with obvious symbolism intended to elevate this imaginary conflict into a statement about the human condition, but it is an interesting anthropological scenario as well, raising many questions. Throughout the ages, for example, humans have expressed a fine democratic and egalitarian spirit in few areas of life, but one of them—to some extent, at least—is in sexual congress: Wherever different "races" have coexisted, they have immediately and continually interbred. Did the Neandertals and other humans mate?

Such a question brings us back to the contrasting models of human origins. As these indicate, some scholars believe that no Neandertal genes are represented in contemporary human populations, while others think that some or even a lot of Neandertal genetic inheritance can be seen in contemporary European populations.

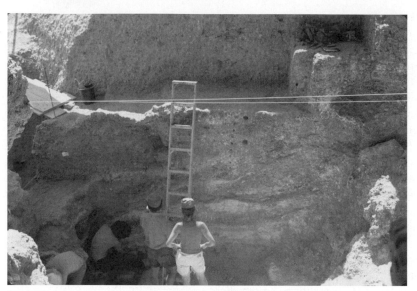

FIGURE 4.20 Overview of the Middle Paleolithic site of Qafzeh, Israel.

Who is right? We begin with the intriguing fact that the Neandertals entirely "disappeared" as a physical type sometime after about 30,000 years ago. No Neandertal bones have been found post-dating this time, and in some sites tool types widely believed to be associated with Neandertals are overlain with levels containing tools different in style. The Neandertals successfully lived over much of Europe and the Middle East for tens of thousands of years—why should they have vanished?

These and other ideas about the relationship of Neandertals to other early *Homo sapiens*, and the relationship of both to ourselves, still cannot be tested systematically and conclusively against the archaeological record because there are so many gaps and biases in this record. But recent discoveries have at least given a sounder empirical basis for some of these debates about the Neandertals. A key site here is Qafzeh (Figure 4.20). Helene Valladas and her colleagues used thermoluminescence to date 20 burnt flint tools from Qafzeh, a cave near Nazareth, in Israel, in strata that contained the bones of a somewhat modern-looking *Homo sapiens*.[97] Other human remains have been found at Qafzeh, and electron spin resonance dating was done on some of these.[98] Various scholars have concluded on the basis of this analysis that a primitive form of modern humans lived here 92,000 years ago, and perhaps earlier—but at least 30,000 years before Neandertals inhabited this region. Valladas and her colleagues speculate that Neandertals came into the Middle East about 60,000 years ago, perhaps migrating into the Mediterranean areas as glaciers expanded during the Pleistocene. Thus, if modern humans evolved in Africa long before they reached Qafzeh, as the DNA evidence might suggest, then the Qafzeh region might have been a contact area between Neandertals and early modern humans—since the Neandertals lived all over Europe 125,000 years ago.

The Qafzeh dates raise many questions. There is no molecular biological or genetic evidence that modern people originated in the Middle East, so it is presumed that any early modern *Homo sapiens sapiens* in this area would have descended from Africans. As Erik Trinkaus noted, if early modern humans reached the Middle East 92,000 years ago, they must have lived there in some relationship to the Neandertals for tens of thousands of years, since Neandertal remains in the Middle East dating to the period between 60,000 and 36,000 are well documented.[99]

The human remains from Qafzeh must be understood in the context of evidence from nearby sites, especially the cave sites of Skhul (early modern *Homo sapiens sapiens*), Tabun (Neandertal), and Kebara (Neandertal). New dates from human remains at Skhul suggest some of the individuals may have lived there as early as 100,000 years ago, and other finds at Skhul and Tabun indicate repeated human occupations between about 60,000 and 40,000 years ago.

So, who were these people in the Levant between 100,000 and 40,000 years ago, and what do they have to do with us?

Advocates of the Total Replacement model see these remains as belonging to two different species, one (*Homo sapiens sapiens*) superior to the other (the Neandertals) and in the process of replacing them, not mating with them. These scholars see "modern" elements in the crania of some of these hominins and very little overlap between these Levantine modern humans and the Neandertals in important elements of the post-cranial skeleton, such as the length of the pubis. But other scholars see these humans as belonging to the same general population and exhibiting anatomical variation that is "less, often considerably less, than normally found in a modern city."[100]

If the replacement of other humans by *Homo sapiens sapiens* occurred after 50,000 years ago, however, then the earliest "modern" *Homo sapiens* at Qafzeh could have been members of a population of archaic humans who were also replaced.

Given these ambiguities of interpretations of anatomy, what about the tools? Even the staunchest advocates of the original versions of the Total Replacement model have difficulty seeing an intrusive culture in the Levantine artifacts. There seems to be great continuity in the kinds of tools made, the species of game hunted, and other aspects of culture.[101]

In some ways the eastern Mediterranean can be considered part of "Africa" during periods of the Pleistocene,[102] given its proximity and similarities of climate and ecology. We might expect, then, these kinds of ambiguities in interpretations of what happened in the eastern Mediterranean. But what about Europe?

The major differences between Neandertals and ourselves are in head and face shapes and sizes, but the Neandertal skeleton, especially the limbs and hip bones, is also different in size and morphology from that of modern humans. The torsional strength of Neandertal leg bones, for example, is about twice that of moderns.[103] Tools may have had a role in changing the selective pressures on the teeth, but how could tools or any other factor have altered the skeletal parts?

We know that Neandertals had a lengthy evolutionary history in Europe, and some scholars have suggested that Neandertals became biologically adapted to resist the cold conditions of glacial Europe. This involved natural selection for features that gave Neandertals a reproductive advantage—"classic" western European Neandertals evolved their distinctive features as part of adapting to cold climates and had so little genetic connection to people living elsewhere in the world that they became distinctive.[104] Eventually, however, they were absorbed or displaced by more modern-looking humans. Other scholars, however, maintain that the fossils from central European Neandertals all exhibit morphological changes in the direction of modern hominins.[105]

If the Neandertals were entirely replaced by modern *Homo sapiens sapiens* moving out of Africa, it is possible that this extinction involved a *social* transformation, not just some slight difference in tool-making ability or other skill. Olga Soffer, for example, argues[106] for the appearance of modern human family structure and the division of labor by sex. She suggests that sites left by Neandertals are small and do not show the clusters of distinct artifacts that we would expect if people in various age and sex groups were doing different tasks in an integrated extended family. Perhaps most important, she sees no evidence of symbolic abilities, as might have been expressed in figurines, cave painting, or other media. In contrast, Soffer suggests that modern *Homo sapiens sapiens* left sites that show substantial evidence of a society in which there was a clear division of labor by sex, that they expressed themselves symbolically to a much greater degree, and, in general, developed the sense of *kinship* that one finds as the basic organizing principle of all known hunter-forager groups.

Determining the presence of a division of labor by sex or of kinship, of course, is very difficult given the types of cultural materials—mainly stone tools and animal bones at most sites—we normally recover from the archaeological record. Much debate about the Mousterian (Middle Paleolithic) and Upper Paleolithic in Europe has thus centered on the types of stone tools characteristic of each tradition, as well as the addition of organic technology, such as points made out of bone or antler, and personal ornamentation and symbolism.

Unlike the sequence of tools at, for example, Qafzeh (in Israel) and Zhoukoudian (in China), the European archaeological record *does* appear to show a relatively sudden change: At many sites levels of "Mousterian" tools dating to the period when Neandertals were here are overlain with occupational debris containing substantially different stone tools and other remains that may or may not be the products of *Homo sapiens sapiens*.[107] But does this reflect replacement of one group by another?

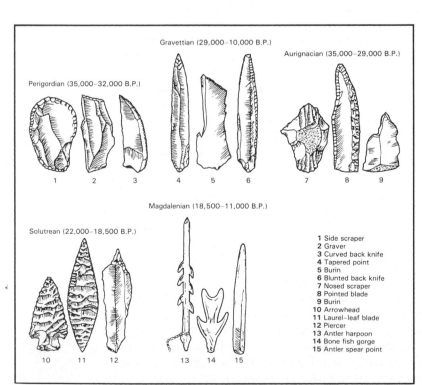

FIGURE 4.21   European tool kits, 35,000–11,000 years ago. The more diversified economies of the late Pleistocene are reflected in increasingly diverse tool kits compared to earlier periods (not drawn to scale).

Much of the debate on this topic has to do with debates about stone-tool technologies. The *Aurignacian* tool kit (Figure 4.21) has been found all over Europe and into the Middle East in sites dated to between about 40,000 to 30,000 years ago (some dates are outside this range).[108] To the specialist, these Aurignacian tools look completely different from the Mousterian tools traditionally associated with Neandertals across this same area, Europe and the Middle East. Mousterian tools are primarily made of flakes, whereas Aurignacian tools include a lot of blades, bladelets, burins, and other distinctive tools. Often the people who made Mousterian tools and those who made the Aurignacian ones used the same sources of flint and they often hunted about the same range of animals, but these two stone-tool industries are made in very different ways and in radically different shapes. There is no evidence that the Mousterian tools were gradually developed into Aurignacian ones[109]—in many sites Aurignacian assemblages lie directly on top of levels containing Mousterian tools. To some scholars, the lack of modern human fossils in western Europe at the time of the appearance of the Aurignacian leaves open the possibility that the earliest Aurignacian may be associated with Neandertals.

Recently, Straus's analysis of the results of intensely dating many Spanish Aurignacian sites with both radiocarbon and uranium-series dates, and comparing them with those from the Europe and the Middle East, revealed that "[f]ew if any other European Aurignacian assemblages have been reliably shown to be as old as the Spanish ones."[110] This pattern of dates may conflict with the idea that the Neandertals were driven into extinction by people who radiated out of Africa and abruptly replaced Neandertals by virtue of a superior technology—as might be represented by the Aurignacian tool kit. If that scenario were accurate, we would expect the Spanish Aurignacian sites to be the youngest, not the oldest, because presumably the modern *Homo sapiens sapiens* coming out of Africa arrived first in the Middle East, after which generations of their descendants and their descendants' descendants moved through eastern Europe, and only eventually into southwestern-most Europe, Spain. Alternatively, if people came out of Africa across the Straits of Gibraltar and arrived in Europe first in Spain, we would expect many Upper Paleolithic sites in southern Spain, and there are virtually none. As Straus notes, "[g]iven the present chronometric situation, it would be necessary for such a migration to have taken place virtually instantaneously to account for the Spanish dates. No possible migration patterns can be confidently reconstructed on the basis of the available chronometric dates for early Aurignacian sites."[111]

Another key site in these debates about the relationship of the Neandertals to ourselves is in France at Saint-Cesaire.[112] Human occupations here date to about 36,000 years ago—precisely the period when Neandertals were disappearing from the archaeological record. The problem is that, while the tools found at this site appear to be Upper Paleolithic in their stylistic and functional attributes, the human body found with them appears to be a Neandertal. As Trinkaus notes:

> If the Chatelperronian industry was produced solely by Neandertals and all the Aurignacian assemblages were the products of early modern humans . . . then there must have been temporal overlap of these two human groups in western Europe. . . . Even if a direct biological-industrial association cannot be assumed, it is still evident that Neandertals were present in western Europe less than [35,000 years ago] and that early modern humans were present there by at least [30,000 years ago].[113]

The significance of this is that 5,000 years is a very short time for the physical changes observed between Neandertals and modern humans to have occurred. The oldest artifacts associated with modern humans in Europe belong to the Aurignacian period. The lowest levels in which Aurignacian-style tools were found at Abric Romaní, in Spain, yielded radiocarbon dates of about 37,000 years ago, but uranium series dates put this site at about 40,000 years ago, and it shows an "abrupt" replacement of earlier levels containing Mousterian remains.[114]

But other anthropologists suggest that the Neandertals were simply evolving into modern humans and that the association of Upper Paleolithic tools with the later forms of

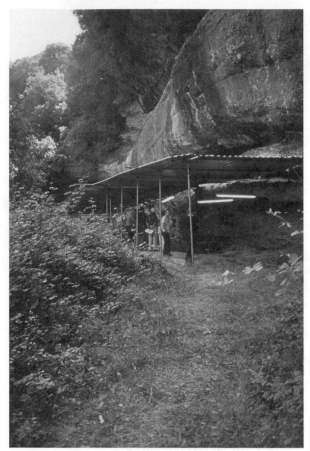

FIGURE 4.22 The Largo Velho rock shelter in Portugal yielded a burial of a child that some reseachers believe represents a "hybrid" between Neandertals and modern humans.

Neandertals is exactly what one would expect if this regional evolution process took place, even if there continued to be gene flow into Europe from outside. Fred Smith, for example, sees clear signs of reduction over time in the size of the brow-ridges of Neandertals at Krapina and Vindija in Yugoslavia, and at other central European sites.[115] Trinkaus and Duarte[116] have even suggested that the child buried at Largo Velho in Portugal (Figure 4.22) around 27,000 years ago is a hybrid between Neandertals and modern humans.

Some scholars have focused on stature and body proportions in debates about the relationship of Neandertals to us. The European Cro-Magnon after 30,000 years ago appears to have, on average, much longer limbs than did the Neandertals. Relatively long limbs are associated with adaptations to heat (as with the Dinka of East Africa today), whereas short limbs are associated with cold adaptation, such as in Eskimos and other north Asians. But it is difficult to make direct equations between stature and height, given that "culture," in the form of clothes, fire, and so on, modify the direct effects of climate. Still, there are many puzzling bits of evidence. The tallest of the post-Neandertal Pleistocene Europeans seem to appear just before 20,000 years ago, in the coldest period of the Pleistocene, when we might have expected natural selection to favor a shorter, stockier body type; and then later, in warmer periods, stature seems to have declined—again, the opposite of what we might expect.[117] Stature is so directly related to diet and other factors, however, that we should not expect to see a clear correlation between it and temperature in every case—except in the long term, and even then the relationship is likely to be modified by migrations, differences in technology and economy, and other factors.

Models of Modern Human Origins: Summary The most recent academic debates about models of modern human origins reveal profoundly different conclusions, with scholars disputing everything from the size and shape of particular characteristics of specific fossil skulls to the nature of basic evolutionary processes. Some see the Neandertals as an archaic form of human who made no significant contribution to ourselves,[118] some believe that modern Europeans represent an admixture of African and Neandertal genes,[119] and some see evidence in the Neandertal fossil record of an evolution toward modern humans and believe that the Neandertals became the modern humans of Europe through regional evolution and genic exchange with other populations outside Europe.[120]

It may be that these disputes are never resolved to everyone's satisfaction on the basis of evidence. For many, however, the recent genetic studies of Neandertal samples from Europe[121] are the final "nail in the coffin" for Neandertals as ancestors to modern humans. The mtDNA differences between Neandertals and modern humans shown in these studies would simply seem to be too numerous for Neandertals to be anything other than extremely distant "cousins" who suffered the fate of many animal species throughout time—extinction.

One thing is absolutely certain. No one in the past 25,000 years has experienced the wonder of encountering a hominin in the landscape who is not us—*Homo sapiens sapiens.*

Life, Art, and Ritual in the Upper Paleolithic

Writing about art is like dancing about architecture.—Anonymous

In 1868, near the Spanish port of Santander, so the story goes, a hunter's dog fell into a crevice in some boulders, and in rescuing the animal the hunter moved some rocks, revealing the opening of a cave. The owner of the land on which the cave (known as Altamira) was located, a Spanish nobleman and amateur archaeologist, eventually began to excavate the cave floor. He found some stone artifacts, but, according to the story, was unaware of the paintings in the cave until his 12-year-old daughter visited the site and glanced at the ceiling. In the glow of her lantern she saw beautiful visions of animals. The central painting is of a group of about 25 animals, mainly bison, with a few horses, deer, wolves, and boars (Figure 4.23). Roughly life-size, these paintings were done in rich browns, yellows, reds, and blacks, and the natural configuration of the cave ceiling had been used to emphasize the shape of the animals. The rounded haunch of a bison, for example, was painted over a natural bulge in the stone ceiling, creating a three-dimensional effect.[122]

Scholarly reception to the Altamira discoveries was almost uniformly negative. Some respected prehistorians even hinted that Don Marcelino, their discoverer, had hired an art student to fake these paintings, while another scholar dismissed them as simply the expression "of a mediocre student of the modern school." So abused by critics was the Don that eventually he padlocked the cave, and he died in 1888 without having seen his discoveries accepted as true Paleolithic expressions. Years later, when many more paintings and other art works had been discovered, Altamira's antiquity was finally acknowledged, and most of these paintings are now given dates between about 17,000 and 12,000 years ago. Analysis shows that the colors were produced by mixing natural mineral pigments, such as ocher and manganese dioxide, with a binder (blood, urine, vegetable juice, or something similar), and that they were either brushed on with an implement made of animal hair or applied by making a kind of crayon from the pigments and lubricant. Some painting may also have been done by using a pipe to blow the powdered pigments on a surface prepared with animal fat. Many of these paintings were executed in the dark

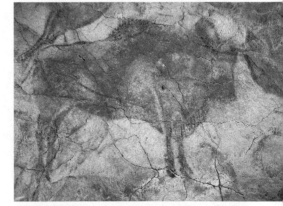

FIGURE 4.23 A bison painted on the ceiling at Altamira, Spain.

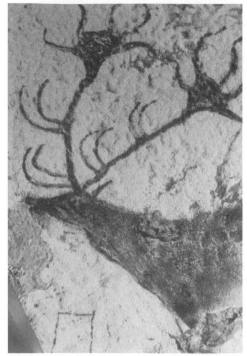

FIGURE 4.24 A painted reindeer from Lascaux, France.

recesses of caves, by light provided by lamps made of stone bowls filled with animal fat, with a wick made of lichens, grass, or juniper.[123]

During World War II, paintings on a scale comparable to those of Altamira were discovered at Lascaux Cave, in France. Researchers estimate that the Lascaux paintings date to about 17,000 years ago, but were done on many different occasions and perhaps over a much longer span. Many varieties of animals are depicted here, including some one hopes were imaginary. The animals are often painted as if they are in motion, and the general effect is very impressive (Figure 4.24). One of the many curious things about these and other Upper Paleolithic cave paintings is that while the animals are depicted in very real, very representational terms, the figures of humans are either simple stick drawings or else weird half-humans, half-animals.

The most stunning recent discovery has been the cave chambers at Chauvet in the Ardèche Valley of southern France, found by three spelunkers in 1994.[124] The wealth of images include both animals commonly shown in cave art—horses, bison, mammoth, and aurochs (an extinct form of wild cattle)—as well as those that are less frequently depicted in the other cave art sites—musk ox, leopard, cave bear, cave lion, rhinoceros, and an owl (Figure 4.25). Incredibly, Chauvet Cave is also the oldest of the cave art sites, dating to about 32,400 years ago—it is some 15,000 years older than the cave art at Lascaux and Altamira.

We must accept at the onset that we can never really know the thoughts of these long-dead Paleolithic artists. The same might be said of Vincent Van Gogh or any other artist, of course, given that aesthetic expressions can never be fully, rationally comprehended, even by the artist. But neither Van Gogh's work nor Paleolithic art can be expected to be random with regard to theme, technique, or style. Art can be expected to tell us something about the artist. And in any case, there is something profoundly unsatisfying about analyses of ancient peoples based only on stone

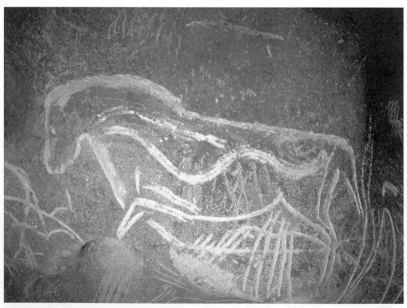

FIGURE 4.25 An engraved horse from Chauvet Cave, France.

tools, hut foundations, and other techno-environmental residues. Most people, including archaeologists, wish to know the "minds" of ancient peoples, and in few ways do these seem so accessible as in their art.

People apply the term Paleolithic art to a great range of materials, including cave paintings, rock carvings, sculpted and carved animal bones, ivory statuettes, and baked clay objects. As Margaret Conkey noted,[125] one should probably not imagine that all these expressions were fundamentally aesthetic in nature, in the sense that we think of aesthetics as removed from economic function. An early interpretation of the great cave paintings was that they were expressions of sympathetic magic, done to ensure success in hunting and other activities. By picturing animals with spears stuck in them or caught in traps, Upper Paleolithic people may have thought they increased their chances of killing and trapping these animals. Many of the paintings are in small, hidden passages where working conditions were very cramped, suggesting that these pictures were not created for the pleasure of the general viewing public. Then again, many paintings are superimposed on one, two, or even more older ones, indicating perhaps that these efforts were ritual in nature, not simply artistic. In fact, the most common themes of these Upper Paleolithic artists were food and sex, with food receiving most of the attention.

These interpretations of Paleolithic art were challenged by Andre Leroi-Gourhan, who plotted the relative frequencies of lions, mammoths, bison, reindeer, and other animals in caves with many such representations; he concluded that these paintings were invested with cosmological significance—reflecting in various ways the patterns in which Paleolithic peoples ordered their world.[126]

The disemboweled bulls, prancing deer, and other hunting scenes, plus the popularity of the penis and vulva motifs, suggest to some that these earliest of Spanish and French impressionists were men. But Elizabeth Fisher has argued that students of cave art have concealed the high frequency of female sex organs represented and thus the implication that many of the artists were probably women.[127] Line markings that some archaeologists have considered calendrical devices, Fisher thinks may be records of menstrual periods.

In recent years various alternative explanations of Paleolithic art have been suggested (Figure 4.26). Lewis-Williams and Dowson have argued that much of Paleolithic art was the product of people in "entopic," or altered, states of consciousness—either through drugs or meditation.[128] They note that ethnographic studies of contemporary hunter-gatherers show wide use of hallucinogens, trances, and such altered states to produce paintings and carvings. They also argue that it seems a feature of human neuroanatomy that images perceived in altered states of consciousness include both "real" representational forms and fantastic nonrepresentational forms and that people tend to project these images on walls and ceilings in their minds. Thus, "Tracing projected

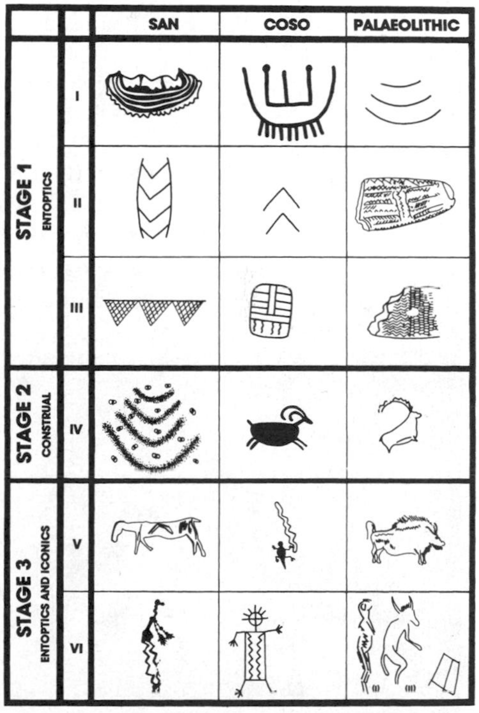

FIGURE 4.26 Entopic forms are images seen during trances and other states of altered consciousness. They are a widespread phenomenon among modern human groups and have been suggested as an explanation for some of the engraved and painted Upper Paleolithic images.

mental images with a finger in the sand or on the soft wall of a cave to experience them more fully would have 'fixed' them and would have been an initial step in the history of art. They were merely touching them and marking *what was already there.*"[129]

The study of Paleolithic visual imagery and art is a demonstration of a point made well by Hodder, that archaeology is not necessarily a neutral discipline in which analyses are scientific and culture-free.[130] Paleolithic art has often been a "Rorschach test," in the sense that modern-day observers have tried to read into it the mind and spirit of primitive humans, but they perhaps have learned more about their own psyches than about the primitives'. In any case, as Conkey notes, "'paleolithic art' [is] an extremely diverse and abundant repertoire of material culture that cannot be accounted for by any inclusive umbrella except perhaps as 'cultural.' "[131]

HUMAN COLONIZATION OF THE WORLD: CIRCA 30,000–10,000 YEARS AGO

One main factor in the upward trend of animal life has been the power of wandering.

Alfred North Whitehead

Unless the earth is truly different from every other known celestial body, any humans left on this lovely green-blue world in a few billion years will be converted to their component atoms—along with the pyramids of Egypt, the Great Wall of China, and all other human artifacts and natural features—and vaporized in a supernova such that they will spend eternity as elements of a timeless universe.

Given our human history, however, we can anticipate that our descendants will have long since colonized other worlds when that fateful day comes. However tenuous our links to these distant successors may become, some portion of "us" may reverberate through space and time until the universe once again collapses on itself.

Thus, "in our beginning is our end," perhaps. For our ancestors have always wandered, always colonized. Generation after generation, they left Africa, probed Europe and Asia, settled the Americas, Australia, the farthest ends of the planet (Figure 4.27). Many of the readers of this book can expect to see human colonies on the moon and perhaps beyond in their lifetimes. Exponential functions are impressive aspects of our universe. In time a single mutated virus turns into uncountable billions and

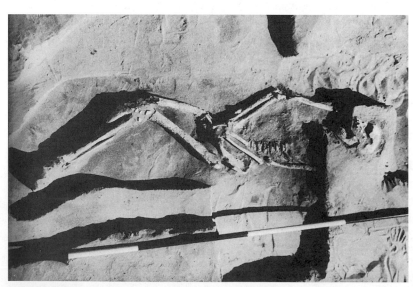

FIGURE 4.27   An early burial at Lake Mungo, Australia.

disperses throughout a system. We may not like the analogy, but we may "infect" the universe in the same way.

All this may seem far from the sturdy human hunter-foragers of the past hundred thousand years, but we are linked to them by the long-term growth functions of which we are all a part.

In various chapters of this book the focus is a major question about a particular human development: Why did culture evolve, how did *Homo sapiens sapiens* emerge as the only remaining hominins? If we ask "why" they colonized the world, we are left with the "because it's there" kind of answer Sir Edmund Hillary gave when asked why he climbed Mt. Everest. Simple demographic models suggest that any population will colonize appropriate environments through growth and migration, and our own ancestors' travels seem adequately "explained" by such formulations. But it is also hard to deny a human "instinct" for travel, an inherent desire to see what's beyond the next hill or valley. Also, as we have noted previously, maintaining genetic variability through genic exchange confers great advantages in terms of long-term survival.

If there is in fact an instinctive human urge to travel, it would be "adaptive" in an evolutionary sense, for long-term evolutionary success comes with dispersal and variation. Our ancestors accomplished both: They penetrated almost all of the world before the end of the Pleistocene, and although they remained a single species, they developed great variety in their physical forms and cultural adaptations.

On the one hand, the superficial variations our ancestors acquired as they colonized the world are the most trivial in all of human evolution; on the other hand, these differences of skin color, facial features, and other characteristics, and the cultural differences that accompanied them, are of the greatest socioeconomic and political importance in today's world—for human variations are inextricably linked to the idea of "race." Despite the rejection of this concept by many scholars, the concept of "race" is likely to remain with us until gene flow is sufficient that obvious differences in physical appearance all but disappear. Most anthropologists do not like the concept of "race" because, aside from the negative social problems associated with it, the characteristics used by most people to define race appear to be superficial, to be crude typologies imposed on a multidimensional underlying variability, and to be poorly correlated in some ways with underlying genetic relationships of various groups.[132] "Black" skin tones, for example, are shared by Australian Aborigines and west Africans—two groups of people whose degree of genetic relatedness may be much less than that between west Africans and Scandinavians. Physical features such as skin tones, degree of hair follicle "curl," nose shape and eyelid shape, and so on, tend to fall on geographic clines—that is, they exhibit variation over space and through time that is continuous, not discrete. And often variations within groups (*polymorphism*) is greater than that between groups (*polytypy*).[133]

For good or ill, however, the migrations and radiations of our ancestors over the past 30,000 years have produced or continued group differences that remain an important part of today's cultural world.[134]

The World at 30,000 Years Ago

Soon after 30,000 years ago the world was inhabited by only one human species, *Homo sapiens sapiens*—ourselves—and our ancestors had penetrated almost every environment of the Old World, and perhaps the New World as well (see chapter 5). Across this great expanse people had developed a great diversity of tools, in stone, bone, and other materials, much of which has probably long since disappeared from the archaeological record. The evidence of fish hooks and barbed spear-points suggests that many people had finally added fish to their diet—a seemingly obvious choice, but one that does not appear to have been made by many people until after 20,000 years ago. In many environments fish can greatly supplement other foods and thereby support much greater human populations with considerable reliability. Other technological advances, such as the atlatl, or throwing stick, probably also greatly extended the hunting prowess of many groups, and exploitation of plant foods was probably also rapidly improving in efficiency.

Late Pleistocene Climates and Geography

If we were ever fortunate enough to find people of about 30,000 years ago well-preserved in some glacier, we would probably see few differences between them and us. Over much of the world human teeth have become smaller during the past 30,000 years and some subtle changes in other aspects of our form and physiology have occurred, but not much else about us physically is different from the people of 30,000 years ago. Human brain size was slightly larger for some of the people at that time, but it is unlikely that they were of a fundamentally different mentality.

By 30,000 years ago people were living in almost every part of the Old World, and in Australia; their arrival in the Americas was certainly before 15,000 years ago, but the evidence for earlier occupations (see chapter 5) is controversial.

Oscillating sea levels had some role in this dispersal, since in some periods land bridges allowed people to walk from Southeast Asia to many areas that are now Indonesian islands, such as Java, Sumatra, and Borneo. Rising sea levels may also have forced people into migrations, even though the rates at which these levels rose were likely slow enough that no single individual had a personal sense of them. Thiel argues that people on islands in danger of being submerged by rising waters made the colonizing trips to Australia 50,000 or more years ago.[135] Elsewhere, people had to abandon many other low-lying areas, such as the shores of the eastern Mediterranean and the broad plains that now lie under the English Channel.

These climatic alterations and ensuing changes in geography and ecology can be thought of as giant engines, acting to mix and move human populations, offering adaptational challenges that elicited human ingenuity in various forms. But people were never simple passive victims of climatic and ecological happenstance: Humans not only developed the technology to make a living in the vast span of the world but also evolved the social systems that were an indispensable part of this adaptation.

Late Pleistocene Europeans

Between about 30,000 and 19,000 years ago, European climates began a long cooling trend, with some periods of extreme cold, but for most of the period the summers were cool and the winters relatively mild. The rich European grasslands and mixed forest habitats supported great numbers of herbivores, including reindeer, deer, bison, wild ox, ibex, woolly rhinoceros, and mammoths. France seems to have been densely occupied during this period, particularly near the confluence of the Dordogne and Vezere rivers

(Figure 4.28). This lovely part of the world is a well-watered, heavily forested limestone formation, honeycombed with caves and rock shelters, which offered excellent places to live. Mammoths, horses, and many other animals were hunted by these Upper Paleolithic peoples, but the reindeer was the staff of life: At many sites 99 percent of all the animal bones found belonged to reindeer; reindeer hides provided clothing and coverings for shelters; reindeer antlers were the hammers used to produce the long elegant blades for which these people are justly famous; and reindeer bone was the raw material for fish gorges, needles, awls, and other important tools.

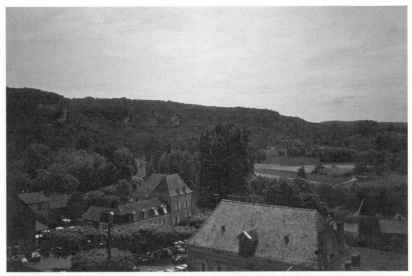

FIGURE 4.28   The Les Eyzies region of southern France is known for its concentration of Upper Paleolithic cave and rock shelter sites, including many famous cave art sites.

Reindeer travel long distances each year as they follow the grazing lands from one climatic zone to another. Thus, through the reindeer herds Upper Paleolithic peoples of southern France could exploit land they had never seen; the reindeer would browse their way to the far north each year and then return to southern France for the winter, at which time they could be harvested.

Average human group size may have been relatively large during the Upper Paleolithic in Europe, the Middle East, and other areas because of the requirements of hunting large gregarious mammals such as reindeer, bison, horses, and wild cattle. With some of these species, an efficient hunting technique is the drive, where many people work together to stampede a herd over a cliff or into a bog. Such mass slaughter also requires many people to process the carcasses, and a large group would also have been advantageous in these circumstances as a means of defending particularly favorable places along the animals' migration routes.

The overall population also increased in some parts of Europe—and probably much of Eurasia—during the last millennia of the Pleistocene. Several factors were probably important in this population growth. The stone-tool technology of this period, with its indirect percussion and pressure techniques, was vastly more efficient than previous industries. Spear throwers, or atlatls, were also in common use—a very significant innovation considering the heavy reliance on big game, since an atlatl can increase the range of a short spear from about 60 m, if thrown by hand, to about 150 m (Figure 4.29). Eventually, the bow and arrow also added significantly to hunting effectiveness. Some of the earliest evidence of bows and arrows comes from the Stellmoor site, near Hamburg, Germany, where about a hundred wooden arrows dating to approximately 10,000 years ago were recovered. But the bow-arrow combination was probably invented independently and

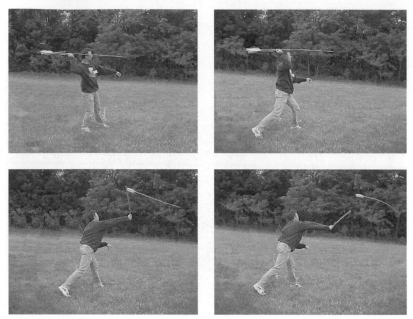

FIGURE 4.29 The atlatl, or spearthrower, was an important new technology in the Upper Paleolithic. Here, John Whittaker of Grinnell College demonstrates how an atlatl is used.

perhaps long before 10,000 years ago, if small stone tools called microliths were used as arrowheads.

Life in the Upper Paleolithic was somewhat more severe than one might imagine. From a sample of 76 Upper Paleolithic skeletons drawn from sites in Europe and Asia, Vallois found that less than half of these individuals had reached the age of 21, that only 12 percent were over 40, and that not a single female had reached the age of 30.[136] In fact, the distribution of ages and sexes represented by these skeletons was not significantly different from what one might expect from a comparable sample of Neandertals.[137] But even worse, many skeletons evidenced rickets, malnutrition, and other diseases and deformities. Not content with nature's provisions for population control, Upper Paleolithic peoples seem also to have occasionally slaughtered each other. At the site of Sandalja II (12,000 B.P.), near Pula, Yugoslavia, for example, the skeletal remains of 29 people were found in a smashed and splintered condition. Elsewhere, there is unmistakable evidence of wounds from arrows and spears.

By about 14,000 years ago, the people of western Europe had developed fish traps to harvest the countless salmon that migrated up the rivers there each year. This relatively late exploitation of fish in Europe has a parallel in prehistoric southeastern North America, where Native Americans lived for thousands of years subsisting primarily on deer, mussels, and a variety of plant foods, almost totally ignoring the myriad fish in nearby lakes and streams. If salmon were present in great numbers in European rivers during the Mousterian and early Upper Paleolithic, their exploitation may have been blocked by the terms of human adaptation to reindeer and other animals. Reindeer and other game would have been a more dependable resource for humans, in the sense that at least some of these animals would have been available year-round, while the salmon would have been sharply seasonal. Salmon runs, in fact, might have conflicted with the scheduling of reindeer hunting, and as a consequence these peoples may have been far from the river, exploiting different resources, at the time the salmon were most available. Perhaps even more important, the successful exploitation of salmon would have required technological readaptation on a major scale. Catching salmon one by one would not have been especially productive: Their real utility probably came only after nets, fish weirs, drying racks, smoking racks, and other largely nonportable technology came into common use.

The slow growth of worldwide human population density through most of the Pleistocene would seem to suggest that Upper Paleolithic populations were not in any sense "driven" by population pressures to exploit new resources, such as reindeer and salmon. Rather, it seems the reverse: As people began to devise ways to exploit rich salmon streams, reindeer herds, and other resources, larger groups could be supported. And just a slight increase in fertility or the number of offspring who lived on the average to reproductive age would in the long run produce vastly greater population densities.

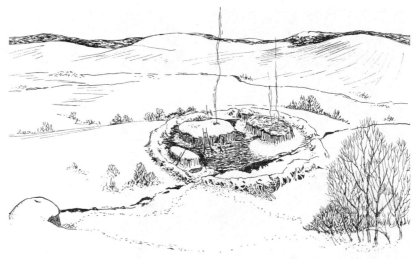

FIGURE 4.30   The reconstruction of a 27,000-year-old settlement at Dolni Vestonice illustrates how people used shelters to colonize the frigid plains of eastern Europe.

And it was not just in France and the ecologically richer parts of Europe that populations were growing in the late Pleistocene. Olga Soffer has documented, for example, the ingenuity of generations of peoples as they adapted to the harsh winters of the central Russian Plain.[138] One of the most amply documented Upper Paleolithic cultures in eastern Europe is the Kostenki-Bershevo culture centered in the Don River Valley, about 470 km southeast of Moscow. About 25,000–11,000 years ago, the Kostenki-Bershevo area was an open grassland environment, with no rock shelters, caves, or other natural habitations, and with very little wood available for fires. People here left a variety of archaeological sites, including base camps, where pithouses were constructed by digging a pit a meter or so deep, ringing the excavation with mammoth bones or tusks, and then draping hides over these supports (Figure 4.30). The savage winters of Pleistocene Russia must have required constantly burning fires, and the great quantities of bone ash found at these sites indicate that these fires were often fed with mammoth bones in lieu of very scarce wood. Some excavated pithouses were relatively large, with many hearths, suggesting that several families may have passed the winter together. The people of Kostenki subsisted primarily through big-game hunting, mainly of herd animals such as horses, with an occasional mammoth, wild cow, or reindeer. Numerous wolf and fox bones at these sites probably reflect the hunting of these animals for their fur for clothing. Like their Upper Paleolithic counterparts elsewhere, the Kostenki people manufactured a variety of decorative items, including "Venus" figurines (representations of women, usually with exaggerated secondary sexual characteristics) (Figure 4.31).

Late Pleistocene Asians

Until recently, few Upper Paleolithic sites were known in East Asia. Excavations at Zhoukoudian revealed levels dating to about 10,000 years ago containing approximately

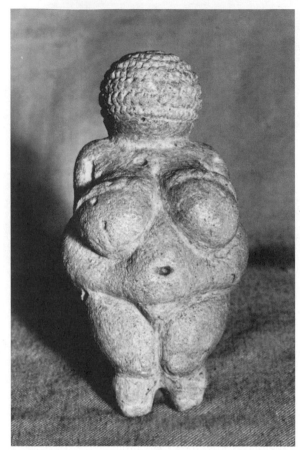

FIGURE 4.31 Cast of Venus figurine from Willendorf, Austria. These figurines are widespread across much of Europe during the Gravettian Upper Paleolithic period, suggesting a shared belief system.

seven individuals—all of whom had been killed, but apparently not eaten. One individual had clearly died from an arrow or small spear wound to the skull, and another had been beaten about the head with a large stone. Elsewhere, two skulls have been retrieved from Wadjak, in central Java, but dating these has proved difficult.

Hundreds of late Pleistocene sites have been found in Japan. Dating these sites is difficult, but the classic European Upper Paleolithic blade and burin industries are well represented in Japan, particularly in the northern areas across from Siberia.

The earliest known stone tools from Southeast Asia may be those of the Sonviian assemblage from northern Vietnam, dating to about 23,000 B.P.,[139] but the Hoabinihian lithics of about 12,000 years ago are the earliest *widespread* Upper Paleolithic lithic industry in this area.

One of the most intriguing problems in Asian prehistory is the initial colonization of Australia. One has to imagine that people who were living in a world in which the Neandertals still had 15,000 years of domination of Europe left somehow managed to float or sail. The geology seems to admit no other possibilities, because even with the most extreme estimates of the extent to which Pleistocene glaciers lowered worldwide sea levels, people could not have got to Australia except over some very deep water. Nor is swimming a realistic possibility. Probably thousands of coastal fisherfolk were washed out to sea and drowned in many millennia of typhoons and floods, before some fortunate castaways finally made it to Australia.

In any case, between 60,000 and 45,000 years ago, the ancestors of the Australian Aborigines somehow managed to cross about 65 km of open ocean to reach Australia. And while it is possible that an occasional boat of fisherfolk was shipwrecked on the New Guinea–Australia coast, computer simulations that take into account normal fertility rates and the genetic diversity of modern populations suggest that more than just a boatload or two of colonists founded that area's present aboriginal population.[140] Two distinct groups of ancient people have been found there,[141] which some scholars believe indicate colonization by two different groups, one a more gracile type, by 50,000 years ago, the other a more robust people, before 20,000 years ago. Like their contemporaries in America, the late Pleistocene Australians lived at a time when many large and small animal species were becoming extinct, and their possible role in this extinction pattern remains a matter of controversy.

The Australian Aborigines offer a wonderful subject for meditations on the nature of humanity. Consider: These people lived in what may have been nearly complete isolation for more than 40,000 years in an ecologically diverse continent, and when first encountered by Europeans in the seventeenth century, their technology hardly approached the sophistication of the Neandertals: just simple stone tools and rudimentary wooden implements. Yet they evolved a kinship system and cosmology that most non-Aborigines can only apprehend dimly after many years of study.

SUMMARY AND CONCLUSIONS

We began this chapter with humans of about 1.5 million years ago spread out along the warm margins of Africa and Asia, making a reasonable living with little more than crude stone tools, intellectual abilities far poorer than our own, and probably only the rudiments of human social organization. We end this chapter, in effect, with ourselves, in the form of our late Pleistocene relatives of just 30,000 years ago. As to what happened in this period of a million and a half years, we have a lot of data, but not enough to describe with certainty some of the most important evolutionary patterns and dynamics. Every year anthropologists meet in conferences around the world to discuss their research, and this year, like last year and every previous year, they will debate the origins of modern humans. Like this chapter, these debates will end with no real resolution. Some anthropologists are convinced that one or another of these models of human origins is accurate, but no one really knows. Even with a tenfold increase in finds of relevant human fossils, these debates would likely continue for years to come. If Richard Klein is correct,[142] for example, the origins of modern humans may have arisen directly from a single mutation, perhaps in a single individual, that allowed one group of East Africans to conceptualize time, space, and human possibilities in a way superior to that of all other humans. Such a mutation could have occurred and left no trace in fragmentary crania. If Frayer, Wolpoff, Thorne, Smith, and Pope—all advocates of multiregional continuity in human evolution—are correct, they apparently will need much additional data to convince their colleagues.

Yet, as noted earlier, it is not necessarily pointless to review evidence and arguments in unresolved debates. In these conflicting ideas about the nature and history of our origins we can see how "science" operates and we can get a sense of the significance of these intellectual problems. Currently, hardly a day passes without the announcement of some new breakthrough in identifying the genetic basis for some aspect of the human condition, from our personalities to our susceptibility to disease. To the extent that we are expressions of our genes, our history and fate, then, are in the selective forces of the past hundreds of thousands of years. These forces and these genetic patterns are, of course, the basic data in these debates about modern human origins.

Given the pace of genetic research, it is not impossible that we will eventually be able to re-create a Neandertal, but until we do and then give him or her the SATs, we will not be able to resolve arguments conclusively about just who these people were, what they were capable of, and how they relate to us.

In searching for causes of the increasing brain size and other changes that took place between 400,000 and 30,000 years ago, we might note that rates of evolutionary change frequently seem to be higher along the margins of a species' range. This may have been the case with *Homo*, as bands of these hominins probed far into England, northern Europe, and perhaps northern Eurasia, and began to specialize in various forms of hunting, scavenging, and gathering. The Swanscombe and Steinheim individuals, with their nearly modern brain size, may be reflections of these developments along the northern periphery. Gene flow in most hunting-and-gathering societies is sufficiently high that these changes in brain size and facial architecture would probably have been quickly disseminated over a wide area.

But the "margins" of a cultural animal like early humans can be culturally and technologically—not just geographically—defined. As noted later, brain sizes may have increased most rapidly in Africa, not on the world's cold periphery. Brain tissue has a relatively high "cost": It consumes great amounts of energy and oxygen. Also, giving birth to large-brained offspring requires a pelvic bone structure that reduces maternal mobility. Since *Homo erectus* was obviously an efficient hunter, forager, and tool-maker, perhaps the increased brain size was related to increasing emotional capacities rather than to improvements in the problem-solving abilities that were important in hunting or tool-making. Great advantages would accrue to a Pleistocene hunting-and-gathering group that could organize itself as part of a social network involving many different bands and hundreds of individuals, and perhaps the increasing brain size had to do with the selective advantage of being able to generalize emotions to scores of "kinsmen."

In any case, the great variability of cranial capacity among "normal" people today, and the fact that human brain size seems generally to have increased quite uniformly up to about 100,000 years ago, should warn against simplistic explanations of this phenomenon.

To explain the relatively slow rate of technological change between 2 million and 100,000 years ago, we must reflect on the fact that our ancestors of this period were many fewer than the large populations of humans that characterized the world even 10,000 years ago. Although technological innovation is not a simple product of the number of minds available to create new ideas, a strong relationship exists between population numbers and innovation in the simple hunting-gathering economies of the early and middle Pleistocene. Even as late as 500,000 years ago, there were probably only a million people in the entire world. Also, people of this era tended to live much shorter lives. Few survived past 30 years of age, and—although few adolescents of any age have believed it—people learn a great deal and retain considerable creativity past 30.

Finally, if we look beyond the bones and stones and the practical analytical questions about our past, we might muse on the implications of the evidence presented here. It is worth noting that the facts and models about the dynamics of our ancestry recounted here and in chapter 3 all but killed a beautiful world- and life-view. The idea of "Nature, red in tooth and claw," as the means by which we emerged from our reptilian past has appalled people since the dark truth of our origins was first made evident by Darwin. It is thus appropriate to end this chapter with a beautifully somber expression of this mortally wounded world and life-view, by Alfred, Lord Tennyson, a contemporary of Darwin, and a man profoundly anguished by Darwin's ideas.

> Are God and Nature then at strife,
>   That Nature lends such evil dreams?
>   So careful of the type she seems,
> So careless of the single life;

That I, considering everywhere
   Her secret meaning in her deeds,
   And finding that of fifty seeds
She often brings but one to bear,

I falter where I firmly trod,
   And falling with my weight of cares
   Upon the great world's altar-stairs
That slope thro' darkness up to God,

I stretch lame hands of faith, and grope,
   And gather dust and chaff, and call
   To what I feel is Lord of all,
And faintly trust the larger hope.

"So careful of the type?" but no.
   From scarpéd cliff and quarried stone
   She cries, "A thousand types are gone:
I care for nothing: all shall go . . ."
. . .

Man, her last work, who seem'd so fair,
   Such splendid purpose in his eyes,
   Who roll'd the psalm to wintry skies,
Who built him fanes of fruitless prayer,

Who trusted God was love indeed
   And love Creation's final law—
   Tho' Nature, red in tooth and claw
With ravine, shriek'd against his creed—

Who loved, who sufferd countless ills,
   Who battled for the True, the Just,
   Be blown about the desert dust,
Or seal'd within the iron hills?

No more? A monster then, a dream,
   A discord. Dragons of the prime,
   That tare each other in their slime,
Were mellow music match'd with him.
         From In Memoriam, 1850

BIBLIOGRAPHY

Adcock, G. J., E. S. Dennis, S. Easteal, G. A. Huttley, L. S. Jermiin, W. J. Peacock, and A. Thorne. 2001. "Mitochrondrial DNA Sequences in Ancient Australians: Implications for Modern Human Origins." *Proceedings of the National Academy of Sciences* 98(2):537–542.

Aiello, L. C. 1993. "The Fossil Evidence for Modern Human Origins in Africa: A Revised View." *American Anthropologist* 95:73–96.

Aiello, L. C., and R. I. M. Dunbar. 1993. "Neocortex Size, Group Size, and the Evolution of Language." *Current Anthropology* 34:184–192.

Arens, W. 1979. *The Man-Eating Myth*. New York: Oxford University Press.

Arensburg, B., and A. Belfer-Cohen. 1998. "Sapiens and Neandertals. Rethinking the Levantine Middle Paleolithic Hominids." In *Neandertals and Modern Humans in Western Asia*, ed. T. Akazawa, K. Aoki, and O. Bar-Yosef, pp. 311–327. New York: Plenum Press.

Arsuaga, J-L., I. Martinez, A. Garcia, J-M. Carretero, and E. Carbonell. 1993. "Three New Human Skulls from the Sima de los Huesos Middle Pleistocene Site in Sierra de Atapuerca, Spain." *Nature* 362:534–537.

Asfaw, B., Y. Beyene, G. Suwa, R. C. Walter, T. D. White, G. WoldeGabriel, and T. Yemane. 1992. "The Earliest Acheulean from Konso-Gardula." *Nature* 360:732–735.

Baffier, D., and M. Julien. 1990. "L'Outillage en Os des Niveaux Châtelperroniens d'Arcy-sur-Cure (Yonne)." In *Paléolithique Moyen Récent et Paléolithique Supérieur Ancien en Europe*, ed. C. Farizy, pp. 329–334. Nemours: Mémoires du Musée de Préhistoire d'Ile de France 3.

Bahn, P. G. 1994. "New Advances in the Field of Ice Age Art." In *Origins of Anatomically Modern Humans*, eds. M. H. Nitecki and V. Nitecki. New York: Plenum Press.

Bahn, P., and J. Vertus. 1988. *Images of the Ice Age*. New York: Viking Press.

Barham, L., and K. Robson-Brown, eds. 2001. *Human Roots: Africa and Asia in the Middle Pleistocene*. Bristol: Western Academic & Specialist Press.

Barton, C. M., G. A. Clark, and A. E. Choen. 1994. "Art as Information: Explaining Upper Paleolithic Art in Western Europe." *World Archaeology* 26(2):185–207.

Bar-Yosef, O. 1994. "The Lower Paleolithic of the Near East." *Journal of World Prehistory* 8:211–265.

———. 2002. "The Upper Paleolithic Revolution." *Annual Review of Anthropology* 31:363–393.

Bar-Yosef, O., and N. Goren-Inbar. 1993. "The Lithic Assemblages of 'Ubeidiya: A Lower Paleolithic Site in the Jordan Valley.'" *Qedem* (Jerusalem) 45:1–266.

Bar-Yosef, O., and B. Vandermeersch. 1993. "Modern Humans in the Levant." *Scientific American* (April):94–100.

Bednarik, R. G. 1992. "Paleoart and Archaeological Myths." *Cambridge Archaeological Journal* 2:27–43.

———. 2003. "A Figurine from the African Acheulian." *Current Anthropology* 44(3):405–413.

Bellwood, P. 1986. *The Prehistory of the Indo-Malaysian Archipelago*. Orlando, FL: Academic Press.

———. 1987. "The Prehistory of Island Southeast Asia: A Multidisciplinary Review of Recent Research." *Journal of World Prehistory* 1(2):171–224.

Bender, M. 1983. "Comment on G. Krantz (*CA* 21:773–79)." *Current Anthropology* 24(1):113.

Berger, T. D., and E. Trinkaus. 1995. "Patterns of Trauma Among the Neandertals." *Journal of Archaeological Science* 22:841–852.

Bermúdez de Castro, J. M., J. L. Arsuaga, E. Carbonell, A. Rosas, I. Martínez, and M. Mosquera. 1997. "A Hominid from the Lower Pleistocene of Atapuerca, Spain: Possible Ancestor to Neandertals and Modern Humans." *Science* 276:1392–1395.

Binford, L. R. 1981. *Bones: Ancient Men and Modern Myth*. New York: Academic Press.

———. 1984. *Faunal Remains from Klasies River Mouth*. New York: Academic Press.

———. 1985. "Human Ancestors: Changing Views of Their Behavior." *Journal of Anthropological Archaeology* 4(4):292–327.

Binford, L. R., and S. Binford. 1966. "A Preliminary Analysis of Functional Variability in the Mousterian of Levallois Facies." In *Recent Studies in Paleoanthropology* (*American Anthropologist* special publication), pp. 238–295.

Binford, L., and N. Stone. 1986. "Zhoukoudien: A Closer Look." *Current Anthropology* 27(5):453–475.

Bischoff, J. L., R. Julià, and R. Mora. 1988. "Uranium-Series Dating of the Mousterian Occupation at Abric Romani, Spain." *Nature* 332:668–670.

Bischoff, J. L., K. Ludwig, J. Francisco Garcia, E. Carbonell, M. Vaquero, T. W. Stafford, and A. J. T. Jull. 1994. "Dating of the Basal Aurignacian Sandwich at Abric Romani (Catalunya, Spain) by Radiocarbon and Uranium-series." *Journal of Archaeological Science* 21:541–551.

Boaz, N. T., R. L. Ciochon, Q. Xu, and J. Liu. 2000. "Large Mammalian Carnivores as an Taphonomic Factor in the Bone Accumulation at Zhoudoukian." *Acta Anthropologica Sinica*. Supplement to Vol. 19:224–234.

Bocquet-Appel, J.-P., and P. Y. Demars. 2000. "Neanderthal Contraction and Modern Human Colonization of Europe." *Antiquity* 74:544–552.

Bordes, F. 1961a. *Typologie du paleolithique ancien et moyen*. Bordeaux: Publication de l'Institut de Prehistoire de l'Universite de Bordeaux.

———. 1961b. "Mousterian Cultures in France." *Science* 134:803–810.

———. 1972. *A Tale of Two Caves*. New York: Harper & Row.

Bordes, F., and D. de Sonneville-Bordes. 1970. "The Significance of Variability in Paleolithic Assemblages." *World Archaeology* 2:61–73.

Boule, M., and H. Vallois. 1932. *Fossil Men*. London: Thames and Hudson.

Bowdler, J. M., R. Jones, and A. G. Thorne. 1970. "Pleistocene Human Remains from Australia: A Living Site and Human Cremation from Lake Mungo, Western New South Wales." *World Archaeology* 2:39–60.

Bower, B. 1988. "An Earlier Dawn for Modern Humans?" *Science News* 133:138.

Brace, C. L. 1975. "Review of *Shanidar: The First Flower People.* by R. Solecki." *Natural History* 80:82–86.

Brace, C. L., D. P. Tracer, L. Allen Yaroch, J. Robb, K. Brandt, and A. Russel Nelson. 1993. "Clines and Clusters Versus 'Race': A Test in Ancient Egypt and of a Death on the Nile." *Yearbook of Physical Anthropology* 36:1–31.

Bräuer, G. 1992. "Africa's Place in the Evolution of *Homo sapiens.*" In *Continuity or Replacement: Controversies in* Homo sapiens *Evolution,* ed. G. Bräuer and F. H. Smith. Rotterdam: A. A. Balkema.

Brennan, M. U. 1991. *Health and Disease in the Middle and Upper Paleolithic of Southwestern France: A Bioarchaeological Study,* Ph.D. Dissertation, New York University, New York.

Brooks, A. S., D. M. Helgren, J. S. Cramer, A. Franklin, W. Hornyak, J. M. Keating, R. G. Klein, W. J. Rink, H. P. Schwarcz, J. N. L. Smith, K. Stewart, N. E. Todd, J. Verniers, and J. E. Yellen. 1995. "Dating and Context of Three Middle Stone Age Sites with Bone Artifacts in the Upper Semliki Valley, Zaire." *Science* 268:548–552.

Brothwell, D. 1961. "Upper Pleistocene Human Skull from Niah Caves, Sarawak." *Sarawak Museum Journal* 9:323.

Brown, K. A., and M. Pluciennik. 2001. "Archaeology and Human Genetics: Lessons for Both." *Antiquity* 75:101–106.

Brown, P., T. Sutikna, M. J. Morwood, R. P. Soejono, Jatmiko, E. Wayhu Saptomo, and R. Awe Due. 2004. "A New Small-Bodied Hominin from the Late Pleistocene of Flores, Indonesia." *Nature* 431:1055–1061.

Cann, R. L., Rickards, O., and J. K. Lum. 1995. "Mitochondrial DNA and Human Evolution: Our One Lucky Mother." In *Origins of Anatomically Modern Humans,* eds. M. H. Nitecki and V. Nitecki. New York: Plenum Press.

Cann, R. L., M. Stoneking, and A. C. Wilson. 1987. "Mitochondrial DNA and Human Evolution." *Nature* 325:31–36.

Caramelli, D., C. Lalueza-Fox, C. Vernesi, M. Lari, A. Casoli, F. Mallegni, B. Chiarelli, I. Dupanloup, J. Bertranpetit, G. Barbujani, and G. Bertorelle. 2003. "Evidence for a Genetic Discontinuity Between Neanderthals and 24,000-Year-Old Anatomically Modern Humans." *Proceedings of the National Academy of Sciences* 100(11):6593–6597.

Carbonell, E., J. M. Bermudez de Castro, J. L. Arsuaga, J. C. Diez, A. Rosas, G. Cuenva-Bescos, R. Sala, M. Mosquera, and X. Rodríguez. 1995. "Lower Pleistocene Hominids and Artefacts from Atapuerca-TD6 (Spain)." *Science* 269:826–830.

Carlisle, R. C., and M. I. Siegel. 1974. "Some Problems in the Interpretation of Neanderthal Speech Capabilities. A Reply to Lieberman." *American Anthropologist* 76:319–322.

Carroll, L. 1920. *Alice's Adventures in Wonderland. Through the Looking Glass and the Hunting of the Snark.* New York: The Modern Library.

Cavalli-Sforza, L. L., P. Menozzi, and A. Piazza. 1994. *The History and Geography of Human Genes.* Princeton, NJ: Princeton University Press.

Chase, P. G. 1986. *The Hunters of Combe Grenal: Approaches to Middle Paleolithic Subsistence in Europe.* Oxford: BAR International Series 286.

Chase, P. G., and H. L. Dibble. 1987. "Middle Paleolithic Symbolism: A Review of Current Evidence and Interpretations." *Journal of Anthropological Archaeology* 6:263–294.

Clark, G. A., ed. 1991. *Perspectives on the Past: Theoretical Biases in Mediterranean Hunter-Gatherer Research.* Philadelphia: University of Pennsylvania Press.

———. 2002. "Neanderthal Archaeology—Implications for Our Origins." *American Anthropologist* 104:50–67.

Clark, G. A., and J. Lindly. 1991. "On Paradigmatic Biases and Paleolithic Research Traditions." *Current Anthropology* 32:577–587.

Clottes, J. 2001. "France's Magical Ice Age Art: Chauvet Cave." *National Geographic* (August) 200(2):104–121.

Clottes, J., A. Beltrán, J. Courtin, and H. Cosquer. 1992. "The Cosquer Cave on Cape Morgiou, Marseilles." *Antiquity* 66:583–598.

Conkey, M. 1980. "The Identification of Prehistoric Hunter-Gatherer Aggregation Sites: The Case of Altamira." *Current Anthropology* 21:609–630.

———. 1987. "New Approaches in the Search for Meaning? A Review of Research in Paleolithic Art." *Journal of Field Archaeology* 14(4):413–430.

Conway, B., J. McNabb, and N. Ashton, eds. 1996. *Excavations at Barnfield Pit, Swanscombe, 1968–72.* London: British Museum.

Coon, C. S. 1962. *The Origin of Races.* New York: Alfred A. Knopf.

Davidson, I., and W. Noble. 1989. "The Archaeology of Perception: Traces of Depiction and Language." *Current Anthropology* 30:125–155.

De Beaune, S. A. 1987. "Paleolithic Lamps and Their Specialization: A Hypothesis." *Current Anthropology* 28(4):569–577.

Dennell, H. M., H. M. Rendell, and A. E. Hailwood. 1988a. "Late Pliocene Artefacts from Northern Pakistan." *Current Anthropology* 29(3):495–498.

———. 1988b. "Early Tool-Making in Asia: Two Million Year Old Artefacts in Pakistan." *Antiquity* 62:98–106.

D'Errico, F., and A. Nowell. 2000. "A New Look at the Berekhat Ram Figurine: Implications for the Origins of Symbolism." *Cambridge Archaeological Journal* 10(1): 123–167.

D'Errico, F., J. Zilhão, M. Julián, D. Baffier, and J. Pelegrin. 1998. "Neanderthal Acculturation in Western Europe? A Critical Review of the Evidence and Its Interpretation." *Current Anthropology* 39(2):S1–S44.

Dibble, H. L. 1995. "Middle Paleolithic Scraper Reduction: Background, Clarification, and Review of the Evidence to Date." *Journal of Archaeological Method and Theory* 2(4):299–368.

de Vos, J., P. Sondaar, and C. Swisher. 1994. "Dating Hominid Sites in Indonesia." *Science* 266:1726–1727.

Dubois, E. 1921. "The Proto-Australian Fossil Man of Wadjak, Java." *Proceedings: Koninklijke Nederlandse Akademie van Wetenschappen* 23:1013.

Falk, D. 1975. "Comparative Anatomy of the Larynx in Man and the Chimpanzee: Implications for Language in Neanderthal." *American Journal of Physical Anthropology* 43:123–132.

Falk, D., C. Hildebolt, K. Smith, M. J. Morwood, T. Sutikna, P. Borwn, Jatmiko, E. W. Saptomo, B. Brunsden, and F. Prior. 2005. "The Brain of LB1, *Homo floresiensis*." *Science* 308:243–245.

Farizy, C. 1990. "The Transition from Middle to Upper Palaeolithic at Arcy-sure-Cure (Yonne, France): Technological, Economic and Social Aspects." In *The Emergence of Modern Humans*, ed. P. Mellars. Ithaca, NY: Cornell University Press.

Ferraro, G., W. Trevathan, and J. Levy. 1994. *Anthropology. An Applied Perspective*. St. Paul, MN: West Publishing Company.

Fisher, E. 1979. *Woman's Creation*. New York: McGraw-Hill.

Frankel, D. 1991. *Remains to Be See: Archaeological Insights into Australian Prehistory*. Melbourne: Longman Cheshire.

Frayer, D. W. 1986. "Cranial Variation at Mladec and the Relationship Between Mousterian and Upper Paleolithic Hominids." *Anthropos* 23:243–256.

Frayer, D. W., and M. H. Wolpoff. 1993. "Comment on 'Glottogenesis and Modern *Homo sapiens*' (R. G. Milo and D. Quiatt)." *Current Anthropology* 34(5):582–584.

Frayer, D. W., M. Wolpoff, A. G. Thorne, F. H. Smith, and G. G. Pope. 1993. "Theories of Modern Human Origins: The Paleontological Test." *American Anthropologist* 95:14–50.

———. 1994. "Getting It Straight." *American Anthropologist* 96:424–438.

Freeman, L. G. 1975. "Acheulian Sites and Stratigraphy in Iberia and the Maghreb." In *After the Australopithecines*, ed. K. W. Butzer and G. L. Isaac. The Hague: Mouton.

———. 1994. "Torralba and Ambrona: A Review of Discoveries." In *Integrative Paths to the Past: Paleoanthropological Advances in Honor of F. Clark Howell*, ed. R. S. Corruccini and R. L. Ciochon. Englewood Cliffs, NJ: Prentice Hall.

Freeman, M. 1971. "A Social and Economic Analysis of Systematic Female Infanticide." *American Anthropologist* 73:1011–1018.

Gabunia, L., and A. Vekua. 1995. "A Plio-Pleistocene Hominid from Dmanisi, Georgia." *Nature* 373:509–512.

Gabunia, L., A. Vekua, D. Lordkipanidze, C. C. Swisher III, R. Ferring, A. Justus, M. Nioradze, M. Tvalchrelidze, S. C. Antón, G. Bosinski, O. Jöris, M-A. de Lumley, G. Majsuradze, and A. Mouskhelishvili. 2000. "Earliest Pleistocene Hominid Cranial Remains from Dmanisi, Republic of Georgia: Taxonomy, Geological Setting, and Age." *Science* 288:1019–1025.

Gambier, D. 1989. "Fossil Hominids from the Early Upper Paleolithic (Auignacian) of France." In *The Human Revolution: Behavioral and Biological Perspectives on the Origins of Modern Humans*, ed. P. Mellars and C. B. Stringer. Edinburgh: Edinburgh University Press.

Gamble, C. 1994. *Timewalkers: The Prehistory of Global Colonization*. Cambridge, MA: Harvard University Press.

Gargett, R. H. 1989. "Grave Shortcomings: The Evidence for Neanderthal Burial." *Current Anthropology* 30(2):157–190.

Garn, S., and W. Block. 1970. "The Limited Nutritional Value of Cannibalism." *American Anthropologist* 72:106.

Gee, H. 1995. "New Hominid Remains Found in Ethiopia." *Nature* 373:272.

Gisis, I., and O. Bar-Yosef. 1974. "New Excavations in Zuttiyeh Cave, Wadi Amud, Israel." *Paléorient* 2:175–180.

Goebel, T. 1995. "The Record of Human Occupation of the Russian Subarctic and Arctic." *Byrd Polar Research Center Miscellaneous Series* M–335:41–46.

Goren-Inbar, N., S. Belitsky, K. Verosub, E. Werker, M. Kislev, A. Heimann, I. Carmi, and A. Rosenfeld. 1992. "New Discoveries at the Middle Pleistocene Acheulian Site of Gesher Benot Ya'aqov, Israel." *Quarternary Research* 38:117–128.

Gould, S. J. 1989. *Wonderful Life*. New York: W.W. Norton.

Halverson, J. 1987. "Art for Art's Sake in the Paleolithic." *Current Anthropology* 28(1):63–89.

Harpending, H. 1994. "Gene Frequencies, DNA Sequences, and Human Origins." *Perspectives in Biology and Medicine* 37:384–394.

Harrold, F. B. 1989. "Mousterian, Châtelperronian, and Early Aurignacian in Western Europe: Continuity or Discontinuity." In *The Human Revolution: Behavioral and Biological Perspectives on the Origins of Modern Humans*, ed. P. Mellars and C. B. Stringer. Edinburgh: Edinburgh University Press.

———. 2000. "The Chatelperronian in Historical Context." *Journal of Anthropological Research* 56:59–75.

Harvati, K., S. R. Frost, and K. P. McNulty. 2004. "Neanderthal Taxonomy Reconsidered: Implications of 3D Primate Models of Intra- and Interspecific Differences." *Proceedings of the National Academy of Sciences* 101:1147–1152.

Hayden, B. 1993. "The Cultural Capacities of the Neandertals: A Review and Re-Evaluation." *Journal of Human Evolution* 24:113–146.

Haynes, C. V. 1992. "Contributions of Radiocarbon Dating to the Geochronology of the Peopling of the New World." In *Radiocarbon After Four Decades*, ed. R. E. Taylor, A. Long, and R. S. Kra. New York: Springer-Verlag.

Herrnstein, R. J., and C. Murray. 1996. *The Bell Curve: Intelligence and Class Structure in American Life*. New York: Simon and Schuster.

Hodder, I. 1986. *Reading the Past: Current Approaches to Interpretation in Archaeology*. Cambridge, England: Cambridge University Press.

Hoffecker, J. G., W. R. Powers, and T. Goebel. 1993. "The Colonization of Beringia and the Peopling of the New World." *Science* 259:46–53.

Holloway, R. L., Jr. 1989. "Comment on 'On Depiction and Language.'" *Current Anthropology* 30(3):331–332.

Howell, F. C. 1961. "Isimila: A Paleolithic Site in Africa." *Scientific American* 205:118–131.

———. 1994. "A Chronostratigraphic and Taxonomic Framework of the Origin of Modern Humans." In *Origins of Anatomically Modern Humans*, ed. M. H. Nitecki and V. Nitecki. New York: Plenum Press.

Hublin, J-J. 1990. "Les Peuplements Paléolithiques de'Europe: Un Point de Vue Géographique." In *Paléolithique Moyen Récent et Paléolithique Supérieur Ancien en Europe*, ed. C. Farizy, pp. 29–37. Nemours: Mémoires du Musée de Préhistoire d'Ile de France 3.

Isaac, G. 1975. "Sorting Out the Muddle in the Middle—An Anthropologist's Post-Conference Appraisal." In *After the Australopithecines*, ed. K. W. Butzer and G. Isaac. The Hague: Mouton.

———. 1984. "The Archaeology of Human Origins: Studies of the Lower Palaeolithic in East Africa, 1971–1981." *Advances in World Archaeology* 3:1–89.

James, S. R. 1989. "Hominid Use of Fire in the Lower and Middle Pleistocene: A Review of the Evidence." *Current Anthropology* 30(1):1–26.

Jelinek, A. J. 1982a. "The Tabun Cave and Paleolithic Man in the Levant." *Science* 216:1369–1375.

———. 1994. "Hominids, Energy, Environment, and Behavior in the Late Pleistocene." In *Origins of Anatomically Modern Humans*, ed. M. H. Nitecki and V. Nitecki. New York: Plenum Press.

Jones, R. 1990. "From Kakadu to Kutikina: The Southern Continent at 18,000 Years Ago." In *The World at 18,000 BP: Low Latitudes*, ed. C. Gamble and O. Soffer. London: Unwin Hyman.

Jorgensen, G. 1977. "A Contribution of the Hypothesis of a Little More Fitness of Blood Group O." *Journal of Human Evolution* 6:741–744.

Klein, R. G. 1973. *Ice-Age Hunters of the Ukraine*. Chicago: University of Chicago Press.

———. 1987. "Reconstructing How Early People Exploited Animals: Problems and Prospects." In *The Evolution of Human Hunting*, ed. M. H. Nitecki and D. V. Nitecki. New York: Plenum Press.

———. 1999. *The Human Career*. Chicago: University of Chicago Press.

———. 1995. "Anatomy, Behavior, and Modern Human Origins." *Journal of World Prehistory* 9(2):167–198.

———. 2003. "Whither the Neanderthals?" *Science* 299:1525–1527.

Klein, R. G., and B. Edgar. 2002. *The Dawn of Human Culture*. New York: John Wiley & Sons.

Krings, M., C. Capelli, F. Tschentscher, H. Geisert, S. Meyer, A. von Haeseler, K. Grossschmidt, G. Possnert, M. Paunovic, and S. Pääbo. 2000. "A View of Neanderthal Genetic Diversity." *Nature Genetics* 26:144–146.

Krings, M., A. Stone, R. W. Schmitz, H. Drainitzki, M. Stoneking, and S. Pääbo. 1997. "Neanderthal DNA Sequences and the Origin of Modern Humans." *Cell* 90:19–30.

Kuzmin, Y. V. 1994. "Prehistoric Colonization of Northeastern Siberia and Migration to America: Radiocarbon Evidence." *Radiocarbon* 36:367–376.

Lahr, M. M. 1994. "The Multiregional Model of Modern Human Origins: A Reassessment of Its Morphological Basis." *Journal of Human Evolution* 26:23–56.

Larichev, V., U. Khol'ushkin, and I. Laricheva. 1987. "Lower and Middle Paleolithic of Northern Asia: Achievements, Problems, and Perspectives." *Journal of World Prehistory* 1(4):415–464.

Laville, H., Rigaud J.-P., and J. Sackett. 1980. *Rock Shelters of the Perigord*. New York: Academic Press.

Leakey, L. S. 1951. *Olduvai Gorge, 1931–1951*. Cambridge, England: Cambridge University Press.

Leroi-Gourhan, A. 1968. "The Evolution of Paleolithic Art." *Scientific American* 209(2):58–74.

———. 1982. *The Dawn of European Art*. Cambridge, England: Cambridge University Press.

Leveque, F., A. M. Backer, and M. Guilband, eds. 1993. *Context of a Late Neandertal: Implications of Multidisciplinary Research for the Transition to Upper Paleolithic Adaptations at Saint-Cesaire, Charente-Maritime, France*. Madison, WI: Prehistory Press.

Leveque, F., and B. Vandermeersch. 1980. "Les Decouvertes de Restes Humains dans un Horizon Castelperronien de Saint-Cesaire (Charente-Maritime)." *Bulletin de la Societe Prehistorique Francaise* 77:35.

Lewis-Williams, J. D., and T. A. Dowson. 1988. "The Signs of All Times: Entopic Phenomena in Upper Paleolithic Art." *Current Anthropology* 29(2):201–246.

Lieberman, D. E. 1995. "Testing Hypotheses About Recent Human Evolution from Skulls." *Current Anthropology* 36:159–197.

Lieberman, L., and F. L. C. Jackson. 1995. "Race and Three Models of Human Origin." *American Anthropologist* 97(2):231–242.

Lieberman, P. E. 1991. *Uniquely Human: The Evolution of Speech, Thought, and Selfless Behavior*. Cambridge, MA: Harvard University Press.

———. 2002. "On the Nature and Evolution of the Neural Bases of Human Language." *Yearbook of Physical Anthropology* 45:36–61.

Lieberman, P. E., and E. S. Crelin. 1971. "On the Speech of Neanderthals." *Linguistic Inquiry* 2:203–222.

Lieberman, P. E., E. S. Crelin, and D. H. Klatt. 1972. "Phonetic Ability and Related Anatomy of the Newborn and Adult Human, Neanderthal Man, and the Chimpanzee." *American Anthropologist* 74:287.

Lindly, J. M., and G. A. Clark. 1990. "Symbolism and Modern Human Origins." *Current Anthropology* 31:233–240.

Littlefield, A., L. Lieberman, and L. T. Reynolds. 1982. "Redefining Race: The Potential Demise of a Concept in Physical Anthropology." *Current Anthropology* 23(6):641–655.

Lourandos, H. 1997. *Continent of Hunter-Gatherers: New Perspectives in Australian Prehistory*. New York: Cambridge University Press.

Lovejoy, O., and E. Trinkaus. 1980. "Strength of Robusticity of the Neanderthal Tibia." *American Journal of Physical Anthropology* 53:465–470.

Lumley, H. de, and M. A. de Lumley. 1971. "Decouverte de restes humains anteneandertaliens dates du debut du Riss la Caune de l'Arago (Tautavel, Pyrenees-Orientales)." *Comptes Rendus de l'Academie des Sciences de Paris* 272:1739–1742.

Lumley, M. A. de. 1975. "Ante-Neanderthals of Western Europe." In *Australopithecus Paleoanthropology: Morphology and Paleoecology*, ed. R. H. Tuttle. The Hague: Mouton.

Macaulay, V., C. Hill., A. Achilli, C. Rengo, D. Clarke, W. Meehan, J. Blackburn, O. Semino, R. Scozzari, F. Cruciani, A. Taha, N. K. Shaari, J. M. Raja, P. Ismail, Z. Zainuddin, W. Goodwin, D. Bulbeck, H.-J. Bandelt, S. Oppenheimer, A. Torroni, and M. Richards. 2005. "Single, Rapid Coastal Settlement of Asia Revealed by Analysis of Complete Mitochondrial Genomes." *Science* 308:1034–1036.

Marks, J. 1995. *Human Biodiversity: Genes, Race, and History*. Hawthorne, NY: Aldine de Gruyter.

Marshack, A. 1976. "Some Implications of the Paleolithic Symbolic Evidence for the Origins of Language." *Current Anthropology* 17:274–282.

McBrearty, S., and A. S. Brooks. 2000. "The Revolution That Wasn't: A New Interpretation of the Origin of Modern Human Behavior." *Journal of Human Evolution* 39:453–563.

Mellars, P. 1985. "The Ecological Basis of Social Complexity in the Upper Palaeolithic of Southwestern France". In *Prehistoric Hunter-Gatherers: The Emergence of Cultural Complexity*, ed. T. D. Price and J. Brown. Orlando, FL: Academic Press.

———. 1989. "Major Issues in the Emergence of Modern Humans." *Current Anthropology* 30:349–385.

———, ed. 1990. *The Emergence of Modern Humans*. Ithaca, NY: Cornell University Press.

———. 1992. "Cognitive Changes and the Emergence of Modern Humans in Europe." *Cambridge Archaeological Journal* 1:63–76.

———. 1993. "Archaeology and the Population-Dispersal Hypothesis of Modern Human Origins in Europe." In *The Origin of Modern Humans and the Impact of Chronometric Dating*, eds. M. J. Aitken, C. B. Stringer, and P. A. Mellars. Princeton, NJ: Princeton University Press.

Mellars, P., and C. Stringer, eds. 1989. *The Human Revolution*. Princeton, NJ: Princeton University Press.

Melnick, D. J., and G. A. Hoelzer. 1993. "What Is mtDNA Good for in the Study of Primate Evolution?" *Evolutionary Anthropology* 2(1):2–10.

Meltzer, D. J. 1993. "Pleistocene Peopling of the Americas." *Evolutionary Anthropology* 1:157–169.

Mercier, N., and H. Valladas. 1994. "Thermoluminescence Dates for the Paleolithic Levant." In *Late Quaternary Chronology and Paleoclimates of the Eastern Mediterranean*. ed. O. Bar-Yosef and R. S. Kra. Tucson: Radiocarbon.

Milo, R. G., and D. Quiatt. 1994. "Language in the Middle and Late Stone Ages: Glottogenesis in Anatomically Modern *Homo sapiens*." In *Hominid Culture in Primate Perspective*, ed. D. Quiatt and J. Itani. Niwot: University Press of Colorado.

Mountain, J. L., A. A. Lin, A. M. Bowcock, and L. L. Cavalli-Sforza. 1993. "Evolution of Modern Humans: Evidence from Nuclear DNA Polymorphisms." In *The Origin of Modern Humans and the Impact of*

Chronometric Dating, ed. M. J. Aitken, C. B. Stringer, and P. A. Mellars. Princeton, NJ: Princeton University Press.

Nitecki, M. H., and D. V. Nitecki, eds. 1995. *Origins of Anatomically Modern Humans*. New York: Plenum Press.

O'Connell, J. F., K. Hawkes, and N. Blurton-Jones. 1988. "Hadza Scavenging: Implications for Plio/Pleistocene Hominid Subsistence." *Current Anthropology* 29:356–363.

Olsen, J. W., and S. Miller-Antonio. 1992. "The Paleolithic in Southern China." *Asian Perspectives* 31:129–160.

Olszewski, D. I. 1999. "The Early Upper Palaeolithic in the Zagros Mountains." In *Dorothy Garrod and the Progress of the Palaeolithic*, ed. W. Davies and R. Charles, pp. 167–180. Oxford: Oxbow Books.

———. in press. "Issues in the Development of the Early Upper Paleolithic, and a 'Transitional' Industry from the Zagros Region." In *Transitional Industries in Europe and Western Asia*, ed. J. Riel-Salvatore and G. A. Clark. British Archaeological Reports International Series. Oxford: Archaeopress.

Ovchinnikov, I. V., A. Götherström, G. P. Romanova, V. M. Kharitonov, K. Lidén, and W. Goodwin. 2000. "Molecular Analysis of Neanderthal DNA from the Northern Caucasus." *Nature* 404:490–493.

Parés, J. M., and A. Pérez-Gonzalez. 1995. "Paleomagnetic Age for Hominid Fossils at Atapuerca Archaeological Site, Spain." *Science* 269:830–832.

Pelcin, A. 1994. "A Geological Explanation for the Berkehat Ram Figurine." *Current Anthropology* 35:674–675.

Petraglia, M. 1999. "The First Acheulian Quarry in India: Stone Tool Manufacture, Biface Morphology, and Behaviors." *Journal of Anthropological Research* 55(1):39–70.

Pope, G. G. 1984. "The Antiquity and Palaeoenvironment of the Asian Hominidae." In *The Evolution of the East Asian Environment*, ed. R . O. I. Whyte. Hong Kong: Center of Asian Studies, University of Hong Kong.

———. 1989. "Bamboo and Human Evolution." *Natural History* 10(89):49–56.

Prideaux, T., and the Editors of Time-Life. 1973. *Cro-Magnon Man*. New York: Time-Life.

Relethford, J. H. 2001. "Absence of Regional Affinities of Neandertal DNA with Living Humans Does Not Reject Multiregional Evolution." *American Journal of Physical Anthropology* 115:95–98.

Renfrew, C. 1988. "Archaeology and Language." *Current Anthropology* 29(3):437–468.

Rice, P. C., and A. L. Paterson. 1985. "Cave Art and Bones: Exploring the Interrelationships." *American Anthropologist* 87(1):94–100.

Rightmire, P. 1990. *The Evolution of* Homo erectus. Cambridge: Cambridge University Press.

———. 1992. "*Homo erectus*: Ancestor of Evolutionary Side Branch?" *Evolutionary Anthropology* 1:43–49.

Rink, W. J., H. P. Schwarcz, F. H. Smith, and J. Radovcic. 1995. "ESR Ages for Krapina Hominids." *Nature* 387:173–176.

Roberts, D. F. 1953. "Body Weight, Race and Climate." *American Journal of Physical Anthropology NS* 11:533–558.

Roberts, M. B., Stringer, C. B., and Parfitt, S. A. 1994. "A Hominid Tibia from Middle Pleistocene Sediments at Boxgrove, UK." *Nature* 369:311–312.

Roberts, R. G., R. Jones, N. A. Spooner, M. J. Head, A. S. Murray, and M. A. Smith. 1994. "The Human Colonisation of Australia: Optical Dates of 53,000 and 60,000 Years Bracket Human Arrival at Deaf Adder Gorge, Northern Territory." *Quaternary Science Reviews* 13:575–586.

Roe, D. A. 1981. *The Lower and Middle Paleolithic Periods in Britain*. London: Routledge & Kegan Paul.

Roebroeks, W. 1994. "Updating the Earliest Occupation of Europe." *Current Anthropology* 35:301–305.

Roebroeks, W., and T. van Kolfschoten. 1994. "The Earliest Occupation of Europe: A Short Chronology." *Antiquity* 68:489–503.

Ruff, C. B. 1993. "Climatic Adaptation and Hominid Evolution: The Thermoregulatory Imperative." *Evolutionary Anthropology* 2:65–107.

Rushton, J. P. 1994. *Race, Evolution, and Behavior: A Life History Perspective*. New Brunswick, NJ: Transaction Publishers.

Russell, M. D. 1987a. "Bone Breakage in the Krapina Hominid Collection." *American Journal of Physical Anthropology* 72:373–380.

———. 1987b. "Mortuary Practices at the Krapina Neandertal Site." *American Journal of Physical Anthropology* 72:381–398.

Schick, K. 1992. "Geoarchaeological Analysis of an Acheulean Site at Kalambo Falls, Zambia." *Geoarchaeology* 7(1):1–26.

Schick, K. D., and D. Zhuan. 1993. "Early Paleolithic of China and Eastern Asia." *Evolutionary Anthropology* 2(1):22–35.

Schwarcz, H. P. 1994. "Chronology of Modern Humans in the Levant." In *Late Quaternary Chronology and Paleoclimates of the Eastern Mediterranean*, ed. O. Bar-Yosef and R. S. Kra. Tucson: Radiocarbon.

Semino, O., G. Passarino, P. J. Oefner, A. A. Lin, S. Arbuzova, L. E. Beckman, G. De Benedicts, P. Francalacci, A. Kouvatsi, S. Limborska, M. Marciki\u00e6, A. Mika, B. Mika, D. Primorac, A. S. Santachiara-Benerecetti, L. L. Cavalli-Sforza, and P. A. Underhill. 2000. " The Genetic Legacy of Paleolithic *Homo sapiens* in Extant Europeans: A Y Chromosome Perspective." *Science* 290:1155–1159.

Serge, A., and A. Asconzi. 1984. "Italy's Earliest Middle Pleistocene Hominid Site." *Current Anthropology* 25(2):230–235.

Sevink, J., E. H. Hebeda, H. N. Priem, and R. H. Verschure. 1981. "A Note on the Approximately 730,000-Year-Old Mammal Fauna and Associated Human Activity Sites Near Isernia, Central Italy." *Journal of Archaeological Science* 8:105–106.

Shapiro, H. 1974. *Peking Man.* New York: Simon and Schuster.

Shea, J. J. 1988. "Spear Points from the Middle Paleolithic of the Levant." *Journal of Field Archaeology* 15(4):441–456.

———. 2003. "Close Encounters: Neandertals and Modern Humans in the Middle Palaeolithic Levant." *The Review of Archaeology* 24(1):42–56.

Sherry, S. T., A. R. Rogers, H. Harpending, H. Soodyall, T. Jenkins, and M. Stoneking. 1994. "Mismatch Distributions of mtDNA Reveal Recent Human Population Expansions." *Human Biology* 66:671–675.

Shipman, P. 1983. "Early Hominid Lifestyle: Hunting and Gathering or Foraging and Scavenging?" In *Animals and Archaeology: Hunters and Their Prey,* ed. J. Clutton-Brock and C. Grigson. Oxford, England: British Archaeological Reports.

Shipman, P., and J. Rose. 1983. "Early Hominid Hunting, Butchering and Carcass-Processing Behaviors: Approaches to the Fossil Record." *Journal of Anthropological Archaeology* 2:57–98.

Singer, R., and J. Wymer. 1982. *The Middle Stone Age at Klasies River Mouth in South Africa.* Chicago: University of Chicago Press.

Singer, R., B. Gladfelter, and J. Wymer. 1993. *The Lower Paleolithic Site at Hoxne, England.* Chicago: University of Chicago Press.

Smith, F. H. 1982. "Upper Pleistocene Hominid Evolution in South-Central Europe: A Review of the Evidence and Analysis of Trends." *Current Anthropology* 23(6):667–703.

———. 1994. "Samples, Species, and Speculations in the Study of Modern Human Origins." In *Origins of Anatomically Modern Humans,* ed. M. H. Nitecki and V. Nitecki. New York: Plenum Press.

Smith, F. H., J. F. Simek, and M. S. Hamill. 1989. "Geographic Variation in Supraorbital Torus Reduction During the Later Pleistocene (c. 80,000–15,000 BP)." In *The Human Revolution: Behavioural and Biological Perspectives on the Origins of Modern Humans,* ed. P. Mellars and C. B. Stringer. Edinburgh: Edinburgh University Press.

So, J. K. 1980. "Human Biological Adaptation to Arctic and Subarctic Zones." *Annual Review of Anthropology* 9:63–82.

Soffer, O. 1985. *The Upper Paleolithic of the Central Russian Plain.* New York: Academic Press.

———. 1993. "Upper Palaeolithic Adaptations in Central and Eastern Europe and Man-Mammoth Interactions." In *From Kostenki to Clovis,* ed. O. Soffer and N. D. Praslov. New York: Plenum Press.

———. 1994. "Ancestral Lifeways in Eurasia—the Middle and Upper Paleolithic Records." In *Origins of Anatomically Modern Humans,* ed. M. H. Nitecki and D. V. Nitecki. New York: Plenum Press.

———, ed. 1987. *The Pleistocene Old World: Regional Perspectives.* New York: Plenum Press.

Soffer, O., and C. Gamble, eds. 1990. *The World in 18,000 B.P.* Edinburgh: Edinburgh University Press.

Soffer, O., and N. D. Praslov, ed. 1995. *From Kostenki to Clovis: Upper Paleolithic–Paleo-Indian Adaptations.* New York: Plenum Press.

Speth, J. D. 1990. "Seasonality, Resource Stress, and Food Sharing in So-Called 'Egalitarian' Foraging Societies." *Journal of Anthropological Archaeology* 9:148–188.

Spoor, F., B. Wood, and F. Zonneveld. 1994. "Implications of Early Hominid Labryinthine Morphology for Evolution of Human Bipedal Locomotion." *Nature* 369:645–648.

Steegmann. A. T., F. J. Cerny, and T. W. Holliday. 2002. "Neandertal Cold Adaptation: Physiological and Energetic Factors." *American Journal of Human Biology* 14: 566–583.

Stoneking, M. 1993. "DNA and Recent Human Evolution." *Evolutionary Anthropology* 2:60–73.

Straus, L. G. 1993/1994. "Upper Paleolithic Origins and Radiocarbon Calibration: More New Evidence from Spain." *Evolutionary Anthropology* 2(6):195–198.

———. 1995. *Iberia Before the Iberians: The Stone Age Prehistory of Cantabrian Spain.* Albuquerque: University of New Mexico Press.

Straus, W., and A. Cave. 1957. "Pathology and the Posture of Neanderthal Man." *Quarterly Review of Biology* 32:348.

Stringer, C., and G. Bräuer. 1994. "Methods, Misreading, and Bias." *American Anthropologist* 96:416–424.

Stringer, C., and C. Gamble. 1993. *The Search for the Neanderthals.* London: Thames and Hudson.

Stringer, C., F. C. Howell, and J. K. Melentis. 1979. "The Significance of the Fossil Hominid from Petralona, Greece." *Journal of Archaeological Science* 6:235–253.

Svoboda, J. 1987. "Lithic Industries of the Arago, Vertesszollos, and Bilzingsleben Hominids: Comparison and Evolutionary Interpretation." *Current Anthropology* 28(2):219–227.

Swisher, C., G. H. Curtis, T. Jacob, A. G. Getty, A. Suprijo, and Widiasmoro. 1994. "Age of the Earliest Known Hominids in Java, Indonesia." *Science* 263:1119–1121.

Taborin, Y. 1990. "Les Prémices de la Parure." In *Paléolithique Moyen Récent et Paléolithique Supérieur Ancien en Europe,* ed. C. Farizy, pp. 335–344. Nemours: Mémoires du Musée de Préhistoire d'Ile de France 3.

Tchernov, E. 1988. "Age of 'Ubeidiya Formation (Jordan Valley, Israel) and the Earliest Hominids in the Levant." *Paléorient* 14(2):63–65.

———. 1994. "New Comments on the Biostratigraphy of the Middle and Upper Plesitocene of the Southern Levant." In *Late Quaternary Chronology and Paleoclimates of the Eastern Mediterranean*, ed. O. Bar-Yosef and R. S. Kra. Tucson: Radiocarbon.

Thackeray, A. I. 1992. "The Middle Stone Age South of the Limpopo River." *Journal of World Prehistory* 6:385–440.

Thiel, B. 1987. "Early Settlement of the Philippines, Eastern Indonesia, and Australia-New Guinea: A New Hypothesis." *Current Anthropology* 28(2):236–241.

Thieme, H. 1997. "Lower Palaeolithic Hunting Spears from Germany." *Nature* 385:807–810.

Thorne, A. 1980. "The Arrival of Man in Australia." In *The Cambridge Encyclopedia of Archaeology*. New York: Crown Publishers/Cambridge University Press.

Thorne, A. G., and M. Wolpoff. 1981. "Regional Continuity and Australasian Pleistocene Hominid Evolution." *American Journal of Physical Anthropology* 55:337–349.

Torroni, A., H.-J. Bandelt, L. D'Urbano, P. Lahermo, P. Moral, D. Sellitto, C. Rengo, P. Forster, M.-L. Savontaus, B. Bonné-Tamir, and R. Scozzari. 1998. "mtDNA Analysis Reveals a Major Late Paleolithic Expansion from Southwestern to Northeastern Europe." *American Journal of Human Genetics* 62:1137–1152.

Trinkaus, E. 1982. "Evolutionary Continuity Among Archaic *Homo sapiens*." In *The Transition from Lower to Middle Palaeolithic and Origin of Modern Man*, ed. A. Ronen. Oxford: BAR International Series 151.

———. 1983. *The Shanidar Neanderthals*. New York: Academic Press.

———. 1985. "Cannibalism and Burial at Krapina." *Journal of Human Evolution* 14:203–216.

———. 1986. "The Neanderthals and Modern Human Origins." *Annual Review of Anthropology* 15:193–218.

———. 1995. "Neandertal Mortality Patterns." *Journal of Archaeological Science* 22:121–142.

Trinkaus, E., and C. Duarte. 2003. "The Hybrid Child from Portugal." *Scientific American Special Edition: New Look at Human Evolution* 13(2):32–33.

Trinkaus, E., and W. W. Howells. 1979. "The Neanderthals." *Scientific American* 241:118–133.

Trinkaus, E., and P. Shipman. 1992. *The Neanderthals: Changing the Image of Mankind*. New York: Alfred A. Knopf.

Turner, A. 1992. "Large Carnivores and Earliest European Hominids: Changing Determinants of Resource Availability During the Lower and Middle Pleistocene." *Journal of Human Evolution* 22:109–126.

Valladas, H., J. Clottes, M.-M. Geneste, M. A. Garcia, M. Arnold, H. Cachier, and N. Tisnérat-Laborde. 2001. "Evolution of Prehistoric Cave Art." *Nature* 413:479.

Valladas, H., J. L. Reyss, J. L. Joron, G. Valladas, O. Bar-Yosef, and B. Vandermeersch. 1988. "Thermoluminescence Dating of Mousterian 'Proto-Cro-Magnon' Remains from Israel and the Origin of Modern Man." *Nature* 331:614–616.

Vallois, H. 1961. "The Social Life of Early Man: The Evidence of the Skeletons." In *Social Life of Early Man*, ed. S. Washburn. Chicago: Aldine.

Van Andel, T. J., and W. Davies, eds. 2003. *Neanderthals and Modern Humans in the European Landscape During the Last Glaciation: Archaeological Results of the Stage 3 Project*. Cambridge, England: McDonald Institute for Archaeological Research.

Vekua, A., D. Lordkipanidze, G. P. Rightmire, J. Agusti, R. Ferring, G. Maisuradze, A. Mouskhelishvili, M. Nioadze, M. Ponce de Leon, M. Tappen, M. Tvalchrelidze, and C. Zollikofer. 2002. "A New Skull of Early Homo from Dmanisi, Georgia." *Science* 297:85–89.

Vértes, L. 1975. "The Lower Palaeolithic Site of Vérteszöllös, Hungary." In *Recent Archaeological Excavations in Europe*, ed. R. Bruce-Mitford, pp. 287–301. London: Routledge and Kegan Paul.

Villa, P. 1991. "Middle Pleistocene Prehistory in Southwestern Europe: The State of Our Knowledge and Ignorance." *Journal of Anthropological Research* 47(2):193–218.

———. 2001. "Early Italy and the Colonization of Western Europe." *Quaternary International* 75:113–130.

Walker, A., and R. E. Leakey, eds. 1993. *The Nariokotome* Homo erectus *Skeleton*. Cambridge, MA: Harvard University Press.

Warren, S. H. 1911. "Palaeolithic Wooden Spear from Clacton." *Quarterly Journal of the Geological Society* (London) 67:cxix.

Weidenreich, F. 1946. *Apes, Giants, and Man*. Chicago: University of Chicago Press.

White, J. P., and J. F. O'Connell. 1982. *A Prehistory of Australia, New Guinea and Sahul*. Sydney: Academic.

White, R. 1982. "Rethinking the Middle/Upper Paleolithic Transition." *Current Anthropology* 23:169–191.

———. 1986. *Dark Caves and Bright Visions*. New York: American Museum of Natural History.

———. 1989. "Production Complexity and Standardization in Early Aurignacian Bead and Pendant Manufacture." In *The Human Revolution: Behavioral and Biological Perspectives on the Origins of Modern Humans*, ed. P. Mellars and C. B. Stringer. Edinburgh: Edinburgh University Press.

———. 1992. "Beyond Art: Toward an Understanding of the Origins of Material Representation in Europe." *Annual Review of Anthropology* 21:537–564.

White, T. D. 1991. "The Question of Ritual Cannibalism at Grotta Guattari." *Current Anthropology* 32(2):103–138.

White, T. D., B. Asfaw, D. Degusta, H. Gilbert, G. D. Richards, G. Suwa, and F. C. Howell. 2003. "Pleistocene *Homo sapiens* from Middle Awash, Ethiopia." *Nature* 423:742–747.

Windels, F. 1965. *The Lascaux Cave Paintings*. London: Faber and Faber.

Wobst, H. M. 1977. "Stylistic Behavior and Information Exchange." In *For the Director: Research Essays in Honor of James B. Griffin*, ed. C. Cleland. Ann Arbor: Museum of Anthropology, University of Michigan, No. 61.

Wolpoff, M. 1968. "Climatic Influence on the Skeletal Nasal Aperture." *American Journal of Physical Anthropology* 29:405–423.

Wolpoff, M. H., J. Hawks, D. W. Frayer, and K. Hunley. 2001. "Modern Human Ancestry at the Peripheries: A Test of the Replacement Theory." *Science* 291:293–297.

Wolpoff, M., Xinzhi Wu, and A. G. Thorne. 1984. "Modern *Homo sapiens* Origins: A General Theory of Hominid Evolution Involving the Fossil Evidence from East Asia." In *The Origins of Modern Humans: A World Survey of the Fossil Evidence*, ed. F. H. Smith and F. Spencer. New York: Alan R. Liss.

Wolpoff, M. H., A. G. Thorne, F. H. Smith, D. W. Frayer, and G. G. Pope. 1994. "Multiregional Evolution: A World-Wide Source for Modern Human Populations." In *Origins of Anatomically Modern Humans*, ed. M. H. Nitecki and V. Nitecki. New York: Plenum Press.

Wu Rukang and Jia Lampo. 1994. "China in the Period of *Homo habilis* and *Homo erectus*." In *History of Humanity*, Vol. 1, ed S. J. De Laet. Londond: Routledge.

Wymer, J. J. 1964. "Excavations at Barnfield Pit, 1955–60." In *The Swanscombe Skull*, ed. C.D. Ovey, pp. 19–61. London: Royal Anthropological Institute.

Yellen, J. E., A. S. Brooks, E. Cornelissen, M. J. Mehlman, and K. Stewart. 1995. "A Middle Stone Age Worked Bone Industry from Katanda, Upper Semliki Valley, Zaire." *Science* 268:553–556.

Zhu, R. X., R. Potts, F. Xie, K. A. Hoffman, C. L. Deng, C. D. Shi, Y. X. Pan, H. Q. Wang, R. P. Shi, Y. C. Wang, G. H. Shi, and N. Q. Wu. 2004. "New Evidence on the Earliest Human Presence at High Northern Latitudes in Northeast Asia." *Nature* 431:559–562.

NOTES

1. Last Poems, 1922, no. 12.
2. Gould, *Wonderful Life*.
3. Although it will be interesting to follow developments in the recent discovery in Indonesia of *Homo floresiensis* (see Brown et al., "A New Small-Bodied Hominin from the Late Pleistocene of Flores, Indonesia"). These hominins, dubbed by some of their discoverers and in the popular press as "hobbits," date to about 18,000 years ago, and thus, at least in this isolated island context, are contemporary with modern forms of humans. *Homo floresiensis* stood only about 3 feet tall and had a brain size in the range of Australopiths, about 380 c³; it was obviously a quite different animal than us.
4. Klein, *The Human Career*, pp. 283–295.
5. Ibid., p. 409.
6. Other names of early hominins include *Homo antecessor* (Spain), *Homo heidelbergensis* (Africa and Europe), *Homo louisleakeyi* (Africa), and *Homo rhodesiensis* (Africa). See Klein, *The Human Career*; McBrearty and Brooks, "The Revolution That Wasn't: A New Interpretation of the Origin of Modern Human Behavior."
7. Reviewed in Klein, *The Human Career*, pp. 333–338.
8. Isaac, "The Archaeology of Human Origins," p. 60.
9. Isaac, "Sorting Out the Muddle in the Middle – An Anthropologist's Post-Conference Appraisal," p. 504.
10. Shipman, "Early Hominid Lifestyle."
11. Impressive numbers of hand-axes at sites could also be the result of taphonomic processes; see, for example, Schick, "Geological Analysis of an Acheulean Site at Kalambo Falls, Zambia."
12. Binford, *Bones, Ancient Men and Modern Myth*, p. 294; idem., "Human Ancestors."
13. Several claims have been made for the early use of fire, perhaps as early as 1.4 million years ago in Africa, but closer analyses of these finds suggest instead that taphonomic processes are responsible. Natural brush fires, for example, leave a scatter of charcoal across both sites and the surrounding region. See, for example, James, "Hominid Use of Fire."
14. Roberts, "Body Weight, Race and Climate."
15. Binford, "Human Ancestors: Changing Views of Their Behavior."
16. Gabunia et al., "Earliest Pleistocene Hominid Cranial Remains from Dmanisi, Republic of Georgia: Taxonomy, Geological Setting, and Age."
17. Zhu et al., "New Evidence on the Earliest Human Presence at High Northern Latitudes in Northeast Asia."
18. de Vos, Sondaar, and Swisher, "Dating Hominid Sites in Indonesia."

19. Bar-Yosef and Goren-Inbar, "The Lithic Assemblage of 'Ubeidiya: A Lower Paleolithic Site in the Jordan Valley"; Tchernov, "Age of 'Ubeidiya Formation (Jordan Valley, Israel) and the Earliest Hominids in the Levant."
20. Klein, "Anatomy, Behavior, and Modern Human Origins."
21. Klein, ibid., p. 178.
22. These are the *Homo antecessor* remains. See Bermúdez de Castro et al., "A Hominid from the Lower Pleistocene of Atapuerca, Spain: Possible Ancestor to Neandertals and Modern Humans."
23. Sevink et al., "A Note on the Approximately 730,000-Year-Old Mammal Fauna and Associated Human Activity Sites Near Isernia, Central Italy"; but see Villa, "Early Italy and the Colonization of Western Europe," who raises questions about the very early date, as well as taphonomic issues in site formation.
24. Wu Rukang and Jia Lampo, "China in the Period of *Homo habilis* and *Homo erectus.*"
25. Ibid.
26. Boaz et al., "Large Mammalian Carnivores as a Taphonomic Factor in the Bone Acumulation at Zhoudoudian."
27. Arens, *The Man-Eating Myth.*
28. Garn and Block, "The Limited Nutritional Value of Cannibalism."
29. Shapiro, *Peking Man.*
30. Freeman, "Acheulian Sites and Stratigraphy in Iberia and the Maghreb," p. 664.
31. Ibid.
32. Evidence for wooden throwing spears has been found elsewhere in Europe, at the site of Schöningen in Germany at 400,000 years ago (see Thieme, "Lower Palaeolithic Hunting Spears from Germany"), and possibly in England at the site of Clacton-on-Sea (see Warren, "Palaeolithic Wooden Spear from Clacton").
33. See Binford, "Human Ancestors," for a scavenging interpretation; but for contrasting view, see Shipman and Rose, "Evidence of Butchery and Hominid Activities at Torralba and Ambrona."
34. Vértes, "The Lower Palaeolithic Site of Vértesszöllös, Hungary."
35. There are some controversial examples of possible figurines from, for example, Berkehat Ram in Israel (see Pelcin, "A Geological Explanation for the Berkehat Ram Figurine"; D'Errico and Nowell, "A New Look at the Berkehat Ram Figurine: Implications for the Origins of Symbolism"), and Tan Tan in Morroco (see Bednarik, "A Figurine from the African Acheulian").
36. Bender, "Comment on G. Krantz (*CA* 21:773–79)."
37. White, "Beyond Art: Toward an Understanding of the Origins of Material Representation in Europe," p. 560.
38. Klein, "Anatomy, Behavior, and Modern Human Origins."
39. *Through the Looking-Glass.*
40. Frayer et al, p. 16.
41. Ibid., p. 17.
42. Ibid., pp. 17–18.
43. Leakey, *Olduvai Gorge.*
44. Weidenreich, *Apes, Giants, and Man.*
45. See also Coon, *The Origins of Races.*
46. Ferraro et al., *Anthropology,* p. 129, presents a simplified description of this issue.
47. Aiello, "The Fossil Evidence for Modern Human Origins in Africa: A Revised View."
48. Melnick and Hoelzer, "What Is mtDNA Good for in the Study of Primate Evolution?" p. 9.
49. Frayer et al., "Theories of Modern Human Origins: The Paleontological Test."
50. Ibid., p. 39.
51. See Krings et al., "Neanderthal DNA Sequences and the Origin of Modern Humans"; Krings et al., "A View of Neanderthal Genetic Diversity"; Ovchinnikov et al., "Molecular Analysis of Neanderthal DNA from the Northern Caucasus"; and Caramelli et al., "Evidence for a Genetic Discontinuity Between Neandertals and 24,000-Year-Old Anatomically Modern Europeans."
52. See, for example, Bräuer, "Africa's Place in the Evolution of *Homo sapiens.*"
53. The following points of evidence are adapted from Frayer et al., "Theories of Modern Human Origins: The Paleontological Test," pp. 19–20.
54. Ibid.
55. Olszewski, "Issues in the Development of the Early Upper Paleolithic, and a 'Transitional' Industry from the Zagros Region."
56. White et al., "Pleistocene *Homo sapiens* from Middle Awash, Ethiopia."
57. McBrearty and Brooks, "The Revolution That Wasn't: A New Interpretation of the Origin of Modern Human Behavior."
58. Singer and Wymer, *The Middle Stone Age at Klasies River Mouth in South Africa.*
59. McBrearty and Brooks, "The Revolution That Wasn't: A New Interpretation of the Origin of Modern Human Behavior."
60. Frayer et al., "Theories of Modern Human Origins: The Paleontological Test," pp. 19–20.

61. McBrearty and Brooks, "The Revolution That Wasn't: A New Interpretation of the Origin of Modern Human Behavior."
62. Klein and Edgar, *The Dawn of Human Culture*, pp. 23–26.
63. Brooks et al., "Dating and Context of Three Middle Stone Age Sites with Bone Points in the Upper Semliki Valley, Zaire."
64. Jones, "From Kakadu to Kutikina: The Southern Continent at 18,000 Years Ago"; Frankel, *Remains to Be Seen*.
65. Pope, "The Antiquity and Palaeoenvironment of the Asian Hominidae"; Wolpoff et al., "Modern *Homo sapiens* Origins: A General Theory of Hominid Evolution Involving the Fossil Evidence from East Asia"; Thorne, "The Arrival of Man in Australia."
66. See table 2 in Frayer et al., "Theories of Modern Human Origins: The Paleontological Test," for their argument that proponents of the Eve hypothesis have systematically misinterpreted the data from Africa with regard to shovelling.
67. Frayer et al., "Theories of Modern Human Origins: The Paleontological Test," p. 22.
68. The one continuity exception that proponents of Total Replacement might allow is the recent discovery of *Homo floresiensis* on Flores Island, Indonesia (see endnote 3). *Homo floresiensis* is thought to be a descendant of the Asian *Homo erectus*.
69. With the possible exception of *Homo floresiensis*, dated to as late as 18,000 years ago.
70. Stringer et al., "The Significance of the Fossil Hominid from Petralona, Greece"; Trinkaus, "Evolutionary Continuity Among Archaic *Homo sapiens*."
71. Conway et al., *Excavations at Barnfield Pit, Swanscombe, 1968–72*; Wymer, "Excavations at Barnfield Pit, 1955–60."
72. Ibid., p. 22.
73. Roe, *The Lower and Middle Paleolithic Periods in Britain*.
74. de Lumley, "Ante-Neanderthals of Western Europe."
75. Svoboda, "Lithic Industries of the Arago, Vértesszöllös, and Bilzingsleben Hominids: Comparison and Evolutionary Interpretation."
76. Tennyson was alluding to Goethe here.
77. White, "Rethinking the Middle/Upper Paelolithic Transition"; others have referred to this as a "revolution" (see Bar-Yosef, "The Upper Paleolithic Revolution").
78. Lieberman, "Testing Hypotheses About Recent Human Evolution from Skulls."
79. Wobst, "Stylistic Behavior and Information Exchange."
80. White, "Rethinking the Middle/Upper Paleolithic Transition."
81. Straus and Cave, "Pathology and the Posture of Neanderthal Man."
82. Trinkaus, "The Neandertals and Modern Human Origins."
83. Ibid., p. 203.
84. Ibid., p. 205.
85. Bordes, *Typologie du Paleolithique Ancien et Moyen*.
86. Binford and Binford, "A Preliminary Analysis of Functional Variability in the Mousterian of Levallois Facies."
87. Dibble, "Middle Paleolithic Scraper Reduction: Background, Clarification, and Review of the Evidence to Date."
88. Lieberman and Crelin, "On the Speech of Neanderthals."
89. Frayer and Wolpoff, "Comment on 'Glottogenesis and Modern *Homo sapiens*.'"
90. Lieberman, "On the Nature and Evolution of the Neural Bases of Human Language," p. 58.
91. For a review of the evidence and dissenting comments on this topic, see Gargett, "Grave Shortcomings: The Evidence for Neandertal Burial"; Chase and Dibble, "Middle Paleolithic Symbolism"; Brace, "Review of *Shanidar: The First Flower People*, by R. Solecki," p. 86.
92. Klein, "Anatomy, Behavior, and Modern Human Origins."
93. Straus, *Iberia Before the Iberians: The Stone Age Prehistory of Cantabrian Spain*.
94. Russell, "Bone Breakage in the Krapina Hominid Collection"; "Mortuary Practices at the Krapina Neandertal Site"; and Trinkaus, "Cannibalism and Burial at Krapina."
95. Trinkaus, "Neandertal Mortality Patterns."
96. Ibid., p. 121.
97. Valladas et al., "Thermoluminescence Dating of Mousterian 'Proto-Cro-Magnon' Remains."
98. Schwarcz, "Chronology of Modern Humans in the Levant."
99. Trinkaus, quoted in B. Bower, "An Earlier Dawn for Modern Humans?" p. 138.
100. Frayer et al., "Theories of Modern Human Origins: The Paleontological Test," p. 37; see also Arensburg and Belfer-Cohen, "Sapiens and Neandertals: Rethinking the Levantine Middle Paleolithic Hominids."
101. Shea, "Spear Points from the Middle Paleolithic of the Levant"; summarized in Frayer et al., "Theories of Modern Human Origins: The Paleontological Test," p. 20.

102. Klein, "Anatomy, Behavior, and Modern Human Origins."
103. Lovejoy and Trinkaus, "Strength of Robusticity of the Neanderthal Tibia."
104. Ruff, "Climatic Adaptation and Hominid Evolution: The Thermoregulatory Imperative"; Steegmann et al., "Neandertal Cold Adaptation: Physiological and Energetic Factors."
105. Smith, "Upper Pleistocene Hominid Evolution in South-Central Europe: A Review of the Evidence and Analysis of Trends"; Wolpoff et al., "Modern Human Ancestry at the Peripheries: A Test of the Replacement Theory."
106. Soffer, "Ancestral Lifeways in Eurasia – the Middle and Upper Paleolithic Records."
107. Reviewed in Straus, "Upper Paleolithic Origins and Radiocarbon Calibration: More New Evidence from Spain."
108. Ibid., p. 197.
109. Olszewski, "The Early Upper Palaeolithic in the Zagros Mountains."
110. Ibid., p. 196.
111. Ibid.; but see Bocquet-Appel and Demars, "Neanderthal Contraction and Modern Human Colonization of Europe" for an alternate model using radiocarbon dates to show the "advancing wave" of Aurignacian-using modern humans.
112. Leveque and Vandermeersch, "Les Decouvertes de Restes Humains."
113. Trinkaus, "The Neandertals and Modern Human Origins," p. 198.
114. Bischoff et al., "Dating of the Basal Aurignacian Sandwich at Abric Romani (Catalunya, Spain) by Radiocarbon and Uranium-Series."
115. Smith, "Upper Pleistocene Hominid Evolution in South-Central Europe: A Review of the Evidence and Analysis of Trends."
116. Trinkaus and Duarte, "The Hybrid Child from Portugal."
117. Frayer et al., "Theories of Modern Human Origins: The Paleontological Test," p. 32.
118. Relethford, "Absence of Regional Affinities of Neandertal DNA with Living Humans Does Not Reject Multiregional Evolution."
119. Trinkaus and Duarte, "The Hybrid Child from Portugal."
120. Wolpoff et al., "Multiregional Evolution: A World-Wide Source for Modern Human Populations."
121. See endnote 51.
122. Prideaux et al., *Cro-Magnon Man*, pp. 93–94.
123. De Beaune, "Paleolithic Lamps and Their Specialization: A Hypothesis."
124. Clottes, "France's Magical Ice Age Art: Chauvet Cave."
125. Conkey, "New Approaches in the Search for Meaning? A Review of Research in 'Paleolithic Art.'"
126. Leroi-Gourhan, "The Evolution of Paleolithic Art."
127. Fisher, *Woman's Creation*.
128. Lewis-Williams and Dowson, "The Signs of All Times: Entopic Phenomena in Upper Paleolithic Art."
129. Ibid., p. 215 (emphasis theirs).
130. Hodder, *Reading the Past*; also see Straus, *Iberia Before the Iberians: The Stone Age Prehistory of Cantabrian Spain*.
131. Conkey, "New Approaches in the Search for Meaning? A Review of Research in 'Paleolithic Art,'" p. 422.
132. Marks, *Human Biodiversity: Genes, Race, and History*.
133. Ibid; Brace et al., "Clines and Clusters Versus 'Race': A Test in Ancient Egypt and the Case of a Death on the Nile."
134. Current news stories (for example, the *Philadelphia Inquirer* of April 17, 2005) report on the start of the five-year Genographic Project that will analyze the DNA of 100,000 people worldwide in an effort to trace, in detail, the migrations of humans after modern humans left Africa. The North American center is at the University of Pennsylvania, under the direction of Dr. Theodore Schurr of the Department of Anthropology.
135. Thiel, "Early Settlement of the Philippines, Eastern Indonesia, and Australia-New Guinea: A New Hypothesis."
136. Vallois, "The Social Life of Early Man: The Evidence of the Skeletons."
137. Ibid.
138. Soffer, *The Upper Paleolithic of the Central Russian Plain*.
139. Bellwood, *The Prehistory of the Indo-Malaysian Archipelago*.
140. White and O'Connell, "Australian Prehistory: New Aspects of Antiquity."
141. Thorne, "The Arrival of Man in Australia."
142. Klein, "Anatomy, Behavior, and Modern Human Origins."

The First Americans

*At break of day the shore was thronged with
people all young . . . all of good stature, fine
looking. . . . I was anxious to learn whether
they had any gold, as I noticed that some of the
natives had rings hanging from holes in their
noses. . . . I tried to get them to go for some, but
they could not understand they were to go.*

Christopher Columbus (13 October 1492)

Columbus and most "discoverers" of the New World were not surprised to find "Indians" there because they thought they had landed in India, or perhaps Japan. But as soon as Europeans realized they were not in the Orient and became aware of the rich diversity of New World cultures, they began to struggle with the problem of the origin of the Native Americans. The Bible, the final authority for most Europeans of this era, was strangely silent on the very existence of this "second-earth," so Europeans began speculating on how the "Indians" could have reached the New World from the Garden of Eden, where they were assumed to have originated. Early explorers were greatly impressed by "similarities" between Egyptian and aboriginal American cultures, such as the great pyramids to be found in Egypt, Mexico, and the Mississippi Valley, and so some concluded that the Native Americans were descendants of Ham, one of Noah's sons, who was also thought to have been the father of the Egyptians.[1] Another popular idea was that the Native Americans were descendants of the "lost tribes of Israel," Jews who had been evicted from Palestine by the Assyrians around 1100 B.C. The "lost tribes" idea eventually was incorporated into the doctrines of the Church of the Latter-Day Saints, whose *Book of Mormon* concludes that Native Americans were remnants of tribes of Israel that had come to the New World by ship hundreds of years before Columbus. Others believed that Native Americans were descendants of people who fled Atlantis or other lost worlds that some think were destroyed thousands of years ago by volcanic eruption.

But by A.D. 1590 a Spanish Jesuit, José de Acosta, had proposed that Native Americans had come from Asia, and by A.D. 1781 Thomas Jefferson could describe the peopling of the New World in terms most scholars today think are accurate:

Late discoveries of Captain Cook, coasting from Kamschatka to California, have proved that if the two continents of Asia and America be separated at all, it is only by a narrow

194

straight. So that from this side also, inhabitants may have passed into America; and the resemblance between the Indians of America and the eastern inhabitants of Asia, would induce us to conjecture, that the former are the descendants of the latter, or the latter of the former: excepting indeed the Eskimaux, who, from the same circumstances of resemblance, and from identity of language, must be derived from the Groenlanders, and these probably from some of the northern parts of the old continent.[2]

10,000 years ago	Beginning of development of later Paleoindian cultures in the Americas
10,500 years ago	Caverna da Pedra Pintada, Brazil, South America
11,500 years ago	Clovis culture, North and Central America
11,600 years ago	Broken Mammoth, Mead, and Swan Point, Alaska, North America
12,500 years ago	Monte Verde, Chile, South America
16,900–10,900 years ago	Cactus Hill, Virginia, North America
19,600 years ago	Meadowcroft Rockshelter, Pennsylvania, North America
20–15,000 years ago	Initial peopling of the Americas begins
25,000 years ago	Earliest known sites in Siberia

In their search for clues to the origins of Native Americans, Jefferson and others of his age were struck by the close physical resemblance between Native Americans and Asians: dark brown eyes; black, coarse, straight hair; and relatively widely spaced cheekbones (Figure 5.1). But differences were also apparent: Except for the Eskimos and Aleuts, most aboriginal Americans had less pronounced epicanthic folds (part of the eyelid) than those that distinguish east Asian populations, and many Native Americans had relatively more prominent noses than east Asians.

Europeans also noted that the New World included an impressive diversity of languages—in some cases people who lived relatively close to one another spoke mutually unintelligible languages—and that none of the languages of Native Americans bore any obvious resemblance to Old World languages. Thus, it seemed certain that although the aboriginal Americans were probably descendants of Asian peoples, they must have lived in America for a long time for such physical and linguistic divergence to have occurred.

That people have lived in the New World for at least 11,000 years has been evident for a long time. In 1908 a cowboy riding along the edge of a gully in New Mexico, near the town of Folsom, discovered some "arrowheads" and animal bones protruding from a layer of soil about 6 m beneath the surface of the plain. Eventually, in 1925, his finds came to the attention of J. D. Figgins, director of the Colorado Museum of Natural History, who began a long series of excavations at this site.[3] A primary find was a long, "fluted" (it had two long strips removed near the base and parallel to the length of the point) "projectile point" that was embedded in the ribs of a species of bison that had been extinct for about 10,000 years (Figure 5.2). Since most archaeologists and others were skeptical of the idea that humans had been in the New World that long, Figgins insisted on excavating the site with a committee of archaeologists on hand to watch his every move so that no one could claim the evidence had been faked.

In 1932 another important find was made, this time near the town of Clovis, New Mexico (Figure 5.3). Here, too, large blade tools were discovered in association with extinct

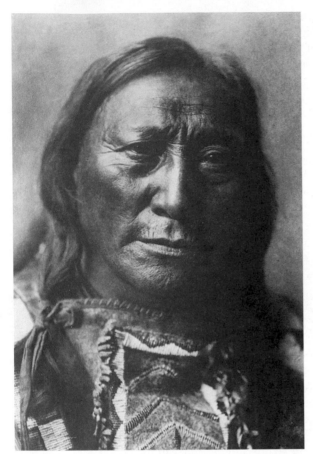

FIGURE 5.1 An early photograph of a Native American. Physical resemblances between Americans and Asian peoples reflect their common origins.

animals. But at this site artifacts somewhat different from those at Folsom were found in a layer beneath some "Folsom points." Analysis suggested a date of about 11,000 years ago for the earliest Clovis-style artifacts, and within a few years artifacts similar in size, shape, and style to the Clovis points were discovered at many different places in North America. Since then, stone points resembling Clovis artifacts have been found in much of North and South America, from the Arctic to the tip of South America.

Disputes about early Americans thus focus on the question of whether or not anyone was here before the Clovis cultures in existence about 11,500 years ago.

For many years, the majority of archaeologists believed that the first Americans came from Asia via a land route. As we shall see, however, there is increasing evidence suggesting that a coastal route may also be a more viable explanation. Some have even suggested a migration from Europe using skin boats across the northern Atlantic, although there are many dubious aspects of this particular hypothesis. Thus, the term "Native American" is something of a misnomer, for on the grand chronology of the human species, the time difference between the arrival of the very first humans in the New World and that of Columbus is relatively trivial. All Americans are immigrants, and evidence suggests that some living Native Americans are descendants of groups that came to the Americas thousands of years after the first immigrants.

ROUTES FOR THE INITIAL COLONIZATION OF THE AMERICAS

Analyses of the initial colonization of the Americas usually focus on four related questions: What Old World people were the ancestors of the first Americans? When did the first people enter the New World and colonize subarctic and temperate zones? What routes did they follow in colonizing North and South America? What kinds of technologies and economies did these initial waves of colonists have?

These questions may seem to be rather simple empirical problems, subjects of speculation studied on the basis of inadequate data about questions that may be intrinsically important but without much wider significance. Whether the first Americans arrived in the New World 30,000 years ago or 13,000 years ago would not seem to make much difference in the grand scheme of things.

But the colonization of the New World does have much greater significance than these simple questions might suggest. Most important is the fact that the subsequent history of these peoples in the New World was largely independent of influences from the Old World. Whenever they first arrived, New World peoples give us a comparative case—a long and rich cultural history that can be compared with that of the Old World. Moreover, the colonization of the New World involves one of the most complex issues in paleolithic archaeology, the nature and processes of human *adaptive radiation*. All animal species seem to radiate across the world "naturally" until they reach the limits of their adaptation. Some tropical species, such as the elephant, evolved cold-adapted subspecies that allowed them penetrate into the far north of both the Old and New Worlds, but even these evolutionary adaptations could not produce an animal capable of supporting its huge bulk in the icy extremes of the poles. Evolutionary change seems to be most rapid along the limits of adaptations, but measuring the tempo of evolutionary change in extinct species is difficult.

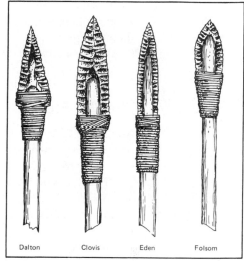

FIGURE 5.2 Some types of early American projectile points.

Human patterns of migration and adaptive radiation are a complex blend of evolving physical characteristics and culture. Thus, the New World archaeological record provides us with an opportunity to study in detail a complex mosaic of human adaptations across a gigantic and highly varied landscape.

Why people came to the Americas has never been an issue. People, like other animal species, seem to penetrate their entire available range "naturally." The "budding-off" process described in the previous chapter is probably applicable to the colonization of the Americas. Ethnographic studies tell us that hunter-forager groups often increase to a certain size level until friction develops among some members of the group, or resources become too scarce, and then the social unit splits, with some members going off into new territory. The long winter nights of northern Asia doubtless offered ample opportunity to brood on what a jerk one's cousin was, or to muse on what Garden of Eden might lie over the horizon, and as a result of tens of thousands of years of group-fissioning, population growth, and small group social interactions, the world was populated.

There remains some doubt about *how* people first got to

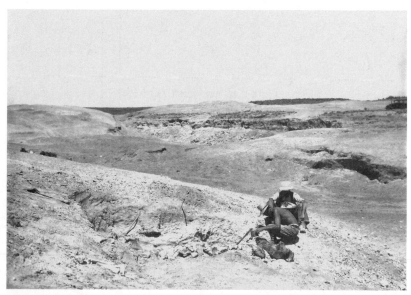

FIGURE 5.3 The Clovis site in New Mexico.

North America because, as we saw in the previous chapter, people were certainly living in Australia long before 30,000 years ago, and there seems no way they could have reached there except by boat. Some archaeologists still believe that the evidence strongly suggests that the first Americans traveled there the old-fashioned way—they walked—although, increasingly, researchers are more convinced that the earliest Americans came by boat.

The "Ice-Free Corridor"

Any explanation of the colonization of the New World from Asia must consider the kinds of physical environments these colonists would have faced, and recent research has challenged many traditional ideas on this point (Figure 5.4).

Today, Eskimos using skin boats easily cross the 90 km of open sea separating Siberia and America, and recently an American woman slathered herself with grease and actually swam from Alaska to Siberia. But such a sea crossing would not have been necessary during much of the Pleistocene. During periods of glacial advance within the last million years, enormous quantities of water were converted to ice, lowering the sea level sufficiently to expose a 1500- to 3000-km-wide expanse of the floor of the Bering Sea. This land bridge— usually referred to as Beringia (Figure 5.5)—was most recently available from about 25,000

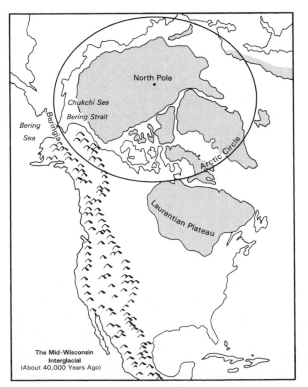 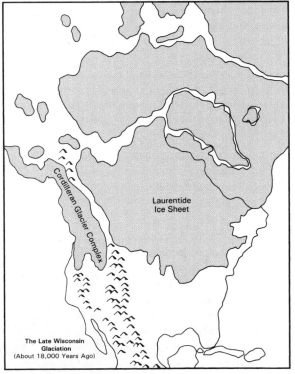

FIGURE 5.4   Between 60,000 and 12,000 years ago, world climate warmed several times, opening routes between the Arctic and more southern latitudes of the New World. Two possible periods of colonization are during the Mid-Wisconsin Interglacial, about 40,000 years ago, and after the Late Wisconsin Glaciation, about 18,000 years ago.

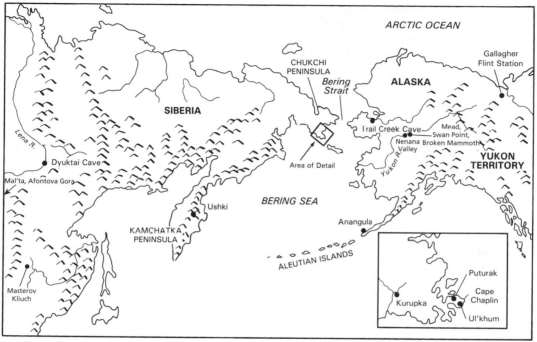

FIGURE 5.5   Several archaeological sites in Siberia may be of cultures ancestral to the first Americans.

to 14,000 years ago. And, for many decades, the majority of archaeologists believed that walking across Beringia from Siberia to Alaska, and then south through Canada using the "ice-free" corridor was the route for the peopling of the Americas.

The kinds of resources Beringia would have offered hunter-foragers would have depended on the period in which the migrants crossed. At various times, ocean currents created an ice-free, tundra-covered connection from eastern Siberia across the land bridge and into central Alaska. These conditions are reflected in the many non-Arctic-adapted animal species that crossed from Asia to America during the Pleistocene. Prior to 10,000 years ago, species of deer, bison, camels, bears, foxes, mammoths, moose, caribou, and even rodents crossed from Siberia into the New World. Going the other way—from America to Asia—were foxes, woodchucks, and, during the early Pleistocene, the ancestors of modern forms of horses, wolves, and other animals.[4] In some periods Beringia would not have been particularly rich—there is even the possibility of dust storms, so dry and barren was most of it.[5] But at other times, migrants on the land bridge in the brief but warm summers of some periods of the Pleistocene would have found musk-oxen and other large herbivores, along with fish, birds, and sea mammals along the shore.

Interior Alaska and Canada were relatively rich environments in the mid Wisconsin interglacial, and at times humans may have had a narrow but clear ice-free run all the way from Alaska into the northern United States. Pollen cores from easternmost Beringia suggest that from 30,000 to 14,000 years ago, the time when most archaeologists think the first Americans arrived, Beringia may have been relatively cool and dry, although some reconstructions of the landscape suggest that it had a mosaic of steppe-tundra, covered mainly in grasses and sedges, along with meadows in valleys.[6] Meadows, of course, would have been attractive grazing habitats for the large Pleistocene herd mammals—woolly mammoths, horses, long-horned bison—that people of this time period hunted.

Southward migrations from Alaska may only have been possible during a few intervals because it is generally thought that for most of the Pleistocene the way would have been blocked by coalescing ice sheets (Figure 5.6). Even if these ice sheets did not completely bar the way south, it is not clear that the "ice-free" corridor would have been habitable for people until after 11,000 years ago.[7] This date is relatively late—as we shall see—compared to the dates of some archaeological sites now known from areas south of the ice sheets, such as in Virginia and Chile. Traveling through the "ice-free" corridor thus remains a viable route, but perhaps it is not the route that the earliest people took to arrive in the Americas south of the glaciers (see later).

The exact path the these early Americans may have taken is not known, but the most likely course would be along the southern coast of the Beringia, then into Alaska north of the Brooks Range, up the Yukon River Valley, then into the Mackenzie River Valley, and from there southward, along the eastern slopes of the Rockies and on into the Dakotas and then farther southward. Along the coast of Beringia were probably abundant resources in the form of fish, birds, eggs, invertebrates, and many plant foods. If groups did come this way, it is unlikely that we shall ever be able to document their journey archaeologically, for the rising seas of the post-Pleistocene era have submerged the ancient shoreline.

If they came across the middle of the land bridge, a reliance on big-game hunting would have been essential, and the migrants were almost certainly not constantly on the move southward. The budding-off process described earlier is the usual one in cases when new species move into empty niches, and many thousands of years may have passed between the time the first human set foot on the land bridge and the year the first groups arrived in the mid-latitudes of North America.

North winds blowing off the northern glacial ice sheets made the climate of Pleistocene North America much different from today's climate. Much of Nevada and Utah was covered by Lake Bonneville, of which only a shrinking remnant (the Great Salt Lake) remains. Wyoming, Iowa, and other parts of the Great Plains were vast pine, spruce, and tamarack forests and lush open grasslands. To the south, the area between the Mississippi River and the Rockies was a verdant mosaic of grasslands, lakes, and birch and alder forests. In eastern North America huge expanses of coniferous forests stretched from the edge of the glacial ice sheets to the lower Ohio River Valley.

The animals inhabiting this wilderness of 14,000–12,000 years ago closely approximate a modern hunter's vision of paradise. Giant moose, 3 m and more in height, could be found in many of the wetter areas, along with *Castoroides*, a species of beaver as large as a modern bear (Figure 5.7). Along the woodland edges of the southeastern United States were large populations of giant ground sloths, ungainly creatures fully as tall as modern giraffes. In more open country were vast herds of straight-horned bison, caribou, musk-oxen, horses, and mammoths—some 4 m high at the shoulders. In the more forested areas of the east and south were the mammoth's cousin, the mastodon, a more solitary animal than the mammoth and apparently a browser rather than a grassland grazer. Amid all these large creatures were rabbits, armadillos, birds, camels, peccaries, and other animals. And the carnivores that such a movable feast attracted were equally impressive. Packs of dire wolves roamed most of the New World, as did panthers as large as modern lions and two species

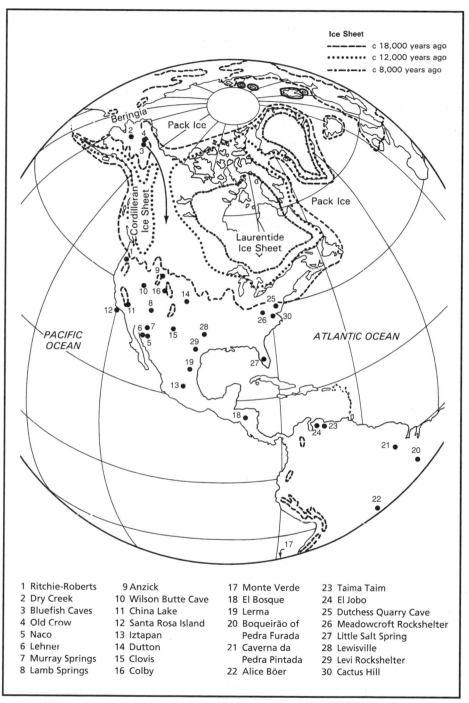

Ice Sheet
- - - - - - - c 18,000 years ago
· · · · · · · · c 12,000 years ago
-·-·-·-·- c 8,000 years ago

Beringia
Pack Ice
Cordilleran Ice Sheet
Pack Ice
Laurentide Ice Sheet
PACIFIC OCEAN
ATLANTIC OCEAN

1 Ritchie-Roberts	9 Anzick
2 Dry Creek	10 Wilson Butte Cave
3 Bluefish Caves	11 China Lake
4 Old Crow	12 Santa Rosa Island
5 Naco	13 Iztapan
6 Lehner	14 Dutton
7 Murray Springs	15 Clovis
8 Lamb Springs	16 Colby

17 Monte Verde	23 Taima Taim
18 El Bosque	24 El Jobo
19 Lerma	25 Dutchess Quarry Cave
20 Boqueirão of	26 Meadowcroft Rockshelter
Pedra Furada	27 Little Salt Spring
21 Caverna da	28 Lewisville
Pedra Pintada	29 Levi Rockshelter
22 Alice Böer	30 Cactus Hill

FIGURE 5.6 Some of the earliest known American sites. Most of these sites range from 20,000 to 10,000 years ago.

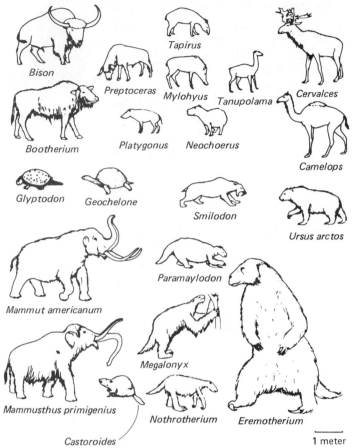

Bison

Tapirus

Preptoceras   Mylohyus   Tanupolama   Cervalces

Bootherium   Platygonus   Neochoerus   Camelops

Glyptodon   Geochelone   Smilodon   Ursus arctos

Mammut americanum   Paramaylodon

Megalonyx

Mammusthus primigenius   Nothrotherium   Eremotherium

Castoroides   1 meter

FIGURE 5.7 Some large mammals of Pleistocene America. The scale preserves relative size.

of saber-toothed cat, one about the size of a lion.[8] Thus, the first Americans were hardly entering an "empty niche," since these ferocious predators no doubt provided stiff competition for people trying to specialize in hunting. Central and South America were also rich game preserves during and just after the Pleistocene.

Coast Hopping from Beringia

We might expect that if the immigrants crossed Beringia primarily along its southern coast, then the groups migrating south would have retained some elements of the generalized hunting, fishing, and foraging economies required in the intertidal zone. The idea that people used watercraft to "hop" along the coastline of what is now Canada at least as far south as the Columbia River —the boundary between the modern states of Washington and Oregon—and perhaps farther still, along the coast into South America, is not new.[9] For many years, however, the main obstacles to accepting this route as a viable idea were a lack of evidence—because sites would lie deep beneath the current coastal seas—and the assumption that the glacial ice sheets extended completely to the sea along the Canadian coast, allowing no possibility for landfall.[10]

Sea waters have not receded in recent years, so why are archaeologists now more willing to accept the coastal route as a better option than the "ice-free corridor?" This shift in viewpoint, which is due to several lines of accumulating evidence, is a good example of how the scientific process works—new data are used to correct, refine, update, and, sometimes, overturn the existing paradigm (model). These new data have come mainly from two sources—securely dated early archaeological sites and paleoenvironmental research.

Although there were occasional claims for early people living in the Americas before about 12,000–15,000 years ago, the vast majority of these claims did not stand up to rigorous scrutiny of either the contexts of the archaeological artifacts or the dating of the sites.[11] A few sites, however, such as Meadowcroft Rockshelter in Pennsylvania (see later), offered tantalizing suggestions that people were in the Americas before the "ice-free" corridor was available for travel between the two Canadian glacial sheets. Since then, several other early sites, such as Cactus Hill in Virginia and Monte Verde in Chile (see later), have been documented. These sites, although somewhat controversial when first discovered, have now been generally accepted as legitimate early sites by most archaeologists.

The presence of these early sites south of the glaciers—in the case of Monte Verde, thousands of kilometers south of the ice sheets—threw a harsh light of reality on the idea that the "ice-free" corridor was the earliest route of entry. And, of course, archaeologists have never had evidence for sites in the "ice-free" corridor area that dated before 11,000 years ago, a fact that was not often mentioned by proponents of the "ice-free" corridor.[12] At best, the archaeology in the "ice-free" corridor was no older than the Clovis archaeological tradition (see later)—long-thought to be representative of the earliest people in the Americas and called the "Clovis-first" model—or was younger than the Clovis phenomenon.

The existence of legitimate pre-12,000-year-old sites south of the glaciers, however, spurred further intensive work by geologists and paleoecologists on two fronts—the context and conditions of the "ice-free" corridor itself and studies of the coastal areas and continental shelf from Alaska to the Northwest coast of the United States. This research has shown that the "ice-free" corridor was a feature created by the retreat of the glaciers. In the period from 30,000 to 11,500 years ago, large parts of the corridor were blocked by glacial ice, so that no one could have used this as a route of entry.[13] Another important consideration comes from paleoenvironmental reconstruction and modeling. These indicate that even those portions of the "ice-free" corridor that might have been penetrated by early Americans in the interval after 18,000 years ago could not have supported people. There simply would have been too few animals to hunt and thus not enough available nutrition to feed people.[14]

These considerations—the late date for the availability of the "ice-free" corridor and its ecological viability—shifted the peopling of the Americas research focus to coastal areas as a route of entry (Figure 5.8). Several remarkable discoveries offer considerable support for the coast-hopping route of entry. Through a combination of deep-sea cores into the Northwest coast continental shelf and digital sounding mapping of the continental shelf to a depth of 150 m below modern sea level, we have an emerging picture of portions of this coast for the period when people may have been present. The deep-sea cores provide pollen data allowing reconstruction of the vegetation of this previously exposed land surface, as well as sediment information crucial to estimating the timing for when this land was submerged by rising sea levels.[15]

The areas of the now submerged coastlines so far investigated were characterized by open tundra, including grasses, sedges, and dwarf willows. Mapping of the continental shelf shows evidence for lakes, rivers, and beaches.[16] Although glaciers would have extended all the way to the sea in some parts of the coastline, other portions were unglaciated not long after the maximum extent of the glaciers (23,000–19,000 years ago) and certainly after 16,000 years ago. These unglaciated locales are sometimes called coastal refugia—attractive areas scattered up and down the northwestern coastline of the Americas that were suitable for landfall in a coast-hopping model of entry, if not also for more extended periods of human habitation. Quite significantly, these coastal refugia were available to humans at least 1,000–2,000 years before the "ice-free" corridor.[17]

The coastal route into the Americas south of the glaciers would also have been much more economically feasible for early people compared to the "ice-free" corridor. Coastal regions provide many attractive resources, including shellfish, marine fish, seals and other

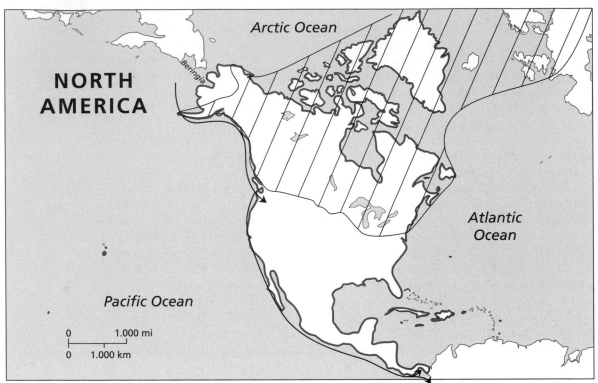

FIGURE 5.8   The coastal route into the Americas from Beringia. Many entry points are possible once south of the glaciated region.

sea mammals, and possibly also migratory waterfowl.[18] How far south did early Americans travel via this route?

At the very least, the coastal route must have been used until somewhere in the vicinity of Washington/Oregon. From this point, people could have moved inland, adopting terrestrial hunting-and-gathering economies to replace coastal fishing, hunting, and gathering. Alternatively, some groups may have continued farther south along the coastal route, with some models hypothesizing touchdown along the Isthmus of Panama[19] and others landfall in South America.[20] However far south people may have used the coastal route before traveling inland, one thing is certain. Within a couple of thousand years of entry south of the glaciers, human groups were nearly everywhere in the Americas.

Despite the attractiveness of the coast-hopping model, however, there remains one obstacle—the lack of an archaeological record. As we saw earlier, the drowning of ancient coastal areas by rising sea levels at the end of the Pleistocene has been the limiting factor for archaeological research. Mandryk and her colleagues, however, note, "Extremely rapid sea-level rise beginning 10,300 BP . . . increases the chances of preservation of any early archaeological sites from this period due to rapid burial."[21] We can anticipate that continued research focused on the continental shelf of the northwest coast may eventually yield this long-sought-after evidence for human presence.

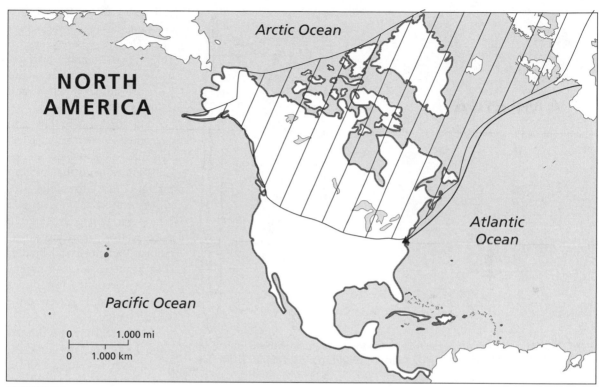

FIGURE 5.9   The Atlantic route proposed for a Solutrean migration from Europe to the Americas.

Across the Atlantic from Europe

Another sea route idea has been recently proposed by Dennis Stanford and Bruce Bradley.[22] They argue that the Americas were reached by people traveling by skin boats across the northern Atlantic from Europe, although they don't claim that these groups were necessarily the first people to arrive in the Americas. In fact, this model is directed explicitly at explaining the origins of the Clovis tradition (see later) in the Americas.

The Atlantic route proposes that permanent sea ice linked Ireland to the Grand Banks area (near Newfoundland) during the period of the maximum extent of the last glacial period, some 23,000–19,000 years ago (Figure 5.9). The presence of this ice front theoretically created conditions that allowed a weak warm sea current that flowed counter-clockwise from the coast of Ireland toward the Grand Banks. Given the existence of maritime adaptations in parts of western Europe, people using skin boats could eventually make the 2,500-km journey along the ice front, hunting sea mammals and fishing to provide food and oil for heating and cooking.[23]

What about archaeological evidence for this route? The primary line of evidence used by Stanford and Bradley is the resemblance of Clovis stone artifacts in North America to those of an Upper Paleolithic tradition from Spain and France called the Solutrean. They note that the stone flaked bifaces—points or spearheads—are very similar in appearance

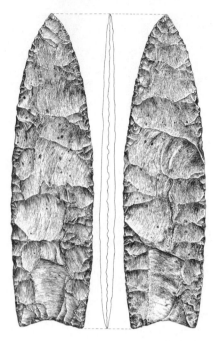

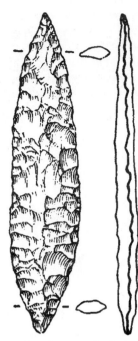

FIGURE 5.10 Proponents of the Atlantic route suggest that there are similarities between New World Clovis points (left) and Old World Solutrean points (right) (not drawn to scale).

and in the technological processes used to manufacture them (Figure 5.10). They also point out that many artifacts made of bone, antler, and ivory are similar in Clovis and Solutrean assemblages.

Stanford and Bradley also cite genetic evidence (see later) that may support their model. This comes from the study of mtDNA and shows the presence of the X haplogroup, a European genetic lineage, in some Native Americans populations.[24] Stanford and Bradley thus argue that the X haplogroup entered the Americas via Solutrean people traveling the Atlantic route.

The Stanford and Bradley model has been heavily criticized by archaeologists and is not accepted as a feasible idea by most. Why is this? It turns out that there are many good arguments that can be made showing major flaws in this model; these have been recently summarized by Lawrence Straus.[25]

The first of these arguments is based on the chronology of the Clovis and Solutrean. Both traditions are well dated using the radiocarbon technique. Solutrean sites in France and Spain fall into the interval between about 21,000 and 17,000 years ago, while Clovis sites are dated to between 11,500 and 10,900 years ago.[26] As Straus notes, the Solutrean bifaces, as well as the techniques used to manufacture them, are about 5,000 radiocarbon years older than their supposed counterpart in the Clovis tradition. There simply were no Solutrean biface-making people in Europe at the time that Clovis appears in the Americas. This same argument would apply to any potential similarities in artifacts made of antler, ivory, or bone.

Straus also points out that at the height of the last glacial period, which is when Stanford and Bradley propose that people crossed the Atlantic along the ice front, there is no evidence for human occupation in Europe north of Paris.[27] Additionally, while Solutrean people are known to have exploited near-shore sea resources such as shellfish, as well as the salmon and trout found in rivers as well as the sea, there is no evidence that Solutreans had adaptations to deep-water fishing or the hunting of sea mammals.

The fact that some techniques used to make bifaces in the Solutrean and Clovis traditions are similar could be no more than independent invention. Making stone artifacts is a reductive process—the person making a stone tool can only fashion it by reducing it, that is, by knocking pieces of stone off the artifact, and there are only so many ways in which this can be done. Making a stone tool is thus quite unlike making pottery vessels, which is an additive process, with all sorts of options ranging from types of handles to types of decoration to types of temper added to ensure that the pots don't break during firing. Similarities in stone artifact techniques are thus often due to the simple fact that there are a limited number of options available to make a particular kind of stone artifact.

Even the genetic evidence of the X haplogroup in some Native American groups can be explained in ways that do not involve the crossing of the Atlantic Ocean by Solutreans. In his discussion of this mtDNA lineage, Theodore Schurr summarizes another possibility: "[T]he lack of haplogroup X mtDNAs in Asian and Siberian groups . . . suggests that these haplotypes originated outside of eastern Siberia, perhaps taken through Beringia by an ancient Eurasian migratory event distinct from the migration(s) that brought the other four mtDNA lineages to the Americas."[28]

Although the coast-hopping model from Beringia to south of the ice sheets is not perfect—and no model ever is—this route appears to be the most likely explanation for how the first people arrived in the Americas.

EVIDENCE FOR THE FIRST AMERICANS

With this sense of the possible entry routes, environments, and resources that the New World offered, we can examine the biological ancestry of the first Americans, the chronology and geography of their colonization, and the economic and technological basis of their colonization. To do this, we can appeal to several categories of evidence involving (1) the biological anthropology of Native Americans and possible ancestral groups in the Old World; (2) linguistic evidence—in the sense of those clues that indigenous New World languages can provide us about the cultural origins, cultural relationships, and migration patterns of the first Americans; and (3) the archaeological records both of the New World and of the areas in the Old World from which the colonists might have come.

Biological Anthropological Evidence

By 100,000 years ago, Old World peoples seem to have had all the skills at making clothes, fire, and tools that would have been necessary for the trek to the New World. But intensive research has failed to turn up any New World human skeletons that cannot be fitted comfortably within our own species, *Homo sapiens sapiens*. And because the first *H. sapiens sapiens* appear in the Middle East and Europe about 35,000–40,000 years ago, we might assume that the aboriginal Americans must have come over since then, but we do not know when the first *Homo sapiens sapiens* appeared in the east Asian areas—early Upper Paleolithic assemblages including bone and antler tools appear in the region from Uzbekistan to Siberian about 40,000–30,000 years ago, but there are no associated human fossils.[29]

With regard to the Old World ancestors of Native Americans, the physical anthropological data strongly suggest that they were, of course, east Asians, and were almost certainly the Pleistocene peoples of the areas near Alaska. Earlier questions focused on whether the genetic ancestors of these east Asian people were, for example, people from coastal areas west of Japan, or north central Chinese, or western Asians who migrated east

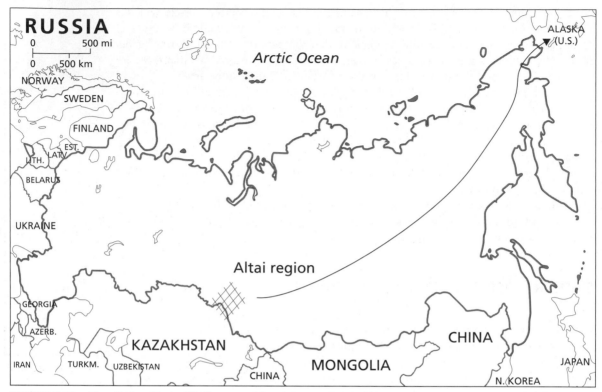

FIGURE 5.11 The Altai region in Siberia, a possible origin area for populations entering the Americas based on genetic data.

from northern Eurasia. Since then, accumulating genetic evidence suggests that the region of the Altai Mountains in Siberia (Figure 5.11) may be the source for these early founding populations.[30]

Many scholars have analyzed the teeth, skulls, and other physical features of early and current Native Americans in hopes of identifying their origins. It is uncertain when some east Asian populations developed epicanthic folds, small noses, and relatively flat facial profiles, but in view of the prominent noses of most Native Americans and their non-Mongolian eye shapes, it is apparent that these differences can be attributed to one or more possibilities: The Americans are only distantly related to these populations, they emigrated before the Asian populations developed their distinctive features, these different characteristics existed in different Asian populations, and what we see in the contrasts of Amerind populations are the results of successive migrations by different human groups. We have very little evidence on which to estimate rates of evolutionary change in these superficial physical characteristics, and variations in them are thus difficult to interpret.[31]

Teeth preserve well, have morphological characteristics that are under relatively simple genetic control, and seem to change relatively quickly under changing selective conditions. Figure 5.12 indicates the relative frequency in various groups of incisor "shoveling"—the degree to which the lingual surface of incisors is curled or ridged. On this trait alone, one

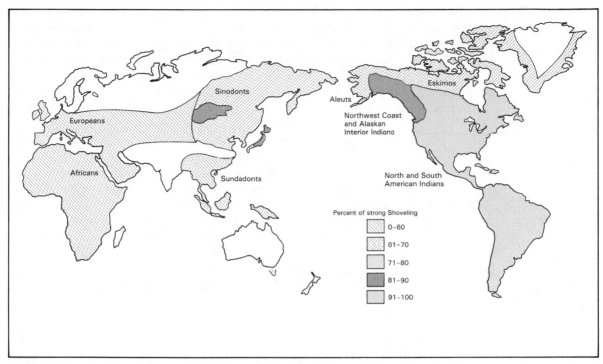

FIGURE 5.12   Variations in human teeth shapes reflect genetic ancestry. Incisor "shoveling"—the curved cross-sectional shape of incisors—occurs most frequently in northeast Asian and New World peoples and distinguishes them from the rest of the world. This evidence supports the view that the New World was colonized by three successive migrations from Asia.

would clearly see north Chinese ancestry for Native Americans.[32] Turner looked at many different features of teeth, including shoveling, and variations in the number of roots of premolars and molars. By comparing large samples of teeth on many different measurements, Turner concluded that (1) New World groups are more like Asians than like Europeans, (2) all New World groups resemble each other more than they do most Old World populations, (3) dental variation is greater in North America than in South America, and (4) there are three "clusters" of New World peoples.[33]

As Turner notes, these characteristics seem to make sense if there were three distinct migrations into the Americas. It is very difficult, however, to estimate rates of change in these kinds of physical features, and thereby to estimate how long ago the migrations to the Americas began, but Turner's calculations estimate a date of about 12,000 years ago for the initial colonization of the New World, with two much later waves of colonizations.

These separate migrations also seem to be reflected in a study by Steele and Powell, who did a complex statistical analysis of measurements on the teeth, skulls, and skeletons of the earliest known Americans and compared them to various other populations. Their results indicate that the earliest Americans were different physically from more recent Native Americans and northern Asians, having longer and narrower braincases and shorter and narrower faces.[34]

Just as DNA has been used to estimate the divergences that mark the early hominin record (see chapters 3 and 4), so too the genetic diversity of Native Americans has been considered as evidence concerning when the New World was colonized and who colonized it. Analyses of DNA from both Siberians and Native Americans have led some scholars to conclude that the original colonization of the Americas occurred sometime between 34,000 and 17,000 years ago, but as always, these estimates are somewhat speculative and disputed.[35] At the very least, this research shows that more than one "wave" of colonists came to the New World and that the earliest of these populations likely was from a population similar to that now found in the Altai Mountains region of Siberia, with contributions from East Asian areas such as Japan and Korea.[36]

It is interesting to note that these various studies of Native American physical anthropology have some relevance for the problem of the origins of modern *Homo sapiens sapiens* (chapter 4). On the basis of their general dental morphology, Turner labeled north Asians and Americans as *sinodonts* and the eastern and southern Asians as *sundadonts*, and he noted that both are very different from Europeans. As we noted in chapter 4, some scholars see traces of these sinodont and sundadont patterns in humans in Asia going back many hundreds of thousands of years, and on that basis they argue against the idea that we are all today descended from Africans who replaced all these very early Asian peoples.

Linguistic Evidence

Various scholars have also tried to estimate the date and patterns of New World colonization by examining Native American languages. Just as the resemblances among English, Greek, Persian, and other languages point toward a common Indo-European original language, the Native American languages have been screened for signs of common origin. One analysis of this problem is made by Joseph Greenberg, who argues that New World languages reflect three periods of colonization—the earliest, which is associated with Amerind, then a group of what are called Na-Dene speakers, and finally, at a later time, Eskimo-Aleut speakers.[37] Each of these three language groups probably originated from separate Old World language families, and there is some (controversial) evidence that all the world's languages can be traced to a single language family.[38] But like studies of teeth, estimates of the time of New World colonization on the basis of language changes must be considered quite speculative.

Archaeological Evidence

One might think that good, solid archaeological data—bones and stones—would be a firm basis for analyzing New World colonization. In fact, at this time there are a growing number of indications that people were in the New World and south of Alaska *before* about 12,000 years ago. That they were there by 11,500 years ago and thereafter is certain, since scores of sites have been dated by many different methods to 11,500 years ago and later.

But the evidence for occupations earlier than 15,000 years ago, and certainly for periods prior to 20,000 years ago, although intriguing, is far from convincing. One might think that, since hundreds of Asian sites have been securely dated to before 13,000 years ago, then, as weak as negative evidence is, this would suggest that there are no American sites of comparably early age. But it is at least possible that people were in the New World long before 13,000 years ago but simply left no traces that have been found yet. In the North American East, for example, exposed land surfaces in what would have been resource-rich areas of Tennessee, Alabama, and the Ohio Valley are extremely old, and artifacts found on them are difficult to date. Crude "pebble-tools" on these land surfaces could conceivably be the only surviving traces of very early occupations here. These pebble-tools show simplicity and extreme patination in comparison to other artifacts. The absence of projectile points and the simplicity of these early artifacts may mean that the earliest immigrants were not highly specialized big-game hunters, which suggests that they came over during the warmer periods of the Pleistocene as generalized hunters and gatherers. We cannot be certain, of course, because successful big-game hunters (like *Homo erectus*) used crude stone tools, but these pebble–tools do not look as if they were specialized killing or butchering implements. Nor have they been found with butchered animal bones or in environmental circumstances suggesting specialized hunting.

Except for this pebble-tool complex, however, to a large degree arguments about the date of New World colonization come down to one's belief in specific radiocarbon dates. And although the radiocarbon dating method has been shown to be broadly accurate around the world (see chapter 2), any single radiocarbon date can be misleading because of any number of factors, ranging from natural contamination through oil seeps or coal deposits to incompetent laboratory technicians. When the first radiocarbon dates were produced on Egyptian materials, for example, Egyptologists rejected these "scientific" dates because they conflicted with a decidedly unscientific farrago of evidence from king-lists, artifact styles, and so on. But the Egyptologists were right. Until archaeologists discovered that radiocarbon dates had to be corrected for past fluctuations in the amounts of radiocarbon in the atmosphere, these radiometric dates were off by centuries.

Because individual radiocarbon dates are sometimes suspect, archaeologists try to work with suites of dates or with comparisons of Asian or Siberian artifact styles and sites and the earliest New World sites and implements. But when we try to do this, we find that similarities between North Asian and early American stone tools are very much in the eye of the beholder.

North Asian Evidence

We might expect to find a long trail of archaeological sites stretching from northeastern Siberia along the sea floor of the now-submerged land bridge into central Alaska, and then southward. If these early immigrants were big-game hunters, we would expect many sites to be concentrations of animal bones, hearths, and flint tools appropriate for killing and preparing these animals. Alas, the gap between the real and ideal—so persistent in all archaeological research—is particularly great in this case. Some sites do fit this pattern, but the evidence is far from conclusive. First of all, it is only recently that adequate surveys of northeastern Siberia have been undertaken. Aside from the rigors of the Arctic climate, the politics of doing surveys amid intercontinental ballistic missile silos and radar stations has, until recently, deterred most Western scholars. Russian archaeologists,[39] nonetheless, have done excellent research in these areas, and now that Siberia is opening to Western scholars, collaborative research is beginning to clarify the cultural relationships of Pleistocene east Asian and North American cultures.

Present evidence suggests that before about 40,000 years ago, Siberia had extremely low population densities or was unsettled altogether—its great frigid interior swamps and forests may have barred human colonization, at least until huts had been developed. In any case, the earliest known sites in northeastern Siberia date to no more than about 25,000 years ago and reflect a life focused on the hunting of mammoths and other large animals. Projectile points, scrapers, and burins—tool types associated with big-game hunters all over the Old World—are the most frequent implements at Siberian sites, such as Mal'ta, Afontova gora II, and other sites of this period (see Figure 5.5). Perhaps most importantly, current paleoecological evidence suggests that human groups in Siberia shifted southward during the height of the last glacial period, and that it was only after 16,000 years ago that they were able to expand northward again and into Beringia.[40]

Stone tools, for example, from Mal'ta in deposits radiocarbon-dated to 14,750 years ago do not include Clovis-style points but seem to show at least similarities to early American assemblages—although there do not appear to be many large, finely crafted projectile points.[41] Haynes has even raised the possibility that Mal'ta represents an intermediate point in migrations of eastern European people across Siberia and into the New World—which he thinks is plausible because of the similarities between Clovis assemblages and late Pleistocene eastern European industries[42]—and which possibly could coincide with the introduction of the X haplogroup mtDNA lineage into the Americas (see earlier).

N. Dikov's work on the shores of Lake Ushki offers at least some evidence about possible links to the Americas. Dikov found the remains of what appears to be a large camp, in which people lived in hide or wood shelters. The center of one camp area was a deep burial pit in which the poorly preserved fragments of a body were found, along with about a thousand soft stone beads, some pendants of the same material, and some amber beads. The whole area of the burial was covered with red ocher, used probably to simulate blood or a living complexion on bodies.

Radiocarbon dating places the Ushki sites about 11,000–12,000 years ago.[43] For purposes of linking this site to the Americas, it is significant that Dikov found stone points in the bifacial, leaf-shape form that resemble those from the North American Great Basin of about the same time period. This might suggest a widespread bifacial point tradition, although the Lake Ushki sites appear to be too late to represent people ancestral to the Clovis tradition in the Americas.

Dikov reviewed the evidence for other sites on the way to what would have been Beringia and concluded that nothing "challenges the conservative view that the significant population movements from Asia occurred after the peak of the last glaciation, which was some 18,000 years ago."[44]

North and South American Evidence

The evidence is also somewhat sketchy on the American side of the land bridge. The Alaskan and northern Canadian climates make surveys very difficult, and farther south the constant waxing and waning of the glacial ice sheets and the vast riverine systems that drained them have thoroughly chewed up much of the land along the Canadian corridor. No doubt many sites in these areas have long since been scoured away by ice or water. The oldest sites currently known in the Alaskan area date to about 11,600 years ago and include Broken

Mammoth, Mead, and Swan Point.[45] They are part of the Nenana complex, with artifacts such as "teardrop-shaped" projectile points, endscrapers and side scrapers, burins, and lanceolate projectile points, as well as the use of red ochre (Figure 5.13). James Dixon notes that all of the Nenana complex sites are small and appear to have been only briefly occupied.[46] They are found mainly in high spots such as bluff tops, giving a panoramic view to the human groups using the camps.

Ironically, the site with perhaps the best claim to a pre-12,000 years ago date in the Americas is among the farthest south, Monte Verde, in south central Chile (Figure 5.14). Here Tom Dillehay and his crew have excavated a camp site that has been radiocarbon-dated to about 12,500 years ago, and below the levels of that age are layers of tools and debris that may be much older, perhaps up to 33,000 years old.[47]

Monte Verde is particularly interesting because, unlike most other sites of this age, it is not a cave or rock shelter. It is an open-air site located in a cold, wet, forested area that was covered by a peat bog and

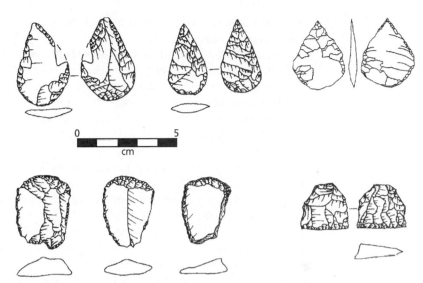

FIGURE 5.13   Examples of Nenana Complex stone artifacts in Alaska.

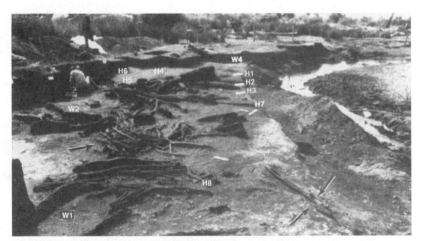

FIGURE 5.14   Excavations at Monte Verde, Chile, yielded remains of ancient dwellings dating to c. 12,500 years ago.

thereby extremely well preserved. A piece of mastodon flesh was found intact, plus a human footprint, log foundations for huts, animal skins, numerous plant remains, and many other remains. Almost all the bones from the site were from seven mastodons, which appear to have been killed elsewhere and carried home in large segments. Scores of plants were eaten, and remains of some plants with medicinal properties were found in the camp debris. Trade with other groups was indicated by the presence of salt, bitumen, non-native plants, and other commodities. Dillehay estimates that 30–50 people lived at Monte Verde at one time, with an impressive degree of occupational specialization in wood-working, stone-tool manufacturing, and other skills.

Monte Verde, is one of the most important sites in the New World. If people were here at 12,500 years ago, they must have been in the New World far earlier; if they lived in the almost sedentary communities that Monte Verde seems to represent, many models of hunting-foraging economies may not apply to much of the New World's earliest populations. And if the layers of the site dated by radiocarbon methods to 33,000 years ago really are that old, then most of the debates about New World colonization have been beside the point.

The evidence for extensive penetration of South America by 10,500 years ago, and perhaps as early as 11,500 years ago, is accumulating, even in difficult environments like the interior of Brazil.[48] Anna Roosevelt and her colleagues have recently described one of these early sites, the Caverna da Pedra Pintada at Monte Alegre, which is in the Amazon region of Brazil.[49] Two strata in the cave contain Paleoindian occupations. These have hearths and carbonized seeds, as well as stone artifacts including triangular bifacial points with stems (Figure 5.15). There are also examples of painted rock art on the walls of the cave. The thousands of pieces of carbonized plants found in these layers show that humans at Monte Alegre gathered tree fruits as part of their diet. These are tropical rain forest

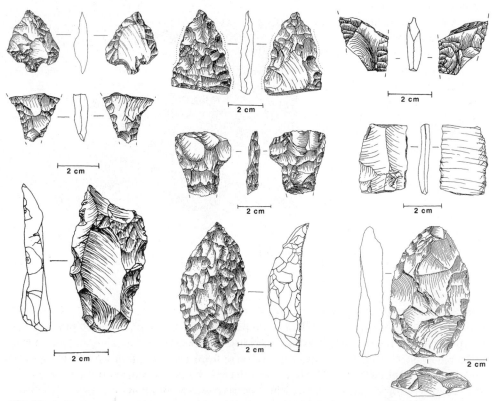

FIGURE 5.15 Stone artifacts from Caverna de Pedra Pintada, Brazil, document human presence in interior South America before 10,500 years ago.

species, including Brazil nuts and various edible palm tree fruits.[50] Paleoindians here also made use of fish, freshwater mussels, tortoise, and aquatic turtles. This type of gathering-and-foraging subsistence economy, which Roosevelt believes is contemporary with Clovis Paleoindians, is quite different from the subsistence economies described for Clovis occupations in North America.

One of the most controversial and potentially important early New World sites is Meadowcroft Rock Shelter, near Avella, Pennsylvania, where many layers of alluvial sediments were deposited by a tributary of the Ohio River (Figure 5.16). Interspersed in these alluvial sediments are many clear indications of human occupation, including prismatic flint blades, basketry, and hearths. Millennia of reoccupation left a 16-foot-thick "layercake" of tools, bones, baskets, and other debris. The question is, how far back does Meadowcroft's earliest occupation date? The site was excellently excavated, and there is no question about the provenience of the artifacts. A bit of charred basketry from near the bottom was radiocarbon-dated to 19,600 +/− 2,400 and 19,150 +/− 800 years B.P. Charcoal from a level beneath the basketry dates to as old as 37,000 years ago, but there were no associated artifacts. Unfortunately, there is some suggestion that the samples may have been contaminated by groundwater and that the site's stratigraphy has been misunderstood.[51] The

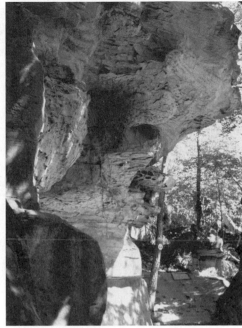

FIGURE 5.16 Meadowcroft Rockshelter, PA, is one of several sites said to contain evidence for pre-Clovis occupations in the New World.

kinds of bones found at the site also pose some problems, in that they do not seem to be from animals one would expect this close to the glaciers that would have pushed far down into the northeastern United States in the late Pleistocene.

The stone tools of Meadowcroft's earliest levels are similar to the typical Clovis assemblage of 11,500 years ago, but some blade sizes and types are different. Adovasio has compared the Meadowcroft lithics to those from other sites and suspects that they may represent a link between Old World tool industries and early North American cultures, such as the Clovis.[52]

But if the earlier dates for Meadowcroft are accepted, it means that people were in the continental United States before the last glacial advance, which implies that the ice sheets were in fact no barrier and that the scarcity of sites found is a matter of inadequate searching, low population densities, and the post-depositional destruction of sites.

If people entered the New World 30,000 or more years ago, it might seem surprising that more archaeological sites have not been found dating to this period; after all, hundreds of Old World sites date to this age. But population densities in Europe and other parts of the Old World had been slowly building for hundreds of thousands of years before people entered the New World. In addition, most European sites of this age are found in caves and rock shelters, and there are relatively few of these along the probable route into the New World. Alternatively, the first Americans may have worked out adaptations to cold climates that did not require caves. Indeed, their ancestors must have done this because there are no caves along the Siberia-Beringia-Alaska route.

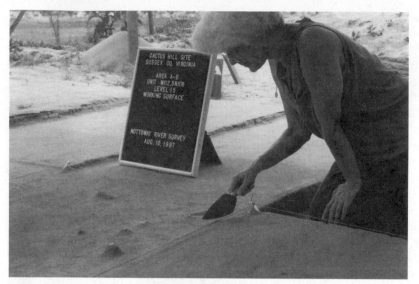

FIGURE 5.17 The site of Cactus Hill, VA, has yielded a pre-Clovis horizon.

Another problem in locating early sites in eastern North America is that in much of the lower Mississippi area, alluviation has been so great that many such sites would be buried under tens of meters of soil. And in the rest of the South and East, where the glacial ice sheets never extended, the present land surface is millions of years old. Thus, soft-drink bottles and ancient artifacts can be found in virtually the same soil because accumulation of soil over these areas has been so slow for millions of years. Additionally, bones and other datable materials do not preserve well under these humid, exposed conditions.

Still, there *are* suitable land surfaces in North America where pre-Clovis occupations could have been preserved. One of these is the recently discovered site of Cactus Hill in Virginia (Figure 5.17).[53] The occupations here are on a relict sand dune and include both a Clovis period occupation and, underneath that, a pre-Clovis horizon named "Blade" by the site's investigators because it yielded quartzite blades.[54] Radiocarbon dates on natural wood particles from the lowest sand deposit show that the sand dune was forming around 19,000 years ago or perhaps slightly earlier. Another date of around 16,900 years ago was obtained from natural charcoal in sterile deposits immediately below the "Blade" occupation. The overlying Clovis horizon is radiocarbon dated to 10,900 years ago. These dates form an age bracket for the "Blade" occupation, which must be somewhere in the interval between 10,900 and 16,900 years ago.

David Whitley and Ronald Dorn evaluated hypothetical migration and fertility rates for a population entering North America through Beringia and compared them with sites whose ages are accepted by nearly all archaeologists, and they conclude that "it is impossible to reconcile the Clovis-first hypothesis with empirical evidence accepted by its own advocates."[55]

THE CALIBRATION OF PALEOINDIAN RADIOCARBON DATES

One of the significant advances in research on Paleoindian complexes in recent years has been the calibration or correction (see chapter 2) of radiocarbon dates for these occupations. Stuart Fiedel has summarized the results, noting that the correction curves indicate that radiocarbon dates for ages in the late Pleistocene are some 2,000 years too young.[56] Although we have used uncalibrated or uncorrected radiocarbon dates in the discussions in this chapter, in actual fact, Clovis period occupations date to between 13,400 and 13,000 calibrated radiocarbon years ago, and the pre-Clovis occupation at Monte Verde to

cal BP	¹⁴C bp	Climate	WESTERN NORTH AMERICA	EASTERN NORTH AMERICA	SOUTH AMERICA
9,000	8,200				
9,500	8,500			bifurcate points	
	8,700				
10,000	9,000		PLANO COMPLEXES		
10,500	9,400				
	9,500			KIRK	
11,000					
	9,900			PALMER, KESSELL	
11,500	10,200		AGATE BASIN		
		–YD ends–			
	10,300				
12,000	10,500			DALTON	MONTE ALEGRE
	10,500				
12,500					
	10,700			MID-PALEO	
	11,000	–YD begins–	FOLSOM	Debert	FELL I
13,000	11,100		GOSHEN?		
	10,300	—	CLOVIS	CLOVIS	
	10,600	IACP			
13,500	11,700				
		Allerød			
	11,800				
14,000	12,000	OD and ACR		(biface/blade industries?)	Monte Verde
	12,300				
14,500					
	12,600	Bølling begins			
15,000					

FIGURE 5.18 The calibration of radiocarbon dates shows that the first people in the Americas arrived 2000 years earlier than previously thought. However, pre-Clovis sites (earlier than 13,500 cal BP) remain controversial. Monte Verde is the most widely accepted site of pre-Clovis occupation (about 14,500 cal BP). However, a few scholars such as Stuart Fiedel (personal communication 2006), noting the peculiarity of stone tools and discrepancies in the site reports, still question this site's authenticity and antiquity.

about 14,400 calibrated radiocarbon years ago (Figure 5.18). Gaining 2,000 years of time also has implications for those researchers who have calculated the timing for the colonization of the New World using genetic "clocks" or even "clocks" based on the length of time it is thought to take for the development of the various Native American languages.[57]

EARLY PALEOINDIAN ECONOMIES

For many thousands of years after people reached mid-continental and southern latitudes in the New World, population densities were probably extremely light, and most bands no

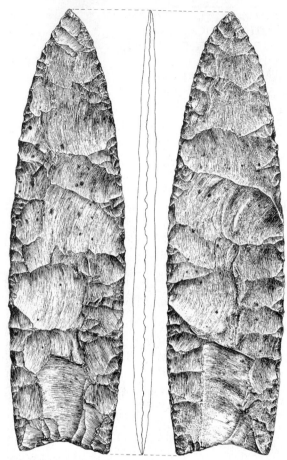

FIGURE 5.19 An cache of extraordinary Clovis points including this example was recovered from the Richie-Roberts site, WA.

doubt stayed in the same general mixed forest and grassland environments their ancestors had adapted to in more northern areas. By about 11,000 years ago, however, they began to display greater diversity in subsistence strategies as they evolved adaptations to a greater range of environments.

Archaeologists think their reconstructions of these early American cultures may be somewhat inaccurate because of the nature of the archaeological record these cultures left. The easiest archaeological sites to find are those with large stone tools and the bones of large animals, and many early New World sites are of this type: dozens of stone tools intermixed with mammoth, bison, and other bones, often near streams or bogs where hunters ambushed these animals. But there may be many less obvious sites—those not yet found because they are not marked by masses of animal bones or impressive stone tools. In 1987, for example, a Clovis site in a Washington State apple orchard (the Ritchie Roberts Site) was found when holes were dug for new trees, and beautiful, exceptionally large stone points were unearthed (Figure 5.19). But if this had been an earlier site containing only crude pebble tools, it is highly improbable that it would ever have been recognized. In short, extreme biases are likely in our recognition of the early American archaeological record. Many archaeologists question, for example, even the presumption that the Clovis and Folsom peoples were mainly big-game hunters, although there is some evidence that groups along the tundra zone, in New York and Massachusetts, specialized in caribou.[58] Meltzer argues that in much of the southeast United States, the people who left the many fluted points in this area were generalized foragers who probably used many of the points as hafted knives, not as spear points.[59] And Dixon points out that the "spectacular and well-publicized Clovis kill sites may be the least typical and the least useful sites for interpreting . . . early New World adaptations."[60]

Numerous surface finds of Clovis fluted points are known from the northern part of Mexico, especially from Sonora.[61] These likely are of comparable age to Clovis occupations in North America, that is, 11,000 years ago or older. But it is the area of Lake Texcoco in the Basin of Mexico that has yielded sites showing an association of mammoths and stone artifacts, indicating hunting and butchering events. The Paleoindians who were responsible for the Lake Texcoco archaeological record, however, were not Clovis groups, but appear to represent later complexes perhaps related to those of the American West.[62] The consistency with which mammoths are found in these sites may seem to reflect an economy specialized in hunting large animals, but most of the people of Mexico at this time were probably generalized hunters and gatherers, and only because of the great size and preservation of the mammoth bones do we find so many of these sites.

But there is no question that some people did kill and eat big animals. Excavations at Iztapan 2, in Mexico, yielded a mammoth skeleton with cut-marks made by stone tools. The base of the skull was smashed, perhaps to get at the brain, a very nutritious resource. A lanceolate and a leaf-shaped projectile point were found with this mammoth.[63]

Perhaps the most direct way to demonstrate hunting of large animals by early Americans is to find residues of animal tissue on the tools themselves, and in a few cases this is possible. At least one of the large fluted points at the Ritchie Site in eastern Washington State was found to have traces of blood on it—in fact, probably from a mammoth.

The earliest distinctive and widely distributed tool complex found in the North American East is distinguished by the presence of large stone projectile points. Most such points are between 12 and 30 cm long and occasionally have been "fluted." Formerly, many archaeologists thought these eastern points were imitations of the Folsom and Clovis points, but it is now evident that these larger points occur as early—and probably earlier—in the eastern woodlands as on the Plains and are more numerous in the East: Alabama alone, for example, has yielded more fluted points than the entire western half of North America.[64]

Other evidence of hunting comes from Arctic sites, such as Dry Creek, Trail Creek, and similar occupations, most of which date to between 11,000 and 8,000 years ago. These sites seem to be hunting camps in unglaciated areas and are marked by bifacial knives, tiny blades, and the bones of horses, bison, hares, ducks, and other animals. By this time, these Arctic hunters may have been pursuing a dying way of life, as the glaciers and the rich animal life they supported were slowly withdrawing.[65]

Shortly after 8,000 years ago at least some groups in the American West were undoubtedly specializing in hunting big game. They often practiced "jump hunting," in which many people cooperated to stampede bison herds or other animals over a precipice, killing them by the score. Where there were no convenient precipices, animals were driven into natural cul-de-sacs, where they could be easily killed (Figure 5.20). In sites reflecting these practices, archaeologists find the bones of hundreds of bison, many showing clear butchering marks. These hunters took cuts of meat from these animals in a way that showed a shrewd appreciation of their nutritional value.[66] By drying the meat, these hunters could accumulate large food reserves, and the skin, hide, and bones of the bison had many uses.

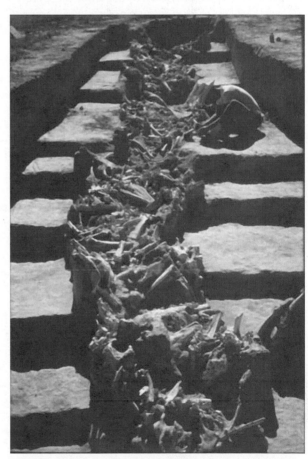

FIGURE 5.20 Overview of the bison kill at the Olson-Chubbuck site, CO.

A good example of the varied nature of early American adaptations is the *Desert West.* The Desert West refers to the area between the Rocky Mountains and the Sierra Nevada and Cascade Mountain range, extending from Canada to southern Mexico.[67] About 12,000 years ago, when the glacial ice sheets were still a kilometer high along the northern border of the United States, some of the Desert West was probably cooler and wetter than it is today and had many large lakes and marshes. Then, between 12,000 and 10,000 years ago, the lakes shrank, rivers ceased to flow, and springs began to dry up.

The Desert West has less diverse flora and fauna than most other parts of North America, but for most of the last 10,000 years it has supported large populations of squirrels, rabbits, marmots, wood rats, peccaries, and other small animals, as well as localized herds of deer, bison, elk, and big-horn sheep. Sunflowers, pickleweed, yucca, piñon nuts, and other vegetable foods are available seasonally in most of this area. Resource diversity is particularly great as one moves up and down the hills and ridges of the Desert West: A single day's climb can take one from a desert environment to Arctic-Alpine environments in the uplands. An especially important element in the subsistence of prehistoric peoples of the Desert West was the lakes and marshes probably present here during much of the Pleistocene. Fish, waterfowl, invertebrates, marsh plants, and many other resources were exploited as soon as colonization began and have played an important part in determining human settlement here to the present. Generally, then, the Desert West offers archaeologists an opportunity to study the many ways prehistoric populations in this area have adapted their subsistence strategies, population densities, technologies, and seasonal movements to the nuances of a somewhat extreme physical environment.

The earliest reliably dated sites are all between 12,000 and 10,000 years old, although remains of earlier occupations will probably be found when the archaeology of the Desert West is better known. Many of the rock shelters and caves in the Desert West were submerged by lakes during the late Pleistocene, so most of the early sites may be "open-air" sites and thus difficult to find and date.

The first well-documented Desert West cultures are represented by lithic artifacts very like the Clovis points that appeared in the Great Plains about 12,000 years ago. These artifacts have been found at many locations in the Desert West, but almost all were surface finds, with no associated animal or plant remains that could tell us much about either the age or the economy of these cultures. Often associated with these points are stone artifacts usually interpreted as gravers, borers, and other types of projectile points.

From about 11,000 to 8,000 years ago, many of the Desert West peoples apparently organized their economies around the resources of lakes and marshes, while groups in more arid areas probably adopted a more generalized hunting-and-gathering strategy. Remains of pole-and-thatch huts have been found in some areas, but the size, location, and contents of most sites of this period suggest that for most of the year Desert West peoples lived in small bands and followed complex seasonal rounds, exploiting different resources as they became available.

Pleistocene Extinctions

The spread of human hunting-and-gathering societies over the New World after 12,000 years ago, at the end of the last glacial period, coincides with the extinction of many animal species, and by about 10,000 years ago, all or most of the mammoths, mastodons, long-horned bison, tapirs, horses, giant ground sloths, dire wolves, camels, and many other creatures had disappeared.[68] Extinction is, of course, a natural evolutionary development and can be accounted for by known biological processes. But the number of animal species that became extinct in the New World and their apparently rapid rate of extinction has led some to conclude that human hunters forced many New World animals into extinction shortly after the Pleistocene.[69]

But people may have had little or nothing to do with these extinctions. Donald Grayson and David Meltzer note that only two animals that became extinct—the mammoth and the mastodon—are known from Clovis kill sites, and of all the Clovis sites, only 14 have this association between an extinct animal and Clovis artifacts.[70] Perhaps even more significant, game species were not the only ones to die out. Grayson has shown that numerous species of birds also became extinct at this time, and it is difficult to believe that people could have played any role in this.[71] Also, some "big-game" species such as the mastodon lived in the North American South and East while humans were there and are known to have died out shortly after the end of the Pleistocene, but their bones have rarely been found in association with evidence of human activities. Thus, it would seem that at least some larger animals became extinct without much human assistance. Finally, we might also note that there is no archaeological evidence that the hunting practices most likely to lead to animal extinctions, such as drives and jumps, were ever used during the period, some 10,000–8,000 years ago, when most of the larger species became extinct.

Kelly and Todd present an alternative to the overkill model, arguing that the Clovis peoples were unlike most known hunter-foragers in that they may have had very little processing technology for food storage, relying instead on proficient hunting using high-quality flint bifacial tools, and shifting their range as they exhausted the resources of an area.[72] They suggest that the pattern of Pleistocene extinctions would have been similar even if people had never entered the New World.

If we rule out human hunting as the most important factor in these extinctions, what alternative explanation can we give? Many have been suggested, but none is really very satisfactory. Clearly, the immediate post-Pleistocene period was one of radical climate change, and no doubt this was of some importance. Of 31 genera of mammals that became extinct, however, only 7 had entered the New World during the last 70,000 years; all the others had managed to adapt to the climatic changes of the previous interglacial periods, which were fully as dramatic as those after the last glacial retreat. Why did they become extinct after the last period?

Some have suggested that New World animals might have been decimated by diseases introduced from the Old World during one of the later intervals when the Bering land bridge route was open—a situation reminiscent of the frightful casualties inflicted on aboriginal Americans by smallpox, measles, and other diseases introduced by the Europeans. Such epidemics, however, usually do not cause species to become extinct: They decimate local populations over a large area but generally leave small pockets of resistant individuals who eventually reestablish the species.

As Grayson has pointed out, it is entirely possible that these Pleistocene extinctions were the results of climatic changes and human interactions of fairly subtle and presently unknown dimensions.[73] Research directed toward this question will likely need to focus on each separate animal and its ecological requirements.[74]

Human population densities rose in many parts of the New World, and, as we will see in chapter 15, by 7,000 years ago some hunting-and-gathering societies were already in the process of domesticating plants and beginning the transition to the agricultural, complex cultures of late prehistoric America.

SUMMARY AND CONCLUSIONS

Evidence for early sites, such as Monte Verde and Cactus Hill, has lent considerable support to the idea that initial peopling of the Americas was via a coastal route from Beringia to at least as far south as Washington and Oregon. This process seems to have been underway by about 13,500 years ago. Use of the "ice-free" corridor as an entry into what is now the United States was simply not feasible before 11,500 years ago because this corridor did not come into existence until then. It is only later human groups who were able to use this route—perhaps traveling in both directions.

We know that people were here in substantial numbers by 11,000 years ago, and within a few thousand years they had occupied most of the more productive New World areas and were beginning to diversify culturally. It seems unlikely that the massive wave of extinctions of large animals after about 11,000 years ago had much to do with human activities.

The initial colonization of the New World may seem to be an epochal development, but it was in fact just one aspect of the great radiation of the human species during the late Pleistocene. From Australia to South America to Siberia and the Arctic, people colonized the world and adapted to its many environments.

BIBLIOGRAPHY

Adovasio, J. M. 1993. "The Ones That Will Not Go Away: A Biased View of Pre-Clovis Occupation in the New World." In *From Kostenki to Clovis: Upper Paleolithic Paleo-Indian Adaptations*, ed. O. Soffer and N. D. Praslov. New York: Plenum Press.

Adovasio, J. M., and R. C. Carlisle. 1987. "The First Americans." *Natural History* 95(12):20–27.

Adovasio, J. M., J. Donahue, and R. Stuckenrath. 1990. "The Meadowcroft Rockshelter Radiocarbon Chronology, 1975–1990." *American Antiquity* 55(2):348–354.

Adovasio, J. M., J. Donahue, J. D. Gunn, and R. Stuckenrath. 1981. "The Meadowcroft Papers: A Response to Dincauze." *Quarterly Review of Archaeology* 2:14–15.

Aikens, C. M. 1978. "Archaeology of the Great Basin." *Annual Review of Anthropology* 7:71–87.

Anderson, D. G. 1995. "Recent Advances in Paleoindian and Archaic Period Research in the Southeastern United States." *Archaeology of Eastern North America* 23:145–176.

Anderson, D. G., and M. K. Faught. 1998. "The Distribution of Fluted Paleoindian Projectile Points: Update 1998." *Archaeology of Eastern North America* 26:163–187.

———. 2000. "Paleoindian Artifact Distributions: Evidence and Implications." *Antiquity* 74:507–513.

Anderson, D. G., and J. C. Gillam. 2000. "Paleoindian Colonization of the Americas: Implications from an Examination of Physiography, Demography, and Artifact Distribution." *American Antiquity* 65(1):43–66.

Arnold, J. E., M. R. Walsh, and S. E. Hollimon. 2004. "The Archaeology of California." *Journal of Archaeological Research* 12(1):1–73.

Aveleyra Arrowyo de Anda, L., and M. Maldonado-Koerdell. 1953. "Assocation of Artifacts with Mammoths in the Valley of Mexico." *American Antiquity* 18:332–340.

Barnosky, A. D., P. L. Koch, R. S. Feranec, S. L. Wing, and A. B. Shabel. 2004. "Assessing the Causes of Late Pleistocene Extinctions on the Continents." *Science* 306:70–75.

Beaudoin, A. B., M. Wright, and B. Ronaghan. 1996. "Late Quaternary Landscape History and Archaeology in the 'Ice-Free' Corridor: Some Recent Results from Alberta." *Quaternary International* 32:113–126.

Beck, C. 1997. "The Terminal Pleistocene/Early Holocene Archaeology of the Great Basin." *Journal of World Prehistory* 11(2):161–236.

Bettinger, R. L. 1977. "Aboriginal Human Ecology in Owens Valley: Prehistoric Change in the Great Basin." *American Antiquity* 42:3–17.

Boldurian, A. T., and J. L. Cotter. 1999. *Clovis Revisited: New Perspectives on Paleoindian Adaptations from Blackwater Draw, New Mexico.* Philadelphia: University of Pennsylvania Museum.

Bonnichsen, R., and K. L. Turnmire, eds. 1991. *Clovis: Origins and Adaptations.* Corvallis: Center for the Study of the First Americans, Oregon State University.

Crawford, M. H. 1993. "DNA Variability and Human Evolution." *Evolutionary Anthropology* 2(4):115.

Cwyner, L. C., and J. C. Ritchie. 1980. "Arctic Step-Tundra: A Yukon Perspective." *Science* 208:1375–1377.

DeJarnette, D. L. 1967. "Alabama Pebbletools: The Lively Complex." *Eastern States Archaeological Federation Bulletin* 26.

Derev'anko, A. P. 1998. *The Paleolithic of Siberia: New Discoveries and Interpretations.* Urbana: University of Illinois Press.

Dikov, N. N. 1977. *Monuments in Kamchatka, Chukotka, and the Upper Reaches of the Kolyma: Asia Joining America in Ancient Times.* Moscow: Nauka.

———. 1987. "On the Road to America." *Natural History* 97(1):12–15.

Dixon, E. J. 1993. *Quest for the Origins of the First Americans.* Albuquerque: University of New Mexico Press.

———. 2001. "Human Colonization of the Americas: Timing, Technology and Process." *Quaternary Science Reviews* 20:277–299.

Dillehay, T. D. 1987. "By the Banks of the Chinchihuapi." *Natural History* 96(4):8–12.

———. 1997. *Monte Verde: A Late Pleistocene Settlement in Chile. Volume 2: The Archaeological Context and Interpretation.* Washington, DC: Smithsonian Institution Press.

Dincauze, D. 1981. "The Meadowcroft Papers." *The Quarterly Review of Archaeology* 2:3–4.

Fiedel, S. 1999. "Older Than We Thought: Implications of Corrected Dates for Paleoindians." *American Antiquity* 64:95–116.

Figgins, J. D. 1927. "The Antiquity of Man in America." *Natural History* 27:229–239.

Fladmark, K. 1979. "Routes: Alternate Migration Corridors for Early Man in North America." *American Antiquity* 44:55–69.

———. 1986. *British Columbian Prehistory.* Chicago: University of Chicago Press.

———. 1987. "Getting One's Berings." *Natural History* 95(11):8–19.

Frison, G. C., M. Wilson, and D. J. Wilson. 1976. "Fossil Bison and Artifacts from an Early Altithermal Period Arroyo Trap in Wyoming." *American Antiquity* 41:28–57.

Frison, G. C., R. L. Andrews, J. M. Adovasio, R. C. Carlisle, and R. Edgar. 1986. "A Late Paleoindian Animal Trapping Net from Northern Wyoming." *American Antiquity* 51(2):352–361.

Goebel, T., M. R. Waters, and M. Dikova. 2003. "The Archaeology of Ushki Lake, Kamchatka, and the Pleistocene Peopling of the Americas." *Science* 301:501–505.

Goebel, T., M. R. Waters, and M. N. Mescherin. 2001. "Masterov Kliuch and the Early Upper Palaeolithic of the Transbaikal, Siberia." *Asian Perspectives* 39(1–2):47–70.

Grayson, D. K. 1977. "Pleistocene Avifaunas and the Overkill Hypothesis." *Science* 195:691–693.

———. 1987. "Death by Natural Causes." *Natural History* 96(5):8–13.

———. 1993. *Desert's Past: A Natural Prehistory of the Great Basin.* Washington, DC: Smithsonian Institution Press.

Grayson, D. K., and D. J. Meltzer. 2003. "A Requiem for North American Overkill." *Journal of Archaeological Science* 30:585–593.

Greenberg, J. H., C. G. Turner II, and S. L. Zegura. 1986. "The Settlement of the Americas: A Comparison of the Linguistic, Dental, and Genetic Evidence." *Current Anthropology* 27(5):477–497.

Guadalupe Sanchez, M. 2001. "A Synopsis of Paleo-Indian Archaeology in Mexico." *Kiva* 67(2):119–136.

Guthrie, R. D. 1980. "The First Americans? The Elusive Arctic Bone Culture." *The Quarterly Review of Archaeology* 1:2.

———. 1984. "Mosaics, Allelochemics, and Nutrients: An Ecological Theory of Late Pleistocene Megafaunal Extinctions." In *Quaternary Extinctions: A Prehistoric Revolution,* ed. P. S. Martin and R. G. Klein, pp. 259–298. Tucson: University of Arizona Press.

Haag, W. G. 1962. "The Bering Strait Land Bridge." *Scientific American* 206:112–123.

Hagelberg, E. 1993. "Ancient DNA Studies." *Evolutionary Anthropology* 2(6):199–207.

Hall, R., D. Roy, and D. Boling. 2004. "Pleistocene Migration Routes into the Americas: Human Biological Adaptations and Environmental Constraints." *Evolutionary Anthropology* 13:132–144.

Haynes, C. V., Jr. 1974. "Elephant Hunting in North America." *New World Prehistory: Readings from Scientific American,* ed. E. Zubrow et al. San Francisco: Freeman.

———. 1987. "Geofacts and Fancy." *Natural History* 97(2):4–12.

Haynes, C. V., Jr., R. E. Reanier, W. P. Barse, A. C. Roosevelt, M. Lima da Costa, L. J. Brown, J. E. Douglas, M. O'Donnell, E. Quinn, J. Kemp, C. Lopes Machado, M. Imazio da Silveira, J. Feathers, and

A. Henderson. 1997. "Dating a Paleoindian Site in the Amazon in Comparison with Clovis Culture." *Science* 275:1948–1952.

Hopkins, D. M., J. V. Matthews, Jr., C. E. Schweger, and S. B. Young. 1982. *Paleoecology of Beringia.* New York: Academic Press.

Jablonski, N. G., ed. 2002. *The First Americans: The Pleistocene Colonization of the New World.* San Francisco: Memoirs of the California Academy of Sciences, No. 27.

Jaffe, A. J. 1992. *The First Immigrants from Asia: A Population History of the North American Indians.* New York: Plenum Press.

Kelly, R. L., and L. C. Todd. 1988. "Coming into the Country: Early Paleoindian Hunting and Mobility." *American Antiquity* 53(2):231–244.

Larichev, V., U. Khol'ushkin, and I. Laricheva. 1987. "Lower and Middle Paleolithic of Northern Asia: Achievements, Problems, and Perspectives." *Journal of World Prehistory* 1(4):415–464.

———. 1993. "The Upper Paleolithic of Northern Asia: Achievements, Problems, and Perspectives III: Northeastern Siberia and the Russian Far East. *Journal of World Prehistory* 6(4):441–476.

Lively, M. 1965. "The Lively Complex: Announcing a Pebble Tool Industry in Alabama." *Journal of Alabama Archaeology* 11:103–122.

Lorenz, J. G., and D. G. Smith. 1996. "Distribution of Four Founding mtDNA Haplogroups Among Native North Americans." *American Journal of Physical Anthropology* 101:307–323.

Lyell, C. 1863. *Principles of Geology.* London: Murray.

Malouf, D. 1993. *Remembering Babylon.* New York: Pantheon Books.

Mandryk, C. A. S., H. Josenhans, D. W. Fedje, and R. W. Mathewes. 2001. "Late Quaternary Paleoenvironments of Northwestern North America: Implications for Inland Versus Coastal Migration Routes." *Quaternary Science Reviews* 20:301–314.

Marks, J. 1995. *Human Biodiversity: Genes, Race, and History.* Hawthorne, NY: Aldine de Gruyter.

Martin, P. S., and J. E. Guilday. 1967. "A Bestiary for Pleistocene Biologists." In *Pleistocene Extinctions: The Search for a Cause,* ed. P. S. Martin and H. E. Wright, Jr. New Haven: Yale University Press.

Martin, P. S., and R. Klein, eds. 1984. *Quaternary Extinctions: A Prehistoric Revolution.* Tucson: University of Arizona Press.

Martin, P. S., and H. E. Wright, Jr., eds. 1967. *Pleistocene Extinctions: The Search for a Cause.* New Haven: Yale University Press.

Mehringer, P., Jr. 1977. "Great Basin Late Quaternary Environments and Chronology." In *Models in Great Basin Prehistory: A Symposium,* ed. D. D. Fowler. *Desert Research Institute Publications in the Social Sciences* 12:113–168.

Meltzer, D. J. 1988. "Late Pleistocene Human Adaptations in Eastern North America." *Journal of World Prehistory* 2(1):1–52.

Meltzer, D. J., D. K. Grayson, G. Ardila, A. W. Barker, D. F. Dincauze, C. V. Haynes, F. Mena, L. Núñez, and D. J. Stanford. 1997. "On the Pleistocene Antiquity of Monte Verde, Southern Chile." *American Antiquity* 62(4):659–663.

Moismann, J. E., and P. S. Martin. 1975. "Simulating Overkill by Paleoindians." *American Scientist* 63:304–313.

Orquera, L. A. 1987. "Advances in the Archaeology of the Pampa and Patagonia." *Journal of World Prehistory* 1(4):333–413.

Osborn, G., and K. Bevis. 2001. "Glaciations in the Great Basin of the Western United States." *Quaternary Science Reviews* 20(13):1377–1410.

Oviatt, C. G., D. B. Madsen, and D. N. Schmitt. 2003. "Late Pleistocene and Early Holocene Rivers and Wetlands in the Bonneville Basin of Western North America." *Quaternary Research* 60(2): 200–210.

Pitulko, V. V., P. A. Nikolsky, E. U. Girya, A. E. Basilyan, V. E. Tumskoy, S. A. Koulakov, S. N. Astakhov, E. Y. Pavlova, and M. A. Anisimov. 2004. "The Yana RHS Site: Humans in the Arctic Before the Last Glacial Maximum." *Science* 303:52–56.

Roosevelt, A. C., M. Lima da Costa, C. Lopes Machado, M. Michab, N. Mercier, H. Valladas, J. Feathers, W. Barnett, M. Imazio da Silveira, A. Henderson, J. Sliva, B. Chernoff, D. S. Reese, J. A. Holman, N. Toth, and K. Schick. 1996. "Paleoindian Cave Dwellers in the Amazon: The Peopling of the Americas." *Science* 272:373–384.

Ruhlen, M. 1987. "Voices from the Past." *Natural History* 96(3):6–10.

Schmitz, P. E. 1987. "Prehistoric Hunters and Gatherers of Brazil." *Journal of World Prehistory* 1(1):53–126.

Schurr, T. G. 2000. "Mitochondrial DNA and the Peopling of the New World." *American Scientist* 88(3):246–253.

Stanford, D., and B. Bradley. 2002. "Ocean Trails and Prairie Paths? Thoughts About Clovis Origins." In *The First Americans: The Pleistocene Colonization of the New World,* pp. 255–271. San Francisco: Memoirs of the California Academy of Sciences, No. 27.

Steele, D. G., and J. F. Powell. 1993. "Paleobiology of the First Americans." *Evolutionary Anthropology* 2(4):138–146.

Stewart, T. D. 1973. *The People of America*. New York: Scribner's.

Stone, A. C., and M. Stoneking. 1993. "Ancient DNA from a Pre-Columbian Amarind Population." *American Journal of Physical Anthropology* 92:463–471.

Straus, L. G. 2000. "Solutrean Settlement of North America? A Review of Reality." *American Antiquity* 65:219–226.

Tankersley, K. B. 1997. "Variation in the Early Paleoindian Economies of Eastern North America." *American Antiquity* 63:7–20.

Taylor, R. E., C. V. Haynes, Jr., D. L. Kirner, and J. R. Southon. 1999. "Radiocarbon Analyses of Modern Organics at Monte Verde, Chile: No Evidence for a Local Reservoir Effect." *American Antiquity* 64:455–460.

Torroni, A., T. G. Schurr, M. F. Cabell, M. D. Brown, J. V. Neel, M. Larsen, D. G. Smith, C. M. Vullo, and D. C. Wallace. 1994. "Asian Affinities and the Continental Radiation of the Four Founding Native American Mitochondrial DNAs." *American Journal of Human Genetics* 53:563–590.

Turner, C. G., II. 1987. "Tell-Tale Teeth." *Natural History* 96(1):6–10.

Vescelius, G. S. 1981. "Early and/or Not-So-Early Man in Peru: Guitarrero Cave Revisited." *Quarterly Review of Archaeology* 2:8–13, 19–20.

Wagner, D. P., and J. M. McAvoy. 25,004. "Pedoarchaeology of Cactus Hill, a Sandy Paleoindian Site in Southeastern Virginia, U.S.A." *Geoarchaeology: An International Journal* 19(4):297–322.

Warren, C., and A. Ranere. 1968. "Outside Danger Cave: A View of Early Men in the Great Basin." In *Early Man in Western North America*, ed. C. Irwin-Williams. Portales: Eastern New Mexico University Press.

Wheat, J. B. 1972. "The Olsen-Chubbuck Site: A Paleo Indian Bison Kill." Washington, DC: *Memoirs of the Society for American Archaeology*, No. 26, pt. 2.

Whitley, D. S., and R. I. Dorn. 1993. "New Perspectives on the Clovis vs. Pre-Clovis Controversy." *American Antiquity* 58(4):626–647.

Yurtsev, B. A. 2001. "The Pleistocene 'Tundra-Steppe' and the Productivity Paradox: The Landscape Approach." *Quaternary Science Review* 20:165–174.

Zegura, S. L. 1987. "Blood Test." *Natural History* 96(7):8–11.

NOTES

1. Stewart, *The People of America*, p. 60.
2. Quoted in Stewart, *The People of America*, p. 70; it should be noted that Jefferson thought it possible for reverse migration from the Americas into Asia and then back again.
3. Figgins, "The Antiquity of Man in America."
4. Haag, "The Bering Strait Land Bridge," p. 269.
5. Cwyner and Ritchie, "Arctic Step-Tundra: A Yukon Perspective"; also see Dixon, *Quest for the Origins of the First Americans*.
6. Yurtsev, "The Pleistocene Tundra-Steppe and the Productivity Paradox: The Landscape Approach."
7. Mandryk et al., "Late Quaternary Paleoenvironments in Northwestern North America: Implications for Inland vs. Coastal Migration Routes."
8. Martin and Wright, *Pleistocene Extinctions: The Search for a Cause*, pp. 32–33.
9. Fladmark, "Routes: Alternate Migration Corridors for Early Man in North America"; Dixon, "Human Colonization of the Americas: Timing, Technology and Process."
10. Fladmark, *British Columbian Prehistory*; idem., "Getting One's Berings."
11. One famous example of this is the site of Calico Hills in California. Among the proponents for the great antiquity of this site, which was claimed to be at least 30,000 years old, was Louis Leakey. Extensive examination of the site's context, however, has shown that while some of the artifacts are real, they are simply deposited on the surface of a very old Pleistocene terrace. In other words, the artifacts are younger than the context with which they are associated (Haynes, "Geofacts and Fancy"; Arnold et al., "The Archaeology of California," p. 9).
12. Beaudoin et al., "Late Quaternary Landscape History and Archaeology in the 'Ice-Free' Corridor: Some Recent Results from Alberta."
13. Mandryk et al., "Late Quaternary Paleoenvironments of Northwestern North America: Implications for Inland Versus Coastal Migration Routes," pp. 303–304.
14. Ibid.
15. Ibid., pp. 305–307; see also Fladmark, "Routes: Alternate Migration Corridors for Early Man in the Americas."
16. Mandryk et al., "Late Quaternary Paleoenvironments of Northwestern North America: Implications for Inland Versus Coastal Migration Routes," pp. 305–307.
17. Ibid., p. 307.
18. Fladmark, "Routes: Alternate Migration Corridors for Early Man in the Americas," p. 61.

19. Anderson and Gilliam, "Paleoindian Colonization of the Americas: Implications from an Examination of Physiography, Demography, and Artifact Distribution."

20. Dixon, "Human Colonization of the Americas: Timing, Technology and Process."

21. "Late Quaternary Paleoenvironments of Northwestern North America: Implications for Inland Versus Coastal Migration Routes," p. 307.

22. This idea was initially available and made widely public only in news stories, and therefore was not subject to peer review typical of professional journal publication (Straus, "Solutrean Settlement of North America? A Review of Reality," p. 219). Since then, one paper by Stanford and Bradley ("Ocean Trails and Prairie Paths? Thoughts About Clovis Origins") has been published in an edited volume.

23. Stanford and Bradley, "Ocean Trails and Prairie Paths? Thoughts About Clovis Origins," pp. 264–265.

24. A haplogroup is an mtDNA lineage that shares the same genetic variants; see Schurr, "Mitochondrial DNA and the Peopling of the New World."

25. Straus, "Solutrean Settlement of North America? A Review of Reality."

26. Dates given here are uncalibrated years ago; see Fiedel, "Older Than We Thought: Implications of Corrected Dates for Paleoindians," for calibrated dates for Clovis and other Paleoindian traditions.

27. Straus, "Solutrean Settlement of North America? A Review of Reality," p. 221.

28. "Mitochondrial DNA and the Peopling of the New World," p. 253.

29. Goebel et al., "Masterov Kliuch and the Early Upper Palaeolithic of the Transbaikal, Siberia"; Pitulko et al., "The Yana RHS Site: Humans in the Arctic Before the Last Glacial Maximum."

30. Schurr, "Mitochondrial DNA and the Peopling of the New World."

31. Marks, *Human Biodiversity: Genes, Race, and History.*

32. Turner, "Tell-Tale Teeth."

33. Turner, "Tell-Tale Teeth"; Greenberg et al., "The Settlement of the Americas: A Comparison of the Linguistic, Dental, and Genetic Evidence," p. 484.

34. Steele and Powell, "Paleobiology of the First Americans."

35. Crawford, "DNA Variability and Human Evolution"; Schurr, "Mitochondrial DNA and the Peopling of the New World."

36. Hall et al., "Pleistocene Migration Routes into the Americas: Human Biological Adaptations and Environmental Constraints"; Schurr, "Mitochondrial DNA and the Peopling of the New World."

37. Greenberg et al., "The Settlement of the Americas: A Comparison of the Linguistic, Dental, and Genetic Evidence." Although Greenberg's linguistic analysis was originally considered controversial, genetic evidence has provided some support for the later migration of the Na-Dene speakers (see Torroni et al., "Asian Affinities and Continental Radiation of the Four Founding Native American mtDNAs"). Unlike Greenberg's notion of three migration waves, however, many scholars believe that the picture is far more complex, with multiple waves of migrants into the New World.

38. Ruhlen, "Voices from the Past."

39. See, for example, Larichev et al., "The Upper Paleolithic of Northern Asia: Achievements, Problems, and Perspectives III: Northeastern Siberia and the Russian Far East"; Derev'anko, *The Paleolithic of Siberia: New Discoveries and Interpretations.*

40. Mandryk et al., "Late Quaternary Paleoenvironments of Northwestern North America: Implications for Inland Versus Coastal Migration Routes," p. 310.

41. Haynes, "Geofacts and Fancy," p. 12.

42. Ibid.

43. Goebel et al., "The Archaeology of Ushki Lake, Kamchatka, and the Pleistocene Peopling of the Americas." Radiocarbon dates in the text are given in uncalibrated radiocarbon years; in articles such as Goebel et al., these ages are expressed in calibrated radiocarbon ages, in this case, to about 13,000 years ago for the earliest occupation at Ushki Lake.

44. Dikov, "On the Road to America," p. 15.

45. Dixon, "Human Colonization of the Americas: Timing, Technology and Process," p. 283.

46. Ibid., p. 284.

47. Dillehay, "By the Banks of the Chinchihuapi"; Meltzer et al., "On the Pleistocene Antiquity of Monte Verde, Southern Chile."

48. Haynes et al., "Dating a Paleoindian Site in the Amazon in Comparison with Clovis Culture."

49. Roosevelt et al., "Paleoindian Cave Dwellers in the Amazon: The Peopling of the Americas."

50. Other fruits come from trees such as the achuá, the muruci da mata, and the apiranga (ibid., p. 379).

51. Dincauze, "The Meadowcroft Papers"; cf. Adovasio et al., "The Meadowcroft Papers: A Response to Dincauze."

52. Adovasio and Carlisle, "Pennsylvania Pioneers."

53. Wagner and McAvoy, "Pedoarchaeology of Cactus Hill, a Sandy Paleoindian Site in Southeastern Virginia, U.S.A."

54. Ibid., p. 297.

55. Whitley and Dorn, "New Perspectives on the Clovis vs. Pre-Clovis Controversy."
56. Fiedel, "Older Than We Thought: Implications of Corrected Dates for Paleoindians."
57. Ibid., p. 110.
58. Meltzer, "Late Pleistocene Human Adaptations in Eastern North America."
59. Ibid., p. 43.
60. "Human Colonization of the Americas: Timing, Technology and Process," p. 294.
61. Guadalupe Sanchez, "A Synopsis of Paleo-Indian Archaeology in Mexico."
62. Ibid., p. 129.
63. Aveleyra Arroyo de Anda and Maldonado-Koerdell, "Association of Artifacts with Mammoths in the Valley of Mexico."
64. Anderson and Faught, "The Distribution of Fluted Paleoindian Projectile Points: Update 1998"; Anderson, "Recent Advances in Paleoindian and Archaic Period Research in the Southeastern United States."
65. Hopkins et al., *Paleoecology of Beringia.*
66. Wheat, "The Olsen-Chubbuck Site: A Paleo-Indian Bison Kill."
67. For surveys of Desert West archaeology, see Grayson, *Desert's Past: A Natural Prehistory of the Great Basin*; Beck, "The Terminal Pleistocene/Early Holocene Archaeology of the Great Basin."
68. Interestingly, the area around Lake Texcoco in Mexico may have been a refugia for at least some of these Pleistocene animals, as late types of Paleoindian points (post-11,000 years ago) are associated with now extinct mammoth and horses at these sites (Guadalupe Sanchez, "A Synopsis of Paleo-Indian Archaeology in Mexico," pp. 129–130).
69. Martin and Wright, *Pleistocene Extinctions*; Haynes, "Elephant Hunting in North America"; Moismann and Martin, "Simulating Overkill by Paleoindians"; Martin and Klein, *Quaternary Extinctions. A Prehistoric Revolution.*
70. "A Requiem for North American Overkill," p. 588.
71. Grayson, "Pleistocene Avifaunas and the Overkill Hypothesis."
72. Kelly and Todd, "Coming into the Country: Early Paleoindian Hunting and Mobility."
73. Grayson, "Death by Natural Causes."
74. Grayson and Meltzer, "A Requiem for North American Overkill," p. 591.

The Origins of Agriculture

*The greatest events come to pass without any
design; chance makes blunders good. . . . The
important events of the world are not
deliberately brought about: they occur.*

George C. Lichtenberg

An alien visitor to earth might understandably conclude that humans naturally and
instinctively cultivate plants, for he, she, or it would see that almost every human
residence and community, from the meanest third world hovel to the lush parks of the
world's richest metropolises, are adorned with flowers and dependent for their very
existence on the farming of plants. It would be manifestly obvious to such a visitor that
human civilizations were largely the product of human abilities to extract energy from
plants.

The systematic cultivation of plants to create an artificial food supply, however, has
never been an instinctive part of the human repertoire. In fact, it is a comparatively recent
human activity, practiced for far less than 1 percent of the time our genus has existed.
And it involved a radical alteration in the way people lived. The several million years
separating the first tool-using hominins of Africa and the French cave artists of just
20,000 years ago encompassed a period of momentous change. Human brain size trebled,
an impressive array of specialized tools replaced the crude stone implements of our
Paleolithic forefathers, and people colonized most of the world. In one important respect,
however, all Pleistocene societies, from the barely human hominins of two million years
ago to the creative hunter-foragers of just 10,000 years ago, were alike: They made their
living by gathering and hunting their food, not by producing it, in the sense that they
did not "farm."

We can look back, perhaps even with a bit of pride, at the adaptability and sheer
resilience of our ancient hunting-gathering forebears. Their generations spanned millions
of years, in every kind of environment, from the high Arctic to the jungles of the Amazon.
They survived and came to inhabit much of the world by means of a profound knowledge
of environments, a sophisticated yet still portable technology, and flexible small-group
social structures that efficiently scaled human groups to available resources. As Robert Kelly
noted, "There are no Gardens of Eden on earth, no single locales, that can provide for all
human needs. Mobility . . . was the first means humans used to overcome this problem."[1]

228

OLD WORLD		NEW WORLD	
3,600 years ago 1600 B.C.	Appearance of domesticated soybeans in north China		
		4,200 years ago 2200 B.C.	Domestication of potatoes in South America
6–5,000 years ago 4–3000 B.C.	Food-producing economies reach northern Europe		
		5,500 years ago 3500 B.C.	Domestication of llamas and guinea pigs in South America
8,000 years ago 6000 B.C.	Beginning of spread of food-producing economies from the Near East into Europe		
		5,500 years ago 3500 B.C.	Domestication of maize in Mexico/Mesoamerica
8,000 years ago 6000 B.C.	Appearance of domesticated pig in the northern Fertile Crescent		
		6–5,000 years ago 4–3000 B.C.	Domestication of beans in Mexico/Mesoamerica
8,500 years ago 6500 B.C.	Appearance of domesticated millet in north China		
		7,700 years ago 5700 B.C.	Domestication of beans in South America
9–8,000 years ago 7–6000 B.C.	Appearance of domesticated rice in south-central China		
		10,700–9,800 years ago 8700–7800 B.C.	Domestication of squash in Mexico
9,000 years ago 7000 B.C.	Appearance of domesticated cattle in the northern Fertile Crescent		
10–8,000 years ago 8–6000 B.C.	Appearance of domesticated goats and sheep in the eastern Fertile Crescent		
10,300–9300 years ago 8300–7300 B.C.	Appearance of domesticated wheat in the western Fertile Crescent		
10,500–7600 years ago 8500–5600 B.C.	Early Neolithic food-producing economies		
12,000 years ago 10000 B.C.	Domestication of the dog		
12,500–10,500 years ago 10500–8500 B.C.	Natufian culture		
14,500–12,500 years ago 12500–10500 B.C.	Geometric Kebaran culture		
22–14,500 years ago 20–12500 B.C.	Kebaran culture		
22,000 years ago 20000 B.C.	Appearance of Epipaleolithic (post-Paleolithic) hunter-gatherers		

Even today, a few hunter-gatherer societies persist on the margins of modern states. But the regions of the world where hunting-gathering was the primary basis of human life began to contract rapidly, soon after the first farmers appeared. Just after 10,000 years ago, people in several widely separated areas of the world began to domesticate a few plant and animal species. At about the same time they built villages, began living in them year-round, and began to subsist mainly on plants they cultivated and animals they kept. In most environments these agricultural economies have been able to produce much greater amounts of food than hunting and gathering could. Today, hunter-gatherers exist only in the Amazon Basin, the Arctic, and the few other places where hunting-gathering is still (or until recently was) more feasible than agriculture, and even in these few areas hunter-gatherers depend in part on their neighbors' agricultural economies.

Two curious facts emerge when we look at the history of human agriculture: First, all of the largest and most complex civilizations throughout history have been based on the cultivation of only a few genera—in fact, just six plant genera—wheat, barley, millet, rice, maize, and potatoes. Other plants, such as sorghum, beans, yams, taro, and thousands more, have been critical to the survival of many peoples, and domesticated animals have also been important sources of calories and power, but the six plant genera listed here have been the main caloric engines of "civilizations." Second, one of the particularly striking characteristics of the "agricultural revolution" is that not only was it rapid and widespread, but it also happened independently in different parts of the world at about the same time. For millions of years our ancestors subsisted solely on the proceeds of hunting and gathering, yet within just a few thousand years, between about 10,000 and 3,500 years ago, people all over the world began growing crops and establishing agricultural economies based on, for example, potatoes in the Andes, maize in Mexico, wheat and barley in Southwest Asia, rice in China, and many other crops in many other places.

The fact that very few species provide most of the world's food, and that plants and animals were domesticated at about the same time at different places in the world, raises important questions. Is there something entirely special, for example, about these particular plants that they became the staples of people around the world, or do they represent chance associations between people and particular plant species at specific times? And why did people make the transition to a life based on these and other plants? Agriculture has had such tremendous importance in human affairs that one is tempted to the logical fallacy of assuming that the factors that first produced agricultural economies must be equally momentous. They may have been; at this point we do not know. Perhaps only slight changes in climate, population density, or technology set off the "agricultural revolution." We know approximately where and when the most important domesticates first appeared but, as we shall see, the reasons *why* they appeared where they did and when they did are still not fully understood. Almost all general explanations of agricultural origins, as we shall see, appeal to the same three basic factors: climate changes, rising population densities, and improving technologies. Yet combining these factors into a compelling explanation of all the world's agricultural origins remains difficult.

In this chapter we review some of the evidence of early domestication and farming and consider more abstract questions concerning why people become farmers after so many long years of hunting-foraging, why agriculture appeared in many different places in the world at about the same time, and how agricultural economies came to dominate the world.[2]

AGRICULTURE, DOMESTICATION, AND SEDENTARY COMMUNITIES

Discussions of agricultural origins involve many specialized terms, and some of these are rather vague and descriptive. The difference between a "crop" and a "weed," for example, is in a sense a cultural construct rather than a precise botanical concept. Luther Burbank, the pioneering American botanist, defined a weed as a plant whose uses to humanity simply had not yet been discovered. Geneticists Blumler and Byrne define a weed as "an uncultivated plant taxon that benefits from human impacts or 'disturbance'";[3] but they note that it also has an economic definition in the sense of weeds as plants that reduce crop yields. Even the species names given to specific plants and animals, as well as cultural terms such as "farming" and "domesticated," are attempts to impose static categories on a dynamic and multidimensional underlying variability. The easy "opposites," too, of "hunter-forager"/"agriculturalist" and "wild"/"domesticated" camouflage underlying continuous variability.[4]

Thus, some precision in terminology is useful. The key concept in the notion of *agriculture* involves human efforts to modify the environments of plants and animals to increase their productivity and usefulness.[5] By weeding, hoeing, watering, fashioning scarecrows, penning pigs, and a thousand other farming activities, people over the millennia have sought to get more food out of their labors. But hunter-gatherers also modify the environments of plants and animals. Some of them, for example, set fires to open up habitats for certain plants and animals; others, simply by collecting and eating wild species, modify the environments of others and have an effect on these gene pools. Agriculture, however, usually involves systematic and purposeful modification of plant and animal environments with the goal of increasing productivity. This definition of agriculture, like that of domestication, is relative. At the one extreme are the simple efforts a group might make to suppress weeds near a stand of wild wheat; at the other are contemporary agri-businesses where crops are grown on precisely leveled fields and treated with pesticides and fertilizers and where chickens live out unremarkable lives in cages until a computer determines that their ratio of food-consumption and growth has reached a critical—and fatal—value.

The term *cultivation* is often used in lieu of, or in combination with, the concept of agriculture. Blumler and Byrne define cultivation as the "growing of plants from seeds, bulbs, shoots, and so on."[6] They note that cultivated plants are not always domesticated and that cultivation may have long preceded domestication in some cases.

The essence of *domestication* in many definitions is *mutualism*. David Rindos, for example, has defined domestication as a "coevolutionary process in which any given taxon diverges from an original gene pool and establishes a symbiotic protection and dispersal relationship with the animal feeding upon it."[7] When people domesticate plants and animals, they do so by active interference in the life cycles of these species in such a way that subsequent generations of these organisms are in more intimate association with, and often of more use to, people. By interfering in these life cycles, people have produced plants and animals that are less "fit," in some ways, than their undomesticated relatives: Domesticated maize, for example, no longer has an effective natural mechanism for seed dispersal, because the seeds are all clustered on a cob that, without human intervention, usually remains tightly attached to the plant. Similarly, a variety of sheep in Southwest Asia has been selectively bred over the last several thousand years so that its tail is a 5- to 8-pound mass of fat, making it necessary, it is said, for people to help some of these animals mate.

In general, humans have intruded in the natural cycles in that they have altered these plants' *dormancy* cycles, *dispersal mechanisms*, and physical and chemical *defenses* against the animals that eat them.[8] People have altered animal genera in ways usually directed at exaggerating characteristics that are useful to humans, such as meat, milk production, fleece, docility, traction power, environmental tolerance, and so forth. People have focused much of their domestication efforts on animals with genetically based aptitude for imprinting dominance hierarchies, such as sheep, cattle, and geese. By intruding on these hierarchical impulses, people have produced the docility that makes animal exploitation simple and efficient.

But the kinds of mutualistic relationships we think of as domestication and agriculture are not unique to humans and their plant and animal food, nor do they depend on human intellect. As Rindos notes, species of African cultivator ants "farm" fungi in a very real sense. They prepare special beds of plant debris and excrement, in special chambers in the ant nest. The ants are meticulous about growth conditions within the chamber; numerous ventilation passages are dug, and these are opened or closed to regulate both temperature and humidity. To construct the beds, the ants chew the substrate material to make a pulpy mass and deposit it in layers in the chamber. The bed is then planted with propagules from previously maintained beds. Constant care is given the beds. The ants remove alien fungi and add anal and salivary secretions, which apparently have a positive effect on the growth of the fungi. These cultivation activities encourage the production, by the fungus, of small whitish round bodies, the so-called kohlrabi structures. These structures are the principal food of the ant colony.[9]

One does not see tiny scarecrows or silos among these ants, but Rindos's point is well taken: In terms of their ecological relationship with the sustaining species, ants do not differ significantly from us. And if this is true, the import of his observation is obvious: What we consider the uniquely human activities of domestication and agriculture are in fact somewhat common ecological relationships that can be "fixed" by natural selection without regard to the intelligence or volition of the organism involved. In fact, "domestication" is to some extent a matter of perspective: If one looks at domestication from the cereals' point of view, for example, people have proved to be excellent devices for cereals to conquer the world. Wheat, which in its undomesticated forms was limited to small areas of the Middle East, has managed to extend its range from South America to central Russia, all by "domesticating" humans in such a way that they became dependent on it. As much as we are the creators of modern plant and animal hybrid domesticates, then, we are their creation; we are locked together in coevolutionary embrace. In these transitions to agriculture and sedentary life we see a subtle evolutionary dynamic in which people were physically changed as they physically changed the plants and animals on which they depended.[10] Agricultural economies allowed the evolution of epidemic diseases such as cholera that "selected out" untold millions of people with genetic susceptibilities to these diseases. Agricultural diets generally increase periodontal and dental diseases and relax selection for robust dentition, so that the spread of agriculture across the world has resulted in a gradual reduction in human teeth size and strength—and in dental health.

This issue of the importance of human intentions remains a major point of contention in studies of agricultural origins. We live in an age in which farmers are constantly and intentionally manipulating plants and animals in order to effect desired changes in them, so it is not surprising that some scholars think this same intentionality was a critical factor in agricultural origins.[11] People may have begun to domesticate many plant and animal genera not out of the desire or intention of making these plants more useful to people, but rather through making relatively minor and unintentional changes in the way they exploited them. Any plant or animal species regularly eaten or used by people will reflect this relationship in its genetic characteristics, and thus all through the Pleistocene hunters and gatherers had some effect on the genetic makeup of various plant and animal species. But the low population densities and mobile way of life of the period before about 10,000 years ago kept people from exploiting plant and animal populations with sufficient intensity to perpetuate the kinds of mutations represented by contemporary maize and fat-tailed sheep.

Domestication seems to have been in most cases a relatively long-term *process*, not something that an occasional genius invented. As discussed later, for example, it took several thousand years to change the wild ancestor of maize into something that looks like an ear of corn. And domestication has usually taken place as a long-term process in which the physical characteristics of plant and animal species change as these species' relationships to their human consumers change. Some scholars believe that domestication of wheat and other plants may have happened over only a few years, while others contend that it took centuries (Figure 6.1). And human intentions to domesticate plants and animals are neither archaeologically retrievable nor logically important to this notion of domestication. As Rindos points out: "People could not create the variation [in plants and animals] that would permit domestication, they could only select; and they could not have known how important the products of their selection would become."[12] According to this point of view, human intentions and goal-oriented behavior, while important, are not archaeologically retrievable and in most cases must be assumed to be constants: That is, there is no reason to believe that agriculture appeared in one place and not another because in the latter case people

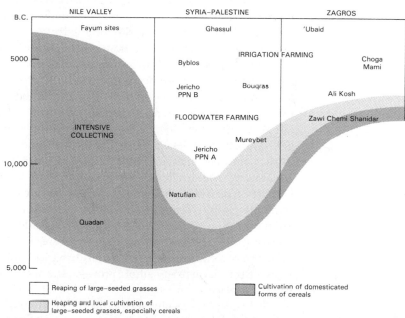

FIGURE 6.1   The world was forever changed by mutualistic relationships that evolved between people and large seeded grasses sometime before about 15,000 years ago. Agriculture was only the last stage of the evolution of these relationships, but the large and reliable harvests made possible by the domestication of wheat and barley were the basis on which ancient and modern civilizations evolved.

just did not successfully analyze the situation and solve the problems of adaptation. And at another level, what people *thought* they were doing in making the adaptations that led to domestication and agriculture does not matter; it is what they actually *did*, in the sense of eating this or that kind of food, moving from one area to another seasonally, and so on, that is important. But other scholars disagree and see the origins of domesticates as processes in which human intentions "speeded-up" the process almost from the beginning.[13]

As noted earlier, another issue in studying the problem of agricultural origins is determining why people chose the particular genera they did to domesticate and cultivate. We will examine this question later in this chapter with regard to the economic equations in specific areas of the world where agriculture appeared independently, such as Southwest Asia. But whatever the importance of human intentionality in producing agricultural economies, it is important to recognize that human food and taste "preferences" seem to have played little role in agricultural origins. In fact, food preferences and other cultural aspects of the diverse human interactions with the foods they eat are a fascinating example of the blend of economic forces and ideologies that govern human actions. One must recognize, for example, that maggoty meat, fresh cow blood, rotted fish-heads, charred goat-intestines, tuna noodle casserole, sheep eyes, pot roasts simmered in packaged onion soup—all these are today savored with as much gusto as anything from the restaurants of Milan or Paris. Economic conditions usually are the major determinants of food preferences and of food production. The reason local supermarkets offer special prices on New Zealand lamb and not Labrador retrievers has more to do with the economics of raising these animals (and the economic conditions of the ancient societies in which they were first domesticated) and with the accidents of cultural ideologies than with the foods' intrinsic tastes. There are few more convincing demonstrations that food preferences are primarily "styles" and cultural constructs, rather than reflections of the inherent subtleties and complexities of tastes and textures, than the crowds of people of all nations who queue for hamburgers at a McDonald's in Rome (near the Spanish Steps), less than 100 m from the competitively priced 37-item antipasto buffet at the Ristorante a la Rampa.

As we shall see later, a complex set of factors seems to have determined why specific genera became domesticated and cultivated while others did not. In terms of historical impact, one of the most important things about agriculture is that it produces not just great amounts of food, it supplies *reliable* and *predictable* amounts of food, and thereby allows population densities to rise and people in many areas of the world to live year-round in the same place—in *sedentary communities*. Such communities probably first appeared in Southwest Asia as much as 1,000 years before domesticated wheat or barley, while in Mesoamerica at least five plant species were in the process of domestication several thousand years before the first sedentary or agricultural communities appeared. But in both cases the transition to agriculture provided strong pressures for permanent residence in one particular place.

Sedentary life usually involves the construction of permanent structures. For a million years and more before agriculture, people built crude shelters and lived in caves, but in almost every case they moved to other camps for part of the year because they had to go to where their food was, and this changed continually as animals migrated, wild plants changed with the seasons, and so forth. In many areas of the world, people probably had to break up into seasonal groups and spend part of the year away from their kinfolk to thin their population density to a level that could be supported in the leanest seasons of the year. By 10,000 years ago, human societies were tied together by trade networks and, probably, by social bonds that extended beyond the group that lived together for most of the year. Traditionally, archaeologists have imagined the people of this period as egalitarian and organized only in simple forms of bands and tribes. But we don't really know if this was true. As we shall see in later chapters, wherever there is plentiful and reliable food and other resources, our ancestors have responded in one way, and one way only: They have social systems that exaggerate differences among themselves and among their social groups in access to wealth, power, and prestige.

When our ancestors began living year-round in the same villages, a complex set of relationships between people, plants, and animals was established that had never existed before. Village life has many effects on the human community. Compared to hunting-foraging societies, village communities usually have higher fertility rates, higher incidences of epidemic diseases, and a basic economic unit based on the family, not the group. Village life also allows the accumulation of material goods. There is a tremendous "inertia" in village agriculture, once it is established. In only a few environments can people move easily from agricultural to other kinds of economies, for the essence of agriculture is that one concentrates one's energies on a very limited number of species that are very reliable. In most agricultural economies, activities that conflict with agricultural production are soon abandoned. In Denmark, for example, analysis of human bone composition shows that in one area along the ocean shore, people before 4,000 B.C. lived mainly on marine resources, but after that time they subsisted almost entirely on agricultural products, even though their villages were within a few hundred meters of the rich fish and other resources of the shore.[14]

The change to village life was a radical shift in the way people dealt with each other and the world, and it produced a completely new social fabric. Here, too, it is probably a mistake to think of these first villagers in terms of consciously trying to identify all problems they encountered in making a living in this new setting and organizing themselves socially, or their developing a wide range of new behaviors to meet these new needs. People cannot always be considered entirely rational consumers who put together economies that are optimally efficient, and we cannot explain agricultural origins simply as the natural outcome of people who search through all the possibilities and put together the best economy based on their technology. But *everything* cultural is subjected to natural selection to some extent, and so we must consider agriculture to be the outcome, at least in part, of behaviors that "worked."

HYPOTHESES ABOUT THE ORIGINS OF DOMESTICATION, AGRICULTURE, AND SEDENTARY COMMUNITIES

> Cursed is the ground for thy sake,
> in sorrow shalt thou eat of it all the days of thy life,
> Thorns also and thistles shall it bring forth to thee
> In the sweat of thy face shalt thou eat bread.
> *Genesis 3:17–18*

To begin with, we can dismiss the idea that people domesticated plants and animals because someone came from outer space and taught them how to do it, or because someone in ancient Syria had a brilliant idea and it spread around the world, or because people simply got sick of chasing animals and wanted an easier way to live.

The roughly contemporary appearance of a vast variety of domesticates, from palm trees to potatoes, across the same approximate latitudes around the world, and the several millennia it took for hunting and gathering to give way to farming in most areas, make any of these scenarios improbable. And, although there is great variability, hunters and gatherers tend to have more leisure time than primitive agriculturists—farming is hard work, as even the suburban gardener knows full well. Moreover, hunters-foragers do not seem to spend their time in continual efforts to improve their lot—or designing cathedrals or composing string quartets. Studies of these groups around the world show that they spend almost all of their spare time talking or sleeping—skills, as Sharp notes, that most of them have already thoroughly perfected.[15]

Even so, the idea that people became farmers because it was an easier way of life than hunting-foraging seems so plausible—particularly to most Westerners—that it is hard to discredit this myth.

The worldwide origins of agriculture constitute a complex *evolutionary* and historical event, and thus cannot be expected to be analyzable in mechanical terms: That is, evolutionary sequences are by definition inherently unpredictable in terms of their specifics. After all, no one could have predicted the evolution of tigers—or of us—from the world's fauna of 100 million years ago. Nothing that has a history in which natural selection has had an effect can be explained in mechanical deterministic terms like those of physics.

But the origins of agriculture tempt one to look at it in somewhat mechanical and deterministic terms because it happened independently, in several places in the Old and New Worlds alike, and at about the same time and in similar environments. Anyone considering the problem of agricultural origins has to be impressed by three major categories of evidence; first, we know that world climates changed greatly just before domestication and agriculture first appeared in the Old World; second, world population densities had also been increasing for hundreds of thousands of years before agricultural origins; and third, human technology seems to have been improving in many ways over the whole history of our genus. Not surprisingly, climate change and population growth are included in most models of agricultural origins, and there is some suggestion in many hypotheses that the accumulation of knowledge about tool-making was an important element in the transition to agriculture.

Early Hypotheses About Agricultural Origins

Among the first hypotheses about agricultural origins was the so-called *Oasis Hypothesis*, an idea associated with the Australian archaeologist V. Gordon Childe,[16] who attempted to explain the origins of agriculture in terms of the climate changes associated with the end of the Pleistocene some 10,000 years ago. Childe and other advocates of this idea suggested that as the world became warmer and drier, people, animals, and plants would be forced into close conjunction and human communities would be under stress to find new food sources, and out of this propinquity and need would arise animal domestication and then farming.[17]

Doubts about the accuracy of the Oasis Hypothesis appeared when it was demonstrated that the wild ancestors of wheat and barley did not grow in the areas where post-Pleistocene oases were thought to have been concentrated, and by evidence that deserts and oases had not formed in most of Southwest and Central Asia at the time domestication began. But more recently, various scholars have reassessed the evidence and find support for the general idea that post-Pleistocene changes in patterns of rainfall and other climatic factors did have a role in the origins of agriculture (see later).[18]

Another early idea about agricultural origins has been termed the *Natural Habitat Hypothesis.* Harold Peake and Herbert Fleure suggested in 1926 that the first domesticates and agriculturalists would have appeared in the upper valley of the Euphrates River because they knew that this is the "natural habitat" of wild species of wheat and barley. In the early 1950s Robert Braidwood of the University of Chicago organized a series of excavations to evaluate post-Pleistocene climatic changes and to look for early farming communities. His expeditions were among the first to include specialists in botany, geology, and zoology as well as archaeology, and this multidisciplinary approach has proven to be a highly successful research strategy. This work redefined the natural zone of plants to include many areas outside the upper Euphrates Valley.

Braidwood's excavations at Jarmo, in the hill country of northern Iraq, revealed an agricultural settlement dating to about 6500 B.C.—much earlier than had been found elsewhere.[19] Jarmo was a settlement of a few dozen mud-walled huts inhabited by people who relied partly on wild plants and animals, such as snails, pistachios, and acorns, but who also seem to have been involved in herding domesticated goats and, perhaps, sheep (Figure 6.2). Braidwood also found at Jarmo the remains of partially domesticated wheat in association with grinding stones, sickle blades, and storage pits. Braidwood suggested that the cumulative effects of generations of interaction between people, plants, and animals in these natural habitat zones led to agriculture.

Braidwood's research into agricultural origins was one of the few systematic investigations into this problem at the time, and he provided crucial evidence for the next stage of research on this problem—trying to understand the precise mechanisms by which agriculture appeared. Evidence that some of the earliest agricultural communities had appeared, not in the middle of the natural habitat, but on the margins or outside of it[20] raised the possibility that agriculture was not just a natural result of people exploiting wild stands of wheat and barley.

Also, a series of experiments was performed by botanist Jack Harlan in eastern Anatolia in 1966 in which, using a crude sickle made with flint blades set in a wooden handle, he was able to harvest wild emmer wheat at the rate of about 6.25 pounds per hour (Figure 6.3).[21] A family of four or five could probably have collected a year's supply of grain with only a few weeks' labor, and this would seem to suggest that the people who lived in the natural habitat of wheat and barley had perhaps the least incentive to domesticate and farm it because they could collect more than enough from wild stands.

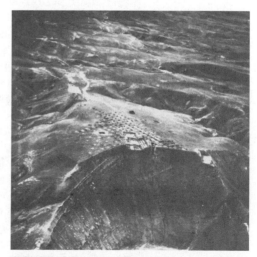

FIGURE 6.2   Aerial view of excavations at Jarmo, Iraq, an important early farming settlement.

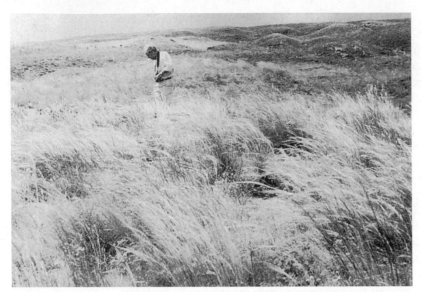

FIGURE 6.3 Prehistoric Near Eastern hunter-gatherers first made use of seeds from wild grass stands, such as those seen in this photograph.

Population growth has also been an important element in most accounts of agricultural origins. Mark Cohen, for example, argues that "the nearly simultaneous adoption of agricultural economies throughout the world could only be accounted for by assuming that hunting and gathering populations had saturated the world approximately 10,000 years ago and had exhausted all possible (or palatable) strategies for increasing their food supply within the constraints of the hunting-gathering life-style. The only possible reaction to further growth in population, worldwide, was to begin artificial augmentation of the food supply."[22]

A major problem in assessing any hypothesis based on ancient population densities is the difficulty of estimating changes in these densities with any precision using archaeological data. One has to locate all the relevant archaeological sites (of which many are certain to have been destroyed or not found), then estimate the numbers of people at each site, and then develop a chronology for these sites that is fine enough to reconstruct changes over fairly short periods of time. Consequently, most population estimates based on archaeological data must be considered extremely speculative; and the relationship between agriculture and demographic change remains complex and not well understood.

Marvin Harris has formulated an explanation of agricultural origins that resembles Cohen's in its stress on increasing human populations, declining worldwide availability of large game animals, and the competition among groups for survival.[23] In addition, Harris considers a fascinating topic—food taboos. In trying to explain food taboos he has illuminated some of the central problems of trying to understand human economic history. Consider, for example, the humble pig. Eventually Islam, Judaism, and some Hindu religions instituted complete bans on pork to the extent that, even today, riots flare in some parts of the world if pigs invade religious areas.

Pigs are one of the most efficient converters of garbage, animal wastes, and other materials discarded by farmers—better in many respects than goats, sheep, or cows. In preindustrial economies and today around the world in Europe, America, and China, the pig is used to convert grains that are not made into food or whisky into portable, storable food. So why should the sturdy farmers of the Middle East reject such a good food source after millennia in which the pig was a staple part of the diet?

Harris dismisses the notion that this prohibition has anything to do with the common infection of pigs with trichinae, parasites that can kill people.[24] Recent studies have shown that pigs raised in hot climates seldom transmit this disease; moreover, Southwest Asian farmers ate cattle, sheep, and goats, which carry anthrax, brucellosis, and other diseases as dangerous or more so than anything pigs can transmit.

Instead, Harris explains prohibitions of pork in terms of the cost-benefit ratio of the animal in early subsistence agricultural systems. Pigs, unlike sheep, goats, and cattle, cannot subsist on husks, stalks, or other high-cellulose foods; their natural diet is tubers, roots, nuts, and fruits. Also, pigs are native to woodlands and swamps and do not tolerate direct sun and open country well. Thus, the clearing of land coincident with the spread of agriculture in Southwest Asia greatly reduced the habitat and natural foods available to pigs, and, increasingly, pigs had to be fed on grain, which brought them into competition with people; they also had to be provided with artificial shade and considerable water. Moreover, Harris points out that, in contrast to some other domesticates, pigs cannot be milked, sheared, ridden, or used to pull a plow. In short, they lost their cost effectiveness relative to sheep, goats, and cattle, and their eventual proscription made excellent economic "sense."

And, as in all instances, it is not important that people ever recognize their motives in cases of such prohibitions: Natural selection "fixes," or perpetuates, economically sound behaviors, regardless of what people think their motives are.

Against Harris and his supporters are many people who believe that Harris is propagating a bastardized version of a misconception of Marxian theory.[25] Sahlins, for example, points to the United States, where millions of cattle are slaughtered every year but where virtually every horse lives out its full life in relative luxury and, usually, enjoying considerable affection. Why, Sahlins asks, do Americans arbitrarily proscribe horsemeat and accept beef? Sahlins answers his own question, arguing that it is because every culture creates its own belief systems from its unique blend of economy, society, and ideology.

All this is rather far from the poor abandoned pigs of Southwest Asia, but the point is an important one. For if archaeologists must seek the causes of changes in the archaeological record (like the succession of pig bones by sheep and goat bones in the levels of a site) in the cultural mediation of "the mode of cultural organization," they will have to apply techniques of archaeological analysis currently not known or, possibly, not within the capacities of any other than a Divine Intellect.

Contemporary Models of Agricultural Origins

Another general explanation of agricultural origins has been proposed by Brian Hayden. He begins with the assumption that ancient hunters and gatherers were, like most people, trying to maintain the reliability and stability with which they could get food.[26] He suggests that for the last several million years our ancestors diversified their "income" by eating a wide range of plant and animal species and developing digging sticks, hand-axes, nets, and all the other implements of pre-agricultural peoples. Rather than a constant drive from population growth or "pressure" which forced these innovations and broadening of diets, Hayden envisions great stability in the population-to-resources balance.

But by the end of the Pleistocene 10,000 years ago, all the larger, more obvious animal species had been exploited, and people faced with the same kinds of cyclical food shortages that always had been humankind's lot could only turn to grasses, seeds, fish, and mice—in other words, the smaller, in some ways less desirable species. Hayden uses here a division of the animal world according to reproductive "strategy": "k"-selected species, like deer, are long-lived, tend to have long maturation periods, have only one or a few offspring each reproductive cycle, and are susceptible to over-exploitation; "*r*"-selected species, on the other hand, like grasses, which reproduce in incalculably large numbers, are genetically plastic, live only a year, are extremely resistant to overexploitation, and quickly reestablish themselves after floods, fires, and droughts.

Switching to a diet of mainly "*r*"-selected species, Hayden argues, would have encouraged a sedentary way of life; stimulated the development of ground-stone tools, wooden implements, and other agricultural devices; stabilized the food supply; and lessened the need for group cooperation and common food storage. In Hayden's view, the rise of agriculture is just a "natural and logical extension of the trends" that led to the late Pleistocene refocusing of exploitation strategies from big-game animals to smaller animals and plants.

As for the timing and location of the first agricultural economies:

> It is especially notable that domestication did not first occur where the environments were rich enough to support sedentary, hunting-gathering-based ranked societies, with wealth competition and primitive valuables, such as those found in California, the Northwest Coast, Florida, and Palestine. According to my model, even though these areas had the highest population densities, their resource bases would have been much more stable and they would have experienced resource stress relatively infrequently. Because sedentism, wealth competition, and ranking in rich environments did not result in domestication in these areas, it is reasonable to conclude that such developments were not sufficient, or perhaps even necessary, conditions for domestication. Instead, domestication can be more usefully linked to the same Paleolithic processes which gave rise to the Mesolithic and Archaic: the effort to increase resource reliability in areas of frequent stress.[27]

Although climatic change does not play a large role in Hayden's explanation for the rise of agriculture, other researchers such as Joy McCorriston and Frank Hole,[28] and Andrew Moore and Gordon Hillman,[29] have suggested that climatic events at the end of the Pleistocene were a critical factor—at least for the origins of agriculture in Southwest Asia, particularly the Levant (Syria, Lebanon, Jordan, and Israel).

Between about 22,000 and 16,000 years ago, glaciers expanded over many areas of America and Eurasia, altering climates around the world. Southwest Asia was generally cooler and drier in this period, but there were shorter cycles of climate change, periods of several thousand years in which the climates became relatively warmer or cooler, drier or wetter.[30] For most of this period, the sea coasts expanded as ocean levels fell. Forests covered coastal areas around the northern and eastern Mediterranean, but many higher areas of Southwest Asia were dry steppe or grasslands.

Then between about 16,000 and 11,000 years ago, as the glaciers retreated, most of Southwest Asia became warmer. Between about 14,500 and 11,000 years ago the eastern Mediterranean appears to have experienced a period of relatively high rainfall, but then between 11,000 and 10,000 years ago there were periods of growing aridity.[31] The rising sea levels of these warmer periods would have submerged from 10 to 20 km of coastal plains around much of Southwest Asia, perhaps forcing people into new areas. The average annual rise would have been only 7–8 mm, so one should not imagine late Pleistocene hunter-foragers scurrying in front of unexpected floods.[32]

It is against this backdrop of climatic change that we can examine the archaeological record to see how patterns of people-plant-animal interactions changed in ways that might explain agricultural origins in this period. Since there were many previous glacial fluctuations and climatic changes in this area that did not produce agriculture, these climatic variations are obviously not a complete explanation of agricultural origins; but it is not without significance for the timing and location of agricultural origins that they coincided with these environmental changes. Subtle changes in seasonality, maximum heat and cold, and other factors have complex impacts on ecologies, and it is difficult to sort these out for periods in the distant past.

Joy McCorriston and Frank Hole,[33] for example, argue that about 10,000 years ago, as the Pleistocene ended, the climates of the Jordan Valley and adjacent areas of the Middle East became much more arid and more sharply seasonal. They suggest that the climate changes of this period encouraged the growth and spread of annual species of cereals and legumes, and that because the summers were hyper-arid and there were few resources available, people began to store more of their food, which in turn required them to become more sedentary—to stay near their stored foods. They note that these climate changes resulted in the establishment of agriculture because at the time they occurred, people in this area had developed tools for processing wild cereals and had partially depleted their environments of some of the wild plants and animals that had sustained Pleistocene hunter-foragers here.

Andrew Moore and Gordon Hillman[34] offer a broadly similar argument, although they focus on the period just prior to the end of the Pleistocene. This climatic episode—known as the Younger Dryas—occurred between 11,000 and 10,000 years ago and represented a return to the cooler and drier settings typical of the last glacial period. After benefiting from the gradual improvement in climate that occurred after 16,000 years ago, a return to conditions more typical of glacial periods was a rude shock to human foraging groups. The consequences are reflected in stresses on their systems of foraging and also in their settlement patterns. People who had been sedentary—at least to some extent—either became more mobile in their search for food resources or developed new and novel ways of exploiting foods such as the wild cereal grasses. The development of these new subsistence systems gave rise to the transition between hunting-gathering and farming about 10,000 years ago.

But there were many periods of climatic alteration in the past hundreds of thousands of years in which agriculture did not emerge, and domestication and agriculture appeared in an extremely diverse range of environments, from cold valleys high in the Andes to the plains of southern Palestine to the humid lowlands of Southeast Asia. If climate change was such a powerful force for agricultural origins, how could it have affected such a diverse range of habitats to produce the same results?

A novel explanation for this phenomenon has been proposed recently by Peter Richerson, Robert Boyd, and Robert Bettinger.[35] Theirs is also a climate-based hypothesis, but one that looks beyond the evidence of selected single regions, such as Southwest Asia, to explain the transition to farming economies throughout the world. Using climatic information derived from ice and ocean cores, as well as mathematical modeling of population and innovation dynamics, Richerson and his colleagues argue that the Pleistocene was, quite simply put, "hostile to agriculture."[36] The data from the cores indicate that the Pleistocene was arid, had low atmospheric CO_2—which impacts plant photosynthesis—and had highly variable short-term climatic fluctuations—human groups could not afford to become dependent on a single food resource under these conditions.

The advent of the Holocene—the geological epoch in which we live today—significantly altered these relationships. Climatic fluctuations became less variable[37] and rainfall and atmospheric CO_2 increased, thus expanding opportunities for plant abundance and reliability. Richerson and his colleagues point out that human groups who adopt the use of efficient subsistence systems that focus on plants will, over the long run, be more successful than other human groups who are less efficient.[38] This is thus the context in which agricultural systems independently came into existence in many different geographical areas, although offset in timing by several millennia in some cases.

And in a quite sobering reflection, Richerson and his colleagues end with the following thoughts:

> Those who are familiar with the Pleistocene often remark that the Holocene is just the "present interglacial." . . . Sustaining agriculture . . . would be a considerable technical challenge. At the very best, lower CO_2 concentrations and lower average precipitation suggest that world average agricultural output would fall considerably. . . . [T]he intrinsic instability of the Pleistocene climate system, and the degree to which agriculture is likely dependent upon the Holocene stable period, should give one pause (Broecker 1997).[39]

With regard to theories of agricultural origins, it is at least plausible that more powerful explanations of this phenomena must somehow take into account social and ideological factors. As Barbara Bender[40] has noted, many groups around the world in the period just before agriculture seem to be different from their predecessors in intriguing ways. They were trading more extensively, and their burials and other artifacts seem to suggest a growing sense of ethnic identity and status differentiation (Figure 6.4). These may have stimulated intensified production and exchange in ways that affected the transition to agriculture. It is tempting to see these changes as *reflections* or results of the economic changes, but societies are integrated functional units in which change is not easily explained strictly in terms of clearly identifiable causes and effects.

Along these lines, Brian Hayden has suggested that ritual feasting was an important driving factor in early complex foraging groups.[41] Control of production by corporate groups in complex hunter-gatherer societies—kinship groups in this case—leads to surpluses that can be used for acquiring labor through marriage, for producing or obtaining prestige items, or for hosting feasts to enhance power and prestige. Once human groups become

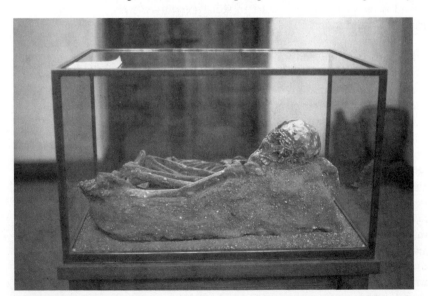

FIGURE 6.4 Natufian hunter-gatherers sometimes buried people in elaborately decorated clothing. Note the marine shell beads adhering to the skull. These were probably sewn onto a cap or hat.

invested in political organization that emphasizes competition between groups, any impacts on acquiring surpluses—such as those caused by climatic change—may lead to the origins of agriculture as people seek methods to acquire surpluses and to maintain these power structures. Hayden's feasting model therefore suggests that agriculture potentially begins not in marginal areas, but in resource-rich regions.

Finally, Ian Hodder has also offered a social explanation for the origins of agriculture.[42] He juxtaposes the notions of nature and culture, with humans acting as the agents of transformation from wild (nature) to domesticated (culture).[43] This is a *symbolic* transition that facilitated competition between groups, and as some people became more sedentary, some aspects of everyday practical activities took on symbolic roles in society. Hodder argues, for example, that the household—the domus—and the activities within it became "a metaphor for the domestication of society."[44] People's fears, emotions, and feelings helped create long-term dependencies that were acted out in a drama that sought to manipulate and control the "wild."[45] Social control of nature is therefore a mechanism to facilitate storage, food processing, food exchange, feasts, and so forth.

In the rest of this chapter we examine in detail two cases of the transition to agriculture —Southwest Asia and Mesoamerica—and attempt to match this evidence to these and other ideas about agricultural origins.

EARLY DOMESTICATION AND AGRICULTURE: THE POST-PALEOLITHIC BACKGROUND

We must assume that, to some extent, the causes of agriculture are to be found in the thousands of years of hunting-gathering that immediately preceded the first agricultural societies. A critical interval may be the period between 22,000 and 8,000 years ago—a time of major climatic changes for much of the world.

In Western Europe, population densities shifted as the herds of reindeer and horses that once supported many hunting bands moved northward with the retreating glaciers. Some people moved with them, but others worked out subsistence strategies stressing plants, smaller game, and fish. Salmon became especially important in Europe as traps, drying racks, and other tools were developed to make salmon exploitation a reliable way to make a living. In Southwest Asia, parts of Africa, and parts of the Americas, some late Pleistocene and early post-Pleistocene peoples began to eat more small game, fish, waterfowl, clams, wild cereals, and similar foods; elsewhere, big-game hunting specializations persisted. In North America, for example, some groups centered their lives around vast bison herds.[46]

Where a shift to smaller, more varied resources was made, technologies also changed. The bow and arrow and throwing stick were important innovations, and new tools were developed to dig plants, trap wild fowl, and prepare and cook this broader diet (Figure 6.5). Small, simple, geometric stone tools predominated in many areas. The world about 12,000 years ago was relatively diverse culturally, as some groups remained big-game hunters while others took up fishing, intensive foraging, and other pursuits. Thus, a great diversity of plants and animals was being exploited with varying intensities and technologies in a wide range of climates. Out of this vast mixture of peoples, plants, animals, and places the first domesticates and farmers appeared (Figure 6.6).

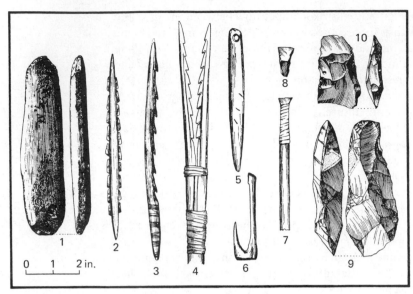

FIGURE 6.5   After about 10,000 years ago, people all over Europe began to exploit a much greater diversity of plants and animals than did their Pleistocene predecessors. This shift is reflected in Mesolithic fishing and hunting equipment: (1) limpet hammer; (2) bone fish-spear with microlith barbs, southern Sweden; (3) barbed point in red deer antler, c. 7500 B.C., Star Carr, Yorkshire; (4) leister prongs of Eskimo fishermen (shows how the barbed point may have been used); (5) net-making needle (?) and (6) bone fish hook, Denmark; (7, 8) microliths or transverse arrowheads, one found in peat hafted in wood with sinew binding, Denmark; (9) core-ax with transversely sharpened edge, Sussex; (10) flake-axe, Denmark.

But which of these groups became agriculturalists and why? Although all the people before about 10,000 years ago were hunter-gatherers, this term covers a wide range of economies.[47] Much of the variability in hunter-gatherer adaptations seems to be linked to *food storage*.[48] Alain Testart notes that some hunter-gatherers store large amounts of food, others do not, and that storing hunter-gatherer societies exhibit three characteristics—sedentism, a high population density, and the development of socioeconomic inequalities —which have been considered typical of agricultural societies and possible only with an agricultural way of life. Furthermore, their economic cycle—massive harvest and intensive storage of a seasonal resource—is the same as that of societies based on the cultivation of cereals. The difference between storing hunter-gatherers and agriculturalists lies in whether the staple food species are wild or domesticated: this proves to be only a minor difference, since it does not affect the main aspects of society. Agriculturalists and storing hunter-gatherers together are neatly in opposition to non-storing hunter-gatherers. The conclusion to be drawn is that it is certainly not the presence of agriculture or its absence which is the relevant factor when dealing with such societies, but rather the presence or absence of an economy with intensive storage as its cornerstone.[49]

Thus, in looking for causes of agricultural economies, we must consider kinds of adaptations where storage is a potential factor. This relates directly to certain types of foods. Cereals store well, but many tubers do not. Sheep, pigs, barnyard fowl, and other animals can also be considered a form of food storage, since one simply feeds them excess or unwanted foods until the need arises to eat them.

In looking for the origins of agriculture, we can look for environments where food storage was an early and important option. It is probably also significant, as Kent Flannery notes, that the major seed crops that supported the first farmers and remain the basis of modern economies, including wheat, barley, millet, and rice, appear to have derived from

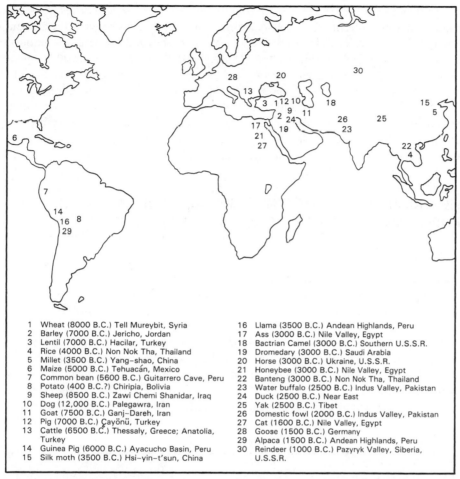

FIGURE 6.6 Early archaeological occurrences of some important Old World and New World domesticates. Domestication is a process, not an event, and these specific sites represent only some early occurrences of species domesticated over wide areas. Many other species have been domesticated.

wild ancestors that were "third-choice" foods: plants that were usually more difficult to gather and process than other wild plants and thus were probably first eaten in quantity because people had to do so, not because they wanted to.[50] On the other hand, most of these third-choice foods are easily storable, plentiful, easy to grow, and, as annuals, genetically malleable—altering the selective forces on them each year can quickly change them genetically.

Aspects of the shift to cereals and other resources may help explain how agriculture— once it was in its initial stages—changed human demographic patterns. In hunting-gathering societies, fertility rates are suppressed significantly simply by maternal mobility: A pregnant woman's chances of spontaneous abortion go up considerably if she walks a lot and works heavily. Thus, those late Pleistocene groups that became less mobile, perhaps because they began to concentrate on salmon runs or wild cereal patches, might have experienced a rise in fertility rates. Also, a direct correlation exists between the amount of carbohydrates in the diet and fertility rates. Studies have shown that it is almost impossible for a woman to become pregnant until she has about 27,000 calories, or 20–25 percent of her body weight, stored as fat[51] (the authors assume no liability for the accuracy of this statistic). Nursing a child requires about 1,000 calories a day, and in many hunter-gatherer societies, the rigors of mobility and their high-protein diet can mean that nursing itself prevents sufficient fat build-up for a successful subsequent pregnancy for about three years. But with the change to a high-carbohydrate, cereal-based diet and restricted mobility of sedentary life, fertility rates may well have risen rapidly.[52]

THE ORIGINS OF DOMESTICATION, AGRICULTURE, AND SEDENTARY COMMUNITIES IN SOUTHWEST ASIA

The best known and perhaps the world's first case of the origins of domestication and agriculture occurred in Southwest Asia and involved peoples and environments ranging from Afghanistan to Greece over a time period of at least 14,000 years. From this region came domesticated sheep, goats, cattle, pigs, wheat, barley, and many other crops on which much of the world today depends.

The environment in which this transition took place is extremely complex. Millions of years ago movements of the earth's crust forced the Arabian Peninsula toward the stable Iranian Plateau, compressing the land in between so that it is pleated like the folds of an accordion. At the end of the Pleistocene, the uplands of the *Fertile Crescent* (Figure 6.7) supported large herds of wild sheep, goats, and cattle and, in many areas, dense stands of

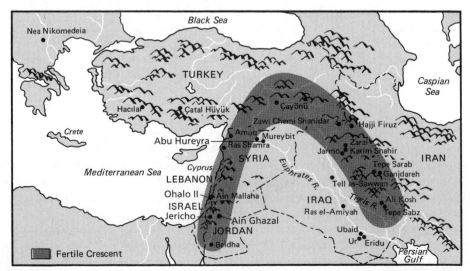

FIGURE 6.7 The "Fertile Crescent" and some important early pre-agricultural and agricultural sites.

wild wheat and barley. In lower elevations and wetter regions, lakes and streams had abundant supplies of waterfowl and fish.

Southwest Asian Domesticates

To understand the origins of agriculture in Southwest Asia, we have to understand the domestication of wheat, barley, cattle, sheep, and goats, for these have been the primary food sources in this area from about 10,000 years ago to the present day. Lentils and other legumes may have been domesticated here earlier,[53] and pigs were more important than cattle, sheep, and goats in some areas and places, but in general it was wheat and barley and cattle, sheep, and goats that supported Southwest Asia's cultural evolution.

If you were a peasant agriculturalist forced to farm the wild ancestors of wheat and barley, you would have had a hard time. Wild wheat, for example, has many limitations as a food crop: Its distribution is sharply limited by temperature, soil, and moisture. As a result, stands of these grains can be widely scattered and therefore difficult to harvest. Much greater efficiency could be attained if these plants could be adapted to a greater variety of temperature, soil, and moisture ranges—especially to the torrid summers of the lowlands, where the rivers offered the potential of irrigation agriculture.

Also, the rachis, the segment of the stalk to which the kernels of wheat or barley are attached, becomes extremely brittle as wild wheat ripens. This brittleness is essential to the successful propagation of these plants because it allows the seeds to be separated from the plant and dispersed by the merest touch of an animal or simply the force of the wind. The head of the plant becomes brittle gradually, from top to bottom, and seed dispersal is spread over one to two weeks. Although this is advantageous for the plant because it prevents the seeds from sprouting in a dense mass of competing seedlings, it poses problems for the human collector. If the grain is gathered when quite ripe, the slightest contact will cause the rachis to fall off, so harvesting with a sickle is difficult—although holding the stalk over a basket and tapping it with a stick works. If, on the other hand, the grain is harvested before it is fully mature, excess moisture in the unripe kernels will cause them to rot in storage. A plant with a tougher rachis and on which the kernels ripen at about the same time would clearly be more useful to people.

Another problem with wild wheat is that the kernels are enclosed in very tough protective husks, called glumes. These protect the seeds from frost and dehydration, but primitive threshing often will not separate the seeds from the glumes, and the human digestive tract cannot break down their tough fibers. Thus a cereal with less tough and less developed glumes would be more digestible.

Also, each stalk of wild grain has only two rows of kernels. Domesticated varieties have six rows, rendering them much more productive as a food resource, and wild species had to change in this direction before it was profitable to invest energy in sowing, cultivating, and harvesting wheat and barley in many areas—particularly in those areas where natural conditions were not optimal for wild cereals.

To base your economy on wheat and barley would also require some specialized tools, for cutting, transporting, threshing, storing, milling, and baking. A full-time cereal farmer is best off living year round in a village or town because of the costs of moving large quantities of grain and because successful harvesting requires that collectors be near stands at very precise times. In contrast to many plants, wild grain can be collected only during

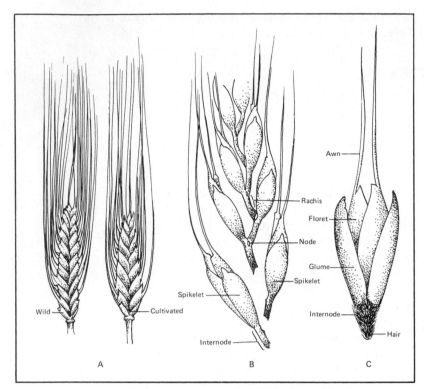

FIGURE 6.8 Domestication of wheat, one of the world's most important crops, involved both human manipulation and natural hybridization between related genera. Human intervention appears to have been aimed at producing free-threshing, nonshattering varieties. The simplest wheats are "diploid," meaning that they have two sets of seven chromosomes. Hybridization with related species produced tetraploid wheats, with six sets of chromosomes, which occur only in cultivated species of wheat. By mixing genetic material from various species, early farmers produced forms of wheat that could adapt to diverse habitats.

the few days when the plants are ripening, and even then there is considerable competition from birds and other predators. Another consideration is that women and children in cereal-gathering societies could contribute a great deal to the food supply, whereas in many societies specializing in hunting, women and children have less direct economic return.

Given all these liabilities and required cultural adjustments, one might wonder why and how these cereals were domesticated. In fact, this seems to have been a relatively rapid process in Southwest Asia, occurring within a few thousand years (and perhaps much less [Figure 6.8]), in several native grasses, including wild barley (*Hordeum spontaneum*), wild einkorn (*Triticum boeoticum*), and wild emmer wheat (*Triticum dicoccum*), each with different habitats and characteristics.

At the same time these plants were being domestic-ated about 10,000 years ago, sheep, goats, pigs, and cattle were also being domesticated. In some areas, such as the southern Mesopotamian alluvial plain, permanent settlement was not possible until domesticated animals were available to supply the fats and proteins that were not readily obtainable from any other source. Domesticated animals also provided a way of converting highland grasses, weeds, shrubs, surplus grain stubble, and other plants into storable, portable, high-quality foods and other usable products. Later, some animals, such as cattle, horses, and donkeys, provided draught and transport power.

Each of the economically most important animals domesticated in Southwest Asia involved somewhat different patterns of change. Cattle, for example, became smaller, perhaps as an adaptation to two factors: the problem of keeping cool in the torrid lowlands where most of the farms eventually were located and the relatively poor diet that was available to cattle there in the leanest seasons. Sheep were bred over time to have a thick multilayered fleece that both protected them from intense temperatures and provided an important product—wool.

The Archaeological Record of Plant and Animal Domestication in Southwest Asia

Archaeological sites throughout Southwest Asia during the late Upper Pleistocene, from about 22,000 to 16,000 years ago, are often concentrations of stone tools, ash, and the bones of large, hoofed mammals (Figure 6.9). Almost all the meat eaten by people came from just a few species of ungulates (hoofed mammals), mainly gazelles, equids (onagers), and aurochs (extinct wild cattle). Based on the tools and other artifacts from South-

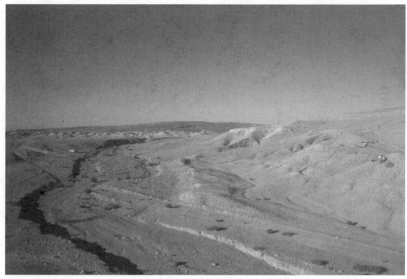

FIGURE 6.9 The Upper Paleolithic site of 'Ain al-Buhayra, Jordan, is on the hillside on the left. The whitish deposits on this hillside represent a fossil spring, while the whitish deposits in the left background are lake bottom sediments.

west Asian sites of this period, it appears that the basic social unit was a band of about 15 or 20 people comprising several families who season after season moved through this area hunting animals and gathering plants.

To understand how these age-old patterns of human adaptation were displaced in just a few thousand years by farmers, we must look in detail at a variety of evidence. The best known archaeological record of this transition is that of the Levant, the area that extends from southeastern Anatolia into the Sinai Peninsula, and east into what is now western Syria and Jordan.

The Levantine cultures of between 22,000 and 14,500 years ago belong to a tradition called *Kebaran* (named, as so many ancient peoples are, after stone tools from a particular site), followed from about 14,500 to 12,500 years ago by the *Geometric Kebaran* cultures, and from 12,500 to 10,500 years ago by the *Natufian* cultures.[54] One aspect that distinguishes each of these is the type of small stone tools—microliths. Kebaran cultures have non-geometric forms, Geometric Kebaran cultures have geometric forms such as triangles and trapezes, and Natufian culture has lunates (half-moon shaped) forms.

If the Kebaran peoples were doing something that inexorably led their remote descendants to become farmers, it is not usually obvious in their archaeological traces. Such traces are almost all small concentrations of bones and stone that reflect a people skilled principally in hunting deer and other large grazing animals. One possible exception to this pattern is the site of Ohalo II— near the Sea of Galilee—which has been radiocarbon–dated to about 19,000 years ago (Figure 6.10). This Kebaran site was wonderfully preserved when it was buried by rising lake levels; a period of low water levels exposed the site in the late 1980s and early 1990s, and it was excavated then. Ohalo II is notable for the preservation of the remains of several brush structures and, most importantly, large quantities of charred

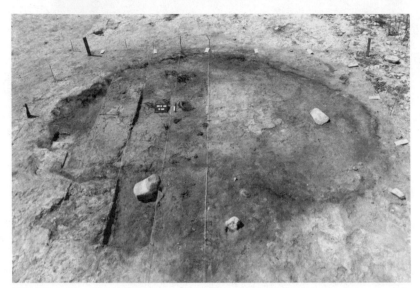

FIGURE 6.10   The Early Epipaleolithic site at Ohalo II, Israel, has excellent organic preservation because the site was submerged when lake levels in the Sea of Galilee rose.

plant foods.[55] We therefore know that people living at Ohalo II were exploiting cereals such as wild barley and wild emmer wheat. They also collected and ate wild almonds, wild olives, wild pistachios, and wild grapes.[56] Ohalo II shows without a doubt that Levantine hunter-gatherer groups used wild cereals as food thousands of years before the advent of agriculture. But Kebaran use of these cereals did not result in the development of agricultural lifeways during this period.

Studies of Kebaran sites and those of later periods led several scholars to the conclusion that there was a "broad spectrum revolution" between 20,000 and 10,000 years ago, in which people in Southwest Asia and many other parts of the world began eating a broader range of foods.[57] In addition to the wide range of plant and animal species found in some sites toward the end of this period, the variety and efficiency of tools used seems to have increased as these millennia passed. Not only do grinding stones appear in quantity, but also barbed spears and arrows, bows, knives made by setting flint flakes into bone or wood, and other tools indicate a greater range of subsistence activities. Some animal species were exploited systematically for the first time, and the grinding stones, "sickles," and other new tools indicate that vegetable foods, including wild cereal grasses, likely were important parts of the diet. Minor local trade in seashells was carried on, and substantial huts appeared in some areas.

But in some ways, the broad spectrum revolution and the agricultural revolution may together form an example of that "great tragedy of Science—the slaying of a beautiful hypothesis by an ugly fact," as Thomas Huxley put it. In a long and thorough review of the evidence from Southwest Asia, archaeologist Donald Henry came to two conclusions:

> First, the proposal of a gradual broadening of the economy leading to a more secure subsistence base, the emergence of sedentary communities, and a growth in population can be rejected. Such a trend is not indicated by the pre-Natufian subsistence evidence. Secondly, the emergence of large sedentary communities, as represented by the Natufian, can best be explained by the intensive exploitation of cereals and nuts. Specialization, as opposed to diversification, characterized the Natufian economy. Although small animal species did form a larger portion of the diet in Natufian times than earlier, these food sources furnished an exceedingly small, almost negligible, part of the overall diet. Instead the specialized hunting of gazelle and the intensive collection of cereals and nuts contributed the greatest part of the subsistence base.[58]

Some evidence of the specialized gazelle hunting that Henry mentions has been provided by Legge and Rowley-Conwy, who have shown that around 11,000 years ago, in the

Euphrates Valley in Syria, at the site of Tell Abu Hureyra people intensively hunted gazelles.[59] Of the 60,000 identifiable animal bones found at this site, about 80 percent are from gazelles—and from gazelles of all sizes and ages and both sexes. Near the site are the traces of stone enclosures, and Legge and Rowley-Conwy have concluded that for thousands of years the people of Tell Abu Hureyra drove herds of gazelle into these enclosures and killed them all. Many of these enclosures have been found and it is possible that eventually the gazelle were driven so close to extinction that people turned to sheep and goats, and in the process domesticated them.

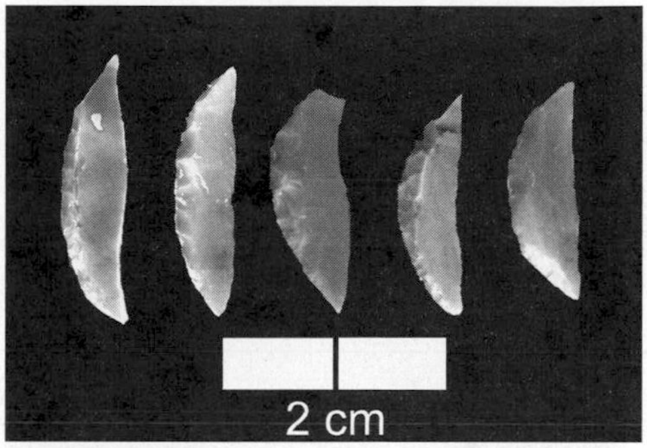

FIGURE 6.11   Lunates (a type of microlith) are common stone tools found during the Natufian period in the Levant.

THE NATUFIAN CULTURE

In the archaeological record of the Natufian period, from about 12,500 to 10,500 years ago, in the Levant, we see clear evidence of agricultural origins. The stone tools of the Natufians include many lunate (i.e., shaped like a segment of the moon) flakes of chert (Figure 6.11), but there is also something new: They used "sickle blades" that show a pattern of wear characteristic of harvesting cereals, rushes, and reeds. Also, querns (milling stones), mortars, pestles, pounders, and other ground stone tools occur in abundance at Natufian sites, and many such tools show signs of long, intensive use. There is also evidence that these heavy grinding stones were transported long distances, more than 30 km in some cases,[60] and this is not something known to have been done by people of preceding periods. Fish hooks and gorges and net sinkers attest to the growing importance of fish in the diet in some areas. Stone vessels indicate an increased need for containers. Studies of attrition—dental wear—of the teeth of Natufians also strongly suggest that these people specialized to some extent in collecting cereals,[61] or at the very least, in eating stone-ground plant foods. But they were also still hunter-foragers, who intensively hunted gazelle and deer in more lush areas and wild goats and equids in more arid zones.

The Natufians had a different settlement pattern from that of their predecessors. Some of their "base-camps" are far larger (over 1,000 m²) than any of the earlier periods, and they may have lived in some of these camps for half the year or even more. In some of the camps people made foundations and other architectural elements out of limestone blocks. Trade in shell and other commodities seems to have been on the rise, and we suspect that exchange of perishables, such as skins, foodstuffs, and salt, was also increasing. Salt probably became for the first time a near necessity: People who eat a lot of meat get many essential salts from this diet, but diets based on cereals can be deficient in salts. Salt was probably also important as a food preservative in early villages.

While some of the later Natufian peoples retained a mobile way of life, others established sedentary communities, such as at 'Ain Mallaha, near Lake Huleh, Israel, which between 12,000 and 10,500 years ago comprised about 50 huts, most of them circular, semi-subterranean, rock-lined, and from 2.5 to 9.0 m in diameter (Figure 6.12). Mortars and pestles litter the site and occur in most huts (Figure 6.13), and storage pits were found both in individual huts and in the compound's interior. These people may have been simply collecting wild cereals instead of cultivating them, but the pattern quickly changed.

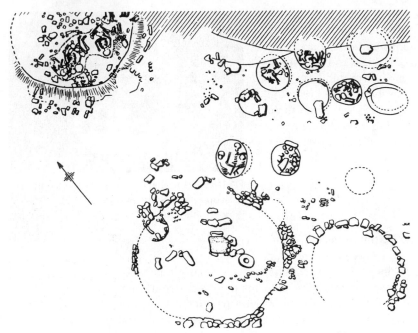

FIGURE 6.12 Simplified plan of an early settlement at 'Ain Mallaha (Israel). Compounds of circular huts such as those at 'Ain Mallaha were widespread in Southwest Asia after about 8000 B.C., but by 6000 B.C. had been superseded largely by villages of rectangular huts.

As always, there is more to a major cultural change than simply a shift in economics. The Natufians made (and presumably wore) beads and pendants in many materials, including marine shells that had to be imported from the Red Sea and from the Mediterranean, and it is possible this ornamentation reflects a growing sense of ethnic identity and perhaps some differences in personal and group status. Cleverly carved figurines of animals and other subjects occur in many sites.[62] More than 400 Natufian burials have been found, most of them simple graves. Grave goods are infrequent, but some burials indicate concern with the philosophical implications of death: At 'Ain Mallaha one elderly person was buried with a young canid—perhaps a puppy (Figure 6.14).[63] In the late Natufian period, some Natufians began burying the body and head of selected people in different but prepared graves. As Belfer-Cohen notes, these burials may reflect an ancestor cult and a growing sense of community emotional ties and attachment to a particular place, and toward the end of the Natufian period people in this area were making a strict separation between living quarters and burial grounds. Compared to the earlier Pleistocene cultures of the Levant, there appears to have been considerable social change in the Natufian.

The question of *why* the Natufians differed in these and other ways from their predecessors, and why they made these first steps toward the farming way of life, remains unclear. There were climate changes, of course, and growing aridity and rising population densities may have forced them to intensify exploitation of cereals, which in turn might have stimulated the development of sickles and other tools and the permanent communities that make agriculture efficient. But precisely how these factors interacted with others is poorly understood.

THE SOUTHWEST ASIAN NEOLITHIC

The earliest farmers of the Middle East appear to have been simultaneously domesticating plants and animals, but animal domestication may have begun slightly earlier and been a longer process than that of cereals. Hillman and Davies,[64] for example, estimate that wheat and barley could have been domesticated in parts of the Middle East in 200 years or less.

So we begin with the animals. The dog[65] is no doubt the oldest animal domesticate in Southwest Asia, probably having been fully domesticated between 22,000 and 10,000 years ago. Hunters and gatherers the world over are known to have remarkably unsentimental ideas about pets, and we should probably see the early domestication of dogs as a result of a symbiotic, utilitarian relationship. Dogs probably served as watchdogs, assisted in the hunt, and were eaten as a starvation food.

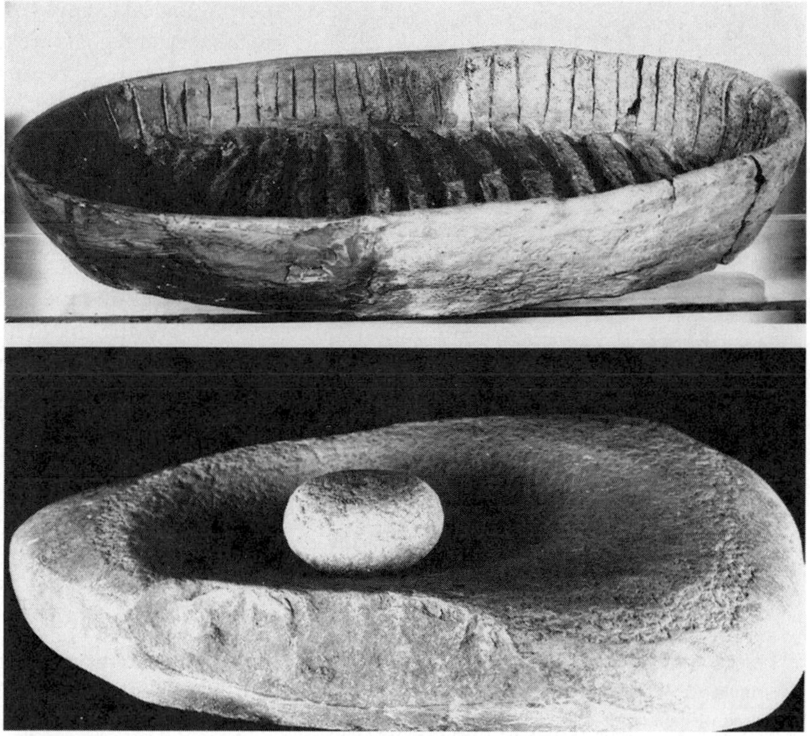

But in economic terms, the most important domesticated animals in Southwest Asia are sheep and goats. Beginning about 8,000 years ago to the present, most meat, milk, and hide products used in the region have come from these animals.

FIGURE 6.13 Common implements for grinding and preparing grain in Iraq, between 7000 and 4000 B.C. The ceramic husking tray (*above*) was used to strip grain from chaff; the heavy stone quern and round pestle (*below*) were used to grind grain to flour.

Detecting the process of animal domestication on the basis of archaeological data is a complex matter on which archaeologists disagree, but the concept of domestication in an archaeological sense usually involves four classes of evidence.[66] Just the presence of an animal species outside its natural range, such as the presence of highland species of sheep in lowland environments, may indicate herding. Second, in most animals, morphological changes occur as domestication progresses. In sheep and goats, the size and shape of horns are major factors in reproductive success, since the larger males fight with their horns to establish breeding hierarchies. As humans domesticated these animals, however, they relaxed selective pressures for large, strong horns (Figure 6.15), and the size and shape of horns changed (morphological changes can also occur at the microscopic level). A third indication of domestication may be evidence of abrupt increases in the number of some species relative to others, which cannot be accounted for by natural causes (e.g. 5 at many Southwest Asian sites the proportion of sheep and goat bones increased dramatically, relative to other animals, at about 8,000 years ago). Finally, age and sex ratios that differ from those of wild herds may also be evidence of domestication.

Early evidence of sheep domestication may be the presence of sheep bones in Neolithic (c. 11,000–8,000 years ago) settlements in the Jordan Valley. These bones reflect no

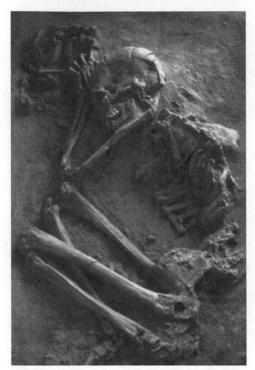

FIGURE 6.14 This Natufian burial from 'Ain Mallaha, Israel, has an elderly person buried with a young canine, possibly a puppy (upper left).

morphological changes in the direction of domestication, but since sheep and goats are not native to this area, their presence here probably reflects intentional introduction.

Ethnographic studies of modern pastoralists suggest that they typically sell or eat 50 percent or more of the animals born each year. Those animals sold or eaten are principally the males, since the females can be kept for reproduction and only a few males are required to service the breeding population. Once a male has reached two years of age, any further investment of food or time in him yields little additional return. Even before the distortions introduced by modern urban markets, the economic importance of sheep and goats was mainly in the milk, cheese, yogurt, and wool obtained from these animals. A well-kept animal can supply many times its own weight in nutritious, storable foods each year for several years, so only young males are regularly slaughtered for meat.

Evidence from two sites near Zawi Chemi Shanidar in Iraq indicates that similar selective slaughtering may have been underway as early as 10,000 years ago. Prior to 14,000 years ago, only about 20 percent of the animals killed and eaten at one of the sites were immature, but by 10,000 years ago, 44–58 percent of the sheep and 25–43 percent of the goats eaten were immature when butchered.[67]

At Ganj Dareh, in the mountains of western Iran, there is evidence that by 10,000 years ago, goats were being herded and managed with selective culling of the subadult males,[68] and there is much other evidence that all over Southwest Asia, sheep, goats, cattle, pigs, and other animal species were well into the process of being domesticated and integrated into a cereal-based farming way of life.

Some of the earliest evidence for domesticated grain cultivation in the Levant comes from the lower levels of Jericho (c. 10,300–9,300 years ago), next to the springs in the center of this oasis. At some time during this period domestic forms of wheat and barley were cultivated in quantity here. Neither wild wheat nor barley appears to have been native to the arid wastelands that surround the site, so these grains were probably brought down from the uplands of the Jordan Valley and grown at Jericho, perhaps as wild species initially. No domestic animals were used in this period, but wild gazelles, goats, cattle, and boars were intensively hunted. Two thousand or more people probably lived at Jericho at any time between 10,300 and 9,300 years ago, and although the earlier communities were apparently unwalled, around 9,300 years ago the inhabitants built a massive stone wall, 3 m thick, 4 m high, and perhaps 700 m in circumference—perhaps to protect the settlement from floodwater erosion. Asphalt, sulfur, salt, and a little obsidian seem to have been traded, but in moderate quantities.

And people living in the northern Levant were making the transition to sedentary communities based on intensive plant collection.

One of these communities was at Tell Abu Hureyra, on the Euphrates River east of Aleppo, Syria. The late Epipaleolithic settlement here consisted of a series of hut pits

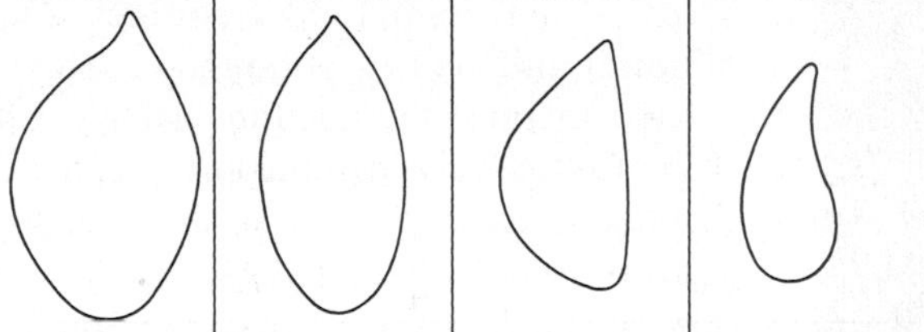

Phase	Site	Zone	Cross section quadrilateral	Cross section lozenge-shaped	Medially flat, but untwisted	Medially concave, helical twist	Too young or too broken to diagnose
Bayat	TS	A₁				1	
Bayat	TS	A₂				1	
Bayat	TS	A₃			1	3	1
Mehmeh	TS	B₁			1		
Mehmeh	TS	B₂				1	1
Mehmeh	TS	B₃					1
Khazineh	TS	C₁					1
Khazineh	TS	C₂					
Khazineh	TS	C₃					3
Sabz	TS	D			2	1	6
Mohammad Jaffar	AK	A₁	4	1		1	7
Mohammad Jaffar	AK	A₂					8
Ali Kosh	AK	B₁		1	2		3
Ali Kosh	AK	B₂	11	7	8		27
Bus Mordeh	AK	C₁	2?	2			
Bus Mordeh	AK	C₂		?			7

Ca. 3700 B.C. (top) — Ca. 7500 B.C. (bottom). Type of Horn Core (header spanning horn core columns).

FIGURE 6.15 The essence of archaeological interpretation is to discern patterns of change in the archaeological record over time. Here, the goat horn cores found at some sites in western Iran indicate that the shape of these horns was changing rapidly between 7500 B.C. and 3700 B.C. One explanation is that in the process of domestication the selective forces that kept these horns quadrilateral—and therefore relatively strong—were being relaxed, probably as a result of the domestication process. Farmers kept goats in herds and selectively bred them, and the strength of the horns apparently was no longer an important determinant of the reproductive success of these goats.

excavated into the virgin subsoil (Figure 6.16). Abu Hureyra is located at the intersection of two vegetation zones—the riverine forest and the woodland-steppe—while a third major zone—the park-woodland—is not far away. Large quantities of charred plant remains were recovered from the site, including wild rye, wild wheat, feather grasses such as *Stipa*

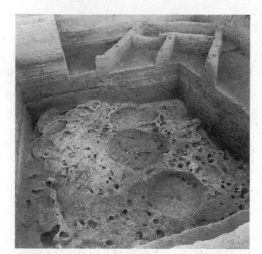

FIGURE 6.16 Epipaleolithic hunter-gatherers constructed several pit-like structures at Tell Abu Hureyra, Syria.

—which have edible seeds—club-rush with edible nutlets, other small grasses that yield edible seeds, and chenopod seeds. Other plant food resources might have included almonds and acorns, although remains of these were not actually found at the site. Interestingly, Gordon Hillman and Susan College have identified a few grains of domesticated rye that have been AMS radiocarbon-dated to about 11,000 years ago. Although whether these represent rye that has been domesticated by people or those grains that represent the genetic variation within the rye gene pool might be an open question for some, Hillman states that the available evidence leads him to conclude that the inhabitants of Abu Hureyra had domesticated rye.[69]

At the same time that agricultural economies were evolving in the Levant, specialized nomadic economies were also probably developing.[70]

Kent Flannery has noted that many contemporary African peoples live in compounds of circular huts and that most such societies share several characteristics: (1) Only one or two people are usually housed in each hut; (2) many of the huts are not residential, but are used for storage, kitchens, stables, and the like; (3) huts are often placed in a circle around a cleared space; (4) food space is usually open and shared by all occupants; and (5) perhaps most important, the social organization of the typical compound, like that of hunting and gathering groups, usually consists of six to eight males, each associated with from one to three women and their respective children, and includes a strong sexual division of labor.[71]

Flannery argues that settlements of adjacent rectangular buildings—which he calls villages—have advantages over settlements of circular buildings—which he calls compounds. The former are more easily enlarged because rooms can simply be added on, whereas increasing the number of circular residences rapidly increases the diameter of the settlement to an unwieldy size.

Villages are also more defensible than compounds for a number of reasons. But the primary difference is in their respective capacities for intensification of production. In compounds, storage facilities are open and shared, and the basic economic unit is the group; but in villages the basic unit is the family, which maintains its own storage of supplies and thus has greater incentives for intensification of production—the seeds, in other words, of private enterprise and the first steps toward capitalist economies.[72]

If Flannery is correct, the transition that occurred between 11,000 and 9,000 years ago from compounds of circular structures to villages of rectangular rooms is a reflection of changes in social organization, with the nuclear family gradually replacing the hunting-and-gathering group as the unit of economic production. And although the circular-building tradition continued for several thousand years in parts of Southwest Asia (Figure 6.17), it was eventually entirely supplanted by rectangular-unit villages.

These kinds of changes appear to be particularly clearly reflected at an early agricultural Levantine community, Beidha, in Jordan. Nine thousand years ago there was a farming community here, set amidst grasslands in adjacent valleys, with forests on the slopes above it.

This community was occupied for hundreds of years, and, as Brian Byrd[73] notes, changes over time in the architecture of the village reflect fundamental changes in social organization, economy, and many other aspects of life (Figure 6.18). In the earliest phases, people lived in small semi-circular buildings with few interior features other than posts. The debris in these houses suggests that many activities of daily life (such as sleeping, tool-making, preparing and eating food, etc.) were done in the same interior spaces. Storage appears to have been communal, as the storeroom is not associated with any particular house. Over time this village organization gave way to one in which people lived in larger rectangular buildings that were subdivided into areas where specialized activities were done. Some of the houses were two-story buildings, with the floors divided into what appear to be separate sleeping areas, tool-making rooms, storage rooms, and so forth. Also, in these later phases, large buildings were constructed that were centrally located and appear to have been public settings for special community activities, or "formal venues for events that integrated the community as a whole."[74]

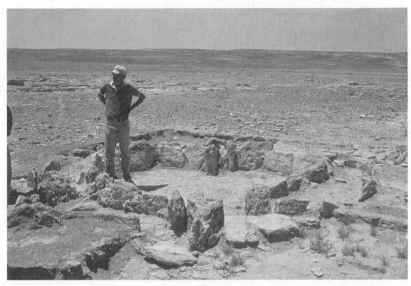

FIGURE 6.17   The base of a Neolithic hut structure at Wadi Jilat 23, Jordan.

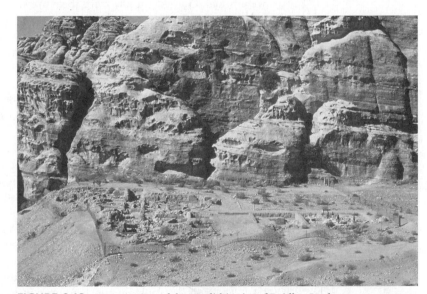

FIGURE 6.18   An overview of the Neolithic site of Beidha, Jordan.

Soon after 10,000 years ago, sedentary communities and domestic plants and animals had appeared at several places along the flanks of the Zagros. At Ali Kosh, situated on the arid steppe of western Iran, at about 9,500 years ago, people hunted gazelles, onagers (wild asses), and pigs; fished in the Mehmeh River; collected shellfish; and snared wild fowl. They also collected vetch and other plants, and between 10,000 and 8,500 years ago they began growing domestic, two-rowed, hulled barley and emmer wheat. These early farmers lived in crude clay huts furnished with reed mats, stone bowls, and a few other small household goods, but this settlement was neither rich nor impressive. Possibly the people came here only in the winter, since summers in the region are unearthly hot and the cooler mountains would have provided many plant and animal products. Wild wheat is not native to the Ali Kosh area, but wild barley is available within a few kilometers, and the people here may have been growing grains that had been domesticated elsewhere.[75]

Archaeologists used to think that the earliest communities of farmers in Southwest Asia and elsewhere remained egalitarian societies for centuries, perhaps millennia, after full-time farming became the subsistence base, but if we look at the early agricultural communities in Southwest Asia, we see very early signs of a changing social world (see also chapter 8). At Jericho, in Jordan, soon after 9,000 years ago, the populace built a stone wall some 1.5 m thick and more than 3.5 m high around a complex of mudbrick houses, even though the populace was still hunting and gathering wild resources to complement their primitive agriculture. If an essential element in cultural complexity is activity specialization to the point that large populations are socially and economically interdependent, Jericho was not a complex community; but the construction of the wall indicates that its people were beginning to direct their energies in a way quite different from that of most hunters and gatherers.

The disposal of the dead, usually an excellent reflection of changing cultural complexity, suggests that people at Jericho and other early Neolithic sites throughout the Levant were much different socially from their predecessors. Forty headless adult bodies were found buried beneath one room at Jericho, and further excavations revealed a cache of skulls that had been reconstructed with plaster, painted, and then decorated with "eyes" made from seashells (Figure 6.19). Whether these represent ancestor worship, war trophies, or some other ritual will probably never be known.

The importance of the bulldozer as an archaeological tool was demonstrated in the late 1970s, when one cut a roadway through a hill in Amman, Jordan, exposing a huge archaeological site. In 1982 archaeologists began excavating this site, now called 'Ain Ghazal ("spring of the gazelles"), one of the largest known Neolithic sites in the Middle East.[76] The first major period of occupation at 'Ain Ghazal began at about 9,400 years ago, and it was probably occupied most or all of the time until about 7,000 years ago. Covering approximately 30 acres, 'Ain Ghazal is about three times larger than Jericho, but it is unclear how much of the site was occupied at any one time. It probably had at one point at least several hundred inhabitants, who lived in mudbrick buildings of various sizes and shapes. For its early age, the community of 'Ain Ghazal has impressive art. Large plaster figures of people were found under house floors. Numerous figures of people and animals have been unearthed (Figure 6.20), and in one cache two clay figures of cattle had flint blades stuck into their heads, necks, and chests.

The diet of the early inhabitants of 'Ain Ghazal is impressive in its diversity. Goats were probably both hunted

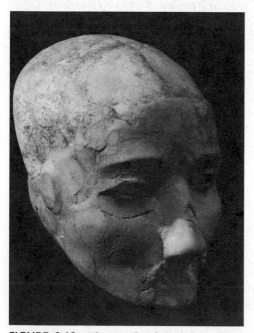

FIGURE 6.19   The people of Neolithic Jericho removed the skulls from some bodies and formed human features on them in plaster.

and herded, and sheep, pigs, gazelles, birds, and many other species were exploited, along with some wheat and barley, peas, lentils, and many wild plants. But toward the end of its occupation, the people of 'Ain Ghazal seem to have fallen on hard times. Late in its history, it seems to have been occupied only seasonally by pastoral peoples.

By 8,000 years ago there is evidence of domestic sheep and goats at sites all over Southwest Asia and even into Greece and southern Europe, and it appears that once domestication was well advanced, the spread of sheep- and goat-raising was very rapid. Most farming villages have hedgerows, patches of weeds and thorny plants, clippings, and stubble that are perfectly acceptable to the rather undiscriminating sheep and goats.

Domestic cattle were herded on the Anatolian Plateau (central Turkey) by about 7,800 years ago and were probably present in the Balkans by 8,500 years ago. As with sheep and goats, cattle domestication seems to have been a widespread phenomenon, probably beginning sometime after 9,000 years ago and occurring in many areas from China to western Europe. Across this vast area, ancient farmers seem to have bred cattle for reduced size, increased docility and milk production, and increased tolerance of climatic conditions. An important step in the evolution of civilizations was the process by which cattle were adapted to the hot lowlands of the river valleys. The cattle found there today are thin, small animals that seem woefully scrawny by comparison to European cattle, but these Mesopotamia varieties are extraordinarily hardy. The late shah of Iran tried to "improve" the cattle in the hot lowland of Iran by importing Dutch and Danish cows that were about four times the size of local varieties and produced vastly more milk and meat—until they strolled out into the hot

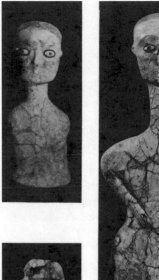
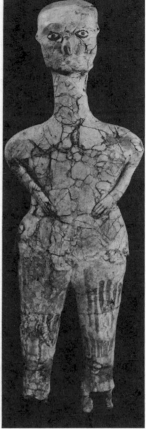
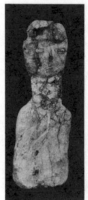

FIGURE 6.20 Figurines from the early agricultural village of 'Ain Ghazal, Jordan.

plains (which we [Wenke] were surveying for archaeological remains), where most of them were felled by heat stroke. These European cattle had to be kept in air-conditioned barns to be productive, whereas the local varieties could do perfectly well on the hottest day, eating poor quality foods that would have killed the larger cattle.

Cattle were probably especially important to the first settlers on the southern Mesopotamian alluvial plain. During the dry, hot summers in this region, few reliable protein sources are available to primitive agriculturalists, and cow meat and milk apparently provided a crucial nutritional component. Oxen (castrated bulls) may also have been used to pull plows and sledges. In many areas of Southwest Asia where rainfall is sufficient for cereal cultivation, plowing is essential because natural vegetation is thick. Later, the horse, donkey, and mule were also used as draught animals, and there is evidence of the use of domesticated horses in the Levant by at least the late fourth millennium B.C.[77]

Another important domesticated animal was the pig, whose bones have been recovered from sites all over Southwest Asia. By 8,000 years ago and even as late as 4,700 years ago, pig bones represented 20–30 percent of all mammal remains at many large sites.

By 8,000 years ago agricultural villages spread over much of Southwest Asia, most of them comprising just a few score mud huts, a few hundred people, and the same essential economic functions. From Greece to Afghanistan, these villages looked very much alike and, taken on the basis of their archaeological remains, they were not impressive in their material wealth. Even sites like Jericho and Çatal Hüyük (see chapter 8), which were larger than most and had relatively impressive art and architecture, were self-sufficient communities without many economic, political, or social ties outside their region. And the vast majority of these villagers were simple farmers without great aesthetic, religious, or social diversions.

As unremarkable as these villages were, however, their inhabitants were the first to focus their lives on agricultural products and to live in the sedentary communities that even today are the basic component of Middle Eastern settlement patterns. And as early as 8,000 years ago, the processes that were to transmute these villages into states and empires were already underway.

OTHER OLD WORLD DOMESTICATES

The domesticates and allied agricultural economies developed in Southwest Asia proved so successful that within centuries of their appearance they had spread far outside the Fertile Crescent. By 7,000 years ago farmers at Argissa-Maghula in Greek Thessaly were subsisting on cultivated emmer wheat and barley as well as domestic cattle and pigs. Recent recalibration of carbon-14 dates for scores of early European sites reveals that the basic wheat-barley/cattle-pigs-sheep complex diffused at the rate of about a mile a year, reaching Bulgaria about 7,500 years ago, southern Italy about 7,000 years ago, and Britain and Scandinavia between 6,000 and 5,000 years ago.[78] To the east, domestic wheat and barley reached the Indus Valley by at least 7,000 years ago (and probably much earlier), and by about 2,500 years ago, domestic wheat was in cultivation in northeastern China.

The processes by which these domesticates and their associated agricultural techniques replaced hunting-and-gathering economies in much of the Old World are not well known but appear to have involved both the replacement of hunters and gatherers by agriculturalists and the conversion of hunters and gatherers to agricultural ways of life (see chapter 12).

The grasslands and forests of temperate Europe and Eurasia contrast sharply with the steppes and arid plains of the Fertile Crescent, and the spread of agriculture northward and westward required new strains of plants and animals and different social and technological adaptations. Methods had to be developed to clear the dense northern forests, and in some areas the rich hunting, gathering, and fishing resources formed such a productive food base that there was considerable "resistance" to the introduction of agriculture. Despite its long-term productivity in most areas, primitive agriculture in even fertile areas of the world was probably marked by famine in seasons of bad harvests and by heavy labor—compared to hunting-foraging—in the best of times.

One interesting aspect of the spread of agriculture may have been the spread of Indo-European languages and culture. Colin Renfrew, in a highly controversial analysis,[79] has suggested that Indo-European languages and culture spread into Europe from Turkey and came with agriculture, which seems to have been established in much of Turkey at least 8,000 years ago. This would explain much about why many of the languages of South and northwest Asia appear to have shared a common ancestry with almost all the native languages of Europe.

Egypt's initial transition to agriculture was based on introductions of wheat, barley, sheep, and goats from outside the Nile Valley, probably both from the Middle East and from North African desert and coastal areas.[80] In the Sudanese part of the Nile Valley, sorghum seems to have been the basis of initial agriculture—although the evidence for its use is scanty.[81]

Many herbs, fruits, and other plants were domesticated in India and Southeast Asia, but it was rice and millet that provided the majority of the food energy for the great Asian civilizations. Imprints from rice-grain husks have been found in potsherds from sites such as Hujiawuchang and Pengtoushan—in the middle Yangtze River Valley of south-central China—by about 8,900 to 8,000 years ago.[82] Additionally, the site of Bashidang—also in the Middle Yangtze and radiocarbon-dated to 8,400–7,700 years ago—yielded more than 10,000 rice grains.[83] The Yangtze River region documents an independent transition to cultivation and agriculture at about the same time that similar events were occurring in the Fertile Crescent of the Near East.

Vegeculture of tubers and other crops probably has a long history in the moist lowlands of Asia. In vegeculture, plants are propagated not from seeds, but from cuttings taken from leaves, stems, or tubers of plants like yams and taro. Bellwood disputes the notion that vegeculture generally preceded cereal agriculture in much of tropical Southeast Asia, but root-crop cultivation may have been the earliest kind of farming in areas like New Guinea.[84]

One of the world's most important cereals—millet—was apparently domesticated and first cultivated on the great Yellow River flood plain in north China (see Figure 6.6). The alluvial soils in this area are extremely fertile and sufficiently arid so that there was little vegetation to clear for agriculture in many areas. By about 8,500 years ago scores of villages existed in north China, most of them subsisting on millet and a few other domesticates and a considerable amount of hunted and gathered food. These villages usually contained about 200 or 300 inhabitants, who lived in wattle-and-daub houses that looked very much like the circular houses and compounds marking the evolution of agricultural communities in Southwest Asia.

Another crop of considerable importance in north China was soybeans; several wild varieties are native to this area. The little evidence available suggests soybeans were in cultivation by at least 3,000 years ago. Soybeans are a remarkably versatile and nutritious crop, and are also good "green manure," enriching the soils on which they grow through nitrogen fixation. The substitution of soybeans for milk and meat in early Chinese diets explains why many Asian populations never evolved the enzymes necessary to digest milk products, causing them to suffer intestinal upsets if they eat these foods. Similar intolerances are found in Africa and South America.

The establishment of agricultural economies in Japan had some similarities to the pattern in Europe. In both areas, rich northern forested environments supported dense populations of hunter-foragers, and, when agriculture came, it supplanted the ancient hunting-foraging economies at different rates in different areas—slowly in areas heavily dependent on marine resources, more quickly in others.[85]

AGRICULTURAL ORIGINS IN THE NEW WORLD

In the New World, the most important domesticates were maize, beans, squash, peppers, potatoes, turkey, guinea pigs (as a food source), and llamas (although some people would add to this list cacao, from which chocolate is derived). Like their Old World relatives, New World peoples complemented their staple domesticates with a wide range of other plants, including avocados, manioc, sunflowers, amaranth, gourds, and cotton, as well as socially valued plants like coca (from which cocaine is derived) and tobacco.

New World peoples, however, did not domesticate any large draught animals suitable for plowing or riding perhaps because there were no suitable native species (although the Rocky Mountain sheep would seem to have possibilities). This fact alone may explain much of the difference between the later cultural histories of the Old and New Worlds: Plowing, even the simple, single blade of a wood plow, opens up many areas to agriculture that cannot be farmed otherwise. In the Old World, human and material transport was dependent from a very early time on domesticated donkeys and, later, horses, and both of these allowed warfare and trade to expand enormously. The llama of South America certainly was an important transport animal, but it does not compare to either donkeys or horses for transport or military uses. Also, no animals equivalent to the Old World pig or sheep were domesticated in the New World.

There were two major centers of plant domestication in the New World, one in Mesoamerica, where maize, beans, squash, and sweet potatoes became the most important crops, and a second center in the Andean highlands, where potatoes and other root crops were grown and llamas were domesticated. But, as in the Old World, these processes of domestication and the transition to agriculture were long-term and occurred over a wide area, involving many different peoples and species. And just as in the Old World, we see the emergence of a very limited range of species as the primary crop plants. Native North Americans, for example, domesticated sunflowers and other plants, and some of these remain commercially important crops even today, but the efficiencies of maize, beans, squash, and potatoes are such that they were—separately or in combination—the basis of life all over the New World when the European colonists first arrived.

Mesoamerica and Central America

The background of New World domestication, like that of the Old World, is many millennia of hunting, gathering, and foraging. Kent Flannery has suggested, for example, that the foods the aboriginal Mexican foragers relied on, such as maguey cactus, prickly pear, and rabbit, were species that could withstand intensive human consumption for many millennia without changing much in their physical characteristics as genera, and that because of the nature of these foragers' seasonal movements, they rarely exerted great pressure on these resources for any length of time.[86] For example, cactus-fruit collecting had to be done during a two- to three-week period, and during this time rabbits would not be hunted. This seasonal concentration on resources kept groups small and dispersed for most of the year, and one wonders why the Spanish found Mesoamerica (roughly from northern Mexico to southern Guatemala) to be a world of cities and farms instead of a domain of hunters and gatherers.

Despite effective mechanisms that maintained the hunting-and-gathering way of life for so long in Mesoamerica, sometime after 8000 B.C. these people—probably unintentionally —began to domesticate maize, beans, squash, peppers, avocados, and other plant species. Why and how this happened is not clear. Climate changes, increasing population densities, and other factors may have been involved, and ecological analyses suggest that in the beginning the shift to agriculture may have involved only a slight change in the way people in Mesoamerica hunted and foraged.[87]

Robert Reynolds's computer simulation[88] of dietary changes reflected in the archaeological record of Guilá Naquitz Cave, in Oaxaca, southern Mexico, between 8750 and 6670 B.C. suggests a subtle pattern of adaptations to the changing conditions in this period. People who lived here eventually focused on a particularly reliable and productive mix of plant and animal foods, one that Reynolds's simulation model linked to complex calculations about travel distances, seasonal availability, and many other factors. He concluded that cultivation here may have begun as a way to increase the density of certain plants and to mitigate the effects of wet-year/dry-year fluctuations, increasing human population densities, and other circumstances.

Eventually maize was domesticated out of millennia of such manipulations and cultural ecological contexts. Domesticated maize was the most important food through much of later Mesoamerican prehistory, and at present it is the only domesticated plant from this area whose evolutionary history we know in any detail. A few fragments of early forms of beans, squash, and peppers have been found, but not enough to reconstruct recent changes in their morphological characteristics. Occasionally there are claims that maize was either brought to or from the Old World at a very early date, usually based on ancient sculptures or other art,[89] but no trace of ancient corn plants has ever been found in the Old World.

Most of our evidence about early plant cultivation in Mesoamerica comes from dry caves in Tamaulipas,[90] Tehuacán, and Oaxaca, so we must immediately suspect biases in preservation: There is little reason to believe that just because the earliest known maize comes from thesesites that these sites were the earliest places to domesticate maize. Also, as Gayle Fritz has noted,[91] there is some evidence that for many years scholars have greatly overestimated the age of maize domestication and agriculture in the New World. Scholars used to believe that maize domestication evolved out of the hunting-foraging groups who lived in this area between 10,000 and 5000 B.C. But more recent evidence and dates[92] raise the possibility that domestication and agriculture first appeared shortly before 3500 B.C. and evolved out of hunter-foragers who had become much less mobile than their ancestors, moving only a few times a year, if at all, and concentrating their efforts on the wild ancestors of plants they eventually domesticated.

Until about 1970 the most widely accepted view of maize domestication was advanced by a geneticist, Paul Mangelsdorf, who argued that domesticated maize evolved from a "wild maize," now extinct, with small cobs topped by small tassels. This would have been a "pod-corn"—that is, the individual kernels would have been enclosed in chaff rather than the cup-like fruit-case of domesticated varieties. Mangelsdorf explains the extinction of this wild maize as the result of two factors: overgrazing by European-introduced cattle and genetic "swamping" from continual hybridization with emerging species of domesticated maize.[93]

In the early 1960s, Richard MacNeish excavated several dry caves near Tehuacán, Mexico, and his findings clarified some aspects of Mesoamerican agricultural origins.

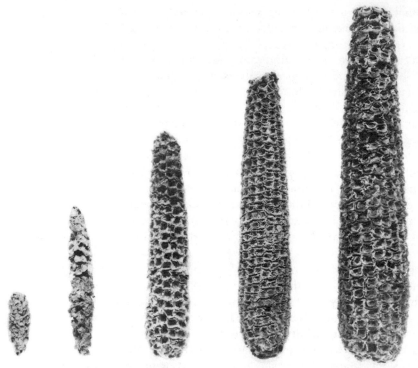

Recent radiocarbon dating results suggest that the plant remains from different strata of Tehuacán were mixed, and thus the site might be less a record of early maize domestication than originally thought. The earliest maize cobs (four samples) are now dated to about 4,700 years ago or younger —much younger, as Gayle Fritz notes,[94] than the fifth and sixth millennium B.C. dates originally ascribed to these remains (Figure 6.21). Despite these revisions and new and interesting evidence from elsewhere, the Tehuacán sequence remains the best archaeological reflection of the sequences of changes in cultural behavior that were involved in the period of the origins of agriculture in Mesoamerica.[95] During the *Ajuereado* phase (c. 10,000–7000 B.C.[96]), people apparently lived in small mobile groups

FIGURE 6.21   The evolution of maize cob size at Tehuacán, from the smallest cob (*left*), which dates to about 3500 B.C., to the cob on the far right, an entirely modern variety dating to about B.C./A.D.

and exploited many wild plants. But they also depended heavily on hunting, exploiting wild horses, antelopes, and jack rabbits at first, and then shifting to deer and cottontail rabbits as post-Pleistocene climates and environments changed, supplementing these resources with gophers, rats, turtles, and birds. In the succeeding *El Riego* phase (c. 7000–5000 B.C.), people appear to have lived much the same nomadic life in bands, but the groups may have been somewhat bigger, and there is evidence that they were exploiting wild squash, chiles, avocados, and other plants that were later domesticated. In the *Coxcatlán* phase (5000–3400 B.C.) the size of the groups that made repeated and probably seasonal visits to Tehuacán seems to have grown significantly, and they exploited more plants and did less hunting. In the *Abeja* phase (c. 3400–2300 B.C.), MacNeish believes that the area was occupied by "central-based bands," people who lived for long periods, and perhaps most of the year, in large camps and relied heavily on cultivated plants. In succeeding periods these Tehuacános used pottery and began to subsist mainly on domesticated maize, beans, squash, and the other staples of Mesoamerica.

The Tehuacán botanical remains seemed to confirm Mangelsdorf's hypothesis: The earliest corn cobs found were very small, and the tassels did indeed emerge from the tops of the fruits. But the early maize found by MacNeish seemed to have many morphological similarities to another wild perennial grass common in the semi-arid, subtemperate regions of Mesoamerica, a grass called teosinte (*Zea mexicana*), and some botanists questioned

Mangelsdorf's reconstruction, partially because the supposed placement of kernels on a cob such as wild and domesticated maize would seem a very inefficient mechanism for seed dispersal.

In 1972 plant geneticist George Beadle reasserted his argument of some decades previous: that there had never been a "wild maize," that domesticated corn instead was a descendant of teosinte.[97] Teosinte is a tall (up to 2 m) annual grass found throughout the semi-arid and subtropical zones of Mexico and Guatemala, where it thrives in disturbed areas and rapidly invades open areas such as abandoned cornfields. Teosinte can be found growing in fields that also include wild beans and squash, sometimes with the beans twining around the teosinte stalk. Thus, the three staffs of life for Mesoamerica—maize, beans, and squash—are a "natural" association.[98] Teosinte plants look like maize, except for the seed structure, where instead of maize's heavy husk-covered cobs of many rows of kernels, teosinte has just two rows of 6–12 triangular kernels enclosed in a very hard covering. Although these seeds look quite different from maize kernels, Beadle was able to produce reasonably good popcorn and mock "Fritos" from teosinte kernels.

Chemical analyses of teosinte and maize and studies of their genetic characteristics support Beadle's view of teosinte as the major ancestor of maize—although Mangelsdorf mounted a spirited counterattack.[99]

Domesticated maize shares several characteristics with teosinte. As Emily McClung de Tapia notes,[100] these include: (1) Teosinte and maize frequently and freely hybridize under natural conditions; (2) they have the same chromosome number, 10, and these chromosome appear nearly identical in structure; (3) maize and teosinte look very much alike in anatomy and morphology; and (4) pollen from maize and teosinte are quite similar in size. She notes, however, that pinpointing where teosinte was transformed into maize, if this did indeed occur, has proven difficult. The type of teosinte that seems most closely related genetically to maize is the Chalco-type (*Zea Mexicana* ssp. *mexicana*), which is native to the Basin of Mexico (modern Mexico City and environs), but this may a result of hybridization.

If teosinte is the ancestor of domesticated maize, the primary changes in the domestication process were (1) the development of a less brittle rachis, followed by the evolution of the cob; (2) the development of a soft fruit-case, so that the kernels could be shelled free of the cob; and (3) the evolution of larger cobs and more rows of kernels. A single gene—the so-called tunicate allele—controls to some extent both the brittleness of the rachis and the toughness of the fruit case, and thus these features could easily have been produced by direct selection of mutants with these characteristics. The third change, increased cob size, was very gradual and probably differed sharply from area to area. If the new dates for the Tehuacán maize remains are accurate (see earlier), maize cobs in this area were selected for larger and larger size in such a way that the average length grew from a little less than 2 cm in length to about 13 cm in length between about 3500 B.C. and A.D. 1500.

Stephen J. Gould accepts Beadle's claim for the derivation of maize from teosinte, but he rejects Beadle's hypothesis of a slow process of gradual genetic change.[101] Gould notes that the Tehuacán maize cobs are smaller than modern varieties, but at least they are cobs, and we do not find intermediate stages between the teosinte "ears," which botanically are radically different from the maize ears. Also, as Gould notes, maize and teosinte are extremely similar genetically, and one would expect that a slow process of domestication toward maize would have resulted in some major genetic differences.

Instead Gould champions Hugh Iltis's hypotheses about maize domestication. Iltis's argument is a complex botanical and genetic scenario that cannot be examined in detail here, but its basic assumption is that there was a small genetic change in teosinte that produced what Iltis called a "catastrophic sexual transmutation."[102] Some minor genetic mutations could transmute male teosinte tassel spikes to female corn ears. This kind of change accords well with Gould's conception of evolution as a series of sudden changes, not the accumulation of gradual changes. But Iltis's scheme requires that people recognize the potential of the "hopeful monsters" a mutant teosinte plant would represent, for it is unlikely this mutant would be able to reproduce easily. In this case, human intentions are an important part of the overall equation of domestication.

While maize is an excellent food source, it is deficient in a number of important proteins and vitamins, and the evolution of agricultural economies in Mesoamerica derived considerable impetus from the domestication of other plant species, the most important of which were beans and squash. In fact, the evidence suggests that beans, squash, pumpkins, and other plants may have been cultivated before maize. Three species of beans (common beans, runner beans, and tepary beans) have wild ancestors in Mesoamerica, and changes in their morphological characteristics began to appear at about the same time as those of maize. But the earliest known domesticated beans did not make their appearance until between 4000 and 3000 B.C.

The domestication of beans seems to have involved (1) increased seed permeability, so that the beans need not be soaked so long in water before being processed; (2) a change from a corkscrew-shaped, brittle pod that shatters easily to a straight, limp, non-shattering pod; and (3) in some cases, a shift from perennial to annual growth patterns.[103] The primary importance of beans is that they are rich in lysine, which maize is deficient in; thus the two are nutritionally complementary.

The domestication of squash and pumpkins, members of the genus *Cucurbita*, seems to have been aimed at improving the seeds (rather than the flesh) since wild cucurbita have flesh so bitter or thin that they have little food value. Squash and pumpkin seeds, on the other hand, like most large seeds are veritable vitamin pills, as they include complex plant starches and other nutrients. Squash and pumpkin seeds, in fact, remain a favorite snack food, especially in less developed countries. The earliest cultivated squash seeds known are from Guilá Naquitz Cave in Oaxaca and date to 8750 to 7840 B.C.[104]

Like all other early farmers, the ancient Mesoamericans were domesticating a variety of other plants, only some of which were eventually developed into staple food sources. Chili peppers, avocados, foxtail grass, "goosefoot" (*Chenopodium*), various kinds of cactus, several root crops, and many other plants were combined in a reliable and highly productive agricultural economy (Figure 6.22).

The species of maize that eventually became the staple crop of North and South America seems to have been derived from species indigenous to central Mexico, perhaps the area around Mexico City, but the stimulus for the adoption and spread of the agricultural and village way of life may also have involved coastal areas. There, rich resources in the littoral/terrestrial interface may have provided sufficient food for non-agricultural but sedentary communities.[105] In time, these sedentary communities could have incorporated the new domesticated plants into their "pre-adapted" economies and social organizations, forming the first agricultural communities. From that point on, the superior productivity of village-based agriculture would have ensured its rapid spread over all the areas where these crops could be grown successfully. Currently we do not have sufficient data to evaluate this reconstruction rigorously, but some evidence indicates it may be correct. Large mounds of shellfish remains, cracked rock, and stone tools have been found on both the Gulf and Pacific coasts of Mesoamerica, but few have been excavated or firmly dated. Many groups of people lived in the rich terrestrial/marine niches along Mexico's coasts after 3000 B.C., and some of them may have lived in villages and farmed some maize and other crops, but the evidence for substantial farming and the spread of villages in Mexico is scanty until shortly after 2000 B.C.[106]

With regard to the question of *why* agriculture appeared in Mesoamerica when and where it did, we are left with the rather unsatisfactory models discussed earlier in this chapter. The sole single factors that seem to have affected most centers of agricultural

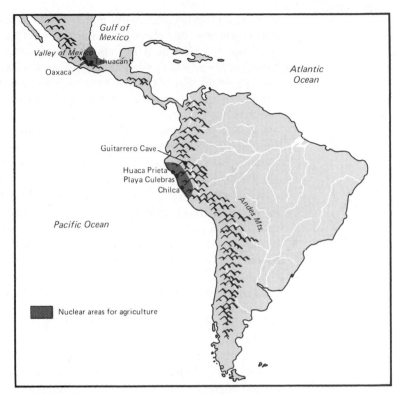

FIGURE 6.22 Some areas of early American domestication and agriculture. Other areas may be buried under coastal waters or undiscovered in dense coastal vegetation zones.

origins, from China to Mesoamerica, are the changes in plant, animal, and human communities that resulted from the change in climates as the glaciers retreated at the end of the last Pleistocene period. If we then pose the standard challenge to the importance of these climate changes—specifically, that they happened many times previously in the Pleistocene without the same effects—we are left with either accepting the Richerson and colleagues, explanation or with the surmise that there was something different about the demography, technological capacities, or some other aspect of human communities 10,000 years ago, compared to earlier groups.

South America

How and when Mexican varieties of domesticated maize spread into Central and South America are not well known. There are some interesting bits of evidence, however, that suggest maize may have been cultivated in Ecuador, Peru, Argentina, and Chile as early as 3000 B.C., and perhaps earlier.[107]

Physical remains of crops would, of course, be the best evidence for the spread of agriculture, but the botanical record of early South American cultivation is poorly known.

Only at sites dated after about 900 B.C. are maize remains commonly found. Deborah Pearsall suggests that maize did not become an important crop until after 1500 B.C.[108]

Maize was just one of the important food crops in Andean South America, and in some areas, potatoes, beans, and quinoa (pronounced "keen-wa") were the staffs of life. There is some evidence that beans may have been domesticated before 8000 B.C., based on a few remains from Guitarrero Cave, and there are fairly secure finds of beans there dating to about 5700 B.C.,[109] but the evidence of the earliest stages of the domestication of beans and many other plants is scanty. The origins of potato domestication, too, are poorly preserved. Domesticated potatoes were found in sites in Peru's Casma Valley in occupations dating to 2250–1775 B.C.,[110] and there are traces of cultivation that may go back as early as about 8000 B.C.[111] This prolific plant, which today is grown in hundreds of varieties in Peru, may not store as well as cereals, but it can be grown in wet cold soils where cereals do not do well— as evidenced by its popularity in Ireland and northern Europe. The ancient South Americans developed a method of storing potatoes by freeze-drying them, and the potato is intrinsically very nutritious, and so this plant could provide the stability and reliability of production for South Americans that cereals did in many other places.

It is an interesting footnote to Peruvian plant domestication that quinoa is becoming increasingly popular in North America. The seeds of this plant can be milled into a flour that has one of the highest protein contents of any plant (but made a miserable chocolate chip cookie in one experiment), and health food enthusiasts are using this plant in growing numbers.

The role of animal domestication in early Peru is unclear, but llamas and guinea pigs were certainly domesticated in central Peru by 3500 B.C. As in Mexico, however, hunting continued to play an important role in many areas until quite late.[112]

The relationship of plants and animals, agriculture, and sedentary communities in northwestern South America in general suggests that domestication and sedentary communities may have preceded specialized agricultural economies in some areas by many centuries, particularly on the coast, where small sedentary communities of fishers, foragers, and part-time bean and squash cultivators were established before maize cultivation was of any importance.

Deborah Pearsall[113] has broken the South American "center" of agricultural origins into three complexes. The origins of the *Lowland Complex* are poorly understood because the remains of some of the most important early plants that may have been native to the tropical forests, such as manioc (*Manihot esculenta*) and sweet potatoes (*Ipomoea batatas*), do not preserve very well archaeologically. Maize eventually became a dominant crop in the lowlands, but it was preceded and eventually complemented by a wide range of other plant foods, ranging from flavoring foods (such as chili peppers) to squash to fruits (including avocado and, later, papaya and pineapple). Pearsall's *Mid-Elevation Complex*, which includes areas between about 1,500 and 3,000 m of elevation, includes amaranths, peanuts, jicama, various beans, and other plants, including coca. Here, too, maize cultivation eventually relegated many of these crops to the status of supplemental foods, but the range of genera domesticated across the Andes and into the lowland coasts and forests underscores just how pervasive and ecologically diverse the domestication process was. Pearsall's *High-Elevation Complex* is found in areas over about 3,000 m of elevation. In this cold and agriculturally demanding zone, potatoes and various other tubers provided the dietary staple, in combination with meat from domesticated llamas and alpacas.

Certainly other plants were cultivated, including quinoa and chenopods, but few traces of these and other plant remains have been found.

SUMMARY AND CONCLUSIONS

Generally, we have no evidence that people of the immediate post-Pleistocene era experienced recurrent periods of starvation, or that they "invented" domesticates and agriculture as a way of addressing their immediate food supply problems. Instead, the situation may well have been one in which, as population densities slowly rose, people gravitated into various niches where the exploitation of wild wheat and barley, teosinte, and other third-choice plants was marginally increased. Even if they were not forced into these areas by expanding population densities and were not under the dire threat of imminent starvation (so that they radically increased their consumption of these third-choice foods), the plasticity of some of these species was such that minimal changes in selective pressures might have quickly and directly rewarded this increased exploitation.

In this sort of reconstruction it does not seem likely that the timing of wheat and barley domestication, for example, was the result mainly of "lucky" mutations. All over the post-Pleistocene world so many diverse animal and plant species were domesticated that explaining them all in terms of "lucky" mutations would require coincidences of a highly unlikely nature. Nor was this a technological revolution: The first intensive cereal collectors required only minimal tools—implements certainly no more complex or imaginative than the fish traps and bows and arrows of the late Pleistocene.

Finally, for the individual with too few things to worry about, we might note that there is a certain danger in the fact that almost all the world's population now depends for most of its subsistence on only about 20 genera of plants. As hybrid strains are replacing local varieties at an ever-increasing rate, the chances for truly catastrophic mutations of new crop diseases are growing, particularly with expected worldwide changes in climate. The Irish potato famine was largely the result of a whole country becoming dependent on a single crop that was cloned from a small genetic population and therefore subject to almost complete destruction by disease. Eventually the world may be at the same risk. The transition to economies based on domesticated plants and animals thus is a process still in operation and one whose future direction is unclear.

Against this uncertain future seed "banks" have been established, such as the one at Washington State University, where seeds of more than 1,700 plant species are kept in special conditions against the day when their genetic resources might be useful. Every species is a unique and complex product of evolution, whose members are in a sense chemical factories able to synthesize the most complex compounds from only air, water, and soil. Not only food but also medicines and many other products are mainly made from plant materials, and we have every reason to believe that the continuing destruction and extinction of plant communities in the Amazon Basin and elsewhere in the developing world will eventually be recognized as irremediable catastrophes. As we have noted previously, in the evolutionary game in which all of earth's life-forms participate, there is usually great advantage to the maintenance of genetic *variability*. We are so mutually interdependent with plants and animals that loss of variety in the nonhuman biological world will almost certainly come back to haunt us.

Perhaps we might also ask ourselves if Jared Diamond is correct in his appraisal of the origins of agriculture:

> Archaeologists studying the rise of farming have reconstructed a crucial state at which we made the worst mistake in human history. Forced to choose between limiting population or trying to increase food production, we chose the latter and ended up with starvation, warfare, and tyranny. Hunter-gatherers practiced the most successful and longest-lasting life style in human history. In contrast, we're still struggling with the mess into which agriculture has tumbled us. . . . [W]ill the plight of famine-stricken peasants gradually spread to engulf us all? Or will we somehow achieve those seductive blessings that we imagine behind agriculture's glittering façade.[114]

Or has an agricultural way of life resulted in changes that led to better distribution of products and access to resources so that life expectancy is now higher and in fact mortality rates lower—at least for first world nations within the last 100 years or so?

BIBLIOGRAPHY

Aitkens, C. M., K. M. Ames, and D. Sanger. 1986. "Affluent Collectors at the Edges of Eurasia and North America: Some Comparisons and Observations on the Evolution of Society Among North Temperate Coastal Hunter-Gatherers." In *Prehistoric Hunter-Gatherers in Japan*, ed. T. Akazawa and C. M. Aikens. Tokyo: University of Tokyo Press.

Akazawa, T., and C. M. Aikens, eds. 1986. *Prehistoric Hunter-Gatherers in Japan*. Tokyo: University of Tokyo Press.

Ammerman, A. J., and L. L. Cavalli-Sforza. 1984. *The Neolithic Transition and the Genetics of Population in Europe*. Princeton, NJ: Princeton University Press.

Anderson-Gerfaud, P. C. 1990. "Experimental Cultivation and Harvest of Wild Cereals: Criteria for Interpreting Epipalaeolithic and Neolithic Artifacts Associated with Plant Exploitation." In *Préhistoires de L'Agriculture: Nouvelles Approches Experimentales et Ethnographiques*, ed. P. C. Anderson-Gerfaud. Valbonne: Monographies du Centre de Recherches Archéologiques.

Aurenche, O., P. Galet, E. Régagnon-Caroline, and J. Évin. 2001. "Proto-Neolithic and Neolithic Cultures in the Middle East—The Birth of Agriculture, Livestock Raising, and Ceramics: A Calibrated ^{14}C Chronology 12,500–5500 cal BC." *Radiocarbon* 43(3):1191–1202.

Bar-Yosef, O. 1991. "The Early Neolithic of the Levant: Recent Advances." *The Review of Archaeology* 12(2):1–18.

Bar-Yosef, O., and A. Belfer-Cohen. 1992. "From Foraging to Farming in the Mediterranean Levant." In *Transitions to Agriculture in Prehistory*, ed. A. B. Gebauer and T. D. Price. Ann Arbor: Prehistory Press.

Bar-Yosef, O., and F. R. Valla, eds. 1990. *The Natufian Culture in the Levant*. Ann Arbor: Monographs in Prehistory, Archaeological Series 1.

Barlow, K. R., and M. Heck. 2002. "More on Acorn Eating During the Natufian: Expected Patterning in Diet and the Archaeological Record of Subsistence." In *Hunter-Gatherer Archaeobotany: Perspectives from the Northern Temperate Zone*, ed. S. L. R. Mason and J. G. Hather, pp. 128–145. London: Institute of Archaeology, University College London.

Barnard, A. 1983. "Contemporary Hunter-Gatherers: Current Theoretical Issues in Ecology and Social Organization." *Annual Review of Anthropology* 12:193–214.

Beadle, G. W. 1972. "The Mystery of Maize." *Field Museum of Natural History Bulletin* 43:2–11.

———. 1980. "The Ancestry of Corn." *Scientific American* 242:112–199.

Belfer-Cohen, A. 1991. "The Natufian in the Levant." *Annual Review of Anthropology* 20:167–210.

Bellwood, P. 1986. *The Prehistory of the Indo-Malaysian Archipelago*. Orlando, FL: Academic Press.

———. 2001. "Early Agriculturalist Population Diasporas? Farming, Languages, and Genes." *Annual Review of Anthropology* 30:181–207.

Bender, B. 1978. "Gatherer-Hunter to Farmer: A Social Perspective." *World Archaeology* 10:204–222.

———. 1985. "Emergent Tribal Formations in the American Midcontinent." *American Antiquity* 50(1):52–62.

Binford, L. R. 1968. "Post-Pleistocene Adaptations." In *New Perspectives in Archaeology*, ed. S. R. Binford and L. R. Binford. Chicago: Aldine.

Bird, R. M. 1990. "What Are the Chances of Finding Maize in Peru Dating Before 1000 B.C.?: A Reply to Bonavia and Grobman." *American Antiquity* 55(4):828–840.

Blumler, M. A., and R. Byrne. 1991. "The Ecological Genetics of Domestication and the Origins of Agriculture." *Current Anthropology* 32(1):23–54.

Boserup, E. 1965. *The Conditions of Agricultural Growth.* Chicago: Aldine.

———. 1981. *Population and Technology.* Chicago: University of Chicago Press.

Boyd, B. 2004. "Agency and Landscape; Abandoning the 'Nature/Culture' Dichotomy in Interpretations of the Natufian and the Transition to the Neolithic." In *The Last Hunter-Gatherers in the Near East*, ed. C. Delage, pp. 119–136. Oxford: Archaeopress, British Archaeological Reports International Series 1320.

Braidwood, R. J. 1960. "The Agricultural Revolution." *Scientific American* 203:130–141.

Braidwood, R. J., and L. S. Braidwood, eds. 1983. *Prehistoric Archaeology Along the Zagros Flanks.* Chicago: The Oriental Institute.

Brocker, W. S. 1997. "Thermohaline Circulation, the Achilles Heel of Our Climate System: Will Man-Made CO_2 Upset the Current Balance?" *Science* 178:1582–1588.

Byrd, B. F. 1989. "The Natufian: Settlement Variability and Economic Adaptations in the Levant at the End of the Pleistocene." *Journal of World Prehistory* 3:159–197.

———. 1994. "Public and Private, Domestic and Corporate; The Emergence of the Southwest Asian Village." *American Antiquity* 59(4):639–679.

———. 2005. "Reassessing the Emergence of Village Life in the Near East." *Journal of Archaeological Research* 13(3):231–290.

Byrne, R. 1987. "Climatic Change and the Origins of Agriculture." In *Studies in the Neolithic and Urban Revolutions: The V. Gordon Childe Colloquium, Mexico, 1986*, ed. L. Manzanilla. British Archaeological Reports International Series 349.

Carneiro, R., and D. Hilse. 1966. "On Determining the Probable Rate of Population Growth During the Neolithic." *American Anthropologist* 68:177–181.

Caton-Thompson, G., and E. W. Gardner. 1934. *The Desert Fayum.* London: Royal Anthropological Institute.

Cavalli-Sforza, L. L., and M. W. Feldman. 1981. *Cultural Transmission and Evolution: A Quantitative Approach.* Princeton, NJ: Princeton University Press.

Childe, V. 1952. *New Light on the Most Ancient East*, 4th ed. London: Routledge & Kegan Paul.

Clark, J. G. D. 1980. *Mesolithic Prelude. The Paleolithic-Neolithic Transition in Old World Prehistory.* Edinburgh: Edinburgh University Press.

Clark, J. D., and S. A. Brandt, eds. 1984. *From Hunters to Farmers.* Berkeley: University of California Press.

Cohen, N. M. 1977. *The Food Crisis in Prehistory.* New Haven and London: Yale University Press.

Cohen, N. M., and G. J. Armelagos. 1984. *Paleopathology at the Origins of Culture.* New York: Academic Press.

Cowan, C. W., and B. D. Smith. 1993. "New Perspectives on a Wild Gourd in Eastern North America." *Journal of Ethnobiology* 13:17–54.

Cowan, C. W., and P. J. Watson, eds. 1992. *The Origins of Agriculture: An International Perspective.* Washington, DC: Smithsonian Institution Press.

Crawford, G. W., and G.-A. Lee. "Agricultural Origins in the Korean Peninsula." *Antiquity* 77:87–95.

Crawford, G. W., and C. Shen. 1998. "The Origins of Rice Agriculture: Recent Progress in East Asia." *Antiquity* 72:858–866.

Crites, G. D. 1993. "Domesticated Sunflower in Fifth Millennium B.P. Temporal Context: New Evidence from Middle Tennessee." *American Antiquity* 58:146–148.

Davis, S., and F. R. Valla. 1978. "Evidence for Domestication of the Dog 12,000 Years Ago in the Natufian of Israel." *Nature* 276:608–410.

Delage, C., ed. 2004. *The Last Hunter-Gatherers in the Near East.* Oxford: British Archaeological Reports International Series 1320, Archaeopress.

Diamond, J. 1991. "The Worst Mistake in the History of the Human Race." In *Applying Cultural Anthropology*, ed. A. Podolefsky and P. J. Brown, pp. 72–75. Mountain View, CA: Mayfield Publishing.

———. 1997. *Guns, Germs, and Steel: The Fates of Human Societies.* New York: W. W. Norton & Company.

Diener, P., and E. E. Robkin. 1978. "Ecology, Evolution, and the Search for Cultural Origins: The Question of Islamic Pig Prohibition." *Current Anthropology* 19:493–540.

Doebley, J. F. 1990. "Molecular Evidence and the Evolution of Maize." In *New Perspectives on the Origin and Evolution of New World Domesticated Plants*, ed. P. K. Bretting. *Economic Botany* 44 (Supplement): 28–38.

Doebley, J. F., and H. H. Iltis. 1980. "Taxonomy of *Zea* [Gramineae]. I. A Subgeneric Classification with Key to Taxa." *American Journal of Botany* 67:982–993.

Dyson-Hudson, R., and N. Dyson-Hudson. 1980. "Nomadic Pastoralism." *Annual Review of Anthropology* 9:15–61.

Ekholm, G. F. 1964. "Transpacific Contacts." In *Prehistoric Man in the New World*, ed. J. D. Jennings and E. Norbeck. Chicago: University of Chicago Press.

Ellen, R. 1982. *Environment, Subsistence and System.* Cambridge, England: Cambridge University Press.

Feldman, M., and E. R. Sears. 1981. "The Wild Gene Resources of Wheat." *Scientific American* 244:102–113.

Fieldel, S. J. 1987. *Prehistory of the Americas.* Cambridge, England: Cambridge University Press.

Flannery, K. V. 1968. "Archeological Systems Theory and Early Mesoamerica." In *Anthropological Archeology in the Americas*, ed. B. J. Meggers. Washington, DC: The Anthropological Society of Washington.

————. 1972. "The Origins of the Village as a Settlement Type in Mesoamerica and the Near East: A Comparative Study." In *Man, Settlement and Urbanism*, ed. P. J. Ucko, R. Tringham, and G. W. Dimbleby. London: Duckworth.

————. 1973. "The Origins of Agriculture." *Annual Review of Anthropology* 2:271–310.

————. 1997. "In Defense of the Tehuacán Project." *Current Anthropology* 38(4):660–672.

Flannery, K. V., and M. D. Coe. 1968. "Social and Economic Systems in Formative Mesoamerica." In *New Perspectives in Archeology*, ed. S. R. Binford and L. R. Binford. Chicago: Aldine.

Friedman, J. 1974. "Marxism, Structuralism, and Vulgar Materialism." *Man* 9:444–469.

Frisch, R., and J. McArthur. 1974. "Menstrual Cycles: Fatness as a Determinant of Minimum Weight for Height Necessary for Their Maintenance or Onset." *Science* 185:949–951.

Frison, G. C. 1978. *Prehistoric Hunters on the High Plains*. New York: Academic Press.

Fritz, G. J. 1994. "Are the First American Farmers Getting Younger?" *Current Anthropology* 35(3):305–309.

Galinat, W. C. 1971. "The Origin of Maize." *Annual Review of Genetics* 5:447–478.

————. 1985. "The Missing Links Between Teosinte and Maize: A Review." *Maydica* 30:137–160.

Garrod, D. 1957. "The Natufian Culture. The Life and Economy of a Mesolithic People in the Near East." *Proceedings of the British Academy* 43:211–217.

Gebauer, A., and T. D. Price, eds. 1992. *Transitions to Agriculture in Prehistory*. Madison, WI: Prehistory Press.

Gould, S. J. 1985. *The Flamingo's Smile*. New York: W. W. Norton.

Grigson, C. 1993. "The Earliest Domestic Horses in the Levant." *Journal of Archaeological Science* 20(6):645–655.

Grun, P. 1990. "The Evolution of Cultivated Potatoes." In *New Perspectives on the Origin and Evolution of New World Domesticated Plants*, ed. P. K. Bretting. *Economic Botany* 44 (Supplement): 28–38.

Haaland, R. 1987. *Socio-Economic Differentiation in Neolithic Sudan*. Oxford, England: British Archaeological Reports, International Series 350.

Halperin, R. 1980. "Ecology and Mode of Production: Seasonal Variation and the Division of Labor by Sex among Hunter-Gatherers." *Journal of Anthropological Research* 36:379–399.

Harlan, J. R. 1967. "A Wild Wheat Harvest in Turkey." *Archaeology* 20:197–201.

————. 1989. "The Tropical African Cereals." In *Foraging and Farming: The Evolution of Plant Exploitation*, ed. D. R. Harris and G. C. Hillman. London: Unwin Hyman.

————. 1992. "Indigenous African Agriculture." In *The Origins of Agriculture: An International Perspective*, ed. C. Cowan and P. Watson. Washington, DC: Smithsonian Institution Press.

Harlan, J., and D. Zohary. 1966. "Distribution of Wild Wheats and Barley." *Science* 153:1074–1080.

Harner, M. 1970. "Population Pressure and the Social Evolution of Agriculturalists." *Southwestern Journal of Anthropology* 26:67–86.

Harpending, H., and H. Davis. 1976. "Some Implications for Hunter-Gatherer Ecology Derived from the Spatial Structure of Resources." *World Archaeology* 8:275–286.

Harris, D., and G. Hillman, eds. 1989. *Farming and Foraging*. Oxford: Clarendon Press.

Harris, M. 1974. *Cows, Pigs, Wars, and Witches*. New York: Random House.

————. 1977. *Cannibals and Kings*. New York: Random House.

Hassan, F. A. 1980. *Demographic Archaeology*. New York: Academic Press.

Hayden, B. 1981. "Research and Development in the Stone Age: Technological Transitions Among Hunter-Gatherers." *Current Anthropology* 22:519–548.

————. 1990. "Nimrods, Piscators, Pluckers, and Planters: The Emergence of Food Production." *Journal of Anthropological Archaeology* 9:31–69.

————. 2001. "Fabulous Feasts: A Prolegomenon to the Importance of Feasting." In *Feasts: Archaeological and Ethnographic Perspectives on Food, Politics, and Power*, ed. M. Dietler and B. Hayden, pp. 23–64. Washington, DC: Smithsonian Institution Press.

————. 2004. "Sociopolitical Organization in the Natufian: A View from the Northwest." In *The Last Hunter-Gatherers in the Near East*, ed. C. Delage, pp. 263–308. Oxford: Archaeopress, British Archaeological Reports International Series 1320.

Helback, H. 1964. "First Impressions of the Çatal Huyuk Plant Husbandry." *Anatolian Studies* 14:121–123.

Henry, D. 1989. *From Foraging to Agriculture: The Levant at the End of the Ice Age*. Philadelphia: University of Pennsylvania Press.

Higham, C., and T. L.-D. Lu. 1998. "The Origins and Dispersal of Rice Cultivation." *Antiquity* 72:867–877.

Hillman, G., and M. S. Davies. 1990. "Measured Domestication Rates in Wild Wheats and Barley Under Primitive Cultivation, and Their Archaeological Implications." *Journal of World Prehistory* 4:157–222.

Ho, P. 1969. "The Loess and the Origin of Chinese Agriculture." *American Historical Review* 75:1–36.

Hodder, I. 1990. *The Domestication of Europe: Structure and Contingency in Neolithic Societies*. Cambridge, MA: Blackwell.

Hole, F. 1971. "Comment on 'Origins of Food Production in Southwestern Asia' by G. Wright." *Current Anthropology* 12:472–473.

————. 1984. "A Reassessment of the Neolithic Revolution." *Paléorient* 10:49–60.

Hole, F., K. V. Flannery, and J. A. Neely. 1969. *Prehistory and Human Ecology of the Deh Luran Plain*. Ann Arbor: Memoirs of the Museum of Anthropology, University of Michigan, No. 1.

Iltis, H. 1983. "From Teosinte to Maize: The Catastrophic Sexual Mutation." *Science* 222:886–894.

———. 1987. "Maize Evolution and Agricultural Origins." In *Grass Systematics and Evolution*, ed. T. R. Soderstrom, K. W. Hilu, C. S. Campbell, and M. E. Barkworth. Washington, DC: Smithsonian Institution Press.

Johannessen, C. L. 1988. "Indian Maize in the Twelfth Century B.C." *Nature* 332:587.

Johnson, F., ed. 1972. *The Prehistory of the Tehuacan Valley*, Vol. 4. Austin: University of Texas Press.

Just, P. 1980. "Time and Leisure in the Elaboration of Culture." *Journal of Anthropological Research* 36:105–115.

Kaufman, D. 1986. "A Reconsideration of Adaptive Change in the Levantine Epipaleolithic." In *The End of the Paleolithic in the Old World*, ed. L. G. Straus. Oxford: British Archaeological Reports International Series 284.

Keene, A. S. 1981. "Optimal Foraging in a Nonmarginal Environment: A Model of Prehistoric Subsistence Strategies in Michigan." In *Hunter-Gatherer Foraging Strategies*, ed. B. Winterhalder and E. A. Smith. Chicago: University of Chicago Press.

Kelly, R. L. 1992. "Mobility/Sedentism: Concepts, Archaeological Measures, and Effects." *Annual Review of Anthropology* 21:43–66.

Kirkbride, D. 1968. "Beidha: Early Neolithic Village Life South of the Dead Sea." *Antiquity* 42:263–274.

Kirkby, A. 1973. *The Use of Land and Water Resources in the Past and Present Valley of Oaxaca, Mexico*. Memoirs of the Museum of Anthropology, University of Michigan, No. 5.

Kislev, M. E., and O. Bar-Yosef. 1988. "The Legumes: The Earliest Domesticated Plants in the Near East?" *Current Anthropology* 29(1):175–178.

Kislev, M. E., D. Nadel, and I. Carmi. 1992. "Epipalaeolithic (19,000 BP) Cereal and Fruit Diet at Ohalo II, Sea of Galilee, Israel." *Review of Palaeobotany and Palynology* 73:161–166.

Köhler-Rollefson, I. 1989. "Changes in Goat Exploitation at 'Ain Ghazal between the Early and Late Neolithic: A Metrical Analysis." *Paléorient* 15(1):141–146.

Kuijt, I., ed. 2000. *Life in Neolithic Farming Communities: Social Organization, Identity, and Differentiation*. New York: Plenum.

Lange, F. W. 1971. "Marine Resources: A Viable Subsistence Alternative for the Prehistoric Lowland Maya." *American Antiquity* 73:619–639.

Legge, A. J., and P. A. Rowley-Conwy. 1987. "Gazelle Hunting in Stone Age Syria." *Scientific American* (August): 88–95.

Lippe, R. N., R. M. Bird, and D. M. Stemper. 1984. "Maize Recovered at La Ponga, an Early Ecuadorian Site." *American Antiquity* 49(1):118–124.

Lynch, T. F. 1980. *Guitarrero Cave: Early Man in the Andes*. New York: Academic Press.

MacNeish, R. S. 1983. "Mesoamerica." In *Early Man in the New World*, ed. R. Shutler, Jr. Beverly Hills, CA: Sage Publications.

———. gen. ed. 1970. *The Prehistory of the Tehuacan Valley: Chronology and Irrigation*, Vol. 4. Austin: University of Texas Press.

Mangelsdorf, P. 1974. *Corn: Its Origin, Evolution, and Improvement*. Cambridge, MA: Harvard University Press.

———. 1983. "The Mystery of Corn: New Perspectives." *Proceedings of the American Philosophical Society* 127(4):215–247.

Martin, L. 2000. "Gazelle (*Gazella* spp.) Behavioural Ecology: Predicting Animal Behaviour for Prehistoric Environments in South-West Asia." *Journal of Zoology London* 250.13–30.

McClung de Tapia, E. 1992. "Origins of Agriculture in Mesoamerica and Central America." In *Origins of Agriculture: An International Perspective*, ed. C. W. Cowan and P. J. Watson, pp. 143–171. Washington, DC: Smithsonian Institution Press.

McCorriston, J., and F. Hole. 1991. "The Ecology of Seasonal Stress and the Origins of Agriculture in the Near East." *American Anthropologist* 93:46–69.

Meggers, B. 1975. "The Transpacific Origins of Mesoamerican Civilization: A Preliminary Review of the Evidence and Its Theoretical Implications." *American Anthropologist* 77:1–27.

Mellaart, J. 1975. *The Neolithic of the Near East*. London: Thames and Hudson.

Milisauskas, S., and J. Kruk. 1989. "Neolithic Economy in Central Europe." *Journal of World Prehistory* 2(3):403–446.

Miller, N. 1996. "Seed Eaters of the Ancient Near East: Human or Herbivore?" *Current Anthropology* 37(3):521–528.

Molleson, T. 1989. "Seed Preparation in the Neolithic: The Osteological Evidence." *Antiquity* 63(239):356–362.

Moore, A. M. T., and G. C. Hillman. 1992. "The Pleistocene to Holocene Transition and Human Economy in Southwest Asia: The Impact of the Younger Dryas." *American Antiquity* 57(3):482–494.

Moore, A. M. T., G. C. Hillman, and A. J. Legge. 2000. *Village on the Eyphrates: From Foraging to Farming at Abu Hureyra*. New York: Oxford University Press.

Mortensen, P. 1972. "Seasonal Camps and Early Villages in the Zagros." In *Man, Settlement and Urbanism*, ed. P. Ucko, R. Tringham, and G. W. Dimbleby. London: Duckworth.

Munchaev, R. M., and N. Y. Merpert. 1971. *New Studies of Early Agricultural Settlements in the Sinjar Valley*. Belgrade: VIII Congress International des Sciences Prehistoriques et Protohistoriques.

Nadel, D. 1995. "The Organization of Space in a Fisher-Hunter-Gatherers Camp at Ohalo II, Israel." In *Nature et Culture*, ed. M. Otte, pp. 373–388. Liège: E.R.A.U.L. 68.

Nesbitt, M. 2002. "When and Where Did Domesticated Cereals First Occur in Southwest Asia?" In *The Dawn of Farming in the Near East*, ed. R. Cappers and S. Bottema, pp. 113–132. Studies in Early Near Eastern Production, Subsistence, and Environment 6. Berlin: *ex oriente*.

Olsen, S. 1985. *Origins of the Domestic Dog*. Tucson: University of Arizona Press.

Olszewski, D. I. 1993. "Subsistence Ecology in the Mediterranean Forest; Implications for the Origins of Cultivation in the Epipaleolithic Southern Levant. *American Anthropologist* 95(2):420–435.

———. 2004. "Plant Food Subsistence Issues and Scientific Inquiry in the Early Natufian." In *The Last Hunter-Gatherers in the Near East*, ed. C. Delage, pp. 189–209. Oxford: British Archaeological Reports International Series 1320, Archaeopress.

Pearsall, D. M. 1992. "The Origins of Plant Cultivation in South America." In *The Origins of Agriculture*, ed. C. W. Cowan and P. J. Watson. Washington, DC: Smithsonian Institution Press.

Pearsall, D. M., and D. R. Piperno. 1990. "Antiquity of Maize Cultivation in Ecuador: Summary and Reevaluation of the Evidence." *American Antiquity* 55:324–337.

Perkins, D., Jr., and P. Daly. 1968. "A Hunter's Village in Neolithic Turkey." *Scientific American* 210:94–105.

Piperno, D. R. and D. M. Pearsall. 1998. *The Origins of Agriculture in the Lowland Neotropics*. New York: Academic Press.

Price, T. D. 1987. "The Mesolithic of Western Europe." *Journal of World Prehistory* 1(3):225–305.

Price, T. D., and A. B. Gebauer, eds. 1995. *Last Hunters First Farmers*. Santa Fe, NM: School of American Research.

Pryor, F. L. 1986. "The Adoption of Agriculture: Some Theoretical and Empirical Evidence." *American Anthropologist* 88(4):879–897.

Pumpelly, R. 1908. *Explorations in Turkey, the Expedition of 1904: Prehistoric Civilization of Anau*. Vol. 1. Washington, DC: Publications of the Carnegie Institution, No. 73.

Redding, R. W. 1988. "A General Explanation of Subsistence Change: From Hunting and Gathering to Food Production." *Journal of Anthropological Archaeology* 7:59–97.

Renfrew, C. 1987. *Archaeology and Language*. London: Jonathan Cape.

Reynolds, R. G. 1986. "An Adaptive Computer Model for the Evolution of Plant Collecting and Early Agriculture in the Eastern Valley of Oaxaca." In *Guilá Naquitz: Archaic Foraging and Early Agriculture in Oaxaca, Mexico*, ed. K. Flannery. New York: Academic Press.

Richards, M. 2003. "The Neolithic Invasion of Europe." *Annual Review of Anthropology* 32:135–162.

Richerson, P. J., R. Boyd, and R. L. Bettinger. 2001. "Was Agriculture Impossible During the Pleistocene but Mandatory During the Holocene? A Climate Change Hypothesis." *American Antiquity* 66(3):387–411.

Rick, J. W. 1980. *Prehistoric Hunters of the High Andes*. New York: Academic Press.

Rindos, D. 1980. "Symbiosis, Instability, and the Origins and Spread of Agriculture: A New Model." *Current Anthropology* 21:751–772.

———. 1984. *The Origins of Agriculture: An Evolutionary Perspective*. New York: Academic Press.

Rollefson, G. O. 1983. "Ritual and Ceremony at Neolithic Ain Ghazal (Jordan)." *Paléorient* 9(2):29–38.

———. 1986. "Neolithic Ain Ghazal (Jordan): Ritual and Ceremony II." *Paléorient* 12(1):45–52.

Roosevelt, A. 1980. *Parmana. Prehistoric Maize and Manioc Subsistence along the Amazon and Orinoco*. New York: Academic Press.

Rosen, S. A. 1988. "Notes on the Origins of Pastoral Nomadism: A Case Study from the Negev and Sinai." *Current Anthropology* 29(3):498–506.

Rosenberg, M. 1990. "The Mother of Invention: Evolutionary Theory, Territoriality, and the Origins of Agriculture." *American Anthropologist* 92(2):498–506.

Rosenberg, M., and M. K. Davis. 1992. "Hallan Çemi Tepesi, An Early Aceramic Neolithic Site in Eastern Anatolia." *Anatolica* VXIII:1–18.

Sahlins, M. 1976. *Culture and Practical Reason*. Chicago: University of Chicago Press.

Simmons, A. H., I. Köhler-Rollefson, G. O. Rollefson, R. Mandel, and Z. Kafafi. 1988. "'Ain Ghazal: A Major Neolithic Settlement in Central Jordan." *Science* 240:35–39.

Smith, B. D. 1994. "The Origins of Agriculture in the Americas." *Evolutionary Anthropology* 3(5):174–184.

———. 1997. "Reconsidering the Ocampo Caves and the Era of Incipient Cultivation in Mesoamerica." *Latin American Antiquity* 8(4):342–383.

Smith, P. E. L. 1967. "New Investigations in the Late Pleistocene Archaeology of the Kom Ombo Plain (Upper Egypt)." *Quaternaria* 9:141–152.

———. 1972. "Ganj Dareh Tepe." *Iran* 10:165–168.

————. 1976. "Early Food Productions in Northern Africa as Seen from Southwestern Asia." In *Origins of African Plant Domestication*, ed. J. R. Harlan, J. M. J. de Wet, and A. Stemler. The Hague: Mouton.

Solecki, R. L. 1981. "An Early Village Site at Zawi Chemi Shanidar." *Bibliotheca Mesopotamica*. Vol. 13.

Solecki, R. S., and R. L. Solecki. 1980. "Paleoecology of the Negev." *Quarterly Review of Archaeology* 1:8, 12.

Spuhler, J. 1985. "Anthropology, Evolution, and 'Scientific Creationism.'" *Annual Review of Anthropology* 14:103–133.

Stark, B., and B. Voorhies, eds. 1978. *Prehistoric Coastal Adaptations: The Economy and Ecology of Maritime Middle America*. New York: Academic Press.

Stothert, K. E. 1985. "The Preceramic Las Vegas Culture of Coastal Ecuador." *American Antiquity* 50(3):613–637.

Takamiya, H. 2001. "Introductory Routes of Rice to Japan: An Examination of the Southern Route Hypothesis." *Asian Perspectives* 40(2):209–226.

Tauber, H. 1981. "13C Evidence for Dietary Habits of Prehistoric Man in Denmark." *Nature* 292:332–333.

Testart, A. 1982. "The Significance of Food Storage Among Hunter-Gatherers: Residence Patterns, Population Densities, and Social Inequalities." *Current Anthropology* 23(5):523–527.

Thorpe, I. J. 1996. *The Origins of Agriculture in Europe*. New York: Routledge.

Tringham, R., D. Drstić, T. Kaiser, and B. Voytek. 1980. "The Early Agricultural Site of Selevac, Yugoslavia." *Archaeology* 33(2):24–32.

Turnball, P. F., and C. A. Reed. 1974. "The Fauna from the Terminal Pleistocene of Palegawra Cave." *Fieldiana* (Chicago Field Museum of Natural History) 63(3):81–146.

Ugent, D., S. Pozorski, and T. Pozorski. 1984. "New Evidence for Ancient Cultivation of *Canna edulis* in Peru." *Economic Botany* 38(4):417–432.

Unger-Hamilton, R. 1989. "The Epi-Palaeolithic Southern Levant and the Origins of Cultivation." *Current Anthropology* 30:88–103.

Upham, S., et al. 1987. "Evidence Concerning the Origin of Maize de Ocho." *American Anthropologist* 89(3):410–419.

Valla, F. 1988. "Les premiers sédentaires de Palestine." *La Recherché* 19:576–584.

Van Zeist, W., and J. A. H. Bakker Heeres. 1986. "Archaeobotanical Studies in the Levant. Late Paleolitic Mureybit." *Palaeohistoria* 26:171–199.

Webster, G. S. 1986. "Optimization Theory and Pre-Columbian Hunting in the Tehuacan Valley." *Human Ecology* 14(4):415–435.

Wenke, R. J., J. E. Long, and P. E. Buck. 1988. "Epipaleolithic and Neolithic Subsistence and Settlement in the Fayyum Oasis of Egypt." *Journal of Field Archaeology* 15(1):29–51.

Wilcox, G. 2002. "Geographical Variation in Major Cereal Components and Evidence for Independent Domestication Events in Western Asia." In *The Dawn of Farming in the Near East*, ed. R. Cappers and S. Bottema, pp. 133–140. Studies in Early Near Eastern Production, Subsistence, and Environment 6. Berlin: *ex oriente*.

Wills, W. T. 1992. "Plant Cultivation and the Evolution of Risk-Prone Economies in the Prehistoric American Southwest." In *Transitions to Agriculture in Prehistory*, ed. A. B. Gebauer and T. D. Price. Madison: Prehistory Press.

Winterhalder, B., and E. A. Smith, eds. 1981. *Hunter-Gatherer Foraging Strategies*. Chicago: University of Chicago Press.

Wright, G. 1971. "Origins of Food Production in Southwestern Asia: A Survey of Ideas." *Current Anthropology* 12:447–477.

Wright, H. T. 1993. "Environmental Determinism in Near Eastern Prehistory." *Current Anthropology* 12:447–478.

Zeder, M., and B. Hesse. 2000. "The Initial Domestication of Goats (*Capra hircus*) in the Zagros Mountains 10,000 Years Ago." *Science* 287:2254–2257.

Zevallos, M. C., W. C. Galinat, D. W. Lathrup, E. R. Leng, J. G. Marcos, and K. M. Klumpp. 1977. "The San Pablo Corn Kernel and Its Friends." *Science* 196:385–389.

Zohary, D. 1989. "Pulse Domestication and Cereal Domestication: How Different Are They?" *Economic Botany* 43:31–34.

Zohary, D., and M. Hopf. 1988. *Domestication of Plants in the Old World*. Oxford: Oxford University Press.

NOTES

1. Kelly, "Mobility/Sedentism: Concepts, Archaeological Measures, and Effects," p. 60.
2. For detailed recent reviews of agricultural origins around the world, see Cowan and Watson, eds., *The Origins of Agriculture: An International Perspective*.
3. Blumler and Byrne, "The Ecological Genetics of Domestication and the Origins of Agriculture," p. 24.
4. Price, "The Mesolithic of Western Europe."

5. R. C. Dunnell is among the first we know to use this definition.
6. Blumler and Byrne, "The Ecological Genetics of Domestication and the Origins of Agriculture," p. 24.
7. Rindos, *The Origins of Agriculture*, p. 143.
8. Blumler and Byrne, "The Ecological Genetics of Domestication and the Origins of Agriculture," p. 24.
9. Rindos, "Symbiosis, Instability, and the Origins and Spread of Agriculture: A New Model," p. 754.
10. Cohen and Armelagos, eds., *Paleopathology at the Origins of Agriculture*.
11. Blumler and Byrne, "The Ecological Genetics of Domestication and the Origins of Agriculture."
12. Rindos, *The Origins of Agriculture*.
13. Others, e.g., Blumler and Byrne, "The Ecological Genetics of Domestication and the Origins of Agriculture," disagree; Rosenberg, "The Mother of Invention: Evolutionary Theory, Territoriality, and the Origins of Agriculture."
14. Tauber, "13C Evidence for Dietary Habits of Prehistoric Man in Denmark."
15. See, e.g., Price and Gebauer, eds., *Last Hunters First Farmers*; Harris and Hillman, *Farming and Foraging*.
16. Childe, *New Light on the Most Ancient East*.
17. Pumpelly, *Explorations in Turkey, the Expedition of 1904: Prehistoric Civilization of Anau*, pp. 65–66; Childe, *New Light on the Most Ancient East*.
18. McCorriston and Hole, "The Ecology of Seasonal Stress and the Origins of Agriculture in the Near East"; Moore and Hillman, "The Pleistocene to Holocene Transition and Human Economy in Southwest Asia: The Impact of the Younger Dryas."
19. Braidwood, "The Agriculture Revolution."
20. See Hole, Flannery, and Neely, *Prehistory and Human Ecology of the Deh Luran Plain*; see also Hole, "Comment on 'Origins of Food Production in Southwestern Asia' by G. Wright."
21. Harlan and Zohary, "Distribution of Wild Wheats and Barley."
22. Cohen, *The Food Crisis in Prehistory*, p. 279.
23. Harris, *Cannibals and Kings*; Harris, *Cultural Materialism*.
24. Harris, *Cows, Pigs, Wars, and Witches*.
25. See, for example, Friedman, "Marxism, Structuralism, and Vulgar Materialism"; Sahlins, *Culture and Practical Reason*.
26. Hayden, "Research and Development in the Stone Age: Technological Transitions Among Hunter-Gatherers."
27. Ibid., p. 530.
28. McCorriston and Hole, "The Ecology of Seasonal Stress and the Origins of Agriculture in the Near East."
29. Moore and Hillman, "The Pleistocene to Holocene Transition and Human Economy in Southwest Asia: The Impact of the Younger Dryas."
30. Henry, *From Foraging to Agriculture: The Levant at the End of the Ice Age*; McCorriston and Hole, "The Ecology of Seasonal Stress and the Origins of Agriculture in the Near East"; Moore and Hillman, "The Pleistocene to Holocene Transition and Human Economy in Southwest Asia: The Impact of the Younger Dryas."
31. Byrd, "The Natufian: Settlement Variability and Economic Adaptations in the Levant at the End of the Pleistocene," p. 170; McCorriston and Hole, "The Ecology of Seasonal Stress and the Origins of Agriculture in the Near East"; Moore and Hillman, "The Pleistocene to Holocene Transition and Human Economy in Southwest Asia: The Impact of the Younger Dryas."
32. Spuhler, "Anthropology, Evolution, and 'Scientific Creationism,'" p. 115.
33. McCorriston and Hole, "The Ecology of Seasonal Stress and the Origins of Agriculture in the Near East."
34. Moore and Hillman, "The Pleistocene to Holocene Transition and Human Economy in Southwest Asia: The Impact of the Younger Dryas."
35. "Was Agriculture Impossible During the Pleistocene but Mandatory During the Holocene? A Climate Change Hypothesis."
36. Ibid., p. 387.
37. There are a few well-known exceptions, such as the "Little Ice Age" that occurred between A.D. 1300 and 1850.
38. "Was Agriculture Impossible During the Pleistocene but Mandatory During the Holocene? A Climate Change Hypothesis," p. 404.
39. Ibid.
40. Bender, "Emergent Tribal Formations in the American Midcontinent."
41. See, for example, "Sociopolitical Organization in the Natufian: A View from the Northwest"; "Fabulous Feasts: A Prolegomenon to the Importance of Feasting"; "Nimrods, Piscators, Pluckers, and Planters: The Emergence of Food Production."
42. Hodder, *The Domestication of Europe*.
43. As Boyd points out, however, this opposition of nature and culture is a Western concept that comes from the Renaissance ("Agency and Landscape: Abandoning the 'Nature/Culture' Dichotomy in Interpretations

of the Natufian and the Transition to the Neolithic," p. 119). How valid is it to apply a modern Western idea to ancient people's ways of conceptualizing the world around them?

44. Hodder, *The Domestication of Europe*, p. 41.
45. Ibid.
46. Frison, *Prehistoric Hunters on the High Plains*.
47. Barnard, "Contemporary Hunter-Gatherers."
48. Ellen, *Environment, Subsistence and System*.
49. Testart, "The Significance of Food Storage Among Hunter-Gatherers," p. 530.
50. Flannery, "The Origins of Agriculture," p. 307.
51. See, for example, Frisch and McArthur, "Menstrual Cycles: Fatness as a Determinant of Minimum Weight for Height Necessary for Their Maintenance or Onset."
52. Harris, *Cannibals and Kings*.
53. Kislev and Bar-Yosef, "The Legumes: The Earliest Domesticated Plants in the Near East?"
54. Henry, *From Foraging to Agriculture. The Levant at the End of the Ice Age*; Bar-Yosef and Belfer-Cohen, "From Foraging to Farming in the Mediterranean Levant"; Aurenche et al., "Proto-Neolithic and Neolithic Cultures in the Middle East—The Birth of Agriculture, Livestock Raising, and Ceramics: A Calibrated ^{14}C Chronology 12,500–5500 cal BC."
55. Nadel, "The Organization of Space in a Fisher-Hunter-Gatherers Camp at Ohalo II, Israel"; Kislev et al., "Epipalaeolithic (19,000 BP) Cereal and Fruit Diet at Ohalo II, Sea of Galilee, Israel."
56. Kislev et al., "Epipalaeolithic (19,000 BP) Cereal and Fruit Diet at Ohalo II, Sea of Galilee, Israel," p. 162.
57. Binford, "Post-Pleistocene Adaptations"; Flannery, "The Origins of Agriculture"; Hayden, "Research and Development in the Stone Age: Technological Transitions Among Hunter-Gatherers."
58. Henry, *From Foraging to Agriculture: The Levant at the End of the Ice Age*, pp. 29–30.
59. Legge and Rowley-Conwy, "Gazelle Hunting in Stone Age Syria," although it should be noted that not all researchers agree with this perspective; see, for example, Martin, "Gazelle (*Gazella* spp.) Behavioural Ecology: Predicting Animal Behaviour for Prehistoric Environments in South-West Asia."
60. Belfer-Cohen, "The Natufian in the Levant," p. 169.
61. Whether Natufians specialized in wild cereals is a matter of some debate. There is growing evidence that the cost-benefit ratio is higher for gathering/processing acorns, a wild food resource widely available in the Mediterranean forest, compared with wild cereals. See, for example, Barlow and Heck, "More on Acorn Eating During the Natufian: Expected Patterning in Diet and the Archaeological Record of Subsistence"; Olszewski, "Plant Food Subsistence Issues and Scientific Inquiry in the Early Natufian."
62. Belfer-Cohen, "The Natufian in the Levant," p. 171.
63. Valla, "Les premiers sédentaires de Palestine," p. 583.
64. Hillman and Davies, "Measured Domestication Rates in Wild Wheats and Barley Under Primitive Cultivation, and Their Archaeological Implications."
65. Olsen, *Origins of the Domestic Dog*.
66. Perkins and Daly, "A Hunter's Village in Neolithic Turkey."
67. Wright, "Origins of Food Production in Southwestern Asia: A Survey of Ideas," p. 463; see also Solecki, "An Early Village Site at Zawi Chemi Shanidar."
68. Zeder and Hesse, "The Initial Domestication of Goats (*Capra hircus*) in the Zagros Mountains 10,000 Years Ago," p. 2256.
69. Hillman in Moore et al., *Village on the Euphrates*, pp. 349–398.
70. Rosen, "Notes on the Origins of Pastoral Nomadism: A Case Study from the Negev and Sinai," p. 504; see also Köhler-Rollefson, "Changes in Goat Exploitation at 'Ain Ghazal Between the Early and Late Neolithic: A Metrical Analysis."
71. Flannery, "The Origins of the Village as a Settlement Type in Mesoamerica and the Near East: A Comparative Study."
72. Ibid., p. 48.
73. Byrd, "Public and Private, Domestic and Corporate; The Emergence of the Southwest Asian Village."
74. Ibid., p. 658.
75. Hole, "Comment on 'Origins of Food Production in Southwestern Asia' by G. Wright," p. 473.
76. Simmons et al., "'Ain Ghazal: A Major Neolithic Settlement in Central Jordan."
77. Grigson, "The Earliest Domestic Horses in the Levant."
78. Ammerman and Cavalli-Sforza, *The Neolithic Transition and the Genetics of Population in Europe*.
79. Renfrew, *Archaeology and Language*.
80. Harlan, "Indigenous African Agriculture"; Wenke et al., "Epipaleolithic and Neolithic Subsistence and Settlement in the Fayyum Oasis of Egypt."
81. Haaland, *Socio-Economic Differentiation in Neolithic Sudan*.
82. Crawford and Shen, "The Origins of Rice Agriculture: Recent Progress in East Asia"; Higham and Lu, "The Origins and Dispersal of Rice Cultivation."

83. Higham and Lu, "The Origins and Dispersal of Rice Cultivation," p. 870.
84. Bellwood, *The Prehistory of the Indo-Malaysian Archipelago*.
85. Akazawa and Aikens, *Prehistoric Hunter-Gatherers in Japan*; Takamiya, "Introductory Routes of Rice to Japan: An Examination of the Southern Route Hypothesis."
86. Flannery, "Archeological Systems Theory and Early Mesoamerica."
87. Webster, "Optimization Theory and Pre-Columbian Hunting in the Tehuacan Valley."
88. Reynolds, "An Adaptive Computer Model for the Evolution of Plant Collecting and Early Agriculture in the Eastern Valley of Oaxaca."
89. Johannessen, "Indian Maize in the Twelfth Century B.C."
90. Recent radiocarbon dates for the Ocampo caves in Tamaulipas show that this area—compared to the evidence from Tehuacan and Oaxaca—was peripheral to the development of agriculture in Mexico. The Ocampo caves are relatively late, dating to between 5,500 to 5,200 years ago. See Smith, "Reconsidering the Ocampo Caves and the Era of Incipient Cultivation in Mesoamerica."
91. Fritz, "Are the First American Farmers Getting Younger?" see, however, Flannery, "In Defense of the Tehuacán Project," who states that the only dates for maize that are getting younger are AMS dates for samples contaminated with a preservative. Flannery purposes that original estimates for early maize are correct.
92. Ibid.
93. Mangelsdorf, *Corn: Its Origin, Evolution, and Improvement*.
94. Fritz, "Are the First American Farmers Getting Younger?" p. 306.
95. See MacNeish, *The Prehistory of the Tehuacan Valley: Chronology and Irrigation*; McClung de Tapia, *The Origins of Agriculture in Mesoamerica and Central America*, pp. 157–158.
96. All of these period dates are now somewhat suspect because of recent AMS dates on these materials (see Fritz, "Are the First American Farmers Getting Younger?"), but additional research will be required to determine if just the botanical remains are mixed or if other occupational debris are mixed as well.
97. Beadle, "The Mystery of Maize"; Beadle, "The Ancestry of Corn."
98. Flannery, "The Origins of Agriculture."
99. See, for example, Galinat, "The Origin of Maize"; but cf. Mangelsdorf, "The Mystery of Corn: New Perspectives."
100. McClung de Tapia, *The Origins of Agriculture in Mesoamerica and Central America*, pp. 148–149.
101. Gould, *The Flamingo's Smile*.
102. Iltis, "From Teosinte to Maize: The Catastrophic Sexual Mutation."
103. Flannery, "The Origins of Agriculture," p. 300.
104. McClung de Tapia, *The Origins of Agriculture in Mesoamerica and Central America*, p. 154.
105. Flannery and Coe, "Social and Economic Systems in Formative Mesoamerica"; Stark and Voorhies, *Prehistorical Coastal Adaptations: The Economy and Ecology of Maritime Middle America*.
106. Stark and Voorhies, *Prehistoric Coastal Adaptations: The Economy and Ecology of Maritime Middle America*; Fiedel, *Prehistory of the Americas*, pp. 160–184.
107. Stothert, "The Preceramic Las Vegas Culture of Coastal Ecuador"; Lippi, Bird, and Stemper, "Maize Recovered at La Ponga, an Early Ecuadorian Site"; Pearsall and Piperno, "Antiquity of Maize Cultivation in Ecuador: Summary and Reevaluation of the Evidence." There are also arguments that the Peruvian evidence is "not good" due to disturbed contexts, shallow deposits, and other factors (see Bird, "What Are the Chances of Finding Maize in Peru Dating Before 1000 B.C.?: Reply to Bonavia and Grobman").
108. Pearsall, "The Origins of Plant Cultivation in South America," p. 192.
109. Lynch, *Guitarrero Cave: Early Man in the Andes*; Flannery, "The Origins of Agriculture," p. 303.
110. Ugent et al., "New Evidence for Ancient Cultivation of *Canna edulis* in Peru."
111. Reviewed in Pearsall, "The Origins of Plant Cultivation in South America," p. 190.
112. Rick, *Prehistoric Hunters of the High Andes*.
113. Pearsall, "The Origins of Plant Cultivation in South America."
114. "The Worst Mistake in the History of the Human Race," p. 75.

The Evolution of Complex Societies

I should like to see, and this will be the last and
most ardent of my desires, I should like to see
the last king strangled with the guts of the last
priest.

J. Messelier (clause in a will, Paris, 1733)

M esselier's vengeful wish was prompted by his feelings of exploitation as a citizen of France during the last period of its monarchy, when France was dominated by oppressive elites and a venal clergy. Societies ruled and exploited by kings and priests have existed for thousands of years, and many of their citizens have echoed Messelier's complaints. In today's world, billions of people subsist on a tiny fraction of the goods and services that the most industrialized countries enjoy, and even within the richest states there are great inequalities.

Why have societies for thousands of years been organized in terms of social classes and economic inequalities? Are these inequities somehow the "natural" order of things? Will they ever be replaced by truly just and equitable societies? What has determined who was rich and powerful and who was poor and weak throughout history?

To answer such questions it is important to recognize that although exploitative political and religious elites have formed the very warp and woof of our concept of "civilization," they are just one of many elements in our sense of "civilization," or what anthropologists call "complex" societies. Scholars, predictably, disagree on exactly what social or cultural "complexity," or a "civilization," or a "state," is, particularly when these terms are applied to the bones, stones, and bricks of the archaeological record. When archaeologists speak of the first "complex" societies, however, most have in mind the kinds of changes we think happened first long ago, for example, in Mesopotamia, on the broad Tigris-Euphrates alluvial plains of what is now Iraq, Syria, and Iran. The evidence suggests that if you were a member of an ordinary community here at about 6000 B.C., you would have lived in a village of a few hundred people, most of whom were your blood relatives. You and almost everyone else in your community would have worked in the fields to produce the grain held in common stores for large extended families and the community as a whole. And if you were an older adult male you would have made most of the decisions for you and your family about every aspect of your life. People much like you and communities very like yours would be found in all directions from your home,

279

but your only contacts with them would have been minor trade in obsidian, flint, semi-precious stone, and a few other commodities, as well as the exchange of young men and women in marriage, and—probably—the occasional fight. For all practical purposes, you and your fellow villagers were on your own in terms of religion, manufacturing tools, defense, and food production; probably you and every other adult in town would know most of the skills necessary for survival; and your extended family—and every other extended family—probably could muster all the technological and social skills necessary for survival.

But if you lived in this same area—perhaps the same town—3,000 years later, at about 3000 B.C., you would have led a very different life. You could have been a slave or a king, depending on accidents of birth. Unlike your ancestors, who were almost all full-time farmers, you may have been a fisherman, potter, weaver, priest, or some other specialist. Unless you were among the elite, however, many of the decisions you made about your job and your life would have been out of your hands—the prerogative of royal administrators. You would have been taxed and expected to fight with the army in any of the numerous wars and revolutions you would have seen in your lifetime. As a farmer or any other semi-skilled or skilled worker, you would have been dependent for your continued existence and way of life on people with skills you yourself did not possess, such as potters, warriors, herdsmen, scribes, doctors, metalsmiths, sailors, and priests. Instead of a village of a few hundred people, you might have lived in a city of thousands, perhaps tens of thousands; you would probably have been a fervent believer in the national religion, and you would probably have been acutely aware of your social class, whether high or low. In these and many other ways, your society would have been "complex," at least in comparison to the simple, cooperative, communistic peasants of your ancient ancestry.

In summary then, when anthropologists speak of sociocultural *complexity*, they are generally ranking particular societies on a single scale but on the basis of several primary variables. For any given society these variables include (1) the degree of *differential access to wealth, power, and prestige*; (2) the extent to which differential access to wealth, power, and prestige are *inherited*, as opposed to earned; (3) the degree to which individuals in a community are *specialized* in their *occupations*, and the extent to which these different occupations are *integrated* and *organized* in the economy as a whole; and (4) the degree to which political power is *centralized* in a government.

The same kinds of changes in these variables that we have described here for Mesopotamia also happened—largely independently—in various other areas of the ancient world, in Egypt, the Indus Valley, China, Peru, Mesoamerica, and a few other places. Later they also occurred in many other times and places, especially in societies that were in contact with the earliest civilizations. By now the reader will not be at all surprised to learn that the question that has fascinated archaeologists for centuries is, *why*? Why did simple agriculturalists give way to socially more complex forms in these specific areas, and not in other areas? Why did our ancestors not remain simple farmers or revert to the ancient security of the hunting-foraging way of life? Why were these early civilizations so much alike in socioeconomic structures and political systems? Moreover, why was this transition so rapid and pervasive? Although complex societies have existed for only the last five or six millennia, they have almost completely replaced the simpler cultural forms in which our ancestors had lived for a million years or more. Today, in the Amazon Valley, the Kalahari Desert, and a few other places, hunting-and-gathering groups still follow some of their ancient ways, but if current trends continue, soon there will be no groups left in the world that resemble our Pleistocene ancestors in society and economy.

To answer all these various questions about the evolution of complex societies, and to understand why today almost all people of the world live in them, we must appeal to a wide range of evidence. Since all largely independent cases of the evolution of cultural complexity happened before any written languages had been developed, much of this analysis must be based on archaeological data. But in many areas of the world written languages were used later in these developmental sequences and these provide fascinating information about the early civilizations.

The fact that complex societies, like agricultural economies, evolved independently in the Old and New Worlds gives us the opportunity for *comparative analyses*. As we shall see, ancient Egypt, for example, had a language completely incomprehensible to the Aztecs, worshipped Gods unknown to the Aztecs, and lived in a riverine ecological system unimaginable to the Aztecs. Egyptian and Aztec culture histories were unique, different, unconnected. But for a century, the idea of a science of history has been based on the idea that the ancient Egyptians and Aztecs were fundamentally alike—that they can both be considered members of the same class of political entities, and that they could be analyzed and understood in the same terms.

Perhaps the most influential general attempt to categorize all cultures and explain their similarities and differences was that by Karl Marx (see later). But there have been scores of other attempts to analyze cultural differences and similarities. Bruce Trigger, for example, compiled a comparative analysis of the ancient civilizations of Egypt, Mesopotamia, China, Mesoamerica, and South America, as well as the early Yoruba state—all chosen because they were class-based societies in which power was derived from control of agricultural production and because there is relatively good archaeological, ethnographic, and textual data for each. In this context, Trigger has come to an interesting conclusion about the results of his many years of study of early civilizations:

> I expected to discover that, because of ecological constraints, the differences in economic systems [among early states] would be limited, and there would be more variation in sociopolitical organization, religious beliefs, and art styles. In fact, I have found that a wide variety of economic behavior was associated with early civilizations, the one constant being the production of surpluses that the upper classes appropriated through a tributary relationship. Yet I have been able to discover only one basic form of class hierarchy, two general forms of political organization, and a single basic religious paradigm. . . . I have documented significant variation from one early civilization to another only in terms of art styles and cultural values.[1]

Trigger's perceptive conclusion expresses clearly the fundamental issues in analyses of ancient civilizations. He sees, for example, extremely little variation among them except in art styles and cultural values. Thus we must ask, why were they so similar? It seems reasonable to assume, as Trigger does, that there is such little variation in some elements in these early civilizations because of these elements' relative "efficiency,"[2] and great variations in other elements because they have little effect on the adaptiveness and competitive success of the social organism of which they are a part. If so, then one aspect of an archaeological analysis can be an examination of the specific factors that may have determined the adaptiveness and efficiency of these cultural elements, and changes in these variables over time and space. This kind of investigation does not require that one ignore the great extent to which the unique and specific values, ideas, and concepts of these ancient civilizations formed the structure of these cultures and, in a sense, determined their history. Trigger suggests that we must examine both the similarities and differences in ancient cultures and try to understand and explain them using a variety of perspectives and methods (see later).

Today, however, the premise that a science of history can be developed on the basis of comparative analyses of cultures is under sustained attack.[3] Some scholars argue that the only similarities between, for example, Egypt and Mexico and others of their supposed class, such as the Sumerians, the Shang Chinese, and the Harappan of the Indus Valley, are simply the products of gross similarities in environments and technologies. They suggest that the more important focus of archaeological analysis should be the ways in which the people in these different cultures constructed different worlds and realities through the use of incommensurable cultural categories. Also, many scholars today are wary of the term "evolution" as applied to cultures because it implies that some cultures are "better," or more evolved, than others. For others, the difference in systems of trait-transmission between biological entities (sexual and asexual reproduction) and cultural systems (e.g., learning) makes any sense of evolution inapplicable to cultures. But other scholars have found Darwinian evolution to be applicable to cultural changes, if one divorces this sense of evolution from biological concepts and focuses on trait-transmission, not any particular *method* of trait-transmission.[4]

We shall examine this issue in detail later in this chapter, and in the remaining chapters, because it is fundamental to all that follows: Do the similarities and differences exhibited by various extinct cultures offer the raw material for some kind of "scientific" analysis of history, or do they simply represent gross analogies among societies that were intrinsically incommensurate and that can only be analyzed in terms of their unique histories and characteristics?

Another difficult issue here involves the obvious problems of trying to analyze the ideologies of extinct human groups on the basis of their material archaeological record. Karl Marx is just one of many scholars who over the millennia have tried to explain the rise of civilization in terms of environments, technologies, economies, and so forth. But can we understand the course of history from this perspective? The rise of Islam, for example, might seem to be a case where a powerful ideology spurred people, who previously had lived in simple tribal groups, to conquer huge areas of Asia and Europe. Is the spread of Islam to be understood as a result of the appearance of this unique inexplicable ideology, or is the ideology just a reflection of powerful underlying historical and economic forces? Similarly, the ancient Egyptian state seems to be something that we can only understand in terms of its national *ideology*: As we shall see in chapter 9, all the temples, tombs, and pyramids of Egypt are reflections of their principle of "divine kingship." Ancient Egyptian civilization was to a certain extent a product of the rich Nile Valley environment, but it was also a sociopolitical construct, an idea. But how does one analyze the power of ideas from the archaeological record, especially since most of Egyptian civilization formed long before the written language began recording its development?

Based on inferences from the archaeological record, ancient texts, and ethnography, one of the fundamental things that apparently all early complex societies evolved was a *coercive sociopolitical elite*—that is, a class of people who took most of the society's power, prestige, and wealth. And they apparently did so without regularly resorting to armed robbery or direct confiscation by their personal militias. These societies evolved *ideologies* that sanctioned this confiscatory behavior and monopolization of power.[5] In ancient Egypt, for example, the pharaoh was considered a manifestation of God, and therefore duly entitled to monopolize political power and much of the country's wealth. Ancient Egyptians might have whined about taxes, but they rarely if ever managed a revolution to dispossess the elites (nor did the Victorian British or many other modern peoples, for that matter). But how are we to study the origins and dynamics of the evolution of these all-important belief systems? We have some traces of this evolution in such things as differences in the wealth of individual burials, but these only indicate (possibly) that coercive sociopolitical elites existed, not how they came about or the ideological basis of their status.

Another issue in analyzing these early civilizations involves our assumptions about how similar they all were in terms of power relationships. It is important to recognize that not every society in history can be placed at some point on a continuum between a simple band of hunter-foragers and the dimensions of complexity described earlier and applied to, for example, ancient Mesopotamia. The term "heterarchy" has been applied by Carol Crumley[6] to aspects of social relationships in early states, particularly those, like ancient Greece, for example, where economic control by elites and many other social interactions were not entirely set within the context of rigid, bureaucratic, hierarchical, administrative institutions. In such cases the activities and interests of the elites do not entirely correspond to the activities and interests of the state. She suggests that states can include social structures that are heterarchical in the sense that elements in these structures are either unranked relative to other elements or possess the potential for being ranked in a number of different ways. In such situations she suggests that power is not ranked, it is "counterpoised."

The concept of heterarchy is linked to ideas about dialectical social relationships that are beyond the scope of this book, but we must assume that the social relationships of ancient societies cannot be fit exactly and simply into traditional notions about dominance and hierarchy.

Many scholars have explored these issues.[7] The development of evolutionary theory as applied to archaeological data remains, however, at a relatively primitive level. Major questions remain about how one can use concepts such as "scale of selection" in cultural analyses. One interesting current trend in these forms of evolutionary analyses involves non-systems analyses and the "emergent" properties of complex systems. The recent book *Complexity*[8] popularizes research done by physicists, biologists, anthropologists, and others on the processes whereby simple systems grow in complexity in an apparently Lamarckian way—able to direct the generation of variety that is then selected. Lansing and Kremer[9] have published one of the first applications of these ideas to an anthropological problem, the evolution of Balinese economic systems.

In part because of the limitations of functionalist explanations, in part because of the great power of modern evolutionary theory, there has been a revival of interest in applying the principles of biological evolution to cultural phenomena.[10] Many scholars argue that the modern theory of evolution has never really been applied to archaeological data. A key difficulty has always been that the objects of the archaeological record do not reproduce in the same way that people do, and thus the rules of genetics cannot be applied; also, whereas change in the biological world is through the relatively slow processes of genetic mutation, drift, selection, and so on, cultural changes can be conveyed quickly and pervasively from one group to another (as in the spread of agriculture).

So how might we apply evolutionary principles to archaeological problems? The answer is not at all clear, but there are a few interesting ideas. As Robert Dunnell has observed, what matters in evolutionary theory is not so much how a characteristic is transmitted—whether by genes or culture—as it is the mechanisms by which traits are perpetuated in an individual.[11] Thus, whether a person gets the allele for sickle cell anemia through genetic inheritance or gets religious beliefs through parental instruction is irrelevant in the sense that both traits have been transmitted. In short, we do not have to concern ourselves overmuch with the fact that the behaviors at the base of cultural complexity are not transmitted genetically.

SOCIAL COMPLEXITY AND HUMAN VALUES

Before considering how societies evolved into different forms, it is worthwhile to muse on the fact that over the centuries people have had a very difficult time coming to terms with their perceptions of the relative virtues of types of societies. One of the oldest and commonest human errors has been to confuse cultural complexity and cultural worth. Already by the time of city-states, a haughty citizen of a city-state in Iraq disparagingly described his nomadic neighbors as "[barbarians], who know no house or town, the boor of the mountains . . . who does not bend his knees [to cultivate the land] . . . who is not buried after his death."[12] Even in our own age, it is difficult to avoid the notions that civilizations have emerged because of the special gifts and vitality of their populaces, that simpler societies are incompletely developed, and that all the world's cultures are at various points along a gradient whose apex is the modern Western industrial community. This attitude was a great advantage in the age of European colonialism because it allowed the Europeans to treat other peoples as hardly human, and therefore undeserving of the full protection of laws and morality. Immanuel Kant said that the essence of immorality is to treat other people as objects, and in a way this is the Original Sin of cultural complexity. Europeans are routinely used as examples of colonialism, but it must be recognized that all cultures that have achieved dominance by virtue of time and circumstance have been equally colonialism.

To classify, as archaeologists do, history's thousands of societies in terms of their inferred social stratification, size, and the complexity of information, matter, and energy exchanges is a research tactic that has as its goal the elucidation of the processes that produced these forms of complexity; but we should not consider these measures as ultimate criteria. If we categorized human societies in terms of piety, social cohesiveness, "justice," or other abstract but important concepts, we would see an ordering of societies very different from the earlier discussion about Trigger's analysis, concerned as it was with "cultural complexity."

Because of the nature of archaeological data, we must limit ourselves primarily to the artifacts of these extinct civilizations, the bones and stones and debris that have survived them. But it is worth reflecting on the tremendous impact the evolution of cultural complexity has had on the way people view themselves and the world. If recent band societies resemble Pleistocene band societies, most Pleistocene individuals were deeply embedded in social and family relationships and had a clear role in society. Marshall Sahlins observed that our hunting-and-gathering ancestors took the "Zen road to affluence": People living in complex sedentary communities seem to live in the eternal economic dilemma of unlimited wants and limited means, but simpler societies have adjusted to their limited means by having few wants.[13] Because they are frequently moving, hunters and gatherers cannot accumulate large quantities of material objects and therefore do not covet air conditioners and trash compactors, and they live in such small and scattered groups that social hierarchies are of little use or relevance. Ethnologist Richard Lee described how one Christmas he supplied a group of Kalahari Bushmen with a 1,200-pound ox for a great feast (Figure 7.1)—the ox represented far more meat than the group could eat.[14] Everyone in the group complained, however, about how scrawny the animal was and how poor his gift was. Lee realized eventually that the cool reception to his generosity was the Bushmen's way of maintaining an egalitarian spirit: Any particularly valuable or productive act or service met the same response because group dynamics worked best if no one could take great personal and public prestige from his accomplishments.

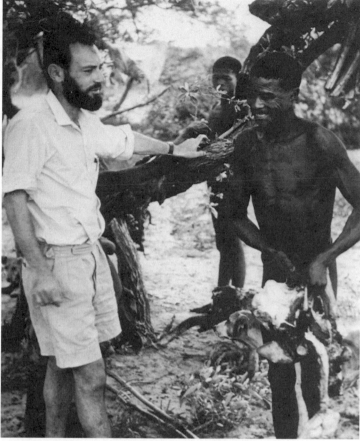

FIGURE 7.1   Richard Lee at a Christmas ox roast for a group of Kalahari Bushmen, southern Africa (see text for discussion of egalitarian principles of band organization demonstrated at this event).

Hunter-gatherers of the recent and contemporary world are probably uncertain guides to what life was like during the millennia when all of our ancestors lived this way. But any romantic visions one might have of this ancient world may well be illusions. We might want to think of our ancestors as generous and sharing, and perhaps they were, but not necessarily. Nicolas Peterson reports, for example, that one aboriginal Australian in the group he was studying said to him, "I want to owe you five dollars." Peterson labels this kind of behavior "demand sharing," in which exchange of resources is stripped of all pretense that people do it because they want to or feel generous.[15] Sharing is to everyone's advantage in some social organizations, particularly band societies, but there is no necessary reason that it has to be cloaked in an aura of generosity and altruism. We will never know how our Pleistocene forebears organized their patterns of sharing and cooperation, but they were probably not the "noble savages" that we sometimes imagine.

All forms of social organization, of course, have their human costs, as well as benefits. In complex societies, from ancient times to the present, people often have felt themselves to be minor replaceable cogs in a machine that operates mainly for the benefit of others. From some of the earliest written documents, those from Mesopotamia in the third millennium B.C., we hear the age-old complaints about poverty, taxes, oppressive rulers, governmental harassment, and other ills of cultural complexity. Little wonder that from these early records we also see the beginnings of Utopian movements, made up of those who yearn for a return to a hypothetical simpler place and time, when political, religious, and economic hierarchies did not exist, when all people were considered of equal worth, where all had an equal share, and where no one had power over anyone else.

Many of the perceived pathologies in modern societies are attributed to greed, but one must at least consider the premise that human selfishness and greed are "engines" that have propelled humanity to ever-more-complex socioeconomic and political forms. The biblical sentiment that "the love of money is the root of all evil" is no doubt true, but the love of money also has had some beneficial side effects. Novelist John LeCarré explores this theme in one of his books[16] in the form of an argument between two characters, one who is sickened by the excesses of greed, waste, and inequity in capitalistic "pigs in clover" societies, and another character who defends the West on the premise that capitalism uses human greed and acquisitiveness to produce goods and services that, ultimately, enhance human life, dignity, and liberty.

In the last couple of decades, eastern Europe has begun a painful transition, from centralized quasi-socialist systems to more capitalistic market-oriented economies—or at least that is the intention of the politicians and planners. The impetus for this change appears to be the simple fact that economies based on self-interest have been far more productive than other forms in terms of goods and services. The last great bastion of communism, China, too has found that it can sustain impressive growth rates by allowing individuals to profit from their own labor and initiative, with the result that barely 20 years after the Maoist Red Guards terrorized any individual not totally subservient to the idea of a pure theoretical communism, Chinese "millionaires" are emerging in ever-greater numbers.

Only the future will reveal if the great complexity and integration that seems to make societies highly productive and "efficient" can be achieved without the stimulus of individual and corporate competitiveness, and without socioeconomic inequalities.

TRADITIONAL SOCIOCULTURAL TYPOLOGIES

Analyzing different kinds of societies and comparing them implies that one can put them into categories that have some analytical significance and then use their similarities and differences to focus on the determinants of cultural variation. Such studies are, for obvious reasons, almost exclusively the products of highly complex societies.

The basic issues here are the concepts of "cross-cultural comparisons" and "ethnographic analogy." To what extent can we extrapolate from recent and present societies to the past? Archaeologists have been heavily influenced in their conceptions of ancient cultural complexity by ethnographers who have studied not just hunter-foragers, but other people who live in social organizations and with economies that may resemble those of our extinct ancestors.

Although the ethnographic categories formulated by anthropologists such as Elman Service and Morton Fried were devised principally to classify the diversity of extant and recent cultures, their ideas have been widely applied by archaeologists to prehistoric societies. The use of ethnographic data to categorize ancient societies that exist only as rubble and discarded artifacts can, of course, be misleading, particularly since "it . . . seems possible that every hunter-gatherer or tribal society in the world was influenced to some degree by contact with technologically more advanced societies prior to ethnographic study."[17]

In some ways social typologies and taxonomies are a hindrance to good archaeological analysis because they inexactly lump together societies on the basis of unstated and sometimes irrelevant criteria.[18] But almost all archaeologists continue to think of the archaeological record in terms of three or four basic *types* of societies. These types are abstractions that may fit precisely no particular case, especially with regard to extinct societies, but they are convenient summaries of the kinds of social differences archaeologists think were involved in the evolution of complex societies.

Egalitarian Societies: Bands and Tribes

As we noted in chapters 3 and 4, the archaeological evidence is undeniable that for the first three million years of our history, we lived in what anthropologists generally—if inexactly —call *band* societies. There is great variation[19] in these societies, and all have been influenced to some extent by industrial cultures. Eskimos who use snowmobiles to hunt bears and Kalahari Bushmen who steal their neighbors' cows, for example, are often seen as distorted remnants of band societies because when first described by explorers and anthropologists, they exhibited far fewer signs of "contamination" by industrial societies.

Archaeologists have developed a sense of what a "band" society is mainly by distilling and combining ethnographic studies of societies in many different parts of the world. The Copper Eskimo, African Pygmies, Kalahari Bushmen, and Australian Aborigines are usually cited as examples of this social form. In contemporary and recent band societies, the most salient characteristic seems to be that there are only minor differences among members of the group in terms of prestige; in these societies no one has any greater claims to material resources than anyone else. In most of these societies, older males who are good providers gain the most respect, but they have little or no power to coerce other band members. This lack of social differentiation is tied to their economy: Band members spend most of their lives in groups of 15–40 people, moving often as they exploit wild plants and animals. Julian Steward concluded that most, perhaps all, bands were patrilineal and patrilocal—that is, people reckoned their descent primarily through their father and newlyweds lived with the husband's band.[20] Whether or not this is true is still a major issue in ethnography, and many ethnologists think that band societies can be extremely flexible in where newlyweds live, for example, based on available resources and other factors.[21] In any case, this is the kind of thing archaeologists can never be sure about when applying the model of a band society to a scatter of stones and bones. The division of labor in bands is generally along basic age and sex lines, and the economic structure is a sort of practical communism: Money is not used, and exchange usually takes place between people who consider themselves friends or relatives. This gift-giving is usually done very casually, and relationships are frequently cemented by offers of reciprocal hospitality.

In the context of the topic of this chapter, the origins of cultural complexity, one of the most important things about bands is that they appear to be largely *functionally redundant*. That is, these individual bands are very much alike in their social organization and economy, and each individual is able to do almost everything needed for the group to survive and reproduce itself. Each band contains, in the form of its members' skills, all of the expertise it needs to function and persist. As we shall see, it is the change from this kind of functional redundancy to functional *interdependence* that seems to be at the heart of the origins of complex societies.

And, in any case, the question remains: How similar are (or were) these ethnographically described groups to our hunter-forager ancestors—whose lives constitute 99 percent of our human past?

Tribe is the rather ambiguous term that anthropologists have used to label social groupings that are larger than band societies but generally not particularly complex in terms of economy, social hierarchies, law, and so forth. People living in tribes are often subsistence farmers, such as the Pueblo Indian maize farmers of the American Southwest or New Guinea yam cultivators. Tribes often have a nominal leader—usually male—who acts to redistribute food and perform a few minor ceremonial activities, but, as in band societies, he has no privileged access to wealth or power. He leads only by example and serves at the pleasure of the tribe. Exchange in such societies is still usually accomplished through reciprocal trading within a kinship structure. Typically, tribal societies are larger and more territorial, have more elaborate ceremonialism and kinship systems, and make more distinctions in terms of prestige than band societies.[22]

In many cases, tribes may have been transitional forms, appearing where farmers were in the transition to more complex forms of social organization, and in some cases tribal societies may have been direct outgrowths of the influences of or contacts with state societies.[23]

Stratified Societies: Chiefdoms

Timothy Earle defines *chiefdoms* as "regionally organized societies with a centralized decision-making hierarchy coordinating activities among several village communities."[24] For many authorities, "chiefdoms" are different from bands and tribes both in degree and in kind. Chiefdoms are based on the concept of hereditary inequality: In a chiefdom, if you are the son of a chief, chances are you will become chief no matter how unsuitable you may be; and if you are able but born a "commoner," your options in life will be narrowly circumscribed.

These differences in prestige usually correlate with preferential access to wealth; chiefs and their families can claim the best farmlands or fishing places as well as more food and more exotic and expensive items than "commoners." They are often regarded as divine and typically marry within noble families. The economies of these societies often show a greater degree of specialization and diversification than those of tribes or bands. Craftsmen exist, but they are usually also farmers, and there is no permanent class of artisans as there is in states. Chiefdoms are much larger than tribes, often involving thousands of people. Examples of chiefdoms include the pre-contact Nootka of British Columbia and early Hawaiian societies.

Earle stresses the ideological bases of chiefdoms. He notes that chiefs typically create sacred places, such as ceremonial areas; they also use symbols of individual power and position in burial cults, and their mortuary symbolism often includes expressions of military might. To some extent, recent archaeological research on chiefdoms has focused on the political and ideological activities of chiefs, rather than just the simple deterministic factors of agriculture and economy that permit the evolution of chiefdoms.[25] In fact, the literature on chiefdoms clearly mirrors a major conceptual trend in contemporary archaeology: Traditional analyses of chiefdoms have concentrated on the functionalist and adaptive aspects of these societies, such as how chiefs may have been responsive to the problem of redistributing resources in rapidly growing societies; but contemporary approaches[26] stress the varieties of ways in which chiefs gain and maintain control.

The archaeology of chiefdoms is a particularly valuable endeavor, as Dick Drennan points out, because in some cases they seem to have been a transitional phase leading to states, and elsewhere they were "terminal," in the sense that the indigenous developmental factors seem to have produced chiefdoms but not states. Drennan defends the use of the concept of chiefdoms on various grounds. He notes that "Their story is, in one respect, the story of the emergence of substantial inequality, but it has a number of other aspects as well, such as spatial and demographic scale, centralization, economic specialization, exchange, supralocal political organization. . . . Very broadly speaking, these aspects are known to be correlated with each other."[27]

Stratified Societies: States

What a *state* is depends to some extent on what an analyst sees as the causal factors in producing cultural complexity. The term "stratified" refers to the division of the society into hierarchically arranged socioeconomic classes and political elites. Generally, states are assumed to have centralized governments composed of political and religious elites who exercise economic and political control. In addition to being larger in population and territory than other societal forms, states are characterized by having full-time craftsmen and other specialists, whose products are distributed in part through an integrated national economy. The state codifies and enforces laws, drafts soldiers, levies taxes, and exacts tribute. States have powerful economic structures, often centered on market systems, and they have a diversity of settlement sizes, such as villages, towns, and sometimes cities.

Wright and Johnson, for example, define the state in terms of a political polity that has at least three levels in the decision-making hierarchy, such as village headmen, provincial governor, and national leader.[28]

Early states formed essentially independently in at least six areas of the ancient world: Mesopotamia, Egypt, the Indus Valley, China, Mesoamerica, and Peru; ethnographic and historical accounts of state formation include cases in Africa, Madagascar, and various other places (Figure 7.2).

Scholars use the same term, "state," to refer both to ancient Egypt and to the United States, for example, despite their gross differences in complexity. Yet in a sense the differences between ancient Egypt and the modern United States are matters of degree. The level of occupational specialization in the contemporary United States is much greater than in ancient Egypt, of course, but it is mainly an elaboration of the same basic economic principle. Some scholars, however, use the term "preindustrial state" to distinguish ancient states from those of the industrial era.

Many of the early states seem to have been involved in competitive relationships with other, adjacent states, and for long periods this apparently limited their size and power. Eventually, however, in all the early centers of state formation these competitive relationships broke down and one state was able to increase its size and influence drastically—usually so rapidly that it had few competitors. In fact, its ultimate size seems to have been limited only by the level of its communications technology and its administrative efficiency.

States of this type first appeared in Mesopotamia, Egypt, and the Indus Valley toward the end of the fourth millennium B.C. and within a thousand years thereafter in China. The

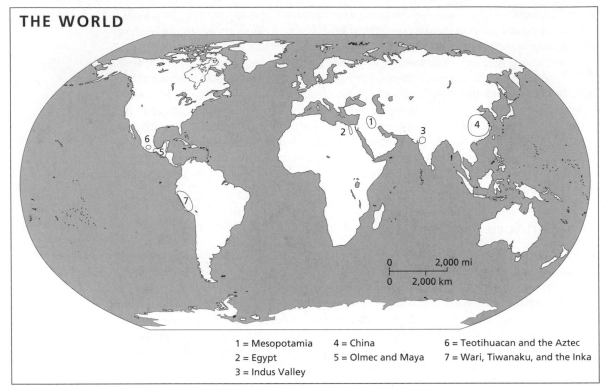

THE WORLD

1 = Mesopotamia   4 = China   6 = Teotihuacan and the Aztec
2 = Egypt   5 = Olmec and Maya   7 = Wari, Tiwanaku, and the Inka
3 = Indus Valley

FIGURE 7.2   Locations of some of the world's first highly complex civilizations and states.

Inka state of Peru and the Aztec state of Mexico also seem to have achieved imperial dimensions just before the arrival of the Europeans, in the sixteenth century A.D.

CONTEMPORARY APPROACHES TO SOCIOCULTURAL TYPOLOGY

Rather than think of the archaeological record primarily in terms of bands, tribes, chiefdoms, and states, it is probably more accurate to see the record as a great continuum of variability, reflecting the unique flexibility that humans bring to any situation. We can be certain the australopiths had no academic conferences on mathematics or international labor federations, and no great ancient state was founded principally on caribou hunting. But most other generalizations about these social typologies are likely to be imprecise.

The important point here is that simple categories such as "bands," "tribes," "chiefdoms," and "states" are static descriptive types that are not of much use in analyzing the origins and functions of the phenomena these labels loosely describe. Labeling ancient Egypt a "state," for example, based on the inferred appearance of characteristics such as centralized government or a class-structured society, is more a description than an analysis. To many scholars such typologies are inexact, atheoretical categorizations of a continuous and multidimensional underlying variability. McGuire argues that such "an approach inevitably degenerates into taxonomic arguments: What is a simple society? What is a state?"[29]

How do we decide where to draw a boundary line that defines a "state" in such a pattern of continuous variability? The critical problem with these archaeological analyses of cultural variability is that there is no powerful theory that tells us what the proper units of analysis are and what principles explain their functions. Compare this situation to biology: Darwinian theory and modern genetics give biology a powerful explanatory theory that reveals much about the history and operations of the biological universe. Darwinian theory and modern genetics tell the researcher what units to use (genes, cells, populations, etc.) and explain change over time and space in the biological universe. Archaeology has no comparable theories and thus has no comparably effective units or principles of analysis. Some scholars argue that because archaeology deals with people (even if they are dead) and unique cultures (even if they are extinct), it will never be possible to have comparably powerful theories. Others argue that we already have the beginnings of powerful theories—a position discussed later in terms of Marxism and Cultural Evolutionary theory.

In the face of these ambiguities, many archaeologists have resorted to trying to break down typologies as exemplified by the "bands," "tribes," "chiefdoms," and "states" paradigm and to examine the underlying variability in selected aspects of societies. Numerous archaeologists, for example, have focused on the concepts of *specialization* and *exchange*. Cathy Costin,[30] for example, has developed a complex categorization of how societies produce and distribute goods and services. Similarly, Elizabeth Brumfiel and Timothy Earle break down the concept of occupational specialization into at least four dimensions: (1) specialists can be *independent* or *attached*, in the sense that a potter, for example, can supply pots for an unspecified, changing market, perhaps just for members of his or her own village, or for the larger region; or the potter can be attached to a particular patron and make ceramics only for a given noble family or governing institution; (2) specialists differ in the *nature of their products*, in that they can produce *subsistence* items, such as grain; *wealth*, such as ritual feather headdresses or gold bracelets; or *services*, such as military duty or religious ceremonies; (3) specialists differ in the *intensity of production*, in that they could be part-time hunters, who contribute an occasional deer to the village economy, or full-time weavers, who do little else but produce textiles for trade; (4) specialists also differ in the *scale* of production, in the sense that in some economies a large group of people, or a village, or even a region may specialize in something, such as salt production, while in other cases, one or two people may produce a particular good or service.[31] Brumfiel and Earle also note that there are many different kinds of exchange: between an elite and its supporting citizenry, among different elites, and in the wide variety of political and social arrangements in which subsistence goods and nonsubsistence "wealth" can be circulated within and among communities, regions, and larger political entities.

Another aspect of contemporary rethinking of typologies of ancient societies has to do with the notion of the "collapse" of civilizations. Many scholars over the centuries have thought of civilizations almost as if these societies were organisms, with a birth, life span, and death, or collapse. And there certainly are some examples in the past of cultures that appear to have quickly and pervasively lost some of their unique, fundamental cultural expressions, such as the Maya civilization of Mesoamerica (see chapter 13). But in most cases the collapse of civilizations seems to involve not a collapse and mass extinction of people and their cultural ideas, but rather adaptation, sometimes in the form of a process—to use Mark Kenoyer's terms[32]—of *decentralization* and *localization*, in which political authorities lose their ability to control people and economies. These periods of decentralization can in fact involve periods of population growth, rather than decline, and in many cases decentralization was followed by a larger, more politically potent polity in the same area. We will return to this point in later chapters.

Recently, archaeologists have also moved beyond the typology of "bands," "tribes," "chiefdoms," and "states" by developing models that feature the actions of people—thereby offering interpretations that cross-cut the static categories of "bands," "tribes," "chiefdoms," and "states." One example is the work of Gary Feinman and his colleagues in the American Southwest.[33] They use the concepts of *corporate* and *network* strategies of political action, which allow for the concurrent presence of equality and hierarchy in any society, regardless of whether it is classified as complex or simple in terms of social organization. A network strategy is characterized by a centralized leadership and access to wealth is held by only a few people in the society. These individuals use their networks to maintain and increase their authority and power and may hold ostentatious displays or adorn themselves ostentatiously with prestige items. A corporate strategy, on the other hand, is typified by much wider access to wealth among the people of that society and power and authority tends to be shared among many individuals. Societies with a corporate strategy have communal projects such as rituals—fertility, rainfall, successful hunts—focused on benefits to all members of society, as well as the construction of public works. Corporate societies are integrated through the use of ideology. But such societies are not necessarily egalitarian; hierarchies do exist, such as differences in influence and authority between various social groups.

Analyses such as that of Feinman and his colleagues demonstrate the potential for considering the highly variable nature of how human societies are organized. We will undoubtedly see additional examples of these cross-cutting sociocultural typologies as archaeologists continue to focus on the issues involved in the origins of and explanations for complex societies.

THE ARCHAEOLOGY OF COMPLEX SOCIETIES

Archaeologists regularly talk about the band societies of the Middle Pleistocene and the early chiefdoms of prehistoric Mesopotamia, but we do not have these societies trapped in amber; we have only their artifacts, and we use the words "bands," "tribes," "chiefdoms," and "states" to describe them only with some license. To deal with this problem, archaeologists typically equate these terms with specific categories of physical evidence.

At the heart of many conceptions of cultural complexity is the idea of changing forms and levels of matter, energy, and information exchange. Each person and each society exists because it is able to divert energy from the natural world, through food sources and technology, and some of these changes are selective advantages. The greater the amount of energy a culture can capture and efficiently utilize, the better its competitive chances. And we can measure this in part by measuring such variables as population density and agricultural and commodity productivity.

Leslie White's equation of cultural evolution, with the amount of energy captured per person per year, has been widely criticized, but it remains of interest.[34] The fundamental data of archaeology are usually the stones and pots and other implements with which people converted energy to their purposes—the very appliances of energy use, in other words, that White stressed. And every early state left a record of its economic basis in the form of such things as irrigation canals, stone tools, and agricultural fields. Yet in essence every ancient state was also an *idea*. The Egyptians viewed their state and culture metaphorically as a living organism, an organism of which they were all a part, from the pharaoh himself to the lowliest slave. As Egyptologist Barry Kemp has noted, for example, the ancient Egyptians' vision of their state as an organism is vividly portrayed on the throne base of Pharaoh Senusret I (1971–1928 B.C.) (Figure 7.3). Here, two potent competing Egyptian deities, Seth and Horus, are shown tying together the plants symbolic of Upper (southern) and Lower (northern) Egypt, the lotus and the papyrus, respectively, reconciling their conflicting powers and thereby forming the Egyptian state. Note that the plants and the column supporting the name of the king (in the "cartouche," or

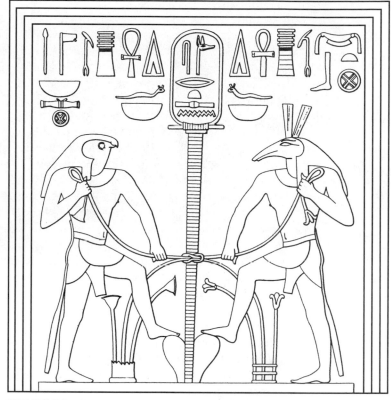

FIGURE 7.3   Two potent competing Egyptian deities, Seth and Horus, shown tying together the plants symbolic of Upper and Lower Egypt.

the oval inscribed around the letters in the king's name) form a vivid representation of a human windpipe and lungs—a person, for all intents and purposes.

All other early states had a similar intellectual foundation—an ideology that embraced the people and elements of the state. For all early states, the process of analyzing them archaeologically requires that the material remains of these cultures be interpreted in the context of their ideologies.

Architecture

Perhaps the most obvious differences between the archaeological record of the Pleistocene and that of the last five or six millennia is the presence in the latter period of massive amounts of residential and public architecture. All early states built palaces and tombs (Figure 7.4); hunter-gatherers occasionally built permanent structures but rarely on the same scale as agriculturalists.

The appearance of substantial houses and other forms of *residential* architecture is mainly a reflection of economic productivity: If a group produces or gathers sufficient resources within a small enough area, it can become sedentary, and in most climates shelter

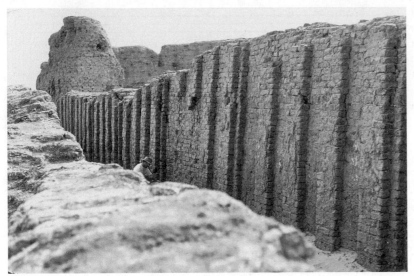

FIGURE 7.4   The mudbrick wall of the Early Dynastic Shunet al-Zebib (the funerary enclosure of King Khasekhemwy) at Abydos, Egypt.

from rain, sun, heat, cold, and other elements is worth the cost and effort required to build it.

Soon after permanent communities appeared in both the Old and New Worlds, the architecture of these settlements began to reflect changing levels of cultural and social complexity. Whereas the first houses in all communities were probably built very much alike and had the same contents, later communities incorporated residences that varied considerably in expense of construction and furnishing. Ethnographic evidence leaves little doubt that this architectural variability reflects economic, social, and political differentiation within the community, but the essential point is that, relative to earlier societies, there was a change in patterns of investment of societal energy and resources.

Similarly, once residential architectural variability appeared in many of these early communities, "monumental" architecture also appeared. Pyramids, earthen or brick platforms, "temples," "palaces," and other constructions protrude from the ruins of ancient settlements from North China to the high mountain valleys of Peru. Here, too, the important thing is that the ability and incentive to make these investments are radically different from the capacities of Pleistocene bands, in that they imply the ability of some members of the society to control and organize others.

Mortuary Evidence

For much of its early history archaeology was almost synonymous with grave-robbing. Its early practitioners were primarily concerned with finding ancient burials so that they could loot the beautiful goods that people so often have lavished on their departed.

Objects carefully enclosed in burials are often much better preserved than those found in houses or tool-making sites. Also, death for our ancestors, as for ourselves, was invested with more ritual than any other cultural aspect. In many burials we have, so to speak, the crystallization of complex religious and social forces, as well as reflections of social status. It is in their great *variability* that mortuary customs are so informative: Corpses can be buried, burned, ritually exposed, or entombed; they can be laid out flat, on their sides, or flexed; they can be oriented to the cardinal points of the compass or to a geographical feature; they can be placed in earth, in caves, in crypts, in trees, or on refuse heaps. Burial contents can range from nothing to enormous quantities of jewelry and furnishings and scores of sacrificed human attendants and animals (Figure 7.5).

It is a fundamental archaeological assumption that a correlation exists between the level of social complexity of a people and the way they treat their dead.[35] Ethnographic studies show that the correlation between subsistence strategy, social organization, and mortuary practices is strong: Bands and tribes differed comparatively little in mortuary practices, while sedentary agriculturalists varied their practices according to a wide range of age, sex, and status distinctions.[36] These correlations are strong but not perfect: In some cultures, including our own, some of the most important and wealthiest people are cremated and leave no material record of their passing, their status, or their wealth.

The presence of juveniles buried with rich grave goods has been given considerable importance in defining the cultural complexity of ancient societies because such burials are considered indications of ascribed status: We assume that young individuals could not have earned these goods on their own. Similarly, some ancient cemeteries have three or four distinct classes of burials. Some types are well constructed of stone, have rich grave goods, and are centrally located, while others are simple graves with little in them except the corpse. And it is a reasonable inference that these divisions correspond to different economic and social classes.[37]

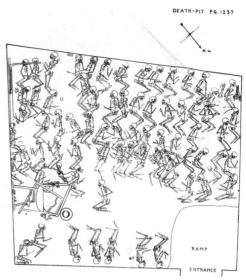

FIGURE 7.5 Excavations at Ur in Mesopotamia by Sir Leonard Woolley revealed the "death pit" in the tomb of Queen Pu-abi, which contained the bodies of dozens of her retainers.

Functional Differentiation and Integration

In chapter 15 we will see that the aboriginal Americans of the Mississippian culture who built the huge mounds that dot the eastern North American river valleys had great trade systems, intensive maize agriculture, thousands of inhabitants, and a mortuary cult that involved human sacrifice and great expenditures of wealth on dead leaders—yet most archaeologists do not consider that these societies constituted "states" because these Native Americans were almost all full-time maize farmers, with only a few specialists: in religion, hunting, warfare, and other areas. In some definitions of cultural complexity, the essential component is the division of a community into functionally interdependent entities of such complexity that no small group of people can maintain all that community's activities. This is important because it produces a situation in which societies survive or die out as *societies*, as groups; in contrast, among hunter-gatherers the focus of selection is usually the *individual*, or at most the 12 or 15 people with whom each individual spends most of the year. In other words, the unit of "selection" changes with cultural complexity. Contemporary North Americans, for example, are extremely interdependent, in the sense that we are all reliant for our continued existence as both physical individuals and social organizations on the 3 or 4 percent of the population that produces nearly all our food.

To translate this sense of functional interdependence into archaeological terms, we must look for concentrations and distributions of artifacts indicating a certain level of activity specialization. In early agricultural villages, each house and each group of houses had approximately the same contents in terms of numbers and types of ceramics, stone tools, figurines, and garbage. But in later, more complex societies we find concentrations of artifacts that clearly represent such things as pottery or stone-tool manufacturing workshops, indicating that people specialized in these activities. Again, we infer that they were specialized, but the significant point archaeologically is that certain classes of artifacts are found in places, volumes, and diversities far different from what would be produced by, say, a hunting-and-gathering group. Certain differences will also be evident if we compare the contents of settlements. Some settlements might specialize in salt-making, or barley agriculture, or pottery manufacture. This variability in the artifacts found within discrete but contemporary sites is a key element in our identification of cultural complexity.

Settlement Patterns

In addition to measuring social complexity by looking at objects excavated at specific sites, we can also look at how settlements are distributed spatially. First, we can examine variability in settlement size and configuration. Early Southwest Asian agricultural villages were almost all approximately the same size, but settlements there several thousand years later were of many different sizes, ranging from a few hundred square meters to several square kilometers. Similarly, the basic shape of the settlements changed; some were apparently fortified rectangular compounds, while others were just five or six mudbrick houses. Thus, any archaeological analysis of cultural complexity will involve measuring the variability in site size and shape in a large sample of contemporary sites.

Second, we can look at the placement of settlements relative to the environment and to each other. A major part of the cost of exploiting any resource is the distance it must be transported. This applies equally to the deer hunted by Paleolithic bands and the irrigated rice of ancient China. It also applies to the cost of making decisions about resource production, movement, and storage. With primitive communications systems, for example, an official in one settlement cannot make many timely decisions about the agriculture or craft production of 30 or 40 other settlements many kilometers away because the cost of gathering the relevant information and accurately and rapidly acting on it is too high: He would need teams of observers and relay runners.

As a consequence, some arrangements of settlements are more common than others under certain conditions, and we can tell something about the relationships between settlements by analyzing their respective locations. On a relatively broad agricultural plain, towns and villages that exchange goods and services tend to be placed so as to form a pattern of interlocking hexagons (Figure 7.6) because this arrangement is especially efficient if there is a high level of movement of goods and people among the various settlements.[38] In our discussion of archaeological evidence relevant to the origins of cultural complexity, we will see several instances where ancient settlements are arranged in a hexagonal pattern or some other form. Here too it is relatively unimportant whether or not the distribution of ancient settlements corresponds exactly to the patterns observed among present ones. What is important is that we know a major change in settlement patterning has occurred over time. Paleolithic hunters and gatherers and early agriculturalists lived in locations determined largely by the availability of material resources. But later, in some areas of the ancient world, settlements began to be located with less regard for natural resources and more concern for trade routes, political frontiers, and administrative networks. Again, these changes occurred in settlements that were also building monumental structures, achieving denser population concentrations, and evolving some or all of the other elements of cultural complexity.

For these reasons, archaeological settlement pattern analyses have provided significant insights into the nature of ancient social, political, and economic changes.[39]

One of the continuing debates in archaeology is the relationship of *urbanism* and state societies. Some civilizations, such as those in Mesopotamia, seemed to have been formed out of cities, while others, such as Egypt, remained largely non-urban for much of their history. Trigger evaluates the attempts to place examples of the pre-industrial city on a single continuum and concludes that, while we can identify key variables that link these examples, the variables combine "to shape an indefinite number of trajectories or paths of pre-industrial urban development, any one of which may be associated with a particular civilization."[40] He identifies three variables of particular importance:

> (1) The degree of economic complexity of the society in which the city is found, as measured in terms of the degree of division of labour in craft production, the increasing number of people divorced from food production . . . , and the increasingly large areas and numbers of people that are effectively linked by routine economic interaction . . . ; (2) the different strategies by which urban dwellers obtain food from their hinterland . . . ; (3) The political context within which cities occur.[41]

It may seem as if the elements of cultural complexity we have sketched here are mainly found in the urban centers and ceremonial centers of early states, but this is not so. In Egypt, for example, the remains of tiny provincial villages appear to reflect a simple agrarian life, undisturbed by the events and forces emanating from the center of the Egyptian state; but a closer look at the remains of these provincial communities reveals many reflections of the state as a whole. Artifact styles are those of every other community in the state, inscribed clay commodity sealings bespeak a commercial connection to the royal court, and trade items reflect standardization and integration into the national and international economy. Similar patterns are observed in most early states.[42]

To summarize archaeological approaches to determining cultural complexity, we have several specific lines of evidence: We can look for changes in architecture, technology, mortuary complexes, and settlement size and location; and we can attempt to link these changes to different levels and forms of energy and information usage and overall thermodynamic capture.

Most of the rest of this book is a summary of how different cultures in various parts of the world made the transition to complexity, and this summary is based on these forms

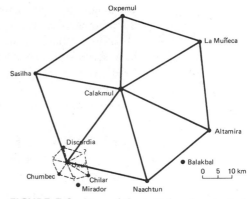

FIGURE 7.6 One of the initial archaeological signs of changing levels of complexity in regional economic and political systems is the appearance of settlement patterns in which settlements are arranged spatially in recognizable patterns. The *Central Place* model suggests that on a flat plain where all resources are uniformly distributed, the settlements will be arranged in different patterns depending on the strength of marketing, transport, administrative, and other factors. No perfectly uniformly endowed plains exist, of course, but actual maps of archaeological settlements can be matched against the theoretical ideal and similarities noted to these ideal models. The hexagonal areas surrounding the settlements in the models here are produced by assuming that on a featureless plain each settlement would have a circular area around it, the inhabitants of which would go to the center for goods and services. But since a plain packed with such circular "demand zones" would leave some areas outside these circles, the theoretical model assumes that the circles are slightly overlapped and that the overlapping areas are bisected. The resulting figures are hexagons. Modern settlement maps as well as archaeological site maps for a given area often roughly approximate the variations of hexagonal distributions illustrated here. Here some of the major settlements of the Maya in lowland Mexico were spaced in an hexagonal arrangement.

of evidence of evolving complexity. But before considering the specifics, let us look first at the general problem of explaining these evolutionary patterns. As in the case of the origins of cultural behavior itself, and the appearance of agricultural economies, we would like to have some kind of theoretical constructs that will help tie all these separate early states together as members of a class and then will account for the time and location of their appearance.

EXPLAINING THE EVOLUTION OF CIVILIZATIONS: THE SEARCH FOR CAUSES

The earliest scholars believed the rise of cities and states and other elements of evolving cultural complexity required no explanation because they assumed these developments to be mainly or entirely the work of the gods. The scholars of the Enlightenment and subsequent centuries usually explained the origins of cultural complexity in evolutionary terms. Drawing a parallel with the biological world, Europeans felt that competition between human societies was inevitable and that to a large extent they had already "won."

Darwin thought that "civilized nations are everywhere supplanting barbarous nations, excepting where the climate opposes a deadly barrier; and they succeed mainly, though not exclusively, through their arts, which are the products of the intellect. It is, therefore, highly probable that with mankind the intellectual facilities have been gradually perfected through natural selection."[43] John Locke saw the cultures of North America as exemplifying a moral and philosophical lesson:

> There cannot be a clearer demonstration of [European cultural superiority] than . . . [the] several nations of the Americans . . . , who are rich in land and poor in all the comforts of life; whom nature having furnished as liberally as any other people, with the materials of plenty, i.e. a fruitful soil, apt to produce in abundance, what might serve for food, raiment, and delight; yet for want of improving it by labor, have not one hundredth part of the conveniences we enjoy; and a king of a large and fruitful territory there, feeds, lodges, and is clad worse than a day-labourer in England.[44]

Even in the early part of the twentieth century, many scholars believed that the process of cultural evolution of the whole world was to some extent a result of the rise of the West. The ancient states of China, India, and even the Americas were thought to have been prodded to higher achievements by contact with the European/Middle Eastern core areas. Thor Heyerdahl's expeditions, for example, perpetuate this notion that all civilizations are derived from a Middle Eastern, or at least Old World, source.

The coincidence of the village farming way of life with the rise of cultural complexity represented to some scholars a sufficient explanation of the evolution of cultural complexity. People then finally had enough leisure time and sedentary habits, it was argued, to develop architecture, art, writing, cities, and the rest of "civilization." The problems with this explanation are apparent even with a superficial examination. Many agricultural groups apparently never developed into "states," while at least one early complex culture (in Peru) may have evolved without a primary agricultural economy. In any case, many hunters and gatherers have more leisure time than did primitive agriculturalists.

Techno-Ecological Hypotheses About the Origins of Civilizations

For many analysts of early civilizations, the search for an explanation of how these cultures evolved in highly similar yet distinctive ways logically should begin with a consideration of these similarities and differences. What, in other words, did these early civilizations share in the way of, for example, climate, ecology, demographics, or any other factors, that might explain why it was Mesopotamia, Egypt, the Indus Valley, China, Mesoamerica, and Andean South America that gave rise to the first great states and civilizations, and not Australia, Polynesia, Scandinavia, California, Japan, or Scotland?

If you knew nothing about the archaeology of early complex cultures and began to compare them, chances are you would be struck by the same facts that so forcefully impressed Julian Steward, V. G. Childe, and other early scholars who studied the problem of cultural complexity origins: Most of these cultures developed in similar physical environments and were based on similar economies.[45] The earliest states and empires arose for the most part in arid or semi-arid environments where crops like wheat and barley could be grown without having to turn over thick grasslands or fight back lots of competing vegetation and where agricultural production could be easily intensified, either by canals, terracing, building up fields in lake beds, or some other method.

Thus, you might look for one or two key factors that had operated in each of these early societies to *cause* civilization in a rather mechanical fashion, in which these civilizations were the outcome of the proper mix of population growth, agricultural intensification, trade, and the peculiarities of the human mind.

In some ways it is easy to imagine societies becoming more complex once the first elements of complexity are in place. A powerful chief, for example, could become a national king if he were successful in battle and conquered a large, exploitable hinterland like the Mesopotamian Alluvium. And once a city had organized its production and distribution of pottery and grain, it seems an easy step to extend these administrative institutions to fish, beer, plows, and tax revenues; and once the first royal tombs filled with grave gifts are constructed, the building of great mortuary pyramids seems a fairly simple extension of the basic idea.

But what could produce the first irrevocable breaks with the strong traditions of practical communism and social equality of the first agricultural communities?

To begin with the most obvious factor, as noted earlier, even though intensive agriculture is the foundation of almost all early complex cultures, it is not a sufficient explanation in and of itself. Therefore most attempts to understand the origins of complexity try to link specific agricultural patterns with other factors. Anthropologist Stephen Athens notes that agriculture is an effort to maintain an artificial ecosystem, and in some climates, such as arid or temperate environments, the plowing, irrigating, and other efforts needed to maintain agricultural ecosystems are so great that it is doubtful that "the more intense forms of agricultural production would be developed or become adopted unless there was a compelling reason to do so."[46] Athens maintains (as does Ester Boserup)[47] that the only reason sufficient to account for the enormous efforts required to maintain agricultural systems would be an imbalance between the population and available food supply.

In both arid and temperate environments, annual agricultural production can vary greatly because of crop disease, weather, and other factors, and there is some incentive to try to stabilize production in these areas by intensive weeding, land leveling, augmenting the irrigation system, and other tasks that require a great deal of labor. In arid, semi-arid, and temperate regions, the growing season is often sharply restricted by the weather, and thus "cultivation . . . does not permit cycling of plantings in such a way as to equalize the labor requirement throughout the year."[48] Each spring, for example, many different activities might have to be performed to avoid poor harvests, and under these conditions, according to Athens, there is a strong selection for certain kinds of cultural complexity. Increasing the territorial size of the cultural system would help meet crises brought on by a flood or some other disaster striking a single village; individuals and villages might also become specialized in trades and crafts to make production more efficient; and, perhaps most important, it would be advantageous to have a hierarchical administrative organization, so that work and production could be closely and efficiently administered.

Many explanations of the evolution of complex societies combine certain forms of agricultural intensification with *population growth*. But what causes human population growth? The immediate cause of population growth is well-known, but the more important question is: What are the causes and effects of the gradual rise in population densities and total population that all early civilizations experienced? George Cowgill remarked that many analysts of cultural evolution have assumed that a pervasive and powerful factor in human history has been the strong tendency of human populations to increase up to the point where serious shortages of important resources are in the offing and that experience or anticipation of such shortages has been a major factor, or even the dominant factor, in stimulating intensification of agricultural production and other technical and social innovations. In extreme versions, the entire history of complex societies and civilizations is seen as hardly more than the outcome of measures that began as ways of coping with problems posed by relentless human fertility—what might be called the "strictly from hunger" point of view of developmental processes.[49]

It is easy to see the attractiveness of these ideas, for if one examines history, a strong positive statistical correlation between population growth and cultural complexity is evident. The relationship between human population growth and cultural complexity may not be one of direct cause and effect, however, for correlation does not necessarily demonstrate causation. Moreover, even if the relationship is in some sense causal, it may be that the evolution of cultural complexity leads to rising population densities, rather than the reverse. Empirically, too, there seem to be some problems with the idea that human population growth somehow caused the evolution of cultural complexity. All societies have evolved mechanisms like migration, abortion, infanticide, marriage rules, and contraceptive techniques to control population growth, and thus we might expect people faced with stresses because of overpopulation to impose population controls rather than "invent" cultural complexity.[50]

It is worth noting that the greatest recent falls in fertility rates come not as the result of food shortages or technical advances in contraception, but as correlates of increasing educational levels for women, greater social mobility, increasing urbanization, the expanding role of women in the work force—in sum, the lessening of women's dependence on husbands and children for support.

The actual causal mechanisms by which these factors are translated into reduced fertility are not clear, however. In any case, there is no evidence human populations have ever increased at anything approaching the biologically feasible rate. If the world's population 5,570 years ago were only 1,000 people and their annual rate of increase since then were 4 per 1,000 people—a relatively moderate growth rate—the world's present population would be between seven and eight trillion. Obviously, human populations in the past have been under fairly stringent natural and cultural controls, and if we are to link population growth to increasing cultural complexity, we must specify additional factors or principles in causal "models" of how these variables were related.

It should be stressed, however, that most of the following "models" of cultural evolution are relatively simple, and many current scholars consider them incomplete or flawed as explanations of early complexity.

IRRIGATION AGRICULTURE AND THE EVOLUTION OF CULTURAL COMPLEXITY

Perhaps the most obvious common denominator of ancient complex societies was extensive irrigation systems. Even today aerial photographs of Mesopotamia, Peru, and most other areas of early state formation clearly show the massive remnants of these ancient structures, and similar constructions were built by early "chiefdoms" in such places as Hawaii and southwestern North America (Figure 7.7). This led some scholars to conclude that the construction and operation of extensive irrigation systems were at the heart of the origins of complex societies. A particularly influential proponent of this view was Karl Wittfogel, whose *Oriental Despotism* is a detailed excursion into comparative history and sociological analysis.[51]

Wittfogel notes that the limiting factors on agriculture are soil conditions, temperature, and the availability of water. Of these, water is the most easily manipulated, but its weight and physical characteristics impose limitations on this manipulation. To divert water to agricultural fields requires canal systems, dams, and drainage constructions that can only be built efficiently with organized mass labor; and, once built, irrigation systems require continued enormous investments of labor and resources to operate, clean, and maintain them. In addition, these systems necessitate complex administration and communication because crucial decisions have to be made about construction and repairs, water allocation, and crop harvesting and storage. Thus, a complex irrigation system under ancient conditions required cooperation and centralized hierarchical decision-making institutions.

Irrigation systems also have the intrinsic capacity to

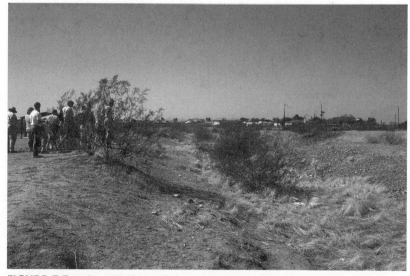

FIGURE 7.7   The Hohokam of Arizona built an extensive canal system to carry water to their agricultural fields. Some of these can still be seen today as large "ditches," only partially filled in after hundreds of years of abandonment.

create another element in the process of the evolution of complex societies: wealth and status differentials. Fields closer to main rivers are better drained and more easily irrigated and possess a higher natural fertility; thus control of such lands would create immediate wealth differentials. Correspondingly, wealth and status would most likely accrue to the elites of the decision-making hierarchies. Wittfogel concludes that irrigation-based agriculture has many other effects on a society. It encourages the development of writing and calendrical systems, so that records can be kept of periods of annual flooding, agricultural production statistics, the amounts of products in storage, and the allocation of water. Construction of roads, palaces, and temples would also be encouraged because the mobilization of labor for the canal works could be generalized to these other endeavors very easily, and roads would contribute to the movement of agricultural produce and to the communication required for efficient operation of the systems. The construction of temples and palaces would also serve to reinforce the position of the hierarchy. The creation of standing armies and defensive works would also likely follow because irrigation systems are extremely valuable but not very portable, and they are easily damaged by neglect or intentional destruction.

Wittfogel's hydraulic hypothesis still has some currency, but there seem to be logical and empirical problems with his ideas as a general model of the origins of cultural complexity. Simple societies in several parts of the world have been observed operating extensive irrigation works with no perceptible despotic administrative systems or rapid increases in social complexity.[52] More damaging to Wittfogel's hypothesis is the scarcity of archaeological evidence of complex irrigation systems dating to before, or to the same time as, the appearance of monumental architecture, urbanism, and other reflections of increasing cultural complexity, in Southwest Asia and perhaps other areas where complex societies appeared independently and early.

Nonetheless, the difficulties of dating irrigation canals, inadequate archaeological samples, and other deficiencies of evidence are such that we cannot conclude that irrigation was unimportant in virtually any case of early cultural complexity.

WARFARE, POPULATION GROWTH, AND ENVIRONMENTAL CIRCUMSCRIPTION

"War is the father of all things," said Heraclitus, and, given its frequency in human affairs, we should not be surprised that many scholars see warfare as a natural adjunct of population growth in driving cultural evolution. In the film *The Third Man*, Orson Welles—justifying his profiteering in postwar Vienna to Joseph Cotton—says, "in Italy for 30 years under the Borgias they had warfare, terror, murder, bloodshed, but they produced Michelangelo, Leonardo da Vinci, and the Renaissance. In Switzerland, they had brotherly love, they had 500 years of democracy and peace. And what did that produce? The cuckoo-clock."

Welles's character was stating what for many is an uncomfortable truth: Human competition seems to be a powerful engine of cultural evolution. No early state—not Mexico, or China, or Sumer, or Peru—was without a background level of organized violence that occasionally erupted into great wars spanning decades.

Why should this be so? Why doesn't "natural selection" favor those cultures that develop institutions to resolve conflicts? Why doesn't cultural selection seem to give the edge to communities that pool their resources to build irrigation canals, establish universities, and work for world peace?

Most scholars consider warfare simply a cultural behavior that is elicited by environmental and cultural conditions. Anthropologist Robert Carneiro argues that warfare was the primary mechanism for the evolution of social complexity in ancient Peru, Mesopotamia, Egypt, Rome, northern Europe, central Africa, Polynesia, Mesoamerica, Colombia, and elsewhere. He believes, however, that "warfare cannot be the only factor. After all, wars have been fought in many parts of the world where the state never emerged. Thus while warfare may be a necessary condition for the rise of the state, it is not a sufficient one. Or, to put it another way, while we can identify war as the mechanism of state formation, we need also to specify the conditions under which it gave rise to the state."[53] Carneiro sees two such conditions as essential to the formation of complex societies in concert with warfare: population growth and environmental circumscription. He notes that human population densities have been increasing in many areas for millennia, but that only in certain environmental zones can population growth join with warfare to produce highly complex early civilizations. These environmental zones are exceptionally fertile areas "circumscribed," or surrounded, by areas of lesser productivity such as deserts, mountains, or oceans. As an example, Carneiro points to the coast of Peru, where approximately 78 rivers run from the Andes to the ocean through an 80-km stretch of some of the driest deserts on earth (Figure 7.8). Here, he says, are fertile, easily irrigated strips of land along the rivers, but in any direction one soon encounters desert, mountains, or the ocean. Similar conditions, he asserts, prevailed in Mesopotamia, Egypt, and the other centers of early civilizations.

Again using Peru as an example, Carneiro suggests that shortly after the appearance of the village farming way of life, these fertile riverine areas were sparsely occupied by small autonomous villages. He assumes that in such conditions populations grew, and, as these populations increased, villages tended to divide because of internal conflicts and pressure on agricultural lands. Some of the inhabitants would then establish a new community some distance away. Such movements were easily accomplished in this early period because there was no shortage of land and little investment in terracing or irrigation systems. As a consequence, the number of villages increased faster than village size, and all communities remained essentially the same in political and social organization.

Eventually, however, given this constant population growth and the proliferation of villages, all the land that could be irrigated and exploited easily became occupied, and the expanding population rapidly began to outrun the available food supplies. Since they could not move into the sea or deserts or easily colonize the mountains, early Peruvian farmers chose agricultural intensification. They built terraces and irrigation canals and tried to keep pace with their population growth rates, but they were caught in the classic Malthusian dilemma: Food supplies can be increased, but not nearly as quickly as population increases. At this point, Carneiro concludes, people turned to warfare as the only alternative. The village under the most stress would attack the weakest adjacent village, and the victor would expropriate the land and harvests of the loser. The conquered people not killed in the fighting could not simply move away and reestablish their villages, and they could not emigrate to the highlands because their whole culture was based on the village farming way of life. They were either taken back to the victors' village, where they became slaves or artisans, or they were left as serfs who were taxed so heavily that they had to reduce their own consumption and intensify their production still further.

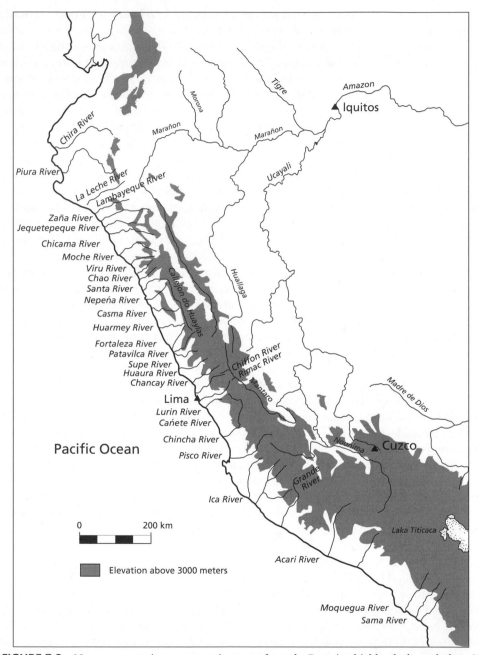

FIGURE 7.8 Numerous semi-permanent rivers run from the Peruvian highlands through the arid coastal zone to the sea. These rivers allowed people to establish agricultural centers in an otherwise inhospitable desert.

These developments encouraged the formation of an institutionalized bureaucracy to administer the taxes and slaves, and the establishment of the bureaucracy in turn intensified wealth and status differentials, as the most successful military leaders were given the administrative posts. In addition, the defeated peoples came to constitute a lower class, and thus the stratification of society increased as the level of warfare rose. Carneiro believes that warfare continued in Peru until all of each river valley was under the control of one integrated authority, a development he terms a "state." Subsequently, again because of the never-ending pressure of population, these states contended with each other until a whole series of river valleys was controlled by a single dominant center. Carneiro's ideas are diagrammed in Figure 7.9.

Since many primitive societies had remarkably precise control of their population-to-resources balance, population growth cannot be regarded as automatic. There is no demonstrated and inevitable reason why these populations could not have maintained their size below the stress level rather than resorting to agricultural intensification or warfare. Thus, to strengthen Carneiro's hypotheses we must stipulate other factors that encouraged or allowed these presumed growth rates.

In a reconsideration of Carneiro's model, David Webster maintains that warfare's principal importance in the evolution of the first states was the role it played in breaking down the kinship ties that organized early chiefdoms.[54] He notes that chiefdoms apparently are kept from evolving into states partially because the chief's power and prestige are tied to his role as a redistributive head, and if the chief begins to hoard wealth or exploit people, he begins to lose the support of his kinsmen and deputy rulers. Webster proposes that warfare produces a potent environment for the evolutionary change to state-level societies by rendering ineffective many of the internal constraints that keep chiefdoms in a stable sociopolitical status. Continued warfare between chiefdoms would place great adaptive value on a stable military leadership, thereby dampening the constant petty squabbles between rival rulers. A chief who is successful in warfare can also claim more wealth in the form of booty than he could on the basis of his redistribution of his own society's production.

Carneiro's ideas have stimulated much research[55] and seem to have broad applicability to various cultures.[56] But in contemporary archaeology there is a widespread sense that the key points of analysis in understanding the origins of early states must be at a socioeconomic and political level, not just demographics, physical environments, and the assumption of warfare.

EARLY MARXIST AND MATERIALIST EXPLANATIONS OF EARLY CULTURAL COMPLEXITY

For much of the twentieth century, Marxist social scientists had few doubts about the proper explanation of the origins of civilization. Friedrich Engels's remarks at Karl Marx's grave expressed this certainty: "As Darwin discovered the law of evolution in organic nature so Marx discovered the law of evolution in human history."[57]

Despite the collapse of Marxist states all over the world, and despite the interweaving of Marx's economic analysis with dubious political polemic, there is no denying the tremendous influence Marx's contributions have had on the analysis of social systems.

Almost any attempt to sum up Marx's theories about the origins of cultural complexity and the dynamics of history necessarily involves great oversimplification and arguable

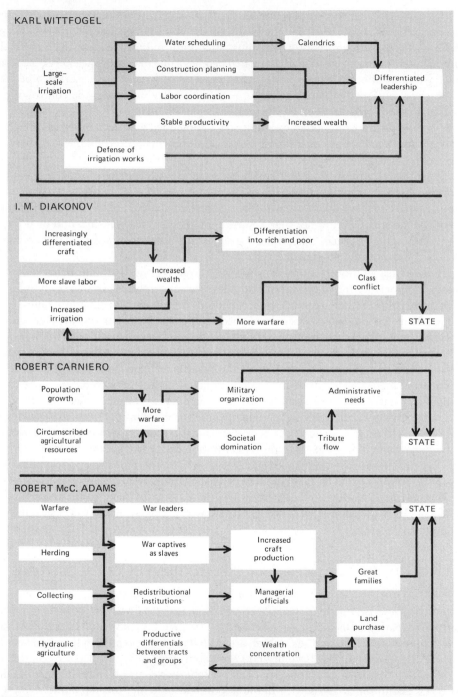

FIGURE 7.9 Several models of the evolution of cultural complexity. In these diagrams Henry Wright (1977) has depicted the most important hypothetical cause-and-effect relationships in several models of the origins of states and urbanism.

interpretations. Marx's famous statement of his basic ideas is worth quoting at length and studying carefully because it is still one of the most astute and revolutionary observations on the nature of cultural evolutionary history:

> In the social production of their subsistence men enter into determined and necessary relations with each other which are independent of their wills—production-relations which correspond to a definite stage of development of their material productive forces. The sum total of these production-relations forms the economic structure of society, the real basis, upon which a juridical and political superstructure arises, and to which definite forms of social consciousness correspond. The mode of production of material subsistence conditions the social, political and spiritual life-process in general. It is not the consciousness of men which determines their existence but on the contrary it is their social existence that determines their consciousness. At a certain stage of their development, the material productive forces of society come in conflict with the existing production relations, or what is merely a juridical expression for the same thing, the property relations within which they operated before. From being forms of development of the productive forces, these relations turn into fetters upon their development. Then comes an epoch of social revolution. With the change in the economic foundation the whole immense superstructure is slowly or rapidly transformed. In studying such a transformation one must always distinguish between the material transformation in the economic conditions essential to production—which can be established with the precision of the natural science—and the juridical, political, religious, artistic, or philosophic, in short ideological forms, in which men become conscious of this conflict and fight it out. As little as one judges what an individual is by what he thinks of himself, so little can one judge such an epoch of transformation by its consciousness; one must rather explain this consciousness by the contradictions in the material life, the conflict at hand between the social forces of production and the relations in which production is carried on.[58]

What all this means in terms of the whole history of complex societies is the point of enough books to fill a large library, and Marx's basic premises are being constantly reinterpreted. Still, many accept as valid the basic tenets of Marxian analyses of history, and there is certainly great power to some of his ideas.[59]

Marx himself, however, had very little to say specifically about the origins of complex societies. Much more attention was paid to the problem by later followers of Marx, particularly Engels and Lenin, and, more recently, V. V. Streuve and I. M. Diakonoff.[60]

Until the origins of agriculture, these scholars suggest, all societies were classless, all goods were shared, no one really owned anything, and all were treated equally. But gradually, after the achievement of domestication and the agricultural way of life, some people managed to control more than their fair share of the land, which is of course the basic source of wealth in an agricultural community. By controlling land, these elites were able to enslave others and force these people to work the land for them. In time the ruling classes developed the state, the laws, and the church to justify, protect, and perpetuate their economic and political privileges. The state is then seen as an exploitative mechanism created by the elites to control and oppress the workers. Marx promulgated a "labor theory of value," according to which capitalists steal much of the value that a worker produces by paying the worker only a fraction of the value his labor confers on goods and produce and appropriating the rest.

According to Marxian theory, every economic system based on the division of society into socioeconomic classes and on exploitation carries within itself the seeds of its own destruction because generally the means of producing wealth constantly improve, technologically and otherwise, and at a certain stage outgrow the social system constructed on them. Thus, slave societies would eventually give way to feudal societies and, eventually, Communist societies will replace capitalist societies.

I. M. Diakonoff has been the most prominent but traditional Marxist. His model of early Mesopotamian state formation rests on the assumption that if wealth differentials can arise, they will, and that once these differentials exist, antagonism between socioeconomic classes will follow and eventually the state will form to promote and protect the vested interests of the ruling class.[61]

Economists and others have challenged many of Marx's ideas, but evidence from early Mesopotamian and Egyptian societies does support some aspects of the Marxian reconstruction: Wealth differentials developed early and were impressive, and slavery existed, as did communal labor pools, warfare, irrigation systems, trade networks, and other elements integral to the Marxian scheme. But that is not to say that this scheme is correct or complete. Much of it was constructed on the basis of evidence from early documents, and some forms of the Mesopotamian state evolved several hundred years prior to writing; thus the textual evidence is most likely of only limited relevance to the origins of social complexity. More important, it is very difficult to test the Marxian reconstruction with archaeological data. Without written records, we cannot conclusively demonstrate class conflict or slavery, and many of the crucial elements of the Marxian paradigm, such as the labor theory of value and the contradictions between economies and their social correlates, seem utterly beyond the reach of archaeological research per se. Zagarell uses documents from Mesopotamia, however, to show that by the time the first extensive texts were written, some correspondences do exist between Marxian ideas and what we know from these texts about property, the rights of women, and so on.[62]

Other scholars have focused on the importance of trade in a Marxian context. Kipp and Schortman, for example, argue that an important factor in some cases of early state formation was the destabilizing effects markets in luxury goods had on early chiefdoms. In chiefdoms personal relationships between elites and the populace are important, but, as market economies evolved, chiefs and other elites had an increasingly difficult time trying to control these markets: "When leadership is undermined by a market blind to everything except profits, policies of systematic impoverishment are as essential to leaders as armies. Economic exploitation joins tyranny, and so states are born."[63]

Marvin Harris has tried to combine some of Marx's ideas with those of Wittfogel, Carneiro, and others to formulate a model that, although many reject it, at least has the advantages of being stipulated and partially testable with the archaeological data.[64]

The big step in Harris's view is the rise of chiefdoms, which he ties to the appearance of "big men," particularly influential older men whose advice and guidance the community seeks. Village big men act as the "nodes" of three important institutional complexes: They intensify production, carry out redistribution of harvest surpluses and trade goods, and use their prestige and position to lead the way in fighting or trading with neighboring villages.

Harris says that simple

> chiefdoms come into being with the first intensifier-redistributor-warrior complexes. The more production is intensified, the more there is to redistribute and to trade, the larger the population, the more intense the warfare, the more complex and powerful the chiefly sector. Other things being equal, all such systems tend to move from symmetric forms of

redistribution (in which the primary producers get back everything they produce) to asymmetric forms (in which the redistributor gets more of what is produced for longer and longer periods). Eventually the retained portion of the harvest surplus provides the chief with the material means for coercing his followers into further intensification.[65]

If all this is a standard developmental trajectory, why did chiefdoms never appear among the Eskimo, while they appeared in Melanesia but stabilized at that level of development, and while they quickly became interregional states in Mesopotamia and many other areas?

Harris turns to basic factors of demography, economy, environment, and technology to answer this question. He suggests that for chiefdoms to appear and then to become states and empires, the appropriate "energy gates" had to be available: Yams and tubers are poor energy gates because they do not store well and have no clearly defined harvest period, so a big man or chief cannot easily shut off the flow of proteins and calories produced by the farmers; but grains store well and have defined periods of harvest, so a chief with command of community grain stores absolutely controls the lives of his associates.[66]

Harris expects the first "pristine" states to arise in areas of sharp ecotones, where there is good potential for intensifying agriculture, but where away from the agricultural lands the environment is such that a family would suffer a sharp drop in standard of living if they moved away.[67] Drawing on the work of Robert Carneiro (see earlier), Harris identifies the sharply circumscribed farmlands of Egypt, Mesopotamia, northern India, the Yellow River Basin, central highland Mexico, the Peruvian coast, and the Andes highlands as areas where pristine states could be expected.[68] And once pristine states form in an area, their expansionist tendencies and economic impact act as a "single gigantic amplifier," as the whole region is caught in cycles of agricultural intensification, population growth, warfare, and so on.

Harris's version of Marxist analysis is rejected by many as being too "vulgar" and "mechanical," in that it focuses on demographic and ecological variables and appeals to these as the primary explanations of differences and similarities in early states.

Contemporary Approaches to the Explanation of the Evolution of Civilizations

It is better to know some of the questions than all of the answers.

James Thurber (1894–1961)

Attempts by Childe, Wittfogel, Harris,[69] and others to formulate general models of cultural evolution, on the basis of correlations between techno-environmental and demographic variables and social and political patterns and processes, stimulated a great deal of creative research, and there is still much of value about these ideas. But many contemporary scholars[70] argue that identifying correlations between these variables, patterns, and processes does not and cannot "explain" all the important aspects of the evolution of ancient civilizations. With the growing appreciation of the limits of techno-ecological analyses and traditional Marxist approaches, contemporary archaeologists have gone in many different directions in their approaches to the problem of the origins of civilizations.

CONTEMPORARY MARXIST PERSPECTIVES

Many contemporary archaeologists continue to draw inspiration from Marx and his theoretical successors. Friedman and Rowlands,[71] for example, have interpreted Marx in such a way that the focus of the analysis is the social relations of production that economies embody, rather than just the blunt forces of technology, environment, and agriculture. Their study defies easy translation and summary, but contains at least the following elements. Friedman and Rowlands assert that we must "reconstruct the structures of reproduction of particular social forms," which they define as the "social structures that dominate the process of production and circulation and which therefore constitute the socially determined form by which populations reproduce themselves as economic entities."[72]

Although Friedman and Rowlands's complex approach includes much of interest, it involves various problems. The primary one is that so much of it seems untestable with the archaeological record. Testability with archaeological data cannot, of course, be taken as the ultimate criterion of social theory, but archaeologists must try to measure the "fit" of their ideas against the reality of the bones and stones they excavate. In Friedman and Rowlands's approach, as in so many Marxist and Structuralist endeavors, causation is expressed in terms of dominances and constraints. Friedman and Rowlands say that the physical environment, technology, and general economic forces impose a system of constraints that make certain kinds of things unlikely to evolve (like a drive-through bank set up and frequented by hunter-gatherers); but, working in the opposite direction, the relations of production dominate the entire functioning of the system, determining its characteristics and developmental pattern. To find "relations of production" archaeologically, however, and then to demonstrate how they were the causes of other cultural phenomena is difficult. In Friedman and Rowlands's approach, something like an organized system of ancestor worship can—in a given society and instance—be the *result* of a complex of economic factors, and in another society and time organized ancestor worship can be a *cause* of economic behavior.

In general, many contemporary Marxist archaeologists are bound together by several basic ideas. One of these involves the rejection of "functionalist" ideas about adaptation. We might conclude, for example, that all early civilizations were rigidly stratified by socioeconomic classes because, in the absence of modern communications technology, an industrial base, and other means of economic production and social integration like those of contemporary societies, ancient civilizations could only organize themselves and function efficiently if their citizens were born into classes that automatically determined what occupational specialty they would perform and what access to wealth, power, and prestige they would have. Many Marxists reject this kind of functionalism and adaptationism on various grounds but particularly because such interpretations are descriptions, not explanations, and because they tend to emphasize the stability of these adaptations— and in so doing, justify them to some extent. Most forms of Marxism are about the necessity and social desirability of radical social change arising out of social conflict and inequities. It is not surprising, thus, that they see any attempt to interpret the appearance of such phenomena as social classes, legal systems, administrative bureaucracies, and so on as adaptive responses to problems societies faced as interpretations that obscure the conflicts and contradictions that are the true forces behind social changes. But contemporary Marxist critiques of traditional archaeology go much deeper than this. Marxists reject the notion that people in any society are just passive players whose actions and ideas are entirely the result of external forces. They focus on the social relationships that are the nexus of interactions among individuals and groups.

Marxism continues to have a strong influence on contemporary archaeology, although Marx himself might not recognize, or might reject, many contemporary applications of his ideas to the archaeological record. A continuing issue for Marxist archaeologists is the testability of their ideas in terms of the material remains of the archaeological record. In the absence of a written language, how are we to know if, for example, overt or institutionalized class conflict, or the subordination of women, or other social behaviors and concepts were part of the origins of the first states in the northern Andes—or anywhere else? If one rejects the notion that the archaeological record offers the possibility of a scientific and empirical test of the validity of *any* theory of history, however, as some archaeologists do, then the apparent difficulties of relating Marxian ideas to the material record of the past disappear.

The details of contemporary Marxist approaches are beyond the scope of this book, but the interested reader is referred to the bibliography of this chapter for additional sources on this topic.

THE THEORY OF CULTURAL EVOLUTION

The term theory of *cultural evolution* is heavily encrusted with past misuse and inappropriate applications, and for many scholars it immediately suggests that the analysis will be based on a false analogy with biology, will invoke sterile social typologies, will rearrange all human history in a sequence leading to the apex of Western civilization, and will apply capitalist and colonialist misperceptions to the analysis of history.

S. Gould summed up this view as follows: "Cultural evolution is not even a good analogue for biological evolution because it proceeds so much more rapidly and, especially, because it works by amalgamation and coalescence across lineages—the very topology precluded on the Darwinian tree of continuous divergence."[73]

The kind of evolutionary theory that some archaeologists now are applying to cultures, however, is different from the Spencerian forms of traditional neo-evolutionism that was, in fact, guilty of many of these sins. Evolutionary theory basically concerns the transmission of traits through time and space, and there is no necessary linkage with biology. As Robert Dunnell (see earlier) has observed, what matters in evolutionary theory is the mechanisms by which traits are perpetuated in an individual.[74] Nonetheless, the objects that comprise the archaeological record do not reproduce in the same way that people do, and thus the rules of genetics cannot be applied; also, whereas change in the biological world is through the relatively slow processes of genetic mutation, drift, selection, and so on (see chapter 3), cultural changes can be conveyed quickly and pervasively from one group to another (as in the spread of agriculture).

One issue in evolutionary models of cultural complexity involves the *scale* of selection. In the biological universe, the transmission of traits takes place at the level of the individual. The individual genes of the plant or animal do or do not get perpetuated, not the species as a whole. Therefore, the most productive point at which to analyze a given evolutionary problem is the transmission of traits from individual to individual. But in cultural situations, many individual traits, specifically behavioral ones, are the products of instruction by the complete community of parents, teachers, and friends. And people act in corporate groups in ways that make these the functional units of the society. For example, in the next chapter we will see that religions appeared[75] early in all great civilizations and that these formed effective ways to get people to act in concert for the corporate good—such as in fighting wars, clearing irrigation canals, and building pyramids. To summarize, in the production and transmission of cultural characteristics, cultural selection can act on groups as well as individuals.

So, to apply evolutionary theory to archaeological data will require analyzing a great diversity of concepts of trait transmission.

It is also important to note that the cases of cultural evolution detailed in the following chapters repeatedly show that cultural evolution is not a continuous, cumulative, gradual change, in most places. "Fits and starts" better describes it. In Mesopotamia, the Indus Valley, and elsewhere, there is clear evidence of communities that seem on the verge of cultural complexity—either to die out without further development or to be overtaken by developments in some core area to which they became the periphery.

The supposed "unification" of the Nile Delta and Valley cultures at about 3200 B.C. provides a useful example here. This pivotal event in Egyptian history apparently involved a process in which the cultural repertoire of the Valley cultures—in terms of artifact styles, political ideology, and so forth—was imposed upon, or was integrated into, or largely replaced those of the Delta cultures.

How are we to understand such a process of trait-transmission? And, at a higher level, how are we to understand similar processes in other early civilizations? Consider again Trigger's conclusion, quoted earlier, concerning the extremely limited variations in what he observed in early states in their most important elements. In trying to account for this lack of variation, Trigger appeals to the apparent "efficiency" that these basic social and political forms must have conferred on their individual cultures. If we accept that supposition, the analytical problem then becomes one of understanding and measuring the relative efficiency of various mechanisms of social forms and phenomena—and the kinds of selection that operate on variability, and how that variability is generated in the first place. If evolutionary theory has any application to the analysis of ancient and modern cultures, it would seem to be precisely with regard to these questions of cultural change.

Most early complex societies, for example, underwent a transition in which labor-intensive, highly decorated pottery was replaced by mass-produced forms of much less aesthetic appeal. Various scholars have seen cultural collapse and dissolution in such changes, but as Trigger notes, this replacement does "not indicate a decline in cultural or aesthetic standards. Instead it suggests that pottery no longer served as a medium of artistic expression."[76] In fact, the appearance of these mass-produced forms of pottery seems to be a prime indicator of increasing complexity in the institutions administering and controlling craft production. G. Johnson, R. McC. Adams,[77] and others have concluded that the rapid development of Southwest Asian states occurred during the period when the beautiful painted wares of the early fourth millennium were largely replaced by the unimpressive, mass-produced unpainted pottery. Egyptian pottery seems to have made a parallel transition in the Early Dynastic and Old Kingdom periods, when various low-fired wares including "bread molds" were the dominant ceramic types.

Several factors may explain these dramatic changes in pottery manufacture. The individual and corporate social groups identified by regional pottery styles, for example, are, in a sense, dangerous expressions of individualism and group distinctiveness that detract from the unity of the larger state, and it is possible that these states suppressed some expressions of group identity not derived from the state structures. The greater efficiency, too, of producing massive quantities of cheap and nearly identical pottery vessels would be best realized in a state organization.

The formulation of a powerful evolutionary theory will require that we avoid the naive "functionalism" of early versions of cultural evolutionism: that is, that evolutionary theory must supply some explanation for cultural change other than that a given cultural characteristic made a positive contribution to a culture's efficiency of adaptation.

CRITIQUES OF COMPARATIVE APPROACHES

Shanks and Tilley, for example, suggest that cross-cultural generalizations are not only misguided but also result from conscious or unconscious attempts to further the cause of Western imperialism.[78] In contrast to materialist deterministic models, Giddens[79] and many others have emphasized the power of sociopolitical factors over economic factors as determinants of the character and histories of pre-industrial class-based societies. "Post-processualists" and "post-modernists," in general, argue that "positivist" scientific epistemologies are fundamentally inappropriate for understanding the past.[80]

Critiques of the methodology of comparative studies have come from a wide variety of sources. Philip Kohl, for example, himself an advocate of a form of materialist theory, suggests that "[l]inear models of class and state formation, which decontextualize social and historical processes, make meaningful comparative studies impossible."[81] Even some traditional Marxists[82] now emphasize how different cultures construct unique and—at some levels—incommensurable social forms and histories.

And it is not just the post-processualists and post-modernists who have challenged the validity of traditional anthropological comparative studies. Contemporary thought in evolutionary theory, as applied to both cultural and biological systems, emphasizes the uniqueness and essential unpredictability of evolutionary trajectories.[83]

If even evolutionists conclude that evolutionary sequences are unpredictable and unique, what is the importance of comparative analyses as applied to, for example, Old Kingdom Egypt and the Inka state?

HOLISTIC AND SYNTHETIC APPROACHES

A holistic perspective, to use Bruce Trigger's term, is a multifaceted one in which any and every form of inquiry that seems to expand one's knowledge of the past is used. Trigger argues[84] that the future of analyses of the origins of civilizations must include combining all our ideas, perspectives, and methods in order to examine all the factors that "constrain" human behavior, in the present and the past. He notes that these constraints can be ecological, such as the great river valleys that were the homes of many of the first great civilizations and which directly determined the kinds of agriculture and settlement patterns that could be effective in this kind of environment, but he notes that these constraining and shaping factors can also be ideologies and cultural traditions.

Trigger dismisses the simplistic materialist determinism of, for example, Wittfogel,[85] and acknowledges the research importance of the unique aspects of early states. But in his concluding essay, he writes:

[My] findings indicate that practical reason plays a greater role in shaping cultural change than many postprocessual archaeologists and postmodernist anthropologists are prepared to admit. This encourages me to accord greater importance to an evolutionist analysis and less importance to a cultural particularist one than I would have done when I began my study. A particularlist approach is necessary to understand many aspects of early civilizations. But it is clearly a mistake to ignore, or even to underestimate, the importance of evolutionism, as those who would privilege cultural reason would have us do.[86]

Trigger acknowledges the power and primacy of cultures to construct their own realities, but he also sees extremely limited worldwide variation in some of the core structures and processes of early civilizations.[87] One can, therefore, usefully study what factors contribute to the "efficiency" of these rather invariant elements of early civilizations, perhaps from the "evolutionist" perspective Trigger suggests. But the baroque variability of "art styles and cultural values" provides ample material for particularistic studies that need not appeal to cross-cultural and comparative analyses for intellectual justification.

Trigger thus provides a justification and rationale for a wide variety of theoretical perspectives in archaeology, embracing both particularist studies and cross-cultural comparative analyses aimed at understanding the selective forces that so greatly constrained variation in some elements of these early civilizations.

Moreover, even in those elements that seem relatively invariant in early civilizations, there is considerable interesting variety in specific expression. Trigger suggests that many archaeologists have assumed "that aspects of civilizations that were shaped most directly by the constraints of environment and technology would display the greatest degree of cross-cultural uniformity."[88] He notes, however, that this is not the case. Metal-working, for example, was a core industry in Mesopotamia, where it was used to produce tools as well as ornaments, whereas in Egypt it was used to make weapons but not often to make agricultural tools, and in the New World it was used extensively to produce ornaments.

There may well be good functional reasons for these patterns (e.g., the scarcity of stone for implements such as hoes in Mesopotamia), but cultural constructs may be equally determinative even in such basic technologies as metallurgy.

In his chapter on religion, Trigger states he initially assumed that, given the flexibility of the human intellect, religious behavior would vary much more greatly in early civilizations than economic behavior, but he concluded that this was not the case. He identifies strong recurrent patterns in many religious systems. Kings, for example, tend to trace their descent to strangers, probably in order to minimize their kinship obligations to the people they dominate. He suggests that all early civilizations had religious systems based on establishing social relationships with unseen forces in the natural world in order to manipulate it. The early civilizations Trigger surveys are all ones, he notes, that existed prior to the appearance of "transcendent religions"—those that make strict distinctions between the social, the natural, and the supernatural.

Some of the commonalties in ideology that Trigger finds in early civilizations seem obviously understandable in functional terms. Most placed their own civilization in the center of a world that had four quarters corresponding to the cardinal directions, political competition was cast in terms of religious struggles, and the universe was once or regularly threatened with extinction and could only be saved by the intercession of gods, who had to be placated by human activities and earthly wealth.

In summary, Trigger's basic goal and strategy is to use many different ideas and techniques to analyze early civilizations—not in a simplistic positivist sense but, still, in a sense that does not admit the possibility that any "reading" of the record of the past is equally valid, equally "true." He stresses that cultural differences are as important in this context as are cultural similarities, and he admits particularistic studies as useful adjuncts in a synthetic approach to the past. But his basic goal is to understand why these similarities and differences appeared, and he invokes materialist and evolutionist ideas in this regard.

All explanations of cultural complexity focus on the similarities and differences that the various forms of cultural evolution exhibit. But what is the significance of these similarities and differences?

Stephen Jay Gould, in his book *Wonderful Life*,[89] emphasizes how every evolutionary sequence is unique; and the state of uniqueness, like that of pregnancy, permits no qualifications or degrees. But if every sequence is unique, what is the significance of the similarities of cultural systems unconnected by genetics or history? The Aztecs and the Egyptians—who knew nothing of each other and lived thousands of years separated in time—did many of the same things, from building pyramids to establishing state religions; but what is the significance of these similarities? Scholarly opinion, of course, remains divided on this point.

Brumfiel and Earle have categorized some of the variability they see in early economic exchange in terms of three "models": (1) *commercial development models*, in which increasing occupational specialization and exchange are seen as the "natural" outgrowth of economic growth; (2) *adaptationist models*, in which political leaders are assumed to have intervened directly in the economy, to redistribute goods, for example, or to manage irrigation systems; and (3) *political models*, in which local rulers intervene in economies but, unlike their role in adaptationist models, these leaders are assumed to be the primary beneficiaries of their efforts.[90] Brumfiel and Earle propose that "political elites consciously and strategically employ specialization and exchange to create and maintain social inequity, strengthen political coalitions, and fund new institutions of control, often in the face of substantial opposition from those whose well-being is reduced by such actions."[91]

It is worth noting here that most of these many kinds of explanations of cultural complexity are *functional arguments*. The basic idea of a functionalist explanation was introduced earlier in the context of contemporary Marxist perspectives on archaeology. Functional arguments attempt to explain the origins of something (e.g., the human heart) in terms of the functions it performs (e.g., blood circulation). To the question, "Why do people have hearts?" the answer that some device is needed to circulate blood is an explanation of sorts, but it does not explain why some other kind of life-support system did not evolve, nor does it explain the evolutionary history of the heart or the selective pressures that shaped this history.

Similarly, to assert that complex societies developed because a leader was needed to coordinate irrigation and redistribute agricultural production is a functional explanation and does not explain why the society did not remain egalitarian, or develop a capitalist economic system, or go off in some other developmental direction.

Yet functional explanations seem to work so well for certain phenomena. The national religious cults that all early states developed, for example, seem so transparently a device for social control. Montaigne said, "Man is certainly stark mad. He cannot make a worm, and yet he will be making gods by the dozen." But for an early state few things are as useful as gods in whom everyone believes. Then one can despise and kill (and take possession of the property of) all nonbelievers, foreign and domestic, without qualms; one is willing to sacrifice oneself in battles, or participate in pyramid building, or accept a social hierarchy, simply because the gods have so decreed. And the best part is that one does all these things without much cost to the state—people fight in wars, work for the common good, or accept life as a disenfranchised slave often on the premise that in the afterlife things will be greatly improved.

Thus, functionalist arguments have the strong heuristic value of suggesting hypotheses about a specific development and indicating crucial variable relationships. Marxist and other scholars see such functionalist interpretations as adequate *descriptions*, perhaps, but not *explanations*, which must involve, in their opinion, an analysis of the social relations out of which arise social changes.

SUMMARY AND CONCLUSIONS

In the rest of this book we will review numerous cases of the evolution of complex societies, but in all these analyses of cultural and social complexity, archaeologists must come to terms with a fundamental problem: Most of the origins and development of ancient societies cannot be fully explained on the basis of the archaeologically retrievable facts of climate, technology, economy, and demography. Cultural evolution instead must be analyzed at some level above these basic conditions—at the higher level of the social, economic, and political relationships of peoples and social entities. But how do we get at these higher-level interactions through the data and methods of archaeology? Some archaeologists have concluded that we cannot do so in any scientific way, and thus archaeology cannot be a science; others argue that only the principles of evolutionary theory will help us understand these patterns of cultural change, but that we can never get at the specifics of the changes in social relations at the heart of the origins of civilizations; still other archaeologists believe that we can make inferences about these kinds of social changes and in various ways incorporate them in a holistic discipline of archaeological analysis.

The following chapters of this book, thus, should be seen as more of a *description* of the problems of analyzing the evolution of civilizations than an *explanation* of these evolutionary processes, for we are still very far from any powerful comprehensive explanation of them—and there is little agreement about how we might analyze these processes or even about the usefulness of trying to analyze them. If that summary sounds somewhat nilhilistic, it is well to recall that there is much about the pyramids of Egypt, the first written texts of Mesopotamian civilization, the glory that was Greece and the grandeur that was Rome, and so on, that is interesting and rewarding to consider, even if we can't ultimately and utterly explain their origins.

BIBLIOGRAPHY

Adams, R. McC. 1966. *The Evolution of Urban Society*. Chicago: Aldine.
———. 1981. *Heartland of Cities*. Chicago: Aldine.
Adams, R. N. 1981. "Natural Selection, Energetics, and Cultural Materialism." *Current Anthropology* 22:603–624.

————. 1988. *The Eighth Day*. Austin: University of Texas Press.

Alexander, R. D. 1975. "The Search for a General Theory of Behavior." *Behavioral Science* 220:77–100.

————. 1979. "Evolution and Culture." In *Evolutionary Biology and Human Social Behavior: An Anthropological Perspective*, ed. N. Chagnon and W. Irons. North Scituate, MA: Duxbury Press.

————. 1987. *The Biology of Moral Systems*. Hawthorne, NY: Aldine de Gruyter.

Algaze, G. 1989. "The Uruk Expansion." *Current Anthropology* 30(5):571–608.

Ammerman, A. J., and L. L. Cavalli-Sforza. 1973. "A Population Model for the Diffusion of Early Farming in Europe." In *The Explanation of Culture Change*, ed. C. Renfrew. Pittsburgh: University of Pittsburgh Press.

Appadurai, A., ed. 1986. *The Social Life of Things*. Cambridge: Cambridge University Press.

Athens, J. S. 1977. "Theory Building and the Study of Evolutionary Process in Complex Societies." In *For Theory Building in Archaeology*, ed. L. S. Binford. New York: Academic Press.

Bard, K. 1994. *From Farmers to Pharaohs*. Monographs in Mediterranean Archaeology 2. Sheffield, UK: Sheffield Academic Press.

Barnard, A. 1983. "Contemporary Hunter-Gatherers: Current Theoretical Issues in Ecology and Social Organization." *Annual Review of Anthropology* 12:193–214.

Bartel, B. 1982. "A Historical Review of Ethnological and Archaeological Analyses of Mortuary Practice." *Journal of Anthropological Archaeology* 1(1):32–58.

Bass, G. F. 1987. "Splendors of the Bronze Age." *National Geographic*, 172(6): 693–732.

Beck, L. A., ed. 1995. *Regional Approaches to Mortuary Analysis*. New York: Plenum Press.

Bender, B. 1985. "Emergent Tribal Formations in the American Midcontinent." *American Antiquity* 50(1):52–62.

Berlinski, D. 1976. *On Systems Analysis*. Cambridge, MA: MIT Press.

Bernal, M. 1987. *The Afroasiatic Roots of Classical Civilization*. New Brunswick, NJ: Rutgers University Press.

Berry, B. 1967. *Geography of Market Centers and Retail Distribution*. Englewood Cliffs, NJ: Prentice-Hall.

Betzig, L. L. 1986. *Despotism and Differential Reproduction: A Darwinian View of History*. Hawthorne, NY: Aldine de Gruyter.

Binford, L. R. 1971. "Mortuary Practices: Their Study and Their Potential." In *Approaches to the Social Dimensions of Mortuary Practices*, ed. J. A. Brown. Memoirs of the Society for American Archaeology 25:6–29. Washington, D.C.: Society for American Archaeology.

Blanton, R. E. 1995. *Houses and Households: A Comparative Study*. New York: Plenum Press.

Boserup, E. 1965. *The Conditions of Agricultural Growth*. Chicago: Aldine.

Boyd, R., and P. J. Richerson. 1985. *Culture and the Evolutionary Process*. Chicago: University of Chicago Press.

Braun, D. P. 1986. "Midwestern Hopewellian Exchange and Supralocal Interaction." In *Peer Polity Interaction and Socio-Political Change*, ed. C. Renfrew and J. F. Cherry. Cambridge: Cambridge University Press.

Bronson, B. 1980. "South-east Asia: Civilizations of the Tropical Forest." *Cambridge Encyclopedia of Archaeology*. pp. 202–266.

Brumfiel, E. M., and T. K. Earle, eds. 1987. *Specialization, Exchange, and Complex Societies*. Cambridge, England: Cambridge University Press.

————. 1987. "Specialization, Exchange, and Complex Societies: An Introduction." In *Specialization, Exchange, and Complex Societies*, ed. E. M. Brumfiel and T. K. Earle. Cambridge, England: Cambridge University Press.

Buck, R. C. 1956. "On the Logic of General Behavior Systems Theory." In *The Foundations of Science and the Concept of Psychology and Psychoanalysis*, ed. H. Feigl and M. Scriven. Minnesota Studies in the Philosophy of Science 1:223–128. Minneapolis: University of Minnesota Press.

Carniero, R. 1970. "A Theory of the Origin of the State." *Science* 169:733–738.

Carr, C. 1995. "Mortuary Practices: Their Social, Philosophical-Religious, Circumstantial, and Physical Determinants." *Journal of Archaeological Method and Theory* 2:105–200.

Carr, C., and J. E. Neitzel, eds. 1995. *Style, Society, and Person: Archaeological and Ethnological Perspectives*. New York: Plenum Press.

Cavalli-Sforza, L. L., and M. W. Feldman. 1981. *Culture Transmission and Evolution. A Quantitative Approach*. Princeton, NJ: Princeton University Press.

Childe, V. G. 1934. *New Light on the Most Ancient East*. London: Kegan Paul.

Clark, J. G. D. 1986. *Symbols of Excellence: Precious Materials as Expressions of Status*. Cambridge: Cambridge University Press.

Cohen, G. A. 1978. *Karl Marx's Theory of History: A Defense*. Princeton, NJ: Princeton University Press.

Cohen, R. 1981. "Evolutionary Epistemology and Human Values." *Current Anthropology* 22:201–218.

Costin, C. L. 1991. "Craft Specialization: Issues in Defining, Documenting, and Explaining the Organization of Production." *In Archaeological Method and Theory*, Vol. 3, ed. M. B. Schiffer. Tucson: University of Arizona Press.

————. 1996. "Ceramic Production and Distribution." In *Empire and Domestic Economy: Transformation in Household Economics of Xauxa Soceity Under the Inkas*, ed. T. D'Altroy and C. Hastorf. Washington, DC: Smithsonian Institution Press.

Costin, C. L., and T. Earle. 1989. "Status Distinction and Legitimation of Power as Reflected in Changing Patterns of Consumption in Late Prehispanic Peru." *American Antiquity* 54(4):691–714.

Cowgill, G. 1975. "On the Causes and Consequences of Ancient and Modern Population Changes." *American Anthropologist* 77:505–525.

Crumley, C. L. 1979. "Three Locational Models. An Epistemological Assessment for Anthropology and Archaeology." In *Advances in Archaeological Method and Theory*, Vol. 2, ed. M. B. Schiffer. New York: Academic Press.

———. 1992. "A Dialectical Critique of Hierarchy." In *Power Relations and State Formation*, ed. T. Patterson and C. Gailey. Salem, WI: Sheffield Publishing Company.

Crumley, C. L., and W. H. Marquardt, eds. 1987. *Regional Dynamics: Burgundian Landscapes in Historical Perspective*. Orlando, FL: Academic Press.

Darwin, C. 1871. *The Descent of Man and Selection in Relation to Sex*. New York: Appleton.

Demarest, A. A., and G. W. Conrad, eds. 1992. *Ideology and Pre-columbian Civilizations*. Santa Fe, NM: School of American Research.

Diakonoff, I. M., ed. 1969. *Ancient Mesopotamia*. Moscow: Nauka.

———. 1991. *Early Antiquity*. Chicago: University of Chicago Press.

Drennan, R. D. 1995. "Chiefdoms in Northern South America." *Journal of World Prehistory* 9(3):301–340.

Drennan, R. D., and C. A. Uribe, eds. 1987. *Chiefdoms in the Americas*. Lanham, MD: University Press of America.

Dunnell, R. C. 1978. "Style and Function: A Fundamental Dichotomy." *American Antiquity* 43:192–202.

———. 1980. "Evolutionary Theory and Archaeology." In *Advances in Archaeological Method and Theory*, Vol. 3, ed. M. B. Schiffer. New York: Academic Press.

———. 1982. "'Science, Social Science, and Common Sense: The Agonizing Dilemma of Modern Archaeology." *Journal of Anthropological Research* 38:1–25.

Dunnell, R. C., and R. J. Wenke. 1980. "An Evolutionary Model of the Development of Complex Societies." Paper presented at the Annual Meeting of the American Association for the Advancement of Science, San Francisco.

Durham, W. H. 1990. "Advances in Evolutionary Culture Theory." *Annual Review of Anthropology* 19:187–242.

Earle, T. K. 1987. "Chiefdoms in Archaeological and Ethnohistorical Perspective." *Annual Review of Anthropology* 16:279–308.

———, ed. 1991. *Chiefdoms: Power, Economy, Ideology*. Cambridge, England: Cambridge University Press.

Earle, T., and R. W. Preucel. 1987. "Processual Archaeology and the Radical Critique." *Current Anthropology* 28(4):501–538.

Eisenstadt, S. N. 1963. *The Political System of Empires*. New York: Free Press of Glencoe.

Ember, C. R. 1975. "Residential Variation Among Hunter-Gatherers." *Behavioral Science Research* 10:199–227.

Evans, S. "Settlement Models in Archaeology." *Journal of Anthropological Archaeology* 1:275–304.

Feinman, G. M., K. G. Lightfoot, and S. Upham. 2000. "Political Hierarchies and Organizational Strategies in the Puebloan Southwest." *American Antiquity* 65(3):449–470.

Feinman, G. M., and J. Neitzel. 1984. "Too Many Types: An Overview of Sedentary Prestate Societies in the Americas." In *Advances in Archaeological Method and Theory* Vol. 7, ed. M. Schiffer. New York: Academic Press.

Flannery, K. V. 1972. "The Cultural Evolution of Civilizations." *Annual Review of Ecology and Systematics* 3:399–426.

———. 1973. "Archeology with a Capital S." In *Research and Theory in Current Archeology*, ed. C. L. Redman. New York: Wiley.

Fried, M. H. 1960. "On the Evolution of Social Stratification and the State." In *Culture in History*, ed. S. Diamond. New York: Columbia University Press.

———. 1967. *The Evolution of Political Society*. New York: Random House.

Friedman, J., and M. J. Rowlands. 1977. *The Evolution of Social Systems*. Pittsburgh: University of Pittsburgh Press.

Gellner, E., ed. 1980. *Soviet and Western Anthropology*. London: Duckworth.

Giddens, A. 1981. *A Contemporary Critique of Historical Materialism, Vol. 1. Power, Property and the State*. London: Macmillan.

———. 1985. *A Contemporary Critique of Historical Materialism, Vol. 2. The Nation-State and Violence*. Cambridge: Polity Press.

Gould, S. J. 1989. *Wonderful Life*. New York: W.W. Norton.

———. 1987. *An Urchin in the Storm*. New York: W.W. Norton.

Graber, R. B. 1994. *A Scientific Model of Social and Cultural Evolution*. Lanham, MD: University Press of America.

Harris, M. 1968. *The Rise of Anthropological Theory*. New York: Crowell.

———. 1977. *Cannibals and Kings*. New York: Random House.

———. 1979. *Cultural Materialism: The Struggle for a Science of Culture*. New York: Vintage Press.

Harris, M., and E. B. Ross. 1990. *Death, Sex and Fertility: Population Regulation in Preindustrial and Developing Societies*. Irvington, NY: Columbia University Press.

Hassan, F. 1988. "The Predynastic of Egypt." *Journal of World Prehistory* 2(2):135–185.

Hastorf, C. A., and S. Johannessen. 1993. "Pre-Hispanic Political Change and the Role of Maize in the Central Andes of Peru." *American Anthropologist* 95(1):115–137.

Hill, J. N. 1977. *Explanation of Prehistoric Change*. Albuquerque: University of New Mexico Press.

Hodder, I., ed., 1982. *Symbolic and Structural Archaeology*. New York: Cambridge University Press.

Hodder, I. 1986. *Reading the Past: Current Approaches to Interpretation in Archaeology*. Cambridge, England: Cambridge University Press.

Johnson, G. A. 1977. "Aspects of Regional Analysis in Archaeology." *Annual Review of Anthropology* 6:479–508.

———. 1980. "Rank-Size Convexity and System Integration: A View from Archaeology." *Economic Geography* 56:234–247.

———. 1981. "Monitoring Complex System Integration and Boundary Phenomena with Settlement Size Data." In *Archaeological Approaches to Complexity*, ed. S. E. van der Leeuw. Amsterdam: University of Amsterdam.

———. 1982. "Organizational Structure Scalar Stress." In *Theory and Explanation in Archaeology*. New York: Academic Press.

———. 1987. "The Changing Organization in Uruk Administration on the Susiana Plain." In *The Archaeology of Western Iran*, ed. F. Hole. Washington, DC: Smithsonian Institution Press.

Kemp, B. J. 1989. *Ancient Egypt: Anatomy of a Civilization*. London and New York: Routledge.

Kenoyer, J. M. 1991. "The Indus Valley Tradition of Pakistan and Western India." *Journal of World Prehistory* 5(4):331–385.

Kipp, R. S., and E. M. Schortman. 1989. "The Political Impact of Trade in Chiefdoms." *American Anthropologist* 91(2):370–385.

Kirch, P. V. 1988. "Circumscription Theory and Sociopolitical Evolution in Polynesia." *American Behavioral Scientist* 31(4):416–427.

———. 1990. "The Evolution of Sociopolitical Complexity in Prehistoric Hawaii: An Assessment of the Archaeological Evidence." *Journal of World Prehistory* 4(3):311–346.

Kohl, P. L. 1987. "The Use and Abuse of World Systems Theory." In *Advances in Archaeological Method and Theory*, Vol. 11, ed. M. B. Schiffer. New York: Academic Press.

Lansing, J. S., and J. N. Kremer. 1993. "Emergent Properties of Balinese Water Temple Networks." *American Anthropologist* 95(1):97–114.

LeCarré, J. 1974. *Tinker, Tailor, Soldier, Spy*. New York: Knopf.

Lee, R. E. 1969. "!Kung Bushmen Subsistence: An Input-Output Analysis." In *Environment and Cultural Behavior*, ed. A. P. Vayda. Garden City, NY: Natural History Press.

Legros, D. 1977. "Chance, Necessity and Mode of Production: A Marxist Critique of Cultural Evolutionism." *American Anthropologist* 79:26–41.

Locke, J. 1980 (orig. A.D. 1690). *Second Treatise of Government*. Indianapolis: Hackett.

Lumsden, C. J., and E. O. Wilson. 1981. *Genes, Mind, and Culture*. Cambridge, MA: Harvard University Press.

Madsen, M., C. Lipo, and M. Cannon. 1999. "Fitness and Reproductive Trade-Offs in Uncertain Environments: Explaining the Evolution of Cultural Elaboration." *Journal of Anthropological Archaeology* 18:251–281.

Madsen, T. 1982. "Settlement Systems of Early Agricultural Societies in East Jutand, Denmark: A Regional Study of Change." *Journal of Anthropological Archaeology* 1:197–236.

Mann, M. 1986. *The Sources of Social Power I: A History of Power from the Beginning to AD 1760*. Cambridge: Cambridge University Press.

Marx, K. 1932 (orig. 1859). *Capital and Other Writings*. New York: The Modern Library.

———. 1973 (orig. manuscript 1857–1858). *Grundrisse: Foundations of the Critique of Political Economy*. New York: Vintage Press.

Marx, K., and F. Engels. 1970. *Selected Works*. 3 Vols. Moscow: Progress Publishers.

May, D. A., and D. M. Heer. 1968. "Son Survivorship, Motivation and Family Size in India: A Computer Simulation." *Population Studies* 22:199–210.

McGuire, R. H. 1992. *A Marxist Archeology*. San Diego: Academic Press.

McGuire, R. H., and R. Paynter, eds. 1991. *The Archaeology of Inequality*. Cambridge, MA: Basil Blackwell.

Miller, D. 1985. "Ideology and the Harappan Civilization." *Journal of Anthropological Archaeology* 4(1):34–71.

Montmollin, O. de 1989. *The Archaeology of Political Structure: Settlement Analysis in a Classic Maya Polity*. Cambridge: Cambridge University Press.

Neiman, F. D. 1995. "Stylistic Variation in Evolutionary Perspective: Inferences from Decorative Diversity and Interassemblage Distance in Illinois Woodland Ceramic Assemblages." *American Antiquity* 60(1):7–36.

O'Shea, J. M. 1984. *Mortuary Variability—An Archaeological Investigation*. New York: Academic Press.

Patterson, T. C., and C. W. Gailey, eds. 1987. *Power Relations and State Formation*. Washington, DC: American Anthropological Association.

Peebles, C. S. 1971. "Moundville and Surrounding Sites: Some Structural Considerations of Mortuary Practices, II." In *Approaches to the Social Dimensions of Mortuary Practices*, ed. J. A. Brown. Society for American Archaeology Memoir No. 25. Washington, D.C.: Society for American Archaeology.

———. 1987. "Moundville from 1000–1500 AD." In *Chiefdoms in the Americas*, ed. R. D. Drennan and C. A. Uribe. Lanham: University Press of America.

Peterson, N. 1993. "Demand Sharing: Reciprocity and the Pressure for Generosity Among Foragers." *American Anthropologist* 95(4):860–874.

Polyani, K., C. M. Arensberg, and H. W. Pearson. 1957. *Trade and Market in the Early Empires*. Glencoe, IL: Free Press.

Price, T. D., and G. M. Feinman, eds. 1995. *Foundations of Social Inequality*. New York: Plenum Press.

Redman, C. L. 1978. *The Rise of Civilization*. San Francisco: Freeman.

Renfrew, C. 1972. *The Emergence of Civilization*. London: Methuen.

———. 1986. "Varna and the Emergence of Wealth in Prehistoric Europe." In *The Social Life of Things*, ed. A. Appaudrai. Cambridge: Cambridge University Press.

———. 1987. *Archaeology and Language*. London: Jonathan Cape.

Renfrew, C., and J. F. Cherry, eds. 1986. *Peer Polity Interaction and Socio-political Change*. Cambridge: Cambridge University Press.

Rindos, D. 1984. *The Origins of Agriculture*. New York: Academic Press.

Roberts, N. 1989. *The Holocene: An Environmental History*. Oxford: Blackwell.

Robins, G. 1986. *Egyptian Painting and Relief*. Aylesbury: Shire.

Rothschild, N. A. 1979. "Mortuary Behavior and Social Organization at Indian Knoll and Dickson Mounds." *American Antiquity* 44(4):658–675.

Roux, G. 1964. *Ancient Iraq*. Baltimore: Penguin.

Sabloff, J. A. 1989. *The Cities of Ancient Mexico*. London and New York: Thames & Hudson.

Sahlins, M. 1968. "Notes on the Original Affluent Society." In *Man the Hunter*, ed. R. Lee and I. DeVore. Chicago: Aldine.

———. 1976. *Culture and Practical Reason*. Chicago: University of Chicago Press.

Saunders, N. 1989. *People of the Jaguar*. London: Souvenir Press.

Schacht, R. M. 1988. "Circumscription Theory." *American Behavioral Scientist* 31(4):438–448.

Schele, L., and M. E. Miller. 1986. *The Blood of Kings: Dynasty and Ritual in Maya Art*. Fort Worth: Kimbell Art Museum.

Schwartz, G. M., and S. E. Falconer, eds. 1994. *Archaeological Views from the Countryside: Village Communities in Early Complex Societies*. Washington, DC: Smithsonian Institution Press.

Service, E. 1962. *Primitive Social Organization*. New York: Random House.

———. 1975. *Origins of the State and Civilization*. New York: Norton.

Shanks, M., and C. Tilley. 1987a. *Re-Constructing Archaeology*. Cambridge, England: Cambridge University Press.

———. 1987b. *Social Theory and Archaeology*. Oxford: Polity Press.

———. 1989. "Archaeology into the 1990s." *Norwegian Archaeological Review* 22(1):1–12.

Shennan, S. J. 1987. "Trends in the Study of Later European Prehistory." *Annual Review of Anthropology* 16:365–382.

———. 1988. *Quantifying Archaeology*. Edinburgh: Edinburgh University Press.

Stein, G. J., and M. J. Blackman. 1993. "The Organizational Context of Specialized Craft Production in Early Mesopotamian States." *Research in Economic Anthropology* 14:29–59.

Steward, J. 1936. "The Economic and Social Basis of Primitive Bands." In *Essays in Anthropology in Honor of Alfred Louis Kroeber*. Berkeley: University of California Press.

———. 1949. "Cultural Causality and Law: A Trial Formulation of the Development of Early Civilizations." *American Anthropologist* 51:1–27.

Streuve, V. V. 1969. "The Problem of the Genesis, Development and Disintegration of the Slave Societies in the Ancient Orient." Trans. I. Levit. In *Ancient Mesopotamia*, ed. I. M. Diakonov. Moscow: Nauka.

Tainter, J. A. 1987. *The Collapse of Complex Societies*. Cambridge, England: Cambridge University Press.

Teltser, P. A., ed. 1995. *Evolutionary Archaeology: Methodological Issues*. Tucson: University of Arizona Press.

Trigger, B. 1972. "Determinants of Urban Growth in Pre-Industrial Societies." In *Man, Settlement and Urbanism*, ed. P. J. Ucko, R. Tringham, and G. W. Dimbleby. London: Duckworth.

———. 1983. "The Rise of Egyptian Civilization." In *Ancient Egypt: A Social History*, ed. B. Trigger, B. J. Kemp, D. O'Connor, and A. B. Lloyd. Cambridge, England: Cambridge University Press.

———. 1984. "Archaeology at the Crossroads: What's New?" *Annual Review of Anthropology* 13:275–300.

———. 1985. "The Evolution of Pre-industrial Cities: A Multilinear Perspective." *Melanges offerts à Jean Vercoutter*. Paris: Editions Recherce sur les Civilisations.

———. 1993. *Early Civilizations: Ancient Egypt in Context*. Cairo: American University in Cairo Press.

———. 2003. *Understanding Early Civilizations: A Comparative Study*. New York: Cambridge University Press.

Waldrop, M. M. 1992. *Complexity*. New York. Touchstone.

Wallerstein, I. 1974. *The Modern World System*. New York: Academic Press.

Webb, M. 1975. "The Flag Follows Trade: An Essay on the Necessary Integration of Military and Commercial Factors in State Formation." In *Ancient Civilization and Trade*, ed. J. Sabloff and C. C. Lamberg-Karlovsky. Albuquerque: University of New Mexico Press.

Webster, D. 1975. "Warfare and the Evolution of the State: A Reconsideration." *American Antiquity* 40:471–475.

Weiss, R. M. 1976. "Demographic Theory and Anthropological Inference." *Annual Review of Anthropology* 5:351–381.

Wenke, R. J. 1981. "Explaining the Evolution of Cultural Complexity: A Review." In *Advances in Archaeological Method and Theory*, Vol. 4, ed. M. B. Schiffer. New York: Academic Press.

White, L. 1949. *The Science of Culture*. New York: Grove Press.

Wittfogel, K. A. 1957. *Oriental Despotism: A Comparative Study of Total Power*. New Haven: Yale University Press.

Wolf, E. R. 1966. *Peasants*. Englewood Cliffs, NJ: Prentice-Hall.

Woodburn, J. 1982. "Egalitarian Societies." *Man* (NS) 17:432–451.

Woodbury, R. B. 1961. "A Reappraisal of Hohokam Irrigation." *American Anthropologist* 63(3):550–560.

Wright, H., and G. A. Johnson. 1975. "Population, Exchange, and Early State Formation in Southwestern Iran." *American Anthropologist* 77:267–289.

Yellen, J. E. 1976. "Settlement Patterns of the !Kung: An Archaeological Perspective." In *Kalahari Hunter-Gatherers: Studies of the !Kung San and Their Neighbors*, ed. R. Lee and I. DeVore. Cambridge, MA: Harvard University Press.

Yoffee, N. 1979. "The Decline and Rise of Mesopotamian Civilization: An Ethnoarchaeological Perspective on the Evolution of Social Complexity." *American Antiquity* 44:5–35.

Yoffee, N., and G. Cowgill, eds. 1988. *The Collapse of Ancient States and Empires*. Tucson: University of Arizona Press.

Yoffee, N., and A. Sherratt, eds. 1993. *Archaeological Theory: Who Sets the Agenda?* Cambridge: Cambridge University Press.

Zagarell, A. 1986. "Trade, Women, Class, and Society in Ancient Western Asia." *Current Anthropology* 27(5):415–430.

NOTES

1. Trigger, *Early Civilizations: Ancient Egypt in Context*, p. 110.
2. Ibid.
3. See, for example, Shanks and Tilley, *Re-Constructing Archaeology*.
4. See, for example, Graber, *A Scientific Model of Social and Cultural Evolution*; Neiman, "Stylistic Variation in Evolutionary Perspective: Inferences from Decorative Diversity and Interassemblage Distance in Illinois Woodland Ceramic Assemblages"; Dunnell, "Science, Social Science, and Common Sense: The Agonizing Dilemma of Modern Archaeology."
5. See, for example, Demarest and Conrad, eds., *Ideology and Pre-columbian Civilizations*.
6. Crumley, "A Dialectical Critique of Hierarchy."
7. See, for example, Dunnell, "Science, Social Science, and Common Sense: The Agonizing Dilemma of Modern Archaeology"; Rindos, *The Origins of Agriculture*; Lumsden and Wilson, *Genes, Mind, and Culture*; Boyd and Richerson, *Culture and the Evolutionary Process*; Wenke, "Explaining the Evolution of Cultural Complexity: A Review"; Ammerman and Cavalli-Sforza, "A Population Model for the Diffusion of Early Farming in Europe"; Kirch, "The Evolution of Sociopolitical Complexity in Prehistoric Hawaii: An Assessment of the Archaeological Evidence"; R. N. Adams, "Natural Selection, Energetics, and Cultural Materialism"; Cavalli-Sforza and Feldman, *Cultural Transmission and Evolution. A Quantitative Approach*; Neiman, "Stylistic Variation in Evolutionary Perspective: Inferences from Decorative Diversity and Interassemblage Distance in Illinois Woodland Ceramic Assemblages"; Teltser, ed., *Evolutionary Archaeology: Methodological Issues*.
8. Waldrop, *Complexity*.
9. Lansing and Kremer, "Emergent Properties of Balinese Water Temple Networks."
10. See, for example, Adams, "Natural Selection, Energetics, and Cultural Materialism"; Alexander, "The Search for a General Theory of Behavior"; Alexander, "Evolution and Culture"; Cohen, "Evolutionary Epistemology and Human Values"; Dunnell, "Style and Function: A Fundamental Dichotomy"; Dunnell and Wenke, "An Evolutionary Model of the Development of Complex Societies"; Kirch, "Circumscription Theory and Sociopolitical Evolution in Polynesia"; Boyd and Richerson, *Culture and the Evolutionary Process*; also see Durham, "Advances in Evolutionary Culture Theory"; Betzig, *Despotism and Differential Reproduction: A Darwinian View of History*; Alexander, *The Biology of Moral Systems*.
11. Dunnell, "Evolutionary Theory and Archaeology."
12. Roux, *Ancient Iraq*, p. 161.

13. Sahlins, "Notes on the Original Affluent Society."

14. Lee, "!Kung Bushmen Subsistence."

15. Peterson, "Demand Sharing: Reciprocity and the Pressure for Generosity Among Foragers."

16. LeCarré, *Tinker, Tailor, Soldier, Spy.*

17. Trigger, "Archaeology at the Crossroads: What's New?" p. 287.

18. Wenke, "Explaining the Evolution of Cultural Complexity: A Review."

19. Recently other typologies have been developed based on food storage and other characteristics.

20. Steward, "The Economic and Social Basis of Primitive Bands."

21. Barnard, "Contemporary Hunter-Gatherers: Current Theoretical Issues in Ecology and Social Organization," pp. 195–197; Ember, "Residential Variation Among Hunter-Gatherers."

22. Flannery, "The Cultural Evolution of Civilizations."

23. Service, *Origins of the State and Civilization.*

24. Earle, "Chiefdoms in Archaeological and Ethnohistorical Perspective," p. 288.

25. Ibid.

26. See, for example, Earle, ed., *Chiefdoms: Power, Economy, Ideology.*

28. Drennan and Uribe, *Chiefdoms in the Americas.*

27. Drennan, "Chiefdoms in Northern South America." Also see Drennan and Uribe, *Chiefdoms in the Americas.*

28. Wright and Johnson, "Population, Exchange, and Early State Formation in Southwestern Iran."

29. McGuire, *A Marxist Archeology*; also see Rindos, *The Origins of Agriculture*; Yoffee, "The Decline and Rise of Mesopotamian Civilization: An Ethnoarchaeological Perspective on the Evolution of Social Complexity"; Wenke, "Explaining the Evolution of Cultural Complexity: A Review."

30. Costin, "Craft Specialization: Issues in Defining, Documenting, and Explaining the Organization of Production."

31. Brumfiel and Earle, "Specialization, Exchange, and Complex Societies: An Introduction," p. 5.

32. Kenoyer, "The Indus Valley Tradition of Pakistan and Western India."

33. Feinman et al., "Political Hierarchies and Organizational Strategies in the Puebloan Southwest."

34. White, *The Science of Culture.*

35. Binford, "Mortuary Practices: Their Study and Their Potential"; Rothschild, "Mortuary Behavior and Social Organization at Indian Knoll and Dickson Mounds"; also see Beck, ed., *Regional Approaches to Mortuary Analysis.* See, however, Carr ("Mortuary Practices: Their Social, Philosophical-Religious, Circumstantial, and Physcial Determinants") for an alternative view. Carr's extensive use of ethnographic files (HRAF) appears to show that there are many determinants involved in mortuary practices, and that these are highly variable from society to society, irrespective of their level of social complexity. As such, one-to-one correspondances do not exist between societal type and mortuary behavior.

36. See also O'Shea, *Mortuary Variability—An Archaeological Investigation*; Peebles, "Moundville and Surrounding Sites"; Bartel, "A Historical Review of Ethnological and Archaeological Analyses of Mortuary Practice."

37. O'Shea, *Mortuary Variability—An Archaeological Investigation.*

38. Berry, *Geography of Market Centers and Retail Distribution.*

39. Johnson, "Aspects of Regional Analysis in Archaeology"; Johnson, "Monitoring Complex System Integration and Boundary Phenomena with Settlement Size Data"; Evans, "Settlement Models in Archaeology"; Crumley and Marquardt, *Regional Dynamics*; Madsen, "Settlement Systems of Early Agricultural Societies in East Jutland, Denmark."

40. Trigger, "The Evolution of Pre-industrial Cities: A Multilinear Perspective," p. 343.

41. Ibid., pp. 344–345.

42. See, for example, Schwartz and Falconer, eds., *Archaeological Views from the Countryside: Village Communities in Early Complex Societies.*

43. Darwin, *The Descent of Man and Selection in Relation to Sex*, p. 154.

44. John Locke, *Second Treatise on Government*, section 41.

45. See, for example, Steward, "Cultural Causality and Law: A Trial Formulation of the Development of Early Civilizations."

46. Athens, "Theory Building and the Study of Evolutionary Process in Complex Societies," p. 375.

47. Boserup, *The Conditions of Agricultural Growth.*

48. Athens, "Theory Building and the Study of Evolutionary Process in Complex Societies," p. 366.

49. Cowgill, "On the Causes and Consequences of Ancient and Modern Population Changes," p. 505.

50. Harris and Ross, *Death, Sex and Fertility: Population Regulation in Preindustrial and Developing Societies.*

51. Wittfogel, *Oriental Despotism.*

52. Woodbury, "A Reappraisal of Hohokam Irrigation."

53. Carniero, "A Theory of the Origin of the State," p. 734.

54. Webster, "Warfare and the Evolution of the State: A Reconsideration."

55. Schacht, "Circumscription Theory."

56. Kirch, "Circumscription Theory and Sociopolitical Evolution in Polynesia."
57. Quoted in Harris, *The Rise of Anthropological Theory*, p. 217.
58. Marx, *Capital and Other Writings*, pp. 10–11.
59. See, for example, G. A. Cohen's excellent *Karl Marx's Theory of History: A Defense*.
60. See, for example, Streuve, "The Problem of the Genesis, Development and Disintegration of the Slave Societies in the Ancient Orient"; or Diakonoff, *Early Antiquity*.
61. Diakanov, *Ancient Mesopotamia*.
62. Zagarell, "Trade, Women, Class, and Society in Ancient Western Asia."
63. For example, Kipp and Schortman, "The Political Impact of Trade in Chiefdoms."
64. Harris, *Cannibals and Kings*; idem., *Cultural Materialism*.
65. Harris, *Cultural Materialism*, p. 92.
66. Ibid., p. 94.
67. Webster, "Warfare and the Evolution of the State: A Reconsideration"; Webb, "The Flag Follows Trade."
68. See Carniero, "A Theory of the Origin of the State."
69. Childe, *New Light on the Most Ancient East*; Wittfogel, *Oriental Despotism: A Comparative Study of Total Power*; Harris, *Cultural Materialism*.
70. For example, Hassan, "The Predynastic of Egypt," p. 166; Trigger, "The Rise of Egyptian Civilization"; Bard, *From Farmers to Pharaohs*; Kohl, "The Use and Abuse of World Systems Theory."
71. Friedman and Rowlands, *The Evolution of Social Systems*; also see Patterson and Gailey, *Power Relations and State Formation*.
72. Friedman and Rowlands, *The Evolution of Social Systems*.
73. *An Urchin the Storm*, pp. 33–34.
74. Dunnell, "Evolutionary Theory and Archaeology."
75. See, for example, Adams, "Natural Selection, Energetics, and Cultural Materialism"; Alexander, "The Search for a General Theory of Behavior"; Alexander, "Evolution and Culture"; Cohen, "Evolutionary Epistemology and Human Values"; Dunnell, "Style and Function: A Fundamental Dichotomy"; Dunnell and Wenke, "An Evolutionary Model of the Development of Complex Societies"; Kirch, "Circumscription Theory and Sociopolitical Evolution in Polynesia"; Boyd and Richerson, *Culture and the Evolutionary Process*; also see Durham, "Advances in Evolutionary Culture Theory"; Betzig, *Despotism and Differential Reproduction: A Darwinian View of History*; Alexander, *The Biology of Moral Systems*.
76. Trigger, "The Rise of Egyptian Civilization," p. 64.
77. Johnson, "The Changing Organization in Uruk Administration on the Susiana Plain"; R. McC. Adams, *Heartland of Cities*.
78. See, for example, Shanks and Tilley, "Archaeology into the 1990s."
79. Giddens, *A Contemporary Critique of Historical Materialism, Vol 1. Power, Property and the State*.
80. See, for example, Shanks and Tilley, *Re-Constructing Archaeology, Social Theory and Archaeology*, "Archaeology into the 1990s"; Hodder, *Symbolic and Structural Archaeology*.
81. Kohl, "The Use and Abuse of World Systems Theory," pp. 10–11.
82. See, for example, Diakonov, ed., *Early Antiquity*.
83. See, for example, Gould, *Wonderful Life*.
84. Ibid., p. 563.
85. Wittfogel, *Oriental Despotism*.
86. Trigger, *Early Civilizations: Ancient Egypt in Context*, p. 112.
87. Ibid., p. 110.
88. Ibid., p. 8.
89. Gould, *Wonderful Life*.
90. Brumfiel and Earle, "Specialization, Exchange, and Complex Societies: An Introduction."
91. Ibid., p. 3.

Origins of Complex Societies in Southwest Asia

And Babylon, the glory of kingdoms, the beauty of the Chaldees excellency, shall be as when God overthrew Sodom and Gomorrah.

It shall never be inhabited, neither shall it be dwelt in from generation to generation: neither shall the Arabian pitch tent there; neither shall the shepherds make their fold there.

But wild beasts of the desert shall lie there; and their houses shall be full of doleful creatures; and owls shall dwell there, and satyrs shall dance there.

And the wild beasts of the islands cry in their desolate houses, and dragons in their pleasant places: and her time is near to come, and her days shall not be prolonged.

Isaiah 13:19–22

The Old Testament presents Isaiah as a dreary, complaining alarmist, but in the case of Babylon he was right. Babylon—once the brightest star in a galaxy of brilliant ancient cities—has for many centuries been a great rubbish heap.

Five thousand years ago, however, when many of the world's people were illiterate marginal farmers, and most were still hunters and gatherers, and when the peoples of the New World were still many centuries from village life, Babylon and its surroundings were a cosmopolitan world of cities, libraries, schools, international trade, roads, taxes, temples, and many of the other elements we collectively call "civilization." Indeed, much of the world's population today is still living the *urban* way of life that first evolved in these ancient Southwest Asian cities.

Southwest Asian cultural history is so rich, so ancient, that even short journeys here take one through complex histories (Figure 8.1). Before recent wars it was possible to drive from the eastern outskirts of Babylon, near Baghdad, Iraq—the heartland of the oldest cities in the world—east to Susa, in Iran, one of the world's first true metropolises at about 3400 B.C. One could then continue north through the area of some of the world's first farms, distributed along the margins of the Zagros Mountains in Iran and Syria, and the foothills of the Taurus Mountains in Turkey. North from Syria through Turkey one crosses the same terrain that Xenophon[1] tells us ancient Greek soldiers traversed as—homesick for Greece —they fought their way to the Black Sea to sail home. South from Turkey through Syria and along the Mediterranean coast one follows a route very close to that taken by European crusaders a millennium later, to effect the fateful collision of Christianity and Islam.

Amidst the ruins of these millennia of civilization, scholars have tried to sort out much about the human condition. This, after all, was the homeland of several of the world's great religions and the place where writing, cities, metallurgy, and many other aspects of civilization first appeared. And all the obvious questions apply: Why here? Why in the particular period of about 5000 to 3000 B.C.? And—perhaps the most intriguing and revealing question—why in forms so strikingly similar to later developments in China, Egypt, Mesoamerica, and elsewhere?

THE ECOLOGICAL SETTING

Two ecological elements are particularly important to analyses of Southwest Asian cultural history: First is the great productivity of agriculture in this area, and second is its role as a nexus, a crossroads, of many cultural influences. As Nicholas Postgate noted, Mesopotamia is quite different from its near neighboring civilization in Egypt (see chapter 9):

1792 B.C.	Babylonian Empire begins
2100–2004 B.C.	Ur III period
2350 B.C.	Sargon of Akkad and the beginning of the Akkadian period
3000 B.C.	Development of cuneiform writing
3000–2350 B.C.	Early Dynastic period (Sumerians)
3000 B.C.	Fortification of most major settlements begins
3300–2800 B.C.	Proto-Elamites
4000 B.C.	Early monumental construction of temples begins
4100–3000 B.C.	Uruk and Jemdat Nasr periods; development of city-states
6000–3700 B.C.	'Ubaid period
5500 B.C.	Samarran and Halafian style pottery appear
6500 B.C.	Ceramic technology appears
8500 B.C. (10,500 years ago)	Neolithic food-producing economies appear

> Egypt, physically constrained within the narrow strip of the Nile Valley and isolated from western Asia, retained its highly idiosyncratic identity with little infusion from elsewhere, and did not export its language or script or other artistic forms, except upstream to Nubia. Mesopotamia was open along both flanks to intrusion from the desert and mountain, and its cuneiform script was exported across thousands of miles.[2]

The first states and cities appeared in a relatively small area of southern Iraq and Iran, but the factors that produced them involved most of the Fertile Crescent and the surrounding lowlands it encompasses, or *Greater Mesopotamia*, as it is known (see Figure 8.1).

The lower elevations of the great arc of mountains of the Fertile Crescent were the natural habitats of wild wheat, barley, sheep, and goats (Figure 8.2). In ancient times this area was covered with vast grasslands and oak and pistachio forests, and, even as late as the nineteenth century, sheep grazing these verdant uplands were brought to lowland markets

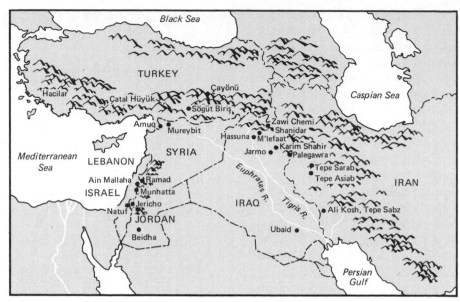

FIGURE 8.1   Southwest Asia. The world's first complex societies evolved in the alluvial plains of the Tigris and Euphrates rivers and their tributaries, but they had their origins in these early agricultural communities.

with their wool stained scarlet by wildflowers in their range. Today the forests are almost entirely gone, and the whole area is severely overgrazed.

From the very beginnings of life on the alluvial lowlands, people there fought and traded for the gold, silver, copper, stone, wheat, sheep, and goats of the mountain areas. Today there is still no better way to integrate the highlands and lowlands economically than this same ancient pattern in which nomads and herders take sheep and goats to these highlands in the lush summer months, using the animals to convert mountain vegetation into milk, meat, and hides, which can then be exchanged for lowland products.

Below the high ridges of the Zagros and Taurus moun-

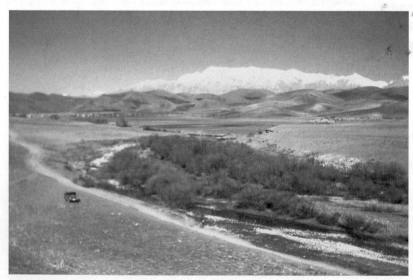

FIGURE 8.2   The Zagros Mountains and foothills region of Iran.

tains, the foothills and rolling plains of the piedmont saw some of the world's earliest agricultural villages. Neolithic settlements are found here almost every place rainfall is sufficient to grow wheat and barley with a reasonable reliability.

Coming down from the piedmont, one finds north and northwest of Baghdad the dry, undulating northern Mesopotamian Plains. The Tigris and Euphrates have cut deeply into the land surface, so that irrigation here requires sophisticated damming and canalization. But with irrigation, the high productivity of this area made these northern plains the "breadbasket" of some of the greatest empires of antiquity.

For the very first cities, however, the heartland is the lower alluvial plains of Mesopotamia. Historian Arnold Toynbee argued that civilizations first evolved in physical circumstances that challenged the inhabitants to overcome severe problems of climate and resources, and he was thinking in part about southern Mesopotamia. Nothing in this region appears to account for its pivotal role in human history. The unprepossessing hot plains have no usable stone or metal, few trees, and a climate whose extremes of heat have been a main topic of conversation for generations of archaeologists.

But most early civilizations are the "gift" of some great river system, and this is particularly true of Mesopotamian cultures ("Mesopotamia" means "between the rivers" in Greek). The Tigris and Euphrates rivers created the alluvial plain—mainly in the area south of Bagdad—with annual deposits of flood-borne fertile silt and clay, and they provide the irrigation water that has made productive farming possible here for many thousands of years. The swamps and wetlands formed by the rivers support a variety of usable wild plants, such as flax for textiles and rushes for basketry, but in addition to these plants and water for irrigation, the major gift of the rivers is fish. The scrub forests along the rivers cannot support many game animals, and thus fish—and later, domestic cattle—furnished the protein indispensable to survival on the alluvial plain. Vegetarianism was not an option for ancient Mesopotamians because the blend of vegetable proteins necessary to substitute for animal protein was not always available. Fish fill this lack admirably, however, and many clues point to their importance for the early inhabitants: "Altars" in buildings dating to the fifth millennium B.C. have been found covered with layer upon layer of fish bones. Mesopotamia's rivers also provided a vital transportation artery. None of these rivers was as navigable as the Nile, for example, but with the proper boats one could move goods, armies, and so forth from ports along the Turkish and Syrian foothills, south through the heart of Mesopotamia.

From May to October, the average daily high temperature is over 40°C (104°F), and hot winds dry the soil to the depth of a meter and darken the sky with choking clouds of dust. Anyone who has spent a summer in Mesopotamia understands why several Middle Eastern religions have envisioned heaven's primary recreation to be sitting by shaded streams in cool palm groves, eating fruit, in complaisant sexual company. The fiery summers, however, are balanced by temperate, lovely, warm autumns, winters, and springs. And with adequate irrigation, the Mesopotamian alluvial plain richly rewards those who farm it, so that throughout history this region has been celebrated for its melons, oranges, pomegranates, dates, wheat, barley, lentils, onions, and other crops.

Part of Mesopotamia's rich agricultural heartland is enclosed in large deserts, from Syria far into the Arabian peninsula. Nomads and pastoralists eventually occupied some of these areas, and trade routes crossed them, but even in our own age some of these desert areas are only sparsely inhabited.

As we saw in chapter 4, Southwest Asia in the Pleistocene can be thought of as an extension of Africa, in terms of its climates, flora, and fauna, and even as late as a few hundred to a thousand years ago such African animals as ostriches, cheetahs, lions, and hartebeest were common in large areas of Southwest Asia.

The climates and physical geography of Southwest Asia have been much the same for the past 9,000 years, with some variations. At times tectonic movements have raised or lowered Mesopotamia, and these movements, in combination with fluctuations in the water level of the Persian Gulf and the deposition of massive amounts of alluvial silts and clays in some areas, have made it difficult to determine where the coastline was during the past 10,000 years. Some areas, for example, that were farmed a millennium ago are now underwater, and it is possible that some important parts of the ancient archaeological record are under the Gulf, too. Human alterations of river courses, deforestation, and climate changes have so greatly altered the landscape (and probably even microclimates) that we may never have an entirely clear picture of what Southwest Asia was like as a natural landscape when its first civilizations began forming.[3]

FUNDAMENTALS OF THE SOUTHWEST ASIAN ARCHAEOLOGICAL RECORD

Southwest Asian peoples have lived in villages for nine millennia, and there is hardly a square meter there that does not contain a few sherds, stone tools, bones, or old irrigation canal banks. Nevertheless, the most common unit of analysis in Southwest Asian archaeology is still the "site," which usually takes the form of a mound, referred to as a *tell* (Arabic) or *teppeh* (Persian). These tells are a result of the construction and continual reconstruction of villages or towns on the same spot (Figure 8.3). For thousands of years, people here have used mudbricks as their basic building material, and their settlements have numerous closely packed, small, rectangular structures. Although ideally suited to the climate and resources of the area, such buildings become so dilapidated after 50 or 100 years that it is easier to rebuild than to repair them, and because there are incentives to rebuild on the same spot (less land is lost to cultivation and higher elevation gives better drainage and protection against floods and attack), settlements become mound-shaped as they are constantly reconstructed on the debris of the previous ones.

Hundreds of thousands of such mounds dot the Southwest Asian landscape, some of them rising 50 m or more above plain level, while others—occupied for only a few decades or so—are only imperceptibly higher than the surrounding plains or are buried beneath the alluvial plain. The mounds are littered with stone tools, bones, broken pottery, broken clay bricks, collapsed walls, eroding ovens and pottery kilns, and

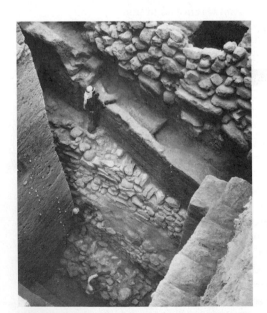

FIGURE 8.3 Millennia of rebuilding at Jericho formed many superimposed layers containing stone walls.

corroding metal. Burrowing animals, well and terrace construction, and erosion often mix the layers of these mounds so that usually one finds the remnants of every phase of a site's occupation on its surface. This allows archaeologists to estimate a site's periods of occupation simply by inspecting the surface artifacts. At some sites bones and floral remains are well preserved, but at other sites, such as those in areas with a high level of salty groundwater, even ceramics do not preserve well.

Besides mounds, the most obvious archaeological features of Southwest Asia are irrigation canals. Seven millennia of irrigation agriculture have resulted in a landscape criss-crossed with canals, and it is not unusual to find abandoned irrigation canals several thousand years old with banks still 2 or 3 m high. Aerial photographs are particularly useful in charting these ancient waterworks.

Because of the time and expense of archaeological excavation and the destruction of sites, far less than 5 percent of all sites dating from 8000 to 2350 B.C., for example, have been, or will ever be, properly excavated, and thus our interpretations must be tempered with some tentativeness. On the other hand, the rich archaeological remains provide an opportunity to use sampling procedures and to test hypotheses; and by using aerial reconnaissance, surface surveys, and regional analyses, archaeologists can determine when and for how long unexcavated sites were occupied. In the case of Mesopotamia, a generation of archaeologists has followed Robert McC. Adams in performing regional surveys.[4] In many of these surveys, archaeologists have used aerial photographs and maps to locate ancient sites, and then made maps of these individual sites and collected ceramics from them to infer their cultural histories. But Southwest Asia's archaeological record is so vast that many hundreds of thousands of ancient towns and villages will probably never be excavated—and many hundreds of thousands more have already been destroyed by agricultural expansion, industrialization, and looting.

THE NEOLITHIC ORIGINS OF SOUTHWEST ASIAN CIVILIZATION (C. 8500–6000 B.C.)

When we left the first farmers of Southwest Asia in chapter 6, they were living in thousands of small villages, from Afghanistan to western Turkey, occupying in small numbers those areas with sufficient rainfall to support wheat and barley without extensive irrigation. In most areas the simple village farming way of life continued largely unchanged into the last few millennia B.C., but in other areas changes were underway by 8500 B.C.

We saw in chapter 6 that people at Jericho, in the West Bank, for example, began building stone walls and other buildings that indicate that they were beginning to direct their energies in a way quite different from that of most hunters and gatherers. Also, the apparent ancestor cult at Jericho and many Levantine sites—in which human skulls were plastered with clay and fitted with eyes made from seashells or otherwise accentuated—and the plaster figures of people and clay animals at sites such as 'Ain Ghazal, in Jordan, suggest a changing social context of village life.

Analogous developments were also underway in Turkey. Recently in the Urfa region (the area in southeastern Turkey just north of the Syrian border) impressive evidence from

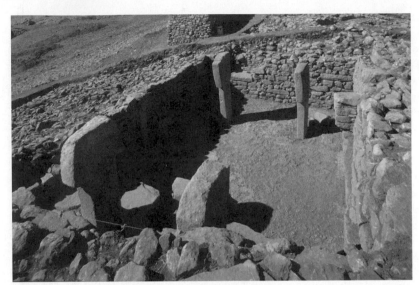

FIGURE 8.4   A Neolithic cult building at Göbekli Tepe, Turkey. Note the unusual T-shaped pillars that may have served as roof supports.

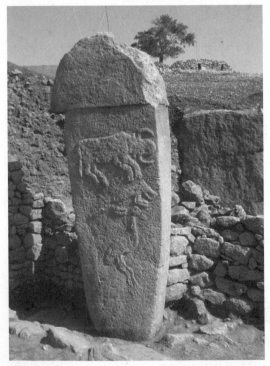

FIGURE 8.5   Many of the T-shaped pillars at the Urfa region Neolithic cult sites are engraved with images of animals. This one shows a cattle (*top*), canine (*middle*), and bird (*bottom*).

about 8400 B.C. for ritual activities at sites such as Nevali Çori, Göbekli Tepe, and Gürcütepe has been found.[5] In many respects, these sites are farming villages similar to many others from this time period. What makes them unusual, however, is the presence of cult buildings —with unusual construction and decoration—and various sculptures.

These cult buildings are nearly square in shape—ranging in size from 13.9-by-13.5 m to 12.1-by-12.8 m at Nevali Çori—and have terrazzo floors as well as benches along the walls covered in stone slabs. All of these building incorporate large "T-shaped" limestone pillars—likely to support the roof of the structure (Figure 8.4)—and, quite remarkably, these pillars are engraved with images of animals such as birds, cattle, lions, and fox (Figure 8.5). Other sculptures—frequently found buried in the these cult buildings—include human and animal heads, birds, and lions.

This dramatic evidence of profound social social changes in Neolithic societies in Turkey continues into later times at sites such as Çatalhöyök (pronounced rather like Chatal Huooyook). James Mellaart, who originally excavated much of this site, suggested that "It may be said without undue exaggeration that Anatolia, long regarded as the barbarous fringe to the fertile crescent, has now been established as the most advanced center of neolithic culture in the Near East. The neolithic civilization revealed at Çatalhöyök shines like a supernova among the rather dim galaxies of contemporary peasant culture."[6] Çatalhöyök may not merit all the superlatives its excavators have showered on it, but it is one of the most interesting sites in Southwest Asia. Located in south central Anatolia (Turkey) and first occupied at about 6250 B.C., Çatalhöyök was probably inhabited continuously until its abandonment at about 5400 B.C. During some of this time it may have extended over 13 hectares and had a population of about 4,000 to 6,000—several times larger than any other known site in this period.

A great fire swept through Çatalhöyök in the middle of its history, nicely preserving the earliest levels, but unfortunately only less than a hectare of the site was excavated before the project was ended by political disputes and other problems several decades ago. Since 1993, Ian Hodder and his colleagues have been able to open new excavations at this site and offer multiple ways of examining and interpreting the information that has been recovered.[7]

Located not far from the first ranges of the Taurus Mountains, Çatalhöyök is near a critical resource: the obsidian sources at the Hasan Dag volcano (Figure 8.6). Because

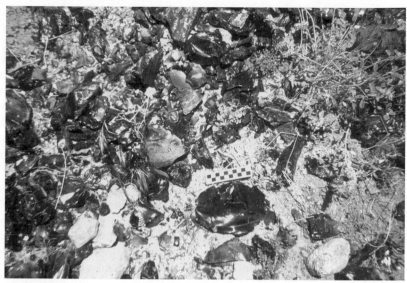

FIGURE 8.6   The volcanic areas of Cappadoccia in Turkey are a source of obsidian. Workshop debris from making stone artifacts litters the surface, as seen in this photograph of a Neolithic period site.

each obsidian source is chemically distinctive, we can track the great quantities of obsidian from this area that were distributed throughout Anatolia, the Levant, and Cyprus (Figure 8.7) after 7000 B.C. Beautiful obsidian artifacts were found in Çatalhöyök itself, but so far

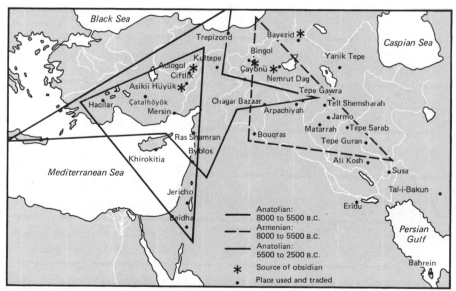

FIGURE 8.7   The circulation of obsidian throughout Southwest Asia was an important economic process that may have contributed to the evolution of political and economic institutions.

no obsidian storage or workshop areas have been discovered in the small fraction of the site that has been excavated. It is possible that most of the workshop activity occurred at the obsidian sources themselves rather than in the village.

Most of the 158 structures uncovered at Çatalhöyök are little different from their contemporaries elsewhere in Southwest Asia: Each is built of shaped mud and composed of rectangular rooms with plastered walls and floors, and most houses are about 25 m square, one story high, and abut one another, except where occasionally separated by an open courtyard. Inside most rooms are two raised platforms, probably for sleeping, and an occasional rectangular bench. Unlike any other community of this period and area, access to the rooms of Çatalhöyök was only by ladder through the roof—there are no front doors—and the close packing of structures is such that much of the movement among the houses must have been on the roofs. The roof access may reflect a need for defense, for once the inhabitants had pulled up the ladders on the outside walls, the settlement would have been difficult to attack. Other Southwest Asian sites had walls at this time, but most settlements were small unfortified hamlets.

The 40 or so shrines at Çatalhöyök have essentially the same floor plan as the other structures, but their walls are richly decorated with paintings, reliefs, and engravings expressing many naturalistic themes, most concentrating on the two favorites of ancient art—fertility and death. Vultures are portrayed ripping apart headless human corpses, women give birth to bulls and ride leopards, and other symbols such as breasts, vultures, bulls, and rams abound. Some of the rooms have intricate arrangements of cattle skulls and horns (Figure 8.8). Walls were plastered and then painted, and periodically the walls were replastered and new designs were painted or engraved on them. One wall was plastered and painted 40 times. These shrines do not seem to have required the expenditure of vast amounts of labor and resources for essentially non-economic purposes, as did the monumental constructions of later periods. Nor do they enclose radically different amounts of expensive goods, indicating great wealth

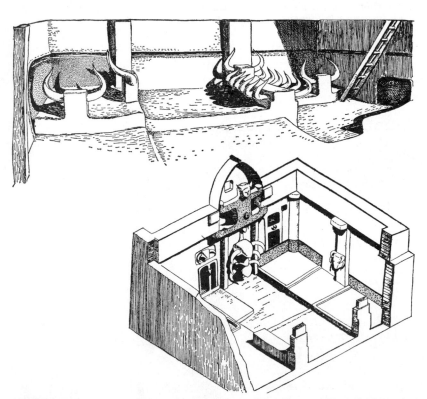

FIGURE 8.8 These reconstructions of "cult-centers" at Çatalhöyök show the importance of the cattle motif. All early complex societies evolved rituals and religions that functioned as organizing and controlling institutions.

disparities. Little about them, in fact, conflicts with the interpretation that they were kinship-cult centers in a simple ranked society.[8]

Such a conclusion would be strengthened if we found only minor variability in mortuary practices, and indeed this seems to be the case. Many corpses appear to have been taken outside the settlement and exposed to the vultures and the elements until the flesh was gone, after which the bones were interred in the house floors. Men, women, and children were buried in much the same way, either in baskets or simply in holes. Most of the graves contained no goods, but some women and children were accompanied by shell and stone necklaces, armlets and anklets, and, occasionally, obsidian mirrors and bone cosmetic implements. Some men were buried with mace heads, flint daggers, obsidian projectile points, clay seals, and other items.

In one complex of rooms, the so-called Vulture Shrine, six individuals were buried in the floor with significantly richer grave goods than were found in the residential burials.[9] However, we do not find any infants at Çatalhöyök buried with disproportionately rich or numerous grave goods, nor is there any significant variation in construction expense of the graves themselves; there are no stone coffins, tombs, or the like.

The people of Çatalhöyök subsisted on the typical late Neolithic combination of agriculture, hunting, and gathering. Emmer, another kind of wheat known as "einkorn," barley, pea vetch, and other crops were grown in quantity, but with simple techniques. Domestic cattle supplied meat, hides, milk, and perhaps traction: Even simple cattle-drawn wood plows that do no more than scratch the surface greatly increase agricultural productivity by suppressing weeds and increasing soil permeability. We do not know when the first plows were used in the Middle East, but the domestication of cattle probably did not precede the development of the plow by more than a millennium or two.

Trade at Çatalhöyök was considerable, but mainly in small quantities of exotic items. Shells from the Mediterranean (160 km distant) and Syrian flint were found here, perhaps taken in trade for obsidian artifacts. But there is no evidence of voluminous trade in agricultural products, or even in large amounts of obsidian, and there are no obvious workshops for goods, no stores of obsidian, and no complex technologies.

Jarmo, in Iraqi Kurdistan, is an example of the drab peasant culture that Mellaart invidiously compared to Çatalhöyök. Jarmo was first settled sometime before 6750 B.C. and was occupied intermittently to 5000 B.C., and thus it overlaps with Çatalhöyök for perhaps as much as 1,000 years. But unlike Çatalhöyök, Jarmo was probably home to no more than 200 people, and for most of its existence it consisted of only about 20 small mud houses. Burials at Jarmo are quite uniform, as are the contents of the houses. There is not nearly the diversity of aesthetic expression found at Çatalhöyök in wall paintings, finely worked obsidian, or the like; there are just a few clay figurines of pregnant women and animals. Jarmo has no fortified walls or large, nonresidential buildings, and the technology seems to have been mainly devoted to the processing of plant foods. Perhaps the most significant difference between the two sites is that Çatalhöyök controlled a localized and important resource (obsidian), whereas Jarmo did not.

Elsewhere in the Zagros, northern Mesopotamia, and the Iranian Plateau, most communities established between 8000 and 6000 B.C. were also farming villages, with little public architecture, elaborate mortuary cults, or occupational specialization.

Charles Redman has pointed out that "Çatal Hüyük exemplifies those communities that may have made many of the crucial advances leading to civilization, but for one reason or another did not become urban societies. In some ways, the town of Çatal Hüyük and its inhabitants should be considered a premature flash of brilliance and complexity that was a thousand years before its time."[10] The various excavations at Jericho, Çatalhöyök, Jarmo, and other sites provide a picture of the kinds of communities that immediately preceded civilization in Southwest Asia, but we still lack many elements of this picture. In a rightly ordered world, the combined international archaeology faculties and their students—funded by the United Nations—would begin surveys in western Anatolia and work their way east into Afghanistan and south into Iraq, mapping and excavating sites along the way. Instead, our evidence for the world's first socially complex societies is gathered mainly from fewer than a hundred well-excavated settlements and perhaps 20 or 30 regional site surveys in this huge area.

INITIAL CULTURAL COMPLEXITY (C. 6000–4000 B.C.)

An early indication of social change in Southwest Asia is evident in the distribution of pottery styles. As with agriculture, the invention of pottery seems to have occurred independently in many areas of Southwest Asia, where clay had been used for centuries for figurines and storage pits. The multiple origins and rapid spread of pottery after about 6500 B.C. no doubt reflect the increasing importance of containers in these agricultural economies—probably for carrying water and for storing, cooking, and serving food.

Soon after ceramic vessels came into general use in Southwest Asia, the first sophisticated pottery styles appeared, and by about 5500 B.C. two distinctive styles, the Samarran and the Halafian, are present (Figures 8.9 and 8.10).[11] Samarran pottery tends to be in simpler shapes than the Halafian and is painted in matte colors, whereas the Halafian colors are glossy. Halafian ceramics are important beyond their aesthetics: They are the first complex style of artifacts to be so widely distributed. These highly stylized ceramics were first made with a tournette, a wooden slab affixed to a peg that could be set in a hole in the ground and act as a pivot around which the slab could be turned by hand. Simple as this sounds, it was a major advance over simply hand-molding a pot; the tournette allowed the potter to turn the pot so as to shape and paint it.[12] So intricate and delicate are the designs that one might assume that specialists produced them. But Frank Hole cautions us not to underestimate the skill of villagers—Persian carpets being just one example of an extraordinarily complex and beautiful product made by simple villagers.[13] And despite the wide geographical distribution of the Halafian designs, there is little evidence that ceramic production was centrally organized and administered.

Exactly what kinds of social changes the spread of these styles may reflect remain obscure. Their distributions tend to overlap and there is no convincing proof that they belong to different time periods or social groups.[14] Yet people of the Halafian era transported decorated pottery over distances of almost 1,000 km, and it is difficult to believe that this was a simple utilitarian and cost-effective adaptation to the growing need for containers in agricultural economies. Pottery is heavy, breaks easily, and can be made from local materials in nearly every part of Southwest Asia, so why transport it in massive quantities? The expanding zones of distribution of Halafian and other decorated ceramics would seem to make the most sense as expressions of a growing sense of social status and political allegiance. At some point in every ancient civilization, elites were able to begin

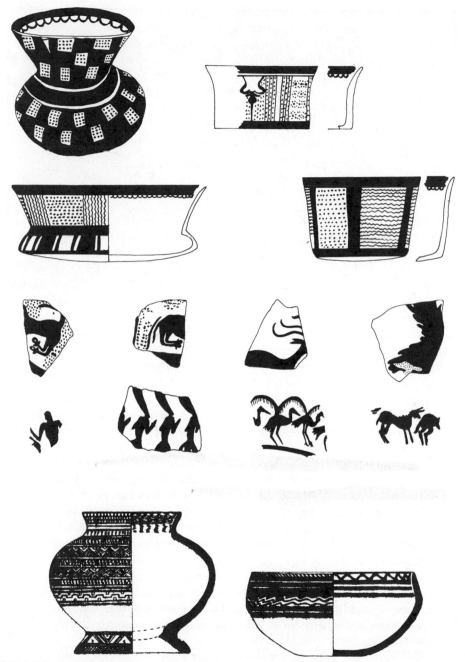

FIGURE 8.9 Halafian and Samarran (bottom two vessels) pottery styles spread over large areas of sixth millennium B.C. Mesopotamia.

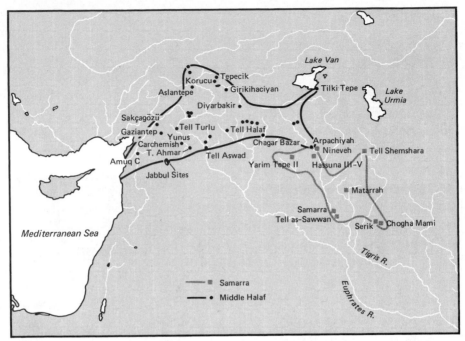

FIGURE 8.10 Distribution of Samarran and Halafian pottery. One of the first steps in the evolution of complex societies seems to be a rapid expansion of an art style over a large area.

appropriating elaborate and exotic goods and use them to indicate their status and power. Perhaps these early pottery styles are early indications of this process of the emergence of elites.

The distribution of Halafian and Samarran ceramics coincides with the extension of cultivation to the arid areas of Mesopotamia, and this involved what may have been the world's first systematic artificial irrigation systems. At sites such as Choga Mami, in the areas just east of Baghdad, for example, people used irrigation canals to grow cereals, linseed (for oil), and other crops. Another significant site of this period is Tell as-Sawwan, located in north central Iraq at the juncture of the northern arid steppe country and the alluvial plains.[15]

Preliminary excavations indicate that from 6000 to 5000 B.C. Tell as-Sawwan was home to a few hundred people, most of whom were engaged in simple irrigation farming of wheat, barley, and linseed. They also kept domestic goats, sheep, and cattle; hunted onagers, antelopes, and other animals; and gathered fish and mussels from the Tigris, which ran close to the site.

In most ways, this settlement resembled other early agricultural villages: Granaries, kilns, ovens, and small mudbrick houses were arranged around open courtyards. In addition, a large ditch or moat was constructed around the site by cutting into the natural conglomerate rock on which the site was located. The discovery of many hardened clay balls (sling missiles) in the ditch led its excavators to conclude it was a defensive structure, reminiscent of the fortifications at Jericho.

The residential architecture of Tell as-Sawwan contrasts somewhat with that of other settlements of the period, consisting mainly of huts with stone foundations and the more common rectangular clay structures, although there is still little variability in building size or apparent construction cost.

At least 128 burials at Tell as-Sawwan date to approximately 5500 B.C., and they contain one of the richest assortment of grave goods for this period of any site known in Southwest Asia. Of the classifiable skeletons, 55 were infants, 16 were adolescents, and 13 were adults. The graves differ little in orientation, location, or construction. Most bodies were placed in a contracted position, facing west, in simple shallow oval pits dug into house floors. Most graves had at least one craft item, mainly carved alabaster, beads in exotic stones, or pottery. Although most rooms had many burials (one had up to 23), one room contained only an adult male's burial, whose relatively rich grave goods may reflect emerging status ascription. But the Tell as-Sawwan burials do not seem to reflect *inherited* status and wealth. As we noted in chapter 7, attempts to draw conclusions about the social systems of extinct societies from examination of burial characteristics is somewhat speculative, but there does seem to be a period in all early civilizations where burials begin to reflect inherited status. An infant buried with massive amounts of wealth that he or she could not possibly have earned personally may reflect nothing more than a wealthy and caring family, but in all known early civilizations wealth and status eventually became largely inherited aspects of everyone's life. Although there are some signs of differences of wealth and status at Tell es-Sawwan, there is nothing to indicate this wealth and status was inherited.

Tell as-Sawwan is just one of many sites of this period, and soon after Halafian, Samarran, and other pottery styles spread through the highlands, the developmental focus shifted to the Mesopotamian alluvial plain.

The few sites on the alluvial plain that may antedate 5500 B.C. are poorly known—most are probably covered by much larger and later sites. The earliest known sites on the alluvial plain are near the estuary of the Persian Gulf, and there is some evidence that with the end of the Pleistocene, the Gulf shoreline moved inland as much as 180 km.[16] Thus, the key settlements in the transition to life on the alluvial plain—and the origins of cultural complexity here—may now be under sea water. Between about 5500 and 3500 B.C. Mesopotamian climates were comparatively humid, with a change to cooler and drier conditions after about 3500 B.C. Subtle changes in climate like this might have had major effects on the settlement history of the area, because the zones in which dry-field rainfall-based grain cultivation was possible may have shifted. Also, changes in sea levels at this time may have meant that lands that previously were flooded were opened to settlement.[17]

Frank Hole has argued that

economic necessity, caused by environmental shocks that were induced by climatic changes, resulted in major dislocations of local [Mesopotamian] populations as early as the second half of the sixth millennium [B.C.], and continued into the fourth, during which there was a qualitative reorientation of society around urban places. These natural events resulted first in the loss of sites and decline of population. Except at a few favorable locations, these conditions discouraged nucleation. However, with the steady flow of dislocated people who could provide labor, larger and more dependable agricultural systems could be built. The first urban-sized places may have been composed of disparate populations who developed an organic interdependence as they filled many . . . ecological and economic niches.[18]

If Hole is correct, then the rise of cities and civilizations was based on ecological factors, and once these developments were underway, very complex patterns of socioeconomic changes would have developed. Subsistence in most parts of the alluvial plain is more complex than in the highlands, requiring many timely decisions in which floods must be anticipated and controlled, land irrigated and drained, and cattle pastured, tended, and milked. Fishing adds to this complexity because it is seasonal to some extent and requires coordination to be maximally effective. Even getting sufficient stone for simple agricultural implements necessitates considerable organization here, for such stone often had to be obtained in the mountains, far from lowland settlements.

If Ali Kosh in Iranian Mesopotamia is typical, the movement onto the alluvial plain required a very generalized diet, in which many small plant seeds eventually were discarded in favor of the wheat-barley-lentil group augmented by sheep-goat-cattle proteins.[19] There is some evidence that the cuisine centered on a variant of the one-pot approach, a stone or clay vessel filled with water, cereals, and other plants, and bits of whatever animals were about. Like the spartan meals of ancient Sparta (described as consisting of two courses, the first a kind of porridge, and a second, which was a kind of porridge), the diets of these Mesopotamian villagers probably relied on blending as many plant and animal nutrients as possible in soups and stews. Breakfasts may have been rather uninspiring, but perhaps these early farmers subsisted on something quite like their modern descendants and ate porridge, bread, cheese, and dates.

The 'Ubaid Period (c. 6000–3700 B.C.)

In the ancient Sumerian account of the creation of the universe, the city of Eridu was the first to have emerged from the primeval sea that covered the world before humans. Eridu is in fact one of the earliest known settlements on the southern Mesopotamian alluvial plain, having been established at about 5700 B.C. The southern Mesopotamian alluvium in fact is characterized by many small communities of farmers by 5700 B.C. These earliest southern communities belong to the 'Ubaid period, named after a small town of this period, and are associated with a particular and distinctive style of ceramics. These people may be identified with their styles of pottery, but they did something much more important than make ceramics: They were the first to establish a productive economy on the basis of a traditional Mesopotamian farming strategy, based on cereals (in this case, barley) and various vegetables and fruits (particularly dates) in combination with the milk and meat of cattle, sheep, and goats. Living in communities that ranged in size from fewer than 50 to a few thousand, the 'Ubaid peoples did small-time irrigation of crops, traded for a few products, and in general were able to produce the base materials out of which the alchemy of cultures produces civilization, namely economic *surpluses*. Anthropologists have long argued about the applicability of the term *surplus* to pre-monetary economies, such as that of the 'Ubaid farmers, but the most important point is that, once established, the agricultural economy of the alluvial lowlands could be intensified in such a way that ever greater populations could be supported and massive amounts of materials and energy could be devoted to monumental construction, warfare, and ever more diversified occupational specialization, from kings to foot-soldiers, from scribes to potters.

Debates continue as to the ethnic origins of the 'Ubaid people—they may have been Iranians who migrated to the river valleys as domesticated wheat, barley, sheep, and goats became adapted to these environments and as changes in climates and river regimes made the alluvium more suitable for simple farming.[20]

If we look at the 'Ubaid archaeological record for the first signs of these fundamental changes, we see only a few indirect reflections. One of the earliest known 'Ubaid sites is at Tell al-Ouell: near Larsa, which dates to at least 5300 B.C., and recent excavations deep into the great site of Uruk suggest that occupations of the earliest 'Ubaid sites are probably deeply buried at many major sites. A major temple dating to after 4000 B.C. at Uruk was found to have been built on the exact same site as a temple of the 'Ubaid period, indicating a great continuity of religious traditions.[21] At Eridu, the earliest known structure is thought to have been a temple. Archaeologists have been accused of bestowing this term on virtually any structure large enough to stand upright in, but the earliest building at Eridu is very similar to others known through texts and other evidence to have been temples. A single small room (3.5-by-4.5 m) with an altar faces the entrance, and a pedestal is in the center; in these specifics the building is nearly identical to the temples of later periods. These temples may reflect a low level of social complexity, and some of the larger 'Ubaid communities included some fairly impressive mudbrick buildings, but for the most part the people of the 'Ubaid period appear to have been small-time farmers; no clear evidence has been found indicating differential access to wealth, power, or prestige, and their economy seems only marginally more diversified and integrated than that of the first Southwest Asian farmers a millennium earlier.

But by 4500 B.C. some signs of cultural changes toward complexity appeared in a large region of the lower alluvial plain, in the foothills of the Zagros, and in some of the larger valleys in the Zagros. Henry Wright notes that, in these areas, "There were large centers with populations of 1,000 to 3,000, which dominated networks of smaller settlements. Excavation on some of these larger centers revealed central platforms, supporting ritual buildings, segregated elite residences with large storage structures, and indications of socially segregated cemeteries."[22] As Wright notes, there is evidence that there had been a *previous* period in which larger centers had emerged, but here too, as in the case described earlier for Çatalhöyök, we see no uniform gradual pattern of increasing complexity. The whole history of early complexity, in fact, seems to be a messy boom-or-bust cycle, with only a very general long-term overall trend toward complexity.

In addition to the central Mesopotamian plains in Iraq, the Susiana Plain (Figure 8.11) in southwestern Iran was also a major developmental center for early complexity— probably because one could do both rainfall agriculture and irrigation farming here and because trade routes from the Gulf to the Iranian plateau ran across the Susiana. By about 4500 B.C.—perhaps much earlier—several large centers may have dominated surrounding areas economically and politically. The people of this era made beautiful hand-painted pottery in such large quantities and with such great similarity that, even given the virtuosity of peasant artisans, some occupational specialization may be reflected.[23]

In summarizing this and other evidence from the Susiana, Gregory Johnson observed:

> In sharp contrast to the pervasive smaller villages of the [earlier] periods, Choga Mish on the Susiana Plain covered an area of some fifteen hectares by 4300 B.C. Most architecture consisted of residences and associated ceramic kilns. The community also contained at least one monumental building, perhaps more. This ten-by-fifteen-meter structure had walls of between one and two meters thick and contained several interior rooms. One of these was stacked with storage jars, while another was apparently used in working flint. A substantial

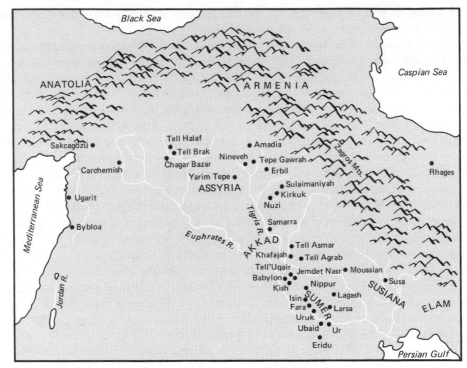

FIGURE 8.11   The first socially complex societies were concentrated in areas of Mesopotamia where rivers allowed great agricultural productivity.

mud-brick platform stood nearby. This period in Susiana and elsewhere saw the introduction of formalized closure of containers using clay sealings that carried the impression of a decorated seal. This practice is ordinarily associated with problems of security in materials storage or shipment.[24]

Johnson goes on to note that the high degree of similarity in ceramics across the plain indicates that not everyone was making these—that their production might already have been somewhat centralized. All this evidence, he says, "[s]trikes me as indicative of a hierarchically organized social system with some degree of influence over labor and resource allocation. The fact that the known major architecture at Choga Mish was destroyed by fire and the community abandoned . . . suggests that elite influence over the population in general was less than elites might have wished."[25] Frank Hole's interpretation of Susiana culture history differs somewhat from Johnson's.[26] Hole suspects that even toward the end of the fifth millennium B.C., the Susiana was loosely tied together by small-scale trade and a regional religious cult, centered at Susa, in which priests and people were in a voluntary mutually supportive relationship dedicated to the continued success of agriculture.[27]

To the west of the Susiana, in central Mesopotamia, the later 'Ubaid period (after about c. 4500 B.C.) saw the gradual settlement of the plain by villagers. By 4350 B.C. the 'Ubaid culture was quite uniform over most of the alluvial plain: All the settlements seem to have been located on reliable water courses, and almost all were less than 10 hectares in size (most of them only 1 or 2).

The spread of the 'Ubaid culture is remarkable for many reasons, particularly its great extent. 'Ubaid-style ceramics are found far into central Turkey, to the southwest in the Arabian Plateau, and in highland Iran—an area much greater than that encompassed within the Halafian and Samarran stylistic zones. The potter's wheel was probably invented by the end of the 'Ubaid period, when the pivoted working surface, or tournette, was altered by setting the wheel's axle in bearings and weighting the wheel in such a way that high speeds could be produced. This allowed delicate vessels to be made, and painted decorations like bands could be easily applied simply by holding a paintbrush steady against a rotating ceramic vessel.[28]

Virtually every 'Ubaid settlement had a large nonresidential building, probably a temple, built of mudbrick on platforms of clay or imported stone. Access typically was by a flight of stairs, to a room about 10 m in length, with a broad platform at one end and a table or small altar at the other. Smaller rooms were built on both sides of the main room, and ladders in these would sometimes give access to a second story. The exteriors of the buildings were often decorated with projections and recesses, where light and shadows created pleasing effects. In later periods, mosaics of colored ceramic cones and bitumen were used as decorations. At Eridu, 17 such temples were found superimposed, giving the later ones considerable elevation. Such structures are found all over Greater Mesopotamia soon after their appearance on the southern alluvial plain.

Until about 5000 B.C., settlements seem to have been located primarily with regard to the availability of resources and the land's agricultural potential, not on the basis of political and economic relationships. People tend to organize their territories in patterns reflecting changing social and economic conditions; thus when the movement of people and goods between settlements becomes important, and the area is agricultural and relatively flat, these settlements often are quite regularly spaced, as is evident in both the Warka area and the Susiana Plain.

By 4000 B.C., the number of small settlements had increased dramatically in many areas, and there was increasing variability in their arrangement and composition.

EARLY STATES: THE URUK AND JEMDET NASR PERIODS (C. 4100–3000 B.C.)

The Uruk period is regarded as the era of primary state formation in Southwest Asia. Cultural forces and processes probably in operation for thousands of years culminated in this interval in the appearance of the complete checklist of civilization: cities, warfare, writing, social hierarchies, advanced arts and crafts, and other elements.

Recently, Guillermo Algaze has proposed a model to explain why complex societies developed first in southern Mesopotamia.[29] He suggests that it is the ecological context of southern Mesopotamia that makes it unusual compared to neighboring regions. The alluvial lowlands are well watered by the Tigris and Euphrates rivers and thus create the potential for enormous agricultural productivity as well as for extensive trade using the rivers for transportation. In Algaze's model, trade is the most significant mechanism that early elite people or groups used as a method to expand their control of resources and power. They also used trade as a way to legitimize unequal access to resources that favor themselves. During the course of the Uruk period, further disparities in resource access, power, and trade arose between regions—including those outside of Mesopotamia—and these disparities favored cities in southern Mesopotamia. Trade thus accentuated differences in localized ecologies and their attendant resources as well as differences in ability to control river transportation routes.

Algaze's model receives some support from the geological work of Galina Morozova.[30] She points out that natural *avulsions*—changes in the courses of rivers—in the delta area of Tigris and Euphrates rivers were the result of a low-gradient floodplain, floods with high water levels, and deposition of sediments within channels. Rivers such as the Euphrates had many channels and networks of channels, and it is along these networks that the earliest southern Mesopotamian cities were built—a situation favorable to control of floodplain agriculture and control of transportation routes. Natural shifts in river channel courses away from the cities could, of course, affect these ecological advantages. [31]

The central Mesopotamian alluvial plain and the Susiana Plain offer our earliest and best known examples of the changes that occurred in Greater Mesopotamia in the Uruk period.

Warka: An Uruk City-State

The ancient settlement of Uruk (known as Warka in Arabic and Erech in the Bible), located in the heart of the southern alluvial plain, is one of the oldest cities in the world and may have been the center of one of the earliest states.

As many as 10,000 people may have lived in the city of Uruk by 3800 B.C., and around the town were many smaller villages and towns whose sizes and distribution suggest they may not have been tightly integrated into Uruk's political and economic systems (Figure 8.12).[32] Then, at about 3000 B.C., the city of Uruk apparently grew rapidly to about 50,000 people, who lived behind substantial defensive walls. There is also evidence of the beginning of abandonment of rural settlements surrounding Uruk—leaving little doubt, Robert McC. Adams suggests, that the growth of the city was a result of the immigration or forcible transference of the population from the hinterlands into the city.[33]

The residential architecture of Uruk reflects a diversity of occupational, economic, and social classes. All the buildings were mudbrick, but some were larger, better built, and more elaborately decorated. Many of the people lived in small rectangular buildings along narrow winding streets through which ran both above- and below-ground drainage canals. Apparently, houses were one story high for the poor and two stories tall for the wealthier, but both types were similar. Built of mudbrick and whitewashed, they represent an ideal architectural adaptation to the climate. Similar houses today are comfortable and attractive, with their whitewashed walls contrasting effectively with beautiful dyed rugs and textiles.

Archaeologists who have excavated Uruk occupations usually have found themselves ankle deep in the remains of millions of bevel-rimmed bowls, surely one of the ugliest ceramic types ever made outside a kindergarten, but also one of the most significant. Gregory Johnson has shown that various measurements of these bowls change over time, so that the Late, Middle, and Early Uruk periods can be defined in part by changes in their form.[34] Hans Nissen has also argued that these bowls, which an associated with temples,

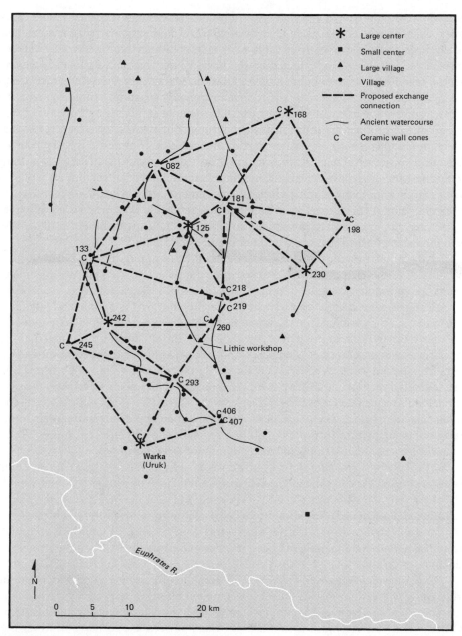

FIGURE 8.12   In simple societies the location of settlements with respect to each other is dictated mainly by ecological factors like water availability. But as societies become more complex, political and economic relationships begin to influence where settlements are located and how large they become. In Gregory Johnson's reconstruction (1975) of exchange networks among Late Uruk period (c. 3200 B.C.) settlements in southern Iraq, the spatial arrangement of the settlements with respect to one another is quite regular (the wall cones were used to decorate administrative centers, and their distribution here may indicate lines of political authority).

probably were ration bowls and were used to pay workers in grain for their labors.[35] Most have a capacity that corresponds to what a laborer's daily ration was asserted to be in ancient texts, and the symbol for to eat in early Mesopotamian writing seems to be that of a person eating from a bevel-rimmed bowl. Others have suggested that these bowls were used to bake bread. The prevailing theory, however, is that they were votives for temple ceremonies. The bowls were mass-produced, probably by simply molding, and they represent one of the first craft items for which the temple administrators organized some aspects of the production and distribution system. But these simple features of mass production and, perhaps, government administration of commodity production and distribution were fateful steps in the evolution of states. To most modern people, few things are more natural than governmental forms of organization and control, but our ancestors lived as farmers for many centuries without government in this sense; these first few steps in the direction of government in Mesopotamia were a long, slow process in these initial stages; later, the process of ancient state-formation was largely one in which the government increasingly intruded on socioeconomic and political life.

By the middle of the fourth millennium B.C., the population of Uruk included specialists in scores of arts and crafts. Potters, using molds and mass-production techniques, turned out enormous quantities of pottery. In earlier periods great numbers of beautifully painted vessels were made at most larger settlements, but by the middle and late fourth millennium, pottery manufacture had become a centralized, administered activity at Uruk and many other settlements. Other specialists included stonecutters, metalsmiths, bricklayers, farmers, fishermen, shepherds, and sailors. Writing did not come into general use in Mesopotamia until the first half of the third millennium B.C., but at Uruk and other sites, in levels dating from the fifth millennium onward, archaeologists find clay tablets and cylinder seals—a distinctive Mesopotamian tradition for 3000 years—which were used to impress clay sealings for containers, bales of commodities, and documents. Some of these seals convey in picture form the economic specialization of the community. Boats, domestic animals, grain, deities, and many other motifs are portrayed.

By the late fourth millennium B.C., Uruk was already an impressive settlement of residences and several large temples. Between about 3200 and 3100 B.C., the "White Temple" at Uruk was built on a platform some 12 m above ground level. Constructed of whitewashed mudbrick and decorated with elaborate recesses, columns, and buttresses, it must have been an impressive sight—especially to peasants coming into the city on market days. Inside the temple were tables and altars, all arranged according to the same ritual plan evident at Eridu some 2,500 years earlier.

The temple architecture and ziggurats of Mesopotamian antiquity raise an important point. As we will see in surveying other early complex cultures around the world, one of the most consistent signs of evolving cultural complexity is the diversion of enormous amounts of energy and materials into pyramids, ziggurats, palaces, platforms, and other huge constructions. Why would people who could just as easily—and certainly more profitably—build irrigation canals or terrace slopes, weave wool, or do other productive tasks instead "waste" their labors on these mammoth construction projects?

The answer to this question may lie precisely in the fact that these constructions are, in a limited sense, "wasteful." They may, for example, have helped prevent high and unstable rates of population growth, perhaps by deflecting investments in food production. As Leslie White suggested: "It would appear that the ruling class was frequently confronted with the problems of over-production and the threat of technological unemployment or a surplus of population among the lower classes. Their great public works programs, the wholesale disposition of wealth in mortuary customs, etc., enabled them to solve both these problems with one stroke."[36]

Just as important, monumental construction programs could reinforce social and political hierarchies. Frankfort speculates:

> The huge building, raised to establish a bond with the power on which the city depended, proclaimed not only the ineffable majesty of the gods but also the might of the community which had been capable of such an effort. The great temples were witnesses to piety, but also objects of civic pride. Built to ensure divine protection for the city, they also enhanced the significance of citizenship. Outlasting the generation of their builders, they were true monuments of the cities' greatness.[37]

SUSIANA PLAIN DURING THE URUK PERIOD

The sequence of Uruk culture history on the Susiana Plain parallels in many ways developments on the central alluvium. Gregory Johnson and Henry Wright have analyzed Susiana cultural history by focusing on the evolution of administrative institutions.[38] They have been principally concerned with the origins of the state, which they define as a society with at least three levels of hierarchically arranged, specialized administrators. For example, in a simple agricultural village, many of the decisions about what crops to plant, how much of the harvest is to be stored, who gets what share of the land, who marries whom, and so forth are made by individuals. Some of those decisions—particularly those that directly affect the whole community—are made by a village headman. We might say that this individual represents the first level of the decision-making hierarchy—he directs the activities of others who do the work. A second level of administrative hierarchy would exist if there were people who coordinate the activities of these village headmen and correct or approve their decisions—perhaps government agents charged with taxing and administering local affairs. Such agents would be under a third administrative level, and additional levels may exist above this.

In addition to suggesting that the ancient Mesopotamian state can be defined as a society with at least three such levels of specialized administrators, Wright and Johnson contend that the effectiveness of such societies and their dominance over other societal forms are tied to their ability to store and process information and make correct decisions at specific points within the control hierarchy.

Wright and Johnson examined several areas where the first Mesopotamian states developed, looking for evidence of this change. One type of evidence was the actual administrative documents themselves. In most of Mesopotamia at this time, the administration of people and goods was facilitated by using pieces of inscribed stone to impress clay with signs of authorization. These stones were usually either in the form of stamps, used like the rubber stamps of today, or cylinders that were rolled across the clay to make an impression, and they varied in size and in the complexity of the symbols incised on them. Fortunately, the clay impressed with these seals and the seals themselves are often preserved in archaeological sites, and they can be used to infer the levels of administration in these extinct societies.

The impressed clay can be divided into two classes. Some were used to certify the contents of a container such as a vessel, basket, bale, or storeroom. They were made by placing a lump of clay over a knot that had to be untied to gain access to the container, so that unauthorized entry could be detected. Discarded sealings of this type indicate the receipt of stored or redistributed goods. Other seals convey or store facts about goods or people. Some are plain counters whose shape indicates a numerical unit, while others (*bullae*) are small spheroidal jackets that were once wrapped around sets of counters, and still others are flat, rectangular tablets stamped with numerical symbols. Writing, as we know it, did not exist until after the state—as defined by Wright and Johnson—emerged, but these stamps and seals obviously conveyed a great deal of information. Clay tokens have also been found in about 10 geometric shapes at many early Mesopotamian sites, and Denise Schmandt-Besserat argues that these tokens, which were usually enclosed in clay envelopes, represented such commodities as pots of grain, numbers of animals, and areas of land and are the direct precursors of later written scripts.[39]

Wright and Johnson used commodity and message sealings found at sites on the Susiana to reconstruct some aspects of the production, transport, and administration of goods. They concluded that they could determine when the change was made from one- and two-level decision-making institutions to the three levels that define the state.

Wright and Johnson also analyzed the locational arrangement of the settlements in southwestern Iran and found that after about 3600 B.C. there were trends toward more regular spacing of settlements and the emergence of distinctive site size groupings—both consistent with the change from a two-level to a three-level control hierarchy. This pattern of developing settlement arrangements that correlate with changes in the technology of administration is apparently not unique to southwestern Iran: "The transition seems to occur in several adjacent regions in Iraq between [2700 B.C. and 3250 B.C.] around the ancient centers of Nippur, Nineveh, and Uruk. . . . Thus rather than one case of state emergence, there was a series of emergences of individual states in a network of politics."[40] Wright and Johnson suggest that decisions involving problems posed by drought, overpopulation, conflict, or some other single factor could probably be handled by a two-level hierarchy—something on the order of a chiefdom, perhaps—but a combination of problems would require additional decision-making capacity. They suspect that one important factor in early Southwest Asian state formation may have been the economic interactions between nomadic pastoralists and lowland farmers, probably in the form of the exchange of cheese, rugs, meat, minerals, and other highland resources for pottery, grain, and other lowland commodities. Economic models suggest that fluctuating demand for certain craft products in relatively simple economies often stimulates the centralization of workshops and economic administration, and Wright and Johnson suggest that in prehistoric Mesopotamia the economic demands of nomads on lowland economies may have fluctuated sufficiently to produce a similar effect, with the eventual emergence of a three-level hierarchy.

Johnson has applied various concepts from what is known as hierarchy theory and the so-called rank-size rule to the Susiana data.[41] Hierarchy theory is essentially a search for explanations of how everything, from molecular structures to world governments, seems to involve hierarchical orderings. The assumption here is that there are principles common to all these forms of hierarchies and that the processes by which hierarchies change and appear can be mathematically analyzed.

The rank-size rule is an empirical observation that many settlement patterns are similar in terms of the relative sizes of their component settlements. Thus, in any region, state, or country, one can expect that the distribution of people will be somewhere between the extreme distributions in which everyone lives in one settlement, or those in which the populace is divided into settlements of exactly equal population size. A rank-size plot is produced by ranking each settlement in terms of its population, assigning the number one to the largest, two to the second largest, and so on, and then graphing the actual population of each settlement against the rank of that settlement on a full logarithmic scale. Geographers have noted that for many developing countries, such as Egypt, the rank-size plot will be a *primate* one. For example, Cairo is much larger than any other settlement and forms such a large proportion of the total Egyptian population that a rank-size plot of Egypt is sharply concave, in contrast to a linear distribution in which the second-ranked city is only slightly smaller than the largest, the third is slightly smaller than the second, and so on. It is sufficient here to note that major shifts in the political and economic organization of an area are usually reflected in its rank-size plot. To use Egypt as an example again, the great growth of Cairo's population to nearly 15 million people recently has correlated with the growing power of the national government and the rapidly industrializing economy. Prior to 1965, a much greater percentage of Egyptians lived in smaller towns and villages than do now.

The archaeological applications of this are obvious. If we know when a site was occupied and how big it was, we can then estimate population sizes, construct rank-size plots, and perhaps detect when great political and economic changes were taking place. The application of this idea to various areas of Mesopotamia yields mixed results. Clearly there were different rank-size patterns at different times, which might signal the origins of state-level societies. This would not *explain* their appearance, but it would help identify them. But it is difficult to estimate the populations of sites in different time periods with precision. Also, no one really knows what the different kinds of rank-size plots mean. They are essentially empirical generalizations without any theory to explain them.

Nonetheless, a fundamental problem of archaeology is to define and interpret patterns in the distribution of artifacts through space and time, and these rank-size plots at least have the virtue of showing us some possible patterns.

Various other archaeologists have proposed alternative models of how the Uruk states formed. Guillermo Algaze,[42] for example, has argued that this development was essentially a process in which the peoples of the resource-deficient Mesopotamian lowlands expanded their state through trade and warfare in order to incorporate resource-rich areas on the periphery and to establish secure trade routes extending far beyond the Uruk heartland. We see, for example, communities in which Uruk styles of architecture and ceramics were used in western Iran, north into Syria, and even as far away as the Nile Delta.[43]

In evaluating the many models of the development of the Uruk and Jemdet Nasr periods, Susan Pollock notes that these models present these ancient people as rather passive elements in these developments and tend to focus on the adaptations large groups made over time and large areas. She suggests that archaeological analyses should attempt to make our appreciation of the Uruk peoples more human and that "archaeological analyses . . . must also highlight internal conflicts generated from acts of daily social life, as well as those deriving from major sociocultural transformations."[44] In making these and other points, Pollock joins numerous other contemporary archaeologists in trying to see the peoples of the Uruk period, and of all other cultures and eras, as individuals—*real, live* people.

In a sense, the rise of Mesopotamian states is the rise of urbanism. As the centuries of the fourth millennium B.C. passed, towns that had once been home to hundreds became cities of thousands of inhabitants. Urbanism does not just increase the size of communities, however: A key element of Mesopotamian urbanism was that proportionately greater numbers of people lived in larger settlements, and the people in these settlements became increasingly specialized in their occupations. All of these people—kings, priests, scribes, farmers, soldiers, farmers, slaves, and so on—became functionally integrated in the sense that they all depended on each other to perpetuate the community, and all derived benefits from the greater efficiency of functional differentiation and integration. Toward the end of the Uruk period, almost all major settlements were fortified, and documents written much later, at circa 2600 B.C., speak at length of conflict between the people of Ur, Uruk, Umma, and the other city-states. In subsequent chapters, we will see that the initial stimulus for urbanization in other parts of the world also seems to be related to defensive needs: Egypt, which was protected from hostile outside forces by the deserts and the sea, developed urban societies only comparatively late; while in the Indus Valley, which was much more of a crossroads for nomadic and other groups, urbanism was present almost from the very first. In this context, Adams argues that early Mesopotamian urbanization may have been imposed on a rural populace by a small, politically conscious superstratum that was motivated principally by military and economic interests.[45]

Because of defensive considerations and the cost of transporting labor and products, agricultural land nearest the urban areas would have been the most intensively exploited, and this may have stimulated the construction of large irrigation systems. Another important possible effect of urbanism is that it might have created—and to some extent have been created by—the large nomadic populations thought to have been present in Southwest Asia as early as 6000 B.C. Most of these people were probably similar to the present-day Bakhtiari of western Iran, who herd sheep and goats in the uplands during much of the year but come down to the lowlands in the winter to sell their animals wool, meat, and milk products and to buy craft items, food, and other products. The relationships between these upland nomadic and lowland sedentary groups are varied and complex.[46] Historically, when central governments have weakened in Southwest Asia, some marginal cultivators revert to nomadic pastoralism in times of war or poor harvests, while other pastoralists become laborers or marginal farmers if they lose too many sheep. One of the effects of urbanism suggested by the archaeological record—the depopulation of the countryside—may have given nomads a new niche. By working the mountain areas and highlands for most of the year, the nomads could have come down and exploited the marginal areas between urban centers—peacefully most of the time, but other times with hostility—and then traded with the townspeople.

Toward the end of the fourth millennium B.C., the Mesopotamian alluvium and adjacent regions were the heartland of a developed sociopolitical and economic organization that most would call a civilization. Writing had been developed, great temples soared up from the centers of large cities, and the economy was both productive and complexly interdependent. Also, the Uruk polity spread far beyond the central alluvial plain. At Habuba Kabira South, in Syria, a large later Uruk settlement is so similar to the great Uruk cities to the south in styles of ceramics and architecture that it may well have been built by people who came directly from the south to found this city.[47]

As noted earlier, this expansion and intensification of the Uruk sphere of cultural interaction undoubtedly involved extension of commercial links between and within communities, but there was also probably a strong element of conflict as well.

THE EARLY DYNASTIC PERIOD (C. 3000–2350 B.C.)

To the modern urbanite, it may seem inappropriate to label as a "state" a collection of 12 or 14 cities with a combined population of perhaps 100,000 and an area of only a few thousand square kilometers, but, as someone once observed, it is the small states, like fifth–century B.C. Athens, Renaissance Florence, and Elizabethan England, that have put posterity most in their debt. To this list can be added Early Dynastic Sumer.

Sumerian Civilization

Approximately 13 city-states made up Sumerian "civilization" between about 3000 and 2350 B.C. Through most of their history, these city-states were politically autonomous, but they belonged to the same cultural tradition, and by 3000 B.C. they had collectively developed many of the classical elements of Southwest Asian civilization, including ziggurats, brick platforms, the potter's wheel, wheeled carts, metal-working, sailboats, and writing.

The fact that the Sumerian language was essentially unlike those of the contemporary but less-developed Semitic cultures that surrounded the Sumerian has led some to place Sumerian origins in Turkey or Bahrain. Sumerian myths speak of origins in some distant land; but we will probably never determine their ethnic origins, and in a sense this is an unimportant question. The achievements of cultures cannot be explained in terms of the special characteristics and mental gifts of the people of these cultures: People are constants in the equations of cultural evolution, and it is their circumstances and position in place and time that determine their cultural "achievements."

SUMERIAN WRITING

We have a detailed picture of life in these Sumerian city-states because shortly before 3000 B.C. they began to develop a written language. What we know about the Sumerian language is derived from the thousands of clay tablets on which they wrote (Figure 8.13). Their script is known as *cuneiform*, from the Latin for "wedge-shaped," a reference to the fact that Sumerian was written by impressing wet clay with the end of a reed, leaving wedge-shaped marks.

The earliest known written documents may be clay tablets and sealings from early occupations at Uruk (c. 3400 B.C.)—although we can't identify their language as written by Sumerians. These documents include signs for carpenter, donkey, boat, copper, and many other things, totaling 1,500 symbols in all (Figure 8.14). Some signs seem to mean "to buy," while others refer to *en*, the title of a lord, and to *unken*, which may have been a people's assembly.[48] The hierarchical nature of Mesopotamian society by the end of the Uruk period is vividly illustrated by one of the oldest documents known, the "Standard Professions List,"

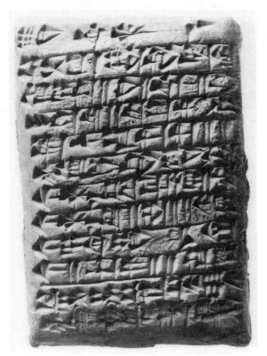

FIGURE 8.13   A cuneiform text on clay.

which gives the titles of officials and names of professions, all arranged according to what is apparently a composite sense of power and prestige.[49]

The ability of this cumbersome writing to convey abstract concepts or the spoken language was initially quite limited, but in the centuries after 2900 B.C. the Sumerians improved it. Phoneticization, by which some signs came to represent distinct words and syllables of the spoken language, was a most important development.[50] Eventually, much of spoken Sumerian was represented by written symbols, and the pictographic elements slowly lost their representational character as the scribes stylized them and reduced the number of directions in which the stylus had to move to write them.[51] Signs were developed for most Sumerian vowels and syllables, but the language was never reduced to an alphabetic system where every distinct sound is represented by a unique sign. Instead, it remained a welter of signs that represented pictographs of concrete objects, signs that represented syllables of speech, and signs that categorized (determinatives). This made reading the script somewhat complicated, requiring the memorization of hundreds of different characters. One sign, for example, which ultimately derived from a pictograph representing a mountain, acquired a total of 10 possible phonetic values and 4 ideographic values as well.[52]

To aid in reading the meaning of the word the Sumerians devised a system of determinatives—signs placed before or after a word to indicate the general category to which the word belonged, such as birds, male proper nouns, or deities.

Over the centuries the Sumerians' successors reduced the complexity of the written language, but even as late as about 1900 B.C., it had between 600 and 700 unique elements. At this stage it was similar to Chinese and a few other modern languages, which faithfully represent the spoken language and are adequate for most purposes, but which, compared to alphabetic systems, are very cumbersome. It is difficult to construct typewriters or computers for languages with hundreds of unique elements, and even minimal literacy in such languages is the product of long and arduous training. (To become literate in modern Chinese, for example, one must memorize several thousand characters.)

The role of writing in early Mesopotamian societies seems largely economic. Simple pictographs and the spoken language cannot efficiently meet the requirements of a society that has surpluses to be stored and redistributed, water to be allocated, land rights to be assigned and adjudicated, ritual prayers to be said, and all the other tasks we find in complex cultures. In fact, only the Inka of Peru managed to develop states and empires without a written language, but they had a fairly efficient substitute in the form of a vast bureaucracy and the *quipu*, a system of knotted strings in which the length of strings and placement of knots was used as a device to assist the memory of the recordkeeper.

The economic element in ancient Mesopotamian scripts is evident in their mathematical notations. Georges Ifrah notes that the Sumerians used a counting system with a base of 60, as well as the base-10 system we have.[53] Different commodities were counted using

EARLIEST PICTOGRAPHS (3000 B.C.)	DENOTATION OF PICTOGRAPHS	PICTOGRAPHS IN ROTATED POSITION	CUNEIFORM SIGNS CA. 1900 B.C.	BASIC LOGOGRAPHIC VALUES		ADDITIONAL LOGOGRAPHIC VALUES		SYLLABARY (PHONETIC VALUES)
				READING	MEANING	READING	MEANING	
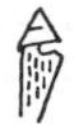	HEAD AND BODY OF A MAN	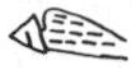	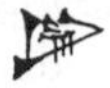	LÚ	MAN			
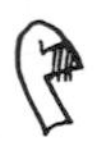	HEAD WITH MOUTH INDICATED	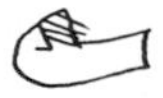	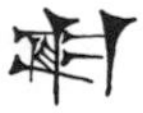	KA	MOUTH	KIRI₃ ZÚ GÙ DUG₄ INIM	NOSE TEETH VOICE TO SPEAK WORD	KA ZÚ
	BOWL OF FOOD			NINDA	FOOD, BREAD	NÍG GAR	THING TO PLACE	
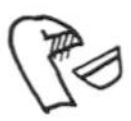	MOUTH + FOOD	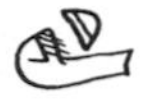	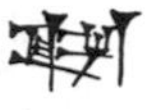	KÚ	TO EAT	ŠAGAR	HUNGER	
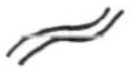	STREAM OF WATER			A	WATER	DURU₅	MOIST	A
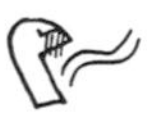	MOUTH + WATER	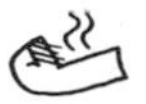	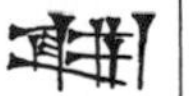	NAG	TO DRINK	EMMEN	THIRST	
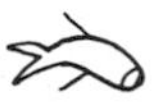	FISH	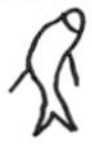	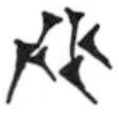	KUA	FISH			KU₆ HA
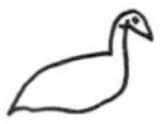	BIRD	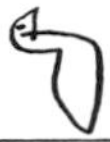	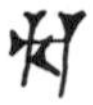	MUŠEN	BIRD			HU PAG
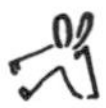	HEAD OF AN ASS	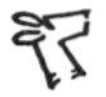	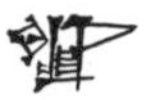	ANŠE	ASS			
	EAR OF BARLEY		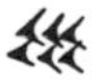	ŠE	BARLEY			ŠE

FIGURE 8.14   The evolution of Sumerian writing. Fourth millennium B.C. tablets were inscribed vertically with pictographs, but in the early third millennium, the direction of the writing and the pictographs were rotated to the horizontal. In succeeding millennia the symbols were stylized and given phonetic meanings.

different systems. It is difficult for most people to accept that there is nothing inherently necessary about a base-10 numbering system. But modern computers employ a base-2 system, for example, using just 1s and 0s to represent all numbers. Whatever base is used, people usually have given a unique name to *each* of the numbers, so a base-2 system is the simplest and a base-60 system is rather unwieldy.[54] The Sumerians got around the problem of having to learn and use a unique name for each number between 0 and 60 by giving a name to each multiple of 10 lower than or equal to 60. As H. W. F. Saggs notes, the ancient Sumerians and their successors used their mathematical systems not only for economic accounting but also for land surveying, calendrical calculations, and astronomical science.[55] By about 1800 B.C. the people of Mesopotamia (1) had calculated the square root of 2 to a value correct to 1 in 2,000,000; (2) had formulated massive tables of reciprocals of sexagesimal numbers; (3) knew how to calculate the length of a hypotenuse from the lengths of the sides of right-angled triangles (1,200 years before Pythagoras); (4) could calculate cube roots; and (5) knew some algebraic operations.[56]

The way of life described by the Sumerian texts, and by texts of other Southwest Asian cultures of the third millennium B.C., is still recognizable to anyone who has traveled in these areas. Sheep, goats, and cattle are tabulated, taxed, and exchanged; children are shepherded to school—as always, much against their will; a council of elders meets to consider grievances against the inhabitants of an adjoining town; and Sumerian proverbs express ideas recognizable in many societies:

> Upon my escaping from the wild ox,
> The wild cow confronted me.

> When a poor man dies,
> do not try to revive him.[57]

But when they turn to mythological and eschatological themes, the ancient Mesopotamians are less accessible—perhaps even a bit bizarre—by our standards, as in this section of the myth of the revival of the goddess Inanna:

> Go to the underworld.
> Enter the door like flies.
> Ereshkigal, the Queen of the Underworld, is moaning
> With the cries of a woman about to give birth.
> No linen is spread over her body.
> Her breasts are uncovered.
> Her hair swirls about her head like leeks.

> When she cries, "Oh! Oh! My inside!"
> Cry also, "Oh! Oh! Your Inside!"
> When she cries, "Oh! Oh! My outside!"
> Cry also, "Oh! Oh! Your outside!"
> The queen will be pleased.
> She will offer you a gift.
> Ask her only for the corpse that hangs from the hook on the wall.
> One of you will sprinkle the food of life on it.
> The other will sprinkle the water of life.
> Inanna will arise.[58]

Western philosophy and theology are deeply influenced by the philosophies first propounded in ancient Greece, philosophies very different from those of ancient Sumer. Thus, most Westerners see the world in terms of beginnings and ends, causes and effects, and the importance and "will" of the individual. We cannot completely reconstruct Sumerian philosophy on the basis of fragmentary texts, but it seems evident that the Sumerians saw a much more static and magical world than we do. Although their technology and complex organizations demonstrate that they were shrewd, rational people, there seems to have been little emphasis or analysis of human motivation or the physical world. They viewed the earth as a flat disk under a vaulted heaven and believed that various gods guided history according to well-laid-out plans and that the world continues without end and with little

Table 8.1 Similarities Between Sumerian Stories and the Noachian Flood Story

Babylonian Cuneiform	Genesis
1. The gods decide to make a flood.	1. The Lord decides to destroy wicked mankind.
2. The God Ea warns Artarhasis to build a ship.	2. The Lord warns Noah to build an ark.
3. Artarhasis is to take his family and animals aboard.	3. Noah is to take his family and animals aboard.
4. The flood turns mankind into clay.	4. The flood destroys all flesh.
5. The ship grounds on Mount Nisir.	5. The ark comes to rest on the Ararat Mountains.
6. Artarhasis learns when the waters have subsided by sending out a dove, a swallow, and a raven.	6. Noah learns when the waters have subsided by sending out a dove, a swallow, and a raven.
7. He offers sacrifice to the gods.	7. He offers sacrifice to the Lord.
8. The gods smell the sweet savor.	8. The Lord smells the pleasing odor.
9. The god Enlil blesses Artarhasis and his wife.	9. God blesses Noah and his sons.

change. Each god was in charge of something—the movements of the planets, irrigation, or brick-making, for example—and each was immortal and inflexible. As with humans, the deities were hierarchically arranged in power and authority and were given to power struggles and many vices.

Like most people, the Sumerians thought that the gods had a special interest in them. Just as every American dollar bill has on the back of it the assertion that *annuit coeptis* ("[God] has favored our undertaking"), almost every official Sumerian pronouncement and inscription invoked the favor of the gods who, it was assumed, favored the city's fortunes.

One way in which Sumerian religion and ideology has influenced modern cultures is in its influence on Judeo-Christian religious traditions. The biblical account of the Noachian flood, for example, is clearly related to Sumerian stories that predated the Old Testament by thousands of years. Finegan has identified some of the similarities[59] (see Table 8.1).

In 1929 S. Langdon, excavating the Sumerian city of Kish, and Sir L. Woolley, excavating at Ur, both announced that they had found thick levels of clean sand that they presumed was evidence of the biblical Flood.[60] Some members of these expeditions are even said to have sold vials of sand labeled "Samples from the Great Flood."

But Spuhler notes that many layers thought to be flood deposits are really sand dunes produced by winds, while others are ordinary river deposits.[61] In any case, radiocarbon dates for levels thought to be of the biblical Flood range from 4500 B.C. to 2700 B.C., and the absence of sand strata at many other nearby sites, and the evidence of life as usual all over Mesopotamia at this time, rule out fairly conclusively any scientific evidence for the biblical Flood—except in the opinion of the people who keep climbing Mount Ararat looking for pieces of the ark. Popular press reports of a Russian pilot who saw the outline of a boat far above the tree line on this mountain have fueled several expeditions to recover the ark, but so far only a few questionable bits of wood have been found. Only the drearily unimaginative archaeologist would be impressed by the fact that all the samples of wood were radiocarbon-dated to about 3,500 years ago—a time for which there is no evidence that the rest of the world was flooded.[62]

SUMERIAN INSTITUTIONS AND ECONOMY

Tantalizing clues in documents suggest that many Sumerian city-states had a public assembly in which, perhaps, people formulated policy and made decisions through consensus and even a form of simple democracy.[63] Cities appear to have been divided into something like modern "wards," but we really don't know the organizing principles. There is some evidence[64] that people were organized in clans, and kinship ties probably remained the connective tissue of Sumerian civilization through most of its history. Yet one of the things that all states do is complement kinship ties with links among and within socioeconomic classes in order to provide effective methods of getting people to operate in useful corporate groups (e.g., serving in military units tied together by kinship and place of origins, as in units in the American Civil War). In the long run, state societies seem to wear away at kinship ties, replacing them with socioeconomic class ties and other kinds of corporate groups.

The Sumerian extended family appears to have been a strong and durable unit, protected by laws governing rights of inheritance, recompense for injuries, and so forth. As Nicholas Postgate notes, women were reasonably well treated both by law and custom in Sumerian society, but there seems little doubt that this was a strongly patriarchal culture, as evidenced by divorce law: "If a wife rejects her husband and says 'You are not my husband', they shall cast her into the river. If a husband says to his wife 'You are not my wife', he shall pay 1/2 mina of silver."[65]

In Sumer, wheat, barley, vegetables, and dates were the major crops, while cattle-raising and fishing were of almost equal importance. Cattle were raised for draft power, hides, and milk and meat. Fish was a staple, as were mutton, goat, and pork. It is interesting in view of their later status as a taboo food in much of the Middle East that pigs were a common sight on Sumerian farms, prized for their fat and grease (although rarely if ever depicted in art, except in figures and ceramics[66]).

Out of each measure of wheat or barley harvested, the Mesopotamian farmer probably fed about 16 percent to his animals, reserved about 10 percent for the next year's sowing, lost about 25 percent in storage, and ate the rest.[67] If ethnographic studies are to be believed, in the absence of modern transport, people did not cultivate fields much more than 4 km from their houses. At any given time, much of the land around a village in ancient times would have been fallow, while other land would have been unirrigatable or of marginal productivity. Adams estimates that each person would need for subsistence about 1 hectare of barley and wheat fields, along with at least some pastures and orchards.

One of the less desirable "firsts" of Sumerian civilization was probably in the field of epidemic diseases. Just as there are certain disastrous things a hunter and gatherer can do (e.g., to presume on too slight evidence that a cave bear is not at home), one of the worst things a villager can do is contaminate drinking water with sewage, and this is hard to avoid in a primitive town. Typhoid, cholera, and many other diseases require certain levels of population density to evolve, to maintain a reservoir of infected individuals, and to perpetuate themselves. These levels were probably reached for the first time in Sumer. Once people started digging wells and irrigation canals in areas with many people and animals, disease and epidemics quickly followed.

Few economies in history or prehistory have been as organized as the Sumerian. Tablet after tablet records endless lists of commodities produced, stored, and allotted. Ration lists, work forces, guild members—all are recorded in numbing detail. Even the city's snake-charmers were organized.

The state and church controlled economic matters through much of Mesopotamian history, but individual merchants and capitalist elements also seem to have been significant fairly early on. This is important for the Marxian scholar because once you have individual wealth and capital, the possibilities for class conflict and the rest of the Marxian paradigm exist. Although Sumerian society was organized on the basis of kinship, people also belonged to and acted through occupational and social classes. In the event of war, for example, members of different "guilds," such as silversmiths or potters, would be under the command of their "guild president." At the pinnacle of Sumerian society was a god-king, assumed to be a descendant of the gods who was also in contact with the gods. Beneath him was a leisure class of nobles. There was also a class of wealthy businessmen who lived in the larger, better houses of the city; of lesser wealth and prestige were the many artisans and farmers, including smiths, leather-workers, fishermen, bricklayers, weavers, and potters. Scribes apparently held fairly important positions, and literacy was an admired accomplishment. At the bottom of society were the slaves, often war captives or dispossessed farmers.

Money, as we know it, did not exist in ancient Sumer; most exchange was "in kind," the trading of products for other products. Local and long-distance trade was voluminous, however, and ships sailed up the rivers from the gulf carrying shell, carnelian, lapis lazuli, silver, gold, onyx, alabaster, textiles, and food and other produce.

One of the most spectacular differences between Sumerian societies after 3000 B.C. and their predecessors is in mortuary practices. At the end of the 'Ubaid period (3800 B.C.), graves varied little, even at the largest settlements; but after 3000 B.C. a radical shift occurred. The famous death pit at Ur is an impressive display of wealth and pomp (Figure 8.15). Excavating here in 1927–1928, Sir Leonard Woolley came upon five bodies lying side by side, each with a copper dagger and other items.[68] Beneath them was a layer of matting on which he encountered the bodies of 10 women, lying in two rows,

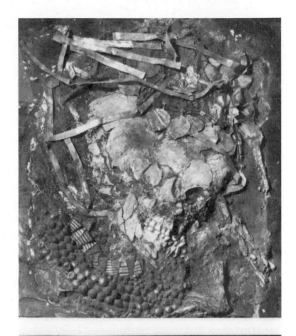

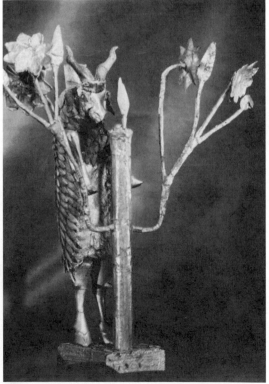

FIGURE 8.15 (*Right*) Crushed skull of a female attendant in the death pit at Ur (*above*). Note the gold jewelry and precious stones. This Sumerian model of a goat and a tree (*below*) is made of wood, lapis, and gold, and is about 51 cm high. It was found at Ur and dates to about 2600 B.C.

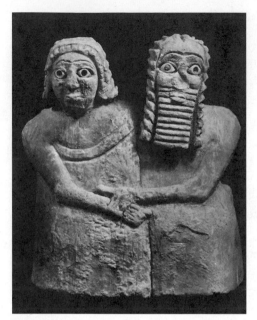

FIGURE 8.16 Gypsum statuettes of an aged couple, residents at about 2500 B.C. of Nippur, one of the largest cities in southern Mesopotamia during this period.

each richly ornamented with gold, lapis lazuli, and carnelian jewelry. Nearby was a gold- and jewel-encrusted harp, across which were the bones of the gold-crowned harpist. The bodies were lying on a ramp, and as the excavators continued down the platform they encountered a heavily jeweled chariot, complete with the remains of oxen and grooms. Then the investigators began unearthing masses of gold, silver, stone, and copper vessels, as well as additional human bodies, weapons, and other items. Nearby, another set of six male skeletons equipped with copper knives and helmets was found, as well as the remains of two four-wheeled wooden wagons—also decorated with harnesses of gold and silver and accompanied by the skeletons of grooms and drivers. Other arrangements of human skeletons, harps, wagons, and model boats appeared as the excavations continued. At the end of the tomb was a wooden bier containing the remains of the queen. The entire upper part of her body was hidden by a mass of beads of gold, silver, lapis lazuli, carnelian, agate, and chalcedony. Her headdress and other furnishings were lavishly ornamented with gold, silver, and precious jewels. Liberally strewn about the chamber were human bodies, jewelry, vessels of precious metals, silver figurines, silver tables, cosmetics, seashell ornaments, and a number of other treasures.

All together some 16 "royal" burials were found at Ur, all of them distinguished from the myriad common graves by the fact that each was not merely a coffin but rather a structure of stone, or stone and mudbrick, and by the inclusion of human sacrifices—up to 80 in one case. At least three categories of burials seemed evident, ranging from the 16 royal graves to less elaborate but still richly furnished graves in which the common people were presumably placed.

As brilliant as Sumerian civilization was, one must realize that it was just one of the states of this era (Figure 8.16). In the southwestern highlands of Iran, for example, between 3300 and 2800 B.C. a great *Proto-Elamite* trading state arose, perhaps on the basis of its ability to dominate trade over the rich routes between Mesopotamia and the Iranian Plateau.[69]

SOUTHWEST ASIA AFTER 2350 B.C.

For centuries after 3000 B.C., the Sumerian city-states engaged in almost constant warfare, with first one and then another gaining temporary ascendancy. With the rise to power of Sargon of Akkad at about 2350 B.C., however, the political fabric of ancient Southwest Asia was forever changed. Sargon and his several immediate successors used the city of Akkad as a military base from which they mounted spectacularly successful attacks in all directions. Akkadian historical documents recount 34 battles fought by Sargon against the southern city-states, during which he moved down the alluvial plain, capturing many kings, smashing city walls, and finally "cleansing his weapons in the sea." Sargon appointed

Akkadians to administrative posts in the conquered city-states and then began expanding his other frontiers, invading Syria, Lebanon, and western Iran.

After 2250 B.C. quarrels arose among rival claimants to the Akkadian throne, and the state fragmented under the onslaught of peoples moving in from the highlands on its margins. This "dark age" lasted until about 2100 B.C., when one or more Sumerian kings were able to evict the invaders and reestablish political control over much of the southern alluvial plain under what is known as the Ur III dynasty. One ruler, Ur-Nammu, based at the ancient city of Ur, aggressively extended his influence into much of the area formally encompassed by the Akkadians. Great volumes of obsidian, lapis lazuli, and copper are thought to have passed into central Mesopotamia from as far away as Afghanistan, Anatolia, and even Cyprus. Legal texts of the late third millennium describe in detail problems of land use, irrigation rights, compensation for bodily injury, penalties for adultery, and many other elements of daily life.

Despite its apparent stability, the Ur III political system of the late third millennium was constantly under pressure from internal political rivalries, as well as from the incursions of semi-nomads and rival groups along the state's frontiers. The coup de grace was administered at about 2004 B.C. with the invasion from western Iran of the Elamites, who led the king of Ur away in captivity.

From about 2000 to 1800 B.C., Greater Mesopotamia was politically fragmented as kings at Isin, Larsa, Susa, and elsewhere established contending states.[70] Eventually, the ancient city of Babylon became the most powerful political entity, and by 1792 B.C. Hammurabi established the Babylonian Empire, based mainly on the southern alluvial plain. The many documents of his reign that have survived reflect a skillful politician adept at bureaucratic, military, and political uses of power: his famous law code, although harsh by modern standards, reflects efficient administration. Both Hammurabi and his successors encountered opposition from southern city-states and from a rival state in Assyria, to the north. As always, the nomads and other peoples on the empire's periphery—in this case the Kassites and Hurrians—made inroads as soon as the central government weakened, and eventually they overran much of the Babylonian Empire.

After about 1600 B.C., the political history of Southwest Asia becomes extremely complicated, with frequent political realignments and, ultimately, the gradual development and extension of imperial power (Figure 8.17). Assyrians, Elamites, Achaemenids, and

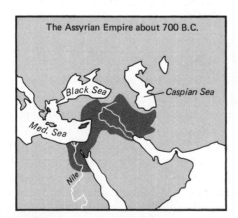
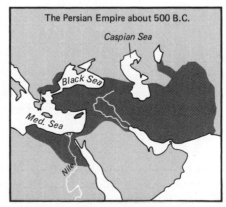

FIGURE 8.17   The extent of the Assyrian and Persian (Achaemenid) empires.

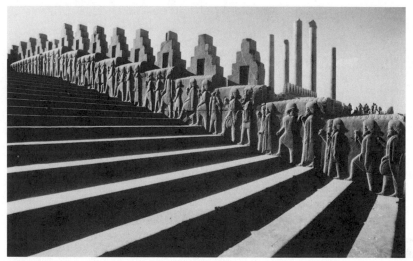

FIGURE 8.18 At about 500 B.C. the capital of the Achaemenid Empire was Persepolis, in central Iran. This grand stairway ascends to the Palace, and along it are reliefs that illustrate real-life processions to pay homage to the king. Some of these sculpted figures carry flowers and other gifts for the ruler.

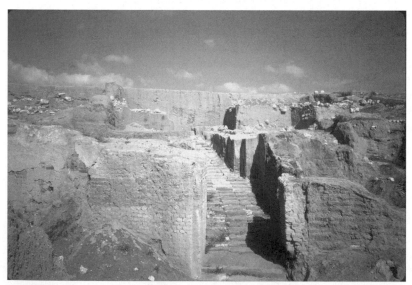

FIGURE 8.19 Important records written on clay tablets were preserved in burnt rooms at Ebla, Syria.

other cultural groups established empires, and eventually the political and military scale became distinctly internal as empires centered in Egypt, Anatolia, and Iran met and, more often than not, came into conflict (Figure 8.18).

SUMMARY AND CONCLUSIONS

It is possible that some archaeologist will, while sweating over a Mesopotamian mudbrick building foundation one day, discover a library of cuneiform tablets that record in great detail a history of the origins of the Mesopotamian state, complete with population statistics, war casualties, changes in the weather, average fertility rates, and a demographic analysis of the whole critical two millennia of state origins.

In fact, discoveries from Syria, dated to the late third millennium B.C., of previously unknown archives of thousands of texts do provide some information of this kind (Figure 8.19). But for the most part, only archaeological data can provide evidence of the long-term and broad-scale factors that form the framework of Southwest Asian cultural history. We have some sense of such factors as the rates of population growth, evolution of trade networks, changing settlement patterns (Figure 8.20), and so on, but excavations are slow and expensive, and political problems continue to hinder research.

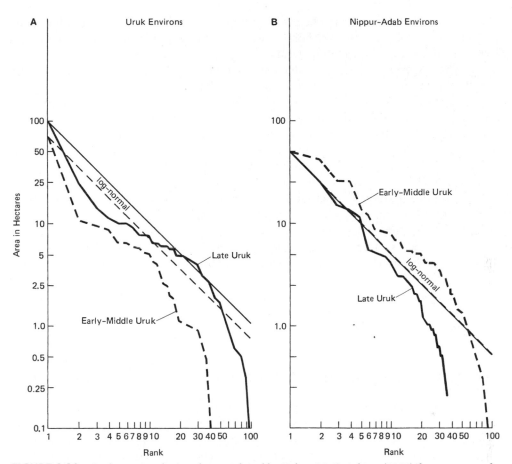

FIGURE 8.20   Settlement rank-size plots produced by Robert McC. Adams (1981) for two areas of Mesopotamia during the early Middle Uruk period (c. 3400 B.C.) and the Late Uruk period (c. 3200 B.C.), the periods when the first "states" were appearing in this part of Mesopotamia. Rank-size plots like these are formed by ranking the settlements from largest to smallest and then plotting a settlement's rank against its size on a log-log scale. Geographers have found that different shapes of such plots correlate with certain kinds of economic and political situations. The "flat-top" plot of the Early Uruk in the Nippur-Adab region (B) often is associated with very loose economic integration, whereas a log-normal distribution (the dotted lines in the graphs) is associated with considerable political and economic integration. The fact that both the plots for the Late Uruk period—when the first developed complex societies here were in operation—changed over time in the same direction from markedly different original plots may reflect the growing economic and political interdependence of settlements in the Late Uruk "state."

With the information now available, however, the evolution of complex societies in Mesopotamia seems to have been the result of multiple factors, operating in complex patterns that differed from place to place. The alluvial plain has the potential to produce tremendous quantities of food, more than is required in most years to sustain millions of people and their domestic animals. Such surpluses do not necessarily create great differences in wealth, but they certainly allow the formation of rich and poor social classes, and it seems to be a pattern that wherever one finds economic systems that produce great surpluses, one also discovers elaborate social hierarchies of administrators to organize, store, distribute, and exploit these surpluses.

What factors stimulate the production of surpluses and thus create the conditions for the establishment of social classes and administrative hierarchies? Our review of the evidence from Southwest Asia suggests that irrigation cannot be said to be the "primary cause" of early Southwest Asian cultural complexity. Occupational specialization, monumental architecture, changes in settlement spacing and size hierarchies, architectural variability, mortuary stratification—in short, the whole range of physical evidence of cultural complexity —appear before evidence of significant extension of irrigation systems. This is true for both the heartland of Sumer and for the Susiana Plain in southwestern Iran—the two areas for which we have the best archaeological data. In much of Southwest Asia, in fact, increased investments in irrigation systems appear to be the result of urbanism, not its cause.[71]

For large cities to form and persist, the areas surrounding them must be particularly productive because it was not feasible for these ancient city-dwellers to farm areas more than a 5 or 10 km from the city. Irrigation was absolutely necessary for any sedentary existence on the alluvial plain, but if the spread, integration, and construction of irrigation systems were the mechanisms whereby complex societies first evolved and developed, we would expect to see a direct and positive correlation between the size and complexity of irrigation systems and the complexity of cultures based on them.

Instead, we find that 'Ubaid, Uruk, and Early Dynastic settlements subsisted on the produce of fields that could be irrigated by relatively simple, autonomous canal works. Only many centuries after the appearance of the first complex societies were complex, integrated irrigation systems in place.

Some scholars have tried to explain the origins of cultural complexity in Southwest Asia and elsewhere as mainly the result of human population growth. The persistence of this view must be seen in large part as a result of the fact that if one graphs the approximate population of Greater Mesopotamia from about 8000 B.C. to about 3000 B.C. against evidence of activity specialization, monumental architecture, agricultural productivity, and other indications of cultural complexity, then an impressively close correlation is apparent. Also, it is difficult not to be impressed by the evidence that warfare was a potent factor in Mesopotamian cultural evolution. Great brick walls ring cities and villages alike in some periods, and there are caches of weapons, chariots, documents, and representational art to tell us that warfare formed the very weft and warp of Mesopotamian history. Nor is this sustained level of warfare merely a historical curiosity: If some adult male citizen in ancient Mesopotamia of almost any century were transported through time to our own age, the thing he would find most familiar, perhaps, is the battle that raged through the 1980s between Iran and Iraq, or the 1990 Gulf War, or the recent Iraq war in 2003. Armies have met here in this same general area in almost every century for more than 5,000 years.

If we apply the principles of evolutionary biology, warfare is simply an expression of competition, which is common to all life-forms. To give it a name, however, is not to explain it, nor is the importance of warfare in *initial* Mesopotamian cultural complexity manifestly evident. One might expect that, with the cheapness of clay construction, there would be many more walled settlements in the early civilizations if warfare were a frequent curse. The walling of towns does occur very soon after the emergence of urbanism, and warfare may have played a significant role in the major increases of cultural complexity that followed the earliest "states," but extensive circumvallation of sites is common on the southern alluvial plain mainly after about 2900 B.C.—some centuries after the appearance of other evidence of cultural complexity. After 2900 B.C. the historical records leave no doubt that warfare was almost continuous throughout Southwest Asia. But can population growth and warfare be shown to have been antecedent conditions to the rise of Mesopotamian states? Robert McC. Adams concludes:

> Possibly the attainment of some minimal population level was necessary to set the process [for urbanization] into motion. But such evidence as there is suggests that appreciable population increases generally followed, rather than preceded, the core processes of the Urban Revolution. Particularly in Mesopotamia, where the sedentary village pattern seems to have been stabilized for several millennia between the establishment of effective food production and the "take-off" into urbanism, it may be noted that there is simply no evidence for gradual population increases that might have helped to precipitate the Urban Revolution.[72]

Adams here is principally concerned with the phenomenon of urbanism rather than complex societies in general, but his "Urban Revolution" includes many of the essential transitions we have defined as the basis for the evolution of complex societies. What about agricultural intensification? In Carneiro's scheme this is a direct result of population pressure; thus we should find evidence of increasingly intensive irrigation and of farming of marginal lands just before, and along with, the evolution of cultural complexity. But major investments in irrigation and land reclamation seem to have occurred after the emergence of urbanism and other evidences of cultural complexity. In addition, as Adams notes, urbanization appears to have involved the widespread abandonment of large areas of formerly intensively farmed lands. Furthermore, there is no evidence that any of the areas of early state formation ever approached their agricultural limits; that is, with only minor investments in additional irrigation systems, they could have enormously increased the numbers of people who could be supported, yet the population size remained quite stable. In short, agricultural intensification seems to have been more a result than a cause of the emergence of complex societies.

Adams nonetheless attributes considerable importance to environment and agriculture in the evolution of Southwest Asian civilization:

> In the largest sense, Mesopotamian cities can be viewed as an adaptation to [the] perennial problem of periodic, unpredictable shortages. They provided concentration points for the storage of surpluses, necessarily soon walled to assure their defensibility. The initial distribution of smaller communities around them suggests primarily localized exploitation of land, with much of the producing population being persuaded or compelled to take up residence within individual walled centers rather than remaining in villages closer to their fields. Tending to contradict a narrowly determinist view of urban genesis as merely the formation of walled storage depots, the drawing together of significantly larger settlements than had existed previously not only created an essentially new basis for cultural and organizational growth but could hardly have been brought about without the development of powerful new means for unifying what originally were socially and culturally heterogeneous groups.[73]

Adams argues "that the primary basis for [political-economic] organization was religious allegiance to deities or cults identified with particular localities, political superordination resting ultimately on the possibility of military coercion, or a fluid mixture of both."[74]

So, as with other areas of early civilization, when we examine the basic factors of environment, ecology, technology, demography, and agriculture, we see strong correlations between these factors and the shape and history of Southwest Asian history. Yet, these correlations do not constitute a powerful explanation or comprehensive understanding of Southwest Asian cultures. At a fundamental level these civilizations were a set of ideas and social relations. The ideology that legitimized the strict hierarchies of power, prestige and wealth and the social relationships among the many peoples in these hierarchies are a crucial focus of analysis in trying to understand why Southwest Asian civilizations evolved and how they functioned. Ancient texts, in combination with other archaeological data, help us understand much about these social relationships, but there is much we still do not understand.

BIBLIOGRAPHY

Abu es-Soof, B. 1968. "Tell Es-Sawwan: Excavations of the Fourth Season (Spring 1967) Interim Report." *Sumer* 24:3–16.

Adams, R. McC. 1965. *Land Behind Baghdad.* Chicago: University of Chicago Press.

———. 1966. *The Evolution of Urban Society: Early Mesopotamia and Prehispanic Mexico.* Chicago: Aldine.

———. 1972. "Patterns of Urbanization in Early Southern Mesopotamia." In *Man, Settlement and Urbanism,* ed. P. G. Ucko, R. Tringham, and G. Dimbleby. London: Duckworth.

———. 1981. *Heartland of Cities.* Chicago: Aldine.

Adams, R. McC., and H. Nissen. 1972. *The Uruk Countryside.* Chicago: University of Chicago Press.

Akkermans, P. P. M. G. 1989. "Tradition and Social Change in Northern Mesopotamia During the Later Fifth and Fourth Millenium B.C." In *Upon This Foundation—The Ubaid Reconsidered,* ed. E. F. Henrickson and I. Thuesen. Copenhagen: Museum Tusculanum Press.

Alden, J. R. 1982. "Trade and Politics in Proto-Elamite Iran." *Current Anthropology* 23(6):613–640.

Algaze, G. 1989. "The Uruk Expansion, Cross-Cultural Exchange in Early Mesopotamian Civilization." *Current Anthropology* 30(5):571–608.

———. 1993. *The Uruk World System.* Chicago: University of Chicago Press.

———. 2001. "Initial Social Complexity in Southwestern Asia: The Mesopotamian Advantage." *Current Anthropology* 42(2):199–233.

Algaze, G., M. E. Evins, M. L. Ingraham, L. Marfoe, and K. A. Yener. 1990. *Town and Country in Southeastern Anatolia.* Vol. 2: *The Stratigraphic Sequence at Kurban Höyük.* Oriental Institute Publications 110. Chicago: Oriental Institute.

Areshian, G. E. 1990. "Further Thoughts on the Uruk Expansion." *Current Anthropology* 31:396–398.

Ball, W., D. Tucker, and T. J. Wilkinson. 1989. "The Tell Al-Hawa Project: Archaeological Investigations in the North Jazira, 1986–87." *Iraq* 41:1–66.

Ballard, R. D. 2001. "Deep Black Sea." *National Geographic* 199(5):52–69.

Behm-Blancke, M. R. 1989. "Mosaiksifte am oberen Euphrat—Wandschmuck aus Uruk-Zeit." *Istanbuler Mitteilungen* 39:73–83.

Boehmer, R. M. 1991. "Uruk 1980–1990: A Progress Report." *Antiquity* 65:465–478.

Breniquet, C. 1989. "Les origines de la culture d'Obeid en Mésopotamie du nord." In *Upon This Foundation—The Ubaid Reconsidered,* ed. E. F. Henrickson and I. Thuesen. Copenhagen: Museum Tusculanum Press.

Byrd, B. F. 1994. "Public and Private, Domestic and Corporate: The Emergence of the Southwest Asian Village." *American Antiquity* 59(4):639–666.

Chase-Dunn, C., and T. D. Hall. 1991. "Conceptualizing Core/Periphery Hierarchies for Comparative Study." In *Core/Periphery Relations in Pre-capitalist Worlds,* ed. C. Chase-Dunn and T. D. Hall. Boulder, CO: Westview Press.

Childe, V. G. 1952. *New Light on the Most Ancient East.* 4th ed. London: Routledge and Kegan Paul.

Cowgill, G. 1975. "On Causes and Consequences of Ancient and Modern Population Changes." *American Anthropologist* 77:505–525.

Crawford, H. 1991. *Sumer and the Sumerians.* Cambridge: Cambridge University Press.

Cribb, R. 1991. *Nomads in Archaeology.* Cambridge: Cambridge University Press.

Crumley, C. L. 1979. "Three Locational Models: An Epistemological Assessment for Anthropology and Archaeology." In *Advances in Archaeological Method and Theory,* Vol. 2, ed. M. B. Schiffer. New York: Academic Press.

Diakonoff, I. M., ed. 1969. *Ancient Mesopotamia*. Moscow: Nauka.

Diringer, D. 1962. *Writing*. New York: Praeger.

Evins, M. A. 1989. "The Late Chalcolithic/Uruk Period in the Karababa Casin, Southeastern Turkey." In "Out of the Heartland: The Evolution of Complexity in Peripheral Mesopotamia During the Uruk Period, Workshop Summary," ed. M. Rothman. *Paléorient* 14:270–271.

Falconer, S. E., and S. H. Savage. 1995. "Heartlands and Hinterlands: Alternative Trajectories of Early Urbanization in Mesopotamia and the Southern Levant." *American Antiquity* 60(1):37–58.

Finegan, J. 1964. *Handbook of Biblical Chronology: Principles of Time Reckoning in the Ancient World and Problems of Chronology in the Bible*. Princeton, NJ: Princeton University Press.

Flannery, K. V. 1972. "The Cultural Evolution of Civilizations." *Annual Review of Ecology and Systematics* 3:399–426.

Frangipane, M., and A. Palmieri. 1987. "Urbanization in Perimesopotamian Areas: The Case of Eastern Anatolia." In *Studies in the Neolithic and Urban Revolutions*, ed. L. Manzanilla, pp. 295–318. Oxford: British Archaeological Reports International Series 349.

Frankfort, H. 1956. *The Birth of Civilization in the Near East*. Garden City, NY: Doubleday.

Friedman, J., and M. J. Rowlands. 1977. *The Evolution of Social Systems*. Pittsburgh: University of Pittsburgh Press.

Gelb, I. J. 1952. *A Study of Writing: The Foundations of Grammatology*. Chicago: University of Chicago Press.

———. 1969. "On the Alleged Temple and State Economics in Ancient Mesopotamia." *Estratto da studi in onore di Edouard Vtoltera* 4:139–154.

Gibson, M. 1972. "Population Shift and the Rise of Mesopotamian Civilization." In *The Explanation of Cultural Change: Models in Prehistory*, ed. C. Renfrew. London: Duckworth.

Goldstein, P. S. 1989. "The Tiwanaco Occupation of Moquegua." In *Ecology, Settlement, and History in the Osmore Drainage, Peru*. ed. D. S. Rice, C. Stanish, and P. R. Scarr. Oxford: British Archaeological Review, International Series 545.

Hamblin, D. J., and the Editors of Time-Life Books. 1973. *The First Cities*. New York: Time-Life.

Hauptmann, H. 1999. "The Urfa Region." In *Neolithic in Turkey: The Cradle of Civilization: New Discoveries*, ed. M. Özdoğan and N. Başgelen, pp. 65–86. Istanbul: Arkeoloji Sanat Yayinlari.

Hodder, I. 1999. "Renewed Work at Çatalhöyük." In *Neolithic in Turkey: The Cradle of Civilization: New Discoveries*, ed. M. Özdoğan and N. Başgelen, pp. 157–164. Istanbul: Arkeoloji Sanat Yayinlari.

———, ed. 2000. *Towards Reflexive Method in Archaeology: The Example at Çatalhöyük*. Cambridge, UK: McDonald Institute for Archaeological Research.

Hodder, I., and C. Cessford. 2004. "Daily Practice and Social Memory at Çatalhöyük." *American Antiquity* 69(1):17–40.

Hole, F. 1978. "The Prehistory of Herding: Some Suggestions from Ethnography." In *L'Archéologie de l'Iraq du début de l'époque Néolitique à 333 avant notre ère*, ed. M. T. Barrelet pp. 119–130. Paris: Éditions de la Centre National de la Recherche Scientifique.

———. 1987. "Settlement and Society in the Village Period." In *The Archaeology of Western Iran*, ed. F. Hole. Washington, DC: Smithsonian Institution Press.

———. 1994. "Environmental Instabilities and Urban Origins." In *Chiefdoms and Early States in the Near East: The Organizational Dynamics of Complexity*. Monographs in World Archaeology 18, pp. 121–151. Madison: Prehistory Press.

Hole, F., K. V. Flannery, and J. A. Neely. 1969. *Prehistory and Human Ecology of the Deh Luran Plain*. Ann Arbor: Memoirs of the Museum of Anthropology, University of Michigan, No. 1.

Hout, J.-L. 1979: "Ubaidian Villages of Lower Mesopotamia." In *Upon This Foundation—The Ubaid Reconsidered*, ed. E. F. Henrickson and I. Thuesen. Copenhagen: Museum Tusculanum Press.

Ifrah, G. 1985. *From One to Zero*. Trans. L. Bair. New York: Viking Penguin.

Jacobsen, T., and R. Adams. 1958. "Salt and Silt in Mesopotamian Agriculture." *Science* 128:1251–1258.

Jawad, A. J. 1965. *The Advent of the Era of Townships of Northern Mesopotamia*. Leiden: Brill.

Johnson, G. A. 1973. *Local Exchange and Early State Development in Southwestern Iran*. Ann Arbor: Museum of Anthropology, Anthropological Papers, University of Michigan, No. 51.

———. 1977. "Aspects of Regional Analysis in Archaeology." *Annual Review of Anthropology* 6:479–508.

———. 1981. "Monitoring Complex System Integration and Boundary Phenomena with Settlement Size Data." In *Archaeological Approaches to the Study of Complexity*, ed. S. E. van der Leeuw. Amsterdam: University of Amsterdam.

———. 1982. "Organizational Structure Scalar Stress." In *Theory and Explanation in Archaeology*. New York: Academic Press.

———. 1987a. "The Changing Organization in Uruk Administration on the Susiana Plain." In *The Archaeology of Western Iran*, ed. F. Hole. Washington, DC: Smithsonian Institution Press.

———. 1987b. "Nine Thousand Years of Social Change in Western Iran." In *The Archaeology of Western Iran*, ed. F. Hole. Washington, DC: Smithsonian Institution Press.

———. 1988–1989. "Late Uruk in Greater Mesopotamia: Expansion or Collapse?" *Origini* 14:595–613.

Kipp, R. S., and E. M. Schortman. 1989. "The Political Impact of Trade in Chiefdoms." *American Anthropologist* 91:370–385.

Kramer, S. N. 1959. *History Begins at Sumer*. Garden City, NY: Doubleday.

Larsen, C. E. 1975. "The Mesopotamian Delta Region: A Reconsideration of Lees and Falcon." *Journal of the American Oriental Society* 95:43–57.

Larsen, C. E., and G. Evans. 1978. "The Holocene History of the Tigris-Euphrates-Karun Delta." In *The Environmental History of the Near and Middle East Since the Last Ice Age*, ed. W. C. Brice. London: Academic Press.

Lees, S. H., and D. G. Bates. 1974. "The Origins of Specialized Nomadic Pastoralism: A Systematic Model." *American Antiquity* 30:187–193.

Loding, D. 1976. *Ur Excavations: Economic Texts from the Third Dynasty*. Philadelphia: Publication of the Joint Expedition of the British Museum and the University Museum, University of Pennsylvania.

Maisels, C. K. 1993a. *The Emergence of Civilization: From Hunting and Gathering to Agriculture, Cities and the State in the Near East*. New York: Routledge.

———. 1993b. *The Near East: Archaeology in the "Cradle of Civilization."* New York: Routledge.

Mallowan, Sir M. E. L. 1965. *Early Mesopotamia and Iran*. London: Thames and Hudson.

Margueron, J-Cl. 1992. "Le bois dans l'architecture." *Bulletin on Summerian Agriculture* 6:79–96.

Mellaart, J. 1965. *Earliest Civilizations of the Near East*. London: Thames and Hudson.

———. 1975. *The Neolithic of the Near East*. London: Thames and Hudson.

Mellink, M. 1989. "Archaeology in Asia Minor, Samsat." *American Journal of Archaeology* 93:114.

Mitchell, W. 1973. "The Hydraulic Hypothesis: A Reappraisal." *Current Anthropology* 4:532–534.

Moghaddam, A., and N. Miri. 2003. "Archaeological Research in the Mianab Plain of Lowland Susiana, Southwestern Iran." *Iran* 41:99–137.

Morozova, G. S. 2005. "A Review of Holocene Avulsions of the Tigris and Euphrates Rivers and Possible Effects on the Evolution of Civilizations in Lower Mesopotamia." *Geoarchaeology* 20(4):401–423.

Nissen, H. 1988. *The Early History of the Ancient Near East, 9000–2000 B.C.* Chicago: University of Chicago Press.

Nutzel, W. 1976. "The Climatic Changes of Mesopotamia and Bordering Areas." *Sumer* 32. pp. 11–24.

Oates, J. 1980. "The Emergence of Cities in the Near East." In *The Cambridge Encyclopedia of Archaeology*. New York: Crown Publishers/Cambridge University Press.

Oppenheim, A. L. 1964. *Ancient Mesopotamia: Portrait of a Dead Civilization*. Chicago: University of Chicago Press.

Özdoğan, M., and N. Başgelen, eds., 1999. *Neolithic in Turkey: The Cradle of Civilization: New Discoveries*. Istanbul: Arkeoloji Sanat Yayinlari.

Palmieri, A. 1989. "Storage and Dsitribution at Arslantepe-Malatya in the Late Uruk Period." In *Anatolia and the Ancient Near East: Studies in Honor of Tahsin Özgüç*, ed. K. Emre et al. Anakara: Türk Tarih Kurumu.

Pattee, H. H. 1973. *Hierarchy Theory. The Challenge of Complex Systems*. New York: Braziller.

Pitman, W., and W. Ryan. 1998. *Noah's Flood*. New York: Simon & Schuster.

Pollock, S. 1983. "Style and Information: An Analysis of Susiana Ceramics." *Journal of Anthropological Archaeology* 2(4):354–390.

———. 1992. "Bureaucrats and Managers, Peasants and Pastoralists, Imperialists and Traders: Research on the Uruk and Jemdet Nasr Periods in Mesopotamia." *Journal of World Prehistory* 6(3):297–336.

Postgate, N. 1994. *Early Mesopotamia: Economy and Society at the Dawn of History*. New York: Routledge.

Redman, C. L. 1978. *The Rise of Civilization*. San Francisco: W. H. Freeman.

Reimer, S. 1989. "Tell Qraya on the Middle Eurphrates." In "Out of the Heartland: The Evolution of Complexity in Peripheral Mesopotamia During the Uruk Period, Workshop Summary," ed. M. Rothman. *Paléorient* 15:273.

Rothman, M. 2004. "Studying the Development of Complex Society: Mesopotamia in the Late Fifth and Fourth Millennia B.C." *Journal of Archaeological Research* 12(1):75–119.

Roux, G. 1976. *Ancient Iraq*. Baltimore: Penguin.

Saggs, H. W. F. 1989. *Civilization Before Greece and Rome*. New Haven: Yale University Press.

Scammell, G. V. 1989. *The First Imperial Age*. London: Unwin Hyman.

Schacht, R. 1987. "Early Historic Cultures." In *The Archaeology of Western Iran*, ed. F. Hole. Washington, DC: Smithsonian Institution Press.

Schmandt-Besserat, D. 1981. "Decipherment of the Earliest Tablets." *Science* 211:283–284.

———. 1992. *Before Writing*. Austin: University of Texas Press.

Simmons, A. H., I. Kohler-Rollefson, G. O. Rollefson, R. Mandel, and Z. Kafafi. 1988. "'Ain Ghazal: A Major Neolithic Settlement in Central Jordan." *Science* 240:35–39.

Smith, P. E. L., and T. C. Young, Jr. 1972. "The Evolution of Early Agriculture and Culture in Greater Mesopotamia. A Trial Model." In *Population Growth: Anthropological Implications*, ed. B. Spooner. Cambridge, MA: MIT Press.

Spuhler, J. 1985. "Anthropology, Evolution, and 'Scientific Creationism.'" *Annual Review of Anthropology* 14:103–133.

Stager, L. 1992. "The Periodization of Palestine from Neolithic to Early Bronze Times." In *Chronologies in Old World Archaeology*, 3d ed., ed. R. Ehrich. Chicago: University of Chicago Press.

Stein, G. J., and M. J. Blackman. 1993. "The Organizational Context of Specialized Craft Production in Early Mesopotamian States." *Research in Economic Anthropology* 14:29–59.

Steward, J. H. 1949. "Cultural Causality and Law: A Trial Formulation of the Development of Early Civilizations." *American Anthropologist* 51:1–27.

Taylor, R. E., and R. Berger. 1980. "The Date of Noah's Ark." *Antiquity* 54:35–36.

Tosi, M. 1984. "The Notion of Craft Specialization and Its Representation in the Archaeological Record of Early States in the Turanian Basin." In *Marxist Perspectives in Archaeology*, ed. M. Spriggs. Cambridge: Cambridge University Press.

Wattanmaker, P. 1990. "On the Uruk Expansion." *Current Anthropology* 31:67–68.

Wattanmaker, P., and G. Stein. 1989. "Leilan 1987 Survey: Uruk Summary." In "Out of the Heartland: The Evolution of Complexity in Peripheral Mesopotamia During the Uruk Period, Workshop Summary," ed. M. Rothman. *Paléorient* 15:273.

Webb, M. 1975. "The Flag Follows Trade: An Essay on the Necessary Integration of Military and Commercial Factors in State Formation." In *Ancient Civilization and Trade*, ed. J. Sabloff and C. C. Lamberg-Karlovsky. Albuquerque: University of New Mexico Press.

Weiss, H. 1977. "Periodization, Population, and Early State Formation in Khuzestan." In *Mountains and Lowlands: Essays in the Archaeology of Greater Mesopotamia*, ed. L. D. Levine and T. C. Young, Jr. Malibu: Undena.

———, ed. 1986. *The Origins of Cities in Dry-farming Syria and Mesopotamia in the Third Millennium B.C.* Guildford, CT: Four Quarters Publishers.

Wenke, R. J. 1975–1974. "Imperial Investments and Agricultural Developments in Parthian and Sasanian Khuzestan: 150 B.C. to A.D. 640." *Mesopotamia* 10–11:31–217.

———. 1981. "Explaining the Evolution of Cultural Complexity. A Review." In *Advances in Archaeological Method and Theory*, Vol. 4, ed. M. B. Schiffer. New York: Academic Press.

———. 1987. "Western Iran in the Partho-Sasanian Period: The Imperial Transformation." In *The Archaeology of Western Iran*, ed. F. Hole. Washington, DC: Smithsonian Institution Press.

White, L. 1949. *The Science of Culture*. New York: Grove Press.

Wilkinson, T. J. 1990a. *Town and Country in Early Southeastern Anatolia*. Vol. 1: *Settlement and Land Use in the Lower Karababa Basin*. Oriental Institute Publications 109. Chicago: Oriental Institute.

———. 1990b. "The Development of Settlement in the North Jazira Region Between the Seventh and First Millennia B.C." *Iraq* 52:49–62.

———. 2000. "Regional Approaches to Mesopotamian Archaeology: The Contribution of Archaeological Surveys." *Journal of Archaeological Research* 8(3):219–267.

Willcox, G. H. 1992. "Timber and Trees." *Bulletin on Sumerian Agriculture* 6:1–31.

Wittfogel, K. A. 1957. *Oriental Despotism: A Comparative Study of Total Power*. New Haven: Yale University Press.

Wolkstein, D., and S. N. Kramer. 1983. *Inanna, Queen of Heaven and Earth*. New York: Harper & Row.

Woolley, Sir L. 1965. *Excavations at Ur*. New York: Crowell.

Wright, H. T. 1969. *The Administration of Rural Production in an Early Mesopotamian Town*. Ann Arbor: Museum of Anthropology, Anthropological Papers, University of Michigan, No. 38.

———. 1986. "The Evolution of Civilizations." In *American Archaeology. Past and Future*, ed. D. Meltzer, D. Fowler, and J. Sabloff. Washington, DC: Smithsonian Institution Press.

———. 1987. "The Susiana Hinterlands During the Era of Primary State Formation." In *The Archaeology of Western Iran*, ed. F. Hole. Washington, DC: Smithsonian Instution Press.

Wright, H. T., and G. A. Johnson. 1975. "Population, Exchange, and Early State Formation in Southwestern Iran." *American Anthropologist* 77:267–289.

Yasin, W. 1970. "Excavation at Tell Es-Sawwan, 1969 (6th Season)." *Sumer* 26:4–11.

Yener, A. K., H. Ozbal, A. Minzoni-Deroche, and B. Alsoy. 1989. "Bokardag: Archaeo-metallurgy Surveys in the Taurus Mountains, Turkey." *National Geographic Research* 5:477–494.

Yener, A. K., E. V. Sayre, E. C. Joel, H. Ozbal, et al. 1991. "Stable Lead Isotope Studies of Central Taurus Ore Sources and Related Artifacts from Eastern Mediterranean Chalcolithic and Bronze Age Sites." *Journal of Archaeological Science* 18:541–577.

Yoffee, N. 1995. "Political Economy in Early Mesopotamian States." *Annual Review of Anthropology* 24:281–311.

Young, C. T., Jr., P. E. L. Smith, and P. Mortensen, eds. 1983. *The Hilly Flanks and Beyond: Essays on the Prehistory of Southwestern Asia*. Chicago: Studies in Ancient Oriental Civilization, No. 36, University of Chicago.

Zagarell, A. 1986. "Trade, Women, Class, and Society in Ancient Western Asia." *Current Anthropology* 27(5):415–430.

NOTES

1. Xenephon, *Anabasis*.
2. Postgate, *Early Mesopotamia: Economy and Society at the Dawn of History*, p. xxi.
3. Reviewed in Postgate, *Early Mesopotamia: Economy and Society at the Dawn of History*.
4. See, for example, Adams, *Land Behind Baghdad*, or Adams and Nissen, *The Uruk Countryside*.
5. Hauptmann, "The Urfa Region."
6. Mellaart, *Earliest Civilizations of the Near East*, p. 77.
7. Hodder, "Renewed Work at Çatalhöyük"; Hodder, *Towards Reflexive Method in Archaeology: The Example at Çatalhöyük*.
8. In Building 1 in the North Area, Hodder's excavations suggest that some of these "shrines" can be linked to the cycle of family life, as a young family (extended family) grows up in the structure and ages. For example, early phases of occupation have an association of the wall paintings with burial of young individuals (deaths of children). This pattern shifts as the family ages and there are less children, so that burials of older individuals are the most common. Eventually the building is abandoned (see Hodder, "Renewed Work at Çatalhöyük").
9. Mellaart, *The Neolithic of the Near East*, pp. 101–105.
10. Redman, *The Rise of Civilization*, p. 187.
11. Wilkinson, "Regional Approaches to Mesopotamian Archaeology: The Contribution of Archaeological Surveys."
12. Mellaart, *Earliest Civilizations of the Near East*, p. 77.
13. Hole, *Settlement and Society in the Village Period*, p. 95, citing Childe, *New Light on the Most Ancient East*, p. 111.
14. Nissen, *The Early History of the Ancient Near East, 9000–2000 B.C.*, p. 57.
15. Abu es-Soof, "Tell Es-Sawwan: Excavations of the Fourth Season (Spring 1967) Interim Report"; Yasin, "Excavation at Tell Es-Sawwan, 1969 (6th Season)."
16. Larsen and Evans, "The Holocene History of the Tigris-Euphrates-Karun Delta."
17. Nutzel, "The Climatic Changes of Mesopotamia and Bordering Areas."
18. Hole, "Environmental Instabilities and Urban Origins," p. 140.
19. Hole, Flannery, and Neely, *Prehistory and Human Ecology of the Deh Luran Plain*.
20. Nissen, *The Early History of the Ancient Near East, 9000–2000 B.C.*
21. Postgate, *Early Mesopotamia: Economy and Society at the Dawn of History*, p. 24.
22. Wright, "The Evolution of Civilizations."
23. Cf. Hole, "Settlement and Society in the Village Period," p. 95.
24. Johnson, "Nine Thousand Years of Social Change in Western Iran," p. 284.
25. Ibid., p. 285.
26. Hole, "Settlement and Society in the Village Period."
27. Ibid., p. 96.
28. Nissen, *The Early History of the Ancient Near East, 9000–2000 B.C.*, pp. 47–48.
29. Algaze, "Initial Social Complexity in Southwestern Asia: The Mesopotamia Advantage."
30. Morozova, "A Review of Holocene Avulsions of the Tigris and Euphrates Rivers and Possible Effects on the Evolution of Civilizations in Lower Mesopotamia."
31. Following Morozova's analysis to its conclusion indicates that avulsions could be "created" by cities upstream from others through channel diversion and blockage. This essentially acts as a way to control cities located downstream (ibid., p. 419) and to shift power balances from one city to another.
32. Adams, "Patterns of Urbanization in Early Southern Mesopotamia."
33. Ibid., p. 739.
34. Johnson, *Local Exchange and Early State Development in Southwestern Iran*; Johnson, "Organizational Structure Scalar Stress."
35. Nissen, *The Early History of the Ancient Near East, 9000–2000 B.C.*, pp. 84–85.
36. White, *The Science of Culture*, p. 383.
37. Frankfort, *The Birth of Civilization in the Near East*, pp. 56–58.
38. Johnson, *Local Exchange and Early State Development in Southwestern Iran*; Johnson, "The Changing Organization of Uruk Administration on the Susiana Plain"; Wright, "The Evolution of Civilizations"; Wright, "The Susiana Hinterlands During the Era of Primary State Formation"; Wright and Johnson, "Population, Exchange, and Early State Formation in Southwestern Iran."
39. Schmandt-Besserat, "Decipherment of the Earliest Tablets."
40. Wright and Johnson, "Population, Exchange, and Early State Formation in Southwestern Iran," pp. 273–274.
41. Johnson, "Aspects of Regional Analysis in Archaeology"; Johnson, "Organizational Structure Scalar Stress." For a description of hierarchy theory, see Pattee, *Hierarchy Theory: The Challenge of Complex Systems*.
42. Algaze, "The Uruk Expansion"; also see Algaze, *The Uruk World System*.

43. Algaze, "The Uruk Expansion, Cross-Cultural Exchange in Early Mesopotamian Civilization"; Algaze, *The Uruk World System*; Frangipane and Palmieri, "Ubranization in Perimesopotamian Areas: The Case of Eastern Anatolia"; Johnson, "Late Uruk in Greater Mesopotamia: Expansion or Collapse?"

44. Pollock, "Bureaucrats and Managers, Peasants and Pastoralists, Imperialists and Traders: Research on the Uruk and Jemdet Nasr Periods in Mesopotamia," p. 330.

45. Adams, "Patterns of Urbanization in Early Southern Mesopotamia," p. 743.

46. Cribb, *Nomads in Archaeology.*

47. Nissen, *The Early History of the Ancient Near East, 9000–2000 B.C.*, pp. 120–121.

48. Oates, "The Emergence of Cities in the Near East."

49. Nissen, *The Early History of the Ancient Near East, 9000–2000 B.C.*, p. 81.

50. Diringer, *Writings.*

51. Nissen, *The Early History of the Ancient Near East, 9000–2000 B.C.*, p. 136.

52. Ibid., p. 40.

53. Ifrah, *From One to Zero.*

54. Ibid., p. 35.

55. Saggs, *Civilization Before Greece and Rome.*

56. Ibid., pp. 225–227.

57. Hamblin et al., *The First Cities*, pp. 103–104.

58. Wolkstein and Kramer, *Inanna, Queen of Heaven and Earth.*

59. Finegan, *Handbook of Biblical Chronology: Principles of Time Reckoning in the Ancient World and Problems of Chronology in the Bible*, pp. 42–43; quoted in Spuhler, "Anthropology, Evolution, and 'Scientific Creationism,'" p. 116.

60. One theory says that Noah's Flood occurred when rising sea levels caused the Mediterranean Sea to breach the Bosporus Valley and flow into the Black Sea (then a freshwater lake) about 7,500 years ago. If this is true, it is not hard to imagine how such a profound event, even though it did not occur in Mesopotamia, might have been preserved initially in oral traditions of the region, later to be recorded in writing (see Ballard, "Deep Black Sea"; Pitman and Ryan, *Noah's Flood*).

61. Spuhler, "Anthropology, Evolution, and 'Scientific Creationism.'"

62. Taylor and Berger, "The Date of Noah's Ark."

63. See Postgate, *Early Mesopotamia: Economy and Society at the Dawn of History*, for an excellent review of Sumerian civlization.

64. Ibid., pp. 82–83.

65. Ibid., p. 105.

66. Ibid., p. 166.

67. Adams, *Heartland of Cities*, pp. 252–254.

68. Woolley, *Excavations at Ur.*

69. Alden, "Trade and Politics in Proto-Elamite Iran."

70. Schacht, "Early Historic Cultures."

71. Adams, "Patterns of Urbanization in Early Southern Mesopotamia."

72. Adams, *Heartland of Cities*, pp. 252–254.

73. Ibid., p. 244.

74. Ibid., p. 78.

The Origins of Complex Societies in Egypt

Concerning Egypt I shall extend my remarks to a great length, because there is no country that possesses so many wonders, nor any that has such a number of works that defy description.

Herodotus (c. 440 B.C.)

gypt's similarities to other early civilizations are obvious: Egypt is yet another variation on an ancient theme, a developmental pattern in which farmers succeeded the hunter-forager-gatherers who had roamed northeast Africa for millennia, and then within a few centuries produced state-level governments, writing, monumental architecture, and the other aspects of "civilization," including a spiral of, first, civil wars, and later, centuries of ever-wider spheres of international warfare. In these and other developmental similarities Egypt is just one of a general class of phenomena —pre-industrial states, one of the six "primary civilizations" (see chapter 7).

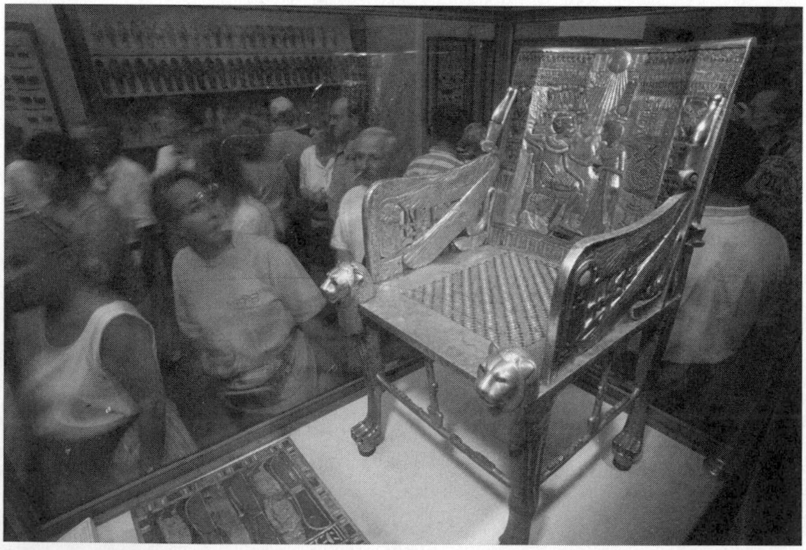

Yet the similarities among ancient civilizations should not blind us to the unique genius of each. Egypt was a distinctive civilization whose excellence in arts, letters, and science can only be dimly glimpsed in its artifacts that lie in museum cases all over the world (Figure 9.1).

Ancient Egypt's most important contributions to the

FIGURE 9.1 Museum visitors gaze at Tutankhamun's throne at the Egyptian Museum in Cairo.

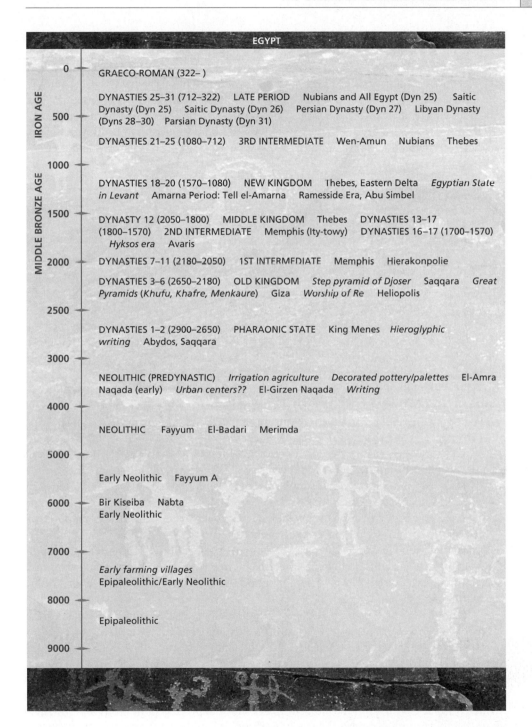

EGYPT

IRON AGE

0 — GRAECO-ROMAN (322–)

DYNASTIES 25–31 (712–322)   LATE PERIOD   Nubians and All Egypt (Dyn 25)   Saitic
Dynasty (Dyn 25)   Saitic Dynasty (Dyn 26)   Persian Dynasty (Dyn 27)   Libyan Dynasty
500 — (Dyns 28–30)   Parsian Dynasty (Dyn 31)

DYNASTIES 21–25 (1080–712)   3RD INTERMEDIATE   Wen-Amun   Nubians   Thebes

1000 —

MIDDLE BRONZE AGE

DYNASTIES 18–20 (1570–1080)   NEW KINGDOM   Thebes, Eastern Delta   *Egyptian State
in Levant*   Amarna Period: Tell el-Amarna   Ramesside Era, Abu Simbel

1500 — DYNASTY 12 (2050–1800)   MIDDLE KINGDOM   Thebes   DYNASTIES 13–17
(1800–1570)   2ND INTERMEDIATE   Memphis (Ity-towy)   DYNASTIES 16–17 (1700–1570)
   Hyksos era   Avaris

2000 — DYNASTIES 7–11 (2180–2050)   1ST INTERMEDIATE   Memphis   Hierakonpolie

DYNASTIES 3–6 (2650–2180)   OLD KINGDOM   *Step pyramid of Djoser*   Saqqara   *Great
Pyramids (Khufu, Khafre, Menkaure)*   Giza   *Worship of Re*   Heliopolis

2500 —

DYNASTIES 1–2 (2900–2650)   PHARAONIC STATE   King Menes   *Hieroglyphic
writing*   Abydos, Saqqara

3000 —

NEOLITHIC (PREDYNASTIC)   *Irrigation agriculture   Decorated pottery/palettes*   El-Amra
Naqada (early)   *Urban centers??*   El-Girzen Naqada   *Writing*

4000 —

NEOLITHIC   Fayyum   El-Badari   Merimda

5000 —

Early Neolithic   Fayyum A

6000 — Bir Kiseiba   Nabta
Early Neolithic

7000 —

Early farming villages
Epipaleolithic/Early Neolithic

8000 —

Epipaleolithic

9000 —

comparative analyses of early civilizations may derive from its variations on the themes evident in other early civilizations. Egypt, for example, was one of the most politically centralized of early states, yet it also seems to have been the least urban; the complexity of its governmental bureaucracy was extraordinary, with rank upon rank of viziers, governors, and other officials, but the vast majority of people seem to have lived in largely self-sufficient villages and towns; and though its political cycles were closely related to a single environmental factor (Nile flood levels), within these environmental limits Egypt's sociopolitical evolution was a baroque interweaving of factors, personalities, and events.

THE ECOLOGICAL SETTING

Egypt . . . is an acquired country, the gift of the [Nile].

Herodotus (c. 440 B.C.)

Egypt is, indeed, in Herodotus's much-repeated phrase, the gift of the Nile, and the Nile in turn is the gift of rainstorms in the mountains of eastern and central Africa. The "White Nile" flows out of the lakes and springs of central Africa and flows northward, where it is joined at Khartoum, in the Sudan, by the "Blue Nile," which is fed by summer monsoonal rains in the Ethiopian savannas and highlands.[1] Further north in the Sudan, the Atbara River, which also drains the Ethiopian highlands, joins the Nile.

The White Nile's volume does not vary much from season to season or year to year, but the Blue Nile and the Atbara fluctuate with the sharply seasonal rainstorms in their watersheds. Thus, until the twentieth century, when huge dams were built in southern Egypt, the torrential spring rains in east Africa annually sent silt-choked floods pulsing down the Nile Valley, depositing along the way a rich layer of fertile silts and clays. Along the river's course this natural alluviation has produced one of the world's richest agricultural niches, which with even the simplest tools supports as many as 450 people per square kilometer.

The Nile itself was an enormous source of food and other resources. The Nile perch,[2] for example, was a favorite food of ancient Egyptians before they became farmers and then throughout the pharaonic period as well. This fish lived in the ancient Nile in huge numbers and it is often found in warm shallow water—where it can easily be harpooned. It regularly grows to 75 kg in weight, and one specimen caught in Lake Nasser in recent times was over 2 m long and weighed 175 kg.[3] The Nile also teemed with wildfowl—a favorite food throughout Egyptian antiquity.

Although highly productive, the Nile Valley is really only an extremely elongated oasis (Figure 9.2) where agricultural lands are sharply circumscribed in most regions by rocky deserts. From the Sudanese border to Cairo, the cultivable strip along both banks of the river is only a few kilometers wide in most places, and so sharp is the demarcation that, as the cliché has it, one can stand with one foot on the red desert sands and the other foot on the black, irrigated croplands (Figure 9.3). The ancient Egyptians called their country *Kemet*, or "black land," after the life-giving dark silts that produced the crops that sustained them. The surrounding deserts they called *Deshret*, or "red land." This distinction between desert and croplands is so marked because Egypt does not get enough precipitation to sustain any agriculture based on rainfall alone. The Nile is a single river through most of

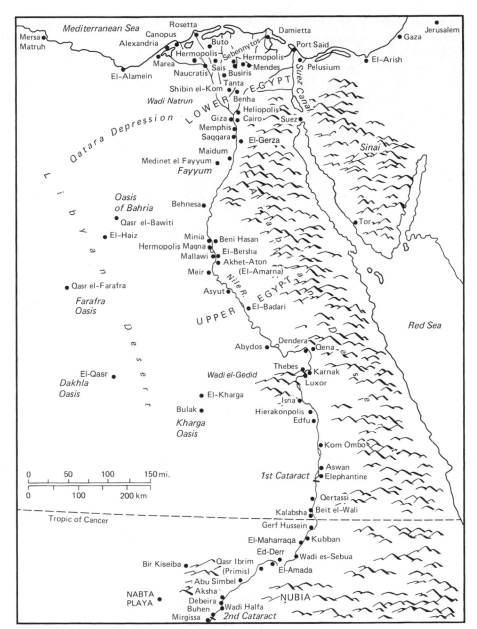

FIGURE 9.2 Some major Egyptian sites. Egypt's desert and mountain frontiers protected it for many centuries against outside influences, but already by 3000 B.C. its trade and military contacts extended into Palestine, Nubia, and the Mediterranean world.

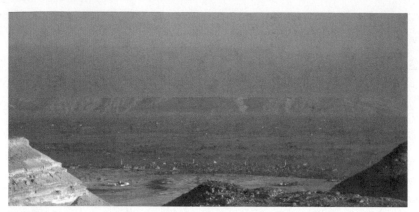

FIGURE 9.3   A dramatic contrast exists between the well-watered, irrigated Nile Valley corridor and the hyper-arid desert regions.

the land of Egypt, but north of Cairo it divides into several main branches, creating a delta of flat, well-watered, fertile land. Although the origins of Egyptian civilization were in the south, near Hierakonpolis, in later Egyptian history the Delta was the agricultural heartland of the country, famed for its wines, wheat, fruit, garden crops, and huge herds of cattle pastured there. As Egypt's political and cultural focus increasingly turned toward Syro-Palestine, the Delta also became a more important staging ground for armies and a crossroads of overland and maritime trade routes.

The ancient Egyptians appreciated the basic geographic dichotomy of the Valley and Delta and thought of their country as composed of two different geographical units: from the Nubian border to the border of the Delta was *ta-shema*, the "land of the *shema* reed"; north of that, the Delta, was *ta-mehu*, the "land of the papyrus plant." Today most archaeologists refer to this division as that between "Upper Egypt" in the south and "Lower Egypt" in the north, the "Upper" and "Lower" reflecting the gradient of the Nile.

Thanks to the Nile, ancient Egyptians could traverse the length of their country in just a week or so of pleasant sailing, providing a rapid, reliable channel for the movement of goods, people, and information. The Egyptians did not use the wheel—either for vehicles, pottery manufacture, or other uses—until quite late, many centuries after it was a mainstay of Asian technology, probably because wheeled vehicles did not have much use in a country where the Nile provides such easy transport and where there is limited advantage to moving products among communities in an ecosystem that is quite similar over its entire length. Egypt's ecological similarity over most of its area and the Nile's efficiency as a transport and communications artery were key factors in the highly centralized governments that developed in later Egyptian antiquity, and it is not surprising that in the southern reaches of the Nile, where five cataracts (steep rapids) constitute impassable barriers to navigation, the power of the Egyptian government often weakened.

Although there have been major fluctuations in the annual volume of the Nile—for example, catastrophically low water levels in some of the years between 2250 and 1950 B.C.—the Nile floodplain has existed in essentially its present form since about 3800 B.C. In ancient times, however, the Mediterranean coastline was farther inland (see Figure 9.2) because the Delta had not sunk nearly as far as it has now under the weight of accumulated silt. The gradient, periodicity, and other attributes of the Nile are such that complex irrigation systems using dams and long feeder canals up river became important only fairly late in Egypt's history. For the most part the Nile forms small flood basins that a few villages could manage successfully.[4] One simply waited for the spring floods to recede, leaving behind their rich sediments, and then scattered seeds on the ground, herded pigs or sheep over the cropland to trample the seeds into the ground, weeded and hoed the crops as they needed it, and then waited for the bountiful harvest. And while the Egyptians faced a lot of competition for grain ripening in fields, especially from birds and rodents, they had the friendly help of cats, which they "domesticated" (and vice versa), and most harvests were bountiful.

The annual floods were usually visible in southern Egypt, near the Nubian border, by late May, and the river rose quickly thereafter, until the beginning of September, when it began a long slow recession to its lowest level the next May. The Egyptian annual calendar was based on this flood cycle, dividing the year into three periods of four months each. The period of flooding, from July to October, was called *akhet*, which may have meant "inundation." Most of the crops were planted between November and February, a season called *peret*, or "time of emergence," in the sense that the farmland emerged as the floods receded. The harvest season, or *shemu*, was from March to June.

By ancient standards, Egypt was a rich country. The Israelites, wandering in the Sinai deserts, bemoaned the rich meals they had enjoyed while living in Egypt: "[A]nd the children of Israel . . . wept again and said, who shall give us flesh to eat? We remember the fish, which we did eat in Egypt for nought; the cucumbers, and the melons, and the leeks and the onions and the garlic."[5] But if the spring floods were too high, then water stayed on the lands too long and crops could not be sown in time to harvest them before the summer heat destroyed them; if the floods were too low, not enough sediment and water were available for good harvests. Ancient Egyptians used tripods to dip water from the river to irrigate crops, and in some cases they trapped water behind dams during low flood years, so that they could use it later for irrigation; but in the long run—and with sensible storing of grains—the Nile Valley was rich enough to support high population densities.

EARLY EGYPTIAN AGRICULTURE

The Nile Valley and Delta are among the richest agricultural niches in the world, and thus the farming way of life may seem to be the "natural" state of human habitation there, but in fact farming came to Egypt only relatively late. For many millennia before farming appeared in Egypt, people lived there simply by hunting, fishing, and gathering the area's rich profusion of indigenous plants and animals. Today the Nile Valley looks like a rather poor place to try to make a living as a hunter-forager because the narrow Nile floodplain runs through one of the harshest deserts on earth, the Sahara; but before about 60,000 years ago rainfall made the deserts bloom for many millennia. In this Pleistocene epoch the Nile itself teemed with fish and wildfowl, and areas that are now deserts along the Nile were for long periods rich grasslands that supported wild cows, gazelles, and many other large animals which, in turn, supported ancient Egyptian hunter-foragers.

This centuries-old way of life began to fade away about 60,000 years ago. The African rainfall patterns shifted, and the deserts replaced grasslands across much of North Africa. And as these deserts expanded, almost all human life in Egypt was concentrated in the Nile Valley and Delta, where until about 8000 B.C., people continued to hunt wild animals, fish, and gather wild plant foods. Sometime between 8000 and 7000 B.C., agriculture and domestication appear for the first time in the Nile Valley area, with some scholars suggesting that people in Egypt might have been in the process of domesticating cattle.[6] But only at about 7500 B.C. did some of them become full-time farmers and make the transition to village life and an economy based mainly on the foods that eventually were to serve as the staples of pharaonic Egypt—emmer wheat, barley, sheep, goats, cattle, and pigs.

How did this transition to agriculture occur in Egypt? Egypt provides an interesting case to study this question because it exhibits both the processes by which people transmuted "wild" species into the ordinary domesticates of the village farm and also the means through which these people came to adopt Southwest Asian domesticates.

There is some suggestion of intensified plant use at late Pleistocene northeast African sites in areas like Kom Ombo in the form of mortars, sickle blades, and other implements, but the adaptation appears to have been a mobile one, based on small groups pursuing a diversified hunting-foraging economy.[7] Sometime after about 10,000 years ago, Egyptians appear to have been domesticating several varieties of local grasses,[8] and they also apparently were in the process of domesticating cattle, and then later some other animals, such as the mongoose (ichneumon), gazelle, oryx, addax, ibex, and hyena—none of which ever became completely domesticated or extensively used as farm or food animals.

The earliest evidence of forms of subsistence, settlement, and technology that differed significantly from those of the late Pleistocene in northeast Africa comes from the desert areas of Bir Kiseiba and Nabta in southwest Egypt (see Figure 9.2). On the basis of evidence from this area, Wendorf, Schild, and Close note that both "cattle and pottery seem to have been known in the Sahara as early as anywhere else in the world."[9] Moreover, they observe that the people of about 6200–5900 B.C. lived in communities in which:

> The houses and pits indicate long term or, at least, recurrent settlement. At the very least, they must have been occupied for most of the year, and it seems likely that the Nile no longer played an important role in the settlement system, suggesting that a different kind of exploitation was now being employed in the desert. Instead of sites representing small family units or task-groups, there are now medium-sized villages, composed of perhaps as many as 14 family units . . . where there was at least sufficient social control to determine the arrangement of the community.[10]

One of the most intriguing discoveries at Nabta is the presence of wild sorghum, an important African cereal—in one structure at Nabta it represents 74 percent of the wild plant foods.[11] Although sorghum was not to become one of the main staples of later Egyptian civilization, the use of this wild cereal by Neolithic people in Egypt clearly shows that—like their early Neolithic counterparts in the Levant—these early Egyptians were focusing intensively on plant foods that would later become domesticated crops. Wild sorghum, along with sheep and goats, has also been found in Neolithic contexts at Farafra, an oasis far out in the Sahara desert in north-central Egypt.[12]

Compared to the glories of pharaonic civilization, these tiny communities described by Wendorf, Schild, and Close might seem of negligible importance and interest, but they demonstrate again the great breadth and pervasiveness of the changes that swept the world after the end of the last Pleistocene era. As we saw in chapter 6, for reasons not altogether clear people around the world after about 10,000 years ago began to interact with plants and animals in ways that led in many cases to domestication and agriculture; and in this same period of transition people all over the world appear to have begun living in larger communities, in which they spent much or all of the year. Not every group around the world changed in these ways, and hunting-foraging in the traditional ways continued throughout most of the world. But when we place these early Egyptian communities in the context of similar changes in Anatolia, Mesoamerica, northern China, and many other places, this pattern of worldwide change appears revolutionary.

These early Egyptian communities also illustrate the nature of cultural evolutionary processes: Cultural change and transformation is a fitful process of dead-ends, failures, extinctions, and only occasionally the kinds of slight changes that result in long-term revolutionary cultural transformation. For example, apparently these early Egyptian communities did not make the transition to a fully agricultural, sedentary way of life in these arid zones. Fekri Hassan and others have argued that eventually climate changes induced people to abandon areas that were slowly turning into deserts and migrate into the richer Nile Valley.[13] Had these climatic changes not forced people out of what are now the deserts of Egypt, perhaps they would have evolved their own agricultural communities on the basis of local grasses, cattle, and other resources—but we will never know: Evolutionary processes are not predictable and only reveal a "pattern" when viewed backward in time.

Sometime between 6000 and 5000 B.C., domesticated wheat, barley, sheep, and goats were introduced from outside Egypt and became the basis for the evolution of Egyptian civilization. Whether these domesticates were introduced for the first time in this millennium or were just successfully farmed for the first time is unknown, as are their ultimate origins. The most likely source of the domestic wheat, barley, sheep, and goats that formed the staples of the Egyptian diet is Syro-Palestine and other areas of Southwest Asia, where they had already been in agricultural use for 2,000 years.

Our most systematic evidence about these early agriculturalists is from the Fayyum Oasis. British archaeologist Gertrude Caton-Thompson conducted excellent excavations along the lake's north shore in the 1930s, Fred Wendorf and Romauld Schild's work there in the 1970s greatly augmented Caton-Thompson's findings, and additional work has been done by other scholars.[14]

Agriculture has such great inertia because once people begin making and using large grinding stones, big grain storage silos, sickles, and all the rest of the primitive farmer's tool kit, there is a strong incentive not to move. Also, cereal grains ripen over a short interval, and a farmer who is out hunting the week they ripen can expect to come back to a field stripped bare by rodents and birds.

Thus it is puzzling that the ancient peoples of the Fayyum left no traces of houses or prolonged occupation. Caton-Thompson found complete sickles in silos full of wheat and barley in Fayyum sites dating to about 5000 B.C., but people here seem to have combined some minor cereal farming with the ancient hunting-foraging ways. Partly for this reason, some scholars see a resistance to the spread of agriculture in Egypt because of the richness of the lake and river environments.[15] But by 4000 B.C. agriculture had spread over much of Egypt, including the southern areas. Some people still depended on fish and wild plants for much of their food, while others were already heavily dependent on the wheat-barley, sheep-goat-cattle-pig combination that underlies so much of Middle Eastern cultural evolution.

THE PREDYNASTIC PERIOD (C. 4000–3000 B.C.)

One of the most impressive and puzzling things about ancient Egypt is the apparent rapidity and comprehensiveness with which hundreds of unconnected and functionally similar villages were transmuted into an organized social, economic, and political unity—the first

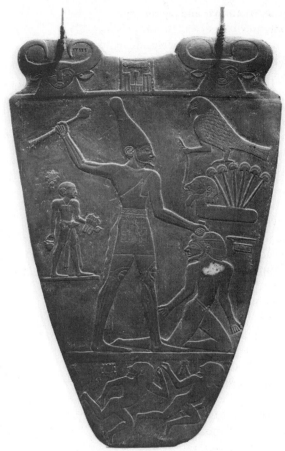

FIGURE 9.4 The Narmer Palette, a thin sheet of stone engraved with symbols that may reflect the political unification of Egypt. King Narmer is shown wearing different crowns on the different sides of the palette, possibly symbolizing the political unification of the Delta and Nile Valley, under the representation of the hawk-headed god Horus. Scenes of battle and what appears to be a beheading suggest a military unification of the country.

Egyptian state. This transformation began at about 4000 B.C. in the south and rapidly spread to the north, encompassing most of Egypt by 3000 B.C.

The rise of the Egyptian "state" after circa 3100 B.C. is really just a bold reconstruction of what we infer happened. These inferences are based on (1) the spread over much of Egypt of pottery and architectural styles that suggest close, continuing contacts among people over large areas of the country; (2) the investment of massive amounts of labor and resources in tombs and monumental buildings in such a way as to imply an unequal distribution of wealth, power, and prestige; and (3) some equivocal signs, like the Narmer Palette (Figure 9.4), that seem to indicate a potentate in the process of exercising kingly authority.

The evolution of Egyptian civilization began in the south, in Upper Egypt. In 1894 Sir Flinders Petrie excavated more than 2,000 graves at the site of Naqada, just north of Luxor, and defined the Predynastic cultural sequence. These graves were filled with pottery in different styles, as well as slate palettes, beautiful flint tools, jewelry made of bone and other materials, untold beads, figurines, and other riches. These graves and other Predynastic sites reveal a society quickly changing in the direction of the class-stratified, religious unity that we know from documents of less than a thousand years later.[16]

The largest and most complex cluster of Predynastic settlements in Egypt are those at Hierakonpolis, the "City of the Hawk," where excavations have gone on for almost a century (until recently under the direction of the late Michael Hoffman).[17]

The Predynastic people of Hierakonpolis lived in rectangular, semi-subterranean houses of mudbrick and thatch; they apparently worshiped in small, perhaps wooden shrines; and they made and distributed regionally several kinds of pottery, some of it very beautiful. They also hunted, herded, fished, and farmed the by now traditional array of Egyptian plants and animals, and they buried their dead in rock and mudbrick tombs of a size and content to reflect the social power and prestige of the individual. The famed Narmer Palette (see Figure 9.4), which traditionally has been interpreted as commemorating the unification of the Nile Valley and Delta into a national state, was found at Hierakonpolis, which may indicate that this city was an early capital of Egypt. But many scholars doubt that the Narmer Palette was a unique record of the first unification of Egypt.[18]

Elsewhere in southern Egypt, excavations by Fekri Hassan at Naqada (see Figure 9.2) suggest that by the middle of fourth millennium B.C. this site was a large town that already was fully dependent on agriculture. Naqada and Hierakonpolis may have been by far the largest communities in all of southern Egypt at this time, with much smaller communities scattered down the valley.

In the north, beginning at about 3650 B.C. there were at least some large and comparatively wealthy communities, such as those at Ma'adi and El-Omari, both of which are just south of what is now Cairo. Stone tools, pottery, and other artifacts show that the people of Ma'adi exchanged products with Palestine, and they may have been part of a large trade network that integrated commodities from the Levant, the Nile Valley, and even the deserts and oases. The bones of donkeys have been found at Ma'adi, and one can imagine these people sending caravans off across the desert to Palestine, while their boats plied the Nile River trade. Burials at El-Omari included some apparently wealthy and perhaps powerful people who were buried in straw mats, along with large stores of pots, stone tools, and other goods.

Other Predynastic communities have been found in northern Egypt, most of them dating to just before 3000 B.C. At Minshat Abu Omar, hundreds of graves have been found containing the distinctive pottery, alabaster jars, slate palettes, and other riches of the late Predynastic. Excavations at Buto, in the northwestern Delta, have revealed clay cones identical to those used to decorate temples in the Uruk state centered in Mesopotamia at about 3200 B.C. Buto may have been one of the most important ports on maritime trade routes over which vast quantities of timber, oil, wine, minerals, pottery, and other commodities passed.[19]

THE ARCHAIC, OLD KINGDOM, AND FIRST INTERMEDIATE PERIODS (C. 3000–2040 B.C.)

Despite the apparent extent of commercial relationships in Predynastic Egypt, the ceramics of northern and southern Egypt remained quite different in style until about 3100 B.C. As we noted in chapter 8 with regard to Southwest Asia, and as we will see in later chapters, one apparently unfailing sign of increasing cultural complexity in ancient societies was a growing uniformity over larger and larger areas of styles of pottery. In fact, around the world, these increases in the area of distribution of certain styles and their growing uniformity correlate precisely with the appearance of other elements of complexity, such as more complex settlement patterns, monumental architecture, agricultural intensification, mortuary cults, and so on. Thus, we might suspect that in Egypt the same pattern would hold, and there is evidence that it did. The distinctive styles of pottery from northern sites like Ma'adi, Buto, and various other sites in the Delta[20] appear to have been quickly and completely replaced by the styles of southern Egypt.

If this pattern of change does reflect the unification of Egypt, we may wonder how it was actually accomplished. As noted earlier, traditional sources suggest that Narmer, a minor official from Upper Egypt, rose to power and conquered Lower Egypt at about 3100 B.C., and that he and his successors established a theocratic political system over the entire navigable length of the Egyptian Nile. Narmer (also known as *Menes*) is recorded as having built a capital at Memphis (near modern Cairo), diverting the stream of the Nile to create a strategic position at the junction of Upper and Lower Egypt. His next several successors were also powerful kings, but there is some evidence of internal dissension at about 2900 B.C. Later, peace appears to have been restored, and major construction projects were undertaken in the centuries before 2700 B.C. We know from tombs and other archaeological evidence that already by the early Old Kingdom (c. 2700 B.C.), Egypt was a complexly organized nation-state, with monumental architecture, a multi-tiered economy, and a centralized and hierarchically arranged bureaucracy.

Fekri Hassan has shown that the evolution of complex societies in Predynastic Egypt was a long, involved process, in which climate changes, warfare, evolving agricultural efficiency, and the development of religions and political institutions were all subtly interrelated. He stresses that no simple ecological model can account for these changes and that Egypt is not likely to have been unified by any single battle or ruler.[21]

And while the Predynastic period saw the first complex Egyptian societies, in trade patterns, occupational specialization, and settlement patterns, the Archaic and Old Kingdom periods were the great formative era of Egyptian civilization, the time when Upper and Lower Egypt were first united politically and Egyptian forms of writing, architecture, administration, and ideology emerged.

By 2700 B.C. the economic sphere was already quite complex, involving long-distance trade to Syria and beyond and considerable local exchange of craft goods and foodstuffs; but most Egyptians of the Old Kingdom period continued to live in unwalled, largely self-sufficient villages. Apart from Memphis there were few towns or cities, which may have contributed to the political integration of the country, since there were no urban power centers to resist incorporation.[22] Large areas of the middle Nile Valley were only sparsely settled, and population growth was quite slow, with little competition for agricultural land or irrigation water (although many new settlements appear to have been established in the Delta). Apparently, the slow population growth during the Old Kingdom (Butzer estimates an annual rate of 0.8 per 1,000 people) eventually did begin to exert some pressure on available resources toward the end of the period, since large game almost disappeared from the Alluvium and contemporary documents describe a shift away from pastoralism to a greater reliance on grain agriculture.[23]

The middle of the third millennium B.C. was for Egypt a marvelous age in which many of the greatest pyramids and palaces were built, an integrated royal bureaucracy was formed, and arts and crafts were brilliantly executed (Figure 9.5). Because of the relatively comprehensive documents from this period, we know many of its political and social details.[24] Economic exchange was apparently controlled almost entirely through the king; there were no "merchants"—in the capitalistic sense at least—until centuries after the end of the Old Kingdom. Craftsmen, scribes, peasants, and everyone else were required to perform some services in the name of the king and were liable for military and civil conscription, but there is a clear contrast here with the partially capitalistic, multi-tiered, highly differentiated economic system characteristic of the later Mesopotamian states.

What Old Kingdom Egypt was like outside the main centers is less well known. Recent excavations and surveys have shown that the Old Kingdom Delta was densely occupied.[25] Many Delta settlements were probably "pious donations," the granting of tax exemptions to certain communities whose revenues were used to support mortuary cults at Giza and elsewhere. Pharaoh Wahkare' Khety III (2070–2040 B.C.), in his instructions to his son, Merykare, forcefully recommended building towns as a means to counteract political fragmentation and inefficient organization, especially in the eastern Delta, which, he lamented, was being subdivided into rival provinces and cities.[26] Old Kingdom Egypt had complex commercial and political relationships to Southwest Asian cultures, and since most of the sea and land routes to these areas were through the Delta, the Delta's importance increased. In fact, by about 2400 B.C. the majority of Egypt's population probably lived north of Saqqara, and the seat of government power remained at Memphis, in the north, through much of Egypt's ancient history. Old Kingdom towns at Hierakonpolis and other southern cities remained important, however. Also, the Old Kingdom fort at Elephantine, near Aswan, guarded the southern approaches to the Kingdom.

Some characteristics distinguish Old Kingdom Egypt from Mesopotamia and other early complex societies. For example, there seem to have been no standing armies during most of the Old Kingdom and no economically significant slavery. In some ways the economic system—although highly administered—was a simple redistributive, almost chiefdom-like system, quite different from that of early Mesopotamian states.

Pyramids

Djoser, the second king of the Third Dynasty who reigned from about 2630 to 2611 B.C., was able to organize Egypt's people and economy to the extent that he, or his grand vizier, Imhotep, could arrange construction of the great step pyramid at Saqqara as his tomb (Figure 9.6). The actual crypt was built inside the pyramid, whose six levels rose over 60 m and were surrounded by large buildings and a stone wall more than 9 m wide with a perimeter of more than 1.6 km. The pyramid complex at Saqqara was the world's first large-scale stone building and remains, despite much deterioration and the looting of its limestone facing, one of the most beautiful. It truly must have been an impressive sight, 45

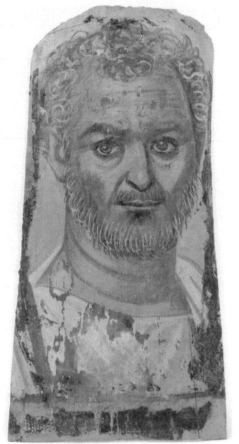

FIGURE 9.5 Lifelike funerary portrait masks such as this one, from the Fayyum, are a highlight in the history of mortuary art.

centuries ago, with its crisp white limestone facing contrasting with the cobalt blue sky, green palm groves, and desert sands.

Djoser's successors, particularly those of the Fourth Dynasty (c. 2575–2465 B.C.)—the beginning of the Old Kingdom Period—also built massive pyramids and experimented with designs and constructions until the "perfect" pyramid form was achieved by King Khufu—as exemplified by the pyramids at Giza (Figure 9.7). It is not just the massive size of this and other pyramids of this era that is so impressive, but also the complex engineering, the deft execution of stone sculpture, and the precise planning such projects would have required.

So much has been said and imagined about the pyramids, yet we can hope to know so little. The minds that designed them and invested them with meaning are these many centuries gone to dust, and not a single ancient Egyptian text of the period when they were built describes how they were constructed or why.

Cairo sprawls out and around the pyramids today in such clamorous ubiquity that the only way to see the pyramids in a manner anything like that of the ancient Egyptian is to

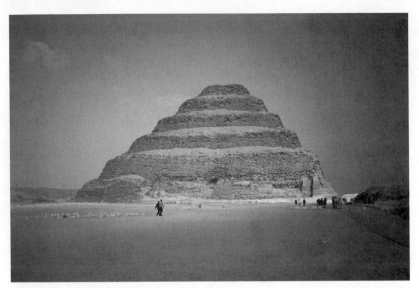

FIGURE 9.6 The stepped pyramid of the Pharoah Djoser at Saqqara is an early forerunner of the Pyramids at Giza.

come in from the west, in the early morning, in the quiet of the desert. The pyramids were all located on the west bank of the Nile, an equation no doubt with death and the setting sun. All are situated on the limestone outcrop near the river, to facilitate the transfer of innumerable blocks of limestone and alabaster, some of which had to be shipped down the Nile and then transported up the bank to the construction area.

Exactly how the blocks were quarried and transported remains unknown, but we have some clues. Quarrying probably involved a combination of hammering with hard stones, chopping with copper adzes, and fracturing by heating the rock with fires and then splashing cold water on it. Mark Lehner has thoroughly analyzed evidence relating to the surveying and construction methods used to build the pyramids, and he has evaluated the various possible combinations of ramps, rollers, and so on against the physical remains.[27] The Great Pyramid of Giza required the quarrying, transport, preparation, and laying of about 2,300,000 stone blocks, each with an average weight of 2.5 tons, and an estimated labor force equivalent to about 84,000 people employed for 80 days a year for 20 years. We do not know how these people were mobilized and administered, but many think the construction was done by the peasantry during the flood seasons, when little agricultural activity was required. The administration, feeding, direction, and planning required to control such a work force, which included many highly trained craftsmen as well as laborers, would obviously argue a high degree of political and bureaucratic centralization. The king was apparently able to call on all the resources of the country, and direct them and the people to virtually any end, and at times the entire national economy was probably focused on these projects. The monarch's absolute control is directly reflected in the texts and in the mortuary complexes of the various levels of high-ranking administrators who served him, many of whose tombs are laid out around the king's, reflecting his control over them even into eternity.

With the construction techniques available to Old Kingdom craftsmen, a pyramid is the only architectural form that could support its own weight when built to the scale that the Old Kingdom pyramids were. But we also have to account for the dimensions and angles used. Engineering considerations obviously constrained the Egyptians to build the pyramids at angles such that stone blocks could be raised to each new level and that the whole could sustain its own weight. But I. E. S. Edwards suggested that this angle (about 52 degrees) parallels that of the slant of light on winter afternoons[28] in Egypt, and he says

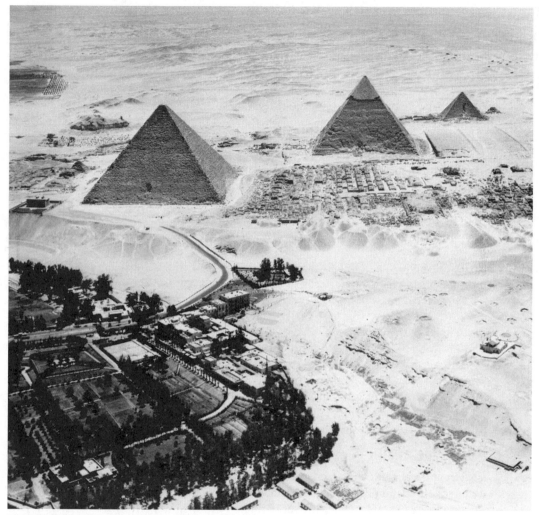

FIGURE 9.7 The Pyramids at Giza are the focal points in a vast mortuary complex of tombs and temples. But outside these mortuary centers Egypt was primarily a rural, agricultural society, with few cities.

the texts hint that the pharaohs ascended into heaven by walking up the rays of light.[29] The pyramids thus would be a first step to the pharaoh's union with the sun god and eternity.

Limited as they were by the lack of electronic survey equipment and precisely engineered tools, we cannot expect Egyptian craftsmen to have been up to modern construction standards. The north corner of the Great Pyramid at Giza, for example, is almost a whole inch higher than the south corner, and there is the famous example of the "bent" pyramid at Dashur, the top of which leans at an odd angle to achieve its apex.

Some of the most impressive features associated with the pyramids were the "solar boats," which are thought to have been buried at the time of the pharaoh's death, to facilitate his sailing into eternity. These boats were disassembled and buried in stone pits near the pyramids, and in the 1960s and 1970s, when one was excavated and reconstructed, the wood, ropes, and other components were found to be almost perfectly preserved by the dark and aridity of the boat pits. In 1987 scientists introduced a camera through an airlock into another boat pit, in the hopes that the atmosphere would be unchanged since the time of burial, but the camera showed dung beetles walking around somewhat decayed segments of the boat.

Earlier versions of boat burials, however, have a long history in Egypt, dating back to the period of the earliest dynasties. They have been found, for example, at Abydos, surrounding a funerary monument to the Second Dynasty Pharoah, Khasekhemwy, but they are stratigraphically earlier than this monument and may actually date to the period of the First Dynasty Pharoah, Djer, around 2920 B.C.[30] The 12 boats at Abydos are "moored" with a small boulder placed either near the prow or the stern to anchor them, and they range in length from 19 to 29 m. Unlike the later Giza boat burials, however, those at Abydos are not complete—they lack decks, cabins, oars, and attached prows and sterns (which are fashioned of mudbrick instead). They are, in David O'Connor's estimation, "proto-types" for the Giza boat pits.[31]

Mark Lehner has argued that the placement of the various elements of the Giza monuments in relation to the geology of the area indicates that the Sphinx, the three main Giza pyramids, and various temples are part of a single unified design, in which the different strata of limestone on the Giza Plateau were carefully used to produce this magnificent ceremonial center.[32]

The pyramids continue to fascinate most people who see them, and numerous ideas have been suggested about what the pyramids meant to the ancient Egyptians and how they were constructed. On hot summer nights some tourists continue experiments to determine if the pyramids retard aging, heighten sexual potency, cure diseases, or in other ways give off powerful emanations.

Egyptian Temples

The Egyptians built thousands of temples, some of which still stand as classics of architectural accomplishment, such as the Temple of Queen Hatshepsut at Deir el-Bahri.

In our own world architecture seems a somewhat chaotic art form and discipline, with the highest adulation often reserved for those who break free from tradition and introduce new forms that express an aesthetic sense but also function well. "Form follows function" and "less is more" are principles that have guided some great architects of the modern world, but new materials and methods allow them a freedom to experiment that was utterly unknown in the ancient world.

Egyptian architects, too, evolved forms and developed new aesthetic expressions, but there was a canon of architectural principles for many buildings that did not permit innovation in certain fundamental aspects. In Ancient Egypt there was no sense of "art for the sake of art," in the sense of a free-form expression of whim and whimsy. Egyptian architects did not, for example, use gigantic stone replicas of papyrus plants as columns for temples because of simple personal aesthetic preference. Everything had a purpose. Egyptian architecture was made to "work" in a profound sense.

The traditional plan of Egyptian temples was based on the belief that the temple was not a place of meditation, as a modern church might be said to be, but, instead, a home of a god. Egyptian temples were static realizations in stone of the creation of the universe and are to be seen as replicas of the universe at this moment of creation. Thus, the temples were aligned on an east-west axis, so that each morning the rising sun, the god Ra, would shine through the double pylon gate, representing two mountains, and penetrate the westernmost chamber of the temple, to illuminate the statue of the god. The temple itself was subdivided into different chambers, so that a person entering would only *gradually* pass through toward the god, reflecting a step-by-step process of purification in preparation for approaching the god. As Nicholas Grimal explains:

> The approach consisted of a gradual movement from light to shadow, achieving total darkness in the holy of holies where the god dwelt. At the same time the ground slowly rose, achieving its highest point under the naos [large carved stone cubicles], which was thus located on the primeval mound emerging from Nun, the lake of chaos. Out of this aqueous environment rose the stems of the papyrus columns, their architraves holding up the sky, which was usually represented on the ceiling. In order to achieve this effect, the temple had to consist of at least three elements: a courtyard, a colonnade, and a pylon entrance.[33]

In this movement from light to dark, low to high, profane to sacred, ancient Egyptian worshippers expressed many elements of their view of the world and the significance of their lives.

The Intellectual Foundations of the Ancient Egyptian State

Wilson notes that the written language of Old Kingdom Egypt had no words for "government" or "state" as impersonal terms, conceived apart from the pharaoh; the Egyptian "theory of government was that the king was everywhere and did everything. . . . The fiction of direct delegation of duty and of a direct report to the king was impossible to maintain in practice; but in the theory of government it was no fiction, it was a working reality."[34] Thus, the Egyptians viewed their state and culture metaphorically as a living organism, an organism of which they were all a part, from the pharaoh himself to the lowliest slave (described in chapter 7 and illustrated in Figure 7.3 using iconography from the throne base of Pharaoh Senusret I—1971–1928 B.C.).

A key concern to the Egyptian theory of government was "divine kingship."[35] The ancient Egyptians viewed their state as a complex blend of human and divine elements that was created and sustained by the interactions of people and gods, particularly through the agency of the pharaoh. The divinity of the pharaoh was a complex idea, however. Various scholars[36] have suggested that the position of pharaoh, his "job," in a sense, was regarded as divine but that the person of the pharaoh was not considered divine. For example, a statue of Chephren, for whom the second pyramid at Giza was constructed, shows the god Horus protecting him by spreading his wings over Chephren. And usually the pharaoh is pictured as confronting the gods, not as one of them. The pharaoh's responsibility was the "containment of unrule"—in other words, he had to ensure domestic tranquility and prosperity. To that end he participated in many religious rituals.

Shortly after 2495 B.C. there was a change in dynasties as well as in the religious and political texture of the Old Kingdom. The worship of the sun god, Ra, emerged as the dominant religion, and the nobility and provincial authorities began to encroach on the king's authority.

The First Intermediate Period (c. 2134–2040 B.C.): Breakup or Transformation?

In a sense the end of the first cycle of dynastic Egypt appears to have occurred between about 2134 and 2040 B.C., when the Old Kingdom state seems to have experienced a short period of disruption and change. Scholars differ on the extent of fluctuations of royal power during the Fourth and Fifth Dynasties. Kemp suggests that in Upper Egypt the control of local affairs by the pharaoh's overseer was gradually diluted during the late Old Kingdom, culminating in the appearance of provincial governors, or *nomarchs*.[37] Trigger raises the possibility that a slow but continuous expansion and elaboration of society and economy in the Old Kingdom may have been accompanied by growing complexity and power of provincial administrative institutions.[38] The apparent emergence of powerful *nomarchs* in the Sixth Dynasty may reflect a reduction of pharaonic power, but the pharaohs of this period were still able to send expeditions to Nubia and Palestine and to exert considerable internal control as well.[39]

The political breakdown of Egypt toward the end of the Old Kingdom may have been in part a result of dramatic climatic changes. Rainfall decreased in much of Egypt after about 2900 B.C., and Butzer notes that decreasing rainfall would have reduced the resources and numbers of desert nomads as well as eliminated much of the seasonal pastoral movements into the deserts.[40]

The concept of societal "collapse," a dominant theme in many analyses of Egypt, Mesopotamia, China, and other early states,[41] has some application to Egypt, but the periodic partial disintegrations of Egyptian polities seem to have been quite different. When its central government weakened, there was a reversion to greater autonomy for the provinces for brief periods. Even during the three "intermediate periods" that are taken as major divisions of Egypt's culture history, the level of disruption may have been less than originally estimated.[42] There was always a base level of expansion-collapse cycles as a result of variations in the Nile's annual flow. Various texts describe social disruptions that may be associated with flood-level fluctuations, but the Egyptian state evolved effective mechanisms to cope with these problems.

To some extent, Egypt's "intermediate periods" may have been periods of reorganization rather than of collapse. For example, the great decline in pyramid construction that marked the end of the Old Kingdom and the beginning of the First Intermediate Period does not necessarily reflect catastrophe; in fact, there is evidence that any economic dislocations in these periods were short-lived and relatively minor.[43]

THE MIDDLE KINGDOM AND SECOND INTERMEDIATE PERIODS (2040–1550 B.C.)

Reconstructing the sociopolitical changes of the Middle Kingdom (c. 2080–1640 B.C.) —Egypt's "Classical" period—is a complex matter. In general, the history of the Middle Kingdom contains the same cycles of expansion and collapse that can be seen in all the great ancient empires. Periods of well-regulated trade, prosperity, and brilliance in art, architecture, and literature were punctuated by periods of revolution, poverty, and political fragmentation. The Middle Kingdom originated in the great civil unrest of the twenty-first century B.C., when, according to a contemporary account:

> [Grain] has perished everywhere. . . . People are stripped of clothing, perfume, and oil. . . . Everyone says, "There is no more." . . . Strangers have come into Egypt everywhere. . . . Men do not sail to Byblos today: What shall we do for fine wood? Princes and pious men everywhere as far as the land of Crete are embalmed with the resins of Lebanon, but now we have no supplies. . . . The dead are thrown in the river. . . . Laughter has perished. Grief walks the land.[44]

In the face of this turmoil, successive rulers sought to increase national integration while directing defense and trade along increasingly active frontiers.[45] The Eleventh Dynasty Pharaoh Nebhepetre' Mentuhotpe (c. 2061–2010 B.C.) and his immediate successors of the Eleventh Dynasty reunified the country. He and his successors of the Eleventh and Twelfth Dynasties reorganized the country with considerable energy, undertaking expeditions into Nubia, Libya, and Syria; reopening trade routes to the Red Sea; and commencing again the construction of monumental buildings. The capital was reestablished near Memphis, from which both Upper and Lower Egypt could be ruled effectively; trade routes were extended; fortresses were built along the country's frontiers; and the tradition of co-regency was established, in which sons were made co-rulers toward the end of their fathers' reigns, thereby eliminating some of the bloody battles for succession that had plagued previous dynasties.

There were also advances in Egyptian art and architecture during this period. Many literary classics were composed, and the cult of Osiris completed its replacement of the colder, sterner religion of Ra and gave the common people some hope of the afterlife that in the past had been restricted to royalty.

From about 1786 to about 1720 B.C., various kings managed to remain in general control of most of Egypt, but gradually people from, it appears, Syro-Palestine, who were collectively referred to as the Hyksos, began to infiltrate the Delta, and they eventually appear to have been absorbed into the lower levels of Egyptian society. Gradually the power of these Asiatic peoples increased. At about 1640 B.C. they captured Memphis, and the Hyksos king adopted the trappings of Egyptian royalty. Artifacts made in the Hyksos manner have been found all along the Nile Valley and as far south as Karnak, but it is not clear how directly they were able to control most of the population. The skull of a ruler of southern Egypt, Seqenenre' Ta'o II (c. ruled at about 1600 B.C.), bears the imprint of a western Asiatic-type battle axe,[46] and there are other evidences of frequent conflict between Egyptians and Asiatics along the eastern Delta border.

THE NEW KINGDOM AND THIRD INTERMEDIATE PERIODS (1550–712 B.C.)

The hated Asiatics were largely expelled from Egypt by Pharaoh Ahmose I (c. 1550–1525 B.C.), who ushered in a new age of political unity. The major cities of the New Kingdom were Memphis, near what is now Cairo, and Thebes, at Luxor. Ahmose, a native of Thebes, expelled the Hyksos from the Delta, and after several battles drove them beyond the eastern frontier. He even captured the rich city of Sharuhen, in Palestine, and he and his successors

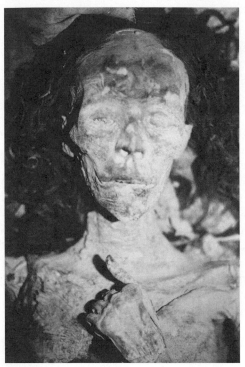

FIGURE 9.8 Mummy of Queen Tiye—her lovely hair still largely intact—who died about 1350 B.C. The position of the left hand is typical of Egyptian royalty.

reformed the bureaucracy, modeling it after that of the Middle Kingdom. He and his immediate successors also undertook massive building projects to restore and expand cult complexes at Abydos, Deir el-Bahari, and other major southern towns.

By the mid-fifteenth century B.C. Egypt probably had a population of many millions of people, whose governmental institutions, religion, language, economy, and most other aspects of life were probably remarkably like those of their ancestors during all of the preceding 2,000 years.[47] This great weight of tradition must be considered when analyzing Egyptian history. Time and time again Egypt would fragment under revolt and invasion, but the ancient order would always persist and reform.

New Kingdom documents, such as the Wilbour Papyrus, describe a highly stratified society, with a king and elite who could draw freely on the country's wealth (Figure 9.8), and under them provincial nobles, who inherited their titles and wealth, lesser bureaucrats, priests, military officers, wealthy farmers, craftsmen, soldiers, and tenant-farmers, with peasants supporting the whole structure (Figure 9.9).[48]

One of the greatest New Kingdom rulers, Thutmosis III, reigned for 54 years (1479–1425 B.C.), and his mummified body suggests that he died still looking quite young for his many years and accomplishments.[49] Thutmosis III established Egypt's Asiatic empire with his conquest of much of the eastern Mediterranean coastal areas. Even powerful Assyria paid material tribute to the Egyptian Empire, as did the Babylonians and the Hittites. His surprise attack on Megiddo in Palestine and his amphibious operation against the Mitanni, a powerful northern Mesopotamian kingdom, established Egypt as a world power. By about 1450 B.C. Egypt had commercial contacts on a large scale, exchanging products with Phoenicia, Crete, the Aegean Islands, and its traditional African trading partners. Military pacification programs were extended far into Nubia, and vast quantities of Nubian gold and building stone were shipped to the Nile Valley.

One of the most famous New Kingdom monarchs was Akhenaten (ruled 1353–1335 B.C.), who introduced a semi-monotheistic religion and tried to eradicate vestiges of older polytheistic cults. He built marvelous temples to Aten, the new god, and constructed a new capital at Tell el-Amarna in central Egypt, complete with magnificent religious and administrative buildings.

Akhenaten's physical appearance suggests he may have been a hermaphrodite, and some suspect that he had physical problems that produced some mental instabilities, but he was a reasonably effective civil and military leader.

Akhenaten started off with certain disadvantages. From statues and portraits medical historians have diagnosed tuberculosis, hyperpituaritism, hypogonadism, and acromegaly. . . . Nor was his emotional life any healthier. His first wife appears to have been his mother,

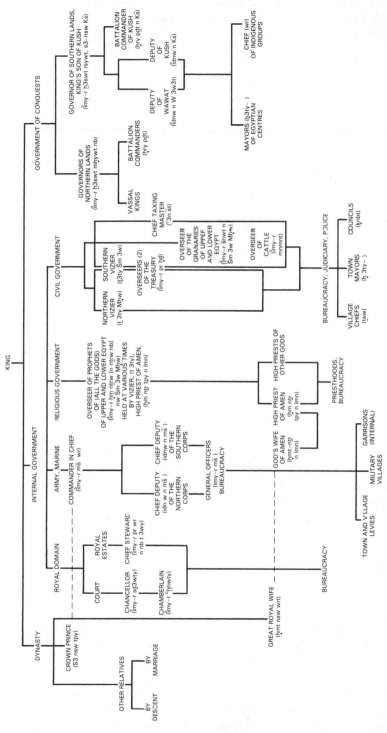

FIGURE 9.9 The bureaucratic organization of Egypt in the New Kingdom period. This reconstruction by David O'Connor (1983) shows the numerous officials who organized most aspects of Egyptian society.

Tiy. . . . [T]hey had one daughter. Then he married his maternal cousin, Nefretiti, and fathered three more daughters. His third and fourth wives were not blood relatives, and there was one son of each marriage, the second of whom was to rule as the boy pharaoh Tutankhamun. Akhenaten's fifth and last marriage was to the third of his own daughters by Nefretiti. . . .[50]

Soon after Akhenaten's death, the old religions were reestablished by Smenkhare and the famous Tutankhamun. Akhenaten's mummy was probably intentionally destroyed by bitter opponents of his attacks on the old religious traditions of Egypt.[51] The "Boy King," Tutankhamun, reigned as a teenager from about 1333 to 1323 B.C.,[52] and powerful members of his court tried to reestablish the power of the central court by reviving the state religion in the classical traditions of the cult of Amun.

When Howard Carter, whose work was funded by a British nobleman, Lord Carnarvon, discovered Tutankhamun's undisturbed tomb in 1922, his find captured the world's attention as no other archaeological discovery has. Lord Carnarvon's death from an infected mosquito bite in 1923 and other bad luck (to which we can add Howard Carter's favorite donkey, who was bitten on the lip by a cobra and died within three hours),[53] inspired the notion of the "Curse of the Pharaohs" and made Lord Carnarvon's son so disenchanted with things Egyptian that he had some of his father's antiquities sealed away in the family castle. In 1988, with the help of a 75-year-old butler, these antiquities were rediscovered, but the most important finds from this tomb had long since been distributed among various museums, principally Cairo's Egyptian Museum.

Between about 1327 B.C. and the accession of Ramesses II (ruled 1290–1224 B.C.), Egypt's fortunes varied, with periods of foreign invasion and some internal breakdowns of the social order. And from Ramesses II on, "[c]ontraction, not expansion, characterized the foreign policy while the disintegration of government became evident."[54] Even in an era of megalomaniacs, Ramesses II is impressive. While invading Palestine, he allowed himself and his army to be ambushed by Hittites. He barely salvaged himself by a strategic retreat, and then proceeded to cover almost every available flat stone surface in Egypt (and much papyri) with heroic accounts of his mighty victory. Ramesses II and his successors were also plagued by court intrigues, probably some assassination attempts, various economic problems, and threats along the frontiers. Some scholars think that it may have been Ramesses II, or his successor, Mer-ne-Ptah, who refused to let the Israelites leave, as related in the biblical Exodus story, but few scholars consider this story to have much—if any— historical basis.[55] There is little if any reliable evidence of major changes in the archaeological record of Palestine at the time the Exodus story is supposed to have occurred, nor are there any evident traces in Sinai, where presumably the million or more Israelites would have wandered. The eastern Delta was a strongly fortified military area at the time the Exodus is supposed to have occurred, and the area of Palestine which they were recorded in the Bible to have invaded was already largely controlled by the Egyptians, so it is difficult to imagine how the Exodus story could have occurred as recorded. Also, the pyramids were built thousands of years before the Israelites arrived in Egypt—or were recognized as a distinct people, and it may be that the building projects described in the Bible as their work were small mudbrick complexes in the eastern Delta.

In any case, the Exodus story is a classic example of the collision of myth and the positivistic view of history. As discussed in chapter 1, all history is interpretation, and the phrase "what actually happened" is to some scholars meaningless.

At about 1000 B.C., Egypt lost military control of Nubia, and the breakup of its Asiatic empire brought it into confrontation with the Israel of David and Solomon. The Egyptians captured a city on the border of Israel and agreed to peace with the marriage of the pharaoh's daughter to Solomon. But five years after Solomon's death Seshonk I invaded Israel, plundered Jerusalem, and reestablished Egypt's control.

During the first millennium B.C., Egypt had various periods of resurgence when various kings reasserted Egyptian influence in Palestine and Africa, and as late as 715 B.C. Shako conquered the Delta and forged a unified country once again. But continued military pressures from Kush and the disintegration of national political and economic systems ate away at the country's structure and stability, and at about 525 B.C. Cambyses, a Persian king, conquered Egypt and reduced it to a vassal kingdom, proclaiming himself pharaoh. In 332 B.C., Alexander the Great marched into Egypt, evicted the Persians, and built the city of Alexandria. Later, the Romans, Arabs, and British would complete the conquest of Egypt, submerging almost entirely this distinctive civilization that was for so many years the light of the ancient world (Figure 9.10). Not until A.D. 1952 was Egypt again ruled by Egyptians.

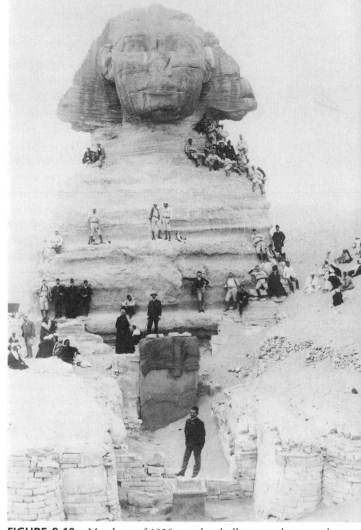

FIGURE 9.10 Members of 1920s-era baseball teams play a road game.

ANCIENT EGYPTIAN ART AND THOUGHT

As we noted in chapter 1, some archaeologists now argue that the archaeological record can only really be interpreted if we shift our attention away from the simplicities of technology, environment, and economy, to the ideas, concepts, and world-views of ancient peoples. Unlike many areas, in Egypt it is in some ways possible to do this because of its rich and early literature. Through most of antiquity, Egyptians believed that their society and life in general had been established by the gods and that they and all their social, political, and economic relationships were part of a divinely designed, immutable world order. To some extent, the Egyptian past makes sense only when viewed in that way.

Certain themes are deeply embedded in ancient Egyptian culture. For one thing, Egyptians seem to have been a "God-intoxicated" people, "half in love with easeful death." Herodotus wrote that they were the most "religious" people he had encountered, given to incessant and elaborate religious rituals and an enormous priestly bureaucracy. Their concern with death, and the vast energies and richness they invested in preparing for it, are manifestly evident, but it is also a testament to a people so passionately alive that they tried everything to perpetuate life into death.

Mummification was an attempt to preserve the body for use in the afterlife, when it would be revived and rehabilitated. Burial in the arid desert sands must have been the first form of mummification, but chemical methods were already developed by the Old Kingdom period. After death, the corpse was placed on a board and washed. The brain was removed by a hooked wire passed through the nose, an incision was made in the abdomen, and all the internal organs except the kidneys and heart were removed. A Greek of the third century A.D. reported that the stomach was then placed in a box and offered to the sun god, with the incantation, "If I have sinned in eating or drinking what was unlawful, the fault was not mine, but of this" (showing the box containing the stomach).

The heart was left in, so that on the final day it could be weighed against a feather, to see if its accumulated sins would tip the balance against eternal life. After the internal organs had been removed, the abdomen and chest cavity were washed in palm wine, and the viscera were placed in a container of natron (hydrated sodium carbonate) for 40 days. The liver, lungs, stomach, and intestines were then placed separately in four "canopic" jars, to be guarded over by four different deities. The body was then stuffed with sand, sawdust, linen, or straw and covered with dry natron crystals to desiccate it for another 40 days. Then it was washed once more and rubbed with wine, spices, and oils. The cheeks were sometimes restored to life-like dimensions with rag stuffing, the incised abdomen was sewn up, and the hair and complexion were touched up with paint. The entire body was protected with a coating of resin, wrapped in linen bandages (up to 324 m² of linen could be used), placed in a coffin or tomb, and carried across to the west bank of the Nile for interment. At the close of ceremonies, the priest would incant: "You live again, you revive always, you have become young again, you are young again, and forever. . . ." It must have been a great comfort to the ancient Egyptians to hear these words and see the extensive care given the dead.

Egyptian deities were conceived of as very human in their behavior, even to the extent that they could be intimidated. Egyptians recited prayers in which they ticked off the services rendered a god, demanding payment in the form of the prayer answered.

For the Westerner, the physical world is a rather neutral place, where a lightning bolt or virus may strike one down, but on the basis of chance, without malevolence. Rocks are rocks, the dark is peopled only by morbid human projections, and death is inevitable, final, complete. For the ancient Egyptian, however, the world teemed with unseen but animate, conscious forces; malignant spirits were everywhere, as were forces for good; and, with sufficient effort, some of the inconveniences of being dead could be mitigated.

Ancient Egyptians seem to have had a monophysitic perspective in that everything in the universe was thought to have been derived from one substance and to be an expression of that substance. The god Amun, for example, might reside in a stone statue, but also in a well-formed ram or a duck, or in all three at the same time. Nor were these considered just different representations; rather, "the image was the god for all working purposes."[56] The symbolic, mythical element seemed to pervade even quite practical areas, such as medicine. One remedy for schistosomiasis (a disease characterized by bloody urine) was to shape some cake dough like a penis, then wrap it in meat, recite an incantation, and feed it to a cat.[57]

In all this supernatural and symbolic content, we should not lose sight of the practical, canny Egyptian. These were not people paralyzed by the Infinite: They built houses, boats, and beautiful buildings, and they enjoyed themselves in a world of color, play, and physical pleasures that still seems attractive and alive, even when viewed only in fragmentary 4,000-year-old paintings on tomb walls. When contemporary tourists see Egyptian wall paintings they are often surprised at the riot of colors—even the great temple columns of Karnak were brightly colored. This seems strange to many because we see beauty in the monochrome simplicity of Egyptian stone reliefs and buildings. But it helps to understand their art if one experiences first-hand the qualities of Egyptian natural light, the sun rolling up redly over the horizon, illuminating the blues and greens of river, sky, and vegetation with a vividness possible only in the thin arid air of the Sahara, with the limestone of the pyramids and temples absorbing and transforming the light into weights and colors and dimensions and textures that constantly change.

To our own, essentially Greek, minds, the Egyptians seem to have been unable to distinguish between things and representations of things. J. Wilson argues that the Egyptians saw no difference between supplying a dead king with real loaves of bread, wooden models of bread, or loaves painted on the walls; it was not the actual thing that mattered, it was the idea.[58] The physical man needed physical bread, but in the spirit world, "spiritual" bread was appropriate.[59]

Similarly, Egyptian art challenges Western notions about aesthetics. For the Egyptians, art was mainly functional and had a purpose—it was done so that people and things could live forever. Wall frescoes, statues, and drawings were all done not just to record an image, but "to create and maintain a perfect world in which the good life . . . could continue to flourish without opposition from the bad."[60] Therefore, decay and imperfection are seldom shown in Egyptian art—people and objects are shown in ideal condition, since they are meant to be part of an ideal afterlife. And given this purpose, people and objects, whether loaves of bread, geese, gardens, or boxes, should be depicted in their most easily recognizable forms and positions, and not necessarily from a single point of view or in perspective.

The ethical basis of Egyptian society was a composite sense of order, fairness, and justice, all expressed in the concept of *maat*, which is usually translated as "justice," "truth," or "right-dealing." It is interesting that English really has no single word equivalent to the sense of *maat*, or to the Greek concept of "virtue," which has a little of the same sense of *maat*. For the Egyptian, *maat* was recognizing the order of the world and universe and the necessity of doing the right thing, which usually meant following religious and civil laws and customs. Justice tempered with mercy, giving to the widow and the orphan but encouraging self-reliance and planning, doing one's share—all these and more were part of *maat*. One could demand justice and respect as a moral right, based on *maat*.

EGYPTIAN WRITING AND LITERATURE

One of the many mysteries of Egypt is the origin of its written language, or hieroglyphs ("sacred carvings") (Figure 9.11). These were first used shortly before 3100 B.C. and continued in use until about A.D. 1100 (and are still used today by the crafty forgers in modern Cairo's tourist traps). Elements of the spoken ancient Egyptian are still used in the liturgy

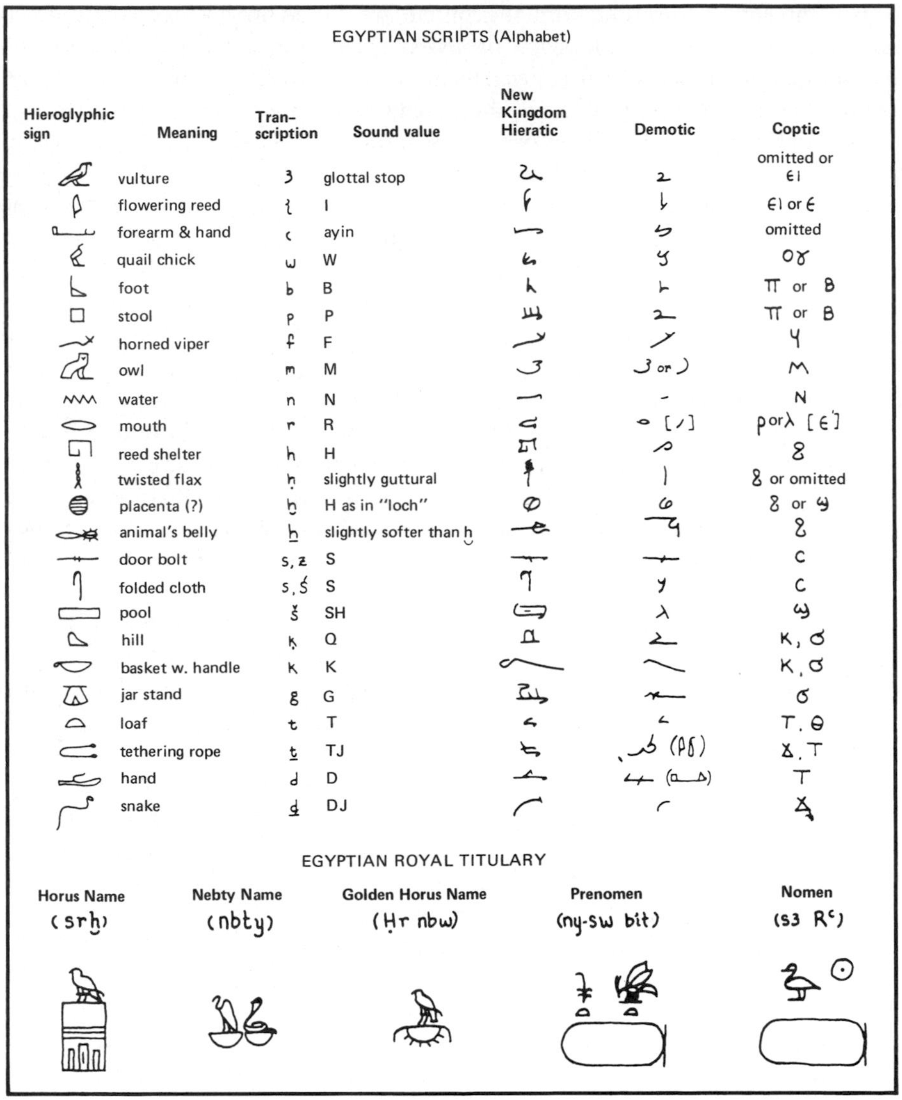

EGYPTIAN SCRIPTS (Alphabet)

Hieroglyphic sign	Meaning	Tran-scription	Sound value	New Kingdom Hieratic	Demotic	Coptic
	vulture	ꜣ	glottal stop	𝒰	𝟤	omitted or ει
	flowering reed	ı̓	I	ƒ	ι	ει or є
	forearm & hand	ꜥ	ayin	⌐	⌐	omitted
	quail chick	w	W	⌐	ꙗ	oγ
	foot	b	B	⋀	⊢	Π or Β
	stool	p	P	⊔⊔	⊥	Π or Β
	horned viper	f	F	⌐	⌐	ϥ
	owl	m	M	ꙅ	ꙅ or)	м
	water	n	N	⌐	-	n
	mouth	r	R	⌐	ο [∕]	ρ or λ [є']
	reed shelter	h	H	⌐	ρ	ϩ
	twisted flax	ḥ	slightly guttural	⌐	⌐	ϩ or omitted
	placenta (?)	ḫ	H as in "loch"	⌀	⌐	ϩ or ϧ
	animal's belly	ẖ	slightly softer than ḥ	⌐	⌐	ϧ
	door bolt	s, z	S	⌐	⌐	c
	folded cloth	s, ś	S	ꙅ	ꙗ	c
	pool	š	SH	⌐	λ	ϣ
	hill	q̱	Q	⌐	⌐	κ, ϭ
	basket w. handle	k	K	⌐	⌐	κ, ϭ
	jar stand	g	G	⌐	⌐	ϭ
	loaf	t	T	⌐	⌐	τ, ⲑ
	tethering rope	ṯ	TJ	⌐	⌐ (ρϛ)	ϫ, τ
	hand	d	D	⌐	⌐ (ⲁ⌐ⲁ)	τ
	snake	ḏ	DJ	⌐	⌐	ϫ

EGYPTIAN ROYAL TITULARY

Horus Name (srḫ)	Nebty Name (nbty)	Golden Horus Name (Ḥr nbw)	Prenomen (ny-sw bit)	Nomen (s3 Rꜥ)

FIGURE 9.11 The hieroglyphic signs in early Egyptian writing were representations of common objects, but they eventually acquired phonetic meaning—sound values—that allowed Egyptians to express their entire spoken language in writing. In later periods the signs were stylized and simplified to facilitate writing. The names of royalty were written in ovals—cartouches—and each ruler used several different names.

of the Coptic Christian church. But hieroglyphic writing first appeared in such a developed form that we cannot see the full transition from what was probably pictographic writing first expressed on papyrus. Some scholars think writing was introduced from Mesopotamia, where it may have been in use some centuries before it appeared in Egypt, but there are great differences between the characters and materials used.

Ancient Egyptian was a mixture of signs and symbols, some of them expressing sounds in the spoken language, others indicating to the reader how a written character with several possible meanings was to be read in that specific context (Figure 9.12). It was not used as a truly alphabetic system, but virtually everything in the spoken language could be efficiently conveyed in the written language.

To a much greater degree than in modern English, hieroglyphs were written in a manner that expressed both contemporary aesthetic styles and the subject matter. Thus, we get simple, grave characters in early religious writings and more overblown, showy characters in later military texts. The beautifully simple hieroglyphic characters were complemented very early on by a *hieratic* script (see Figure 9.11), which was much more abstract and cursive and thus could be written easily on papyrus with a reed pen and ink.

Various scholars had tried to decipher ancient Egyptian writing in the eighteenth century and had guessed correctly about the sound values and of some of the characters, but they were also wrong about most of the characters. One key to the eventual decipherment of the language was the discovery of the Rosetta Stone, which had been found by Napoleon's soldiers in 1799 in the northern Delta. We now know that its text is an unimportant tribute to the Pharaoh Ptolemy V, written at about 196 B.C., but it is significant because the same text was written in Greek as well as in two forms of ancient Egyptian, hieroglyphic and demotic—a cursive form of handwriting that was easier to write on papyrus than the hieroglyphic script. The English scholar Thomas Young, for example, recognized the names of Ptolemy, Cleopatra, and Berenice—in parts of the Rosetta Stone inscriptions.

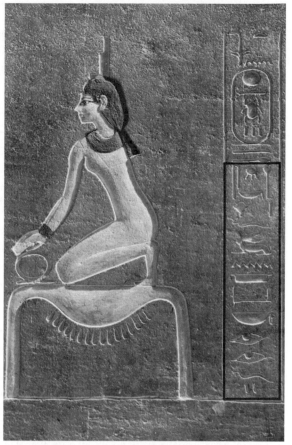

FIGURE 9.12 Reading hieroglyphic writing required recognizing symbols that convey sound values, symbols that are determinatives—which clarify meanings in ambiguous contexts—and symbols that are grammatical markers. The inscription outlined in this figure is on the sarcophagus of Amenhotep II (died c. 1412 B.C.) and reads "Illumine his face, open his eyes."

It was Jean-François Champollion, however, to whom we are most indebted for the decipherment of ancient Egyptian. Champollion was born in France in 1790, and by the age of 16 he was fluent in Latin, Greek, Coptic, and at least five other languages; and from boyhood his physical features were such that eventually he was nicknamed "The Egyptian." To enter a Parisian school he was asked to write a paper on the subject of his choice, and he wrote on *Egypt under the Pharaohs* with such obvious intelligence that he was immediately asked to join the faculty.

A key to Champollion's success in deciphering Egyptian script was his extensive knowledge of the many ancient Egyptian texts, and a major breakthrough was when he

. . . became the first man in fourteen centuries to recognize the dual principle behind the Egyptian hieroglyphic script. . . . The name Ramses illustrates most clearly the dual principle: Ra means 'sun' in Coptic, and in the cartouche [the name of the king written in an oval] Champollion recognised the sun-disk, clearly representing the sense or idea 'sun', with the sound-value *ra* in Egyptian. The sign at the end of the cartouche was used to write the letter *s* in the name Ptolemy (Greek form in full Ptolemaios) on the Rosetta Stone, and so Champollion could read *ra-?-s-s*; he was then able to guess that the middle sign should read *m*, and he had the name Ramses, which he could explain from his knowledge of Coptic as 'Ra-mise' or 'Ra is the one who gives birth to him'.[61]

By extending these principles to other names and inscriptions, and by using the work of previous scholars, Champollion eventually became the first person in centuries to be able to read an Egyptian text. He made mistakes, and later scholars greatly extended his work (and this work continues), but after Champollion the meaning of many ancient Egyptian texts could be understood.

The ancient written Egyptian language was different from ancient Mesopotamian scripts in a significant structural element. Sumerian nouns and verbs did not vary in their written forms depending on grammatical context, so that the word for mouth (*ka*), for example, was always the same, whether it was the subject, direct object, or some other grammatical element; but in ancient Egyptian the first letter in the word for mouth, *r*, was followed by a different vowel, depending on the grammatical position of the word.[62] As H. W. F. Saggs notes, an important consequence of this is that the ancient Egyptians "already had an alphabet within their grasp." Ancient Egyptians could have written all or most of their spoken language with just 24 signs. Saggs points out, however, that the Egyptians never simplified their written language to this alphabetic format—probably, as he says, because it would have been against the interest of the scribes who had mastered the difficult and more cumbersome syllabic forms to use a system anyone could have mastered in just a few months—a reaction similar to that of print unions throughout history.[63]

Since hieroglyphs give us only consonantal sound values (and not vowels), we will never know what ancient Egyptian really "sounded" like precisely, although no cat lover would have any problem with the fact that the ancient Egyptian word for cat was written with the sound values "MIW."

Egyptian literature took many forms. Dedicatory inscriptions recording the activities and histories of the kings and priests predominate, but there are also many poems, songs, financial records, letters, medical texts, astronomical accounts, and so on. As ancient and strange as pharaonic culture may seem, there are many signs that these were very human people and would be recognizable to us in many ways.

The theme of one love poem of the New Kingdom, for example, is the timeless lament of a young man prostrated by the adolescent passions that poetry celebrates in all cultures. He proclaims that the absence of the object of his desires (where she's gone we don't know) has so sickened him that doctors and priests are helpless. But if his girlfriend could only visit!

> Why, that girl's better than any prescription,
>   more to me than the Pharmacopoeia—
> My own secret Hathor Home Remedy?—
>   Her slipping into my room from the road!

(have *her* examine me, *then* watch my energy!)
And just let her look me full in the eye,
   every bit of my body is back in its prime.
At the sound of her voice my heart leaps to her tune,
And then when I kiss her, feel her length breast to thigh,
   Love's evil spirits fly clean from my system—
      God, what a girl, what a woman!
And that bitch has been gone for a week![64]

WHO WERE THE ANCIENT EGYPTIANS?

Victory has a thousand fathers; defeat is an
orphan.

Chinese proverb

This chapter is mainly a review of ancient Egyptian cultural history, but the ancient Egyptians offer an opportunity to consider some larger issues about such difficult topics as cultural "achievement" and the nature of historical interpretation. History is not only kind to "winners," most of history is written by them; also, most people like to be associated with cultural "achievements": Thus, it is not surprising that, as with the Sumerians (chapter 8), many people have tried to claim the ancient Egyptians as their physical or intellectual ancestors.

Beyond this, there is the question of Egyptian contributions to Western civilization. The traditional academic view is that the origins of Western civilization are mainly in the classical Greek world, with some influences from Southwest Asia, but few if any from Egypt.[65] But the historian I. Bernal has argued that Western scholars have had anti-Jewish, anti-Arab, and anti-Black African biases that resulted in their intentionally ignoring the contributions of Egypt and Africa to Greek and Western civilization. Few scholars give much credence to Bernal's claims, but in this politically sensitive era they have achieved a level of debate far beyond their rather esoteric academic subject.

Various studies strongly suggest that ancient Egyptians were a distinctive people early in the pharaonic period, but with much of the same variations of physical characteristics that one sees in modern Egypt. The ancient Egyptians, of course, considered themselves different from all other peoples and superior to them. They disparaged all other peoples, particularly those with whom they had the most interactions, such as the "Asiatics" of Syro-Palestine and the Nubians beyond their southern border.

Their artistic representations of their neighbors are demeaning, and they clearly show that the ancient Egyptians considered themselves physically different from Nubians and other sub-Saharan Africans in facial features and skin tones, and from "Asiatics" as well. Egyptian men were painted a darker color than women to underscore gender differences, misleading some to conclude that most ancient Egyptians were very dark in skin tone; but there is no evidence that they were much different in this regard from modern Egyptians, with a wide range from the very light Mediterranean types to sub-Saharan African tones.

SUMMARY AND CONCLUSIONS

Many simplistic notions about the origins of cultural complexity have foundered on the evidence from Egypt. Population growth, for example, may have produced fairly dense concentrations of people in favorable agricultural areas, but the long-term pattern of population growth was probably one of very slow increase through most of antiquity. Karl Wittfogel's notion of large-scale irrigation as a powerful impetus to empire (chapter 7) may have some application to Egypt, for irrigation no doubt was important early on, and some of the first Egyptian stone engravings apparently show royalty in the process of opening irrigation canals.[66] But irrigation in ancient Egypt was primarily through the passive blessings of the Nile flood, and such irrigation works as were constructed seem to have been small, local installations that did not require a lot of people or "paperwork" to run them.

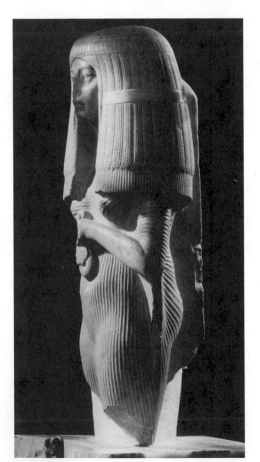

FIGURE 9.13 This late second millennium B.C. Egyptian sculpture of a noble woman has the vibrant, sensual quality typical of some later periods but in great contrast to archaic forms.

Similarly, the Egyptians were fond of murals showing their kings defeating hordes of foreigners, and people in the competing areas of pre-state Egypt may well have been given to bloody civil wars. But the location of settlements, the lack of walled towns and forts, and the art and literature do not support the notion that the critical factor in Egyptian state origins was Menes or someone else strapping on his sword, massing his troops, and marching to the Mediterranean, leaving a unified political state in his wake. Warfare was part of state formation processes, but probably as a mechanism, not a primary cause.

Nor is there much solace for the orthodox Marxian searching for the power of class conflict to produce states. Many scholars can and do see Egypt as an example of the validity of Marxian theory, but Egyptian literature and iconography seem to exhibit more mutually supportive bonds of kinship and religion than naked class struggle.

The pressure of nomads and others on the Egyptian periphery seems to have been a factor occasionally, but there is not much of a parallel here with the situation in ancient Mesopotamia or in China, where nomad-farmer relationships were a central theme in imperial developments.

A comparison of Mesopotamian and Egyptian settlement patterns underscores that urbanization is just one strategy, not an indispensable condition of cultural complexity. Whereas the people of Mesopotamia early and dramatically aggregated into fortified towns and cities, from which they conducted agricultural, industrial, religious, and administrative operations, the Egyptians did not even have a permanent capital until late in the second millennium, when Thebes emerged as a center—although recent excavations reveal a greater degree of urbanization than was previously thought to have existed. The comparatively slow development of Egyptian urbanism probably had many causes, including (1) the absence of any powerful foreign peoples on Egyptian borders, and thus relatively little need for large walled defensive cities; (2) the uniformity of the environment all along the Nile, so that there was little to be gained from large-volume, inter-regional exchange of food or craft products; and (3) the pronounced political centralization, which inhibited development of secular, economic differentiation.

When the largest pyramids and other structures were built, population growth rates were slow, there was apparently little pressure on the country's resources, and large areas of uninhabited but fertile land existed. If we view these pyramids as mechanisms to mobilize and train a large work force, we must ask why such a work force would be an advantage, since when the first pyramids were built there were few large irrigation works and little demand for a standing army. If we view the vast expenditures of wealth in the funerary complexes as a means of "balancing" the economy by taking out of circulation inordinate amounts of gold, silver, or craft items, there is some difficulty in explaining why this would have been necessary in a society whose economic system and long-distance trade were strictly controlled by the monarchy and where there were few large markets and almost no free enterprise or capitalism of any kind.

In conclusion, it has proven remarkably difficult to prise apart the many causes and effects that make up Egyptian cultural history, but we are beginning to understand at least some aspects of this history. And, like other early civilizations, there is much about Egypt that is interesting and rewarding at a level beyond that of the mechanics of its history (Figure 9.13).

BIBLIOGRAPHY

Aldred, C. 1961. *The Egyptians.* New York: Praeger.
Allen, R. O., H. Hamroush, and D. J. Stanley. 1993. "Impact of the Environment on Egyptian Civilization Before the Pharaohs." *Analytical Chemistry* 65(1):36–43.
Anderson, W. 1992. "Badarian Burials: Evidence of Social Inequality in Middle Egypt During the Predynastic Era." *Journal of the American Research Center in Egypt* xxix:51–66.
Asante, M. K. 1990. *Kemet, Afrocentricity, and Knowledge.* Trenton, NJ: Africa World Press.
Badawy, A. 1967. "The Civic Sense of the Pharaoh and Urban Development in Ancient Egypt." *Journal of the American Research Center in Egypt* 6:103–109.
Baer, K. 1960. *Rank and Title in the Old Kingdom.* Chicago: University of Chicago Press.
Baines, J. 1990. "Restricted Knowledge, Hierarchy, Decorum: Modern Perceptions and Ancient Institutions." *Journal of the American Research Center in Egypt* xxvii:1–23.
Bakr, M. 1988. "The New Excavations at Ezbet el-Tell, Kufur Nigm: The First Season (1984)." In *The Archaeology of the Nile Delta: Problems and Priorities,* ed. E. C. M. van den Brink. Amsterdam: Netherlands Foundation for Archaeological Research in Egypt.
Bard, K. A. 1987. "The Geography of Excavated Predynastic Sites and the Rise of Complex Society." *Journal of the American Research Center in Egypt* 24:81–93.
———. 1992. "Toward an Interpretation of the Role of Ideology in the Evolution of Complex Society in Egypt." *Journal of Anthropological Archaeology* II:1–24.
———. 1994. *From Farmers to Pharaohs.* Sheffield, UK: Sheffield Academic Press.
Bard, K. A., and R. L. Carneiro. 1989. "Patterns of Predynastic Settlement Location, Social Evolution, and the Circumscription Theory." *Societes Urbaines en Egypte et au Soudan, Cahiers de Recherches de l'Institut de Papyrologie et d'Egyptologie de Lille* 11:15–23.
Barich, K., and F. Hassan. 2000. "A Stratified Sequence from Wadi el-Obeiyd, Farafra. New Data on Subsistence and Chronology of the Egyptian Western Desert." In *Recent Research into the Stone Age of Northeastern Africa,* ed. L. Kryzaniak, K. Kroeper, and M. Kobuciewicz, pp. 11–20. Studies in African Archaeology, Vol. 7. Poznan: Poznan Archaeological Museum.
Bernal, M. 1987. *Black Athena: The Afroasiatic Roots of Classical Civilization,* Vol. 1: *The Fabrication of Ancient Greece.* New Brunswick, NJ: Rutgers University Press.

Bokonyi, S. 1985. "The Animal Remains of Maadi, Egypt: A Preliminary Report." In *Studi di Paletnologia in Onore di S. M. Puglisi.* Rome: Universita di Roma "La Sapienza."

Bonani, G., H. Haas, Z. Hawass, M. Lehner, S. Nakhla, J. Nolan, R. Wenke, and W. Wölfli. 2004. "Radiocarbon Dates of Old and Middle Kingdom Monuments in Egypt." *Radiocarbon* 43(3):1297–1320.

Bourriau, J. 1981. *Umm el-Ga'ab: Pottery from the Nile Valley Before the Arab Conquest.* Cambridge: Fitzwilliam Museum.

Bradley, D. G., D. E. MacHugh, P. Cunningham, and R. T. Loftus. 1996. "Mitochondrial Diversity and the Origins of African and European Cattle." *Proceedings of the National Academy of Sciences* 93(10):5131–5135.

Brewer, D. J. 1991. "Temperature in Predynastic Egypt Inferred from the Remains of the Nile Perch." *World Archaeology* 22(3):288–303.

Brewer, D. J., and R. Friedman. 1989. *Fish and Fishing in Ancient Egypt.* Warminster: Aris & Phillips.

Brewer, D. J., and R. J. Wenke. 1992. "Transitional Late Predynastic-Early Dynastic Occupations at Mendes: A Preliminary Report." In *The Nile Delta in Transition: 4th–3rd Millennium BC, Proceedings of the Seminar Held in Cairo, 21–24 October, 1990,* ed. E. C. M. van den Brink. pp. 191–197. Jerusalem: R. Pinkhaus.

Brothwell, D. R., and B. A. Chiarelli, eds. 1973. *Population Biology of the Ancient Egyptians.* London: Academic Press.

Butzer, K. W. 1976. *Early Hydraulic Civilization in Egypt.* Chicago: University of Chicago Press.

———. 1980. "Pleistocene History of the Nile Valley in Egypt and Lower Nubia." In *The Sahara and the Nile,* ed. M. Williams and H. Faure. Rotterdam: Balkema.

———. 1984. "Long-Term Nile Flood Variation and Political Discontinuities in Pharaonic Egypt." In *From Hunters to Farmers,* ed. J. D. Clark and S. A. Brandt. Berkeley: University of California Press.

Caneva, I., M. Frangipane, and A. Palmieri. 1987. "Predynastic Egypt: New Data from Maadi." *The African Archaeological Review* 5:105–114.

———. 1989. "Recent Excavations at Maadi (Egypt)." In *Late Prehistory of the Nile Basin,* ed. L. Krzyzaniak and M. Kobusiewicz. Poznan: Polish Academy of Sciences.

Cavalli-Sforza, L., and M. Feldman. 1981. *Cultural Transmission and Evolution.* Princeton, NJ: Princeton University Press.

Close, A. E., ed. 1980. *Loaves and Fishes: The Prehistory of Wadi Kubbaniyya.* New Delhi: Pauls Press.

———, ed. 1987. *Prehistory of Arid North Africa. Essays in Honor of Fred Wendorf.* Dallas: Southern Methodist University Press.

Coutellier, V., and D. J. Stanley. 1987. "Late Quaternary Stratigraphy and Paleogeography of the Eastern Nile Delta, Egypt." *Marine Geology* 77:257–275.

Cruz-Uribe, E. 1985. *Saite and Persian Demotic Cattle Documents.* Chico, CA: Scholars Press.

Davis, W. 1989. *The Canonical Tradition in Ancient Egyptian Art.* Cambridge, England: Cambridge University Press.

———. 1992. *Masking the Blow.* Berkeley: University of California Press.

Decker, W. 1992. *Sports and Games of Ancient Egypt.* Trans. A. Guttmann. New Haven: Yale University Press.

Diop, C. A. 1974. *The African Origin of civilization: Myth or Reality.* New York: L. Hill.

Edwards, I. E. S. 1961. *The Pyramids of Egypt.* London: Parrish.

Eiwanger, J. 1987. "Die Archaologie der spaten Vorgeschichte: Bestand und Perspektiven." In *Problems and Priorities in Egyptian Archaeology,* ed. J. Assmann, G. Burkard, and V. Davies. London: Routledge & Kegan Paul.

Fairservis, W. 1972. "Preliminary Report on the First Two Seasons at Hierakonpolis." *Journal of the American Research Center in Egypt* 9:7–27, 67–99.

———. 1991. "A Revised View of the *Na'rmr* Paletette." *Journal of the American Research Center in Egypt* XXVIII:1–20.

Farooq, M. 1973. "Historical Development." In *Epidemiology and Control of Schistosomiasis (Bilharziasis),* ed. N. Ansari. Baltimore: University Park Press.

Fattovich, R. 1979. "Trends in the Study of Predynastic Social Structure." *First International Congress of Egyptology, Cairo, Actes* (Berlin): 17–39.

Foster, J. L., illus. and trans., and Davies, Nina M., illus. 1992. *Love Songs of the New Kingdom* (Reprint ed.). Austin: University of Texas Press.

Frank, A. G. 1993. "Bronze Age World System Cycles." *Current Anthropology* 34(4):383–430.

Frankfort, H., J. Wilson, and T. Jacobsen. 1949. *Before Philosophy.* Baltimore: Penguin.

Friedman, J., and M. J. Rowlands. 1977. *The Evolution of Social Systems.* Pittsburgh: University of Pittsburgh Press.

Gautier, A. 1984. "Archaeozoology of the Bir Kiseiba Region, Eastern Sahara." In *Cattle-Keepers of the Eastern Sahara. The Neolithic of Bir Kiseiba,* ed. A. E. Close. pp. 49–72. New Delhi: Pauls Press.

———. 1987. "Prehistoric Men and Cattle in North Africa: A Dearth of Data and a Surfeit of Models." In *Prehistory of Arid North Africa,* ed. A. E. Close. Dallas: Southern Methodist University.

Ghoneim, W. 1977. "Die Okonomische Bedeutung des Rindes im Alten Agypten." *Lexikon der Agyptologie* 5:259.

Goedicke, H. 1967. *Konigliche Dokumente aus dem alten Reich*. Wiesbaden: Harrasowitz.

Grimal, N. 1991. *A History of Ancient Egypt*. Trans. I. Shaw. Cambridge, MA: Blackwell.

Haaland, R. 1987. *Socio-Economic Differentiation in the Neolithic Sudan*. Oxford, England: British Archaeological Reports International Series 350.

Haas, H., J. Devine, R. J. Wenke, M. E. Lehner, W. Wolfli, G. Bonani. 1987. "Radiocarbon Chronology and the Historical Calendar in Egypt." In *Chronologies in the Near East*, ed. O. Avrenche, J. Evin, and P. Hours. *British Archaeological Reports* 379:585–606.

Haas, J. 1982. *The Evolution of the Prehistoric State*. New York: Columbia University Press.

Hamilton, E. 1930. *The Greek Way*. New York: Norton.

Harlan, J. R. 1982. "The Origins of Indigenous African Agriculture." In *The Cambridge History of Africa*, Vol. 1, ed. J. D. Clark. Cambridge, England: Cambridge University Press.

Harlan, J. R., J. M. de Wet, and A. B. Stemler, eds. 1976. *Origins of African Plant Domestication*. The Hague: Mouton.

Harris, J. E., and K. R. Weeks. 1973. *X-Raying the Pharaohs*. New York: Scribner's.

Hassan, F. 1986. "Desert Environment and Origins of Agriculture in Egypt." *Norwegian Archaeological Review* 19:63–76.

———. 1988. "The Predynastic of Egypt." *Journal of World Prehistory* 2(2):135–185.

———. 1992. "Primeval Goddess to Divine King. The Mythogeneis of Power in the Early Egyptian State." In *The Followers of Horus: Studies Dedicated to Michael Allen Hoffman*, ed. R. Friedman and B. Adams. Oxford: Oxbow.

———. 1993. "Town and Village in Ancient Egypt: Ecology, Society, and Urbanization." In *The Archaeology of Africa*, ed. T. Shaw, P. Sinclair, B. Andah, and A. Okpoko. London: Routledge & Kegan Paul.

Hassan, F. A., and S. W. Robinson. 1987. "High-Precision Radiocarbon Chronometry of Ancient Egypt and Comparisons with Nubia, Palestine and Mesopotamia." *Antiquity* 61(231):119–135.

Helck, W. 1971. *Die Beziehungen Agyptens su Vorderasien im 3. und 2. Jahrtausend v. Chr.* Wiesbaden: Harrasowitz.

———. 1974. *Die altagyptische Gaue*. Weisbaden: Harrassowitz.

———. 1975. *Wirtschaftsgeschichte des alten Agyptens im 3. und 2. Jahrtausend vor Chr.* Leiden-Koln: Brill.

Herodotus. 1972. *Books I and II*. Trans. A. D. Godley. London: Loeb Classical Library.

Hess, R. 1993. *Amarna Personal Names*. ASOR Diss. Series 9. Winona Lake, Indiana: Eisenbrauns.

Hoffman, M. 1980. *Egypt Before the Pharaohs: The Prehistoric Foundations of Egyptian Civilization*. New York: Knopf.

———. 1982. *The Predynastic of Hierakonpolis—An Interim Report*. Egyptian Studies Association, Publication No. 1. Cairo: Cairo University Herbarium and the authors.

———. 1989. "A Stratified Predynastic Sequence from Hierakonpolis (Upper Egypt)." In *Late Prehistory of the Nile Basin and the Sahara*, ed. L. Krzyzaniak and M. Kobusiewicz. Poznan: Poznan Archaeological Museum.

Hoffman, M. A., H. A. Hamroush, and R. O. Allen. 1986. "A Model of Urban Development for the Hierakonpolis Region from Predynastic Through Old Kingdom Times." *Journal of the American Research Center in Egypt* 23:175–187.

Hoffmeier, J. K. 1994. "The Structure of Joshua 1-11 and the Annals of Thutmoses III," in *Faith, Tradition and History*. Winona Lake: Eisenbrauns.

Jacquet-Gordon, H. 1962. *Les Noms des Domaines Funeraires sous l'Ancien Empire Egyptien*. Cairo: Institut Francais d'Archeologie Orientale.

Janssen, J. J. 1978. "The Early State in Egypt." In *The Early State*, ed. H. J. M. Claessen and P. Skalnik. The Hague: Mouton.

Janssen, R., and J. Janssen. 1989. *Egyptian Household Animals*. Aylesbury, England: Shire.

Jeffreys, D. G. 1985. *The Survey of Memphis I*. London: The Egypt Exploration Fund.

ben-Jochannan, Y. B. 1972. *Cultural Genocide in the Black and African Studies Curriculum*. New York: ECA Associates.

Joffee, A. 1991. "Early Bronze I and the Evolution of Social Complexity in the Southern Levant." *Journal of Mediterranean Archaeology* 4(1):3–58.

Johnson, A. L., and N. C. Lovell. 1994. "Biological Differentiation at Predynastic Naqada, Egypt: An Analysis of Dental Morphological Traits." *American Journal of Physical Anthropology* 93:427–433.

Kaiser, W. 1964. "Einige Bermerkungen zur agyptische Fruhzeit." *Zeitschrift agyptische Sprache Altertumskunde* 91:86–125.

———. 1985. "Zur Sudausdehnung der vorgeschichtlichen Deltakulturen und zur fruhen Entwicklung Oberagyptens." *Mitteilungen des Deutschen Archaeologischen Instituts Abteilung Kairo* 41:61–87.

Kanawati, N. 1977. *The Egyptian Administration in the Old Kingdom: Evidence on Its Economic Decline*. London: Warminster, Aris & Phillips.

Kaster, J., trans. and ed. 1968. *Wings of the Falcon*. New York: Holt.

Kees, H. 1961. *Ancient Egypt: A Cultural Topography*. Chicago: University of Chicago Press.

Kemp, B. J. 1977. "The Early Development of Towns in Egypt." *Antiquity* 51:185–200.

———. 1982. "Old Kingdom, Middle Kingdom and Second Intermediate Period in Egypt." In *The Cambridge History of Africa*, Vol. 1, ed. J. D. Clark. Cambridge, England: Cambridge University Press.

———. 1993. *Ancient Egypt: Anatomy of a Civilization.* New York: Routledge.

Kitchen, K. A. 1989. "The Rise and Fall of Covenant, Law, and Treaty." TynBul 40.

———. 1995. "The Patriarchal Age-Myth or History?" BAR 21(2). *Biblical Archaeology Review* 21(2):48ff.

Kitto, H. D. F. 1951. *The Greeks.* Harmondsworth: Pelican.

Knapp, A. B. 1988. *The History and Culture of Ancient Western Asia and Egypt.* Chicago: Dorsey.

Kroeper, K. 1988. "The Excavations of the Munich East-Delta Expedition in Minshat Abu Omar." In *The Archaeology of the Nile Delta: Problems and Priorities*, ed. E. C. M. van den Brink. Amsterdam: Foundation for Archaeological Research in Egypt.

———. 1989. "Settlement in the Nile Delta to the End of the Old Kingdom." Doctoral dissertation. Warsaw: Uniwersytet Warszawski Wydzial Historcyczny.

———. 1990. "Tell Ibrahim Awad North-eastern Delta." *Bulletin de Liaison* 14:6–8.

Kroeper, K., and D. Wildung. 1985. *Minshat Abu Omar.* Munich: Staatliche Agyptischer Kunst.

Kromer, K. 1978. "Siedlungsfunde aus dem fruhen Alten Reich in Giseh." *Denkschriften, Oesterreichische Akademie der Wissenschaften, Philosophisch-historische Klasse* 136:1–130.

Krzyzaniak, L. 1977. *Early Farming Cultures on the Lower Nile: The Predynastic Period in Egypt.* Warsaw: Polish Academy of Sciences.

———. 1988. "Research on the Location of the Predynastic Settlement at Minshat Abu Omar." Paper presented at the Fifth International Congress of Egyptology, Cairo.

Krzyzaniak, L., and M. Kobusiewicz, eds. 1989. *Late Prehistory of the Nile Basin and Sahara.* Poznan: Poznan Archaeological Museum.

Lehner, M. 1983. "Some Observations on the Layout of the Khufu and Khafre Pyramids." *Journal of the American Research Center in Egypt* 20:7–29.

———. 1985. *The Pyramid Tomb of Hetep-heres and the Satellite Pyramid of Khufu.* Mainz am Rhein: Philipp von Zabern.

Leprohon, R. Personal communication.

Lovell, N. 1990. "Biosocial Consequences of the Development of Complex Societies in the Nile Valley and Delta." Proposal to the Social Sciences and Humanities Research Council of Canada. Manuscript on file with the author, Seattle, WA.

Lubell, D., P. Sheppard, and M. Jackes. 1984. "Continuity in the Epipaleolithic of Northern Africa with Emphasis on the Maghreb." *Advances in World Archaeology* 3:143–168.

Maisels, C. K. 1990. *The Emergence of Civilization.* London: Routledge Routledge & Kegan Paul.

Marshall, F., and E. Hildebrand. 2002. "Cattle Before Crops: The Beginnings of Food Production in Africa." *Journal of World Prehistory* 16(2):99–143.

McDonald, M. M. A. 1991. "Technological Organization and Sedentism in the Epipaleolithic of Dakhleh Oasis, Egypt." *African Archaeological Review* 9:81–109.

Midant-Reynes, B. 2003. *Aux origines de l'Égypte: du Néolithique à la emergence de l'État.* Fayard.

Millet, N. B. 1990. "The Narmer Macehead and Related Objects." *Journal of the American Research Center in Egypt* 27:53–59.

Mills, A. 1984. "Research in the Dakhleh Oasis." In *Origin and Early Development of Food-Producing Cultures in North-Eastern Africa*, ed. L. Krzyzaniak and M. Kobusiewicz. Poznan: Poznan Archaeological Museum.

Moens, M., and W. Wetterstrom. 1989. "The Agricultural Economy of an Old Kingdom Town in Egypt's West Delta: Insights from the Plant Remains." *Journal of Near Eastern Studies* 3:159–173.

Morenz, S. 1973. *Egyptian Religion.* Trans. A. E. Keep. Ithaca, NY: Cornell University Press.

O'Connor, D. 1982. "New Kingdom and Third Intermediate Period, 1552–664 B.C." In *Ancient Egypt. A Social History*, ed. B. G. Trigger, B. J. Kemp, D. O'Connor, and A. B. Lloyd. Cambridge, England: Cambridge University Press.

———. 1987. "The Old Kingdom Town at Buhen." Paper presented at the Annual Meeting of the American Research Center in Egypt.

———. 1989. "New Funerary Enclosures (*talbezirke*) of the Early Dynastic Period at Abydos." *Journal of the American Research Center in Egypt* 26:51–86.

———. 1991. "Boat Graves and Pyramid Origins: New Discoveries at Abydos, Egypt." *Expedition* 33(3):5–17.

O'Connor, D., and D. Silverman, eds. 1994. *Ancient Egyptian Kingship.* New York: E. J. Brill.

Oren, E. D. 1989. "Early Bronze Age Settlement in Northern Sinai: A Model for Egypto-Canaanite Interconnections." In *Proceedings of The Colloque d'Emmaus, British Archaeological Reports* (527I):389–405.

Patterson, T. C., and C. W. Gailey, eds. 1987. *Power Relations and State Formation.* Washington, DC: American Anthropological Association.

Paynter, R. 1989. "The Archaeology of Equality and Inequality." *Annual Review of Anthropology* 18:369–399.

Petrie, W. M. F. 1900. "The Royal Tombs of the First Dynasty, Part 1." *Egypt Exploration Fund Memoir* 18. London.

Porten, B., and A. Yardeni. 1993. *Textbook of Aramaic Documents from Ancient Egypt.* 2 Vols. Jerusalem: The Hebrew University; Winona Lake: Eisenbrauns.

Posener-Krieger, P. 1976. *Les Archives du Temple Funeraire de Neferirkare-kaki.* 2 Vols. Cairo: Institut Francais d'Archeologie Orientale du Caire.

Quirke, S. 1990. *The Administration of Egypt in the Late Middle Kingdom: The Hieratic Documents.* New Malden: Sia.

———. 1992. *Ancient Egyptian Religion.* London: British Museum Press.

Quirke, S., and J. Spencer, eds. 1992. *The British Museum Book of Ancient Egypt.* New York: Thames and Hudson.

Redding, R. W. 1992. "Egyptian Old Kingdom Patterns of Animal Use and the Value of Faunal Data in Modeling Socioeconomic Systems." *Paleorient* 18(2):99–107.

Redford, D. B. 1986. "Egypt and Western Asia in the Old Kingdom." *Journal of the American Research Center in Egypt* 23:125–143.

———. 1989. "Prolegomena to Archaeological Investigations of Mendes." Manuscript on file with Wenke, Seattle, WA.

———. 1992. *Egypt, Canaan, and Israel in Ancient Times.* Princeton, NJ: Princeton University Press.

Reeves, C. 1992. *Egyptian Medicine.* Buckinghamshire, England: Shire.

Reeves, N. 1990. *The Complete Tutankhamun.* New York: Thames and Hudson.

Reeves, N., and J. H. Taylor. 1992. *Howard Carter Before Tutankhamun.* London: British Museum Press.

Rice, M. 1990. *Egypt's Making: The Origins of Ancient Egypt.* London: Routledge & Kegan Paul.

Rindos, D. 1984. *The Origins of Agriculture.* New York: Academic Press.

Rizkana, I., and J. Seeher. 1984. "New Light on the Relation of Maadi to the Upper Egyptian Cultural Sequence." *Mitteilungen des Deutchen Archaologischen Instituts Abteilung Kairo* 40:237–252.

Saggs, H. W. 1991. *Civilization Before Greece and Rome.* New Haven: Yale University Press.

Seidlmayer, S. 1987. "Wirtschaftliche und gesellschaftliche Entwicklung im Ubergang vom Alten zum Mittleren Reich: Ein Beitrag zur Archaologie der Graberfelder der Region Qau-Matmar in der Ersten Zwischenzeit." In *Problems and Priorities in Egyptian Archaeology*, ed. J. Assman, G. Burkhard, and V. Davies. London: Routledge & Kegan Paul.

Service, E. 1975. *Origins of the State and Civilization.* New York: Norton.

Shafer, B. E., ed. 1991. *Religion in Ancient Egypt: Gods, Myths, and Personal Practice.* Ithaca, NY: Cornell University Press.

Shaw, I. 1991. *Egyptian Warfare and Weapons.* Aylesbury, England: Shire.

Sjoberg, G. 1960. *The Preindustrial City.* New York: The Free Press.

Smith, H. S., and D. G. Jeffreys. 1986. "A Survey of Memphis, Egypt." *Antiquity* LX:88–95.

Spencer, A. J. 1982. *Death in Ancient Egypt.* Harmondsworth: Penguin.

Strudwick, N. 1985. *The Administration of Egypt in the Old Kingdom: The Highest Titles and Their Holders.* London: KPI.

Tannahill, R. 1982. *Sex in History.* Briarcliff Manor, NY: Scarborough Books.

Teeter, E. 1993. Personal communication.

Trigger, B. G. 1979. "Egyptology and Anthropology." In *Egyptology and the Social Sciences*, ed. K. Weeks. Cairo: American University in Cairo Press.

———. 1982a. "The Rise of Civilization in Egypt." In *The Cambridge History of Africa*, Vol. 1, ed. J. D. Clark. Cambridge, England: Cambridge University Press.

———. 1982b. "Archaeological Analysis and Theories of Causality." *Culture* 2(2):31–42.

———. 1984. "The Mainlines of Socioeconomic Development in Dynastic Egypt to the End of the Old Kingdom." In *Origin and Early Development of Food-Producing Cultures in North-Eastern Africa*, ed. L. Krzyzaniak and M. Kobusiewicz. Poznan: Poznan Archaeological Museum.

———. 1985. "The Evolution of Pre-industrial Cities: A Multilinear Perspective." *Melanges offerts Jean Vercoutter.* Paris: Editions Recerce sur les Civilisations.

———. 1990. "Monumental Architecture: A Thermodynamic Explanation of Symbolic Behavior." *World Archaeology* 22:119–131.

Uphill, E. P. 1988. *Egyptian Towns and Cities.* Aylesbury, England: Shire.

Van den Brink, E., ed. 1988. *The Archaeology of the Nile Delta: Problems and Priorities.* Amsterdam: Amsterdam Foundation for Archaeological Research in Egypt.

Vinogradov, I. V. 1982. "The Predynastic Period and the Early and the Old Kingdoms in Egypt." In *Early Antiquity*, ed. I. M. Diakonoff. Chicago: University of Chicago Press.

Von der Way, T. 1987. "Tell el-Fara'in-Buto, 2 Bericht mit einem Beitrag von Klaus Schmidt zu den lithischen Kleinfunden." *Mitteilungen des Deutschen Archaologischen Instituts Abteilung Kairo* 3:241–250.

———. 1988. "Investigations Concerning the Early Periods in the Northern Delta of Egypt." In *The Archaeology of the Nile Delta: Problems and Priorities*, ed. E. C. M. van den Brink. Amsterdam: Netherlands Foundation for Archaeological Research in Egypt.

————. 1992. "Indications of Architecture with Niches at Buto." In *The Followers of Horus: Studies Dedicated to Michael Allen Hoffman*, ed. R. Friedman and B. Adams. Oxford: Oxbow.

Waldrop, M. M. 1992. *Complexity*. New York: Touchstone.

Wasylikowa, K., J. Mitka, F. Wendorf, and R. Schild. 1997. "Exploitation of Wild Plants by the Early Neolithic Hunter-Gatherers of the Western Desert, Egypt: Nabta Playa as a Case-Study." *Antiquity* 71:932–941.

Watson, R. A. 1990. "Ozymandias, King of Kings: Postprocessual Radical Archaeology as Critique." *American Antiquity* 55(4):673–489.

Wegner, J. 2000. "A Hundred Years at South Abydos: Reconstructing the Temple of Pharoah Senwosret III." *Expedition* 42(2):9–18.

Wendorf, F., R. Said, and R. Schild. 1980. *Prehistory of the Eastern Sahara*. New York: Academic Press.

Wendorf, F., R. Schild, and Associates. 2002. *Holocene Settlement of the Egyptian Sahara, Vol. 1: The Archaeology of Nabta Playa*. New Youk: Kluwer Academic/Plenum.

Wendorf, F., R. Schild, and A. Close. 1984. *Cattle-Keepers of the Eastern Sahara. The Neolithic of Bir Kiseiba*. New Delhi: Pauls Press.

————. 1989. *The Prehistory of Wadi Kubbaniya*, Vols. 2 and 3. Dallas: Southern Methodist University Press.

Wenke, R. J. 1981. "Explaining the Evolution of Cultural Complexity: A Review." In *Advances in Archaeological Method and Theory*, ed. M. B. Schiffer. New York: Academic Press.

————. 1986. "Old Kingdom Community Organization in the Western Egyptian Delta." *Norwegian Archaeological Review* 19(1):15–33.

————. 1989. "Egypt: Origins of Complex Societies." *Annual Review of Anthropology* 18:129–155.

————. 1991. "The Evolution of Early Egyptian Civilization: Issues and Evidence." *Journal of World Prehistory* 5(3):279–329.

Wenke, R. J., and D. J. Brewer. 1996. "The Archaic—Old Kingdom Delta: The Evidence from Mendes and Kom el-Hisn." *In House and Palace in Egypt*, ed. M. Bietak. Vienna: Austrian Archaeological Institute.

Wenke, R., J. Long, and P. Buck. 1988. "Epipaleolithic and Neolithic Settlement in the Fayyum Oasis of Egypt." *Journal of Field Archaeology* 15(1):29–51.

Wenke, R. J., R. Redding, P. Buck, H. A. Hamroush, M. Kobusiewicz, and K. Kroeper. 1988. "Kom el-Hisn: Excavations of an Old Kingdom West Delta Community." *Journal of the American Research Center in Egypt* xxv:5–34.

White, L. 1949. *The Science of Culture*. New York: Grove Press.

Wilson, H. n.d. *Egyptian Food and Drink*. Princes Risborough, England.

Wilson, J. A. 1946. "Egypt: The Nature of the Universe." In *Before Philosophy*, ed. H. A. Frankfort et al. Baltimore: Penguin.

————. 1951. *The Culture of Ancient Egypt*. Chicago: University of Chicago Press.

————. 1960. "Civilizations Without Cities." In *City Invincible*, ed. C. H. Kraeling and R. McC. Adams. Chicago: University of Chicago Press.

Wittfogel, K. A. 1957. *Oriental Despotism: A Comparative Study of Total Power*. New Haven: Yale University Press.

Wright, H. T. 1986. "The Evolution of Civilizations." In *American Archaeology, Past and Future*, ed. D. J. Meltzer, D. D. Fowler, and J. A. Sabloff. Washington, DC: Smithsonian Institution Press.

Yoffee, N. 1979. "The Decline and Rise of Mesopotamian Civilization: An Ethnoarchaeological Perspective on the Evolution of Social Complexity." *American Antiquity* 44:5–35.

Yoffee, N., and G. Cowgill, eds. 1988. *The Collapse of Ancient States and Empires*. Tucson: University of Arizona Press.

Younger, K. L. 1990. *Ancient Conquest Accounts: A Study in Ancient Near Eastern and Biblical History Writing*. JSOT Supp. 98. JSOT Press: Sheffield, England.

NOTES

1. The film *Mountains of the Moon* is an entertaining story of the search for the origins of the Nile.
2. *Lates niloticus*.
3. Brewer and Friedman, *Fish and Fishing in Ancient Egypt*, p. 74.
4. Butzer, "Long-Term Nile Flood Variation."
5. Numbers 11:4–6.
6. The archaeological argument for domestication of cattle was ecological. In the early Holocene, cattle bones are found at seasonal lake sites far out into the hyper-arid Sahara Desert. These sites are present because of wetter periods during the early Holocene that permitted human exploitation of areas away from the Nile Valley. The aridity of the desert, except for the seasonal lake areas, is thought to be a barrier to wild cattle being part of the local fauna; wild cattle are present, however, in the well-watered Nile Valley. Thus, the presence of cattle at these early Holocene desert sites is thought to be the result of people bringing these animals

to these locales (for example, see Wendorf et al., *Holocene Settlement of the Eastern Sahara, Vol. 1: The Archaeology of Nabta Playa*). Recently, studies of cattle DNA indicate that the archaeological interpretations of local domestication of cattle are likely correct (see Bradley et al., "Mitochondrial Diversity and the Origins of African and European Cattle"), and other scholars are increasingly accepting the local domestication of cattle in Africa (for example, Marshall and Hildebrand, "Cattle Before Crops: the Beginnings of Food Production in Africa").

7. Wendorf et al., *Cattle-Keepers of the Eastern Sahara. The Neolithic of Bir Kiseiba*; Wendorf et al., *The Prehistory of Wadi Kubbaniya*, Vols. 2 and 3; Close, *Prehistory of Arid North Africa: Essays in Honor of Fred Wendorf*; Lubell et al., "Continuity in the Epipaleolithic of Northern Africa with Emphasis on the Maghreb."

8. *Aristida, Eragrostis, Panicum,* and *Echinoclou.*

9. Wendorf, Schild, and Close, *Cattle-Keepers of the Eastern Sahara: The Neolithic of Bir Kiseiba*, p. 428.

10. Ibid., p. 425.

11. Wasylikowa et al., "Exploitation of Wild Plants by the Early Neolithic Hunter-Gatherers of the Western Desert, Egypt: Nabta Playa as a Case-Study."

12. Barich and Hassan, "A Stratified Sequence from Wadi el-Obeiyd, Farafra. New Data on Subsistence and Chronology of the Egyptian Western Desert," cited in Midant-Reyes, *Aux origines de l'Égypte: du Néolithique à l'émergence de l'État.*

13. Hassan, "Desert Environment and Origins of Agriculture in Egypt"; Hassan, "The Predynastic of Egypt."

14. Reviewed in Wenke et al., "Epipaleolithic and Neolithic Settlement in the Fayyum Oasis of Egypt."

15. Although it should be pointed out that early Neolithic farmers in the Levant also incorporated many wild plant foods and wild animals in their diet (chapter 8). This combination of wild and domesticated subsistence economies merely reflects the lengthy transition from reliance mainly on wild foods to reliance mainly on domesticated foods. The Fayyum case in Egypt may thus reflect this type of transition rather than a resistance to the spread of agricultural lifeways.

16. Hassan, "The Predynastic of Egypt." Also see Bard, *From Farmers to Pharaohs.*

17. Hoffman, *Egypt Before the Pharaohs*; Hoffman, *The Predynastic of Hierakonpolis—An Interim Report*; Hoffman et al., "A Model of Urban Development for the Hierakonpolis Region from Predynastic Through Old Kingdom Times."

18. Reviewed in Wenke, "The Evolution of Early Egyptian Civilization: Issues and Evidence."

19. von der Way, "Investigations Concerning the Early Periods in the Northern Delta of Egypt"; van den Brink, ed., *The Archaeology of the Nile Delta: Problems and Priorities.*

20. See van den Brink, ed., *The Archaeology of the Nile Delta: Problems and Priorities*; Wenke, "The Evolution of Early Egyptian Civilization: Issues and Evidence."

21. Hassan, "The Predynastic of Egypt."

22. Service, *Origins of the State and Civilization*, p. 228.

23. Butzer, *Early Hydraulic Civilization in Egypt.*

24. Trigger, "The Rise of Civilization in Egypt."

25. Wenke et al., "Kom el-Hisn: Excavations of an Old Kingdom West Delta Community."

26. Badawy, "The Civic Sense of the Pharaoh and Urban Development in Ancient Egypt," p. 105.

27. Lehner, "Some Observations on the Layout of the Khufu and Khafre Pyramids."

28. See Emily Dickinson's "There's a certain slant of light . . ." for a lovely meditation on this light and, of course, death.

29. Edwards, *The Pyramids of Egypt.*

30. O'Connor, "Boat Graves and Pyramid Origins: New Discoveries at Abydos, Egypt."

31. Ibid., p. 14.

32. Lehner, "Some Observations on the Layout of the Khufu and Khafre Pyramids."

33. Grimal, *A History of Ancient Egypt*, pp. 264–265.

34. Wilson, *The Culture of Ancient Egypt*, p. 79. See also Kemp, "Old Kingdom, Middle Kingdom and Second Intermediate Period c. 2686–1552 B.C."; Trigger, "Egyptology and Anthropology," pp. 32–50.

35. See O'Connor and Silverman, eds., *Ancient Egyptian Kingship.*

36. Ibid.; R. Leprohon, personal communication.

37. Kemp, "Old Kingdom, Middle Kingdom and Second Intermediate Period c. 2686–1552 B.C.," p. 108.

38. Trigger, "The Mainlines of Socioeconomic Development in Dynamic Egypt to the End of the Old Kingdom," p. 107. See also Kanawati, *The Egyptian Administration in the Old Kingdom. Evidence on Its Economic Decline*, pp. 69–77; Goedicke, *Konigliche Dokumente aus dem Alten Reich.*

39. Butzer, "Pleistocene History of the Nile Valley in Egypt and Lower Nubia," p. 278; Kemp, "Old Kingdom, Middle Kingdom and Second Intermediate Period c. 2686–1552 B.C.," p. 113.

40. Butzer, *Early Hydraulic Civilization in Egypt*, pp. 26–27.

41. Yoffee, "The Decline and Rise of Mesopotamian Civilization: An Ethnoarchaeological Perspective on the Evolution of Social Complexity"; Yoffee and Cowgill, *The Collapse of Ancient States and Empires.*

42. Strudwick, *The Administration of Egypt in the Old Kingdom: The Highest Titles and Their Holders.*

43. Ibid.
44. Aldred, *The Egyptians*, p. 102.
45. Kemp, "Old Kingdom, Middle Kingdom and Second Intermediate Period c. 2686–1552 B.C."
46. Quirke and Spencer, *The British Museum Book of Ancient Egypt*, p. 40.
47. O'Connor, "New Kingdom and Third Intermediate Period, 1552–664 B.C.," p. 190.
48. Ibid., pp. 194–195.
49. Ibid., p. 219.
50. Tannahill, *Sex in History*, pp. 77–78.
51. O'Connor, "New Kingdom and Third Intermediate Period, 1552–664 B.C.," p. 222.
52. The fascination with all things Egyptian is clearly seen in the many recent stories in the newspapers that have focused on the "mystery" of Tutankhamun's death at such an early age. Earlier surmises, based on pieces of skull bone found inside his brain case, suggested to some that Tutankhamun was murdered by a blow to the head. Recent CT scans, however, do not confirm this; these broken pieces of skull are due to mishandling of the mummy when it was discovered in the early 1960s. Tutankhamun does appear to have suffered a badly broken leg prior to his death, and some speculation suggests that he succumbed to an infection related to the break.
53. Carter's donkey was named San Toy, and reportedly would wander through the excavation camp until she found Carter and then "bray with delight." Reeves and Taylor, *Howard Carter Before Tutankhamun*, p. 60.
54. O'Connor, "New Kingdom and Third Intermediate Period, 1552–664 B.C.," p. 222.
55. This issue remains contentious. See Hess, *Amarna Personal Names*; Younger, *Ancient Conquest Accounts: A Study in Ancient Near Eastern and Biblical History Writing*; Kitchen, "The Rise and Fall of Covenant, Law, and Treaty"; Kitchen, "The Patriarchal Age-Myth or History?"; Hoffmeier, "The Structure of Joshua 1–11 and the Annals of Thutmoses III."
56. Wilson, "Egypt: The Nature of the Universe," p. 73.
57. Farooq, "Historical Development," p. 2.
58. Wilson, "Egypt: The Nature of the Universe," p. 72.
59. Ibid.
60. Quirke and Spencer, *The British Museum Book of Ancient Egypt*, p. 150.
61. Ibid., p. 129.
62. Saggs, *Civilization Before Greece and Rome*, pp. 73–74.
63. Ibid.
64. Translation by John Foster, *Love Songs of the New Kingdom*, pp. 58, 61.
65. See Frankfort, *The Birth of Civilization in the Near East*; Hamilton, *The Greek Way*; Kitto, *The Greeks*.
66. Wittfogel, *Oriental Despotism: A Comparative Study of Total Power*; Hoffman, *Egypt Before the Pharaohs: The Prehistoric Foundations of Egyptian Civilization*, p. 315.

The Evolution of Complex Societies in the Indus Valley

Enough has been said to show that India confronts Egypt and Babylonia in the third millennium [B.C.] with a thoroughly individual, and independent civilization of her own, technically the peer of the rest. And plainly it is deeply rooted in India soil.

V. Gordon Childe[1]

Ancient texts bring the people of the past to life much more vividly than do their bricks, bones, and pots, and thus it is particularly frustrating that the written language of the first great civilization of South Asia, the Harappan State (c. 2600–1900 B.C.) (Figure 10.1), continues to defy decipherment. Since the discovery of its archaeological remains early in the twentieth century, the Harappan civilization that flourished in the Indus Valley, in what is now Pakistan and India, in the third millennium B.C., has been unfairly considered a sort of poor relation to the great states and empires that graced the Mesopotamian alluvial plain and the Nile Valley. Not only did the Indus Valley cultures mature many centuries later than those in Egypt and Southwest Asia, they also neglected to leave much in the way of the pyramids, tombs, and palaces so prized by archaeologists. Nor was the Harappan a particularly long-lived civilization; its mature phase lasted only about five or six centuries[2] (Figure 10.2).[3] Perhaps the most important factor in the relative neglect of Harappan culture by scholars is that until its first great cities were discovered in the first half of the twentieth century (many by Sir John Marshall), no one had any idea of its existence. Scholars knew that Alexander the Great invaded the northwestern Indus Valley in 326 B.C., but they had no idea that 2,000 years earlier a great civilization had flourished and died in this area. As Gregory Possehl noted,[4] we "do not know what these people called themselves or their cities. . . . We have no king lists, no internal chronology . . . no historical account of commerce, production . . . no historical record of the internal social organization."

On the basis of its archaeological record, however, we know that the Harappan culture is yet another example of the appearance of a pre-industrial "state," whose major evolutionary dynamics now appear to have been primarily self-contained, with only minor

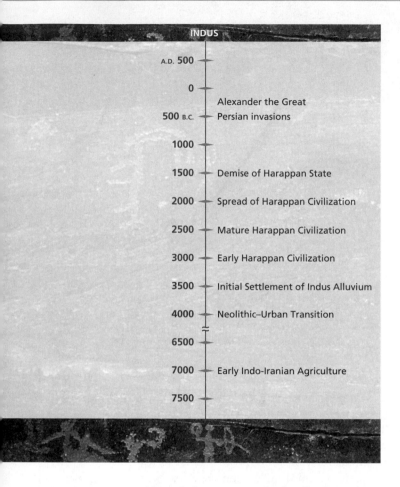

INDUS

A.D. 500

0

500 B.C. — Alexander the Great
— Persian invasions

1000

1500 — Demise of Harappan State

2000 — Spread of Harappan Civilization

2500 — Mature Harappan Civilization

3000 — Early Harappan Civilization

3500 — Initial Settlement of Indus Alluvium

4000 — Neolithic–Urban Transition

6500

7000 — Early Indo-Iranian Agriculture

7500

aspects that were the results of outside influences. In fact, the Indus Valley cultures are of great interest for the study of the origins of cultural complexity for several reasons: (1) Backed brick architecture, prototypes of the Indus square stamp seal, and town planning—characteristics that help define Mature Harappan civilization—may have appeared very rapidly beginning during a transitional phase between the Early and Mature Harappan stages, with a highly urbanized society developing out of a rather simple one in perhaps as little as 100–150 years[5]—although others dispute this view;[6] (2) they constructed massive cities with perhaps the most advanced sense of town planning and provision of city services (e.g., a municipal water and sewage system) in the ancient world until the advent of the Romans; (3) their area of cultural and political influence and control extended over almost 1.3 million km^2—considerably more territory than any other Old World civilization of this period; (4) Harappan culture over this large area appears very homogenous, compared to Mesopotamia; and (5) although there were undoubtedly elite rulers, and other social classes, Harappan civilization has left us very little in the way of archaeological materials that point to unequal distribution of wealth and resources—lacking are sumptuous burials and accompanying burial good wealth, numerous images of rulers and their exploits, and concentrations of palaces and large residential houses for the ruling elite within the cities.[7]

It is not an uncommon archaeological irony that the Indus civilization, so interesting in various ways, is one of the most archaeologically inaccessible. Some critical phases of its archaeological record are buried beneath meters of alluvium and beneath the water table. Along with the pleasures of sloshing through mud against a background whine of pumps, the archaeologist working on early complex societies in the Indus must be prepared for the collapse of huge walls of debris as he or she cuts down through the alluvium to the earliest levels. For this and other reasons, our knowledge of Harappan civilization is in some ways less than that of Egypt and Mesopotamia. One effect of this has been that interpretations of Harappan civilization have suffered the effects of "received wisdom": In the absence of adequate data, characterizations of Harappan civilizations made in the 1950s and before have been repeated and recycled long past the time they have been shown to be inaccurate. Thus, as Jim Shaffer notes, Stuart Piggot's characterization in 1950 of the Harappan

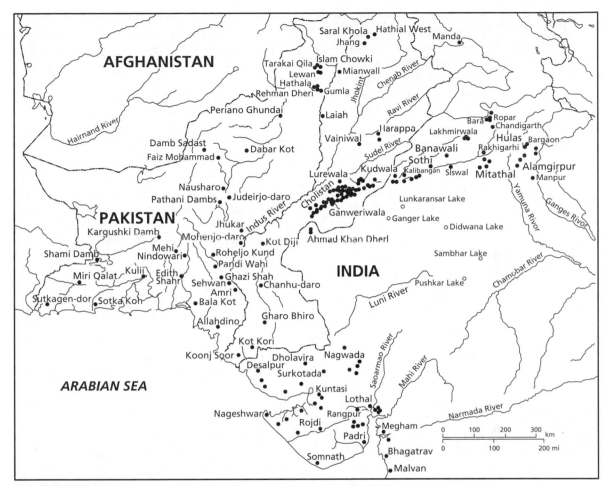

FIGURE 10.1   The heartland of the Harappan civilization is the Indus Valley.

civilization as rigidly stratified, centralized, and authoritarian has been "repeated in nearly every synthesis on the culture to date,"[8] despite evidence that challenges these characterizations.[9]

THE ECOLOGICAL SETTING

Aristobulus . . . says that when he was sent upon a certain mission [to Pakistan and India] he saw a country of more than a thousand cities, together with villages, that had been deserted because [a great river] had abandoned its proper bed.

Strabo (c. 63 B.C.–24 A.D.)[10]

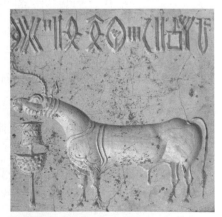

FIGURE 10.2   Harappan writing.

Millions of years ago, movements of the earth's crust forced the Indian subcontinent against the main Eurasian land mass with such pressure that the land in between was squeezed upward, creating the Himalayan Mountains. Every spring, melting snow in these mountains sends floods down the rivers that cross the lowlands to the sea. Of these rivers, the Indus and its floodplain form a large segment of the area between the borders of present-day Pakistan and India (see Figure 10.1). During the early Holocene, the large floodplains of this region apparently stabilized, when the development of soil occurred at a faster rate than *alluviation* (the process of sediment deposition by flowing water).[11]

So little rain falls on this plain during the average year that reliable agriculture is possible only through irrigation from the river, although geological work in the Lower Indus Valley suggests that—like Egypt—flood inundation may have been the main way that agricultural areas received their water.[12] The Indus civilizations, thus, are—like those in all other "pristine" cases except Mexico—the gift of large rivers. The stabilized floodplains that existed during the earlier part of the Holocene likely also contributed to the success of early settlements located here.

Indus Valley cultures are really the products of two rivers, the Indus and the Ghaggar-Hakra, which is now extinct. In ancient times these two rivers ran roughly parallel to each other, creating a vast alluvial plain with great potential for farming and herding. The Ghaggar-Hakra was the legendary Saraswati River mentioned in later Sanskrit texts—and it may have been the river that had supported the settlements that Aristobulus (quoted earlier) saw abandoned. According to the archaeologist M. Mughal,[13] the Ghaggar-Hakra supported many communities, including two cities that were as large as the two largest known Indus Valley cities, Mohenjo-daro and Harappa.

Compared to the Nile, the Indus River, and probably the Ghaggar-Hakra River as well, were relatively unpredictable, with great annual fluctuations in their volume and course. Frequently, the rivers flowed across the countryside in devastating floods. Centuries of this flooding have left the Indus floodplain a maze of old river channels and great deposits of silt, all smoothed down by the action of wind and water. The great fertility of these soils is complemented by the arid, hot climate, which, like that of Egypt and Mesopotamia, supports several crops a year and a great diversity of plant species.

Recent research on *avulsions*—natural changes—in the course of the Indus River has yielded important information about the placement of its ancient course(s). Louis Flam has identified three major courses, the earliest of which is the Jacobabad (Early Holocene), followed by the Sindhu Nadi (Middle Holocene), and the Kandhkot (Late Holocene).[14] At the time of the Early and Mature Harappan stages, the Sindhu Nadi Course was the path of the Indus River, and it ran considerably to the west of the modern course. Flam suggests that the placement of Harappan sites can be understood in part by examining their distance from the Sindh Nadi Course—for example, Mohenjo-daro is some 25 km to the southeast and thus outside the area of the worst of the unpredictable annual flooding of the floodplain. The shift of the Sindhu Nadi Course to the east toward the end of the third millennium B.C.—about the same time that Mohenjo-daro declined—may have subjected this city to annual flood ravages that persuaded people to relocate elsewhere.[15]

Because the Indus River is navigable over much of its length, ships could sail between Harappan cities with goods and, presumably, transport the bureaucrats sent by the central government to collect taxes and administer the provinces.

Like those of ancient Mesopotamia, the ancient cultures and polities of the Indus Valley must be seen as the products of a wide sphere of long-term cultural interactions of people far beyond the river plain itself. To the west of the hot Indus plains the arid foothills and mountains of Pakistan, Afghanistan, and Iran sharply limit the extension of agriculture, but they also provide valuable minerals, metals, animal products, and other goods and are the homelands of pastoral and nomadic peoples who exerted great influence on lowland civilizations. Because the Himalayas to the north posed a formidable barrier to transport, the diffusion of new ideas, objects, and peoples into and out of the Indus Valley was mainly along routes through these western borderlands, or along the thin coastal strip on the Arabian Sea. The Great Indian Desert to the east of the Indus Valley reduced contacts with the rest of the subcontinent. As a result, the Indus Valley was, like Egypt and Peru, an area of rich agricultural lands sharply bounded by highlands, desert, and ocean.

THE NEOLITHIC BACKGROUND TO SOUTH ASIAN CULTURAL COMPLEXITY (C. 7000–4300 B.C.)

One of the primary archaeological discoveries of the past decade in South Asia is that the village farming way of life, which was once thought to have been a rather recent development in this area, actually has deep and extensive roots.[16] The ancestors of the people who built the Indus civilizations spent thousands of years as small-time farmers and herders in the highlands above the Indus; most of the plain was perhaps only lightly occupied during these centuries. Domesticated wheat and the remains of domesticated sheep and goats have been found in levels dating to about 7000 B.C. in several sites in Afghanistan and Baluchistan, and the evidence suggests that thereafter the agricultural and pastoral ways of life spread gradually, from west to east, throughout highland areas where rainfall and streams provided sufficient water.

The Neolithic background to Harappan civilization has been clarified by recent work at several sites, including Kili Ghul Mohammad in the Quetta Valley, Baluchistan; Ghar-i-Mar and Aq Kupruk II in Afghanistan; and especially at Mehrgarh, on the Kachi Plain, in Pakistan.

Mehrgarh was first occupied shortly after 7000 B.C. by people who lived in simple, multi-roomed mudbrick buildings and seem to have subsisted on a blend of cereal farming and hunting (Figure 10.3). This community is the first known example in the Indus area of the basic domesticated plants, animals, agricultural technologies, and the village form of community organization, all appearing together as a functioning entity—a form of economy and society that would be the basic building block of all the civilizations that followed in this part of Asia. Around the world, pottery is usually found at locales where economies were based on domesticated cereals since pottery is so useful in making the soups, stews, and porridges (and beer) that take maximum advantage of cereals. But like the earliest Neolithic peoples of Southwest Asia, the people of early Mehrgarh did not use pottery to store their domesticated wheat and barley. Archaeologists have found

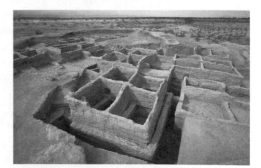

FIGURE 10.3 Possible mudbrick storage structures from Mehrgarh, Pakistan.

ovens in these buildings, so the people of Mehrgarh may have used these cereals for making bread. They also hunted extensively. Most of the bones from the earliest levels of Mehrgarh are from gazelle, deer, antelope, wild water buffalo, wild sheep and goat, wild cattle, wild pig, and even elephant.

Soon after about 5500 B.C., however, the people of Mehrgarh had begun to specialize mainly on sheep, goat, and cattle, which Richard Meadow, a faunal analyst, thinks is an indication that these animals were being kept and in the process of domestication. He notes that some evidence from Mehrgarh indicates that they were using domesticated hump-backed cattle ("zebu"), and he suggests that the keeping and herding of zebu (*Bos indicus*) appeared on the eastern margins of the Middle East as early as non-humped cattle (*Box taurus*) were kept and herded the western areas of the Middle East.[17] Moreover, beginning at about 5500 B.C. the people of Mehrgarh began to use a crude but serviceable kind of pottery. They also used copper tools and imported turquoise and lapis lazuli from Iran and Afghanistan and marine shell from the Arabian Gulf area—and they used some of these exotic items in the form of beads to decorate the corpses of their deceased.

As the farming way of life spread over South Asia, people seem to have domesticated other animals, such as the pig, water buffalo, and the distinctive hump-backed cattle still found all over this area.[18] And like their neighbors in Southwest Asia, they complemented wheat and barley with many other crops, including peas, lentils, and other legumes, which people all over the world discovered could provide the vegetable proteins so often needed in the uncertain circumstances of primitive agriculture.

Like other early agriculturalists around the world, the early farming peoples of southern Asia solved the problem of clothing by domesticating a plant for fiber, specifically, cotton. Just as linen and wool were the staple textiles in Egypt and Mesopotamia, respectively, cotton became the primary source of cloth for South Asia—as it did in Peru and elsewhere. Textiles are by no means the invention only of agriculturalists, however: Various hunter-foragers around the world wove natural plant fibers into clothing. The growing populations of early farming cultures, however, and the need for seasonally adaptable and cheap clothing seems to have resulted in the domestication of a plant that could be grown intensively and easily converted to textiles. Cotton was probably domesticated in several areas of southern Asia between about 7000 and 5000 B.C., but the evidence of precisely when and where this occurred is unclear.

As humble as these beginnings of South Asian civilization might seem, they clearly involve the same elements that we have already seen in Egypt and Mesopotamia. By about 7000 B.C. people from all over this area, though just a few thousand years removed from their hunter-forager ancestors, were experimenting with various economic strategies. Within a few thousand years these people had achieved a reliable, productive blend of economic activities that particularly suited their circumstances. They all solved the same basic problems of living. They found that cattle, pigs, sheep, and goats were a particularly productive mix of large domesticated animals, that wheat and barley could form the core of their food-production, that ceramic containers were ideal food-processing and storage vessels, that textiles could be made from a diversity of plants and animals, and that mudbrick buildings and permanent villages made effective residences.

All of these developments may seem natural, almost inevitable, but they were not. We should not imagine that these people—from North Africa to India —fine-tuned their economies from generation to generation until they all converged on essentially the same solutions to these problems of living. People experimented with various aspects of these economies to solve personal needs, and some solutions proved better than others. The process for making durable pottery, for example, may well have been independently "invented" scores, perhaps hundreds, of times in South and West Asia and North Africa. Textile production, too, was probably independently "invented" many times.

One gets the sense that necessity really was the mother of invention in many of these developments. Pottery's uses are probably most obvious. Primitive farmers in general had to find a way to water their plants effectively, store the grain, boil it, and serve it, and although animal skins, wooden bowls, and other containers can meet some of these uses, only pottery is cheap, durable, available everywhere, and reasonably effective at meeting all these needs. Textiles, too, offer obvious advantages over animal skins and other possible sources for clothing, bags, ropes, nets, and so forth. To make clothing out of animal skins, which we have reason to believe were the primary source of clothing for almost all hunter-foragers, one must truly "cut one's coat to fit one's cloth," as the old maxim has it. But cotton, linen, or wool textiles can be mass-produced in variable sizes and textures in relatively cheap and reliable fashion, as opposed to the exigencies of antelope or tiger hunting. Moreover, although people could certainly have worn clothing of leather and other forms of animal skin in the hot river valleys of the Nile, the Indus, the Tigris-Euphrates, and elsewhere in the area, life must have been much more comfortable in the linens, cottons, and thin wools that these people eventually wore.

THE NEOLITHIC–URBAN TRANSITION (C. 4300–3200 B.C.)

Harappan civilization, like those of the Nile Valley and Mesopotamia, seems so much a creation of its specific environment that it is easy to lose sight of the wider ecological and cultural contexts in which it was set. Harappan civilization, in particular, can be seen as a direct product of the village farming tradition that spread all over the uplands of Iran, Afghanistan, and Pakistan after 5000 B.C.[19]

At this time, many settlements in the highlands west of the Indus were probably based on simple wheat farming supplemented by sheep- and goat-raising and some hunting and gathering. These farmers made pottery and used a few copper tools, but the sites of some villages are so insubstantial that they suggest a relatively mobile population and perhaps only seasonal occupation.[20] Slowly, however, these villages grew and farming became the way of life over an ever-larger area. To the south and east, too, Neolithic cultures were forming. Rice may well have been cultivated on the Ganges Plain by 4500 B.C.; indeed, all over South Asia at this time people made intensive use of many cereals, although most of these never became staples like wheat and rice.[21] In a sense, it is as if all of these farming traditions coalesced on the Indus floodplain. Boosted by the great agricultural productivity of this area and its easy riverine transport, these village-farming adaptations were subsequently transformed into an urban civilization.

Like the origins of farming itself, the cultural transformation of a simple agricultural society into a state might appear in retrospect to be an automatic and inevitable outcome of a favorable mix of agricultural economies and particularly productive conditions for farming, but this is not the case. The Indus Valley civilizations seem another classic demonstration of the discontinuous nature of cultural evolution. Rather than a smooth building process wherein Neolithic villages added the components of civilization trait by trait, we see in the Indus area the same pattern evident in Mesopotamia, where initial moves toward complexity stalled and disappeared, while areas that were once on the periphery became the core developmental regions.

As Kenoyer notes,[22] early interpretations of Indus civilizations were that these people derived from a single ethnic group, but the evidence suggests that the Indus civilizations —like those of Mesopotamia—were built of mosaics of ethnic groups, languages, and adaptations.

Harappan civilization was much like Mesopotamia in its pattern of core-periphery relationships, and very much unlike Egypt, for example. Egypt was sheltered by poor harbors on the north, steep rapids in the south, and large and largely unpopulated deserts on the east and west; thus, the idea of a "core" and a "periphery" is not really applicable, except in the sense of the differences between the central government and provincial authorities and towns. In Mesopotamia, in contrast, hundreds of distinctive cultures and economies flourished in the area from Anatolia to highland Iran and the Persian Gulf, although states centered in Mesopotamia repeatedly dominated these other cultures.[23]

Daniel Miller sees a similar pattern of core-periphery relationships between the edge of the highlands bordering the Indus Plain and the plain itself. He notes that by 4000 B.C. communities all over what is now Pakistan traded in marine shells, lapis lazuli, and other goods; had a degree of overall planning evident in the architecture; and produced pottery in regional styles that may reflect competitive political entities.[24]

Unfortunately, the first critical steps toward complexity, in the form of growing differences in the size and socioeconomic and political power of some communities, are difficult to document with settlement pattern data[25] and other evidence. [26]

Miller observes that several regions on the Indus Plain and in eastern Iran at this time were "moving toward a greater degree of social complexity and urbanization,"[27] although eventually the Indus Plain became the developmental center. And although some of the mature Harappan civilization can be found in these developments of the fifth and fourth millennia B.C., the cultural changes that occurred as part of the Harappan civilization after about 2600 B.C. seem to have an indigenous and in some ways revolutionary character.[28]

EARLY HARAPPAN CULTURE (C. 3200–2500 B.C.)

As Possehl has noted,[29] the emergence of Harappan civilization seems to have involved great continuity over thousands of years in such things as the production and use of items for basic subsistence, local trade, and personal decoration (such as chert knives, clay female figurines, and copper rings), but also considerable discontinuity in cultural trends: These discontinuities appear most pronounced in such things as degree of urbanism, social stratification, and occupational specialization.

These discontinuities—relatively abrupt changes in core aspects of these societies between about 3200 and 2600 B.C.—have been archaeologically exposed at only a few sites (e.g., Amri, Nausharo, and Harappa), but there are many other sites that date to this period. Possehl[30] lists 463 sites of this period and notes that they do not seem to vary greatly in size (and therefore, by inference, in population). Most are about 5 hectares in area, although there are a few much larger communities in the 22- to 30-hectare range. As we noted in chapter 8, one of the things archaeologists look at to infer changes in the sociopolitical nature of a society is the degree of diversity in the population size of the communities in a particular polity. States tend to have a wide range of communities of different sizes, ranging from large cities to many tiny villages. But communities in areas that are not politically and economically integrated and administered tend to be about the same size.

There may have been only two general size groups, big cities and smaller towns and villages,[31] but overall, the population in the region appears to have more than tripled between about 3200 and 2600 B.C. In addition, more remote areas, such as the Kuli complex in Baluchistan, were brought into the Harappan cultural sphere. Between 3000 and 2400 B.C., settlements appeared at Kot Diji, Harappa, Kalibangan, and elsewhere, perhaps founded by people moving in from the western highlands. The few excavated settlements of this period reveal simple mudbrick houses in small villages scattered in areas where no extensive irrigation would have been necessary. Some villages were walled, though there was certainly no shortage of land or pressure on other resources at this time. These various lowland settlements prior to 2600 B.C. show some stylistic uniformity and a great deal of economic and architectural similarity, but they appear to have been economically and politically independent and self-sufficient and reflect none of the rigid planning typical of later settlements here.

When we look at the changes in the composition of these communities during this same period of settlement pattern changes (i.e., between 3200 B.C. and 2600 B.C.), we see some interesting developments. As noted in chapter 7, in every one of the world's early civilizations there was a gradual elaboration of "public," often monumental, architecture, in the form of pyramids, forts, temples, plazas, warehouses, municipal waterworks, and so on. Given this, it is not surprising that until about 2600 B.C. few of the communities found in the Harappan area have much evident public architecture. A few possible defensive walls at Kot Diji and a few other sites have been found, but as Possehl notes, only 3 of the 463 known pre-urban sites of this formative period have walls around the community. Nor is there much evidence of social stratification, as would be indicated by elaborate tombs, expensively constructed residences, and so forth. But after 2600 B.C. the major Harappan cities are marked by large buildings, such as "citadels" and "warehouses," and by differences in residential structures that probably correlate with wealth and status.

If we look for factors in the evolution of Harappan civilization, we find the usual correlates of early civilizations: an ecological setting that permitted relatively high agricultural productivity with simple technology; a riverine system that facilitated transport and command/control mechanisms; and a highly varied mix of cultures and natural resources concentrated in a relatively small area by natural terrain features. But the Harappan civilization may be one of the few cases where foreign trade was a powerful stimulus to the development of this culture and many of its forms. Harappan communities extracted minerals, metals, animal products, and many other commodities from the surrounding foothills and mountains and circulated these not only through local and regional trade, but also with Mesopotamian states via the sea lanes of the Persian Gulf (Figure 10.4). The cities of Harappa, Mohenjo-daro, and Lothal, for example, seem to be evenly spaced and optimally placed to exploit specific resources found in the areas around them; they may have been "central places" (see chapter 7) in a commercial network of

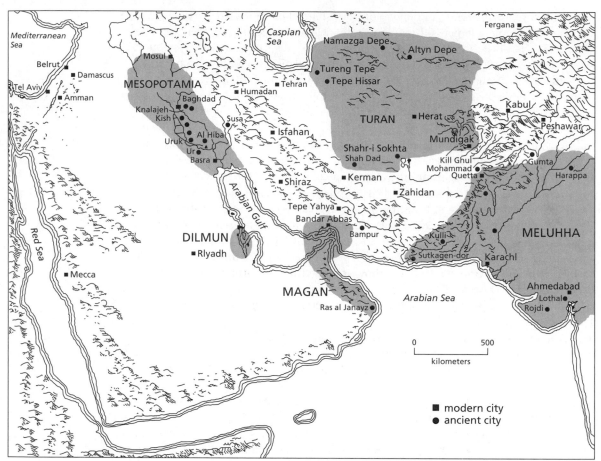

FIGURE 10.4 The Indus Valley region maintained trade contacts over a wide area of Middle Asia.

integrated local, regional, and foreign trade.[32] Mesopotamian texts suggest that states in this area regularly received commodities from far to the east, as well as from Magan and Meluhha, two ports whose location is not certain but which may have been in the Indus Valley. Gold, silver, copper, carnelian, lapis lazuli, ivory, oils, and many other commodities probably flowed west from the Indus to Mesopotamian towns, most of which were located far from natural sources of these exotic goods. But the Mesopotamians could reciprocate with cereals, leather, wool, and other products of their prolific agricultural system. The details of such trading patterns are poorly preserved in the archaeological record because the foodstuffs would have been consumed, leaving no traces (not even pollen), while the exotics, such as gold and precious stones, were fungible wealth: They could exchange hands hundreds of times and be converted to many different kinds of wealth, obscuring their original point of production and entry into the initial exchange network.

In the contemporary world there are great "economies of scale" and other advantages to international trade that are directly economic in impact. If individual nations concentrate on what they do best economically and exchange products in an integrated network, great advantages accrue to all—at least according to classical economic theory. Modern Japan and Singapore have few resources, but they have concentrated on highly efficient production of goods for export. In today's world, oil from the Persian Gulf, fruit from Central America, metals from Africa, financial services from the United Kingdom, and tens of thousands of other goods and services lock most of the world's people into inter-dependent economies that offer at least some benefits to all, despite the exploitative labor they stimulate and the destruction of rain forests and other environments that they cause directly.

But trade in the ancient world was not entirely the same thing. If the only transport available is pack animals and primitive sailing ships, there is little advantage to shipping dates from the Indus Valley to the Tigris-Euphrates Valley. Nor does it make much sense to move pottery from Egyptian kilns to Mohenjo-daro. The pattern of trade we infer between Harappan and Mesopotamian civilizations included some useful functional items, but much was in the form of exotics such as gold, whose most direct use was in reinforcing and elaborating the social distinctions between elites and commoners. One cannot consider these exotics to be functionally worthless on this account, however, because class-stratification seems to have been a basic functional element in constructing the competitive expansionist societies that all early states were.

Trade may have been an important stimulus to the rise of Harappan civilization, but Harappan civilization seems to have "taken off" at a time when there is some evidence (in the form of burned buildings) of regional warfare.[33]

MATURE HARAPPAN CIVILIZATION (C. 2500–1900 B.C.)

The appearance of large cities shortly after 2600 B.C., and the associated spread of a distinctive constellation of artifacts and architectural styles over much of the Indus Valley, marked the emergence of Harappan civilization. This system survived only about 600 years, but managed to integrate much of the Indus Plain in a cultural unit.

In the Indus area the sites that date to the Mature Harappan period (after about 2600 B.C.) include three relatively huge communities (c. 80–85 hectares). These cities—Mohenjo-daro, Harappa, and Ganwariwala—are evenly spaced, as we would expect on the basis of locational theory of state-level settlement patterns (see chapter 7), but there are also clusters of sites in other size categories. Whether or not these corresponded to the traditional sense of terms like *capital, regional capital, provincial center, town, village, hamlet,* and so on is unclear. More than 800 Mature Harappan sites are known, and these are spread over an area that at 1.25 million km^2 is larger than the first Egyptian state and the total area of Sumer, Akkad, and Assyria.[34]

Miller notes that Harappan civilization is not really a strictly riverine civilization, for Harappan settlements are found in many ecological zones, and only after the main Harappan developments were well underway did settlements begin to cluster along the river. Most research on Indus sites has been devoted to the largest settlements, especially Mohenjo-daro, Harappa, Chanhu-daro, Pathiani Kot, Judeirjo-daro, Kalibangan, and Lothal. Doubtless many smaller Harappan settlements are buried beneath silt or have been washed away by floods.

The largest Harappan settlement, Mohenjo-daro (Figure 10.5), covers at least 2.5 km² and may have had 40,000 inhabitants. M. Jansen has argued that Mohenjo-daro was not so regularly constructed as archaeologists once thought, and that only the central "platform mound" area (about 100 hectares)[35] of the city was planned—although there were many more hectares of suburban unplanned residential areas around the main city center. Compared to the jumbled anarchy of most Mesopotamian city plans, however, Mohenjo-daro was quite orderly.[36] M. A. Fentress has questioned the overall similarity of Mohenjo-daro and Harappa, but here too, by Mesopotamian standards, these settlements are quite similar.[37] Miller, in fact, notes that even tiny Harappan hamlets seemed to try to emulate the grid pattern and other designs of the major Harappan metropolises.[38]

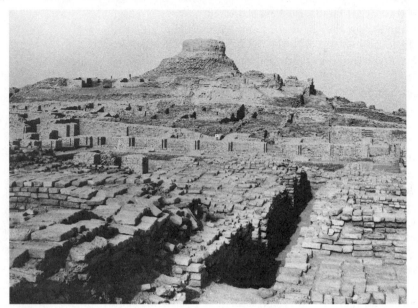

FIGURE 10.5 Some elements of the "Citadel" at Mohenjo-daro are evident in this photograph (the large circular Buddhist shrine in the background was built many centuries after Mohenjo-daro was abandoned).

Mohenjo-daro was bisected by a north-south street some 9 m wide that was flanked by drainage ditches. Public toilets and sewers and bathrooms in houses were connected to the main sewage lines. Most residences were made of fired brick, comprising several rooms arranged around an open courtyard, and the majority appear to have had private showers and toilets drained by municipal sewage systems. Some houses were two stories high and larger and more elaborate than others, but the overall impression is one of uniformity. In fact, A. Sarcina found that almost all houses at Mohenjo-daro were of two basic patterns: those having a courtyard at one corner that was flanked by rooms on two sides, or those with a courtyard in the center and rooms on three sides.[39] Also, almost all the houses were of the same approximate size and construction: 77 percent of the buildings seem to have been ordinary houses, while the rest were small shops and businesses distributed throughout the living areas.[40] If gross differences in wealth divided the inhabitants, these inequities are not reflected in residential architecture, at least not to the extent that they were in Mesopotamia.

At Mohenjo-daro and some other large sites, such as Harappa, the carefully arranged residential areas were flanked on the west by a large raised mound with a wall around it. This mound (sometimes called a *citadel* or *Mound of the Great Bath*) is about 150 m to the north of the area of settlement known as the *Lower Town*. These residential areas appear to have been adjacent to areas that were devoid of any settlement and perhaps were regularly flooded by a branch of the river. It has even been suggested that this flooding may have been deliberate, to create a pool of water for bathing, fishing, or some other activity.

One of the most interesting structures on the high mound itself is the *Great Bath*, a swimming-pool-like building about 12-by-7 m and 2.5 m in depth with a sunken enclosure, constructed of baked brick and lined with bitumen. Flanking the pool are what appear to have been dressing rooms, carefully staggered to give maximum privacy.[41] The Great Bath may have figured in some religious activities, but it contained no obvious icons or other religious elements and may have been mainly just a public bathing facility.

Adjacent to the bath are various mudbrick platforms and rooms, variously—and imaginatively—interpreted as granaries, assembly halls, and garrisons, but there is little evidence with which to infer their functions. Overall, the Mound of the Great Bath was about 450 m long and 90 m wide at its maximum extent—representing a major investment of labor and materials. Thus, while there is nothing at Mohenjo-daro or any other Indus city to compare with the Egyptian pyramids or the White Temple at Uruk, the Indus city-dwellers nonetheless diverted considerable energy and resources to building projects. The major difference seems to have been that, in contrast to the largely ceremonial public architecture in Mesopotamia and Egypt, the Indus Valley constructions provided some return in the way of administrative buildings, better defenses, and more storage space.

There is at least a possibility that Harappan civilization was "cut off" in the midst of its development by invasion, flood, interrupted trade routes, or some other factor, and that more "wasteful" monumental architecture might eventually have appeared in the Indus cities had they been allowed to develop for a longer period. The absence of easily accessible building stone may also account for the comparatively utilitarian and drab Harappan monumental architecture—although such limitations did not hamper Mesopotamian monumental building efforts (see chapter 8).

The thousands of people who lived at Mohenjo-daro included many craftsmen, such as goldsmiths, potters, weavers, brick masons, architects, and many other specialists, and streets were lined with stores and shops. Cereals—particularly barley, but also wheat—were the basis of the economy, supplemented by dates, melons, sesame, peas, mustard, and other crops. Cattle, sheep, goats, pigs, and domestic fowl were the major animal foods, and buffaloes, camels, asses, dogs, and cats were also kept. A few elephant bones have even been found. The horse apparently was rarely used until the very end of the Harappan period.

Most of the larger Harappan settlements were similar to Mohenjo-daro in architecture and economy, but the site of Lothal, although only about 250–300 m in size, shows an impressive complexity for a relatively small settlement[42] (Figure 10.6). A large tank, which the excavator, S. R. Rao, and others have interpreted as a dock,[43] may not be[44]—its function is unclear. There was a factory for making beads from carnelian, crystal, jasper, and other stones and facilities for making ornaments out of bronze, elephant tusks, and many other commodities. Possehl sees in Lothal's precise layout and concentrations of exotic commodities an entrepôt, a frontier settlement of entrepreneurs who were processing raw materials from the hinterlands and sending products on to the great Harappan cities. He also notes that Harappan urbanites and hunter-gatherers probably not only coexisted, they were likely continually trading products, with such things as copper knives, pottery, and steatite beads from Harappan communities, while hunter-gatherers supplied stone, meat, beeswax, wood, charcoal, string, rope, reeds, and so on.[45]

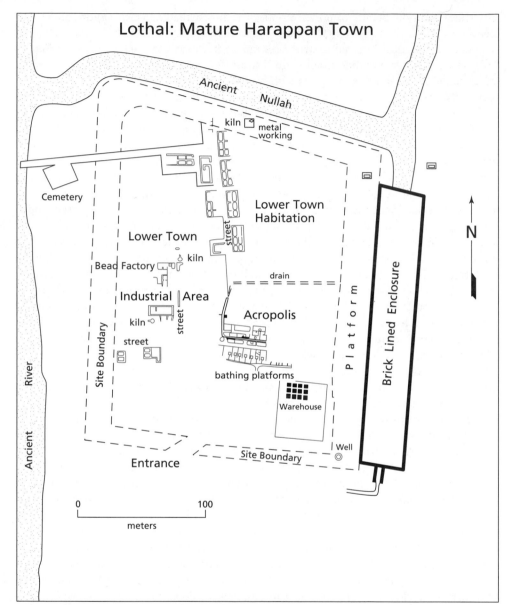

FIGURE 10.6   A plan map of the settlement at Lothal, India.

We know little about the smaller Harappan settlements. The few that have been examined seem to have brick walls around a district within the site, perhaps in imitation of the citadels at the larger cities, and the basic arts and crafts and subsistence practices also appear to have been patterned after those of the larger cities.

Relatively few Harappan cemeteries have been found, but the bodies so far excavated were buried with far fewer evidences of social differentiation than in Mesopotamia and Egypt.[46]

Harappan settlements, with their precisely administered character, would seem to be excellent subjects for the systematic analysis of settlement patterns. Such an analysis might help archaeologists discern the economic and political forces that dictated where people lived, but generally, archaeologists have not competed with each other for a chance to do systematic surveys on the intensely hot, heavily populated Indus Plain.

Scholars have debated whether Harappan civilization was a *chiefdom*, *state*, or *empire*. As is discussed at length in chapter 7, such debates are usually unresolvable because few people agree on what these political types are, and what kinds of archaeological evidence reflect them. What we do know of Indus settlement patterns suggests at least four different size categories (see chapter 7), comparable to, for example, those of Mesopotamia in the third millennium B.C. If we consider three or more administrative levels to be evidence of state-level political organization, then the Harappan civilization was certainly a state.

If we discard political typologies and concentrate on things we can measure archaeologically, such as the size of the area over which we find similar artifact styles, or differences in the sizes of communities that existed at the same time, or the existence of a script, or a standardized system of weights and measures, and so forth, the evidence from Harappa civilization might be best interpreted within the context of the rise of urbanism or perhaps as a reflection of the power of ideology.[47] In fact, the Harappan population at the beginning of the second millennium B.C. probably totaled at least 200,000 people, and the tightly organized fabric of their lives suggests perhaps an empire-like political system, but we may never know how complex the socioeconomic and political institutions of this culture were.

The Indus Script and Weights and Measures

The similarity of Harappan cities, towns, and villages probably reflects a nation in which various settlements were in regular and diverse communication with each other. Clay and metal models of wheeled carts and river boats are the only artifacts remaining of a transportation system that once probably moved large quantities of flint tools, pots, and other artifacts, some mass-produced at a few locations. The considerable degree of occupational specialization evident in these artifacts suggests intensive local trade, but there is a strong possibility that this was a kind of administered, noncapitalistic redistribution, rather than a free-enterprise or peasant marketing system. One possible key to the Harappan economic system is the hundreds of Harappan stamps and seals (Figure 10.7) that have been found; these may have been used to denote ownership or make records of transactions. The apparently ritual scenes depicted in so many of these might argue against this interpretation, but the question will remain unresolved as long as the Harappan script is undeciphered.

Much of Harappan writing is in the form of inscriptions on these stamp seals. Many other documents could have been written on palm leaves or some other long-since decayed medium. The estimated number of unique symbols is between 350 and 425, which means that the writing is almost certainly not alphabetic: Alphabetic languages use one symbol for each unique sound in the spoken language, and no known language has more than about 50 alphabetic characters. Since the Indus script contains about 400 unique characters, it is probably made up of symbols indicating syllables in the spoken language, plus some determinatives and other marks to aid interpretation.

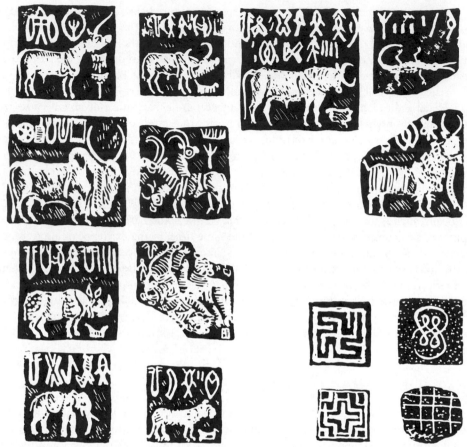

FIGURE 10.7 Harappan seals were inscribed with many different symbols in complex arrangements, suggesting a form of written language, but this language has not yet been deciphered.

Parpola[48] used a computer analysis to try to find a language that fit the apparent structure of the Indus script, but he concluded that it is not related to any known writing system. One of the Indus languages may have been Dravidian, from southern India, but no links have been conclusively demonstrated. Various scholars have suggested that the ancient Indus language was part of a group that extended from the Elamite-speakers of Iran into northern India, and that the Indus script represents this language family—not Dravidian itself.

If other early scripts are any guide, the majority of these Indus documents and those that presumably have been lost may have had to do with such mundane matters as Farmer A selling 18 cows to Farmer B and paying the appropriate taxes; others may include a ritual prayer or blessing on the ruler, followed by some record of events and transactions of ordinary daily life. Computers now hum away, trying to find patterns of co-occurrence among the 400 Indus symbols, and some day we may have a clear sense of what they mean.

But the texts are so few and the characters so stylized that it will not be easy to decipher them.

The most common form[49] of Indus writing was on intaglio seals (i.e., an engraving on stone or some other hard material so that when clay or some soft material is impressed with it the engraved elements appear in shallow relief). Impressions of seals have been found on pottery, lumps of wet clay, and other materials. The script also appears as graffiti, scratched or painted on clay surfaces. Examination of these reveals that the script was often written from right to left, and from top to bottom, but in some longer inscriptions the lines are *boustrophedonic*, meaning that the lines alternated (i.e., first line from right to left, second line from left to right, and so on). Most inscriptions are short, containing just five or six signs—far fewer elements than most Egyptian or Mesopotamia documents.

Archaeologists have tried to correlate the locations where these seals were found with some notions of their use, but they seem to be distributed throughout the communities in which they were used. George Dales and Mark Kenoyer[50] have recently suggested that the spatial distribution of the seals may suggest that the people who used them were restricted to certain areas, such as along main streets and access routes.

Unlike Mesopotamian writing, there is no evidence that Harappan writing evolved out of the gradual elaboration of a simpler system. This writing seems to have appeared rapidly and in full form—something like the ancient written Egyptian language. This might suggest that the idea of writing was introduced from western Asian cultures and adapted to local styles, but there are no clear similarities between the Indus script and others. Also, as with ancient written Egyptian, we do not know whether the "suddenness" of the appearance of the Indus script is simply a result of archaeological biases: Early forms of these languages may have been written on materials that did not preserve or on materials that have not been found in sufficient numbers to trace the origins of these languages.

The writing system was complemented by a standardized system of weights and measures. Small, precisely cut pieces of chert in both binary and decimal arrangements were used as counterweights in balances, and several measuring sticks marked off in units of about 33.5 cm have been found; apparently this unit was the common measurement of length, much like the English foot, for many of the buildings are precisely constructed to this scale.[51]

The writing, seals, and weights suggest substantial interregional—perhaps international—trade, and we have some reports of Harappan colonies as far away as Afghanistan and Oman.[52] But as Miller claims, "It can, however, by now be asserted that there is a remarkable lack of evidence for external trade in Harappan material."[53] Harappan peoples may have traded principally in raw materials rather than the finished goods that would allow identification of trade patterns, but the overall evidence of foreign trade is slight when compared with Mesopotamia at the same period of development.

The Harappan art and religious architecture so far discovered seem less varied, complex, and beautiful than that of the same period in Mesopotamia, but they have a certain affecting quality (Figure 10.8). The most popular art was in the form of terra cotta figurines, the majority of which were standing females, heavily adorned with jewelry. For reasons that will probably forever remain unclear, the Harappan people simply did not produce large amounts of "art" in the form of sculpture, figurines, paintings, or even bodily adornment—or at least few such things have been preserved into our own time (Figure 10.9).

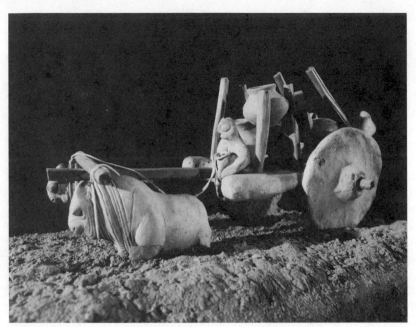

FIGURE 10.8　This Harappan toy cart is one of the earliest known models of wheeled vehicles.

THE DECLINE OF HARAPPAN CIVILIZATION (C. 1900–1000 B.C.)

As we have noted, most civilizations do not die the same way that biological organisms do. Civilizations are transmuted by time and circumstance so that they change, but usually complexes of their constituent elements live on for millennia in languages, art, and other forms.

The Harappan civilization is part of the cultural stream that connects even the present-day inhabitants of the Indus to their long and complex ancestry, but archaeologists have long wondered if the Indus might really be that rare civilization that, rather than being transformed, was obliterated, perhaps by flood, drought, invasion, or some other calamity. The principal archaeological evidences relating to the demise of Harappan civilization are (1) the increasing heterogeneity of pottery and other artifact styles within the same area that in earlier centuries had been so uniform stylistically; (2) the "degradation" of art and architecture toward the end of the Harappan period—which has led some imaginative scholars to suppose that the Harappans had lost their sense of central unity and purpose; and (3) the discovery of about a score of human skeletons "sprawled" in the streets and buildings of Mohenjo-daro (Figure 10.10), thought by some to be perhaps the aftermath of an invasion.

Hydrologist Robert Raikes suggests that Harappan civilization was terminated by destruction of their fields and settlements as a result of floods brought on by major shifts of the earth's crust near the mouth of the Indus River.[54] Raikes notes the lack of settlements in the area near the mouth of the river and points out that the fossil beaches are many miles inland from the present coast. This is what one would expect if the river's route to the sea were blocked by an uplift of land near the mouth, since water would have been backed up into a large lake that eventually could have inundated the Harappan area. Other viable geological explanations include Flam's work on the shift in the course of the Sindhu Nadi which may have placed major Harappan cities more directly in the pathway of extensive and damaging annual floods.[55]

Alternatively, Possehl notes that several strains of domesticated African millet were introduced to South Asia at about the time of the Harappan decline. He suggests that these domesticates were better suited to areas south of the Harappan homeland and that populations might have thus shifted to those areas.[56]

B. K. Thapar[57] sees the demise of Harappa in a destructive combination of several factors, including (1) tectonic movements that made the Indus and other rivers in this area prone to shifting courses and flooding at destructive levels; (2) wholesale destruction of forests and overgrazing in the Himalayan foothills that led to erosion and subsequent changes in stream courses as these channels built up their beds with silt; and (3) tectonic movements and marine regressions that stranded major ports several kilometers inland and lowered the water table in many areas.

A more romantic suggestion is that the Harappan civilization was destroyed by repeated invasions of semi-nomadic peoples coming out of Central Asia and Iran. The *Rig Veda*, the oldest surviving Vedic Sanskrit text, describes the conquest of the dark-skinned natives of the Indus Plain by lighter-skinned Aryan invaders, and the Harappans have traditionally been associated with the former. The translation of Sanskrit literature, first accomplished in the sixteenth century, revealed major similarities between Sanskrit, Greek, and European and Central Asian language families. These similarities were eventually traced to origins in the Caucasus Mountains of southern Russia and adjacent areas and associated with tall, long-headed, fierce peoples collectively referred to as Aryans or Indo-Europeans. Some believe that shortly after 1900 B.C., these peoples apparently invaded and influenced the cultures of India, Central Asia, Western Asia, and Europe.

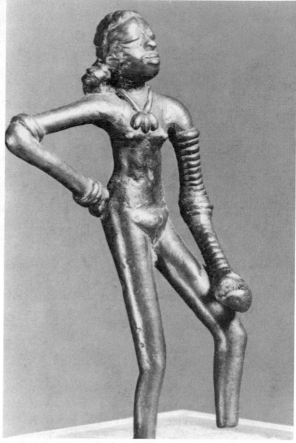

FIGURE 10.9 This lovely bronze figure from Mohenjo-daro is one of the few examples of Harappan art.

Bronze weapons and other artifacts traditionally associated with the Indo-Europeans have been found in the upper levels of some Harappan sites, and some scholars have identified these with the invaders referred to in the *Rig Veda*. It is difficult to substantiate these invasions, and many now believe that such invasions are either at most only a minor part of the Harappan collapse or were simply migrations spread out over many millennia and in the absence of major armed conflict.[58] Kennedy specifically rejects the notion that the bodies Sir Mortimer Wheeler found at Mohenjo-daro were massacred.[59]

Overall, there may have been a gradual shift of power away from the Harappan heartland to peripheral groups in the south and east, where the evolutionary potential may have been higher because of the emergence there of rice or millet agriculture. Political and cultural influence may well have gravitated to those areas outside the primarily wheat-growing regions of the Harappan sphere of influence.[60] Colin Renfrew has challenged the old notion of Indo-European invaders who sacked the Indus civilizations and suspects that

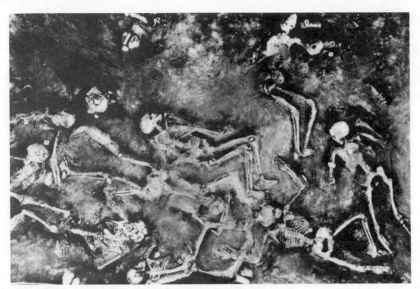

FIGURE 10.10   These skeletons found lying in a public area of Mohenjo-daro were interpreted by some as evidence of an invasion, but there is little proof of this.

the people of the Indus Plain were already Indo-European speakers.[61] Rather than a violent spread of Indo-European storm-troopers, there may well have been a spread of the Indo-European *languages*, along with elements of crops and agriculture.

The end of Harappan civilization was probably a result of many factors. Continued pressure from peripheral groups, the altering courses of the Indus River and the drying up of other rivers as their courses and sources changed, droughts, floods, earthquakes —all may have contributed to the gradual abandonment of Harappan centers.

After the Harappan downfall, many diverse cultures appeared throughout India and Pakistan, ranging from hunters and gatherers to highly sophisticated urban-based civilizations. The centers of power and influence gradually shifted from the Indus Valley to the great Ganges River Valley where, after about 1100 B.C., large cities were built and state-level political systems were formed. Many Harappan elements appeared in these later societies, including aspects of metallurgy, architecture, pottery styles, and agriculture.

SUMMARY AND CONCLUSIONS

Scholars dispute general interpretations of the Indus culture history. Some stress the ecological, demographic, and technological bases of life on the Indus Plain,[62] while others emphasize sociopolitical factors.[63]

It is difficult to see an obvious equation between the simple ecological circumstances of life on the ancient Indus Plain and the differences that distinguish Harappan settlements from those in Mesopotamia or Egypt. The planning and execution of Harappan settlements bespeak a powerful centralized authority, perhaps rivaling that of ancient Egypt, but there is no evidence in Harappa of the great tombs, palaces, and pyramids that accompanied theocratic states in Egypt and elsewhere.[64]

Because of its brevity, lack of monumental architecture, and absence of obvious wealth differential and militarism, the Harappan civilization, some have argued, was not a true state, merely a chiefdom.[65] But as Jacobson notes, recent discoveries cast doubt on this interpretation.[66] Settlement pattern studies show considerable variation in the sizes of communities and rates of population growth that are consistent with changes to state-level societies.[67] The Harappan civilization also featured a form of writing that, even if not developed, may have conveyed a great deal of administrative and economic information—should we be able to decipher it someday—and recent excavations show a degree of military fortification and economic stratification not previously suspected.

Shaffer concludes that in some ways the analytical models applied to Mesopotamia and other early states are not really applicable to Harappan culture.[68] He notes, for example, that compared to Mesopotamia, the Harappan culture did not seem to exhibit the same degree of cyclical rise and fall of state governments, and that in the Indus Valley, a technologically advanced, urban, literate culture was achieved without the usually associated social organization based on hereditary elites, centralized political government (states, empires), and warfare.[69]

Kenoyer suggests that

the Indus state was composed of several competing classes of elites who maintained different levels of control over the vast region of the Indus and Ghaggar-Hakra Valley. Instead of one social group with absolute control, the rulers or dominant members in the various cities would have included merchants, ritual specialists, and individuals who controlled resources. . . . These groups may have had different means of control, but they shared a common ideology and economic system. . . . This ideology would have been shared by occupational specialists and service communities, who appear to have been organized in loosely stratified groups."[70]

Long-distance trade, particularly the flow of goods from the Indus Valley to Mesopotamia, has frequently been suggested as a key factor in the development—and decline—of Harappan civilization. Harappan seals and seal impressions have been found in limited quantities in Mesopotamia and along the Persian Gulf, and there clearly was some commerce between these areas, perhaps by way of ships sailing along the coast and caravans traversing the Iranian Plateau. Exactly which commodities would have been shipped from the Indus Valley westward is unknown, although steatite and a few kinds of semi-precious stones and other minerals would have been likely trade items. Commerce appears to have been very one-sided, however, with little going from Southwest Asia to the Indus area, and this has suggested to some that Harappan civilization may have been established and maintained mainly by Mesopotamian or Iranian states. Indeed, some Mesopotamian elements exist in the Indus cultures—carved stone boxes, dice, faience, wheeled vehicles, shaft-hole axes, religious art motifs, and the "ram-style" sculptural motif. But taken as a whole, long-distance trade seems to have had little importance in the evolution of cultural complexity in the Indus Valley. The volume of product exchange was very low and mainly in luxury items, and the movement of goods appears to have been accomplished through intermediaries in the Iranian Plateau, rather than through deliberate and directly administered trade between Harappans and Mesopotamians.

As in the case of Egypt and Mesopotamia, rates of population growth in the Indus Valley appear to have been slow, and there is no evidence of pressure on the agricultural systems until long after the Harappan civilization had collapsed.

So in the case of the Indus civilizations we again see the divergence in modern archaeological interpretation. For some, the ecological, technological, and demographic factors are primary, and interpretations are limited quite closely to aspects of administration, class differences, trade, and other aspects of the society that can be related directly to artifacts. But others consider such analyses to be limited, and they stress, instead, the ideological elements that determine a society.

BIBLIOGRAPHY

Adams, R. McC. 1979. "The Natural History of Urbanism." In *Ancient Cities of the Indus*, ed. G. L. Possehl. New Delhi: Vikas Publishing House.

Agrawal, D. P. 1971. *The Copper Bronze Age in India*. New Delhi: Manoharlal.

———. 1982. *The Archaeology of India*. Guildford: Curzon Press.

———. 1984. "Metal Technology of the Harappans." In *Frontiers of the Indus Civilization*, ed. B. B. Lal and S. P. Gupta. New Delhi: Books and Books.

Agrawal, D. P., and S. D. Kusumgar. 1974. *Prehistoric Chronology and Radiocarbon Dating in India*. New Delhi: Manoharlal.

Allchin, F. R. 1960. *Piklihal Excavations*. Hyderabad, India: Government of Andhra Pradesh.

———. 1961. *Utnur Excavations*. Hyderabad, India: Government of Andhra Pradesh.

———. 1963. *Neolithic Cattle-Keepers of South India*. Cambridge: Cambridge University Press.

———. 1968. "Early Domesticated Animals in India and Pakistan." In *Man, Settlement and Urbanism*, ed. P. J. Ucko, R. Tringham, and G. W. Dimbleby. London: Duckworth.

———. 1969. "Early Cultivated Plants in India and Pakistan." In *The Domestication and Explanation of Plants and Animals*, ed. P. J. Ucko and G. W. Dimbleby. London: Duckworth.

———. 1974. "India from the Late Stone Age to the Decline of Indus Civilization." *Encyclopaedia Britannica* 9:336–348.

———. 1989. "City and State Formation in Early Historic South Asia." *South Asian Studies* 5:1–16.

Allchin, B., and F. R. Allchin. 1968. *The Birth of Indian Civilization*. Baltimore: Penguin.

———. 1983. *The Rise of Civilization in India and Pakistan*. Cambridge: Cambridge University Press.

Allchin, F. R., and D. K. Chakrabarti, eds. 1979. *A Source Book of Indian Archaeology*, Vol. 1. New Delhi: Munshirman Maroliarlal.

Bhan, K. K. 1989. "Late Harappan Settlements of Western India, with Specific Reference to Gujurat." In *Old Problems and New Perspectives in the Archaeology of South Asia*, ed. J. M. Kenoyer. Madison: Wisconsin Archaeological Reports, Vol. 2.

Bisht, R. S. 1984. "Structural Remains and Town Planning of Banawali." In *Frontiers of the Indus Civilization*, ed. B. B. Lal and S. P. Gupta. New Delhi: Books and Books.

Buchanan, B. "A Dated Seal Impression Connecting Babylonia and Ancient India." In *Ancient Cities of the Indus*, ed. G. L. Possehl. New Delhi: Vikas Publishing House.

Chakrabarti, D. K. 1984. "Origins of the Indus Civilization: Theories and Problems." In *Frontiers of the Indus Civilization*, ed. B. B. Lal and S. P. Gupta. New Delhi: Indian Archaeological Society.

Childe, V. G. 1953. *New Light on the Most Ancient East*. New York: Praeger.

———. 1979. "The Urban Revolution." In *Ancient Cities of the Indus*, ed. G. L. Possehl. New Delhi: Vikas Publishing House.

Cunningham, A. 1979. "Harappa." In *Ancient Cities of the Indus*, ed. G. L. Possehl. New Delhi: Vikas Publishing House.

Dales, G. F. 1964. "The Mythical Massacre at Mohenjo Daro." *Expedition* 6(3):36–43.

———. 1965. "New Investigations at Mohenjo Daro." *Archaeology* 18(2):145–150.

———. 1966. "The Decline of the Harappans." *Scientific American* 214(5):93–100.

———. 1968. "Of Dice and Men." *Journal of the American Oriental Society* 88(1):14–23.

———. 1979. "The Balakot Project: Summary of Four Years of Excavations in Pakistan." In *South Asian Archaeology 1977*, ed. M. Taddei. Naples: Instituto Universitario Orientale.

Dales, G. F., and J. M. Kenoyer. 1990. "Excavation at Harappa—1988." *Pakistan Archaeology* 24:68–176.

Durante, S. 1979. "Marine Shells from Balakot, Shahr-i Sokhta and Tepe Yahya: Their Significance for Trade and Technology in Ancient Indo-Iran." In *South Asian Archaeology 1977*, ed. M. Taddei. Naples: Instituto Universitario Orientale.

During-Caspers, E. L. C. 1984. "Sumerian Trading Communities Residing in Harappan Society." In *Frontiers of the Indus Civilization*, ed. B. B. Lal and S. P. Gupta. New Delhi: Books and Books.

Dyson, R. H. 1982. "Paradigm Changes in the Study of the Indus Civilization." In *Harappan Civilization: A Contemporary Perspective*, ed. G. L. Possehl. New Delhi: AIIS.

Fairservis, W. A., Jr. 1956. Excavations in the Quetta Valley, West Pakistan. NY: Anthropological Papers of the American Museum of Natural History 45(2).

———. 1967. "The Origin, Character and Decline of an Early Civilization." *Novitates* 2302:1–48.

———. 1975. *The Roots of Ancient India*. 2nd ed. rev. Chicago: University of Chicago Press.

———. 1984. "Archaeology in Blauchistan and the Harappan Problem." In *Frontiers of the Indus Civilization*, ed. B. B. Lal and S. P. Gupta. New Delhi: Books and Books.

Fairservis, W. A., and F. C. Southworth. 1989. "Linguistic Archaeology and the Indus Valley Culture." In *Old Problems and New Perspectives in the Archaeology of South Asia*, ed. J. M. Kenoyer. Madison: Wisconsin Archaeological Reports, Vol. 2.

Fentress, M. A. 1976. *Resource Access, Exchange Systems and Regional Interaction in the Indus Valley: An Investigation of Archaeological Variability at Harappa and Mohenjodaro.* Ann Arbor: University Microfilms.

———. 1979. "Indus Charms and Urns, a Look at the Religious Diversity at Harappa and Mohenjodaro." *Man and Environment* 3:9–104.

———. 1985. "Water Resources and Double Cropping in Harappan Food Production." In *Recent Advances in Indo-Pacific Prehistory*, ed. V. N. Misra and P. Bellwood. New Delhi: Oxford and IBH.

Flam, L. 1991. "Excavations at Ghazi Shah, Sindh, Pakistan." In *Harappan Civilization: A Contemporary Perspective*, 2nd ed., ed. G. L. Possehl. New Delhi: Oxford and IBH.

———. 1999. "The Prehistoric Indus River System and the Indus Civilization in Sindh." *Man and Environment* 24(2):35–69.

Frankfort, H.-P., and M.-H. Pottier. 1978. "Sondage Preliminaire sur l'Establissement Protohistorique Harapeen et Post-Harapeen de Shortugai." *Ars Asiatique* 34:29–86.

Gadd, C. J. 1979. "Seals of Ancient Indian Style Found at Ur." In *Ancient Cities of the Indus*, ed. G. L. Possehl. New Delhi: Vikas Publishing House.

Gadd, C. J., and S. Smith. 1979. "The New Links Between Indian and Babylonian Civilization." In *Ancient Cities of the Indus*, ed. G. L. Possehl. New Delhi: Vikas Publishing House.

Gupta, S. P. 1978. *Archaeology of Soviet Central Asia and the Indian Borderlands*, Vol. 1. New Delhi: B. R. Publishing Co.

Jacobson, J. 1979. "Recent Developments in South Asian Prehistory and Protohistory." *Annual Review of Anthropology* 8:467–502.

Jansen, M. 1979. "Architectural Problems of the Harappa Culture." In *South Asian Archaeology 1977*, ed. M. Taddei. Naples: Instituto Universitario Orientale.

———. 1981. "Settlement Patterns in the Harappa Culture." In *South Asian Archaeology 1979*, ed. H. Hartel. Berlin: Dietrich Reimer.

———. 1987. "Mohenjo-Daro—Stadt am Indus." In *Vergessen Städt am Indus*, ed. M. Jansen and G. Urban. Mainz am Rhein: Phillip von Zabern.

Jarrige, J. F. 1981. "Economy and Society in the Early Chalcolithic/Bronze Age of Baluchistan." In *South Asian Archaeology 1979*. Berlin: Dietrich Reiner.

———. 1984. "Chronology of the Early Period of the Greater Indus as Seen from Mehrgarh, Pakistan." In *South Asian Archaeology 1981*, ed. B. Allchin. Cambridge: Cambridge University Press.

Jarrige, J. F., and M. Lechevaleier. 1979. "Excavations at Mehrgarh, Baluchistan: Their Significance in the Prehistorical Context of the Indo-Pakistan Borderlands." In *South Asian Archaeology 1977*, ed. M. Taddei. Naples: Instituto Universitario Orientale.

Jarrige, J. F., and R. H. Meadow. 1980. "The Antecedents of Civilization in the Indus Valley." *Scientific American* 243(2):122–133.

Johnson, G. A. 1973. *Local Exchange and Early State Development in Southwestern Iran.* Ann Arbor: Museum of Anthropology, Anthropological Papers, University of Michigan, No. 51.

Joshi, J. P., and M. Bala. 1981. "Manda: A Harappan Site in Jammu and Kashmir." In *Harappan Civilization: A Contemporary Perspective*, ed. G. L. Possehl. New Delhi: Oxford and IBH.

Kelly, D. H., and B. Wells. 1995. "Recent Progress in Understanding the Indus Script." *The Review of Archaeology* 16(1):15–23.

Kennedy, K. 1982. "Skulls, Aryans and Flowing Drains: The Interface of Archaeology and Skeletal Biology in the Study of the Harappan Civilisation." In *Harappan Civilization*, ed. G. Possehl. Warminster, England: Aris & Phillips.

———. 1984. "Trauma and Disease in the Ancient Harappans." In *Frontiers of the Indus Civilization*, ed. B. B. Lal and S. P. Gupta. New Delhi: Books and Books.

Kennedy, K., and G. L. Possehl, eds. 1976. *Ecological Backgrounds of South Asian Prehistory.* South Asia Occasional Papers and Theses, No. 4. Ithaca, NY: Cornell University South Asia Program.

Kenoyer, J. M. 1991. "The Indus Valley Tradition of Pakistan and Western India." *Journal of World Prehistory* 5(4):331–385.

———. 1998. *Ancient Cities of the Indus Valley Civilization.* New York: Oxford University Press.

Kohl, P. L. 1979. "The 'World Economy' of West Asia in the Third Millennium B.C." In *South Asian Archaeology 1977*, ed. M. Taddei. Naples: Instituto Universitario Orientale.

———. 1987. "State Formation: Useful Concept or Idée Fixe?" In *Power Relations and State Formation*, ed. T. C. Patterson and C. W. Gailey. Washington, DC: American Anthropological Association.

Lamberg-Karlovsky, C. C. 1967. "Archaeology and Metallurgical Technology in Prehistoric Afghanistan, India and Pakistan." *American Anthropologist* 69:145–162.

———. 1975. "Third Millennium Modes of Exchange and Modes of Production." In *Ancient Civilization and Trade*, ed. J. Sabloff and C. C. Lamberg-Karlovsky. Albuquerque: University of New Mexico Press and the School of American Research.

————. 1979. "Trade Mechanisms in Indus-Mesopotamian Interrelations." In *Ancient Cities of the Indus*, ed. G. L. Possehl. New Delhi: Vikas Publishing House.

Lambrick, H. T. 1967. "The Indus Flood Plain and the 'Indus' Civilization." *Geographical Journal* 133(4):483–495.

————. 1979. "Stratigraphy at Mohenjo Daro." In *Ancient Cities of the Indus*, ed. G. L. Possehl. New Delhi: Vikas Publishing House.

Leshnik, L. S. 1968. "The Harappan 'Port' at Lothal: Another View." *American Anthropologist* 70:911–922.

Loftus, R. T., D. E. MacHugh, D. G. Bradley, P. M. Sharp, and P. Cunningham. 1994. "Evidence for Two Independent Domestications of Cattle." *Proceedings of the National Academy of Sciences* 91: 2757–2761.

Mackay, E. J. H. 1979. "Further Links Between Ancient Sind, Sumer and Elsewhere." In *Ancient Cities of the Indus*, ed. G. L. Possehl. New Delhi: Vikas Publishing House.

Mahadevan, I. 1979. "Study of the Indus Script through Bi-lingual Parallels." In *Ancient Cities of the Indus*, ed. G. L. Possehl. New Delhi: Vikas Publishing House.

Mallory, J. P. 1988. *In Search of the Indo-Europeans.* New York: Thames and Hudson.

Marshall, J. 1979. "Harappa and Mohenjo Daro." In *Ancient Cities of the Indus*, ed. G. L. Possehl. New Delhi: Vikas Publishing House.

Meadow, R. H. 1984. "Animal Domestication in the Middle East: A View from the Eastern Margin." In *Animals and Archaeology*, ed. J. Clutton-Brock and C. Grigson. Vol. 3. Oxford: British Archaeological Reports, S-202.

————. 1993. *Harappan Civilization: A Recent Perspective*, 2nd ed., ed. G. Possehl. New Delhi: Oxford and IBH Publishing.

Miller, D. 1985. "Ideology and the Indus Civilization." *Journal of Anthropological Archaeology* 4(1):34–71.

Mughal, M. R. 1970. "The Early Harappan Period in the Greater Indus Valley and Northern Baluchistan." Doctoral dissertation, University of Pennsylvania.

————. 1974. "New Evidence of the Early Harappan Culture from Jalilpur, Pakistan." *Archaeology* 27:106–113.

————. 1990. "Further Evidence of the Early Harappan Culture in the Greater Indus Valley: 1971–90." *South Asian Studies* 6:175–200.

Oppenheim, A. L. 1979. "The Seafaring Merchants of Ur." In *Ancient Cities of the Indus*, ed. G. L. Possehl. New Delhi: Vikas Publishing House.

Pande, B. M. 1973. "Inscribed Copper Tablets from Mohenjo Daro: A Preliminary Analysis." In *Radiocarbon and Indian Archaeology*, ed. D. P. Agrawal and A. Ghosh. Bombay: Tata Institute of Fundamental Research.

Parpola, A. 1986. "The Indus Script: A Challenging Puzzle." *World Archaeology* 17(3):399–419.

————. 1994. *Deciphering the Indus Script*. Cambridge: Cambridge University Press.

Piggott, S. 1950. *Prehistoric India*. London: Pelican.

Possehl, G. L. 1974. "Variation and Change in the Indus Civilization." Doctoral dissertation, University of Chicago.

————. 1976. "Lothal: A Gateway Settlement of the Harappan Civilization." In *Ecological Backgrounds of South Asian Prehistory*, ed. A. P. Kennedy and G. L. Possehl. *South Asia Occasional Papers and Theses* 4:118–131. Ithaca, NY: Cornell University South Asia Program.

————. 1977. "The End of a State and the Continuity of a Tradition in Proto-Historic India." In *Realm and Region in Traditional India*, ed. R. Fox. Durham NC: Duke University Program in South Asian Studies.

————, ed. 1979. *Ancient Cities of the Indus*. New Delhi: Vikas Publishing House Pvt Ltd.

————. 1980. "African Millets in South Asian Prehistory." Mimeographed.

————. 1990. "Revolution in the Urban Revolution: The Emergence of Indus Urbanism." *Annual Review of Anthropology* 19:261–282.

————. 1992. "The Harappan Civilizations in Gujarat: The Sorath and Sindhi Harappans." *The Eastern Anthropologist* 45(1 & 2):117–154.

————, ed. 1993. *Harappan Civilization: A Recent Perspective*, 2nd ed. New Delhi: Oxford and IBH Publishing.

————. 1999. "Transformation of the Indus Civilization." *Man and Environment* 24(2):1–33.

————. 2002. *The Indus Civilization: A Contemporary Perspective*. Walnut Creek, CA: Altamira.

Possehl, G. L., and M. H. Raval. 1989. *Harappan Civilization and Rojdi*. New Delhi: Oxford and IBH and AIIS.

Raikes, R. L. 1964. "The End of the Ancient Cities of the Indus." *American Anthropologist* 66(2):284–299.

————. 1965. "The Mohenjo-Daro Floods." *Antiquity* 39:196–203.

Raikes, R. L., and R. H. Dyson, Jr. 1961. "The Prehistoric Climate of Baluchistan and the Indus Valley." *American Anthropologist* 63(2):265–281.

Ralph, E. K., H. N. Michael, and M. Han. 1979. "Radiocarbon Dates and Reality." In *Ancient Cities of the Indus*, ed. G. L. Possehl. New Delhi: Vikas Publishing House.

Ramaswamy, C. 1968. "Monsoon over the Indus Valley During the Harappan Period." *Nature* 217(5129):628–629.

Rao, S. R. 1968. "Contacts Between Lothal and Susa." *Proceedings of the Twenty-sixth International Congress of Orientalists*, Vol. II, pp. 35–37.

————. 1973. *Lothal and the Indus Civilization*. Bombay: Asia House.

————. 1979. "A 'Persian Gulf' Seal from Lothal." In *Ancient Cities of the Indus*, ed. G. L. Possehl. New Delhi: Vikas Publishing House.

Ratnagar, S. 1981. *Encounters, The Westerly Trade of the Harappan Civilization*. Delhi: Oxford University Press.

Renfrew, C. 1988. "Archaeology and Language." *Current Anthropology* 29(3):437–468.

Sankalia, H. 1974. *The Prehistory and Protohistory of India and Pakistan*. Pune, India: Deccan College.

————. 1979. "The 'Cemetery H' Culture." In *Ancient Cities of the Indus*, ed. G. L. Possehl. New Delhi: Vikas Publishing House.

Sarcina, A. 1979a. "The Private House at Mohenjodaro." In *South Asian Archaeology 1977*, ed. M. Taddei. Naples: Instituto Universitario Orientale.

————. 1979b. "A Statistical Assessment of House Patterns at Mohenjodaro." *Mesopotamia* 13/14:155–199.

Schuldenrein, J., R. P. Wright, M. R. Mughal, and M. A. Khan. 2004. "Landscapes, Soils, and Mound Histories of the Upper Indus Valley, Pakistan: New Insights on the Holocene Environments Near Ancient Harappa." *Journal of Archaeological Science* 31:777–797.

Service, E. 1975. *Origins of the State and Civilization*. New York: Norton.

Shaffer, J. G. 1978. *Prehistoric Baluchistan*. Delhi: B. R. Publishers.

————. 1982. "Harappan Culture: A Reconsideration." In *Harappan Civilization*, ed. G. L. Possehl. New Delhi: Oxford and IBH.

————. 1984. "The Indo-Aryan Invasions: Cultural Myth and Archaeological Reality." In *The People of South Asia*, ed. J. R. Lukacs. New York: Plenum Press.

————. 1988. "One Hump or Two: The Impact of the Camel on Harappan Society." In *Orientalia Iosephi Tucci Memoriae Dicata*, ed. G. Gnoli and L. Lanciotti. Rome: IsMEO.

————. 1991. "The Indus Valley, Baluchistan and Helmand Traditions: Neolithic Through Bronze Age." In *Chronologies in Old World Archaeology*, 3rd ed., ed. R. Ehrich. Chicago: University of Chicago Press.

Singh, G. 1979. "The Indus Valley Culture." In *Ancient Cities of the Indus*, ed. G. L. Possehl. New Delhi: Vikas Publishing House.

Thapar, B. K. 1975. "Kalibangan: A Harappan Metropolis Beyond the Indus Valley." *Expedition* 17(2):19–32.

Tosi, M. 1984. "The Notion of Craft Specialisation and Its Representation in the Archaeological Record of Early States in the Turanian Basin." In *Marxist Perspectives in Archaeology*, ed. M. Spriggs. Cambridge: Cambridge University Press.

Trigger, B. 1972. "Determinants of Urban Growth in Pre-Industrial Societies." In *Man, Settlement and Urbanism*, ed. P. J. Ucko, R. Tringham, and G. W. Dimbleby. London: Duckworth.

Van Lohnizen-de Leeuw, J. E., and J. M. M. Ubagns, eds. 1974. *South Asian Archaeology*. Leiden, Netherlands: Brill.

Vishnu-Mittre. 1977. "Discussion on Local and Introduced Crops." In *The Early History of Agriculture: A Joint Symposium of the Royal Society and the British Academy*, organized by J. Hutchinson. London: Oxford University Press.

Wheatley, P. 1972. "The Concept of Urbanism." In *Man, Settlement and Urbanism*, ed. P. J. Ucko, R. Tringham, and G. W. Dimbleby. London: Duckworth.

Wheeler, Sir M. 1979. "Harappan Chronology and the Rig Veda." In *Ancient Cities of the Indus*, ed. G. L. Possehl. New Delhi: Vikas Publishing House.

Wheeler, R. E. M. 1950. *Five Thousand Years of Pakistan*. London: Royal India and Pakistan Society.

Wolpert, S. A. 1977. *A New History of India*. London: Oxford University Press.

Wright, H. T. 1986. "The Evolution of Civilizations." In *American Archaeology Past and Future*, ed. D. J. Meltzer, D. D. Fowler, and J. A. Sabloff. Washington, DC: Smithsonian Institution Press.

Wright, H. T., and S. Pollock. 1985. "Regional Socio-economic Organization in Southern Mesopotamia: The Middle and Late Fifth Millennium B.C." In *La Mesopotamie: Pre- et Protohistoire*, ed. J.-L. Huot. Paris: C.N.R.S.

Wright, R. P. 1989. "The Indus Valley and Mesopotamian Civilizations: A Comparative View of Ceramic Technology." In *Old Problems and New Perspectives in the Archaeology of South Asia*, ed. J. M. Kenoyer. Madison: Wisconsin Archaeological Reports, Vol. 2.

Yule, P. 1982. *Lothal*. Munich: C. H. Beck.

Zide, A. R. K. 1979. "A Brief Survey of Work to Date on the Indus Script." In *Ancient Cities of the Indus*, ed. G. L. Possehl. New Delhi: Vikas Publishing.

NOTES

1. Childe, *New Light on the Most Ancient East*, p. 183; cited by Possehl, "Revolution in the Urban Revolution: The Emergence of Indus Urbanism," p. 267.

2. Viewed from the perspective of its entire sequence (including development and demise), however, Harappan civilization has a much lengthier history, lasting from about 3200 through 1000 B.C. (see Possehl, *The Indus Civilization: A Contemporary Perspective*, p. 29).

3. Kenoyer's chronological divisions (see Kenoyer, *Ancient Cities of the Indus Valley Civilization*, p. 24) are somewhat different from those proposed by Possehl (see Possehl, *The Indus Civilization: A Contemporary Perspective*, p. 29). Possehl's chronology is followed in this chapter.

4. Possehl, "Revolution in the Urban Revolution: The Emergence of Indus Urbanism," p. 262.

5. Possehl, *The Indus Civilization: A Contemporary Perspective*, p. 51.

6. Kenoyer, "The Indus Valley Tradition of Pakistan and Western India"; Kenoyer, *Ancient Cities of the Indus Valley Civilization*, p. 49.

7. Kenoyer, *Ancient Cities of the Indus Valley Civilization*, pp. 81–82.

8. Shaffer, "Harappan Culture: A Reconsideration."

9. Also see Possehl, "Revolution in the Urban Revolution: The Emergence of Indus Urbanism."

10. Strabo and many other Greek historians wrote about the eastern lands Alexander had conquered, but few of them appear to have seen them in person, and thus their accounts were based on travelers' accounts and second-hand knowledge.

11. Schuldenrein et al., "Landscapes, Soils, and Mound Histories of the Upper Indus Valley, Pakistan: New Insights on the Holocene Environments Near Ancient Harappa."

12. Flam, "The Prehistoric Indus River System and the Indus Civilization in Sindh," pp. 61–64.

13. Mughal, "Further Evidence of the Early Harappan Culture in the Greater Indus Valley: 1971–90."

14. Flam, "The Prehistoric Indus River System and the Indus Civilization in Sindh," pp. 54–55.

15. Ibid., pp. 64–65.

16. Possehl, "Revolution in the Urban Revolution: The Emergence of Indus Urbanism," p. 261.

17. Meadow, *Harappan Civilization: A Recent Perspective*, p. 311.

18. The local domestication of the hump-backed cattle, *Bos indicus*, is supported by research on the DNA of cattle (see Loftus et al., "Evidence for Two Independent Domestications of Cattle").

19. Fairservis, "The Origin, Character and Decline of an Early Civilization."

20. Allchin, "India from the Late Stone Age to the Decline of Indus Civilization," p. 337.

21. Vishnu-Mittre, "Discussion on Local and Introduced Crops."

22. Kenoyer, "The Indus Valley Tradition of Pakistan and Western India," p. 332.

23. Miller, "Ideology and the Indus Civilization," p. 38.

24. Ibid., p. 39; Jarrige and Lechevaleier, "Excavations at Mehrgarh, Baluchistan: Their Significance in the Prehistorical Context of the Indo-Pakistan Borderlands"; Gupta, *Archaeology of Soviet Central Asia and the Indian Borderlands*; Durante, "Marine Shells from Balakot, Shahr-i Sokhta and Tepe Yahya"; Fairservis, *The Roots of Ancient India*.

25. Wright, "The Evolution of Civilizations."

26. Ibid., p. 337. In comparing the Indus Valley and Mesopotamia, Wright concludes that by the late fifth and early fourth millennia B.C. some areas of the Indus Plain had settlements of such different sizes that we may suspect that they reflect hierarchically organized societies.

27. Miller, "Ideology and the Harappan Civilization," p. 40.

28. Mughal, "The Early Harappan Period in the Greater Indus Valley and Northern Baluchistan."

29. Possehl, "Revolution in the Urban Revolution: The Emergence of Indus Urbanism," p. 270.

30. Ibid., p. 270.

31. Ibid., p. 271.

32. Possehl, ed., *Harappan Civilization: A Recent Perspective*.

33. Wright, "The Evolution of Civilizations," p. 340.

34. Jansen, "Settlement Patterns in the Harappa Culture," p. 252; Agrawal, *The Archaeology of India*, p. 135; Miller, "Ideology and the Harappan Civilization," p. 40.

35. Jansen, "Settlement Patterns in the Harappa Culture."

36. Shaffer, "Harappan Culture: A Reconsideration."

37. Fentress, *Resource Access, Exchange Systems and Regional Interaction in the Indus Valley*, pp. 136–137.

38. Miller, "Ideology and the Harappan Civilization."

39. Sarcina, "The Private House at Mohenjodaro"; Sarcina, "A Statistical Assessment of House Patterns at Mohenjodaro."

40. Miller, "Ideology and the Harappan Civilization," p. 48; Sarcina, "The Private House at Mohenjodaro"; Sarcina, "A Statistical Assessment of House Patterns at Mohenjodaro."

41. Fairservis, *The Roots of Ancient India*, pp. 246–247.

42. Possehl, "The End of a State and the Continuity of a Tradition in Proto-Historic India."

43. Rao, *Lothal and the Indus Civilization*.

44. Possehl, "The End of a State and the Continuity of a Tradition in Proto-Historic India."

45. Ibid. For Possehl's analysis of the interactions between Harappans and hunter-foragers, see his "The Harappan Civilization in Gujarat: The Sorath and Sindhi Harappans," especially pp. 125–126.
46. Miller, "Ideology and the Harappan Civilization," pp. 56–57; but also see Fentress, "Indus Charms and Urns, a Look at the Religious Diversity at Harappa and Mohenjodaro."
47. Possehl, *The Indus Civilization: A Contemporary Perspective*, pp. 249–250.
48. Parpola, "The Indus Script: A Challenging Puzzle." Wenke is indebted to Gregory Possehl (personal communication) for references and a summary of current interpretations for this paragraph on the language affiliation of the Indus script.
49. The following description of Indus writing is taken mainly from Kenoyer, "The Indus Valley Tradition of Pakistan and Western India." Also see Kelly and Wells, "Recent Progress in Understanding the Indus Script."
50. Dales and Kenoyer, "Excavation at Harappa—1988"; Kenoyer, "The Indus Valley Tradition of Pakistan and Western India."
51. Allchin, "India from the Late Stone Age to the Decline of Indus Civilization."
52. Frankfort and Pottier, "Sondage Preliminaire sur l'Establissement Protohistorique Harapeen et Post-Harapeen de Shortugai"; Miller, "Ideology and the Harappan Civilization," p. 54.
53. Miller, "Ideology and the Harappan Civilization," p. 55.
54. Raikes, "The Mohenjo-Daro Floods."
55. Flam, "The Prehistoric Indus River System and the Indus Civilization in Sindh."
56. Possehl, "African Millets in South Asian Prehistory."
57. Tharpar, "Kalibangan: A Harappan Metropolis Beyond the Indus Valley."
58. Possehl, *The Indus Civilization: A Contemporary Perspective*, p. 249.
59. Kennedy, "Skulls, Aryans and Flowing Drains: The Interface of Archaeology and Skeletal Biology in the Study of the Harappan Civilisation."
60. Fairservis, *The Roots of Ancient India*, p. 311.
61. Renfrew, "Archaeology and Language."
62. Shaffer, *Prehistoric Baluchistan*; Possehl, "African Millets in South Asian Prehistory."
63. Miller, "Ideology and the Harappan Civilization."
64. Service, *Origins of the State and Civilization*, p. 246.
65. Ibid.
66. Jacobson, "Recent Developments in South Asian Prehistory and Protohistory."
67. Johnson, *Local Exchange and Early State Development in Southwestern Iran*.
68. Shaffer, "Harappan Culture: A Reconsideration."
69. Ibid., p. 49; Miller, "Ideology and the Harappan Civilization."
70. Kenoyer, "The Indus Valley Tradition of Pakistan and Western India," p. 369.

The Evolution of Complex Societies in China

Let the past serve the present.

Mao Zedong

Shortly after 3000 B.C., just a century or so after Harappan civilization began in the Indus region, the people of North China began a period of development that was to take them from simple agricultural tribes to one of the most brilliant and complex civilizations of antiquity (Figure 11.1). Because scientific archaeology in China is only a few decades old, however, and because much of the literature on Chinese archaeology has not been accessible to foreign scholars, ancient Chinese civilization has not had the place in Western scholarship that it deserves.

Like ancient Egypt, China was, superficially at least, intensely self-absorbed and inward looking, and it saw itself as the center of the world whose periphery was populated by vicious barbarians. But China has a far larger and more varied physical landscape than Egypt—or Mesopotamia, for that matter—and this and other factors made its civilization a rich amalgam of many diverse ethnic groups and cultures.

Mesopotamia, Egypt, and Europe gave the world many great technological inventions, but ancient East Asia's contributions include such fundamental advances as the magnetic compass, gunpowder, printing, paper, paddle-wheel propulsion, and many other inventions.[1] China's traditions, for example, its writing system, are also the only ones that have lasted until today.

In analyzing history it is interesting that, although the Chinese invented gunpowder, they used it exclusively for fireworks. Europeans quickly saw other interesting potential uses for it. China, thus, provides an object lesson in a rather brutal historical dynamic: China was once among the largest, most powerful, and most innovative civilizations in the world, but it too was eventually dominated by the rise of the West, which exploited it for centuries. As the twenty-first century begins, however, there are indications that the world's center of power is shifting back toward China. The world has become so interconnected politically and economically that the kinds of massive imbalances of power of nations that marked the nineteenth and early twentieth centuries may never occur again, but China's enormous population, strong national sense of identity and culture, and rich natural resources may support a great expansion of its economy and power in this century. It would be truly

	CHINA
AD 618	Tang dynasty unifies China empire based on Chang'an, world's largest city (1 million inhabitants)
AD 220	Collapse of Han dynasty, China divided into three independent states
AD 150	Buddhism reaches China
AD 105	Paper comes into use in China
50 BC	Chinese silk traded to Romans
108 BC	Chinese take control of Korea establishing military outposts
119 BC	Chinese iron industry becomes state monopoly
206 BC	Accession of the Han dynasty
210 BC	Emperor Shih Huang-ti interred in vast mausoleum with terracotta army
	Shih Huangh-ti first Qin emperor builds the Great Wall
221 BC	Unification of China by the Qin dynasty
350 BC	Crossbow invented
403 BC	Warring States Period finds of bronze and iron weapons and city defenses
500 BC	Beginning of coinage
550 BC	First significant iron production
770 BC	Beginning of Eastern Zhou
1046 BC	Zhou dynasty replaces the Shang
1400 BC	First written inscriptions on oracle bones and bronze ritual vessels
1600 BC	Emergence of Shang civilization in northeast China
1900 BC	Erh-li-t'ou culture
2000 BC	Urban settlements
2500 BC	
	First bronze artifacts
2700 BC	Evidence of silk weaving
3000 BC	Early Complex Societies Longshan Culture
5000 BC	Yangshao Culture Bampo Jiangzhai
6500 BC	Early Farmers Cishan Peiligang Dadiwan

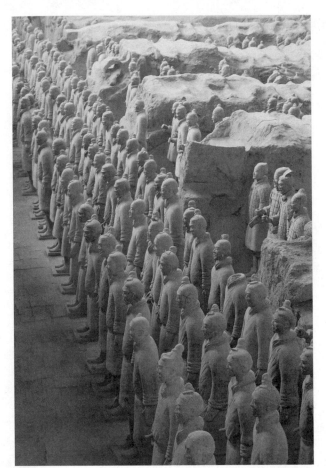

FIGURE 11.1 A portion of the terracotta army interred with Emperor Shih Huang-ti.

ironic, but it is entirely plausible that the archaeologists of the future will need to know Mandarin in order to participate fully in their discipline.

THE ECOLOGICAL SETTING

Modern China incorporates an area slightly larger than the contemporary United States. Within this territory are vastly different environments, ranging from the Himalayas to the Pacific shore, and ethnic groups throughout this vast expanse played formative roles in shaping Chinese civilization. K. C. Chang—whose work and writings until recently provided much of what is known about China in the West—defined three ecological zones as crucial areas in the evolution of ancient Chinese civilization: the Huanghe (formerly transliterated, under the Wade-Giles system, as "Hwang Ho") valley; the southern deciduous zone; and the northern forests and steppes.[2] He also notes that for some thousands of years after the end of the Pleistocene at about 12,000 years ago, China's climate was somewhat warmer and moister than it is today, and much of the country was probably heavily forested, from the temperate forests of the north to the jungles in the south. Chang observes that because of China's mountainous nature and heavy post-Pleistocene vegetative cover, people were probably restricted to the river valleys at first, since these would have been the richest sources of food and would have offered the most open land for farming. Developments in these three ecological zones eventually overlapped, and in later periods of antiquity the vast populations of nomads on the northern and western frontier of China greatly influenced the character of Chinese civilization.

During the Holocene, when Neolithic and later societies were present in China, paleoclimate and paleoenvironment were influenced by the strength of the East Asian monsoon.[3] The East Asian monsoon is a precipitation—rainfall—belt that shifts gradually northward during the period from winter to summer each year. Precisely where the heaviest precipitation associated with this rainfall belt fell during different points in the past changed over time because of changes in solar radiation and the conditions of the surface of the Northern Hemisphere—for example, 9,000 years ago, the maximum northerly extent of the monsoon belt was just to the north of some of the early Neolithic cultures of the Huanghe River area.[4] By 6,000 years ago, the maximum extent of the rainfall belt reached only as far north as just north of the Yangtze River area. The East Asian monsoon is thus an important feature of the ecological setting of various Neolithic and later societies, as well as in the levels of lakes, river flooding, and growth of vegetation.

Geological processes that likely had an impact on people living in the Huanghe area include shifts in the course of the Huanghe River[5]—similar to avulsions seen in the Mesopotamian Euphrates and Tigris rivers.

Other geological factors that may have influenced some societies in China include rising sea levels, perhaps acting in combination with increased rainfall during the middle Holocene.[6] In the delta of the Yangtze River, for example, Stanley and his colleagues have documented a major inundation of the central delta area. This removed previously dry land from the territory available to people for settlement and use for agriculture. Stanley and his colleagues believe that this inundation is partly responsible for the disappearance of the local Neolithic culture—the Liangzhu—about 4,200 years ago. After 3,900 years ago, when shifts in climate resulted in some of the delta land being reexposed, a few of the Liangzhu sites were reoccupied by people of the early Bronze Age—known locally as the Maqiao culture.[7]

Wheat and barley supplied much of the energy that ran Mesopotamian and Egyptian societies, but in China rice and millet were in many instances as important as wheat or barley. North China's developmental leadership was closely tied to its agricultural potential. Pleistocene winds blowing off the Gobi Desert covered parts of North China with a layer of loess (a fine grain sediment) that reached a depth of several hundred meters. The Huanghe River (or "Yellow River"—from the color given it by the loess it carries) cuts through these loess plains, frequently changing its course, and through flooding and draining it has created a rich agricultural zone of lakes, marshes, and alluvial fields. Loess is the agricultural soil par excellence: It is organically rich, requires little plowing, and retains near the surface much of the sparse rain that falls on North China. Moreover, it can yield large crops with little fertilization, even under intensive cultivation. The southern alluvial plains, with their hot, humid climate, eventually became the great rice heartlands.

Early farmers around the world converged in finding, through domestication and agriculture, four key ingredients to the village-farming way of life: They all found (1) a source for textiles; (2) a productive, high carbohydrate, main crop plant; (3) an edible oil for cooking; and a (4) a reliable source of animal protein. The initial northern Chinese solutions to these problems were hemp for textiles, millet for a main crop plant, rapeseed and soybeans for edible oils, and pigs for meat. But east Asia—including Japan, Southeast Asia, Korea, and other areas peripheral to the mainland—domesticated an impressive range of other plants, perhaps more than any other area of the world. Wheat, barley, and perhaps other plants may have been introduced from western Asia, but east Asian domesticates and/or early cultivars include apricot, peach, pear, persimmon, and plum trees; soybeans, mung beans, peas, and other legumes; buckwheat, various kinds of millet, barley, and rice; safflower, rape, and other producers of edible oils; Chinese cabbage, radishes, and other vegetables; and a variety of special-purpose plants such as the lacquer tree (lacquer), hops (flavoring agent), hemp (fibers and drugs), and the bottle gourd (containers).

EARLY FARMERS (C. 7000–5000 B.C.)[8]

K. C. Chang suggested that one of the most significant discoveries in the prehistoric archaeology of North China is the discovery in eastern Shensi Province and other areas of

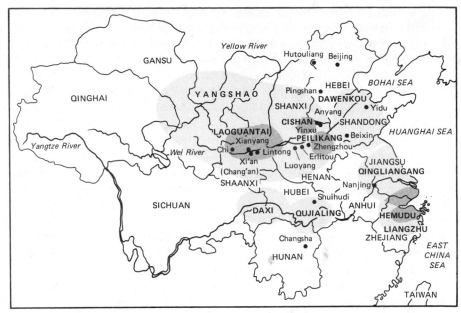

FIGURE 11.2   The earliest Neolithic cultures of North China appeared in several distinct regions, shown here in darker shading, with the approximate boundaries of their artifact style distributions shown in lighter shading.

microlithic stone tools dating perhaps (the dating is uncertain) to about 13,000 years ago. These finds are important because little is known about the people of China as the Pleistocene ended or about their descendants, whose hunting-foraging culture gave way to the first farmers. The distinctive artifact styles of these stone tools and other finds indicate that a large population of pre-agricultural peoples were widely distributed over much of China about 10,000 years ago. Most of these people were hunter-gatherers, with some groups specializing in fishing near the coasts and large lakes.

Although there are gaps in the archaeological record in the centuries just after these microlithic industries were in use, during the past decade many sites have been found that appear to have been the earliest Chinese farming communities. These villages date to between about 6500 and 5000 B.C. and have been grouped into regional clusters (Figure 11.2). These include the Cishan, Peiligang, and Dadiwan, as well as several other cultures.[9] These settlements were located along the lower terraces of the western highlands, in the valleys of the Wei, Huanghe, and a few other rivers. This warm, moderately rainy area has great agricultural potential, especially in the alluvial plains, the loess plateau, and the hilly lands of the Shangdong peninsula. Early farmers in this area took advantage of these zones by staking their subsistence on several highly reliable and stable resources. Probably the most important food source was millet, a cereal grass (both foxtail millet [*Setaria italica*] and broomcorn millet [*Panicum miliaceum*]) that produces a very nutritious grain. Nutritionally as rich as wheat, millet is also quick-maturing and drought-resistant—making it admirably suited to North China—and its stems can be used for food, fuel, and fodder. Stone sickle blades, grinding stones, and other tools indicate that much farming was devoted to millet, which was complemented with vegetables, an edible vegetable oil (in the form of rapeseed [*Brassica*]), and meat from domesticated pigs and chickens. The farmers also collected walnuts, hazelnuts, and other wild plant foods and hunted deer. Like many other peoples around the world, their first domesticate was probably the dog, skeletons of which have been found at various sites. These early farmers lived mainly in small (2–3 m in diameter) subterranean houses. They already knew how to make pottery at this time, and used an impressive diversity of ground stone grinders, bone needles, and many other implements of stone, bone, and wood.

The earliest agricultural sites in South China are only a bit later than those in the north, but our knowledge of them is much less advanced. Several caves in China and Thailand have deeply buried remains from this period, and some of these early levels contain cord-marked pottery and what may be the remains of domesticated plants.

REGIONAL NEOLITHIC DEVELOPMENTS IN NORTH CHINA (5000–3000 B.C.)

The largest and best-known early agricultural Chinese communities are those of the Yangshao culture (see Figure 11.2). The Yangshao covered the same approximate area as did the earlier P'ei-li-kang culture, and the similarities between these two indicate cultural continuity. Most of the Yangshao settlements were distributed along the banks of the Huanghe and other river systems in central China. Bones of most of the larger animals native to this part of China, from rabbits to rhinos, have been found in Yangshao settlements, but millet probably provided most of the calories, while sorghum and a few other crops were also cultivated. Like their counterparts in the forests of temperate Europe, early Chinese farmers probably cleared land for farming by slashing down vegetation with stone axes and then burning it off when it had dried.[10]

And like other early cultivators they took full advantage of game animals, wild plants, and fishing—as evidenced by the hundreds of hooks, fish gorges, and net weights found. Pigs, domestic fowl, and, later, cattle, sheep, and goats were favored sources of meat.

In a real sense, the first ancestors of the civilization we know imprecisely as "China" were probably the sturdy peasants of the Yangshao period (radiocarbon-dated to c. 5100–2950 B.C.,[11] who lived in villages like Bampo (formerly "Pan-p'o"). Wearing rough clothes made of hemp, bunkered down in houses with floors dug several feet below ground (Figure 11.3) to shield themselves from winter snows and summer heat, the people of Bampo followed the familiar agricultural cycle of China. Other Yangshao sites have evidence for above-ground houses (Figure 11.4). Millet was the staple; pigs and ducks recycled wastes into the basic meats of what was even then perhaps a world-class cuisine; and cattle, sheep, and goats contributed their all in the form of meat, milk, draft power, leather, and wool. The few hundred people at Bampo, like most of their neighbors, were probably self-sufficient in everything that really mattered except marriageable women.

Another Yangshao village that has been extensively excavated is Jiangzhai, in Shaanxi Province.[12] Over an area of about 50,000 m² the people here built a neatly organized community that was surrounded by a defensive moat and was arranged in five complexes, each with a large house surrounded by 10–20 smaller ones. Most of the houses were semi-

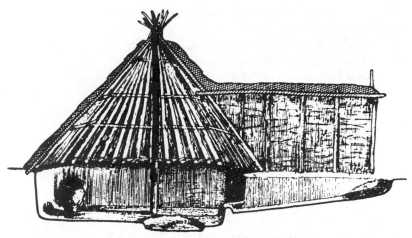

FIGURE 11.3 This reconstruction of a Neolithic house at Bampo (Pan-p'o-ts'un) illustrates how early Chinese farmers protected themselves against the harsh north China winters by living in pithouses.

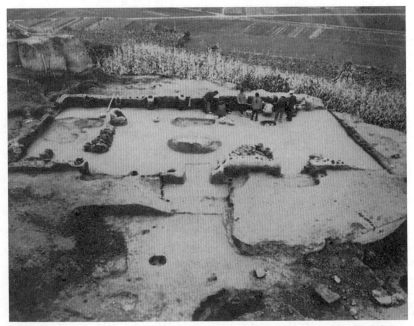

FIGURE 11.4 The foundation of a Yangshao culture house at Dadiwan, China.

subterranean with wood super-structures. Like other early farmers, the people of Jiangzhai buried their dead with household objects, which suggests a belief in a life after death that was something like their life in this world. Children were buried in ceramic urns—an ancient practice that still continues in parts of Asia.

Yangshao villages seem to have been abandoned and reoccupied periodically—probably because these people practiced slash-and-burn farming, wearing out the soil in the area around their community, then relocating the village, and eventually returning to the abandoned areas when the fertility was renewed by regrowth of vegetation.

Already by the time of Bampo the Chinese aesthetic sense is evident in the designs and color of pottery, jade carvings, and other artifacts. Stylized fish and animals grace some of the burnished pottery, and some pots were marked with symbols that may be early expressions of written Chinese. Around the houses were many deep pits, presumably for storing millet and other commodities. No doubt most villagers were full-time agriculturalists, but some engaged in silkworm cultivation, pottery manufacture, jade carving, and leather and textile production.

Bampo has been converted into an impressive museum, and more than 200 of the original inhabitants of this community are still there, their skeletons protruding from house floors and pits. Most of the site has been enclosed in a building, with some of the most important houses and artifacts left in place. At some Yangshao sites the bodies of people seem to have been reburied in groups. K. C. Chang notes that at Yuan-chun-miao, 57 graves were arranged "in six north-south rows, the earliest being the first and fourth rows, the latest the third and sixth rows. . . . This layout and chronological order have led to the reasonable speculation that the cemetery was divided into two moieties, reflecting the two-clan composition of the village."[13]

In the middle of Bampo was a distinctive building, much larger than the typical house and of different construction. To the Chinese excavators, this building seems most likely to have been a communal meeting hall; but one might also suspect that a bit of capitalistic inequality had infected the Yangshao culture and that this was the house of a "big man" or chief.[14] However, there are no evident signs of varying status in other artifacts at the site.

There are, however, some indications that Yangshao peoples occasionally buried individuals with grave goods and other furnishings that might be interpreted as indicating status differences. One example is found at the site of Xishuipo in Henan Province. The site, which extends over 50,000 m², contains house foundations, pits for storage, and burials.[15] In Tomb 45, an adult male is buried in an extended position. Surrounding him are three younger individuals. The most significant aspect of this burial, however, is the presence of two animal mosaics made of mollusk shells, as well as a triangular mosaic of mollusk shells and two human tibia—lower leg bones.[16] The animal mosaics include a dragon and a tiger (Figure 11.5). One interpretation of this burial is that the adult male was a shaman—a ritual specialist—with the animal images representing helpers in communicating with the supernatural.[17]

More than a hundred Neolithic sites (c. 5000–3000 B.C.) have been found in the Lake T'ai-hu area, southeast of Nanjing. Rice cultivation provided the main staple, but the range of animals hunted was impressive, including boars, elephants, alligators, deer, and many other species. One example of an early southern Neolithic community is at Hemudu, in northern Zhejiang Province, where excavations in 1973 through 1978 revealed a 7,000-year-old village of wooden houses built on piles along the shore of a small lake (Figure 11.6). The preservation of objects at this site is spectacular. Excavators found bone hoes, wooden shuttles for weaving, ivory carvings, and many plant and animal remains, including rice, bottle gourds, water chestnuts, domesticated water buffalo, pigs, dogs, and wild animals such as tigers, elephants, and rhinoceroses.

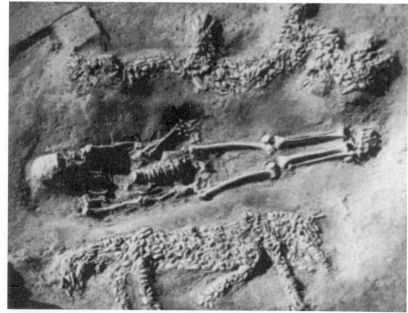

FIGURE 11.5 This Yangshao culture burial from the site of Yangshao, China, is accompanied by shell mosaics of a dragon (*top*) and tiger (*bottom*).

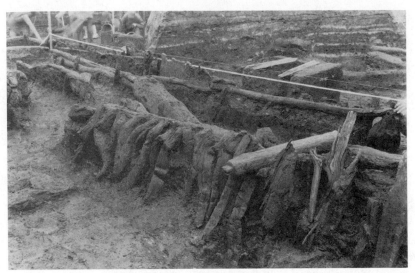

The extension of pottery styles over much of North China during the period between 5000 and 3000 B.C. is probably the clearest early sign that by this time people were developing the integrated economic and political institutions on which the later Chinese states were constructed.

FIGURE 11.6 Good organic preservation yielded the wooden structural remains from the site of Hemudu, China.

EARLY COMPLEX CHINESE SOCIETIES (3000–1900 B.C.)

In the early third millennium B.C., the people of North and Central China—at least on the basis of our limited archaeological evidence—seem the very picture of egalitarian, peaceful villagers; but by the beginning of the second millennium B.C., signs of social rank and violence are everywhere.

Chinese legend relates that the first Chinese emperor was Huang Di, a northern Chinese warlord who is reputed to have established a dynasty in 2698 B.C. Whatever the validity of this legend, the archaeological record indicates rapidly increasing social complexity, with the emergence of the Longshan and related cultures (Figure 11.7). Longshan cultures, like the Yangshao, are defined on the basis of similar styles of artifacts—in the Longshan case by highly burnished, wheel-made, thin-walled black pottery in many different vessel forms; these pots are found, with minor stylistic variations, from the southeastern coast of China to the northern provinces. Very early Longshan pottery and other diagnostic artifacts are found over most of the old Yangshao heartland. And while Yangshao communities in some places seem to have given rise almost directly to Longshan communities, the linkages between these periods and peoples are still quite obscure.[18]

As with the Yangshao, the Longshan peoples lived mainly in villages made up of pithouses arranged around a central "long house," and virtually every Longshan adult male was probably still a millet farmer who supplemented the family fortunes with hunting, collecting, and part-time craft production of pottery, jade, or another commodity. But Longshan villages were, on the average, significantly larger than those of the Yangshao period, and were likely occupied for longer periods of time.

Like their counterparts in other early civilizations, ancient Chinese farmers eventually made a momentous transition: Instead of the slash-and-burn agriculture practiced in the Yangshao period, shifting fields from year to year, they began in Longshan times to cultivate the same fields each year. The costs of doing this are high: One has to use animal manure, clovers, and discarded plants to renew fertility, or else irrigation water must be led to the

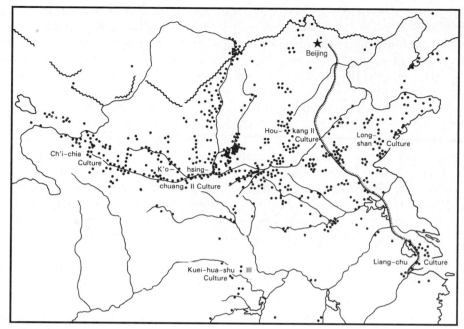

FIGURE 11.7 Archaeological sites of the Longshan and related cultures.

fields through canals to replenish soil fertility. In some places, of course, in China as in Egypt, the annual floods renew soil fertility, but in all ancient civilizations a point was eventually reached where intensification of agriculture was required to sustain life. Longshan agriculture, although still based on millet and a few domesticated animals, seems to have been more intensive than that of the Yangshao. Domestic poultry, sheep, and cattle became more important, and there is evidence of the increasing significance of rice agriculture in some southern areas.

There are also signs of change in social organization. Compared with Yangshao graves, Longshan burials seem to differ between those of richer and those of poorer people, at least as reflected in the pots, metal implements, and other items buried with these people. One of the best examples is from the Taosi cemetery in southern Shanxi.[19] The excavators identified three groups of burials—the "richest" were all males, each of whom had a wooden coffin, powdered cinnabar (a bright red mineral), and 100–200 grave goods. The very largest of these rich tombs had alligator drums and jade ritual objects, suggesting trade in exotic items among the elite members of Longshan culture.[20] In contrast, the "poorest" group of burials were only narrow vertical burial pits and contained few if any burial goods.[21]

Longshan pottery and jade ornaments are so technologically sophisticated and beautiful that they suggest the existence of at least some semi-specialized craftsmen.

Based on an analysis of pig skulls in burials at several Neolithic sites, Seung-Og Kim has argued[22] that pigs were used as important status and wealth markers. Pigs were supremely adapted to Neolithic Chinese agriculture. Evidence suggests that pigs were even kept in household latrine areas and subsisted in part on human waste products—an early indication of the extraordinary practicality of Chinese cuisine and their ability to convert materials from every stage of the food chain into appealing foods. Kim found that the Chinese Neolithic graves with the most wealth in the form of ivory and jade ornaments, pottery, and other goods also, on average, had more pig skulls and carved pig tusks in them. Kim suggests that these interred pig bones reflect a society in which the great economic value of the pig as the most important domestic animal (in terms of its popularity as a food) was complexly linked to the social context of ritual, wealth, and political prestige. He hypothesizes that pigs could be used as a form of exchangeable wealth and that some individuals could have risen in wealth and prestige by using pigs to acquire exotic prestige goods such as jade and turtle shell through long-distance trade. As Kim notes, ethnographic studies of Melanesian and other societies show that pigs often are viewed as a form of wealth and that pig slaughtering and meat distribution are important parts of the competition for power, wealth, and prestige in these "big-man" or tribal societies. Kim argues that between about 4000 and 2000 B.C. the elites in many Chinese communities used pigs as "concentratable and productive internal wealth in order to establish political authority."[23]

Longshan people sought knowledge through *scapulimancy*, the art of writing signs on bones, applying heat to the bone to crack it, and then interpreting the pattern of cracking to foretell the future. Archaeologist K. C. Chang interprets the appearance of this art in Longshan times as a reflection of the rise of at least a semi-professional class of shamans—an interpretation made credible by the fact that the character meaning "book" already appears on these bones and may signify the existence of specialized scribes.

Chang also notes that the first traces of town walls—which became a standard feature of later communities—are found at the Longshan site of Ch'eng-tzu-yai. It was built with the "stamped-earth" technique, in which layer after layer of fine loess silts and clays were stamped by workers into a compact wall. The wall at Ch'eng-tzu-yai has now largely deteriorated, but from its traces the excavators estimate it was 6 m high and 9 m wide at the top.

Longshan and related communities were probably still largely self-sufficient and independent. Researchers such as Li Liu,[24] however, have described the medium and large sites of the Longshan period as possible regional centers. Some of these sites are fortified while others are not. Evidence for residential segregation within larger communities consists of large well-constructed buildings, some of which are associated with human sacrifice, and all of which are separated from the houses of commoners. And there appears to be craft specialization and production in items such as textiles, pottery, stone tools, and maybe metallurgy. Another key aspect—like the situation in Mesopotamia—is that these regional centers are often located near river channels that are important water transportation routes.[25]

The transition to life in permanent villages and established agricultural fields was made over much of North China in the Longshan period, from the western highlands into the northern Manchurian highlands and well into southern China.

K. C. Chang has summarized the overall developments of China in the third millennium B.C. in terms of eight features that, taken together, indicate evolving cultural interaction and complexity: (1) the beginnings of copper metallurgy; (2) the widespread use of sophisticated potters' wheels and presumably the emergence of a specialized class of potters; (3) the stamped-earth walls found at some sites, and their implication of the need for civil defense; (4) burials of bodies in wells, mass graves, and other conditions that suggest warfare; (5) the use of animal and other motifs in art works in ways that indicate emerging status differences; (6) decorated jade masks and other objects that suggest an emerging ritual system practiced over a large part of the country; (7) the widespread use of scapulimancy, also suggesting ritual interaction over a large area; and (8) signs of social ranking and wealth differences in burials.[26]

We can easily draw parallels here with Egypt, Mesopotamia, and the Indus Valley: the Chinese use of jade, scapulimancy, and so forth are distinctive in their specifics, but the general pattern is one of emerging and evolving class-consciousness, functional specialization, and administrative complexity.[27]

ERH-LI-T'OU CULTURE (C. 1900–1500 B.C.)

After about 2000 B.C., large towns and cities began to replace or emerge from the tens of thousands of villages that marked earlier, simpler times. During the second millennium B.C. China really became "China," in the sense that this period marked the first widespread use of the distinctively Chinese forms of writing, architecture, art, and ideology. Also during this period all the correlates of cultural complexity—such as monumental architecture; large population concentrations; occupational specialization; written records; gross differences in wealth, power, and prestige; and large public-works projects—appeared in full measure.

Legends and early texts suggest that the first Shang kings established seven or more capital cities in the central area of the Huanghe River basin. One of the earliest sites of this transitional period to complexity is Erh-li-t'ou (Yen-shih) (Figure 11.8). Here lies a vast complex of ruins, scattered over an area about 1.5-by-2.5 km, and extending to a depth of 4 m in some places (Figure 11.9).

Among the most impressive features at Erh-li-t'ou are the foundations of two buildings that some have called "palaces": One is 108-by-100 m and is associated with a large earthen platform. In one area of its foundation was a group of burials, including one person who seems to have been buried with his hands bound. The other, smaller palace was drained with a system of pottery pipes and associated with a large earthen tomb—long since plundered of most of its wealth. The richness of Erh-li-t'ou's jade, bronze, pottery, and other artifacts; the indications of human sacrifice; and the large buildings all suggest a level of emerging cultural complexity greater than that of previous periods.

The Erh-li-t'ou culture is important because it documents the advent of the Bronze Age in China at a period earlier than the Shang, with which the earliest Bronze Age formerly was associated.[28] In fact, some Chinese scholars have attributed the Xia Dynasty to the Erh-li-t'ou culture, perhaps with the site of Erh-li-t'ou as the Xia capital.[29] More than 200 sites of the Erh-li-t'ou culture have been found, and the settlement pattern is suggestive of a four-tiered hierarchy characteristic of civilizations elsewhere—such as Mesopotamia—with a major center at Erh-li-t'ou, two smaller regional centers, several large villages, and numerous small villages.[30]

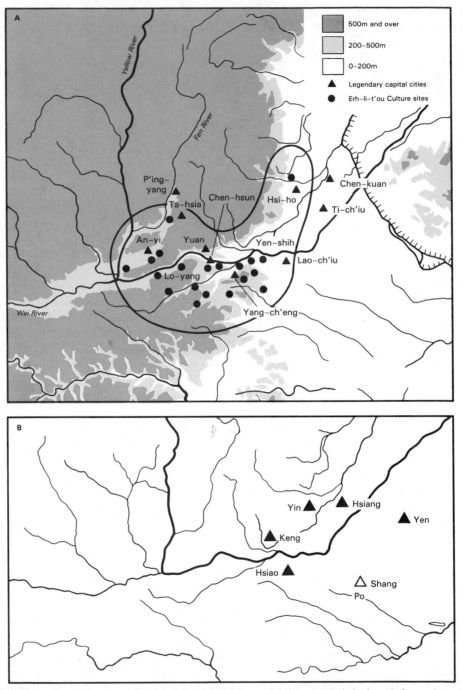

FIGURE 11.8   K. C. Chang's (1986) reconstructions of (A) major Erh-li-t'ou Culture sites and traditional Hsia Dynasty capitals; (B) traditional Shang Dynasty capitals.

SHANG CIVILIZATION AND ITS CONTEMPORARIES (C. 1600–1046 B.C.)

The Early Shang phase (or Erh-li-kang phase) is best documented archaeologically at the cluster of settlements largely buried under the modern city of Zhengzhou (formerly "Chengchou"). The central area of Erh-li-kang phase settlement was a roughly rectangular arrangement of buildings extending about 3.4 km², much of which was enclosed by a pounded-earth wall some 36 m wide at the base and 9.1 m in height—as estimated from the segments still remaining.[31] The northeastern area of the site is

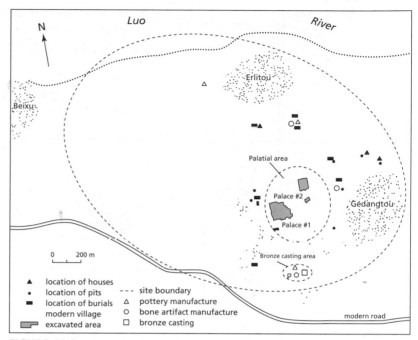

FIGURE 11.9   A sketch map of the urban center at Erh-li-t'ou, China.

thought to have been the residence and ceremonial center of the ruling elite,[32] and around it were thousands of pithouses, animal pens, shops, storage pits, and other features that make it clear that many of the people of Shang China lived lives radically different from those of Neolithic times. Hundreds of skilled, full-time craftsmen probably resided at Zhengzhou. In one area thousands of pieces of animal and human bone were recovered, much of it already fashioned into fish hooks, awls, axes, and hairpins. In another area were more than a dozen pottery kilns, each surrounded by masses of broken and overfired pottery.

But the Zhengzhou craftsmen really displayed their skill in working bronze (Figure 11.10). Large areas were given over to workshops for casting fish hooks, axes, projectile points, and various ornaments. A kind of mass-production was achieved by using multiple molds, made by impressing a clay slab with the forms of six arrowheads, with each impression connected by a thin furrow to a central channel. A second clay mold was placed over the first, the two bound together, and then molten bronze was poured in. After cooling, the individual points could be sawed off from the central stem.

In Western societies especially, there is a tendency to think of cultural change as often being driven by technological change. The invention of the locomotive, for example, radically altered nineteenth-century Western society. When we look at ancient China, there is a temptation to see a culture shaped and formed by the invention of bronze-working and iron-working. Bronze-working seems to have been an indigenous development, probably made possible by the high-temperature kilns first used to fire pottery. The requisite copper and tin could be found within several hundred kilometers of the Shang homeland, and various processes using clay models and the lost-wax process were known. The first great

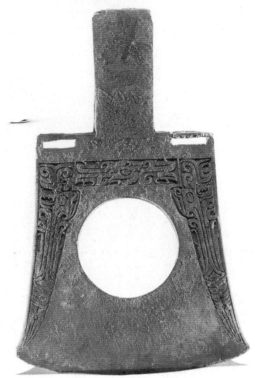

FIGURE 11.10   A bronze axe from the early
Shang period.

diffusion of Shang culture, which probably marked both the rise of national consciousness and the ramifying of political and economic networks that underlay the emergence of Shang civilization, was also marked by the spread of bronze artifacts.

But the use of bronze seems to have been mainly a stylistic phenomenon rather than a great technological advance. Though lovely to look at, the myriad bronze Shang vessels offer few culinary advantages over ceramics, and there is no evidence that bronze weapons revolutionized Shang-period warfare. And for clearing forests—an important part of the Shang expansion—stone axes and hoes would probably have worked at least as well as bronze tools, which were, in any case, a luxury item.

Bronze-making may have been invented at different times by different people. Already by 4500 B.C. people in Southeast Asia, at sites like Ban Chiang, in Thailand, were using cast-bronze spearheads and ornaments.[33] We know relatively little about these early Southeast Asian bronze-using cultures, but it seems likely that their precocious use of bronze was a result of the proximity of copper and tin deposits. Their evolution to cultural complexity followed that of the north in all essential elements and occurred much later.

Both archaeological evidence and ancient documents written after the Shang period indicate that Shang society was headed by a king, who ruled through a hierarchically arranged nobility. Commoners were conscripted for public works and military service, there were highly organized and incessant military campaigns, and many settlements were apparently integrated into an organized intervillage system of commerce.[34] It has not been determined if there were large-scale irrigation systems, but at Zhengzhou at least a canal system was in use, perhaps to carry water to the settlement or else to remove drainage water or sewage from the complex.[35]

The great mass of Shang people, however, probably lived much as their ancestors had, in villages of pithouses located along river systems, subsisting on the same kinds of crops and agricultural technology as people of previous millennia.

The last and most brilliant phase of Shang civilization, the Yinxu phase, seems to have begun about 1300 B.C., when the Shang King P'an-keng is reported to have moved his capital to the city of Angang (formerly "An-yang"), in Henan Province.

Excavations at Angang and contemporary sites in this area have been conducted intermittently since the 1920s, but the publication of this research is far from complete. Scores of sites within an area of about 24 km² have been tested, and the evidence suggests that the complex at Angang includes a large ceremonial and administrative center surrounded by smaller dependent hamlets and craft centers.[36] True to tradition, most peasants still lived in small pithouses—not very different from those of 2,000 years earlier. Scattered throughout the settlement were granaries, pottery kilns, storage pits, bone and bronze workshops, animal pens, ditches, and other familiar features of ancient Chinese life.

No city wall has been found at Angang, but monumental buildings were constructed. The largest of these was about 60 m long, rectangular in form, with large stone and bronze column bases, and founded on a large platform of compacted earth. There were at least 53 structures of this type (though somewhat smaller) in one group at Angang, arranged in three main clusters. Although not lavish in construction, these buildings were surrounded by scores of human and animal sacrificial burials, as well as many pits containing royal records written on oracle bones and numerous small structures thought to be for service personnel.[37] Near the cluster of buildings a cemetery held 11 large graves, replete with lavish, expensive burial goods and many human sacrificial burials—the whole complex surrounded by 1,200 smaller, much less lavish burials.

Elsewhere, a complex of ceremonial buildings at Hsiao-T'un was dedicated with what appears to have been the sacrifice of 852 people, 15 horses, 10 oxen, 18 sheep, 35 dogs, and 5 fully equipped chariots and charioteers.[38] A recent bumper sticker declared "If I can't take it with me, I ain't going"—a sentiment probably very agreeable to Shang rulers. Tomb after tomb was stocked with everything from chariots to rice. Like the early Mesopotamian peoples, the Chinese probably believed that burying a ruler's wives, servants, guards, and other staff with him would provide him with full services in the afterlife. The Shang may also have employed that most efficient of all incentives to a devoted domestic staff—the ritual murder of a king's staff on the occasion of his own death. Unlike feudal European nobility, few Shang nobles probably feared poisoning by members of their households. In some Shang tombs bodies were found decapitated or dismembered, and some of them had been bound before they died. How others of these people were killed—if they were—before burial is not clear, but their orderly arrangement in these and other tombs would be certain to arouse the suspicions of a coroner.

The Shang ceremonial and administrative structures are perhaps not as impressive in size or cost as the temples of Mesopotamia or the pyramids of Egypt and Mesoamerica, but the level of occupational specialization, the immense wealth of the burials, and the intensity of organization of the agricultural and economic systems remind one of the Mesopotamian city-states of the late fourth millennium B.C.

Outside the immediate Shang region were other Bronze Age cultures that have been less intensively excavated and studied. These include the site of Sanxigdui in Sichuan Province. A walled city covering some 3 km^2 was discovered here and extensive excavations were undertaken beginning in the late 1980s.[39] In the south part of the walled city, two sacrificial pits were found. These contain literally thousands of artifacts of all kinds—jade, pottery, seashells, gold and bronze masks, bronze vessels, bronze human heads, elephant tusks, and more. Study of the artifacts suggests that they were made locally, but some have features that indicate contact with Erh-li-t'ou and Shang cultures.[40]

Late in the Shang period (about 1200 B.C.), the written language had evolved (perhaps quite rapidly) to the point that texts from this period give us a detailed portrait of Shang life. Over 3,000 phonetic, ideographic, and pictographic characters were in use—of which about 1,200 have been identified—and more than 160,000 inscribed shells (of which only some have been translated) and numerous inscriptions in bronze or stone date to this period.[41]

According to the texts, the late Shang rulers held sway over a territory extending from the Pacific shore to Shensi Province in the west, and from the Yangtze River in the south to southern Hupeh in the north. At the apex of Shang society was the king, who ruled directly on many affairs of state and was assisted by a complex hierarchy of nobles possessing considerable local autonomy in their respective territories. These lords were charged with defending the homeland, supplying men for armies and public-works projects, and collecting and contributing state taxes. Toward the end of the Shang period, many nobles apparently achieved almost feudal status and were virtually independent in their own domains. But the king was still considered to have superior supernatural powers and to be the pivot of all ritual procedures. The kingdom was viewed in the traditional Chinese fashion, with itself as the center of the universe but ringed by non-Shang "barbarians," whom the Shang kings manipulated through force and diplomacy.[42]

On occasion, royal armies of up to about 30,000 men were conscripted and led by the nobles against insurgent "barbarians" and neighboring principalities. The basis of the army was the horse-drawn chariot, supported by infantrymen armed with powerful laminated wood and bone bows and bronze-tipped arrows and equipped with small knives and/or halberds, which were large knives or axes mounted on the end of a wood shaft about 6 feet long. Royal records indicate that military campaigns often incurred and inflicted frightful casualties. No doubt many hundreds of thousands of people died in ferocious wars of which history no longer has any record. Staggering quantities of plunder were often taken, along with thousands of prisoners, most of whom were apparently sacrificed or enslaved.[43]

The agricultural system seems to have been essentially the same as previously, with millet, wheat, rice, and vegetables the major crops; cattle, sheep, pigs, and poultry the main livestock; and water buffalo the only "new" domestic animal. The proportions of these crops and animals may have shifted somewhat, with wheat and rice expanding their range at the expense of millet, but the evidence for this is questionable. There is little record of large irrigation systems anywhere in the Shang domain, and hunting and gathering still supplied a substantial part of the diet. The mammalian faunal remains from Angang include massive quantities of boar, deer, bear, and other hunted animals, including a few elephants, rhinoceroses, leopards, and even part of a whale.[44] Apparently intravillage trade in foodstuffs was voluminous.

Local occupational specialization was considerable. Many villages lacked one or more of the more important handicraft workshops, suggesting that products were exchanged among these settlements.[45] The discovery of large caches of agricultural implements (3,500 stone sickles, new and used, in a single pit at one site, for example) may indicate a degree of centralized management of both agriculture and craft production.[46] The Shang even had a type of money, in the form of strings of cowrie shells.

Toward the end of the Shang period, there were many walled towns and villages in North and Central China, and, compared to earlier periods, a much greater proportion of the populace lived in these semi-urban settings. But if we compare the settlement size distribution of late Shang China—or rather what we estimate it to have been—with those of Mesopotamia or Mesoamerica at a comparable level of development, it is clear that Shang China was a much less urbanized society. There were no settlements the size of Ur or Teotihuacán.

We cannot know the minds of the Shang Chinese in any detailed sense, but their artifacts give us clues as to what they thought of the world. Like many ancient peoples, they seem to have sought a basic symmetry in all things. All temples and tombs were oblong or square and oriented to the four cardinal directions. Bronzes were always symmetrical, and even the messages inscribed on turtle shells for divinations were repeated on the right and left sides. The world was conceived of as square, the wind as blowing from four quarters, and four groups of foreigners were thought to live on China's borders. Throughout their art, architecture, and literature, elements appear two by two, four by four, and in other intricate but symmetrical arrangements.

The texts and inscriptions tell us that the Shang nobles felt in constant and clear communication with their ancestors, whom they consulted through oracles about the best actions to take in multitudes of situations.

EARLY IMPERIAL CHINA (1046 B.C.–A.D. 220)

The early phases of Chinese civilization are often called the "Three Dynasties"—the Erh-li-t'ou being the first, the Shang the second, and the Zhou (formerly known as "Chou") the third. Yet these three dynasties overlapped somewhat, and, as K. C. Chang notes, the developmental pattern was one of "Early Shang, interacting with Erh-li-t'ou, and proto-Zhou, interacting with Shang."[47]

Chang goes on to quote a poem dating to the Zhou Dynasty that ascribes the dynasty's origins to divine will:

> August is God on high;
> Looking down, he is majestic;
> He inspected and regarded the [states of] the four quarters,
> He sought tranquillity for the people.
> These two kingdoms [of Hisa and Shang],
> Their government had failed;
> Throughout those states of the four [quarters] he investigated and estimated;
> God on high brought it to a settlement;
> Hating their extravagance,
> He looked about and turned his gaze to the West,
> And there he gave an abode.[48]

The "West" of this lyric, chosen by God, was the Zhou state. Had we the means to see it in all its splendor, ancient imperial China under the Zhou and later states may well have appeared to us as the most complex and colorful civilization of all antiquity. After 1046 B.C., the Zhou Empire (Figure 11.11) and its successors arranged much of China in a feudal system that led to the growth of cities, great cycles of peace followed by warfare, and minutely differentiated administrative hierarchies.[49] Again and again particular families of nobles or commoners would rise to power, make war on their neighbors, extend their kingdoms, and then collapse under the onslaught of competing warlords. Through it all, exquisite bronzes, porcelains, pots, and jewelry were made and lavished on the rich; untold thousands of people were sacrificed to be buried with their rulers; and millions lived and died in the eternal agricultural cycle of rural China (Figure 11.12).

By 500 B.C. iron-working became widespread, and iron agricultural tools were in common use. Iron weapons, mass burials, and military annals tell of a savage form of warfare, not at all like the depersonalized modern combat of tanks, missiles, and automatic weapons. Men in armor fought at close quarters with swords and knives on battlefields swarming with chariots, cavalry, and bowmen.

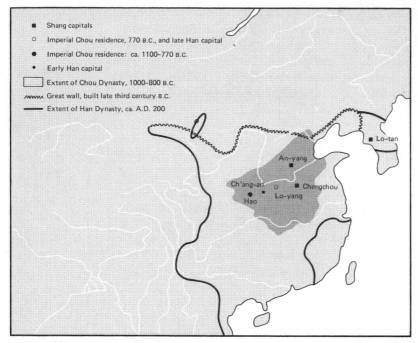

Shang capitals
Imperial Chou residence, 770 B.C., and late Han capital
Imperial Chou residence: ca. 1100–770 B.C.
Early Han capital
Extent of Chou Dynasty, 1000–800 B.C.
Great wall, built late third century B.C.
Extent of Han Dynasty, ca. A.D. 200

Lo-tan
An-yang
Ch'ang-an   Chengchou
Hao   Lo-yang

FIGURE 11.11 From the original Shang-period state, China evolved into true empires during the Zhou and Han dynasties, whose extents are indicated here.

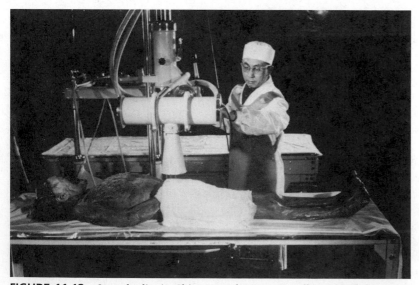

FIGURE 11.12 Some bodies in Chinese tombs were so well preserved that autopsies can reveal causes of death. Here a Chinese radiologist X-rays Lady Dai, a Han Dynasty noblewoman who died in 141 B.C. of a heart attack.

At about the time iron was introduced, Confucius (551–479 B.C.) lived and taught and, together with the spread of Buddhism in the third century A.D., moved much of Chinese thought beyond the reach of the foreigner.

Amid the panoply of arts, crafts, and religion, the prosaic elements of agriculture were also changing. After 500 B.C. great irrigation works were brought into use, allowing the intensive cultivation of wet-rice species as well as many other crops. This in turn supported the tremendous population densities of China. Along with the introduction of the ox-drawn plow and the evolution of precise crop-rotation practices, Chinese agriculture underwrote the impressive cultural elaborations we associate with the Qin (221–206 B.C.) and Han (206 B.C.–A.D. 220) dynasties.

The great richness and opulence of the Qin Dynasty is lavishly displayed in the Museum of Qin Shi Huang, in Shaanxi Province. In a project worthy of Egyptian pharaohs, the emperor Qin Shi Huang drafted 700,000 people to build a huge mausoleum and palace complex. The work lasted for 39 years, and when it was finished it was full of rare and beautiful objects. Historical records of the time say that the complex was lighted with lamps fueled by the fat of giant salamanders. In 206 B.C. the whole complex was burned in a popular revolt. When archaeologists excavated they found 56.25 km^2 of buildings and features, including "tombs of immolated slaves, table pits, stone material processing workshops, tombs of criminals, pits for the execution of slaves, pits of life-size terra cotta warriors and horses, and pits of bronze chariots and horses."[50] The site so far has revealed thousands of life-size statues of warriors and horses, all rendered in exquisite detail.

One of the world's first imperial censuses was conducted in China in A.D. 1–2 and tallied 57.7 million people, at least 10 percent of whom lived in rectangular wooden buildings in towns with populations of up to about 250,000. Coins circulated, schools flourished, and a rich store of literature was created.

Through it all, along the northern and western frontiers, the nomadic horsemen and herders of Asia pressed on the periphery of successive empires. The Great Wall, begun during the Warring States period and unified under Qin Shi Huang (246–209 B.C.) was meant to keep the nomad out and the farmer in, but it was probably not too successful. Throughout Chinese history there was a constant interchange between sedentary and nomadic cultures.

Westerners tend to think of China as a static civilization with ancient and fixed forms. But from the long-term perspective, it has been a varied, ineffably complex cultural pageant.

SUMMARY AND CONCLUSIONS

If we look at Chinese civilization for the standard markers of early civilizations, as described in chapter 7, they are all evident: (1) an initial spread of regional styles of ceramics and artifacts reflecting increasing intensity and scope of cultural interactions among Neolithic farmers; (2) the appearance of burials indicating inherited wealth, power, and prestige (Figure 11.13); (3) the gradual development of towns and cities, often ringed with defensive walls, in which administrative bureaucracies and craft-production facilities were concentrated; (4) a rising level of regional and national warfare; (5) an elaboration over time in monumental architecture, writing, and other arts and crafts and the development of a national religion and ideology; and, (6) throughout the whole sequence, an overall increase in the population density, technological production, and size of competing nation-states.

Chinese civilization also offers some contrasts to other civilizations. Compared to Mesopotamia, for example, early Chinese societies were less urban than the Sumerian peoples, although in later Chinese history the country

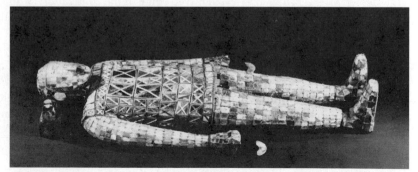

FIGURE 11.13 Like their contemporaries in Egypt and Mesopotamia, early Chinese complex societies expended enormous amounts of wealth in mortuary cults. This Chinese princess of the late second millennium B.C. was entombed in a suit made of 2,000 jade tiles tied together with gold wire.

became heavily urbanized. Many hypotheses have been suggested for why people aggregate in settlements of different sizes under different conditions. Unfortunately, the archaeological evidence from China during the critical periods is not sufficiently complete to evaluate the several possibilities. Some have thought that warfare was important in determining the settlement size distribution in ancient China, and in fact warfare did have a profound influence on Chinese developments. But warfare, too, seems to be simply another—and somewhat variable—expression of more fundamental changes going on within societies as their complexity and differentiation increase.

One factor of continual importance in all Chinese developments was the great spread of the nomadic and semi-nomadic peoples who lived on the borders of the agricultural heartland. Some of the earliest documents attesting to the rise of the Chinese state, for example, imply that the Zhou Empire was initiated by the movement of the warlord Tai Wang to the central Shaanxi Province under pressure from his nomadic neighbors.[51] And Owen Lattimore's comprehensive history of relationships between nomad and farmer in China illustrated the crucial role of this relationship in the formation of all later Chinese empires.[52]

Chinese civilization also appears to have placed women in positions of power to a much greater degree than some other civilizations. In all known ancient civilizations women of elite and royal families had special status and prerogatives, but in ancient China women were important bureaucrats, served as royal envoys, and in at least one instance commanded an army.[53]

K. C. Chang suggests that Chinese civilization was extraordinarily absorbed with *shamanism*—the connection to another world, a world of the gods and magical powers, through priests. Chang also offers this condensed hypothesis about Chinese cultural evolution: "[T]he wealth that produced the civilization was itself the product of concentrated political power, and the acquisition of power was accomplished through the accumulation of wealth."[54] Chang suggests that Chinese civilization operated on a profoundly religious basis, with kings, nobles, and commoners arranged in a layered universe, under a pantheon of gods, with communication between the physical and spirit worlds channeled through priests. Hence the abiding concern with divining the will of the gods through oracles—the king himself was credited with oracular powers. And, as Chang notes, technology has a reduced importance in such a fundamentally religious and abstract cosmology, which may explain even some of the contemporary differences between East and West.

China eventually became locked in the same cyclical pattern of expansion and collapse we documented in other ancient civilizations. Indeed, the apparent cyclicity of Chinese history has been the basis for many general models of cultural complexity, ranging from Marx to Marvin Harris.[55] In these ancient empires it is as if some internal limiting factors exist that restrain growth past a certain point, at least until certain evolutionary conditions are present. Perhaps these were primarily technological limits in these early empires. Without modern means of information collection, storage, retrieval, and dissemination, political systems have very definite limits in terms of the numbers of people, projects, and provinces they can successfully integrate.

BIBLIOGRAPHY

Akazawa, T., and C. M. Aikens, eds. 1986. *Prehistoric Hunter-Gatherers in Japan*. Tokyo: University Museum, University of Tokyo, Bulletin No. 27.

An, Zhimin. 1994. "China During the Neolithic." In *History of Humanity, Vol. 1: Prehistory and the Beginnings of Civilization*, ed. S. J. De Laet. New York: Routledge.

Anonymous. 1982. *Neolithic Site at Banpo Near Xian*. Trans. Du Youliang [sic]. Guide to the Banpo Museum, printing data written in Chinese.

Barnard, N. 1961. *Bronze Casting and Bronze Alloys in Ancient China*. Canberra: Australian National University.

Barnes, G. L. 1990. *Bibliographic Reviews of Far Eastern Archaeology 1990: Hoabhinian, Jomon, Yayoi*. Oxford, England: Oxbow Books.

———. 1993. *China, Korea, and Japan*. London and New York: Thames and Hudson.

Bayard, D. 1979. "The Chronology of Prehistoric Metallurgy in North-East Thailand: Silabhumi or Samrddhabhumil." In *Early South-East Asia*, ed. R. B. Smith and W. Watson. London: Oxford University Press.

———. 1986. "Agriculture, Metallurgy, and State Formation in Southeast Asia." *Current Anthropology* 25(1):103–105.

Bellwood, P. 1986. *The Prehistory of the Indo-Malaysian Archipelago*. Sydney: Academic Press.

Chang, K. C. 1976. *Early Chinese Civilization: Anthropological Perspectives*. Cambridge, MA: Harvard University Press.

———. 1977. *The Archaeology of Ancient China*, 3rd ed. New Haven: Yale University Press.

———. 1980. *Shang Civilization*. New Haven, CT: Yale University Press.

———. 1981. "In Search of China's Beginnings: New Light on an Old Civilization." *American Scientist* 69:148–158.

Chang, S. 1963. "The Historical Trend of Chinese Urbanization." *Annals of the Association of American Geographers* 53:109–143.

Chang, T. 1957. *Archaeological Studies in Szechwan*. Cambridge, England: Cambridge University Press.

———. 1963. *Archaeology in China, Vol. 3: Chou China*. Cambridge: Heffer.

De, Zhou Shi. 1987. "Classical Chinese Contributions to Shipbuilding." *Endeavour* NS. 11(1):2–4.

Harris, M. 1977. *Cannibals and Kings* . New York: Random House.

Higham, C. 1989. *The Archaeology of Mainland Southeast Asia*. Cambridge, England: Cambridge University Press.

Kim, S. O. 1994. "Burials, Pigs, and Political Prestige in Neolithic China." *Current Anthropology* 35(2):119–142.

Lattimore, O. 1951. *Inner Asian Frontiers of China*. Boston: Beacon Press.

Li, C. 1957. *The Beginnings of Chinese Civilization*. Seattle: University of Washington Press.

Liu, L. 2003. "'The Products of Minds as Well as of Hands': Production of Prestige Goods in the Neolithic and Early State Periods of China." *Asian Perspectives* 42(1):1–40.

———. 2004. *The Chinese Neolithic: Trajectories to Early States*. New York: Cambridge University Press.

Meacham, W. 1977. "Continuity and Local Evolution in the Neolithic of South China: A Non-Nuclear Approach." *Current Anthropology* 18:419–440.

Nelson, S. M., ed. 1995. *The Archaeology of Northeast China: Beyond the Great Wall*. New York: Routledge.

Olsen, S. J. 1987. "The Practice of Archaeology in China Today." *Antiquity* 61(232):282–290.

Skinner, G. W. 1964. "Marketing and Social Structure in Rural China." *Journal of Asian Studies* 24:3–43.

Stanley, D. J., Z. Chen, and J. Song. 1999. "Innundation, Sea-Level Rise and Transition from Neolithic to Bronze Age Cultures, Yangtze Delta, China." *Geoarchaeology* 14(1):15–26.

Stover, L. E. 1974. *The Cultural Ecology of Chinese Civilization*. New York: Pica Press.

Toynbee, A., ed. 1973. *Half the World*. New York: Holt.

Triestman, J. 1972. *The Prehistory of China*. Garden City, NY: Natural History Press.

Trigger, B. G. 1993. *Early Civilizations: Ancient Egypt in Context*. Cairo: American University in Cairo Press.

———. 1999. "Shang Political Organization: A Comparative Approach." *Journal of East Asian Archaeology* 13(1):43–62.

Wangping, S. 2000. "The Longshan Period and Incipient Chinese Civilization." *Journal of East Asian Archaeology* 2(1–2):195–226.

Watson, W. 1971. *Cultural Frontiers in Ancient East Asia*. Edinburgh: Edinburgh University Press.

———. 1974. *Ancient China*. Greenwich, CT: New York Graphic Society.

Wheatley, P. 1971. *The Pivot of the Four Quarters*. Chicago: Aldine de Gruyter.

Wittfogel, K. A. 1957. *Oriental Despotism: A Comparative Study of Total Power*. New Haven: Yale University Press.

Wu, Z. 1985. "The Museum of Qin Shi Huang." *Museum* 147:140–147.

Yang, X., ed. 2004a. *New Perspectives on China's Past: Chinese Archaeology in the Twentieth Century. Volume 1: Cultures and Civilizations Reconsidered*. New Haven, CT: Yale University Press, and Kansas City: The Nelson-Atkins Museum of Art.

———, ed. 2004b. *New Perspectives on China's Past: Chinese Archaeology in the Twentieth Century. Volume 2: Major Archaeological Discoveries in Twentieth-Century China*. New Haven, CT: Yale University Press, and Kansas City: The Nelson-Atkins Museum of Art.

NOTES

1. De, "Classical Chinese Contributions to Shipbuilding."
2. Chang, *The Archaeology of Ancient China*, pp. 95–99.
3. Liu, *The Chinese Neolithic: Trajectories to Early States*, p. 22.
4. Ibid., pp. 23–24.
5. Ibid., pp. 20–21.
6. Stanley et al., "Inundation, Sea-Level Rise and Transition from Neolithic to Bronze Age Cultures, Yangtze Delta, China."
7. Ibid., pp. 20–24.
8. Recent work appears to show that "transitional" cultures between the late Paleolithic and Neolithic have evidence for very early pottery, as well as rice and millet—these sites date between 10,000 to 14,000 years ago, depending on the specific site (see Yang, *New Perspectives on China's Past: Chinese Archaeology in the Twentieth Century. Volume 2: Major Archaeological Discoveries in Twentieth-Century China*, pp. 34–37). This is some of the earliest pottery in the world, comparable in age to Jomon in Japan, where pottery is found associated with complex hunter-gatherers about 12,000 to 13,000 years ago (see Akazawa and Aikens, *Prehistoric Hunter-Gatherers in Japan*).
9. An, "China During the Neolithic"; Yang, *New Perspectives on China's Past: Chinese Archaeology in the Twentieth Century. Volume 1: Cultures and Civilizations Reconsidered*, p. 12.
10. Triestman, *The Prehistory of China*.
11. Yang, *New Perspectives on China's Past: Chinese Archaeology in the Twentieth Century. Volume 2: Major Archaeological Discoveries in Twentieth-Century China*, pp. 46–59.
12. Ibid.
13. Chang, "In Search of China's Beginnings: New Light on an Old Civilization," pp. 152–153.
14. Watson, *Ancient China*.
15. Yang, *New Perspectives on China's Past: Chinese Archaeology in the Twentieth Century. Volume 2: Major Archaeological Discoveries in Twentieth-Century China*, p. 53.
16. Ibid.
17. Liu, *The Chinese Neolithic: Trajectories to Early States*, p.155.
18. The following discussion of early complex Chinese societies is taken mainly from Chang, *The Archaeology of Ancient China*.
19. Liu, *The Chinese Neolithic: Trajectories to Early States*, p. 135.
20. Ibid., p. 136.
21. Ibid.
22. Kim, "Burials, Pigs, and Political Prestige in Neolithic China."
23. Ibid., p. 120.
24. See also Wangping, "The Longshan Period and Incipient Chinese Civilization."
25. Liu, *The Chinese Neolithic: Trajectories to Early States*, pp. 111–113.
26. See Chang, *The Archaeology of Ancient China*, for a review of the archaeological record of these cultural elements.
27. In addition to Chang, *The Archaeology of Ancient China*, see also Triestman, *The Prehistory of China*.
28. Yang, *New Perspectives on China's Past: Chinese Archaeology in the Twentieth Century. Volume 2: Major Archaeological Discoveries in Twentieth-Century China*, p. 114.
29. Ibid.
30. Liu, *The Chinese Neolithic: Trajectories to Early States*, p. 226.
31. Chang, *The Archaeology of Ancient China*, pp. 286–294.
32. Yang, *New Perspectives on China's Past: Chinese Archaeology in the Twentieth Century. Volume 2: Major Archaeological Discoveries in Twentieth-Century China*, p. 121.
33. Bayard, "The Chronology of Prehistoric Metallurgy in North-East Thailand: Silabhumi or Samrddhabhumil."
34. Chang, *Early Chinese Civilization: Anthropological Perspectives*.
35. Wheatley, *The Pivot of the Four Quarters*.
36. Ibid.
37. Chang, *Early Chinese Civilization: Anthropological Perspectives*, p. 10.
38. Wheatley, *The Pivot of the Four Quarters*, p. 93.
39. Limited excavations and surveys in the 1930s originally identified the site (Yang, *New Perspectives on China's Past: Chinese Archaeology in the Twentieth Century. Volume 2: Major Archaeological Discoveries in Twentieth-Century China*, pp. 144–146).
40. Ibid., p. 145.
41. Chang, *Early Chinese Civilization: Anthropological Perspectives*, p. 48.
42. Wheatley, *The Pivot of the Four Quarters*.
43. Ibid., p. 63.

44. Ibid.
45. Chang, *The Archaeology of Ancient China*, pp. 138–139.
46. Wheatley, *The Pivot of the Four Quarters*, p. 76.
47. Chang, "In Search of China's Beginnings: New Light on an Old Civilization," p. 156.
48. Ibid.
49. Wu Zilin, "The Museum of Qin Shi Huang," p. 141.
50. Chang, "In Search of China's Beginnings: New Light on an Old Civilization."
51. Lattimore, *Inner Asian Frontiers of China*.
52. Ibid.
53. Trigger, *Early Civilizations: Ancient Egypt in Context*, p. 37.
54. Chang, *The Archaeology of Ancient China*, p. 414.
55. See, for example, Harris, *Cannibals and Kings*.

Later Complex Societies of the Old World

*The day may come when, contemplating a
world given back to the primeval forest, a
human survivor will have no means of even
guessing how much intelligence Man once
imposed upon the forms of the earth, when he
set up the stones of Florence in the billowing
expanse of the Tuscan olive-groves. No trace
will be left then of the palaces that saw
Michelangelo pass by, nursing his grievances
against Raphael; and nothing of the little Paris
cafes where Renoir once sat beside Cezanne,
Van Gogh beside Gauguin. Solitude, vicegerent
of Eternity, vanquishes men's dreams no less
than armies, and men have known this ever
since they came into being and realized that
they must die.*

Andre Malraux

To imply that the rich ancient civilizations of Greece, Ghana, Germany, Japan, Thailand, and other areas beyond the "primary civilizations" we have considered in earlier chapters were "secondary" in some sense is to imply an inappropriate sense of a hierarchy of importance. In many ways these later states and empires were largely independent developments—creations of their own environments, peoples, and unique histories, even if they incorporated elements from earlier civilizations. Interactions among the world's many different cultures, moreover, have gradually increased in the past two millennia, with the balance of power and wealth frequently shifting from place to place and time to time.

But ancient cultures of temperate Europe, Sub-Saharan Africa, Southeast Asia, and many other areas were, in fact, influenced by the first civilizations, and to some extent were derivatives of them. And while European cultures, for example, eventually came to dominate the civilizations of Egypt, China, and Mesopotamia, they did so partly on the basis of the forms of agriculture and technology invented by these earlier civilizations.

It is beyond the scope of this book to review these later states and empires in great detail,[1] and, with the exception of Europe, only a few of them are described briefly at the end of this chapter to illustrate the diversity of ancient cultures and the extent to which after about 3000 B.C. the Old World became a mosaic of evolving cultures, none of which developed in isolation. From the last few millennia B.C. onward, Old World history is a dizzyingly complex tapestry in which to separate individual strands and even discern patterns is sometimes difficult. The reader may also wish to consider anew the biblical prophecy that "the last shall be first," a sentiment repeatedly demonstrated in Old World culture history, where "peripheral" political systems often rose to imperial power.

Old World prehistory after about 4000 B.C. is in a sense an account of the division of the world into fewer and fewer great empires and the slow economic intermeshing of Europe, Asia, and Africa. At about 2700 B.C. a citizen of Memphis, the capital of the Egypt state, and a hunter-forager working the north coast of France probably had not the slightest impact on each other's lives, not even as the end points of trading networks in the most exotic of commodities. But by about A.D. 200, northern France and Egypt were provinces in the Roman Empire, and French veterans of Roman armies were sometimes paid their pensions in the form of farms in Egypt. That process of growing interconnection occurred all over Europe, Asia, and Africa, but it was greatly modified by environments, transport routes, and specific historic events. Ships plying the Mediterranean coast linked millions of people in Asia, Europe and Africa, but the Sahara desert cut much of Africa off from this intense interaction; the mountains of central and western Europe had a similar effect for a time, as did the deserts, tundra, and other barriers to the east.

A.D. 600	Settlers from the Society and Marquesas islands reach Hawai'i in the Pacific
15 B.C.	Roman Conquest of central and western Europe
200 B.C.	Settlers from Fiji and Samoa reach the Society and Marquesas islands in the Pacific
475–15 B.C.	La Tène period in Europe
800–475 B.C.	Halstatt period in Europe
1000 B.C.	Iron Age begins in Europe
1000 B.C.	Fortified hilltop settlements appear in Europe
1000 B.C.	Mycenaean civilization begins
1000 B.C.	Lapita pottery reaches Fiji and Samoa in the Pacific
1500 B.C.	Lapita pottery appears in the Bismarck Archipelago in the Pacific
2000 B.C.	Minoan civilization begins
2700 B.C.	Troy established as a city in the Aegean
3000 B.C.	Beginning of the Beaker culture in Europe
3500–2300 B.C.	Battle-axe culture in Europe
4000 B.C.	Gold and copper tools appear in central Europe
4500 B.C.	Megalith construction in western Europe begins
5000 B.C.	Food-producing economies well-established in the Aegean
5600–5000 B.C.	Bandkeramik culture in central Europe
5600 B.C.	Food-producing economies reach central Europe
6000–2000 B.C. (8,000–4,000 years ago)	Neolithic food-producing economies spread in Europe

Today, however, nearly the whole world is interconnected and everywhere there are indications of a worldwide homogenization of cultures: Eskimos drive snowmobiles, Chinese drink American soft drinks, and a financial tremor in the money markets of, say, Singapore, reverberates powerfully through the world's economies. The rapid growth of the Internet and worldwide communications systems now links peoples in what can be considered a new form of organism, whose nervous system transcends distances and cultural differences. As different as our world today seems from the world of, say, 5,000 years ago, however, what we see today is the continuation of the same basic trends that were evident already by 3000 B.C., when ships were beginning to sail the Mediterranean and farming was being extended into Europe, Asia, and Africa.

TEMPERATE EUROPE

Until about the seventh millennium B.C., "Barbarian Europe"—the great forests, grasslands, and mountain ranges beyond the Aegean Sea and extending north to Britain, Scandinavia, and Russia—was inhabited only by hunters and foragers. In succeeding millennia, Europeans developed complex forms of subsistence and adaptation and a rich cultural repertoire of technology and social systems, but throughout prehistory and well into the early centuries of the first millennium A.D., European cultures were not the equal of those of Egypt, Mesopotamia, China, and other areas in most of the characteristics of cultural "complexity" (see chapter 7).

One of the great questions of comparative history is how it happened that for thousands of years much of the creativity of the world was centered in Mesopotamia, China, the Indus, and the Mediterranean, and then, after the middle of the second millennium A.D., the cultural center of the world seemed to shift so decisively to Western Europe. Europeans seem to have incorporated many cultural elements of older, foreign cultures and then developed them in unique ways in an environment very different from that of these older civilizations. Karl Marx and others have argued that one key element in the eventual dominance of Western Europe was that its societies were based on rainfall agriculture, instead of the large riverine-canal systems of the older civilizations of Egypt, Mesopotamia, and China. Central governments can control every aspect of life, if their citizens are inextricably tied to an irrigation system fed by a great river through canal systems controlled by the government. In Western Europe, however, a central government could try to conquer smaller polities but it could not control the rainfall that was the indispensable element in farming the rich lands of temperate Europe. Marx used this environmental fact to explain much of the transition to feudalism and capitalism that made Western Europeans masters of so much of the world.

Yet the economic and political history of the Old World cannot be easily or simply explained. Steven Shennan notes that many early scholars, especially V. Gordon Childe and the Marxists, saw history as a case in which "the Olympic torch of development was passed from East to West."[2] During the past several decades, research has suggested that many innovations were, in fact, independently invented in Europe, and in general there has been a critical reevaluation of the notion that to understand European prehistory one should look first and always at Mediterranean civilizations.[3]

Temperate Europe: Early Agriculture

As was discussed in chapter 6, the rough distinction between "farmers" and "hunter-foragers" obscures great variations within and between these abstract socioeconomic types. But debates about the origins of European agriculture have often been thought of in these terms. Between about 6000 and 2000 B.C. hunting-foraging economies in most of temperate Europe were replaced by agricultural economies based on cereals that had first been domesticated in the Middle East and introduced into Europe, including einkorn wheat, barley, and rye; these crops were complemented by sheep and cattle—which also were introduced as domesticates from the Middle East.[4] As Robin Dennell notes, the only major cereal crop domesticated in Europe was probably oats, which did not become economically important until late in prehistory.[5]

As with most such long-term, widespread, and radical processes of culture change, archaeologists have tended to focus on the *mechanisms* of these cultural changes. One traditional model offered to explain these mechanisms is that farmers from southern Europe and the Middle East colonized temperate Europe over several millennia and displaced hunter-foragers (Figure 12.1). As Marek Zvelebil and Paul Dolukhanov have noted,[6] this view focuses almost entirely on the circumstances and the processes of colonization, but largely ignores the response of the hunter-foragers who were presumably displaced. Other more recent models for the agricultural transition in Europe posit a greater role for the indigenous hunter-foragers.[7] Robin Dennell[8] suggests that the climate changes in Europe after the end of the ice ages favored the growth of grasses such as einkorn and barley, and Europeans may have begun exploiting them in ways that led to domestication and cereal agriculture—a largely indigenous development, in other words, that may have involved some introduced plants, and animals from Southwest Asia, but was not simply the transplanting of Asians or their agricultural systems into Europe. Emmer wheat, bread wheat, sheep, and other crops and animals, nonetheless, seem certainly to have been domesticated in Southwest Asia and then introduced to Europe.

Unfortunately, the archaeological evidence with which to evaluate some of these contrasting ideas, especially the archaeology of post-glacial hunter-foragers of Mesolithic Europe, has only recently begun to be treated systematically.[9] The European Mesolithic is defined in terms of a shift in stone tool types to an emphasis on smaller geometric forms—which may reflect primarily the introduction and improving efficiency of bows and arrows.[10]

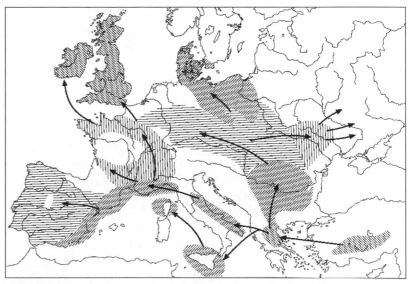

FIGURE 12.1   The spread of agriculture into Europe from the Middle East.

As Douglas Price has noted, this transition may have been mainly the result of different raw materials available as the glaciers retreated and of the evolution of tool-making skills, rather than profound social or cultural changes.[11] He also points out that we have lost much of the Mesolithic archaeological record because sea levels in northern Europe did not reach current levels until about 6000 B.C.; thus many regions available for settlement by Mesolithic peoples are now submerged.[12]

Among the earliest evidence for cereal farming comes from Argissa-Maghula in Greece, where people were cultivating emmer wheat and barley and raising cattle, sheep, and pigs by 6800 B.C.

On the Mediterranean fringes of European farming communities, agricultural villages were established on a reliable, productive mixture primarily of cereals, olives, and grapes in combination with sheep and goats. The processes by which domesticates and farming spread from the Middle East and Mediterranean areas into the great temperate forests of northern Europe remains one of the most interesting and intensively researched subjects in contemporary archaeology. Bogucki's analysis of agricultural origins in the northern European Plain, particularly in the region of Poland, for example, suggests that for centuries Mesolithic foragers and primitive agriculturalists were increasingly symbiotic in their economies and that the first agriculturalists, the Funnel Beaker People, involved the "selective incorporation of cultigens and domestic animals into an essentially Mesolithic way of life."[13] He also suggests that the great stone monuments and tombs that eventually appeared all over Europe were in fact territorial markers, which became important considerations as agriculture spread.

There are great environmental differences between the semi-arid Mediterranean zone and the wetter, cooler regions of Britain, the Low Countries, northern Germany, and southern Scandinavia. A prehistoric farmer in southern Italy needed only a few hand-tools to farm successfully, but a peasant in northern Germany required capital-intensive equipment, such as the horse-drawn mouldboard plow. As Graeme Barker has observed,

> The object of Mediterranean plowing has always been to conserve the moisture content of the soil by scuffling the surface, whereas in northern Europe heavy equipment is needed to break up the thick mass of roots in order to release the soil nutrients from the lower depths. . . . The analysis of the early history of agriculture in particular, and of the productive economy in general, in the two areas has been characterized by a definite sense of entrepreneurial risk takers in the Mediterranean contrasting with their honest but stolid contemporaries in the north, rather like the familiar contrast between the respective football teams of southern and northern European countries today.[14]

The rate and pattern of agriculture's spread across Europe raise some interesting questions. To a certain extent, this spread can be assumed to be determined by the blunt forces of environment, technology, and demography. The genetic composition of cereals sets a strict limit to the rate at which species adapt to different environments, and without artificial fertilizers the yields of crops—and therefore human population densities—are narrowly constrained. But when we look at the problem of how small-time European farmers eventually produced complex societies here, we can begin to see how complexly interrelated are four dimensions of these ancient societies: climate-environment, farming technology, human population fluctuations, and sociopolitical institutions.[15] By 5600 B.C., a Mediterranean complement of domestic grains, cows, and sheep—and the technology to exploit them—had moved up the Danube into central Europe (see Figure 12.1). People lived in small clusters of wooden huts, often with their animals, and farmed narrow plots near rivers and streams. Some of the spread of this form of agricultural settlement in Europe is marked by pottery decorated with incised, linear patterns—the Bandkeramik style. The Bandkeramik peoples and their agricultural way of life appear first along the Danube in central Europe, and by shortly after 5000 B.C. had settled as far north as southern Holland. These sturdy farmers lived in small homesteads composed of

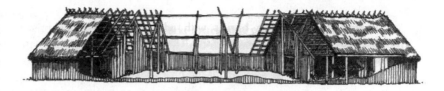

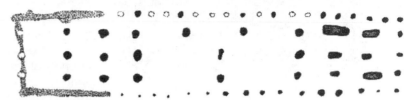

FIGURE 12.2   Reconstruction (*top*) and plan view (*bottom*) of a Linear Bandkeramik longhouse in Europe.

timber-and-thatch houses (Figure 12.2) and subsisted on barley, einkorn, wheat, cattle, sheep, goats, and a variety of other crops and animals.

Unlike that of the semi-arid plains of the Middle East and the Mediterranean littoral, however, the agricultural way of life in Europe proper required clearing thick forests and grasslands, at first by cutting down the trees, later by plowing.

Alasdair Whittle has reviewed the evidence for the variations in the location and composition of Neolithic European sites and has shown that the distribution of loess and alluvium and the forces of trade and social stratification produce considerable variations in the density and sizes of settlements across the European Plain.[16] Marek Zvelebil and Peter Rowley-Conwy[17] have argued that the transition to agriculture in much of Europe involved a continuum of social and economic changes in which, at first, hunter-foragers and farmers encountered each other and traded a few products but were largely independent of each other; over time, however, hunter-foragers and farmers began to compete directly, as farmers moved into areas that had been exploited by hunter-foragers; eventually, the superior economic resources of farmers probably enabled them to displace hunter-foragers in the most productive areas—although crop failures and other disasters probably forced farmers to rely on hunting and foraging to survive on many occasions.

The Zvelebil and Rowley-Conwy hypothesis represents the "traditional view" of the settlement of Europe by Neolithic farmers. Recently, a wide variety of archaeologists working on the origins of agriculture and the Neolithic in Europe have come to a somewhat different conclusion.[18] While acknowledging that certain plants and animals were introduced from the Middle East into Europe and that there were also some Neolithic colonists who entered and spread throughout portions of Europe,[19] archaeologists today believe that local Mesolithic populations had a much greater role in the transition to food-production and the appearance of Neolithic lifeways. The notion that hunter-gatherers were simply displaced by or absorbed into groups of Neolithic immigrants is clearly far too simplistic an explanation. As Douglas Price points out, indigenous Mesolithic populations were the likely the main agents in the adoption and spread of agriculture especially for most areas of Europe outside of southeastern and southern Europe.[20]

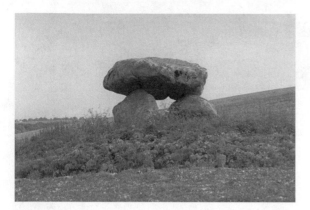

FIGURE 12.3 A dolmen type of megalith. These structures number in the tens of thousands in the maritime areas of Western Europe.

After about 5000 B.C., as populations grew and farmers adapted their crops and technologies to the diverse European environments, larger communities formed, some with apparent fortifications of earthworks and enclosure walls of timber. Some people were buried in large communal graves, marked by earthen mounds and megaliths—large stone monuments (Figure 12.3).

By 3000 B.C. agricultural villages were to be found from Great Britain far into eastern Russia. There were hundreds of local resource specializations, but most of these settlements subsisted mainly on domesticated cereals and cattle. Copper axes and ornaments were widely distributed, especially in central Europe and the Balkans.

Population densities were heaviest in the central European areas where rivers supplied broad alluvial fields, but after 3000 B.C. villages appeared in light to heavy densities over almost every area where the environment permitted stock-raising and cereal agriculture. The areas where this kind of subsistence was possible were greatly expanded by the introduction (perhaps from the Middle East) of the animal-drawn plow. In the absence of an arid climate or alluvial soils, it is difficult for the agriculturalist to compete with wild vegetation and renew the fertility of the soil. But the plow gave these early European farmers a way to expose the soil for seeding, and it contributed to weed control and soil fertility by plowing under vegetation (although the deep plowing of modern times was a later invention).

Much of the archaeological work on the Neolithic in Europe has been focused on the economic transformations, the interactions of colonists with local Mesolithic populations, and the involvement of Mesolithic hunter-gatherers in the adoption and spread of the Neolithic way of life. There are, however, other perspectives on the Neolithic transition in Europe. These are post-processual in orientation and they focus on ideological aspects involved in the transition of society. Prominent among these have been the work of Hodder, Thorpe, Tilley, and Edmonds, as well as others.[21] While the aspects emphasized vary somewhat from scholar to scholar, they all share in common a focus on ideas, symbols, and the way in which people view the world around them.

As we saw in chapter 6, for example, Hodder has stressed the notion of a contrast between wild and tame, nature and culture, field (*agrios*) and household (*domus*). These concepts interact to create a social domestication of people as well as a domestication of wild plants and animals. On the other hand, Tilley emphasizes the interactions and interplay between people and material culture. In his viewpoint, items of material culture are used by people to build, manipulate, and change the world around them. This results, over time, in a different worldview and, in the case of the Neolithic, the introduction of social inequality, the transformation of how the dead are treated via rituals, and how one perceives the landscape around them.

Whichever pathway is used to better understand or explain the Neolithic, one aspect is quite important—once most Europeans became agriculturalists, the stage was set for the evolution of complex forms of social organization. Some of the factors that transformed Europe were local, others international.

Temperate Europe: Later Neolithic Through Bronze Age Developments

Some of the earliest signs of social change in temperate Europe are, predictably, in southern Europe, on the fringes of the Mediterranean world. For example, the Varna cemetery near the Black Sea coast of Bulgaria, dating to about 4000 B.C., contained massive hoards of golden and copper tools, suggesting not only great differences in economic classes in this society, but also the existence of a metallurgical industry of considerable sophistication.[22] Varna may well have flourished on the basis of a Black Sea trade.

Because they are so common and preserve well, metal and ceramic objects have been used as the defining characteristics of European peoples before the Romans. The *Battle Axe People*, for example, is the general term for people who lived between about 3500 and 2300 B.C., whose copper and stone axes are found all over temperate Europe, mainly in graves, along with their distinctive cord-marked pottery. These people seem to have originated in central and eastern Europe, and they may have begun using the domestic horse and wheeled carts as early as 3000 B.C. As usual, it is difficult to determine if people in eastern Europe physically migrated westward en masse, or if their art styles and economic impact spread across Europe much in advance of any actual population movements.

Another spread of artifact styles involved the *Beaker Culture*, named after the distinctive pottery they produced. The Beaker Culture was evident in much of western and central Europe just after 3000 B.C., and eventually the Battle Axe and Beaker cultures seem to have coalesced.

In talking about these cultures we must remember, of course, that nearly all the people of this era were simple agriculturalists, with a few families living together in tiny hamlets. Most would have lived out their lives in small houses and farms. Houses were simple structures of logs, clay, and thatch.

Another indication of the social changes that accompanied the spread of farming in Western Europe are megaliths. By about 4500 B.C.—1,500 years and more before the Egyptians began to build large stone buildings—farmers in Spain were using large stones weighing many tons to build tombs, and over the next several millennia people all over western Europe built large megalithic tombs. These tombs were often composed of several interior rooms with stone walls, with large blocking stones covering entrances to the complex and to its various compartments. These tombs were usually communal, with numerous corpses in them, and there is some evidence that the dead were exposed to the elements for a time and then their bones were entombed. Many tombs were covered by earth and thus formed long "barrow" mounds (Figure 12.4).

Tombs were not the only megalithic structures in Europe. Huge stones were raised in complex designs in areas of France—for example, the thousands of standing stones in the alignments that stretch over some three-quarters of a mile at Carnac. Stonehenge (Figure 12.5), in England—the final arrangement we see today dates to the Bronze Age— is the most famous example of the circular arrangements of European megaliths.

Like the pyramids of Egypt, the megalithic structures of Europe have elicited many speculations about the societies and ideologies of which they were a part. Their spatial arrangements in some cases suggest that they were positioned to mark boundaries of some kind. Stonehenge and similar arrangements were probably ritual centers, and some, perhaps, were used for astronomical observations and calculations. The long "barrow" mounds that enclose megalithic tombs may have been evocations of the long

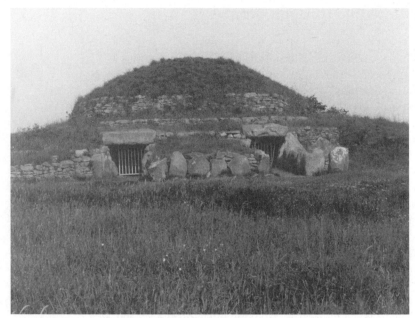

FIGURE 12.4   A passage grave type of megalith.

houses in which these early farmers lived[23]—and thus perhaps were a reflection of the ties of community and kinship that united these people in life and death. Like the Egyptians, these monuments no doubt reinforced social hierarchies of power and ideology and maintained the connections between generations past, present, and future.[24]

A somewhat different question is, aside from what the people who built these monuments thought about them, why did these structures appear when they did and where they did? As noted in chapter 9, with regard to the

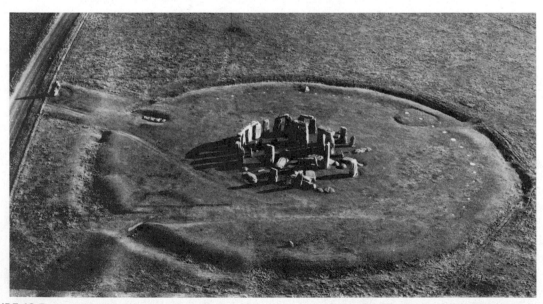

FIGURE 12.5   Stonehenge began as a series of ritual excavations about 2700 B.C. and was greatly elaborated between 2000 and 1000 B.C. The arranged stones probably had astronomical significance. Stonehenge is just one example of thousands of stone monuments built in this period in western Europe.

Egyptian pyramids, these colossal monuments around the world (similar forms are considered in later chapters on Mexico, Peru, and North America) seem to appear at times of particular stress and rapid change. In North America, for example, as Robert C. Dunnell has noted,[25] great communal tombs not unlike the megalithic tombs of Europe appeared in the Ohio and Mississippi river valleys just at the time when maize-beans-squash-based agriculture was being established in these areas, and these monuments seem to appear on the edges of the area where that agricultural adaptation was effective.[26] Perhaps these great "wastes" of energy and resources stabilized these societies by reducing population growth and economic expansion. Viewed from this perspective, what the ancient Europeans actually thought about these monuments is not just unknowable, it is not particularly important: What is important is that these monuments had profound socioeconomic impact on these societies. The prehistoric natives of Mississippi and of England may have had vastly different ideas about the significance of their monuments—yet each built them at similar points in their cultural evolutionary history.

The organization and planning required to build monuments like Stonehenge probably reflect a society with at least incipient rank, class, and occupational specialization, and all through the last few millennia B.C. expanding trade between Europe and the Mediterranean and Aegean regions would have provided some stimulus to cultural change.

Lewthwaite used the term *Mafia model* to describe views of the emergence of complex societies in Europe in which "the motor for social change is the ambition of certain individuals to dominate and control their fellow human beings, an ambition that can be realized in certain ecological . . . circumstances."[27]

From burials not only of bodies but also of hoards of precious metals and artifacts, we can speculate that warrior tribes contended all across Europe in the late second millennium B.C., with their fortunes rising and falling to some extent with their success in maintaining trading links with the Mediterranean and Aegean societies. Baltic amber, salt, metal tools, and hundreds of other products flowed along these ancient trade routes. By the end of this period, fortified hilltop settlements were a characteristic of many parts of Europe, including central Europe.[28]

Temperate Europe: Iron Age Developments: Hallstatt and La Tène

Until about 1000 B.C. the secret of iron-making was a monopoly of the Hittite state in Anatolia, but after this time knowledge of the technique spread north and west into Europe. Iron is a much more utilitarian metal than bronze or gold: Iron tools could make a major difference in efficiencies of plows, hoes, awls, knives, swords, arrowheads, and a thousand other products.

One early European iron-working culture, the Hallstatt, is reflected in the distinctive artifacts of this tradition from Austria, southern Germany, the Czech Republic, and Slovakia, between about 800 and 475 B.C. Archaeological evidence recovered in the past several decades indicates that a number of earlier settlements, such as Heuneburg and Hochdorf, grew into important manufacturing and trade centers during the Hallstatt period, as well as the subsequent La Tène period[29] (Figure 12.6). Differences between people also became more accentuated during the Iron Age, with a proliferation of different design elements and patterns on items such as belt plates.[30] There is also ample evidence of status

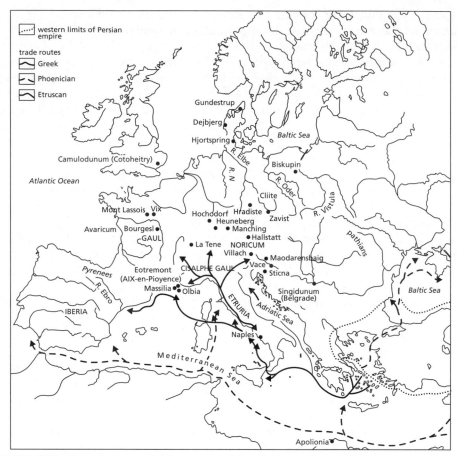

FIGURE 12.6 Some important Hallstatt and La Tène sites.

differences between people, with some of the most notable examples coming from burial contexts. At Hochdorf, in Germany, for instance, a late Hallstatt burial of a 30-year-old male included a large mound with a burial chamber built of oak, abundant gold, feasting paraphernalia—drinking horns of iron and of aurochs (wild cattle) horn, bronze dishes, a bronze cauldron, a gold bowl, and so forth—elaborate textiles, a four-wheeled wagon, and a bronze couch (on which the deceased was laid).[31]

Another well-known and impressive late Hallstatt burial is the so-called princess at Vix, Mont Lassois, in France (Figure 12.7).[32] The 35-year-old woman laid to rest here was covered with a leather blanket and placed on the bed of a cart in the center of a large square chamber dug into the earth. The burial chamber was lined with wooden planks and covered with an earthen mound. Inside the chamber were a wealth of grave goods, including an enormous bronze cauldron—made in Greece and decorated with Greek warriors and chariots—used for serving and storing wine, bowls made of silver, gold, and bronze—one of which was from the Etruscan area of Italy—a gold collar, bronze brooches, and other items of personal adornment. Not far from this tomb is another structure containing life-size stone statues of a richly dressed woman and a male warrior. Some have speculated that the female stature is a representation of the "princess."[33]

An interesting reinterpretation of the Vix burial has recently been offered by Christopher Knüsel.[34] He argues that the traditional interpretation of Vix contextualizes the richly adorned female in terms of male society, thus, a "princess." Knüsel, however, sees the combination of exotic goods, ritual treatment, and physical characteristics of the woman—which include skeletal evidence for a waddling gait and a wry-neck deformity that resulted in her head held tilted to the right—as evidence that she was a ritual specialist, perhaps placed in a socially powerful or leadership position with respect to control of trade relationships with the Mediterranean region. Richly adorned female ritual specialists are known from later La Tène contexts such as Gündlingen in Germany.[35]

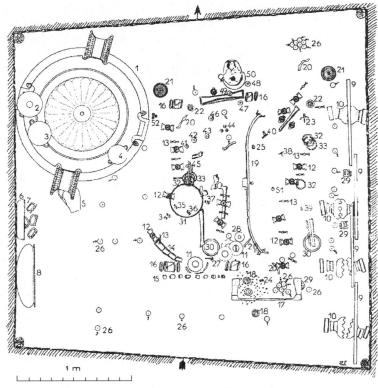

1 m

FIGURE 12.7 Plan map of the tomb of the "princess" at Vix, France.

Although trade relationships continued to be important in the following La Tène period—from about 475 B.C. to the Roman Conquest in the last few years B.C.—the nature of the goods imported from the Mediterranean area appears to have changed rather radically.[36] Hallstatt burial assemblages include unique and "expensive" Greek bronze vessels that were the result of extraordinary craftsmanship. La Tène burial assemblages, on the other hand, contain the everyday Mediterranean items typical of the households of wealthy Greek and Etruscan social classes. The emphasis on the unique in La Tène society is instead on local products such as gold neck and arm jewelry, leading to the development of distinctive Celtic art and ornamentation. Quite interestingly, there is less and less evidence for individual identity through time in La Tène culture, and burials change from single inhumations to modest cremations or no evidence for burial at all.[37] What seems to replace an emphasis on burial of humans is a greater focus on landscape features such as water, where "hoards" of swords, iron tools, gold coins, and gold rings have been found in numerous places.[38]

At about the same time as the decreased emphasis on individuals and individual identities, and the florescence of indigenous Celtic art styles, is the appearance of sites known as *oppida*—enormous settlements, such as Manching, fortified by massive walls built of earth, stone, and timber, and located in natural defensive positions. These vary in population size from place to place, as well as in overall size, with some covering only 10 hectares and others, 500 hectares.[39] The oppida represent massive investments of time and labor, and thus are similar in effort and organization of work forces to monumental construction projects in Egypt, China, Mesoamerica, South America, and other early complex societies, civilizations, and states.

The Hallstatt and La Tène cultures of first millennium B.C. Europe flourished in a period of rapid population expansion, migrations of various ethnic groups, reformation of trade routes along lines dictated by Mediterranean cultures, and other major social changes. The prehistoric European Iron Age, however, came to a relatively abrupt end with the Roman Conquest, which is conventionally dated to 15 B.C.[40]

A BRIEF OVERVIEW OF OTHER LATER OLD WORLD COMPLEX SOCIETIES

Earlier in this chapter we mentioned that there are numerous later states and empires in the Old World, all of which provide quite interesting examples of the many and varied trajectories in the development of complex societies. Each is certainly deserving of extended discussion, although here we can offer only a brief description of a few.

The Aegean

The "wine dark sea" of which Homer rhapsodized is the lovely expanse of the Aegean between Greece and Anatolia that encloses Lemnos, Lesbos, and hundreds of other islands. These islands and much of the mainlands of Asia and Europe that border on the Aegean and the Mediterranean seas are relatively arid, but they became very productive farmlands and also were an abundant source of metals, woods, and other materials.

Domesticated wheat, barley, sheep, goats, grapes, olives, and other crops were established all over the Mediterranean by 5000 B.C., and by 3000 B.C. great volumes of commodities were flowing throughout the eastern Mediterranean world. By about 2700 B.C. Troy, Poliochni on the island of Lemnos, and other communities were already cities, with impressive stone buildings, efficient roads, and a diversified economy that included specialized and lucrative production of objects in gold, tin, and other metals.

These metals were, in a sense, not economically indispensable to the economies of the Aegean world of this age. Some bronze tools and weapons were no doubt useful, but much of this trade seems to have been in luxury goods without direct economic utility—gold figurines, for example. But a lot of the other products were basic staples and commodities. Probably the greatest volumes of trade were in commodities long since consumed and therefore archaeologically invisible, such as the millions of gallons of wine no doubt shipped all over the Mediterranean. In any case, it is really not quite accurate to think of golden figurines as economically useless: Status and the pursuit and social reinforcement of status were primary economic stimuli all over the ancient world.

By about 2500 B.C., the Aegean islands, including Crete, and the Anatolian and Greek mainlands were dotted with hundreds of towns and villages. And while gold was a central element in trade among these communities, painted pottery, obsidian bowls, marble statues and figurines, dyed textiles, and hundreds of other products were not only widely traded, but also important as mortuary goods in the rich tombs here that indicate societies already stratified into the rich and the poor, the powerful and the weak. Hissarlik, the "Troy" of the Classical world, was a city at 2300 B.C., with fortress walls and many larger stone buildings, is probably a good example of a typical large and powerful community of this era.

Crete eventually came to dominate much of the Aegean world. By about 1900 B.C. the many small towns and villages on Crete seem to have become linked increasingly into a state-level political, economic, and religious system. This general pattern of change is similar to that of all the other early civilizations: monumental architecture, increasingly interdependent economies, rising population densities, and everywhere the signs of rank, wealth, and power. The settlement at Knossos included a large palace that probably functioned as a production center for many commodities, such as pottery, gold-work, and lovely vessels in serpentine and other hard stones. A writing system, known as Linear A, was developed, probably as a way to manage this complex economy.

The culture of Crete of the second millennium B.C. is generally known as the Minoan civilization, and throughout this era the wealth and power of Crete seems to have increased. Minoan goods are found all over the Aegean and the Greek and Anatolian mainlands, and as far away as the Levant and Egypt. Knossos probably had a population of 10,000 people just in the central areas of the settlement. Great palaces and rich tombs are the most obvious signs of the character of this society, but it was all based on a thriving economy. The warehouses at Knossos held hundreds of huge pottery storage vessels with enough capacity to hold tens of thousands of gallons of wine and olive oil.[41]

Toward the end of the second millennium B.C., Minoan culture and power were supplanted over most of the Aegean world by Mycenaean civilization. The origins of Mycenaean culture seem to have been on the Argos Plain on the Greek mainland. The stone fortress at Mycenae (Figure 12.8) appears to have been the center of a warrior kingdom, based on an extensive trade network. The rich shaft-graves found at Mycenae reflect a luxurious yet violent society, caught up in competition for economic and political dominance of not only the mainland but the Aegean islands and western Anatolia as well.

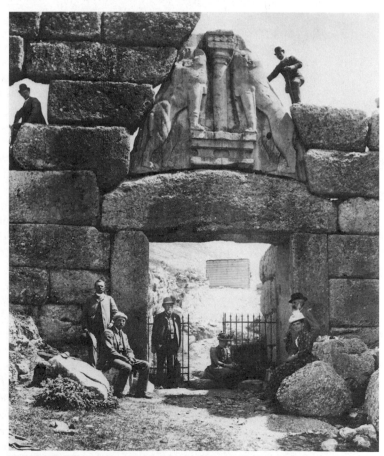

FIGURE 12.8 Heinrich and Sophia Schliemann seated to the right of the legendary Lion Gate at Mycenae in 1876.

Scholars will never be able to resolve how much of Homer's *Iliad* and *Odyssey* is fiction and how much fact, but these epics probably reflect much of the character of late Mycenaean civilization.

Africa

Africa is so rich in gold, silver, iron, jewels, ivory, palm oil, and other resources that one might expect it to have been a center of initial origins of cultural complexity, as it was for the first three million years of hominin development. But Africa has formidable barriers that afflict the agriculturalist more than the hunter-gatherer.[42] The enormous Sahara Desert, expanding and contracting with Pleistocene and post-Pleistocene climatic changes, has almost always isolated most of Africa from the critical mass of Middle Eastern and Mediterranean cultures. And even in the more humid Sub-Saharan regions the dense vegetation, poor soils, and unpredictable rainfall make large-scale intensive agriculture unproductive for the primitive cultivator. Nor do the great rivers, like the Niger, have the regular regimes, large semi-arid alluvial plains, or latitude that make the Nile, Tigris and Euphrates, and Yellow river valleys so productive. To make matters worse, Africa has a veritable horror show of diseases, including a tsetse fly–borne cattle illness that barred pastoralists from many areas and malaria, which recurrently wiped out human populations in the more tropical areas.

Given these and other ecological problems, early African societies are an object lesson in human inventiveness and adaptability in the face of an extreme environment.

Sub-Saharan Africa of the last few millennia B.C. was probably a rich blend of hunting, foraging, fishing, and agricultural societies, with extensive trade networks in gold, salt, and foodstuffs. We know comparatively little about the earliest phases of these societies because of the problems of preservation and inadequate archaeological research—although the intensity of research is increasing.[43] The character of all these cultures was changed radically, however, by the introduction (beginning about 500 B.C.) of an iron-working technology. Complex societies quickly followed the introduction of iron in west Africa, and first-millennium B.C. tombs in Nigeria and Senegal reflect great differences in wealth. At Igbo-Ukwu in Nigeria, one burial chamber contained cast-bronze objects and thousands of glass and carnelian beads.[44] Arab accounts of these societies in the eighth through the eleventh centuries A.D. describe complex empires, with armies, kings, and massive craft industries.[45] Many scholars have concluded that it was Arab commerce that stimulated west African cultural complexity, but McIntosh and McIntosh conclude that the spread of Arab goods and culture "reflects the grafting of Arab commerce onto a preexisting infrastructure of Saharan and Sub-Saharan networks. Such an explanation implies that earlier phases of development at Igbo-Ukwa were characterized by indigenous processes of trade expansion and increasing social stratification."[46]

The first five centuries A.D. saw the rapid spread over much of Africa of agriculturalists using iron tools and weapons and subsisting in part on indigenous domesticates like sorghum and squash and on domestic cattle and other animals (Figure 12.9). Only in a few arid wastelands were these agriculturalists unsuccessful in displacing the stone-age hunters who were the heirs of the millions-of-years-old tradition of African hunting-foraging.

In contrast to the earlier-held view that the first African states were "contact-states," created by the economic and political "touch" of the established North African and Egyptian states, it now seems more reasonable to see Sub-Saharan indigenous states as

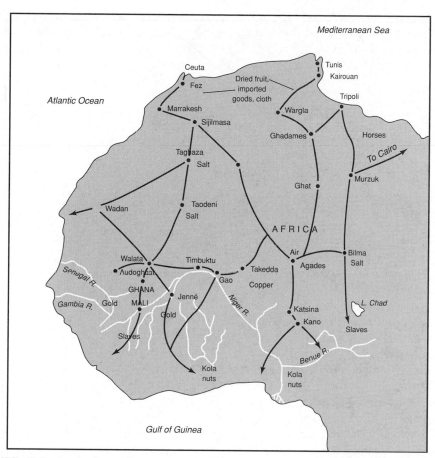

FIGURE 12.9   In the first millennium A.D. trade routes in various commodities connected west African kingdoms with each other and with coastal traders from the Middle East, Europe, and the Mediterranean.

products of their own cultural matrix. The rapid population growth associated with the introduction of agriculture to these areas; the rising spiral of trade in gold, copper, salt, and slaves; and the sporadic influences of distant Mediterranean and Asian empires probably all combined to produce the rich second millennium A.D. African chiefdoms and states. Most seem to have been marked by some public buildings and were composed of a ruler and an upper class who organized and taxed a complex economic system comprised of farmers, herders, miners, iron-workers, traders, and religious leaders. Cemeteries often show great variations of wealth and, presumably, social status.

COLONIZATION OF THE WESTERN PACIFIC ISLANDS

In one of the last great migrations in human prehistory, people colonized the southern Pacific (Figure 12.10), and the subtle variations of local climates and different times of

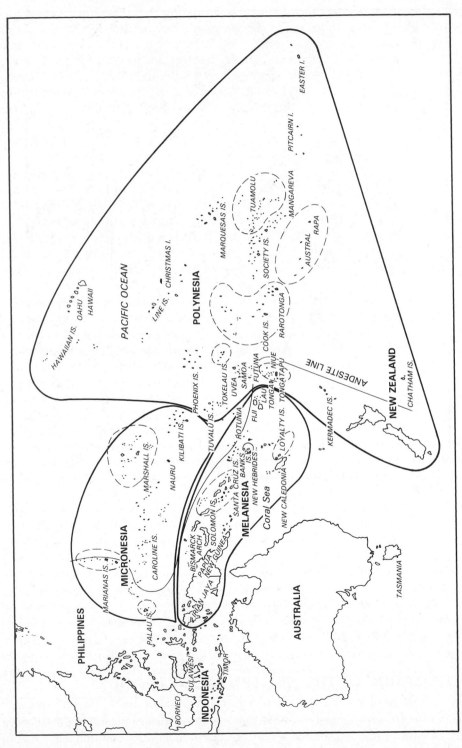

FIGURE 12.10 Cultural areas of Micronesia, Melanesia, and Polynesia.

colonization have produced a varied cultural landscape that is, in the cliché, a giant cultural laboratory.[47] These areas have great significance for a truly evolutionary analysis of the past. In Polynesia, for example, during the last three millennia peoples spread out from island to island, and the development of their languages, adaptations, and physical types reflects the workings of basic evolutionary mechanisms.[48] Patrick Kirch has argued that, in some ways, the evolution of complex societies in Hawaii, Tonga, and other areas of Polynesia agrees well with the "circumscription hypothesis" of Robert Carneiro[49] (see chapter 7).

Scholars have long wondered how ancient peoples sailed across the tropical Pacific from west to east, when the prevailing winds and ocean currents move from east to west. Various simulation models have been considered,[50] and different colonizing rates and processes are possible. Finney reports a voyage during 1986–1988 of the *Hokule'a*, a 19-m double-hull canoe under the command of Hawaiian navigator Nainoa Thompson.[51] By exploiting occasional spells in which the prevailing winds shifted, the canoe was sailed from American Samoa east to Tahiti, along the track the ancient settlers of these islands might have traveled. Subsequent voyages of the *Hokule'a*, as well as a second ocean-going canoe, the *Hawai'iloa*, have made voyages from the Marquesas Islands to Hawaii and back, as well as to Easter Island (*Rapa Nui*).

As always in human colonization, the timing and nature of the colonization depended on the evolution of technologies and cultural adaptations that could provide sufficient food. Even Pacific Islands with rich resources of animals and plants tended to be small enough that hunting and foraging of wild plants and animals would not support many people. The key to colonization was in the form of several domesticated plants and animals that together provided a stable source of food. Domesticated pigs and chickens were primary meat sources, along with fish and birds, but the mainstays of the diet were cultivated tubers. One of the most important of these is taro, a perennial tropical plant with large, starchy, tuberous roots. Lowland taro roots generally are prepared by heating them to destroy the chemicals that give them a bitter taste, then they are ground and fermented into an edible paste called poi (very much an acquired taste for most non-islanders). Taro species native to dry lands produce corms that are eaten like potatoes in Japan, China, the West Indies, and elsewhere.

Another Pacific Island staple is breadfruit, the globular fruit of the breadfruit tree. The breadfruit tree grows to heights of 18 m (60 feet) or more. The yellow-green fruit is up to 30 cm (12 inches) in diameter, and its starchy pulp can be cooked in various ways to supply a good source of carbohydrates.

Among the most important foods of the Pacific are yams, the tuberous roots of several species of vines. Yams are grown and eaten much like potatoes and have a similar role as a dietary staple and source of vitamins and carbohydrates. Yams look something like sweet potatoes, but the two are not even distantly related. Some species of Pacific yams produce tubers weighing up to an impressive 45 kg (100 lb). These tubers have brown or black skin and white, purple, or red flesh. Like potatoes, yams are usually propagated by planting the crowns of the large tuberous root or small whole small tubers. The climbing vines of yam plants are supported on stakes or trellises to maximize yields.[52]

One of the most interesting patterns in the colonization of the Pacific is the spread of the *Lapita Cultural Complex*. The people associated with this culture made a particularly

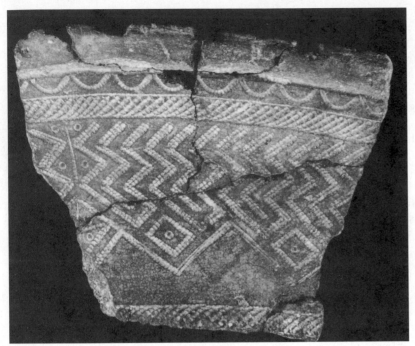

FIGURE 12.11 An example of Lapita pottery.

elaborately decorated pottery that has come to define them, in a sense. Lapita pottery appears at about 1500 B.C. in the Bismarck Archipelago (Figure 12.11), an island group in the southwest Pacific that includes part of Papua New Guinea, New Britain, New Ireland, the Admiralty Islands, and other islands to the east of Australia. These hot, humid, volcanic islands form the core of *Melanesia* (from the Greek for "black islands") and are home to an impressive variety of peoples, languages, and cultures.

Lapita pottery occurs over an area more than 5,000 miles (8,100 km) long, encompassing hundreds of islands stretching as far east as Samoa and Fiji, and the rapid spread—occurring in about 500 years—of this pottery style over such a large area poses the same kinds of questions we have seen elsewhere: Does this spread of a particular artifact style represent people who migrated and carried with them their pottery and the rest of their culture? Or were indigenous peoples incorporated into a growing exchange network in which they eventually came to use pottery in Lapita styles, as well as obsidian and other commodities traded among these many islands? Islands, like all varied environments, have the potential for economic expansion through the exchange of commodities. If the costs of extracting or producing goods and transporting them and exchanging them with neighbors is less than their value in these exchanges, everyone—producers and consumers alike—is richer than if they consumed only the resources they themselves produce. And it is not only food and other utilitarian objects that have value. In the Pacific as in every other human society of our recent past, people used objects as status markers and ceremonial items. In the Pacific shells, pearls, and other commodities were circulated and used in ways that seem to have defined, facilitated, and maintained exchange networks and social hierarchies.

After reaching islands such as Samoa and Fiji, Lapita pottery "disappears" in the sense that the archaeological sites of the islands colonized to the east and north do not have pottery. Use of pottery for containers is likely replaced by investment in making wooden bowls and jars, as well as containers of other organic materials. Sometime after about 200 B.C., some groups from the area of Samoa and Fiji reached the Society and Marquesas Islands to the east. And from there, they expanded outward to Hawaii, Easter Island, and New Zealand.

One of the most interesting examples of the evolution of sociopolitical complexity is Hawaii. Hawaii was probably settled sometime around A.D. 600 or so, by settlers from the

Marquesas or Society islands. Although one might think that Hawaii was isolated after this initial wave of colonization —after all, the trip to Hawaii is more than 3,300 km (2,100 miles) from the Marquesas and Society islands and takes a minimum of 30 days of open ocean voyaging—the oral traditions of Native Hawaiians say otherwise. Until as late as about the mid-1200s A.D., these oral traditions document long-distance ocean voyages between Tahiti and Hawaii, with newcomers from Tahiti sometimes becoming ruling chiefs in Hawaii.[53] Tahitian settlers also introduced new

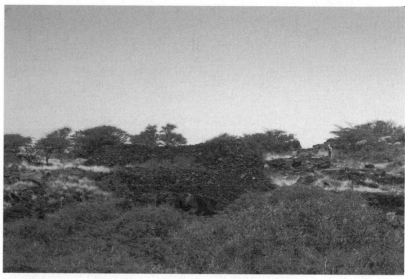

FIGURE 12.12   A small heiau (temple) at the site of Kaunolu, island of Lana'i, Hawaii.

religious elements such as the war god, Ku, and the building of the *luakini heiau*—a special type of Hawaiian temple that is associated with Ku. For reasons not recorded in the oral traditions, these long-distance voyages appear to have ceased after the mid-1200s A.D.— perhaps koa trees large enough to build the ocean-voyaging boats were no longer available in the Hawaiian islands after this time.

When Captain Cook and his crew "discovered" the Hawaiian Islands in 1778, they found a society on the verge of becoming a state. Eighteenth- and nineteenth-century ethnographic accounts provide a detailed account of this highly stratified society with inherited power, prestige and wealth, a diversified economy—including intensification of food-production through the use of aquaculture (trapping of fish in both freshwater and seawater fishponds)—complex trade relationships, monumental architecture (Figure 12.12), and many other elements associated with complex societies. The many different ideas about how the ancient Hawaiians developed these cultural complexities reflect theoretical trends in archaeology in general.[54] Some scholars see population growth and various cultural ecological features as primary factors in Hawaii's cultural evolution; others appeal to sociopolitical causes.

SUMMARY AND CONCLUSIONS

The cultures on the periphery of the Old World, from northern Scandinavia to Hawaii, repeat the common fact that most aspects of cultural complexity are the partial products of technology and agricultural productivity. Battle Axe culture in Europe and ruling chiefs in Hawaii represent gradients of cultural complexity, and in all these Old World areas we see great diversity in the archaeological manifestations of these societies. Many are characterized by monumental architecture, highly stratified social classes, and great disparities in wealth and access to other resources. Some had towns and regional political centers, while others are not recognizably urban at all. And, while all are indigenous developments, each was also influenced by peoples or events from other regions where complex societies had been in existence for some time.

BIBLIOGRAPHY

No attempt is made here to provide a comprehensive bibliography for the many secondary states and empires of the ancient world.

Aikens, C. M., K. M. Ames, and D. Sanger. 1986. "Affluent Collectors at the Edges of Eurasia and North America: Some Comparisons and Observations on the Evolution of Society Among North-Temperate Coastal Hunter-Gatherers." In *Prehistoric Hunter-Gatherers in Japan*, ed. T. Akazawa and C. M. Aikens. Tokyo: University of Tokyo Press.

Akazawa, T. 1982. "Cultural Change in Prehistoric Japan." *Advances in World Archaeology* 1:151–212.

Akazawa, T., and C. M. Aikens, eds. 1986. *Prehistoric Hunter-Gatherers in Japan*. Tokyo: University Museum, University of Tokyo, Bulletin No. 27.

Anderson, A. 1987. "Recent Developments in Japanese Prehistory: A Review." *American Antiquity* 61(232):270–281.

Barber, R. L. N. 1988. *The Cyclades in the Bronze Age*. Iowa City: University of Iowa Press.

Barker, G., and C. Gamble. 1985. "Beyond Domestication: A Strategy for Investigating the Process and Consequence of Social Complexity." In *Beyond Domestication in Prehistoric Europe*, ed. G. Barker and C. Gamble. New York: Academic Press.

———, eds. 1985. *Beyond Domestication in Prehistoric Europe*. New York: Academic Press.

Bellwood, P. 1986. *The Prehistory of the Indo-Malaysian Archipelago*. Sydney, Australia: Academic Press.

Bellwood, P., and J. Koon. 1989. "Lapita Colonists Leave Boats Unburned." *Antiquity* 63(240):613–622.

Bintliff, J., ed. 1984. *European Social Evolution*. Bradford, England: Bradford University Press.

Bogucki, P. 1987. "The Establishment of Agrarian Communities on the North European Plain." *Current Anthropology* 28(1):1–24.

———. 1988. *Forest Farmers and Stockherders*. Cambridge, England: Cambridge University Press.

Bradley, D. G., D. E. MacHugh, P. Cunningham, and R. T. Loftus. 1996. "Mitochondrial Diversity and the Origins of African and European Cattle." *Proceedings of the National Academy of Sciences* 93:5131–5135.

Bronson, B. 1980. "South-east Asia: Civilizations of the Tropical Forest." In *Cambridge Encyclopedia of Archaeology*, pp. 262–266. New York: Crown Publishers/Cambridge University Press.

Castleden, R. 1993. *Minoans: Life in Bronze Age Crete*. New York: Routledge.

———. 1994. *The Making of Stonehenge*. New York: Routledge.

Cavalli-Sforza, L. L., and E. Minch. 1997. "Paleolithic and Neolithic Lineages in the European Mitochondrial Gene Pool." *American Journal of Human Genetics* 61:247–251.

Charoenwongsa, P., and D. Bayard. 1983. "Non Chai: New Dates on Metalworking and Trade from Northeastern Thailand." *Current Anthropology* 24(4):521–523.

Childe, V. G. 1958. *The Prehistory of European Society*. Baltimore: Penguin.

Clist, B. 1987. "Early Bantu Settlements in West Central Africa: A Review of Recent Research." *Current Anthropology* 28(3):380–382.

Collis, J. 1984. *The European Iron Age*. London: Batsford.

Connah, G. 2001. *African Civilizations: An Archaeological Perspective*. New York: Cambridge University Press.

D'Arcy, P. 2003. "Warfare and State Formation in Hawaii: The Limits of Violence as a Means of Political Consolidation." *Journal of Pacific History* 38(1):29–52.

Davidson, J. 1985. "New Zealand Prehistory." *Advances in World Archaeology* 4:239–292.

Dennell, R. C. 1983. *European Economic Prehistory: A New Approach*. New York: Academic Press.

———. 1992. "The Origins of Crop Agriculture in Europe." In *The Origins of Agriculture*, ed. C. W. Cowan and P. J. Watson. Washington, DC: Smithsonian Institution Press.

Dickinson, O. 1994. *The Aegean Bronze Age*. Cambridge, England: Cambridge University Press.

Donohue, R. E. 1992. "Desperately Seeking Ceres: A Critical Examination of Current Models for the Transition to Agriculture in Mediterranean Europe." In *Transitions to Agriculture in Prehistory*, ed. A. B. Gebauer and T. D. Price, pp. 73–80. Madison, WI: Prehistory Press.

Edmonds, M. 1999. *Ancestral Geographies of the Neolithic: Landscapes, Monuments and Memory*. New York: Routledge.

Ekholm, K. 1981. "On the Structure and Dynamics of Global Systems." In *The Anthropology of Pre-Capitalist, Societies*, ed. J. Kahn and J. Lobera. London: Macmillan.

Fagan, B. 2004. *People of the Earth,* 11th ed. Upper Saddle River, NJ: Pearson Prentice Hall.

Finney, B. 1988. "Voyaging Against the Direction of the Trades: A Report of an Experimental Canoe Voyage from Samoa to Tahiti." *American Anthropologist* 90(2):401–405.

Fischer, A., P. V. Hansen, and P. Rasmussen. 1984. "Macro and Micro Wear Traces on Lithic Projectile Points." *Journal of Danish Archaeology* 3:19–46.

Fornander, A. 1999a. *Fornander Collection of Hawaiian Antiquities and Folk-lore. Vol. IV* (with T. G. Thrum). Honolulu: 'Ai Pohaku Press [facsimile publication; original publication 1916–1917, Honolulu: Bishop Museum Press].

———. 1999b. *Fornander Collection of Hawaiian Antiquities and Folk-lore. Vol. V* (with T. G. Thrum). Honolulu: 'Ai Pohaku Press [facsimile publication; original publication 1918, Honolulu: Bishop Museum Press].

———. 1999c. *Fornander Collection of Hawaiian Antiquities and Folk-lore. Vol. VI* (with T. G. Thrum). Honolulu: 'Ai Pohaku Press [facsimile publication; original publication 1919, Honolulu: Bishop Museum Press].

Gilman, A. 1981. "The Development of Social Stratification in Bronze Age Europe." *Current Anthropology* 22:1–8.

Graves, M. W., and D. J. Addison. 1995. "Polynesian Settlement of the Hawaiian Archipelago: Integrating Models and Methods in Archaeological Interpretation." *World Archaeology* 26(3):380–399.

Green, M. 1993. *Symbol and Image in Celtic Religious Art.* New York: Routledge.

Gregg, S. A. 1988. *Foragers and Farmers.* Chicago: University of Chicago Press.

Grigg, D. B. 1982. *The Dynamics of Agricultural Change.* London: Hutchinson.

Hagelberg, E. 1993. "Ancient DNA Studies." *Evolutionary Anthropology* 2(6):199–207.

Hagelberg, E., S. Quevedo, D. Turbon, and J. B. Clegg. 1994. "DNA from Ancient Easter Islanders." *Nature* 369:25–26.

Hall, M. 1987. *The Changing Past: Farmers, Kings, and Traders in Southern Africa, 200–1860.* Cape Town, South Africa: David Phillip.

Harding, A. F. 1984. *The Myceneaeans and Europe.* New York: Academic Press.

Harlan, J., J. DeWet, and A. Stemler, eds. 1976. *Origins of African Plant Domestication*. The Hague: Mouton.

Higham, C. 1988. *The Archaeology of Mainland Southeast Asia.* Cambridge, England: Cambridge University Press.

———. 2000. "The Origins of the Civilization of Angkor." *Antiquity* 74:27–28.

Hodder, I. 1990. *The Domestication of Europe.* Oxford. Blackwell.

Hood, S. 1973. *The Minoans.* London: Thames and Hudson.

Irwin, G. 1992. *The Prehistoric Exploration and Colonisation of the Pacific.* Cambridge, England: Cambridge University Press.

Isager, S., and J. E. Sydsgaard, eds. 1995. *Ancient Greek Agriculture: An Introduction.* New York: Routledge.

Ivanov, I. S. 1978. "Les fouilles archéologiques de la nécropole chalcolithique à Varna (1972–1975)." *Studia Praehistorica* 1–2:13–26.

Joffroy, R. 1962. *Le Trésor de Vix. Historie et porteé d'une grande decouverte.* Paris: Fayard.

Keeley, L. H. 1992. "The Introduction of Agriculture to the Western North European Plain." In *Transitions to Agriculture in Prehistory*, ed. A. B. Gebauer and T. D. Price, pp. 81–95. Madison, WI: Prehistory Press.

Kinnes, I. 1982. "Les Fouaillages and Megalithic Origins." *Antiquity* 56:24–30.

Kirch, P. V. 1984. *The Evolution of Polynesian Kingdoms.* Cambridge, England: Cambridge University Press.

———. 1988. "Circumscription Theory and Sociopolitical Evolution in Polynesia." *American Behavioral Scientist* 31(4):416–427.

———. 1990. "The Evolution of Sociopolitical Complexity in Prehistoric Hawaii: An Assessment of the Archaeological Evidence." *Journal of World Prehistory* 4(3):311–345.

———. 2003. "New Archaeological Insights into Food and Status: A Case Study from Pre-Contact Hawaii." *World Archaeology* 34(3):487–497.

Kirch, P. V., ed. 1986. *Island Societies.* Cambridge, England: Cambridge University Press.

Kirch, P. V., and R. C. Green. 1987. "History, Phylogeny, and Evolution in Polynesia." *Current Anthropology* 28(4):431–454.

Kirch, P. V., and T. L. Hunt. 1988. *Archaeology of the Lapita Cultural Complex: A Critical Review.* Seattle: Burke Museum.

Knüsel, C. J. 2002. "More Circe Than Cassandra: The Princess of Vix in Ritualized Social Context." *European Journal of Archaeology* 5(3):275–308.

Kolb, M. J. 1994. "Monumentality and the Rise of Religious Authority in Precontact Hawaii." *Current Anthropology* 35(5):521–548.

Kristiansen, K. 2002. "The Tale of the Sword—Swords and Swordfighters in Bronze Age Europe." *Oxford Journal of Archaeology* 21(4):319–332.

Lawson, A. 2001. "Recent Archaeological Research on Gambian Iron Age Habitation." *Nyame Akuma* 55:32–35.

Lewis, D. 1972. *We the Navigators.* Honolulu: University of Hawaii Press.

Lewthwaite, J. 1981. "Comment on A. Gilman, 'The Development of Social Stratification in Bronze Age Europe.'" *Current Anthropology* 22:14.

McIntosh, S. K., and R. J. McIntosh. 1983. "Current Directions in West African Prehistory." *Annual Review of Anthropology* 12:215–258.

————. 1988. "From Stone to Metal: New Perspectives on the Later Prehistory of West Africa." *Journal of World Prehistory* 2(1):89–133.

Nishida, M. 1983. "The Emergence of Food Production in Neolithic Japan." *Journal of Anthropological Archaeology* 2(4):305–322.

Nygaard, S. E. 1989. "The Stone Age of Northern Scandinavia: A Review." *Journal of World Prehistory* 3(1):71–116.

Pawley, A., ed. 1991. *Man and a Half.* Auckland, New Zealand: Polynesian Society, Memoir 48.

Pikirayi, I. 2001. *The Zimbabwe Culture: Origins and Decline of Southern Zambezian States.* Walnut Creek, CA: Altamira Press.

Pfeiffer, J. E. 1977. *The Emergence of Society.* New York: McGraw-Hill.

Price, T. D. 1986. "The Earlier Stone Age of Northern Europe." In *The End of the Paleolithic in the Old World*, ed. L. G. Straus. Oxford: B.A.R. International Series 284.

————. 1987. "The Mesolithic of Western Europe." *Journal of World Prehistory* 1(3):225–305.

————. 2000. "Lessons in the Transition to Agriculture." In *Europe's First Farmers*, ed. T. D. Price, pp. 301–318. New York: Cambridge University Press.

Price, T. D., ed. 2000. *Europe's First Farmers.* New York: Cambridge University Press.

Price, T. D., and A. B. Gebauer. 1992. "The Final Frontier: First Farmers in Northern Europe. In *Transitions to Agriculture in Prehistory*, ed. A. B. Gebauer and T. D. Price, pp. 97–116. Madison, WI: Prehistory Press.

Renfrew, C. 1973. *Before Civilization: The Radiocarbon Revolution and Prehistoric Europe.* New York: Knopf.

————. 1978. "Varna and the Social Context of Early Metallurgy." *Antiquity* 52:199–203.

Richards, M., V. Macaulay, A. Torroni, and H.-J. Bandelt. 2002. "In Search of Geographical Patterns in European Mitochondrial DNA." *American Journal of Human Genetics* 71:1168–1174.

Rowlands, M., M. Larsen, and K. Kristiansen, eds. 1987. *Center and Periphery in the Ancient World.* Cambridge, England: Cambridge University Press.

Rowley-Conway, P., M. Zvelebil, and H. P. Blankholm. 1987. *Mesolithic Northwest Europe: Recent Trends.* Sheffield, England: John R. Collis.

Semino, O., G. Passarino, P. F. Oefner, A. A. Lin, S. Arbuzova, L. E. Beckman, G. De Benedictis, P. Francalacci, A. Kouvatsu, S. Limborska, M. Marcikiae, A. Mika, B. Mika, D. Primorac, S. Santachiara-Benerecetti, L. L. Cavallis-Sforza, and P. A. Underhill. 2000. "The Genetic Legacy of Paleolithic *Homo sapiens sapiens* in Extant Europeans: A Y Chromosome Perspective." *Science* 290:1155–1159.

Shennan, S. J. 1987. "Trends in the Study of Later European Prehistory." *Annual Review of Anthropology* 16:365–382.

Sievers, S. 2002. "Manching Revisited." *Antiquity* 76:943–944.

Stahl, A. 1994. "Innovation, Diffusion, and Culture Contact: The Holocene Archaeology of Ghana." *Journal of World Prehistory* 8(1):51–112.

Terrell, J. 1986. *Prehistory in the Pacific Islands.* New York: Cambridge University Press.

Thomas, J. 1991. *Rethinking the Neolithic.* Cambridge: Cambridge University Press.

Thorpe, I. J. 1996. *The Origins of Agriculture in Europe.* New York: Routledge.

Tilley, C. 1996. *An Ethnography of the Neolithic.* Cambridge: Cambridge University Press.

Trump, D. 1980. *The Prehistory of the Mediterranean.* New Haven: Yale University Press.

Weissleder, W. 1978. *The Nomadic Alternative: Models and Models of Interaction in the African-Asian Deserts and Steppes.* The Hague: Mouton.

Weisler, M. 1990. "Sources and Sourcing of Volcanic Glass in Hawai'i: Implications for Exchange Studies." *Archaeology in Oceania* 25:16–23.

Wells, P. 1994. "Changing Models of Settlement, Economy, and Ritual Activity: Recent Research in Late Prehistoric Central Europe." *Journal of Archaeological Research* 2(2):135–163.

————. 1998. "Identity and Material Culture in the Later Prehistory of Central Europe." *Journal of Archaeological Research* 6(3):239–298.

————. 2001. *Beyond Celts, Germans and Scythians.* London: Duckworth.

Whittle, A. 1987. "Neolithic Settlement Patterns in Temperate Europe." *Journal of World Prehistory* 1(1):5–52.

————. 1996. *Europe in the Neolithic.* Cambridge: Cambridge University Press.

Zvelebil, M., ed. 1986. *Hunters in Transition.* Cambridge, England: Cambridge University Press.

Zvelebil, M., and P. Rowley-Conwy. 1984. "Transition to Farming in Northern Europe: A Hunter-Gatherer Perspective." *Norwegian Archaeological Review* 17:104–128.

Zvelebil, M., and P. Dolukhanov. 1991. "Transition to Farming in Eastern and Northern Europe." *Journal of World Prehistory* 5(3):233–278.

NOTES

1. See Fagan, *People of the Earth*, for a more detailed coverage of these later states and empires.
2. Shennan, "Trends in the Study of Later European Prehistory"; see also Childe, *The Prehistory of European Society.*
3. See, e.g., Harding, *The Myceneaeans and Europe.*

4. Bradley et al., "Mitochondrial Diversity and the Origins of African and European Cattle."

5. Dennell, "The Origins of Crop Agriculture in Europe," p. 91.

6. Zvelebil and Dolukhanov, "Transition to Farming in Eastern and Northern Europe."

7. See, for example, articles in Price, *Europe's First Farmers*; and Thorpe, *The Origins of Agriculture in Europe*.

8. *European Economic Prehistory: A New Approach.*

9. See, e.g., Rowley-Conwy et al., *Mesolithic Northwest Europe: Recent Trends*; Price, "The Mesolithic of Western Europe"; Nygaard, "The Stone Age of Northern Scandinavia: A Review."

10. Fischer et al., "Macro and Micro Wear Traces on Lithic Projectile Points."

11. Price, "The Earlier Stone Age of Northern Europe," p. 3. Although it should be noted that the shift to small backed microlithic stone tools is a widespread phenomenon throughout the Middle East and much of Europe in the late Pleistocene and early Holocene. This shift occurs earlier in the Middle East—about 20,000 years ago—but appears to be an independent innovation in Europe some 10,000 years later.

12. A good example of this phenomenon is the English Channel. Prior to about 8,000 or 9,000 years ago, Mesolithic hunter-gatherers in England could walk to what is now France over dry land. Rising sea levels eventually cut England off from the continent and undoubtedly submerged many Mesolithic sites in the process.

13. Bogucki, "The Establishment of Agrarian Communities on the North European Plain," p. 11.

14. Barker and Gamble, *Beyond Domestication in Prehistoric Europe*, p. 9.

15. Grigg, *The Dynamics of Agricultural Change*; Barker and Gamble, *Beyond Domestication in Prehistoric Europe*, p. 22.

16. Whittle, "Neolithic Settlement Patterns in Temperate Europe."

17. "Transition to Farming in Northern Europe: A Hunter-Gatherer Perspective"; see also Zvelebil, *Hunters in Transition*.

18. See, for example, articles in Price, *Europe's First Farmers*; and Thorpe, *The Origins of Agriculture in Europe*.

19. Genetic research has shown that there is some contribution of Middle Eastern genes to the European gene pool, suggesting that a population expansion from the Middle East did occur. See, for example, Cavalli-Sforza and Minch, "Paleolithic and Neolithic Lineages in the European Mitochondrail Gene Pool"; Semino et al., "The Genetic Legacy of Paleolithic *Homo sapiens sapiens* in Extant Europeans: A Y Chromosome Perspective"; but see Richards et al., "In Search of Geographical Patterns in European Mitochondrial DNA," for a somewhat contrasting viewpoint.

20. Price, "Lessons in the Transition to Agriculture," p. 302.

21. Hodder, *The Domestication of Europe*; Thorpe, *The Origins of Agriculture in Europe*; Tilley, *An Ethnography of the Neolithic*; Edmonds, *Ancestral Geographies of the Neolithic*; Whittle, *Europe in the Neolithic*; Thomas, *Rethinking the Neolithic*.

22. Ivanov, "Les fouilles archéologiques de la nécropole chalcolithique à Varna (1972–1975)"; Renfrew, "Varna and the Social Context of Early Metallurgy."

23. Hodder, *The Domestication of Europe*.

24. Renfrew, *Before Civilization*.

25. Personal communication to Wenke.

26. Also see Kinnes, "Les Fouaillages and Megalithic Origins."

27. Lewthwaite, "Comment on A. Gilman, 'The Development of Social Stratification in Bronze Age Europe.'"

28. Wells, "Changing Models of Settlement, Economy, and Ritual Activity: Recent Research in Late Prehistoric Central Europe," p. 138.

29. Ibid., p. 139.

30. Wells, "Identity and Material Culture in the Later Prehistory of Central Europe," pp. 250–251.

31. Wells, *Beyond Celts, Germans and Scythians*, pp. 46–47.

32. Joffroy, *Le Trésor de Vix. Historie et porteé d'une grande decouverte*.

33. Wells, *Beyond Celts, Germans and Scythians*, p. 48.

34. "More Circe Than Cassandra: The Princess of Vix in Ritualized Social Context."

35. Wells, *Beyond Celts, Germans and Scythians*, pp. 58–60.

36. Ibid., pp. 60–61.

37. Wells, "Identity and Material Culture in the Later Prehistory of Central Europe," pp. 251–254.

38. Ibid.

39. Wells, *Beyond Celts, Germans and Scythians*, pp. 84–90.

40. Wells, "Changing Models of Settlement, Economy, and Ritual Activity: Recent Research in Late Prehistoric Central Europe," p. 151.

41. Pfeiffer, *The Emergence of Society*, p. 282.

42. Harlan et al., *Origins of African Plant Domestication*.

43. Stahl, "Innovation, Diffusion, and Culture Contact: The Holocene Archaeology of Ghana."

44. Mcintosh and McIntosh, "From Stone to Metal: New Perspectives on the Later Prehistory of West Africa," p. 110.

45. Ibid.

46. Ibid., p. 120.

47. See Pawley, *Man and a Half.*

48. Kirch and Green, "History, Phylogeny, and Evolution in Polynesia"; Kirch and Hunt, *Archaeology of the Lapita Cultural Complex: A Critical Review.*

49. Kirch, "Circumscription Theory and Sociopolitical Evolution in Polynesia."

50. Reviewed in Terrell, *Prehistory in the Pacific Islands.*

51. Finney, "Voyaging Against the Direction of the Trades: A Report of an Experimental Canoe Voyage from Samoa to Tahiti."

52. These descriptions of Pacific Islands and crops are based on entries in the Grolier Electronic Publishing, www. gme. grolier.com.

53. See, for example, the three volumes by Fornander, *Fornander Collection of Hawaiian Antiquities and Folk-lore.*

54. Reviewed in Kirch, "The Evolution of Sociopolitical Complexity in Prehistoric Hawaii: An Assessment of the Archaeological Evidence."

13

The Evolution of Complex Societies in Mesoamerica

*During the morning we arrived at a broad
causeway and continued our march towards
Iztapalapa, and when we saw so many cities
and villages in the water and other great towns
on dry land and that straight and level
causeway going towards Mexico, we were
amazed and said it was like the enchantments
they tell of in the legend of Amadis, on account
of the great towers . . . and buildings rising from
the water, all built of masonry. And, some of
our soldiers asked whether the things we saw
were not a dream.*

Bernal Diaz del Castillo[1]

In Easter week of 1519, the Spanish conquistador Hernan Cortés landed on the coast of Veracruz, Mexico, and began a military campaign that would end in the crushing defeat of the indigenous Aztec civilization. (Figure 13.1) For tens of thousands of years before Cortés's arrival, the peoples of the Old and New Worlds had had so little contact that they were physically different, spoke entirely different languages, and had no idea that the others even existed. But here is the intriguing thing: When Cortés traveled the road from Veracruz to the Aztec capital near Mexico City, he passed through cities, towns, villages, markets, and irrigated fields, and he saw slavery, poverty, potentates, farmers, soldiers, temples, massive pyramids, roads, boats, pottery, gold jewelry, and textiles; in short, he encountered a world whose almost every aspect he could understand in terms of his own experience as an urban Spaniard of the sixteenth century.

There were, of course, many dissimilarities between the Spanish and Aztec peoples. And the ideological differences between the Aztecs and their European conquerors were also profound. The Spanish, despite their imperialism and murderous ferocity in warfare, viewed the Aztecs' preoccupations with death and human sacrifice with abhorrence, and the Aztecs found many aspects of Roman Catholic Christianity both evil and incomprehensible.

Yet despite profound differences in their respective morals and ideas, the Spanish and the Aztecs were fundamentally alike in cultural respects: They lived in hierarchically

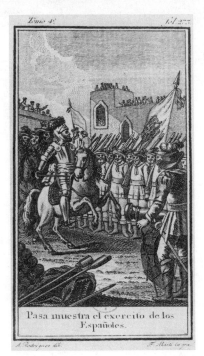

FIGURE 13.1 Cortés haranguing his troops.

organized, class-structured, expansionist empires in which state religions provided much of the context of life, supported by an economy of intensive agriculture and highly specialized and integrated systems of craft production.

Spanish military technology, coupled with diplomacy with non-Aztec groups and the diseases the Spanish introduced, effectively ended the indigenous developments of Mesoamerican civilizations, and it is interesting to speculate about what the Europeans would have found in the Americas if they had come a few centuries later—would there have been a great Pan-American empire to rival that of Spain? Or is it possible that in, say about A.D. 1850, people living on the coast of England (or France or Spain) might have awakened to the sight of Aztec warships in their harbors? The latter scenario is unlikely because New World peoples did not develop two technologies fundamental to the powerful imperialism of Old World societies—iron in the form of tools and weapons and large domesticated animals capable of providing traction and transport (although New World peoples used metals in ornaments and had domesticated some beasts of burden, mainly the llama, in South America).

In any case, scholars have assumed for centuries that the rise of agricultural and complex societies in the New World offered them a "Second Earth," a comparative case, and that by examining these cultural developments in two somewhat different environments and times, the causes of these forms of cultural evolution might be more clearly revealed. Despite contemporary reassessment of that premise,[2] the early Mesoamerican states, in combination and comparison with the Inka of the Andes, Sumerian Mesopotamia, Old Kingdom Egypt, and other early polities, all illustrate that, whatever the factors are that produced these societies, they operated similarly around the world and at different times. Beyond these fundamental similarities of early civilizations, their unique arts and ideologies provide ample material for particularistic studies that need not appeal to cross-cultural and comparative analyses for intellectual justification. In this regard, the early states of Mesoamerica are some of the most fascinating in the world.

In previous chapters we have considered the issue of ethics and history: A central issue here is the political consequences of interpretations of different cultures and their histories. The European conquerors of the New World, for example, pointed to the prevalence of warfare, human sacrifice, and ritual murder as evidence that the New World peoples were barbarians who could only benefit from the imposition of Western "civilization." In this chapter and in chapters 14 and 15 the evidence for these New World practices is reviewed, and to some this may seem to perpetuate the stigmatization of New World peoples. But the fact is that warfare, human sacrifice, and ritual murder, as well as every other kind of gross exploitation of people, were common elements of cultures all over the world, from China to England. The point of discussing the evidence here is not to titillate the morbidly inclined reader; it is to confront the problem of the origins of ideologies and the nature of their transformations—and to emphasize how cultures can make any behavior, no matter how reprehensible in our own view, into a virtue that facilitates the workings of their political systems.

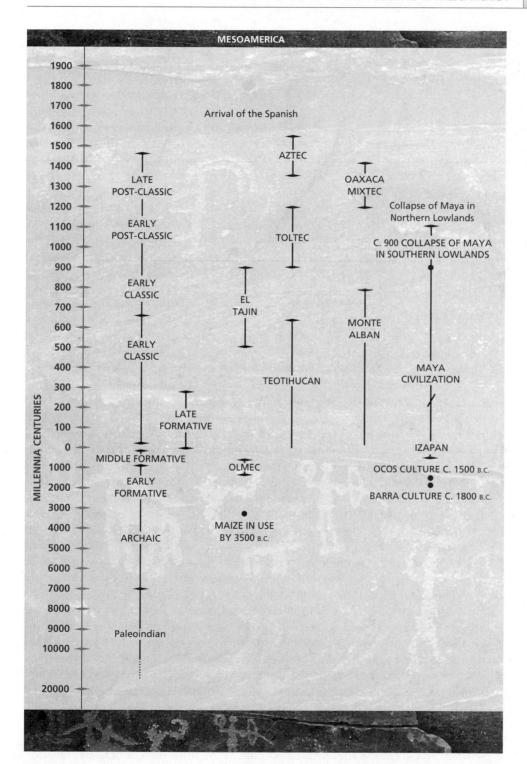

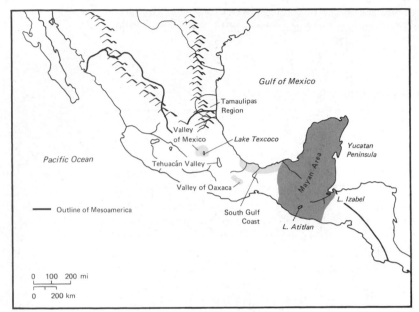

FIGURE 13.2 The geography of Mesoamerica. The darker shading identifies developmental centers of early cultural complexity.

THE ECOLOGICAL SETTING

As in other areas of early civilization, the first complex societies did not appear in just one area of Mexico and then gradually expand to occupy Mesoamerica; instead, there were several developmental centers, including the South Gulf Coast, the Valley of Mexico, the Valley of Oaxaca, and the Maya lowlands and highlands (Figure 13.2). Eventually some of these regions coalesced into larger polities, but only after centuries of competition, cooperation, expansion, and collapse.

In each of these Mesoamerican areas, cultural evolution was much influenced by three general ecological conditions: (1) the millions of years of mountain-building volcanic activity that left Mesoamerica a still-trembling land of towering mountains and circumscribed valleys, and which in many areas compressed extremely different flora, fauna, and climates into proximity, thereby rewarding inter-regional exchange, even though it made transport and communication difficult; (2) the absence of any domesticable animal suitable for providing milk, transport, or draft power; and (3) the relative scarcity of large rivers with extensive alluvial plains in warm latitudes: Unlike Egypt, Mesopotamia, the Indus Valley, North China, and Andean South America, for example, Mesoamerica has few large, navigable rivers in the semi-arid environments where primitive agriculture is highly productive.

All civilizations can be understood to a limited extent purely in thermodynamic terms. From the food that keeps our bodies at proper metabolic temperature to the draft animals, engines, or nuclear reactors that propel our vehicles, the connection between energy and culture is close and causal. And, as in all early civilizations, in ancient Mesoamerica a few plant and animal species were, in effect, the power base of cultural evolution. Not just any domesticated plants and animals would do: There had to be a reliable, voluminous carbohydrate source and nutritionally complementary plants and animals. In Mesoamerica these foods were, principally, maize, beans, and squash, augmented by protein from rabbits, deer, dogs, and, in some places, fish and shellfish.[3] The combination of maize and beans was particularly important because it allowed populations to overcome significant short falls in protein that resulted from the small numbers of available hoofed animals. These rather plain foodstuffs were enlivened in antiquity by the use of cacao (from which chocolate is derived), incendiary peppers, numerous herbs and spices, and several natural hallucinogens.

And like all ancient farmers, they used the magic of fermentation to improve the food products of various high-sugar plants—cactus being the principal source of alcohol in Mesoamerica.

EARLY MESOAMERICAN FARMING (C. 3500–1300 B.C.)

Between 9,000 and 4,000 years ago most of Mesoamerica was inhabited mainly by hunter-foragers who lived in small bands that moved with the seasons to exploit cactus fruits, deer herds, nuts, and the hundreds of other plant and animal species in their range, depending on the season. Since these bands were small in size and never stayed in one place for a sufficient period of time to have much long-term effect on the plant and animal populations on which they subsisted, the hunter-foragers' overall impact on their environment was low. Some groups along the margins of the lake in the Valley of Mexico may have been sedentary villagers, as were some groups along the coasts. They are likely to have had an important role in the domestication of plants and animals and the eventual spread of agriculture. Kirkby suggests that by about 4,000 years ago, maize cob size was large enough that people over large areas of the Mexican highlands could subsist mainly on maize.[4] Grinding corn and making tortillas out of it may not seem to be a great technological leap forward from hunting-foraging, but maize, along with beans, squash, and a variety of other plants, provided the reliable and productive source of food required for people to be able to live in one place permanently.

The recent redating of some of the supposedly earliest domesticated maize in Mesoamerica to about 3500 B.C. raises the possibility, as Gayle Fritz notes,[5] that initial agriculture evolved out of intensified foraging by groups of people who were relatively sedentary, perhaps living all or most of the year in one or a few places, and that they were perhaps even in the process of developing social differences that increased the intensity of their foraging. However maize was domesticated, and by whom, maize appears to have reached sufficient productivity to permit the village-farming way of life soon after about 2000 B.C., and agricultural communities appeared at about this time in many different areas.[6]

From the hot, wet Guatemalan lowlands to the arid Tehuacán Valley, the earliest villages were quite similar in size and contents.[7] Almost all houses (Figure 13.3) were built using the wattle-and-daub method—sticks, branches, and cane were woven in-and-out between vertical wall poles, then covered with a mud plaster, which was dried by the hot sun. Houses, which were seldom larger than 4-by-6 m, featured thatched roofs and tamped clay floors on which fine sand was scattered.

Most of the earliest farming communities were tiny hamlets, villages of 10–12 houses that were home to about 50–60 people, but some communities were larger. Most houses that have been excavated have yielded the same remains, mainly grinding stones, storage pits, pieces of large ceramic storage jars, bones of cottontail rabbits, carbonized maize fragments, and broken pieces of ceramic charcoal braziers.[8] In addition, ovens, middens, and graves are very common. While the proportion of plant and animal foods varied somewhat, all villages probably grew maize, beans, squash, peppers, and some other crops and hunted deer and rabbits. Each village, or each extended family, may have

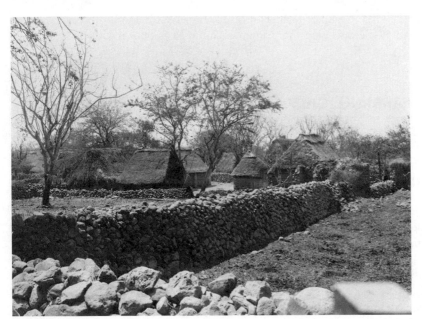

had a specialist who did pressure flaking of stone, leatherworking, or a similar craft, and individual villages may have concentrated on specialties like salt production, featherweaving, shell-working, grinding stone manufacture, and the like.

THE ARCHAEOLOGICAL RECORD OF EARLY COMPLEX MESOAMERICAN SOCIETIES (C. 1300–500 B.C.)

FIGURE 13.3 Mexico's first agriculturalists lived in wattle-and-daub houses much like these contemporary homes in Morelos, Mexico. The people in this village speak Nahuatl, which is derived from the language of the Aztecs.

As in Mesopotamia, China, and elsewhere, the background to the origins of complex society in Mesoamerica was a great scatter of relatively simple agricultural villages in which the mechanics of producing a reliable, expandable food supply had been mastered. Many areas of Mesoamerica contributed to the overall rise of the first Mesoamerican states, but four areas appear to have been particularly important: the South Gulf Coast, the Valley of Mexico, the Valley of Oaxaca, and the Maya highlands and lowlands. The Maya are considered separately later in this chapter.

Early Complex Societies on the South Gulf Coast

An early and radical break with the simple village farming tradition of Mesoamerica occurred in the sweltering lowlands of the South Gulf Coast. Here, beginning at about 1300 B.C., people built massive clay pyramids and platforms, lived in small-town groups of hundreds or even thousands, intensively farmed a variety of ecological zones, and produced what is one of the world's most valued examples of stone sculpture.

These people are known to us as the Olmec, a name derived from an ancient American word for rubber—doubtless a reference to the rubber trees that grow in this area—but a name they themselves probably did not use.

Some scholars have considered the possibility that the Olmec culture was the *cultura madre* (mother culture) of all later complex societies in Mesoamerica, and that they were directly responsible for transforming their neighbors by military, political, religious, or economic means into complex societies.[9] Other scholars, however, have argued convincingly that the Olmec represent only one of several largely independent cases of the evolution of social complexity in Mesoamerica.[10] As we have seen in other areas of the world, civilizations seem not to have developed, in general, because of the behavior of a particular group or the actions of a few particularly gifted individuals: Civilizations all appear to be the products of broad regional and long-term historical processes that manifest themselves differently at different places and times.

The Olmec heartland is a coastal strip approximately 350 km in length, extending inland about 100 km (Figure 13.4). It was created by the alluviation of several rivers that run to the sea from the

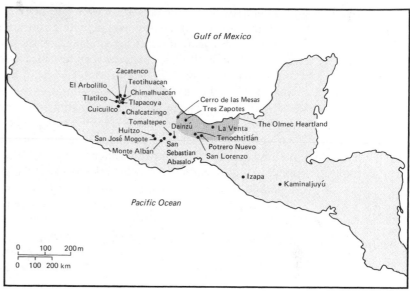

FIGURE 13.4   Centers of initial cultural complexity in first millennium B.C. Mesoamerica.

highlands. Except for a few areas, the region is thickly forested. Torrential rains fall during the summer, but the area is dry in the winter, which permits swidden, or slash-and-burn, agriculture, as it is sometimes called. Swidden agriculture involves cutting down all the vegetation in a particular area and then waiting for the dry season so that the cut vegetation can be burned. Nutrients are thus returned to the soil—an important contribution since manure and artificial fertilizers were not available (unlike the peasants of Mesopotamia, the Olmec had no manure-producing cattle to graze on and replenish fields). After burning, the land is sown, and the crops germinate and come to maturity in the rainy season. After 1 or 2 years of exploitation, however, the land must be left fallow, sometimes for 20 years or more. If the cycle is accelerated, productivity falls rapidly. Until recent times, in the flat lowlands of the Olmec heartland as much as 70–90 percent of the land was fallow at any one time.[11]

Maize, beans, and squash were agricultural staples in early formative times, supplemented by hunting and fishing and collecting wild plant foods. In coastal areas, mussels and other rich marine resources could also be collected. And while much of Olmec agriculture may have been swidden-based, very productive farming was possible on the river levees. Some river levees near the coast are annually inundated with water-borne silt of such fertility that it was possible to raise two crops a year using swidden techniques. Indeed, the precocity of the Olmec in developing one of the first complex Mesoamerican cultures was probably tied directly to the great agricultural potential and rich floral and faunal resources of these riverine environments. The economic basis of Olmec culture is still relatively poorly known. Although plant remains do not preserve well in the South Gulf Coast, we know that most of the people were maize farmers. They ate some peccary and deer, but fish and domestic dogs provided most of their protein. Human bones found at San Lorenzo with obvious burning and butchering marks suggest cannibalism, undertaken for either ritual or more secular motives. Obsidian, imported in large volumes from the Mexican highlands to the west, was used for arrowheads, knives, and many other tools.

After many years of research, we finally have substantial data about the early formative cultures of the South Gulf Coast, although we will probably never know with great precision the population densities in the countryside in many periods because the tiny hamlets they apparently lived in are covered by vegetation and easily missed in archaeological surveys.[12]

As a result, we know the Olmec primarily from their larger ceremonial centers, and on this basis they are an impressive culture. People had been living since about 1500 B.C. on the San Lorenzo plateau in southern Veracruz, for example, exploiting its good soil and natural springs. Then, sometime after about 1250 B.C., the inhabitants of this area began moving tons of earth and clay in baskets to level the plateau's upper surface over an area some 600-by-100 m. At first, perhaps, they were simply trying to raise the elevation of their residential areas above the flood levels of the seasonally inundated plains on which they lived. Within a century or two, however, they began to build pyramids and ceremonial platforms adorned with monumental stone sculptures and other impressive monuments.[13]

San Lorenzo actually is a group of sites within about a 5-km area, a complex that reached its peak between about 1150 and 900 B.C., when several thousand people probably lived there; but after about 900 B.C. construction of monuments ceased and population densities appear to have declined.

San Lorenzo's florescence was followed by that of another Olmec site, La Venta, located on a small island in a coastal swamp near the Tonal River (Figure 13.5). At this location the Olmec constructed a series of mounds, platforms, courts, and pyramids covering more than 5 km². Much of this has been destroyed by looters and an oil well/processing installation, but excavations have revealed a large portion of this site's plan. Dominating the area is a pyramid of clay, 128-by-73 m at the base and 33.5 m high. Two long, low mounds extend out to the north from the pyramid, with a circular mound between them. All these mounds are oriented eight degrees west of true north.

A particularly striking remnant of Olmec culture at both San Lorenzo and La Venta are the Olmec "heads" and other monumental sculptures (Figure 13.6). The most impressive art works at La Venta are four "Olmec heads," some of which are over 8 feet tall. They often depict a human with a stern, not to say sneering, facial expression, and usually are shown wearing a "helmet." Presumably these sculptures are of Olmec rulers, but we will probably never know for certain. Since the Olmec

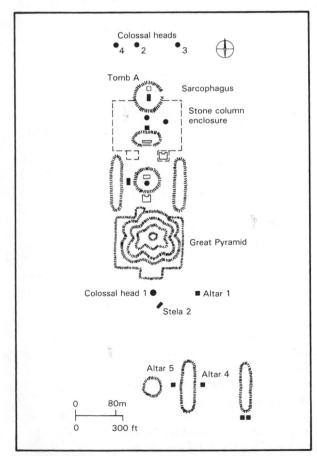

FIGURE 13.5 The Olmec complex at La Venta included a 30-m-high pyramid and several other lower mounds.

had no metal tools, we assume they worked with grinding and pecking stone implements, and it is difficult to believe that these sculptures were made by anyone other than skilled specialists. Major Olmec sites often also included other monumental stone carvings, such as those of free-standing figures of kneeling men and carved stelae and "altars," all carefully executed from massive basalt blocks. On some of them are engraved fantastic mythical creatures representing hybrids of snakes, jaguars, and humans. The basalt for these carvings was imported from 80 km or more away, probably by being floated down rivers on rafts. Some of the heads weigh more than 20 tons, so scores of people must have been involved in quarrying, transporting, carving, and then erecting the stone blocks in monumental compositions.

The Olmec also decorated their ceremonial complexes with many other kinds of expensive and exotic goods, such as the "pavements" at La Venta. To form these mosaic-like pavements, hundreds of serpentine (a green hard stone) blocks about the size of small construction bricks were laid out in a traditional Olmec design—a jaguar mask—and then carefully buried (Figure 13.7).

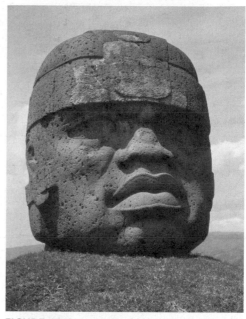

FIGURE 13.6   An Olmec stone head sculpture.

Unfortunately, the acidic, damp soils of the Olmec region do not preserve bones well, and we have only meager knowledge of Olmec burial practices. At La Venta a tomb in a large mound near the central pyramid was elaborately constructed of basalt columns, and on its limestone floor two juveniles were laid out in fabric bundles heavily coated with red paint. Buried with the bodies were jade figurines, beads, a shell ornament, a stingray spine, and a few other items, and

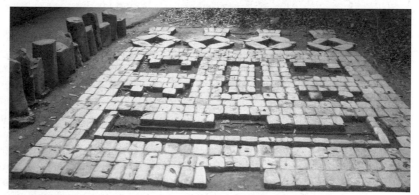

FIGURE 13.7   Mosaic jaguar mask pavement at La Venta, Mexico.

these burials may reflect inherited wealth and prestige. Other types of evidence relating to social complexity, such as residential architecture and settlement patterns, are not well represented at La Venta. And while there is little residential debris there (except for pottery and a few clay figurines), scholars now believe that the people who built La Venta did live there permanently.[14]

Other Olmec ceremonial centers were built at Laguna de los Cerros and elsewhere, and between about 900 B.C. and 400 B.C. It is possible to have large buildings and other trappings of social complexity on the basis of a very simple economic system, but the Olmec also had an intensive and productive agricultural system. In addition, they traded jade, iron

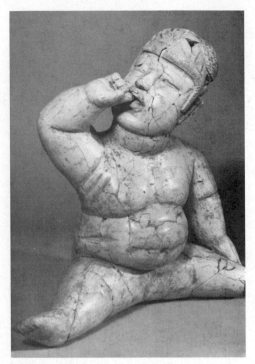

FIGURE 13.8 These Olmec ceramic "baby" figurines were distributed over a large region of central Mesoamerica.

ore, obsidian, bitumen, magnetite mirrors, shark teeth, stingray spines, perhaps cacao and pottery, and many other goods in complex patterns between the Olmec heartland and highland Mexico and as far south as Guatemala.

As we have seen in other civilizations, a key element in the development of most of them was some formative *idea*, some set of religious or philosophical ideology that people over a large area adopted and expressed in ways that linked them in complex interrelationships. The core ideology of the Olmec is hard to discern and decipher, however. Judging from their art style, the Olmec seem to have believed that at some distant time in the past a woman mated with a jaguar and gave issue to a line of half-human/half-feline monsters, or "were-jaguars." These were portrayed in pottery, stone, and other media in a highly stylized way, usually as fat infants of no discernible sexuality (Figure 13.8). Their snarling mouths, long canine teeth, and cleft heads give them a strikingly bizarre quality that some scholars have explained as an imitation of a birth defect of the neural tubes, or as the deformities one would expect of a mating between a human and a jaguar.[15]

"Olmec" ceramic and sculptural designs have also been found far outside the borders of the South Gulf Coast. Some bas-relief rock carvings at Las Victorias in highland El Salvador strongly resemble those at La Venta, and similar sculptures have been discovered in the highlands of Guerrero and Morelos in western Mexico. At Chalcatzingo, in Morelos, cliff sculptures include a standard Olmec motif of a human (probably male) seated in what may have been meant as the mouth of a cave or a steaming monster (Figure 13.9). Olmec styles of pottery, worked stone, jade, and other artifacts have also been found at several sites in the Valley of Oaxaca, at Tlatilco and Tlapacoya near Mexico City, in Guatemala, and elsewhere in Mesoamerica.

The later Olmec and their immediate successors may have formulated some of the ideology that formed the basis of the Maya (see later), but the evidence is controversial. In 1902 a small jadeite figure of a person with what appears to be the bill of a duck was found at San Andres Tuxtla. On it were engraved some glyphs that appeared to be a date, but without the signs that would allow it to be converted to our calendar, and other glyphs, some of which resembled those of later Maya writing but many others that did not. Scholars disputed the significance of this figure for many years, and in 1986 another find helped clarify its significance. This was the La Mojarra Stela 1, found in southern Veracruz, where writing was found that appeared to be the same script as that of the Tuxtla duck-billed figurine. John Justeson and Terrence Kaufman[16]—whose work is controversial—have argued that these inscriptions are in the Zoquean language, which is only distantly (if at all) related to the language of the later Maya, and consists of separate glyphs for each combination of the 11 consonants and 6 vowels of Zoquean (thus, 66 possible consonant-vowel combinations). What is particularly important, however, is that this Epi-Olmec script contains logograms that are semantically equivalent to very similar-looking Maya glyphs[17] and that the Olmec were using essentially the same calendar. These Epi-Olmec inscriptions refer to the accession of various rulers, to what seems to be a war between brothers-in-law, and to other dynastic and calendrical matters.

Perhaps the most important recent discovery of early writing, however, comes from San Andrés, not far from La Venta. Pohl and her colleagues[18] report finding a cylinder seal and a greenstone plaque that contain glyphs. These artifacts are from contexts that date to about 650 B.C. and show that some of the features of later Mesoamerican writing systems, as well as the use of the sacred 260-day calendar and the association of glyphs with rulers, were definitely present in Olmec society.

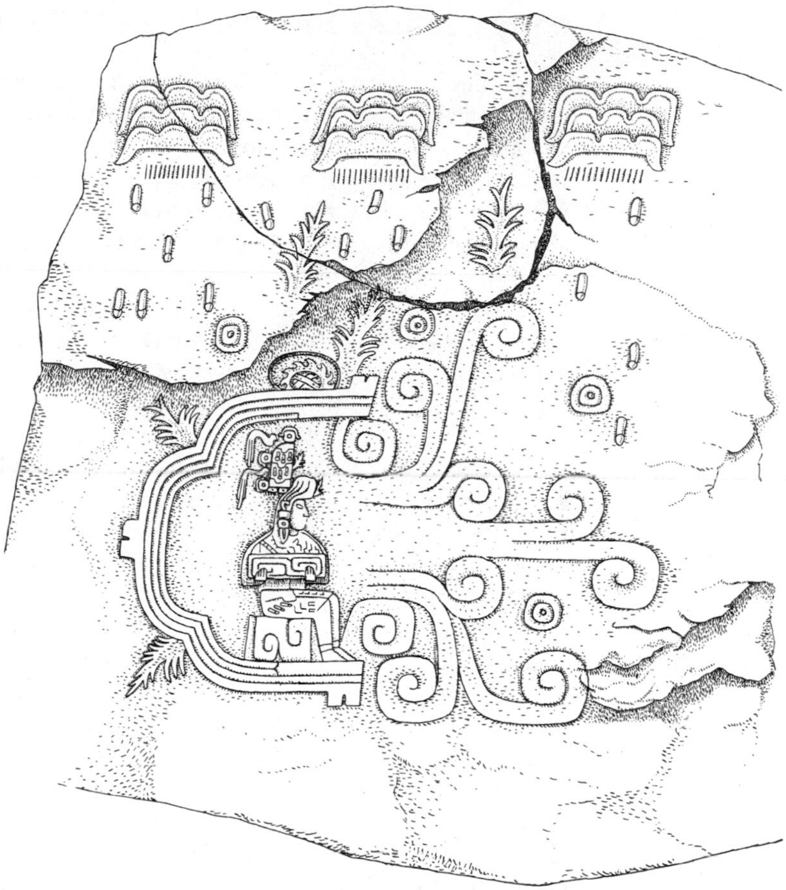

Whether or not the Olmec can be credited with the origins of Maya ideology, the Olmec were far different from their hunter-forager ancestors, and if we match them against the checklist

FIGURE 13.9   Relief 1, Chalcatzingo, Morelos. One interpretation of this Olmec motif is that it is a ruler within a cave or a stylized monster's mouth, which gives off steam or smoke, while raindrops fall from above.

of monumental architecture, burials of juveniles with wealth, voluminous craft production and trade, writing, and so on, the Olmec were clearly a complex society. Their relatively low population densities and small population numbers in centers is probably a direct result of the constraints of their agricultural methods, although we may have an inaccurate sense of their agriculture, which may have been more intensive than many scholars think.

La Venta appears to have been intentionally destroyed soon after about 400 B.C., or at least we might infer this from the fact that some of its greatest stone monuments were intentionally defaced. The history of the Olmec appears to have been one in which small centers of power and prestige, such as San Lorenzo and La Venta, alternately became dominant. And while the people of these centers probably shared core cultural elements, ranging from language to theology, it is not certain that they ever formed a united, integrated political unit over the entire Olmec region.

Early Complex Societies in the Valley of Mexico

The Valley of Mexico is a large basin with no external drainage that is rimmed on three sides by high mountain walls cut by only a few passes; even in the north where there are no mountains, the valley is delimited by a series of low hills (see Figure 13.2). The valley has often been considered a "natural" analytical unit, bounded as it is by such impressive natural barriers, but archaeological research has revealed that almost from their arrival here the people of this area interacted with cultures far beyond the valley itself.[19]

Although much of the Valley of Mexico lies beyond the temperature limits of maize agriculture, people were able to successfully pursue maize cultivation for several thousand years. They also benefited from a large lake, which until the last 400 years, covered the low central portion of the valley, providing rich resources in the form of fish, fowl, turtles, algae, and reeds.

There is not a single navigable stream or river in the whole Valley of Mexico today, and agriculture in most places in the valley would have depended on rainfall and small streams.[20] Rainfall is sharply seasonal and varies considerably from north to south. Today, as in the past, the upper slopes of the Valley of Mexico provide many wood products, and in earlier times the slopes supported large deer herds that were an important part of the prehistoric and early historic diet.

Modern urbanization in the Valley of Mexico has probably destroyed many of the earliest villages and towns there. What we do know suggests that by about 1000 B.C. there were small villages and hamlets in several areas of the valley. Only a few larger sites have been found, such as Tlatilco and Cuicuilco.[21] The valley's apparent two-tiered site size hierarchy, with a few large towns like Tlatilco and Cuicuilco and many small villages, suggests a simple, perhaps tribal, organization, and the distribution of settlements does not point to any political or social spacing. Settlements seem to be located principally around the edge of the great lake, although a few small villages have also been found in highland areas where the soil is particularly rich and deep. Differences in settlement size seem to be a result of local variations in agricultural potential.

Nor is there much evidence of complex architecture at these settlements. A few small mounds and platforms may date to before 800 B.C., but none is on the scale of the pyramids, platforms, and other structures found later on the South Gulf Coast and in the Maya areas. No evidence of elaborate residential structures or monumental sculptures has been found.

The cemetery at Tlatilco provides little evidence that the occupants of the Valley of Mexico were living in complex cultures. Burial goods include pottery, shell ornaments, obsidian tools, figurines, bone tools, and jade and serpentine objects. Some women seem to have been buried with more numerous and more expensive objects than other people in the cemetery, perhaps even with sacrificed men and children. But there is no evidence of lavish mortuary cults.

From about 800 B.C. to about 500 B.C., the population density of the Valley of Mexico increased considerably. At least 10 sites were larger than 50 hectares (each inhabited by about 1,000 people), and one, Cuicuilco, probably had a population of about 2,500. All the larger sites are located along the lake margin, while scattered small hamlets have been found in the highlands. The larger settlements along the lake are fairly evenly spaced at 8- to 10-km intervals, and they all used similar styles of pottery, suggesting some degree of social or political integration, but probably at a low level.

Early Complex Societies in Oaxaca[22]

In the Olmec area the basis of cultural evolution was the productivity of the coastal zone and river alluvium, while in the Valley of Mexico it was the lake shore and adjacent areas, but in the Valley of Oaxaca, cultural evolution seems to have been based on the diversity of ecological zones and the presence of some small river valleys (see Figure 13.2). On the valley floor are large, fertile, flat alluvial areas with a water table sufficiently high for irrigation to be easily accomplished. Grading up into the mountains, the piedmont areas are less fertile than the alluvium, but they can be productively farmed by diverting water from the perennial streams that run toward the valley floor. The higher mountains are cooler and wetter than the other zones and are still covered with pine and oak trees. Frost here is not nearly the limiting factor on agriculture that it is in the Valley of Mexico, although it can be a significant determinant of productivity. Since formative times, irrigation by means of canals and wells has been an important aspect of agriculture in Oaxaca.

Some of the most important resources of Oaxaca were the native iron ores, including magnetite, ilmenite, and hematite. Small pieces of these materials were polished and used as mirrors and ornaments, which were then traded widely over Mesoamerica and used as marks of status.

Shortly after 1400 B.C., the most productive areas of the piedmont and the alluvium in the Valley of Oaxaca were occupied by small villages composed of perhaps 50 people living in tiny wattle-and-daub structures. The first significant deviation from this pattern of egalitarian farmers occurred sometime between 1350 B.C. and 1150 B.C., when the inhabitants of at least one site (San José Mogote) at different times built several "public buildings" of earth and adobe construction.[23] Although these structures average only 5.4-by-4.4 m each, they are interpreted as public buildings because the floors were carefully covered with a distinctive white lime plaster and swept clean, in contrast to the average house of this period, the floors of which were usually stamped clay and sand and covered with household debris.

Other evidence suggests that these buildings at San José Mogote may have been intended for special functions: They were repaired and reused over longer periods of time than the obviously residential structures; at least one of them had an "altar" or step against one wall; and they are oriented eight degrees west of true north, about the same as the major monumental constructions at La Venta, in the Olmec heartland, which suggests that the strong Mesoamerican tradition of imputing magic to place and arrangement (see later) was already in force.

Most of the other formative villages in Oaxaca lack such public structures, although one, Tomaltepec, was found to have a large prepared mudbrick platform.[24] In the floor of this structure was a storage pit, considerably larger than any of the others at the site, containing relatively large quantities of obsidian, ornamental seashell, and deer and rabbit bones.[25] Between 1400 and 1000 B.C., overlapping in time with the construction of this platform, a large cemetery was created at Tomaltepec. Eighty burials containing a total of about 100 individuals were found at the cemetery, and most of these burials had almost the same goods, mainly ceramics and a few other small items. In four of the burials, small quantities of obsidian, magnetite, and jade were found, but these differences in grave goods seem fairly small in view of the overall similarity. And, interestingly, no juveniles or infants were buried here; all the bodies were of adults, suggesting that this society had not yet achieved significant social stratification.

Analysis of trade items in the valley between 1400 B.C. to 1000 B.C. also reinforces this impression of low-level community organization. A few items, such as obsidian, were traded, but in small amounts, and the trade was probably organized through individual households.[26]

But archaeological evidence suggests that major changes were in process in the cultural organization of Oaxacan society between about 1400 B.C. and 1100 B.C. More crafts were apparently performed at San José Mogote than at other settlements in the valley at this time. Debris from working obsidian, jade, magnetite, shell, and other substances has been found here in concentrations proportionately greater than at other sites. There was a major increase in the volume of "exotic" traded materials in Oaxaca at this time also, perhaps in response to increasing social stratification: These materials seem to have been used most frequently to make ornaments that reflect differences in social rank.

As is discussed later in the context of the Maya, a widespread religious practice in Mesoamerica was ritual self-mutilation to produce blood—often in the form of cutting one's tongue or (for men) penis with obsidian blades or stingray spines. This practice is thought to have been a way of materializing the gods and invoking their powers, and the presence of these materials at San José Magote may reflect this practice. The spread of common elements of ideology over Mesoamerica also seems reflected in other ways. There are clear resemblances between Olmec figurines and ones of comparable age from Oaxaca, for example, and some pottery with Olmec motifs reminiscent of the South Gulf Coast has been found in Oaxaca. Certainly, magnetite and obsidian were moved in substantial volumes between Oaxaca and the South Gulf Coast between 1100 B.C. and 850 B.C.

Kent Flannery and Joyce Marcus have challenged[27] the notion that "Olmec" motifs on early Oaxaca pottery support the contention that somehow the South Gulf Coast cultures stimulated cultural developments in Oaxaca. They note that Oaxaca seems to have been more influenced by cultures in the Valley of Mexico than the South Gulf Coast and that Oaxaca society was, in any case, among the earliest in Mesoamerica to develop public architecture and other evidence of increasing cultural complexity.

After about 850 B.C., variation in settlement size in Oaxaca increased; by 550 B.C., San José Mogote, for example, grew to 15 times the size of the next largest community (Figure 13.10). Many settlements excavated have public architecture, and their distribution seems to mirror the growing importance of social and political factors in determining site location.

It seems unlikely that cultural evolution in either Oaxaca or the Valley of Mexico was directly instigated by the Olmec through military imposition, economic exploitation, or slavish imitation.[28] The wide distribution of Olmec styles of ceramics, figurines, and sculpture and the construction in Oaxaca and elsewhere of public buildings with astronomical orientations similar to those of the Olmec buildings seem to reflect interregional trade networks and perhaps the circulation of important people, but the archaeological evidence does not support the idea of unified political and military control of these three regions.[29]

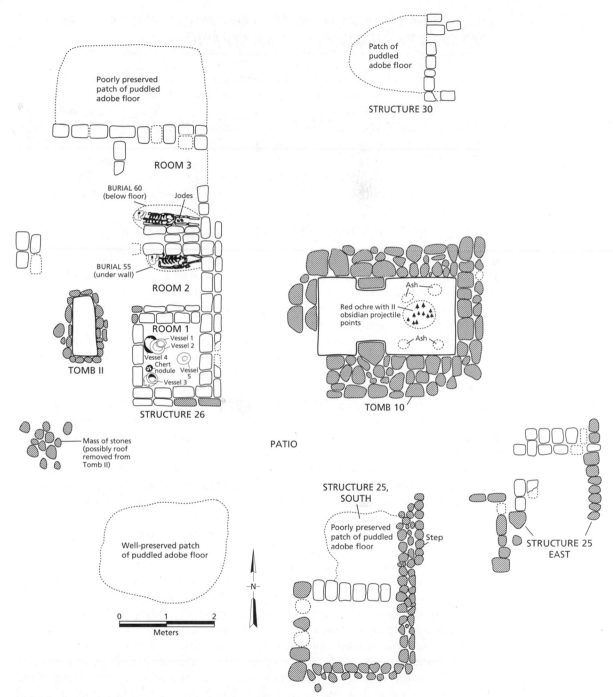

FIGURE 13.10   A plan view of structures at San José Mogote, Oaxaca, Mexico.

THE ARCHAEOLOGICAL RECORD OF MESOAMERICAN STATES IN THE VALLEYS OF MEXICO AND OAXACA

As discussed in chapter 7, applying a static concept such as *state* to complex multi-dimensional cultural changes involves many difficulties, but as an informal descriptive term the notion of *state* implies a society based in part on socioeconomic classes; a centralized, hierarchically arranged bureaucratic structure; and the economic and functional integration of many settlements over a comparatively large area. Cuicuilco, with its early stone monuments, intensified agricultural system, and other developments, may be Mesoamerica's first state in this sense, but it is clear that other areas of Mesoamerica, especially the Valley of Oaxaca, were undergoing roughly contemporaneous and similar processes of state-formation.

Early States in the Valley of Mexico (C. 500 B.C.–A.D. 800)

Thanks to the hard work of William Sanders, Jeffrey Parsons, George Cowgill, Rene Millon, and many others in the Valley of Mexico, we can now reconstruct over 4,000 years of settlement history and other evidence related to the process of state-formation here.[30] Elizabeth Brumfiel, for example, attempted to test the hypothesis that "population pressure" was an important factor in cultural evolution in the Valley of Mexico between 500 B.C. and A.D. 1—the important interval just before the florescence of Teotihuacán.[31] She did this by estimating the agricultural productivity and the potential for intensification of each settlement known for this period. Her argument is complex and mathematical, but one of her conclusions is quite simple: An important factor in the growth of smaller towns and villages was the imposition of tribute by elites in the largest communities. She found little convincing evidence of "population pressure" at the critical period—although, the data are not conclusive.[32]

Several other analyses of these Valley of Mexico settlement patterns have been set in mathematical-locational geographical terms,[33] and the results have stimulated a great deal of discussion about Mesoamerican cultural history and the applicability of these kinds of analytical techniques. The settlement pattern data we have here come from archaeological surveys where the procedure was to collect a sample of pottery from each site and then estimate the site size, periods of occupation, and distinctive architectural features. The limitations of such data have been intensively reviewed by Tolstoy and others, but this information can be quite useful.[34]

For the period between about 500 B.C. and 200 B.C., there is persuasive evidence of changing cultural complexity in the Valley of Mexico. The population of the valley grew substantially in this period, and in most of Mesoamerica as well,[35] and people were now living in larger settlements. Cuicuilco may have had as many as 7,500 people at this time —an unmanageable size without considerable social organization and control. Many other settlements of 80–100 hectares existed, intermediate and small settlements also increased in number, and there are some early signs of irrigation agriculture. Small "temple" platforms of stone and clay, some 3–4 m high, appeared in several areas, and Cuicuilco and other sites had large stone structures. Cuicuilco had the largest early pyramid structure in central Mexico, an anticipation of the great stone pyramids at Teotihuacán (see later).

As we saw in the case of Mesopotamia (chapter 8) and Egypt (chapter 9), early polities that were developing centralized political authority, class-based social organizations, and other elements of social complexity often seemed to begin building massive ceremonial structures very early in this evolutionary process. That so many people around the world chose the pyramid form has nothing to do with instinctive human aesthetics or the mystical power of pyramids and everything to do with the simple engineering reality that people with primitive tools who try to build a monumental structure capable of bearing its own weight can only construct a few basic shapes. Of these, the pyramid is the easiest to build in terms of raising materials to the top of the structure and the amount of materials and labor needed. As discussed in previous chapters, monumental structures are functionally efficient in early complex societies, despite their apparent "waste" of resources and labor, because they legitimize and focus the religious and social hierarchies of which they are an expression, and they may also act to dampen unstable rates of population growth and economic expansion.

Before 200 B.C. the Teotihuacán area of the Valley of Mexico had been relatively unimportant culturally, but it has large areas suitable for irrigated agriculture and possesses large springs capable of supplying irrigation systems. Obsidian is also available nearby, and the area is thought to have supported large stands of maguey cactus, used for its fiber and to make *pulque* (a kind of beer), as well as edible nopal cactus, a plant species that is home to an insect that can be rendered into a red dye highly prized in pre-Hispanic Mexico. Moreover, Teotihuacán stands along a natural trade route to eastern Mesoamerica—an important advantage given the difficult terrain of this region.

Between 150 B.C. and 1 B.C. the population growth rate exceeded that of any other period, and Teotihuacán grew to some 6–8 km², reaching about one-third its eventual maximum size.[36] Between about A.D. 1 and A.D. 150 Teotihuacán's growth rate was still high but had slowed; the average population during this period was probably between 60,000 and 80,000, and rose to 100,000 or more by A.D. 300.[37]

During this time work was completed on the massive Pyramids of the Sun and the Moon (Figure 13.11) and on at least 20 other important temple complexes.[38] The Pyramid of the Sun is 198 m long on each side of its base—as large an area as the Great Pyramid of Khufu in Egypt—and rises 64 m (half the height of the Khufu pyramid). The pyramid seems to have been built over an earlier, smaller structure made of sun-dried bricks and is filled with an additional one million cubic meters of earth, stone, and rubble. In volume, this probably equaled two million cubic meters of uncompressed fill, which would have required the excavation, transport, and shaping of the soil in an area 1.4 km² to a depth of 1 m—a considerable effort by any standards. The Pyramid of the Moon is somewhat smaller (150 m at the base, 45 m high), but of greater architectural sophistication, with a series of inset trapezoidal platforms. Pottery fragments in the fill of these pyramids indicate that the pyramids were constructed by using material from earlier occupations near the city. Considering the size of these structures, it is little wonder that the later Aztecs believed that the pyramids had been constructed by giants and that some of the gods were buried beneath them.

By about A.D. 100 Teotihuacán had hundreds of workshops, with perhaps as much as 25 percent of its population employed as craft specialists, making products in obsidian, ceramics, precious stones, slate, basalt, seashells, feathers, basketry, leather, and other materials. Craft production was also extensive within households, and may have been taxed

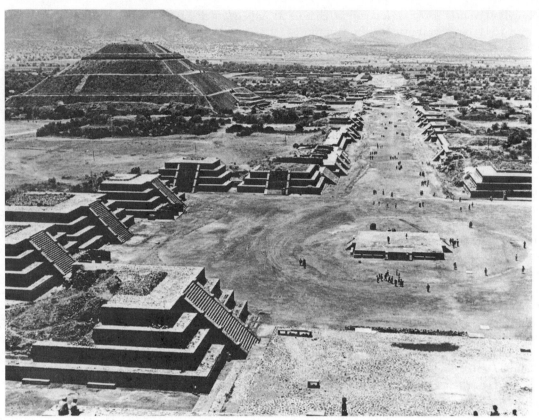

FIGURE 13.11   The Pyramid of the Sun (*upper left*) and the Pyramid of the Moon (from which this photograph was taken) were the ceremonial center of Teotihuacán. At times the city probably had a population of more than 100,000, and there were hundreds of workshops and houses.

by the state.[39] Massive public constructions were underway, considerable variability existed in mortuary complexes and residential architecture, and the settlement patterns in the surrounding areas were heavily influenced by the city.

The rest of the city is perhaps even more significant in terms of its evidence of cultural complexity (Figure 13.12). It was laid out in quadrants, formed by the Street of the Dead intersected by streets running east to west. Some of the quadrants were more densely occupied than others, and very different architectural styles and artifacts were found in various zones of the city. Along the main north-south street were elaborate residences, presumably for societal elites, as well as large and small temple complexes. Many of the more impressive buildings were built on platforms and often faced inward on patios and courtyards. Most buildings were one story high. In some temple complexes the walls were decorated with beautiful murals depicting religious themes, warfare, imaginary animals, and scenes from daily life.

The basic residential unit of Teotihuacán appears to have been large, walled, often windowless compounds made of adobe bricks and chunks of volcanic rock. Many such compounds measured 60 m or more on a side and internally were divided into many rooms, porticoes, patios, and passageways. In some, open patios let in sun and air and drained the compounds through underground stone troughs. Many walls were decorated with frescoes of jaguars, coyotes, trees, gods, and people in naturalistic settings.

Some residential complexes at Teotihuacán were found to have concentrations of artifacts characteristic of distant areas of Mesoamerica, with at least two enclaves with "foreign" associations.[40] The Oaxaca Barrio, for example, included ceramics, funeral urns, burials, and other elements indistinguishable from the artifacts used in Oaxaca—over 400 km to the south—and very much in contrast to the distinctive artifacts of the Teotihuacán natives. These foreign "barrios" appear to have remained culturally distinct and intact for at least several centuries and may have been trade entrepôts or ethnic "ghettos," but no persuasive explanation for these features has been made.

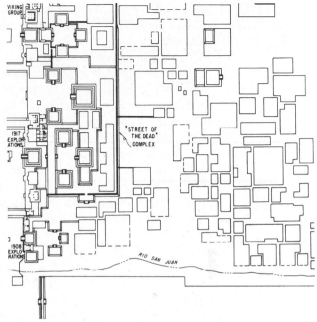

FIGURE 13.12 A plan map of the central area of Teotihuacán, Mexico.

The city's people apparently ate large quantities of nopal and other kinds of cactus, as well as maize, beans, squash, and a variety of other domesticated and nondomesticated plants and animals. Deborah Nichols has shown how extensive was the irrigation system that supported the intensive agriculture that fed Teotihuacán's tens of thousands of people.[41] Even at Teotihuacán's peak, however, there was considerable hunting, as evidenced by the fact that about 80 percent of the animal remains found were deer bones.

By the time Teotihuacán reached its maximum size, it had apparently depopulated much of the rest of the Valley of Mexico: Only one other major settlement appears in the valley at about A.D. 500, and it is but a small fraction of the size of Teotihuacán. In fact, the abandonment of rural sites correlates so closely with Teotihuacán's growth that it appears likely that populations were either drawn or coerced directly into the city.[42] By A.D. 500 Teotihuacán-style ceramic vases were placed in the richly furnished burials of apparently high-status individuals on the Gulf Coast, in Oaxaca, and elsewhere.

Teotihuacán so dominated the Valley of Mexico that some have wondered if its power extended far beyond the valley itself. It seems unlikely that the few hundred thousand people at Teotihuacán were able to extend military control over the millions of people living in the rest of Mesoamerica: Fighting a military campaign in the rough terrain of these distant areas would have been suicidal. More likely, the Teotihuacános were tied to the many other areas through trade networks. The city has no major defensive fortifications, but it does have what appear to be large market areas, and the ecological diversity of Mesoamerica would have put a high premium on large-volume trade in basic agricultural and technological commodities. By circulating these many products, people would have had a much higher standard of living and much greater protection against food shortages.

As we will see later, Teotihuacán was quite different from other Mesoamerican cities of the Classic period. In many respects, Teotihuacán was more comparable to Mesopotamian or Chinese cities.

Sometime before A.D. 600, Teotihuacán's size and influence began to decline. As the city shrank in population, new centers and settlements appeared throughout the Valley of Mexico, particularly on its edges. Significantly, after A.D. 600 Teotihuacán styles in pottery, architecture, and other artifacts disappeared from the rest of Mesoamerica. It is as if a complicated exchange network had been beheaded, and local cultures began developing their own distinct traditions.

Various factors appear to have diminished Teotihuacán's population growth and influence after A.D. 600.[43] Teotihuacán may have been eclipsed by other political systems based on more productive agricultural and economic resources: There is some evidence that at least part of its sphere of influence was encroached on by emerging states in the Maya areas. Even closer to home, political systems centered at Tula, Xochicalco, and elsewhere in the Valley of Mexico may have begun to block Teotihuacán's access to needed raw materials and foodstuffs.

There is some evidence that Teotihuacán was selectively burned down at about A.D. 650, with the targeted destruction of temples and elite residences, along with the smashing of idols.[44] Whether this was an internal revolt or resulted from the actions of populations from other regional centers is not entirely clear. Some 40,000 people or so, however, did reinhabit the city after its destruction, although it never regained its former prominence or influence. Whatever malignant conjunction of wars, fires, droughts, and other factors that destroyed it, Teotihuacán was one of the first great states of the New World.

Early States in the Valley of Oaxaca (C. 500 B.C.–200 B.C.)

The rise of early states in Oaxaca paralleled that in the Valley of Mexico in many ways. Many years of intensive survey, for example, have shown that the settlement patterns changed from one in which small villages predominated to one in which villages proliferated in number but were also complemented by larger towns and villages.[45]

Richard Blanton notes that shortly after about 500 B.C., Oaxaca experienced at least the following transformations: (1) Population density increased at a more rapid rate than in any previous period; (2) agricultural intensification in the form of canal irrigation became important; (3) pottery manufacture became specialized and perhaps was part of the Valley's first market system; and (4) the settlement at Monte Albán, on a high plateau in the center of the Valley, grew to become a major regional center (Figure 13.13).[46] Blanton has argued that the capital at Monte Albán was founded in an unpopulated area between various important settlements as an expression of a new confederation between people who previously may have been linked by rather low-level social and economic ties.[47]

Blanton and his colleagues estimate that Monte Albán grew from an unoccupied, waterless mountaintop to a great religious and political complex of 5,000 people in fewer than 200 years.[48] To accomplish this rate of increase, they suggest, people would have had to move up from settlements in the valley to their new home on the plateau, and agriculture in the valley and piedmont would have had to be intensified to support the town.

By 200 B.C. the population of Monte Albán reached about 17,000—a great city, by ancient standards. Agriculture was intensified around Monte Albán as well, and rural population densities soared. Craft specialization in pottery and other commodities was sharpened, and the location and products of kilns indicate some degree of regional administrative control, although Blanton concludes that Monte Albán itself remained mainly a ceremonial center with few economic functions.[49]

One of the main plaza buildings at Monte Albán contains a gallery of carved stone reliefs whose main theme seems to be the commemoration of military conquests. Scores of bodies are depicted with open mouths, closed eyes, and blood streaming from them in flowery patterns.[50] These depictions have many parallels in themes around the ancient world, such as in the Egyptian Narmer Palette (chapter 9).

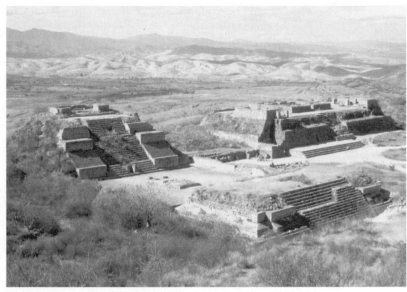

FIGURE 13.13   Overview of Monte Alban, Valley of Oaxaca, Mexico.

In succeeding centuries, population densities and settlement patterns varied considerably, but the investments in monumental architecture, the hierarchical arrangements of towns in terms of the distribution of goods and services, and other markers of cultural complexity persisted and became more elaborate. Thus, by 200 B.C. or shortly thereafter, a state, by almost any definition, appears to have been operating in Oaxaca.

It may be overstating the case to say that by 200 B.C. we have also moved from prehistory to history in Mesoamerica, but the engraved signs and symbols at Oaxaca and elsewhere in Mexico seem to be well on the way to the development of a true writing system.

Although the rough outlines of Oaxacan cultural history have been established, scholars argue about what forces determined this history. Sanders and Nichols stressed the importance of irrigation agriculture and population growth as factors in the valley's florescence.[51] Kowalewski and Feinstein, in a lengthy assessment of the development of economic systems in Oaxaca, conclude that much of this "economic variation was largely determined by the changing functions and degrees of chiefly or state power."[52] They reconstruct a situation in which the power and predilections of elites changed, and with them the permeability of the borders of Oaxacan political systems.[53]

THE MAYA

In Mexico the gods ruled, the priests interpreted and interposed, and the people obeyed. In Spain, the priests ruled, the king interpreted and interposed, and the gods obeyed. A nuance in an ideological difference is a wide chasm.

Richard Condon

At about the same time the civilization of Teotihuacán was developing in the Valley of Mexico, Maya civilization was emerging in southern Mexico, Guatemala, Belize, and Honduras (see Figure 13.2).

Early Maya civilization may have been influenced to some minor degree by Teotihuacán, but it was largely its own creation. The Maya devised a complex writing system, built temples and palaces that are spectacularly beautiful monumental constructions, and are thought to have organized vast areas and many peoples in a series of independent states. The Maya were a civilization with cities although these cities were quite different in layout than our stereotypic notion of a city because Maya cities incorporated much farmland into their boundaries. Maya centers such as Tikal and Dzibilchaltun had thousands, perhaps tens of thousands, of people in permanent residence[54]—although these settlements never attained the population or physical size of Teotihuacán, and they had less diversity in residential architecture and perhaps less occupational specialization than existed in Teotihuacán or Oaxaca at a comparable time.

It is difficult to fault archaeologists who spend most of their time excavating the spectacular Maya ceremonial centers instead of surveying the snake-infested jungles for the rural settlements that supported these centers, but in recent years an increasing amount of research has focused on surveys of nonurban areas, and the general picture is much clearer than previously.[55]

Much of the Maya homeland is hot, semitropical forest, but large areas are highlands created by a string of snow-capped volcanoes that extend from southeastern Chiapas toward lower Central America. In the highlands volcanic ash and millennia of wind and water erosion have created a rich thick layer of soil spread over a convoluted landscape of ravines, ridges, and valleys. Hard seasonal rains make this a fairly productive agricultural zone.

The tropical lowlands at the steamy heart of Maya civilization cover the Petén and the Yucatan Peninsula, a massive limestone shelf lifted out of the seas over millions of years by tectonic movements. The land is rugged toward the southern part of the Petén, but most of the peninsula is flat. There are few rivers or lakes because the porous limestone quickly drains away surface water.

The lowland climate is hot and humid for most of the year, but drought can be a severe problem because the rainfall is seasonal and localized. In early spring a period of drought sets in, and the agricultural cycle slows. Trees are burned to open fields for crops, and the land dries. In May and June the rains begin, and the lowland landscape is transformed into a riot of life as plants green and animals multiply.

Recent research has revealed large irrigation systems in some Maya areas and, during at least some periods, permanent field agriculture with annual cropping, which was probably very important economically in the lowlands. Irrigation, however, was an exception. Labor intensive soil and water management for agriculture by the Maya mainly involved techniques such as slope terracing, water diversion, and wetland reclamation. In much of the Maya area, the fields used for maize, beans, squash, tomato, and pepper cultivation must be fallow for four to eight years after about three years of production. The Maya also converted land that today might be considered "unusable" through innovative techniques such as raised fields and seasonal use of bajos—swamp lands. Raised fields are created in bajos by digging channels and piling the excavated dirt between the channels. This produces a series of artificial areas on which agricultural crops can be grown year-round, although the raised field technique is only viable where water levels remain relatively stable.[56] Seasonal use of the bajos occurs when they are dry—in other words, not during the rainy season—and it is possible to grow one crop a year under these conditions.[57]

When all the evidence of canals, raised fields, botanical remains from sites, and other data are considered, it is clear that a variety of agricultural techniques, adapted to each local ecology and regime, must be seen as the basis for Maya civilization.[58] Most peasant cultivators use animals, whether wild or domestic, to convert brush and hedgerow vegetation into usable form, and the small Yucatec deer—which was intensively hunted—apparently filled this role in the Maya lowlands, along with domestic dogs, rabbits, and wildfowl. The Maya were sophisticated farmers who blended field cultivation with a form of tropical-forest management in which they were able to use foods from both in a complementary, productive, and highly stable way.[59]

Maya Ideology

In Karl Marx's somewhat self-contradictory and ambivalent view, state religions were seen almost as by-products of state economies. He saw religions as ideologies that evolved as a way of legitimizing state authority and of controlling the masses after the real causes of state-formation—changes in the economic and technological base of the society—had produced the socioeconomic classes and governmental structures of states.

The case of the Maya, however, is one of many in history where one might argue for the primacy of the *idea* of the state. The great agricultural productivity of the Maya area was, of course, the base of Maya civilization and not only provided its energy but also shaped its culture. But little about Maya civilization seems understandable apart from their ideas of the divinity of kings and the nature of the cosmos.

It is a truism, a cliché, that we can really never fully enter into the ideology of another culture, whether that cultural ideology be the "dream time" of the Australian Aborigines, the Marxist-Confucian ethos of modern China, or the spirit world of the ancient Maya. And, unfortunately, much of a culture makes little "sense" unless one can share the cultural perspective from which it derived. This is particularly true of the Maya, whose beautiful monuments and intricate written language derive from a world-view and life-view that is in so many ways fundamentally different from our own. So, we can only *try* to see the world and time through the perspective of other cultures—try to get some sense of the fundamental ideas that bound people together in time and place and community.

For the Maya, the world manifested itself in two complementary dimensions—one in which they lived out their lives, the other (the Otherworld) in which gods, ancestors, and other supernatural beings existed—that were inextricably locked together.[60] The Maya apparently saw their dimension as three layered domains, "the starry arch of heaven, the stony Middleworld of earth made to flower and bear fruit by the blood of kings, and the dark waters of the Underground below."[61] This world-view was highly structured, with 13 levels in the heavens and 9 levels in the underworld, each overseen by a particular god.[62]

The Maya believed that these three regions—heavens, earth, and underworlds—were interrelated, that shamans and rulers, for example, could penetrate the Underground world via ecstatic trances. Above all, in the sky, was a great crocodilian monster who "made the rains when it shed its blood in supernatural counterpoint to the royal sacrifices on the earth below."[63] The human world was envisioned as floating in a primordial sea and was sometimes represented as the back of a caiman (a crocodile-like animal) or a turtle. These various interrelated worlds and planes of existence, including the earth, were imbued by the gods with a sacredness that was especially concentrated at special points, such as caves and mountains. As Schele and Freidel note:

> The principal pattern of power points had been established by the gods when the cosmos was created. Within this matrix of sacred landscapes, human beings built communities that merged with the god-generated patterns and created a second human-made matrix of power points. These two systems were perceived to be complementary, not separate. . . . [The] world of human beings was connected to the Otherworld along the *wacah chan* ["six sky," or "raised up sky"—a tree-like axis whose base was in the watery underworld and whose top was in the highest heavens of the Otherworld] which ran through the center of existence. This axis was not located in any one earthly place, but could be materialized through ritual at any point in the natural and human-made landscape. Most important, it was materialized in the person of the king, who brought it into existence as he stood enthralled in ecstatic visions atop his pyramid-mountain."[64]

Through proper ritual, the Maya believed that the power points on the earthly plane, whether they be places, people, or objects, could be intensified and become charged with accumulated energy. Kings, for example, rebuilt temples on the same spot time after time, thereby compounding the sacred power within them. These kings or holy rulers—K'uhul Ajaw—may have originally risen from the role of shaman in Maya society.[65]

Blood-letting was a "focus ritual of Maya life."[66] The Maya believed that beings of the Otherworld could be materialized through the ritual shedding of blood. Men are shown in inscriptions using obsidian blades and other implements to pierce their tongues or penises, and women are shown piercing their tongues. Through blood-letting one could, in a sense, give "birth" to a god or ancestor, enabling it to materialize in physical form on the earthly plane of existence. Ritual blood-letting apparently was practiced not just by elites and priests but even by lowly peasant farmers in remote villages.

Like many other cultures, the Maya rationalized and justified the great inequities of wealth, power, and prestige in their society by setting these inequities in a divine context. The king and his relatives *deserved* their wealth and power because the king was the pinnacle of the population and it was through him that contact could be made with the sacred, the Otherworld. Every Maya, from highest to lowest, benefited from the king's intercession with the divine world, and they all shared in the material wealth that the king provided the community through successful performance of his powers.[67]

Like most early states, the Maya appear to have been strongly patriarchal—if the sex of people commemorated in royal inscriptions accurately reflects this society. But Maya royalty included women of high status. As Joyce Marcus notes,[68] an inscribed stela records an occasion in which a royal woman from Calakmul improved the prestige of a particular lineage at El Perú by marrying the local ruler, who was socially beneath her.

To the modern mind, the entire Maya world-view and life-view may seem bizarre and to represent a patent misunderstanding of how the cosmos operates. But by means of their ideology, the Maya in a sense invented a civilization. Schele and Freidel observed, "They invented ideas that harnessed social energy. . . . They invented political symbols that transformed and coordinated such age-old institutions as the extended family, the village, the shaman, and the patriarch into the stuff of civilized life."[69]

Thus Maya civilization was as much an idea as a physical manifestation in towns and villages, farms and monuments. The beginning of Maya ideology and its physical manifestations go back deep into the Mesoamerican past.[70]

For the earliest Maya, as with the many other cultures we have considered in this book, we come back to some basic and difficult questions. Why and how did kings, priests, writing, pyramid-building, and all the other facets of ancient civilization arise out of these unprepossessing communities of farmers? For most Westerners it is difficult to rid one's mind of the assumption that "civilization" is the "natural" outcome of agricultural life and that complex societies will somehow develop out of societal competition, individual strivings, the accumulation of technological advances, and other factors in all environments (except for those in areas such as the Arctic, where there simply are not enough people and not enough food and wealth to be expropriated). But archaeology shows us many examples of cultures that did not automatically progress to "civilizations," even in environments where it would seem technically possible for them to have done so (e.g., aboriginal Australia).

The early agricultural economy of the Maya shows that it had the potential for at least one of the major common denominators of all ancient civilizations: agricultural production of sufficient quantity and diversity that it could be intensified, administered, and expropriated.

The Preclassic Maya (1000 B.C.–A.D. 300)

Earlier views on the development of Maya civilization stressed explanations such as the migration of people from the periphery of the Maya areas into the core areas of the lowlands and highlands, the necessity for a political elite to manage trade, warfare, or population pressures.[71] Research since the 1980s, however, has considerably revised the chronology of the Maya and has shown that these earlier explanations are simply no longer supported by accumulating data. Monumental public architecture and flourishing regional centers are present by at least 600 B.C., with the best known example at Nakbe in the northern Petén.[72] By 400 B.C., there are numerous examples of such centers in both the lowlands and highlands, for example, at el Mirador, Kaminaljuyu, Calakmul, and Cuello.[73]

Because these discoveries have been only recently made, and in many cases are ongoing, scholars are reexamining earlier explanations, and undoubtedly there will be many exciting hypotheses put forward in the next several years. How important, for example, was irrigation agriculture? Some Maya canals are an impressive 1.6 km in length, 30 m in width, and 3 m deep.

Does the significance lie instead in the development of Maya ideology? One element may have been the growing Maya belief that dead ancestors could be conduits for power from the Otherworld and that their relationship to the dead extended beyond just their immediate families. All early states appear to have made a transition wherein people began thinking of themselves as belonging to entities that extended far beyond the immediate family. The first suggestions we have that these changes were underway are found in burial practices: Like ancient Chinese, Mesopotamians, and many others, the early Maya farmers buried their closest relatives under their house floors, perhaps to retain in some remote way the intimacy of family connections to house and home and to lay claim forever to the land of their ancestors. At about 600 B.C., however, some Maya, such as those at K'axob,[74] began burying their dead in the core of large stone and earth platforms—which themselves are an

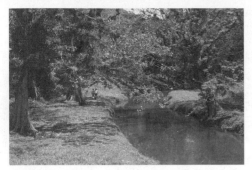

FIGURE 13.14 A jungle river in Central America.

architectural reflection of important changes occurring in these formerly simple small villages.

As we saw earlier, some of the first great stone Maya buildings, such as pyramids and platforms, appeared in the Maya area by at least 600 B.C. (at Nakbe). For the Maya as for many other ancient civilizations, monumental architecture appears as one of the first signs of the transformation of the society. Between 600 B.C. and 400 B.C. people at Nakbe[75] and other sites built lovely stone and masonry buildings on huge platforms and depicted gods and ancestors on building façades, stelae, masks, and other objects. If the people of Nakbe and other Preclassic Maya communities were already enmeshed in the formal Maya theology that we know from the later Maya, they probably regarded these buildings as important points from which to tap into the power of the cosmos and amplified their sacredness by building and rebuilding these impressive complexes.

The largest Preclassic Maya community was El Mirador, in the jungles (Figure 13.14) of the Guatemalan part of the Petén—an area so remote that even though the site had been sighted from an airplane in the 1930s, its inaccessibility prevented exact location and excavation until the 1970s. El Mirador is remarkable for its early dates, its massive size, and its anticipation of many core elements of later Classic Maya culture—including pyramid complexes, stucco mask representations of Maya gods, and Maya writing. Some of the earliest examples of Maya writing have been found here in the form of an inscribed pot sherd and inscribed symbols on stone sculpture.

Several pyramidal mounds 18–20 m high at El Mirador appear to date to between 600 B.C. and 300 B.C. Between about 150 B.C. and A.D. 50 the people of El Mirador built hundreds of large stone constructions, including buildings, pyramids, plazas, and causeways. The *Tigre* complex, for example, includes a pyramid that rises more than 50 m above the jungle floor, set amidst a temple and other buildings.[76] Most of these buildings were coated with a white plaster and then painted deep red.[77] To modern aesthetics the great stone buildings of the Maya, the Greeks, the Egyptians, and others have an elegant and simple beauty in their natural light stone colors, but ancient peoples undoubtedly had different aesthetic preferences, and they probably also painted their buildings in primary colors for cultic and ideological reasons, and not primarily, if at all, because of aesthetic preferences.

Shortly before about 50 B.C. at Cerros, where the New River, which runs through the eastern part of the Yucatán Peninsula, empties into Chetumal Bay, the Maya established a small community of farmers, fishermen, and traders. At this time Cerros was unremarkable, just one of the hundreds of others like it in the Petén. But within the space of two generations, perhaps 40 or 50 years, the people of Cerros experienced a revolution: "The Coming of Kings." As Linda Schele and David Freidel note, this transition appears to have been so rapid that many individuals probably personally experienced the transition from life in a simple village to one in which they became citizens of a large ceremonial city, living amid great stone temples, plazas, and other monuments and initiated into the full ideology of the Maya world-view and life-view.[78]

We will never know exactly what happened to effect this transformation at Cerros, but the archaeological evidence suggests that this was a conscious reformulation of a community: They apparently broke their pottery, jade ornaments, and other objects into small bits and scattered them over their simple houses, buried flowers and other talismanic objects in the rubble, and then proceeded to build a new, vastly larger community around and over the remains of their abandoned village. They began by building a temple at the water's edge (edges in the natural world were places of power in the Maya view[79]) and then proceeded to build a large complex of temples, plazas, pyramids, stairways, causeways, and other monuments—all laid out on the axis that connected this world to the other planes of reality (see earlier). Decorating many of these structures were stucco representations of the gods. Artisans made these by applying wet plaster to a wall and modeling the plaster, as well as some appliqué pieces, into extremely complex designs. Few if any of these designs were actual texts, but they can be read and they portray complex Maya religious ideas. On one temple, for example, representations of the Jaguar Sun God on a south-facing wall would, when lighted by the sun, present the sun "rising" on the east side of the wall and "setting" on the west side as the sun made its daily trek across the sky.

Despite all its beauty and magic, Cerros declined and all but disappeared as a community after only a few generations of glory—another example of a fundamental rhythm of Maya political history, in which small communities all over their world were rapidly transformed into great gleaming ceremonial settlements, home to tens of thousands of people, only to fade and die in a relatively short time. Where many of the greatest Old World cities, such as Memphis in Egypt and Warka in Mesopotamia, counted their histories of dominance in millennia, most Mesoamerica centers ruled their particular worlds for only 400–600 years at most.

The Classic Maya (A.D. 300–A.D. 900)

As we have seen in the case of the Harappan (Indus Valley) and 'Ubaid (Mesopotamian) ceramics, the spread of a distinctive, uniform artifact style over large areas often precedes rapid and fundamental cultural change. By about A.D. 1, a distinctively styled pottery was in use over the entire 250,000 km² of the Maya lowlands, and pyramids, platforms, and other large public buildings were being constructed at Dzibilchaltun, Uaxactun, and elsewhere. Between A.D. 300 and A.D. 900, Maya civilization reached its climax as hundreds of beautiful pyramids, temples, and other buildings were completed, and painting and sculpture flourished (Figure 13.15).

The first part of this period corresponds to the florescence of Teotihuacán, and the extent to which interactions between the Maya area and Teotihuacán occurred is not entirely clear. It is likely that this relationship included trade and alliances through marriages, while other contacts might have been military or shared/adopted aspects of religion or other ideological features.[80] After A.D. 600, when Teotihuacán rapidly began to lose influence and population, the Maya began a 300-year period of intense development. Hundreds of temple complexes were constructed and beautiful stone sculptures executed—many dated and inscribed.

Stephen Houston has used archaeological evidence and interpretations of Maya writing to estimate that most Maya polities were organized within areas of 70 km diameter or less—with most of the settlements within a day's walk of the major center.[81] These dispersed agricultural hamlets were grouped around small ceremonial centers that included a small temple pyramid and a few other stone constructions. Several districts of small

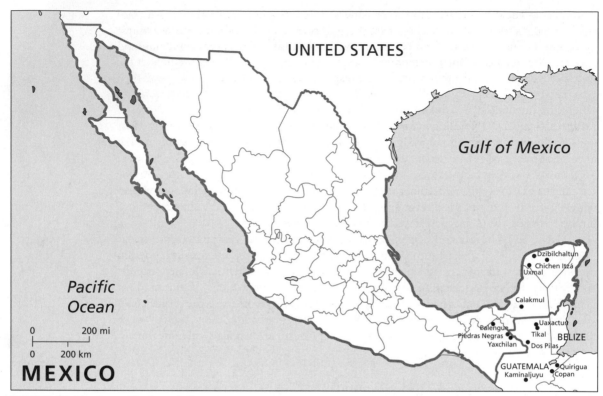

FIGURE 13.15   Some Classic period Maya sites.

ceremonial centers were congregated around the major ceremonial centers of Tikal, Uaxactun, Palenque, Uxmal, and other sites. By this time much of southern Mesoamerica featured beautiful, gleaming, white limestone pyramids and temples that were surrounded by marvelously executed stone sculptures and decorated with wall paintings.

Most centers also had ball courts made of stucco-faced rock. We know little about how the ball game was played.[82] Apparently the objective of the game, played by two opposing teams, was to try to get a rubber ball through a goal, probably not by throwing or batting it, but by using knees, elbows, or torso. The ball apparently could not be held in the hands when it was in play. As played by the Mesoamericans, this game was not a sport: The ball may have represented the sun, and the court and play were imbued with ritual and cosmological imagery. Losing players were sometimes executed. A relief panel from a ball court at El Tajín, in Veracruz, Mexico, shows the captain of the losing team being stretched out over a sacrificial stone while the victor drives a knife into his chest.[83] Maya representations of this ball game show a ball that, if the proportions are correct, would be larger than a basketball, but the Maya may have simply been exaggerating these representations to focus attention on the ball.

John Fox has argued that these ball courts were imbued with great and complex ideological and social significance and that they were the focus of feasts, competitions, and other rituals that provided "strategic settings for the negotiations of power relations. These rituals centered on the redistribution of food and wealth and the symbolic renewal of agricultural fertility." He concludes that the ball courts, as places with "supernatural associations, served as [stages] for rituals in which political conflict was mapped onto and resolved through cosmological drama."[84]

TIKAL AND UAXACTÚN[85]

Tikal and Uaxactún, two great Classic Maya communities, provide in their individual elements and the history of their relationship to each other both an illustration of all the essential elements of Maya civilization and also an object lesson regarding the political history of early states in many parts of the world.

Tikal and Uaxactún are located about 40 miles south of El Mirador in the hot lowland jungles of the Petén, and much of their destiny was determined by the fact that they were built only about 12 miles apart: Much of the social interactions of the ancient world were determined by the distance a person could walk in a day or so—distances that linked cultures in conflict and cooperation—and Tikal and Uaxactún were less than a day's walk for both traders and soldiers. In the end, it was the soldiers whose efforts shaped most of the history of these communities.

Tikal originated at about 600 B.C. in the form of a small farming village set on a small hill in the middle of a swamp. Simple peasants these people may have been, but in one of the burials of this period a severed human head was placed next to the corpse of a man— perhaps an anticipation of the ritual decapitation of later Maya court rituals. Over succeeding centuries the people of Tikal built one of the greatest ceremonial centers of the New World. Temple I at Tikal (Figure 13.16), built about A.D. 700, captures much of the architectural brilliance of the Maya. In previous centuries the people of Tikal had covered the original village with a massive complex of temples, plazas, causeways—all the standard elements of Maya ceremonial centers, but realized in particularly beautiful form. Well-preserved tombs at Tikal included the bodies of kings and elites and rich offerings of pottery, food, stingray spines, and other goods. One of the richest tombs, Burial 85, contained a headless and thighless body wrapped in a cinnebar-impregnated bundle along with a marine shell and a stingray spine—common tools in ritual blood-letting. Schele and Friedel suggest that the Maya may have kept some of the bones of dead kings as relics and talismans; they also note that the bodies of kings and elites show that they were larger and more robust than the commoners of this community.[86]

Computer simulations have been used to suggest that as many as 77,000 people may have lived in Tikal's immediate environs at its peak,[87] and probably 300,000 or more people lived in the entire 965 square miles that this center dominated.

Uaxactún's florescence generally paralleled that of Tikal, and by about A.D. 320 they were both the centers of large, powerful kingdoms. Then an extraordinary Tikal king named Great-Jaguar-Paw—Maya king names are based on the visual imagery of their name signs, a device used prior to the

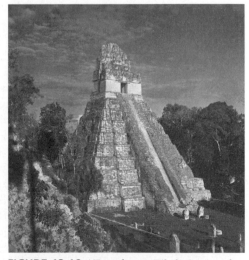

FIGURE 13.16 Temple 1 at Tikal, Guatemala.

phonetic decipherment of Maya signs in recent years—ascended the throne, and on January 16, A.D. 378, he conquered Uaxactún and installed a warrior from Tikal named Smoking-Frog as ruler. As Schele and Freidel note, before the ascension of Great-Jaguar-Paw, Maya warfare had a personal, almost formal quality: The Maya fought not to kill their enemies but to capture them, usually in hand-to-hand combat, so that the captured ruler and nobles could be carried back to the victorious city to be tortured and sacrificed in public rituals. But Great-Jaguar-Paw fought a war not of stylized, formalized combat aimed at taking captives for sacrifice for personal glory. Instead, he fought a war of conquest when he attacked Uaxactún: "This was war on an entirely different scale, played by rules never before heard of and for stakes far higher than reputations or lives of individuals. In this new warfare of death and conquest, the winner would gain the kingdom of the loser".[88] Great-Jaguar-Paw and his warriors not only physically killed the Uaxactún elites, but they also killed this community spiritually, cutting off the people from the guidance and protection of their ancestors and gods.

Tikal and Uaxactún were two of the most prominent Classic Maya communities, but there were many others of interest. Some of the greatest of all known Maya frescoes are at Bonampak, dating to the end of the eighth century A.D. Here, in several rooms of murals, the paintings tell a story of warfare, torturing of prisoners of war, and celebration. The carefully drawn murals, which depict mutilated bodies, marching bands, richly dressed figures, and men with weapons, convey an extraordinarily vivid sense of militarism, royalty, and religion. Mary Ellen Miller has argued that these scenes are in part a depiction of raids to take prisoners. Unfortunately, these murals have been obscured by seepage through the composite limestone, so that they are only clearly visible when they are splashed with water or kerosene.[89]

Themes of military triumph, the torture of captives, and the power of the ruling classes were also commonly depicted in bas-relief sculpture throughout the Classic period—even in the Valley of Oaxaca and the peripheral areas of the Maya sphere of influence. Individuals of presumably higher status were juxtaposed in stone carvings with persons of lower status, and differences of dress, bearing, and position sharpened the contrast. In some cases, representations of prisoners were carved into the facings of stone steps, so that they were trod on by the nobility—a not too subtle visual pun.[90]

MAYA POLITICAL ORGANIZATION

Scholars have advanced several different competing ideas about the political organization of the Maya. Joyce Marcus,[91] for example, has suggested that the various Maya centers constituted a political hierarchy, with some royal families at particular centers being more powerful and prestigious than others, but with these various dynasties linked through marriage alliances and other ties. Stephen Houston, however, challenges this view, suggesting that the "Maya Lowlands may have consisted not only of centralized polities, with control some 30 km in any direction, but of 'buffer zones' in which smaller polities switched allegiance at will while remaining essentially independent. . . . Yet other areas may have been politically 'neutral' centers of pilgrimage."[92]

However, emerging data suggest that Maya polities were far more varied than center-dominated regions surrounded by buffer zones. Edward Schortman and Patricia Urban,[93] for example, examined the relationship of Maya communities on the periphery of the central Maya lowlands to centers such as Copán and Quirigua and concluded that these relationships varied depending on whether one considers politics, economy, or ideology. They suggest that despite the signs of great military domination by the most powerful communities in the central Maya area, no community could dominate to the extent that there was severe interregional exploitation in all dimensions of these relationships.

These and other views of how the Maya were organized politically raise fundamental questions about the nature of human societies in general. From the perspective of our own world and time we can look back and see the cultures of the world inexorably being linked closer and closer and ever more intensively. The United Nations, the European Union, and other political and commercial organizations now affect the flow of goods and ideas in even the most distant corners of the world. But this long-term evolutionary pattern has been a fitful one, with frequent reversals and great variations through time and space. And it is not clear that increasing complexity in these forms of organization are necessary or even "good." The various foreign conquests of the ancient Greek city-states, for example, are traditionally attributed to the Greeks' apparent inability to forge durable commercial, military, and political ties and unite against their aggressors, but this lack of unity did not seem to cripple these cultures intellectually—quite the opposite, in fact, when we consider their cultural contributions.

Basic geography certainly seems to explain part of the differences in level of political organization that we see in the ancient world. The Maya, like the Greeks, did not have the easy transport and communication channel that the Nile provided the ancient Egyptians, for example. And the Maya did not have the domestic horses and donkeys that allowed Middle Eastern societies to move goods, people, and information across a complex and vast social landscape. As discussed in chapter 7, ancient civilizations are in essence *ideas*: Maya ideology appears to have linked the many different centers that constituted this civilization, but there is little evidence that this ideological unity ever culminated in political or economic integration that extended beyond small regions.

MAYA WRITING

Maya writing is in many ways a more impressive achievement than their pyramids and temples. Fortunately, we have many Classic Maya texts in the form of inscriptions on stone and pottery, written in the same writing system as the "books" that followed 1,000 years later. These books consist of long strips of bark paper covered with a layer of plaster and folded like screens. Only a few of these "books" survive, but three are quite long and informative: the Dresden, Madrid, and Paris codices.

The sixteenth-century Spanish cleric Bishop Landa thought Maya writing (Figure 13.17) at first to be entirely alphabetic. Scholars quickly realized, however, that Maya writing was to be read in double columns, from left to right and from top to bottom, and by the turn of the last century Maya glyphs had been identified for the "zero" and "twenty" signs, the cardinal points of the compass, the basic colors,

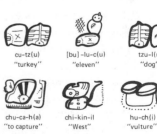

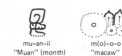

FIGURE 13.17 Some Mayan glyphs and the phonetic values assigned to them by Y. V. Knorosov. Research in the last two decades has shown that ancient Maya writing is a finely nuanced, beautiful orthography that probably records the entire spoken language of these people.

Venus, the months of the year, and the "Long Count," the system of reckoning by which the Maya figured how many years had elapsed since the beginning of their time.

Unlike the case with Egyptian hieroglyphs and Mesopotamian cuneiform, Maya writing had to be deciphered without the aid of "parallel scripts"—that is, the expression of the same text in two different languages, one of which is known.[94] As noted in chapter 8, *phoneticization* is a key step in the evolution of a written language, for once the elemental sounds of the spoken language are represented by abstract characters, the complete language can be written. The Russian linguist Yuri Knorosov was the first to demonstrate that Maya writing was indeed a phonetic system, and since his initial translations, many inscriptions have been almost entirely translated.[95] Building on the work of Tatiana Proskouriakoff, Henrich Berlin, and Yuri Knorosov, a new generation of Mayanists has made great progress: David Stuart, Peter Mathews, Steve Houston, Karl Taube, James Fox, John Juteson, and Michael Coe are just some of the scholars of the past several decades whose combined efforts have shown that ancient Maya writing is a finely nuanced, beautiful orthography that probably records the entire spoken language of these people.[96]

Maya script is somewhat similar to Egyptian hieroglyphs (chapter 9) in that it includes a mixture of signs, some representing whole words or ideas, others expressing syllables, sounds, and determinatives that clarify meanings.

In the Middle East the first writings are almost unrelievedly economic, but in Mesoamerica the surviving documents are primarily calendrical and historical, recording, for example, when a temple was begun, when a king defeated a rival, and what lands were under the control of the state. About the dull details of maize and men, they seemed much less concerned.[97] Recently, however, the inscriptions on hundreds of ceramics have been translated, and they do provide a great deal of economic information. Michael Coe, Steve Houston, and others[98] have shown that these texts recorded such information as the class of vessels a particular pot belonged to, its methods of adornment, the contents (e.g., chocolate or flavored maize gruel[99]), and occasionally the person who made or owned the vessel and its contents. As Houston also notes, the inscribed dates for the birth, accession, death, and other primary events in the lives of elites offer at least a speculative basis for estimating basic anthropological data about life spans. Justifying the fulsomeness of inscriptions on headstones and mortuary monuments, Samuel Johnson said, "In lapidary inscriptions a man is not upon oath," and it may be that there is a fictional element in the life-histories recorded for elite Maya. But the inscriptions fit rather well with some anthropological data that indicate that the Maya rarely lived past 55-65 years.[100]

The Maya were sophisticated mathematicians. They used a base-20 system in which they expressed the quantity 39, for example, as 19 numbers after 20, and the value 60 as three 20s.[101] They discovered the concept of zero and used a place-value notation system that allowed them to express numbers beyond 100,000,000. They had no way to express fractions in mathematical notation, but they computed the length of the solar year to 365.242000 days, compared to our own Gregorian calendar figure of 365.242500 days (the true value is approximately 365.242198 days). The Maya used two calendars. One was the familiar solar calendar in which a year equaled 365 days, but whereas we intercalate an extra day every four years to compensate for the year being actually 365.24 days long, the Maya blithely ignored this and let the seasons creep around the calendar. And in contrast to our system of 12 months of from 28 to 31 days, the Maya had 18 named months of 20 days each, with 5 days, which were considered highly unlucky, added to the end.

The second calendar (which appears to have been in use by the Olmec, a millennium or so prior to the Maya) involved a 260-day year, composed by intermeshing the sequence of numbers from 1 to 13 with 20 named days (Figure 13.18). These two calendars ran parallel, and thus every particular day in the 260-day calendar also had a position in the solar calendar. The calendars' permutations are such that each named day would not reappear in the same position for 18,980 days, or 52 of our solar years. Every day on the Maya calendar had

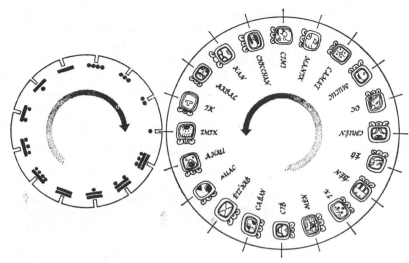

FIGURE 13.18   One of the Maya calendars was calculated from the correlation of the numbers from 1 to 13 and 20 named days.

its omens, and activities were rigorously scheduled in accordance with their astrological significance.

In some of the later adaptations of the Maya calendar, it appears that people were named after the day on which they were born and could not marry if they shared a numerical coefficient (e.g., Mr. "8 deer" could not marry Ms. "8 flower").[102] The Maya were thoroughly attuned to these calendrical cycles and used them to schedule many aspects of daily life and ritual. The Maya's "zero day," from which they counted time (and which they perhaps believed was the date on which the world was created) was August 13, 3114 B.C. Contrary to some speculations, the Maya apparently did not believe the world will end on December 24, A.D. 2011, but this date does mark the point at which the Long Count will return to the symmetry of its beginning. Pacal, king of Palenque, predicted in one of his inscriptions that the eightieth Calendar Round of his accession will be celebrated on October 15, A.D. 4772—a man who took the long view, indeed.[103]

The End of the Classic Maya (C. A.D. 760–A.D. 1100)

For decades scholars have debated the "collapse" of Maya civilization. It is in part a Western view of the world to see periods of rise and collapse in nations' histories and to search for causes. But the collapse of states, ancient and modern, never seems easily explained, and this is especially true of the Maya.

"Collapse" in the sense of what happened to the Maya has many meanings, since hundreds of thousands of people who spoke Mayan and were the direct genetic descendants of the classic first millennium A.D. Maya were there to greet the first Europeans on their arrival in the sixteenth century. And as Andrews and others have noted, the "collapse" of the Maya may be more apparent than real. A decline in temple construction and in the production of lavish goods does not necessarily mean societal collapse. As we noted in the discussion of changes in Egypt and elsewhere in the ancient world, declines in certain kinds of "waste" seem to be more indicative of a changing economic basis and administrative structure than the destruction of a culture. Had the Spanish not arrived when they did, the people of the Maya areas might have been reformulated by time and circumstance into a larger, more powerful, nation-state.

But Classic Maya culture did change—it lost many of its most important elements, and many formerly great communities were abandoned. One of the last kings of the Maya, Can-Ek, ruler of Itzá, met Cortés as he and his expedition crossed the Petén in A.D. 1525. But Maya culture was in decline long before that. As Anthony Andrews notes:

> In the eighth and ninth centuries the Maya area was a densely populated mosaic of large and small city-states ruled by regal and ritual dynasties who oversaw the great achievements of what we now call Classic Maya Civilization. These polities were also crossing the threshold of their demographic and ecological limits, which when coupled with managerial shortcomings, warfare, and the breakdown of political structure, led to a spectacular process of societal collapse. Cities throughout the southern lowlands were abandoned— some quickly. . . . Small populations survived in pockets . . . but for the most part they had severed their ties with the Classic past.[104]

Until about A.D. 910, the Maya usually accompanied any new monumental building with a stone stela engraved with the date of its construction, and thus we know that while many buildings were completed during the eighth and ninth centuries A.D., by A.D. 889 only three sites were under construction, and by about A.D. 900, construction seems to have ended for good. On the basis of ceramics and other information, we know that depopulation of the countryside and centers apparently followed quickly.

We know from inscriptions at Palenque, Dos Pilas, and other sites that the ninth century A.D. was a time of intense warfare and conquest, but there were also sporadic attempts to reestablish control and build communities in the ancient traditions. But the last king to erect a *tree-stone*, a traditional royal inscription to celebrate the end of a calendrical cycle, did so on January 20, A.D. 909, and after that the Maya traditions in the southern lowlands contracted and all but disappeared in the next few centuries.

But in the northern lowlands the ninth and tenth centuries A.D. were a time of great expansion. Cities such as Chichén Itzá established empires that transcended in size and power those of the earlier Classic period. Despite these periods of regional florescence and empire, however, Maya writing fell out of use and, with it, perhaps, the central ideology of the Maya world—the complex ideas about the universe and human affairs that melded these people into a culture and inspired them to build their civilization.

Many factors have been suggested as causes of the collapse, and also the development, of Maya civilization, and new interpretations sporadically appear. Not surprisingly, many involve the ecology of the Maya homeland, which seems at first glance to be a major barrier to cultural evolution.

A traditional archaeological approach to explaining the development of something is to imagine a set of problems to which the development is a solution. We might ask, given the Maya environment, under what conditions would it have been advantageous to organize into larger political and social units? Perhaps the answer lies in the necessity of local exchange to meet the threat of drought, disease, or disturbance. Rainfall is quite variable within the Maya area, and many other factors can adversely affect each community's agricultural system. Because the communities were all so similar in the crops they grew and their techniques for growing them, a major drought, such as happens in this area every 8–10 years, could result in the starvation of many people in hundreds of hamlets. But this could be avoided if many villages established exchange networks that spread the risks. Each year earthquakes, droughts, disease, floods, warfare, or some other combination of calamities might wipe out some sectors of the subsistence system, but if a village belonged to an organization that included many hamlets, it could get help or give help, depending on its fortunes. Population-control regulators were very important, hence the monumental construction projects in this most unlikely of places.

Whatever was at the root of the Maya cultural evolution, the collapse of this culture poses equally interesting questions. We have argued that the evolution of Maya society could probably be tied to the necessity of spreading the "risk" of life in this area by integrating many different settlements under a centralized authority. But by the same token, such an integrated system might eventually have encountered a series of catastrophes and internal problems that were spaced so closely together and in such a sequence that their effects could not be successfully fought off. "Murphy's Law" stipulates that if anything can go wrong, it will. This is especially true for cultural systems spanning millennia. Earthquakes, disease, warfare, drought, crop disease—all have certain periodicities, and unfavorable conjunctions must necessarily arise if the system is sufficiently long-lived.

For the Maya lowlands, accumulating data suggest that drought played a significant role in the demise of much of the Classic Maya world.[105] As we discussed earlier, the lowlands are characterized by seasonal rainfall, with about 90 percent of the rain falling in the interval between June and September.[106] Exacerbating this ecological factor is the rarity of surface water —water dissolves the limestone substrate in the Yucatan, forming caves and underground rivers. Maya settlements, whether large or small, had to build reservoirs to trap rainfall or, occasionally, where possible, dig into the bedrock to reach underground sources of water. Throughout this period, dry conditions were always more prevalent in the northern lowlands compared to the south. If less rainfall fell during the wet seasons for an extended period of time, then reservoirs would not be sufficiently full to support both the water needs of people and the water needed for irrigation and crop growing.

Richardson Gill[107] recently suggested that three major periods of drought occurred during the latter part of the Classic Maya period: 760 to 810 A.D., around 860 A.D., and about 910 A.D. These would have differentially affected Maya settlements, with sites in the southern lowlands being the earliest to suffer the consequences of reduced rainfall. This periodicity of major droughts has recently received independent confirmation from climatic data from sediments off the shore of Venezuela.[108]

While major droughts likely were an important factor, the demise of the Classic Maya should be seen as a period when people began to restructure their society and culture to meet various challenges, such as failure of rulership, increasing populations, and warfare, as well as major droughts.[109] Restructuring often results in archaeological signatures that are different from what came before, and thus appear to be striking changes in the archae-ological record. We see these most dramatically in the southern Maya lowlands, where the Classic Maya "disappears." It is now clear, however, that societal adaptations among the Maya were quite variable. Chichén Itzá (see earlier) in the northern lowlands is a good case in point. The great droughts occurred here, but Chichén Itzá grew in power, prestige, and influence. Bruce Dahlin[110] has provided one explanation for this pattern, suggesting that the northern lowlands had access to a much wider diversity of resource zones. Chichén Itzá capitalized on this access by intensifying trade networks and also through conquests. Chichén Itzá also may have benefited from the endemic warfare between Tikal and Calakmul in the southern and central lowlands. Emphasis on obtaining a diversity of resources, especially those related to subsistence, and providing labor in the form of the military and services related to trade, led to some restructuring of society, particularly in political and economic organization. Chichén Itzá is now viewed by scholars as the last of the Classic Maya capitals—rather than as a phenomenon of the Postclassic period—not reaching its demise until sometime between A.D. 1000–1100, long after the abandonment of Classic Maya centers in the southern lowlands.[111]

Global explanations for societal changes are rarely satisfactory. In the case of the Maya, regional variability in ecology, settlement, population, aptitude of individual rulers, droughts, warfare, and a host of other factors all appear to have contributed in varying degrees to the end of the Classic period. As we have seen, however, this demise did not occur over all the Maya region simultaneously, but took place over some 250 years.

POSTCLASSIC MESOAMERICA (A.D. 900–A.D. 1521)

As Maya political power in the lowlands was beginning to wane, much of highland Puebla, Mexico, and Hildago was apportioned among several competing power centers. One group, the Toltecs, began to dominate the Valley of Mexico after about A.D. 900. According to Aztec legends (the Aztecs claimed descent from the Toltecs), the Toltecs came to central Mexico from northwestern Mexico. The desert plateaus of northwestern Mexico were for many millennia the home of the *Chichimeca*, groups of nomadic hunter-foragers, and it is possible that some of these people migrated south and did, in fact, join with (or displace) local cultures to produce the Toltec culture. One of the major centers of the Toltec polity was at Tula, just north of the Valley of Mexico. Shortly after about A.D. 900, the Toltec built two stone pyramids and a ball court at Tula. On one of the pyramids they placed a temple dedicated to the Serpent god, Quetzalcóatl. On top of the pyramid (which is just over 10 m high) they placed stone statues of warriors (Figure 13.19), which are about 4.6 m high, as supports for a temple, and these figures continue to dominate the site. The base of the pyramid is decorated with reliefs of prowling jaguars and coyotes and eagles eating hearts.[112]

The Toltecs established trade and military outposts in many areas of northern and western Mexico and exported metal, gemstones, and other commodities as far north as Arizona and New Mexico. To the south, the Toltecs interacted with Chichén Itzá.

Eventually, Toltec power weakened. Under the onslaught of the invading Chichimec from the north, the Toltecs broke up into many smaller, competitive groups. Tula itself was almost entirely destroyed by invaders at about A.D. 1156. Succeeding centuries saw the rise of various other cultural traditions in central Mexico, such as the Tarascan state.[113] Chichén Itzá also went into a period of decline, to be replaced by a loose confederation of provinces, called the *League of Mayapán*, and the island of Cozumel, on Yucatan's east coast, which was a major trading center between A.D. 1250 and the arrival of the Spanish in A.D. 1519.[114] But by the time of the arrival of the Spanish, the community at Mayapán had been abandoned and the Maya areas were a welter of small chiefdoms at war with one another.[115]

The Aztec
(c. A.D. 1150–1521)

One of the last tribes to invade central Mexico from the north and west was the Aztecs. Aztec histories and legends, as recorded by the Spanish, tell of their arrival in the Valley of Mexico as rag-tag foragers and primitive agriculturalists who at first were forced by the established residents of the valley to live in the swamps around the lake, subsisting on flies, snakes, and vermin. According to legend, rival political groups in the valley enlisted the Aztecs in their campaigns but avoided other contacts with them because of the Aztecs' predilections for human sacrifice and other barbarisms. At war with various groups, the Aztecs were forced to take refuge on islands in the lake where, according to legend, they built their first

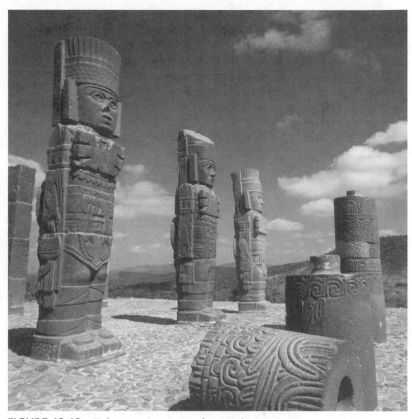

FIGURE 13.19   Toltec warrior statues from Tula, Mexico.

city, Tenochtitlán (Figure 13.20). In time Tenochtitlán grew to become a massive complex of pyramids, courts, and other buildings (now largely buried beneath the streets of Mexico City).

As allies of the Tepanec kingdom of Atzcapotzalco, the Aztecs conquered many of the surrounding cities, and at about A.D. 1427 they turned on their erstwhile allies and through savage warfare brought most of central Mexico under their control. Military expeditions conquered peoples all the way to the Guatemalan border, and garrison towns were established from the Pacific Coast to the Gulf of Mexico. Considerable investment in monumental construction characterized the capital at Tenochtitlán, but outside the capital, as Mary Hodge points outs, "the Aztec Empire has been described as nearly 'invisible' because it did not invest in roads, administrative buildings, or walls."[116]

Although the Aztecs are usually associated with militarism, they also created an impressive civil and commercial administration. Between about A.D. 1300 and A.D. 1520 they drained large areas of the Valley of Mexico, transforming them into productive agricultural plots. Michael Smith has argued that the Valley of Mexico settlement pattern during Aztec times was a hierarchically arranged marketing system of products with intense local specialization in goods and services.[117] Many commodities, including salt, reeds, fish, stone, cloth, various crops, ceramics, gold, and wood, were exchanged among hundreds of

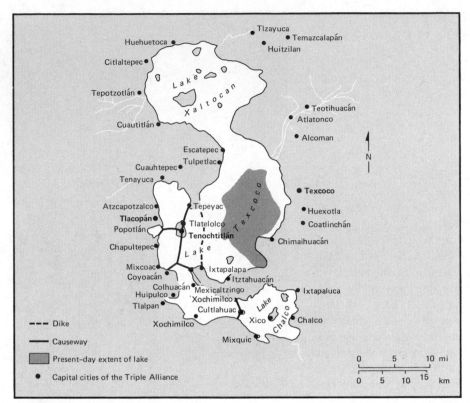

FIGURE 13.20   The most important Aztec cities were built around the lake that used to cover part of the Valley of Mexico. The lake margins were intensively farmed, and boats conveyed great quantities of food and craft products among these cities.

communities (Figure 13.21). In fact, the improbable location of Tenochtitlán—on an island in the middle of the lake—is probably best understood in terms of its central role in these redistributive networks.[118] In A.D. 1519 Tenochtitlán is estimated to have had about 200,000–300,000 inhabitants, five times the population of London at that period, and there were many other large cities within the Aztec domain.[119] Many cities had broad avenues, causeways, temples, pyramids, and other large buildings, often interspersed with gardens, courtyards, and large markets.

It is estimated that between one and two million people lived in the Valley of Mexico in late Aztec times.[120] The lake provided great and reliable quantities of food in the form of fish, waterfowl, and salamanders. In the southern areas of the valley's lake system, maize, beans, squash, tomatoes, and other crops were grown on *chinampas*, long rectangular plots of ground created out of the lake bed by piling up layers of aquatic weeds, mud, human feces, garbage, and other materials. According to ancient documents, the Aztecs initially made the chinampas by braiding grass and reeds into thick mats that could float, and thus they were able to float entire fields from one place to another—an agricultural system unparalleled in the ancient world.[121] The Aztecs and their successors planted trees, including the *ahejote* (a kind of willow), that eventually anchored most plots. Farmers who

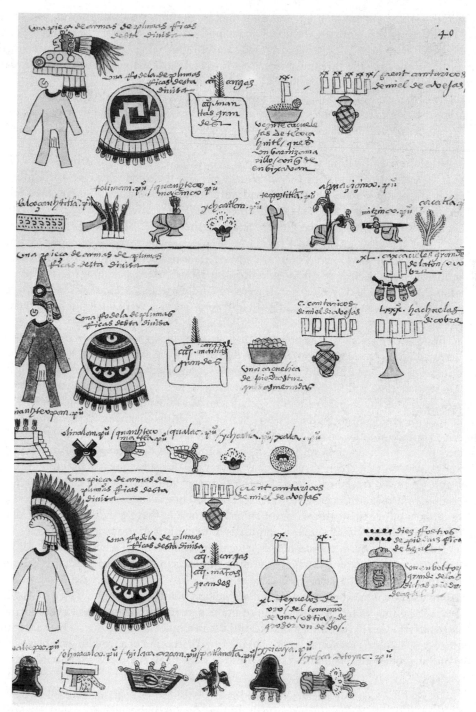

FIGURE 13.21 A Mexican tribute list (from the Codex Mendoza) describing the tribute paid to the government by towns in Guerrero Province. Among the commodities described are uniforms, shields, jade, gourds, sage, and amaranth.

still cultivate chinampas water the plots until they are the consistency of pudding and then use a rake to grid them into squares about an inch on a side. Seeds are placed in each square and covered with organic material to provide a greenhouse effect, and once the seedlings are at the proper size they are transplanted to other fields. As many as four crops per year can be grown on these exceptionally fertile plots of land.

The Aztecs were organized into a highly stratified class system headed by a divine king. Beneath the king were the nobles, the *pillitin*, all of whom belonged to the royal house, while the great mass of the populace were commoners who were organized in large clans, called *calpulli* ("big house"). The *calpulli* were the basic units of Aztec society. Each was composed of several lineages, totaling several hundred people, one of whom was designated the *calpule*, or leader. Members of a *calpulli* usually lived in the same village or ward, fought together as a unit if drafted for war, held and worked land in common, paid taxes as a unit, and worshiped at the shrine maintained by the *calpulli*. The leaders of the *calpulli* were the direct link between the imperial government and the people. There was also a class of professional merchants called *pochteca*.

The *calpulli* differed from one another in social rank. There was some social mobility for individuals—usually by virtue of extraordinary service to the state in warfare, trade, or religion. At the bottom of the social scale were the landless peasants and slaves, who worked the fields, performed other menial tasks, and were sacrificed in enormous numbers to various gods.

The Aztecs believed that the present world was just one in a succession of creations by the gods and that constant effort was required to forestall the extinction of the sun and the utter disappearance of humanity. Human blood was an essential part of the ritual (Figure 13.22) whereby the end of the world was postponed, and each time a human heart was ripped from a sacrificed person, another small step was taken toward prolonging the daily rebirth of the sun.[122] At times long lines of sacrificial victims snaked down the steps of the major pyramid mounds, on the top of which priests spent hour after hour engaged in the bloody process of heart removal. After the heart and blood had been offered to the gods, the body was thrown down the steps of the pyramid and subsequently flayed and then, perhaps, eaten. Other victims slated for sacrifice were pitted in gladiatorial contests, or beheaded, or drowned, or cast into fires. The Spanish conquistadors may have exaggerated the numbers of people sacrificed, but it seems inescapable that the Aztecs annually killed many tens of thousands and perhaps hundreds of thousands of people. This slaughter was accepted by the common people; in fact, it seems to have been widely supported. All war captives knew their fate, and it was an act of honor to accept a sacrificial death. In addition, young men were selected each year to lead a life of luxury in which they were surrounded by complaisant young women and feasted on the best of food, realizing full well that at the end of the year they would be sacrificed. In addition, parents throughout the land turned over infants and children to government officials for use in annual sacrificial rites. One sixteenth-century (apparently) eyewitness account of the ritual execution of a woman who played the role of the goddess Uixtociuatl gives us a sense of what these rites may have been like:

> And after they had slain the captives, only [then] Uixtociuatl ['s impersonator] followed; she came only at the last. They came to the end and finished only with her.
>
> And when this was done, thereupon they laid her down upon the offering stone. They stretched her out upon her back. . . . They laid hold of her; they pulled and stretched out

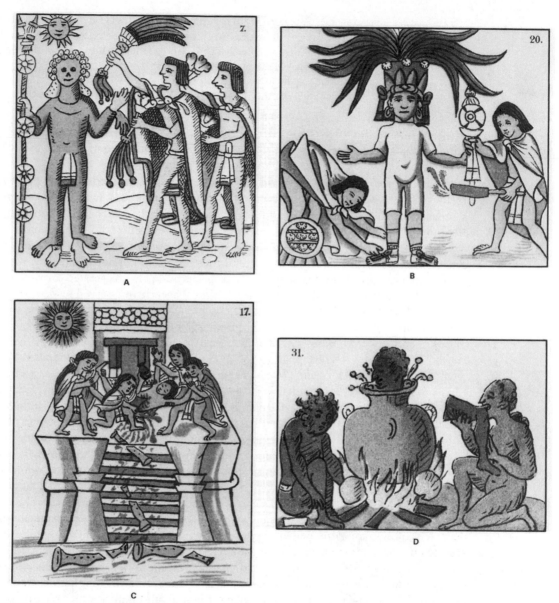

FIGURE 13.22   These early drawings (from the Codex Florentino) describe the sequence of ritual human sacrifice. (A) The priest is dressed in the skin of a sacrificed person; another person (B) was given a shield, mirror, and other ritual items and played the part of the god Tezcatlipoca; the individual was then sacrificed (C) and eaten (D).

her arms and legs, bending [up] her breast greatly, bending down her head taut, toward the earth. And they bore down upon her neck with the tightly pressed snout of a sword fish, barbed, spiny, spined on either side.

And the slayer stood there; he stood up. Thereupon he cut open her breast.

And when he opened her breast, the blood gushed up high; it welled up far as it poured forth, as it boiled up.

And when this was done, then he raised her heart as an offering [to the god] and placed it in the green jar, which was called the green stone jar.

And as this was done, loudly were the trumpets blown. And when it was over, then they lowered the body and the heart of [the likeness of] Uixtociuatl, covered by a precious mantle.[123]

Many of the sacrificial victims, as well as soldiers who died in battle, people struck by lightning, and mothers who died in childbirth, were thought to spend eternity in various paradises, cosseted with the pleasures of this world and the next.

With its emphasis on death, blood, and cosmic cataclysm, it is little wonder that Aztec theology struck the Spanish as somewhat heterodox (Figure 13.23). Even anthropologists, renowned for their cultural relativism, are impressed with the violence of Aztec religion. But human sacrifice is an old and recurrent theme in the evolution of complex cultures: In Mesopotamia, China, North America, and most other places, examples of warfare and slaughter can be found that equaled that of the Aztecs in form, if not in intensity. Also, as noted at the beginning of this chapter, the Europeans probably exaggerated the violence of Mesoamerican life, for the Europeans had a political agenda well-served by depicting the Native Americans as savages.

But human sacrifice and blood-letting *were* important elements in Mesoamerican cultures, and it is an interesting anthropological problem to explain why these acts, so repugnant to the modern mind, became so celebrated by the ancients of Mesoamerica, China, Mesopotamia, and elsewhere. It is not difficult to posit "functional" explanations that are plausible, if largely untestable. Michael Harner, for example, has argued that the key to Aztec sacrifice is the contribution the cannibalism of sacrificial victims made to the Aztec diet.[124] Mesoamerica lacks any large domesticated animals that could have been effectively integrated with Aztec agricultural strategies, and this animal protein and fat deficiency may have been compensated for by cannibalism. But the Mesoamerican diet is generally a rich one, with a nutritionally adequate basis of maize, beans, squash, fish, frogs, birds, deer, dogs, and other animals. This diet was sufficient to have supported long-term population growth and the needs of hundreds of thousands of people who lived around what is now Mexico City. There is little doubt that the Aztecs engaged in cannibalism, since several sixteenth-century Europeans described it as it happened, but we have insufficient evidence with which to evaluate Harner's thesis.

Despite their death cults, the Aztecs in everyday life were a colorful and in some ways engaging people. The Spanish remarked on their love of flowers and natural beauty, and their poetry contains many references to the joys of the natural world. The Spanish were amazed to find that Aztecs bathed their entire bodies most days—a level of personal cleanliness

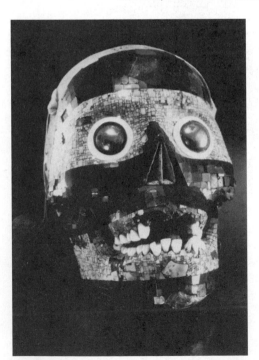

FIGURE 13.23   The supreme Aztec divinity was Tezcatlipoca, whose skull is modeled here in jade and crystal.

that would have struck even most eighteenth- and nineteenth-century Europeans as bizarre and unhealthy.

Dress for men and women often consisted of a loincloth and a woven cloak, and brightly colored cotton fabrics were used for ornamentation. In the countryside women often went about naked to the waist, but middle- and upper-class urban women wore decorated blouses.[125]

The diet of the Aztecs centered on maize, beans, squash, and tomatoes, although the wealthier people could eat various fruits, nuts, meats, and other exotic foods. The relatively unvaried diet was enlivened with peyote and other natural hallucinogens and by tobacco and *pulque*, a cactus-derived alcoholic drink with impressive powers to revive the weary.

THE SPANISH CONQUEST

> The captain Alonso Lopez de Avila . . . captured during the war . . . a young Indian woman of lovely and gracious appearance. She had promised her husband, fearful lest they should kill him in the war, not to have relations with any other man but him, and so no persuasion was sufficient to prevent her from taking her own life to avoid being defiled by another man; and because of this they had her thrown to the dogs.[126]

The melancholy history of the conquest of Mesoamerica by Spanish adventurers in the early sixteenth century was recorded in detail by the Spanish themselves. Accounts on both sides of this meeting of worlds provide a fascinating look at the clash of cultures.[127]

In A.D. 1519 Corte's left Cuba with a sizable force of ships, men, armaments, and horses and sailed to the coast of Veracruz. With the advantage of diplomacy with non-Aztec groups, horses, cannons, war dogs, and an extraordinary esprit de corps, Cortés and his men were able to march directly into the Aztec capital at Tenochtitlán, where they were at first welcomed by the Aztec king, Moctezuma, who was under the delusion that the Spanish were gods returning to their ancestral homeland. He could hardly have been more wrong. Within a short time, the Spanish had kidnapped and jailed him and were forming alliances with local non-Aztec peoples, who were only too happy to help the Spanish displace the Aztecs. Moctezuma and many of his people were eventually killed in a fierce battle at Tenochtitlán, after which Aztec resistance stiffened; but within a few years the Spanish had captured most of the Aztec heartland. In 1524 they hanged the last Aztec king, and thereafter Spanish domination of Mexico was rapid. When the Spanish first arrived, the population of the heartland of the Aztec empire was probably more than a million; 150 years later it probably held fewer than 70,000 people—the survivors of war, European diseases such as smallpox, slavery, and the other plagues of this epic clash of cultures.

SUMMARY AND CONCLUSIONS

As in all the other cases of early cultural complexity we have considered, it is clear that aspects of economy, ecology, and demography explain much of what happened in the New World. The Olmec, Teotihuacán, Oaxacan, Maya, Aztec, and other Mesoamerican societies appeared where they did and not in Newfoundland or Nebraska because of the exceptional productivity of the South Gulf Coast, Oaxaca, and other areas of Mesoamerica, given a simple farming technology and the maize-beans-squash complex.

We see in Mesoamerica, too, the stimulus to development provided by irrigation agriculture, environmental circumscription, interregional exchange, and other factors.

Once we get beyond an ecological level of analysis, we encounter a welter of variability in sociopolitical forms, economic histories, settlement patterns, and the other elaborations in these complex societies. In the absence of sufficient written documents, it is difficultto apply Marxian or other sociopolitical models to Mesoamerica. So we are left with a case of cultural evolution that is so striking a parallel to what happened in, for example, Mesopotamia, that we must consider both areas examples of a single developmental pattern.

From a nonscientific point of view, in some ways the most interesting thing about early Mesoamerican societies is the psychological contrast they make with ourselves. We may be sure that the average Olmec town of 500 B.C. had a full range of human personality types and an agricultural existence that we can all imagine. But in their cosmologies, world-views, and life-views, ancient Mesoamericans were profoundly different from the Spanish who first met them. Indeed, their views were probably profoundly different from those of any of the other western European traditions.

BIBLIOGRAPHY

Adams, R. E. W., ed. 1977. *The Origins of Maya Civilization.* Albuquerque: University of New Mexico Press.

Adams, R. E., W. E. Brown, Jr., and T. P. Culbert. 1981. "Radar Mapping, Archaeology, and Ancient Mayan Land Use." *Science* 213:1457–1463.

Alden, J. R. 1979. "A Reconstruction of the Toltec Period Political Units in the Valley of Mexico." In *Transformations: Mathematical Approaches to Culture Change,* ed. C. Renfrew and K. L. Cooke. New York: Academic Press.

Anderson, A. O., and C. Dibble, eds. 1978. *The Florentine Codex.* Salt Lake City: University of Utah Press.

Andrews, A. P. 1990. "The Fall of Chichen Itza: A Preliminary Hypothesis." *Latin American Antiquity* 1(3):258–267.

———. 1993. "Late Postclassic Lowland Maya Archaeology." *Journal of World Prehistory* 7(1):35–70.

Andrews, A. P., E. W. Andrews, and F. R. Castellanos. 2003. "The Northern Maya Collapse and its Aftermath." *Ancient Mesoamerica* 14:151–156.

Andrews V, E. W. 1990. "Early Ceramic History of the Lowland Maya." In *Vision and Revision in Maya Studies,* ed. F. S. Clancy and P. D. Harrison, pp. 1–19. Albuquerque: University of New Mexico Press.

Andrews V, E. W., and N. D. C. Hammond. 1990. "Redefinition of the Swasey Phase at Cuello, Belize." *American Antiquity* 54:570–584.

Armillas, P. 1971. "Gardens on Swamps." *Science* 174:653–661.

Arnold, J. E., and A. Ford. 1980. "A Statistical Examination of Settlement Patterns at Tikal, Guatemala." *American Antiquity* 45:713–726.

Ashmore, W., ed. 1981. *Lowland Maya Settlement Patterns.* Albuquerque: University of New Mexico Press.

Bell, E. B., M. A. Canuto, and R. J. Sharer. eds. 2004. *Understanding Early Classic Copan.* Philadelphia: University of Pennsylvania Museum of Archaeology and Anthropology.

Berlo, J. C., ed. 1992. *Art, Ideology and the City of Teotihuacan: A Symposium at Dumbarton Oaks 8th and 9th October 1988.* Washington, DC: Dumbarton Oaks.

Berrin, K., and Pasztory, R., eds. 1994. *Teotihacan.* London: Thames and Hudson.

Blanton, R. E. 1972. "Prehistoric Adaptation in the Ixtapalapa Region, Mexico." *Science* 175:1317–1326.

———. 1978. *Monte Albán: Settlement Patterns at the Ancient Zapotec Capital.* New York: Academic Press.

———. 1980. "Cultural Ecology Reconsidered." *American Antiquity* 45:145–151.

———. 1983. "Advances in the Study of Cultural Evolution in Prehispanic Highland Mesoamerica." In *Advances in World Archaeology,* Vol. 2, ed. F. Wendorf and A. E. Close. New York: Academic Press.

Blanton, R. E., S. A. Kowalewski, G. Feinman, and J. Appel. 1981. *Ancient Mesoamerica, a Comparison of Change in Three Regions.* Cambridge: Cambridge University Press.

Blomster, J. P., H. Neff, and M. D. Glascock. 2005. "Olmec Pottery Production and Export in Ancient Mexico Determined Through Elemental Analysis." *Science* 307:1068–1072.

Braswell, G., ed. 2003. *The Maya and Teotihuacan: Reinterpreting Early Classic Interaction*. Austin: University of Texas Press.

Brumfiel, E. 1976. "Regional Growth in the Eastern Valley of Mexico: A Test of the 'Population Pressures' Hypothesis." In *The Early Mesoamerican Village*, ed. K. V. Flannery. New York: Academic Press.

———. 1983. "Aztec State Making: Ecology, Structure, and the Origin of the State." *American Anthropologist* 85(2):261–284.

Chase, D. V. 1990. "The Invisible Maya: Population History and Archaeology at Santa Rita Corozal." In *Prehistoric Population History in the Maya Lowlands*, ed. T. P. Culbert and D. S. Rice, pp. 199–214. Albuquerque: University of New Mexico Press.

Chippendale, C., N. Hammond, and J. Sabloff. 1988. "The Archaeology of Maya Decipherment." *Antiquity* 62(234):119–122.

Clancy, F. S., and P. D. Harrison, eds. 1995. *Vision and Revision in Maya Studies*. Albuquerque: University of New Mexico Press.

Clark, J. E. 1997. "The Arts of Government in Early Mesoamerica." *Annual Review of Anthropology* 26:211–234.

Clendinnen, I. 1991. *The Aztecs: An Interpretation*. Cambridge: Cambridge University Press.

Coe, M. D. 1965. "The Olmec Style and Its Distribution." *Handbook of Middle American Indians* 3:739–775.

———. 1968. *America's First Civilization: Discovering the Olmec*. New York: American Heritage.

———. 1970. "The Archaeological Sequence at San Lorenzo Tenochtitlán, Veracruz, Mexico." *Contributions of the University of California Archaeological Research Facility* 8:21–34.

———. 1992. *Breaking the Maya Code*. London and New York: Thames and Hudson.

———. 1994. *Mexico*, 4th ed. New York: Thames and Hudson.

Coe, M., and R. Diehl. 1980. *The Land of the Olmec: The People of the River*, Vol. 2. Austin: University of Texas Press.

Coe, M., D. Snow, and E. Benson. 1986. *Atlas of Ancient America*. New York: Facts on File.

Coe, W., and W. A. Haviland. 1982. *Introduction to the Archaeology of Tikal, Guatemala*. Philadelphia: University Museum, University of Pennsylvania.

Coggins, C. 1985. *The Sacred Cenote of Sacrifice*. Austin: University of Texas Press.

Collier, G. A., R. I. Rosaldo, and J. D. Wirth, eds. 1982. *The Inca and Aztec State*. New York: Academic Press.

Conrad, G. W., and A. A. Demarest. 1984. *Religion and Empire: The Dynamics of Aztec and Inca Expansionism*. Cambridge: Cambridge University Press.

Cook, S. 1946. "Human Sacrifice and Warfare as Factors in the Demography of Precolonial Mexico." *Human Biology* 18:81–102.

Cordova, C., A. L. M. del Pozzo, and J. L. Camacho. 1994. "Palaeolandforms and Volcanic Impact on the Environment of Prehistoric Cuicuilco, Southern Mexico City." *Journal of Archaeological Science* 21:585–596.

Cowgill, G. 1974. "Quantitative Studies of Urbanization at Teotihuacán." In *Mesoamerican Archaeology: New Approaches*, ed. N. Hammond, pp. 363–396. Austin: University of Texas Press.

———. 1997. "State and Society at Teotihuacan, Mexico." *Annual Review of Anthropology* 26:129–161.

Cowgill, U. 1971. "Some Comments on Manihot Subsistence and the Ancient Maya." *Southwest Journal of Anthropology* 27:51–63.

Culbert, T. P. 1973. *The Classic Maya Collapse*. Albuquerque: University of New Mexico Press.

———. 1988. "Political History and the Decipherment of Maya Glyphs." *Antiquity* 62(234):135–152.

Culbert, T. P., and D. S. Rice, eds. 1995. *Precolumbian Population History in the Maya Lowlands*. Albuquerque: University of New Mexico Press.

Dahlin, B. H. 2002. "Climate Change and the End of the Classic Period in Yucatan." *Ancient Mesoamerica* 13:327–340.

Demerest, A. 2004. *Ancient Maya: The Rise and Fall of a Rainforest Civilization*. New York: Cambridge University Press.

Demarest, A., and G. W. Conrad, eds. 1992. *Ideology and Pre-Columbian Civilizations*. Santa Fe, NM: School of American Research Press.

DePalma, A. 1993. "Mexico City Restoring Area Tilled by Aztecs," *New York Times*, Sept. 14, 1993, p. B7.

Diaz del Castillo, B. 1928. *The Discovery and Conquest of Mexico*. London: Routledge.

Dickson, D. B. 1981. "Further Simulations of Ancient Agriculture and Population at Tikal, Guatemala." *American Antiquity* 46:922–926.

Diehl, R. A., and M. D. Coe. 1996. "Olmec Archaeology." In *The Olmec World: Ritual and Rulership*, pp. 10–25. Princeton, NJ: The Art Museum of Princeton University.

Dunning, N. P. 1996. "An Examination of Regional Variability in the Prehispanic Maya Agricultural Landscape." In *The Managed Mosaic: Ancient Maya Agriculture and Resource Use*, ed. S. L. Fedick, pp. 53–68. Salt Lake City: University of Utah Press.

Dunning, N. P., T. Beach, P. Farrell, and S. Luzzadder-Beach. 1998. "Prehispanic Agrosystems and Adaptive Regions in the Maya Lowlands." *Culture and Agriculture* 20:87–101.

Dunning, N. P., T. Beach, and D. Rue. 1997. "The Paleoecology and Ancient Settlement of the Petexbatun Region, Guatemala." *Ancient Mesoamerica* 8:255–266.

Fash, W. L. 1991. *Scribes, Warriors and Kings: The City of Copan and the Ancient Maya.* New York: Thames and Hudson.

Fedick, S. L. 1994. "Ancient Maya Agricultural Terracing in the Upper Belize River Area." *Ancient Mesoamerica* 5:107–127.

———, ed. 1996. *The Managed Mosaic: Ancient Maya Agriculture and Resource Use.* Salt Lake City: University of Utah Press.

Feinman, G. M., and L. M. Nicholas. 1990. "At the Margins of the Monte Alban State: Settlement Patterns in the Ejutla Valley, Oaxaca, Mexico." *Latin American Antiquity* 1(3):216–246.

Flannery, K. V. 1968. "The Olmec and the Valley of Oaxaca: A Model for Inter-Regional Interaction in Formative Times." In *Dumbarton Oaks Conference on the Olmec,* ed. E. P. Benson. Dumbarton Oaks, Washington, DC: Dumbarton Oaks.

———. 1976a. "The Early Mesoamerican House." In *The Early Mesoamerican Village,* ed. K. V. Flannery. New York: Academic Press.

———. 1976b. "Evolution of Complex Settlement Systems." In *The Early Mesoamerican Village,* ed. K. V. Flannery. New York: Academic Press.

———. 1976c. "Contextual Analysis of Ritual Paraphernalia from Formative Oaxaca." In *The Early Mesoamerican Village,* ed. K. V. Flannery. New York: Academic Press.

———, ed. 1982. *Maya Subsistence: Studies in Memory of Dennis E. Puleston.* New York: Academic Press.

Flannery, K. V., and J. Marcus. 1976. "Evolution of Public Building in Formative Oaxaca." In *Cultural Change and Continuity,* ed. C. E. Cleland. New York: Academic Press.

———. 1994. *Early Formative Pottery of the Valley of Oaxaca, Mexico* (with a technical ceramic analysis by W. O. Payne). Memoirs of the Museum of Anthropology 27. Ann Arbor: University of Michigan Press.

———. 2000. "Formative Mexican Chiefdoms and the Myth of the 'Mother-Culture.'" *Journal of Anthropological Archaeology* 19:1–37.

Flannery, K. V., J. Marcus, and S. A. Kowalewski. 1981. "The Preceramic and Formative of the Valley of Oaxaca." In *Supplement to the Handbook of Middle American Indians,* pp. 48–93. Austin: University of Texas Press.

Flannery, K. V., and M. C. Winter. 1976. "Analyzing Household Activities." In *The Early Mesoamerican Village,* ed. K. V. Flannery. New York: Academic Press.

Folan, W. J., E. R. Kintz, and L. A. Fletcher. 1983. *Coba: A Classic Maya Metropolis.* New York: Academic Press.

Fox, J. G. 1996. "Playing with Power. Ballcourts and Political Ritual in Southern Mesoamerica." *Current Anthropology* 37(3):483–509.

Fox, J. W. 1987. *Maya Postclassic State Formation.* Cambridge: Cambridge University Press.

Freidel, D. A., and J. A. Sabloff. 1984. *Cozumel: Late Maya Settlement Patterns.* New York: Academic Press.

Fritz, G. J. 1994. "Are the First American Farmers Getting Younger?" *Current Anthropology* 35(3):305–309.

Fry, R., and S. Cox. 1974. "The Structure of Ceramic Exchange at Tikal, Guatemala." *World Archaeology* 6:209–225.

Gill, R. B. 2000. *The Great Maya Droughts: Water, Life, and Death.* Albuquerque: University of New Mexico Press.

Grennes-Ravits, R., and G. Coleman. 1976. "The Quintessential Role of Olmec in the Central Highlands of Mexico." *American Antiquity* 41:196–205.

Grove, D. C. 1992. "Ideology and Evolution at the Pre-State Level." In *Ideology and Pre-Columbian Civilizations,* ed. A. Demarest and G. W. Conrad. Santa Fe, NM: School of American Research Press.

Grove, D. C., ed. 1987. *Ancient Chalcatzingo.* Austin: University of Texas Press.

Hammond, N. 1995. *Ancient Mayan Civilization.* New Brunswick, NJ: Rutgers.

Hansen, R. D. 1990. *Excavations in the Tigre Complex, El Mirador, Petén, Guatemala.* Papers of the New World Archaeological Foundation 62. Provo, UT: New World Archaeological Foundation.

———. 2001. "The First Cities: The Beginnings of Urbanization and State Formation in the Maya Lowlands." In *Maya: Divine Kings of the Rainforest,* ed. N. Grube. Cologne, Germany: Könemann.

Harner, M. 1977. "The Ecological Basis for Aztec Sacrifice." *American Ethnologist* 4:117–135.

Harris, M. 1977. *Cannibals and Kings: The Origins of Cultures.* New York: Random House.

Hodge, M. 1991. "Land and Lordship. The Politics of Aztec Provincial Administration in the Valley of Mexico." In *Land and Politics in the Valley of Mexico: A Two-Thousand Year Perspective,* ed. H. R. Harvey. Albuquerque: University of New Mexico Press.

———. 1995. "Polities Composing the Aztec Empire's Core." In *Economies and Polities in the Aztec Realm,* ed. M. E. Smith and M. G. Hodge. Albany: State University of New York.

———. 1998. "Archaeological Views of Aztec Culture." *Journal of Archaeological Research* 6(3):197–238.

Houston, S. D. 1988. "The Phonetic Decipherment of Mayan Glyphs." *Antiquity* 62(234):126–135.

———. 1989a. "Archaeology and Maya Writing." *Journal of World Prehistory* 3(1):1–32.

———. 1989b. *Maya Glyphs.* Berkeley: University of California Press.

Hunt, R. C., and E. Hunt. 1976. "Canal Irrigation and Local Social Organization." *Current Anthropology* 17:389–411.

Ifrah, G. 1985. *From One to Zero.* Trans. L. Bair. New York: Viking Penguin.

Johnston, K. J. 2004. "The 'Invisible' Maya: Minimally Mounded Residential Settlemnt at Itzán, Petén, Guatemala." *Latin American Antiquity* 15(2):145–175.

Joyce, R. A. 1986. "Terminal Classic Interaction on the Southeastern Maya Periphery." *American Antiquity* 1986:313–329.

Joyce, R. A., and J. S. Henderson. 2001. "Beginnings of Village Life in Eastern Mesoamerica." *Latin American Antiquity* 12(1):5–24.

Justeson, J. S., and T. Kaufman. 1993. "A Decipherment of Epi-Olmec Hieroglyphic Writing." *Science* 259:1665–1796.

Kelley, D. H. 1993. "The Decipherment of Epi-Olmec Script as Zoquean by Justeson and Kaufman." *The Review of Archaeology* 14(1):29–32.

Killion, T. W., and J. Uraid. 2001. "The Olmec Legacy: Cultural Continuity and Change in Mexico's Southern Gulf Coast Lowlands." *Journal of Field Archaeology* 28(1–2):3–25.

Kirkby, A. 1973. *The Use of Land and Water Resources in the Past and Present Valley of Oaxaca, Mexico.* Ann Arbor: Memoirs of the Museum of Anthropology, University of Michigan, No. 5.

Kowalewski, S. A. 1990. "The Evolution of Complexity in the Valley of Oaxaca." *Annual Review of Anthropology* 19:39–58.

Kowalewski, S. A., and L. Feinstein. 1983. "The Economic Systems of Ancient Oaxaca: A Regional Perspective." *Current Anthropology* 24(4):413–441.

Knorozov, Y. 1982. *Maya Hieroglyphic Codices.* Trans. S. D. Cole. Austin: University of Texas Press.

Kunen, J. L., T. P. Culbert, V. Fialko, B. R. McKee, and L. Grazioso. 2000. "Bajo Communities: A Case Study from the Central Petén." *Culture and Agriculture* 22(3):15–31.

Kurtz, D. V. 1987. "The Economics of Urbanization and State Formation at Teotihuacán." *Current Anthropology* 28(3):329–353.

Landa, D. de. *The Maya Account of Affairs of Yucatan.* Chicago: J. O'Hara.

Lees, S. H. 1973. *Sociopolitical Aspects of Canal Irrigation in the Valley of Oaxaca.* Ann Arbor: Memoir of the Museum of Anthropology, University of Michigan, No. 6.

Lounsbury, F. G. 1991. "Distinguished Lecture: Recent Work in the Decipherment of Palenque's Hieroglyphic Inscriptions." *American Anthropologist* 93(4):809–825,

Lowe, J. W. G. 1982. "On Mathematical Models of the Classic Maya Collapse: The Class Conflict Hypothesis Reexamined." *American Antiquity* 47:643–652.

Manzanilla, L. 1996. "Corporate Groups and Domestic Activities at Teotihuacan." *Latin American Antiquity* 7(3):228–246.

———. 1999. "Emergence of Complex Urban Societies in Central Mexico: The Case of Teotihuacan." In *Archaeology in Latin America*, ed. G. G. Politis and B. Alberti, pp. 93–129. New York: Routledge.

Marcus, J. 1973. "Territorial Organization of the Lowland Classic Maya." *Science* 180:911–916.

———. 1974. "The Iconography of Power Among the Classic Maya." *World Archaeology* 6:83–94.

———. 1976a. "The Origins of Mesoamerican Writing." *Annual Review of Anthropology* 5:35–68.

———. 1976b. "The Iconography of Militarism at Monte Albán and Neighboring Sites in the Valley of Oaxaca." In *The Origins of Religious Art and Iconography in Preclassic Mesoamerica*, ed. H. B. Nicholson. Los Angeles: Latin American Center, UCLA.

———. 1993. *Mesoamerican Writing Systems: Propaganda, Myth, and History in Four Ancient Civilizations.* Princeton, NJ: Princeton University Press.

Masson, M. A., and D. A. Freidel, eds. 2002. *Ancient Maya Political Economies.* Walnut Creek, CA: Altamira.

Matheny, R. T. 1986. "Early States in the Maya Lowlands During the Late Preclassic Period: Edzná and El Mirador." In *City-States of the Maya*, ed. E. P. Benson, pp. 1–44. Denver: Rocky Mountain Institute for Pre-Columbian Studies.

Matheny, R. T., and D. L. Gurr. 1983. "Variation in Prehistoric Agricultural Systems of the New World." *Annual Review of Anthropology* 12:79–103.

McAnany, P. 1994. *Living with the Ancestors: Kinship and Kingship in Ancient Maya Society.* Austin: University of Texas Press.

Miller, M. E. 1986. *The Murals of Bonampak.* Princeton: Princeton University Press.

Miller, M., and K. Taube. 1993. *The Gods and Symbols of Ancient Mexico and the Maya.* London and New York: Thames and Hudson.

Millon, R. 1974. "The Study of Urbanism at Teotihuacán, Mexico." In *Mesoamerican Archaeology: New Approaches*, ed. N. Hammond. Austin: University of Texas Press.

Millon, R., R. B. Drewitt, and G. L. Cowgill. 1973. *Urbanization at Teotihuacán, Mexico*, Vol. 1, Parts 1 and 2. Austin: University of Texas Press.

Moctezuma, E. M. 1988. *The Great Temple of the Aztecs.* New York: Thames and Hudson.

Murdy, C. N. 1981. "Congenital Deformities and the Olmec Were-Jaguar Motif." *American Antiquity* 46:861–869.

Nations, J. D. 1980. "The Evolutionary Potential of Lacondon Maya Sustained-Yield Tropical Forest Agriculture." *Journal of Anthropological Research* 36:1–30.

Nichols, D. L. 1982. "A Middle Formative Irrigation System Near Santa Clara Coatitlan in the Basin of Mexico." *American Antiquity* 47:133–144.

———. 1988. "Infrared Aerial Photography and Prehispanic Irrigation at Teotihuacán: The Tlajinga Canals." *Journal of Field Archaeology* 15:17–27.

———. 1995. "The Organization of Provincial Craft Production and the Aztec City-States of Otumba." In *Economies and Polities in the Aztec Realm*, ed. M. Hodge and M. Smith, Albany: Institute for Mesoamerican Studies, State University of New York.

Niederberger, C. 1979. "Early Sedentary Economy in the Basin of Mexico." *Science* 203:131–146.

O'Brien, M. J., J. A. Ferguson, T. D. Holland, and D. E. Lewarch. 1989. "On Interpretive Competition in the Absence of Appropriate Data: Monte Albán Revisited." *Current Anthropology* 30(2):191–199.

O'Brien, M. J., R. D. Mason, D. E. Lewarch, and J. A. Neely. 1982. *A Late Formative Irrigation Settlement Below Monte Albán.* Austin: University of Texas Press.

Offner, J. A. 1981. "On the Inapplicability of 'Oriental Despotism' and the 'Asiatic Mode of Production' to the Aztecs of Texcoco." *American Antiquity* 46:43–61.

Parsons, J. R. 1971. *Prehistoric Settlement Patterns in the Texcoco Region, Mexico.* Ann Arbor: Memoir of the Museum of Anthropology, University of Michigan, No. 3.

———. 1974. "The Development of a Prehistoric Complex Society: A Regional Perspective from the Valley of Mexico." *Journal of Field Archaeology* 1:81–108.

Pelzer, R. J. 1945. *Pioneer Settlement in the Asiatic Tropics.* Special Publications, No. 29. New York: American Geographical Society.

Pendergast, D. M. 1993. "Late Postclassic Maya Archaeology." *Journal of World Prehistory* 7(1):35–70.

Peterson, L. C., and G. H. Haug. 2005. "Climate and the Collapse of Maya Civilization." *American Scientist* 93:322–329.

Pires-Ferreira, J. W. 1975. *Formative Mesoamerican Exchange Networks with Special Reference to the Valley of Oaxaca.* Ann Arbor: Memoirs of the Museum of Anthropology, University of Michigan, No. 7.

Pohl, M. E. D., K. O. Pope, and C. van Nagy. 2002. "Olmec Origins of Mesoamerican Writing." *Science* 298:1984–1987.

Pollard, H. P. 1980. "Central Places and Cities: A Consideration of the Protohistoric Tarascan State." *American Antiquity* 45:677–697.

Porter, M. N. 1953. *Tlatilco and the Pre-Classic Cultures of the New World.* New York: Viking Fund Publications in Anthropology, No. 19.

Puleston, D. E., and O. S. Puleston. 1971. "An Ecological Approach to the Origins of Maya Civilization." *Archaeology* 24:330–336.

Rathje, W. L. 1971. "The Origin and Development of Lowland Classic Maya Civilization." *American Antiquity* 36:275–285.

———. 1973. "Classic Maya Development and Denouement: A Research Design." In *The Classic Maya Collapse*, ed. T. P. Culbert. Albuquerque: University of New Mexico Press.

Reilly, K. 1991. "Olmec Iconographic Influences on the Symbols of Maya Rulership: An Examination of Possible Sources." In *Sixth Palenque Round Table, 1986*, ed. V. M. Fields, pp. 151–74. Norman: University of Oklahoma Press.

Robertson, R. A., and D. A. Freidel, eds. 1988. *Archaeology at Cerros, Belize, Central America. Volume I: An Interim Report.* Dallas: Southern Methodist University Press.

Rust, W., and R. Sharer. 1988. "New Settlement Data from La Venta." *Science* 242:102–104.

Sabloff, J. A. 1990. *The New Archaeology and the Ancient Maya.* New York: Scientific American Library.

Sabloff, J. A., and D. A. Freidel. 1984. *Cozumel: Late Maya Settlement Patterns.* New York: Academic Press.

Sahagun, F. B. de. 1976. *A History of Ancient Mexico.* Trans. F. R. Bandelier. Glorieta, NM: Rio Grande Press.

Sanders, W. T., and D. L. Nichols. 1988. "Ecological Theory and Cultural Evolution in the Valley of Oaxaca." *Current Anthropology* 29(1):33–80.

Sanders, W. T., J. R. Parsons, and R. S. Santley. 1979. *The Basin of Mexico: Ecological Processes in the Evolution of a Civilization.* New York: Academic Press.

Sanders, W. T., and D. Webster. 1978. "Unilinealism, Multilinealism, and the Evolution of Complex Societies." In *Social Archaeology*, ed. C. L. Redman et al., pp. 249–302. New York: Academic Press.

Schele, L., and D. Freidel. 1990. *A Forest of Kings.* New York: Morrow.

Schele, L., and E. Miller. 1986. *The Blood of Kings.* Austin: University of Texas Press.

Schortman, E. M., and P. A. Urban. 1994. "Core and Periphery in Southeastern Mesoamerica." *Current Anthropology* 35(4):401–430.

Sempowski, M. L., and M. W. Spence. 1995. *Mortuary Practices and Skeletal Remains at Teotihuacán*, ed. R. Millon. Salt Lake City: University of Utah Press.

Sharer, R., and D. Grove, eds. 1989. *Regional Perspectives on the Olmec.* Cambridge: Cambridge University Press.

Sheets, P. D. 1979. "Environmental and Cultural Effects of the Ilopango Eruption in Central America." In *Volcanic Activity and Human Ecology*, ed. P. D. Sheets and D. K. Grayson, pp. 525–564. New York: Academic Press.

———. 2000. "Provisioning the Ceren Household: The Vertical Economy, Village Economy, and Household Economy in the Southeastern Maya Periphery." *Ancient Mesoamerica* 11:217–230.

Sheets, P. D., ed. 1983. *Archeology and Volcanism in Central America*. Austin: University of Texas Press.

Siemens, A. H., and D. E. Puleston. 1972. "Ridged Fields and Associated Features in Southern Campeche: New Perspectives on the Lowland Maya." *American Antiquity* 37:228–239.

Sisson, E. B. 1970. "Settlement Patterns and Land Use in the Northwestern Chontalpa, Tabasco, Mexico: A Progress Report." *Ceramica de Cultura Maya* 6:41–54.

Smith, M. E. 1979. "The Aztec Marketing System and Settlement Pattern in the Valley of Mexico: A Central Place Analysis." *American Antiquity* 44:10–24.

———. 2003. "A Quarter-Century of Aztec Studies." *Mexicon* 25(1):4–10.

Smith, M. E., and L. Montiel. 2001. "The Archaeological Study of Empires and Imperialism in Pre-Hispanic Central Mexico." *Journal of Anthropological Archaeology* 20:245–284.

Soustelle, J. 1961. *Daily Life of the Aztecs*. Trans. P. O'Brian. Stanford: Stanford University Press.

Stark, B., L. Heller, F. W. Nelson, R. Bishop, D. M. Pearsall, D. S. Whitley, and H. Wells. 1985. "El Balsamo Residential Investigations: A Pilot Project and Research Issues." *American Anthropologist* 87(1):100–111.

Steponaitis, V. P. 1981. "Settlement Hierarchies and Political Complexity in Non-market Societies: The Formative Period in the Valley of Mexico." *American Anthropologist* 83:320–363.

Stoltman, J. B., J. Marcus, K. V. Flannery, J. H. Burton, and R. G. Moyle. 2005. "Petrographic Evidence Shows That Pottery Exchange Between the Olmec and Their Neighbors was Two-Way." *Proceedings of the National Academy of Sciences* 102(32):11213–11218.

Storey, R. 1985. "An Estimate of Mortality in a Pre-Columbian Urban Population." *American Anthropologist* 87(3):519–535.

———. 1992. *Life and Death in the Ancient City of Teotihuacán*. Birmingham: University of Alabama Press.

Symonds, S. C. 1997. "Settlement System and Population Development at San Lorenzo." In *Olmec to Aztec*, ed. B. L. Stark and P. J. Arnold III. Tucson: University of Arizona Press.

Thomas, P. M. 1981. *Prehistoric Maya Settlement Patterns at Becan, Campeche, Mexico*. New Orleans: Middle American Research Institute, Tulane University.

Todorov, T. 1984. *The Conquest of America*. Trans. R. Howard. New York: Harper & Row.

Tolstoy, P. 1981. "Advances in the Basin of Mexico, Pt. 1." *The Quarterly Review of Archaeology* 2:33–34, 36.

Tolstoy, P., and A. Guinette. 1965. "Le Placement de Tlatilco dans le Cadre du Pre-Classique du Basin de Mexico." *Journal de la Societe des Americanistes* (Paris) 54:47–91.

Tolstoy, P., and L. Paradis. 1970. "Early and Middle Preclassic Culture in the Basin of Mexico." *Science* 167:344–351.

Townsend, R. F. 1992. *The Aztecs*. London and New York: Thames and Hudson.

Trigger, B. G. 1993. *Early Civilizations: Ancient Egypt in Context*. Cairo: American University in Cairo Press.

Turner, B. L., and P. D. Harrison, eds. 1978. *Prehispanic Maya Agriculture*.

———. 1984. *Pulltrouser Swamp: Ancient Maya Habitat, Agriculture, and Settlement in Northern Belize*. Austin: University of Texas Press.

Urban, P. A., and E. M. Schortman, eds. 1986. *The Southeast Maya Periphery*. Austin: University of Texas Press.

Webster, D. 1988. "Copan as a Classic Maya Center." In *The Southeast Classic Maya Zone*, ed. E. Boone and G. Willey. Washington, DC: Dumbarton Oaks.

———. 1992. "Maya Elites: The Perspective from Copan." In *Mesoamerican Elites*, ed. D. Chase and A. Chase. Norman: University of Oklahoma Press.

Webster, D., and N. Gonlin. 1988. "Household Remains of the Humblest Maya." *Journal of Field Archaeology* 15(2):169–190.

Whalen, M. E. 1976. "Zoning Within an Early Formative Community in the Valley of Oaxaca." In *The Early Mesoamerican Valley*, ed. K. V. Flannery. New York: Academic Press.

———. 1981. *Excavations at Santo Domingo Tomaltepec: Evolution of a Formative Community in the Valley of Oaxaca, Mexico*. Ann Arbor: Museum of Anthropology, University of Michigan, No. 12.

Wilcox, V. L., and D. R. Scarborough, eds. 1993. *The Mesoamerican Ballgame*. Tucson: University of Arizona Press.

Wilk, R. R., and W. Ashmore, eds. 1987. *House and Household in the Mesoamerican Antiquity* 62(237):703–707.

Winter, M. 1972. "Tierras Largas: A Formative Community in the Valley of Oaxaca, Mexico." Doctoral thesis. Tucson: University of Arizona.

———. 1976. "The Archaeological Household Cluster in the Valley of Oaxaca." In *The Early Mesoamerican Village*, ed. K. V. Flannery. New York: Academic Press.

NOTES

1. Bernal Diaz del Castillo, *The Discovery and Conquest of Mexico*, pp. 190–191.
2. Reviewed in Trigger, *Early Civilizations: Ancient Egypt in Context.*
3. Harner, "The Ecological Basis for Aztec Sacrifice."
4. Kirkby, *The Use of Land and Water Resources in the Past and Present Valley of Oaxaca, Mexico.*
5. Fritz, "Are the First American Farmers Getting Younger?"
6. See, for example, Joyce and Henderson, "Beginnings of Village Life in Eastern Mesoamerica."
7. Flannery, "The Early Mesoamerican House," pp. 13–15.
8. Flannery and Winter, "Analyzing Household Activities," p. 36.
9. For example, Diehl and Coe, "Olmec Archaeology." Recently, Blomster et al., "Olmec Pottery Production and Export in Ancient Mexico Determined Through Elemental Analysis," have provided some support for the notion of Olmec priority. Not all Mesoamerican researchers agree, however. See Stoltman et al., "Petrographic Evidence Shows That Pottery Exchange Between the Olmec and Their Neighbors was Two-Way," for a different viewpoint.
10. A good review of this can be found in Flannery and Marcus, "Formative Mexican Chiefdoms and the Myth of the 'Mother Culture.'"
11. Pelzer, *Pioneer Settlement in the Asiatic Tropics.*
12. Sisson, "Settlement Patterns and Land Use in the Northwestern Chontalpa, Tobasco, Mexico: A Progress Report."
13. Coe and Diehl, *The Land of the Olmec: The People of the River.*
14. Rust and Sharer, "New Settlement Data from La Venta."
15. Murdy, "Congenital Deformities and the Olmec Were-Jaguar Motif."
16. Justeson and Kaufman, "A Decipherment of Epi-Olmec Hieroglyphic Writing."
17. Kelley, "The Decipherment of Epi-Olmec Script as Zoquean by Justeson and Kaufman," p. 31.
18. "Olmec Origins of Mesoamerican Writing."
19. Sanders, Parsons, and Santley, *The Basin of Mexico: Ecological Processes in the Evolution of a Civilization.*
20. Nichols, "A Middle Formative Irrigation System Near Santa Clara Coatitlan in the Basin of Mexico."
21. Parsons, "The Development of a Prehistoric Complex Society: A Regional Perspective from the Valley of Mexico," p. 91.
22. This section relies heavily on Kowalewski's review article, "The Evolution of Complexity in the Valley of Oaxaca."
23. Flannery, "Contextual Analysis of Ritual Paraphernalia from Formative Oaxaca," p. 335; Flannery and Marcus, "Evolution of Public Building in Formative Oaxaca," in *Cultural Change and Continuity.*
24. Whalen, "Zoning Within an Early Formative Community in the Valley of Oaxaca."
25. Whalen, *Excavations at Santo Domingo Tomaltepec: Evolution of a Formative Community in the Valley of Oaxaca, Mexico.*
26. Winter, "The Archaeological Household Cluster in the Valley of Oaxaca."
27. Flannery and Marcus, *Early Formative Pottery of the Valley of Oaxaca, Mexico.*
28. Despite some evidence to the contrary (Coe, "The Olmec Style and Its Distribution").
29. Blanton et al., *Ancient Mesoamerica, A Comparison of Change in Three Regions*, pp. 180–183; Flannery, "The Olmec and the Valley of Oaxaca: A Model for Inter-Regional Interaction in Formative Times"; Grennes-Ravits and Coleman, "The Quintessential Role of Olmec in the Central Highlands of Mexico"; Flannery, Marcus, and Kowalewski, "The Preceramic and Formative of the Valley of Oaxaca."
30. See, for example, the works of William Sanders (Sanders, Parsons, and Santley, *The Basin of Mexico: Ecological Processes in the Evolution of a Civilization*), Jeffrey Parsons (Parsons, *Prehistoric Settlement Patterns in the Texcoco Region, Mexico*; idem., "The Development of a Prehistoric Complex Society: A Regional Perspective from the Valley of Mexico"), and Richard Blanton (Blanton, "Prehistoric Adaptation in the Ixtapalapa Region, Mexico"); O'Brien et al., "On Interpretive Competition in the Absence of Appropriate Data."
31. Brumfiel, "Regional Growth in the Eastern Valley of Mexico: A Test of the 'Population Pressure' Hypothesis."
32. Ibid. See Tolstoy, "Advances in the Basin of Mexico, Pt. 1."
33. Alden, "A Reconstruction of the Toltec Period Political Units in the Valley of Mexico."
34. Tolstoy, "Advances in the Basin of Mexico, Pt. 1."
35. Grove, "Ideology and Evolution at the Pre-State Level."
36. Cowgill, "Quantitative Studies of Urbanization at Teotihuacan."
37. Cowgill, "State and Society at Teotihuacan, Mexico," pp. 129–130.
38. Millon, "The Study of Urbanism at Teotihuacan, Mexico," p. 42.
39. Cowgill, "State and Society at Teotihuacan, Mexico," p. 144; see also Manzanilla, "Coporate Groups and Domestic Activities at Teotihuacan."

40. Cowgill, "State and Society at Teotihuacan, Mexico," p. 139.
41. Nichols, "Infrared Aerial Photography and Prehispanic Irrigation at Teotihuacán."
42. Parsons, "The Development of a Prehistoric Complex Society: A Regional Perspective from the Valley of Mexico."
43. Kurtz, "The Economics of Urbanization and State Formation at Teotihuacan"; Blanton, "Advances in the Study of Cultural Evolution in Prehispanic Highland Mesoamerica."
44. Cowgill, "State and Society at Teotihuacan, Mexico," pp. 156–157.
45. Kowalewski, "The Evolution of Complexity in the Valley of Oaxaca," p. 44.
46. Blanton, "Advances in the Study of Cultural Evolution in Prehispanic Highland Mesoamerica," pp. 261–262; Blanton et al., *Ancient Mesoamerica, A Comparison of Change in Three Regions*, p. 67.
47. Blanton, "Cultural Ecology Reconsidered."
48. Blanton et al., *Ancient Mesoamerica, A Comparison of Change in Three Regions*.
49. Ibid. See also Blanton, "Advances in the Study of Cultural Evolution in Prehispanic Highland Mesoamerica," p. 2.
50. Marcus, "The Iconography of Militarism at Monte Albán and Neighboring Sites in the Valley of Oaxaca."
51. Sanders and Nichols, "Ecological Theory and Cultural Evolution in the Valley of Oaxaca."
52. Kowalewski and Feinstein, "The Economic Systems of Ancient Oaxaca: A Regional Perspective," p. 425.
53. See *Current Anthropology* 29(1):52–80 for a discussion of this point.
54. Culbert and Rice, *Precolumbian Population History in the Maya Lowlands*.
55. Flannery, *Maya Subsistence. Studies in Memory of Dennis E. Puleston*; Ashmore, *Lowland Maya Settlement Patterns*; Dunning, "An Examination of Regional Variability in the Prehispanic Maya Agricultural Landscape." In recent years we have seen greatly increased research on the smaller Maya sites. See Robertson and Freidel, *Archaeology at Cerros, Belize, Central America: Volume I: An Interim Report*; Sheets, "Provisioning the Ceren Household: The Vertical Economy, Village Economy, and Household Economy in the Southeastern Maya Periphery"; Chase, "The Invisible Maya: Population History and Archaeology at Santa Rita Corozal"; Johnston, "The 'Invisible' Maya: Minimally Mounded Residential Settlement at Itzán, Petén, Guatemala." See also Clancey and Harrison, eds., *Vision and Revision in Maya Studies*.
56. Fedick, "Ancient Maya Agricultural Terracing in the Upper Belize River Area"; Dunning, "An Examination of Regional Variability in the Prehispanic Maya Agricultural Landscape"; Dunning et al., "The Paleoecology and Ancient Settlement of the Petexbatun Region. Guatemala."
57. Kunen et al., "Bajo Communities: A Case Study from the Central Petén."
58. Fedick, The Managed Mosaic: Ancient Maya Agriculture and Resource Use"; Turner and Harrison, *Pulltrouser Swamp: Ancient Maya Habitat, Agriculture, and Settlement in Northern Belize*; Dunning et al., "Prehispanic Agrosystems and Adaptive Regions in the Maya Lowlands."
59. Coe and Diehl, *The Land of the Olmec*.
60. Ibid., p. 65.
61. Ibid., p. 66.
62. Demarest, *Ancient Maya: The Rise and Fall of a Rainforest Civilization*, p. 179.
63. Schele and Freidel, *Forest of Kings*, p. 66.
64. Ibid., pp. 67–68.
65. Demarest, *Ancient Maya: The Rise and Fall of a Rainforest Civilization*, p. 206.
66. Schele and Freidel, *Forest of Kings*, p. 70.
67. Ibid., p. 98.
68. Marcus, *Mesoamerican Writing Systems*.
69. Schele and Freidel, *Forest of Kings*, p. 97.
70. See Andrews, "Early Ceramic History of the Lowland Maya," and Schele and Freidel, *A Forest of Kings*.
71. For example, articles in Adams, *The Origins of Maya Civilization*; Rathje, "Classic Maya Development and Denouement: A Research Design"; Sheets, "Environmental and Cultural Effects of the Ilopango Eruption in Central America."
72. Hansen, "The First Cities: The Beginnings of Urbanization and State Formation in the Maya Lowlands."
73. Demarest, *Ancient Maya: The Rise and Fall of a Rainforest Civilization*, pp. 83–86.
74. McAnany, *Living with the Ancestors: Kinship and Kingship in Ancient Maya Society*.
75. Hansen, "The First Cities: The Beginnings of Urbanization and State Formation in the Maya Lowlands."
76. Hansen, *Excavations in the Tigre Complex, El Mirado, Petén, Guatemala*.
77. Matheny, "Early States in the Maya Lowlands During the Late Preclassic Period: Edzná and El Mirador"; Coe, *Breaking the Maya Code*, p. 63.
78. Schele and Freidel, *A Forest of Kings*, p. 103.
79. Ibid., p. 102.
80. Braswell, *The Maya and Teotihuacan: Reinterpreting Early Classic Interaction*.
81. Houston, "Archaeology and Maya Writing," p. 26.
82. Wilcox and Scarborough, eds., *The Mesoamerican Ballgame*.

83. This scene is well illustrated in Coe, Snow, and Benson, *Atlas of Ancient America*, pp. 108–109.
84. Fox, "Playing with Power: Ballcourts and Political Ritual in Southern Mesoamerica."
85. The following discussion is based largely on Schele and Freidel, *A Forest of Kings*.
86. Ibid., p. 135.
87. Dickson, "Further Simulations of Ancient Agriculture and Population at Tikal, Guatemala."
88. Schele and Freidel, *A Forest of Kings*, p. 145.
89. Miller, *The Murals of Bonampak*.
90. Marcus, "The Iconography of Power Among the Classic Maya," p. 92.
91. Marcus, "The Origins of Mesoamerican Writing."
92. Houston, "Archaeology and Maya Writing," p. 26.
93. Schortman and Urban, "Core and Periphery in Southeastern Mesoamerica."
94. Chippindale, Hammond, and Sabloff, "The Archaeology of Maya Decipherement"; Demarest, *Ancient Maya: The Rise and Fall of a Rainforest Civilization*, pp. 47–48.
95. Knorosov, *Maya Hieroglyphic Codices*.
96. Reviewed in Coe, *Breaking the Maya Code*.
97. See Houston, *Maya Glyphs*.
98. Reviewed in Houston, "Archaeology and Maya Writing."
99. Ibid., p. 13.
100. Reviewed in Houston, "Archaeology and Maya Writing."
101. Ifrah, *From One to Zero*, p. 404.
102. Marcus, "The Origins of Mesoamerican Writing."
103. Schele and Freidel, *A Forest of Kings*, p. 82.
104. Andrews, "Late Postclassic Lowland Maya Archaeology," p. 54.
105. Gill, *The Great Maya Droughts: Water, Life, and Death*; Peterson and Haug, "Climate and the Collapse of Maya Civilization"; Dahlin, " Climate Change and the End of the Classic Period in Yucatan."
106. Peterson and Haug, "Climate and the Collapse of Maya Civilization," p. 322.
107. Gill, *The Great Maya Droughts: Water, Life, and Death*.
108. Peterson and Haug, "Climate and the Collapse of Maya Civilization," pp. 326–328.
109. Andrews et al., "The Northern Maya Collapse and Its Aftermath."
110. Dahlin, "Climate Change and the End of the Classic Period in Yucatan."
111. Andrews et al., "The Northern Maya Collapse and Its Aftermath."
112. Tula is well illustrated in *The Atlas of Ancient America*, Coe, Snow, and Benson, eds., pp. 134–135.
113. Pollard, "Central Places and Cities: A Consideration of the Protohistoric Tarascan State."
114. Freidel and Sabloff, *Cozumel: Late Maya Settlement Patterns*.
115. Andrews, "Late Postclassic Lowland Maya Archaeology," p. 55.
116. Hodge, "Archaeological Views of Aztec Culture," pp. 199–200.
117. Smith, "The Aztec Marketing System and Settlement Pattern in the Valley of Mexico: A Central Place Analysis."
118. Parsons, "The Development of a Prehistoric Complex Society: A Regional Perspective from the Valley of Mexico," p. 107.
119. Coe, *Mexico*, p. 151.
120. Parsons, "The Development of a Prehistoric Complex Society: A Regional Perspective from the Valley of Mexico."
121. Some of this description is taken from DePalma, "Mexico City Restoring Area Tilled by Aztecs."
122. Soustelle, *Daily Life of the Aztecs*, p. 97.
123. Quoted in Harris, *Cannibals and Kings*, p. 101.
124. Harner, "The Ecological Basis for Aztec Sacrifice."
125. Soustelle, *Daily Life of the Aztecs*, p. 135.
126. Diego de Landa, *Relacion de las Cosas de Yucatan*, p. 32 (quoted in Todorov, *The Conquest of America*).
127. Todorov, *The Conquest of America*; Collier, Rosaldo, and Wirth, *The Inca and Aztec State*.

The Evolution of Complex Societies in Andean South America

*In the lands assigned to Religion and to the
Crown, the Inka kept overseers and
administrators who took care in supervising
their cultivation, harvesting the products and
putting them in storehouses. The labor of
sowing and cultivating these lands and
harvesting their products formed a large part of
the tribute which the taxpayer paid to the king.
. . . The people assembled to cultivate them in
the following way. If the Inka himself . . . or
some other high official happened to be present
he started the work with a golden [spade] . . .
and following his example, all did the same.
However the Inka soon stopped working, and
after him the other officials and nobles stopped
also and sat down with the king to their
banquets and festivals which were especially
notable on such days.*

*The common people remained at work . . .
each man put into his section his children and
wives and all the people of his house to help
him. In this way, the man who had the most
workers finished his suyu first, and he was
considered a rich man; the poor man was he
who had no one to help him in his work and
had to work that much longer.*

Father Bernabe Cobo (c. A.D. 1653)[1]

Father Cobo's observations remind us of a point reviewed in detail in chapter 7 and
other previous chapters: Ancient civilizations varied greatly in many respects, but
one of the fundamental ways in which they were all profoundly similar is that each and
every one evolved social institutions that not only permitted the pervasive exploitation of

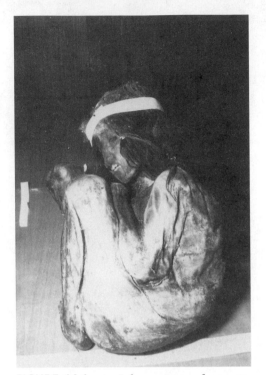

FIGURE 14.1 An Inka mummy of a seven-year-old boy, Mount Aconcagua, Argentina.

the many by the few, but also made that exploitation into a religious and civil virtue. Few "artifacts" demonstrate this "exploitation" more vividly than the well-preserved corpse (Figure 14.1) of a seven-year-old Inka boy whose body was found in the high Andes.[2] He was dressed in beautifully woven cotton clothes—embroidered with geometric and other designs—and was wearing a plume headdress, a turquoise and *Spondylus* shell necklace, and woven sandals. Ritual offerings found nearby include six small statues of gold and carved *Spondylus* shells. The statues of humans were clothed and adorned with ornaments, while the others have camelid features—likely representing animals such as the llama and alpaca. Perhaps this was a ritual sacrifice to some deity associated with the mountains. We simply shall never know—but this boy and many similar finds in ancient civilizations around the world exemplify behavior that we think of as exploitation, but which the boy and his culture probably saw as necessary and virtuous acts of faith that kept the cosmos in order.

When European explorers reached Peru and the other countries of Andean South America, they found a civilization that was very strange to them in many ways, including ritual human sacrifice, but they recognized immediately that the Inka were organized in a rigidly stratified class society under a supreme monarch—just as the Europeans themselves of that era were.

As with other New World political systems, one has to wonder how it would all have turned out had the Spanish not beheaded this civilization in the sixteenth century through murder, warfare, and the spread of European diseases. The Spanish themselves did not know about the origins of smallpox and other diseases that so terribly afflicted aboriginal Americans, but their imposition of slavery and intentional destruction of South American civilizations (see later) seem particularly barbaric in retrospect, even in the context of the bloody sixteenth and seventeenth centuries.

Andean South American civilizations paralleled other early complex cultures in their intensive farming systems, massive pyramids and temples, large cities, powerful armies, and hierarchies of wealth, power, and prestige. But they were different from other early civilizations in interesting ways. The Inka Empire, for example, was the only one of the six "primary" (see chapter 7) ancient civilizations that did not develop a written language, despite the fact that it was the largest political system ever to evolve in the pre-Columbian New World. The Inka and some of their predecessors compensated to some extent for the lack of a written language by using the knot-system for transmitting information (see later) and by building a massive system of roads that linked people to the central government and to each other (Figure 14.2). Neither the Inka nor any other New World people, however, ever developed the wheeled chariots, wagons, and other vehicles that were a major reason why Old World civilizations were able to dominate the world for centuries.

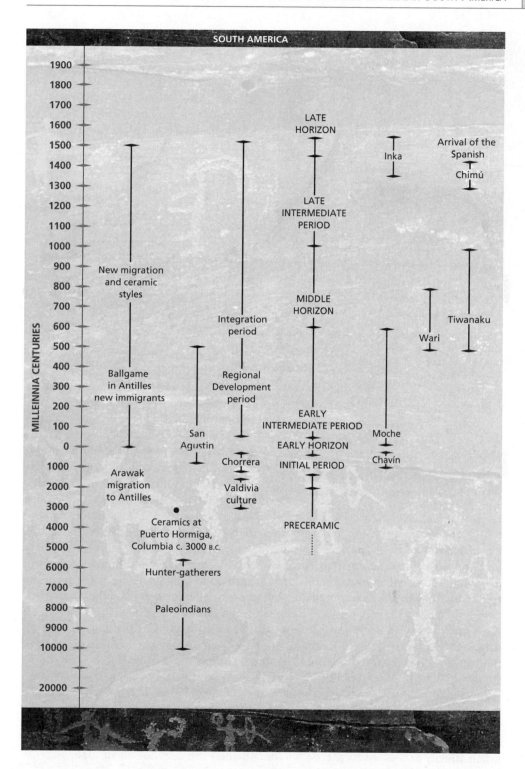

SOUTH AMERICA

MILLEINNIA CENTURIES

1900
1800
1700
1600
1500
1400
1300
1200
1100
1000
900
800
700
600
500
400
300
200
100
0
1000
2000
3000
4000
5000
6000
7000
8000
9000
10000

20000

New migration
and ceramic
styles

Ballgame
in Antilles
new immigrants

Arawak
migration
to Antilles

Ceramics at
Puerto Hormiga,
Columbia c. 3000 B.C.

Hunter-gatherers

Paleoindians

San
Agustin

Chorrera

Valdivia
culture

Integration
period

Regional
Development
period

LATE
HORIZON

LATE
INTERMEDIATE
PERIOD

MIDDLE
HORIZON

EARLY
INTERMEDIATE PERIOD

EARLY HORIZON

INITIAL PERIOD

PRECERAMIC

Inka

Wari

Moche

Chavín

Tiwanaku

Arrival of the
Spanish

Chimú

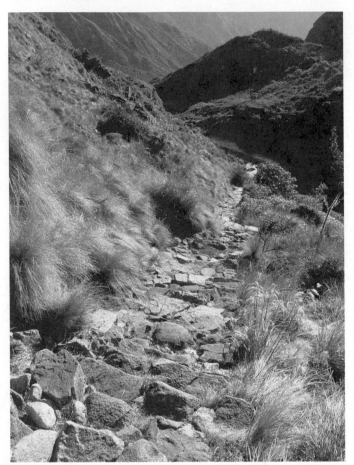

FIGURE 14.2 A stone-lined trail that served as part of the Inka road system.

THE ECOLOGICAL SETTING

> Ecological complementarity was a major human achievement, forged by Andean civilizations to handle a multiple environment, vast populations, and hence high productivity. It helps us understand the unique place of the Andean achievement in the repertory of human histories; it may even point to future possibilities.
>
> *John Murra*[3]

Like most other complex societies that developed independently, Andean South American civilization was possible because of—indeed, to an extent it can be defined as—the economic integration of the resources from highly varied physical environments.[4] Ancient Egypt (chapter 9) is something of an exception to this pattern, in that its resources were quite similar over the length of the Nile Valley and Delta, but in Andean South America there were great economic advantages to integrating the different natural resources of highlands and lowlands, ocean and farm. The Andes rise so sharply from the Pacific that only a thin strip of land, less than about 60 km at its widest point, separates the mountains from the sea. And because the Andes shield the coast from the rain-bearing air currents crossing the continent from the Atlantic, most of this coastal strip is one of the world's driest deserts, a region where rain falls only once or twice every five years. In a few places winter fogs along the coast keep skies overcast and in most years this phenomenon provides enough moisture through condensation to support vegetation zones (called *lomas*). But most of the coastal strip is utterly dry, and when the wind blows, dunes can quickly cover houses and choke irrigation canals.

This desert is habitable only because of the 50 or so small rivers that flow down from the mountains, across the plain, and into the sea. Many contain water during only part of the year, but the larger, permanent ones support forests and shrubs and their attendant wildlife, and in some areas the rivers keep the water table sufficiently high so that cultivation is possible without irrigation. Near the mouths of the rivers are fish, freshwater shrimp, and other resources, and in some valleys rivers have created broad alluvial plains of potentially rich farmlands. The coast has extraordinarily rich concentrations of fish, birds, birds' eggs, sea mammals, mollusks, crustaceans, kelp, and other plant foods. Human life along the coast is tied directly to these rivers and streams because they provide the only drinking water.

These rich marine resources are produced by a fascinating interplay of wind and ocean currents in which winds drive water north along the coast while the earth's rotation from east to west pushes the water westward, creating an upwelling of water from the ocean floor. Carried with these deep waters are tremendous concentrations of phosphates and other nutrients that support countless billions of microscopic plants, and these form the basis of a complex food chain comprising anchovies and other small fish that eat the plants; larger fish, birds, and sea mammals that eat the anchovies; and, ultimately, people, who exploit many links in the chain.

Occasionally, shifts in wind and water change the water temperatures and the plants die, cutting off the base of the food chain. When this happens, rotting plant and animal life fill the air with clouds of hydrogen sulfide that can blacken ships and houses.[5] Several years may pass before the fertility of the sea is restored. The frequency in prehistory of *el Niño* (a reference to the Christ child), as this disturbance is called, is unknown, but it has occurred somewhat regularly in historical times, and recently it has been recurring about once every two to seven years and usually lasts about a year. By late 1995 this area had been experiencing el Niño continuously for nearly four years, which seems exceptionally long. Recent research using sedimentary cores from land and lake deposits, however, indicates that major el Niño events in prehistory were not that common. The work of Fontugne and his colleagues, for example, documents a major el Niño at 8980 B.C. and another one sometime after 3380 B.C.[6] In the interval between these events were 10 humid episodes separated by dry phases. During the humid periods, the upwelling was stronger and there was increased moisture condensation in the form of fogs—these correlate with increased evidence for human occupation.

In the mountains are lush valleys, large basins, and high grassy plateaus (called *punas*). Hunters and gatherers here were succeeded after 4000 B.C. by farmers of potatoes, maize, quinoa, and other crops and by herders of llama and alpaca (domesticated New World camels).

The eastern slopes of the Andes, the *montaña,* are wet and heavily forested, and the combination of steep slopes and intense rain apparently limited exploitation by prehistoric peoples. East of the Andes is the Amazon Basin, a tropical rain forest from which feathers and other products were harvested and brought into early Andean South American economic systems, but which was never directly controlled by Andean peoples. The earliest known pottery in the New World dates to between 6000 B.C. and 5000 B.C. and comes from the lower Amazon Basin, in Brazil, where it was apparently made by hunter-foragers who specialized in shellfishing.[7] But ceramics were independently invented many times in the New World, and the extent to which these tropical cultures may have influenced those of the Andean regions remains unclear.

EARLY HUNTERS AND GATHERERS

A few South American sites have been dated (controversially) to 20,000–15,000 years ago, but not until about 10,000 years ago is there substantial evidence of people in the mountains and coasts of Andean South America. John Rick has surveyed large areas of these uplands, and in caves and rock shelters he has found projectile points, scrapers, knife blades, and other traces of these early Peruvians: They ate a lot of deer, guanaco, and vicuña (an animal related to the llama, both of which are New World forms of camels), and in some cases were perhaps even able to live year-round in small areas.[8] In the beginning they also hunted giant ground sloths and a few other animals that became extinct about 10,000 years ago.

Some of these people were probably "transhumant," meaning that they moved up and down the mountains to exploit various resources as they came in season. Many people made these seasonal moves once alpacas and llamas were domesticated because these animals require constant tending and frequent moves to new pasturages, thus making it possible for people to exploit the different environments at different times of year. The "thin" air, intense cold, blizzards, and thick fogs of the highlands make movement difficult, and over millennia of adapting to these conditions, natural selection has produced Andean peoples with extraordinary cardiovascular systems. Genetics and life-long exposure to the strains of life at high altitudes have produced people who can work hard in air extremely low in oxygen, while others unadapted to this environment can hardly function.

We may never know if coastal Andean South America was occupied before or at the same early date as the mountains because long stretches of what were beaches and inland areas before 3000 B.C. have been flooded by rising sea levels.[9] In areas that escaped flooding there is evidence of communities as early as 10,000 years ago, so some scholars suspect that coastal populations may have been substantial at an early date.[10]

THE AGRICULTURAL BASIS OF ANDEAN CIVILIZATION

As was discussed in chapter 6, maize phytoliths (the microscopic hard remains of some plant cells) and pollen have been found at a few South American sites that date earlier than 1500 B.C. In reviewing the evidence, though, Deborah Pearsall concluded that maize probably did not become an important crop until after 1500 B.C.[11]

Maize was just one of the important food crops in Andean South America, and in some areas potatoes, beans, and quinoa were the staffs of life. Quinoa seeds has one of the highest protein contents of any plant, and this plant was grown in many Andean regions. Domesticated potatoes were found in sites in Peru's Casma Valley mountains in occupations dating around 2250 B.C. to 1775 B.C.,[12] and there are traces of cultivation that may go back as early as about 4400 B.C.[13] This prolific plant is well suited to wet, cold soils where cereals do not do well, and the ancient South Americans partially solved a major problem of any agricultural system based on tubers—specifically, that tubers do not store well for long periods—by developing a method of storing potatoes by freeze-drying them.

The domestication of cotton between about 4000 B.C. and 1200 B.C. provided a relatively cheap source of textiles, and cotton textiles were complemented by a highly developed weaving craft in which reeds and other grasses were woven into sandals, clothes, and many other products. Ancient Andean cotton textiles are a lovely fusion of form and function. Many Andean textiles of various periods have survived because human corpses were frequently wrapped in them and buried in the coastal deserts, which desiccated and preserved both the textiles and the bodies. Using mineral and plant-derived dyes, ancient Andeans decorated many of their textiles with a wide variety of motifs, including geometric figures and stylized people and animals.

The role of animal domestication in early Peru is unclear, but llamas and guinea pigs were certainly domesticated in central Peru by 3500 B.C. As in Mexico, however, hunting continued to play an important role in many areas until quite late.[14] Evidence from several highland sites suggests that by about 4000 B.C. guinea pigs had been domesticated—if they were not domesticated by this time, then these Andean peoples were formidable hunters of these rodents, for guinea pig bones are thickly spread through many layers of occupational refuse. Guinea pigs do so well in captivity, are so prolific and easy to feed, and are so suitable in terms of size for the modern diet that one wonders why international food conglomerates have not yet renamed and successfully marketed them.

THE FIRST COMPLEX SOCIETIES IN ANDEAN SOUTH AMERICA

The formative period of Andean South American civilization can be thought of in terms of two periods, the Late Preceramic period (c. 3200 B.C.–1800 B.C.) and the Initial period (c. 1800 B.C.–900/600 B.C.).[15]

Like their archaeological colleagues working on early civilizations in other parts of the world, archaeologists in Peru have tried to identify when ancient Peruvian societies first made those fateful transitions in the direction of cultural complexity—complexity in the sense of the evolution of the kind of society represented by the Inka, with its bureaucratic hierarchies, class divisions, monumental architecture, economic differentiation and integration, expansionistic militarism, and elaboration of arts, crafts, and ideology.

As we have seen in other chapters, every early civilization around the world solved similar problems of nutrition and adaptation. Each found a reliable and productive plant to provide carbohydrates (rice, wheat, potatoes, maize, etc.), a legume to provide high-quality vegetable proteins (beans, peas, vetch, etc.), an animal protein source (usually a blend of hunting, fishing, and herding), and a textile to provide clothing (wool, linen, cotton, etc.). Not every society that evolved these adaptations became a great civilization (e.g., Polynesian societies based on tubers, pigs, and bark cloth), but all that did converged in their solutions to essentially the same problems of adaptation.

Peru offers an interesting possible variation on this theme because its sea coasts offer such a prolific source of food, in the form of many species of birds, shellfish, and fish—particularly schooling fish, such as anchovies. Even without farming, or with some minimal gardening, these coasts may have proffered enough reliable food to support many people—people who could live for all or much of the year in the same communities.

In the 1970s archaeologist Michael Moseley suggested that the initial stage of the rise of Andean societies was based on people who lived in villages and began to evolve some simple social stratifications on the basis of a fishing and foraging economy along the marine coasts rather than agriculture—at least at first. At one level this suggestion might not seem particularly radical. We know that all that is required for sedentary communities and the first appearances of complex societies is a highly productive and reliable blend of animal and plant foods, and it is not important whether these foods are agricultural (chapter 6) or not. Native Americans on the northwest coast of North America managed to live in non-agricultural sedentary communities that were stratified by wealth and an elementary sense of class, for example, as did many others, including the hunter-foragers of Southwest Asia, whose descendants became the denizens of the great Sumerian and Babylonian empires (chapter 8).

Also, the Inka Empire managed to tie together a great diversity of upland and lowland environments in an economy that was fundamentally agricultural when the Spanish encountered it, so it is interesting to see what role maritime resources played in the overall cultural evolution of this area, both before agriculture became the dominant source of food and afterward.

We know that by at least 6000 B.C. quite a few people lived on the Pacific coast, probably moving between the river valleys, the *lomas* (fog-oases), and the coast.[16] For several millennia thereafter, these societies seemed to change little as they adapted to this rich complex of environments. Anyone who has had the good fortune to live at the interface between sea, plains, and mountains, where oysters, clams, and fish can be combined with the wealth of terrestrial foods, can appreciate the stability and diversity of such economies, and the Andean coast is among the richest such zones in the world.

The Late Preceramic Period in Andean South America (c. 3200 B.C.–2000 B.C.)

Just prior to the beginning of the third millennium B.C., the appearance of sedentary, complex societies becomes a feature of both the coastal and highland areas. As we have seen in other areas of the world, one feature of such cultures is monumental construction–plazas, pyramids, and courts (discussed later). These sites also appear to be politically organized at a level above egalitarian villages.[17]

Excavations at Paloma,[18] on the coast of the Chilca Valley, 65 km south of Lima, illustrate some aspects of life in such regions (Figure 14.3). Paloma was located about 3.5 km from the ocean and 7.5 km from the Chilca River, on the edge of the *lomas* zone, where fogs supported some vegetation. Beginning about 8,000 years ago, people were living there in reed huts, probably already putting together a varied economy of plant collecting, hunting, and foraging. But shortly before 3000 B.C., some people apparently moved from the *lomas* in order to concentrate on the interface of coast and river valley, and small, dispersed settlements began to appear in these zones.[19] By about 2500 B.C., many small sedentary communities had appeared along the Andean coast. In some cases, the diet of these communities seems to have been based mainly on marine resources, with wild or domestic plants of only secondary importance,[20] but there was great variability from site to site.

At Alto Salaverry,[21] which was occupied from about 2500 B.C. to 1800 B.C., people cultivated and subsisted mainly on plants, but a lot of the calories in their diet came from sharks, bonito, mussels, and many other types of marine foods. In several communities of this period, skeletons show a pattern of bone growth in the inner ear that is common among people who spend a lot of time diving in cold water.[22]

At Chilca, the primary meat source appears to have been sea lions, but mussels, other invertebrates, and a variety of collected plants were also important. At other sites the remains of sharks, rays, cormorants, gulls, pelicans, and other animals attest to the importance of the resources of the coastal shallows, as does the presence of fish hooks, nets, and lines. No boats have been found at any of these sites, but the kinds of fish and invertebrates usually eaten along the coast are easily taken with simple nets.

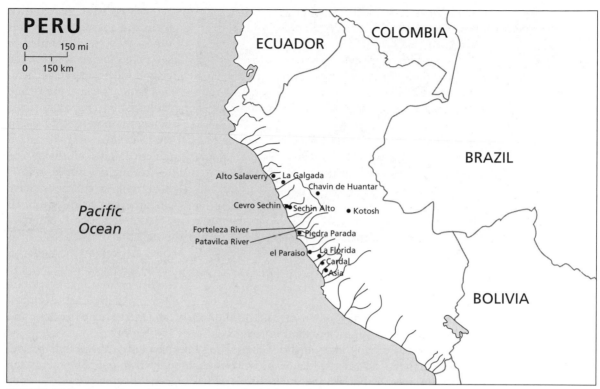

FIGURE 14.3   Some sites of the Preceramic and Initial periods.

By about 2000 B.C., numerous communities dotted the Andean coastline, many of them on river deltas and bays. Most of these seem to have been quite simple foraging-based communities, and few had more than several hundred inhabitants. At Chilca, examination of the burials of 30 adults and 22 children and adolescents indicated only minor differences in grave goods or positioning of the corpses. Some people were interned with spindles and spindlewhorls, others with fish hooks and lines, still others with cotton and weaving tools or a pointed stick and spatula kit that may have been used in shellfish gathering.

Once the Andean coast was fairly thickly settled, people here, like those in Egypt, Mesopotamia, China, and other early developmental centers, began building monumental architecture. It is absurd to think that people generally have some innate desire to build big stone buildings, but in Andean South America, too, no sooner had people devised economies of some reasonable reliability and richness than they began "wasting" massive amounts of their wealth in temples, tombs, and pyramids.

As was discussed in chapter 7 and other earlier chapters, the appearance of monumental architecture was one of the earliest signs of social transformations of cultures around the world. Andean South American civilization also followed this pattern. In the third millennium B.C., people in dozens of communities along the coast began to build impressive stone buildings and complexes of plazas, sunken pits, courts, truncated pyramids, and other large and formally arranged architecture.

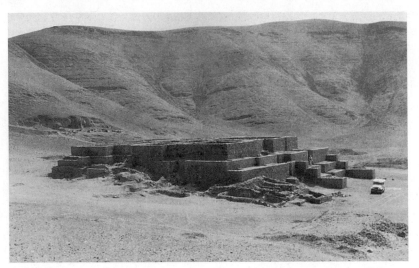

FIGURE 14.4 A structure at el Paraiso, Peru.

Many sites are known from the coastal area at this time—they are distributed in several ecological zones in the coastal valleys, and inland sites continue to have maritime resources as an important component of their subsistence. In the Pativilca and Fortaleza River Valleys in the Norte Chico region, for example, Haas and his colleagues have documented a minimum of 16 sites with late Preceramic occupations.[23] Each of these is characterized by monumental architecture, large plazas, and large ceremonial structures. The rectangular, terraced pyramids (mounds) range in size from 3,000 to 100,000 m², and there are between one and seven mounds present at each of the 16 sites.

Of the other early monumental buildings along the coast in the Preceramic period, most seem to have had a clear ritual purpose. Their alignment with mountain peaks, small inner rooms, internal burials, and other characteristics suggests ritual purposes, although like other early ceremonial structures around the world, they probably were centers for economic exchange and administration. Religion and economy, as we have noted, are inextricably intertwined throughout human history.

At the end of the late Preceramic period, a new form of construction appears in the coastal regions, the U-shaped mound complexes.[24] An example of this development is El Paraíso, on the banks of the Rio Chillón, about 2 km inland from the sea (Figure 14.4). This site is dominated by seven mounds that form a U-shape covering some 58 hectares, with a large plaza situated between the mounds. The structures were built over a period of several centuries and contain some 100,000 tons of stone masonry; the two largest structures rise to a height of over 5 m.[25] One structure is reported to have been painted a bright red and has evidence of burning on the floor, perhaps as a result of rituals.

There is much variability in early Andean South American monumental architecture, but there are also regularities that suggest that the builders of these structures shared a complex ideology and aesthetic. In previous chapters we have noted that early civilizations seem to have been built around a core of fundamental beliefs that integrated peoples over large areas and motivated them to work in concert within and between communities. Traces of this ideology seem to be expressed at El Paraíso. As Jeffrey Quilter noted,[26] the principal mounds at both El Paraíso and another coastal site, Piedra Parada,[27] are oriented to north 25 degrees east. This orients the sites

toward the NE and SW maxima of the Milky Way, and the axis perpendicular to this orientation is directed to the rising of the sun at the Summer Solstice (December) in the east and the setting of the sun [at] the Winter Solstice (June), as calculated for the years ca. [1450 b.c.].[28] . . . This suggests that the astrocosmological concepts known to have been important for the Inka were established in Preceramic times.[29]

Other complexes of this period have different orientations, but most of them have a formal, almost stylized use of specific architectural elements and arrangements. Ancient Peruvians used the interplay of rectilinear arrangements with circular or rounded elements, as well as the placement of sunken courts, terraces, and other constructions at different levels of elevation. These arrangements may have been intended, like those of Egyptian temples, to take the individual who enters the complex through a progression of "sacred" spaces.[30] At El Paraíso, Huaca Florida, and other sites, people built complexes in a U pattern, in which people presumably entered the open part of the U-shaped complex of platforms and buildings and then proceeded through interior forecourts, sunken courts, and other structures.

People in the Andean highlands also built monumental structures. At Kotosh, at about the 1,800-m level on the eastern slopes of the Andes, a large complex may have been begun before 1800 b.c. The earliest structure—a temple—was built on a stone-faced platform some 8 m high. At least 10 superimposed building levels were found. A good example of one of these structures is the Temple of the Crossed Hands, which is approximately square in shape—just over 9 m on a side—and about 2 m high. A stylized white serpent is painted on the staircase leading to this temple, and its entrance is plastered and painted red. A circular firepit, built into the floor, has subfloor flues to facilitate complete burning of materials placed into the firepit. Other features include five wall niches, and just below the two niches that flank a large central niche are clay-sculpted pairs of crossed hands—the feature used to name this temple.[31] Richard Burger estimates that perhaps as many as 100 such chambers are present at the site, and interestingly these chambers appear to have been deliberately buried—for example, the Temple of the Crossed Hands was filled in with river cobbles.[32]

Richard Burger and Lucy Salazar-Burger have suggested[33] that much of the architecture of Andean South America between about 1900 b.c. and 1000 b.c. expresses a common religious ideology, the *Kotosh Religious Tradition* (named after the site of Kotosh). We will never know precisely what this religion comprised, but an important element appears to have been ritual fires, placed in the firepits of the temple chambers. Quilter notes[34] that El Paraíso's sunken pit, a rectangle about 4.5-by-4.25 m, shows evidence of considerable burning. Benches around these pits are common in constructions of this period, and Quilter suggests that in ritual use 10–12 adults sat around these ritual fires and offered marine shells, meat, quartz, or other goods in sacrifices—perhaps while under the influence of coca or alcohol. As Charles Stanish[35] points out, however, the architectural constructions of the highlands and the coastal areas are considerably different. This makes it somewhat unlikely that the Kotosh Religious Tradition was widely shared across this entire region, especially in the context of little overall site planning or formal designs for sites in the highlands as compared to those in the coastal areas.

Contacts between highlands and lowlands, however, were important and included marine fish and shellfish. Another aspect appears to have been trade in salt. At the site of La Galgada in the highlands, for example, one burial yielded a salt crystal that had been placed under a woman's head, while two other burials were underlain by a bed of salt crystals.[36]

The Maritime Foundations of Andean South American Civilization?

As noted earlier, Michael Moseley has argued that early Andean South American complex societies, as represented by El Paraíso and similar sites, were initially based on an essentially non-agricultural economy.[37] If so, this would be interesting but would not alter our basic understanding of cultural complexity, for what is important in cultural evolution at this stage is the overall productivity of an environment rather than the specific ways in which it is productive.

As Quilter and Stocker[38] point out, fish can be dried or converted to a paste that has at least some shelf life. People who know anchovies only from the oversalted horrors on pizzas may underestimate the appeal and nutritive potential of this staple of Andean South American life. This fish was served fresh, dried, or as a kind of paste that, as every cook knows, is a marvelous addition to many tomato-based sauces. And anchovies are only one of many species of fish available in great numbers on the Peruvian coast. Sea mammals, too, can be rendered into storable oil, and they provided a reliable source of meat in ancient times.

Although inhabitants in coastal sites relied heavily on marine resources, they also used wild and domesticated plant crops. These include gourds, legumes, squash, *achira*, beans, sweet and white potatoes, peanuts, and cotton.[39] Sites that were a bit farther inland obtained marine resources through exchange, while cultivating agricultural crops and collecting wild plant foods. Trade with the highland sites allowed coastal groups to obtain potatoes, *oca*, and *ullucu*.[40]

Moseley's hypothesis for the maritime origins of Andean complex societies, however, is not applicable to developments in the highlands, where, as we saw earlier, sites with monumental architecture are of similar age to sites in the coastal region. While highlands inhabitants received some marine resources through trade, their subsistence economies were based on rainfall and small-scale irrigation agriculture—potatoes, oca, ullucu, quinoa, and some maize—as well as hunting of wild animals such as deer, guanaco, and vicuña.[41]

As these various sites indicate, cultural evolution rests not on any particular form of economy—all that is required is sufficient and reliable production.

The Initial Period in Andean South America (c. 1800 B.C.–900/600 B.C.)

During the Initial period, settlements in the coastal and highlands regions increased in size and complexity of architectural construction. U-shaped construction becomes a common feature along both the coast and in the central part of the highlands. In the south-central highlands—the Titicaca Basin—public architecture makes its first appearance.[42] Construction of centers, changes in settlement patterning, and population growth appear to have resulted from the construction of irrigation systems in the upper coastal valleys.

A particularly important Initial period area is the Casma Valley, located on the north-central coast. Eight important centers were present here during the Initial period, including Sechin Alto, Cerro Sechin, and Pampa de las Llamas-Moxeke. At about 1400 B.C. or earlier, Sechin Alto had the largest monumental architecture to be found anywhere in the New World.[43] Its U-shaped construction is anchored by an adobe-block pyramid mound that measures 250-by-300 m and stands 44 m high.[44] Several large plazas, some of which have sunken circular courts, are associated with the pyramid.

Some 2 km away is the site of Cerro Sechin, with a three-tiered stepped platform with two smaller buildings on each side.[45] A possible sunken circular court is present in front of the platform. As noted by several researchers, one of the most striking aspects at Cerro Sechin are the 302 small and large basalt sculptures that were originally placed in alternating sizes—large and small—along the outer wall of the platform-pyramid. These sculptures depict military scenes of war, victims of captivity, and victors. Some of the defeated are shown decapitated or cut so that their intestines are spilling out, while other sculptures simply show severed heads, legs, arms, and so forth.[46] There would seem to be little doubt that some level of violence was a part of life during the Initial period, although Initial period sites do not appear to have defensive constructions such as walls. Perhaps such gruesome scenes were not the fabric of everyday life, but rather—as suggested by some archaeologists—a record of a mythological event that helps establish and sustain the ceremonial or ritual nature of these monumental constructions.[47]

Farther inland in the Casma Valley lies the site of Pampa de las Llamas-Moxeke (Figure 14.5). This site has two massive platform-pyramid mounds that are separated by an enormous terraced plaza, as well as more than 70 smaller aligned platforms and buildings that were likely residences. The two platform-pyramids are aligned along the site's central axis, and the larger of the two—the Moxeke mound—has painted clay sculptures and geometric designs along the sides of the third platform terrace, about 10 m above ground surface.[48] The clay sculptures show humans wearing tunics, short skirts, and loose mantles—some hold two-headed snakes with forked tongues in upraised hands—or massive heads.[49] This frieze would have been quite visible to people in the plaza below the platform-pyramid, likely reinforcing the ideology common to Initial period culture in the Casma Valley.

These developments in the Casma Valley have been variously interpreted. Jonathan Haas and Sheila and Thomas Pozorski favor a relatively complex sociopolitical organization—perhaps even a theocratic state—that features distinct, highly stratified social classes.[50] Richard Burger,[51] on the other hand, believes that the evidence best supports a variety of small societies that have social divisions that are weakly developed. He points to a lack of economic specialization, as well as variability in the layout of the ceremonial centers, as indicative of independent local groups rather than a single political entity. Their religious traditions are, however, well developed, and may have served to loosely connect the various centers through shared symbols.

Another example of Initial period U-shaped constructions

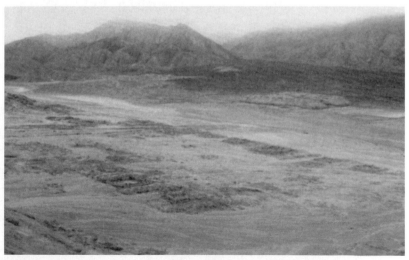

FIGURE 14.5 Overview of Pampas de las Llamas-Moxeke, Peru.

comes from the coastal area site of Caral in the Lurín Valley. This ceremonial center was built and occupied in the late Initial period, from about 1300 to 900 B.C.[52] It contains a ceremonial road that travels between two enormous enclosures and two sunken circular courts, leading to the raised central plaza. From the plaza level is a 34-step staircase leading to the top of the central pyramid. One of the most impressive decorations is arranged so that one would pass through it when reaching the top of the staircase and is described as a "massive mouth band with interlocking teeth and large upper fangs on either side of the entryway into the central atrium. This awesome motif is clearly visible from the central plaza."[53]

Caral also contains evidence for habitation, with most house structures located to the south of the ceremonial central area. The population is estimated to be no more than 300 people.[54] As Burger and Salazar-Burger observe, this is a relatively small number of people considering the size of the ceremonial complex and the labor required to build and maintain that complex. They hypothesize that most of the population served by this ceremonial center lived in scattered farmsteads around Cardal. A small number of residences and burials were also found on top of the platform-pyramid—these may have been the homes for people of elite status, but few burial goods are present, suggesting that inequities in access to resources were not significant during the Initial period.

In summary of the Initial period, we see clear evidences of important social changes in these monumental complexes in the highlands and along the coast, but it seems likely that these communities remained relatively simply organized compared to the cultures that followed them. When we look at mortuary practices, for example, the small amount of very sketchy evidence we have shows a certain formalization of burial practices and some elaboration of them, but there is no clear evidence of massive disparities in wealth, power, or prestige. At the site of Asia, for example, 49 funeral bundles were recovered in which bodies and a few utilitarian goods were wrapped in reed mats and placed below the floor of a rectangular compound.[55] Differences in these burials may indicate some status differences, and there are a few "trophy heads" and headless bodies in this group that may indicate raiding or warfare, but overall the burial practices until about 900 B.C. suggest a society that is somewhat non-egalitarian, perhaps, but one that is not organized on the basis of class.

More important, insofar as the scanty evidence indicates, while these people traded products and evolved common ideologies, these communities were not functionally integrated to any great extent. There is little evidence of functional specialization within and among communities.

THE EARLY HORIZON (C. 900/600 B.C.–A.D. 1)

It is a fallacy of historical analysis to assume that increasing complexity is a natural, inherent quality in human societies. The idea of "progress" is so much a part of Western culture that it sometimes blinds people to the fits and starts of cultural evolution. Such is the case with the apparent collapse of many of the coastal complex societies just before the beginning of the Early Horizon.[56] Yet at the same time, sites in the central highland areas show considerable new investment in monumental construction, shared artistic and religious motifs, and perhaps power and influence.

The monumental constructions at El Paraíso, Cerro Sechin, Cardal, Kotosh, and other sites anticipate the cultural changes underway in this period, and there are many other signs that the Andean world was changing after about 1000 B.C. As we saw in the cases of Egypt, Mesoamerica, and elsewhere, "art" was not just a minor peripheral part of the rise of ancient civilizations: Art was an integral part of this process. In all early states, the cities, rank-wealth hierarchies, and functionally interdependent economies that arose were presaged by the spread of an art style that was usually expressed mostly directly in pottery. In the case of Andean South America, novel religious elements also appear to have been quite pervasive in this process.

Peru was no exception to this pattern. After about 900 B.C., people living at Chavín de Huántar (Figure 14.6) and other sites in the highlands of northern Andean South America began to use the same styles of decoration in their pottery, architecture, and other artifacts. Over succeeding centuries, tens of thousands of people over a great area participated in the Chavín Horizon, as this complex of stylistic elements is called.

The main motifs of Chavín art include fantastic depictions of hybrid combinations of people and jaguars, as well as snakes, bats, fish, crabs, and crocodile-like figures (Figure 14.7). In its fusion of tropical forest elements, such as snakes, jaguars, and caiman, Chavín art may reflect earlier cultural influences from the forests east of the Andes, but the "story" of Andean South American civilizations is that of integrating different zones—coasts, mountains, and lowland forests. The spread of Chavín styles is probably a harbinger of the functional integration of these areas in later periods. In some areas these motifs spread at about the same time as apparent increases in product exchange, activity specialization, population densities, and investments in monumental buildings, but the general tenor of the Chavín diffusion is reminiscent of the initial spread of Olmec art in Mesoamerica—a relatively simple extension of aesthetic and perhaps religious traditions in the absence of elaborate political hierarchies or economic elites.

Chavín de Huántar, the site after which the art style is named (though it is probably not the earliest or even most important Chavín settlement), was occupied for all or most of the period between about 900 B.C. and 200 B.C.[57] It boasts a ceremonial complex composed of two low platform mounds, a massive terraced platform, and a sunken circular plaza, 21 m in diameter and paved with stone. This complex is arranged in the U-form (discussed earlier) that was established some centuries earlier at El Paraíso. The most prominent feature of this complex is the Old Temple (remodelled during the Early Horizon into the New Temple), which was built of alternating thick and thin slabs of granite, sandstone, and limestone. These large stone blocks form the exterior of the temple, while the interior was filled with earth and rock fill into which were built numerous narrow passageways, canals, ducts for ventilation, and underground rooms.[58] The best known of these galleries is the Lanzón Gallery—named after the granite sculpture with a lance-like shape, carved as a fanged deity. Aspects of the sculpture's position in the chamber and its associated features—such as a vertical channel from the gallery above and a depression located at the top of the Lanzón sculpture—have led to interpretations such as pouring the blood of human sacrifices into the vertical channel and letting it drip into the depression and run down the Lanzón sculpture, as well as the use of the Lanzón sculpture as an oracle.[59]

By the fourth century B.C. as many as 2,000–3,000 people may have lived in and around the monumental complex at Chavín de Huántar—a large number of people—and there was probably some significant craft-specialization. Gold was the medium of the finest art

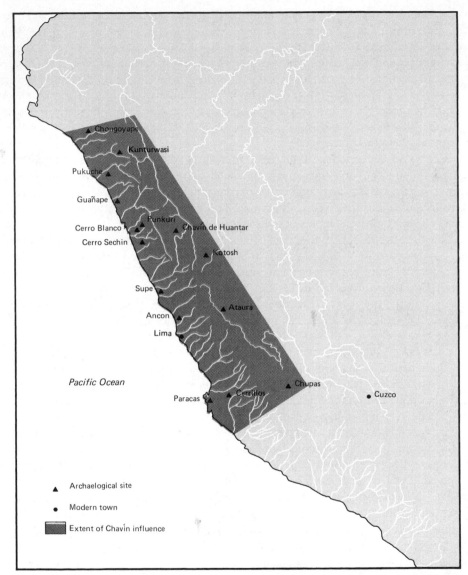

FIGURE 14.6   As in other early civilizations, initial cultural complexity in Andean South America was prefaced by the rapid spread of particular styles of pottery and other artifacts. Chavín-style artifacts have been found throughout the area indicated here.

in the Chavín era, as craftsmen cut, embossed, annealed, cast, and welded it into ear spools, nose ornaments, plaques, crowns, and face coverings for corpses. Copper and silver were also extensively used for making ornaments, and weaving became a fine art as well.

The central religious symbols of Chavín were widely distributed over the northern and central coasts, and Chavín-style ceramics and architecture are found even in small villages.

The Chavín cult, like other early religions, may have been an effective means of stimulating people to act in coordinated ways. After all, the expenses of large buildings and the "furs and feathers" of office are cheap compared to their power in directing the population toward specific economic and political goals. The Amazonian animals typical of Chavín designs and the distribution of these designs suggest that the center at Chavín de Huántar may have been an intermediate point on routes connecting the coasts with the exotic, rich world of the interior Amazon.

But were Chavín and its contemporaries a state-level form of political organization? Archaeologists have disagreed in their interpretations on this point. Some see the large Early Horizon sites as well-organized pilgrimage centers, regional cult complexes, or oracle centers. Others believe that these Early Horizon polities represent complex chiefdoms. Still others would attribute the classification of "secondary state" to Chavín, in part, because these scholars think that earlier sites, such as Pampa de las Llamas-Moxeke, represent primary states.[60]

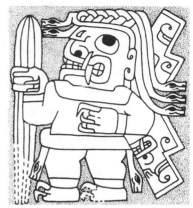

FIGURE 14.7   An example of an artistic motif from the Chavín art style.

THE EARLY INTERMEDIATE PERIOD (A.D. 1–A.D. 600): EARLY STATES

In the first millennium A.D., Andean South American societies were transformed from relatively simple, small political units that we might call chiefdoms into much larger and more populous militaristic cultures that we can legitimately term states.[61] Within this period the population of Andean South America rose from a few hundred thousand to approximately four or five million, large cities appeared in scores of places, armies conquered thousands of square kilometers, irrigation systems brought rich harvests to the desert and mountains, and the ceramic, architectural, metallurgical, and textile arts reached great heights.[62]

This transformation seems to have arisen out of the disintegration of the Chavín cult at about 200 B.C., which was followed by the emergence of as many as 15 different centers of regional development. Ceremonial centers can be found in many places in the southern Andean South American highlands at this time, as well as in the Nazca Valley and other coastal regions. Some of these were sizable towns, such as Tambo Viejo in the Acari Valley (Nazca area), which contains hundreds of rectangular rooms, most of which seem to have been residences. But the Nazca polity probably remained a mix of villages and towns.[63] Also numerous along the northern coast were great fortresses of terraced adobe platforms with room complexes and defensive peripheral walls.

One of the best known examples of Early Intermediate period cultures are the Moche whose area appears to have contained two political units—one to the north and one to the south. The Moche culture was concentrated in about a 400-km coastal strip that extended about 50 km inland and used an elaborate irrigation system. The population of the Moche Valley itself was likely more than 50,000 people (Figure 14.8). By 200 B.C. the community at Cerro Arena, for example, contained hundreds of houses and public buildings that extended over an area of about a square mile. The economic basis of this and other

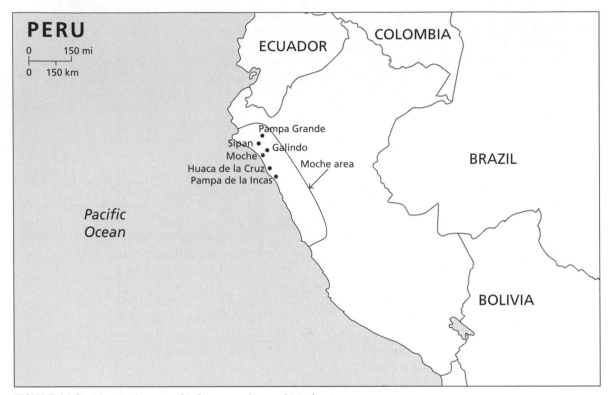

FIGURE 14.8 The Moche area of influence and several Moche sites.

communities was an irrigation system in which mud canals were built high in the hills, diverting water through kilometers of canals that snaked along the mountainside and down to the valleys. Because the Moche worked only with mud, the construction of these canal systems had to be done with great precision; if the water flowed too slowly, silt would accumulate so rapidly as to make the canal a vast waste of effort, while if it flowed too quickly, the whole system could be eroded. Cleaning the wind-blown sand from these systems probably required the annual orchestration of thousands of laborers.

In chapter 7 the premise that irrigation systems like these are primary *determinants* of cultural evolution was discussed and, for the most part, rejected. Often in prehistory, great irrigation systems seem more the products of states than their immediate cause. But in the case of the Moche Valley and many other examples, irrigation agriculture and cultural evolution are perhaps better viewed as closely interrelated, with an increase in the complexity of administrative and economic systems going step by step with increases in the complexity of irrigation systems.[64]

We know much about life in Andean South America during this period because the people recorded their activities in great detail in ceramics, sculpture, paintings, and tapestries. Pottery vessels depict people hunting deer with spears and clubs, fishermen putting to sea in small canoes, blowgun hunters taking aim at birds, weavers working under the direction of a foreman, and many people engaging in war, human sacrifice, and violence. People are also shown being carried on sedan chairs, seated on thrones, receiving tribute, and presiding at executions.

One of the most spectacular archaeological discoveries of the last decade of the twentieth century was the Moche royal burial complex at Sipán, about 420 miles northwest of Lima. These burials are particularly important because, unlike most known Moche sites, they had not been completely looted (the tomb was rescued and protected from local thieves by Walter Alva) and also because they express many elements of Moche culture. By now the reader, having surveyed Egypt, Mesopotamia, Mesoamerica, and other early civilizations in previous chapters, will not be surprised to learn that ancient Moche culture was based on massive inequalities in wealth, power, and prestige; that warfare was glorified and celebrated with the ritual executions of captives; that loving skill and precious materials were lavished on making beautiful objects—many of which were buried with dead elites— and that the entire society comprised an expansionistic and militaristic state.

The Sipán burials that reflect these aspects of Moche culture were found in the interior of a large mudbrick pyramid. In one burial a man identified by archaeologist Christopher Donnan[65] as a "warrior-priest" was found lying on his back in a wooden coffin. He was wearing gold nose and ear ornaments, turquoise bead bracelets, and copper sandals and was surrounded by other exotic goods, including spears, war clubs, shields, atlatl darts, seashells, feather ornaments, lovely cotton fabrics, hundreds of pots, a dog, two llamas, and other goods (Figure 14.9). This man was also buried with what one might consider the most valuable of all commodities, three young women and two men. As we have seen in other ancient cultures, many of these societies were based on ideologies that sanctioned these sacrifices and probably promised the participants an eternal and joyful afterlife. Although we will never know for certain what was going on in the minds of these nonliterate peoples, it seems a reasonable speculation that the Moche believed that by supplying this man with a few female and male attendants, food, tools, and some personal ornaments, they were assuring him of a reasonably comfortable eternity.

Depictions on Moche pots provide a "text," of sorts, for hundreds of them show similar scenes, apparently recording rituals in which warrior-priests slit the throats of war-captives, distributed the blood to be drunk, and then dismembered the bodies.

Among the other ideological expressions in ceramics of this period are the frank depictions of sexual practices. While every conceivable sexual variation is amply illustrated, oral sex and heterosexual coitus are common themes. Pots representing sexual themes in the most explicit terms may have been used in ordinary daily life, and to drink from them is to perform, symbolically at least, acts still considered illegal in some states in the United States. If the sexual practices depicted in pottery are in any way a reflection of the proclivities of the people—and reports of the Spanish and the Inka suggest this was the case—then the Moche may have devised a very efficient system of birth control.[66]

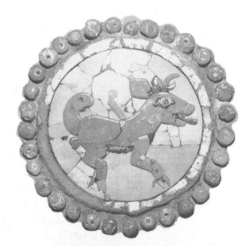

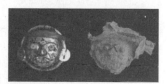

FIGURE 14.9 Some of the burial objects from Sipán, Peru.

If Moche pottery is an accurate reflection of daily life, men hunted, farmed, fished, and fought in wars, while women cooked food and performed other basic domestic services. Based on pottery representations and later ethnographic accounts, women also produced all or most of a primary kind of wealth in the form of textiles. Ethnographic evidence from the time of European contact to the present suggests that nearly all women wove textiles, and even the most elaborate fabrics may have been produced by peasant women working individually in villages.

The overall archaeological record of the Moche reveals the central patterns of all early complex societies. The evidence of warfare, for example, in ceramic depictions is supported by settlement patterns: Every well-surveyed coastal valley has been found to have fortresses and fortified settlements dating to this period, and weapons are common in these sites, particularly along the southern coast. Trophy heads and mummified corpses showing signs of violence are frequently found in cemeteries.

Occupational specialization was still at a rather simple level, but skilled craftsmen must have been full-time specialists to be able to produce the intricate objects in gold, silver, copper, and many other commodities found here.

The economic productivity of the Moche, their class-based society, and their ideology were also expressed in monumental architecture. At various places in the Moche Valley they built large clay platforms, ramps, temples, pyramids, and other constructions. One Moche pyramid, Huaca del Sol, was 340-by-160 m at the base, stood 40 m high, and comprised an estimated 140 million mudbricks.

In general, the Moche and other small states of this period appear to have been caught up in spirals of warfare, but they were also linked by trade mechanisms. Like other early states around the world, they seem to have expanded and contracted as the fortunes of war changed and as differences in the agricultural potential of various regions took effect.

THE MIDDLE HORIZON (C. A.D. 600–A.D. 1000): COMPETING STATES

At about A.D. 600, the many rival "states" and other competing polities of Andean South America began to give way to several larger competing political systems, one centered at Wari in the Manteco Basin; another at Tiwanaku, at the southern end of Lake Titicaca; and a third in the Moche-Chimú area. In these and perhaps other areas, wars of conquest may have brought large territories under the control of centralized, hierarchically-organized governments and lessened regional isolation.[67]

Tiwanaku is one of the first and largest "states" to be based in large part on potatoes, which were intensively cultivated with other crops on raised fields reclaimed from the lake marshes. The people of Tiwanaku also herded vast numbers of llamas—invaluable beasts of burden in this high country of thin air, and where in the classic Andean tradition the resources of highlands and lowlands could best be exploited via voluminous trade.

The people of Tiwanaku included master stonecarvers, who produced monumental gates, statues, and other buildings that are some of the most impressive in all Andean South America. Tiwanaku itself—from A.D. 100 to 700 or later—is an enormous and planned urban capital with state buildings, palaces, pyramids, temples, and streets (Figure 14.10). At its height, the population of the Tiwanaku state may have been approximately 100,000.[68]

Unlike the wars of conquest model (see earlier), the work of Juan Albarracin-Jordan[69] examines the rise of the Tiwanaku state from the perspective of how local hierarchies became integrated into a larger political entity. He uses ethnohistoric information to suggest that local hierarchies were developed to manage the exploitation of the resources from multiple ecological zones. Through reciprocity relationships, shared ideologies, and aggregation of population in

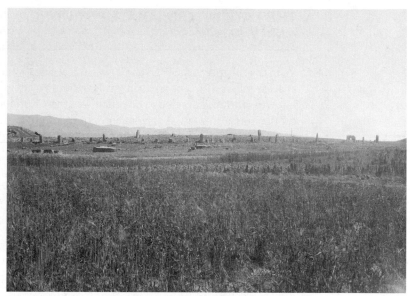

FIGURE 14.10   Stone pillars at the North and East Sides of Agapana, Tiwanaku, Bolivia.

larger centers, leaders of these local hierarchies—which may have represented distinct ethnic groups—began to participate in larger political organizations as intensification in management of the resources of the multiple ecological zones occurred. There is some evidence that some of these groups concentrated on certain specializations, such as particular crafts or the production of specific staples.

Wari existed as a political system for only a century or two, but at its high point it carried out political and economic activities over most of the coast and highlands between Cajamarca in the north and Sicuani in the south. The evidence for the Wari "empire" comes mainly from the distribution of specific art styles and religious symbols over a wide area of the central highlands and from its roads and provincial centers. Significantly, the art motifs show up most frequently in the burials of individuals whose associated mortuary goods appeared to reflect particularly high status. The city of Wari expanded to an impressive 15 km² —making it one of the largest residential sites in the ancient New World—and the proportion of its domestic and nondomestic architecture along with its overall size are similar to Tiwanaku.

It is probably significant that some of ancient Peru's major roadways may have been constructed during this period, for such roads would have been very important in facilitating the exchange of goods and services over an area as large as the one apparently administered from Wari.

The worldwide pattern of early states is one in which ever-larger polities compete with each other, with many expansions and contractions, but with a long-term increase in the size of the polities and the scale of the conflict. Wari, Tiwanaku, and other early states probably reflect this evolutionary paradigm, although Tiwanaku and Wari seem to have had little interaction except for their shared ideology.

THE LATE INTERMEDIATE PERIOD (C. A.D. 1000–A.D. 1476): EARLY EMPIRES

With the collapse of the Wari and Tiwanaku political systems between A.D. 800 and A.D. 1000, at least seven different areas in Andean South America became power centers, the best known and most developed of which was the Chimú state centered in the Moche Valley on the northern coast. A major center of the Chimú political system was the beautiful city of Chan-Chan, a partially planned settlement covering nearly 11 km²—one of the largest pre-Columbian cities in the New World. It contained 10 major compounds, each with houses, terraces, reservoirs, parks, roads, and public buildings. By the time Chan-Chan was built, Andean societies were rigidly stratified: Fiedel notes that in one area of Chan-Chan the skeletons of between 200 and 300 young women were found, "probably members of the royal harem, [who] were sacrificed either at the time of the deceased ruler's funeral or at later commemorative ceremonies."[70]

Gold-working, silver-working, ceramics, weaving, and sculpture were all highly developed crafts. Chimú society seems to have been rigidly stratified according to wealth and prestige, and the extension of political and economic control appears to have been based on a highly efficient army.[71]

Perhaps the most significant development in Andean South America during this period was the multiplication of urban centers. Much of southern Peru remained largely rural, but in the northern half of the country some of the greatest cities of the pre-conquest period were built.[72]

THE LATE HORIZON (C. A.D. 1476–A.D. 1532): THE IMPERIAL TRANSFORMATION

The largest and most highly integrated ancient political system ever to appear in the New World evolved in Andean South America within the space of only 87 years. Centered in the Cuzco Valley, the Inka Empire (more properly known as the Empire of Tawantinsuyu ["the four parts together"]) eventually stretched from Colombia to central Chile and from the Pacific to the eastern jungles, tying together under the administration of a single royal lineage many diverse regional economic and political systems. At its height, as many as 10–12 million people may have been living under Inka rule in one of the most intricately ordered societies of all time.[73] Like Egypt, the Inka polity was a "hegemonic-territorial" state[74]—one that dominated other polities—with its population spread rather thinly over a large area but with effective government control over most aspects of life.

Native and Spanish accounts say that the Inka began their rise to power out of the dissolution of the many small competing Andean South American states of the thirteenth and fourteenth centuries A.D. The people of Cuzco were attacked by a rival ethnic group— the Chankas—at about A.D. 1438 and managed to prevail. Succeeding monarchs at Cuzco added new provinces to the empire by conquest, treaty, and simple annexation. The Inkas' oral histories—recorded by the Spanish—speak of military campaigns in which Inka kings smashed the rival power of Chan-Chan in the 1460s, put down large-scale revolts in the 1470s, and greatly expanded the empire in the 1480s.[75]

The backdrop to this story of the development of the Inka as a state, however, is more complex than these accounts, and likely took place over a greater period of time. Alan Covey,[76] for example, has recently proposed that the Inka began their rise to regional domination in the period just after the fall of the Wari state—about A.D. 1000–1200. During this time, the Inka strengthened their control of the Cuzco Basin and some of the areas to the south of Cuzco. Using marriage alliances, they also established close relationships to the north and west of the Cuzco Basin. Two benefits were immediately available: Alliances and warfare created a labor supply for tending agricultural fields and construction work, and consolidation of the region opened opportunities for agricultural intensification. Another major factor was a dramatic population increase in the Cuzco Basin as people migrated in from surrounding areas.

As Covey[77] points out, Cuzco Basin elites capitalized on the need for administration of this growing polity, and these rulers began to practice nepotism—appointing their relatives to various positions of power in the military, religious, and administrative hierarchy. The Inka rulers also legitimized their rulership through control of commodities such as coca, cloth, and precious metals; through feasting (see later); and through the redistribution of some of these precious commodities to their allies and subjects. During the fourteenth century A.D., the Inka continued to expand their territories and establish long-distance diplomatic relationships. Eventually, the Inka began military campaigns against groups outside their region as they sought to enlarge their empire.

The economic basis of the Inka Empire was a highly integrated system of fishing, herding, farming, taxation, textile production, metallurgy, and so on. Rivers were channeled through stone-lined canals, while lowland irrigation systems, which had existed for thousands of years, were extended and brought under a centralized authority. Llamas and alpacas were raised for wool, while dogs, muscovy ducks, and guinea pigs provided most of the meat. But the staple foods were maize, beans, potatoes, quinoa, oca, and peppers.

The food-storage methods used by the Inka were very important in establishing imperial food reserves. Potatoes were alternately dried and frozen to produce a black, pulpy product called *chuño*; meat was turned into jerky; and grain was brewed into *chicha*, a nutritious beer. Archaeologists familiar with this combination say it is not as bad as it sounds.

Christine Hastorf and Sissel Johannessen have studied changes in the use of maize as the political system of Andean South America changed between A.D. 500 and 1500, particularly among the Inka. The Inka and their immediate predecessors converted maize into beer and then defined this beer as a prestige item and associated it with imperial power and the theology of the Inka state. People were brought together in communal feasts in which beer was consumed, and at these feasts the elites could reinforce their position: By providing beer in this context they could underscore the indebtedness of the peasantry to them and put the labor that the peasantry did for the elites in the context of the national religion and the highly stratified class system.[78]

The people of the empire were organized in a complex way according to a decimal system in which there were administrators for every unit of taxpayer from 10 to 10,000. Most people were members of large kin groups, called *ayllu*; marriages were between members of the same *ayllu*. The *ayllu* were usually economically self-sufficient units that held land in common, and their members were bound together by complex patterns of reciprocal obligations, such as requiring members to work in each other's place when one was absent

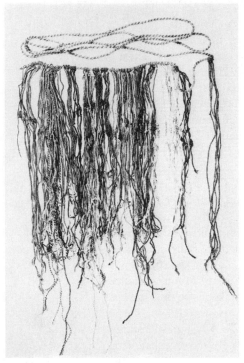

FIGURE 14.11   The Inka never developed a written language, but administrators used the *kipu*, a set of knotted strings, to keep records.

and to support widows and the infirm. Farmers worked a certain amount of time on state-owned plots, while craftsmen and specialists such as runners, weavers, and goldsmiths contributed according to their particular talents.

Records of taxes, transactions, and census figures were kept with the aid of the *kipu*, a set of strings tied into knots at different levels (Figure 14.11) and used by a special hereditary class of accountants to memorize the information.[79] A writing system of the type used in early Mesopotamia would no doubt have conveyed more religious and philosophical information, but for simple information storage and retrieval, the *kipu* appears to have been an adequate substitute for writing, when complemented by the enormous Inka bureaucracy.[80]

Gold, fabrics, and other luxury goods were collected from around the empire for distribution among the elites. Women, too, were treated as commodities. Government agents visited each village periodically and took selected girls of about age 10 back to provincial capitals where they were taught spinning, weaving, and cooking. They were then apportioned out as wives for the emperor and the nobles.

The Inka Empire both created and was created by its system of roads (Figure 14.12).[81] Most villages were largely self-sufficient, but the flow of goods and information and, most important, armies required to create the empire were dependent on the road system, comprising an overall network of about 40,000 km of paved roads. Road beds were excavated through hillsides, swamps were crossed by drained causeways, walls were built along roadways to protect the traveler from the fierce gales of the uplands, and wide rivers and ravines were crossed by suspension bridges made of woven vines hung from stone towers. All along the roads were storehouses and administrative outposts, and runners stationed about a kilometer apart were reputed to carry messages over distances as great as 2,400 km in just five days.[82]

Although they were master builders, most Inka lived in rural villages, not great metropolises. Typical Inka residential units were rectangular walled houses of stone or adobe, subdivided into smaller units. Most public constructions were in the form of palaces, temples, granaries, fortresses, barracks, and highway stations. The skill used in these constructions is amazing, considering the simple tools employed. The Inka cut stones into huge blocks simply by chipping and abrading them with harder stones, and they then fitted them together (without the use of mortar) so precisely that, as the cliché goes, a knifeblade could not be inserted between them.

The cultural order and social structure of the Inka were expressed not only in its public monuments, but even in its domestic architecture. Susan Niles has catalogued how, in one particular case, the buildings constituting the fifteenth-century estate of a noble family were arranged to reflect the rigid class hierarchy of the Inka polity.[83]

The capital city of Cuzco was an orderly arrangement of houses, monumental buildings, and streets, well-provided with a municipal water and drainage system. The great temple of Qori Kancha here had exterior walls measuring 68-by-59 m and a semi-circular annex that rose to a height of more than 34 m. A gold frieze about a meter wide ran along the exterior wall, and the entranceway was heavily sheathed in gold plate. Many other structures at the capital were lavishly decorated with gold and silver.

The comparatively great internal security of the empire made it unnecessary to defend most settlements, except with occasional hilltop forts. The heart of the Inka army was the common foot-soldier, who was armed with club, mace, battle axe, or lance. Slings, bolas, and spear throwers were used prior to the main attack, but brutal hand-to-hand combat usually decided the issue. One successful tactical innovation of the Inka was the practice of holding back a large body of troops who were thrown in at a critical juncture—a simple tactic similar in a way to Napoleon's successful use of reserves.

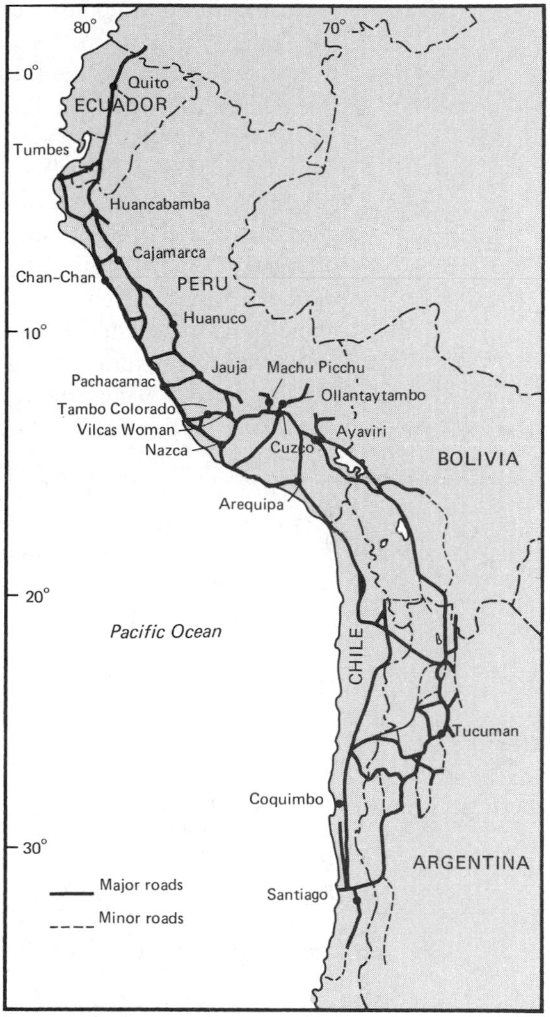

THE EUROPEAN CONQUEST

Archaeological research in some areas of Andean South America was interrupted in the 1980s and early 1990s by peasant revolutions and armed conflict between the government and rebels. The colonial history of Andean South America explains a lot about the origins of these conflicts.

After sporadic, occasionally hostile contacts with the Inka people in the A.D. 1520s, the Spanish under Francisco Pizarro set out toward the provincial capital at Cajamarca, the residence of Atawallpa, the Inka king. The Inka sent a reception force of 20,000 to meet the Spanish, but did not seem to have appreciated the threat that the Spanish represented. In any case, the Andean South Americans soon had cause to regret their

FIGURE 14.12 The Inka road system connected almost every settlement to two main north-south routes and facilitated voluminous transports of goods and effective administration.

diffidence. Pizarro and his men entered the city on November 15, 1532, and found it to be surprisingly nearly deserted. After establishing himself with a couple of cannons and his few score of soldiers, Pizarro and de Soto—accompanied by a troop—visited the Inka king at Konoj. The next day the emperor came to Cajamarca, borne on a litter and preceded by thousands of soldiers, attendants, and subjects. The first Spaniard to approach the king was the chaplain who, as part of Pizarro's contract with the king of Spain and the Pope, was charged with spreading the Christian faith. The chaplain immediately began to harangue the king, through an interpreter, about the creation of the world, the fall of Adam and Eve, the Virgin Birth, the establishment of the papacy, and other dogma, culminating his speech with the announcement that the Pope had given the Inka Empire to King Charles of Spain.

Not surprisingly, the Inka king took exception to parts of the chaplain's speech. He wanted to know how the Pope could give away something that was not his, and how it had happened that the god of the Christians had died, since the Inka deity, the Sun, was immortal.[84] When Atawallpa asked how the chaplain knew all these things, he was handed a breviary. The king looked briefly and no doubt uncomprehendingly inside, and then threw it away. At this point the Spanish attacked, and then the inexplicable happened: Instead of killing the Spanish, the Inka fled, dropping their weapons and killing themselves in their panicked flight, and the Spanish were able to dispatch thousands and capture the king with little trouble. They remained in Cajamarca for some months, detaining the king, who tried to win his release by offering to fill a room (supposed to have been 6.5-by-4.5 m in size) once with gold and twice with silver. The Spanish, meanwhile, took masses of gold and silver in ransom payments for the king, as well as from the sack of Cuzco, most of it in the form of exquisitely wrought figures, which they melted into ingots.

Rumors of insurrections in the countryside convinced the Spanish to execute the Inka king. They did so, but considered themselves enlightened for giving him the option of being garroted rather than burned at the stake—a reward to the king for allowing himself to be baptized. Atawallpa's death and the ensuing factionalism among rival claimants to the throne, as well as the devastation brought on by introduced diseases and the horror wrought on the populace through warfare and the destruction of the irrigation system, proved crippling. The population of Andean South America is thought to have dropped from 10–12 million to about six million within a 50 years of the conquest.

SUMMARY AND CONCLUSIONS

The reader by now will not be surprised to learn that most scholars interpret the rise of civilization in Andean South America to be the result of a multiplicity of factors.

Robert Carneiro's hypotheses linking warfare, population growth, and environmental circumscription (chapter 7) to the rise of states seems particularly applicable to Andean South America. There are some suggestions that warfare was in fact an important "stress" that stimulated some kinds of complexity (though perhaps not in the manner suggested by Carneiro).[85] But sustained warfare seems to have been more of an important factor well *after* the appearance of such things as monumental buildings, the coordination of regional economies, craft specialization, and the rise of great religious traditions.

How, then, are we to account for Andean South American complex societies? Obviously, the rich maritime and agricultural resources were essential ingredients in this development. In only a few areas of the world is it possible to produce and gather enough food to run complex cultures on the basis of primitive technologies, and Andean South America is one of these regions.

An important "negative" element in the evolution of Andean South America appears to have been the fact that, unlike ancient China, Egypt, Mesopotamia, or the Indus Valley, Andean South America was geographically isolated from other highly complex political systems. Evolving Old World civilizations soon came into contact with one another, and their political, economic, and social interchanges appear to have transformed each of them to some degree. But, except for Mesoamerica—which was very distant and cut off by ocean and jungle—Andean South America evolved alone.

The absence of a domesticable draft animal also was a limit on Andean South American development. Llamas compensated for this to a degree, but they cannot compare with the transport or plowing abilities of horses, mules, or oxen. It is difficult to judge the effects the presence of a domesticable draft animal in Andean South America would have had, but it may be significant that almost all agricultural areas of Andean South America today are plowed.

Thus, in summary of Andean South American prehistory, we see that cultural developments there paralleled those in other centers of independent complex society formation in most important details, including the initial spread of a religious cult, the presence of a highly productive economy, the widespread occurrence of monumental architecture, and the gradual emergence of highly stratified, economically integrated state and imperial political systems.

BIBLIOGRAPHY

Albarracin-Jordan, J. 1996. "Tiwanaku Settlement System: The Integration of Nested Hierarchies in the Lower Tiwanaku Valley." *Latin American Antiquity* 7(3):183–210.

Alva, W., and C. Donnan. 1993. *Royal Tombs of Sipán.* Los Angeles: Fowler Museum of Cultural History, UCLA.

Ascher, M., and R. Ascher. 1982. *Code of the Quipu: A Study in Media, Mathematics, and Culture.* Ann Arbor: University of Michigan Press.

Bauer, B. S. 1992. *The Development of the Inca State.* Norman: University of Oklahoma Press.

Bawden, G. 1995. "The Structural Paradox: Moche Culture as Political Ideology." *Latin American Antiquity* 6(3):255–273.

Bennfer, R. A. 1982. "The Lomas Site of Paloma (5000 to 7500 B.P.), Chilca Valley, Peru." In *Andean Archaeology,* ed. R. Matos, pp. 27–54. New York: Academic Press.

———. 1984. "The Challenges and Rewards of Sedentism: The Preceramic Village of Paloma, Peru." In *Paleopathology and the Origin of Agriculture,* ed. M. N. Cohen and G. J. Armelagos. New York: Academic Press.

Billman, B. R. 2002. "Irrigation and the Origins of the Southern Amoche State on the North Coast of Peru." *Latin American Antiquity* 13(4):371–400.

Browman, D. L. 1974. "Pastoral Nomadism in the Andes." *Current Anthropology* 15:188–196.

———. 1975. "Trade Patterns in the Central Highlands of Peru in the First Millennium B.C." *World Archaeology* 6:322–330.

Burger, R. L. 1992. *Chavin and the Origins of the Andean Civilization.* London and New York: Thames and Hudson.

Burger, R. L., and L. Salazar-Burger. 1980. "Ritual and Religion at Huaricoto." *Archaeology* 33:26–32.

———. 1985. "The Early Ceremonial Center of Huaricoto." In *Early Ceremonial Architecture in the Andes,* ed. C. B. Donnan. Washington, DC: Dumbarton Oaks.

———. 1986. "Early Organizational Diversity in the Peruvian Highland: Huaricoto and Kotosh." In *Andean Archaeology, Papers in Memory of Clifford Evans, Monograph 27,* ed. M. R. Matos, S. A. Turpin, and H. H. Eling, Jr. Los Angeles: University of California, Institute of Archaeology.

———. 1991. "The Second Season of Investigations at the Initial Period Center of Cardal, Peru." *Journal of Field Archaeology* 18(3):275–296.

Burger, R. L., and N. Van Der Merwe. 1990. "Maize and the Origin of Highland Chavin Civilization: An Isotopic Perspective." *American Anthropologist* 92(1):85–95.

Carneiro, R. 1970. "A Theory of the Origin of the State." *Science* 169:733–738.

Cobo, Bernabe. 1990 (orig. c. A.D. 1639). *Inca Religion and Customs.* Trans. and ed. Roland Hamilton. Austin: University of Texas Press.

Collier, G. A., R. I. Rosaldo, and J. D. Wirth, eds. 1982. *The Inka and Aztec States, 1400–1800.* New York: Academic Press.

Conlee, C. A. 2003. "Local Elites and the Reformation of Late Intermediate Period Sociopolitical and Economic Organization in Nasca, Peru." *Latin American Antiquity* 14(1):47–65.

Covey, R. A. 2003. "A Processual Study of Inka State Formation." *Journal of Anthropological Archaeology* 22:333–357.

D'Altroy, T. N. 1992. *Provincial Power in the Inka Empire.* Washington, DC: Smithsonian Institution Press.

Dillehay, T. D. 1990. "Mapuche Ceremonial Landscapes, Social Recruitment and Resource Rights." *Journal of World Archaeology* 22(2):223–241.

Dillehay, T. D., P. Netherly, and J. Rossen. 1989. "Early Preceramic Public and Residential Sites on the Forested Slope of the Western Andes, Northern Peru." *American Antiquity* 54(4):733–758.

Donnan, C. B. 1973. *Moche Occupation of the Santa Valley, Peru.* University of California Publications in Anthropology, No. 8. Berkeley: University of California

———. 1976. *Moche Art and Iconography.* Los Angeles: UCLA Latin American Center Publications.

———. 1990. "Master Works Reveal a Pre-Inca World." *National Geographic Magazine* 177(6):34–49.

———. 2001. "Moche Burials Uncovered." *National Geographic Magazine* 199(3):58–73.

Donnan, C. B., ed. 1985. *Early Ceremonial Architecture in the Andes.* Washington, DC: Dumbarton Oaks.

Engl, L., and T. Engl. 1969. *Twilight of Ancient Peru.* Trans. A. Jaffe. New York: McGraw-Hill.

Feldman, R. A. 1980. *Aspero, Peru: Architecture, Subsistence Economy, and Other Artifacts of a Preceramic Maritime Chiefdom.* Ph.D dissertation, Department of Anthropology, Harvard University.

Fernández, J., H. O. Panarello, and J. Schobinger. 1999. "The Inka Mummy from Mount Aconcagua: Decoding the Geographic Origin of the 'Messenger to the Deities' by Means of Stable Carbon, Nitrogen, and Sulfur Isotope Analysis." *Geoarchaeology* 14(1):27–46.

Fiedel, S. J. 1987. *Prehistory of the Americas.* Cambridge: Cambridge University Press.

Fontugne, M., P. Usselmann, and C. Hatté. 1999. "El Niño Variability in the Coastal Desert of Southern Peru During the Mid-Holocene." *Quaternary Research* 52:171–179.

Haas, J. 1987. "The Exercise of Power in Early Andean State Development." In *The Origins and Development of the Andean State,* ed. J. Haas, S. Pozorski, and T. Pozorski. New York: Cambridge University Press.

Haas, J., W. Creamer, and A. Ruiz. 2004. "Dating the Late Archaic Occupation of the Norte Chico Region in Peru." *Nature* 432:1020–1023.

Haas, J., S. Pozorski, and T. Pozorski, eds. 1987. *The Origins and Development of the Andean State.* New York: Cambridge University Press.

Hastorf, C. A., and S. Johannessen. 1993. "Pre-Hispanic Political Change and the Role of Maize in the Central Andes of Peru." *American Anthropologist* 95(1):115–137.

Hoopes, J. W. 1994. "Ford Revisited: A Critical Review of the Chronology and Relationships of the Earliest Ceramic Complexes in the New World, 6000–1500 B.C." *Journal of World Prehistory* 8(1):1–49.

Hyslop, J. 1984. *The Inka Road System.* New York: Academic Press.

Idyll, C. P. 1973. "The Anchovy Crisis." *Scientific American* 228:22–29.

Isbell, W. H. 2004. "Mortuary Preferences; A Wari Culture Case Study from Middle Horizon Peru." *Latin American Antiquity* 15(1):3–32.

Japanese Scientific Expedition to Nuclear America. 1979. *Excavations at La Pampa in the North Highlands of Peru, 1975.* Tokyo: University of Tokyo Press.

Jennings, J., and W. Y. Alvarez. 2001. "Architecture, Local Elites, and Imperial Entanglements: The Wari Empire and the Cotahuasi Valley of Peru." *Journal of Field Archaeology* 28(1/2):143–159.

Jennings, J., and N. Craig. 2001. "Politywide Analysis and Imperial Political Economy: The Relationship Between Valley Political Complexity and Administrative Centers in the Wari Empire of the Central Andes." *Journal of Anthropological Archaeology* 20:479–502.

Jones, G. D., and R. R. Kautz, eds. 1981. *The Transition to Statehood in the New World.* Cambridge: Cambridge University Press.

Kaplan, L., T. Lynch, and E. E. Smith, Jr. 1973. "Early Cultivated Beans (*Phaseolus vulgaris*) from an Intermontane Peruvian Valley." *Science* 179:76–77.

Keatinge, R. W. 1974. "Chimú Rural Administration Centers in the Moche Valley, Peru." *World Archaeology* 6:66–82.

———. 1988. *Peruvian Prehistory: An Overview of Pre-Inka and Inka Society.* New York: Cambridge University Press.

Lanning, E. P. 1967. *Peru Before the Inkas.* Englewood Cliffs, NJ: Prentice-Hall.

Lathrap, D. W. 1973. "The Antiquity and Importance of Long-Distance Trade Relationships in the Moist Tropics of Pre-Columbian South America." *World Archaeology* 5:170–186.

Lynch, T., ed. 1980. *Guitarrero Cave: Early Man in the Andes.* New York: Academic Press.

MacNeish, R. S., R. K. Vierra, A. Nelken-Terner, R. Lurie, and A. G. Cook. 1983. *Prehistory of the Ayacucho Basin, Peru, Volume IV: The Preceramic Way of Life.* Ann Arbor: University of Michigan Press.

Masuda, S., I. Shimada, and C. Morris, eds. 1985. *Andean Ecology and Civilization.* Tokyo: University of Tokyo Press.

Milliaire, J.-F. 2004. "The Manipulation of Human Remains in Moche Society: Delayed Burials, Grave Reopening, and Secondary Offerings of Human Bones on the Peruvian North Coast." *Latin American Antiquity* 15(4):371–388.

Morris, C. 1985. "From Principles of Ecological Complementarity to the Organization and Administration of Tawantinsuyu." In *Andean Ecology and Civilization*, ed. S. Masuda, I. Shimada, and C. Morris. Tokyo: University of Tokyo Press.

Moseley, M. E. 1975. *The Maritime Foundations of Andean Civilization*. Menlo Park, CA: Cummings.

———. 1985. "The Exploration and Explanation of Early Monumental Architecture in the Andes." In *Early Ceremonial Architecture in the Andes*, ed. C. Donnan, pp. 28–58, Washington, DC: Dumbarton Oaks.

———. 2001. *The Incas and Their Ancestors*. London and New York: Thames and Hudson.

Moseley, M. E., and K. C. Day, eds. 1982. *Chan Chan: Andean Desert City*. Albuquerque: University of New Mexico Press.

Murra, J. 1958. "On Inka Political Structure." In *Systems of Political Control and Bureaucracy in Human Society*, ed. V. F. Ray. Seattle: University of Washington Press.

———. 1965. "Herds and Herders in the Inka State." In *Man, Culture and Animals*. Washington, DC: American Association for the Advancement of Science.

———. 1985. "The Limits and Limitations of the 'Vertical Archipelago' in the Andes." In *Andean Ecology and Civilization*, ed. S. Masuda, I. Shimada, and C. Morris. Tokyo: University of Tokyo Press.

Murra, J., and C. Morris. 1976. "Dynastic Oral Tradition, Administrative Records, and Archaeology in the Andes." *World Archaeology* 7:269–279.

Niles, S. A. 1988. *Callachaca*. Iowa City: University of Iowa Press.

Ortloff, C. R., M. E. Moseley, and R. A. Feldman. 1982. "Hydraulic Engineering Aspects of the Chimú/Chicama-Moche Intervalley Canal." *American Antiquity* 47:572–595.

Parsons, J. 1968. "An Estimate of Size and Population for Middle Horizon Tiahuanaco, Bolivia." *American Antiquity* 33:243–245.

———. 1977. Personal communication to Wenke.

Parsons, M. 1970. "Preceramic Subsistence on the Peruvian Coast." *American Antiquity* 35:292–303.

Patterson, T. C. 1971. "Central Peru: Its Population and Economy." *Archaeology* 24:316–321.

———. 1983. "The Historical Development of a Coastal Andean Social Formation in Central Peru, 6000 to 500 B.C." In *Investigations of the Andean Past, Papers from the First Annual Northeast Conference on Andean Archaeology and Ethnohistory*, ed. D. H. Sandweiss. Ithaca, NY: Cornell University Latin Studies Program.

———. 1985. "The Huaca La Florida, Rimac Valley, Peru." In *Ceremonial Architecture in the Andes*, ed. C. B. Donnan. Washington, DC: Dumbarton Oaks.

———. 1992. *The Inca Empire*. London: Berg.

Pearsall, D. M. 1992. "The Origins of Plant Cultivation in South America." *In The Origins of Agriculture. An International Perspective*, ed. C. W. Cowan and P. J. Watson. Washington: Smithsonian Institution Press.

Pearsall, D. M., and D. R. Piperno. 1990. "Antiquity of Maize Cultivation in Ecuador: Summary and Reevaluation of the Evidence." *American Antiquity* 55(2):324–337.

Pickersgill, B. 1969. "The Archaeological Record of Chile Peppers (*Capsicum spp.*) and the Sequence of Plant Domestication in Peru." *American Antiquity* 34:54–61.

Pickersgill, B., and A. Bunting. 1969. "Cultivated Plants and the Kon-Tiki Theory." *Nature* 222:225–227.

Pozorski, S. 1987. "Theocracy vs. Militarism: The Significance of the Casma Valley in Understanding Early State Formation." In *The Origins and Development of the Andean State*, ed. J. Haas, S. Pozorski, and T. Pozorski. New York: Cambridge University Press.

Pozorski, T. 1987. "Changing Priorities Within the Chimu State: The Role of Irrigation Agriculture." In *The Origins and Development of the Andean State*, ed. J. Haas, S. Pozorski, and T. Pozorski. New York: Cambridge University Press.

Pozorski, S., and T. Pozorski. 1979. "Alto Salaverry: A Peruvian Coastal Preceramic Site." *Annals of the Carnegie Museum of Natural History* 49:337–375.

———. 1986. "Recent Excavations at Pampa de las Llamas-Moxeke, A Complex Initial Period Site in Peru." *Journal of Field Archaeology* 13(4):381–401.

———. 1987. "Chavín, the Early Horizon, and the Initial Period." In *The Origins and Development of the Andean State*, ed. J. Haas, S. Pozorski, and T. Pozorski. New York: Cambridge University Press.

———. 1988. *Early Settlement and Subsistence in the Casma Valley, Peru*. Iowa City: University of Iowa Press.

———. 1990. "Huaynun, a Late Cotton Paraceramic Site on the North Coast of Peru." *Journal of Field Archaeology* 17(1):17–26.

———. 1994. "Early Andean Cities." *Scientific American* 270(6):66–72.

Prescott, W. H. 1908. *History of the Conquest of Peru*. London and New York: Everyman's Library.

———. 1989. *Life and Death at Paloma: Society and Mortuary Practices in Preceramic Peruvian Village*. Iowa City: University of Iowa Press.

Protzen, J.-P. 1986. "Inca Stonemasonry." *Scientific American* 254(2):94–105.

Quilter, J. 1985. "Architecture and Chronology at El Paraíso, Peru." *Journal of Field Archaeology* 12(3):274–298.

————. 1991a. "Late Preceramic Peru." *Journal of World Prehistory* 5(4):387–438.

————. 1991b. "Problems with the Late Preceramic of Peru." *American Anthropologist* 93(2):450–454.

————. 2002. "Moche Politics, Religion, and Warfare." *Journal of World Prehistory* 16(2):145–195.

Quilter, J., and T. Stocker. 1983. "Subsistence Economies and the Origins of Andean Complex Societies." *American Anthropologist* 85(3):545–562.

Ramenovsky, A. 1987. *Vectors of Death*. Albuquerque: University of New Mexico Press.

Raymond, J. S. 1981. "The Maritime Foundations of Andean Civilization: A Reconsideration of the Evidence." *American Antiquity* 46:806–820.

Reitz, E. J. 1988. "Faunal Remains from Paloma, an Archaic Site in Peru." *American Anthropologist* 90(2):310–322.

Richardson, J. B., III. 1981. "Maritime Adaptations on the Peruvian Coast: A Critique and Future Directions." Paper presented at the 47th Annual Meeting of the Society for American Archaeology, San Diego, California.

Rick, J. W. 1980. *Prehistoric Hunters of the High Andes*. New York: Academic Press.

Rodbell, D. T., G. O. Seltzer, D. E. Anderson, M. B. Abbott, D. B. Enfield, and J. H. Newman. 1999. "A 15,000-Year Record of El Niño-Driven Alluviation in Southwestern Ecuador." *Science* 283:516–520.

Rowe, J. H. 1946. "Inka Culture at the Time of the Spanish Conquest." *Bureau of American Ethnology Bulletin* 143:183–331.

————. 1967. "Form and Meaning in Chavín Art." In *Peruvian Archaeology: Selected Readings*. Palo Alto: Peek Publishers.

Schreiber, K. J. 1987. "Conquest and Consolidation: A Comparison of the Wari and Inka Occupation of a Highland Peruvian Valley." *American Antiquity* 52(2):266–284.

Scott, R. J. 1981. "The Maritime Foundations of Andean Civilization: A Reconsideration." *American Antiquity* 46:806–821.

Shady, R., and A. Ruiz. 1979. "Evidence for Interregional Relationships During the Middle Horizon on the North-Central Coast of Peru." *American Antiquity* 44:670–684.

Silverman, H. 1988. "Cahuachi: Non-Urban Cultural Complexity on the South Coast of Peru." *Journal of Field Archaeology* 15(4):403–430.

Stanish, C. 2001. "The Origin of State Societies in South America." *Annual Review of Anthropology* 30:41–64.

Ugent, D., S. Pozorski, and T. Pozorski. 1984. "New Evidence for Ancient Cultivation of *Canna edulis* in Peru." *Economic Botany* 38(4):417–432.

Von Hagen, V. W. 1952. "America's Oldest Roads." *Scientific American* 187:17–21.

Willey, G. R. 1962. "The Early Great Art Styles and the Rise of Pre-Columbian Civilizations." *American Anthropologist* 64:1–14.

Wilson, D. J. 1981. "Of Maize and Men: A Critique of the Maritime Hypothesis of State Origins on the Coast of Peru." *American Anthropologist* 83:93–114.

————. 1983. "The Origins and Development of Complex Prehispanic Society in the Lower Santa Valley, Peru: Implications for Theories of State Origins." *Journal of Anthropological Archaeology* 2:209–276.

Wing, E. S. 1977. "Animal Domestication in the Andes." In *Origins of Agriculture*, ed. C. A. Reed. The Hague: Mouton Publishers.

NOTES

1. Father Cobo's description here is from various sections of his *Inca Religion and Customs*.
2. Fernández et al., "The Inca Mummy from Mount Aconcagua: Decoding the Geographic Origin of the 'Messenger to the Deities' by Means of Stable Carbon, Nitrogen, and Sulfur isotope Analysis," pp. 30–32.
3. Murra, "Andean Ecology and Civilization," p. 11, in Masuda et al., eds., *Andean Ecology and Civilization*.
4. Masuda et al., eds., *Andean Ecology and Civilization*.
5. Idyll, "The Anchovy Crisis."
6. Fontugne et al., "El Niño Variability in the Coastal Desert of Southern Peru During the Mid-Holocene."
7. Hoopes, "Ford Revisited: A Critical Review of the Chronology and Relationships of the Earliest Ceramic Complexes in the New World, 6000–1500 B.C.," p. 41.
8. Rick, *Prehistoric Hunters of the High Andes*.
9. Richardson, "Maritime Adaptations on the Peruvian Coast: A Critique and Future Directions," pp. 140–45.
10. Quilter and Stocker, "Subsistence Economies and the Origins of Andean Complex Societies," p. 547.
11. Pearsall, "The Origins of Plant Cultivation in South American," p. 192.
12. Ugent et al., "New Evidence for Ancient Cultivation of *Canna edulis* in Peru."
13. Reviewed in Pearsall, "The Origins of Plant Cultivation in South America," p. 190.
14. Rick, *Prehistoric Hunters of the High Andes*.
15. See Quilter, "Late Preceramic Peru," p. 387, for a discussion of these dates; see also Stanish, "The Origins of State Societies in South America," and Haas et al., "Dating the Late Archaic Occupation of the Norte Chico Region in Peru."

16. Patterson, "Central Peru: Its Population and Economy."
17. Stanish, "The Origins of State Societies in South America," p. 45.
18. Benfer, "The Challenges and Rewards of Sedentism: The Preceramic Village of Paloma, Peru"; Reitz, "Faunal Remains from Paloma, an Archaic Site in Peru."
19. Quilter and Stocker, "Subsistence Economies and the Origins of Andean Complex Societies," p. 545.
20. Parsons, "Preceramic Subsistence on the Peruvian Coast," p. 297.
21. Pozorski and Pozorski, "Alto Salaverry: A Peruvian Coastal Preceramic Site."
22. Benfer, "The Challenges and Rewards of Sedentism."
23. Haas et al., "Dating the Late Archaic Occupation of the Norte Chico Region in Peru," p. 1021.
24. Ibid., p. 1022.
25. Quilter, "Architecture and Chronology at El Paraíso, Peru."
26. Quilter, "Late Preceramic Peru," p. 417.
27. Quilter, "Late Preceramic Peru," citing Feldman, *Aspero, Peru: Architecture, Subsistence Economy, and Other Artifacts of a Preceramic Maritime Chiefdom*, p. 89.
28. Quilter, "Late Preceramic Peru," citing Urton, personal communication, 1991.
29. Quilter, "Late Preceramic Peru."
30. Moseley, "The Exploration and Explanation of Early Monumental Architecture in the Andes."
31. Burger, *Chavin and the Origins of Andean Civilization*, pp. 46–48.
32. Ibid., p. 48.
33. Burger and Salazar-Burger, "Ritual and Religion at Huaricoto," and "The Early Ceremonial Center of Huaricoto."
34. Quilter, "Late Preceramic Peru," pp. 420–421.
35. Stanish, "The Origins of State Societies in South America," p. 47.
36. Burger, *Chavin and the Origins of Andean Civilization*, p. 32.
37. Moseley, *The Maritime Foundations of Andean Civilization*.
38. Quilter and Stocker, "Subsistence Economies and the Origins of Andean Complex Societies."
39. Moseley, *The Maritime Foundations of Andean Civilization*, p. 105.
40. Burger, *Chavin and the Origins of Andean Civilization*, pp. 28–33.
41. Ibid., pp. 42–43.
42. Stanish, "The Origins of State Societies in South America," pp. 48–50.
43. Ibid., p. 49.
44. Burger, *Chavin and the Origins of Andean Civilization*, p. 80.
45. Ibid., p. 77.
46. Ibid., p. 78.
47. Ibid., p. 79.
48. Stanish, "The Origins of State Societies in South America," p. 49; Burger, *Chavin and the Origins of Andean Civilization*, p. 82.
49. Burger, *Chavin and the Origins of Andean Civilization*, p. 83.
50. Haas, "The Exercise of Power in Early Andean State Development"; Pozorski and Pozorski, "Early Andean Cities."
51. Burger, *Chavin and the Origins of Andean Civilization*, pp. 75, 87–88.
52. Ibid., pp. 66–68; Burger and Salazar-Burger, "The Second Season of Investigations at the Initial Period Center of Cardal, Peru."
53. Burger, *Chavin and the Origins of Andean Civilization*, p. 68.
54. Burger and Salazar-Burger, "The Second Season of Investigations at the Initial Period Center of Cardal, Peru," p. 278.
55. Quilter, "Late Preceramic Peru," p. 414.
56. Stanish, "The Origins of State Societies in South America," p. 51.
57. Burger, *Chavin and the Origins of the Andean Civilization*.
58. Ibid., pp. 130–135.
59. Ibid., pp. 135–137.
60. Stanish, "The Origins of State Societies in South America," p. 52.
61. Reviewed in Keatinge, *Peruvian Prehistory*; also see Haas, Pozorski, and Pozorski, *The Origins and Development of The Andean State*; Donnan, ed., *Early Ceremonial Architecture in the Andes*. But see Quilter, "Moche Politics, Religion, and Warfare," for a viewpoint that questions whether or not the Moche can be considered a state-level society.
62. Lanning, *Peru Before the Inkas*, pp. 114–115.
63. Silverman, "Cahuachi: Non-Urban Cultural Complexity on the South Coast of Peru."
64. Although see Billman, "Irrigation and the Origins of the Southern Moche State on the North Coast of Peru," who argues that canals and their construction early in the Moche would not have required organization above the level of the village or community. Billman instead contends that it was the production of subsistence

surplus brought about by the use of irrigation that gave certain individuals the opportunity to accumulate wealth and power.

65. Donnan, "Master Works Reveal a Pre-Inca World." Additional unlooted tombs were located at Dos Cabezas, about 40 miles south of Sipán. A description of these can be found in Doonan, "Moche Burials Uncovered."
66. Donnan, *Moche Art and Iconography.*
67. Lanning, *Peru Before the Inkas*, p. 127.
68. Stanish, "The Origins of State Societies in South America," pp. 53–54.
69. "Tiwanaku Settlement System: The Integration of Nested Hierarchies in the Lower Tiwanaku Valley."
70. Fiedel, *Prehistory of the Americas*, p. 333.
71. Keatinge, "Chimú Rural Administration Centers in the Moche Valley, Peru," p. 79.
72. Moseley and Day, *Chan Chan: Andean Desert City.*
73. Collier et al., *The Inka and Aztec States, 1400–1800.*
74. D'Altroy, *Provincial Power in the Inka Empire.*
75. Lanning, *Peru Before the Inkas*, pp. 159–160.
76. Covey, " A Processual Study of Inka State Formation."
77. Ibid.
78. Hastorf and Johannessen, "Maize and Politics in the Pre-Hispanic Andes."
79. Lanning, *Peru Before the Inkas*, pp. 166–167.
80. Ascher and Ascher, *Code of the Quipu: A Study in Media, Mathematics, and Culture.*
81. Hyslop, *The Inka Road System.*
82. Von Hagen, "America's Oldest Roads."
83. Niles, *Callachaca.*
84. Engl and Engl, *Twilight of Ancient Peru*, p. 119.
85. Carneiro, "A Theory of the Origin of the State"; see also Wilson, "The Origins and Development of Complex Prehispanic Society in the Lower Santa Valley, Peru."

15

Early Cultural Complexity in North America

You must explain to the natives of [North America] that there is only one God in heaven, and the emperor on earth to rule and govern it, whose subjects they must all become and they must serve.

Instructions of the viceroy to Fray Marcos de Ninza (A.D. 1538)

As Europeans invaded North America in the sixteenth and seventeenth centuries, they encountered what looked to them like the relics of ancient civilizations: hundreds of large earthen mounds, some nearly as large as the Egyptian pyramids, dominated the Ohio and Mississippi river valleys; and in Arizona, Colorado, and New Mexico large, neatly planned but abandoned towns that had obviously once been inhabited by hundreds, if not thousands, were found along the major rivers and even in the arid highlands (Figure 15.1).

The Europeans of this age were, like the citizens of all world powers, highly ethnocentric. It is not surprising, therefore, that they assumed that these impressive works had been constructed by their own ancestors—the Celts, Romans, or perhaps the Vikings; they simply could not believe that the ancestors of the poor and "degenerate" Native Americans they saw about them might have had something to do with these great monuments. Some Europeans even blamed the Native Americans for massacring what the Europeans believed to be an ancient and extinct "superior" American race—the ultimate in adding insult to injury, given the Native Americans' eventual fate.

The truth, of course, is that these mounds and abandoned settlements had indeed been built by Native Americans many centuries before the Europeans arrived, and we now know that these ancient Americans had a rich culture history going back more than 10,000 years in the New World.

Some of the people of "pre-Columbian" North America were influenced by contact with the complex cultures of ancient Mesoamerica, and it is also true that, according to some criteria, aboriginal American cultures never reached the level of complexity attained in "independent" ancient centers of cultural evolution, such as Mesoamerica and Mesopotamia.

565

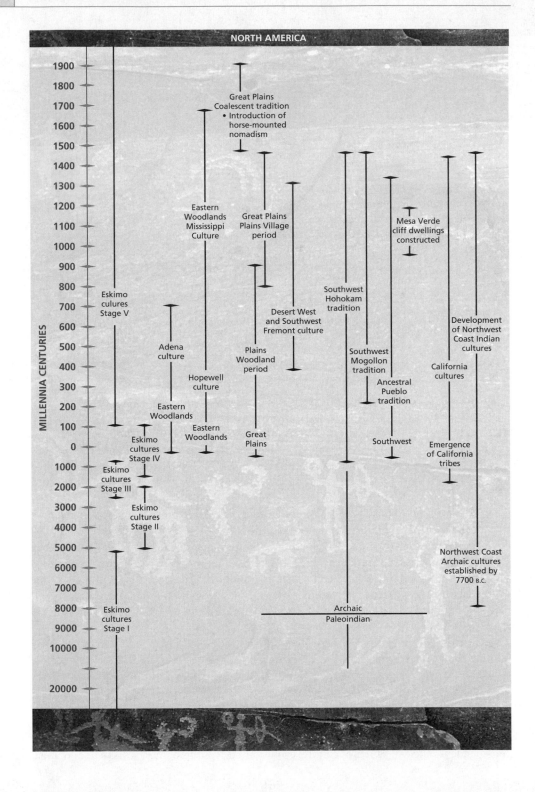

NORTH AMERICA

MILLENNIA CENTURIES

1900
1800
1700
1600
1500
1400
1300
1200
1100
1000
900
800
700
600
500
400
300
200
100
0
1000
2000
3000
4000
5000
6000
7000
8000
9000
10000

20000

Eskimo culures Stage V

Eskimo cultures Stage IV

Eskimo cultures Stage III

Eskimo cultures Stage II

Eskimo cultures Stage I

Adena culture

Eastern Woodlands

Hopewell culture

Eastern Woodlands

Great Plains Coalescent tradition
• Introduction of horse-mounted nomadism

Eastern Woodlands Mississippi Culture

Great Plains Plains Village period

Desert West and Southwest Fremont culture

Plains Woodland period

Great Plains

Southwest Hohokam tradition

Southwest Mogollon tradition

Ancestral Pueblo tradition

Southwest

Mesa Verde cliff dwellings constructed

Development of Northwest Coast Indian cultures

California cultures

Emergence of California tribes

Northwest Coast Archaic cultures established by 7700 B.C.

Archaic Paleoindian

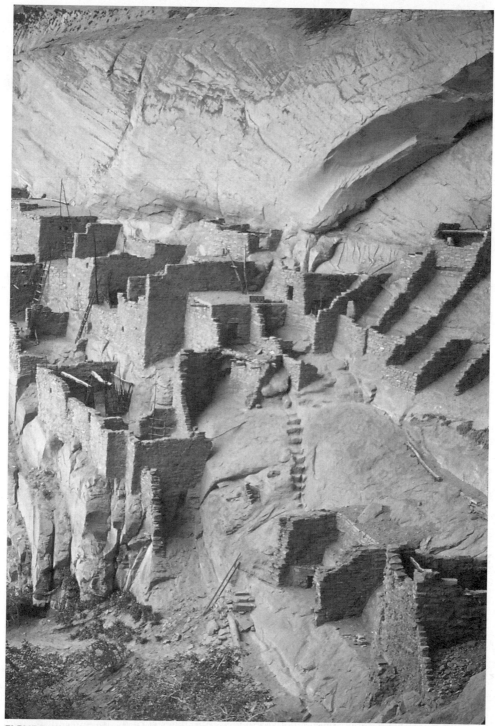

FIGURE 15.1   Betatakin, an Ancestral Puebloan settlement in Arizona, was inhabited for only about 50 years before being abandoned.

But the native North Americans did develop some aspects of cultural complexity, and they did so largely independently. Moreover, the ecological and cultural reasons North American cultures did not exactly parallel those of Mexico or Peru provide some insights into all of these cultures.

For more than a century archaeologists have been systematically digging North American sites, from Alaska to southern Texas, and we should know more about developments here than virtually anywhere else in the world, given the high ratio of archaeologists per square kilometer. But, unfortunately, early American archaeologists also yielded to the temptations of excavating mainly rich tombs and large towns, resulting in a very biased view of the American past. And because of decades of turning ancient Native American cultural resources into parking lots and hamburger stands and because of the looting that continues today, so much of the archaeological record of North America has been destroyed that much of the American past will forever remain a mystery.

The old, sometimes pejorative myths about "Indians" are now giving way in some circles to new ones stressing the social harmony, ecological purity, and superior metaphysics of ancient Native Americans. As with all cultures, there is much to admire about ancient North Americans. But the evidence suggests that for much of their antiquity, aboriginal Americans were like prehistoric peoples in every other part of the world—harried small-time foragers or farmers, worrying about this year's drought and next year's deluge, shifting their crops from year to year as they exhausted the resources in one place after another, and as enmeshed in slavery, exploitation, and warfare as any ancient Chinese, Egyptian, or European.

The term "Native American" is gradually replacing the wildly imprecise "Indian" of bygone years, but it is well to remember that all Americans are immigrants, and rather recent ones at that. The people who colonized the New World and became "Native Americans" were, in fact, northern Asians who came in several episodes of colonization (chapter 5)— the first of many waves of immigration to the New World.

THE ECOLOGICAL SETTING

We saw in chapter 5 that about 12,000 years ago the huge glacial ice sheets that once covered much of eastern North America retreated into Canada, and the distribution of plant and animal species in this region became similar to that of the recent past. Between about 8000 and 6500 B.C., the annual temperature of much of the North American East was probably 2.5°C cooler than at present, and after that time aboriginal Americans were likely directly affected by a number of climate fluctuations. Subtle shifts of climate and effective rainfall may have had important effects on the distribution of nut-bearing trees, which were a very important food source, and also on the size and stability of rivers and lakes—rich environments around which early Americans often built their hunting-foraging economies.

Temperate eastern North America is a rich niche for hunter-foragers, but its abundant agricultural potential can only be realized with technologies such as draught animals and the plow. The American Southwest and West also include some very rich areas, but none of these areas has the same agricultural potential—given primitive technologies—as that, for example, of the Nile Valley or Mesopotamia. The modern U.S. agricultural economy is so productive that it is somewhat surprising just how poor a place it was for pre-industrial subsistence farmers. First, most of it is far from the equator and therefore has less solar radiation and fewer frost-free days, and thus lower absolute agricultural potential, than more southern environments—such as the one in Mesoamerica. Second, those areas of North America that are today the fertile fields of Iowa, Missouri, and other areas of the Plains and Middle West were for the most part unavailable to the Native American farmer because they lacked the plows and draft animals that can rip through thick grasses and other vegetation to reveal these fertile soils and the other machines that are needed to suppress the competition to crops from weeds. Third, much of the area between the Atlantic Coast and the western reaches of the Mississippi River drainage were thickly forested and relatively cool, "closed-canopy climax forests," which could be exploited for nuts and a few other resources but were in most areas an unprepossessing place for the maize-beans-squash farming that became the basis for Native American cultivation in North America. Fourth, the areas of California and other parts of the West that are today food suppliers to the world were far too arid for anything but basic subsistence agriculture until modern irrigation systems were installed.

THE NORTH AMERICAN EAST

The most complex ancient cultures in North America evolved in the great river valleys of the North American East, especially the Mississippi and Ohio Rivers and the lands they drain (Figure 15.2).

Agricultural Origins: The Late Archaic Period (c. 4000–800 B.C.)

Untangling the processes by which many Native Americans became farmers is difficult. One might consider maize and beans to be the most important domesticated plants in North America because they were the basis of the largest and most complex cultures in this area. But maize was a late introduction and only became an important source of food over most of eastern North America after about A.D. 1000. Maize pollen found in sediments of Lake Shelby in coastal Alabama seems securely dated to about 1500 B.C., but it is not clear that this plant was an important food resource at this time. One of the earliest and securely dated samples of maize in eastern North America is a collection of carbonized maize kernels found at the Icehouse Bottom site in eastern Tennessee and directly dated by radiocarbon methods to about A.D. 75; but until well into the first millennium A.D. maize remained a minor source of food.

The productive patches of maize, beans, and squash that eventually allowed Native Americans to live in great numbers all over North America were only the last, most productive stages of a long, slow shift—away from simple plant collecting and hunting and toward an ever-growing reliance on fewer and fewer kinds of plants. Long before maize reached temperate North America, people there had specialized in exploiting several kinds of plants in early forms of agriculture. So, the questions about North American agriculture are the same as those we asked about other areas. Why did agricultural economies appear

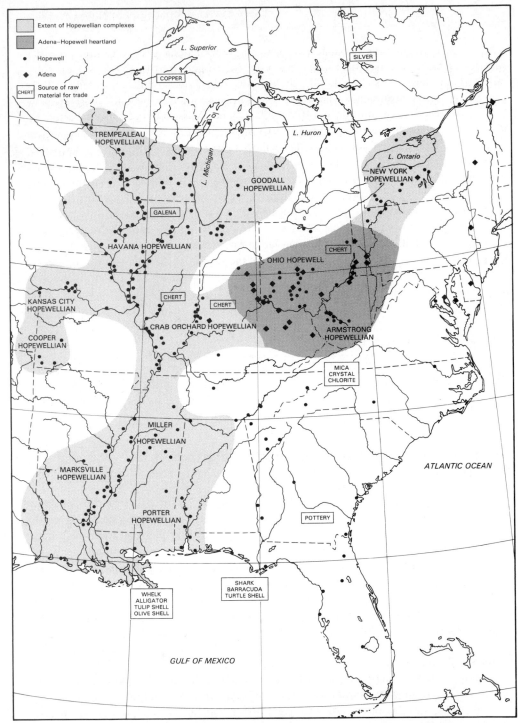

FIGURE 15.2 Adena-Hopewell and related cultures. The Adena culture was centered in Ohio, but Adena trade networks reached as far away as New York. Adena culture appears to have peaked at about 100 B.C. and was waning by A.D. 400. By about 100 B.C. Adena cultures in Ohio were being replaced by Hopewell cultures and for the next nine centuries the Hopewell cultures spread over much of the East.

when and where they did, through what processes, and with what results? And what was the long-term relationship between local domesticates and those introduced from elsewhere?

It was the oil- and starch-rich seeds of a variety of plants that formed the basis of initial agriculture in eastern North America. Among the primary domesticated plants were goosefoot (*Chenopodium*), sumpweed (*Iva annua*), sunflowers (*Helianthus annus*), wild gourds (*Cucurbita*), maygrass (*Phalaris*), little barley (*Hordeum pusillum*), and knotweed (*Polygonum erectum*). Until late in the first millennium B.C., hunting and foraging continued to be the way of life for most people, but through these many millennia after the Ice Age, the overall trend was toward increasing numbers of sedentary communities that specialized first in hunting and intensive plant collecting and later in maize and bean agriculture.

As in all other areas of early agriculture, climatic changes cannot be disregarded. Complex climatic changes between about 5000 and 2000 B.C., for example, changed the flow characteristics of streams and rivers across the eastern woodlands so that backwater swamps and lakes created by obstructions in river channels greatly expanded the abundance and accessibility of shellfish and other aquatic resources; and they also produced greater and more varied "disturbed" habitats—areas of the floodplain where floodwaters disturbed vegetation—which offered ecological niches for "pioneer" plants such as goosefoot, sumpweed, sunflowers, marsh elder (*Sambucus*), wild gourds, and other plants,[1] which Native Americans exploited. They could have encouraged the growth of hickory trees, for example, by "girdling" (cutting through the bark and growth layers) other species of trees in stands of hickory, and they could have burned off other areas to encourage the growth of chenopods, sunflowers, and other edible plants.[2]

Among the earliest domesticates found in the North American woodlands are gourds and squash, which appear shortly after 3,500 years ago.[3] Species of gourds may have been introduced from Mexico or washed ashore—for example, in Florida—and eventually become locally domesticated. They were probably used as containers and for seeds, and occasionally eaten directly, and we may suppose that their use goes back many millennia before we have archaeological evidence of them. There is also a problem in distinguishing between species of gourds based on their few traces in the archaeological record.[4]

The first clear evidences of changes in the direction of domestication of native food plants in North America, however, appears in the period between about 2050 and 1050 B.C. The primary evidence is in the form of changes in the morphology of the seeds of sunflowers, goosefoot, and other disturbed-habitat plants. As we saw in chapter 6, one of the ways in which people all over the world domesticated plants was to increase their usefulness by increasing seed size and number (for example, from two-row to six-row barley) and by altering the dormancy cycle of plants. When sunflowers, goosefoot, and other plants germinated in the spring, they would have faced tremendous competition because these plants release many seeds in a small area. In such conditions, plants that are the earliest to sprout and are larger and more vigorous than others would be at an advantage. One key to early sprouting is the thickness of the seed coat, the *testa*. As Bruce Smith notes,[5] the average testa thickness on goosefoot seeds shows marked decline over a large area of the eastern woodlands after about 2,500 years ago, based on specimens retrieved from cave sites and other occupations in Illinois, Arkansas, Kentucky, and adjacent areas. Other changes indicative of domestication appeared at about this same time in a variety of plants, but, as Smith notes, "it also appears likely that indigenous cultigens and domesticates did not become substantial food sources, and food production did not play a major economic role until . . . a full 1,000 years after their initial domestication."[6]

Nonetheless, various scholars have tried to explain how the transition to initial agriculture might have occurred. Michael O'Brien has developed a "Coevolutionary" model to account for the transition to agriculture in one area, near the Illinois/Missouri border.[7] Based on David Rindos's work on plant domestication,[8] O'Brien suggests that the consistent but low-intensity use of sunflower seeds, goosefoot, marsh elder, and other native annuals during the period up to about 300 B.C. created a relationship between these plants and people that resulted in a form of domestication and agriculture. He argues that initial exploitation of these plants would not have been of great significance in the overall economy, but the costs of exploiting them were very low, since they did not conflict with other activities and one could carry these seeds as a minor food without too much effort. But then he says, "by 200 B.C. the interaction between human groups and their resource base had reached the point that sedentism became a viable option."[9] He notes that the risks of concentrating on these plants were considerable, in the way of droughts and floods. But they also had potential for supporting increased population densities.

Many of the seeds of native North American domesticates could be eaten simply by drying and cracking them, but they also appear to have been staples in processed foods (Figure 15.3). David Braun has shown that during the Middle and Late Woodland periods

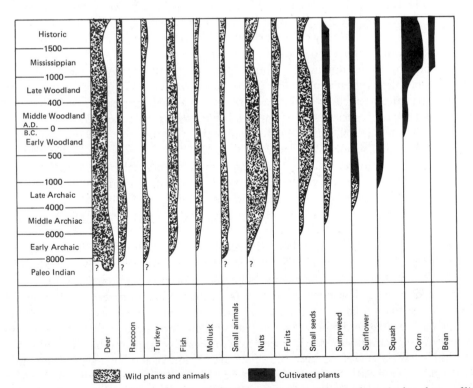

FIGURE 15.3 In the prehistoric American Middle West the transition to the agricultural way of life was a process in which native crops and wild plant foods were replaced by maize, beans, and squash (the thickness of the shaded and black areas reflects relative importance of the different resources).

people began to make more and more pottery in ways that seem particularly designed to cook starchy seeds, such as those of goosefoot.[10] Such pottery has to withstand high heat and sudden temperature changes, and all over the world people making these kinds of pots invented the same globular shapes and kinds of tempering and wall thicknesses that facilitate the long, slow simmering of seeds and other foods in liquids. Stews and soups are extraordinarily nutritious—and, more than that, they make excellent foods out of things that normally people cannot profit from much, such as dry goosefoot seeds and a picked-over rabbit skeleton: The best way to increase the nutrition of these annuals is to boil them, which "may increase palatability as well".[11]

The collection and domestication of these various plant species seem always and everywhere to have been combined with relentless hunting, fishing, and nut gathering. There is little evidence that much energy was invested in modifying the environments of sunflowers and these other plants through hoeing, watering, or weeding, although cultivation must have been practiced at least in the sense that seeds were selected and planted. Melvin Fowler noted that most of the native plants apparently domesticated in the East are species that prefer open, disturbed areas, such as would have been provided by the refuse piles that must have become increasingly available as hunters and gatherers cluttered the landscape with snail and clam shells, fish bones, and other debris.[12] When and to what extent the kind of natural association between these plants and human disturbances was converted into farming, in the sense of people planting and caring for these crops, will probably always be difficult to measure.

EARLY CULTURAL COMPLEXITY IN THE NORTH AMERICAN EAST

Like other hunter-foragers around the world, the people of the North American East began to show signs of increasing social differentiation as they intensified their exploitation of plants and as they became less mobile and spent more time in particular places.[13] One of the earliest signs of these changes is in burials. Beginning at about 2000 B.C., people all over the East began burying their dead with exotic items, such as copper, marine shells, and ground stone jewelry—often covering the corpse with red ocher, a mineral pigment.[14] Yerkes suggests that these "individuals would go to their graves with the exotic materials that they had accumulated, but it is unlikely that they were able to pass their achieved status on to their descendants."[15] As we noted in chapter 4, even the Neandertals of 100,000 years ago may have had at least some slight sense of death as a transition to another plane of existence, so it is not surprising that some burials in the North American East after 2000 B.C. contain exotic commodities and that cremation was practiced in some areas. But, as in many other areas of the world, this early sense of ceremonialism was transmuted over time into elaborate mortuary cults in which social differentiations and other signs of increasing complexity are evident.

One of the earliest and most dramatic indications that American cultures were becoming more complex than those of the previous millennia is the Poverty Point culture of the lower Mississippi Delta. This culture is named after the Poverty Point site in Louisiana (Figure 15.4), where large earthworks were constructed sometime between 1200 and 600 B.C. The six nested ranks of earthen mounds at Poverty Point average about 25 m wide and 3 m high and are set about 40 m apart. Near them stands an artificial mound more than 20 m high and more than 200 m across.[16] It is estimated that more than three

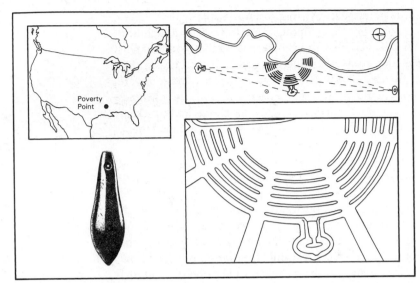

FIGURE 15.4 One of the most impressive Archaic sites in North America is the complex of earthworks at Poverty Point, Louisiana. Between about 1500 and 700 B.C. hunter-gathering peoples in this area built six nested octagons of piled earth. The outer octagon is about 1,300 m in diameter. Part of this complex was later eroded away by a river. A small mound near these earthworks and other occupations produced many beautiful artifacts, as well as thousands of fired clay balls that were apparently heated and then dropped into containers to boil foods.

million man-hours of labor were required to build this complex, with hundreds, perhaps thousands, of people hauling dirt in baskets in an organized, planned effort. If each basket contained a cubic foot of dirt, about 1,236,007 loads would have been required.[17] Burials suggest that this complex was a mortuary cult, but its overall significance is difficult to assess. Some of the Poverty Point people were skilled artisans who made vessels out of steatite and sandstone, pipes out of clay and stone, and axes, adzes, saws, and weights from hard kinds of stone—importing these raw materials, in some cases, from sources more than 600 miles away. In fact, trade in exotic commodities and the production of craft goods from them may be the reason for Poverty Point's prominence, since it is located at the confluence of six major rivers. Like any other large earthworks, those of Poverty Point offer points for astronomical observation: A person standing on the large mound at Poverty Point can see the vernal and autumnal equinoxes on a line across the center of the mound, looking east.[18] But, as with Stonehenge, any large monument offers a great array of possible observation points, and it is not difficult to find some astronomical regularity that may or may not have been the object of constructing that particular observation point.

As we have seen elsewhere in the ancient world, at sites such as Jericho and el Paraíso, agriculture is not a prerequisite for substantial architecture—all that is required is sufficient productivity. The Poverty Point people may have practiced some limited agriculture with native plants, but it was probably a rich blend of hunting and foraging that supported these mound-builders.

In any case, the people of Poverty Point did what people at a similar level of cultural organization around the world did: They built monumental architecture, they expanded and intensified regional trade in exotic commodities (and probably subsistence ones as well) and apparently used these to mark differences in social status and other social and ethnic identification, and then, again like these other cultures, their culture began to decline in importance as that of other cultures began to increase. The Poverty Point culture began to contract at about 650 B.C. and went into decline as other areas to the northeast became more powerful.

Evolving Cultural Complexity: The Early, Middle, and Late Woodland Periods (c. 800 B.C.–A.D. 750)

Between about 800 B.C. and A.D. 750, population densities in many parts of eastern North America increased sharply, thousands of gigantic earthworks were constructed, inter-regional trade expanded, and large villages were built. This era of change, usually referred to as the Woodland period, is associated with two major cultural manifestations: the *Adena* (centered in southern Ohio, and extending into Indiana, Kentucky, Pennsylvania, and West Virginia), and the *Hopewell* (centered in southern Ohio but extending widely over much of eastern North America). These cultures overlapped in time, with the Adena somewhat earlier than the Hopewell in some areas. Both are defined on the basis of styles of pottery, engraved stone tablets, textiles, and worked bone and copper.

THE ADENA CULTURE

Adena mound-building and artifact styles seem concentrated in the interval between about 500 B.C. and A.D. 700, and the richness of some of these sites, in the burial goods found in the mounds as well as the scale of the mounds themselves (Figure 15.5), originally led some scholars to suppose that these people already lived in chiefdoms, built on the sweat and labor of exploited farmers.

But the Adena seem to have been still mainly hunter-forager peoples who moved seasonally. Maize may have been cultivated on a small scale, but it was probably not very important.[19] And as impressive as the mounds are, they could easily have been built by small groups adding a layer or two each year, without much supervision,[20] perhaps as bodies were interred in layers that covered earlier burials.

Many of the mounds were mortuary centers in which one or more corpses were placed in log tombs or clay pits in communal burials, sometimes with beautiful stone tools and other goods, and then covered with earth. If the relative richness of these burials accurately reflects social differentiation in Adena society, then there were elites who could command in death special treatment in the form of log tombs, ocher and graphite decorations of their bodies, and expensive grave goods in copper, stone, and shell. Lower-status individuals appear to have been cremated with little ritual. These mounds may have

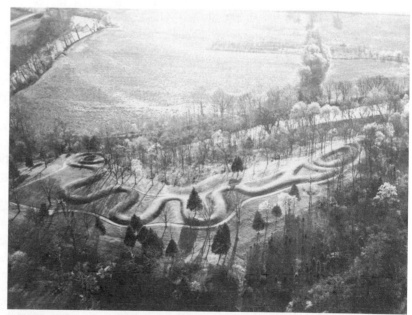

FIGURE 15.5   Great Serpent Mound, an Adena construction near Cincinnati, Ohio.

been ceremonial sites or centers for the exchange of goods, but they also could have served as territorial markers.[21]

Stone tobacco pipes are found in some Adena sites, and smoking probably played an important role in rituals. The native strains of tobacco were much more powerful than modern strains and could have produced narcotic effects much stronger than modern cigarettes.[22]

It is unfortunate that so many Adena sites were destroyed by modern constructions, and also that archaeologists excavated scores of mounds but almost no ordinary Adena settlements. Those few settlements that have been excavated suggest simple, somewhat temporary structures, probably made by setting series of posts in the ground and covering them with hides or wood—the *wigwam*.[23]

THE HOPEWELL CULTURE

The Hopewell culture—which was riverine in its adaptation—dominated parts of the Middle West from about 200 B.C. to A.D. 750. The Ohio Hopewell was centered in southern Ohio, and the Havana Hopewell dominated the central and lower Illinois River Valley, while various Hopewell groups extended up the Missouri River as far west as Kansas City. Hopewell religious traditions were practiced as far north as Wisconsin, south into Louisiana, and east into New York.

While grave goods are not usually profuse in Adena mounds, Hopewell tombs often contain finely worked copper, pipestone, mica, obsidian, meteoric iron, shell, tortoise shell, shark and alligator teeth, bear teeth, ceramics, and other commodities; there is also evidence of the ultimate grave good—sacrificed humans. Hopewell settlements and mounds increased in size and number in the centuries before about A.D. 400, and major earthworks were often built near the burial mounds.

These burials may reflect something about the dead person's rank and status within the community—though burials are an uncertain guide to the actual prestige and power relationships of any community. Joseph Tainter carried out a statistical analysis of more than 500 Hopewell burials and concluded that there were six discrete levels of status within the Hopewell community, corresponding to six different forms of burial, ranging from simple holes in the ground to massive mounds in which the corpse was accompanied by the finest goods.[24] In some Adena and Hopewell mounds, infants and juveniles were found buried with great ceremony and rich goods, suggesting the inheritance of rank and prestige and the control of the society's resources by a limited number of its people.

To understand these mound complexes we need to place them in the context of a local economy—and about this we know comparatively little. Because many later Hopewell buildings and earthworks were precisely planned and relatively expensive to construct, we must suspect that at least some people had become specialized labor-organizers and engineers of sorts, perhaps even constituting a privileged social group. But one of the many puzzling things about these mound complexes is that in many areas they do not seem to have any associated domestic houses. Some archaeologists assumed that any society capable of building such impressive works must certainly have been composed of sedentary agriculturalists, but Hopewell peoples for the most part probably hunted and gathered essentially the same plant and animal species as did their ancestors, with deer, ducks, small mammals, fish, snails, mussels, pigweed, lambsquarter, sunflowers, and nuts providing much of their nutrition.

In any case, the Hopewell heartland was in no sense so poor that hunters and gatherers were desperately trying to become full-time maize farmers. Estimates of resources around the Hopewell settlement at Scoville, in the lower Illinois Valley, indicate that "within a half-hour's walk . . . there would annually be from 182,000 to 426,000 bushels of nuts and 48,000 to 484,000 bushels of acorns, 100 to 840 deer, 10,000 to 20,000 squirrels, and 200 turkeys. Not computed were seeds, fruits, smaller animals, fish, mussels, and migratory birds (6 million mallards were estimated to be in the Illinois River Valley in 1955)."[25] Given these abundant resources, it is not surprising that maize agriculture apparently appeared first in poorer, more marginal environments and displaced hunting and gathering in the lushest environments only much later.

Hopewell peoples traded extensively in exotic commodities, such as obsidian and grizzly bear teeth from Montana, silver from Ontario, copper from northern Michigan, and shark teeth and many marine shells and products from the Gulf Coast. By the first few centuries A.D., people all over eastern North America were participants in a great trading network, and by "consuming" these goods by lavishing them on the dead and burying them deeply in mound-tombs, the demand for these treasures was kept high and the trading system in constant operation.

Although the conspicuous consumption of the Hopewell era, with its great mounds, rich burials, and wide variety of arts and crafts, indicates that Archaic egalitarian social structures were changing, these societies seem to have been less complexly organized than, for example, Mesoamerican cities like Teotihuacán.[26] Most of the Hopewell and Adena communities were small sedentary groups of hunter-collectors who built the burial mounds and ceremonial complexes for reasons that may fundamentally have had to do with distributing resources. Whereas Archaic hunters and gatherers met their needs by following seasonal rounds and exploiting a diversity of resources, Hopewell communities probably accomplished the same thing by exchanging products among themselves. Like the Adena mounds, however, these constructions could have also been territorial markers.

But we know comparatively little about daily life for the mass of the Hopewell or Adena peoples. The few houses excavated seem to be rectangular or ovoid constructions supported on posts and covered with bark or mats. Most people apparently lived in small hamlets composed of a few such houses and a few storage pits and garbage dumps. Some people were obviously specialists in flint working and a few other arts and crafts, and some of these communities may have been organized around a "big-man" and his favored lineage. But at the Murphy site, in Licking County, Ohio—one of the few Hopewell sites that has been excavated and analyzed for evidence of functional specialization—William Dancey and Paul Hooge found little evidence of complex economic or social organization. This site was occupied in the first few centuries A.D., probably intermittently or annually during the summer and fall.[27] They found no evidence of craft-specialization or farming, although these people did use pottery.

THE LATE WOODLAND PERIOD

After about A.D. 400 there is some evidence of a decline in mound-building and other changes in settlement patterns that used to be considered evidence of a Hopewellian "collapse." But it is not at all certain that there was, in fact, a collapse, at least in the sense of disintegrating economic relationships and declining productivity and population densities.

Richard Yerkes has reviewed studies by David Braun and others that suggest that although the people who lived toward the end of the Hopewell era, indeed, seem to have invested comparatively little effort in rich burials, pottery decoration, and trade of exotic goods, these cultural changes may be reflections of evolving—not disintegrating—cultural complexity.[28] At this time populations seem to have increased, people began producing more of their food through cultivation of native plants, and they seem to have moved into most of the major river valleys and established small settlements, perhaps in small nuclear family groups. As we have seen elsewhere, monumental architecture may be a response to stress and a device to control societal growth, rather than just an expression of societal wealth and extravagance.

The Mississippian Culture (A.D. 800–1650)

From about A.D. 600 to about 1650, the agricultural way of life spread over much of eastern North America, and in the North American East the Mississippian culture appeared—the high point of cultural evolution in aboriginal North America, particularly in terms of geographical extent of influence, ceremonialism, public works, technology, population density, and social stratification.[29]

Stoltman has listed some characteristics that define Mississippian culture, including (1) intensive maize-beans-squash agriculture; (2) apparent complex social organization—perhaps with chiefs and elites who could expropriate great amounts of societal wealth and power; (3) a theocratic social organization, with elites having both religious and political power; (4) towns in which 100, or in some cases 1,000 or more, people lived year-round, often behind fortifications; (5) monumental architecture, including mounds and tombs; (6) some occupational specialization in farming, trading, ritual, and administration; (7) mortuary cults involving certain patterns of burying the dead with "status goods" under earthen mounds; (8) distinctive pottery in shell-tempered wares, sometimes in the form of animals, and often beautifully incised, polished, or in other ways decorated; (9) use of the bow and arrow, with distinctive small, triangular stone arrowheads; and (10) certain kinds of houses, built by digging wall trenches and then using clay and thatch to form rooms.[30]

The florescence of Mississippian culture may have been linked with the continuing domestication and improvement of maize. The sensitivity of maize to daylight duration and temperature is vividly demonstrated each summer along the northern fringe of its present range—such as in Seattle, where except in the warmest summers few maize varieties can be coaxed into production. But in more suitable environments, maize is a prolific source of food. Maize probably first became an agricultural staple in North America only in those southern zones where there are at least 200 frost-free days a year, but during the Mississippian era newer strains appeared that could be farmed productively with just 120 frost-free days. And so adaptable is the plant that it was a staple as far north as Ontario, Canada, by the time the Europeans arrived in the sixteenth century. Primitive strains of maize had such small cobs when first introduced from Mexico that considerable selective breeding was required before it was worthwhile to do all the work of clearing land, weeding, and harvesting necessary for successful maize agriculture here. Once domesticated beans were combined with maize in North American fields, thereby supplying the critical amino acids lacking in maize, people could live in dense concentrations all over the North American East. The spread of maize farming has been detected by analyzing carbon isotope concentrations in the skeletons of ancient Native Americans. Maize contains relatively high amounts of ^{13}C, so people who eat maize also have high concentrations of this isotope. Several studies have shown that in Missouri, Arkansas, and other areas, skeletons of people who lived before about A.D. 1000 tend to have little ^{13}C, but beginning at about A.D. 900 to A.D. 1000, this isotope is found in radically higher concentrations.[31]

But to identify maize agriculture as an economic foundation of the Mississippian culture does not explain its emergence: Here, too, as in every other case of early complex societies considered in this book, we must consider how elite groups manage to appropriate a society's resources and perpetuate their domination. And for the Mississippian culture, as for other complex societies, there are many well-worn and largely unsatisfactory ideas about how this happened, ranging from the presumed economic benefits that would be provided by a "redistributor-chief" who could facilitate the circulation of goods to the effects of increasing occupational specialization.[32]

Artifacts and mounds of the Mississippian type first appeared in the lower Mississippi Valley, but they soon spread into the Tennessee River drainage and by A.D. 800–A.D. 900 occurred over much of the Ohio and Missouri river valleys. Between A.D. 900 and A.D. 1600, large towns with impressive ceremonial centers were built from Florida to northern Illinois, and from Ohio to eastern Oklahoma, but the heartland of this culture was in the central Mississippi Valley (Figure 15.6).

The largest prehistoric settlement north of Mexico was Cahokia, in East St. Louis, Illinois. Beginning at about A.D. 600 the people of Cahokia began building mounds and other features, and by about A.D. 1250 there were over 100 mounds within the 13 km² of the site. Monk's Mound, an earthen pyramid in the center of Cahokia, is over 30 m high, 241-by-316 m at the base, and covers an area of more than 6.5 hectares (Figure 15.7). Thirty to forty thousand people are estimated to have lived in the environs of Cahokia at about A.D. 1200 in several large towns, a few smaller towns, and more than 40 villages; no doubt people living within a large surrounding area had some contact with Cahokia.[33]

The beginnings of a class-based society in which elites could control community wealth is evident at Cahokia. One adult male was buried with 20,000 shell beads, 800 arrowheads, and sheets of mica and copper.[34] In addition, there were many burials, including 4 mutilated men and 118 women, many of whom appear to have been ritually strangled; we can only surmise that, like their Chinese, Mesopotamian, Mesoamerican, and other counterparts, these ritual killings and entombments were

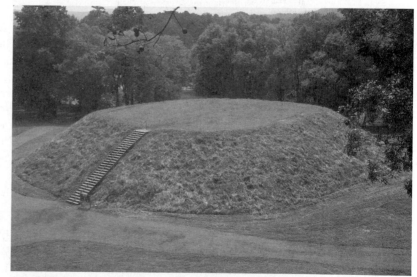

FIGURE 15.6 Mound B at Etowah, Georgia, is an example of a Mississippian structure.

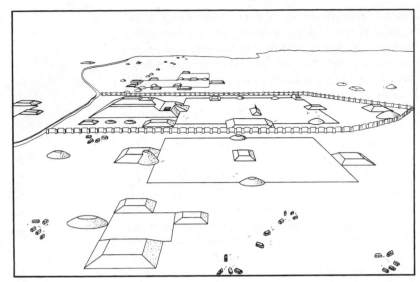

FIGURE 15.7   This reconstruction of Cahokia shows the palisade that enclosed the center of the site and some of the other major structures that existed at about A.D. 1200. The base of Monk's Mound, the largest pyramid, is larger than the Great Pyramid at Giza, Egypt.

attempts to provide elites in death with the same personal services they enjoyed in this life.

Some elite groups were permanent residents of Cahokia, but most of the people who built and sustained this center were probably maize farmers who lived in surrounding hamlets and who supplemented their farm incomes with hunting and gathering.

The mounds and burials at Cahokia and other sites are impressive monuments to status and power, but like other early complex societies, Mississippian society expressed these social dynamics in many ways. Timothy Pauketat and Thomas Emerson, for example, have argued that a particular kind of Mississippian pottery, called Ramey Incised (which is incised with figures of eyes, fish, arrows, abstract objects, and various designs), served to legitimize and communicate the authority of rulers:

> [These] pots were imbued with symbolism of order, hierarchy, and religiosity. . . . In the context of the rites of intensification, like the Green Corn ceremony, the Ramey Incised jar would have been a vehicle not only for the "redistribution" of comestibles, but also for the diffusion of elite ideas. Even the rudimentary actions of commoners, using Ramey Incised pots (after they had been ceremonially distributed from the administrative center[s]) may have provided a living metaphor of the role of elites—the source of the pots—as mediators of cosmic forces.[35]

Archaeologists have long debated the kind of sociopolitical entity that Cahokia represents. Some think Cahokia was a highly centralized, densely populated polity that can be thought of as a "chiefdom" (see chapter 7), perhaps even an embryonic state. Others think it was much less complex. George Milner, for example, suggests it was a "comparatively decentralized, geographically and socially segmented, less populous, and more dynamic cultural system."[36]

Cahokia is an impressive site, but it was probably not functionally similar to Teotihuacán or similar cities in prehistoric complex societies, at least in the degree of occupational specialization or the volumes and diversity of products produced, the class-stratification of the society, or the overall productivity of the economy.

At another great Mississippian site—Moundville, Alabama—a central earthen mound was the focus of a settlement in which elaborate burials, fortifications, and other structures were found. Christopher Peebles's statistical analysis of the grave goods unearthed with these burials suggests a society with considerable internal ranking.[37] Moundville had a complex history, and one gets the impression that here was a society with the potential to become a true urban metropolis, the center of a state.[38] Here too, however, the straight ecological arguments are quite convincing as to why this never happened: In a temperate forested environment, with an economy based on extensive cultivation of maize and a few other plants and on considerable hunting and foraging, there was not the stimuli of irrigation agriculture, interactions with nomads, and the other features of life present in early agricultural Mesopotamia, Egypt, or China. The environment simply does not permit or allow agricultural intensification on the scale possible in the tropical Olmec river basins, the Nile Valley, and other areas of advanced complexity.

Many late Mississippian and later period mounds and burials contain ornaments, pottery, and other artifacts decorated with motifs almost identical to some Mesoamerican motifs, including plumed serpents, eagles, jaguars, and warriors carrying trophy heads, as well as the 52-year calendar round. Collectively, they are taken as evidence of a southern (Mesoamerican) religious cult. Opinions differ on their significance in terms of contacts with Mesoamerica; some consider them evidence of quite direct and sustained contacts, while others see them as minor borrowings with little more than an accidental connection to Mesoamerican cultures. The southern cult, as well as the Adena and Hopewell mortuary ceremonialism, likely achieved importance in North America only after cultural complexity in the north had reached a stage where these elements "made sense" for northern societies.

Outside the great ceremonial centers, Mississippian villages were dispersed settlements of a few score of wattle-and-daub structures, supported by internal wooden beams, with floors of packed earth.[39] The highest Mississippian population densities were along the rich river bottoms where it was possible to combine maize and bean farming with waterfowl exploitation.[40] In some areas the river annually renewed the fertility of the soil through alluviation, and permanent field agriculture was possible. Without plows or an advanced technology, the Native Americans in many areas relied on a form of swidden cultivation in which they burned off the vegetation on rich, well-drained alluvial plains, then planted maize and a few other crops, invested some effort in weeding and cultivation during the growing season, and then harvested and stored as much maize as they could. After one or two seasons a given plot of swidden land would lose its fertility, and the areas of cultivation—and perhaps the whole village—would have to be shifted elsewhere.

Where maize was most productive the people probably planted two crops a year in the richest lands, with beans planted next to the maize and encouraged to grow up its stalks. Squash, sunflowers, and other crops were interspersed among the maize fields. The Mississippians were more gardeners than farmers compared to, for example, the wheat farmers of Southwest Asia. There is little evidence that Mississippian peoples ever did much in the way of flood control or irrigation, but they certainly used hoes and intensive weeding to boost crop yields.

Warfare among competing Mississippian chiefdoms may have been frequent and brutal, particularly as the best lands were overexploited and fertility began to fall.[41]

Our view of Mississippian life comes from both archaeological and ethnological sources, as Mississippian communities were still extant when the Europeans arrived in the sixteenth century. Initial accounts of the aboriginal Americans by Europeans must be viewed with suspicion because there is every reason to believe that European diseases sped quickly through aboriginal populations—far faster in fact than the spread of the Europeans.

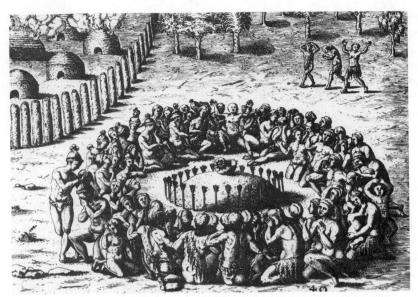

FIGURE 15.8   A sixteenth-century illustration by Jacques le Moyne of the burial of a Florida Indian chief. Arrows have been driven into the ground around the grave, and the chief's houses (upper left) are being ceremonially burned.

Moreover, it was to the advantage of the Europeans to portray Native Americans as savages who could be legitimately displaced and to suggest that they had a moral duty to subdue and instruct these savages in the mores of civilized life.

Ethnographic accounts of Mississippian communities as they existed in the sixteenth and seventeenth centuries—long after the culmination of Mississippian culture—describe an intensely class-conscious society in which nobles and warriors alternately exploited and abused the "stinkards," commoners and slaves who made up most of these societies. The upper classes were slavishly obeyed and respected. They frequently married the lower classes, but the aristocrat could divorce or kill the lower-ranking spouse, given even minor cause. In A.D. 1720 the French explorer Le Page du Pratz witnessed the funeral of "Great Sun," a ruler of the Natchez Mississippian people. On the occasion of his death, Great Sun's wives, servants, and relatives were drugged and then clubbed to death and buried with him[42] (Figure 15.8).

In contrast to most other ancient cultures, there is little question about the immediate cause of the decline of Mississippian culture. These people had no natural immunities to measles, smallpox, and cholera, and the densely settled Mississippian areas provided an ideal medium for the rapid spread of these highly contagious diseases.[43] Le Page du Pratz, who lived with the Natchez from 1718 to 1734, found that even "minor" diseases were devastating:

> Two distempers, that are not very fatal in other parts of the world, make dreadful ravages among them; I mean small-pox and a cold, which baffle all the arts of their physicians, who in other respects are very skillful. When a nation is attacked by the small-pox, it quickly makes great havock; for as a whole family is crowded into a small hut, which has no communications with the external air, but a door about two feet wide and four feet high, the distemper, if it seizes one, is quickly communicated to all. The aged die in consequence of their advanced years, and the bad quality of their food; and the young, if they are not strictly watched, destroy themselves, from an abhorrence of the blotches on their skin. . . . Colds, which are very common in winter, likewise destroy great numbers of the natives. In that season they keep fires in their huts day and night; and as there is no other opening but the door, the air within the hut is kept excessively warm without any free circulation; so that when they have occasion to go out, the cold seizes them, and the consequences of it are almost always fatal.[44]

Ann Ramenofsky has analyzed the archaeological evidence from several regions of the North American East and found that in each area there are significantly fewer settlements that date to the decades *just prior* to European invasion of these areas, which suggests that epidemic European diseases spread rapidly inland from the first physical encounters between most Native Americans and Europeans.[45] Native Americans died by the hundreds of thousands from diseases introduced by people they never saw.

Within a few decades of European contact in the sixteenth century, the once highly integrated and proud Mississippian people, and other cultures as well, were a much-reduced and poverty-stricken group, living amid thousands of abandoned settlements and eroding mounds attesting to their former greatness.

In summary of cultural developments in the North American East, we see the familiar script of cultural evolution. From a hunting-and-gathering base, specialized hunting and minor plant exploitation gradually gave way to intricate hunting-foraging economies in which fishing, nut collecting, shellfishing, and other activities were added to the subsistence repertoire according to what was probably a largely unrecognized but very precise "cost-benefit" analysis; then, after centuries of manipulation and selection, maize-based agriculture displaced less-productive economies in many areas, with consequent increasing population densities and the establishment of large sedentary communities. Once food-production reached certain levels, the familiar harbingers of increasing cultural complexity, such as the spread of religious and stylistic traditions, monumental architecture, mortuary cults, and increasingly diverse and interdependent arts and crafts, also appeared. Social and religious hierarchies emerged as "efficient" ways to make the decisions necessary for the perpetuation of these increasingly complex economies, and the institutionalization of prestige and privilege may have arisen as an effective way of reducing competition between these populations and of maximizing administrative efficiency.

In these essentials, little differentiates the sequence of cultural evolution in North America from that in Mesoamerica, except that, given the available domesticates and technology, most of eastern North America had less agricultural potential than Mesoamerica, causing these northern cultures to stabilize at a much lower level of complexity. Had the Europeans not invaded and introduced their diseases, true state-level societies might well have evolved from the remnants of the Mississippian climax, but only if food-production could have been increased drastically through technological, agricultural, or administrative innovations.

THE NORTH AMERICAN SOUTHWEST

The dramatic mountains, crystal skies, and primary colors of the Southwest make it an attractive place to live—especially if one has access to a municipal water system and a modern market and transport system. But from the perspective of a hunter and gatherer or subsistence farmer, most of the Southwest is not a lush environment: There are few large rivers or streams, and the combination of low rainfall and high elevation renders much of the Southwest a land of searing summers and bitterly cold winters.

In some prehistoric periods the Southwest was wetter than it is today, but for most of the last 10,000 years the Southwest has usually been at least as hot and dry as it is today, and there were short periods of extreme drought.

As a consequence, although people have lived here for at least 10,000 years, and although they eventually adopted maize-based agriculture, aggregated into large towns, and evolved some occupational and administrative specialization, they never produced class-structured, hierarchically organized, economically differentiated societies. Periodic food shortages stimulated the development of small-scale cooperation among groups, but neither the economic inducements nor basic productivity were there to make such elaborate cultural forms necessary or possible.[46]

Yet the archaeological record of the American Southwest is an extraordinary cultural resource. Its proximity to major universities and excellent aridity-related preservation has meant that the archaeology of this region is among the best known in the world. Many important methodological advances in archaeology have developed in part out of research in the Southwest, including tree-ring dating, regional statistically based sampling designs, analyses of site formation processes, and paleobotanical and paleoenvironmental research. Contemporary Native Americans living in the Southwest are in some cases direct descendants, both physically and culturally, of ancient groups, and thus the archaeology of the Southwest can be related to a well-studied ethnographic record.[47] Also, the fact that early Southwest cultures developed political and economic systems that, while less "complex" than those of, for example, Maya Mesoamerica, had sufficient complexity to offer an opportunity to study the kinds of cultural changes that in more productive environments are obscured archaeologically by the great states and empires that followed.[48] Moreover, there are some clear indications of cultural contacts between Southwest cultures and those of Mesoamerica, providing a "test case" in a sense for varying ideas about the nature of cultural contacts between more- and less-powerful groups in the ancient world.[49] And as Steadman Upham has shown, the American West provides an example of one of the enduring themes of human history, the relationship of nomads and agriculturalists. For, as people in some areas became farmers, they developed complex economic and social relationships with the many groups around them that continued to pursue the ancient hunting-foraging way of life.[50]

Agricultural Origins: The Late Archaic Period

As we saw in chapter 6, people have been in the Southwest for at least 12,000 years, and up to about A.D. 1, people here worked out a marvelous array of arid-land adaptations based on hunting and foraging. Late Archaic foragers, heirs to a tradition thousands of years old of desert plant collecting, may have been exploiting maize for a long time. The apparent presence of maize pollen in samples dated to about 2000 B.C. suggests that this plant may have been used for some millennia before it became the staple food crop,[51] but the earliest evidence for substantial use of maize—at Sheep Rock Shelter, Bat Cave, numerous sites in the Tucson and Tonto Basins, as well as several sites in the Mogollon highlands and on the Colorado Plateau—seems to cluster around 1000 B.C.[52] Domesticated varieties of beans and squash also appear in the archaeological record at about this time, but the diet was still probably based on a broad range of other plants and animals. Even today Native Americans in the Southwest still hunt deer, rabbits, and other animals and augment their farm produce with high-calorie nuts, berries, and seeds.

The earliest maize variety used in the Southwest was the Chapalote variant found much earlier at Tehuacán, and thus there was a long time lag before it was in significant use in the Southwest. It used to be thought that early varieties of maize had to be adapted to local Southwest environments, but as Paul Minnis notes, the recent recovery of Archaic maize from the deserts around Tucson does not support this idea. He suggests that the modern maize variety morphologically closest to Archaic maize, Chapalote, was well adapted to high and low environments and could be grown under many conditions.[53] In any case, just as we have seen prehistoric people in the Middle East, Mesoamerica, and other parts of the world combine cultivated and wild food resources, so did the people of the Southwest adapt maize to their lifestyle and combined it with beans, squash, and a wide variety of other resources in an economy with sufficient productivity to permit the village-farming way of life and the beginnings of cultural elaboration.

The Hohokam Culture: 1000 B.C.–A.D. 1450

The Hohokam peoples flourished in southern Arizona—particularly in the Salt and Gila river valleys, as well as secondary river systems[54] (Figure 15.9). For many decades, archaeologists wrestled with the question of the origins of the Hohokam. Were they local peoples whose culture was transformed by contacts with the high civilizations of Mexico? Or, on the basis of similarity in styles of architecture, construction, ceramics, turquoise ornaments, and other artifacts, were they were so similar to Mesoamerican examples that they could only be the result of an immigration of Mexican people who transplanted their way of life directly to the Hohokam area?[55] The considerable amount of research that has been undertaken in the Hohokam area since the 1990s has put to rest some of the intensity of this debate because it indicates that local origins for the Hohokam are the more plausible explanation.[56] Additionally, those traits that appear to have derived—at least in part—from Mesoamerican influences are most notable in Hohokam society only after about A.D. 800[57] Sedentary villages and reliance on maize agriculture were present in this region long before Hohokam culture.

One of the most interesting aspects of the Hohokam is their agricultural system. Their homeland is set in some of the driest deserts of North America, where summer temperatures have impressed even archaeological veterans of the Middle East. Canal irrigation is known from sites as early as 1200–1100 B.C.,[58] although the large, impressive networks of canals that channeled water from the Salt and Gila rivers to irrigate gardens of maize and other crops were mainly built after A.D. 700. Modern buildings have erased much of the Hohokam irrigation system, but two canals near Phoenix were over 16 km long, several meters wide, and about 60 cm deep when first constructed. Tightly woven grass mats were probably used as gates to open and close canal segments, and earthen dams on the rivers in some places diverted water through canals for more than 50 km across the desert floor, with many small branches serving individual fields.

In the recent past, Southwestern Native American irrigation systems, as well as comparable agricultural systems elsewhere in the world, have been operated by a few thousand people in relatively simple tribal organizations in which no coercion, permanent authorities, or police agencies were necessary, and this might well have been the case among the Hohokam.

In areas away from the major rivers, Hohokam groups used *akchin*—floodwater—farming, taking advantage of natural events that irrigated areas alongside small seasonal streams, or farmed alluvial fans where moisture essential for plant growth was retained for

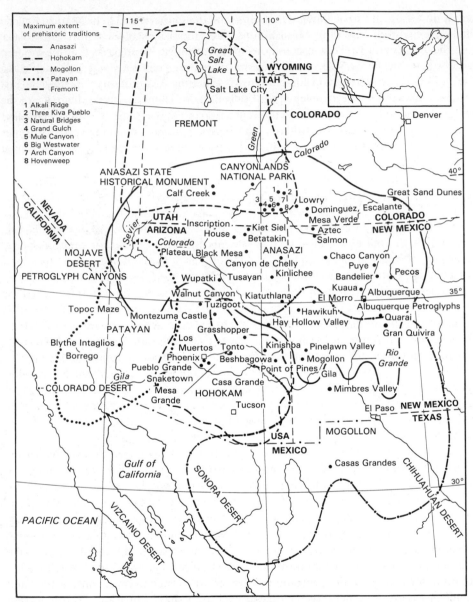

FIGURE 15.9   Major cultural traditions of the North American Southwest. These cultures are shown at their maximum extent, which they did not reach simultaneously.

longer periods of time. Ethnohistoric and ethnographic accounts document akchin farming among some groups of the Tohono O'odham,[59] who may be descendants of the Hohokam.

Although the largest irrigation systems were apparently built sometime after A.D. 800, by about A.D. 300 there were already indications of minor increases in the complexity of Hohokam cultures. Some low platform mounds, about 29 m long, 23 m wide, and 3 m high, were built at the Snaketown site, and here and elsewhere people built large sunken ball courts like those found in Mesoamerica. The Hohokam ball courts were east-west oriented oval depressions about 60 m long, with 4.5- to 6-m-high sloping earth embankments on a side. Apparently the objective of the game, played by two opposing teams, was to try to get a rubber ball (several of which have been found in the Southwest) through a goal, probably not by throwing or batting it, but by using knees, elbows, or torso. The ball apparently could not be held in the hands when it was in play. As played by the Mesoamericans, this activity was not a sport: The ball may have represented the sun, and the court and play were imbued with ritual and cosmological imagery. Losing players were sometimes executed (see chapter 13).

The Southwestern ball courts were probably not stops on the northern road trips of the Mexican major leagues, but they do indicate very close southern affinities, as do the platform mounds. And between A.D. 900 and A.D. 1200, many other Mesoamerican elements were imported, including cotton textiles, certain ceramic motifs, pyrite mirrors, effigy vessels, cast copper bells, ear plugs, etched shell ornaments, and even parrots and macaws—kept and prized for their feathers.

Generally, however, there is little evidence in subsistence practices, settlements, or mortuary ceremonies of evolving rank and wealth differences. Most of the Hohokam lived in small square pithouses roofed with clay and grass domes supported by a wooden pole framework. Early dwellings appear large enough for several families, but single-family residences became more popular in later periods. This is not to say, however, that elites did not exist in Hohokam society, particularly during the Classic period from A.D. 1150–1450. Platform mound burials clearly show that some individuals were differentially treated—including, at times, a few women.[60] The degree to which these elites managed labor and resources or established political connections within the Hohokam area or with other groups remains an open and vigorously debated question.

Research in the last two decades of the twentieth century, particularly by cultural resource management (CRM) firms investigating areas prior to the building of roads, housing developments, pipelines, and other modern projects, has greatly expanded our understanding of Hohokam settlement patterns. While there are few indications of a master plan in village layouts or of economic specialization of villages, by A.D. 700 and later, patterns in intracommunity and intercommunity organization emerge. Within village sites, domestic houses are arranged around courtyards, and these groupings have communal cemeteries, cooking ovens, and trash areas.[61] On a larger scale, villages along the same irrigation canal may have been grouped into "irrigation communities" and linked together in terms of social organization, economies, labor efforts related to canal construction, and maintenance and shared public ceremonies at ball court sites.[62] After A.D. 1150, irrigation communities appear to have been linked to a series of major platform mound sites— ball courts are no longer the integrative ceremonial mechanism—and at some sites, such as Casa Grande, "great houses" were constructed (Figure 15.10). Most villages, however, probably repeated all the economic activities of other villages, except that some favored locations allowed a greater reliance on maize, beans, squash, and other crops. Nonetheless, many atlatl dart points and arrowheads have been found at each Hohokam site, and botanical remains indicate that almost every community supplemented its diet with wild mustard, amaranths, chenopods, cactus fruits, mesquite, screwbeans, and other wild products.[63]

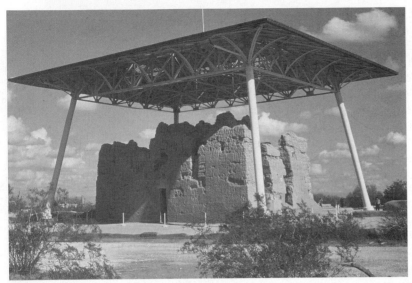

FIGURE 15.10 The "Great House" at Casa Grande, Arizona, is an example of large-scale construction by the Hohokam. The large shelter over the Great House was built in the 1930s.

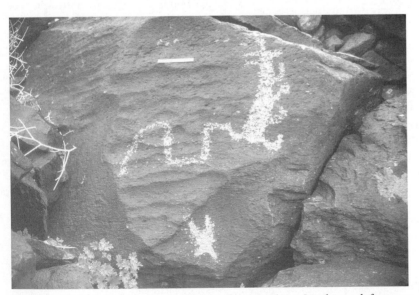

FIGURE 15.11 Prehistoric peoples in the American Southwest left many examples of petroglyphs (*pecked images*). Some appear to represent animals, while others are more enigmatic. These are from an outcrop on a ridge above the Classic period Hohokam site of Verbena Village, Arizona.

Artifacts in the Hohokam style have been found over a wide area—73,000 km²—encompassing a core Hohokam area (centered on the Salt and Gila rivers) and its surrounding regions (such as the Tucson and Tonto basins), as well as more peripheral areas such as the Papagueria (the southwestern corner of Arizona) (Figure 15.11). This interaction sphere included groups of people who were Hohokam, those who were new immigrants into the region, as well as those who participated only marginally in Hohokam social life. Evidence for supra-political control over this region—for example, along the lines of Moche, Tiwanku, or Maya—is lacking, making it likely that the Hohokam were sociopolitically organized along less complex lines.

The archaeological signature of the Classic Hohokam fades from the record after about A.D. 1450. Archaeologists have struggled with various explanations for this "disappearance," and it will come as no surprise that the most favored causes are ecological—particularly flooding episodes along the major rivers—and European diseases spreading in advance of the actual arrival of the Spanish.

The Mogollon:
A.D. 200–1450

The Mogollon peoples (pronounced something like "Mug-ee-yone"), who also were heirs to the Archaic desert foraging cultures of the last several millennia B.C., lived mainly in the mountains of east central Arizona and west central New Mexico. Sedentary villages and ceramics of the Mogollon type may have already been established by the last few centuries B.C., but the distinctive Mogollon red-and-brown pottery is securely dated to about the third century A.D., at which time villages of about 15 pithouses each were scattered along ridges, bluffs, and terraces. Like their contemporaries in much of the Americas, they relied on the maize-beans-squash complex, supplemented by many wild plants and game. Mogollon burials of this period were often simple inhumations in house floors, accompanied by a few pottery vessels, turquoise ornaments, and stone tools typical of unstratified societies.

At the important Mogollon site of Swarts Ruins, in the Mimbres Valley, New Mexico, river boulders set in adobe were used to construct a large complex of conjoined rectangular rooms, access to which was apparently possible only through the roof, since there were no exterior doors. Inside walls were plastered with mud, and doorways led from one room to another. Storage bins, shelves, fireplaces, and benches constituted the essential furnishings. Corpses were frequently interred in the floors of abandoned rooms, in occupied rooms, or within the village compound; most burials were very simple.

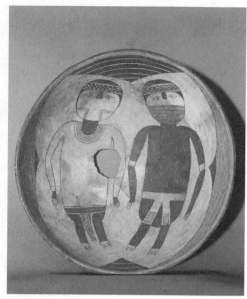

FIGURE 15.12 Some of the most beautiful painted pottery in the American Southwest is from the Mimbres Mogollon culture in New Mexico and Arizona.

The Mogollon built no pyramids, ball courts, or major irrigation systems, but they did produce an extraordinarily beautiful array of ceramics. Their "Mimbres" ceramic forms, decorated with vivid figures of frogs, insects, fish, deer, and other animal life painted against black backgrounds, are particularly notable (Figure 15.12). Stephen Jett and Peter Moyle have shown that many of the fish species illustrated on Mimbres pottery are marine species that could be found no closer to the Mimbres area than 1,500 km southwest, in the Gulf of California.[64] The beauty of Mogollon pottery has resulted in widespread looting, a sickening destruction of yet another Native American culture.

Mogollon settlement patterns show some evidence of minor emerging social ranking. Mogollon villages seem to be of two types: a small cluster of fewer than 5 pithouses, without any large ceremonial kivas-pithouses-and larger collections of 100 or more pithouses associated with "great kivas." The largest pithouses in these communities tend to have the greatest amount of storage space, larger numbers of exotic trade items, and evidence of greater consumption of agricultural products. Lightfoot and Feinman interpret this evidence and other data to mean that a "suprahousehold" decision-making organization had developed among the Mogollon, perhaps as a result of competition among rival political leaders.[65] But it is hard to link changing distributions of artifacts like these to the fairly subtle social changes that would have been involved in the rise of suprahousehold administrative positions. In any case, there is little about the Mogollon to suggest profound social changes in the direction of complexity. Natural limitations on agricultural intensification seem to have restricted the complexity of social and political organization here.[66]

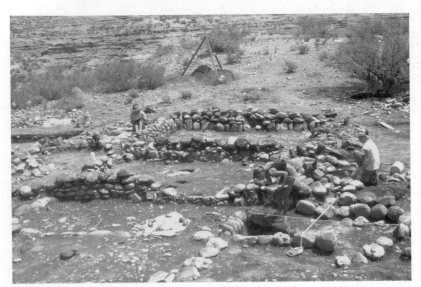

FIGURE 15.13 A small pueblo structure of the Mogollon period at the Powers Ranch Ruin, Arizona.

One of the major settlement pattern transitions in Southwestern cultural history occurred during the first millennium A.D., when people gradually, generation by generation, stopped living in relatively small villages of semi-subterranean pithouses and began building their communities in the "pueblo" style of blocks of contiguous above-ground rooms (Figure 15.13).

For the archaeologist, of course, such a change is immediately seen in adaptive terms: What conditions would induce this sort of long-term, regional change? In a consideration of this question from the perspective of Mogollon settlements in western Texas, Michael Whalen notes that the change is associated with an increase in regional population densities, the appearance of larger community size, a growing reliance on plant cultivation as the main subsistence source, and an increasingly elaborate ceremonialism, as expressed in the design and contents of structures.[67]

Whalen suggests that as populations grew, climates fluctuated, and settlements spread into different microenvironments, people tried to maintain their traditional way of life by extending agriculture into the margins of basins where water was more available. The greater productivity of these basin margins fostered certain kinds of economic agricultural specialization in which the community rather than the family was the basic social and economic unit. McGuire and Schiffer show that the transition from pithouses was the outcome of a long period of experimentation.[68]

Some Mogollon sites, such as Paquimé—A.D. 1250–1450—in northern Mexico, have what appear to be Mogollon-style artifacts along with Mesoamerican items, such as ball courts, platform mounds, and jewelry in turquoise and shell. As Stephen Lekson[69] notes, Paquimé is one of the best candidates in the Southwest for status as politically complex, and few archaeologists have disputed this attribution. The degree of this complexity, however, has been debated, ranging from a Mesoamerican central authority who controlled trade to a Mesoamerican authority based on ritual and religion to a local elite using ritual as a power base.[70]

Like the Hohokam, the "disappearance" of the Mogollon as an archaeological culture has been variously explained, with emphasis on ecological factors, particularly droughts. Other researchers have stressed a shift to a more dispersed settlement pattern characterized by small hamlets[71] or the relocation of some Mogollon people to puebloan communities and a subsequent restructuring of society.

The Ancestral Pueblo: A.D. 100–1300

Like the Mogollon and Hohokam, the Ancestral Pueblo[72] developed out of desert-foraging cultures, and their earliest pre-pottery representatives are widely known as the Basketmaker cultures. It is not entirely certain how mobile early Ancestral Pueblo groups were, but by the first few centuries A.D. they were apparently living in many sedentary settlements located on old river terraces and mesa tops or in river valleys in the high plateau country of the central Southwest.[73] The earliest houses were circular structures of wattle and daub set on log bases, or semi-subterranean houses. These early Ancestral Pueblo did not use pottery and, although they ate maize, beans, and squash, they invested little labor in cultivating these crops, relying instead on wild foods, such as roots, bulbs, grass seeds, nuts, acorns, berries, cactus fruits, sunflowers, deer, rabbits, antelopes, and wild sheep.

After about A.D. 400, the Ancestral Pueblo began to use pottery and to build large pithouses, most of which were circular or rectangular, from 3 to 7.5 m in diameter, and covered by log and mud roofs supported on center posts. Interior walls were plastered with mud or faced with stone, access was through a descending passageway, and fireplaces and benches were standard furnishings. At some sites, large ceremonial pithouses, or kivas, were built. After about A.D. 700, above-ground masonry houses were erected in some Ancestral Pueblo communities, but the pithouse and kiva combination continued to be the basic village type until the end of the thirteenth century A.D. (Figure 15.14).

Defensive considerations, greater exploitation of more productive strains of maize, and climatic changes beginning about A.D. 700 may have spurred the Ancestral Pueblo into constructing the "cliff cities" for which they are famous[74] (Figure 15.15). Pollen and geological studies suggest that summer rainfall, in the form of torrential storms, increased after A.D. 700, while winter rainfall decreased, and the resulting changes in water tables and stream flows may have forced the Ancestral Pueblo to congregate around larger, permanently flowing rivers.[75] Hillsides were terraced to control erosion, and diversion canals and dams were constructed to control and store as much of the vital summer rainwater as possible. On Chapin Mesa, for example, in the Mesa Verde area, the older agricultural fields were extended by an elaborate checkdam system that added 8 or 12 hectares of cultivable land.

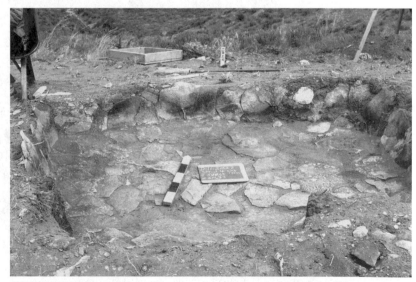

FIGURE 15.14 Small pueblo structures were also typical of the Ancestral Puebloan culture. This room from a site on Black Mesa, Arizona, was used to store corn. When the room burned, the corn cobs were preserved when they carbonized. Note the evidence of burning on the slab walls.

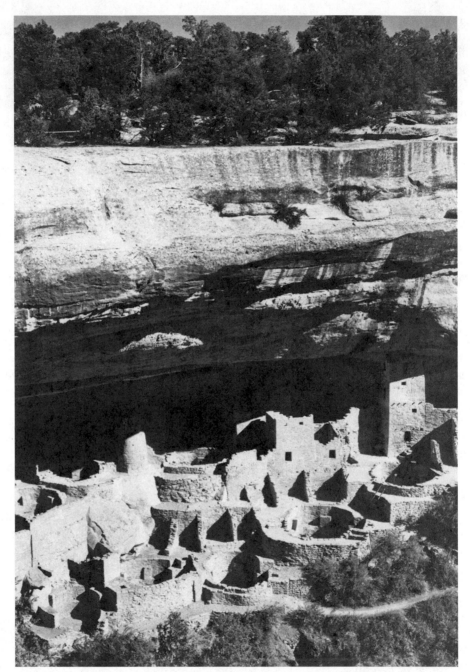

FIGURE 15.15   Cliff Palace, Mesa Verde, Colorado, is one of the most impressive settlements built under massive cliffs in the American Southwest.

In some areas erosion forced frequent settlement relocations, and some communities met the changing agricultural conditions by scattering into small family groups; but the prevailing response was to aggregate into large towns along the major rivers. By about 1100 A.D., prosperous enclaves were established at Mesa Verde, Chaco Canyon, Canyon de Chelly, and elsewhere, and in some ways these communities represent the high point of Southwestern culture.

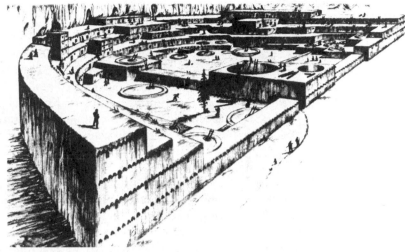

FIGURE 15.16   Reconstruction of Pueblo Bonito, as it may have appeared at about A.D. 1050.

The developments at Chaco Canyon are often cited as the best example of sociopolitical complexity in the Ancestral Pueblo region, a not surprising outcome given the many unusual features found here and throughout the greater Chacoan interaction sphere. There were 12 large towns ("Great Houses") in Chaco Canyon, of which Pueblo Bonito was the largest, with almost 700 rooms (Figure 15.16)—built over a period of almost 300 years (A.D. 850–1125). The Great Houses were relatively elaborate, planned elements in the landscape of Chaco Canyon, and it is of some interest that sites such as Pueblo Bonito, with its hundreds of rooms, appear to have been the residence for only a small number of families.[76] In addition to these large, multi-story pueblos, there were smaller pueblo units and many single-story and apparently unplanned villages—these are the likely residences for most of Chaco's population.

Vivian[77] has shown that the Chaco Canyon was part of a large organized system that included a unified irrigation system (using rainfall runoff from the canyon cliffs, as well as water from the Chaco wash) and about 600 km of roads that linked scores of Chacoan outliers—smaller-sized Great Houses built in the Chaco style—and other small communities. Some 150–200 outlying Great Houses are linked by this road system to Chaco and sometimes to other Chacoan outliers, reaching as far as 140 km away from Chaco Canyon, and perhaps as far as southern Utah, some 240 km away.[78]

The roads were long and straight constructions, sometimes cut into bedrock as stairways when obstacles to the most direct route were encountered—analogous perhaps to how we construct tunnels through hills and mountains to maintain the shortest distances for roads. These ancient roads facilitated movement of people between the various Chacoan settlements, as well as the transport of resources into Chaco Canyon. The hundreds of thousands of pine logs[79] used as roof beams and ceilings in the pueblos there, for example, came from mountain areas at least 60 km away and represent a relatively major transport labor investment. Other resources that entered Chaco Canyon include most of the pottery—made at various Chacoan outliers—associated with the Great Houses, as well as exotic items from much farther away, including copper bells and macaws from Mexico, and turquoise, likely from mines near Santa Fe.[80]

Whether sociopolitical complexity is associated with the Chacoan "phenomenon" is a subject, as Barbara Mills[81] observes, that is of less interest to archaeologists today than in past decades. As she notes, Chacoan research has instead posed new and interesting questions about how complexity may have been organized rather than seeking to simply determine its presence. Chief among the recent explanations have been models stressing prestige-good economies (elite dominated consumption of exotic materials), ritual leadership (Chaco as a pilgrimage center), and communal feasting (rather than competitive feasting).

Sometime around A.D. 1125 or shortly thereafter, the Chaco system seems to disintegrate (possibly due to a prolonged drought), although some people continue to live in Chaco Canyon and a number of the outlier sites become more important, for example, Aztec Ruin—its name does not, however, denote contact with the Aztec. There are, in fact, many indications of continuity with the earlier Chaco "phenomenon," although the social structure of Ancestral Pueblo communities after A.D. 1125 undergoes reorganization.[82]

As beautiful as many Ancestral Pueblo settlements were, they do not appear to have been the work of a highly complex society. There may have been minor occupational specialization in ceramic manufacture, weaving, and turquoise carving, but most if not all of the people were subsistence farmers. Nor is there much evidence of differential rank expressed in domestic architecture or in grave goods—one exception being the burial of two possible elite males at Pueblo Bonito.[83] Even the irrigation system, while intricate and efficient, was probably administered through simple kinship systems.

Shortly before A.D. 1300, many once-prosperous Ancestral Pueblo communities began to be abandoned, and when the Spanish arrived in the sixteenth century, they found some of the descendants of the Ancestral Pueblo living along the Rio Grande in small villages, each a largely autonomous political and economic unit. The Hopi, Zuñi, and Rio Grande pueblos are the descendants of the Ancestral Pueblo peoples.

SUMMARY AND CONCLUSIONS

Illegal aliens have always been a problem in the
United States. Ask any Indian.

Robert Orben

The New World was truly a "second earth," where long millennia of indigenous cultural development produced a rich spectrum of peoples and cultures unaffected by contact with European and Asian peoples. The spectacular Mississippian and Southwestern sites dominate the North American archaeological record, but all over North America there were divergent cultural traditions, many of them interacting economically, but also remaining distinctive in essential ways, from language to social organization. To the northeast, the Iroquois peoples adapted maize-beans-squash farming to the colder uplands of New York State, New England, and southeastern Canada. Their shifting pattern of swidden agriculture seems to have created land shortages and recurrent warfare, forcing people to live in well-fortified villages. To the west, marginal cultivators lived in the richer river valleys of Nebraska, South Dakota, and the other north-central states, with bison-hunting groups on the grasslands, where maize agriculture could not be practiced until the introduction by Europeans of deep-bottom plows. The horse-mounted nomadic hunters who range through thousands of Hollywood epics have some basis in reality, but only after the Europeans reintroduced the horse in America. Most of the desert regions of the west were thinly settled by hunter-foragers until European colonization, but rich and sedentary communities were established along the Pacific Northwest Coast and areas of California, where marine and terrestrial resources were so naturally productive that low-level complex societies could be sustained by simple fishing-foraging-hunting.

In some ways it is less than satisfying to conclude that the temperate latitudes of North America never produced states and empires because of the simple absence of draft animals, developed metallurgy, extensive warm arid alluvial plains, and a few other techno-environmental factors—but this conclusion seems inescapable. From the perspective of the present, the violent collision between Old and New World cultures also seems an inevitable outcome of the competition dynamic of evolutionary processes and the demographic, techno-environmental, and other conditions of both areas. But to rank Old and New World cultures in this sense of an evolutionary scale is only a useful research device; it should not obscure the great richness of the ancient cultures of both areas.

BIBLIOGRAPHY

Anderson, D. G., and G. T. Hanson. 1988. "Early Archaic Settlement in the Southeastern United States: A Case Study from the Savannah River Valley." *American Antiquity* 53(2):262–286.

Baby, R., and S. Langlois. 1977. "Prehistoric Agriculture: A Study of House Types in the Ohio Valley." *Ohio Historical Society Echoes* 16(2):1–5.

Barker, A. W., and T. R. Pauketat, eds. 1992. *Lords of the Southeast: Social Inequality and the Native Elites of Southeastern North America*. Washington, D.C.: Archeological Papers of the American Anthropological Association Number 3.

Baugh, T. G., and J. E. Ericson. 1995. *Prehistoric Exchange Systems in North America*. New York: Plenum Press.

Bayman. J. M. 2001. "The Hohokam of Southwest North America." *Journal of World Prehistory* 15(3):257–313.

Betancourt, J. L., J. S. Dean, and H. M. Hull. 1986. "Prehistoric Long-Distance Transport of Construction Beams, Chaco Canyon, New Mexico." *American Antiquity* 51:370–375.

Blitz, J. H. 1999. "Mississippian Chiefdoms and the Fission-Fusion Process." *American Antiquity* 64(4):577–592.

Braun, D. P. 1983. "Pots as Tools." In *Archaeological Hammers and Theories*, ed. A. Keene and J. Moore. New York: Academic Press.

———. 1987. "Comment on M. J. O'Brien, 'Sedentism, Population Growth, and Resource Selection in the Woodland Midwest: A Review of Coevolutionary Developments.'" *Current Anthropology* 28(2):189–190.

———. 1988. "The Social and Technological Roots of 'Late Woodland.'" In *Interpretations of Culture Change in Eastern Woodlands During the Late Woodland Period*, ed. R. W. Yerkes. Department of Anthropology, Ohio State University, Occasional Papers in Anthropology 3:17–38.

Brose, D. S., and N. Greber, eds. 1979. *Hopewell Archaeology: The Chillicothe Conference*. Kent, OH: The Kent State University Press.

Brown, J. A. 1985. "Long-Term Trends to Sedentism and the Emergence of Complexity in the American Midwest." In *Prehistoric Hunter-Gatherers: The Emergence of Cultural Complexity*, ed. T. D. Price and J. A. Brown. Orlando, FL: Academic Press.

Bush, D. E. 1975. "A Ceramic Analysis of the Late Adena Buckmeyer Site, Perry County, Ohio." *Michigan Archaeologist* 21:9–23.

Cleland, C. E. 1966. *The Prehistoric Animal Ecology and Ethnozoology of the Upper Great Lakes Region*. Ann Arbor: Museum of Anthropology, Anthropological Papers, University of Michigan, No. 29.

Cobb, C. R., and P. H. Garrow. 1996. "Woodstock Culture and the Question of Mississippian Emergence." *American Antiquity* 61(1):21–37.

Coe, M., D. Snow, and E. Benson. 1986. *Atlas of Ancient America*. New York: Facts on File.

Cordell, L. S. 1984. *Prehistory of the Southwest*. New York: Academic Press.

Cordell, L. S., and G. J. Gumerman, eds. 1989. *Dynamics of Southwest Prehistory.* Washington, DC: Smithsonian Institution Press.

Crown, P. L. 1990. "The Hohokam of the American Southwest." *Journal of World Prehistory* 4(2):223–255.

———. 1995. *Ceramics and Ideology: Salado Polychrome Pottery.* Albuquerque: University of New Mexico Press.

Crown, P., and S. Fish. 1996. "Gender and Status in the Hohokam Pre-Classic to Classic Transition." *American Anthropologist* 98:803–813.

Crown, P. L., and J. W. Judge. 1991. *Chaco and Hohokam: Regional Systems in the American Southwest.* Santa Fe, NM: School of American Research.

Dancey, W. S. 2005. "The Enigmatic Hopewell of the Eastern Woodlands." In *North American Archaeology,* ed. T. R. Pauketat and D. D. Loren, pp. 108–137. Malden, MA: Blackwell Publishing.

Dickson, D. B. 1975. "Settlement Pattern Stability and Change in the Middle Northern Rio Grande Region, New Mexico: A Test of Some Hypotheses." *American Antiquity* 40:159–171.

———. 1981. "The Yanomamo of the Mississippi Valley? Some Reflections on Larson . . . Gibson . . . and Mississippi Period Warfare in the Southeastern United States." *American Antiquity* 46:909–916.

Diehl, M. W. 1997. "Changes in Architecture and Land Use Strategies in the American Southeast: Upland Mogollon Pithouse Dwellers, A.C. 200–1000." *Journal of Field Archaeology* 24(2):179–194.

Ericson, J. E., and T. G. Baugh, eds. 1995. *The American Southwest and Mesoamerica.* New York: Plenum Press.

Fagan, B. M. 1995. *Ancient North America,* 2nd ed. New York: Thames and Hudson.

Farnsworth, K. B., and T. E. Emerson, eds. 1986. *Early Woodland Archaeology.* Kampsville Seminars in Archaeology, No. 2. Kampsville, IL: Kampsville Archeological Center, Center for American Archeology.

Fiedel, S. J. 1992. *Prehistory of the Americas,* 2nd ed. Cambridge: Cambridge University Press.

Fish, S. K. and P. R. Fish. 1994. "Prehistoric Desert Farmers of the Southwest." *Annual Review of Anthropology* 23:83–108.

Ford, R. I. 1981. "Gardening and Farming Before A.D. 1000: Patterns of Prehistoric Cultivation North of Mexico." *Journal of Ethnobiology* 1(1):6–27.

Fowler, M. L. 1969. *Explorations into Cahokia Archaeology.* Illinois Archaeological Survey Bulletin 7. Urbana: University of Illinois.

———. 1971. "Agriculture and Village Settlement in the North American East: The Central Mississippi Valley Area, a Case History." In *Prehistoric Agriculture,* ed. S. Struever. Garden City, NY: Natural History Press.

———. 1975. "A Pre-Columbian Urban Center on the Mississippi." *Scientific American* 233(2):93–101.

Fritz, G. 1990. "Multiple Ways to Farming in Precontact Eastern North America." *Journal of World Prehistory* 4(4):387–436.

Glassow, M. A. 1980. *Prehistoric Agricultural Development in the Northern Southwest: A Study in Changing Patterns of Land Use.* Socorro, NM: Ballena Press.

Gumerman, G. J., ed. 1988. *The Anasazi in a Changing Environment.* Cambridge: Cambridge University Press.

Haury, E. W. 1976. *The Hohokam Desert Farmers and Craftsmen.* Tucson: University of Arizona Press.

Hegmon, M. 2005. "Beyond the Mold: Questions of Inequality in Southwest Villages." In *North American Archaeology,* ed. T. R. Pauketat and D. D. Loren, pp. 212–234. Malden, MA: Blackwell Publishing.

Hill, J. N. 1970. *Broken K Pueblo: Prehistoric Social Organization in the American Southwest.* Tucson: University of Arizona Press.

Hines, P. 1977. "On Social Organization in the Middle Mississippian—States or Chiefdoms?" *Current Anthropology* 18:337–338.

Houart, G. L. 1971. *Koster—A Stratified Archaic Site in the Illinois Valley.* Springfield: Illinois State Museum Reports of Investigations, No. 22.

Iseminger, W. R. 1996. "Mighty Cahokia." *Archaeology* 49(3):30–37.

Jennings, J. D. 1974. *Prehistory of North America,* 2nd ed. New York: McGraw-Hill.

Jett, S. C., and P. B. Moyle. 1986. "The Exotic Origins of Fishes Depicted on Prehistoric Mimbres Pottery from New Mexico." *American Antiquity* 51(4):688–720.

Kantner, J. 1996. "Political Competition Among the Chaco Anasazi of the American Southwest." *Journal of Anthropological Archaeology* 15:41–105.

Keegan, W. F., ed. 1987. *Emergent Horticultural Economies of the Eastern Woodlands.* Occasional Paper No. 7. Carbondale, IL: Center for Archaeological Investigations, Southern Illinois University.

Lekson, S. H. 2005. "Chaco and Paquimé: Complexity, History, Landscape." In *North American Archaeology,* ed. T. R. Pauketat and D. D. Loren, pp. 235–272. Malden, MA: Blackwell Publishing.

Lightfoot, R. G., and G. M. Feinman. 1982. "Social Differentiation and Leadership Development in Early Pithouse Villages in the Mogollon Region of the American Southwest." *American Antiquity* 47:64–81.

Lynott, M. J., T. W. Boutton, J. E. Price, and D. E. Nelson. 1986. "Stable Carbon Isotopic Evidence for Maize Agriculture in Southeast Missouri and Northeast Arkansas." *American Antiquity* 51(1):51–65.

Madsen, D., and D. Rhode, eds. 1995. *Across the West: Human Population Movement and the Expansion of the Numa.* Salt Lake City: University of Utah Press.

Marquardt, W. H. 1985. "Complexity and Scale in the Study of Fisher-Gatherer-Hunters: An Example from the Eastern United States." In *Prehistoric Hunter-Gatherers: The Emergence of Cultural Complexity*, ed. T. D. Price and J. A. Brown. Orlando, FL: Academic Press.

Mathien, F. J., and R. H. McGuire, eds. 1986. *Ripples in the Chichimec Sea: New Considerations of Southwestern-Mesoamerican Interactions*. Carbondale: Southern Illinois University Press.

Mabry, J. B. 1999. "Las Capas and Early Irrigation Farming." *Archaeology Southwest* 13:14.

McGuire, R. H. 1992. *Death, Society, and Ideology in a Hohokam Community*. Boulder, CO: Westview Press.

McGuire, R. H., and M. B. Schiffer. 1982. *Hohokam and Patayan: Prehistory of Southwestern Arizona*. New York: Academic Press.

McGuire, R. H., and M. B. Schiffer. 1983. "A Theory of Architectural Design." *Journal of Anthropological Archaeology* 2:277–303.

Mehrer, M. W. 1995. *Cahokia's Countryside: Household Archaeology, Settlement, Patterns, and Social Power*. Dekalb: Northern Illinois University Press.

Milanich, J. T., and C. H. Fairbanks. 1987. *Florida Archaeology*. New York: Academic Press.

Mills, B. J. 2002. "Recent Research on Chaco: Changing Views on Economy, Ritual, and Society." *Journal of Archaeological Research* 10(1):65–117.

Milner, G. 1990. "The Late Prehistoric Cahokia Cultural System of the Mississippi River Valley: Foundations, Florescence, and Fragmentation." *Journal of World Prehistory* 4(1):1–44.

Minnis, P. E. 1985. *Social Adaptation to Food Stress*. Chicago: University of Chicago Press.

———. 1992. "Earliest Plant Cultivation in the Desert Borderlands of North America." In *The Origins of Agriculture*, ed. C. W. Cowan and P. J. Watson. Washington, DC: Smithsonian Institution Press.

Morse, D. F., and P. A. Morse. 1983. *Archaeology of the Central Mississippi Valley*. New York: Academic Press.

Muller, J. 1986. *Archaeology of the Lower Ohio River Valley*. New York: Academic Press.

Nassaney, M. S. 1992. "Communal Societies and the Emergence of Elites in the Prehistoric American Southeast." In *Lords of the Southeast: Social Inequality and the Native Elites of Southeastern North America*, ed. A. W. Barker and T. R. Pauketat, pp. 111–143. Washington, D.C.: Archeological Papers of the American Anthropological Association, No. 3.

Nelson, M. C., and M. Hegmon. 2001. "Abandonment Is Not as It Seems: An Approach to the Relationship Between Site and Regional Abandonment." *American Antiquity* 66(2):213–235.

O'Brien, M. J. 1987. "Sedentism, Population Growth, and Resource Selection in the Woodland Midwest: A Review of Coevolutionary Developments." *Current Anthropology* 28(2):177–197.

Pauketat, T. R. 2004. *Ancient Cahokia and the Mississippians*. New York: Cambridge University Press.

Pauketat, T., and T. Emerson. 1991. "The Ideology of Authority and the Power of the Pot." *American Anthropologist* 93(4):919–941.

Peebles, C. S. 1977. "Moundville and Surroundings Sites: Some Structural Considerations of Mortuary Practices, II." In *Approaches to the Social Dimensions of Mortuary Practices*, ed. J. A. Brown. Washington, D.C.: Society for American Archaeology Memoir, No. 25.

Phillips, J., and J. Brown, eds. 1983. *Archaic Hunter-Gatherers in the Midwest*. Orlando, FL: Academic Press.

Porter, J. W. 1969. *The Mitchell Site and Prehistoric Exchange Systems at Cahokia: A.D. 1000–300*. Illinois Archaeological Survey Bulletin, No. 7. Urbana: University of Illinois.

Powell, S. 1983. *Mobility and Adaptation: The Anasazi of Black Mesa, Arizona*. Carbondale: Southern Illinois University Press.

Price, T. D., and G. M. Feinman, eds. 1995. *Foundations of Social Inequality*. New York: Plenum Press.

Prufer, O. H. 1964. "The Hopewell Cult." *Scientific American* 211:90–102.

Ramenofsky, A. F. 1987. *Vectors of Death: The Archaeology of European Contact*. Albuquerque: University of New Mexico Press.

Redman, C. L. 1993. *People of the Tonto Rim: Archaeological Discovery in Prehistoric Arizona*. Washington, DC: Smithsonian Institution Press.

Reid, J. J., and D. E. Doyel, eds. 1986. *Emil W. Haury's Prehistory of the American Southwest*. Tucson: University of Arizona Press.

Rice, G. E. 1975. "A Systemic Explanation of a Change in Mogollon Settlement Patterns." Unpublished doctoral dissertation, University of Washington.

Riley, T. J., R. Edging, and J. Rossen. 1990. "Cultigens in Prehistoric Eastern North America." *Current Anthropology* 31(5):525–541.

Rindos, D. 1984. *The Origins of Agriculture: An Evolutionary Perspective*. New York: Academic Press.

Rothschild, N. A. 1979. "Mortuary Behavior and Social Organization at Indian Knoll and Dickson Mounds." *American Antiquity* 44:658–675.

Simmons, A. H. 1986. "New Evidence for the Early Use of Cultigens in the American Southwest." *American Antiquity* 51(1):73–89.

Smith, B. 1974. "Middle Mississippi Exploitation of Animal Populations—A Predictive Model." *American Antiquity* 39:274–291.

———. 1985. "The Role of *Chenopodium* as a Domesticate in the Pre-Maize Garden System of the Eastern United States." *Southeastern Archaeology* 4:51–72.

———. 1986. "The Archaeology of the Southeastern United States: From Dalton to de Soto, 10,500–500 B.P." *Advances in World Archaeology* 5:1–92.

———. 1992. "Prehistoric Plant Husbandry in Eastern North America." In *The Origins of Agriculture: An International Perspective*, ed. C. W. Cowan and P. J. Watson, pp. 101–119. Washington, DC: Smithsonian Institution Press.

Smith, B. D., ed. 1990. *The Mississippian Emergence*. Washington, DC: Smithsonian Institution Press.

———. 1992. *The Rivers of Change: Essays on Early Agriculture in Eastern North America*. Washington, DC: Smithsonian Institution Press.

Spielmann, K. A., M. J. Schoeninger, and K. Moore. 1990. "Plains-Pueblo Interdependence and Human Diet at Pecos Pueblo, New Mexico." *American Antiquity* 55(4):745–765.

Steponaitis, V. P. 1983. *Ceramics, Chronology, and Community Patterns: An Archaeological Study at Moundville*. New York: Academic Press.

Stoltman, J. B. 1983. "Ancient Peoples of the Upper Mississippi River Valley." In *Historic Lifestyles of the Upper Mississippi River Valley*, ed. J. Wozniak. New York: University Press of America.

———. 1986. *Prehistoric Mound Builders of the Mississippi Valley*. Davenport, IA: Putnam Museum.

Struever, S., and K. D. Vickery. 1973. "The Beginnings of Cultivation in the Midwest-Riverine Area of the United States." *American Anthropologist* 75:1197–1220.

Tainter, J. 1975. "Social Inference and Mortuary Practices: An Experiment in Numerical Classification." *World Archaeology* 7:1–15.

Upham, S. 1994. "Nomads of the Desert West: A Shifting Continuum in Prehistory." *Journal of World Prehistory* 8(2):113–168.

Upham, S., K. G. Lightfoot, and G. M. Feinman. 1981. "Explaining Socially Determined Ceramic Distributions in the Prehistoric Southwest." *American Antiquity* 46:822–836.

Utah Museum of Natural History. 1995. *Treading in the Past: Sandals of the Anasazi*. Salt Lake City: University of Utah Press.

Vivian, G. 1990. *The Chacoan Prehistory of the San Juan Basin*. San Diego: Academic Press.

Vogel, J. C., and N. J. Van Der Merwe. 1977. "Isotopic Evidence for Early Maize Cultivation in New York State." *American Antiquity* 42:238–242.

Washburn, D. R. 1975. "The American Southwest." In *North America*, ed. S. Gorenstein et al. New York: St. Martin's Press.

Watson, P. J. 1974. *Archeology of the Mammoth Cave Area*. New York: Academic Press.

Webb, C. H. 1977. *The Poverty Point Culture*. Baton Rouge: The School of Geoscience, Louisiana State University.

Whalen, M. 1981. "Cultural-Ecological Aspects of the Pithouse-to-Pueblo Transition in a Portion of the Southwest." *American Antiquity* 46:75–91.

Willey, G. R. 1966. *An Introduction to American Archaeology, Vol. 1: North and Middle America*. Englewood Cliffs, NJ: Prentice-Hall.

Wills, W. H. 1996. "The Transition from the Preceramic to Ceramic Period in the Mogollon Highlands of Western New Mexico." *Journal of Field Archaeology* 23(3):335–359.

Wills, W. H., and R. D. Leonard, eds. 1995. *The Ancient Southwestern Community: Models and Methods for the Study of Prehistoric Social Organization*. Albuquerque: University of New Mexico Press.

Woosley, A. I., and J. C. Ravesloot, eds. 1995. *Culture and Contact: Charles C. DiPeso's Gran Chichimeca*. Albuquerque: University of New Mexico Press.

Yerkes, R. W. 1988. "The Woodland and Mississippian Traditions in the Prehistory of Midwestern North America." *Journal of World Prehistory* 2(3):307–358.

NOTES

1. Smith, *The Rivers of Change: Essays on Early Agriculture in Eastern North America*, pp. 102–106.
2. Ibid., p. 106.
3. Smith, "Prehistoric Plant Husbandry in Eastern North America," p. 106.
4. Fritz, "Multiple Ways to Farming in Precontact Eastern North America," p. 399.
5. Smith, *The Rivers of Change: Essays on Early Agriculture in Eastern North America*, p. 107.
6. Smith, "Prehistoric Plant Husbandry in Eastern North America," pp. 107–108.
7. O'Brien, "Sedentism, Population Growth, and Resource Selection in the Woodland Midwest: A Review of Coevolutionary Developments."
8. Rindos, *The Origins of Agriculture*.

9. O'Brien, "Sedentism, Population Growth, and Resource Selection in the Woodland Midwest: A Review of Coevolutionary Developments," p. 186; also see Keegan, ed., *Emergent Horticultural Economies of the Eastern Woodlands.*

10. Braun, "Pots as Tools," and "Comment on M. J. O'Brien, 'Sedentism, Population Growth, and Resource Selection in the Woodland Midwest: A Review of Coevolutionary Developments.'"

11. Braun, "Comment on M. J. O'Brien, 'Sedentism, Population Growth, and Resource Selection in the Woodland Midwest: A Review of Coevolutionary Developments,'" p. 189.

12. Fowler, "Agriculture and Village Settlement in the North American East: The Central Mississippi Valley Area, a Case History."

13. Price, and Feinman, eds., *Foundations of Social Inequality.*

14. Stoltman, *Prehistoric Mound Builders of the Mississippi Valley*; Marquardt, "Complexity and Scale in the Study of Fisher-Gatherer-Hunters"; Rothschild, "Mortuary Behavior and Social Organization at Indian Knoll and Dickson Mounds."

15. Yerkes, "The Woodland and Mississippian Traditions in the Prehistory of Midwestern North America," p. 315.

16. Fiedel, *Prehistory of the Americas*, p. 111.

17. Fagan, *Ancient North America*, p. 331.

18. Ibid.

19. Murphy, *An Archaeological History of the Hocking Valley*, pp. 161–163; Yerkes, "The Woodland and Mississippian Traditions in the Prehistory of Midwestern North America," p. 317.

20. Yerkes, "The Woodland and Mississippian Traditions in the Prehistory of Midwestern North America," p. 317.

21. Brown, "Long-Term Trends to Sedentism and the Emergence of Complexity in the American Midwest," p. 219.

22. Coe, Snow, and Benson, *Atlas of Ancient America*, p. 50.

23. Bush, "A Ceramic Analysis of the Late Adena Buckmeyer Site"; Baby and Langlois, "Prehistoric Agriculture," p. 3.

24. Tainter, "Social Inference and Mortuary Practices: An Experiment in Numerical Classification."

25. Jennings, *Prehistory of North America*, p. 232.

26. Brose and Greber, *Hopewell Archaeology: The Chillicothe Conference.*

27. Yerkes, "The Woodland and Mississippian Traditions in the Prehistory of Midwestern North America," p. 323.

28. Braun, "The Social and Technological Roots of 'Late Woodland.'"

29. For varied considerations of Mississippian America, see Smith, ed., *The Mississippian Emergence.*

30. Stoltman, "Ancient Peoples of the Upper Mississippi River Valley," pp. 232–233.

31. Lynott et al., "Stable Carbon Isotopic Evidence for Maize Agriculture in Southeast Missouri and Northeast Arkansas."

32. Reviewed by Brown, Kerber, and Winters, in Smith ed., *The Mississippian Emergence.* See also Nassaney, "Communal Societies and the Emergence of Elites in the Prehistoric American Southeast."

33. Porter, *The Mitchell Site and Prehistoric Exchange Systems at Cahokia: A.D. 1000–300.* See also Yerkes, "The Woodland and Mississippian Traditions in the Prehistory of Midwestern North America."

34. Iseminger, "Mighty Cahokia," pp. 34–35.

35. Pauketat and Emerson, "The Ideology of Authority and the Power of the Pot," p. 935.

36. Milner, "The Late Prehistoric Cahokia Cultural System of the Mississippi River Valley: Foundations, Florescence, and Fragmentation," p. 2; also see Smith, "The Archaeology of the Southeastern United States: From Dalton to de Soto, 10,500–500 B.P."

37. Peebles, "Moundville and Surrounding Sites."

38. Steponaitis, *Ceramics, Chronology, and Community Patterns: An Archaeological Study at Moundville.*

39. Ramenofsky, *Vectors of Death.*

40. Smith, "Middle Mississippi Exploitation of Animal Populations—A Predictive Model."

41. Dickson, "The Yanomamo of the Mississippi Valley? Some Reflections on Larson . . . Gibson . . . and Mississippi Period Warfare in the Southeastern United States."

42. Fagan, *Ancient North America*, p. 338.

43. Mehrer, *Cahokia's Countryside: Household Archaeology, Settlement Patterns, and Social Power*; Pauketat, *Ancient Cahokia and the Mississippians.*

44. Le Page du Pratz.

45. Ramenofsky, *Vectors of Death.*

46. Minnis, *Social Adaptation to Food Stress.*

47. See, for example, Redman, *People of the Tonto Rim: Archaeological Discovery in Prehistoric Arizona.*

48. For example, Cordell and Gumerman, eds., *Dynamics of Southwest Prehistory*; Wills and Leonard, eds., *The Ancient Southwestern Community: Models and Methods for the Study of Prehistoric Social Organization.*

49. Woosley and Ravesloot, *Culture and Contact*.
50. Upham, "Nomads of the Desert West."
51. Cordell, *Prehistory of the Southwest*; Simmons, "New Evidence for the Early Use of Cultigens in the American Southwest."
52. Fish and Fish, "Prehistoric Desert Farmers of the Southwest," p. 85.
53. Minnis, "Earliest Plant Cultivation in the Desert Borderlands of North America," pp. 128–129.
54. Bayman, "The Hohokam of Southwest North America."
55. Haury, *The Hohokam Desert Farmers and Craftsmen*.
56. Bayman, "The Hohokam of Southwest North America," p. 266.
57. See Bayman, "The Hohokam of Southwest North America," for a discussion of the competing definitions of what constitutes "Hohokam Culture."
58. Mabry, "Las Capas and Early Irrigation Farming."
59. These Native Americans were fomerly called the Papago in various publications.
60. Crown and Fish, "Gender and Status in the Hohokam Pre-Classic to Classic Transition"; Hegmon, "Beyond the Mold: Questions of Inequality in Southwest Villages."
61. Bayman, "The Hohokam of Southwest North America," p. 271.
62. Ibid.
63. Ibid., pp. 275–276, 283–284.
64. Jett and Moyle, "The Exotic Origins of Fishes Depicted on Prehistoric Mimbres Pottery from New Mexico."
65. Lightfoot and Feinman, "Social Differentiation and Leadership Development in Early Pithouse Villages in the Mogollon Region of the American Southwest," p. 81.
66. Minnis, *Social Adaptation to Food Stress*.
67. Whalen, "Cultural-Ecological Aspects of the Pithouse-to-Pueblo Transition in a Portion of the Southwest."
68. McGuire and Schiffer, "A Theory of Architectural Design."
69. "Chaco and Paquimé: Complexity, History, Landscape."
70. Ibid., p. 264.
71. See, for example, Nelson and Hegmon, "Abandonment Is Not as It Seems: An Approach to the Relationship Between Site and Regional Abandonment."
72. The "Ancestral Pueblo" classification has been used by some scholars in recent years to replace the term "Anasazi," which is regarded by many modern Puebloan groups as an inaccurate descriptor for their ancestors.
73. Powell, *Mobility and Adaptation: The Anasazi of Black Mesa, Arizona*.
74. Dickson, "Settlement Pattern Stability and Change in the Middle Northern Rio Grande Region, New Mexico: A Test of Some Hypotheses."
75. Washburn, "The American Southwest," p. 114; but see Rice, "A Systematic Explanation of a Change in Mogollon Settlement Patterns."
76. Lekson, "Chaco and Paquimé: Complexity, History, Landscape," p. 243.
77. Vivian, *The Chacoan Prehistory of the San Juan Basin*.
78. Lekson, "Chaco and Paquimé: Complexity, History, Landscape," pp. 247–248.
79. Betancourt et al., "Prehistoric Long-Distance Transport of Construction Beams, Chaco Canyon, New Mexico."
80. Ibid., pp. 244–246.
81. "Recent Research on Chaco: Changing Views on Economy, Ritual, and Society."
82. Ibid., p. 97.
83. Lekson, "Chaco and Paquimé: Complexity, History, Landscape," p. 247.

Prehistory in Perspective

[W]hat's past is prologue.

Shakespeare[1]

Having followed in this book our past, from the three-million-year-old hominin footprints of Laetoli through the sixteenth-century A.D. European invasion of the Americas, the reader is invited to return to the questions posed in the first chapter: Does the world's archaeological record tell us why history has turned out as it has? Can we predict our future from our past? Does the human past appear to have some "meaning" that transcends the sum of the individual lives of the billions of people who have comprised humanity? Who "owns" the past, in the sense of who gathers evidence about it and interprets it, and decides how the past is preserved and presented?

These are, of course, ancient questions, and by now the reader will not expect an ultimate answer from this book. It is perhaps a bad pedagogical tactic to raise questions, review the evidence, and then conclude weakly that "we don't really know," but most contemporary archaeologists find themselves in this predicament. The world's archaeological record seems to provide a general sense of potentially important causes of various ancient cultural changes, but there is no single, powerful, comprehensive explanation of the past. Thus, rather than demonstrating the power and accuracy of any specific models of culture and history, we have simply explored the limitations and potentials of some of the more obvious ideas about the past. Moreover, as we have seen, the very possibility of a unified, objective, "scientific" understanding or explanation of the past has been rejected by some archaeologists and questioned by most.

OUR INTELLECTUAL HERITAGE

One of the earliest casualties of our review here was the Enlightenment and nineteenth-century view of mechanical cultural evolutionism, with its belief in the gradual improvement of people and their societies, generation after generation, as we "progressed" from rude savagery to the better, brighter world of industry, liberalism, and democracy. The Victorian proponents of cultural evolutionism—who number among their ranks some of the greatest intellects of all time—can be forgiven, perhaps, for this belief in progress because they lived in an age of marvelous change. Just Darwin's insights alone revolutionized the way people viewed the world and themselves. It is not surprising that people of the nineteenth century believed in the possibility of a science of history, for throughout their lives they saw "progress" in almost every kind of human endeavor. Consider, for example, the changes in both technology and dominant ideologies witnessed by someone like Oliver Wendell Holmes (1841–1935), father of the great American jurist: Holmes wrote his senior thesis at Harvard in the provincial America of the decade before Abraham Lincoln's election to the presidency; he then served in the Civil War; in later life he broadcast on the radio during Franklin Roosevelt's presidency.[2] Holmes and others of his generation saw a world transformed by science and technology in a way few other generations have experienced.

But, as Simone Weil said: "The great mistake of the nineteenth century was to assume that by walking straight on one mounted into the air." Two of the nineteenth century's greatest proponents of progressive evolution, Herbert Spencer and Karl Marx, today lie across from each other in death, on opposites sides of a gravel path in London's Highgate Cemetery. Herbert Spencer is now remembered by only a few, and even Karl Marx—whose ideas transformed the twentieth century—will probably soon join Spencer in being more cited than read, and increasingly unregarded.

"Change" is scientific, "progress" is ethical;
change is indubitable, whereas progress is a
matter of controversy.

Bertrand Russell[3]

It is difficult to discard entirely the notion of history as describing a "progressive" trajectory, leading to ourselves, and this idea is embedded in many cultures. Our review of the archaeological records reveals, however, that instead of a smooth rising curve of social, physical, technological, and moral evolution, our past has been a series of fitful cycles, where social forms and technologies have reached their limits of growth and then failed, to be replaced by new social forms and technologies, more complex in some ways than their predecessors, but neither permanent nor "better" in any evident moral or philosophical sense. Clearly, there is nothing in the archaeological record to indicate that we are on a straight path to an earthly paradise. Today, many people are "involuntary vegetarians,"[4] whose diet, morbidity and mortality rates, and general standard of living probably compare poorly with those of most ancient hunting-and-gathering bands. Even in the most industrialized countries, the vast majority labors longer for sustenance than did many of the people of prehistory. Moreover, the misery, poverty, wars, and generic atrocities of our current world make it difficult to argue that our past is one of "moral evolution."[5]

But this lack of "progress" in the Victorian sense should not be taken as a complete indictment of the general notion of history as reflecting long-term directional change. Despite repeated local reversals and long plateaus, the past three million years can be seen as directional change in many aspects of humanity, from average brain size to the complexity of cultures, as measured by changes in the size, differentiation, and interdependence of social, political, and economic systems—and by such basic dynamics as the ability to divert energy to human use, and the degree of economic interdependence of the world's people.

Perhaps nowhere in the human past is there more convincing evidence of powerful general determinants of cultural evolution operating than in the appearance of early civilizations. As noted in chapter 7, the six earliest civilizations seem independently to have evolved in extraordinarily similar ways and with nearly identical characteristics. All were based economically on comparatively productive agricultural systems, the "surplus" production of which was expropriated by elites. All evolved national religious cults, monumental architecture, complex bureaucratic hierarchies, and many other character-istics in common.

Given this, the world's archaeological record cannot be understood accurately as the reflection simply of the vagaries of human intentions or of unrelated and random cultural constructs. We have identified many patterns and parallels. Cross-cutting cultural developments all over the world are the same essential expressions of religion, warfare, population growth, emerging social stratification, and evolving economic productivity.

But when we try to dissect the causal processes that produced the past, our explanations seem incomplete and simplistic. We have seen, for example, that human population growth has been correlated with almost every cultural transformation, from initial tool use to the appearance of industrial empires. This relationship may even be thought of as possibly causal: The rate of technological change might be linked simply to the number of minds available to solve problems and produce innovations. But this is clearly an incomplete explanation of our past. Time and time again the archaeological record discloses that the relationship between population growth and cultural change is neither consistent nor direct, and it remains for archaeologists to demonstrate the direct causal connections—if there are any—between the world's increasing population size and the specific, crucial transformations of prehistory and history.

This inability even to understand the impact of basic demographic factors on cultural change does not augur well for a deterministic science of culture and history, for basic demography would seem to be potentially the most easily understood aspect of change over time in the human past, compared to changes in technology, society, and ideology.

To consider another example of the complexity of unraveling the causal patterns of the past, the recurrent nature of human interspecies violence—from the cannibalism of some of our early hominin ancestors to the war in Iraq—clearly suggests that conflict is an evolutionary mechanism of considerable power; conflict must do something for societies, or it would be difficult to explain its depressing ubiquity in human affairs (Figure 16.1). But here, too, the actual mechanisms in most past societies whereby conflict interacted with other variables to produce cultural change are unknown.

It is the nature of evolutionary patterns that they only appear to have a direction when one looks backward. As many have observed, "real life seems to have no plots," and in the same sense, evolutionary accounts have no plots, except in retrospect. The first hunter-gatherers who made wild wheat part of their diet, for example, could have had no inkling their activities would eventually lead to vast stretches of North America being devoted to highly mechanized cultivation of distant genetic descendants of those wild Southwest Asian cereals.

We can look back and discern many similar evolutionary sequences in the past. To identify a long span of connections that link developments, however, is not the same as explaining history—no general theory has won universal acceptance. Most archaeologists employ a vaguely evolutionary perspective: They assume that cultural innovations are constantly arising in human societies and that some of these innovations confer an adaptive advantage and are "fixed" within cultural systems and perpetuated until they too are

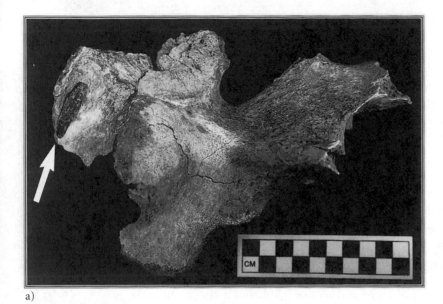

a)

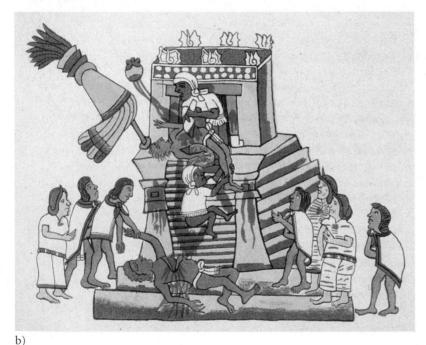

b)

FIGURE 16.1   Examples of violence throughout time a) a stone point embedded in human bone; b) a depiction of a human sacrifice; c) a suicide bomber.

outmoded and replaced. Many archaeologists also adopt a rather "vulgar" materialist determinism in that they assume that cultural forms and dynamics are to some extent constrained and shaped by technological, environmental, and economic variables. Great cities like Babylon could not have arisen in pre-industrial Alaska, and there seems to be no great mystery that the first productive agricultural economies appeared in fertile, easily farmed river valleys close to the natural habitat of the wild ancestors of domesticated plants. Similarly, contrasting cultural forms, such as the social egalitarianism of hunters and gatherers in the Pleistocene and the rigid social stratification of emerging states, are generally understood in part as results of their respective economic bases. Nonetheless, many contemporary archaeologists see such links between primary economics and environments and socioeconomic and political systems as only the starting points of analysis. Most now recognize that even if they are able to demonstrate a strong correlation in time and space between, say, population growth, warfare, and urbanism, they will still not have explained in a powerful way any of these factors or their relationships to each other.

In the face of these analytical ambiguities, many contemporary archaeologists have become profoundly sociological and behavioral in their theoretical approach, in the sense that they have focused on the ways people and societies have culturally constructed the specifics of their socioeconomic and political systems and ideologies. In previous chapters we have reviewed many attempts to analyze and interpret the social structures, dynamics, and ideologies of extinct societies. A great variety of sociological and political theories have been developed to explain how different cultures used the same organizational mechanisms to produce the worldwide and historical patterns we see in power relations, ethnicity, gender relationships, social reproduction, and so on.

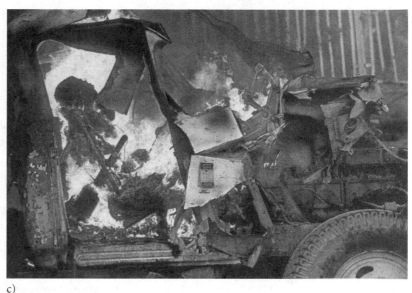

c)

FIGURE 16.1   (*cont'd*)

In contrast to these approaches, as we noted in previous chapters, other scholars have argued that it is not possible to formulate a true science of the behavior of extinct peoples and that the long chains of inference that must be constructed to link the existing archaeological remains with such concepts as "class conflict" and "political domination" cannot be measured in the archaeological record and treated scientifically. Robert Dunnell argues that archaeology can never be a science of behavior because behavior does not exist—artifacts exist—and because any science must deal with phenomena, a scientific archaeology must deal with artifacts, not with inferred behavior. Yet such a science of artifacts cannot be like physics, Dunnell has argued, because the artifactual record is primarily one created by evolutionary processes, in contrast to the uniform timeless laws that govern the physical universe.

Dunnell and numerous other scholars[6] are investigating applications of Darwinian evolutionary theory to history and humanity, and recent advances in such related fields as "complexity theory" and "chaos theory," and in studies of artificial intelligence, may eventually have great impact on the theory of archaeology. One interesting current trend in these forms of evolutionary analyses involves nonlinear systems analyses and the "emergent properties" of complex systems.[7] The most vivid example is that of biological organisms, such as ourselves, in which somehow there is a complete set of information in our genes such that as we are formed from the division of a single cell, subsequent cells are formed into skin, hair, bones, blood, and all the other tissues and organs that comprise us. We cannot, however, draw an accurate and direct analogy between the formation of a human being and the evolution of an ancient state. In each of these systems there is a growing complexity that seems in some sense inherent in the simpler earlier stages of these processes of evolution—a "Lamarckian" sense of evolution, in other words, instead of simply a Darwinian one.

But, as we have noted (chapter 1), attempts to make archaeology into a Darwinian or positivist science of any kind have been dismissed by other archaeologists, who reject the entire notion that "science" has any application to the explanation of the past—arguing that archaeology can never be a neutral, value-free, empirical science of artifacts. As discussed in chapter 1, the post-processualists[8] and others have contended that, just as one cannot assign a definitive single meaning to a text, one cannot make an empirically verifiable and definitive interpretation of the archaeological record. We create the past, they argue, and our interpretations of the past are limited by, and arise out of, our own cultural context. As discussed in chapter 1 and elsewhere, some contemporary archaeologists believe that there is no one "past;" rather, there is a continuing dialectical process in which each person confronts the past and comes to a unique understanding of it.

The general perspective taken in this book—a "holistic" approach, to use Bruce Trigger's phrase (chapter 1), or "cognitive processualism," to use Colin Renfrew and John Bintliff's term[9] (chapter 1)—may seem like a sensible moderate course. In this kind of archaeology one can use any analytical techniques that seem to increase understanding of the past, and one need not shrink from nonscientific interpretations of ancient ideologies, on the one hand, or abandon scientific rigor in evaluating evidence and competing hypotheses, on the other. But to many post-processualists, positivist science has no place in archaeology beyond technical applications (for example, radiocarbon dating), and to Darwinian evolutionists and other scientifically inclined archaeologists, the nonscientific interpretations of ancient ideologies and "meanings" may be a form of personal expression or art, but it is not scientific analysis.

These theoretical debates will no doubt continue for many years to come. In the meantime most archaeologists will do what they have always done, whatever their theoretical perspective, and that is to study the remains of the past—struggling to understand what they meant to the people of the past as well as what they mean to the archaeologist.

Bill Nye described Wagner's music as "better than it sounds," and in a way archaeology is like this: Its limitations are obvious, but its achievements are also obvious—we understand human antiquity today to an extent unimaginable just a century ago.

LESSONS OF PREHISTORY

To think of time—of all that retrospection,
To think of to-day, and the ages continued henceforward.
Have you guess'd you yourself would not continue?
Have you dreaded these earth-beetles?
Is to-day nothing? is the beginningless past nothing?
If the future is nothing they are just as surely nothing.
Walt Whitman[10]

It would be gratifying if we could extract from our review of world prehistory some important predictions about the future of humankind, but, as we have noted, archaeology should not be considered a predictive science. It is not that we cannot look at the past and extrapolate trends we see into the future. It is that there is no necessity to these trends: Evolutionary histories are what happened, not what had to happen or what has to happen, and they are unique.

This is especially true when we consider the long-range future, particularly now that humanity has instruments with which to terminate all life on this planet. But even should we survive as a species for millions of future generations, the virtuosity of culture as an adaptive device makes extrapolation into the far future an act of either ignorance or hubris. None of the human ancestors who strolled through Olduvai Gorge some Sunday morning two million years ago could have had even the dimmest vision of the gaudy technology and kaleidoscopic social and political forms of twentieth-century civilization, and this civilization was not a necessary outcome of our Olduvai forebears.

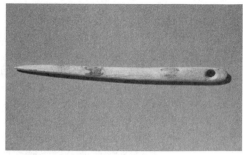

FIGURE 16.2 An eyed bone needle from the Upper Paleolithic site at Creswell Crags, England.

No student of the past, however, can overlook the persistent, powerful trends that tie the present—and perhaps the future—to the past. These trends extend beyond the simple cumulative increases in world population density and the technology of energy capture. The increasing functional differentiation and integration of the world's economies and societies can be seen in any food market, any airport. It may seem like a tenuous link between the development of, say, tailored clothing in the Upper Paleolithic (chapter 4) (Figure 16.2), which allowed human radiation into more demanding environments, and today's rapidly mutating and world-invading Internet, but they are both part of an increasing "complexity" of human society and adaptation.

Nor are these changes just technological. In chapter 1 the Darwinian revolution in world-views and life-views was discussed, but there is no reason to suspect that any ideology will be the final, definitive perspective for all humanity. Consider, for example, religion. We will let those with more confidence in their omniscience than we have pronounce upon the ultimate nature of human religiosity; it is always sobering to recollect that neither the study of world prehistory nor any other art or science has much to offer in the way of a reason why we are out here, on a small planet in an incomprehensibly infinite universe, and to all evidence very much alone.

Religion and Cultural Values

I remember, I remember
The fir-trees dark and high;
I used to think their slender tops
Were close against the sky:
It was a childish ignorance,
But now 'tis little joy
To know I'm further off from heav'n
Than when I was a boy.

Thomas Hood

Taken solely on the level of its effects on other aspects of culture, religion appears to operate principally as a highly adaptable, thermodynamically efficient mechanism of social control. We have in the archaeological and historical record an irrefutable demonstration that there is no act so repellent—be it sacrificing thousands of one's own countrymen to the gods or incinerating hundreds of thousands of one's "enemies"—that it cannot be made not only acceptable, but entirely virtuous within the context of religious systems. The exploitation of the many by the few to build massive pyramids, the complete catalogue of sexual "perversions," the avoidance of this or that food—all have been incorporated into state religions with no more difficulty than Christian faith, hope, and charity.

Recent wars illustrate that, despite the apparent decline of formal theistic religions in some parts of the industrialized world, the power of ideology to set societies into conflict has not changed. These conflicts may stem in part from long-term underlying economic forces, but no observer of modern politics can help but be profoundly impressed by the awesome power of ideas about history and ethnicity to stimulate both genocide against one's perceived enemies and identification with one's kin.

The late-twentieth-century societies of the West are almost obsessed with social and economic inequalities, and it would be significant if the study of world prehistory had anything to tell us about the future of differences in class, gender, and ethnicity. But the lessons of the archaeological record concerning the origins and significance of social and economic inequalities are not as clear as they might seem at first glance. It is inescapable that there has never been an economically powerful, sociopolitically complex society—especially the supposedly "classless" societies of Marxist Russia and China—that was not also stratified into groups having differential access to wealth, power, and prestige. It remains to be demonstrated, however, that cultural functional complexity and integration are inextricably linked to social stratification. It would appear that in the past the complexity of managing an economy based on agriculture, and later agriculture in combination with fossil fuels, could work effectively only through administrative and social hierarchies and class-structured societies. These social and cultural forms allowed great stability and predictability because people's functional roles in society and their contributions and consumption of goods and services were largely determined by the class into which they were born. But if in future centuries population densities are stabilized and perhaps reduced, if control of energy and food sources is decentralized and the production of material wealth made highly automated, it would seem at least possible that human societies will someday approximate the "social justice" of the late Pleistocene.

Perhaps the archaeological record's bleakest implication concerning our short-term future has to do with that ambiguous concept, "the quality of life." We have already noted that today most of the world's people have a diet and standard of living in many ways inferior to that of Pleistocene hunters and gatherers, and although medical technology, solar power, and contraceptives may change this by bringing the Western industrial standard of living to all parts of the world, this is by no means a certainty. Even given sufficient energy and rapid industrialization, fundamental questions remain about the short-term prospects for the quality of life on this planet. In the wealthiest countries today the abundance of luxury goods seems to convey a sense of ease and fulfillment, but modern economics work only because the vast majority of the population are coerced or induced to spend most of their lives at hard labor. And it is not only the poorer, laboring class whose quality of life is questionable. It has been observed that a citizen of Athens in the fifth century B.C. would consider today's professionals—physicians, politicians, professors, and football players alike—to be in the main incomplete, undeveloped people whose "success" has required them to devote so much of their lives to their specialty that they are grotesquely incompetent at the oratorical, conversational, athletic, philosophical, agricultural, and aesthetic skills that the ancient Greeks, for example, would insist on as necessary components of a "whole" person.[11]

THE FUTURE OF ARCHAEOLOGY

When I was a boy of fourteen, my father was so ignorant I could hardly stand to have the old man around. But when I got to be twenty-one, I was astonished at how much the old man had learned in seven years.

Mark Twain

The energy produced by the breaking down of the atom is a very poor kind of thing. Anyone who expects a source of power from the transformation of these atoms is talking moonshine.

Ernest Rutherford (1871–1937), physicist, after he had split the atom for the first time[12]

History teaches us that it is often a fundamental mistake to extrapolate immediate experience and situations far into the future. Contemporary archaeology and the historical disciplines are in such a state of flux and ideological rivalry that we may have no sense of what these fields of inquiry will be like in a century or two.

In any case, the archaeological record is disappearing at such a rapid rate that the future of field archaeology on the problems of prehistory is very much in doubt. The worldwide wave of industrialism—the major destroyer of archaeological materials—seems destined to expand at ever-increasing speed.

Dismal as the loss of the archaeological record is, it may be that the major progress in archaeology in the next several generations will come not so much from the discovery of new bones and stones, but rather from a reconsideration of theoretical and methodological approaches and a reanalysis of existing data. We have recounted in this book the prospects of current analytical approaches, and these and other perspectives are likely to increase considerably our knowledge about our past. Does this mean that the general problem of, for example, the origins of cultural complexity will someday be as precisely solved as the formulae for making plastics? Probably not. These are very different kinds of questions with different criteria for solution. Yet, the history of science is replete with examples in which a seemingly impossible problem was not only solved but made routine: The general problems of prehistory we have discussed here may well fall into this category, to be solved in succeeding centuries in terms and with techniques that we now only dimly perceive. After all, people of only a few centuries ago no doubt would be astounded not only by our science and lush technology, but also by our knowledge of prehistory and the dynamics of culture.

*Requiem aeternam dona eis, Domine, et lux
perpetua luceat eis (Grant them eternal rest, O
Lord, and may perpetual light shine on them)
Mozart Requiem*

Requiem Mass in D. Minor (K. 624)

BIBLIOGRAPHY

Alexander, R. D. 1987. *The Biology of Moral Systems.* Hawthorne, NY: Aldine de Gruyter.

Bintliff, J. 1986. "Archaeology at the Interface: An Historical Perspective." In *Archaeology at the Interface,* ed. J. L. Bintliff and C. F. Gaffney. Oxford: BAR International Series 300.

———. 1993. "Why Indiana Jones is Smarter Than the Post-Processualists." *Norwegian Archaeological Review* 26(2):91–100.

Diamond, J. 2004. *Collapse: How Societies Choose to Fail or Succeed.* New York: Viking.

Dunnell, R. C. 1982. "Science, Social Science, and Common Sense: The Agonizing Dilemma of Modern Archaeology." *Journal of Anthropological Research* 38:1–25.

———. 1992. "Is a Scientific Archaeology Possible?" In *Metaarchaeology,* ed. L. Embre, pp. 73–97. The Netherlands: Kluwwer.

Durham, W. H. 1990. "Advances in Evolutionary Culture Theory." *Annual Review of Anthropology* 19:187–242.

Gamble, C. 1994. *Timewalkers: The Prehistory of Global Colonization.* Cambridge, MA: Harvard University Press.

Harris, M. 1977. *Cannibals and Kings: The Origins of Cultures.* New York: Random House.

Hern, W. M. 1993. "Is Human Culture Carcinogenic for Uncontrolled Population Growth and Ecological Destruction?" *Bioscience* 43(11):768–773.

Hodder, I., M. Shanks, A. Alexandri, V. Buchli, J. Carman, J. Last, and G. Lucas. 1995. *Interpreting Archaeology: Finding Meaning in the Past.* New York: Routledge.

Lansing, J. S., and J. N. Kremer. 1993. "Emergent Properties of Balinese Water Temple Networks." *American Anthropologist* 95(1):97–114.

Neiman, F. D. 1995. "Stylistic Variation in Evolutionary Perspective: Inferences from Decorative Diversity and Interassemblage Distance in Illinois Woodland Ceramic Assemblages." *American Antiquity* 60(1):7–36.

Palgrave, F. T. 1965. *The Golden Treasury,* p. 234. NY: Oxford University Press.

Pile, S. 1979. *The Book of Heroic Failure.* London: Macdonald Futura Publishers.

Russell, B. 1950. *Unpopular Essays.* New York: Simon & Schuster.

Trigger, B. 1991. "Distinguished Lecture in Archaeology: Constraint and Freedom." *American Anthropologist* 93(3):551–569.

———. 1993. *Early Civilizations: Ancient Egypt in Context.* Cairo: American University in Cairo Press.

Waldrop, M. M. 1992. *Complexity.* New York: Touchstone.

NOTES

1. Clear for 10 Shakespeare, *The Tempest,* Act II, Scene I.
2. *Brief Lives.*
3. *Unpopular Essays,* "Philosophy and Politics."
4. Harris, *Cannibals and Kings,* p. x.
5. Trigger, *Early Civilizations: Ancient Egypt in Context,* p. 110.
6. See, for example, Dunnell, "Science, Social Science, and Common Sense: The Agonizing Dilemma of Modern Archaeology," and "Is a Scientific Archaeology Possible?"; also see Neiman, "Stylistic Variation in Evolutionary Perspective: Inferences from Decorative Diversity and Interassemblage Distance in Illinois Woodland Ceramic Assemblages."
7. Lansing and Kremer ("Emergent Properties of Balinese Water Temple Networks"), for example, have published one of the first applications of these ideas to an anthropological problem, the evolution of Balinese economic systems.
8. See, for example, Hodder et al., *Interpreting Archaeology: Finding Meaning in the Past.*
9. See, for example, Bintliff, "Archaeology at the Interface," and "Why Indiana Jones Is Smarter Than the Post-Processualists."
10. From Whitman's "To Think of Time."
11. Kitto.
12. Quoted by Pile, *The Book of Heroic Failure,* p. 216.

Art Credits

FRONTISPIECE

From *Touching the Mekong* by Andrea Baldeck, reprinted by permission of University of Pennsylvania Press.

CHAPTER 1

1.1 Image of a Paleolithic site near Les Eyzies, France, courtesy the Library, American Museum of Natural History; **1.2** Collections of The New York Public Library/Rare Books Division; **1.3** Copyright: Griffith Institute, Oxford; **1.4** Copyright: Griffith Institute, Oxford; **1.5** Reprinted with the permission of Barry D. Kass; **1.6** Hirmer Fotoarchiv, Munich; **1.7** Courtesy Deborah I. Olszewski; **1.8** Neg./Trans. No. 326795, courtesy the Library, American Museum of Natural History; **1.9** Reproduced by permission of the Syndics of Cambridge University Library; **1.10** Reprinted with the permission of Hulton Archive/Getty Images, Inc.; **1.11** Courtesy Deborah I. Olszewski.

CHAPTER 2

2.1 figure on right: Courtesy Deborah I. Olszewski; **2.2** John Reader/Photo Researchers; **2.3** Courtesy Deborah I. Olszewski; **2.4** Courtesy Deborah I. Olszewski; **2.5** Courtesy Deborah I. Olszewski and the Abydos Survey for Paleolithic Sites; **2.6** Courtesy Deborah I. Olszewski and the Abydos Survey for Paleolithic Sites; **2.7** Courtesy Deborah I. Olszewski; **2.8** Reprinted with the permission of Clark Erikson; **2.9** Lennart Larsen, The National Museum of Denmark; **2.10** Reprinted with the permission of Cambridge; University Press; **2.11** Courtesy Deborah I. Olszewski; **2.12** Courtesy Deborah I. Olszewski and the Abydos Survey for Paleolithic Sites; **2.13** From F. Hole, K. V. Flannery, and J. Neely, *Prehistory and Human Ecology of the Deh Luran Plain*, Mem. Of the Museum of Anthropology, No. 1 (U. of Michigan, 1969) Fig. 15. Reproduced by permission of Museum of Anthropology Publications; **2.14** University of Pennsylvania Museum (image #S8-8995); **2.15** Photo by Pat Shipman; **2.16** Courtesy Deborah I. Olszewski; **2.17** Hirmer Fotoarchiv, Munich; **2.18** Victor R. Boswell, Jr./National Geographic Image Collection; **2.19** Courtesy Deborah I. Olszewski; **2.20** Courtesy Deborah I. Olszewski and the Abydos Survey for Paleolithic Sites; **2.21** From J. D. Jennings, *Prehistory of North America*, McGraw Hill, Inc., all rights reserved. Reproduced by permission of McGraw-Hill Book Co.; **2.22** From *Invitation to Archaeology* by James Deetz, copyright © 1967 by James Deetz. Used by permission of Doubleday, a division of Random House, Inc.; **2.23** Débenath & Dibble, Handbook of Paleolithic Typology, 1994, Vol. 1, p. 73, Fig. 6.19 and p. 106: Fig. 8.10 University Museum Publications; Upper Paleolithic and Epipaleolithic figures Courtesy Deborah I. Olszewski.

CHAPTER 3

3.1 Photograph by Jean-Baptiste Leca; **3.2** Reinisches Landmuseum; **3.3** Neg./Trans. No. 335795, courtesy the Library, American Museum of Natural History; **3.4** Reprinted with the permission of Cambridge University Press; **3.5** Reprinted with the permission of Cambridge University Press; **3.6** Reprinted with the permission of the Zoological Society of San Diego; **3.7** Courtesy Deborah I. Olszewski; **3.8** National Geographic map/NG Image Collection; **3.9** Reprinted with the permission of Cambridge University Press; **3.10** From J. B. Birdsell, *Human Evolution: An Introduction to the New Physical Anthropology, 2nd, ed.* (Rand McNally, 1975), Fig. 6.7. Reproduced by permission of the estate of J. B. Birdsell; **3.11** Courtesy Deborah I. Olszewski; **3.12** Reprinted with permission of Anthro-Photo File; **3.13** Reprinted from Journal of Human Evolution, Vol. 27 Issue 2, Blumenschine, Carvallo, and S. D. Capaldo, "Competition for Carcasses and Early Hominid," Pages 197–213, copyright 1994, with permission from Elsevier; **3.14** From W. Howells, *Evolution of Genus Homo* (Benjamin/Cummings Pub. Co., copyright © 1973), p. 47. Reproduced by permission of W. W. Howells.

CHAPTER 4

4.1 Figure 17.7, p. 263 From *Humankind Emerging*, 4th Edition by Bernard G. Campbell. Copyright © 1985 by Bernard G. Campbell. Reprinted by permission of HarperCollins Publishers, Inc.; **4.2** Reprinted with the permission of Cambridge University Press; **4.3** Photo Alan Walker © National Museum of Kenya; **4.4** Courtesy Deborah I. Olszewski and the Abydos Survey for Paleolithic Sites; **4.5** Courtesy Deborah I. Olszewski; **4.6** *Glynn Ll. Isaac;* **4.7** Reprinted with permission from Vekua et al., *Science* 297:85–89, Fig. 2 views a, b and c. Copyright 2002 AAAS; **4.8** Courtesy of Naama Goren-Inbar; **4.9** Courtesy Deborah I. Olszewski; **4.10** Reprinted with the permission of Cambridge University Press; **4.11** Courtesy Deborah I. Olszewski; **4.12** Reprinted with the permission of Cambridge University Press; **4.13** One fig from Singer & Wymer, *The Middle Stone Age at Klasies River Mouth in South Africa*. Reprinted with the permission of the University of Chicago Press; **4.14** National Geographic map/NG Image Collection; **4.15** Photo provided by John Yellen; **4.16** Henri de Lumley, Centre nationale de la recherche scientifique, Marseile; **4.17** © Erik Trinkaus; **4.18** From F. Bordes, *The Old Stone Age* (Weidenfeld and Nicolson, 1968). Reproduced by permission of Weidenfeld and Nicolson; **4.19** Dibble, The Interpretation of Middle Paleolithic Scraper Reduction Patterns, 1998, L'Homme de Néandertal vol. 4, p. 57: Fig. 1; **4.20** Photo Courtesy of Paul Goldberg; **4.21** Reprinted with the permission of Cambridge University Press; **4.22** Courtesy Deborah I. Olszewski; **4.23** Bridgeman-Giraudon/Art Resource, NY; **4.24** *New York Times*, January 22, 1995; **4.25** Ph. Carole FRITZ/équipe Grotte Chauvet/Ministère de la Culture; **4.26** Fig. 4 from "The Signs of All Times: Entroptic Phenomena in Upper Paleolithic Art" *Current Anthropology* 29:2 (1988) pp. 201–245. Reprinted with the permission of the University of Chicago Press; **4.27** From Flood, *The Archaeology of Dreamtime*, copyright 1991, reprinted with the permission of Yale University Press; **4.28** Courtesy Deborah I. Olszewski; **4.29** Photos by Jeff Lindon; **4.30** Reprinted with the permission of Scribner, a Division of Simon & Schuster Inc. from *The Threshold of Civilization* by Walter A. Fairservis, Jr., drawings by Jon Fairservis. Copyright © 1975 Walter A. Fairservis, Jr.; **4.31** Courtesy Austrian Cultural Institute of New York.

CHAPTER 5

5.1 Philadelphia Museum of Art: Purchased with funds from the American Museum of Photography; **5.2** From J. J. Hester, Introduction of Archaeology(Holt, Rinehart, and Winston, 1976), compiled from A. Krieger, "Early Man in the New World," in J. D. Jennings and E. Norbeck, eds., Prehistoric Man in the New World (University of Chicago Press, 1964). Reproduced with the permission of the University of Chicago Press; **5.3** Photo courtesy of Anthony T. Boldurian, Clovis Archives; **5.4** Joe LeMonnier, courtesy of Natural History Magazine, (11), (87); © the American Museum of Natural History, 1987; **5.5** Modified from Joe LeMonnier, courtesy of Natural History Magazine, (1), (87); © the American Museum of Natural History, 1987; **5.6** Modified from *The Great Journey* by Brian Fagan, © 1987. Thames & Hudson, Inc. Reprinted by permission of the publisher; **5.7** Reprinted with permission of John Wiley & Sons, Inc.; **5.8** National Geographic map/NG Image Collection; **5.9** National Geographic map/NG Image Collection; **5.10** figure on left: From Gramly, Guide to the Palaeo-Indian Artifacts of North America, 1990. Illustration by Valerie Waldorf; **5.11** National Geographic map/NG Image Collection; **5.12** From *Natural History*, 1/1987, © Natural History, American Museum of Natural History, Courtesy of C.G. Turner and American Museum of Natural History; **5.13** Original drawings by Ted Goebel. Reprinted by permission of John Hoffecker; **5.14** Tom D. Dillehay; **5.15** Reprinted with permission from Roosevelt, *Science* 272:373–384, Fig. 6. Copyright 1996 AAAS; **5.16** Photo Courtesy of Paul Goldberg; **5.17** Nottoway River Survey—Archaeological Research; **5.18** Courtesy Deborah I. Olszewski; **5.19** From Gramly, Guide to the Palaeo-Indian Artifacts of North America, 1990. Illustration by Valerie Waldorf; **5.20** University of Colorado Museum of Natural History, Joe Ben Wheat.

CHAPTER 6

6.1 Reprinted with the permission of Cambridge University Press; **6.2** Courtesy of the Oriental Institute of the University of Chicago; **6.3** Courtesy Deborah I. Olszewski; **6.4** Courtesy Deborah I. Olszewski; **6.5** Fig. 39 from Oakley, *Man the Toolmaker*. Reprinted with the permission of the University of Chicago Press; **6.6** Robert Wenke and Oxford University Press; **6.7** Robert Wenke and Oxford University Press; **6.8** Robert Wenke and Oxford University Press; **6.9** Photo by Nancy R. Coinman; **6.10** Photo by D. Nadel, Zinman Inst. Of Archaeology, University of Haifa; **6.11** Courtesy Deborah I. Olszewski; **6.12** Robert Wenke and Oxford University Press; **6.13** State Antiquities Organization, Baghdad; **6.14** From F. Valla and Centre de Recherche Français de Jérusalem; **6.15** From F. Hole et al., *Prehistory and Human Ecology of the Deh Luran Plain*, Mem. Of the Museum of Anthropology, No. 1 (University of Michigan, 1969) Fig. 11.5. Reproduced by permission of Museum of Anthropology Publications; **6.16** Courtesy Deborah I. Olszewski; **6.17** Courtesy Deborah I. Olszewski; **6.18** Courtesy Deborah I. Olszewski; **6.19** Reprinted with the permission of Council for British Research in the Levant; **6.20** Courtesy Deborah I. Olszewski; **6.21** The Evolution of Maize from the Tehuacan Valley, copyright © Robert S. Peabody Museum of Archaeology, Phillips Academy, Andover, Massachusetts. All rights reserved; **6.22** Fagan, Brian M., *People of the Earth: An Introduction to World Prehistory w/CD*, 11th Edition, © 2004, p. 305. Adapted by permission of Pearson Education, Inc., Upper Saddle River, NJ.

CHAPTER 7

7.1 Reprinted with the permission of Anthro-Photo File; **7.2** National Geographic map/NG Image Collection; **7.3** Courtesy Deborah I. Olszewski; **7.4** Courtesy Deborah I. Olszewski; **7.5** University of Pennsylvania Museum (image #141592); **7.6** Reprinted from *The Early Mesoamerican Village* by K. V. Flannery figure 6.5, copyright 1982, with permission from Elsevier; **7.7** Courtesy Deborah I. Olszewski; **7.8** Courtesy Deborah I. Olszewski; **7.9** Reprinted with the permission of Henry Wright.

CHAPTER 8

8.1 Robert Wenke and Oxford University Press; **8.2** Private collection, Dr. Elizabeth Ann Morris, research assoc. American Museum of Natural History NYC, 48 Pine Place, Bayfield, CO 81122 USA; **8.3** Reprinted with the permission of Council for British Research in the Levant; **8.4** Reprinted with the permission of Harald Hauptmann; **8.5** Courtesy Deborah I. Olszewski; **8.6** Courtesy Deborah I. Olszewski; **8.7** Robert Wenke and Oxford University Press; **8.8** From J. Mellaart, Catal Huyuk (McGraw-Hill, 1967), pp. 118, 125 © Thames & Hudson Ltd. Reproduced by permission of J. Mellaart; **8.9** From J. Mellaart, *The Neolithic of the Near East* (Charles Scribner's Sons, 1975) Figs. 97, 91, 93, 94. © Thames & Hudson Ltd., Lon. Reproduced by permission of Charles Scribner's Sons and Thames & Hudson.; **8.10** From J. Mellaart, *The Neolithic of the Near East* (Charles Scribner's Sons, 1975) Figs. 97, 91, 93, 94. © Thames & Hudson Ltd., Lon. Reproduced by permission of Charles Scribner's Sons and Thames & Hudson.; **8.11** Robert Wenke and Oxford University Press; **8.12** From Sabloff & Lamberg-Karlovsky, *Ancient Civilization and Trade* 1975, University of New Mexico Press; **8.13** State Antiquities Organization, Baghdad; **8.14** From S.N. Kramer, "The Sumerians," *Scientific American*, Oct. 1957, p. 76. Copyright © 1957 by *Scientific American*; **8.15** (top) Hirmer Fotoarchiv, Munich. (bottom) University of Pennsylvania Museum, Philadelphia; **8.16** Courtesy of the Oriental Institute of the University of Chicago; **8.17** Robert Wenke and Oxford University Press; **8.18** Georg Gerster/Photo Researchers; **8.19** Courtesy Deborah I. Olszewski; **8.20** From Robert McC Adams, *Heartland of Cities*, Fig. 17, 1981, University of Chicago Press.

CHAPTER 9

9.1 Robert Wenke and Oxford University Press; **9.2** Robert Wenke and Oxford University Press; **9.3** Courtesy Deborah I. Olszewski and the Abydos Survey for Paleolithic Sites; **9.4** Munich East Delta Expedition, D. Wildung; **9.5** Seattle Art Museum, Eugene Fuller Memorial Collection; **9.6** Courtesy Deborah I. Olszewski; **9.7** TWA; **9.8** Image of the Mummy of Queen Tiye from Harris & Wente, An X-Ray Atlas of the Royal Families. Reprinted with the permission of the University of Chicago Press; **9.9** Reprinted with the permission of Cambridge University Press; **9.10** Collection of Peter B. Rathbone; **9.11** Permission granted from Arelene Wolinski; **9.12** Victor R. Boswell, Jr/National Geographic Image Collection; **9.13** Victor R. Boswell, Jr./National Geographic Image Collection.

CHAPTER 10

10.1 Fig. 1.1 from Possehl, The Indus Civilization, 2002, p. 1. Reprinted with the permission of Altamira Press; **10.2** Copyright Harappa Archaeological Research Project, Courtesy Dept. of Archaeology and Museums, Govt. of Pakistan; **10.3** Courtesy Deborah I. Olszewski; **10.4** Fig. 12.1 from Possehl, The Indus Civilization, 2002, p. 215. Reprinted with the permission of Altamira Press; **10.5** Josephine Powell-Rome; **10.6** Fig. 3.20 from Possehl, The Indus Civilization, 2002, p. 81. Reprinted with the permission of Altamira Press; **10.7** Jan Fairservis; **10.8** James P. Blair/National Geographic Image Collection; **10.9** Courtesy National Museum, New Delhi; **10.10** University of Pennsylvania Museum, Philadelphia.

CHAPTER 11

11.1 Robert Wenke and Oxford University Press; **11.2** Reprinted by permission of American Scientist, Magazine of Sigma Xi, The Scientific Research Society; **11.3** From *Ancient China* by William Watson (New York Graphic Society, 1974) Fig. 12; **11.4** From Yang, *Perspective's on China's Past: Chinese Archaeology in Twentieth Century China* vol. 2, copyright 2004, reprinted with the permission of Yale University Press; **11.5** From Yang, *Perspective's on China's Past: Chinese Archaeology in Twentieth Century China* vol. 2, copyright 2004, reprinted with the permission of Yale University Press; **11.6** From Yang, *Perspective's on China's Past: Chinese Archaeology in Twentieth Century China* vol. 2, copyright 2004, reprinted with the permission of Yale University Press; **11.7** From K.C. Chang, *The Archaeology of Ancient China, 4th edition*, copyright 1987. Reprinted with the permission of Yale University Press; **11.8** From K.C. Chang, *The Archaeology of Ancient China, 4th edition*, copyright 1987. Reprinted with the permission of Yale University Press; **11.9** Reprinted with the permission of Dr. Li Liu; **11.10** From Yang, *Perspective's on China's Past: Chinese Archaeology in Twentieth Century China* vol. 2, copyright 2004, reprinted with the permission of Yale University Press; **11.11** Robert Wenke and Oxford University Press; **11.12** Institute of Archaeology, Academia Sinica, Peking; **11.13** Robert Wenke and Oxford University Press.

CHAPTER 12

12.1 Courtesy Deborah I. Olszewski; **12.2** Courtesy Deborah I. Olszewski; **12.3** Photo Courtesy of Phillip Charles Lucas; **12.4** Photo Courtesy of Phillip Charles Lucas; **12.5** Aerofilms Ltd., London; **12.6** Reprinted with the permission of Cambridge University Press; **12.7** Reproduced with permission from Christopher J. Knüsel's "More Circe Than Cassandra: The Princess of Vix in Ritualized Social Context" in *European Journal of Archaeology* vol. 5 #3 pp. 275–308. Copyright © SAGE Publications and European Association of Archaeologists, 2002, by permission of Sage Publications Ltd.; **12.8** Courtesy of Deutsches Archaeologisches Institut; **12.9** From M. Shinnie, Ancient African Kingdoms, 1965, St. Martin's Press. Reprinted with permission of St. Martin's Press, Incorporated; **12.10** Reprinted with the permission of Cambridge University Press; **12.11** Reprinted with permission of Patrick V. Kirch; **12.12** Courtesy Deborah I. Olszewski.

CHAPTER 13

13.1 Reproduced by permission of Equinox (Oxford) Ltd., Oxford England and first published in Atlas of Ancient America (Facts on File Inc./New York and Phaidon Press/Oxford); **13.2** Robert Wenke and Oxford University Press; **13.3** Image of village of Morelos, Mexico, courtesy the Library, American Museum of Natural History; **13.4** Robert Wenke and Oxford University Press; **13.5** Reprinted with the permission of Michael Coe; **13.6** Werner Forman/Art Resource, NY; **13.7** Reprinted with the permission of Philip Baird/AnthroArcheArt.Org; **13.8** The Michael C. Rockefeller Memorial Collection, Bequest of Nelson A. Rockefeller, 1979 (1979.206.1134); **13.9** Reprinted with the permission of Michael Coe; **13.10** Reprinted from The Cloud People, Flannery & Marcus, Page 59, 1983, with permission from Elsevier; **13.11** Mexican National Tourist Council; **13.12** Courtesy Deborah I. Olszewski; **13.13** Reprinted with the permission of Barry D. Kass; **13.14** Courtesy Deborah I. Olszewski; **13.15** National Geographic map/NG Image Collection; **13.16** University of Pennsylvania Museum (image #65-4-1094); **13.17** Reprinted with the permission of Michael Coe; **13.18** Reprinted with the permission of Michael Coe; **13.19** SEF/Art Resource, NY; **13.20** Robert Wenke and Oxford University Press; **13.21** Image of a Mexican tribute list, courtesy the Library, American Museum of Natural History; **13.22** Image of early drawings describing sequence of ritual human sacrifice, courtesy the Library, American Museum of Natural History; **13.23** Reprinted with the permission of The Bridgeman Art Library International.

CHAPTER 14

14.1 Reproduced by permission of Equinox (Oxford) Ltd., Oxford England and first published in *Atlas of Ancient* America (Facts on File Inc./New York and Phaidon Press/Oxford); **14.2** Vladimir Korostyshevskiy; **14.3** National Geographic map/NG Image Collection; **14.4** Courtesy Deborah I. Olszewski; **14.5** Reprinted from *Early Settlement and Subsistence in Casma Valley* by the University of Iowa Press; **14.6** Reprinted from *Cultures of Ancient Peru*, by F. G. Lumbreras, Smithsonian Institution Press © 1974, Fig. 5.4; **14.7** Courtesy Deborah I. Olszewski; **14.8** National Geographic map/NG Image Collection; **14.9** Courtesy Deborah I. Olszewski; **14.10** University of Pennsylvania Museum (image #G5-18729); **14.11** National Museum of Natural History, Smithsonian Institution; **14.12** Reprinted from *Cultures of Ancient Peru*, by F. G. Lumbreras, Smithsonian Institution Press © 1974, Fig. 218.

CHAPTER 15

15.1 Courtesy Deborah I. Olszewski; **15.2** Reproduced by permission of Equinox (Oxford) Ltd., Oxford England and first published in *Atlas of Ancient America* (Facts on File Inc./New York and Phaidon Press/Oxford); **15.3** Reprinted, with permission, from the Annual Review of Anthropology, Volume 3 © 1974 by Annual Reviews www.annualreviews.org; **15.4** Reproduced by permission of Equinox (Oxford) Ltd., Oxford England and first published in *Atlas of Ancient America* (Facts on File Inc./New York and Phaidon Press/Oxford); **15.5** Reprinted with the permission of the Ohio Historical Society; **15.6** Courtesy Deborah I. Olszewski; **15.7** Collections of The New York Public Library/Rare Books Division; **15.8** Reproduced by permission of Equinox (Oxford) Ltd., Oxford England and first published in *Atlas of Ancient America* (Facts on File Inc./New York and Phaidon Press/Oxford); **15.9** Reproduced by permission of Equinox (Oxford) Ltd., Oxford England and first published in Atlas of Ancient America (Facts on File Inc./New York and Phaidon Press/Oxford); **15.10** Courtesy Deborah I. Olszewski; **15.11** Courtesy Deborah I. Olszewski; **15.12** Werner Forman/Art Resource, NY; **15.13** Courtesy Deborah I. Olszewski; **15.14** Courtesy Deborah I. Olszewski; **15.15** National Park Service; **15.16** From J. D. Jennings, Prehistory of North American, 2nd ed. (McGraw Hill, 1974). All rights reserved. Reproduced by permission of McGraw-Hill Book Co.

CHAPTER 16

16.1a reprinted with the permission of James C. Chatters; **16.1b** reprinted with the permission of Instructional Resources Corporation; **16.2** Copyright of the Trustees of the British Museum, reprinted with permission.

Index

Note: Pictorial representations are in **bold** type.